THIRD EDITION

TORTS
Personal Injury Litigation

THIRD EDITION

TORTS
Personal Injury Litigation

William P. Statsky

WEST PUBLISHING

an International Thomson Publishing company IP®

Albany • Bonn • Boston • Cincinnati • Detroit • London • Madrid
Melbourne • Mexico City • Minneapolis/St. Paul • New York • Pacific Grove
Paris • San Francisco • Singapore • Tokyo • Toronto • Washington

NOTICE TO THE READER

Publisher does not warrant or guarantee any of the products described herein or perform any independent analysis in connection with any of the product information contained herein. Publisher does not assume, and expressly disclaims, any obligation to obtain and include information other than that provided to it by the manufacturer.

The reader is notified that this text is an educational tool, not a practice book. Since the law is in constant change, no rule or statement of law in this book should be relied upon for any service to any client. The reader should always refer to standard legal sources for the current rule or law. If legal advice or other expert assistance is required, the services of the appropriate professional should be sought.

The publisher makes no representation or warranties of any kind, including but not limited to, the warranties of fitness for particular purpose or merchantability, nor any such representations implied with respect to the material set forth herein, and the publisher takes no responsibility with respect to such material. The publisher shall not be liable for any special, consequential, or exemplary damages resulting, in whole or part, from the readers' use of, or reliance upon, this material.

COPYRIGHT © 1995
By West Publishing
an imprint of Delmar Publishers
a division of International Thomson Publishing
The ITP logo is a trademark under license.

Printed in the United States of America

For more information, contact:

Delmar Publishers
3 Columbia Circle , Box 15015
Albany, New York 12212-5015

International Thomson Editores
Campos Eliseos 385, Piso 7
Col Polanco
11560 Mexico D F Mexico

International Thomson Publishing – Europe
Berkshire House
168-173 High Holborn
London, WC1V 7AA
England

International Thomson Publishing GmbH
Königswinterer Strasse 418
53227 Bonn
Germany

Thomas Nelson Australia
102 Dodds Street
South Melbourne, 3205
Victoria, Australia

International Thomson Publishing – Asia
221 Henderson Road
#05 -10 Henderson Building
Singapore 0315

Nelson Canada
1120 Birchmount Road
Scarborough, Ontario
Canada M1K 5G4

International Thomson Publishing – Japan
Hirakawacho Kyowa Building, 3F
2-2-1 Hirakawacho
Chiyoda-ku, Tokyo 102 Japan

 2 3 4 5 6 7 8   XXX   02 01 00 99 98 97

Library of Congress Cataloging-in-Publication Data

Statsky, William P.
    Torts, personal injury litigation / William P. Statsky. — 3rd ed.
        p.   cm
    Incuded index.
    ISBN 0-314-04384-5 (hard : acid-free paper)
    1. Personal injuries—United States.   2. Torts—United States.
3. Actions and defenses-United States.   I. Title
KF1257.S73 1994
346.7303'23—dc20   94-37746
[347.306323]   CIP

For Pat, Jess, Gabe,
and Pani

Also by William P. Statsky

Case Analysis and Fundamentals of Legal Writing, 4th ed. St. Paul: West Publishing Company, 1994 (with J. Wernet)

Essentials of Paralegalism, 2d ed. St. Paul: West Publishing Company, 1993

Essentials of Torts. St. Paul: West Publishing Company, 1994

Family Law, 3d ed. St. Paul: West Publishing Company, 1991

Inmate Involvement in Prison Legal Services: Roles and Training Options for the Inmate as Paralegal. American Bar Association, Commission on Correctional Facilities and Services, 1974

Introduction to Paralegalism: Problems, Perspectives and Skills, 4th ed. St. Paul: West Publishing Company, 1992

Legal Desk Reference. St. Paul: West Publishing Company, 1991 (with B. Hussey, M. Diamond & R. Nakamura)

The Legal Paraprofessional as Advocate and Assistant: Roles, Training Concepts and Materials. Center on Social Welfare Policy and Law, 1971 (with P. Lang)

Legal Research and Writing: Some Starting Points, 4th ed. St. Paul: West Publishing Company, 1993

Legal Thesaurus/Dictionary: A Resource for the Writer and Computer Researcher. St. Paul: West Publishing Company, 1985

Legislative Analysis and Drafting, 2d ed. St. Paul: West Publishing Company, 1984

Paralegal Employment: Facts and Strategies for the 1990s, 2d ed. St. Paul: West Publishing Company, 1993

Paralegal Ethics and Regulation, 2d ed. St. Paul: West Publishing Company, 1993

Rights of the Imprisoned: Cases, Materials and Directions. Indianapolis: Bobbs-Merrill Company, 1974 (with R. Singer)

What Have Paralegals Done? A Dictionary of Functions. National Paralegal Institute, 1973

Contents in Brief

Preface

1 ■ Introduction to Tort Law   1

2 ■ Sources of Tort Law and Litigation   11

3 ■ Legal Analysis in Tort Law   37

4 ■ Legal Interviewing and Investigation in Personal Injury Litigation   61

5 ■ Pre-Trial Litigation   88

6 ■ Discovery Law and Techniques   120

7 ■ Trial and Appeal   164

8 ■ The Judgment Creditor: Enforcement of the Judgment   185

9 ■ Negligence: A Summary   196

10 ■ Foreseeability in Tort Law   203

11 ■ Negligence: Element I: Duty   212

12 ■ Negligence: Element II: Breach of Duty   230

13 ■ Negligence: Element III: Proximate Cause   282

14 ■ Negligence: Element IV: Damages   302

15 ■ Negligence: Defenses   317

16 ■ Survival and Wrongful Death   333

17 ■ Products Liability   342

18 ■ Infliction of Emotional Distress   386

19 ■ False Imprisonment and False Arrest   402

20 ■ Misuse of Legal Proceedings   418

21 ■ Defamation   429

22 ■ Invasion of Privacy   442

23 ■ Battery   453

24 ■ Assault   465

25 ■ Misrepresentation   474

26 ■ Torts Against the Family   484

27 ■ Torts Connected with Land   495

28 ■ Conversion and Trespass to Chattels   535

29 ■ Business Torts   544

30 ■ Worker's Compensation   560

31 ■ Privileges and Immunities: Defenses that Avoid Tort Liability   579

32 ■ Settlement   618

Appendix A · Nonfault Insuraance   686

Appendix B · Accident Reports and Financial Responsibility   699

Appendix C · Verdicts and Settlements   705

Appendix D · Basic Medical Anatomy   714

Appendix E · Product Liability Class Action Settlement Notice   735

Glossary · 737

Index · 750

Contents

Preface   xxix

1

Introduction to Tort Law   1

Major Types of Personal Injury Tort Litigation   1
Elements of all the Torts   2
Categories of Torts   2
  Intentional Torts   2
  Negligence   7
  Strict Liability   7
The Relationship Between Tort Law and Other Areas
  of The Law   8
  Contract Law   8
  Criminal Law   8
  Civil Procedure Law   8
  Evidence Law   8
  Family Law   8
  Conflicts of Law   9
  Constitutional Law   9
  Estate Law   9
  State and Local Government Law   9
  Business Law   9
  Real Property Law   9
  Insurance Law   9
  Environment Law   9
The Skills Assignments in this Book   10
Summary   10
Key Terms   10

2

Sources of Tort Law and Litigation   11

Introduction   11
Primary Authority   11
  Opinions   13
  Statutes   15
  Constitutions   16
  Administrative Regulations   16
  Administrative Decisions   17
  Charters and Ordinances   17
  Rules of Court   17

Secondary Authority   17
  Legal Encyclopedia   18
  Legal Treatise   18
  Legal Periodical Literature   21
  Annotations   21
Riding the Cartwheel: A Basic Technique for Using all Law Books   22
The Importance of Digest in Tort Law   25
General Instructions for Torts Research Assignments   26
Summary   35
Key Terms   36

3
Legal Analysis in Tort Law   37

Structure of Legal Analysis   37
Issue   38
Rule   38
Analysis and Counteranalysis   40
  Preliminary Assessment   40
  Legal Analysis and Legal Research   42
  Legal Analysis, Investigation, and Interviewing   42
  Breaking a Rule Down into Its Elements   44
  Definitions of the Elements   46
  Connecting Facts with Elements of the Rule   50
  Legal Analysis and Further Research, Investigation, and
    Interviewing   55
  Factor Analysis   55
  Counteranalysis   56
  Length of Legal Analysis   57
Conclusion   58
Summary   59
Key Terms   60

4
Legal Interviewing and Investigation in Personal Injury Litigation   61

Interviewing in a Personal Injury Case   61
  Liability   61
  Damages   62
  Collectibility   62
Obtaining the Facts   62

Background Information Checklist   63
Communications Checklist   74
Client Intake Memorandum   76
Introduction of Investigation   78
Evidence Law   79
Tort Law   79
Common Sense   80
Fact Analysis: Organizing the Options   81
Fact Particularization   82
Taking a Witness Statement   85
Summary   87
Key Terms   87

5
Pre-Trial Litigation   88

Court Systems   88
Jurisdiction   88
State Court Systems   90
Federal Court System   91
Jurisdiction over Persons   95
Service Within the State   96
Domicile   98
Consent   98
Long-Arm Statutes   99
Venue   99
Venue in State Courts   100
Venue in Federal Courts   100
Choice of Law in State Courts   101
Parties   103
Real Party in Interest   103
Capacity to Sue and Be Sued   103
Joinder of Parties   103
Pleadings   104
Complaint   105
Answer   116
Ending the Case Without a Trial   116
Default Judgment   116
Voluntary Dismissal by the Plaintiff   117
Involuntary Dismissal   117
Jury Selection   117
Pre-Trial Conference   118
Summary   118
Key Terms   119

6

Discovery Law and Techniques   120

Goals of Discovery   120
Overview of Discovery Devices   122
Drafting Interrogatories   131
Drafting Answers to Interrogatories   143
Preparing for Deposition   144
Digesting and Indexing Discovery Data   157
    Digest by Person   161
    Digest by Subject Matter   162
Summary   162
Key Terms   163

7

Trial and Appeal   164

Trial   164
    Opening Statement by Plaintiff to Jury   165
    Defendant's Motion to Dismiss   165
    Opening Statement by Defendant to Jury   166
    Burden of Proof   167
    Burden of Production   167
    Presentation of Plaintiff's Case   169
    Defendant's Motion for a Directed Verdict   169
    Defendant's Opening Statement to the Jury if it Was Reserved   171
    Presentation of Defendant's Case   171
    Rebuttal Evidence by Plaintiff   171
    Rebuttal Evidence by Defendant   171
    Motions for Directed Verdict by Plaintiff and Defendant   171
    Closing Argument of Defendant to Jury   172
    Closing Argument of Plaintiff to Jury   172
    Instructions to Jury by Judge   172
    Kinds of Verdicts   172
    Motions for Judgment Notwithstanding the Verdict (NOV)   173
    Remittitur and Additur   173
    Entry of Judgment   174
    Motion for a New Trial   174
    Motion to Trial Court for Relief from Judgment   176
Res Judicata and Collateral Estoppel   178
    Res Judicata   178
    Collateral Estoppel   180

Appeal   181
Summary   183
Key Terms   184

8
The Judgment Creditor: Enforcement of the Judgment   185

Introduction   185
Locating the Assets of the Judgment Debtor   186
  Categories of Assets   187
  Formal Methods of Discovering Assets and Liabilities   191
Collection of the Judgment Award   192
Summary   194
Key Terms   195

9
Negligence: A Summary   196

Introduction   196
Negligence and Breach of Duty   197
Negligence and Insurance   197
Shorthand Definition   197
Negligence Checklist   197
Summary   202
Key Terms   202

10
Foreseeability in Tort Law   203

Introduction   203
Defining Foreseeability   204
Foreseeability Spectrum   204
Objective Standard   205
Phrasing the Foreseeability Question   205
Foreseeability Determination "Formula"   207
  Area Analysis   208
  Activity Analysis   208
  People Analysis   208
  Preparation Analysis   208
  Assumptions About Human Nature   208
  Historical Data   209

Specific Sensory Data   209
Common Sense   209
Review of Steps to Determine Foreseeability   210
Summary   211
Key Terms   211

11

Negligence: Element I: Duty   212

General Rule on Duty   212
Unforeseeable Plaintiff   213
Nonfeasance and Special Relationships   216
Gratuitous Undertaking   223
Summary   228
Key Terms   229

12

Negligence: Element II: Breach of Duty (Unreasonableness)   230

Standard of Care: Reasonableness   230
Totality of Circumstances   231
Comparative Standard   231
Reasonableness vs. Perfection   231
Breach of Duty (Unreasonableness) Equation   234
Danger/Caution Hypothesis   235
Foreseeability   236
Burden or Inconvenience   237
Importance or Social Utility   237
Objective or Subjective Standard?   238
Physical Characteristics   239
Mental Characteristics (When the Defendant is an Adult)   239
Mental Characteristics (When the Defendant is a Child)   240
Res Ipsa Loquitur   240
More Likely Than Not Due to Someone's Unreasonableness   241
More Likely Than Not Due to Defendant's Unreasonableness   243
Plaintiff is Not a Responsible Cause of the Accident   245
Custom and Usage   248
Violation of Statute, Ordinance, or Regulation (S/O/R)   249
Was the S/O/R Violated?   250
Did the Violation Cause the Accident?   250
Is Plaintiff Within the Class of Persons Protected by the S/O/R?   251
Was the S/O/R Intended to Avoid this Kind of Harm?   252

Negligence Per Se? Presumption of Negligence? Some Evidence of
  Negligence?   253
Compliance with Statute, Ordinance, or Regulation (S/O/R)   256
Gross Negligence (Unreasonableness) and Willful, Wanton, and
  Reckless Conduct   256
Vicarious Liability   257
  Who Can Be Sued?   258
  Vicarious Liability and Independent Liability   259
Medical Malpractice   266
  Physician-Patient Relationship   266
  Warranty   266
  Negligence   267
  Informed Consent   269
Legal Malpractice   273
  Mistakes   274
  Causation   276
Summary   279
Key Terms   281

13

Negligence: Element III: Proximate Cause   282

Introduction   282
Cause in Fact   283
  Evidence of Causation   285
  Causation by Market Share   290
Cut-Off Test of Proximate Cause   291
  Exceptions to Test   292
  Unforeseeable Plaintiff   295
  Intervening Causes   295
Overview of Steps Needed to Analyze Proximate Cause   297
Summary   300
Key Terms   301

14

Negligence: Element IV: Damages   302

Kinds of Damages   302
Pain and Suffering   309
Property Damage   310
Doctrine of Avoidable Consequences   311
Collateral-Source Rule   311
Joint Tortfeasors   312

Persons Acting in Concert   312
Persons Not Acting in Concert   313
Release   313
Contribution   314
Indemnity   315
Summary   315
Key Terms   316

15
Negligence: Defenses   317

Introduction   317
Contributory Negligence   318
Plaintiff's Negligence (Unreasonableness)   318
Cause in Fact   321
Last Clear Chance   322
Plaintiff in Helpless Peril   322
Plaintiff in Inattentive Peril   322
Comparative Negligence   323
Pure Comparative Negligence   323
Restricted Comparative Negligence   324
Assumption of the Risk   324
Understanding the Risk   325
Voluntarily Confronting the Risk   325
Summary   331
Key Terms   332

16
Survival and Wrongful Death   333

Survival   333
Kinds of Torts That Survive   333
Common Law and Statutory Law   334
Characteristics of Actions That Survive   335
Wrongful Death   336
Common Law   336
Recovery for Wrongful Death   336
Avoiding Double Recovery   337
Summary   340
Key Terms   341

17
Products Liability 342

Introduction   342
Negligence   345
Manufacturer   347
Nonmanufacturer   348
Defenses   349
Misrepresentation   350
Warranty and Strict Liability   350
Express Warranty   350
False Statement of Fact   351
Intent or Expectation the Statement Will Reach the Plaintiff   351
Reliance on Statement   352
Damage and Causation   352
Sales vs. Service   356
Implied Warranties   358
Implied Warranty of Merchantability   359
Implied Warranty of Fitness for a Particular Purpose   360
Privity   360
Defenses to Warranty Actions   362
Strict Liability in Tort   362
Seller   366
Defective Product that is Unreasonably Dangerous   367
Use or Consumer   377
Physical Harm   377
Causation   378
Defenses to Strict Liability in Tort   378
A Federal Products-Liability Law?   383
Summary   384
Key Terms   385

18
Infliction of Emotional Distress 386

Intentional Infliction of Emotional Distress   386
Intentional Infliction of Emotional Distress Checklist   386
Extreme or Outrageous Conduct   390
Intent   391
Severe Emotional Distress   392
Causation   393

Negligent Infliction of Emotional Distress (NIED)   396
   Traditional Negligence   396
   No Physical Harm or Injury   396
   Later Physical Harm or Injury   397
   Witnessing Someone Else's Injury   397
Summary   401
Key Terms   401

19
False Imprisonment and False Arrest   402

False Imprisonment   402
   False Imprisonment Checklist   402
   Confinement   406
   Intent   408
   Causation   408
   Consciousness or Harm   409
False Arrest   411
   Peace Officer's Privilege to Arrest   411
   Private Citizen's Privilege to Arrest   412
Summary   417
Key Terms   417

20
Misuse of Legal Proceedings   418

Malicious Prosecution   418
   Malicious Prosecution Checklist   418
   Initiate or Procure the Initiation of Criminal Proceedings   422
   Without Probable Cause   422
   With Malice   422
   Criminal Proceedings Terminate in Favor of the Accused   423
Wrongful or Unjustified Civil Proceedings   424
Abuse of Process   424
Summary   428
Key Terms   428

21
Defamation   429

Two Torts   429
Defamation Checklist   429
Defamatory Statement   434

Fact   434
Opinion   434
Extrinsic Facts   434
Falsity of the Statement   435
Of and Concerning the Plaintiff   436
Publication   436
Damages   436
Libel   436
Slander   437
Privilege   437
Absolute Privilege   437
Qualified Privilege   437
Summary   441
Key Terms   441

22
Invasion of Privacy   442

Four Torts   442
Invasion of Privacy Checklist   442
Intrusion   446
Appropriation   447
Public Disclosure of Private Fact   447
False Light   448
Summary   452
Key Terms   452

23
Battery   453

Introduction   453
Battery Checklist   453
Act   456
Person   457
Consciousness   457
Intent   457
Transferred Intent   458
Motivate   458
Harmful or Offensive Contact   458
Consent and Privilege   460
Summary   463
Key Terms   464

24
Assault   465

Introduction   465
Assault Checklist   465
Act   469
Apprehension   469
Harmful or Offensive   469
   Reasonable   469
   Imminent   470
Transferred Intent   470
Summary   472
Key Terms   473

25
Misrepresentation   474

Introduction   474
Misrepresentation Checklist   474
Statement of Fact That Is False   478
Scienter   478
Negligent Misrepresentation   478
Justifiable Reliance   479
Summary   483
Key Terms   483

26
Torts Against the Family   484

Torts Derived from Other Torts   484
   Loss of Consortium   484
   Loss of Services   485
Torts Not Derived from Other Torts   486
   Alienation of Affections   486
   Criminal Conversation   486
   Enticement of Spouse   487
   Abduction or Enticement of a Child   487
   Seduction   487
Wrongful Life, Birth, Pregnancy   488
Summary   493
Key Terms   494

27
Torts Connected with Land   495

Introduction   495
Trespass to Land   496
  Trespass to Land Checklist   496
  Land   499
  Damages   499
Strict Liability for Abnormally Dangerous Conditions or Activities   499
  Strict Liability for Abnormally Dangerous Conditions or Activities Checklist   499
  Abnormally Dangerous Condition or Activity   503
  Knowledge of the Condition or Activity   505
  Causation: Cause in Fact and Proximate Cause   505
  Defenses   505
Nuisance   509
  Private Nuisance   510
  Public Nuisance   518
Traditional Negligence Liability   523
  Persons Outside the Land   524
  Trespassers, Licensees, and Invitees   525
  The Special Problems of the Seller and Buyer of Land (Vendor and Vendee)   531
  The Special Problems of the Landlord and Tenant (Lessor and Lessee)   531
Summary   532
Key Terms   534

28
Conversion and Trespass to Chattels   535

Introduction   535
Conversion and Trespass to Chattels Checklist   535
Damages   539
Kind of Interference   539
Mistake Defense   540
Summary   543
Key Terms   543

29
Business Torts   544

Introduction   **544**
Disparagement   **545**
  False Statement of Fact   545
  Disparaging the Plaintiff's Business or Property   546
  Publication   547
  Intent   547
  Special Damages   547
  Causation   547
  Privilege to Disparage   548
Injurious Falsehood   **548**
Interference with Contract Relations   **549**
  Existing Contract   549
  Interference   550
  Intent   550
  Damages   550
  Causation   551
  Privilege to Interfere with Contract Relations   551
Interference with Prospective Advantage   **554**
Prima Facie Tort   **555**
Bad Faith Liability   **556**
Dram Shop Liability   **557**
Tortious Interference with Employment   **558**
Summary   **558**
Key Terms   **559**

30
Worker's Compensation   560

On-the-Job Injuries at Common Law   **560**
Worker's Compensation Statutes   **561**
Injuries and Diseases Covered   **563**
  In the Course of Employment   564
  Arising Out of Employment   568
Filing a Claim   **574**
Benefits Available   **576**
Summary   **577**
Key Terms   **578**

31
Privileges and Immunities: Defenses That Avoid Tort Liability   579

Introduction   579
Consent in Tort Law   580
  Capacity to Consent   580
  Manifestation of Willingness   581
  Voluntariness   581
  Reasonable Belief   582
  Knowledge   582
  Substantially the Same Conduct   583
Self-Help Privileges   588
  Introduction   588
  Self-Defense   589
  Defense of Others   591
  Necessity   593
  Abating a Nuisance   595
  Defense of Property   595
  Recapture of Chattels   599
  Retaking Possession of Land Forcibly   601
  Discipline   601
  Protecting Safety or Morals of a Close Relative, Friend, or
    Client   602
  Arrest   602
Sovereign Immunity   602
  Federal Government   603
  State Government   605
  Local Government   607
**Official Immunity: The Personal Liability of Government
  Employees   609**
Charitable Immunity   613
Intrafamily Tort Immunity   614
Summary   616
Key Terms   617

32
Settlement   618

Introduction   618
Settlement Precis   619

Settlement Precis—Illustration 619
Settlement Brochure 621
Summary 685
Key Terms 685

Appendix A: Nonfault Insurance 686
**Appendix B: Accident Reports and Financial
Responsibility 699**
Appendix C: Verdicts and Settlements 705
Appendix D: Basic Medical Anatomy 714
**Appendix E: Product Liability Class Action Settlement
Notice 735**

Glossary 737

Index 750

Table of Cases

■ CHAPTER 11

Soldano v. O'Daniels, 141 Cal. App. 3d 443, 190 Cal. Rptr. 310 (1983)   **219**

Riss v. City of New York, 22 N.Y.2d 579, 240 N.E.2d 860, 293 N.Y.S.2d 897 (1968)   **225**

■ CHAPTER 12

Ward v. Forrester Day Care, Inc., 547 So. 2d 410 (Alabama 1989)   **246**

Potts v. Fidelity Fruit & Produce Co., Inc., 165 Ga. App. 546, 301 S.E.2d 903 (1983)   **255**

Fein v. Permanente Medical Group, 38 Cal. 3d 137, 211 Cal.Rptr. 368, 695 P.2d 665 (1985)   **270**

Smith v. Lewis, 13 Cal. 3d 349, 118 Cal. Rptr. 621, 530 P.2d 589 (1975)   **277**

■ CHAPTER 13

Parra v. Tarasco, Inc. d/b/a Jiminez Restaurant, 230 Ill. App.3d 819, 172 Ill. Dec. 516, 595 N.E.2d 1186 (1992)   **288**

Mussivand v. David, 45 Ohio St. 3d 314, 544 N.E.2d 265 (1989)   **299**

■ CHAPTER 14

O'Shea v. Riverway Towing Co., 677 F.2d 1194 (7th Cir. 1982)   **303**

■ CHAPTER 15

Hendricks v. Broderick, 284 N.W.2d 209 (Iowa 1979)   **329**

■ CHAPTER 16

Cassano v. Durham, 180 N.J. Super. 620, 436 A.2d 118 (1981)   **339**

■ CHAPTER 17

Cipollone v. Liggett Group, Inc., 893 F.2d 541 (3rd Cir. 1990)   **352**

Patterson v. Gesellschaft, 608 F. Supp. 1206 (N.D. Texas 1985)   **371**

■ CHAPTER 18

White v. Monsanto Co., 585 So. 2d 1205 (Louisiana 1991)   **393**

Thing v. LaChusa, 48 Cal. 3d 644, 771 P.2d 814 (1989)   **398**

▪ **CHAPTER 19**

Andrews v. Piedmont Air Lines, 297 S.C. 367, 377 S.E.2d 127 (1989) **410**

▪ **CHAPTER 20**

Raine v. Drasin, 621 S.W.2d 895 (Kentucky 1981) **425**

▪ **CHAPTER 21**

Van Duyn v. Smith, 173 Ill. App. 3d 523, 527 N.E.2d 1005 (1988) **438**

▪ **CHAPTER 22**

Peoples Bank and Trust Co. of Mountain Home, Conservator of the Estate of Nellie Mitchell, an Aged Person v. Globe International Publishing, Inc. doing business as "Sun", 978 F.2d 1065 (8th Cir. 1992) **449**

▪ **CHAPTER 23**

Funeral Services by Gregory, Inc., v. Bluefield Community Hospital, 186 W. Va. 424, 413 S.E.2d 79 (1991) **461**

▪ **CHAPTER 24**

Allen v. Walker, 569 So. 2d 350 (Alabama 1990) **471**

▪ **CHAPTER 25**

Vokes v. Arthur Murray, Inc., 212 So. 2d 906 (Florida District Court of Appeal 1968) **479**

▪ **CHAPTER 26**

Berman v. Allen, 80 N.J. 421, 404 A.2d 8 (1979) **489**

▪ **CHAPTER 27**

Foster v. Preston Mill Co., 44 Wash. 2d 440, 268 P.2d 645 (1954) **506**

Armory Park Neighborhood Assn v. Episcopal Community Services, 148 Ariz. 1, 712 P.2d 914 (1985) **520**

▪ **CHAPTER 28**

Moore v. The Regents of the University of California, 51 Cal. 3d 120, 793 P.2d 479, 271 Cal. Rptr. 146 (1990) **540**

▪ **CHAPTER 29**

Texaco, Inc. v. Pennzoil Co., 729 S.W.2d 768 (Court of Appeals of Texas 1987) **552**

■ **CHAPTER 30**

Seitz v. L&R Industries, 437 A.2d 1345 (Rhode Island 1981)   **571**

■ **CHAPTER 31**

Peterson v. Sorlien, 299 N.W.2d 208 (Minn. 1980)   **584**

Katko v. Briney, 183 N.W.2d 657 (Iowa 1971)   **597**

Preface

Tens of thousands of injuries occur every day on the road, at work, in department stores, on the playground, and at home. The incidence of property damage is even higher. While most of these mishaps never find their way into the legal system, many of them constitute potential torts. This is one of the reasons that tort law has a large impact on our lives. In addition to providing compensation to victims, one of the major objectives of tort law is behavior modification. A premise of personal-injury litigation is that one of the most effective ways to force people to avoid injuring others is to hang the threat of a tort lawsuit over their heads. These are some of the dynamics we will explore in this book.

It is an exciting time to study tort law. Throughout the country there is considerable controversy on whether our system of tort litigation is causing more societal ills than it is solving. Horror stories abound on the editorial pages of our morning newspapers. An example is the seventeen-year old Michigan high school student who is suing Nintendo and Toys 'R Us where she bought a Nintendo video game machine. Her suit claims that she has an inflamed thumb from playing too much Nintendo. Her doctor calls her condition, "Nintendinitis," which prevents her from writing, from typing—and, of course, from playing video games! Such cases have prompted calls for reform. The chapters of this book will help place these calls in perspective.

Tort law is one of the first subjects taught to future attorneys in law school because the course can provide an excellent insight into the legal system, the practice of law, and legal analysis. Paralegal students can also gain this insight. In a personal-injury practice of law, the attorney-paralegal team makes an important contribution. In many offices, the team is inseparable. To achieve this work environment, one of the first steps is to understand the principles of tort law that the attorney applies in a personal-injury practice. This understanding is one of our major goals.

▪ CHAPTER FORMAT

Each chapter includes features designed to assist students in understanding the material:

- A chapter outline at the beginning of each chapter provides a preview of the major topics in each chapter.
- Tables are used extensively to clarify concepts and present detailed information in an organized chart form.
- Assignments are included within each chapter that ask students to apply concepts to particular fact situations.
- A chapter summary at the end of each chapter provides a concise review of the main concepts discussed.
- Key terms are printed in bold face type the first time they appear in the text. Also, a list of key terms is found at the end of each chapter to help students review important terminology introduced in that chapter.

▪ CHANGES TO THE THIRD EDITION

- Selected court opinions has been added to the book. The opinions have been edited to highlight the tort issue covered in the chapters. Following most of the opinions, there is an assignment that will test the student's grasp of the principles in the opinion. The opinions cover important issues facing our courts today such as the tort liability growing out of the AIDS crisis, biotechnology, cohabitation, abortion, sex discrimination, invasion of privacy, and interference with business contracts.

- The chapters on legal interviewing and investigation have been combined into a new chapter 4.
- The focus of chapter 2 has been changed from legal research to the sources of tort law and an introduction to the primary authorities in tort law and litigation.
- Medical malpractice and attorney malpractice is covered in the expanded breach-of-duty chapter (chapter 12) rather than in separate chapters.
- The anatomy material has been moved to an appendix.
- The automobile insurance chapter has been updated and moved to an appendix.
- A glossary has been added to the book.

▪ INSTRUCTOR'S MATERIALS

In addition, an Instructor's Manual and Test Bank accompanies this text. The Instructor's Manual by William Statsky contains suggested answers to the assignments in the text, as well as teaching suggestions. The Test Bank is prepared by Anna Boling of Athens Area Technical College. The Test Bank contains an average of thirty true/false, multiple-choice, and discussion questions for each chapter. The questions are designed to test a student's knowledge of major chapter concepts.

▪ ACKNOWLEDGMENTS

I wish to thank the following people at West who were most helpful in the emergence of this book: Elizabeth Hannan, Patricia Bryant, Deborah Aspengren Meyer, and Michelle McAnelly.

Finally, a word of thanks to the reviewers who made valuable suggestions:

Dr. Melody K. Brown
College of Great Falls, MT

Todd E. Carlson
Robert Morris College, IL

Christine S. DeBoer
Rancho Santiago College, CA

Wendy Geertz
Kirkwood Community College, IA

Paul J. Sinopoli
Mississippi Gulf Coast Community College—Jefferson Davis Campus

Cynthia Weishapple
Chippewa Valley Technical College, WI

CHAPTER 1

Introduction to Tort Law

CHAPTER OUTLINE

- MAJOR TYPES OF PERSONAL INJURY TORT LITIGATION
- ELEMENTS OF ALL THE TORTS
- CATEGORIES OF TORTS
- THE RELATIONSHIP BETWEEN TORT LAW AND OTHER AREAS OF THE LAW
- THE SKILLS ASSIGNMENTS IN THIS BOOK

■ MAJOR TYPES OF PERSONAL INJURY TORT LITIGATION

Tort litigation is an important part of our legal system. The estimated total nationwide expense for tort litigation in state and federal courts is between $29 billion and $36 billion a year. This litigation falls roughly into three categories, although there is some overlap among them:[1]

1. Routine Personal Injury

The clearest example is the automobile accident. About 500,000 automobile cases are filed each year.

2. High-Stakes Personal Injury

Products liability, medical malpractice, and business torts are the main high-stakes personal injury cases. The growth in this kind of case has been substantial. Over a twenty-four-year period, the increase in the average award ranged from 200 percent to 1,000 percent. Between 1980 and 1987 there were over 1,300 jury awards of $1 million or more. A number of factors account for these statistics. The injuries are more serious, defendants have "deep pockets", and plaintiffs' attorneys have invested more of their energies and hence stand to earn more (a **deep pocket** is a defendant who has resources with which to pay a judgment).

---

[1]Rand Corporation, *Trends in Tort Litigation* (1987). See also "An Enigma Wrapped in a Riddle," 74 *ABA Journal* 38 (Oct. 1, 1988).

3. Mass Latent Injury

Most of these cases are also products liability cases, but on a broader scale. The injury is usually not discovered immediately. Once it is discovered, however, the number of potential suits can become enormous. In 1981, for example, there were 7,500 cases pending over Dalkon Shields. By 1986, A. H. Robins, manufacturer of Dalkon Shields, filed for protection under a Chapter 11 reorganization plan in which more than 325,000 claims were submitted to the bankruptcy court. Similarly, over the same period, the number of asbestos worker claims rose from 16,000 to 30,000.

Before examining the litigation of these and related kinds of torts, we need to cover some fundamentals.

▪ ELEMENTS OF ALL THE TORTS

What is tort law? What is a tort? As in so many aspects of the law, it is easier to say what a tort is *not* than to provide a comprehensive definition of what it is. A tort is not a crime (although criminal conduct is often also a tort). It is not a breach of contract (although there are circumstances in which it can be a tort to cause or induce a breach of contract). A **tort** is a civil wrong that has caused harm to person or property for which the courts will provide a remedy. The wrongdoer is called the **tortfeasor.**

Perhaps a more fruitful way to approach the topic is to look at what the torts are. Figure 1.1 provides an overview. This table will be our guide throughout this book.

Every tort is a **cause of action,** which is simply a legally acceptable reason for bringing a suit. To state a cause of action, a party must allege facts that support every component of the cause of action. We call these components **elements.** When a party has alleged facts that cover every element of the cause of action, that party has stated a **prima facie case.** Hence, for each cause of action listed in Figure 1.1, you are told what elements must be supported by facts in order to state a prima facie case for that cause of action. The list covers tort causes of action plus closely related causes of action that litigating parties often use along with the torts.

▪ CATEGORIES OF TORTS

There are three main categories of torts:

- the intentional torts
- negligence
- the strict liability torts

These categories are not ironclad. There are some torts that overlap the categories.

Intentional Torts

For **intentional torts** such as battery and false imprisonment, the defendant either desired to bring about the result or knew with substantial certainty that the result would follow from what he or she did, or failed to do.

Figure 1.1   Torts and Related Causes of Action: The Elements
(the page numbers in the first column tell you where the cause of action is discussed in this book)

The Cause of Action	Its Elements
1. Abuse of Process (p. 424)	i. Use of civil or criminal proceedings ii. Improper or ulterior purpose
2. Alienation of Affections (p. 486)	i. Intent to diminish the marital relationship between spouses ii. Affirmative conduct iii. Affections between spouses are in fact alienated iv. Causation of the alienation

3. Assault (Civil) (p. 465)	i. Act
	ii. Intent either
	  a. to cause a harmful or offensive contact, or
	  b. to cause an apprehension of a harmful or offensive contact
	iii. Apprehension of an imminent harmful or offensive contact to the plaintiff's own person
	iv. Causation of the apprehension

4. Battery (Civil) (p. 453)	i. Act ii. Intent to cause harmful or offensive contact iii. Harmful or offensive contact with the plaintiff's person iv. Causation of the harmful or offensive contact
5. Civil Rights Violation (p. 610)	i. A person acting under color of state law ii. Deprives a citizen of federal constitutional or federal statutory rights
6. Conversion (p. 535)	i. Personal property (chattel) ii. Plaintiff is in possession of the chattel or is entitled to immediate possession iii. Intent to exercise dominion or control over the chattel. iv. Serious interference with plaintiff's possession v. Causation of the serious interference
7. Criminal Conversation (p. 486)	Defendant has sexual relations with the plaintiff's spouse (adultery)

Defamation (two torts)
(p. 429)

8. Libel	i. Written defamatory statement by the defendant ii. Of and concerning the plaintiff iii. Publication of the statement iv. Damages: a. In some states, special damages never have to be proven in a libel case

Figure 1.1   cont'd.

The Cause of Action	Its Elements
	b. In other states, only libel on its face does not require special damages. In these states, libel per quod requires special damages v. Causation

9. Slander	i. Oral defamatory statement by the defendant
	ii. Of and concerning the plaintiff
	iii. Publication of the statement
	iv. Damages:
	  a. Special damages are not required if the slander is slander per se
	  b. Special damages must be proven if the slander is not slander per se
	v. Causation

10. Disparagement (p. 545)	i. False statement of fact ii. Disparaging the plaintiff's business or property iii. Publication of the statement iv. Intent v. Special damages vi. Causation

11. Enticement of a Child or Abduction of a Child (p. 487)	i. Intent to interfere with a parent's custody over his or her child
	ii. Affirmative conduct by the defendant:
	  a. to abduct or force the child from the parent's custody, or
	  b. to entice or encourage the child to leave the parent, or
	  c. to harbor the child and encourage him or her to stay away from the parent's custody
	iii. The child leaves the custody of the parent
	iv. The defendant caused the child to leave or to stay away

12. Enticement of Spouse (p. 487)	i. Intent to diminish the marital relationship between the spouses
	ii. Affirmative conduct by the defendant:
	  a. to entice or encourage the spouse to leave the plaintiff's home, or
	  b. to harbor the spouse and encourage him or her to stay away from the plaintiff's home
	iii. The spouse leaves the plaintiff's home
	iv. Causation

13. False Imprisonment (p. 402)	i. An act that completely confines the plaintiff within fixed boundaries set by the defendant ii. Intent to confine plaintiff or a third person iii. Causation of the confinement iv. Plaintiff was either conscious of the confinement or was harmed by it

Figure 1.1   cont'd

The Cause of Action	Its Elements
14. Intentional Infliction of Emotional Distress (p. 386)	i. An act of extreme or outrageous conduct ii. Intent to cause severe emotional distress iii. Severe emotional distress is suffered iv. Causation of this distress
15. Interference with Contract Relations (p. 549)	i. An existing contract ii. Interference with the contract by defendant iii. Intent iv. Damages v. Causation
16. Interference with Prospective Advantage (p. 554)	i. Reasonable expectation of an economic advantage ii. Interference with this expectation iii. Intent iv. Damages v. Causation

Invasion of Privacy (four torts)

17. Appropriation (p. 447)	i. The use of the plaintiff's name, likeness, or personality ii. For the benefit of the defendant
18. False Light (p. 448)	i. Publicity ii. Placing the plaintiff in a false light iii. Highly offensive to a reasonable person
19. Intrusion (p. 446)	i. An act of intrusion into someone's private affairs or concerns ii. Highly offensive to a reasonable person
20. Public Disclosure of a Private Fact (p. 447)	i. Publicity ii. Concerning the private life of the plaintiff iii. Highly offensive to a reasonable person
21. Malicious Prosecution (p. 418)	i. Initiation or procurement of the initiation of criminal proceedings ii. Without probable cause iii. With malice iv. The criminal proceedings terminate in favor of the accused
22. Misrepresentation (p. 474)	i. a. Statement of fact, or b. Statement of opinion, if a fiduciary relationship exists between the parties ii. The statement is false iii. Scienter (intent to mislead) iv. Justifiable reliance v. Actual damages

Figure 1.1   cont'd

The Cause of Action	Its Elements
23. Negligence (p. 196)	i. Duty ii. Breach of duty iii. Proximate cause iv. Damages
Nuisance (two torts) (p. 509)	
24. Private Nuisance	An unreasonable interference with the use and enjoyment of private land
25. Public Nuisance	An unreasonable interference with a right that is common to the public
26. Prima Facie Tort (p. 555)	i. Infliction of harm ii. Intent to do harm (malice) iii. Special damages iv. Causation
27. Seduction (p. 487)	The defendant has sexual relations with the plaintiff's daughter, with or without consent
28. Strict Liability for Harm Caused by Animals (p. 509)	Domestic Animals: i. The owner had reason to know the animal has a specific propensity to cause harm ii. Harm is caused by the animal due to that specific propensity Wild Animals: i. Keeping a wild animal ii. Causes harm
29. Strict Liability for Abnormally Dangerous Conditions or Activities (p. 499)	i. The existence of an abnormally dangerous condition or activity ii. Knowledge of the condition or activity iii. Damages iv. Causation
30. Strict Liability in Tort (p. 362)	i. Seller ii. A defective product that is unreasonably dangerous to person or property iii. User or consumer iv. Physical harm v. Causation
31. Trespass to Chattels (p. 535)	i. Personal property (chattel) ii. Plaintiff is in possession of the chattel or is entitled to immediate possession iii. Intent to dispossess or to intermeddle with the chattel iv. Dispossession or intermeddling v. Causation of element (iv)

Figure 1.1   cont'd

The Cause of Action	Its Elements
32. Trespass to Land (p. 496)	i. An act ii. Intrusion on land iii. In possession of another iv. Intent to intrude v. Causation of the intrusion

Warranty (three causes of action)

The Cause of Action	Its Elements
33. Breach of Express Warranty (p. 350)	i. A statement of fact that is false ii. Made with the intent or expectation that the statement will reach the plaintiff iii. Reliance on the statement by the plaintiff iv. Damage v. Causation
34. Breach of Implied Warranty of Fitness for a Particular Purpose (p. 360)	i. Sale of goods ii. Seller has reason to know the buyer's particular purpose in buying the goods iii. Seller has reason to know the buyer is relying on the seller's skill or judgment in buying the goods iv. The goods are not fit for the particular purpose v. Damage vi. Causation
35. Breach of Implied Warranty of Merchantability (p. 359)	i. Sale of goods ii. By a merchant of goods of that kind iii. The goods are not merchantable iv. Damage v. Causation

Negligence

Negligence is a category unto itself. It covers harm due to actions or inactions that were unreasonable under the circumstances.

Strict Liability

The general meaning of **strict liability** is liability without fault. If the defendant engages in a certain kind of conduct that causes harm, liability will result irrespective of intent, negligence, or innocence. An example would be performing an abnormally dangerous activity such as blasting. If the plaintiff is injured because of the explosion of the defendant's dynamite, the latter will be responsible (i.e., **liable**), regardless of whether the defendant desired to injure the plaintiff (intent), and regardless of whether the defendant acted unreasonably in setting off the explosives (negligence). As we shall see, however, it is sometimes difficult to distinguish strict liability from negligence, especially in the area of products liability.

Terminology must be used with considerable caution. The most dangerous definitions are the ones that give the appearance of universality. The meaning of a word or phrase may change when the context changes. As courts struggle to do justice, they sometimes stretch the definitions of words and phrases to accommodate the result they want to reach on the facts before them. Hence in the practice of law, great care is needed to *localize* your definitions by determining what a particular court in your state meant by a word or phrase. Many of the assignments in this book will ask you to translate some general principles of tort law into specific applications, or modifications, of those principles by your state.

■ THE RELATIONSHIP BETWEEN TORT LAW AND OTHER AREAS OF THE LAW

The study of tort law will involve us in many other areas of the law:

Contract Law

When you buy a toaster, you have entered a contract of purchase. If the appliance explodes in your face when you try it for the first time, you may have an action for a breach of contract *and* an action for a tort. Most of the law of products liability grows out of such situations. Furthermore, as we shall see, it can be a tort to induce someone to breach a contract.

Criminal Law

When Ted punches Bob in the face, two wrongs have probably been committed. Bob has been *personally* injured. He can bring a tort action against Ted for civil battery. In addition, *the state* has been injured. The public peace has been violated. The state prosecutor can bring a criminal action against Ted for a crime that might be called "assault and battery." The tort action and the criminal action are separate proceedings. We need to examine the relationship between torts and crimes. For example, is it a tort to encourage the prosecutor to bring a criminal action that turns out to be groundless? We will answer this question when we study the tort called malicious prosecution.

Civil Procedure Law

When a tort has been committed, one of the major options of the injured party is to sue. Bringing a lawsuit requires an understanding of civil procedure law governing jurisdiction, pleading, discovery, trial, appeal, collection, etc.

Evidence Law

The law of evidence is as important as the law of civil procedure in understanding how attorneys use tort law in court. Initially, *facts* are uncovered through the skills of interviewing and investigation. Interviewers and investigators must have an appreciation of the difficulties that might exist in establishing these facts as evidence in a court of law.

Family Law

Family members can commit torts against each other, but they may not always be allowed to sue for such torts. We will examine what tort suits can and cannot be brought under the topic of intrafamily tort immunity.

Conflicts of Law

Each state has its own tort law. Suppose a person brings a tort suit in one state on the basis of a wrong that was committed in another state. What tort law applies, the law of state where the tort was committed or that of the state where the suit is brought? Suppose that the wrong or the tort was committed in more than one state. Which state tort law applies? These are conflicts-of-law questions.

Constitutional Law

Here the central question shall be: if a particular tort action is allowed, will constitutional rights be violated? Does traditional tort law conflict with the United States Constitution? One of the difficult problems faced by courts today is when to allow a libel action to be brought against a newspaper or other media entity. Such a case involves the interrelationship between tort law and the freedom-of-the-press clause in the First Amendment.

Estate Law

What happens when the wrongdoer dies before being sued by the injured party? Can the wrongdoer's estate be sued? Suppose the injured party dies before suing the wrongdoer. Can the estate of the injured party sue the wrongdoer? If so, what happens to the assets collected in the suit? We will examine these questions under the topic of survival and wrongful death.

State and Local Government Law

Can a city or state be sued in tort? Can a tort action be brought against the United States government? Answers to such questions involve the doctrine of sovereign immunity.

Business Law

We need to explore the torts that can be committed by or against businesses. Except for automobile accident cases, most defendants in tort cases are businesses.

Real Property Law

There are a number of torts that are committed by or against landowners and land occupiers. Such torts sometimes raise questions like these: What is land? What is the possession of land?

Insurance Law

Insurance law has a major impact on tort litigation, particularly on the question of whether the parties will settle their dispute. Also, in many states, insurance companies can be sued for "bad faith" in how they handle claims made against them.

Environmental Law

Environmental rules and regulations can have an important impact on certain negligence and nuisance cases.

▪ THE SKILLS ASSIGNMENTS IN THIS BOOK

Working in a law office with a litigation practice requires a number of important skills in addition to knowing the basic tort principles. For example:

1. Legal Analysis: applying rules of law to facts
2. Legal Interviewing: obtaining facts from clients of the office
3. Investigation: obtaining further facts and verifying the facts that you have
4. Drafting: preparing drafts of tort complaints, interrogatories, etc.
5. Digesting: compiling case summaries from litigation files
6. Legal Research: identifying the tort law of your state
7. Monitoring: becoming familiar with proposed legislation relevant to an area of practice

We will examine these skills in greater detail in the following chapters. Most of the assignments in the book will ask you to demonstrate these skills.

SUMMARY

There are three main kinds of tort litigation: routine personal injury, high-stakes personal injury, and mass latent injury. A tort is a civil wrong that has caused harm to person or property for which the courts will provide a remedy. To state a tort cause of action is to allege enough facts to support every element of the tort. When this is done, the plaintiff has stated a prima facie case. Torts fall into three categories. First, intentional torts cover cases in which the defendant either desired the result or knew with substantial certainty that the result would follow from what he or she did or failed to do. Second, negligence covers cases in which harm was caused because of actions or inactions that were unreasonable under the circumstances. Third, strict liability covers torts without regard to whether the defendant was at fault. Tort litigation often involves other areas of law, such as insurance, contracts, civil procedure, evidence, real property, and criminal law. Hence, we cannot study tort law in isolation.

Key Terms

deep pocket
tort
tortfeasor
cause of action

elements
prima facie case
intentional torts

negligence
strict liability
liable

CHAPTER 2

Sources of Tort Law and Litigation

CHAPTER OUTLINE

- INTRODUCTION
- PRIMARY AUTHORITY
- SECONDARY AUTHORITY
- RIDING THE CARTWHEEL: A BASIC TECHNIQUE FOR USING ALL LAW BOOKS
- THE IMPORTANCE OF DIGESTS IN TORT LAW
- GENERAL INSTRUCTIONS FOR TORTS RESEARCH ASSIGNMENTS

■ INTRODUCTION

Where does tort law come from? What are its sources? Who writes the rules for establishing tort liability through litigation? Where are these rules found? These are our concerns in this chapter.

As we study the meaning of primary and secondary authority, we will also focus on the kinds of law books and materials that contain this authority. While many of these themes will be covered in a legal research course, it is helpful to reinforce them in the context of personal injury litigation.

Our final goal will be to present the general instructions for the assignments in this book that will allow you to use the law library to find the tort law of your state. Throughout the remaining chapters of the book, we will be referring back to these general instructions.

■ PRIMARY AUTHORITY

Primary authority is any law that a court could rely on in reaching a decision. Examples include opinions, statutes, constitutions, administrative regulations, ad-

Figure 2.1   Categories of Primary Authority Involved in a Personal Injury Practice

Category	Definition	Example
(a) Opinion	A court's written explanation of how it applied the law to the facts before it to resolve a legal dispute. Also called a case.	The case of *Smith v. Jones* rules that Jones negligently injured Smith in an automobile collision.
(b) Statute	A law passed by the legislature declaring commanding, or prohibiting something.	Davis is injured in one of the elevators at Macy's Department Store. In the suit, Davis alleges that Macy's violated § 236 of the State Code, which requires a monthly safety inspection of all elevators.
(c) Constitution	The fundamental law that creates the branches of government and identifies basic rights and obligations.	A story in *Time* magazine links Harris with the illegal drug trade. Harris sues for libel. *Time* argues that the suit violates the First Amendment right to freedom of the press.
(d) Administrative Regulation	A law of an administrative agency designed to explain or carry out the statutes and executive orders that govern the agency.	Simpson suffers food poisoning after eating a product of General Foods Inc. The suit alleges that General Foods failed to follow § 137.3, a regulation of the Food and Drug Administration on proper food labeling.
(e) Administrative Decision	An administrative agency's resolution of a specific controversy involving the application of the agency's regulations or its government statutes and executives orders.	In *Perry v. Commissioner,* the State Worker's Compensation Board rules that Perry is not entitled to benefits because his injury did not arise out of his employment.
(f) Charter	The fundamental law of a municipality or other local unit of government, authorizing it to perform designated governmental functions.	Adams can sue Portland for the injury caused by a city police officer because § 26 of the Portland charter waives sovereign immunity for injuries wrongfully caused by municipal employees in the course of employment.

Figure 2.1 con't

(g) Ordinance	A law passed by the local legislative branch of government (e.g., city council, county commission).	Kelly sues Parker for trespass when Parker's cows damage Kelly's land. Parker argues that Kelly did not have the kind of fencing around his land required by § 22(g) of the County Ordinance on farm animal control.
(h) Rules of Court	The procedural laws that govern the mechanics of litigation before a particular court. Also called court rules.	Richardson sues his doctor for negligence. Under Superior Court Rule 38, all medical malpractice cases must be first heard by a magistrate, who must prepare a pretrial order before the case can commence in Superior Court.

ministrative decisions, charters, ordinances, and rules of court. See Figure 2.1 for the definitions of these categories of primary authority and examples of how they can be involved in personal injury litigation.

Opinions

Court opinions are the foundation of tort law. In fact, the major way in which tort law comes into existence is through what is called **common law.** This is judge-made law created in the absence of statutes or other controlling law.[1] In effect, the courts create tort law when there is a vacuum. If, for example, the court has a dispute before it that is not governed by any statute or constitutional provision, the court can create law to govern that dispute. What it creates is

---

[1]There are four interrelated meanings of the term *common law,* the last of which will be our primary concern in this book.

At the broadest level, common law simply means case law as opposed to statutory law. In this sense, all case law develops and is part of the common law.

The term common law also refers to the legal system of England, America, and countries adopting or based on this legal system. Its counterpart is the civil law system of many Western European countries other than England, e.g., France. The origins of civil law include the jurisprudence of the Roman Empire set forth in the Code of Justinian. (Louisiana is unique in that its state law is in large measure based on the civil law—the ***Code Napoléon***—unlike that of the remaining forty-nine common law states.) While there is overlap between the two systems, there is generally a greater reliance on case law in common law systems than in civil law systems. The latter tend to place a greater emphasis on code or statutory law than common law systems.

More narrowly, common law refers to all of the case law *and* statutory law in England and the American colonies before the American Revolution. The phrase **at common law** will often refer to this colonial period.

The most prevalent definition of common law is judge-made law in the absence of statutes or other controlling law.

called the common law. In doing so, the court will rely primarily on the unwritten customs and values of the community from time immemorial.

Court opinions are printed in volumes called **reporters.** For example, in Figure 2.2 you will find the first page of the opinion called *Austria v. Bike Athletic Co.,* printed in volume 810 of the Pacific Reporter, 2d Series. This is a products liability case in which a high school student sued a helmet manufacturer after

Figure 2.2   Excerpt from a Court Opinion on a Torts Issue: *Austria v. Bike Athletic Co.,* 810 P.2d 1312, 107 Or. App. 57 (1991)

1312 Or.   810 PACIFIC REPORTER, 2d SERIES

107 Or.App. 57

John AUSTRIA, as guardian ad litem for Richard Austria, a minor, and John Austria and Perla Austria, husband and wife, Respondents,

v.

BIKE ATHLETIC CO., a foreign corporation, Colgate-Palmolive Co., a foreign corporation, and Kendall Research Center, a foreign entity, Appellants,

and

Renato Pizarro, M.D., Defendant.

A8707–044789; CA A63376.

Court of Appeals of Oregon.

Argued and Submitted Nov. 21, 1990.

Decided May 1, 1991.

Parents of football player severely injured by blow to head during football practice brought suit against designer and manufacturer of football helmet, alleging defective design. The Circuit Court, Multnomah County, Richard L. Unis, J., entered judgment for plaintiffs, and defendants appealed. The Court of Appeals, Deits, J., held that there was evidence from which jury could conclude that player's injuries were caused by defects in football helmet.

Affirmed.

1. Products Liability ⬅ 60

In order to prove that football player's injuries were caused by defects in football helmet, it was not necessary to prove amount of force received by player as result of blow, amount of force that he would have received had he been wearing helmet of alternative design or amount of force required to cause type of head injury he suffered.

2. Products Liability ⬅ 83

Evidence, when combined with inferences drawn therefrom, was sufficient to allow jury to conclude that defective helmet caused football player's head injury; there

was evidence about how and why player was struck, what a football helmet is supposed to do to reduce consequences of collision, that hematoma resulted from precisely the kind of trauma that helmets are designed to prevent, that properly designed helmet would have greatly reduced likelihood of hematoma and that helmet was not adequately designed to reduce that likelihood.

3. Products Liability ⬅ 88

There was sufficient proof to submit to jury allegation that football helmet was improperly designed or manufactured so that it would allow energy of blow to be transmitted to head of user without absorbing sufficient amounts of energy so as to prevent closed head injuries.

James N. Westwood, Portland, argued the cause for appellants.

W. Eugene Hallman, Pendleton, argued the cause for respondents.

Before RICHARDSON, P.J., and NEWMAN and DEITs, JJ.

DEITS, Judge.

Richard Austria was severely injured by a blow to the head during football practice. This guardian ad litem, he sued the designer and manufacturer of the football helmet that he was wearing, alleging that its defective design was the cause of his injury. The jury returned a verdict for plaintiffs and defendants appeal, arguing, primarily, that the trial court erred in denying their motions for directed verdict, because there was insufficient evidence of causation. We affirm.

In September, 1985, Richard Austria was a sixteen year old high school junior. He was injured during football practice when the knee of another player forcefully struck the front of his helmet. Although he was dazed by the collision, he walked off the field on his own and seemed to suffer few ill effects. Approximately two weeks later, however, he experienced severe headaches. On October 1, he collapsed during football practice. A CT scan indicated that Richard had a subdural hematoma. . . .

being severely injured in the head during football practice. Hundreds of thousands of tort opinions such as this can be found in the many sets of reporter volumes in the law library.

Statutes

The statutes passed by legislatures affect tort litigation in two significant ways:

Statutes Can Change the Common Law

Generally, statutes are superior in authority to court opinions. If the legislature desires to change the common law that has been developed by the courts, it can pass a statute making this change. Such a law is called a statute in **derogation of the common law.**

Statutes Sometimes Define the Standard of Care

When a defendant is sued for negligence, one of the claims that is often made by the plaintiff is that the defendant violated a statute, e.g., a traffic statute or a license statute. In such cases, the court must examine the relationship between the common law of negligence and the statute that has allegedly been violated. As we will see later, the specific question is whether the statute will be used by the court to define the standard of care to which the defendant will be held.

Statutes are printed in volumes called **statutory codes** or **annotated statutes.** For example, in Figure 2.3 you will find the beginning of § 2-621 in *Illinois Annotated Statutes.* This section of the statute provides some of the requirements

Figure 2.3   Excerpt from a Page in a Statutory Code on a Torts Issue: *Illinois Annotated Statutes,* chapter 110, section 2-621 (Smith-Hurd 1983)

110 ¶ 2–621
Code Civ.Proc. § 2–621

CODE OF CIVIL PROCEDURE

2–621. Product liability actions

§2–621. Product liability actions. (a) In any product liability action based in whole or in part on the doctrine of strict liability in tort commenced or maintained against a defendant or defendants other than the manufacturer, that party shall upon answering or otherwise pleading file an affidavit certifying the correct identity of the manufacturer of the product allegedly causing injury, death or damage. The commencement of a product liability action based in whole or in part on the doctrine of strict liability in tort against such defendant or defendants shall toll the applicable statute of limitation and statute of repose relative to the defendant or defendants for purposes of asserting a strict liability in tort cause of action.

(b) Once the plaintiff has filed a complaint against the manufacturer or manufacturers, and the manufacturer or manufacturers have or are required to have answered or otherwise pleaded, the court shall order the dismissal of a strict liability in tort claim against the certifying defendant or defendants, provided the certifying defendant or defendants are not within the categories set forth in subsection (c) of this Section. Due diligence shall be exercised by the certifying defendant or defendants in providing the plaintiff with the correct identity of the manufacturer or manufacturers, and due diligence shall be exercised by the plaintiff in filing an action and obtaining jurisdiction over the manufacturer or manufacturers. . . .

for bringing products liability litigation against manufacturers and other defendants.

Constitutions

Most state constitutions establish the state court system and define the kinds of cases that each court can hear. For your state, you must know what court(s) can take personal injury cases, i.e., what court(s) have **subject matter jurisdiction** over tort actions. This is one way in which constitutional law affects tort law. Another major impact of the constitution is felt when there is a conflict between the common law of torts and a particular provision in the constitution. For example, a newspaper may libel a citizen according to the traditional common law definition of libel. The problem of using this definition, however, is that the result may violate the constitutional freedom of the press. By resolving such conflicts, the constitution has a profound effect on the development of tort law.

Constitutions are usually printed within the same sets of books that contain statutes. For example, the Illinois constitution is printed in *Illinois Annotated Statutes,* and the United States Constitution is printed in *United States Code Annotated.*

Administrative Regulations

In a number of areas, administrative agencies and their regulations have a large role in personal injury litigation. At the state level, the best example is the worker's compensation agency or board that covers occupational accidents. At the federal level, the Consumer Product Safety Commission is a major player, as we will see when we examine products liability.

Administrative regulations are printed in volumes often called **administrative codes** or **codes of regulations.** For example, in Figure 2.4 you will find § 1118.1

Figure 2.4   Excerpt from an Administrative Regulation on a Torts Issue: 16 Code of Federal Regulations § 1118.1 (1993)

Consumer Product Safety Commission

PART 1118—INVESTIGATIONS, INSPECTIONS AND INQUIRIES UNDER THE CONSUMER PRODUCT SAFETY ACT
Subpart A—Procedures for Investigations, Inspections, and Inquiries
Sec.
1118.1 Definitions, initiation of investigations, inspections, and inquiries delegations.
1118.2 Conduct and scope of inspections.
1118.3 Compulsory processes and service.
1118.4 Subpoenas.
1118.5 Investigational hearings.
1118.6 Depositions.
1118.7 Rights of witnesses at investigatonal hearings and of deponents at depositions.
1118.8 General or special orders seeking information.
1118.9 Motions to limit or quash subpoenas and general or special orders and delegation to modify terms for compliance.
1118.10 Remedies for failure to permit authorized investigation.

1118.11 Nonexclusive delegation of power.
Subpart A—Procedures for Investigations, Inspections, and Inquiries
§1118.1 Definitions, initiation of investigations, inspections, and inquiries and delegations.
(a) *Definitions.* For the purpose of these rules, the following definitions apply:
(1) *Act* means the Consumer Product Safety Act (15 U.S.C. 2051, et seq.).
(2) *Commission* means the Consumer Product Safety Commission.
(3) *Firm* means a manufacturer, private labeler, distributor, or retailer of a consumer product, except as otherwise provided by section 16(b) of the Act.
(4) *Investigation* is an undertaking by the Commission to obtain information for implementing enforcing, or determining compliance with the Consumer Product Safety Act and the regulations, rules, and orders issued under the Act.

in *Code of Federal Regulations.* This section covers investigations conducted by the Consumer Product Safety Commission on products alleged to be unsafe, such as athletic equipment used in school sports.

Administrative Decisions

If an administrative agency has jurisdiction over a case, an injured party may be required to resort to it before going to court. This is known as **exhausting administrative remedies.** You pursue all available methods of resolving a dispute within the administrative agency before asking a court to take action. For example, a court will not want to determine whether an injured worker is entitled to worker's compensation until the appropriate agency or board has rendered its administrative decision on the case. If the worker tries to go into court before such a decision has been rendered, the court will dismiss the case for failure to exhaust administrative remedies.

Administrative decisions are not as easy to find in the law library as the other categories of primary authority listed in Figure 2.1. Check with the law librarian to determine whether the agency has its own set of volumes containing the decisions, or whether other publishers print them, in full or in summary format.

Charters and Ordinances

At the local level of government, charters are the equivalent of constitutions at the state and federal levels. The same is true of ordinances passed by a local legislature—they are the equivalent of state and federal statutes. If an injured party wants to sue the government for its role in causing an injury, the suit might be blocked by the defense of **sovereign immunity.** Simply stated, this defense means that no one can sue the sovereign—the government—unless the sovereign consents to be sued. This consent is known as a waiver of sovereign immunity. If your suit is against a city or county government, your research must include the city or county's charter and ordinances, to determine whether it has waived sovereign immunity for the kind of suit you want to bring. (In addition, check statutes to determine if the legislature has waived this immunity.) Ordinances are also extremely important in automobile accidents in which traffic laws may have been violated. Charters and ordinances are often printed in their own special sets of books, called **municipal codes.**

Rules of Court

Rules of court (also called court rules) govern the procedural steps of litigation. In many states, such rules are found both in the statutes of the legislature and in the rules of court of a particular court. Separate sets of rules usually exist for trial courts, for probate courts, for criminal courts, for appellate courts, etc. The rules govern matters such as how attorneys can make an appearance for a party in a court, the duties of the court clerk, the mechanics of filing motions, etc.

▪ SECONDARY AUTHORITY

Secondary authority is any nonlaw that a court could rely on to reach its decision. Examples include legal encyclopedias, legal treatises, and legal periodical literature. There are two main values of secondary authorities. First, they often contain extensive footnotes that will lead you to court opinions and other primary authorities on the tort (or other) topic you are examining. Second, they are usually written in a clear, basic writing style. Since they often cover the fundamentals, they are excellent starting points for the novice who needs a quick overview or summary of the law. This background can be very valuable in understanding the sometimes more difficult-to-read primary authority.

Assume that you are working on a products liability case and that you want to find relevant discussions of the law in secondary authority. Here are some examples of law books you might use:

Legal Encyclopedia

A **legal encyclopedia** is a multivolume set of books that alphabetically summarizes almost every legal topic. Two of the major legal encyclopedias are *Corpus Juris Secundum,* published by West (see Figure 2.5 for a sample page), and *American Jurisprudence 2d,* published by Lawyers Co-op (see Figure 2.6 for a sample page).

Legal Treatise

A **legal treatise** is a book written by a private individual (or by a public official writing as a private citizen) that provides a summary or commentary on a legal

---

Figure 2.5   **Excerpt from a Page in a Volume of Corpus Juris Secundum on a Torts Issue:** 72 Corpus Juris Secundum Supplement § 66 (1975)

72 C.J.S.Supp.

Assuming facts favorable to plaintiff suing a cigarette manufacturer for cancer or death resulting from cancer because of cigarette smoking, recovery might be grounded on negligence,[67] fraud for misrepresentation,[68] implied warranty,[69] or strict liability in tort.[70] While a manufacturer of cigarettes is strictly liable for foreseeable harm resulting from a defective condition in the product when the consumer uses the product for the purposes for which it was manufactured and marketed,[71] there is no absolute liability for the harmful effects of which no developed skill or foresight can avoid.[72] Thus the manufacturer of cigarettes cannot be held absolutely liable for cancer, or a consumer's death from cancer, allegedly caused by smoking cigarettes,[73] where plaintiff's claim negatives scientific foreseeability, peculiar defects in cigarettes, and cancer consequences to a substantial segment of the public.[74]

§66. Toys, Games, and Athletic or Recreational Equipment

The concept of products liability applies to a manufacturer of toys, games, and athletic or recreational equipment.

PRODUCTS LIABILITY §§65–66

Library References

Products Liability ⬖ 60.

The concept of products liability applies to a manufacturer of toys, games, and athletic or recreational equipment.[75] Thus, the manufacturer may be liable under the doctrine of strict liability in tort for injury caused by a defective condition unreasonably dangerous to the user or consumer of such products.[76] Liability may also be grounded on negligence.[77] The manufacturer is not an insurer of safety of the equipment[78] and does not guarantee that it will not wear out and will last forever.[79] The manufacturer should anticipate the reasonably foreseeable risks in the use of the product.[80]

The manufacturer of toys, games, and athletic or recreational equipment, is under a duty to test and inspect the products for safety before marketing them,[81] but a wholesaler or retailer has been held not to have a duty to inspect products packaged by, and received from, a reputable manufacturer.[82] While a manufacturer has a

67. U.S.—Lartigue v. R. J. Reynolds Tobacco Co., C.A.La., 317 F.2d 19, certiorari denied 84 S.Ct. 137, 375 U.S. 865, 11 L.Ed.2d 32.
68. U.S.—Lartigue v. R. J. Reynolds Tobacco Co., C.A.La., 317 F.2d 19, certiorari denied 84 S.Ct. 137, 375 U.S. 865, 11 L.Ed.2d 92.
69. U.S.—Lartigue v. R. J. Reynolds Tobacco Co., C.A.La., 317 F.2d 19, certiorari denied 84 S.Ct. 137, 375 U.S. 865, 11 L.Ed.2d 92.
70. U.S.—Lartigue v. R. J. Reynolds Tobacco Co., C.A.La., 317 F.2d 19, certiorari denied 84 S.Ct. 137, 375 U.S. 865, 11 L.Ed.2d 92.

71. U.S.—Lartigue v. R. J. Reynolds Tobacco Co., C.A.La., 317 F.2d 18, certiorari denied 84 S.Ct. 137, 375 U.S. 865, 11 L.Ed.2d 92.
72. U.S.—Lartigue v. R. J. Reynolds Tobacco Co., C.A.La., 317 F.2d 19, certiorari denied 84 S.Ct. 137, 375 U.S. 865, 11 L.Ed.2d 92.
73. U.S.—Hudson v. R. J. Reynolds Tobacco Co., C.A.La., 427 F.2d 541—Green v. American Tobacco Co., C.A.Fla., 409 F.2d 1166, certiorari denied 90 S.Ct. 912, 397 U.S. 911, 25 L.Ed.2d 93—Lartigue v. R. J. Reynolds Tobacco Co., C.A.La., 317 F.2d 19, certiorari denied 84 S.Ct. 137, 375 U.S. 865, 11 L.Ed.2d 92.
74. U.S.—Hudson v. R. J. Reynolds Tobacco

Co., C.A.La., 427 F.2d 541.
75. Ind.—Dudley Sports Co. v. Schmitt, 279 N.E.2d 266, 151 Ind.App. 217.
Golf cart
Purchaser of allegedly defective golf carts could maintain action against manufacturer to recover for loss of his bargain and cost of making repairs, even though parts were purchased from a dealer and not directly from the manufacturer.
Mich.—Cova v. Harley Davidson Motor Co., 812 N.W.2d 800, 26 Mich.App. 602.
76. Baseball sunglasses
U.S.—Filler v. Rayex Corp., C.A.Ind., 435 F.2d 336.

Figure 2.6   Excerpt from a Page in a Volume of American Jurisprudence 2d on a Torts Issue: 63 American Jurisprudence Second § 4 (1984)

63 Am Jur 2d   PRODUCTS LIABILITY

"Express warranty," as defined by the model act, means any positive statement, affirmation of fact, promise, description, sample, or model relating to the product.[53]

§4. The nature of a products liability case.

Although "products liability" is currently regarded as a more or less distinct area of law, it should be kept in mind that a products liability case shares the basic characteristics of many other lawsuits which, although presenting fact patterns totally unrelated to product-caused injury, fall within an analogous classification. Thus, if the foundation of a products liability case is negligence, there must be proof on all of the elements of actionable negligence common to any such action.[54] If the foundation is breach of warranty, there must be some elements of any action grounded on a breach of contract;[55] accordingly, there must be an adequate showing of the existence of the warranty, its breach, and the injured party's right to recover for the breach, particularly in the light of the Uniform Commercial Code or other governing statutes.[56] Similarly, if the foundation of the action is strict liability in tort, there must be an adequate showing of the injured party's right to recover under all the requirements of that doctrine,[57] and the same problems of proof of the right to recover exist where the action is grounded upon allegations of fraud and deceit, misrepresentation, nuisance, or wilful or intentional wrong.[58]

53. Model Uniform Product Liability Act §102(K); 44 Fed Reg p. 62718.
54. For discussion of liability predicated on negligence, see §§284 et seq.
55. Breach of warranty actions involving personal injury or loss also have some elements of an action in tort.
56. As to liability predicated on breach of warranty, see §§450 et seq.
57. As to liability predicated on nuisance, attractive nuisance, and willful or intentional wrong, see §§585–587.
As to liability based on negligent misrepresentation, see §§583, 584.

As to liability predicated on strict liability, see §§528 et seq.
58. As to liability based on fraud and deceit, see §§570–577.
As to liability based on negligent misrepresentations, see §§ 583, 584.
59. Averbach, Handling Accident Cases, vol 3B §§2, 4 (discussing the effect of technology and the complexity of modern products).
60. §§528 et seq.
61. For discussion of privity of contract, see §§588 et seq.
62. Cova v. Harley Davidson Motor Co. 26 Mich App 602, 182 NW2d 800, 8 UCCRS 1258

topic. Perhaps the most famous and widely used legal treatise is *Prosser and Keeton on Torts* (see Figure 2.7 for a sample page).

Another extremely important legal treatise is *Restatement of Torts 2d,* published by a private organization of scholars, the American Law Institute. Many courts are greatly influenced by the *Restatement,* particularly when these courts are dealing with questions or issues that are relatively new for their states. Prod-

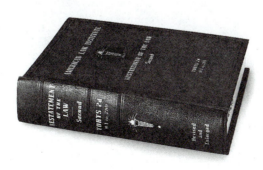

Figure 2.7   Excerpt from a Page of a Legal Treatise on a Torts Issue:
Prosser & Keeton on Torts § 95 (5th ed. 1984)

Chapter 17
PRODUCTS LIABILITY

Table of Sections

Sec.
95. Theories of Recovery and Types of Losses.
95A. Warranty and Intangible Economic Losses.
96. Negligence and Liability for Physical harm to Persons and Tangible Things.
97. Strict Liability in Warranty for Physical Harm to Persons and Tangible Things.
98. Strict Liability in Tort for Physical Harm to Persons and Tangible Things.
99. Meaning of Dangerously Defective or Unsafe Products.
100. Parties.
101. Summary—Interests Protected and Theories of Recovery.
102. Contributory Negligence, Misuse, and Other Intervening Misconduct.
103. Proof.
104. Other Suppliers.
104A. Real Estate Transactions.

§95. Theories of Recovery and Types of Losses

Products liability is the name currently given to the area of the law involving the liability of those who supply goods or products for the use of others to purchasers, users, and bystanders for losses of various kinds resulting from so-called defects in those products.

At the very outset, it is important to make a distinction between two types of product conditions that can result in some kind of loss either to the purchaser or a third person. One is a dangerous condition of the product or, if one prefers, a product hazard;[1] the other is the inferior condition or . . .

1. A recent government estimate placed the number of consumer product injuries (both in and out of the home) at 36 million for 1977. See Prod.Saf. & Liab.Rep. (BNA), June 29, 1979, 511. The total cost of such injuries to the nation has been estimated at $20 billion or more per year. Owen, Punitive Damages in Products Liability Litigation, 1976, 74 Mich.L.Rev. 1258–59 n. 2.

677

ucts liability litigation is a major example of this; a large number of courts have agreed with and have adopted positions of the *Restatement* on strict liability in tort.

Legal Periodical Literature

A **legal periodical** is an ongoing publication (e.g., published six times a year) containing articles, case notes, and other information on legal topics. When published by law schools, legal periodicals are often called **law reviews** or **law journals**, e.g., *Harvard Law Review, Yale Law Journal*. Three of the main indexes to legal periodical literature are the *Current Law Index,* the *Legal Resource Index,* and the *Index to Legal Periodicals.* See Figure 2.8 for a sample page from the *Index to Legal Periodicals.*

Annotations

An **annotation** is a set of notes and commentary on issues in court opinions. The major annotations are published by Lawyers Co-op in books called *American*

Figure 2.8   Excerpt from a Page from the Index to Legal Periodicals that Provides Citations to Legal Periodical Literature on a Torts Issue

---

SUBJECT AND AUTHOR INDEX   199

Prodan, Pamela
The legal framework for Hydro-Quebec imports, 28 *Tulsa L.J.* 435–75 Spr '93
Products liability
See also
Strict liability
Tobacco industry
Apportionment of damages—Third Circuit predicts Pennsylvania courts would not allow jury to apportion liability in a cigarette smoking, asbestos exposure case—Borman v. Raymark Industries, Inc., 960 F.2d 327 (1992). R. K. Shuter, student author. 66 *Temp.L.Rev.* 223–38 Spr '93
Cipollone v. Liggett Group, Inc. [112 S.Ct. 2608 (1992)]: one step closer to exterminating the FIFRA presumption controversy. C. E. Boeh, student author. 81 *Ky.L.J.* 749–78 Spr '92/'93
Constitutional law—pre-emption—the Federal Cigarette Labeling and Advertising Act's express pre-emption provision defines the pre-emptive reach of the Act and must be construed narrowly. Cipollone v. Liggett Group, Inc., 112 S.Ct. 2608 (1992). M. A. Bakris, student author. 70 *U.Det.Mercy L.Rev.* 487–512 Wint '93
Dangerous products and injured bystanders. R. F. Cochran, Jr. 81 *Ky.L.J.* 687–725 Spr '92/'93

Drugs
California
Kill or cure? Pogash. 13 *Cal.Law.* 48–51+ Je /'93
Motor vehicles
The tide has turned. L. E. Cohen. 29 *Trial* 75–9 Ja '93
Alaska
Products liability in Alaska—a practitioner's overview. T. A. Matthews. 10 *Alaska L.Rev.* 1–32 Je '93
California
Don't kill the messenger 'till you read the message: products liability verdicts in six California counties, 1970–1990. S. Daniels, J. Martin. 16 *Just.Sys.J.* 69–95 '93
European Community countries
The asbestos problem and the European Economic Community. E. R. Bothwell, student author. 31 *Column. J. Transnat'l L.* 205–30 '93
Michigan
Uniform Commercial Code—Article 2—the economic loss doctrine bars an action in tort and a buyer's sole remedy is found under Article 2, where a product purchased for commercial purposes causes economic loss. Neibarger v. Universal Cooperatives, Inc., 486 N.W.2d 612 (Mich.1992). C. W. Fabian, student author. 70 *U.Det.Mercy L.Rev.* 513–29 Wint '93

Law Reports. These books print the annotations and the court opinions that contain the issues treated in the annotations. The main units of *American Law Reports* are *ALR, ALR2D, ALR3D, ALR4TH, ALR5TH,* and *ALR Fed.* Annotations provide excellent leads to case law on thousands of issues. For an example, see Figure 2.9.

▪ RIDING THE CARTWHEEL: A BASIC TECHNIQUE FOR USING ALL LAW BOOKS

A major reason law books are sometimes difficult to use is that the indexes to the books are confusing and incomplete. The **CARTWHEEL** is a technique of overcoming some of this difficulty. It has the following objective: to develop the habit of phrasing every word involved in the client's problem *fifteen to twenty different ways!* When you go to the index of a law book, you naturally begin looking up the words you think should lead you to the relevant material in the book. If you do not find anything on point, two conclusions are possible:

· There is nothing on point in the law book.
· You looked up the wrong words in the index.

Figure 2.9   Excerpt from a Page Containing an Annotation on a Torts Issue: Lee R. Russ, *Products Liability: Competitive Sports Equipment,* 76 *American Law Reports,* 4th Series 201 (1990)

Products Liability—Sports   76 ALR4th
76 ALR4th 201

ANNOTATION

PRODUCTS LIABILITY: COMPETITIVE SPORTS EQUIPMENT

by

Lee R. Russ, J. D.

§7. Football helmets—liability of manufacturers and sellers
[a] Failure to protect against spinal injury—liability supportable
In the following products liability cases involving claims that a football helmet was defective in failing to protect its wearer against injuries to the spine, the courts held that, under the particular circumstances presented, there was sufficient evidence of liability to support a judgment in favor of the plaintiff or to reverse a judgment in favor of the manufacturer of the helmet at issue.
Finding several evidentiary rulings to have been erroneous, the court in

Galindo v. Riddell, Inc. (1982, 3d Dist) 107 Ill App 3d 139, 62 Ill Dec. 849, 437 NE2d 376, CCH Prod Liab Rep ¶ 9374, reversed a judgment for the maker of a "TK-2" football helmet who was sued by a high school football player for spinal injuries sustained while attempting to make a tackle in a varsity football game. The helmet consisted of a plastic shell on the outside, with a grey rubber pad and cloth strap suspension system on the inside. The plaintiff was paralyzed from the neck down as a result of a dislocation fracture at the fifth and sixth cervical vertebrae. The plaintiff sued on theories of strict liability. . . .

Figure 2.10   The CARTWHEEL

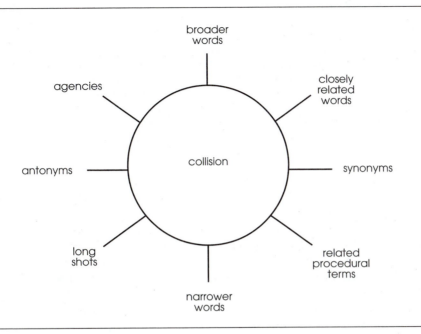

Too often we make the mistake of thinking that the first conclusion is accurate. Nine times out of ten, the second conclusion is more accurate. The solution is to be able to phrase a word in as many different ways and in as many different contexts as possible. Hence, the CARTWHEEL.

Suppose that the problem of the client involved, among other things, a collision. The structure for one of the CARTWHEELs in this case is presented in Figure 2.10.

The first step is to look up the word "collision" in the index of any law book you are checking. Assume you are not successful with this word, either because the word is not in the index, or because the pages or section references after the word in the index do not lead you to relevant material in the body of the book. The next step is to think of as many *different* phrasings and contexts of the word "collision" as possible. Here is where the steps of the CARTWHEEL can be useful:

The CARTWHEEL: Using the Index of Law Books

1. Identify all the *major words* (e.g., collision) from the facts of the client's problem (most of these facts can be obtained from the intake memorandum written following the initial interview with the client.) Place each word or small set of words in the center of the CARTWHEEL.
2. In the index, look up all of these major words.
3. Identify the *broader* categories of the major words.
4. In the index, look up all of these broader categories.
5. Identify the *narrower* categories of the major words.

6. In the index, look up all of these narrower categories.
7. Identify all of the *synonyms* of the major words.
8. In the index, look up all of these synonyms.
9. Identify all of the *antonyms* of the major words.
10. In the index, look up all of these antonyms.
11. Identify all words that are *closely related* to the major words.
12. In the index, look up all of these closely related words.
13. Identify all *procedural* terms related to the major words.
14. In the index, look up all of these procedural terms.
15. Identify all *agencies,* if any, that might have some connection to the major words.
16. In the index, look up all of these agencies.
17. Identify all *long shots.*
18. In the index, look up all of these long shots.

There may be some overlapping of the categories; they are not mutually exclusive. Also, it is *not* significant whether you place a word in one category or another as long as the word comes to your mind as you comb through the index. The CARTWHEEL is, in effect, a *word association game,* which should become second nature to you with practice. Perhaps you might think that some of the word selections in the categories of the CARTWHEEL are a bit farfetched. The problem, however, is that you simply will not know for sure whether a word will be fruitful until you try it. To be imaginative, you must be prepared to take some risks.

If we were to apply the 18 steps of the CARTWHEEL to the word "collision," here are some of the words and phrases that you would check in the index of *every* law book that deals with tort law:

Broader words: Accident, occurrence, event, mishap, contact, bump, hit, encounter, casualty, etc.

Narrower words: Pileup, smashup, train collision, car collision, bus collision, plane collision, bike collision, boat collision, minor collision, major collision, etc.

Synonyms: Impact, crash, dash against, etc.

Antonyms: Safety, care, accident-free, etc.

Closely related words: Motor vehicle, car, negligence, unexpected, intentional, unintentional, injury, fall, lane, speeding, speed limit, traffic, transportation, smash, brittle, damage, destroy, ruin, dent, driving, license, curve, contingency, fortuitous, foreseeable, unforeseeable, weather, noise, strike, shock, cause, unusual, change, money, hospital, careless, road, bleeding, conscious, unconscious, attention, tourniquet, death, insurance, tort, doctor, emergency, malpractice etc.

Procedural terms: Suit, civil action, action, damages, trial, litigation, statute of limitations, defense, discovery, evidence, petition, jurisdiction, court, liability, etc.

Agencies: Police Department, Motor Vehicle Department, Weather Bureau, Highway Department, etc.

Long shots: Criminal law, violence, battery, etc.

Some of the above words may be *subheadings* of other words. For example, you may find nothing directly under the heading of "accident" when you are checking the "a" section of the index. Yet, "accident" could be a subheading of "motor vehicle" in the "m" section. Words and phrases, therefore, must be checked as headings, as subheadings, and sometimes as sub-subheadings.

Again, do not be afraid to check something that does not appear to be directly relevant to the problem you are researching. You may be surprised by what you will "bump" into!

▪ ASSIGNMENT 2.1 ▪

Prepare a CARTWHEEL for the following:

a. duty
b. settlement
c. fraud
d. trespass
e. lawn mower

▪ THE IMPORTANCE OF DIGESTS IN TORT LAW

So much of tort law is common law found in court opinions. It is extremely important, therefore, that you become familiar with digests as soon as possible. **Digests** are volumes of small-paragraph summaries of court opinions. They serve as a massive index system to these court opinions. West Publishing Company is the major publisher of digests. The summaries of the opinions are organized under key topics and numbers such as the following, which are subtopics of the topic of negligence:

⇾**10. Unintended consequences.**   ⇾**74. Danger incurred to save life.**   ⇾**82. Contributory negligence as proximate cause of injury.**

You can use any of the digests of West Publishing Company to try to locate opinions that are summarized under such key topics (or subtopics) and numbers.

The following assignments deal only with digests. Later we will review other techniques of locating case law in addition to using the digests.

▪ ASSIGNMENT 2.2 ▪

There are two (and possibly three) digests that cover the court opinions of your state: the *American Digest System* (covering every court in the country), a regional digest (covering a cluster of states in the same region of the country), and an individual digest that covers only your state. This assignment asks you to identify these digests.

a. Does your library have a complete set of the *American Digest System?*
b. What is the name of the regional reporter that gives the complete text of court opinions for your state? Ask your librarian if West Publishing Company publishes a regional digest that covers opinions in your regional reporter. If so, does your library subscribe to that regional digest?
c. Is there a West digest that covers opinions for your state only? If so, what is its name, and does your library subscribe to it?
d. Ask your librarian if there is any other digest that covers the opinions of your state court, whether or not it is published by West Publishing Company.

▪ ASSIGNMENT 2.3 ▪

In this assignment you will trace a key topic and number in all of the West digests that you identified in Assignment 2.2. Proceed as follows:

a. Go to the Descriptive Word Index (DWI) of your state digest *or* of any West digest that you identified in Assignment 2.2. Turn to the portion of the Index covering the topic of Negligence. Select any two key topics and numbers. What are they? (The Index references in the DWI are to key topics or subtopics, and to numbers rather than to pages or sections.)

b. Go to the digest that covers only your state. Go to the parts of the digest where cases are summarized under the two key topics and numbers you selected. Give the citation to the first case digested under these key topics and numbers. If there are no cases there, write ''none'' in your answer.

c. Go to the pocket part of the volume(s) you used to answer question b. Look up your two key topics and numbers in the pocket part. Give the citation to the first case, if any, digested under these key topics and numbers in the pocket part.

d. Go to the regional digest, if any, that covers your state. Go to the parts of the digest where cases are summarized under the same two key topics and numbers. Give the citation of the first case, if any, *written by a court in your state* that is digested under these key topics and numbers.

e. Do the same for the pocket parts of the digest volumes you used for question d.

f. Go to the *American Digest System.* We will trace these same two key topics and numbers through several of the Decennials and General Digest volumes of the *American Digest System.* For each of the units referred to below, find the first case, if any, *written by a court in your state* under both key topics and numbers you selected in the first question above. Do this:
   1. for the Fourth Decennial
   2. for the Fifth Decennial
   3. for the Sixth Decennial
   4. for the Seventh Decennial
   5. for the Eighth Decennial
   6. for the Ninth Decennial (part 1)
   7. for the Ninth Decennial (part 2)
   8. for the Tenth Decennial (part 1)
   9. for the Tenth Decennial (part 2)
   10. for any three General Digest volumes.

▪ GENERAL INSTRUCTIONS FOR TORTS RESEARCH ASSIGNMENTS

Throughout the chapters of this book, you will find a number of assignments that require you to use the law library. The general instructions for these assignments are on the following pages. You will be referred back to these instructions as the assignments are given in the chapters.

The general instructions can also serve as useful checklists in doing any research.

General Instructions for the State Court Opinion Assignment

1. The starting point in this assignment is a set of facts. You are asked to find court opinion(s) from your state on this set of facts. It is unlikely that you will find an opinion **on all fours,** i.e., an opinion with exactly the same facts (or overwhelmingly the same facts) as the set of facts in the assignment. Find opinions as close as possible to the set of facts in the assignment.

2. Applying case law is essentially a process of fact comparison. How close are the facts of the opinion to the facts of the assignment? How different from them? The more similar the facts are, the more likely it is that the opinion will apply.

3. Digests are useful starting points for finding court opinions. In the Descriptive Word Index of West digests, try to find key topics and numbers that cover your facts.

4. When examining digests and every set of books mentioned below, use the CARTWHEEL as an aid in getting into the indexes of the books.

5. Shepardize every opinion that you find that is on point or that is in the ball park. Shepardizing may lead to other opinions that could be used. To **shepardize** something means to use the volumes of *Shepard's Citations* to check the history and validity of what you are shepardizing, and in the process, to obtain leads to other relevant material.

6. Check annotations in *ALR, ALR2D, ALR3D, ALR4TH,* or *ALR5th* on the same subject matter as the problem you are researching in the set of facts. These annotations might lead you to relevant case law of your state.

7. Go to *Corpus Juris Secundum* and *American Jurisprudence 2d.* Use the indexes to find the area of law covering your facts. See if any of the footnotes in these national encyclopedias lead you to relevant case law of your state. (Some states have their own state encyclopedia. If your state has one, check it for leads.)

8. Go to *Words and Phrases,* the multivolume legal dictionary. Look up words from your set of facts to see if there are any definitions in this dictionary written by courts from your state.

9. Go to the *Index to Legal Periodicals,* the *Legal Resource Index,* or the *Current Law Index* to try to find legal periodical literature that might cover your set of facts. In the footnotes of such literature, you might find a reference to relevant case law of your state.

10. Determine whether a state statute might be involved in the set of facts you are given in the assignment. To find this out, check the state code. If a state statute is applicable, check the summaries of case law interpreting that statute immediately after the statute in the code. These summaries are often called Notes to Decisions. This route may lead you to relevant case law.

General Instructions for the Federal Court Opinion Assignment

1. In this assignment you will be asked to locate federal court opinions interpreting federal statutes such as the Consumer Product Safety Act or the Federal Tort Claims Act. The following instructions are techniques for finding federal court opinions.

2. Concentrate on locating federal opinions relevant to your state:
   • opinions written by a U.S. District Court sitting in your state
   • opinions written by a U.S. Court of Appeals (or Circuit Court) with jurisdiction over your state.
   If you cannot find federal cases from these two courts, search for cases from *any* federal court.

3. Use the CARTWHEEL as an aid in getting into the law books mentioned below.

4. The starting point should be the federal statute itself. Go to that statute in the *U.S.C.A.* (*United States Code Annotated*) or the *U.S.C.S.* (United States Code Service). Beneath the text of this statute in *U.S.C.A.* and *U.S.C.S.*, check the summaries of court opinions, if any, that have interpreted the statute.

5. Check the pocket parts of *U.S.C.A.* and *U.S.C.S.* for later opinions, if any, interpreting the statutes. Check supplemental pamphlets of *U.S.C.A.* and *U.S.C.S.*, for later opinions, if any, interpreting the statute.

6. Digests can also be used as case finders. Check the following digests: *American Digest System, Federal Practice Digest 3d*, and *Federal Practice Digest 4th*. These digests may help you locate the federal case law you need.

7. Shepardize the federal statute in order to locate cases interpreting the statute.

8. Once you find one opinion on point, or potentially on point, shepardize that opinion in order to try to find more opinions.

9. Check annotations in *ALR, ALR2D, ALR3D,* and especially in *ALR Fed.* These annotations may lead you to case law.

10. Go to *Corpus Juris Secundum* and *American Jurisprudence 2d.* Use the indexes to find the area of law covered by your facts. See if any of the footnotes in these national encyclopedias lead you to federal case law.

11. Are there any loose-leaf services that cover the topic of the statute you are examining? If so, they may lead you to case law.

12. Go to *Words and Phrases,* the multivolume legal dictionary. Look up words from your statute to see if there are any definitions in this dictionary written by federal courts.

13. Go to the *Index to Legal Periodicals,* the *Legal Resource Index,* or *Current Law Index* to try to find legal periodical literature on the subject matter of the federal statute. In the footnotes of such literature you will often find references to federal case law.

As pointed out earlier, there are a number of times when statutes (state and federal) are relevant to personal injury litigation. The following two sets of instructions should help you locate such statutes.

General Instructions for the State Code Assignment

1. The first step is to make sure that you know the name of the statutory code for your state. Some states have more than one code—each from a different publisher.

2. Be sure that you are using the latest edition of the state code.

3. Use the CARTWHEEL technique to help you use the various indexes in the code. (There is often a general index at the end of the code as well as smaller indexes after each volume or set of volumes covering the same topic area.)

4. When you need help in understanding a statute, use the following four approaches:

   a. See if there are definition statutes that define some of the words in the statute you are examining (such definition statutes usually precede the statute you are examining at the beginning of the cluster of statutes on the same topic).

   b. Examine cases that have interpreted the statute. You can get leads to these cases by checking the Notes to Decisions, which are summaries of cases. These Notes are found immediately after the text of the statute in many codes. You can also find cases interpreting the statute by shepardizing the statute.

   c. Trace the legislative history of the statute.

   d. Find out if there is any legal periodical literature on the statute. Leads to such literature may be found as references in the code itself. Also check the *Index to Legal Periodicals,* the *Current Law Index,* and the *Legal Resource Index.*

5. Statutes can be changed or repealed, and new statutes can be added. Be sure that you are aware of such modifications by:

   a. checking the pocket part, if any, of every volume you use

   b. checking replacement volumes, if any

   c. checking supplement volumes or pamphlets, if any

   d. shepardizing the statute

6. Give a complete citation to every statute you mention. The citation must include:

   a. the title or chapter number of the statute

   b. the abbreviated name of the code

   c. the section number of the statute

   d. the subsection number, if any

   e. the date of the code (use the year you find on the spine of the volume, or the year you find on the title page, or the latest copyright year—in this order of preference).

7. When you quote from a statute, always use quotation marks around the language you are quoting.

8. If you are asked to interpret or apply any statutory language to the facts of a hypothetical problem, review the material on legal analysis in Chapter 3.

9. If you cannot find what you are looking for in the statutory code, proceed as follows:

   a. Repeat step 3 above. Frequently, the difficulty is the failure to use the indexes creatively. Do the CARTWHEEL exercise again to try to come up with more words and phrases to be checked in the indexes of the statutory code.

   b. Check the rules of court of your state courts to determine whether they treat the topic you are pursuing.

   c. Check the constitution of your state to determine whether it treats the topic you are pursuing.

General Instructions for the Federal Code Assignment

1. There are three main sets of federal statutes: the *United States Code (U.S.C.), the United States Code Annotated (U.S.C.A.), and the United States Code Service (U.S.C.S.).* Your starting point in this assignment should be to locate any one of these sets.

2. Be sure that you are using the latest edition of the code.

3. Use the CARTWHEEL technique to help you use the various indexes in the code. There is often a general index at the end of the entire code as well as smaller indexes after each volume or set of volumes covering the same topic area.

4. Many of the federal statutes you will be examining have popular names, such as the Federal Tort Claims Act. Each of the three sets of federal statutes has a Tables volume that contains a Popular Name Table. Use this Table as one of the ways of locating the text of such statutes.

5. When you need help in understanding a statute, use the following four approaches:

   a. See if there are definition statutes that define some of the words in the statute you are examining (such definition statutes usually precede the statute you are examining at the beginning of the cluster of statutes on the same topic).

   b. Examine cases that have interpreted the statute. You can get leads to these cases by checking the Notes to Decisions, which are summaries of cases. These Notes are found immediately after the text of the statute in the *U.S.C.A.* and the *U.S.C.S.* You can also find cases interpreting the statute by shepardizing the statute.

   c. Trace the legislative history of the statute.

   d. Find out if there is any legal periodical literature on the statute. Leads to such literature may be found as references in the code itself. Also check the *Index to Legal Periodicals,* the *Current Law Index,* and the *Legal Resource Index.*

6. Statutes can be changed or repealed, and new statutes can be added. Be sure that you are aware of such modifications by:

   a. checking the pocket part, if any, of every volume you use

   b. checking replacement volumes, if any

   c. checking supplement volumes or pamphlets, if any

   d. shepardizing the statute

7. Give a complete citation to every statute you mention. The citation must include:

   a. the title number of the statute

   b. the abbreviated name of the code

   c. the section number of the statute

   d. the subsection number, if any

   e. the date of the code edition you are using

8. When you quote from a statute, always use quotation marks around the language you are quoting.

9. If you are asked to interpret or apply any statutory language to the facts of a hypothetical problem, review the material on legal analysis in Chapter 3.

10. If you cannot find what you are looking for in the statutory code, proceed as follows:

   a. Repeat step 3 above. Frequently, the difficulty is the failure to use the indexes creatively. Do the CARTWHEEL exercise again to try to come up with more words and phrases to be checked in the indexes of the statutory code.

   b. Check federal rules of court to determine whether they treat the topic you are pursuing.

   c. Check the federal constitution to determine whether it treats the topic you are pursuing.

General Instructions for the Annotated Bibliography Assignment

Objectives: • to reinforce the need to check a variety of sources in the library on any given topic

• to provide you with a checklist of sources on any legal topic for your state

1. You will be given a topic on which to compile the annotated bibliography.
2. In this assignment, "annotated" simply means that you provide some description of everything you list in the bibliography—not a long analysis, just a sentence or two explaining why you included it.
3. Hand in an outline that will cover what you find on the topic in the sets of books mentioned in the following instructions.
4. Statutes. Go to your state code. Make a list of the statutes on the topic. If there are none, say so in your answer. For each statute, give its citation and a brief quotation showing that it deals with the topic.
5. Constitutions. Go to your state constitution (usually found within your state code). Make a list of the constitutional provisions on the topic. If there are none, say so in the answer. For each provision, give its citation and a brief quotation showing that it deals with the topic.
6. Cases. If you found statutes or constitutional provisions on the topic, check to see if there are any cases summarized after these statutes or provisions as Notes to Decisions. Select several cases that deal with the topic. Also, use the digests to try to find other cases that deal with the topic. Select several. If you find no cases, say so in the answer. For each case you find, give its citation and a brief quotation from the opinion showing that it deals with the topic.
7. Key topics and numbers. In instruction #6, you went to the digests. Make a list of the key topics and numbers that you found most productive.
8. Rules of court. Go to the rules of court that cover courts in your state. Make a list of several rules, if any, that deal with the topic. For each rule, give its citation and a brief quotation showing that it deals with the topic.
9. Ordinances. Go to the ordinances that cover your city or county. Make a list of several ordinances, if any, that deal with the topic. For each ordinance, give its citation and a brief quotation showing that it deals with the topic.
10. Administrative regulations. Are there any agencies that have jurisdiction over any aspect of the topic at the federal, state, or local level? If so, list the agencies. If your library has the regulations of the agencies, make a list of several regulations, if any, that deal with the topic. For each regulation, give its citation and a brief quotation showing that it deals with the topic.
11. *ALR, ALR2D, ALR3D, ALR4th, ALR5th, ALR Fed.* Go to these six sets of books. Try to find one annotation in each set that deals with your topic. Give the citation of the annotation in each set. Flip through the pages of each annotation to try to find the citation of one case from your state court or from a federal court with jurisdiction over your state. Give the citation of the case.
12. Legal Periodical Literature. Use the *Index to Legal Periodicals,* or the *Current Legal Index,* or the *Legal Resource Index* to locate three articles that deal with the topic. Give the citation of the articles. Put a check mark next to the citation if your library has the legal periodical in which the article is printed.
13. Legal treatises. Go to your card (or computer) catalog. Find any two legal treatises that cover your topic. Give the citations of the treatises. Sometimes you may not find entire books on the topic. The topic may be only one of the many subjects in the treatise. If the catalog does not give you this information, you may have to examine the treatise itself on the library shelves.
14. Loose-leaf texts. Are there any loose-leaf services on this topic? Check the catalog and ask the librarian. For each loose-leaf, give its citation and explain how it covers the topic.

15. Words and Phrases. Go to this multivolume legal dictionary. Locate definitions from court cases, if any, of the major words and phrases involved in your topic. Limit yourself to definitions from court opinions, if any, of your state.
16. Shepardize every case, statute, or constitutional provision you find. State whether *Shepard's Citations* has any data indicating that the case, statute, or constitutional provision may no longer be valid.
17. Other material. If you come across other material not covered in the above instructions, include it in the bibliography as well.
18. There is no prescribed format for the bibliography. One possible outline you can use is as follows:
    Topic: _____
    a. Statutes (instruction 4)
    b. Constitutions (instruction 5)
    c. Cases (instruction 6)
    d. Key topics and numbers (instruction 7)
    e. Rules of court (instruction 8)
    f. Ordinances (instruction 9)
    g. Administrative regulations (instruction 10)
    h. *ALR, ALR2d, ALR3d, ALR4th, ALR5th, ALR Fed.* annotations (instruction 11)
    i. Legal periodical literature (instruction 12)
    j. Legal treatises (instruction 13)
    k. Loose-leaf texts (instruction 14)
    l. *Words and Phrases* (instruction 15)
    m. Other material (instruction 17)

Occasionally, you will be asked to **monitor a bill** currently before the legislature that has relevance to the torts practice of the firm where you work, e.g., a proposed comparative negligence statute, a revised no-fault insurance statute. To monitor the bill means to find out its current status in the legislature and to keep track of all the forces that are trying to enact, defeat, or modify the bill.

Monitoring Proposed Torts Legislation

1. Begin with the legislature. Find out what committee in each house of the legislature (often called the Senate and House) is considering the proposed legislation. Also determine whether there is more than one committee considering the entire bill or portions of it in each house.
2. Ask committee staff members to send you copies of the bill in its originally proposed form and in its amended form(s).
3. Determine whether the committees considering the proposed legislation have written any reports on it and, if so, whether copies are available.
4. Determine whether any hearings have been scheduled by the committees on the bill. If so, try to attend. For hearings already conducted, see if they have been transcribed (a word-for-word account or recording of what was said).
5. Find out the names of people in the legislature who are working on the bill, e.g., legislators "pushing" the bill, legislators opposed to it, staff members of the individual legislators working on the bill, staff members of the committees working on the bill.

6. The local bar association may have taken a position on the bill. Call the association. Find out what committee of the bar is involved with the subject matter of the bill. This committee may have written a report on the position of the bar on the bill. If so, try to obtain a copy.

7. Is there an administrative agency of the government involved with the bill? Do any of these agencies have jurisdiction over the subject matter of the bill? If so, find out who in the agency is working on the bill and whether any written reports of the agency are available.

8. Who else is lobbying for or against the bill? (Check local newspaper stories, if any, about the bill.) What organizations are interested in it? Find out if they have taken any written positions.

9. What precipitated consideration of the bill by the legislature? Was there a court opinion that prompted the legislative action? If so, find out what the opinion said.

10. Are any other legislatures in the country contemplating similar legislation? There are several ways of finding out:

    a. Look for legal periodical literature on the subject matter of the bill (check the *Index to Legal Periodicals,* the *Current Law Index,* and the *Legal Resource Index*).

    b. Check loose-leaf texts covering the subject matter of the bill—these texts often cover proposed legislation in the various legislatures.

    c. Contact organizations such as bar associations, public interest groups, business associations, etc. to find out if they have assigned staff members to conduct this kind of state-by-state research on what the legislatures are doing—such organizations may be willing to share this research with you.

    d. Find out if there is a Council of State Governments in your area—it may have done the same research mentioned above.

The following two charts outline the steps that need to be taken to trace the **legislative history** of state statutes and of federal statutes relevant to tort law. Unfortunately, it is very difficult to obtain the documents of legislative history of state statutes, either because they are poorly organized or because they simply do not exist. The situation is otherwise for federal statutes such as the Federal Tort Claims Act.

Tracing the Legislative History of State Statutes Relevant to Tort Law

1. To trace the legislative history of a state statute means to find out what steps were taken and what documents were filed prior to the enactment of the statute in the state legislature (see Instruction 12 below). The theory is that when you find out what the individual legislators said and what the legislative committees said while they were considering the bill, you will obtain clues on what they were trying to do, what they were trying to accomplish, what their legislative intent was in passing the statute. Such clues may be found in committee reports, if any, transcripts of floor debates, if any, etc.

2. Review the steps for monitoring proposed torts legislation. These steps (particularly steps 1–4) can be helpful in uncovering the documents of legislative history after the statute has been enacted.

3. Contact the committees of both houses of the legislature that passed the statute. Ask staff members for leads to the documents of legislative history.
4. Is there a state law library in your area? If so, ask librarians there for leads to legislative history.
5. Does the legislature have its own law library? If so, check it for leads.
6. Does the legislature have a separate drafting office? If so, check it for leads.
7. Is there a law revision commission in your state? If so, check it for leads.
8. The annotated code (in which the statute is now located) may contain leads to the statute's legislative history. For example, after the text of the statute, you will usually find the date the statute was enacted, a summary of amendments to the statute since its date of enactment, etc.
9. Try to find the original (uncodified) version of the statute when it was first enacted. This version may be called a Statute at Large or a Session Law. The statute in this version might give you some leads.
10. Cases interpreting the statute sometimes discuss the legislative history of the statute. To find cases that have interpreted the statute, look at the Notes to Decisions after the text of the statute in annotated state codes. Also, shepardize the statute.
11. Legal periodical literature on the statute might give leads to legislative history. See *Index to Legal Periodicals,* the *Current Law Index,* and the *Legal Resource Index.*
12. Your legislative history should contain the following information:
    a. the current citation of the statute and its date of enactment
    b. a list of every change in the statute, with dates the changes were enacted
    c. names and dates of committee reports
    d. names and dates of hearing transcripts
    e. cations to the transcripts of floor debates
    f. other materials relevant to the passage of the legislation

---

Tracing the Legislative History of Federal Statutes Relevant to Tort Law

1. To trace the legislative history of a federal statute means to find out what steps were taken and what documents were filed prior to the enactment of the statute in Congress (see Instruction 11 below.) The theory is that when you find out what the individual legislators said and what the legislative committees said while they were considering the bill, you will obtain clues on what they were trying to do, what they were trying to accomplish, what their legislative intent was in passing the statute. Such clues may be found in committee reports, if any, transcripts of floor debates, if any, etc.
2. Review the steps for monitoring proposed torts legislation. These steps (particularly steps 1–4) can be helpful in uncovering the documents of legislative history after the statute has been enacted.
3. Contact the committees in both the House and Senate that passed the statute. Ask staff members for leads to the documents of legislative history.
4. Is there a public law library in your area (e.g., in a courthouse)? If so, ask librarians there for leads to legislative history.
5. Congress has its own law library within the Library of Congress. You might obtain leads by calling this library. There is a special section of the library that collects legislative histories.

6. The three sets of codes containing all the statutes of Congress *(U.S.C., U.S.C.A., U.S.C.S.)* give leads to a statute's legislative history. For example, after the text of the statute, there will usually be the date the statute was enacted, a summary of the amendments to the statute since its date of enactment, etc.

7. Examine the text of the statute in its uncodified form in United States Statutes at Large for possible leads.

8. Cases interpreting the statute sometimes discuss the legislative history of the statute. To find cases that have interpreted the statute, look at the case summaries immediately following the text of the statute in *U.S.C.A.* and in *U.S.C.S.* Also, shepardize the statute.

9. Legal periodical literature on the statute might give leads to legislative history. Check the *Index to Legal Periodicals,* the *Current Law Index,* and the *Legal Resource Index.*

10. In addition, the following sets of books are major sources of information on the legislative history of federal statutes:
   a. *U.S. Code Congressional and Administrative News* (use Table 4)
   b. *CCH Congressional Index*
   c. *Congressional Record—History of Bills and Resolutions*
   d. *Congressional Information Service*
   e. *Digest of Public General Bills and Resolutions*
   f. *Congressional Quarterly*
   g. *Congressional Monitor*

11. Your legislative history should contain the following information:
   a. the current citation of the statute with its date of enactment
   b. a list of every change in the statute, with dates the changes were enacted
   c. names and dates of committee reports
   d. names and dates of hearing transcripts
   e. citations to the transcripts of floor debates
   f. other materials relevant to the passage of the legislation

---

SUMMARY

Primary authority is any law that a court could rely on in reaching a decision. The major categories of primary authority are opinions, statutes, constitutions, administrative regulations, administrative decisions, charters, ordinances, and rules of court. If tort law is created by the courts, it is part of common law; if it is created or modified by the legislature, it is part of statutory law. Statutes sometimes change the common law. They might also set the standard of care in negligence cases. Constitutions often determine what courts have subject matter jurisdiction over tort cases. Constitutions may also set limits on bringing certain kinds of tort cases, such as defamation actions against the media. Administrative regulations and decisions have a large role in certain kinds of personal injury cases, such as worker's compensation. Charters and ordinances are critical in cases in which the local government is being sued. Rules of court govern the procedural steps of personal injury litigation.

Secondary authority is any nonlaw that a court could rely on to reach its decision. Examples include legal encyclopedias, legal treatises, and legal periodicals. Secondary authority can be useful to help find and understand primary authority. When searching for primary or secondary authority, the indexes to the books containing this authority can sometimes be difficult to use. The CARTWHEEL can be of assistance in using these indexes by helping you to think of a large variety of words to look up in them. Digests are volumes of small-paragraph summaries of court opinions. Digests are important because the common law is such a large part of tort law.

Key Terms

primary authority
opinion
statute
constitution
administrative
    regulation
administrative
    decision
charter
ordinance
rules of court
common law
Code Napoléon
at common law
reporters

derogation of the
    common law
statutory codes
annotated statutes
subject matter
    jurisdiction
administrative codes
codes of regulations
exhausting
    administrative
    remedies
sovereign immunity
municipal code

secondary authority
legal encyclopedia
legal treatise
legal periodical
law review
law journal
annotation
CARTWHEEL
digests
on all fours
shepardize
monitor a bill
legislative history

CHAPTER 3

Legal Analysis in Tort Law

- STRUCTURE OF LEGAL ANALYSIS
- ISSUE
- RULE

- ANALYSIS AND COUNTERANALYSIS
- CONCLUSION

■ STRUCTURE OF LEGAL ANALYSIS

The foundation of all the other skills in the delivery of legal services is the skill of **legal analysis.** There is no better way to *mis*prepare oneself to work in a law office than by memorizing a lot of law or by learning to go through the steps of a task by rote. The danger is somewhat similar to signing a contract without understanding the fine print. The fact that it is frequently done makes it no less dangerous.

Simply stated, *legal analysis is the application of rules to facts in order to solve a legal problem or to prevent one from arising.* Legal analysis tells you which law governs an actual or potential problem. In the area of torts, legal analysis tells you whether the defendant is legally responsible (i.e., **liable**) for torts such as battery, negligence, trespass to land, etc.

More specifically, legal analysis will help you achieve the objectives listed in Guideline #1.

Legal analysis always has four components:

1. a question—often called an issue
2. a rule
3. the analysis and the counteranalysis
4. the conclusion

37

Legal Analysis Guideline #1

Legal analysis is the application of rules to facts. There are five objectives in legal analysis:

1. To help you identify what further facts are needed through investigation and additional legal interviewing
2. To state the most reasonable argument on how a rule applies to the facts in a way that will be most helpful to the client on whose behalf you are working (advocacy)
3. To anticipate and state the most reasonable argument on how this same rule applies to the facts in a way that will be most helpful to the opponent of the client (counteranalysis)
4. To state your own position on which side has the better argument on how this rule applies to the facts
5. To make an educated guess on what decision a particular court would make if it had to decide the applicability of this rule to the facts

As a device to remember these components, a new term has been invented: **IRAC.** IRAC stands for issue (I), rule (R), analysis of the rule in light of the facts, (A), and conclusion (C). They are all often found in a written document called a **legal memorandum,** which is an in-house presentation of your legal analysis to a colleague or supervisor. Often the organization of the **memo** consists of four parts corresponding to the four components listed above. Some of the examinations you will take in school will follow the same organizational format, although your examination answer may not be as formally structured as a memo. Even less formal will be the legal reasoning that you will do in your own head, yet the same analytical structure is needed.

Legal Analysis Guideline #2

Legal analysis must have four components:

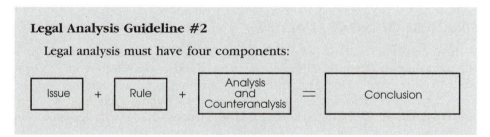

▪ ISSUE

A legal **issue** (also called a **question of law**) is a question about how one or more rules apply to facts. Issues are often stated very broadly:

- Who will win?
- Was Tom negligent?
- What causes of action might be available to Helen?
- What defenses to the trespass action can we raise?
- What result?

This question, given to you by your supervisor or teacher, must guide your entire analysis.

Yet you can and must *narrow* the question as much as possible. At the very least, make sure the question deals with only one cause of action or one defense. (By this standard, only the second question above is in the ballpark.) Break a broad question down into several questions so that each contains no more than one cause of action or one defense. Hence, the question, "Who will win?" becomes:

- Was the seller negligent? and
- Is the seller strictly liable in tort? and
- Did the seller commit deceit?

And the question, "What defenses to the trespass action can we raise?" becomes:

- Did the plaintiff consent to the entry on the land? and
- Did the defendant have the privilege of necessity?

Legal Analysis Guideline #3

If the question or issue you are given is stated broadly, break it down into more narrow questions so that each question covers only one cause of action (i.e., one tort) or one defense.

As we shall see later, there are times when you will need an even narrower statement of the issue.

▪ RULE

The second component of legal analysis is the **rule** to be applied to the facts. Of course, the statement of the question already contains a reference to a rule. Negligence, for example, is a rule, or more accurately, the definition of negligence is a rule. This book deals primarily with the thirty-five torts and related causes of action outlined in Figure 1.1 of Chapter 1, plus their major defenses. These are the rules that you will be studying in this course. In addition, there are a large number of procedural rules that govern the conduct of litigation, e.g., the jurisdiction of a court, the scope of pre-trial discovery.

As we saw in Figure 2.1 of Chapter 2, there are eight major categories of rules that can be involved in a personal injury practice:

- opinions (containing the common law)
- statutes
- constitutions
- administrative regulations
- administrative decisions
- charters
- ordinances
- rules of court

The first two predominate in this area of practice. Law firms interpret and apply the rules to the facts of client cases in order to reach conclusions that are the basis of legal advice (see Figure 3.1).

Figure 3.1   Legal Analysis in Torts

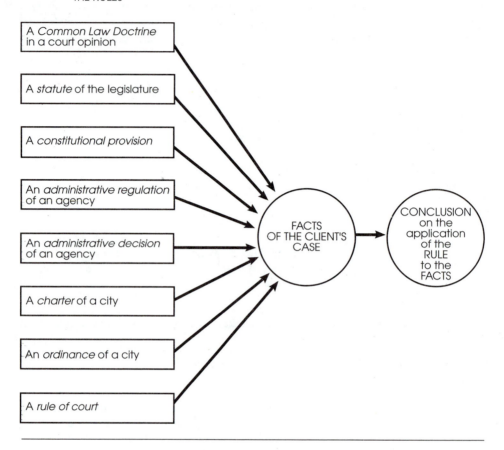

▪ ANALYSIS AND COUNTERANALYSIS

We now come to the heart of the process: the analysis itself. We will examine this subject through the following topics:

1. preliminary assessment
2. legal analysis and legal research
3. legal analysis, investigation, and interviewing
4. breaking a rule down into its elements
5. definitions of the elements
6. connecting facts with elements of the rule
7. legal analysis and further research, investigation, and interviewing
8. factor analysis
9. counteranalysis
10. length of legal analysis

1. Preliminary Assessment

The starting point in legal analysis is always a set of facts. In the law office, these facts come from the initial client interview. (In school, the facts come from the teacher's **hypothetical,** given orally in class or in a written question.[1]) Your first responsibility is to make a preliminary assessment of the facts. This is done in your own mind or on a scrap piece of paper before you start giving a formal answer. The preliminary assessment has the following focus: What rules *appear* to apply to this fact situation? You are searching for reasonable categories of *possibilities.*

Of course, you must be guided by the question asked by your supervisors or teachers. There are two kinds of such questions:

- the open-ended question
- the directed question

The open-ended question broadly asks, in effect, who is liable for what. What torts have been committed? What defenses are available? What remedies can be used? Make a list of possible causes of action and defenses. You are not looking for *the* answer yet; you are searching for possibilities that need to be further explored. As indicated earlier, every separate tort should be formulated into a separate issue. The same is true of every defense. If there is a reasonable possibility that the tort or defense might apply, include it in the list you make for the preliminary assessment. Obviously, this preliminary assessment cannot be done unless you know a fair amount of tort law. At a minimum, you must know the basic elements of the major torts (see Figure 1.1 at the beginning of Chapter One).

The directed question is more specific or narrow. (Was Dr. Davis the proximate cause of Smith's death? Did the accountant intend to deceive the broker? Did Franklin violate the "due diligence" provision of § 23.5 of the statutory code?) The directed question focuses on one of the *elements* of a rule in contention and makes that element the centerpiece of a more narrow issue. We will examine elements in greater detail later in the chapter.

> **Legal Analysis Guideline #4**
>
> Do a preliminary assessment of open-ended questions in order to list the possible tort causes of action and defenses that might be involved in the fact situation. Do a preliminary assessment of directed questions by focusing on the elements of the tort, defense, or other rule that will probably be most in contention.

This preliminary assessment of the open-ended or directed question has three purposes:

- to help you organize your thinking about the next stage of legal analysis
- to help you decide what legal research must be done
- to help you decide what further facts you must check through investigation and further client interviewing

---

[1]The word *hypothetical* has two meanings. As a noun, it means a set of facts that are assumed to exist for purposes of discussion. (The teacher asked the students to analyze the hypothetical she gave them). As an adjective, it means assumed or based on conjecture. (The lawyer asked the witness a hypothetical question).

2. Legal Analysis and Legal Research

Once you have done a preliminary assessment, you have before you a list of the torts and defenses that might be applicable to the facts of the problem, or a list of elements that are most likely to be in dispute. When you are working on a client's case, the next step is to take this information to the law library. Legal research must be undertaken to locate the latest court opinions, statutes, rules of court, etc. You need to determine what *your state* has said about the problem you are analyzing. The facts of the problem should be CARTWHEELed (see Figure 2.10 in Chapter 2) in order to help you find the law in digests, codes, and other reference materials. Your guide in undertaking this research is the list of possibilities that you compiled through a preliminary assessment of the legal analysis problem. While doing the research, the likelihood is that you will come across new options that need to be added to your list. Other tort and defense possibilities, for example, might be revealed by this research.

Following the research,

- You are in a position to evaluate the validity of your preliminary assessment. Did you initially identify the right torts and defenses? Did you initially identify the elements of the torts or defenses that will pose the most difficulty in litigation? Your preliminary assessment must be revised according to what you uncover in the law library.
- You have before you research notes containing citations to the major court opinions, statutes, regulations, etc. These are all rules that must be subjected to the IRAC legal analysis process.

3. Legal Analysis, Investigation, and Interviewing

During the initial stages of legal analysis, you will find yourself saying: "In order to provide an answer to the problem, I need to know more facts." This should happen often while you are still doing your preliminary assessment and legal research. It is rare that the initial client interview will have covered every fact that is relevant to the analysis. It is rare that your supervisor will have given you every fact that you need. The same is true of a fact situation in a school exam.

Assume, for example, that you are analyzing an automobile accident case. In your preliminary assessment and initial research, you are pursuing the possibility of a negligence action. You know that it will be important to determine the foreseeability of the accident. As you start the legal analysis, you realize that foreseeability is a complex topic involving the examination of numerous factors:

- condition of the road
- weather
- visibility
- speed of defendant's car and other cars
- posted speed limit
- other traffic signals
- distance between the two cars
- distractions
- time of day
- defendant's and plaintiff's familiarity with the area
- when defendant first saw plaintiff

- whether anyone used a horn before the accident
- etc.

As you read negligence opinions in the library, you may come across other factors that courts considered relevant to the foreseeability of the accidents discussed in the opinions. Also, as you think more carefully about what foreseeability means, other factors may come to you.

The likelihood is that your initial statement of facts is not adequate to enable you to give an intelligent answer to the question of whether the accident in question was foreseeable; you simply do not have enough facts. The deeper you get into the legal analysis and research of the problem, the wider the gap may become between the facts you have and the facts you need to discover. *Indeed, this is one of the functions of legal analysis: to help you identify facts you need to pursue through investigation and additional client interviewing.* Analysis and research regularly feed into investigation and interviewing in this way.

Of course, if you are taking an examination in school, you do not have the opportunity to obtain more facts through investigation and interviewing. All you have is the set of facts in the exam question. What do you do when you feel that more facts are needed to answer the exam question? First, you answer the question as best you can with the facts that you have. Second, while you are analyzing the facts that you have, you also point out what further facts you need to know in order to answer the question, and why you need to know these facts. For example, you might say, "We are not told in the facts how close the defendant's car was to the plaintiff's car just before the accident. The distance could have a significant bearing on foreseeability. The closer they were, the more foreseeable the accident was or should have been." In other words, you discuss the facts that you *do not have* when they would be relevant to the analysis. You must be reasonable in discussing missing facts. There must be a logical reason why you need the fact. That reason must always be related to the rule under discussion. If the rule you are analyzing is the foreseeability of the accident, it is logical to inquire about the factors that go into a determination of foreseeability. Common sense is also a guide. If, for example, you are not told how fast the defendant was driving, logic and common sense would tell you that questions about speed must be raised because of its high relevance to foreseeability.

| NOTE | **The Relationship between Legal Analysis and the Initial Client Interview** |

Legal services begin with the interview, where the law office obtains the basic facts of the case from the client. There are two main aspects of the initial client interview. First, background information on the client is obtained, e.g., name, address, employment history, etc. Second and most important, facts relevant to the client's legal problem are obtained. But how does the interviewer know what facts are relevant to the client's legal problem? How does the interviewer know what questions to ask? The main guideline to follow is to ask questions that will help determine the existence or nonexistence of each *element* (see next section on elements) of every cause of action and each element of every defense that might be raised. Checklists may help guide the interviewer. Also, the interviewer's prior experience with this kind of legal problem will suggest the kind of questions that should be asked.

What does the legal interviewer do when something comes up during the interview that does not fit into the pigeonholes of a checklist or of prior experience? The danger is that the interviewer will block out anything unfamiliar. Unfortunately, many interviewers have tunnel vision. They tend to avoid that which falls outside the checklist or that which is different from all other cases on which they have worked. What is the antidote? How does one avoid being a one-dimensional interviewer? In part, the answer is to have some comprehension of legal analysis. The more the interviewer knows about *why* a question is asked on a checklist and *how* particular answers might be used in solving the problems of clients, the less likely will the interviewer be so tied to the format and content of the question that everything else will be blocked out.

4. Breaking a Rule Down into Its Elements

One of the most important skills of legal analysis is the ability to break down a rule—any rule—into its elements. An **element** is a component of a rule that is one of the preconditions of the applicability of the rule. If one of the elements of the rule does not apply, the entire rule cannot apply. There are many examples of the importance of "element analysis" in the law:

- In drafting a tort complaint in many states, a plaintiff makes sure that the facts alleged cover every element of the tort.
- When giving instructions to a jury, judges must cover all the elements of the tort and all the elements of the defenses raised.
- When conducting a deposition, attorneys frequently organize questions around the elements of the torts and defenses in the case.
- The organization of a memorandum of law often follows the list of elements of the torts and defenses.
- An exam answer is often effectively organized around the list of elements of the rules being discussed.

A major characteristic of sloppy legal analysis is that it fails to take the reader through the elements of a rule clearly. Suppose that you are analyzing the following statute:

> § 100. A company that keeps or suffers to be kept upon premises owned or occupied by it within 50 yards of an inhabited building of another more than 50 pounds of nitroglycerine shall be subject to a fine of $500 per day.

The first step is to break this rule down into its elements:

1. a company
2. keeps or suffers to be kept more than 50 pounds of nitroglycerine
3. upon premises owned or occupied by the company
4. within 50 yards of an inhabited building of another

The fine of $500 will not apply until each of these four elements is established. It is the nature of an element that if one of the elements falls, the entire rule falls. For example, if a *private citizen* (not engaged in a business of any kind) keeps 51 pounds of nitroglycerine within 50 yards of another, there is no fine, since the first element calls for a *company.*

Legal Analysis Guideline #5

The legal analysis of a rule begins when you break it down into its elements. An element is a portion of a rule that is a precondition to the applicability of the entire rule.

Some rules are already broken down for you into their elements. See, for example, Figure 1.1 in Chapter 1, which lists the elements of the major tort causes of action. For many other rules, however, *you* must break them into their elements. This is particularly true of statutes and administrative regulations.

Use logic and common sense as your guide. In § 100, for example, notice that in the second element, we have included "nitroglycerine" with the verbs "keeps or suffers to be kept," even though "nitroglycerine" does not appear until the end of § 100. This is done because it is impractical to discuss a verb separate from its object. (Keep what?) Do not be reluctant to re-group words and phrases in a sentence so that the elements will consist of logical units. Often the more complex the rule, the more unraveling you will have to do to achieve such units.

When a rule states *alternative* conditions, the alternatives should be kept in the same element. Hence, when you see "or," "either," or like words, be alert to the existence of alternatives. The second and third elements in the above nitroglycerine statute contain alternatives ("keeps or suffers to be kept") ("owned or occupied"). When the alternatives deal with the same topic, they should be kept together so that the element is a self-contained unit.

Legal Analysis Guideline #6

Keep alternative conditions covering the same topic within one element.

There are often two parts in a rule:

- the conditions of the applicability of the rule
- the consequences of the applicability of the rule

The consequence of the nitroglycerine statute is a $500 fine. When consequences are stated in a rule, many different kinds are possible:

- the granting of an injunction
- the establishment of a tort
- the establishment of a defense
- the granting of an extension of time to file a motion
- etc.

When identifying the elements of a rule, you are focusing on the conditions (or preconditions) of the rule's applicability. The consequences follow if all the elements are present. Hence, do not include consequences as part of the elements if consequences are stated in the rule.

■ ASSIGNMENT 3.1 ■

The following rules come from statutes, regulations, and opinions. They are exact quotations. Break them into their elements.

a. In short, where an internal operation is indicated, a surgeon may lawfully perform, and it is his duty to perform, such operation as good surgery demands, even when it means an extension of the operation further than was originally contemplated, and for so doing he is not to be held in damages as for an unauthorized operation.

b. The term safety belt interlock means any system designed to prevent starting or operation of a motor vehicle if one or more occupants of such vehicle are not using safety belts.

c. The constitutional guarantees require, we think, a federal rule that prohibits a public official from recovering damages for a defamatory statement relating to his official conduct unless he proves that the statement was made with actual malice—that is, with knowledge that it was false or with reckless disregard of whether it was false or not.

d. Privacy is invaded only if the information sought is of a confidential nature and the defendant's conduct was unreasonably intrusive.

e. When the mental or physical condition (including the blood group) of a party, or of a person in the custody or under the legal control of parties, is in controversy, the court in which the action is pending may order the party to submit to a physical or mental examination by a physician or to produce for examination the person in his custody or legal control. The order may be made only on motion for good cause shown and upon notice to the person to be examined and to all parties and shall specify the time, place, manner, conditions, and scope of the examination and the person or persons by whom it is to be made.

f. An owner of premises is prohibited from willfully or intentionally injuring a trespasser by means of force that either takes life or inflicts great bodily injury.

5. Definitions of the Elements

As indicated earlier, one of the most important observations you need to learn to make in legal analysis is, "In order to answer your question, I need the following additional facts because . . . ." We come now to another critical inquiry that the student of legal analysis must constantly make: *What is the definition of that word or phrase?* Legal analysis, in large manner consists of the application of definitions to facts. More precisely, it consists of the application of definitions of the *elements* of the rules to facts. Hence, once you have broken a rule into its elements, the next step is to seek definitions of the major words and phrases in those elements.

Refer back to the nitroglycerine example (§ 100) discussed earlier. The definitional questions that need to be asked are as follows:

▪ What is a "company"?
▪ What is meant by "keeps or suffers to be kept"?
▪ What is "nitroglycerine"?
▪ What are "premises"?
▪ What does "owned or occupied" mean?
▪ What is an "inhabited building"?
▪ What does "another" mean?

You must challenge the elements by demanding of yourself and of others that definitions be provided. The same is true if you are listening to a lecture or discussion about the law: Insist that the major terms be defined.

You will note that we did not list a number of words and phrases from the nitroglycerine statute as definitional questions, such as "or," "more than 50 pounds," "upon," "within 50 yards." They do not appear to be unclear and in need of definitions. There may, however, be circumstances where there *will* be a need to have such words or phrases defined. It would not be unusual for a court to spend time defining a conjunction or a preposition! Trespass, for example, requires an intrusion, or an entry *on* land. Litigation has been necessary to define what is meant by "on." If you throw a rock across someone's land and the rock never touches the ground, has there been an entry *on* the land? The answer depends on the definition of "on" as well as the definition of "land."

Your goal is to define every *major* word and phrase in an element. The two tests to use to determine whether something is major are common sense and whether you anticipate that the word of phrase will be the center of a dispute between the parties. When in doubt about whether something is major, provide the definition.

In applying these two tests, you may decide that words such as "nitroglycerine" and "premises" do *not* need to be defined. Both parties may agree, for example, that the substance that exploded was nitroglycerine and that this occurred on premises. If so, time does not have to be wasted defining such terms. Be careful, however, in coming to such conclusions. If you must err, do so on the side of providing too many definitions.

Legal Analysis Guideline #7

Define every major word and phrase in every element of a rule, so that the definitions can be applied to the facts. When in doubt about whether a word or phrase is major, resolve the doubt in favor of providing a definition. Whenever you anticipate a dispute that centers on a word or phrase in an element, that word or phrase is always major.

You may think it is an easy task to know when to ask for a definition. Quite the contrary. Time and again you will see and hear people analyzing the law without defining major terms. *They make the assumption that readers or listeners already know the definitions of the words or phrases being used or that the definitions are obvious from the context of the analysis.* That is a very dangerous assumption to make. You are urged to avoid making this assumption in your own analysis, even though you will be surrounded by courts, legislatures, lawyers, teachers, paralegals, etc. who regularly make the assumption. Sloppy analysis does not cease to be sloppy simply because it appears that everyone is doing it!

To be sure, there is such a thing as shorthand analysis, in which people communicate through short summarizations of legal principles without providing all the definitions. Such analysis plays an important role in a busy law office. In your own career, however, it is much too early for you to attempt such summarizations. You must first learn how to do complete analysis before you start using shorthand analysis. Also, when people talk shorthand *to you,* do not be reluctant to slow them down so that you can better understand what is being said. This understanding comes primarily when you inquire about definitions. Take the risk that someone will think that you do not know a lot of law. At this stage in your career, you don't.

Of course, simply because you have a definition, you are not home free. It frequently happens that you need a definition of the definition. Suppose that you are given the following definition of "hazardous substance": "Any substance that is toxic, corrosive or an irritant." While it is helpful to have this definition, you obviously cannot stop there. What is "toxic"? What is "corrosive"? What is an "irritant"?

Legal Analysis Guideline #8

Provide definitions for the major words or phrases contained *within* definitions.

It is important that you train your ears and eyes to recognize legal analysis that fails to provide definitions of major words or phrases. For example, suppose you hear or read the following:

> The defendant acted reasonably because every safety precaution was taken before the fireworks were exploded, e.g., the area was roped off, the fireworks were inspected for defects, extra personnel were added. Furthermore, the explosion was not the proximate cause of the injury suffered by the plaintiff. The case should be dismissed.

Such a passage should give you intellectual indigestion. There are a number of significant concepts that are not defined: "reasonably," "safety precaution," "exploded," "inspected," "defects," "proximate cause," etc. The author of the passage assumes that you know what they mean. Again, this is a dangerous assumption to make in the law.

▪ ASSIGNMENT 3.2 ▪

Examine the following passages taken from legal analysis found in memos, court opinions, appellate briefs, etc. Identify words or phrases, if any, in each passage that are not defined and that you think may have to be defined:

a. Each tenant in common is equally entitled to share in the possession of the entire property and neither may exclude the other from any part of it.
b. In that case, judgment for the plaintiffs was reversed where it appeared that the odors emanating from defendant's building were necessarily incident to its operation, that the business was properly operated, and that plaintiffs were not substantially injured. It appeared that disinterested witnesses had not found the odors particularly offensive. The Appellate Court said, "In the instant case, we have nothing more than unpleasant and disagreeable odors, and those only occasionally perhaps sickening to a few who seem to be unduly sensitive or might we say allergic to such smells."
c. The interest in emotional and mental tranquility is not one that the law will protect from invasion in its own right.
d. It is not enough that the act itself is intentionally done even though the actor realizes or should realize that it contains a very grave risk of bringing about the contact or apprehension. They must realize that to a substantial certainty the contact or apprehension will result.

Having recognized the need for definitions, the next question is: Where do you get them? Can you go to a standard nonlegal dictionary such as *Webster's?* It is important to understand that there are many **terms of art** in the law. A term of art is a word or phrase that has a special or technical meaning. In the law of battery, for example, the word "act" means a voluntary movement of the body, and in the law of defamation, "publication" means a communication to at least one person other than the plaintiff. To obtain the definition of a term of art, you would *not* go to *Webster's*. Unfortunately, you will not always know whether a word or phrase is a term of art or whether its ordinary "lay" definition was intended. To be safe:

• know the "lay" definition of the word or phrase (check it in *Webster's* or another standard nontechnical dictionary)
• assume, however, that the word or phrase is a term of art until you establish for yourself otherwise
• use the basic research techniques (listed below) to determine whether the word or phrase is a term of art, and if so, what it means

Legal Analysis Guideline #9

Assume that all words and phrases in the law are terms of art until you satisfy yourself that a nontechnical meaning was intended. Know the nontechnical as well as the technical definition of such words and phrases.

Basic Techniques of Locating Definitions

Here are some ways to try to locate definitions of a word or phrase in an element of a rule that needs a definition.

If the word or phrase is in an element of a statute, follow steps 1 through 6:

1. Check whether there is a definitions section in the statutory code. The legislature may have defined the word or phrase in another statute (often called a definitions section) that is part of the same cluster of statutes.
2. Check whether the word or phrase has been interpreted or defined in court opinions. Examine the Notes to Decisions that follow the text of the statute in the annotated code. Also Shepardize the statute.
3. Check whether an agency has written administrative regulations that define the word or phrase.
4. Check whether an agency has written administrative decisions that define or interpret the word or phrase.
5. Check whether the legislative history of the statute gives any clues to the meaning intended by the legislature for the word or phrase.
6. On finding statutes, see also the General Instructions for the State Code Assignment, and the General Instructions for the Federal Code Assignment, both at the end of Chapter Two.

If the word or phrase is in an element of a common law doctrine, you need to find court opinions that have interpreted or defined the word or phrase. To find such opinions on the common law doctrine, follow steps 7 through 12:

7. Check the digests, such as the *American Digest System* and the digest that covers the state court opinions of your state.
8. Check annotations in *ALR, ALR2d, ALR3d, ALR4th, ALR5th,* and *ALR Fed.* Annotations provide extensive references to court opinions.
9. Check the legal encyclopedias such as *Corpus Juris Secundum* and *American Jurisprudence 2d.* The footnotes in them will often lead you to case law.

10. Check the footnotes in legal periodical literature for leads to case law.
11. Check the footnotes in legal treatises for leads to case law.
12. Once you find one court opinion on point through these techniques, Shepardize it to try to find more. On finding statutes, see also the General Instructions for the Court Opinion Assignment (State Court and Federal Court) at the end of Chapter 2.

6. Connecting Facts with Elements of the Rule

By this stage, you have identified a series of rules. Each rule has been broken down into its elements, and the definitions of the major words and phrases in the elements have been obtained. For each rule, the next step is to connect the facts of the problem with the elements of the rule. In your own mind or on a piece of paper, make a series of columns, one column per element. In each column, place those facts that are relevant to the establishment or disestablishment of the element covered by that column. For example, suppose you are analyzing the following fact situation:

> Tom lives in a residential neighborhood. He plants a new tree along the edge of his property, two feet from Jim's land. He finishes planting at 7 A.M. on a Tuesday morning. Before Tom goes to work at 8 A.M., he turns on his hose in front of the tree to water it. He sees that the water quickly collects around the tree and starts draining toward Jim's land. Tom decides to leave the hose on while he is at work. When he returns at 6 P.M. that day, Jim's yard is flooded by the water. Jim sues Tom for trespass to land. What result?

The elements of trespass to land are:

- an act
- intrusion on land
- in possession of another
- intent to intrude
- causation of the intrusion

Once you have obtained the definitions of the major words or phrases in these elements, the next step is to line up the facts of the problem with each of the elements. It is recommended that you do this on a piece of paper. When you acquire practice in doing it, you will eventually do it in your head. Make five columns to correspond with the five elements of trespass to land. Under each column, make a note of the facts that are relevant to that column. A fact is relevant to an element if it may help to prove or disprove that element. Facts that are relevant to more than one element should be repeated under each appropriate column. If you need more facts to help you analyze an element, make a note of the missing facts under the column for that element. (See Figure 3.2.)

You are now ready to write out your legal analysis of the problem. The guide or checklist for the writing will be the information you collected under the columns. In our example, note that the organization of the written analysis follows the listing of the elements. There are five elements, so there will be five sections in our analysis.

In the model answer that follows Figure 3.2, we will assume that you are writing an answer to an examination question. Following the answer, we will discuss the differences between an exam answer and a legal memorandum on the same problem.

Legal Analysis Guideline #10

Before you start writing your final analysis of a problem, make a row of column headings to cover each element of the rule being analyzed (e.g., the tort or defense). Under each column heading, make a list of every fact that may be relevant to proving that the element does or does not apply. If one fact is relevant to more than one element, place the fact in the appropriate column for each of the elements involved. If there are missing facts you need to know, make a list of them in the appropriate column(s). The columns will become a checklist of what you need to discuss when you begin your written analysis.

Figure 3.2 Connecting Facts to Elements
Jim v. Tom
(Trespass to Land)

Act	Intrusion on Land	In Possession of Another	Intent to Intrude	Causation of the Intrusion
• Tom decided to keep the hose on. • There is no indication in the facts that Tom was coerced into turning on the hose.	• The water from the hose flooded Jim's yard.	• The yard and land (where the water went) was Jim's. • We do not know if Jim was living on the land, or whether anyone else was claiming the land.	• Tom saw the water start draining toward Jim's land. • We do not know whether Tom wanted the water to go on Jim's land. • The tree was two feet from Jim's yard. • The water collected quickly. • We do not know whether the land was flat or inclined toward (or away from) Jim's land. • Tom decided to leave the hose on while he is at work. • Ten hours passed with the hose on. • We do not know whether Tom saw the water go onto Jim's land.	• The yard was flooded from Tom's hose. • There is no indication that the water came from any other source.

Jim v. Tom (Trespass to Land)

There are five elements to trespass to land:

- an act
- intrusion on land
- in possession of another
- intent to intrude
- causation of the intrusion

Act

An act is a voluntary movement of the body. Jim will argue that there is no indication in the facts that Tom was coerced into turning on the hose. Everything that Tom did appeared voluntary, as indicated by the fact that he decided to keep the hose on. People who decide things usually act under their own will power. Tom will concede that the first element applies.

Intrusion on Land

Intrusion means physically going onto land. Jim will argue that water is a physical thing that went to the surface of his land, since we are told, the "yard was flooded by the water." Tom will concede that the hose water is something physical that entered the land, and that the second element applies.

In Possession of Another

Possession means actual occupancy of the land with the intent to have exclusive control over it, or the right to immediate occupancy when no one else is actually occupying it with intent to control it. We are told that the land is "Jim's." We do not know, however, whether Jim or anyone else was occupying the land at the time of Tom's intrusion. For example, we do not know whether Jim had a tenant living on the land at the time. Hence, we cannot tell from the facts whether Jim was in possession. I will assume, however, that Jim was in possession, since the facts indicate that Jim owned the land and there is no indication that anyone else was occupying it with the intent to control it. Hence, the third element has been established.

Intent to Intrude

This element poses the most difficulty. Intent to intrude is the desire to intrude or the knowledge with substantial certainty that the intrusion will result from what the defendant does or fails to do. The facts do not tell us whether Tom wanted the water from his hose to enter Jim's yard. Jim would argue, however, that there was an intent to intrude, because Tom knew with substantial certainty that the water would physically enter his land. Presumably, Tom knew that the new tree was two feet from the property line. He knew, therefore, that the water would not have far to travel. He saw the water quickly collect around the tree and start draining toward Jim's land. Tom knew, therefore, that all the water was not being absorbed into his own land. He knew that the water was headed toward Jim's land. (The facts do not tell us if the land was flat or on an incline.) Tom knew that the water was going to run from 8 A.M. until he returned from work—some ten hours later. Furthermore, since the water collected "quickly," Tom probably had it turned on high. Since Tom knew that the water was headed toward Jim's land two feet away and that it would be kept on high for ten hours,

Jim will argue that Tom knew with substantial certainty that the water would enter Jim's land. Therefore, Tom intended the entry or intrusion.

Tom disagrees. The facts do not say that he desired the water to enter. Nor do they say that he saw the water enter. He may have been negligent in causing the water to enter, or maybe even reckless, but there was no intent to have it enter. There may have been carelessness in allowing the water to drain into Jim's yard, but there was no knowledge with substantial certainty that it would enter. Tom admits that it may have been stupid to leave the water on, but there was no intent.

Causation of the Intrusion

There are two definitions of causation: "but for" and substantial factor. Plaintiff must establish causation by either definition. "But for" what the defendant did, the harm would not have occurred; or, the defendant was a substantial factor in producing the harm. Jim argues that "but for" Tom's leaving the hose on for ten hours, his land would not have been flooded. The facts say that the land was flooded "by the water," referring to the water from the hose. There is no indication that the water came from any other source. (Since no other causal entity is involved, Jim does not need to use the substantial factor test. But it would be easy to show that Tom was a substantial factor in producing the flooding.) Tom will concede that he caused the intrusion on Jim's land.

Conclusion

I believe that Jim will win this case. The only element in contention is intent. I do not think that Tom can deny that he knew with substantial certainty that the water would enter Jim's land. He saw the water go toward the yard even before he left for a long time with the hose on. Hence, I think Jim has the stronger argument on intent.

The characteristics of the above answer are outlined in the following guideline:

Legal Analysis Guideline #11

1. The analysis is organized according to the elements of the rule (here, trespass to land). The columns were used as a checklist in writing the answer.
2. Definitions of the major words and phrases in the elements are provided at the beginning of the discussion of each element.
3. The definitions are then applied to the facts. This is done by making a *specific* connection between the language of the definition and the facts. A rehashing of rules without an extensive discussion of facts is weak analysis.
4. Most of the discussion centers on the elements that are most likely to be in contention (here, the element of intent).
5. The writer is not afraid of identifying missing facts where they are relevant to a particular element.
6. If assumptions must be made about missing facts, they are labeled as assumptions (see the discussion on possession).
7. For each element, the positions of both sides are provided, even if one of the positions amounts to a concession on an element (here, most of the counteranalysis centers on the element of intent).
8. The writer's conclusion is provided at the end of the analysis.

▪ ASSIGNMENT 3.3 ▪

Mary and Cindy are walking on the sidewalk beside Lena's home. The home is seven inches from the sidewalk. Suddenly Mary and Cindy start a violent argument. They are shouting at each other. Mary pushes Cindy. Cindy loses her balance and falls on Lena's home. Lena sues Mary and Cindy for trespass to land.

a. Analyze Lena's action against Mary.
b. Analyze Lena's action against Cindy.

Do the column exercise for each case and write your answer according to the guidelines discussed thus far in this chapter. (Do not do any legal research on the problem.)

In the model answer for the case involving Jim v. Tom, the analysis was done in the format of a school examination. A number of major differences would exist in the answer if you were presenting it as a legal memorandum. First of all, there would be a heading to the memo (see Figure 3.3).

The major difference between an exam answer and a legal memorandum is that the memo is supported by research from the law library. For example, court opinions and statutes are cited and applied as authority for the elements of the torts or defenses, as well as for the definitions of the major words and phrases in the elements. No such research is given in the exam answer. The format of the analysis, however, is the same: Rules are broken down into their elements, definitions are given, specific connections between definitions and facts are made, most of the analysis is devoted to the elements most in contention, etc.

It is usually good practice to begin a legal memo with a statement of the assignment that the supervisor has given you.

Figure 3.3   Heading of Legal Memorandum

MEMO TO: Supervisor's name
FROM: Your name   RE: Jim v. Tom
DATE: Today's date   Trespass to Land

                                  OFFICE FILE NO.
                                  82105

     You have asked me to prepare a memo on whether Tom committed trespass to land against Jim.

     Issue: Did Tom commit trespass to land when he flooded Jim's land after leaving his hose on for an extended period of time, knowing that the water was headed toward Jim's land two feet away?

     Conclusion: Yes.

     There are five elements to trespass to land in this state according to the recent case of . . . .

Note also that there is a statement of the issue at the beginning of the memo. The issue contains within it some of the critical facts. There are supervisors, however, who prefer a much shorter statement of the issue, e.g., "Has there been a trespass to land?"

The issue is stated at the beginning of the memo, but is usually written last, after the analysis has been done. First, you do all your thinking and research. You then write out your analysis by the elements. Leave a space at the beginning of the memo for the issue. When you finish the analysis, you will have a better idea of how you want to phrase the issue. At that time, insert it at the beginning of the memo. Of course, the memo may have a number of issues. For long and relatively complex memos, it is recommended that you insert all of the issues at the beginning of the memo so that they serve as a kind of table of contents of what is to come.[2]

There is also a brief conclusion stated after the issue. This summary conclusion should not replace the longer conclusion that will go at the end of the memo and at the end of your analysis of each issue.

7. Legal Analysis and Further Research, Investigation, and Interviewing

It must be emphasized that you will often find yourself redrafting the legal memorandum. New facts may be uncovered, e.g., through discovery. The ongoing research may raise factual gaps that need to be pursued through further investigation and client interviewing. You may even be asked to do research and investigation while the trial is going on, due to the facts revealed by witnesses on the stand. Analysis, legal research, and fact gathering constantly feed into each other as the case unfolds.

8. Factor Analysis

Thus far we have concentrated on the analysis of the *elements* of rules. Elements are preconditions to the applicability of a rule; if one of the elements does not apply, the entire rule does not apply. We now turn to a different kind of analysis: *factor* analysis.

A **factor** is simply a consideration that a court will examine to help it decide whether an element applies. A factor is not a precondition of applicability. It is simply one of a series of items that a court will weigh. In negligence, for example, the determination of reasonableness, as we will see in Chapter 12, is made through an assessment of the following factors:

- the foreseeability of an accident occurring
- the foreseeability of the kind of harm resulting if an accident occurs
- the extent of the burden or inconvenience on the defendant to take precautions against the accident occurring
- the importance or social utility of the defendant's conduct before the accident

Furthermore, the determination of foreseeability itself requires an analysis of a series of factors, as we will see in Chapter 10:

---

[2]On the variety of formats for a memorandum of law, see W. Statsky and J. Wernet, *Case Analysis and Fundamentals of Legal Writing,* 4th ed. (St. Paul: West Publishing Co., 1994). 180ff.

- the area
- the activity
- the people
- preparation
- assumptions about human nature
- historical data
- specific sensory data
- common sense

We will also be examining other rules in this book for which a factor analysis will be required.

No one factor will usually be determinative for a court. All of the factors are examined and weighed. The question is not "Was Jones reasonable?" or "Was the fire foreseeable?", but "How reasonable was Jones?", or "How foreseeable or unforeseeable was the fire?" Factor analysis is most often used when the court is considering the *degree* or the *extent* of something. Hence there is a need to carefully explore everything before concluding where something falls on the scale.

You do a factor analysis by listing the factors that a court will consider and by examining one factor at a time in much the same way that you would analyze each element. State the factor, define it, list the specific facts that appear to support or not to support the applicability of the factor, integrate questions about missing facts into the discussion of each factor, etc.

Legal Analysis Guideline #12

Factors are often used by courts to help decide whether a rule (or an element within a rule) applies. Examine each factor separately and then make a collective assessment of how the totality of factors helps to establish or disestablish the rule (or an element within the rule).

---

9. Counteranalysis

In discussing the model answer above, we looked at the need for a counter-analysis—what the other side will say. Students of law tend to overly identify with clients for whom they are working, or with the side they think should win. *The more you personally believe in an argument, the greater the danger that you will have a weak counteranalysis to that argument.* This is not to say that you must invent a counterargument for the sake of having one. The safest state of mind you can have is to assume that there is a better counterargument than the one you have identified to date. Keep thinking. The worst kind of analysis hits the reader over the head with only one perspective. The test of whether to include a counterargument is whether a reasonable advocate would present that argument. When in doubt, include it.

Legal Analysis Guideline #13

To construct a counteranalysis, put yourself in the shoes of the opponent and ask whether he or she would warmly embrace or would raise objections to the conclusions of your analysis. The objections to your arguments constitute the counteranalysis.

10. Length of Legal Analysis

There are two basic kinds of legal analysis:

- conclusory
- demonstrative

Conclusory Legal Analysis

The following is an example of conclusory legal analysis:

> Reasonable care is the conduct of an ordinary prudent person under the same or similar circumstances. The truck driver took his eyes off the road and it was at this time that his truck swerved into the opposite lane. It cannot be said that the driver was unreasonable simply because he took his eyes off the road in this manner.

This analysis begins with a rule: the definition of reasonable care. The application of this rule to the facts is conclusory because we are told only that the truck driver was not unreasonable; we are not told *why* he was not unreasonable. Conclusory analysis fails to give any reasons why a rule applies or does not apply to the facts, or gives only cursory reasons.

Demonstrative Analysis

The following is an example of demonstrative legal analysis:

> Reasonable care is the conduct of an ordinary prudent person under the same or similar circumstances. The truck driver took his eyes off the road and it was at this time that his truck swerved into the opposite lane. The truck driver will argue that it is not uncommon for a truck driver to take his eyes off the road. Ordinary and prudent truck drivers do not keep their eyes on the road every second. For example, truck drivers look at their gas gauges, their rearview mirrors, etc. Trucks are designed with instrument panels that can be checked only by being looked at, at least momentarily. Hence, it cannot be said that the truck driver acted unreasonably simply because he took his eyes off the road. We need to determine why he took his eyes off the road in order to. . . .

This analysis also begins with a rule: the definition of reasonable care. The analysis is demonstrative, however, because we are taken through at least some of the steps the writer used to conclude that the truck driver was reasonable (or was not unreasonable). We are given *reasons* for this conclusion. For elements in contention, demonstrative analysis will be essential. Such analysis takes the reader by the hand to point out why a rule applies to the facts in a certain way. The assumption of the author of demonstrative analysis is that an argument is rarely, if ever, self-evident.

How long should your answer or memo be? Common sense is an important guide. The more complex the issues being analyzed, the longer the analysis must be. Also, what has your supervisor told you? Has a page limitation been set? Is the analysis needed in a few hours? Will the supervisor have only ten or fifteen minutes to read your analysis before dashing off to court? Questions such as these are relevant to the length of what you write. You do not want to belabor the obvious in your writing, nor write something so long that no one will want to read it.

Early in your legal career, however, it is recommended that you be demonstrative as often as you can. Conclusory analysis is shorthand analysis. As indicated earlier, before you learn how to "talk in shorthand," you should learn how to be demonstrative.

Legal Analysis Guideline #14

Whether you provide conclusory or demonstrative analysis depends on the complexity of the problem and the instructions of your supervisor. When in doubt, be demonstrative.

■ CONCLUSION

The fourth and final component of legal analysis is the conclusion. In the model answer given earlier on the trespass case, you saw an example of a conclusion. It gives your own personal opinion as to which side has the better argument on a question. In a legal memorandum, you will also be predicting how a particular court will rule on the question.

Another function of the conclusion is to list the next steps that should be taken to:

- initiate a lawsuit
- do further investigation on . . .
- do further research on . . .
- etc.

Generally, the conclusion should be brief and should not raise arguments that were not discussed in the analysis or counteranalysis.

Legal Analysis Guideline #15

State a brief conclusion of your personal views at the end of the analysis and counteranalysis. Include any next steps you recommend. Do not state any new arguments in the conclusion.

Throughout this book there are many legal analysis assignments that ask you to apply some rules to sets of facts in the manner in which this chapter has covered this skill. The general instructions for these assignments are as follows:

General Instructions for the Legal Analysis Assignment

1. The most important part of legal analysis is *fact* analysis. Carefully read each fact in this assignment. Give detailed attention to *every* word covering *every* fact. Hence, the first instruction is to know the facts thoroughly.
2. Review the material in this introductory chapter on legal analysis. Give particular attention to the fifteen legal analysis guidelines in this chapter (some of which are repeated and summarized here).
3. Most of the legal analysis assignments will ask you to apply an entire tort

or defense, or will ask you to apply one of the elements of the tort or defense.

4. The rules you will be applying will be found on the pages immediately preceding the assignment. Do not do any legal research unless specifically asked to do so in the assignment.

5. Place a heavy emphasis on the application of definitions of words or phrases in the elements. All of the arguments in your analysis should relate to the definitions of these words or phrases. In effect, it is these definitions that you will be applying to the facts. In your application, draw specific, explicit connections between the language of the element (or the definitions of the words or phrases in the element) and the individual facts of the problem you are analyzing.

6. Where necessary, try to stretch the definition of a word or phrase to fit the facts of the assignment.

7. When you need more facts to do the analysis and counteranalysis, state what facts you need, explain why you need them, and integrate these missing facts into your writing, always making clear that such facts are assumptions only.

8. Use the example of the trespass analysis in this chapter as a model.

9. Use demonstrative rather than conclusory analysis.

10. There are times when two advocates will agree on how a certain rule (or more accurately, how the definition of an element in a rule) applies to the facts, *but such times are rare.* Give both sides of the analytical picture. If you think that one of the parties will concede an argument, say so. For most arguments, however, put yourself in the shoes of both advocates and argue both sides. Do not hit the reader over the head with an analysis that insists on one interpretation. Resist the temptation of constantly telling the reader that an argument "clearly" points in one direction. Legal analysis is rarely that clear.

SUMMARY

Legal analysis is the application of rules to facts in order to solve a legal problem or to prevent one from arising. The structure of legal analysis is the statement of an issue and a rule, the analysis and counteranalysis of the rule, and the reaching of a conclusion (IRAC). The issue is a question about how one or more rules apply to facts. It should be phrased as narrowly as possible. The main rules in personal injury litigation are common law doctrines and statutes. Also important are constitutions, administrative regulations, administrative decisions, charters, ordinances, and rules of court.

Your preliminary analysis should make broad or general issues out of every possible tort cause of action and defense. Then try to narrow the issues to be more specific by focusing on the element(s) of the rule in contention. Next, undertake legal research on the issues you have identified during the preliminary analysis. While going through these steps, you will often be identifying additional facts that you will need to try to uncover through further client interviewing and investigation. Next break down every rule under examination into its elements, noting each of the elements that have words or phrases that require definitions. Do legal research to obtain such definitions. Then line up your facts with each of the elements of the rules under analysis—connect the facts with the elements. Your written analysis should be organized by elements of the rules. Most of the writing should focus on the elements that will probably raise the most contention. Where needed, a factor analysis is also undertaken. The perspective of the other side is presented as a counteranalysis. Avoid conclusory analysis early in your career. For elements in contention, provide demonstrative analysis. The conclusion should state your personal opinion on which side has the better argument, your prediction of what a court might decide, and any next steps you recommend.

Key Terms

legal analysis	memo	hypothetical
liable	issue	element
IRAC	question of law	terms of art
legal memorandum	rule	factor

CHAPTER 4

Legal Interviewing and Investigation in Personal Injury Litigation

---

CHAPTER OUTLINE

- INTERVIEWING IN A PERSONAL INJURY CASE
- OBTAINING THE FACTS
- COMMUNICATIONS CHECKLIST
- CLIENT INTAKE MEMORANDUM
- INTRODUCTION TO INVESTIGATION
- FACT ANALYSIS: ORGANIZING THE OPTIONS
- FACT PARTICULARIZATION
- TAKING A WITNESS STATEMENT

■ INTERVIEWING IN A PERSONAL INJURY CASE

When a new client walks into the office with a personal injury case, three major concerns must be explored:

- liability
- damages
- collectibility

The client interview is usually the most important way in which the office starts collecting facts pertaining to all three concerns.

Liability

The client claims that the defendant caused an injury. Under our system, this does not automatically make the defendant responsible even if the client can prove the defendant caused the injury. *We are not responsible for every harm we cause.* We are responsible only for the harm we *wrongfully* cause. The law makes us *liable* for such harm. **Liability** means being legally responsible for

61

something. In the law of torts, liability occurs when a plaintiff has successfully stated and proven a **cause of action,** which is simply a legally acceptable reason for bringing a suit. For our purposes, the causes of action are the thirty-five tort and related causes of action outlined in Figure 1.1 of Chapter 1. The interview must start identifying facts that are relevant to the *elements* of these causes of action.

Damages

Damages consist of an amount of money awarded to the plaintiff upon establishing a cause of action against the defendant for personal injury or other harm. The amount in damages can range from $1 (which would be considered **nominal**—in name only—damages) to millions of dollars. How much is awarded depends primarily on the extent of the harm proven. An attorney will probably turn away a case where liability is clear, but where the harm suffered is relatively small. For example, it may be easy to establish liability against a bottling company that left a nail in its soda bottle. But if the plaintiff suffered no significant injury upon discovering the nail, the case may not be worth litigating. Most personal injury attorneys are paid a **contingent fee.** They take a percentage of the award *if* an award is given, or a percentage of the settlement *if* the case is settled. In short, the attorney is paid contingent on the client's receiving something. But even a large percentage of a small amount is not very attractive to an attorney. Of course, the client can always offer to pay the lawyer an hourly fee rather than a contingent fee. Few clients, however, are willing to do so when the injury suffered is comparatively small. Hence, the question of damages will be a major theme discussed during the interview.

Collectibility

As the interview proceeds, the attorney may feel that the prospects for establishing liability are very good, and that the injury suffered is so substantial that the likelihood of a high damages award is also very good. A dream case for every **PI** (personal injury) attorney? Not necessarily. What good is a multimillion-dollar judgment against a bankrupt defendant with no liability insurance? (In Chapter 8 we will discuss the enforcement of judgments after trial.) It is during the client interview that the office starts gathering information on the financial health of prospective defendants. Soon into the interview, the attorney will want to know if there are any defendants with **deep pockets,** i.e., defendants who have sufficient personal or insurance assets from which a large judgment award might be satisfied.

▪ OBTAINING THE FACTS

This chapter is not intended to cover every aspect of legal interviewing.[1] Rather, the aim is to cover certain basic concepts of the format and content of a legal interview with particular reference to a personal injury case.

---

[1]For more on interviewing, see R. Gorden, *Interviewing Strategy: Techniques and Tactics* (1969, The Dorsey Press), and W. Statsky, "Legal Interviewing," in *Paralegalism: Perspectives, Problems, and Skills,* 4th ed. 365ff. (West Publishing Co., 1992).

Figure 4.1   Retainer

RETAINER[2]

_____ County
State of _____
    I/We hereby employ _____ as attorney(s) to represent _____ in __
claim for damages against _____ on account of personal injuries and/
or property damage sustained by _____ on the _____ day of _____
19__.
    I/We agree to give my attorney(s) a sum equivalent to _____ (__%)
of any amount that may be recovered after suit is instituted either by
settlement or trial, or _____ (__%) of any sum that may be recovered
by settlement prior to filing suit, as a fee, the same to be deducted from
such recovery after deduction of necessary expenses.
    In the event I/We do not prevail in the above matter I/We understand
and agree that costs of court are to be borne by me/us.

                                          _____ L.S.
                                          _____ L.S.

                                          Accepted By:

                                          _____
                                          By _____
                                              A Member Of The Firm

---

SOURCE: [2]E. Elliott and A. Elliott, *Tort Resume for Use in Prosecution and Defense of All Damage Claims,* 27.

The basic objective of the legal interview is to obtain the facts from the client once the **retainer** (i.e., the agreement to hire someone) has been signed. See Figure 4.1 for a sample retainer.

Background Information Checklist

Law firms differ on the amount of background information they seek from every client. The following checklist of questions will give you some idea of the kind of background information that can be sought.

- name of client
- ever used other names (aliases)?
- ever been through a formal change-of-name procedure?
- birth name
- other married names
- current address and phone (home)
- length of time lived at this address
- current address and phone (work)
- prior residences
- nationality/citizenship/place of birth

- addresses and phones where spouse (or closest relative) can be reached
- date of birth
- religion, race (may be relevant in jury selection process)
- how was client referred to this office?
- has client hired any other attorney on this case?
- has client spoken to any other attorney about this case?
- if client is a minor, is there a legal guardian?
- marital status
- prior marriages (information on divorces)
- date of present marriage
- date of divorce(s)
- names of children, if any
- ages/addresses
- name of other parent of each child
- current status of property settlement alimony/lump sum/child support payments
- current employer(s) of client and spouse
- job title/salary
- length of employment there
- prior employment history
- self-employment/business ventures
- tax data (filing status, gross income, availability of copies of returns, etc.)
- real property client owns in own name
- real property owned in joint names
- personal property (cash, bank accounts, furniture, motor vehicles, etc.)
- education
- prior litigation involvement (dates, courts, attorneys, outcomes, etc.)
- present state of health
- names and addresses of doctors currently treating client
- nature of treatment
- medical problems for which no treatment has been sought
- prior medical history (for the last _____ years)
- prior hospital treatment (dates, addresses, doctors, care provided, outcomes)
- name of every insurance company (past/present) that has covered medical care
- list of every insurance claim client has ever filed for medical care
- names of people who could verify client's prior medical condition

Figure 4.2 presents another checklist for a legal interview (and for later investigation) based upon an automobile accident. Elsewhere in the book you will find other checklists and techniques of identifying facts you need to inquire about. For example,

- Chapter 3 on legal analysis shows how to identify further facts that need to be pursued, particularly in a subsequent client interview
- the process of particularization is critical to formulating questions (see Figure 4.6 in this chapter)
- the sample interrogatories in Chapter 6 on discovery contain numerous questions, many of which could become a guide in asking questions of your own client
- Chapter 10 on foreseeability provides a series of questions that need to be asked when foreseeability is relevant to the case
- Etc.

Figure 4.2   Automobile Accident Interview and Task Checklist[3]

Parties—General Information
( )   Plaintiff _____ Age _____ Sex _____ Phone _____
( )   Address _____ City _____ County _____ State _____ Z.Code _____
( )   Bus. Address _____ City _____ County _____ State _____ Phone _____
( )   Ins. Carrier _____ Address _____ Phone _____
        Amount of Insurance: Liability _____ Property Damage _____
        Medical _____ Collision _____ Uninsured Motorist _____
        Any Coverage Deductible? Which? _____

( )   Defendant 1. _____ Age _____ Sex _____ Phone _____
( )   Address _____ City _____ County _____ State _____ Z.Code _____
( )   Bus. Address _____ City _____ County _____ State _____ Phone _____
( )   Ins. Carrier _____ Address _____ Phone _____
        Amount of Insurance: Liability _____ Property Damage _____
        Medical _____ Collision _____ Uninsured Motorist _____
        Any Coverage Deductible? Which? _____

( )   Co-Defendants 2. _____ Age _____ Sex _____ Phone _____
                        3. _____   _____   _____   _____
( )   Address 2. _____ City _____ County _____ State _____ Z.Code _____
                  3. _____   _____   _____   _____   _____
( )   Bus. Address 2. _____ City _____ County _____ State _____ Phone _____
                        3. _____   _____   _____   _____   _____
( )   Ins. Carrier 2. _____ Address _____ Phone _____
                        3. _____   _____   _____
        Amount of Insurance:
        Liability 2. _____ Property Damage _____ Medical _____ Collision _____
                    3. _____   _____   _____   _____
        Uninsured Motorist 2. _____ Any Coverage Deductible? Which?
                                3. _____
                  2. _____
                  3. _____

Facts of Accident
( )   Date of Accident _____ Time _____ Material Facts _____
        _____
        _____
        _____

( )   Statements Made Immediately Prior to, During, or After the Incident _____
        _____

( )   Type of Case (Check Applicable Subject Matter)
        ( ) Animals ( ) Assault & Battery ( ) Drainage & Pollution
        ( ) Employer, Employee and Independent Contractor ( ) False
        Imprisonment ( ) Fraud and Deceit ( ) Invitees and Licensees
        ( ) Malicious Arrest or Prosecution ( ) Malpractice ( ) Municipal
        ( ) Products Liability ( ) Real Estate ( ) Slander or Libel
        ( ) Transportation—Airplane, Automobile, or Train ( ) Trespass
        ( ) Wrongful Death ( ) Worker's Compensation ( ) Other _____

( )   Attach Diagram of Accident Scene if Physical Facts are Important
        _____
        _____

( )   Indicate and Note on Diagram:
        ( )   Width of Streets or Roads Measured _____

(   ) Number of Lanes _____ Any Peculiar Curves or Hills _____
(   ) Yellow Lines _____ Stop Signs or Traffic Devices _____
(   ) Skid Marks _____ Position of Vehicles after Accident _____
(   ) Type of Road Surface. Asphalt or Concrete _____
(   ) Dry or Wet _____ Weather—Fog, Rain, Drizzle, Sleet, or Snow
_____

(   ) Visibility—Good or Bad _____ Day, Night, Dusk or Dawn _____
_____

(   ) Clear or Cloudy _____ Other _____
(   ) Were Pictures Taken of Accident Scene? _____
(   ) When? _____ By Whom? _____
(   ) Address _____ Phone _____
(   ) If Not, Take Pictures of Accident Scene Immediately
(   ) Place Pictures Obtained or Taken in Evidence File
(   ) Miscellaneous Comments _____
_____

(   ) Automobile Information
    (   ) Plaintiff Vehicle
        (   ) Year _____ Make _____ Model _____ Color _____
        (   ) Cylinders _____ Horsepower _____ Weight _____
             Manuf. I.D. _____
        (   ) Tag No. _____ Power or Regular Steering _____
             Brakes _____
        (   ) Defects of Vehicles—Brakes _____ Lights _____
             Motor _____ Steering _____ Tires _____
             Other _____
             Comments as to Condition _____
        (   ) Seat Belts in Use at Time? _____
             Air Bags Available and Functioning? _____
        (   ) Location of Vehicle—Garage _____
             Address _____ Phone _____
             Were Pictures Taken of Automobile? _____
             When? _____ By Whom? _____
             Address _____ Phone _____
        (   ) If Not, Take Pictures at Garage and Place in Evidence File
             Taken By _____ When _____ Address _____
        (   ) Note Alleged Speed Prior to Collision _____
             _____
        (   ) Indicate Impact Points on Vehicle Diagram and Note Interior
             Damage

Right Side
Length _____ ft.

Front
Width _____ ft.

Rear

Left Side

        (   ) Owner of Plaintiff Vehicle _____ Age _____ Sex _____
        (   ) Address _____ City _____ State _____ Phone _____
        (   ) Business Address _____ City _____
             State _____ Phone _____
        (   ) Ins. Carrier _____ Address _____
             Phone _____
             Amount of Insurance: Liability _____
             Property Damage _____
             Medical _____ Collision _____
             Uninsured Motorist _____ Any Coverage

Deductible? Which? _____
_____
(　) Driver Plaintiff Vehicle _____
(　) Relationship to Owner _____
　　Driving with Permission? _____
(　) Destination and Purpose _____
(　) Impediments of Driver—Intoxication _____
　　Glasses _____
(　) Hearing _____ Other Physical Defects _____
(　) **Passengers　　　Seat Location in Vehicle**
_____
_____
_____

(　　) Defendant Vehicle
(　) Year _____ Make _____ Model _____ Color _____
(　) Cylinders _____ Horsepower _____ Weight _____
　　Manuf. I.D. _____
(　) Tag No. _____ Power or Regular Steering _____
　　Brakes _____
(　) Defects of Vehicle—Brakes _____ Lights _____
　　Motor _____ Steering _____ Tires _____
　　Other _____
　　Comments as to Condition _____
(　) Seat Belts in Use at Time? _____
　　Air Bags Available and Functioning? _____
(　) Location of Vehicle—Garage _____
　　Address _____ Phone _____
(　) Were Pictures Taken of Automobile? _____
　　When? _____ By Whom? _____
　　Address _____ Phone _____
(　) If Not, Take Pictures at Garage and Place in Evidence File
　　Taken By _____ When? _____
(　) Note Alleged Speed Prior to Collision _____
(　) Indicate Impact Points on Vehicle Diagrams & Note Interior
　　Damage

Right Side
Length ____ ft.

Front
Width ____ ft.

Rear

Left Side

(　) Owner of Defendant Vehicle _____ Age _____ Sex _____
(　) Address _____ City _____ State _____ Phone _____
(　) Business Address _____ City _____ State _____
　　Phone _____
(　) Ins. Carrier _____ Address _____ Phone _____
　　Amount of Insurance: Liability ___ Property Damage _____
　　Medical _____ Collision _____ Uninsured Motorist _____
　　Any Coverage Deductible? Which? _____
_____
(　) Driver Defendant Vehicle _____
(　) Relationship to Owner _____
(　) Driving with Permission? _____
(　) Destination and Purpose _____
(　) Impediments of Driver—Intoxication _____ Glasses _____
　　Hearing _____ Other Physical Defects _____

Passengers   Seat Location in Vehicle

_____

_____

_____

(   ) Traffic Violations by Plaintiff and Defendant
Charges Against   Court   Hearing Date   Result

_____

(   ) Get Copy of Traffic Court Testimony if Recorded and Place in Evidence File

(   ) Witnesses to Accident, Including Parties

Witnesses   Address   County   State   Age   Phone

_____

_____

_____

_____

_____

(   ) Statements Taken from Witnesses, Including Parties

Name   Who Took   When?   Do We Have a Copy?
**   Statement?**

_____

_____

_____

_____

_____

_____

_____

(   ) Place All Statements in Evidence File

(   ) Impeachment of Parties and Witnesses (Note Unfavorable Military Record)

Name   Crime Conviction   Date   Good or Bad Character

_____

_____

_____

_____

(   ) Parties' Prior Accidents

Plaintiff _____

_____

Defendant _____

_____

Medical

(   ) Plaintiff—Summary of Injuries (Indicate Degree Of Disability) (Restriction of Activities in Work, Sports, Etc.) _____

_____

_____

_____

_____

_____

_____

_____

_____

_____

_____

_____

_____

_____

_____

_____
_____
_____
_____
_____
_____
_____
_____
_____
_____
_____

( )   Note Injuries on Diagram

( )   Indicate Plaintiff's Area of Pain

( )   Symptoms
    ( ) Headaches
    ( ) Dizziness
    ( ) Nausea
    ( ) Nervousness
    ( ) Insomnia
    ( ) Appetite

( )   Head
    ( ) Brain
    ( ) Forehead
    ( ) Ears
    ( ) Eyes
    ( ) Nose
    ( ) Mouth
    ( ) Teeth

( )   Neck
    ( ) Muscles
    ( ) Spine
    ( ) Throat

( )   Chest
    ( ) Heart
    ( ) Lungs
    ( ) Ribs

( )   Abdomen

( )   Internal Injuries
    ( ) _____
    _____

( )   Arms (Right or Left)
    ( ) Upper
    ( ) Forearms
    ( ) Elbows
    ( ) Wrists
    ( ) Hands
    ( ) Fingers

( )   Trunk
    ( ) Shoulders
    ( ) Spine
    ( ) Thoracic
    ( ) Scapula
    ( ) Lumbar
    ( ) Sacrum
    ( ) Coccyx
    ( ) Pelvix
    ( ) Hips

( )   Legs (Right or Left)
    ( ) Thighs
    ( ) Upper
    ( ) Lower
    ( ) Knees
    ( ) Ankles
    ( ) Feet
    ( ) Toes

Diagram labels: Parietal, Temporal, Zygomatic, Occipital, Frontal, Maxilla, Mandible, Cervical vertebrae (7), Clavicle, Scapula, Sternum, Ribs, Thoracic vertebrae (12), Humerus, Lumbar vertebrae (5), Ulna, Radius, Ilium, Sacrum, Pubis, Carpals (8), Metacarpals (5), Phalanges (14), Ischium, Femur, Patella, Tibia, Fibula, Tarsals (7), Metatarsals (5), Phalanges (14)

(   ) Indicate Radiations of Pain.
(   ) Indicate Cuts, Bruises, Burns, Bumps, Sutures, Fractures, Missing Teeth, Swelling, Contusions, Points of Bleeding, Unconsciousness, etc.
(   ) Same Information for Defendant's Injuries (if any)
(   ) Ambulance, Hospital and Doctor Service, Findings, and Treatment

    (   ) Ambulance Service—By Whom? _____ Other _____
            Any First Aid Administered? If So What? _____
            Note Time Ambulance Arrived at Accident Scene _____

    (   ) **Hospitals   Address   Phone   Period of Treatment   Surgery**
            1. _____
            Treatment _____
            _____ X-Rays Taken? When? _____
            2. _____
            Treatment _____
            _____ X-Rays Taken? When? _____
            3. _____
            Treatment _____
            _____ X-Rays Taken? When? _____

    (   ) **Doctors   Address   Phone   Period of Treatment   Surgery**
            1. _____
            Diagnosis, Treatment, and Prognosis _____
            _____ X-Rays Taken? When? _____
            2. _____
            Diagnosis, Treatment, and Prognosis _____
            _____ X-Rays Taken? When? _____
            3. _____
            Diagnosis, Treatment, and Prognosis _____
            _____ X-Rays Taken? When? _____
            4. _____
            Diagnosis, Treatment, and Prognosis _____
            _____ X-Rays Taken? When? _____

(   ) Summary Comments as to Percent of Disability and Patient Prognosis
    _____
    _____

Prior Medical Treatment—Plaintiff and Defendant
(   ) Plaintiff—Prior Medical Treatment
    Doctors and Hospitals   Address   Phone   Period of Treatment
    1. _____
    2. _____
    3. _____
    Treatment _____

    (   ) Note Relationship of Prior to Present Injuries _____
            _____

    (   ) Prior Claims of any Nature? When? Where? _____
            _____

(   ) Defendant—Prior Medical Treatment
    Doctors and Hospitals   Address   Phone   Period of Treatment
    1. _____
    2. _____
    3. _____
    Treatment _____

    (   ) Note Relationship of Prior to Present Injuries _____
            _____

(   )   Prior Claims of any Nature? When? Where? _____
_____
_____

(   )   Summary Degree of Prior Disability
      (   ) Plaintiff _____
      (   ) Defendant _____

Damages—Plaintiff
(   ) Plaintiff Employment Subsequent and Prior to Accident

Subsequent to	Dates	Position	Annual Earnings	Per Diem

Prior to (Last 2 Yrs.)	Dates	Position	Annual Earnings	Per Diem

(   ) Education and Job Training—(   ) Elementary (   ) High School
     (   ) College (   ) Graduate (   ) Other _____

(   ) Family

Spouse and Children	Relationship	Age

(   ) Computation of General Damages—Note Age of Injured Party _____
     (   )   Pain and Suffering (Past, Present, and Future) Estimate
           of Party—
           Value Assessed Per Day $ _____ × _____ Days
           $ _____ × Life Expectancy _____ $ _____
     (   )   Diminution Capacity to Labor as Element of Pain and Suffering
           (Past, Present, and Future) Estimate of Party—
           Value Assessed Per Day $ _____ × _____
     (   )   Days $ _____ × Life Expectancy _____ $ _____
           Loss of Consortium—Estimate of Party—
           Value Assessed Per Day $ _____ × _____
           Days $ _____ × Life Expectancy _____ $ _____
(   ) Computation of Special Damages (Date Accident _____)
     (   )   Loss of Earnings
           (   )   Past and Present to Date of Trial—(Days
                   in Hospital _____)
           (   )   Past and Present Continued—(At Home
                   _____ Returned To Work—
                   Date _____)
                   Total Days _____ × Per Diem
                   Wages
                   $ _____ $ _____
           (   )   Annual Average Earnings $ _____
                   (Capacity Reduced _____ % Disability
                   $ _____) × _____ (Use Annuity
                   table _____ % Column to Reduce to
                   Present Case Value) or × _____ Life
                   Expectancy (For Gross when Reduction
                   not Required)
                   $ _____
           (   )   Hospitals, Nurses, Doctors, Drugs (Supports and
                   Braces), and Ambulance Expenses

Hospitals	Period	Amount	
			$ _____

_____
_____
_____
_____

		$ _____	$ _____
Nurses	**Period**	**Amount**	
		$ _____	

		$ _____	$ _____
Doctors	**Period**	**Amount**	
		$ _____	

_____
_____
_____
_____

		$ _____	$ _____
Pharmacy	**Period**	**Amount**	
		$ _____	

| | | $ _____ | $ _____ |
| **Ambulance** | **Period** | **Amount** | |

| | | $ _____ | $ _____ |

(   ) Funeral Expenses—Mortician's
Name and Address _____
_____ $ _____

(   ) Property Damage
    (   ) Automobile—Fair
        Market Value before
        Accident $ _____
        Less Fair Market
        Value after Accident $ _____
        Diminution in Value $ _____ $ _____
    (   ) Reasonable Hire _____
        Days × Rental Value $ _____ $ _____
    (   ) Real Estate—
        Fair Market Value
        before Accident $ _____
        Less Fair Market Value
        after Accident $ _____
        Diminution in Value $ _____ $ _____
    (   ) Damages to Building—
        Reasonable Repair
        Repairs by _____
        Address _____
        Estimate $ _____
        Repairs Completed $ _____ $ _____

(   ) Punitive Damages
(   ) Attorney Fees
(   ) Court Costs _____
_____ $ _____

(   ) Other Miscellaneous Damages
_____
_____ $ _____

(   ) Total Damages Sued For $ _____
_____

Summary Reminder
(   ) Client
    (   ) Obtain a Fee Contract (Retainer) from Client
    (   ) Obtain Signed Medical Authorizations from Client

( ) Obtain Financial Statements to Support Special Damages
( ) Obtain Income Tax Returns for Last Two Years
( ) Remind Client to Notify Own Insurance Carrier and File Accident Reports Required by Law
( ) Investigation
   ( ) Obtain Medical Information from Doctors, Hospitals, and Other Sources
   ( ) Take Statements from All Witnesses
   ( ) Obtain or Take Pictures and Place Newspaper Clippings in Evidence File of:
      ( ) Accident Scene
      ( ) Vehicles
      ( ) Visible Injuries To Client
      ( ) Other _____
   ( ) Obtain Appraisals of Property, Warranty Deeds, Plats, and Surveys
   ( ) Obtain Engineer's Drawing of Accident Scene
   ( ) Obtain Copy of Accident Reports and Testimony of Traffic Hearing
   ( ) Obtain Copy of Death Certificate Where Applicable
   ( ) Notice Preparatory to Filing Suit
      ( ) Write Letter of Notice to Opposite Party or Party's Insurance Carrier if Known
   ( ) Office Information
      ( ) File Handled This Office _____
      ( ) Associate Attorney _____
          Address _____ Phone _____
      ( ) Referral by _____
          Address _____ Phone _____
   ( ) Obtain Letter in File as to Fee Arrangement in Associate and Referral Matters

SOURCE: [3]E. Elliott and A. Elliott, *Tort Resume for Use in Prosecution and Defense of All Damage Claims,* 1ff.

▪ ASSIGNMENT 4.1 ▪

Every state has **practice books** designed to help busy practitioners, particularly when handling their first cases in an area of law. The books contain checklists, sample forms, and other practical information needed in the day-to-day handling of a case. They may also provide summaries of the law, but they are more than mere summaries. Go to law libraries available to you in your city. Locate practice books that cover torts or personal injury litigation. These practice books may come in different formats, such as bound single volume, bound multivolume, three-ring or loose-leaf, etc. Try to locate practice books written exclusively for your state as well as ones published from a national perspective. For each practice book you find (up to a maximum of five),

a. state the author, title, publisher, and date of publication;
b. photocopy any two pages from the book that illustrate its practical dimensions;
c. find a checklist in the book that is similar to the checklist in Figure 4.2 of this chapter and summarize some of the similarities and differences in the checklists.

▪ COMMUNICATIONS CHECKLIST

There are no absolute rules on how to interview. There are, however, a number of considerations you should have in mind while interviewing. The following questions are designed to increase your sensitivity about the manner in which an interview is conducted. *The more aware an interviewer is of the factors that might affect communication, the greater the likelihood that an effective interview will result.* The checklist items are not mutually exclusive. Nor is there universal agreement on how some of these questions should be answered.

- Do I fully understand the purpose of this interview? Do I know what my supervisor wants me to accomplish?
- How do I prepare for this interview? From an office manual checklist? By talking with others who have conducted similar interviews in the past? By trial and error?
- Do I want to conduct this interview? Do I view this interview as my thousandth? Do I wish someone else would do this interview? Do I feel that I am doing the office a favor in conducting the interview? Do I feel that I am doing the client a favor? Do I view each interview as a potential learning experience?
- Do I have enough time to conduct this interview? If not, what rescheduling options are available?
- Where should the interview be conducted? In my office? At the client's home or place of work? Would it make any difference?
- How am I dressed? Do I dress to suit *my* personal taste? Have I thought about the impact my clothes and appearance may have on the client and on the effectiveness of the interview? Am I secure enough to ask the opinion of a colleague? How could I encourage a colleague to give me an honest opinion on how I come across to people?
- How should I introduce myself to the client? I understand my title and everyone else in the law office understands my title. Does this automatically mean that the client will understand my title? Should I assume that the client won't care? Does the client think I am an attorney? Does the client think that I am experienced and competent in this kind of case? After the interview, if the client were asked by a friend or relative who I was, what would the client say other than "someone who works in the office"? To what extent does the client need to know my job description and background?
- How is my office arranged? Professionally? Casually? How private is the interview? Can anyone overhear my conversation with the client?
- Do I know what client confidentiality means? Do I have a clear understanding of when confidentiality is violated? Do I appreciate the gray areas? Does the client understand his or her confidentiality rights? Should I make specific assurances to the client about confidentiality?
- Do I know what legal advice is? Do I know how to politely give a *no* answer to questions that directly or indirectly ask me for legal advice?
- Do I use a questionnaire in the interview? If so, do I know why each question is on the questionnaire? How closely do I follow the questionnaire? Do I know when I can deviate from it? Is it only a guide or is it something I must follow rigorously?
- What should I say, if anything, to the client about the questionnaire?
- Do I take notes on what the client says? If so, what do I say to the client, if anything, about the fact that I am taking notes?

- How extensive are my notes? What am I doing to increase the speed of my note-taking?
- In answering questions, clients are certain about some facts, but uncertain about others. Do I know how to take notes about *both* kinds of answers? Do I fall into the trap of taking notes on only concrete answers of the client? Do I understand the importance of articulating on paper (in my client intake memo) when the client *thinks* something happened, or *probably* did something on a given date?
- How do I help the client recall factual details?
- How do I help the client unravel complicated facts so that the "story" of the case can be told coherently—for instance, chronologically?
- Do I know how to *particularize* a fact by asking all the appropriate who-what-where-why-when-how questions concerning the fact? Am I scrupulous about dates, places, verification details, etc.?
- Do I ask follow-up questions to help the client give more specific factual detail? Or do I let the interview wander from topic to topic, question to question, answer to answer?
- When the client answers a question by saying, "I'm not sure," or "Maybe," do I ask questions designed to help the client remember with greater specificity? If no greater specificity is possible at this time, do my notes indicate which facts the client was ambiguous or unsure about?
- Do I make the distinction between facts that establish what happened and facts that help verify someone's version of what happened? Do I ask questions that elicit both kinds of facts?
- Is the client answering my questions? If not, is it due to the manner in which I am asking the questions?
- Am I condescending to the client? Do I know when I am condescending?
- Do I talk distinctly?
- Do I use words the client cannot understand, such as legal jargon or terms of art? Since most people do not want to admit they don't understand a word or phrase, how do I know whether the client understands everything I am saying?
- Interviewers have a mental picture or at least a general idea of the topic of the interview, such as a car accident. What do I do when something comes up during the interview that does not fall into the pigeonhole of this mental picture or general idea? Do I block it out of my mind? How do I know that I *don't* block it out?
- Have I made the client feel welcome?
- Am I aware of the impact and importance of attentive listening? Am I one of the few attentive listeners around? How do I know?
- Do I build the client's ego? Do I understand that ego building is not achieved merely by praising someone?
- Am I offended if the client does not build my ego? Am I aware of my ego needs in an interview?
- Am I willing to say to the client, "I don't know"?
- How do I handle the client's embarrassment over one of my questions?
- How do I handle my own embarrassment over one of my questions or over one of the client's answers? Am I aware of the embarrassment?
- How do I handle the client's irritation over one of my questions?
- How do I handle my own irritation over an answer to one of my questions? Am I aware of the irritation?
- How do I handle a client who is telling me something I do not believe?

- When I have personal knowledge of some aspect of what the client is saying, do I record the client's perspective or my own? Do I know the difference?
- When, if ever, should I role-play with the client? (For example, if I am trying to help the client recall a conversation, I take the role of the other party in the conversation to see if this exercise aids recollection.)
- Have I determined what the client wants? Do I know what his or her expectations are?
- At the conclusion of the interview, have I made it clear to the client what I will do, what the office will do, and what the client is to do as the next step?
- Am I am a good interviewer? How do I know? Who has evaluated me? How can I obtain feedback on the quality of my interviewing skill? Who is available whom I respect enough to give me this feedback? How can I approach this person? For 99 percent of us, intensive criticism is unsettling and threatening to us—even if it is constructive. What makes me think that I fall into the 1 percent category?

▪ CLIENT INTAKE MEMORANDUM

The client **intake memorandum** is the written report of the interviewer on the interview. It should have five parts:

Heading
The heading provides the following information at the top of the first page:

- Name of the person who wrote the memo (you)
- Name of the supervisor in charge of the case
- Date the memo was written
- Date the interview was conducted
- Name of the case
- Office file number of the case
- Kind of case (general area of the law)
- Subject matter of the memo following the notation "RE"

Personal Data
- Name of the client
- Client's home address
- Phone numbers where client can be reached
- Age of the client
- Marital status
- Place of employment of the client
- Etc.

Statement of the Assignment
The first paragraph of the memo should state the precise objective you were given in conducting the interview.

Body of the Memo
Here the facts are presented in a coherent, readable manner according to a number of possible organizational principles:

- A chronological listing of the facts so that the events are unfolded as a story with a beginning, middle, and end

- A categorizing of the facts according to the major topics or issues of the case, each with its own subject heading under which the relevant facts are placed
- Any other format called for by the supervisor

Conclusion

Here a number of things could be included:

- A brief summary of the major facts listed in the body of the memo
- Your impressions of the client, such as how knowledgeable and believable the client appeared to be.
- A list of the next steps, for example, what further facts should be sought through investigation, what legal research should be undertaken, what else should be done on the case based on what was learned during the interview.
- A list of anything you told the client to do, for example, bring in specified documents relevant to the case, check on further facts and call back, return for another interview, etc.

Figure 4.3 presents a sample of the introductory parts of an intake memo:

Figure 4.3   Intake Memo

Inter-Office Memo

To: Ann Fuller, Supervisor   **Case:** John Myers vs. Betsy Myers
From: Jim Smith, Paralegal   **File Number:** 95-102
Date of Memo: March 13, 1995   **Kind of Case:** Negligence
Date of Interview: March 12, 1995   **Re:** Intake Interview of John Myers

Personal Data:

Name of Client: John Myers
Address: 34 Main Street, Salem, MA, 02127
Phone: 966-3954 (H) 297-9700 ($\times$ 301) (W)
Age: 37
Marital Status: Married but separated from his wife,
Betsy Myers
Employment: ABC Construction Co., 2064 South Street, Salem,
MA, 02127

   You asked me to conduct a comprehensive intake interview of John Myers, our client, in order to obtain information on his background and on the facts of the accident.

   A. BACKGROUND

     John Myers lives . . . .

▪ **ASSIGNMENT 4.2** ▪

The Hazard Interview

In this assignment you will be interviewing someone about a hazard. Ask a friend, a neighbor, a relative, another student, or another employee about a hazard where they live, work, study, or play. The hazard should have the following characteristics:

- It should be a hazard about which the interviewee has personal knowledge.
- It should be a hazard about which you (the interviewer) have *no* personal knowledge.
- It should be a hazard that involves a specific thing, object, or condition—preferably relating to a building, an appliance, a motor vehicle, a sidewalk, a street area, etc. It should not deal with anything as general or vague as "the hazards of city living," "the hazards of smoking," etc.

Do not impose on the interviewee any rigid definition of a hazard. In the process of conducting the interview, you will want to find out what technical or common-sense definition of hazard the *interviewee* is using.

After you conduct the interview, write out your notes in the format of a client intake memorandum.

The assignment will be evaluated according to the following criteria:

- factual detail (for suggestions on achieving factual specificity in the related context of investigation, see Figure 4.6 later in this chapter)
- organization (no particular organization is required; select an organization that will make the memo easy to read)
- spelling, grammar, and composition (including the structure and sequencing of sentences and paragraphs)

Type the memo—double-spaced with generous margin space. There is no minimum or maximum length for the memo. The length should be appropriate for the nature of the hazard being described.

▪ INTRODUCTION TO INVESTIGATION

The objective of investigation is, of course, to uncover facts. More specifically,

- Investigation provides a way to verify what the client said during the initial client interview.
- Investigation will be helpful in deciding whether to settle the case and for how much.
- Investigation will be helpful in preparing for trial.

Fact-gathering is usually done by personnel within the law office—the attorney, the paralegal, the full-time investigator, the free-lance investigator, the secretary. In complex cases, the office may use outside experts to help investigate and to provide testimony at trial. Many such experts are available, as indicated by the following ads from trade journals read by trial attorneys:

How do you know what facts need to be investigated in personal injury litigation? The three main guides are presented on the next page in Figure 4.4.

Evidence Law

A general understanding of the law of evidence will be of assistance in understanding how to verify facts and why they need to be verified. Assume a client tells you that he or she suffered $100,000 in lost wages due to the injury that is now the subject of litigation. Some of the evidentiary questions relating to these facts are as follows:

- Are there documents, e.g., past wage slips, that will help document the loss?
- Are these documents admissible in court? Would they be allowed in?
- Are witnesses available to testify about the loss?
- Would the testimony of these witnesses be admissible?

It is not enough, therefore, to know that a $100,000 loss has been suffered. The "evidentiary context" of this fact must always be considered. This evidentiary context helps guide the investigation.

Tort Law

Your knowledge of tort law will be another major guide to investigation in personal injury cases. As we explore the basic principles of tort law in this book,

Figure 4.4   Guides for Investigation

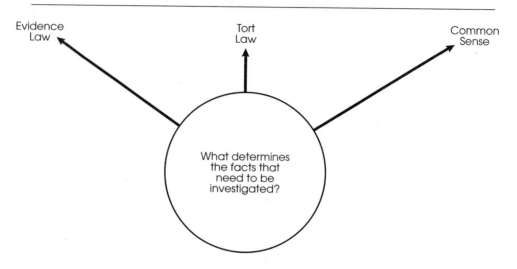

we will regularly focus on the facts that need to be sought in order to determine whether a particular tort has been committed. In Chapter 3 on legal analysis, we saw how the analysis of tort law can help you determine what additional facts should be sought through investigation.

Common Sense

While a knowledge of evidence law and of tort law is important to investigation, *it is probably not as important as common sense.* In fact, once you are in practice, you will be surprised to discover the high degree to which so many legal problems are solved by the use of common sense. Indeed, you must be careful to avoid letting your knowledge of law interfere with the exercise of your common sense! The most effective attorneys and paralegals are those who came to the study and practice of law *already equipped* with:

- a sense of responsibility
- inquisitiveness
- common sense

Facts do not have legs that are simply waiting for an opportunity to walk into the office of the investigator to reveal themselves. Common sense tells investigators that they must be aggressive and imaginative in going out to find the facts. This reality is reflected in the following comments by an investigator who must investigate road conditions in an accident case:

> Sometimes I don't know what I am looking for until I find it. You've got to keep an open mind in this business. I need to find out the road conditions on the day of the accident. I can call the client—that's OK as a starter. I'm going to get a copy of the newspaper for the day of the accident to see if it

has a weather report. I think copies of old newspapers are available. Also, there must be some way to get a governmental weather bureau to give us something official. I think I'll give Fred a call. He once had a case like this. Maybe he can give me a lead. I wonder if the city highway department keeps a record of road conditions and road repairs. I can always ask my supervisor if she wants me to go to some of the people who live in that area to see what they might be able to tell me about the road. Sometimes you can turn up good leads just by talking to people.

An investigator with this kind of determination would be a prized employee in any law office.

■ FACT ANALYSIS: ORGANIZING THE OPTIONS

The process of organizing fact options may initially appear to be complex and cumbersome. But the process can become second nature to you once you understand it, try it out, evaluate it, modify it, and find it helpful. It is, of course, perfectly proper to adopt any process that you find effective. Whatever method you use, the need is to develop the *discipline* of fact analysis as soon as possible.

There are a number of fundamental characteristics of facts that should be kept in mind:

- Events take place.
- Events mean different things to different people.
- Different people, therefore, have different versions of events.
- Inconsistent versions of the same event do not necessarily indicate fraud or lying.
- Although someone's version may claim to be the total picture, it probably will contain only a piece of the picture.
- In giving a version of an event, people usually mix statements of *why* the event occurred with statements of *what* occurred.
- Whenever it is claimed that an event occurred in a certain way, one can logically expect that certain signs, indications, or traces (evidence) of the event can be found.

Given these truisms, the investigator should analyze the facts along the lines indicated in Figure 4.5. It is possible for a single client's case to have numerous individual facts that are in dispute. Furthermore, facts can change, or people's versions of facts can change in the middle of a case. Each new or modified fact demands the same comprehensive process of fact analysis outlined in Figure 4.5.

Obtaining different versions of a fact may be difficult because the differences may not be clear on the surface. Of course, every fact will not necessarily have multiple versions. It is recommended, however, that you assume there will be more than one version until you have demonstrated otherwise to yourself. Undoubtedly, you must do some probing in order to uncover the versions that exist. Better to do so now than to be confronted with a surprise at trial or at an agency hearing.

People will not always be willing to share their accounts or versions of facts with you. If you are not successful in convincing them to tell their story, you may have to make some assumptions of what their story is *likely* to be and to check out these assumptions.

Figure 4.5   Fact Analysis in Investigation

Starting Point:
All the facts you presently have on the case.

Procedure:

- Arrange the facts chronologically.
- Place a number before each fact that must be established in a legal proceeding.

State the Following Versions of Each Fact:

- Version I: The client's
- Version II: The opponent's (as revealed to you or as assumed)
- Version III: A witness's
- Version IV: Another witness's
- Version V: Any other reasonable version (e.g., from your own deductions)

As to Each Version:

- State precisely (with quotations if possible) what the version is.
- State the evidence or indications that tend to support the version according to persons presenting the version.
- State the evidence or indications that tend to contradict this version.
- Determine how you will verify whether the evidence or indications exist.

■ FACT PARTICULARIZATION

The hallmark of the professional is to view people, objects, and events as unique. The bureaucrat or administrator, on the other hand, sees people, objects, and events in categories. The focus of the professional is on differences and individuality. The focus of the bureaucrat is on similarities and groupings.[4]

Professionalism in investigation means to *particularize* the facts so that there is an exploration of all or almost all the details that make the facts unique. (See Figure 4.6.) **Fact particularization** involves collecting more facts in order to obtain a comprehensive picture of what happened. Your guide in accomplishing particularization is common sense.

Figure 4.6   Fact Particularization

The investigator must *particularize* facts collected thus far:

1. By assuming that these facts are woefully incomplete, and
2. By assuming that there is more than one version of the facts, and
3. By identifying a large number of basic who, what, where, why, when, and how questions, which, if answered, would provide as complete a picture of what happened as is possible to obtain at this time.

---

[4]W. Statsky & P. Lang, *The Legal Paraprofessional as Advocate and Assistant: Roles, Training Concepts and Materials,* 159 (1971).

Example: You are working on an automobile negligence case. Two cars collide on a two-lane street. They were driven by Smith and Jones. Jones is a client of your law office. One of the facts in the file is that, according to Jones, Smith's car "veered into Jones's lane moments before the collision." Your job is to particularize this fact. *Design an investigation strategy consisting of questions you would like answered in order to obtain a much more detailed picture of what happened.* This is done by elaborating on the facts already collected. You ask the following common sense questions: who, what, where, why, when, and how.

- What does Jones mean by veering into the other lane?
- How much veering was done? An inch? A foot? The entire car in the other lane? How much of an angle was there?
- Who saw this happen? The file tells us that Smith's car veered, "according to Jones." Did Jones see this happen himself? Who else saw it, if anyone? Any passengers in Jones's car? Any passengers in Smith's car? What about bystanders? Has the neighborhood been checked for witnesses, e.g., people who live or work in the area, people who frequently sit on public benches in the area?
- Were the police called after the accident? If so, who was the officer? Was a report made? If so, what does it say, if anything, about the car veering into the other lane? Where is this report? How can you obtain a copy?
- How fast was Jones's car going at the time of the veering? Who would be able to substantiate the speed? Who might have different views of how fast Jones was going?
- How fast was Smith's car going at the time of the veering? Who would be able to substantiate the speed? Who might have different views of how fast Smith was going?
- Have there been other accidents in the area? If so, how similar have they been to this one?
- What was the condition of the road at the time Smith started to veer? At the time of the collision?
- What was the weather at the time?
- How was visibility?
- What kind of a road is it? Straight? Curved at the area of the collision? Any inclines? Any hills that will affect speed and visibility?
- What kind of area is it? Residential? Commercial?
- Is there anything in the area that would distract drivers, e.g., potholes?
- Where is the nearest traffic light, stop sign, or other traffic signal? How, if at all, did they affect traffic at the time of the accident?
- What is the speed limit of the area?
- What kind of car was Smith driving? Were there any mechanical problems with the car? Would these problems help cause the veering? What prior accidents has Smith had, if any?
- What kind of car was Jones driving? Were there any mechanical problems with the car? What prior accidents has Jones had, if any?
- Etc.

The above list of questions is by no means exhaustive. Many more could be asked to try to complete the picture of what happened and to collect as many new and substantiating facts as possible on what happened. You need to develop the *habit* of generating such factual questions. Not all of the questions will turn out to be productive. Some—or perhaps many—will lead to dead ends. Be willing to take this risk.

Throughout the chapters of this book, there are a number of investigation strategy assignments in which you will be asked to particularize facts relevant to the area of law discussed in the chapters.

General Instructions for the Investigation Strategy Assignment

Objectives of Assignment: ·   To demonstrate the close connection between common sense and investigation
       ·   To assist you in developing an investigation plan based on the need for more factual detail

---

1. The starting point is a set of facts that you are given in the assignment. Assume that you have entered the case after these facts have been collected by someone else.
2. Assume further that these facts are inadequate because *many* more facts are needed.
3. Closely examine the facts you have. Are they arranged chronologically? If not, rearrange them chronologically so that the facts tell a story with a beginning, middle, and ending. Of course, there will be many gaps in the story. Your task will be to identify these gaps and to raise the questions that the investigator would have to pursue in order to try to fill or close the gaps. These questions will become the investigator's plan for further investigation.
4. The focus of these questions will be on what you *don't* know about the facts that you have.
5. Isolate the facts that you have into small clusters of facts, e.g., the soda bottle exploded. For each small set of facts that you identify or isolate in this way, make a *large* list of questions that fall into two categories:
   - questions that you would ask in order to obtain additional facts that will help you compile a much more detailed picture of what happened; to aid you in this list, ask the basic who, what, where, why, when, how questions about every fact
   - questions that you would ask in order to obtain additional facts that will help you substantiate (or prove) the facts that you already have

   There is no rigid formula to follow in order to make these lists of questions. The goal is a comprehensive list of questions, that, if answered, would provide a comprehensive picture of what happened. Do not worry about the answers to these questions. The need now is to identify the questions that will later become the strategy or plan for the investigator.
6. Be scrupulous about dates. Ask questions about the dates you have and also about the dates that are missing.
7. Do a ''people analysis'' of the facts. Make a list of every person who is involved or who could be involved in the facts. Assume that each person potentially has a different version of the facts. Structure your questions for this assignment around these different versions.
8. Preceding most of the assignments there will be a discussion of some legal principles governing certain torts or defenses. Include questions that would be relevant to the elements of these torts or defenses. (On generating such questions, see also p. 43 in Chapter 3 on legal analysis.) If there is no such discussion, simply ask the basic who-what-where-etc. questions that

you would like answered as a matter of common sense, in order to obtain a complete picture of what happened.

9. The list of questions in this assignment does not have to be written in any particular order. You select your own format of presenting the questions so that they are readable. A possible model for writing out your questions would be to cluster all the questions under the elements of the tort or defense being examined in the chapter.

▪ ASSIGNMENT 4.3 ▪

Assume you are working on the following cases. Prepare an investigation strategy. Follow the general instructions for the investigation strategy assignments, except for instruction 8. There is no need to examine elements at this time.

a. Mr. Flint was in the XYZ Supermarket, on his way out. He slipped on a wet floor just inside the exit door.

b. George and Ted are students in the same class. One day during a break, George said to Ted in a very loud voice, ''You are a thief.''

▪ TAKING A WITNESS STATEMENT

There are four major kinds of **witness statements:**

1. Handwritten statement
2. Recorded statement in question-and-answer format (on audio or video tape)
3. Responses to a questionnaire that is mailed to the witness to answer
4. Statement taken in question-and-answer format before a court reporter

The most common kind of statement is the first, which we will consider here.

In a handwritten statement, the investigator writes down what the witness says, or the witness writes out the statement himself or herself. There is no formal structure to which the written statement must conform. The major requirements for the statement are clarity and accuracy.

The statement should begin by identifying (1) the witness (name, address, place of work, names of relatives, and other identifying data that may be helpful in locating the witness later); (2) the date and place of the taking of the statement; and (3) the name of the person to whom the statement is being made. See the example of a witness statement in Figure 4.7.

Then comes the body of the statement, in which the witness provides information about the event or circumstance in question (an accident that was observed, what the witness did and saw just before a fire, where the witness was on a certain date, etc.). It is often useful to have the witness present the facts in a chronological order, particularly when many facts are involved in the statement. It is important that the witness give detailed facts that demonstrate the witness was in a good position to observe the event. This will lend credibility to the statement.

At the end of the statement, the witness should say that he or she is making the statement of his or her own free will, without any pressure or coercion from anyone. The witness then signs the statement. The signature goes on the last page. Each of the other pages is also signed or initialed. If others have watched the witness make and sign the statement, they should also sign an **attestation clause,** which simply states that they observed the witness sign the statement.

Figure 4.7   Witness Statement

Statement of John Wood

I am John Wood. I am 42 years old and live at 3416 34th Street, N.W., Nashua, New Hampshire 03060. I work at the Deming Chemical Plant at region circle, Nashua. My home phone is 966-3954. My work phone is 297-9700 x301. I am married to Patricia Wood. We have two children, Jessica (twenty-two years old) and Gabriel (eighteen years old). I am making this statement to Rose Thompson, a paralegal at Fields, Smith and Farrell. This statement is being given on March 13, 1986 at my home, 3416 34th Street, NW.

On February 15, 1986, I was standing on the corner of . . . .

Before the witness signs, he or she should read the entire statement and make any corrections that need to be made. Each correction should be initialed by the witness. Each page should be numbered with the total number of pages indicated each time. For example, if there are four pages, the page numbers would be "1 of 4," "2 of 4," "3 of 4," and "4 of 4." The investigator should not try to correct any spelling or grammatical mistakes made by the witness. The statement should exist exactly as the witness spoke or wrote it. Just before the signature of the witness at the end of the statement, the witness should say (in writing), "I have read all _____ pages of this statement, and the facts within it are accurate to the best of my knowledge."

Investigators sometimes use various tricks of the trade to achieve a desired effect. For example, if the investigator is writing out the statement as the witness speaks, the investigator may *intentionally* make an error of fact. When the witness reads over the statement, the investigator makes sure that the witness catches the error and initials the correction. This becomes added evidence that the witness carefully read the statement. The witness might later try to claim that he or she did not read the statement. The initialed correction helps rebut this position.

Not all witness statements are eventually admitted into evidence at trial. They may be admitted to help the attorney demonstrate that the pretrial statement of the witness is inconsistent with the testimony of this witness during the trial itself. The main value of witness statements is thoroughness and accuracy in case preparation. Trials can occur years after the events that led to litigation. Witnesses may disappear or forget. Witness statements taken soon after the event can sometimes be helpful in tracking down witnesses and in helping them recall the details of the event.

▪ ASSIGNMENT 4.4 ▪

Select any member of the class and take a witness statement from this person. The statement should concern some accident in which the witness was a participant or an observer. The witness, however, should not be a party to any litigation growing out of the accident. You write out the statement from what the witness says in response to your questions. Do not submit a statement hand-written by the witness except for his or her signature, initials, etc. Assume that you (the investigator–paralegal) work for the law firm of Davis and Davis, which represents someone else involved in the accident.

SUMMARY

A major goal of the initial client interview is to collect facts that will help the office determine whether the elements of one or more cause of action can be established, whether significant damages are possible, and whether the defendant has assets from which a judgment can be satisfied. After the retainer is signed, the interviewer seeks extensive background information on the client. Further details are sought on the accident, the extent of injuries, medical expenses, loss of income, property damage, etc. Knowing the purpose of the interview, pre-paring properly, having the right attitude, and being in the right setting are im-portant considerations in achieving effective communication with a client. After the interview, the intake memorandum records what took place during the interview.

Investigation helps verify facts obtained in the client interview. What is uncov-ered will also help the attorney prepare for trial and make settlement decisions. The three guides for the investigator in a personal injury case are evidence law, tort law, and common sense. People often have different perspectives on what did or did not happen, particularly in regard to emotionally charged events. When different versions of facts exist, the investigator must seek them out. Fact partic-ularization is a technique to help the investigator formulate who-what-where-why-when-how questions that need to be investigated. The purpose of a witness statement is to preserve the testimony of a potentially important witness.

Key Terms

liability	PI	intake memorandum
cause of action	deep pockets	fact particularization
damages	retainer	witness statements
nominal	practice books	attestation clause
contingent fee		

CHAPTER 5

Pre-Trial Litigation

CHAPTER OUTLINE

- COURT SYSTEMS
- JURISDICTION OVER PERSONS
- VENUE
- CHOICE OF LAW IN STATE COURTS
- PARTIES

- PLEADINGS
- ENDING THE CASE WITHOUT A TRIAL
- JURY SELECTION
- PRE-TRIAL CONFERENCE

This chapter covers pre-trial litigation except for discovery, which is covered in the next chapter.

■ COURT SYSTEMS

- Jurisdiction
- State Court systems
- Federal Court Systems

One of the early concerns of a plaintiff's attorney is to identify the court in which to bring a tort action. To address this concern, we need to know something about judicial systems.

1. Jurisdiction

There are fifty state court systems and a federal court system. Each court within a system is identified by its **jurisdiction.** This important word has three meanings.

First, it often refers to the geographic area over which a particular court has authority. A state trial court, for example, has **geographic jurisdiction** to hear cases arising in a specific county or district of the state. A state supreme court, in contrast, may have geographic jurisdiction to hear appeals in cases arising anywhere in the state. Thus a state supreme court will often say "in this jurisdiction" when referring to its own state. The phrase has the same meaning as "in this state."

Secondly, the word jurisdiction refers to the *power* of a court to adjudicate a dispute. **Adjudication** is the process by which a court (or administrative agency) resolves a legal dispute through litigation. In order for the court to have power to order the defendant to do anything (or to refrain from doing something), the court must have **personal jurisdiction** over the defendant. This is also called **in personam jurisdiction.**

Thirdly, jurisdiction means the power that a court must have over the subject matter or over the particular kind of dispute that has been brought before it. Some of the more common classifications of **subject matter jurisdiction** are:

- Limited jurisdiction
- General jurisdiction
- Exclusive jurisdiction
- Concurrent jurisdiction
- Original jurisdiction
- Appellate jurisdiction

Limited Jurisdiction

A court of **limited** (or *special*) **jurisdiction** can hear only certain kinds of cases. A criminal court is not allowed to take a noncriminal case, and a small claims court is authorized to hear only cases in which the plaintiff claims less than a certain amount of money as damages from the defendant.

Another way to look at a court of limited jurisdiction is to say it has a specified *subject matter jurisdiction.* Its subject matter jurisdiction is limited to cases that deal with designated subject matters only, such as criminal cases.

General Jurisdiction

A court of **general jurisdiction** can, with some exceptions, hear any kind of case, as long as the case arises within the geographic boundaries of that court. A *state* court of general jurisdiction can handle any case that raises **state questions** (i.e., questions arising from or based on the state constitution, state statutes, state regulations, or state common law); a *federal* court of general jurisdiction can handle any case that raises **federal questions** (i.e., questions arising from or based on the federal constitution, federal statutes, federal regulations, or other federal laws).

Exclusive Jurisdiction

A court of **exclusive jurisdiction** is the only court that can handle a certain kind of case. For example, it may be that the Juvenile Court has exclusive jurisdiction over all cases involving children under a certain age who are charged with acts of delinquency. If this kind of case is brought in another court, there could be a challenge on the ground that the court lacked jurisdiction over the case.

Concurrent Jurisdiction

Sometimes two courts have jurisdiction over a case; the case could be brought in either court. In such a situation, both courts are said to have **concurrent jurisdiction** over the case. For example, it could be that both the Family Court and a County Court have jurisdiction to enforce a child-custody order.

Original Jurisdiction

A court of **original jurisdiction** is the first court to hear and decide a case. It is also called a trial court or a **court of first instance.** In addition, it can be classified as a court of limited jurisdiction (if it can try only certain kinds of cases), or of general jurisdiction (if it can try cases involving any subject matter), or of exclusive jurisdiction (if the trial can take place only in that court), or of concurrent jurisdiction (if the trial can take place either in that court or in another kind of court).

Appellate Jurisdiction

A court with **appellate jurisdiction** can hear appeals from lower tribunals. An appeal is a review of what a lower court or agency has done, to determine if there was any error. Sometimes a party who is dissatisfied with a lower court ruling can appeal as a matter of right to the appellate court (the court must hear the appeal); in other kinds of cases, the appellate court has discretion on whether it will hear the appeal.

2. State Court Systems

There is considerable variety in the court systems that exist in our states:

Courts of Original Jurisdiction

Depending on the particular state, there may be one or more levels of trial courts (courts of original jurisdiction). These courts hear the dispute, determine the facts of the case, and make the initial determination or ruling. In addition, they may sometimes have the power to review cases that were initially decided by an administrative agency.

The most common arrangement is a two-tier system of trial courts. At the lower level are courts of limited or special jurisdiction, the so-called **inferior courts.** Local courts, such as city courts, county courts, or justice of the peace courts, often fall into this category. These courts may have original jurisdiction over relatively minor cases, such as violations of local ordinances and lawsuits involving small sums of money. Also included in this category are special courts that are limited to specific matters, such as surrogate courts or probate courts that hear matters involving the estates of deceased or mentally incompetent persons.

Immediately above the trial courts of limited jurisdiction are the trial courts of general jurisdiction, which usually handle more serious cases, such as violations of state laws or lawsuits involving large sums of money. The name given to the trial courts at this second level varies greatly from state to state. They are known as superior courts, courts of common pleas, district courts, or circuit courts. New York is especially confusing. There the trial court of general jurisdiction is called the *supreme court,* a label reserved in most states for the court of final appeals, the highest court in the system.

This two-tier system is not invariable. Some states may have only one court of original jurisdiction. Moreover, the individual levels may be segmented into divisions. A court of general, original jurisdiction, for example, may be broken up into specialized divisions such as landlord-tenant, family, juvenile, and criminal divisions.

Courts of Appeal

These courts rarely make the initial decision in a case. Their primary function is to **review** decisions made by lower courts in order to correct **errors of law.** That is, they will look to see if the lower court correctly interpreted and applied the law to the facts of the dispute. In this review process, appellate courts do not make their own findings of fact. No new evidence is taken, and no witnesses are called. The court limits itself to an analysis of the **trial court record** (transcripts of testimony, copies of the pleadings and other documents that were filed, etc.) to determine if that lower court made any errors of law. Attorneys submit **appellate briefs** containing their arguments on the correctness or incorrectness of what the lower court did.

Some states have two levels of appellate courts. The first level is the court of middle appeals, sometimes called an **intermediate appellate court.** The decisions of this court may in turn be reviewed by a second-level appellate court, the court of final appeals. This latter court, often known as the supreme court, is the highest court in the state, the **court of final resort.**

Figure 5.1 illustrates the lines of appeal in many state court systems.

▪ ASSIGNMENT 5.1 ▪

In Figure 1.1 of Chapter 1, thirty-five causes of action relating to tort law were listed. Pick any ten of these. What state courts in your state have subject matter jurisdiction over these causes of action? Prepare a chart of the courts in which these causes of action can be tried in your state. Consult your state constitution, your state code, and the rules of court of individual courts.

3. Federal Court System

The federal court system, like those of the states, consists of two basic kinds of courts: courts of original jurisdiction (trial courts) and appellate courts.

Courts of Original Jurisdiction

The basic federal court at the trial level is the **United States District Court.** There are districts throughout the country, at least one for every state, the District of Columbia, Guam, the Virgin Islands, and Puerto Rico. The District Courts exercise original jurisdiction over most federal litigation and also serve as courts of review for many cases that were initially decided by federal administrative agencies.

In addition to the District Courts, there are several federal courts that exercise original jurisdiction over specialized cases. These include the United States Tax Court, the United States Claims Court, and the Untied States Court of International Trade. (See Figure 5.2.)

Figure 5.1   Hierarchy of State Judicial Systems

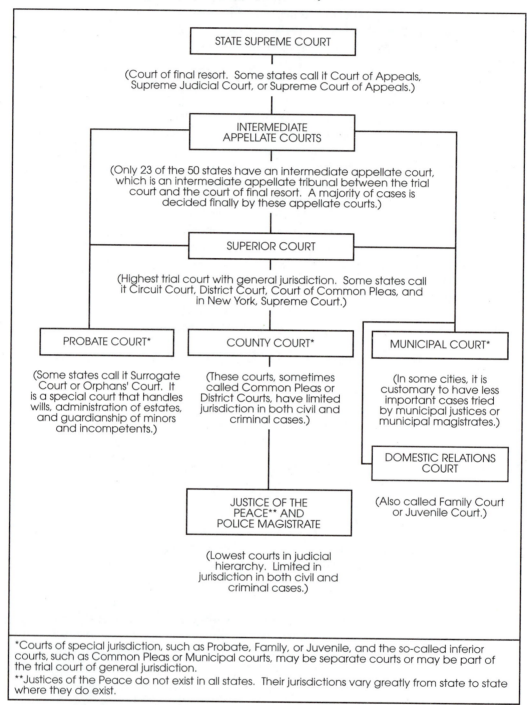

STATE SUPREME COURT

(Court of final resort. Some states call it Court of Appeals,
Supreme Judicial Court, or Supreme Court of Appeals.)

INTERMEDIATE
APPELLATE COURTS

(Only 23 of the 50 states have an intermediate appellate court,
which is an intermediate appellate tribunal between the trial
court and the court of final resort. A majority of cases is
decided finally by these appellate courts.)

SUPERIOR COURT

(Highest trial court with general jurisdiction. Some states call
it Circuit Court, District Court, Court of Common Pleas, and
in New York, Supreme Court.)

PROBATE COURT*

(Some states call it Surrogate
Court or Orphans' Court. It
is a special court that handles
wills, administration of estates,
and guardianship of minors
and incompetents.)

COUNTY COURT*

(These courts, sometimes
called Common Pleas or
District Courts, have limited
jurisdiction in both civil and
criminal cases.)

MUNICIPAL COURT*

(In some cities, it is
customary to have less
important cases tried
by municipal justices or
municipal magistrates.)

DOMESTIC RELATIONS
COURT

(Also called Family Court
or Juvenile Court.)

JUSTICE OF THE
PEACE** AND
POLICE MAGISTRATE

(Lowest courts in judicial
hierarchy. Limited in
jurisdiction in both civil and
criminal cases.)

*Courts of special jurisdiction, such as Probate, Family, or Juvenile, and the so-called inferior
courts, such as Common Pleas or Municipal courts, may be separate courts or may be part of
the trial court of general jurisdiction.
**Justices of the Peace do not exist in all states. Their jurisdictions vary greatly from state to state
where they do exist.

SOURCE: *Law and the Courts,* 20 (American Bar Association, 1974).

Figure 5.2 Hierarchy of Federal Judicial System

```
                    ┌─────────────────────────┐
                    │    SUPREME COURT        │
                    │  OF THE UNITED STATES   │
                    └─────────────────────────┘
```

SUPREME COURT OF THE UNITED STATES

United States Courts of Appeals 12 Circuits	United States Court of Appeals for the Federal Circuit

Appeals from State Courts in 50 States, the Supreme Court of Puerto Rico, and the District of Columbia Court of Appeals	United States Tax Court and various Administrative Agencies Federal Trade Commission National Labor Relations Board Immigration and Naturalization Service	United States District Courts with Federal and Local Jurisdiction Guam Virgin Islands Northern Mariana Islands	United States District Courts with Federal Jurisdiction Only 89 Districts in 50 States 1 in District of Columbia 1 in Puerto Rico	United States Court of Federal Claims	United States Court of International Trade	United States Court of Veterans Appeals

SOURCE: Administrative Office of the United States Courts.

Courts of Appeals

The federal system, like almost half of the fifty state judicial systems, has two levels of appellate courts: middle appeals and final appeals. The primary courts at the middle level are the **United States Courts of Appeals.** These courts are divided into twelve geographic circuits, eleven of which are made up of groupings of various states and territories, with a twelfth for the District of Columbia. Their primary function is to review the decisions of the federal courts of original jurisdiction. In addition, the decisions of certain federal agencies, notably the National Labor Relations Board, are reviewed directly by the court of appeals without first going to the district court. Finally, there is a specialized court of appeals called the Court of Appeals for the Federal Circuit. This court, created in 1982, reviews decisions of the United States Claims Court, the United States Court of International Trade, and the United States Court of Veterans Appeals. It also reviews rulings of the Patent and Trademark Office, and some decisions of the federal district courts where the United States government is a defendant.

The federal court of final appeals is, of course, the **United States Supreme Court,** which provides the final review of the decisions of all federal courts and agencies. The Supreme Court may also review certain decisions of the state courts, when these decisions raise questions involving the Untied States Constitution or a federal statute. (See Figure 5.2.)

Figure 5.3 illustrates the division of the federal court system into twelve geographic circuits. Each circuit has its own United States Court of Appeals. The United States District Courts exist within these circuits.

As we shall see, most tort cases are brought in state courts. In federal courts, two main categories of tort cases can be brought: those based on special federal statutes, and diversity cases.

Figure 5.3   United States Courts of Appeals and United States District Courts

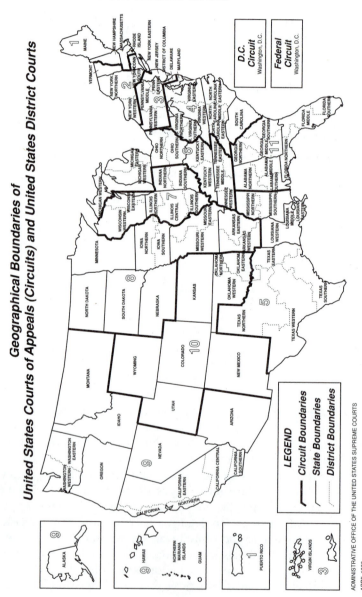

SOURCE: Administrative Office of the United States Courts.

Cases Based on Special Federal Statutes

Congress has passed a number of statutes that have the effect of allowing tort and related cases to be litigated in federal courts such as the United States District Court:

- **Federal Tort Claims Act**   The United States can be sued for money damages when a federal employee commits a tort designated in the Act.
- **Civil Rights Act**   Damages can be obtained against a defendant who deprives the plaintiff of federal rights under the color of law.
- **Federal Employers' Liability Act**   This Act covers injuries received by railroad employees engaged in interstate commerce (similar to worker's compensation covering nongovernmental employees).
- **Consumer Product Safety Act**   Damages can be obtained for a knowing violation of rules under this Act.

We will examine some of these Acts in greater detail later.

Diversity Cases

Mary lives in New York. Tom lives in California. They are citizens of different (or diverse) states—there is **diversity of citizenship** between them. If they want to sue each other for a tort or for any other civil action, they can, of course, use a state court. Since diversity exists, they can also sue in federal court if the amount in controversy exceeds an amount designated by statute of Congress. If one party wants to sue another for negligence, for example, the action can be brought in the United States District Court if:

- there is diversity of citizenship among all the parties, and
- the amount in controversy exceeds the statutory minimum

For "diversity jurisdiction," there is no need to show that the case arises out of a special federal statute. Diversity represents its own independent ticket of entry into the federal courts. Conversely, for a case based on a special federal statute, there is no need to show diversity.

Citizenship is determined by **domicile.** Diversity requires that no plaintiff be domiciled in the same state as any of the defendants. A person can have only one domicile. Domicile is the place where you have been physically present and where you intend to stay indefinitely. If a Texan and a New Yorker bring a negligence action against a Californian, a Georgian, and a Texan, the action cannot be brought in a federal court since there is no complete diversity—a defendant and a plaintiff are from Texas. In a class action, diversity need exist only between the defendants and the representative of the class.

▪ JURISDICTION OVER PERSONS

Assuming that a court has subject matter jurisdiction over a case, the next problem is to obtain jurisdiction over the person of the defendant. Personal jurisdiction over the defendant is usually referred to as *in personam jurisdiction.* A judgment by a court that has such jurisdiction is enforceable against any property of the defendant, whether or not the property was directly involved in the litigation.

Statutory and constitutional requirements must be met before a court can acquire personal jurisdiction. The *statutory* requirements usually involve the technical rules of service of process, discussed below. These statutory requirements must meet the following *constitutional* standards:

- the method of notifying the defendant about the contemplated litigation must be reasonably calculated to reach him or her
- the defendant must have sufficient minimum contacts with the state so that it is reasonable and fair to require the defendant to appear and be subjected to full personal jurisdiction in the state

We will examine some of the statutory and constitutional requirements for jurisdiction over the person through the following topics:

1. service within the state
2. domicile
3. consent
4. long-arm statutes

1. Service Within the State

A civil action begins when the plaintiff files a complaint with the clerk of the court. A **complaint** is a pre-trial document filed in court by the plaintiff that tries to state a claim or cause of action against the defendant. The clerk then issues a **summons** that directs the defendant to answer the complaint and to defend the action. (See Figure 5.4.) Delivery of the summons to the defendant (usually with a copy of the complaint) constitutes **service of process.**

States differ on who can serve process (e.g., a marshal, a sheriff, any adult), when service can be made, etc. If the defendant is a corporation or business, service of process is usually made by delivering the summons to an officer of the company or to any other agent who is authorized to accept service of process.

Full in personam jurisdiction is acquired over an individual defendant by service of process on the defendant who is *physically* within the state.

When personal service cannot be made on a defendant physically in the state, **substituted service** is sometimes authorized, e.g., certified mail, or publication of the summons and complaint in a newspaper. States are reluctant to allow substituted service because of the danger that defendants will never learn about the proposed litigation against them. Hence, specific rules exist on when substituted service can be used and how it must be accomplished.

- ASSIGNMENT 5.2 ·

Answer the following questions for any state trial court of your state. Summarize the major rules on the following topics. Assume that the defendant is being sued for negligence and that the defendant lives, works, or has a business in the state. (See General Instructions for the State Code Assignment in Chapter 2.)

a. Who can serve process?
b. When can process be served?
c. What happens if the defendant is not at home or at work when service is attempted?
d. How is a business or corporation with an office in your state served?
e. When can service by mail and service by publication be used? How is substituted service accomplished?
f. How is service made on a minor or on an incompetent person?
g. Once service has been made, what steps must the process server take, e.g., file a statement with the clerk of court?

Figure 5.4   Sample Summons and Return of Service

COURT OF COMMON PLEAS
FRANKLIN COUNTY, OHIO
SUMMONS

John Jones
221 E. West Street
Columbus, Ohio 43215
          Plaintiff, No. _____
          v.
Robert Farrell
122 Sun Street
Columbus, Ohio 43214
          Defendant,
To the following named defendants:

Name	Address
Robert Farrell	122 Sun St.
	Columbus, OH 43214

  You have been named defendant(s) in a complaint filed in Franklin County Court of Common Pleas, Franklin County Court House, Columbus, Ohio, 43215 by

Name	Address
John Jones	221 E. West St., Columbus, OH 43215

plaintiff(s). A copy of the complaint is attached hereto. The name and address of the plaintiff's attorney is <u>Mary Fin, Esq. 3 Davis St. Columbus, OH 43214</u>

  You are hereby summoned and required to serve upon the plaintiff's attorney, or upon the plaintiff, if he has no attorney of record, a copy of an answer to the complaint within twenty-eight days after service of this summons on you, exclusive of the day of service. Your answer must be filed with the Court within three days after the service of a copy of the answer on the plaintiff's attorney.

  If you fail to appear and defend, judgment by default will be rendered against you for the relief demanded in the complaint.

_____
Clerk, Court of Common Pleas
Franklin County, Ohio

Date _____

By _____
          Deputy

RETURN OF SERVICE

Fees	
Service $	_____
Mileage	_____
Copy	_____
Docket	_____
Return	_____
Totals	_____

I received this summons on _____, 199___, at _____ o'clock, ___ m. and made personal service of it upon _____ by locating him-them [*cross out one*] and tendering a copy of the summons and accompanying documents, on _____, 199___, _____

_____

Sheriff-Bailiff-Process Server

By _____
   Deputy

---

2. Domicile

There is usually little difficulty obtaining personal jurisdiction over a defendant who is *domiciled* in the state, even if he or she is absent from the state at the time of the litigation.

As we have seen, domicile is the place where you have been physically present and where you intend to stay indefinitely. A person domiciled in a state is called a **domiciliary.** One can have several residences, e.g., a summer home in addition to a permanent home, but only one domicile. If the domiciliary is in the state, in-person service of process will, of course, confer personal jurisdiction on the court. If the domiciliary is out of the state, various forms of substituted service of process are often permitted (e.g., mail, publication), as long as they are reasonably calculated to provide notice of the contemplated litigation.

3. Consent

A defendant can consent to a court's assertion of personal jurisdiction. An out-of-state corporation, for example, as a condition of doing business in the state, may have to appoint someone in the state as its agent for receiving service of process. In some states, simply by doing business in the state, the company is held to have impliedly appointed a state official (e.g., the secretary of state) to be its agent for service of process on causes of actions that are based on its in-state activities. A similar form of implied consent exists for out-of-state motorists who drive in the state. Most states say these motorists impliedly appoint a state official (e.g., the registrar of motor vehicles) as their agent to receive service of process on causes of action that are based on their use of the state's roads. An example would be a negligence action following a highway collision.

4. Long-Arm Statutes

Long-arm statutes (like the implied consent rules discussed above) are aimed at the out-of-state defendant over whom the plaintiff wants a local court to assume personal jurisdiction. There are various kinds of long-arm statutes among the states:

- Some statutes assert jurisdiction over non-residents who drive into the state and have an accident.
- Some statutes assert jurisdiction over non-residents who transact business in the state.
- Some statutes assert jurisdiction over non-residents who commit any tort (any "tortious act") in the state.
- Etc.

In a few states, the statute is extremely broad: Any activity of out-of-state defendants will lead to the assertion of jurisdiction as long as the activity amounts to the necessary minimum contacts required by the Constitution.

- ASSIGNMENT 5.3 •

Does your state have a statute on the assertion of jurisdiction against out-of-state defendants who cannot be served within the state? If so, give its citation and summarize its terms. (See General Instructions for the State Code Assignment in Chapter 2.)

Even though a court may be able to acquire personal jurisdiction over a defendant through a device such as long-arm statute, the court may decide, in the interest of fairness and justice, that another state (or forum) would be more convenient for the litigation, e.g., because of where the parties live and the accessibility of witnesses. The power of a court to decline the exercise of jurisdiction for such reasons is referred to as **forum non conveniens.** The court declines to exercise the jurisdiction that it could assert, and, in effect, forces the plaintiff to search out a more convenient forum in which to bring the suit. As we will see, the rules of venue are designed to help identify a convenient forum.

▪ VENUE

Venue means the place of the trial. When more than one court within a judicial system has jurisdiction to hear a case, the rules of venue will tell you which of these courts is the proper place or venue for the litigation. To resolve (i.e., adjudicate) a dispute, a court should have proper jurisdiction *and* proper venue.

Jurisdiction concerns the power of the court to act, while venue is primarily a matter of convenience. Assume that there is a state trial court within each of twenty-five counties in the state. All of these courts may have subject matter jurisdiction over the controversy, and it may be possible for each court to acquire personal jurisdiction over the defendant. Yet it may be quite inconvenient for the defendant and his or her witnesses to travel hundreds of miles across the state to the county where the plaintiff decides to initiate the action. The rules of venue will determine whether the plaintiff selected the proper place for the trial.

Another distinction between jurisdiction and venue concerns waiver. Defective subject matter jurisdiction cannot be waived, whereas defective venue can be waived. A judgment against a defendant from a court that had no subject matter jurisdiction is void and cannot be enforced, even if the defendant agreed to having the trial in that court. Improper venue, however, *can* be waived without affecting the validity of the judgment. If only county X has proper venue, but the defendant agrees to have the trial in county Y, the judgment of the latter court is valid as long as there were no defects in its jurisdiction.

Venue in State Courts

What is the proper venue of a case? There are different rules among the various states. The following is a list of the most commonly used criteria for proper venue:

- where the defendant resides (the most common test)
- where the cause of action arose
- where the defendant does business
- where the defendant has an office or representative
- where the plaintiff resides
- where the seat of government is located
- wherever the defendant can be found

The above rules apply mainly to what are called **transitory actions,** meaning simply that it is possible to bring the action in more than one place. **Local actions,** on the other hand, can be brought only in one place because the subject matter or **res** is located in that place. A suit over the ownership of land, for example, is a local action that must be brought in the county where the land is located.

▪ ASSIGNMENT 5.4 ▪

An automobile accident occurs in your state between two residents of the state. The plaintiff and the defendant do not live in the county where the accident occurred. Nor do they live or do business in the same county. What trial court is the proper venue for this action? What alternatives, if any, exist? Check your state constitution, your state code, and the rules of court that govern the courts with subject matter jurisdiction over such a negligence action. (See also the General Instructions for the State Code Assignment in Chapter 2.)

Venue in Federal Courts

Venue must also be determined within the federal judicial system. As we saw earlier, there are United States District Courts scattered throughout the United States. Any one of them may be able to acquire subject matter and personal jurisdiction. How is venue determined?

In diversity-of-citizenship cases and in cases based on special federal statutes (federal-question cases), venue is proper in the following situations:

- in a district where any defendant resides, if all defendants reside in the same state
- in a district where a substantial part of the events or omissions giving rise to the claim occurred
- in a district where a substantial part of the property that is the subject of the action is situated

In diversity cases, venue is also proper in a district where the defendant is subject to personal jurisdiction when the suit is commenced, if there is no district in which the action may otherwise be brought. In federal-question cases, venue is also proper in a district in which any defendant may be found, if there is no district in which the action may otherwise be brought. In these venue rules, residence is usually interpreted to mean domicile.

■ CHOICE OF LAW IN STATE COURTS

Assume that the plaintiff brings a tort action in a state court that has proper jurisdiction and venue. If all the parties live in the state and all the alleged facts constituting the tort occurred within the state, there is no choice-of-law or conflicts-of-law problem. The state simply applies its own tort law to the dispute.

Suppose, however, that more than one state is involved in the controversy:

New York: Plaintiff and defendant have an automobile collision in New York; defendant lives in New York; plaintiff lives in Massachusetts.

Massachusetts: Plaintiff sues the defendant for negligence in a Massachusetts state court (assume that personal jurisdiction over the defendant is no problem since the defendant is personally served in Massachusetts).

Massachusetts is the **forum** state—the state where the action is brought. What law does Massachusetts apply to the case? Its own law or that of New York?

First of all, as to **procedural law,** the forum state will apply its own law—in this case, that of Massachusetts. The rules on how the litigation will be conducted will be those of the forum state, e.g., scope of discovery, number of days within which the defendant must file an answer to a complaint, propriety of service of process, competency of witnesses, forms of verdicts, etc.

Substantive law, however, is a different matter. It consists of the nonprocedural rules that govern rights and duties. There can be major differences in the substantive law of the various states:

- A defense might be available in one state but not another, e.g., in one state, contributory negligence may be a complete defense, while another state may impose a form of comparative negligence.
- One state may impose strict liability for certain conduct, while another state may require proof of negligence.
- One state may have more liberal rules on damages than another.
- One state may have different survival and wrongful death rules than another state in the event that the plaintiff or the defendant dies before the litigation is over.

A forum does not automatically apply its own substantive law to the case before it. Some states apply the following test to determine which substantive law to apply:

*Lex Loci Deliciti: **Lex loci delicti*** means the state (place) of the wrong. The forum state will apply the substantive law of the state where the wrong occurred. This is the state where the last event occurred that was necessary to make the defendant liable.

In the case above involving the Massachusetts resident suing the New York resident in a Massachusetts state court, the *lex loci delicti* is, of course, New York. All the facts of alleged negligence occurred in New York. Hence, if Massachusetts is following *lex loci delicti,* its state court will apply the New York substantive law of negligence to the facts of the case.

Another example could involve three states:

California:	Tom in California sends a letter to Bill in Florida. The letter libels George, who lives in Ohio.
Florida:	Bill opens the letter in Florida.
Ohio:	George finds out about the letter and sues Tom for defamation (libel) in Ohio.

Assume that when Tom is visiting Ohio, George personally serves him with process so that the Ohio court has personal jurisdiction over Tom. An Ohio court will apply its own procedural law to the case. What substantive law of libel will the Ohio court apply? Ohio's? California's? Florida's? Where is the place of the wrong? As we shall see in the chapter on defamation, the defamatory statement must be "published," which simply means communicated to a person other than the plaintiff. The libel was published in Florida when it was read by a third person—Bill. Assuming that the case does not pose any special damages problems, the publication was the last event necessary to establish the liability of Tom. This last event occurred in Florida. Hence, the *lex loci delicti* is Florida, even though part of the tort was committed in California. The Ohio court will apply the libel law of Florida.

A number of states have developed an alternative test for determining what substantive tort law to apply. Instead of the place of the wrong, these states try to identify the state with the "most significant relationship" to the occurrence and to the parties.[1] Several factors are considered by the forum state, e.g., the policy of the forum state, the policies of other involved states, the basic policies underlying the particular field of law, etc. Also considered are the following contacts:

- the place where the injury occurred
- the place where the conduct causing the injury occurred
- the domicile, residence, nationality, place of incorporation, and place of business of the parties
- the place where the relationship, if any, between the parties is centered

To decide which substantive law of torts to apply, the forum state tries to analyze these factors in order to identify the "center of gravity" in the case, which is the state with the most significant contacts with the matter in dispute.

▪ ASSIGNMENT 5.5 ▪

Tom lives in your state. While traveling in a neighboring state, he is killed in an automobile accident caused by the negligence of Sam, who lives in this neighboring state. Personal service of process on Sam is completed in your state.

---

[1] *Restatement (Second) of Conflicts of Law* §§ 6, 145 (1971).

Assume that your state has full personal jurisdiction over Sam. The suit is for wrongful death (see Chapter 16). Which wrongful death law will your state apply? Its own or that of the neighboring state where Sam lives and where Tom died? (See General Instructions for the State Court Opinion Assignment in Chapter 2.)

▪ PARTIES

The simplest kind of tort litigation would be a negligence action by the plaintiff against the defendant, who denies being negligent. The litigation, however, can become considerably more complex: (1) the defendant may claim that the plaintiff is the wrong party to bring the suit; (2) other parties may want to join the plaintiff in the suit against the defendant; (3) the plaintiff may want to join other defendants; (4) the defendant may have claims against the plaintiff; (5) the defendant may want to force additional parties to be defendants; (6) the defendant may have claims against other defendants already in the litigation, etc.

Real Party in Interest

The plaintiff must be the **real party in interest.** This is the person who, according to the substantive law of torts, has the right to sue. The suit must be brought by this person or by his or her legal representative, e.g., executor, administrator, guardian.

An **assignee** can be a real party in interest. An **assignment** is a transfer of rights. If Tom has a right to collect $100 from Mary, Tom can assign this right to Jim so that Jim will have the right to sue Mary for the $100. Many tort claims are also assignable. If Tom has a tort claim against Mary which he assigns to Jim, the latter is a real party in interest who can sue Mary for that tort. Jim is the assignee (the person who receives someone else's right). Tom is the **assignor** (the person who transfers his or her right to another).

Capacity to Sue and Be Sued

The plaintiff and the defendant must have the legal capacity to sue and be sued. Minors and incompetent persons, for example, cannot be parties to litigation. Guardians or other appointed representatives must bring the suit or defend it on behalf of the minor or incompetent person.

Joinder of Parties

> **Indispensable party:** Someone without whom the action cannot proceed. Someone whose interests would inevitably be directly affected by the outcome of the controversy. The action will be dismissed if an indispensable party is not joined.
>
> **Necessary party:** Someone whose interests might be affected by the outcome of the action. A necessary party should be joined if it is possible or feasible to do so. The action will not be dismissed if a necessary party is not joined, e.g., because the court could not obtain personal jurisdiction over him or her.
>
> **Compulsory joinder:** The joinder of indispensable parties or necessary parties.

Permissive joinder: The joinder of a proper party at the option of one of the existing parties. A proper party is someone with a close interest in the litigation. Proper parties may be joined if the right to relief to be asserted by or against them arises out of the same transaction or occurrence involved in the main action, or if there is a common question of law or fact between the original parties and the parties to be joined.

Impleader: The defendant's right to bring in or join (implead) a third party not part of the original action, when the third party is or may be liable to the defendant if the latter is found liable in the original action. The impleaded party is called the **third party defendant.**

Intervenor: Someone who is not part of the original action but becomes a party at his or her own initiative in order to protect his or her interest, which will be affected by the outcome of the litigation.

Interpleader: The practice whereby someone who holds property joins all claimants to the property in one action in order to avoid multiple liability if all the claimants sued separately. The holder of the property (called the **stakeholder**) usually is making no claim to the property.

Class Action: One or more persons who are members of a class bring a suit or are sued on behalf of every member of that class. To have a class action, the members must be too numerous to allow each of them to litigate individually. The case must involve a common question of law or fact concerning all members of the class. The representative who will be bringing (or defending) the action for the class must adequately and fairly represent all members of the class. And the claims or defenses of the representative must be typical of the claims or defenses that other members of the class will have. *Example:* a resident brings a nuisance action against a chemical plant on behalf of neighbors who live in the immediate area of the plant.

▪ ASSIGNMENT 5.6 ▪

Mary is a newspaper reporter. She writes a story that defames John. John wants to sue Mary, her editor, and the owner of the newspaper for libel in your state. Can John join all three as defendants in the same action in your state? (See General Instructions for the State Code Assignment in Chapter 2.)

▪ PLEADINGS

Pleadings are formal, pre-trial documents filed by parties to litigation that contain their claims, defenses, or other responses. The function of the pleadings is to help define the controversy and give everyone involved, including the court, notice of what the controversy is all about. The major pleadings are as follows:

Complaint (also called a **petition**): The plaintiff's statement of claims against the defendant.

Answer: The defendant's response to the complaint. The allegations of the complaint are admitted or denied, and defenses are presented.

Reply: The plaintiff's response to the affirmative allegations in the answer. (Required in a minority of states.)

Counterclaim: The defendant's statement of a claim or cause of action against the plaintiff. Counterclaims are often stated in the defendant's answer.

Cross-claim: The defendant's statement of a claim against a co-defendant.

Cross-complaint: In some states, claims by a defendant against any other party; would include what other states refer to as counterclaims and cross-claims.

Third-party Complaint: A complaint filed by the defendant against a third party (who is not now in the suit). This complaint alleges that the third party may be liable for all or part of the damages the plaintiff may win from the defendant.

One of the most common challenges to pleadings is the **demurrer.** It states that even if all the facts alleged by the other side can be proven at trial, those facts do not legally add up to or constitute the necessary elements of a claim or cause of action. (Some states and the federal courts no longer use the term demurrer. In its place, motions are used that have the same effect, e.g., motion to dismiss for failure to state a claim on which relief can be granted.)

Complaint

Our main focus in this section will be on the complaint. A number of assignments in this book will ask you to draft a complaint.

The basic structure of many complaints is found in Figure 5.5.[2]

Caption

The **caption** is the heading of the pleading. It should contain the name of the court, the name of the parties, and the number assigned to the case by the court.

Designation of the Pleading

The title of the pleading should be clearly stated at the top. In Figure 5.5, the pleading is a Complaint for Negligence.

Statement of Jurisdiction

Every state does not require a statement of the court's subject matter jurisdiction—its power or authority to hear this kind of case. A complaint filed in federal court, however, usually contains a statement of the United States District Court's subject matter jurisdiction.

For purposes of determining venue—the place of the trial—the complaint may also have to allege the residence of the parties, where the accident or wrong allegedly occurred, etc.

Body

The claims of the plaintiff are presented in the body of the complaint. A claim is a cause of action. Every separate cause of action used by the plaintiff should be stated in a separate "count," e.g., Count I, Count II, or simply as First Cause

---

[2]Adapted from MacDonald, Pick, DeWitt & Volz, *Wisconsin Practice Methods* § 1530, p. 239 (2d ed. 1959).

Figure 5.5   Structure of a Complaint

Caption	STATE OF _____ COUNTY OF _____ _____ COURT John Doe, Plaintiff Civil Action No. _____ v. Richard Roe, Defendant
Designation of Pleading →	COMPLAINT FOR NEGLIGENCE
Statement of Jurisdiction →	Plaintiff alleges that: 1. The jurisdiction of this court is based on section _____ , title _____ of the [State] Code. 2. Plaintiff is a plumber, residing at 107 Main Street in the City of _____ , _____ County, State of _____ .
	3. Upon information and belief, defendant is a traveling salesman, residing at 5747 Broadway Street in the City of Chicago, Cook County, Illinois.
Body	4. On or about the second day of January, 1989 an automobile driven by defendant, on Highway 18 in the vicinity of Verona, _____ , struck an automobile being driven by the plaintiff on said highway. 5. Defendant was negligent in the operation of said automobile as to: a. Speed, b. Lookout, c. Management and control. 6. As a result of said negligence of defendant, his automobile struck plaintiff's automobile and caused the following damage: a. Plaintiff was subjected to great pain and suffering. b. Plaintiff necessarily incurred medical and hospital expense. c. Plaintiff suffered a loss of income. d. Plaintiff's automobile was damaged.
Prayer for Relief →	Wherefore plaintiff demands judgment in the amount of one hundred thousand dollars ($100,000), together with the costs and disbursements of this action.
Subscription →	_____ Plaintiff's Attorney 1 Main Street _____ , _____
Verification	State of _____ SS County of _____ John Doe, being first duly sworn on oath according to law, deposes and says that he has read the foregoing complaint and that the matters stated therein are true to the best of his knowledge, information, and belief. _____ John Doe Subscribed and sworn me on this _____ day of _____ , 19 _____ . _____ Notary Public My commission expires:

of Action, Second Cause of Action, etc. The paragraphs should be consecutively numbered. Each paragraph should contain a single fact or a closely related small grouping of facts.

With what factual detail must the complaint state the cause of action? There are two main schools of thought on this question.

Fact Pleading.   In **fact pleading,** there must be a statement of the **ultimate facts** that set forth the cause of action. Not every detail that the plaintiff intends to try to prove at trial is pleaded. The complaint need not contain a catalog of the evidence that the plaintiff will eventually introduce at the trial. Only the ultimate facts are pleaded. There is, however, no satisfactory definition of an ultimate fact. Generally, it is one that is essential to the establishment of an element of a cause of action.

The complaint must *not* state conclusions of law, such as "Jones assaulted Smith" or Jones "violated section 23 of the state code." The problem, however, is that it is as difficult to define a conclusion of law as it is to define an ultimate fact. Some statements are mixed statements of fact and law—for example, "Jones negligently drove his car into. . . ." As a matter of common sense and practicality, if the conclusion of law (here, "negligently") is also a convenient way of stating facts, it will be permitted.

The only reliable guide for a pleader is to determine what the prior decisions of the courts in the state have concluded are proper and improper statements of fact in a complaint.

Notice Pleading.   Under the federal system and under states that have followed the lead of the federal courts, the goal of the complaint is to say enough to notify or inform the defendant of the nature of the claims against him or her. This is the essence of **notice pleading.** There is no requirement that ultimate facts be alleged. The plaintiff must simply provide a "short and plain statement of the claim showing the pleader is entitled to relief."

It is not improper to fail to plead an ultimate fact. The critical point is that the complaint will not be thrown out if it *fails* to plead an ultimate fact or if it *includes* conclusions of law—as long as the complaint gives adequate notice of the nature of the claim. The technicalities of pleading facts, conclusions of law, etc. are unimportant in notice pleading.

Notice pleading does not necessarily require a different kind of pleading from fact pleading; notice pleading is simply more liberal or tolerant in what is acceptable.

When the plaintiff lacks personal knowledge of a fact being alleged, the fact should be stated "upon information and belief," as in the third paragraph of Figure 5.5.

There are times when the law requires specificity in the pleading. For example, allegations of fraud must be stated with specificity or particularity. Also, when special damages are required in defamation cases, the facts must be pleaded with some specificity.

Prayer for Relief

In the **prayer for relief,** the complaint must ask for a specific amount in damages, or other form of relief, such as an injunction against a nuisance. As we shall see, if the defendant fails to appear and answer the complaint, a default judgment is entered against the defendant. The relief given the plaintiff in a default judgment cannot exceed what the plaintiff asked for in the prayer for relief.

Subscription

The **subscription** is the signature of the attorney who prepared the complaint and who represents the plaintiff. If the plaintiff wrote the complaint and is acting as his or her own attorney in the case, the plaintiff signs.

Verification

A **verification** is an affidavit that is submitted with the pleading. It is signed by parties on whose behalf the pleading was prepared, who swear that they have read the pleading and that it is true to the best of their knowledge, information, and belief. (Not all states require that complaints be verified.)

In Figures 5.7–5.11, you will find other examples of tort complaints. It is frequently helpful to examine sample documents, or what are called *standard* forms. Caution is needed, however, in the use of such forms. See Figure 5.6 on avoiding abuse of standard forms.

▪ ASSIGNMENT 5.7 ▪

Assume that you want to draft a complaint for negligence in your state. Select any court in your state with subject matter jurisdiction over negligence actions. (See assignment 5.1.) Examine your state code and the rules of court governing that court in order to identify the requirements for such a complaint. (You may or may not find rules specifically governing complaints to be filed in negligence actions; the rules may refer more generally to civil actions.) Identify whatever requirements you can find as to the caption, statement of jurisdiction, statement of claim, verification, etc. You do not have to draft a complaint for this assignment. You must simply cite and summarize whatever requirements you find on the format of a complaint for negligence in your state.

▪ ASSIGNMENT 5.8 ▪

Examine the complaints found in Figures 5.5 and 5.7 to 5.11. Assume that all of these complaints are to be filed in state courts of your state. What defects in form, if any, do you find in these complaints in the light of the requirements for complaints in your state? What, if anything, is missing from these forms? Review your answer to assignment 5.7 on negligence complaints in your state. For the other causes of action covered in the complaints, e.g., slander, you will have to determine whether there are any other requirements on format imposed by your state that differ from those governing negligence complaints. Do not concentrate on the substantive law of torts dealt with in the complaints. Focus on the procedural law of format. (The substantive law of these torts will be covered in later chapters.)

Figure 5.6 How to Avoid Abusing a Standard Form

1. A standard form is an example of the document or instrument you need to draft, such as a pleading, contract, or other agreement.
2. Standard forms are found in a number of places—for example, in formbooks, in manuals, practice texts, in some statutory codes, and in some court rules.
3. Most standard forms are written by private attorneys. Occasionally, however, a standard form will be written by the legislature or by the court as the suggested or required format to use.
4. Considerable care must be exercised in the use of a standard form. Such forms can be deceptive in that they appear to require little more than filling in the blanks. The intelligent use of these forms usually requires much more.
5. The cardinal rule is: *adapt* the form to the particulars of the client's case.
6. Do not be afraid of changing the printed language in the form if you have a good reason. Whenever you make such a change, bring it to your supervisor for approval
7. You should never use a standard form unless and until you have satisfied yourself that you know the meaning of *every* word and phrase on the form. This includes **boilerplate,** which is standard language often used in the same kind of document. The great temptation of most form users is to ignore what they do not understand because the form has been used so often in the past without any apparent difficulty. Do not give in to this temptation. Find out what everything means by:
   - Using a legal dictionary
   - Asking your supervisor
   - Asking other knowledgeable people
   - Doing other legal research
8. You need to know whether the entire form or any part of it has ever been litigated in court. To find out, do some legal research in the area of the law relevant to the form.
9. Once you have found a form that appears useful, look around for another form that attempts to serve the same purpose. Analyze the different or alternative forms available. Which one is preferable? Why? The important point is: keep questioning the validity of the form. Be very skeptical about the use of any form.
10. Do not leave any blank spaces on the form. If a question does not apply, make a notation to indicate this, such as N.A. (not applicable)
11. If the form was written for another state, be sure that the form is adapted to the law of your state.
12. Occasionally you may go to an old case file to find a document that might be used as a model for a similar document you need to draft on a current case. All the above cautions apply to the adaptation of documents from closed case files.

Figure 5.7 Sample Complaint

**SUPERIOR COURT OF ALASKA FIRST JUDICIAL DISTRICT
AT JUNEAU**

B-E-C-K CONSTRUCTORS, a Joint
Venture Consisting of Koon-Boen,
Inc. and Cummins-Egge, Inc.,
                            Plaintiff,

vs.

STATE OF ALASKA,
DEPARTMENT OF HIGHWAYS,
                            Defendant.

NO. 72–361

COMPLAINTS FOR DAMAGES

FILED in the Superior Court
State of Alaska, First District
at Juneau

OCT. 5 1972

D. V. Dungan, Clerk

By B. Marlow Deputy

Plaintiff alleges:

1. Plaintiff is and at all times material hereto was a joint venture consisting of Koon-Boen, Inc. and Cummins-Egge, Inc., both of which are foreign corporations holding certificates of authority to transact business in the state of Alaska, and both of which have paid their last annual corporation tax and have filed annual reports for the current year and have complied with all the laws relative to the contractor's registration in the state of Alaska.

2. Plaintiff is general contractor for defendant for the construction of bridges on Copper River at Flagg Point and Round Island, project number ER-38(1) to be constructed in accordance with plans and specifications furnished by defendant.

3. An existing bridge at Flagg Point which had undergone earthquake damage paralleled the work and with the knowledge of defendant and by its invitation plaintiff used it in connection with its work. Said bridge was inherently dangerous in that some of its foundations were in extremely bad repair, but defendant negligently failed to disclose this dangerous situation although it knew from previous investigations of the dangerous condition and negligently failed to include in its specifications any warning as to said dangerous condition.

4. Defendant impliedly warranted the safety of said bridge by permitting and inviting plaintiff to use the same in its construction activities.

5. On or about the 21st day of July, 1971, while plaintiff was making use of said existing bridge, the same collapsed precipitating equipment and personnel of plaintiff into the river, causing loss of life and equipment and thereafter changing the conditions under which the remainder of the contract had to be performed because said bridge became thereafter unavailable, thereby substantially increasing the costs to plaintiff of the completion of the job and substantially delaying completion.

6. Plaintiff has duly made claim in accordance with the provisions of the contract for its extra costs by reason of the changed conditions and the negligence and breach of warranty by defendant, but defendant has declined to entertain said claim and all remedies under the contract have been exhausted by plaintiff.

7. Plaintiff has been damaged by the collapse of said bridge and the changed conditions under which it has thereafter had to perform its contract in the sum of $908,488, and its subcontractor, Central Construction Company, has been damaged in a sum exceeding $449,702, for which amount it has asserted a claim against plaintiff.

Wherefore, plaintiff prays for judgment against defendant in the sum of $1,358,150, or such larger sum as may be proved at the trial, together with plaintiff's costs and disbursements incurred herein, and plaintiff's reasonable attorneys fee.

Dated September 28, 1972.

> ROBERTSON, MONAGLE,
> EASTAUGH & BRADLEY
> Coattorneys for Plaintiff
> By _____
>   J. B. BRADLEY
>
> LYCETTE, DIAMOND &
> SYLVESTER
> Coattorneys for Plaintiff
> By _____
>   LYLE L. IVERSEN
>
> LAW OFFICES
> LYCETTE, DIAMOND
> & SYLVESTER
> HOGE BUILDING, SEATTLE
> 98104 MAIN 3-1330

Figure 5.8   Sample Complaint

SUPREME COURT OF THE STATE OF NEW YORK
County of New York

A. B., Plaintiff,

     -against-   COMPLAINT

C. D., and E. F. Defendants,   Index No. _____

1. On June 1, 1966, on a public highway called Broadway in New York City, defendant C. D. negligently drove a motor vehicle against plaintiff who was then crossing the highway.

2. That motor vehicle was then owned by defendant E. F. and driven by defendant C. D. with defendant E. F.'s permission.

3. Solely as a result of defendant C. D.'s negligence, plaintiff was personally injured, lost earnings and incurred expenses for [e.g., care and treatment].

Wherefore plaintiff demands judgment against C. D. and E. F. for the sum of twenty thousand dollars, and costs and disbursements.

> [Print Name]
> _____
> Attorney for Plaintiff
> Address:
> Telephone Number:

Figure 5.9 Sample Complaint

COMPLAINT FOR NEGLIGENCE

[Where plaintiff is unable to determine definitely whether the person responsible is C. D. or E. F. or whether both are responsible and where plaintiff evidence may justify a finding of willfulness or of recklessness or of negligence]

A. B., Plaintiff

(address)

     v.

C. D. and E. F., Defendants

(addresses)

No. _____

COMPLAINT

  1. On June 1, 19 ___ , on a public highway called High Street in Columbus, Ohio, defendant C. D. or defendant E. F., or both defendants C. D. and E. F. willfully or recklessly or negligently drove or caused to be driven a motor vehicle against plaintiff who was then crossing said highway.

  2. As a result plaintiff was thrown down and had his leg broken and was otherwise injured, was prevented from transacting his business, suffered great pain of body and mind, and incurred expenses for medical attention and hospitalization in the sum of thirty thousand dollars.

  Wherefore plaintiff demands judgment against C. D. or against E. F. or against both in the sum of _____ dollars and costs.

Figure 5.10 Sample Complaint

COMPLAINT FOR SLANDER[3]

[Add title of court and cause]

  Plaintiff, by his attorney, _____ , for his complaint, respectfully shows to the court and alleges as follows:

  1. That at all times hereinafter mentioned the plaintiff was and still is engaged as a plumbing contractor in the Town of _____ , County of _____ , State of New York; that he has conducted said business and trade in said town and in and about _____ County and adjoining counties for many years prior to the utterance of the false and defamatory words hereinafter set forth and has always borne a good reputation for honesty and uprightness in his dealings with the public and a good reputation and credit as a businessman and otherwise.

  2. That during the past several years the plaintiff has done plumbing work and furnished plumbing materials to the defendants, _____ and others.

  3. That heretofore and on or about the _____ day of _____ , 19___ , at _____ in the County of _____ , State of New York, the defendant _____ in connection with the plumbing work done and the plumbing materials furnished to the defendant and others and in the presence of several persons maliciously spoke of and concerning the plaintiff, and his business and trade as a plumbing contractor the following words, "you are a crook and thief."

4. That at the same time and place and before the same persons and in connection with the plaintiff's plumbing business and trade aforesaid, the defendant maliciously spoke of and concerning the plaintiff and plaintiff's plumbing business and trade the following false and defamatory words, "you are a liar."

5. That the words so spoken were false and defamatory, were known to the defendant to be false and defamatory and were spoken willfully and maliciously with the intent to damage the plaintiff's good name, reputation, and credit as a plumbing contractor.

6. That by reason of the words so spoken by the defendant, plaintiff has been injured in his good name and reputation as a plumbing contractor and has suffered great pain and mental anguish and has been held up to ridicule and contempt by his friends, acquaintances and the public, all to his damage in the sum of _____ ($ _____) Dollars.

Wherefore, plaintiff demands judgment against the defendant in the sum of _____ ($ _____) Dollars, together with the costs and disbursements of this action.

_____
Attorney for Plaintiff
P.O. Address
Tel. No.

Figure 5.11   Sample Complaint

COMPLAINT FOR CONVERSION[4]

Plaintiff, A. B., sues defendant, C. D., and alleges:
1. This is an action for damages of (insert jurisdictional amount).
2. On or about _____ , 19__ , defendant converted to his own use (insert description of property converted) that was then the property of plaintiff of the value of $ _____ .
Wherefore plaintiff demands judgment for damages against defendant.

Many of the assignments in this book will ask you to draft complaints on the torts being discussed. The general instructions for these assignments are as follows:

General Instructions for the Complaint-Drafting Assignments in Personal Injury Litigation

Objectives of Assignment: • To introduce you to some of the basic principles of complaint drafting

_____
[3]A *McKinney's Forms* §p 4:3242 (1972).
[4]*Florida Statutes Annotated*, Form 1.938 (West, 1988).

- To show how complaint drafting can help increase your understanding of substantive tort law
- To show the relationship between legal research and complaint drafting

1. The goal is to write a personal injury complaint that would be acceptable in a trial court of your state.
2. Go to your statutory code and read everything you can about complaints, about pleadings in civil actions generally, and about complaints and pleadings on the particular torts involved in the assignment you are doing. (On finding material in codes, use the CARTWHEEL technique. See Figure 2.10 in Chapter Two.)
3. Go to the rules of court of the court before which you expect to bring the complaint you will be drafting. Read everything you can about complaints and pleadings in civil actions generally and about complaints and pleadings on the particular torts involved in this assignment. (On finding material in these court rules, use the CARTWHEEL technique.) If the case can be brought in more than one court, select one of them.
4. In some state codes and in some sets of rules of court there are standard form complaints that may be helpful. Caution, however, must be exercised in using standard forms. See "How to Avoid Abusing a Standard Form" in Figure 5.6.
5. There are many practice texts or manuals written by attorneys. These books often have standard form complaints. See "How to Avoid Abusing a Standard Form" in Figure 5.6.
6. For more on the procedural aspects of complaints, review the discussion on Figure 5.5.
7. In the complaint-drafting assignments of this book, you will often need additional facts to do the complaint, e.g., the full names of the parties, their addresses, some of the basic facts that prompted the plaintiff to file the complaint, etc. Whatever facts are missing should be made up by you as long as your facts are consistent with the limited facts provided in the assignment.
8. The caption of the complaint should conform to local practice. Normally, it contains:
   a. the name of the court
   b. the parties' names and litigation capacity (plaintiff, defendant, etc.)
   c. the docket number assigned by the court, which will usually be a number such as Civil Action No. 90–6483. (You make up this number.)
9. The designation of the pleading should be given. Place a title on the pleading, e.g., COMPLAINT FOR SLANDER.
10. If your state requires a statement of jurisdiction, provide it early in the complaint. This is the statutory cite that gives the court the subject matter jurisdiction over this kind of complaint.
11. If residency, place of the alleged wrong, etc. must be alleged in order to establish proper venue, make the necessary statements.
12. Number each paragraph of the complaint separately. Limit the amount of information you place in each paragraph to a single topic, such as the

statement of jurisdiction. When you are alleging facts, limit each paragraph to one fact or to a small cluster of related facts.

13. Complaints often have more than one legal theory. For example, a products liability complaint may sue on the theories of strict liability, negligence, breach of warranty, and misrepresentation. Each theory is a separate cause of action. Cover each theory separately in the complaint under the heading, CAUSE OF ACTION FOR . . . or FIRST CAUSE OF ACTION, or FIRST COUNT, or COUNT 1, etc.

14. The complaint should be written in readable English. Avoid excessive boilerplate language. Avoid long recitations of the facts. Be brief and concise. There are a number of reasons for this. First, it is common sense to make the complaint readable. Second, in some courts, the jury members are allowed to take the complaint with them into the jury room or to have portions of it read to them during the trial. In such cases, the complaint obviously ought to be clear and interesting! Third, some judges will use the complaint as a reference document during the trial as a way of keeping track of the major facts introduced at the trial. A judge is as much in need of an uncluttered, well-written document as anyone else.

15. The body of the complaint covers the claims made. You will have to determine whether your state is a fact-pleading state or a notice-pleading state. When in doubt, use fact pleading so that ultimate facts are alleged for each element of the tort or cause of action involved.

16. Where do you obtain the law on the causes of action alleged in the complaint? Do research on the torts for your state. This will usually involve searching for court opinions, since most of the tort law is common law. For guidelines on finding common law, see General Instructions for the State Court Opinion Assignment in Chapter 2. Use the elements of torts listed in this book as a guide against which you will compare the law of your state.

17. Where the same facts need to be used to allege elements in more than one cause of action, repetition can be avoided by cross-referencing to the facts mentioned earlier in the complaint. Facts reused in this way are said to be *incorporated*. This can be done with ease if the paragraphs are numbered as indicated in instruction # 12. (For example: "Plaintiff refers to paragraph numbers 6–9 above and incorporates them here.")

18. Very rarely is there a need to give citations to statutes, cases, etc. in a complaint. The one exception is the citation to the law (usually a statute) giving the court subject matter jurisdiction. See instruction # 10 above. This citation should be given in the complaint.

19. Do not fill the complaint with overstatements. At the trial, the allegations in the complaint must be proven. Do not plead facts in the complaint you know cannot be proven at trial. On the other hand, you do not have to limit yourself to facts you will be able to prove beyond a reasonable doubt.

20. Use a separate paragraph for the *prayer for relief* in which you state what you want. This will usually be a specific amount in damages, although other remedies can also be sought, e.g., an injunction. In some courts, there are jurisdictional limits on the amount in damages that can be claimed. If so, be sure your statement of damages is within these limits.

21. The *verification* is a sworn statement that the contents of the complaint are true. Check the law in your state to determine whether your tort complaint must be verified.

Answer

The defendant's answer must respond to the complaint. It must admit or deny the allegations of the complaint. The failure to deny an allegation constitutes an admission by the defendant so that the latter will not be able to deny that the allegation is true at the trial.

General denials are denials of each allegation of the complaint through a single statement of denial. Specific denials are addressed to specific paragraph numbers of the complaint.

Affirmative defenses must be raised by the defendant in the answer. Unlike a denial which simply refutes an allegation in the complaint, an affirmative defense raises new facts, e.g., assumption of the risk, contributory negligence, privilege.

The answer must also allege the **statute of limitations** as a defense if it applies. The statute specifies the time within which the cause of action must be brought. The failure to bring the action within this time will defeat the action.

Counterclaims that the defendant has against the plaintiff are often raised in the answer or in a separate pleading.

▪ ASSIGNMENT 5.9 ▪

Prepare an annotated bibliography for pleadings in civil cases in your state. (See General Instructions for the Annotated Bibliography Assignment in Chapter 2.)

▪ ENDING THE CASE WITHOUT A TRIAL

A **motion for summary judgment** is a request to the court that it conclude that "there is no genuine issue as to any material fact," and that the **movant** (the party making the motion) is entitled to a judgment without the need for a trial. The summary judgment may cover the entire case or may be limited to specific claims, counterclaims, defenses, etc. The granting of a partial summary judgment, in effect, removes a portion of the case from the trial. Either side can ask for a summary judgment. The request is usually made after discovery.

To win a motion for summary judgment, there must be no important or material factual disputes relating to the case or to that portion of the case involved in the motion. The opponent of the motion must show that there *are* genuine factual disputes for which a trial will be needed, e.g., the opponent will present excerpts from interrogatory answers or deposition answers demonstrating the factual disputes.

If the judge decides there are no genuine disputes as to material facts, he or she can decide what law applies to the undisputed facts. The judge does not need a trial to apply the law. The main purpose of a trial is to resolve *factual* disputes.

There are other ways that the case can end without a trial:

Default Judgment

A **default judgment** is entered for the plaintiff when the defendant fails to answer the complaint or to defend the action before the trial has begun.

Voluntary Dismissal by the Plaintiff

In a **voluntary dismissal,** the plaintiff drops the case and decides not to pursue it. The goal of the plaintiff is to end the case **without prejudice,** which means he or she can bring the action at another time. A dismissal **with prejudice** is a judgment on the merits subject to the res judicata rules to be examined later. If the plaintiff acts early in the case, e.g., before the answer of defendants is filed, there is usually no problem in obtaining a dismissal without prejudice.

Involuntary Dismissal

If the plaintiff waits an undue amount of time to bring the case to trial after the complaint has been answered, there may be an **involuntary dismissal** of the case for "lack of prosecution." Another ground for such a dismissal is the failure to obey an order of the court, e.g., an order to answer questions at a deposition. An involuntary dismissal is with prejudice.

▪ ASSIGNMENT 5.10 ▪

a. Prepare an annotated bibliography on summary judgment in your state.
b. Prepare an annotated bibliography on default judgment in your state. (See General Instructions for the Annotated Bibliography Assignment in Chapter 2.)

▪ JURY SELECTION

The function of the **jury** is to resolve the factual disputes in the case; the judge's role is to decide the questions of law. The judge's instructions will give the jury guidelines in resolving the factual disputes. If the case is tried without a jury, the judge determines both the facts and the law.

In most tort cases, the parties have a right to a jury trial. When an equitable remedy is sought, such as an injunction against a nuisance, the case is usually tried by the judge without a jury.

The party seeking a jury trial must request it within the time period prescribed by law, e.g., within ten days after a certain pleading is filed. The demand for a jury is frequently made in the complaint (if the plaintiff wants the jury) or the answer (if the defendant wants a jury).

A **voir dire** examination then occurs. It consists of a series of questions put to a group of prospective jurors that have been summoned for jury duty. The examination is conducted by the trial judge, by the attorneys, or by both judge and attorneys, depending on local practice. Voir dire is designed to identify possible **bias** or prejudice through questions such as:

- Do you know the plaintiff or the defendant?
- Have you already heard about the case and formed an opinion about who should win?
- Have you ever been involved in the same kind of litigation?

The attorneys are allowed to present two kinds of challenges to the prospective jurors:

Challenge for cause: Attorneys can bring an unlimited number of challenges for cause. Each such challenge alleges that a prospective juror is biased in some way (e.g., is related to a party's boss.) The judge then rules on each challenge.

Peremptory challenge: Attorneys can bring a limited number of peremptory challenges (e.g., five) without having to establish potential bias. No reason need be given and the judge will usually not have to rule on the challenge. All jurors subject to peremptory challenges are dismissed automatically. Once an attorney uses all allowed peremptory challenges, other prospective jurors can be dismissed only if cause is shown.

Most juries consist of twelve citizens. In some states, however, a jury of six is permitted.

▪ PRE-TRIAL CONFERENCE

Before the trial actually begins, there is a **pre-trial conference,** which is usually conducted in the judge's chambers with the attorneys; no witnesses or jurors are present. The conference will often cover the following topics:

- the possibilities of settlement
- amendments to the pleadings
- matters that can be agreed upon (i.e., **stipulated**) by attorneys
- the need for additional discovery
- exchange of witness lists and various reports that will be introduced at the trial
- setting the date for the trial to begin

The results of the pre-trial conference will be embodied in a pre-trial order, which the judge will sign.

SUMMARY

Geographic jurisdiction specifies an area of the country over which a court can exercise its power. Personal jurisdiction is the court's power to order a particular defendant to do something or to refrain from doing something. Subject matter jurisdiction specifies the kind of case over which a court can exercise its power. There are six main kinds of subject matter jurisdiction: limited, general, exclusive, concurrent, original, and appellate. Some judicial systems have two levels of trial courts and two levels of courts with appellate jurisdiction. Most tort cases are brought in state courts. The federal courts become involved in cases based on special federal statutes and in diversity cases. Personal jurisdiction is obtained through proper service of process. This is usually easy to accomplish on domiciliaries. Consent and the long-arm statute are additional bases of personal jurisdiction. When more than one court has jurisdiction to hear a case, the rules of venue will determine which is the proper court. In conflicts-of-law cases, the forum state will follow its own procedural law. It will apply the substantive law of the lex loci delicti or of the state with the most significant relationship to the occurrence and to the parties. The suit must be brought by the real party in interest who is an indispensable party with the legal capacity to sue. The major pleadings are the complaint, answer, counterclaim, cross-claim, cross-complaint, and third-party complaint. The main components of many complaints are the caption, designation, statement of jurisdiction, body, prayer for relief, subscription, and verification. The answer should admit or deny the allegations of the complaint. It often also states counterclaims against the plaintiff. The case can end without a trial if the judge grants a motion for summary judgment, default judgment, voluntary dismissal (with or without prejudice), or involuntary dismissal (with prejudice). A jury is selected during voir dire, where prospective jurors are subject to peremptory challenge or to challenge for cause. The final event before the trial begins is often the pre-trial conference.

Key Terms

jurisdiction
geographic jurisdiction
adjudication
personal jurisdiction
in personam
    jurisdiction
subject matter
    jurisdiction
limited jurisdiction
general jurisdiction
state questions
federal questions
exclusive jurisdiction
concurrent jurisdiction
original jurisdiction
court of first instance
appellate jurisdiction
inferior courts
review
errors of law
trial court record
appellate briefs
intermediate appellate
    court
court of final resort
United States District
    Court
United States Courts of
    Appeals
United States Supreme
    Court
diversity of citizenship
domicile

complaint
summons
service of process
substituted service
domiciliary
long-arm statutes
forum non conveniens
venue
transitory actions
local actions
res
forum
procedural law
substantive law
lex loci delicti
real party in interest
assignee
assignment
assignor
indispensable party
necessary party
compulsory joinder
permissive joinder
impleader
third party defendant
intervenor
interpleader
stakeholder
class action
pleadings
complaint
petition
answer

reply
counterclaim
cross-claim
cross-complaint
third-party complaint
demurrer
caption
fact pleading
ultimate facts
notice pleading
prayer for relief
subscription
verification
boilerplate
general denials
affirmative defenses
statute of limitations
motion for summary
    judgment
movant
default judgment
voluntary dismissal
without prejudice
with prejudice
involuntary dismissal
jury
voir dire
bias
challenge for cause
peremptory challenge
pre-trial conference
stipulated

CHAPTER 6

Discovery Law and Techniques

CHAPTER OUTLINE

- GOALS OF DISCOVERY
- OVERVIEW OF DISCOVERY DEVICES
- DRAFTING INTERROGATORIES
- DRAFTING ANSWERS TO INTERROGATORIES

- PREPARING FOR DEPOSITION
- DIGESTING AND INDEXING DISCOVERY DATA

▪ GOALS OF DISCOVERY

Discovery consists of a series of out-of-court, pre-trial devices designed to help attorneys prepare for trial. The six formal discovery devices are:

1. written interrogatories
2. oral deposition
3. written deposition
4. production of documents and things; entry on land for inspection
5. physical or mental examination
6. request for admission

All are designed to force an exchange of pre-trial information about the litigation. Our primary emphasis in this chapter will be on interrogatories and depositions.

Discovery devices, of course, are not the only methods used by litigants to obtain pre-trial information. Other methods include:

- Information alleged in the complaint and answer.
- Information obtained in response to a **bill of particulars,** which is still used in some states. The bill of particulars asks the other side for more particular factual information than is contained in the pleadings filed to date.
- Information obtained in the client interview.

- Information obtained through investigation.
- Information obtained through informal meetings, phone conversations, and letters between counsel of both sides.
- Information obtained from an insurance company based on its own investigation that it is willing to share.

As we examine the discovery devices, our goals will be:

- an understanding of the purposes of each device
- an understanding of the law governing each device; what each can and cannot do
- an understanding of some of the major drafting and strategy techniques involved in each device
- an ability to summarize, digest, or index the data obtained through each device

We begin with an overview of the objectives of discovery. See Figure 6.1.

Figure 6.1   Objectives of Discovery

---

1. Information Gathering

At the beginning of a relatively complex suit, there is a great deal that each side does not know about the other's case. Who are the parties? What is their background? What facts are being alleged to support claims and defenses? What witnesses might be called at trial? What documents or other physical things are involved in the claims or defenses? Rather than wait and be surprised at trial, each side uses discovery to obtain answers to such questions beforehand. Every claim (cause of action) and every defense has elements, or legal components. Discovery is a way of obtaining more facts that both sides are likely to use to prove or disprove these elements at trial.

---

2. Strategy Formulation

A major objective of gathering the information is to formulate strategies for settlement and for trial.

What a person says during discovery can usually be used against that person at trial if there are inconsistencies. One way to **impeach** (i.e., discredit) a witness at trial is to introduce into evidence inconsistent statements the witness made during discovery.

In addition, discovery gives attorneys the chance to observe each other's skills. Strategies are based in part on perceived strengths and weaknesses of opposing counsel. Discovery is one place to gather these perceptions.

More importantly, attorneys use discovery to "size up" parties and other witnesses on both sides in order to determine how well they present their position, how well they communicate. Attorneys may decide not to use witnesses at trial based on how they "come across" during deposition.

Finally, attorneys may want to use discovery to let the other side know how strong their case is, and how correspondingly weak the other side's case is, as a strategy to pressure the other side into a favorable settlement.

---

3. Case Valuation

How much is this case "really" worth? What are the chances of a judgment imposing liability? What are the chances of a high damages award? What obstacles will exist in overcoming expected objections to crucial evidence? How much time, effort, and money will be needed to win this case? These questions are uppermost in the attorney's mind from the moment the client walks in the door. They are also of paramount importance during discovery, where an attorney may begin to obtain clear answers to these questions for the first time.

Figure 6.1   continued

Very often attorneys will present data obtained from discovery to insurance carriers in order to help the latter decide whether to settle, and, if so, for how much. (See Chapter 32 on the settlement brochure.)

---

4. Narrowing the Focus of the Trial

Once the parties have been through discovery, they may be able to agree on what is *not* in dispute. In effect, they stipulate such matters out of the trial. The request for admissions, for example, is a discovery device designed to exert pressure for such agreements that have the effect of narrowing the trial so that time does not have to be wasted on matters the parties are not contesting. Absent such pressure, one party may force another to prove something solely for the purpose of harassment.

---

5. Preserving Evidence

Suppose it is impossible for witnesses to appear at trial, e.g., due to other commitments or illness. If their testimony has been obtained through discovery, the discovery testimony can sometimes be introduced at trial in substitute for an actual appearance at trial. Normally, such a substitution is not allowed. The major exception is when the testimony would otherwise be unobtainable.

---

6. Laying a Foundation for Summary Judgment

One of the early motions made by a party at trial is often the motion for summary judgment. The basis of the motion is that there is no need to go to trial because there are no genuine issues of material fact. In support of the motion, attorneys will refer to the contents of the pleadings and to what is revealed through discovery. Hence, as attorneys go through discovery, an important objective will be to determine whether a basis exists for a summary judgment motion.

A constant problem in the law of discovery is determining how far you can go in seeking information. Courts do not want to unduly burden litigants with expensive and time-consuming discovery devices; yet courts dislike unnecessary surprise at the trial itself. Most courts feel that broad or liberal discovery rules will result in better-prepared attorneys. Hence, you will tend to find relatively few restrictions on what you can try to obtain through discovery. There is a very broad test on the **scope of discovery** applied by almost every court: is your inquiry reasonably calculated to lead to admissible evidence? The test is not whether what you seek would be admissible at a trial, but whether it would tend to *lead to* what would be admissible. Hence, you can ask questions that would call for hearsay, as long as it can reasonably be said that the questions might lead you to other evidence that would not be inadmissible hearsay. There are other limitations such as the attorney work-product rule, the privilege against self-incrimination, the attorney-client privilege, and the doctor-patient privilege. You cannot seek information that violates these privileges. By and large, however, discovery presents a lot of room within which to roam.

▪ OVERVIEW OF DISCOVERY DEVICES

Most of the states have adopted discovery rules modeled after the Federal Rules of Civil Procedure (FRCP) found in title 28 of the United States Code. As we look at each device in Figure 6.2, reference will be made to the federal rule (designated in the last column of the chart as FRCP #___) that governs. In Assignment 6.1 (on page 131), you will be asked to identify the state counterpart of the federal rule.

Figure 6.2 Pre-Trial Discovery Devices

Discovery Device	Who Must Submit to Device?	Description	How Initiated	Time Limits	Legitimate Reasons for not Complying	Sanctions for Noncompliance	Role of the Litigation Assistant	Federal Rules of Civil Procedure
1: Written interrogatories	Parties only. Non-party witnesses do not have to answer and cannot send interrogatories.	A series of written questions is sent by one party to the other. (There may be a maximum number of questions that can be asked, e.g., 25, unless the court grants permission to ask more.) The attorney for the party receiving the questions prepares written answers, which are returned to the sending party. The answers are given under oath, i.e., the answering party swears the answers are true. In many states there is a continuing duty to answer questions *after* the answers have been mailed in order to correct or supplement prior	No court order is involved. The parties begin the process by simply sending the questions to each other.	Parties must usually wait until after the action has been commenced before sending the questions. States differ on how much time the receiving party has to answer, e.g., 30 days, 45 days.	**a.** The question is improper because it is not reasonably calculated to lead to admissible evidence. **b.** The information asked about in the question is protected by privilege (e.g., privilege against self-incrimination, attorney/client privilege, doctor/patient privilege, husband/wife privilege). **c.** The question will lead to annoyance, embarrassment, oppression, or undue burden, or expense. **d.** The answer is protected by the attorney work-product rule, and no showing of substantial need has been made. The rule	**a.** Go to court to move that the other side be ordered to answer. **b.** Ask the court to require the non-complying party to pay the expenses of the motion listed in (a) above. **c.** Ask the court to rule that the other side be deemed to have admitted the matters involved in the questions not answered, or answered incompletely or evasively. **d.** Ask the court for a contempt order. Parties disobeying court orders imposing sanctions may be held in contempt.	**a.** Prepare a draft of the interrogatories. **b.** Prepare a draft of answers to interrogatories received from the other side. **c.** Read all pleadings, interview reports, and investigation reports as background for the drafting tasks listed in (a) and (b) above. **d.** Arrange conference with client to go over questions and answers. **e.** Draft a motion to compel a response to interrogatories. **f.** Draft a motion to have matters not answered be deemed admitted. **g.** Index and digest interrogatories and answers	FRCP #33 (interrogatories to parties) FRCP #37 (sanctions for noncompliance)

Figure 6.2 Continued

Discovery Device	Who Must Submit to Device?	Description	How Initiated	Time Limits	Legitimate Reasons for not Complying	Sanctions for Noncompliance	Role of the Litigation Assistant	Federal Rules of Civil Procedure
1: Written interrogatories— Continued		answers based on later-acquired information.			protects ideas, memos, etc. put together or prepared in anticipation of litigation by attorneys and their assistants.		for office file. **h.** Enter due dates in office tickler to serve as reminders.	
2: Oral deposition	A deposition can be taken of a party to the suit. It is also possible to take the deposition of a nonparty witness. The party being *deposed* (i.e., asked questions) is called the **deponent.**	A deposition is a question-and-answer session usually conducted in the office of one of the attorneys. The attorney asks the questions and all answers are **transcribed** (recorded word for word) by a stenographer or court reporter who administers an oath to the deponent. (The proceeding might also be recorded on video or audio tape recorder.) The opposing attorney is allowed cross-	A court order is generally not needed. The deponent is simply sent a notice of the time and place of the deposition. Some courts allow a **subpoena duces tecum** to be served if the requesting party wants the deponent to bring documents or materials to the deposition. (See Figure 6.3.) Such a subpoena is used mainly when the deponent bringing such documents or materials is a nonparty wit-	Parties must usually wait until the action has been commenced before taking a deposition. (A court order may be needed to take the deposition sooner, e.g., because the deponent may not be available after the action has commenced.)	**a.** The question is improper because it is not reasonably calculated to lead to admissible evidence. **b.** The information asked about in the question is protected by privilege (e.g., privilege against self-incrimination, attorney/client privilege, doctor/patient privilege, husband/wife privilege). **c.** The question will lead to annoyance, embarrassment, oppression, or undue burden or	**a.** Go to court to move that the deponent be forced to appear at the deposition, to answer a question that was objected to, or to bring documents or other materials to the deposition as requested. **b.** Ask the court to require the deponent to pay the expenses of the motion listed in (a) above. **c.** Ask the court to rule that the other side be deemed to have admitted the matters involved in the deposition questions not answered or an-	**a.** Schedule time and place for the deposition. **b.** Prepare subpoena duces tecum. **c.** Prepare a list of suggested questions for attorney to ask deponent. **d.** Arrange for scheduling and payment of stenographer or reporter. **e.** Order transcript of deposition. **f.** Read all pleadings, interview reports, investigation reports, and prior answers to interrogatories, if any,	FRCP #30 (oral depositions) FRCP #37 (sanctions)

Figure 6.2 Continued

Discovery Device	Who Must Submit to Device?	Description	How Initiated	Time Limits	Legitimate Reasons for not Complying	Sanctions for Noncompliance	Role of the Litigation Assistant	Federal Rules of Civil Procedure
2: Oral deposition—Continued		examination questions. If the deponent refuses to answer a question, the deposition moves on to other matters after the reason for the refusal and the objection thereto is noted in the record. (Later, a court may be asked to compel the answer.) Once the transcript is typed, the deponent reads it and signs it if accurate, or states why it is inaccurate.	ness. Note: some states will not allow more than 10 depositions in the litigation without special court permission.		expense. **d.** The answer is protected by the attorney work-product rule, and no showing of substantial need has been made. The rule protects ideas, memos, etc. put together or prepared in anticipation of litigation by attorneys and their assistants.	swered incompletely or evasively. **d.** If the court makes any of the above orders, the deponent may be held in contempt for continued noncompliance.	in order to prepare indexes, digests and draft questions (see (c) above) for the attorney. **g.** Take notes at the deposition. **h.** Prepare motion to force compliance by other side. **i.** Prepare motion to have matters not answered deemed admitted. **j.** Read transcript of deposition to index it, digest it, compare it to interrogatory answers, look for inconsistencies, etc. **k.** Make entries in office tickler on due dates.	
3: Written deposition	Same as oral deposition.	Same as oral deposition, except that both attorneys are not present. The at-	Same as oral deposition.	Same as oral deposition.	Same as oral deposition.	Same as oral deposition.	Same as oral deposition.	FRCP #31 (depositions on written questions)

Figure 6.2 Continued

Discovery Device	Who Must Submit to Device?	Description	How Initiated	Time Limits	Legitimate Reasons for not Complying	Sanctions for Noncompliance	Role of the Litigation Assistant	Federal Rules of Civil Procedure
3. Written deposition— Continued	torneys prepare the questions on behalf of their clients who are the deponents. But the questions are asked by a stenographer or reporter.							FRCP #37 (sanctions)
4: Production of documents and things; entry on land for inspection and other purposes	This device is directed at parties only. The party must be in possession or control of the document, thing, or land in question. If you want a *nonparty* to turn over documents and other materials, you can seek a deposition of this nonparty and use a *subpoena duces tecum* to specify what should be brought to the deposition.	A party wants to inspect, test, or copy documents (e.g., photos, drawings) or other tangible things, or go upon land to inspect, photograph, or measure. This is allowed as long as the requesting party proceeds in a reasonable time and manner. If a party has made a statement about the case, e.g., to the insurance adjuster, this discovery device may be a way to ob-	In most courts, no court order is needed to start the process. A party simply sends a notice to the other party making a reasonable request for access to the document, thing, etc. (See Figure 6.4.) Some courts, however, require a court order and a showing of good cause to use this discovery device.	Parties must usually wait until the action is commenced. After the request is made, the other side has a designated time, e.g., 30 days, in which to respond to the request and allow the inspection, copying, etc.	a. The inspection, copying, or testing is improper because it is not reasonably calculated to lead to admissible evidence. b. The items to be inspected, copied, or tested are protected by privilege, e.g., privilege against self-incrimination, attorney/client privilege, doctor/patient privilege, husband/wife privilege. c. The inspection, copying, or testing will lead	a. Go to court to move that the inspection, copying, etc., be ordered against a noncooperating party. b. Ask the court to require the other side to pay the expenses of the above motion, listed in (a). c. Ask the court to rule that the other side is deemed to have admitted the matters related to the document, thing, etc. in a manner favorable to the requesting party. d. If the court makes any of the	a. Prepare a draft of a request for production of documents, etc. specifying what you want to copy, inspect, or test, and when you want to do so. b. Arrange who will do the inspecting, copying, etc., payment of costs involved, etc. c. Draft a motion to compel the inspection, copying, etc. d. File, digest and index the report(s) that come back	FRCP #34 (production of documents, etc.) FRCP #37 (sanctions)

Figure 6.2 Continued

Discovery Device	Who Must Submit to Device?	Description	How Initiated	Time Limits	Legitimate Reasons for not Complying	Sanctions for Noncompliance	Role of the Litigation Assistant	Federal Rules of Civil Procedure
4. Production of documents and things; entry on land for inspection and other purposes—Continued		tain a copy of the statement.			to annoyance, embarrassment, oppression, or undue burden or expense. **d.** The items to be inspected, copied, or tested are protected by the attorney work-product rule and no showing of substantial need has been made. The rule protects ideas, memos, etc. put together or prepared in anticipation of litigation by attorneys and their assistants.	orders that are not obeyed, the nonconforming party may be held in contempt.	from the inspection. **e.** Enter scheduled dates for inspection, copying, etc. in the office tickler.	
5. Physical or mental examination	Limited to parties only and to persons under the control of parties e.g., the child of a party (In a few courts, the employees of a party can also be forced to un-	The person to be examined is given the name and address of the doctor who will conduct the physical or mental exam. Some states do not allow that per-	A court order is required. There must be a showing of *good cause* for the examination. (Parties, however, may informally agree to have the exam done	The court must approve the time and place of the exam unless the parties mutually agree on their own.	**a.** The person to be examined is not within the control of the responding party. **b.** The person's mental or physical condition is not in controversy.	Ask a court to rule that the party who refused to submit to the ordered examination be deemed to have admitted matters that are in controversy (concerning the physical or mental	**a.** Schedule doctor's appointment and payment. **b.** Enter appointment date in office tickler. **c.** Prepare court motion to order the examination.	FRCP #35 (physical or mental examination) FRCP #37 (sanctions)

Figure 6.2 Continued

Discovery Device	Who Must Submit to Device?	Description	How Initiated	Time Limits	Legitimate Reasons for not Complying	Sanctions for Noncompliance	Role of the Litigation Assistant	Federal Rules of Civil Procedure
5: Physical and mental examination— Continued	dergo a physical or mental examination.)	son's attorney to be present. All parties, including the person examined, are given a copy of the doctor's report.	without asking for a court order.)		**c.** There is no *good cause* for the examination. **d.** The examination would be unduly burdensome.	examination) in a manner favorable to the requesting party.	**d.** Prepare court motion to have matters relevant to the examination be deemed admitted for failure to submit to examination.	
6: Request for admissions	Limited to parties only.	One party sends the other statements of fact and asks that the truth of the statements be admitted so that the requesting party does not have to prove the facts at trial. (See Figure 6.5.) A similar request may be made to admit the genuineness of certain documents or other things. The responding party must either agree to the admission or disagree, with reasons why he or she is denying the	No court order is involved. The requests for admission are simply sent to the other party.	The requests are made after the suit has begun. The responding party has a set number of days in which to reply, e.g., 30.	**a.** The requests for admission call for matters protected by privilege, e.g., the privilege against self-incrimination, attorney/client privilege, doctor/patient privilege, husband/wife privilege. **b.** The requests for admission will lead to annoyance, embarrassment, oppression, or undue burden or expense. **c.** The requests for admission call for matters protected by the attorney work-	**a.** Ask a court to rule that the party who failed to respond to the request within the designated time be deemed to have made the admissions. **b.** Ask the court to require the offending party to pay the expenses the aggrieved party had to bear in proving the truth of the facts or the genuineness of the documents or things at trial.	**a.** Read everything in the file (interview and investigation reports, interrogatory answers, deposition transcript, etc.) in order to prepare a list of facts the other side will be requested to admit. **b.** File, index, and digest the responses from the other side in the office file. **c.** Enter due dates in office tickler.	FRCP #36 (requests for admission) FRCP #37 (sanctions)

Figure 6.2 Continued

Discovery Device	Who Must Submit to Device?	Description	How Initiated	Time Limits	Legitimate Reasons for not Complying	Sanctions for Noncompliance	Role of the Litigation Assistant	Federal Rules of Civil Procedure
6: Request for admissions— Continued		request for admission.			product rule and no showing of substantial need has been made. The rule protects ideas, memos, etc., put together or prepared in anticipation of litigation by attorneys and their assistants.			

Figure 6.3 *Subpoena Duces Tecum* **for Deposition**

THE STATE OF FLORIDA

To: _____

You are commanded to appear before a person authorized by law to take depositions at _____ in _____ , Florida, on _____ , 19___ , at _____ , for the taking of your deposition in this action and to have with you at that time and place the following: _____ _____ .

If you fail to appear, you may be in contempt of court.

You are subpoenaed to appear by the following attorneys and unless excused from this subpoena by these attorneys or the court, you shall respond to this subpoena as directed.

Witness my hand and the seal of this Court on _____ , 19___ .

(Name of the Clerk)
As Clerk of the Court
By _____
        As Deputy Clerk

_____
Attorney for _____
_____
Address

Figure 6.4   Request for Production of Documents and Things; Entry on Land for Inspection and Other Purposes

Plaintiff A. B. requests defendant C. D. to respond within _____ days to the following requests:

(1) That defendant produce and permit plaintiff to inspect and to copy each of the following documents:

[*Here list the documents either individually or by category and describe each of them.*]

[*Here state the time, place, and manner of making the inspection and performance of any related acts.*]

(2) That defendant produce and permit plaintiff to inspect and to copy, test, or sample each of the following objects:

[*Here list the objects either individually or by category and describe each of them.*]

[*Here state the time, place, and manner of making the inspection and performance of any related acts.*]

(3) That defendant permit plaintiff to enter [*here describe property to be entered*] and to inspect and to photograph, test, or sample [*here describe the portion of the real property and the objects to be inspected*].

[Here state the time, place, and manner of making the inspection and performance of any related acts.]

Signed: _____
            Attorney for Plaintiff
Address: _____

Figure 6.5   Request for Admission

Plaintiff A. B. requests defendant C. D. within 30 days [or within such other time as the court may have ordered], after service of this request, to make the following admissions for the purpose of this action only and subject to all pertinent objections to admissibility which may be interposed at the trial:

1. That each of the following documents, a copy of which is attached to this request, is genuine.

[*Here list and describe each document.*]

2. That each of the following statements is true.

[*Here list the statements.*]

Signed _____
                          Attorney for Plaintiff
Address _____
Telephone Number _____

• ASSIGNMENT 6.1 •

The discovery rules for your state will be found in two major places: your state code and your state rules of court. Consult both of these sources to compile a chart similar to the one in Figure 6.2. Fill in the information for each column with the laws found in your state code and in your rules of court. If needed, you can add other columns to your chart to contain information not covered in Figure 6.2. Do not simply photocopy the statutes and rules of court governing your state. Summarize the information and present it in a format that will facilitate comparisons among the various discovery devices authorized in your state. (See also General Instructions for the State Code Assignment in Chapter 2.)

▪ DRAFTING INTERROGATORIES

Attorneys differ on the value of interrogatories. On the plus side, they are inexpensive. They are a potentially efficient way of finding out what witnesses the other side may call, what their trial testimony is likely to be, and what physical evidence might be used at trial. On the other hand, interrogatories can be overused, and most attorneys agree that they are not a substitute for a deposition. The answers to interrogatories are "sanitized" by the answering attorney in order to minimize the quantity and quality of information provided. At a deposition, on the other hand, the questioning attorney can try to catch the deponent off guard and can evaluate how effective the deponent might be at trial if called as a witness. These advantages, of course, are not possible by reading answers to interrogatories.

Below, you will find a series of practical suggestions on drafting interrogatories for your state. (See Figure 6.6 for a set of sample interrogatories in a personal injury case.) Throughout the chapters of this book, you will find assignments requiring the drafting of interrogatories. The suggestions below will also serve as General Instructions for these assignments.

How to Draft Interrogatories; General Instructions for the Interrogatories Assignments

Objectives of Assignments:
- To help develop your general investigation skills
- To help develop the skill of drafting interrogatories
- To help develop the skill of *answering* interrogatories on the theory that if you know how to ask the questions, you will later be in a better position to know how to answer interrogatories directed at clients of your office

1. Particularize. Review the material on how to particularize a fact. See Figure 4.6 in Chapter 4. You must know how to pursue the basic who, what, where, when, why, and how inquiries.
2. Review the material on how to prepare an investigation strategy as a further aid in developing interrogatories for this assignment, p. 84.
3. Review the sample interrogatories later in this chapter (see Figure 6.6). They can be a guide to the kind of specificity desired. On the dangers of using standard forms, however, see "How to Avoid Abusing a Standard Form" in Figure 5.6 of Chapter 5.
4. In your law office or in a law library available to you, you may find other sample interrogatories in closed case files, computer databases, legal treatises, and formbooks. On the dangers of using standard forms, however, see "How to Avoid Abusing a Standard Form."
5. The interrogatories you draft should be acceptable in your state. You must know if restrictions exist in your state statutes and in the rules of court of your state on the scope and format of interrogatories. Review your answers to assignment 6.1, which required you to examine such statutes and rules of court.
6. The scope of questions you can ask is usually quite broad. The test is whether the question is reasonably calculated to lead to evidence that will be admissible in court. This is much broader than whether the answer itself would constitute admissible evidence.
7. Avoid unduly long or oppressive questions.
8. Avoid questions that violate the privilege against self-incrimination (e.g., "Did you steal the car?").
9. Avoid questions that violate the attorney-client privilege (e.g., "What did you tell your attorney about the accident?").
10. Avoid questions that violate the doctor-patient privilege (e.g., "What did you tell your doctor about the pain?").
11. Avoid questions that violate the husband-wife privilege (e.g., "What did you tell your wife after the accident?").
12. Avoid questions that violate the attorney work-product rule (e.g., "In what order will you call your witnesses at trial?").
13. In many states it is permissible to ask a question that would involve the application of law to fact—sometimes called **contention interrogatories,** e.g., "Do you contend that Mr. _____ was driving in excess of the speed limit at the time of the accident?" or, "Is it your position that Ms. _____ was not driving within the scope of her

employment at the time of the accident?" If you ask such a question, be sure to follow it with a series of detailed questions covering the factual reasons for the possible answers that could be given.

14. Be careful about the verb tense used in questions. Present tense (e.g., "is") is used to determine facts that are still current. Past tense (e.g., "was") is used to determine events that are over. If a topic relates to the past *and* present, cover the topic in several questions.

15. Before you draft your interrogatories, you should know the client's case inside and out. You should read all pleadings filed to date (e.g., complaint, answer), all the correspondence in the file, the intake memorandum, etc. Many ideas for questions will come from this knowledge. (Of course, for purposes of most of the assignments in this book, you will not have access to such data since the assignments will be based on hypothetical cases.)

16. Litigation involves causes of action and defenses. Each cause of action and defense can be broken down into the elements discussed throughout this book. (See also Figure 1.1 in Chapter 1.) Each element should be part of a checklist. Ask questions that seek facts that might support each of the elements.

17. It is sometimes useful to ask your questions in such a way that the "story" of the facts comes out chronologically.

18. Be constantly concerned about dates, full names, addresses, exact amounts, etc.

19. Ask what witnesses the other side intends to rely on to support its version of the facts at the trial.

20. Ask for the names and addresses of such witnesses.

21. Ask what documentation, physical things, or exhibits the other side will rely on to support its version of the facts. You may want to ask that such items be sent along with the answers to the interrogatories (or that such items be brought to a later deposition).

22. Avoid questions that call for simple "yes" or "no" answers unless you immediately follow up such questions with other questions asking for details.

23. Include a definition or abbreviation section at the beginning of the interrogatories to avoid confusion and undue repetition in the later questions.

24. Phrase the questions so that the person answering will have to indicate whether he or she is talking from first-hand knowledge, second-hand knowledge (hearsay), etc.

25. As to each fact, ask questions calculated to elicit the respondent's ability to comment on the fact, e.g., how far away was the respondent, does he or she wear glasses, etc.

26. Avoid complicated and difficult-to-read questions. Be direct and concise.

The sample interrogatories in Figure 6.6 are very extensive. They cover a typical personal injury case involving an automobile collision.[1] Of course, all interrogatories for such cases will not be this extensive. Some attorneys will want to use a much shorter version of the questions and rely instead on other discovery

---

[1]The interrogatories are adapted from those found in W. Smith, "Form Interrogatories in Personal Injury Actions," 32 *Insurance Counsel Journal* 453, 458ff (1965). Reprinted with permission granted by the International Association of Insurance Counsel. Some of the questions come directly from interrogatories that have been used in recent litigation.

devices to obtain the kind of detail sought here. Indeed, in some states a much shorter version may be *required.*

In addition to being a guide for drafting interrogatories, the sample questions in Figure 6.6 have a number of other advantages:

- The questions can serve as a guide for investigators in a personal injury case.
- The questions can serve as a guide for the legal interviewer conducting an intake interview of new clients.
- The questions can serve as a guide for the attorney preparing for and conducting a deposition.

Figure 6.6   Sample Interrogatories

STATE OF _____
County of _____
Civil Court Branch

Dennis Diamond   Plaintiff
346 Redgrove Street
City of _____ ,
State of _____   CIVIL ACTION NO. _____
                          V.
Janet McDonald   Defendant
781 4th Street
City of _____ ,
State of _____

Interrogatories to Plaintiff

   Pursuant to section _____ , _____ hereby submits the following interrogatories to _____ . These interrogatories are to be answered by _____ under oath and served on the attorney for _____ within _____ days.

Instructions:

A. All information is to be divulged that is in the possession of individuals or corporate parties, their attorneys, investigators, agents, employees, or other representatives of the named parties and their attorneys.

B. A "medical practitioner" as used in these interrogatories is meant to include any medical doctor, osteopathic physician, podiatrist, doctor of chiropractic, naturopathic physician, or other person who performs any form of healing art.

C. Where an individual interrogatory calls for an answer that involves more than one part, each part of the answer should be clearly set out so that it is understandable.

D. Where the terms "you," "plaintiff," or "defendant" are used, they are meant to include every individual party, and separate answers should be given for each person named as a party, if requested.

E. Where the terms "accident" or "the accident" are used, they are meant to mean the incident or occurrence that is the basis of this lawsuit, unless otherwise specified.

Name

   1. State your full name, age, and place of birth.

   2. Have you ever been known by any other name? If so, give the other name or names and state where and when you used such names.

   3. Has your name ever been legally changed? If so, state when, where, and through what procedure.

Residence

4. State your present residence address and the period during which you have resided at this address.

5. List all other addresses at which you have resided during the past ten years and the dates of the use of each.

Marriage

6. Are you married at the present time? If so:
a. give your spouse's full name,
b. if a female, your spouse's birth name if different.
c. your spouse's address for the five years before your marriage,
d. the date and place of your marriage,
e. state whether your spouse is now living with you,
f. if not, state when the separation occurred, and
g. your spouse's present address.

7. If you were previously married, state for each previous spouse:
a. the name and present residence address of each spouse:
b. the dates of commencement and termination of each marriage,
c. the place where you were married to each spouse,
d. the manner in which each marriage was terminated,
e. if any marriage was terminated by divorce, state for each such divorce the county and state or place where the action was filed and the grounds alleged in said action and whether the divorce was filed by you.

Past Employment

8. For the ten years immediately preceding the date of the incident referred to in the complaint, state:
a. names and addresses of each of your employers,
b. dates of commencement and termination of each employment,
c. detailed description of the services or other work performed for each employment,
d. your average weekly wages or earnings from each employment,
e. whether a physical examination was required, and if so, state the date, place, and person giving the physical examination,
f. whether you gave your employer any statements or representations in writing or answered in writing any questions concerning your physical condition,
g. names of your immediate boss or other superior to whom you were responsible at each of the places of employment listed above.

Present Employment

9. What was your business or occupation at the time of the incident referred to in the complaint? Are you still engaged in such business or occupation? If not, state:
a. when you ceased working in such business or occupation,
b. your present business or occupation, the date entered, and present income from such business or occupation,
c. any other business or occupation prior to your present one, the dates entered and income from such businesses or occupations.

10. Have you lost any time from your business or occupation since the incident referred to in the complaint? If so, state:
a. the cause of such loss of time,
b. the number of days lost and the dates,
c. the amount of any wages or income lost.

11. If employed at the time of the incident referred to in the complaint, state:
a. the name and address of the employer,
b. the position held and the nature of the work performed,

c. average weekly wages for the preceding year.
12. If employed since the incident referred to in the complaint, state:
a. name and address of present employer,
b. position held and nature of work being performed,
c. hours worked per week,
d. present weekly wages, earnings, income, or profit,
e. name of your immediate boss or other superior to whom you are responsible,
f. whether a physical examination was required, and, if so, state the date, place, and person giving the examination,
g. whether you gave your employer any statements or representations in writing or answered in writing any questions concerning your physical condition.

Social Security, Worker's Compensation, or Other Disability Payments
13. What is your social security number?
14. Have you ever drawn social security benefits for disability? If so, state:
a. your residence at the time,
b. the social security office through which you filed your claim,
c. the nature and extent of the disability,
d. the length of time of such disability and the beginning date.
15. Are you now receiving or have you ever received any disability pension, income, or insurance or any worker's compensation from any agency, company, person, corporation, state, or government? If so, state:
a. the nature of any such payment,
b. dates you received the payments,
c. for what injuries or disability you received the payments, and how such injury occurred or disability arose,
d. by whom they were paid,
e. whether you now have any present disability as a result of such injuries or disability,
f. if so, the nature and extent of such disability.
g. whether you had any disability at the time of the incident referred to in the complaint,
h. if so, the nature and extent of such disability.

Income and Tax Returns
16. With respect to each of the past five years, state:
a. your yearly gross income,
b. your yearly net income,
c. the name and address of the person, firm, or corporation having custody of any papers pertaining to your income.
17. Did you file income tax returns with the Internal Revenue Service (IRS) for any of the past five years or with any state tax authority or department? If so, state:
a. The IRS office with which each federal return was filed.
b. the amount reported in each federal return as earned income,
c. the years filed,
d. the amount of tax shown to be due on each federal return,
e. the state tax authority or department with whom state returns were filed,
f. the years filed,
g. the amount of tax shown to be due on each state return.

Education
18. State the name and address of each school, college, or educational institution you have attended or completed, listing the courses of study, dates of attendance, and dates of completion (if completed).

Armed Forces

19. Have you ever served in the armed forces or performed military services for any branch of any governmental agency? If so, state:
   a. the name of each organization and the particular branch for which you performed services,
   b. the dates and places of services,
   c. your serial or identification number,
   d. a detailed description of the services performed,
   e. whether a physical exam was required, and if so, the dates and places of the exams,
   f. the date of termination of the services,
   g. a detailed description of reasons the services were discontinued.
20. Have you ever been rejected for military service for physical reasons? If so, state:
   a. the date thereof,
   b. the condition for which rejected,
   c. the agency rejecting you.
21. Have you ever received a discharge from military or government service for physical reasons? If so, state:
   a. the date thereof,
   b. the condition for which discharged,
   c. the agency discharging you.

Hobbies and Recreation

22. List all hobbies and forms of recreation in which you have participated in the last ten years.
23. State all social clubs, lodges, or associations of any nature in which you have participated or of which you were a member in the last ten years.

Other Claims

24. Have you made claim for any benefits under any medical pay coverage or policy of insurance relating to injuries arising out of the incident involved in the complaint? If so, state:
   a. the name of the insurance company or organization to which the claim was made,
   b. the date of the claim,
   c. the claim number and policy number.
25. Have you ever made claim for any benefits under any insurance policy, or against any person, firm, or corporation for personal injuries or physical condition you have not heretofore listed in your answers to these interrogatories? If so, state:
   a. the injury or condition for which such claim was made,
   b. the name and address of the person, firm, or corporation to which or against which it was made,
   c. the date it was made,
   d. the nature and amount of any payment received.

Prior or Subsequent Injuries and Diseases

26. Have you ever suffered any injuries in any accident either prior or subsequent to the incident referred to in the complaint? If so, state:
   a. date and place of such injury,
   b. detailed description of all the injuries you received,
   c. name and addresses of any hospitals rendering treatment,
   d. names and addresses of all medical practitioners rendering treatment,
   e. nature and extent of recovery, and, if any permanent disability was suffered, the nature and extent of the permanent disability,
   f. if you were compensated in any manner for any such injury, state the names and addresses of each and every person or organization paying such compensation and the amount thereof.

27. Have you ever had any serious illness, sickness, disease, or surgical operations, either prior or subsequent to the incident referred to in the complaint? If so, state:
   a. date and place,
   b. detailed description of your symptoms,
   c. names and addresses of any hospitals rendering treatment,
   d. names and addresses of all medical practitioners rendering treatment,
   e. approximate date of your recovery,
   f. if you did not recover fully, give the date your condition became stationary and a description of your condition at that time.

Life Insurance
28. Have you ever been turned down or rated by any company for accident, health, or life insurance? If so, state:
   a. the name and address of such company or companies,
   b. the date thereof,
   c. the reason therefor.

Weight
29. Please give your average weight for the two years preceding the injuries complained of, your weight at the time of such injuries, and your weight at this time.

Crimes or Imprisonment
30. Have you ever been convicted, by plea of guilty, by plea of no contest, or by trial, of any crime other than traffic violations? If so, state:
   a. the nature of the offense,
   b. the date,
   c. the county and state in which you were convicted,
   d. the sentence given you.

31. Have you ever entered or been committed to any institution, either public or private, for the treatment or observation of mental conditions, alcoholism, narcotic addiction, or disorders of any kind? If so, state:
   a. the name and address of such institution,
   b. the length of your stay and the dates thereof,
   c. the purpose or reason for your entry into such institution,
   d. the name and address of each of the doctors who treated you for such condition.

Traffic Violations
32. Please list all violations of the motor vehicle or traffic laws or ordinances to which you have pleaded guilty or no contest and to which you have been found guilty. For each violation, state the date, the court in which the case was heard, and the nature of the violation charged.

Driver's License
33. At the time of the incident referred to in the complaint, did you have a valid license to operate a motor vehicle? If so, state:
   a. the state issuing it,
   b. the expiration date,
   c. the number of such license,
   d. whether there were any restrictions on said license, and, if so, the nature of the restrictions.

34. Have you ever had a license to operate a motor vehicle suspended or revoked? If so, state:
   a. when and where it was suspended or revoked,
   b. the period of the suspension or revocation,
   c. the reasons for the suspension or revocation,
   d. whether the suspension or revocation was lifted, and if so, when.

Purpose of Trip

35. State the point of origin and the point of destination of the particular travel in which you were engaged on the date and time of the incident referred to in the complaint, and state the following:
    a. the date and time on which you left your point of origin,
    b. the names and addresses of all passengers who may have been with you between the point of origin and the point of accident,
    c. the date, time and specific location of each place you may have stopped between the point of origin and the point of accident,
    d. the number of miles between the point of origin and the point of accident,
    e. the estimated time you were expecting to arrive at your intended point of destination,
    f. the purpose of your travel.

Facts of Accident

36. State in detail the manner in which you assert the incident referred to in the complaint occurred, specifying the speed, position, direction, and location of each vehicle involved during its approach to, at the time of, and immediately after the collision.

Preceding Forty-Eight Hours

37. Did you consume any alcoholic beverage of any type, or any sedative, tranquilizer, or other drug, medicine, or pill during the forty-eight hours immediately preceding the incident referred to in the complaint? If so, state:
    a. the nature, amount, and type of item consumed,
    b. the amount of time during which consumed,
    c. the names and addresses of any and all persons who have any knowledge as to the consumption of these items.

Repairs to Vehicle

38. State whether the vehicle in which you were riding was repaired. If so, state:
    a. the date thereof,
    b. the name and address of the person or corporation making such repairs,
    c. the nature of the repairs,
    d. the cost of the repairs,
    e. if written records or memoranda were made of the repairs, state where and when they were made, the names and addresses of the persons making them, their present whereabouts, and the name and address of the persons now in possession or custody of them.

39. If the vehicle was not repaired, state whether an estimate of the necessary repairs was made. If so, state:
    a. the name and address of the person making such estimate,
    b. if it was written, the name and address of any person presently having custody of a copy thereof.

Statements by Plaintiff

40. State whether you have made any statement or statements in any form to any person regarding any of the events or happenings referred to in your complaint. If so, state:
    a. the name and addresses of the person or persons to whom such statements were made,
    b. the date such statements were made,
    c. the form of the statement, whether written, oral, taken by recording device, by court reporter, or by stenographer,
    d. whether such statements, if written, were signed,
    e. the names and addresses of the persons presently having custody of such statements.

Witnesses

41. State the full name and last known address, giving the street, street number, city, and state of every witness known to you or to your attorneys who has any knowledge regarding the facts and circumstances surrounding the incident referred to in the complaint or your alleged injuries including, but not being limited to, eyewitnesses to such event, as well as medical witnesses and other persons having any knowledge thereof.

42. If any of the witnesses listed above or whom you propose to use at the trial are related to you or to each other, please state the nature of such relationship.

Defendant's Statement

43. State the full name and last known address, giving the street, street number, city, and state, of every witness known to you or to your attorneys who claims to have seen or heard the defendant make any statement or statements pertaining to any of the events or happenings alleged in your complaint.

44. For each individual whose name you have given in the answer to the preceding interrogatory, state:
   a. the location or locations where the defendant made any such statement or statements,
   b. the name and address of the person or persons in whose presence the defendant made any such statement or statements,
   c. the time and date on which the defendant made any such statement or statements,
   d. the name and address of any other person present at the time and place the defendant made such statement or statements,
   e. whether you or anyone acting on your behalf obtained statements in any form from any persons who claim to be able to testify to the statement or statements made by the defendant.

45. If the answer to question 44(e) is in the affirmative, state:
   a. the names and addresses of the persons from whom any such statements were taken,
   b. the date on which said statements were taken,
   c. the names and addresses of the employers of the persons who took such statements,
   d. the names and addresses of the persons having custody of such statements,
   e. whether such statements were written, oral, taken by recording device, by court reporter, or by stenographer.

Written Statements of Witnesses

46. State whether you, your attorney, your insurance carrier, or anyone acting on your or their behalf obtained statements in any form from any persons regarding any of the events or happenings that occurred at the scene of the incident referred to in the complaint immediately before, at the time of, or immediately after said incident. If so, state:
   a. the name and address of the person from whom any such statements were taken,
   b. the dates on which such statements were taken,
   c. the names and addresses of the persons and employers of such persons who took such statements,
   d. the names and addresses of the persons having custody of such statements,
   e. whether such statements were written, oral, taken by recording device, by court reporter, or by stenographer.

Expert and Medical Evidence

47. State the names and addresses of any and all proposed expert witnesses, and the technical field in which you claim they are an expert.

48. Do you intend to rely on any medical text in your cross-examination of this defendant's medical experts? If so, state:
    a. the exact title of each medical text on which you intend to rely,
    b. the name and address of the publisher of each such medical text,
    c. the date on which each such medical test was published,
    d. the name of the author of each such medical text.

Diagrams, Photos, Surveys, and Other Descriptions

49. Do you, your attorney, your insurance carrier, or anyone acting on your or their behalf, have or know of any photographs, motion pictures, maps, drawings, diagrams, measurements, surveys, or other descriptions concerning the events and happenings alleged in the complaint, the scene of the accident, or the areas or persons or vehicles involved made either before, after, or at the time of the events in question, including any photographs or other recordings made of the plaintiff at any time since the incident referred to in the complaint? If so, as to each such item, state:
    a. its nature,
    b. its specific subject matter,
    c. the date it was made or taken,
    d. the name and last known address of the person making or taking it,
    e. what each such item purports to show, illustrate, or represent,
    f. the name and address of the person having custody of such item.

Injuries

50. Please state in detail the nature of the injury or injuries you allege you suffered as a result of the incident referred to in the complaint.

51. With respect to the injuries allegedly suffered, state:
    a. the extent and nature of any disability,
    b. the location of any pain suffered and the duration and intensity of such pain,
    c. whether you suffered any restraint of your normal activities due to the injuries allegedly suffered, and, if so, describe in detail the nature of such restraint and the dates you suffered the pain.

52. If you receive any treatment with respect to the injuries allegedly suffered, state:
    a. the name and address of each hospital at which you were treated or admitted,
    b. the dates on which said treatment was rendered, including the dates of entry and discharge into and from said hospital or hospitals,
    c. the charges rendered by each of the hospitals listed above,
    d. the name and address of each medical practitioner who examined, treated, or conferred with you with respect to the injuries alleged,
    e. the cost and expenses of such examinations or treatments by the medical practitioners listed above.

53. State the treatment, procedures, or operation performed in connection with the alleged injuries at any hospital and give the name of the hospital and the name of the medical practitioners giving the treatment or performing the procedures, and the dates upon which they were given or performed.

54. Since the date of the incident referred to in your complaint, have you been treated by or examined by or conferred with or consulted with any other medical practitioner whose name you have not heretofore supplied? If so, state:
    a. the name and address of each medical practitioner who examined, treated, conferred, or consulted with you and the dates of the same,
    b. the condition for which the examination, treatment, or attention was rendered.

55. If you have incurred any medical bills in connection with the alleged injuries not heretofore listed, please state:
    a. the total amount of each such bill,
    b. the person to whom such amount was paid,

c. the service or thing for which the bill was rendered.

56. If you are still receiving medical services or treatment of any nature whatsoever, state:

a. the name or names of the person or persons serving or treating you,

b. the approximate frequency of said service or treatment,

c. the date you last received said service or treatment.

57. State the dates following your discharge from the hospital during which you were confined:

a. to your bed,

b. to your home.

Orthopedic Appliances

58. Have you worn any brace or other type of orthopedic appliance? If so, state:

a. the name of the medical practitioner who fitted or prescribed said appliance,

b. the nature of the appliance and its cost,

c. when you started wearing said appliance,

d. when you stopped wearing said appliance,

e. was said appliance worn constantly or intermittently during the fore-going period? If both, state the period in which it was worn constantly.

59. At the time of the incident referred to in the complaint, did you have any condition for which you wore eyeglasses or for which eyeglasses had been prescribed for you? If so, state:

a. the nature of the condition,

b. whether you were wearing glasses at the time in question,

c. the name and address of the person who prescribed eyeglasses for you.

Medicine

60. Please list all medicine purchased or used by you in connection with the treatment of the injuries complained of, the cost thereof, and the store from which purchased or obtained.

Charge Based on the Incident Complained of

61. Were you charged with any violation of law arising out of the incident referred to in your complaint? If so, state:

a. the plea entered by you to such charge,

b. the court in which the charge was heard,

c. the nature of the charge,

d. whether the testimony at any trial on said charge was transcribed or recorded in any manner whatsoever.

62. If such testimony was recorded, state by whom it was recorded and whether a transcript has been made of such recording.

a. If a transcript has been made, state who has possession of the tran-script at this time,

b. If there was a hearing or trial on any such charge, state:

(1) the date of the hearing or trial,

(2) the names and addresses of the person or persons who were sub-poenaed or who appeared as witnesses,

(3) the final disposition of the hearing or trial.

Other Actions

63. Have you ever been involved in any other legal action, either as a defendant or as a plaintiff? If so, state:

a. the date and place each action was filed, giving the name of the court, the name of the other party or parties involved, the court docket num-ber of the action, and the names of the attorneys representing each party,

b. a description of the nature of each action,

c. the result of each action, whether there was an appeal, the result of the appeal, whether the case was reported, and, if so, the name, volume number, and page citation of the report.

Losses Not Otherwise Covered

64. Have you sustained any additional financial losses as a result of the incident complained of, other than those covered by the preceding interrogatories? If so, state:

a. the nature and amount of such losses,

b. the date thereof,

c. the names and addresses of any persons to whom any money claimed as an additional loss was paid.

Witnesses and Exhibits

65. List the names, addresses, official titles (if any), and other identification of all witnesses, including expert witnesses, who, it is contemplated, will be called upon to testify in support of your claim in this action, indicating the nature and substance of the testimony that is expected to be given by each witness, and state the relationship, if any, of each witness to the plaintiff(s).

66. List specifically and in detail each exhibit you propose to utilize at the trial in this matter. This interrogatory is directed both to exhibits you have already decided to use at the trial and exhibits you might use.

67. With reference to each exhibit listed in the previous interrogatory, state the source of the exhibit, the nature of the exhibit (e.g., whether the exhibit is documentary, a picture, etc.), who prepared the exhibit, and the date on which it was prepared.

Continuing Interrogatories

68. These interrogatories shall be deemed continuing so as to require supplemental answers if you or your attorneys obtain further information between the time answers are served and the time of trial.

▪ DRAFTING ANSWERS TO INTERROGATORIES

Here are some guidelines on drafting answers to interrogatories.

1. Obtain instructions from the supervising attorney. Drafting answers to interrogatories can involve complex strategy decisions. Meet with the supervisor as soon as possible for specific instructions on how you are to prepare the first draft of the answers for the supervisor's later review.

2. Some law firms ask the client to take the interrogatories home in order to prepare the first draft of the answers. The client should be reminded that all questions should be answered truthfully. Also tell the client to give complete, detailed answers. The client should be told not to try to hide information nor to be evasive. Before the answers go out, the attorney will carefully edit each answer so that nothing inappropriate is said.

3. In other firms, the client is asked to come to the office so that the answers can be compiled in a conference with the attorney and with the attorney's litigation assistant. If so, arrange for this conference. Be sure to instruct the client to bring all documents or supporting papers to the conference if they are not already in the possession of the firm.

4. For some questions, you may simply have to say that the client does not know the answer. Caution, however, is necessary for such answers. There is usually a duty on the client to take reasonable steps to obtain the answers to questions. This can include taking reasonable steps to investigate the client's own files and records. Non-responsive, incomplete, or evasive answers can lead to sanctions. The other side, for example, can ask the court to force the client to answer if the court is convinced that the answers are within the reasonable means of the client to provide.

5. If your client is a corporation or business, send the questions to those members of the corporation or company with relevant information. It is inappropriate to answer, "I don't know," when someone else in the company would be able to provide the answer.

6. Some interrogatories are excessively long, burdensome, or expensive to answer. You may have legitimate reason to refuse to answer such interrogatories.

7. If the interrogatories ask for detailed information from records, an option to consider is to require the requesting party to come and examine the records on its own. If this tactic is used, of course, you will have to provide reasonable access to the records.

8. Know the other objections you can raise to interrogatories. You do not have to answer questions whose answers are protected by privilege (e.g., attorney-client privilege, doctor-patient privilege, husband-wife privilege) or by the attorney work-product rule. You may have to do some research on the discovery laws of your state to determine the scope of such objections.

9. Before you draft any answers, carefully review the entire file of the case to date: complaint, answer, other pleadings, interview and investigation reports, etc. You must know all of the facts already in these documents.

10. Every answer you prepare must be backed by supporting facts. This can include prior statements of client and witnesses, documents, tests made, etc. For every answer, ask yourself what oral, written, or other tangible evidence could be used to support the answer. Every answer must have a source. Your supervising attorney will decide if the support data is sufficient to justify an answer you propose. Your initial task is to collect this data for the attorney's evaluation.

11. Enter all due dates in the office tickler system, e.g., the date when the interrogatory answers must be sent to the other side, and the date when the client conference will be held.

12. It is very difficult to object to a question on the ground that it is irrelevant. The test is very broad: Is the question reasonably calculated to lead to the discovery of admissible evidence? If you think that a question violates this test, check with your supervisor.

13. In many states, there is a continuing duty to answer interrogatories. This means that if you find that an answer you already sent turns out to be incorrect or incomplete (e.g., because of later-discovered information), you must send the corrected or more complete answer to the other side.

Later, when you digest or index information and documents from the client's file in the office, you will want to include the questions and answers from the interrogatories. These questions and answers must be carefully collated and cross-referenced with all the other data in the file, so that all the data will be quickly retrievable.

▪ PREPARING FOR DEPOSITION

At the deposition, the attorney asks questions of opposing parties or witnesses for the other side. As indicated in Figure 6.2, the oral deposition is an out-of-court question-and-answer session usually conducted in the office of one of the attorneys. The roles of the litigation assistant in a deposition include:

- scheduling the deposition
- helping the attorney prepare a checklist of questions
- taking notes at the deposition
- digesting the deposition transcript and collating it with other data and documents in the office file

We turn now to a set of instructions that can be given to a client about to be deposed in a personal injury case. The instructions provide a good overview of the deposition process as well as a series of practical "do's" and "don't's" for the client.

Preparing for Deposition In a Automobile Negligence Case: Instructions for Client

Lawyers & Judges Publishing Company,
About Your Deposition (1979)

INTRODUCTION

You, as a client, have either filed a lawsuit or have been sued by someone. Your attorney tells you that your deposition will be taken at a certain date and place. You have heard the word "deposition" used by your attorney and possibly you have heard some reference to it from friends or other sources. This is the point in your particular lawsuit where you first become directly involved in the adversary system of our judicial process.

Section I: General Information

1. What is a deposition?

> *Answer:* A deposition is sometimes called a *discovery procedure.* It is a lawful method whereby the opposing attorney discovers what you know about your own case through your answers to a series of questions he or she will ask you. The main difference between just talking about your case and giving a deposition is that you will take an oath and swear to tell the truth. A deposition is generally taken after your case has been filed in court but before the actual trial.

2. Why is my deposition taken?

> *Answer:* Your deposition is taken so that the opposing attorney can determine what you know about the facts and details of your case. A deposition enables attorneys to form an impression and to make an appraisal of *you,* *what* you have to say about your case, and *how* you say it.

3. Who will be present when my deposition is taken?

> *Answer:* Your attorney will accompany you. The attorney or attorneys representing the other parties will be there. An official court stenographer will also be present. Frequently the court stenographer is called a "court reporter." This does *not* mean the court reporter is a *newspaper* reporter. Here, the word "reporter" means "stenographer."

4. Will there be any publicity in connection with my deposition?

   Answer: In the vast majority of cases there is no newspaper or television publicity. If your case is one of public interest, your attorney will protect you from unnecessary publicity.

5. Does the taking of my deposition mean my case is going to trial soon?

   Answer: Not necessarily. Your attorney will estimate the expected trial date.

6. Is the deposition conducted like a trial?

   Answer: Not exactly. There will be no judge or jury present, but you will be testifying in somewhat the same manner as you would during a trial.

7. Will the deposition take place in a courtroom?

   Answer: No. It usually takes place in an attorney's office. If it takes place in a courtroom, it just happens to be the most convenient place for everyone to meet.

8. How does the deposition begin?

   Answer: The official court stenographer will ask you to raise your right hand and take an oath to tell the truth. The general language of the oath is: "Do you swear to tell the truth, the whole truth and nothing but the truth as you shall answer to God?" You will, of course, answer, "Yes." If, for reasons of religious belief, you cannot take an oath, you will not be required to do so. Your attorney will explain this to you and will answer any questions you might have on this subject. After the oath has been administered, you will be questioned by the other attorney.

9. If a deposition is not the actual trial of my case, why will an official court stenographer be there?

   Answer: Everything you are asked and the answers you give will be taken down in shorthand or by machine. By law, only an official court stenographer is permitted to do this. The deposition may later be transcribed (typed word for word) by the stenographer. It is important that you answer truthfully and to the best of your knowledge. It will be difficult for you to make any major changes in your testimony once you have testified and the court reporter has recorded it.

10. Will any other person connected with my case be present during the taking of my deposition?

    Answer: Not ordinarily.

11. Will I be told about the attorney who will ask me the questions?

    Answer: Yes. Your attorney will discuss with you the type of questioning usually conducted by the opposing attorney. Your attorney may even tell you about his or her personality, attitudes, tone of voice, speed of questioning, and so on. If the opposing attorney asks questions in rapid-fire order, do not let him or her cause you to give rapid-fire answers. You should answer questions at your own pace.

12. Will more than one attorney be asking me questions?

    Answer: This will depend on how many parties you have sued. If each of the parties you sued is represented by a different attorney, each one of them may be permitted to ask you questions.

13. Will a deposition be taken from anyone else connected with my case?

    Answer: Probably. Your attorney will take depositions if and when he or she feels it is necessary.

14. How long does a deposition take?

Answer: This depends on the particular case and the attorney posing the questions. Ask your attorney to estimate the time for your particular deposition. You should arrange your schedule so that you will not be hurried or rushed for time when you testify.

15. Is there some special way I should be dressed at the deposition?

Answer: Yes. Wear plain, neat, and comfortable clothing—similar to what you would wear if you were going to church. Women should avoid using heavy facial make-up and wearing costume jewelry. If you have suffered scar formations from your injury, *do not* cover them with cosmetics.

16. If the deposition is unusually long, will I be permitted to go to the washroom or just take a break?

Answer: Yes. You should be as comfortable as possible at all times. Tell your attorney *in advance* of the deposition, about any personal problems or physical conditions that require special attention. He or she will arrange the necessary recess.

17. Can I bring anyone with me to the deposition?

Answer: Ask your attorney in advance if anyone may accompany you during the deposition.

18. Is there some special way I should conduct myself at the deposition?

Answer: Yes. Be courteous. Never become angry, antagonistic, hostile, or sarcastic. *Avoid asking questions in answer to questions.* Do not become overly friendly with, or tell jokes to, the opposing attorney or the court stenographer. A deposition is an important and a serious proceeding. Even if the attorneys sometimes engage in informal talk among themselves or with the court stenographer, you should avoid taking part in these conversations.

19. Will there be some special order to the questions I will be asked?

Answer: The deposition will cover about eight to ten general areas of information:
   a. Your personal history and background
   b. The facts of the accident
   c. The injuries you claim to have suffered as the result of the accident
   d. The medical treatment and care you received
   e. The complaints you now have resulting from the injuries
   f. Your ability or lack of ability to engage in your usual daily activities
   g. The effect your injuries have had on your ability to work and to enjoy your off-work activities such as hobbies and sports (bowling, swimming, hunting, etc.)
   h. The damages (money) you lost, paid, or owe as the result of the injuries
   i. A complete history of all illnesses or injuries you have suffered before and after the date of the present accident

20. At the deposition should I relate any conversation I heard about the character of the party I am suing, or anything anyone has told me about the accident?

Answer: No. Privately you should relate these details to your attorney, who will decide how to cover such matters at the deposition.

21. What if the opposing attorney interrupts the completion of my answer to a question by asking me another question?

Answer: Your attorney will keep the record straight. He or she will recognize that you have not been permitted to complete your answer and will make the necessary comments for the record. Your attorney may not be interested in having you complete your answer. He or she may ask you if you care to complete your answer, or may decide that your interrupted answer is all the opposing attorney is entitled to receive under the circumstances. If completing your answer is vital to your case, your attorney will make it possible for you to finish. Listen carefully to what your attorney says during the deposition. Be guided by your attorney's instructions to you and remarks to the stenographer or the opposing attorney.

22. How will the insurance company know about me, my case, or my testimony?

Answer: The opposing attorney will furnish the insurance company with a review of your testimony and his or her personal appraisal of you, your injury, how you testified, and his or her opinion of the value of your case. The opposing attorney and the insurance company will decide whether to settle your case or wait for a trial and a verdict.

23. What if the court stenographer makes a mistake in recording my testimony?

Answer: If your deposition is transcribed, you and your attorney will be able to read it and check it for errors. Your attorney will know what to do if the deposition is inaccurate. Stenographic errors can be avoided if you are careful not to talk at the same time someone else is talking. It is almost impossible for the court stenographer to record overlapping conversations. Speak loudly enough to be heard and clearly enough to be understood. Occasionally, the court stenographer may ask you to spell a word or a name in order to prevent errors.

24. Will the opposing attorney try to trick or confuse me with questions?

Answer: This is a general misconception brought about by what you may have seen on television or at the movies. If the opposing attorney's questions are of this nature, your attorney will be quick to recognize it and will take proper measures to prevent the continuation of this method of questioning.

25. Would it be a good idea to memorize my testimony so I won't forget what to say?

Answer: *Do not memorize your testimony.* A deposition is not a memory contest. Do not bring papers or lists of items you want to remember. If your attorney wants you to bring anything to the deposition, he or she will ask you to do so.

26. Is there some special way I should answer questions?

Answer: Yes. You should be truthful. If you adhere to the truth, you will be better able to remember the details. *Think* before you answer. Consider every question in three steps. First, you hear it. Second, you think about the answer in your own mind. Third, you give the answer audibly. Answers should be brief and in direct response to the question. Do not ramble on. Do not give answers to questions that have not been asked. Many questions can be answered with a simple "yes" or "no." Take your time. *Listen and understand the question. Consider the answer. Then state the answer.* Speak clearly and loudly enough for those in the room to hear you. *Do not nod your head in answer to a question.* The court stenographer may not know what you mean.

27. Must I answer every question the opposing attorney asks?

Answer: Yes, unless your attorney enters an objection, or if you do not know or remember the details involved in the question. *Do not make up answers.*

28. If I do not remember certain facts or figures and I am asked about them, what should I say?

Answer: Say that you do not remember, or words to that effect. If you can give a reasonable approximation, then you may do so. For example: "about 20 feet,'' ''about 35 miles per hour,'' ''about 2 P.M.'' If your answer is based on an estimate, then say that it is an estimate. If you cannot make a reasonably accurate estimate or you do not recall the particular fact or facts, then simply say so.

29. What is an objection?

Answer: If you are asked a question that your attorney considers improper, he or she will say, ''I object.'' The word ''object'' when spoken by either attorney is your signal to stop talking. *You must never volunteer to give an answer if your attorney has made an objection.* The attorneys may want to clear up a point or make certain the question or answer is proper. This is not a signal for you to attempt to explain something. You should remain silent until you are instructed by your attorney to continue with your testimony.

30. What if I think I should not answer the question, but my attorney does not make an objection?

Answer: Answer the question. Your attorney is present in order to protect your interests, and knows when to enter objections. You should never say ''I object'' or ''off the record'' in order to explain answers.

31. What if the opposing attorney fails to ask me certain questions that I think are important?

Answer: The opposing attorney will ask you those questions he or she feels are important. *Do not volunteer facts or answers to questions you have not been asked.* For example:

Q: What is your present residence address?
A. My present residence address is 5 West Elm. I have lived there for 10 years. I work at 5674 West Broadway, and my employer is Henry Hopkins. I have worked there for four years.
You were asked to give only your *present residence address*. The answer should be given simply: ''5 West Elm.'' Stop talking. Wait for another question. If you continue giving answers to questions you have not been asked, the deposition will be unduly long and disorganized.

32. Will I be permitted to talk to my attorney during the deposition, and before I answer certain question?

Answer: Avoid doing this. Everything said at the deposition will be recorded by the court stenographer. If you do ask your attorney questions, he or she, will undoubtedly say ''off the record'' to the court stenographer and will talk to you; however, you may create doubt and suspicion where none should exist. Your attorney will tell you to answer the question to the best of your ability. If you do not know the answer, then say so.

33. What should I do if I did not hear the question or did not understand what the opposing attorney meant?

Answer: Simply say that you didn't hear or that you didn't understand the question. Either the opposing attorney will then ask the court stenographer to reread the question to you, or he or she will rephrase it until you do understand it.

34. What if during the deposition I realize I have given an incorrect or inaccurate answer to a previous question?

Answer: You may ask that the particular question you are concerned about be read back to you. You should also ask that the answer you gave be read back. Then think carefully about any change you wish to make in your testimony. The opposing attorney may ask questions about the change in your testimony in an attempt to discredit your corrected answer.

35. If I am asked: "Did you talk to your attorney before coming to this deposition?", what should I say?

Answer: The truth. "Yes" if you did, and "No" if you did not. It is most probable that you went over the details of your case with your attorney. There is absolutely no reason for you to hide the fact that you did talk to your attorney before coming to the deposition.

36. What if the opposing attorney says: "Did your attorney tell you what to say at this deposition?"

Answer: Your attorney will not tell you *what* to say but will tell you to testify truthfully and to the best of your ability and knowledge. Your attorney will prepare you for your deposition by referring to reports, notes, and other documents in your file, and will review the facts in order to refresh your recollection.

37. Is it permissible for me to talk outside of the deposition room during a break or when there is a lull in the questioning?

Answer: It is best not to talk about your case at any time except in answer to questions during the deposition. Do not discuss your case in lobbies, waiting rooms, washrooms, and so forth. Some things you say may be misinterpreted by others. When the deposition is concluded, stop talking.

Section II: Personal History and Background

38. What has my personal background to do with this case?

Answer: A great deal. A deposition is a search for truth. You may be asked questions concerning your marital and divorce history, how many children you have, their names and ages, your age, where you were born, where you have resided in the past, your schooling and educational background, your employment history, if you have ever been in jail—and many similar questions. Your attorney will object to any improper questions.

39. If there is something in my personal history that happened a long time ago, how can I keep the incident from coming out?

Answer: Confide in your attorney. Unburden yourself of any worry you may have regarding incidents that occurred in your life. It is quite possible the incidents have nothing to do with the issues in your case and can be kept out as a matter of law. Disclose your concern to your attorney, who will evaluate the problem, review its importance, and advise you how the matter can best be handled. Obviously, *if you fail to tell your attorney,* the matter may come out during the deposition and he or she will be unprepared, and thus unable, to come to your assistance.

40. This accident was not my fault. Why are these questions concerning my personal life so important?

Answer: A lawsuit makes some areas of your life an open book. The questions about your personal life may have nothing to do directly with the accident. Indirectly, they may have significance. These questions have to do with who you are, how your accident has presently affected your life, and how your life may be affected in the future.

41. What is so important about my past divorce or remarriage history?

Answer: You must accept the fact that certain information you consider "your business" is no longer completely private and may be significant and proper areas for questioning. You should keep in mind that your attorney must know these details *before* your deposition is taken. *All information given to your attorney is confidential.* If you fail to tell your attorney everything, he or she may be unable to enter an objection to information that would ordinarily be inadmissible, and will not be able to fully protect your rights at the deposition if he or she is not fully informed.

42. What significance is attached to the places I have lived in the past?

Answer: The purpose of learning your past residences (in some cases all the way back to your date of birth) has to do, among other things, with any possible claim or accident you may have had in the past. *Any previous injuries may affect this case.* You must reveal these previous injuries to your attorney so he or she will know how to handle them. Insurance companies maintain a thoroughly documented index of all claims and lawsuits. This information is cross-referenced under your name, place of residence, and other similar categories.

43. Will I be asked if anyone ever sued me or if I was ever a party in a lawsuit?

Answer: Yes. If you are asked such questions, be prepared to answer truthfully. Be sure you tell your attorney about any lawsuits in which you were either the suing party or the person against whom the lawsuit was filed. Do not allow your attorney to be surprised at your deposition by the fact that you were sued or sued someone else. *Discuss any of these facts in advance of the deposition.*

Section III: Facts of the Accident

44. What will the opposing attorney ask me regarding the facts of the accident?

Answer: The questioning regarding the accident will probably start with the date, time, and place it occurred. Thereafter, the questions will relate to *how* it occurred and *what* happened to you personally. Be prepared to answer questions about everything you know about the accident. *Do not attempt to fill in details you do not know.*

45. Will the opposing attorney skip from one subject to another?

Answer: Every attorney develops a particular style of asking questions. Some skip from one subject to another and others follow a definite pattern. You can avoid confusion by paying close attention to the questions asked. Remember, you always have the right to have a question repeated or clarified if you do not hear or understand it. If you stick to the facts as you know them, no amount of skipping around should confuse you.

46. How specific will the questions be?

Answer: This, of course, will depend upon the attorney taking the deposition. Whenever possible, you should answer specific questions with specific answers. Some attorneys may be purposely vague; others may be very specific. Some attorneys will dwell at great length upon what appear to be minor details. Your attorney will know when to enter an objection to answers that are vague. If the opposing attorney asks detailed questions, your own attorney may determine it best not to enter objections. He or she may be learning a lot about your case that otherwise might not be learned.

47. Before my deposition is taken, is it proper for me to visit the place where the accident happened?

Answer: Yes, if it is conveniently located. However, do not travel out of town to visit the place of your accident without first checking with your attorney. If you do visit the scene of the accident, estimate the distances involved (e.g., how far certain points were from you and from other points). Observe the location of highway and road markings, signs, places of business, street lights, traffic lights, and all other such objects.

48. The accident happened so quickly, I can't remember all the details. What should I do about that?

Answer: Take time to think about how the accident happened. Review the details in your own way. Retrace your activities. Take yourself back as far as necessary to piece together the events before, at the time of, and after the accident.

49. The accident happened so long ago I can't remember all the details. What should I do?

Answer: Your attorney has many details in your file you are probably unaware of. With your permission, he or she has obtained police, hospital, medical, employment, and other records. When reviewing your case with you, he will go over these items and will assist you in recalling the details you may have forgotten. Do not panic. Be calm. Refresh your memory.

50. How should I review what happened in my accident?

Answer: Go over such things as where you were before the accident. What was the weather like? What were you doing? Where were you going? Why were you going there? What route did you take? How did you get to the place of the accident? How long did it take you to get there? How far did you travel? How were traffic conditions? As you think about these general questions, the details will probably come back to you.

51. Will I be asked technical questions about the car I was operating or was riding in?

Answer: Yes. Be prepared to answer such questions if you know the answers. If not, your attorney will probably have this information in your file. It is likely that you will be asked if the car had an automatic transmission, seatbelts, airbags, a stick shift, power steering, power brakes; if the lights were on or off; if the car was four-door or convertible; and other similar questions relating to the type of car and its condition. You may be asked about the tires on the car and if the windshield wipers were working. Was the radio on? Was the heater or air conditioner working? Which windows were up or down? When and where did you purchase the car? Was it in good working condition before the accident?

52. What measurements should I be prepared to talk about?

Answer: Generally—the length and width of your car, the width of the streets involved, the distance you were from certain objects such as intersecting streets, traffic lights, other vehicles, crosswalks, street markings, traffic signs, curbs, edges of the pavement, etc. You should be aware of the posted speed limits at the time of the accident, how fast or slow you were traveling, if you were stopped and for what length of time, etc.

53. I didn't measure these things when the accident happened. How can I know them at the time of the deposition?

Answer: Answers to distance and other measurement questions need not be exact. Your best estimate will be sufficient if you can be reasonably accurate. Your attorney may have exact measurements, but will not expect you to memorize and know them to the inch. When preparing you for your deposition, your attorney will review these details with you.

54. If the center of the roadway was not marked, how can I tell where I was in the roadway at the time of the accident?

Answer: How close was your vehicle to the curb or edge of the roadway on the right? How far from the curb or edge was it? Compare the width of your own car to the width of the roadway. Recall (if you can) cars that approached, passed, or were behind you before, at the time of, or after the accident.

55. Is it important to recall sounds (like horns or the squealing of tires) or other such matters?

Answer: Yes. Tell your attorney what you saw, heard, and even smelled. He or she will determine the importance of every detail, and will relate these details to your whole case.

56. What should I be prepared to say about the police officer or officers who came to the scene of the accident?

Answer: What the police officers said to you and to the other parties will be important. Did the officers take photographs or make measurements of skid marks? Did they obtain the names and addresses of witnesses? *Before* your deposition, tell your attorney about the investigations made by the police officers. Be sure to include when and if you signed anything for the police or any other person at the scene, in the hospital, or at your home. If you did write or sign a statement for the police or any other investigator, try to remember what was written in the statement—and tell your attorney all about it. If you have a copy of the statement you signed, be sure to give it to your attorney.

57. Must I know the exact compass directions like east, west, north, and south?

Answer: If you cannot recall the directions, your attorney will be able to assist you. Were you headed uptown, downtown, or crosstown? Were you going in the direction of a certain community or away from it? If you can read a map, you should use one when reviewing the details of the accident at home or with your attorney. By doing so, you will be able to pinpoint your location and direction, as well as the other streets or roadways in the area where the accident occurred.

58. I realize you cannot cover every single question I might be asked, but are there other areas of questioning about the accident I should know about?

Answer: Yes. There are other general areas you should think about when you review your case in your own mind.
   a. Where in the roadway or in the intersection did the impact occur?
   b. Where did the vehicles come to rest after the impact?
   c. Did you see any dirt or debris in the roadway from the vehicles after the collision?
   d. Where was the debris located?
   e. Where was the damage to your vehicle?
   f. Where was the damage to the other vehicle or vehicles?
   g. Were the vehicles moved from the place of collision before the police arrived?
   h. Did you notice any skid marks from the vehicle or vehicles involved (including your own)?
   i. Where were these skid marks? What was the length of the skid marks?
   j. What were you doing and where were you looking just before the collision occurred?
   k. Was there any change in the speed or movement of your vehicle before the collision?
   l. Was your vehicle moved in any direction because of the impact? Which way? How far?
   m. Were there other vehicles at or near the scene of the collision? If so, where were they and what were these vehicles doing?
   n. If you were stopped before the collision, how long were you stopped? Pretend you are stopped, look at the second sweephand (or counter) on your wristwatch or clock and try to judge the time lapse.
   o. Do you remember the type of road surface? If so, describe it.
   p. What parts of the vehicles contacted each other?

q. Did you apply your brakes? Did you blow your horn? Did you swerve? Did you go straight ahead?

r. Was the contour of the roadway hilly, level, curving, or straight?

Section IV: Injuries and Medical Treatment

59. Will the opposing attorney know what injuries I received in the accident?

Answer: In some cases, yes. In others, no. Assume that he or she does not know about your injuries. You will then be better prepared to discuss them in detail.

60. How will this topic be covered in my deposition?

Answer: There are several key questions, one or two of which will probably be asked: "What happened to you?" or "Were you injured?" or "What injuries do you claim you received as the result of this accident?"

61. What questions will I be asked concerning my injuries?

Answer: There are approximately four general categories of information relating to your injuries that you will be questioned about:
a. The specific areas of your body you claim were injured.
b. The hospital, medical, and other care you received.
c. Your pain and disability.
d. Your present condition.

62. Is there some special order I should follow in discussing my injuries?

Answer: Yes. If you sustained injuries to several areas of your body, discuss them in a vertical anatomical order—from your head on down to your toes. You will be better able to recall the injuries you suffered if you follow this anatomical order.

63. What if the particular injury or injuries no longer give me any difficulty? What do I say about that?

Answer: The truth. For example:

Q: How long did you have these pounding headaches?
A: They lasted for about three months following the accident.
Q: And I take it you have had no trouble with headaches since that time, is that correct?
A: That is correct.

64. Will the attorney go through each of my injuries?

Answer: Yes. The attorney will probably take each area of the injury and go through the same process of questioning you about it. Answer truthfully to every question regarding each injury. Do not exaggerate or minimize your injuries or complaints.

65. If an injury still bothers me and I am not asked fully about it, what do I say or do?

Answer: Follow the questions carefully. If you have described each injury and the attorney fails to ask you about any particular one of them, do not be disturbed for example:

Q: Does your fractured knee still bother you?
A: Yes.

If the attorney asks no further questions regarding your knee, *do not offer* to give any further answers. Your attorney will cover your medical condition thoroughly at the time of trial if the case is not settled. Assume you will be asked to describe your complaints fully and be prepared to do so.

66. How thorough should my answers be if the particular injury does bother me and I am asked about it?

Answer: As thorough as the question requires you to be. For example:

Q: How does your knee bother you now?
A: It is painful to bend it. The pain shoots up my thigh and down my leg. I am unable to kneel—at work or at church. It swells up at the end of the day. I can't climb ladders as I did before. At times it gets so painful, I limp.
Q: Does your knee ache every day?
A: No.
Q: When doesn't the knee ache?
A: When I am off my feet. Usually on my days away from work.

If the particular injury no longer bothers you, say so. For example:

Q: How is your right shoulder now?
A: It no longer bothers me.
Q: When did it stop giving you difficulty?
A: It cleared up about two weeks after the accident.
Q: What difficulty did you have with the right shoulder during the two-week period following the accident?
A: It ached and I had pain when I lifted it or moved it.

67. Will I be required to show scars or injuries if exposing that part of my body may be embarrassing to me?

Answer: No. If the opposing side desires to know about such scars or injuries, they will request a medical examination. But as embarrassing as it might be, you should answer questions truthfully and honestly regarding these areas of your body. Every effort will be made to avoid sensitive situations. You must bear in mind that injuries that you refuse to discuss cannot be evaluated by the opposing attorney or the insurance company.

68. If I have an injury that is best demonstrated by walking or going through some particular motion, should I do so?

Answer: Only if you are asked to do so by the attorney asking you the questions and by your attorney .

69. If my injury is visible and can be shown without disrobing or creating an embarrassing situation, should I offer to exhibit it?

Answer: You should *not offer* to do so. If asked, you may show it without hesitation. Anything that will help the attorneys understand your problem will assist them in assessing the injury and the effect it may have on the value of your case.

70. If the opposing attorney wants to feel the lump, scar, or deformity, should I comply?

Answer: It depends on its location and your willingness to permit it. There is a sincere desire to know the extent of your injuries, and if feeling the injured area will add to the attorney's knowledge of the problem, it should be permitted. Your attorney will object if the request is inappropriate.

71. If, at the time my deposition is being taken, I have pain as the result of any of my injuries, should I say so?

Answer: Yes, if that is the truth.

72. Will I be asked about the medical or hospital treatment I received?

Answer: Yes. Questions relating to this subject usually follow a discussion of your injuries. You will probably be asked when you received medical or hospital treatment, who or what institution gave it, and the type of treatment given.

73. Must I know the names of the doctors and hospitals and exact dates of confinements, visits, and treatments?

Answer: Yes, if the information is requested. Your attorney will verify the dates for you from the information in your file before you go to the deposition. If you cannot recall exact dates of treatment, give an estimate of the date of the initial examination, the number of subsequent visits, and the general period of time covered.

74. If my attorney referred me to a doctor for examination, should I tell about that if I am asked to do so?

Answer: Yes. Your attorney has a right to send you to doctors to help evaluate your injuries. If it was a friend, relative, or your family doctor who recommended another doctor, say so. If it was your attorney, say so.

75. If I am asked what the doctors did for me, am I permitted to answer?

Answer: Yes, you may tell what they did for you and the treatment recommended, as well as all medicine prescribed or administered.

76. Should I see my doctor and talk over any injuries or have another examination before I go to the deposition?

Answer: Only if your attorney recommends that you do so.

77. Will I be asked about medical examinations performed by doctors who are not involved in the treatment and care of my injuries?

Answer: Yes. Answer truthfully about such examinations. Be sure you tell your own attorney about any examinations done at work, for life insurance, health insurance, accident insurance, or other reasons.

78. Will I be asked how I got to the hospital or the doctor's office.

Answer: Yes. If someone took you or you were taken by ambulance, say so. If you drove yourself to the doctor, do not hesitate to admit it. If you went by taxi or public transportation, say so.

79. Will I be asked about illnesses or operations that had nothing to do with accidents?

Answer: Yes. But do not *volunteer* information about such operations or illnesses. Discuss them only if you are asked questions about them.

80. What questions will I be asked about injuries I suffered before or after the date of the present accident?

Answer: You may be asked to describe the injuries you received, the complaints of pain you had, and how long the pain persisted.

81. If I was injured before or after the present accident *and I did not file a lawsuit but was paid by the insurance company,* how should I answer if I am asked?

Answer: The manner in which you answer the question will depend on exactly what you are asked. For example, the opposing attorney asks:

> Q: Have you ever *filed* a lawsuit in which you claimed damages for personal injuries?
> A: No.
> Q: Have you ever suffered any injury before or after the date of this accident?
> A: Yes.

If you *deny* having filed a lawsuit or made a claim when in fact you did, you may needlessly impair or completely destroy your right to recover damages in the present case. Search your memory carefully and thoroughly for any lawsuits, claims, or injuries you suffered (regardless if you were or were not paid), and report them to your attorney.

Section V: The Damages Claimed

82. What does the word "damages" mean?

Answer: Damages are the dollars you lost, paid, or owe as the result of the accident. Be prepared to talk about the cost of first aid, ambulances, medical and hospital treatment, drugs and appliances (crutches, braces, etc.), nurses, lost income or wages, property damage (your automobile, personal effects, clothing, luggage, etc.), therapy treatments, transportation expense to and from the doctors, and special help at home during the period you were confined or unable to care for yourself or family.

83. Are bills I have not yet paid counted in adding up the damages I incurred?

Answer: Yes.

84. At the time of the accident I carried insurance that paid my hospital and doctor bills. Can I still claim these bills as damages in my case?

Answer: Yes. Any exceptions will be explained by your attorney.

85. If I lost time from work, but my employer paid me, what should I say?

Answer: If you are asked specifically, "Were you paid for the time you claim you lost from work?" your answer should be, "Yes." (If you used up vacation or accumulated sick leave time, be sure to tell your attorney before going to the deposition.)

86. Will I be asked about how I am paid?

Answer: Yes. In answering questions regarding your pay, your answers should be based on your *gross* paycheck (the amount of your check before deductions for income tax, social security, union dues, etc.). For example, if your paycheck before deductions is $850 per week, you should say "My weekly pay is $850 per week." *Your take-home pay may be $700 or less,* but in discussing your wage loss at the deposition, you should always refer to your weekly, semi-monthly, or monthly *gross* paycheck. Be prepared to answer with detailed information regarding your loss of income. Cover the days, weeks, or months you lost from work plus overtime pay or bonus losses.

87. The time I lost was not lost all at once. I lost some time right after the accident, and then I lost a day every now and then. Will I be required to give exact dates?

Answer: Yes. The more accurate you are, the more reliable will be the damages you claim. Your employer keeps an attendance record to prepare the payroll. Ask your supervisor to give you a letter stating the exact days or hours you were off, the reason for the particular absence, and your rate of pay at the time of the absence.

88. Will I be paid for the time I lost from work to come to the deposition?

Answer: If you are the one who filed the lawsuit, you will not be paid.

89. Will I have to bring my tax returns to prove my loss of income?

Answer: Only if your attorney says you should.

90. Should I bring all of my bills to the deposition?

Answer: No. You should give all bills connected with your accident, whether they are paid or unpaid, to your attorney.

▪ DIGESTING AND INDEXING DISCOVERY DATA

To **digest** a document, you summarize it according to a given organizational principle. To **index** a document, you state where certain topics are covered in the document. The complexity of the task depends on the complexity of the case and the volume of paper generated before and during discovery.

Some of the basic objectives of digesting and indexing include:

- Creating order out of what might be hundreds or thousands of pages of data
- Providing ready access to selected topics in these pages once the summaries are correlated by subject matter
- Providing a way of comparing testimony, verifying facts, spotting inconsistencies, and identifying evidentiary holes that need to be filled by further interviewing, investigation, and discovery
- Assisting the attorney in organizing the trial, particularly by suggesting questions to be used in the direct and cross-examination of witnesses on the stand; such strategy considerations will often go into the attorney's trial notebook, which you may be asked to help prepare.

The starting point in *indexing* any document is to find out what topics in the document your supervisor wants you to index, such as leg injuries, wage history, medical payments, or tax assessments. Every time these topics appear in the document, you note the page number so that someone else can find these topics easily in that document. For an example of an index of a deposition, see Figure 6.7a.

Figure 6.7a   Deposition Index

INDEX OF DEPOSITION OF IAN SMITH
3/13/94

Topic	Pages in Deposition Topic Is Mentioned
Leg injuries	2, 24, 33, 35, 45
Medical payments	1, 7, 19
Tax payments	40, 43, 50
Wage history	1, 2, 4, 7, 25, 29

The method of *digesting* or summarizing data is also fairly simple. Suppose, for example, you are reading page 65 of the transcript of the deposition of Mr. Smith:

Figure 6.7b   Deposition Transcript Excerpt

Line
1. Q. Could you tell me please exactly how long after the accident you first felt the
2.   pain in your leg?
3. A. Well, it's hard to say precisely because everything happened so fast and my
4.   head was spinning from . . .
5. Q. Was it an hour, a day, a week?
6. A. Oh no, it wasn't that long. I'd say the pain started about ten minutes after the
7.   collision.

Figure 6.7c shows how the seven lines of this deposition transcript could be digested into a single line:

Figure 6.7c   Digested Deposition Testimony

Began feeling pain in leg about 10 min. after collision: page 65, lines 1–7

Your supervisor might want you to present this digest in a three-column format. Figure 6.7d contains an example:

Figure 6.7d   Digested and Tabulated Deposition Testimony

Page/Lines	Summary	Topic
65:1–7	Began feeling pain in leg about 10 min. after collision	Injury, Leg Pain

As you can see, considerable space is saved by eliminating the question-and-answer format and by focusing directly on the information sought. Such summaries can be placed on small file cards under the heading "Injury" or on summary sheets categorized by such headings. Alternatively, the summaries can be entered into computer programs. You then can collate all statements made by the same witness on a particular topic. You can compare what this deposition witness said about a particular topic in his or her answers to interrogatories. You can compare what other witnesses have said about the same topic. The possibilities are endless once you have prepared careful, readable summaries.

Before examining some of the major kinds of digesting performed in a law office, read the general guidelines on digesting in Figure 6.8.

Figure 6.8   Guidelines for Digesting Discovery Documents

1. Obtain clear instructions from your supervisor. What precisely have you been asked to do? What have you expressly or by implication been told not to do? It is a good idea to write down the supervisor's instructions. If you have never worked with a particular supervisor before, show him or her your work soon after you begin the assignment in order to make sure you have understood the instructions.

2. Know the difference between paraphrasing testimony and quoting testimony. To *paraphrase* is to put the testimony into your own words. To quote is to use the exact words of the witness even though you may leave out part of what the witness said. Supervisors may not want you to do any paraphrasing. They may want to do their own paraphrasing. Again, you need to know precisely what is expected.

3. Know the client's case inside and out. You cannot digest something you do not understand. You must understand the causes of action and the defenses so that you can grasp the meaning of the testimony. Read the case file, including interview and investigation reports, pleadings, all discovery documents, etc.

4. Keep a list (or know where to find a list) of every piece of paper in a case file. Some digesting/indexing assignments will require you to examine everything in the file.

5. The answers witnesses give in a deposition often ramble. (This may also be true of some interrogatories.) Given this reality, act on the assumption that the same topic is covered in more than one place in the discovery document. Look for this diversity and record it in your summary by pointing out *each* time the same topic is mentioned.

6. Don't expect the answers to be consistent—even from the same witness. Do not consciously or unconsciously block out potential inconsistencies. If on page 45 the witness said she saw a "car" but on page 104 said she saw a "van," do not blur the distinction by saying she saw a "motor vehicle," or by failing to mention both. The danger of doing this is more serious than you think, particularly when you are reading hundreds of pages and are getting a little red in the eyes.

7. Always think in terms of categories as you summarize. The categories may be as broad as the name of a given witness, which would require you to find every reference on any topic pertaining to this witness. More narrow categories might include:
   - Education
   - Past employment
   - Present employment
   - Medical history
   - Insurance
   - Prior claims
   - Facts of the accident
   - Medical injuries from this accident
   - Damage to property
   - Prior statements made

   Your supervisor will probably tell you what categories or topics to use in organizing your summaries. If not, use your common sense to create your own.

8. Each summarized item of information should include the specific document you used (e.g., deposition), the page, and, if possible, the lines on the page that you used to obtain that item of information.

9. Find out if the law firm has an office manual that gives instructions on digesting. If not, check closed case files for samples of the kind of digesting and indexing that the firm has done in the past. Ask your supervisor if you should use such samples as models.

10. Prepare summaries of your summaries whenever you have an extensive digesting assignment that requires the examination of numerous documents for numerous topics.

11. Update the summaries. After you finish your digest, more facts may become known through further investigation and discovery. Supplement your earlier summary reports by adding the new data.

There are two major kinds of digests:

- *Digest by person*
- *Digest by subject matter*

Digest by Person

In a digest by person, you focus on a particular witness, such as the person questioned in a deposition. Your instructions may be to provide a page-by-page summary of everything the witness said. If so, you simply go through the entire document and summarize every page. Include a table of contents at the beginning of the report you prepare (see Figure 6.9).

Figure 6.9   Digest by Person with Table of Contents

DIGEST OF DEPOSITION OF JOHN R. SMITH

CASE: Jones v. XYZ Factory   **OFFICE FILE NUMBER:** 90-341
DEPONENT: John R. Smith,   **COURT DOCKET NUMBER:** Civ. 2357-1
  supervisor of plaintiff   **ATTORNEY ON CASE:** Linda Stout

DATE OF DEPOSITION: 2/24/91
DATE SUMMARY PREPARED: 5/16/91
SUMMARY PREPARED BY: George Henderson, Paralegal

Table of Contents

TOPIC	PAGES IN DEPOSITION
Background Information	1–4, 9
Smith's Knowledge of Accident	2–3, 5, 7–10
Company Report Filed by Smith	23
Smith's Instructions to Plaintiff Just Before Accident	15–17

Page/Line	Summary	Topic
1:1–35	John R. Smith, 12 Main St. Buffalo N.Y. 14202; 456-9103.	Personal Data
1:36–40	Mechanic, XYZ Factory, 3/13/73; became supervisor 3/87.	Employment
2:1–28	Met plaintiff 7/31/81 at factory; was plaintiff's superior; trained plaintiff to operate equipment.	Relationship to Plaintiff
2:29–47	Was working on date of accident (9/1/90); saw plank fall on plaintiff.	Accident

Digest by Subject Matter

In a digest by subject matter, you are asked to focus on a particular topic only. For example:

- Everything a particular witness said about the dismissal
- Everything all witnesses said about the condition of the car after the accident
- Everything all witnesses said about events after 6 P.M. on 5/30/90
- All statements made to the police after the accident
- All references to the meeting of 7/23/90

The subject matter digest can be limited to a particular discovery document, such as a deposition, or it can cover a large number of documents:

- Complaint
- Answer
- Interrogatory answers
- Deposition transcript
- Responses to requests for admission
- Reports obtained via a motion to produce documents or other things
- Medical examination reports
- Other investigation reports
- Etc.

Hence, one digest summary can pull together everything on a particular topic from many sources so that comparisons, correlations, and commentaries can be made.

SUMMARY

The major discovery devices assist a party to prepare for trial by collecting information, preparing strategy, evaluating the case, narrowing the focus of the trial, preserving evidence, and laying the foundation for a possible summary judgment. The scope of discovery is whether an inquiry is reasonably calculated to lead to admissible evidence. Written interrogatories are questions sent by one party to another. An oral deposition is a question-and-answer session involving parties or witnesses. A written deposition is the same as an oral deposition, except that both attorneys are not present. Production of documents and things requires a party to turn over specific tangible items. Also available is entry on land for inspection and other purposes. Courts can order a physical or mental examination of a party. In a request for admissions, one party asks another to admit or deny certain facts; those admitted do not have to be established at trial. When drafting interrogatories, a primary guide is to phrase questions designed to obtain details relevant to each element of every cause of action and defense that might be raised in the litigation. Two important tasks are digesting and indexing discovery documents. To digest a document means to summarize it according to a given organizational principle. When you index it, you state where certain topics are covered in the document. The two main kinds of digests are digests by person and digests by subject matter.

Key Terms

discovery
bill of particulars
impeach
scope of discovery
written interrogatories
oral deposition
deponent
transcribed

subpoena duces tecum
written deposition
production of
    documents and
    things
entry on land for
    inspection and other
    purposes

physical and mental
    examination
request for admissions
contention
    interrogatories
digest
index

CHAPTER 7

Trial and Appeal

CHAPTER OUTLINE

- TRIAL
- RES JUDICATA AND COLLATERAL ESTOPPEL
- APPEAL

■ TRIAL

Our starting point is the opening day of a jury trial in a personal injury case. Assume that the jury has been selected, discovery is over, a pre-trial conference has been held, and all of the pre-trial motions have been made and resolved. We now examine the following topics:

1. opening statement by plaintiff to jury
2. defendant's motion to dismiss
3. opening statement by defendant to jury
4. burden of proof
5. burden of production
6. presentation of plaintiff's case
7. defendant's motion for a directed verdict
8. defendant's opening statement to the jury if it was reserved
9. presentation of defendant's case
10. rebuttal evidence by plaintiff
11. rebuttal evidence by defendant
12. motions for directed verdict by plaintiff and defendant
13. closing argument of defendant to jury
14. closing argument of plaintiff to jury
15. instructions to jury by judge
16. kinds of verdicts
17. motion for judgment notwithstanding the verdict (NOV)

18. remittitur and additur
19. entry of judgment
20. motion for a new trial
21. motion to trial court for relief from judgment

See Figure 7.1 for an overview of these steps, plus the appeal and enforcement stages.

1. Opening Statement by Plaintiff to Jury

The party with the burden of proof (to be discussed below) makes the first **opening statement** to the jury. This is usually the plaintiff. The opening statement is made by the attorney to the jury before any witnesses are called or evidence presented. It is a critical time. Studies of juries have indicated that many jurors make up their mind on who should win after hearing the opening statements!

The opening statement gives a summary of what the trial will be about. An overview is provided of the "story" that will later unfold through the evidence introduced at the trial. In some states, visual aids such as photographs and diagrams can be used as part of the opening statement.

2. Defendant's Motion to Dismiss

At the close of the plaintiff's opening statement, the defendant can move for a dismissal on the ground that even if the plaintiff were able to prove all of the facts alleged in the opening statement, these facts would not be enough to sup-

Figure 7.1   Flow Chart of Jury Trial, Appeal, and Enforcement Process

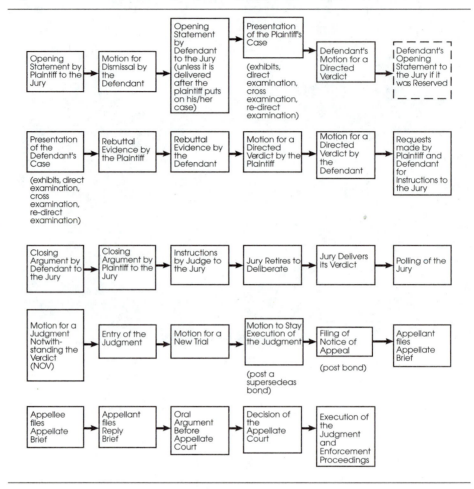

port all of the elements of the cause of action being asserted. When this motion is made, it is argued before the judge by both attorneys, out of the hearing of the jury.

3. Opening Statement by Defendant to Jury

The defendant often has a choice on when to deliver an opening statement: either immediately after the plaintiff's opening statement, or after the direct evidence of the plaintiff has been presented. The latter option is infrequently exercised, since it delays the time when the defendant will be able to give the jury an overview of the evidence. The longer the delay, the longer the "danger" that the jurors will remain predisposed to the version of the case left in their minds by the plaintiff's opening statement.

4. Burden of Proof

The **burden of proof** is also called the burden of persuasion. Two separate questions need to be examined: first, *who* has the burden, and second, *what* is the burden?

Who has the burden of proof? The general rule is that plaintiffs have the burden of proof on all the facts necessary to establish each element of their causes of action, and defendants have the burden of proof on all the facts necessary to establish each element of their defenses. Of course, if a defendant asserts a counterclaim against a plaintiff, the defendant has the burden of proof on all the facts necessary to establish each element of the cause of action raised in the counterclaim, and the plaintiff has the burden of proof as to defenses to that cause of action.

In most cases, the burden of proof follows the burden of pleading. Parties who are required to plead an issue have the burden of proof on that issue. Plaintiff pleads the cause of action in the complaint; defendant pleads defenses in the answer.

What is the burden of proof? It is the standard that tells the trier of fact how believable a party's evidence must be on a fact in order to accept that fact as true. If the standard is not met, the trier of fact is required to reject the party's version of the fact. (In a jury trial, the trier of fact is the jury, while in a non-jury trial, the judge decides both the questions of law and the questions of fact.) Believability, of course, is a very fluid concept. As a starting point in understanding it, examine the range in Figure 7.2.

Do not confuse believability with admissibility. The admissibility of the evidence is determined by the judge according to the rules of evidence. Evidence is **admissible** if it will be allowed in for consideration. The burden of proof is the standard of believability the trier of fact uses to evaluate *admissible* evidence. The burden of proof is applied only to evidence that is admissible. Also, do not confuse the standard of proof with the burden of production, to be considered next.

5. Burden of Production

The **burden of production** is the burden of coming forward with enough admissible evidence. In effect, the party with the burden of production is required to introduce *some* evidence. A plaintiff, for example, cannot bring a negligence complaint against the defendant and then introduce no evidence of any of the elements of negligence at the trial, in the hope that the jury will find the defendant's evidence so weak that it will grant the plaintiff a verdict. So too, when a defendant raises the defense of privilege in the answer, he or she cannot sit back and offer no evidence on the issue of privilege at the trial and hope that the jury will somehow find the facts that constitute the defense of privilege. Initially, the party with the burden of proof on an issue has the burden of coming forward with evidence on that issue.

Figure 7.2   Burden of Proof: The Spectrum of Believability

How Convincing Is the Version of the Fact?	Use of This Standard
Totally Believable: The evidence leaves no doubt whatsoever that the version of the fact is true.	This is never the standard used at trial. It may be that the trier of fact will conclude that a version of the fact offered by a party is totally believable, but it is never *required* that the evidence meet this standard to be accepted as true at trial.
Beyond a Reasonable Doubt: There may be some doubt that the version of the fact is true, but none of these doubts are reasonable.	This is the standard used in a criminal trial. The prosecution must prove the existence of every fact necessary to constitute the crime beyond a reasonable doubt. This standard is *not* used in tort cases.
Clear and Convincing: There is a high probability that the version of the fact is true.	Only rarely is this high standard of believability used in tort cases. One example of its use is the requirement in a defamation case against a media defendant that the plaintiff prove by clear and convincing evidence that the defendant knew the statement about the plaintiff was false or was reckless with regard to its truth or falsity. The standard is also used in many contract or will cases to prove fraud or duress.
Preponderance of the Evidence: It is more likely than not that the version of the fact is true.	This the standard of believability that is used in the vast majority of tort cases.
Fifty/Fifty Possibility: The evidence is evenly balanced on the fact. It is as likely that the version of the fact is true as it is that the version is false.	If the evidence establishes a fifty/fifty possibility of truth, then the fact cannot be established as true. The trier of fact would be acting on mere speculation or conjecture (guessing) if only a fifty/fifty possibility is shown.
A Possibility: The evidence establishes no more than a possibility that the version of the fact is true.	Anything is possible. Hence, to show a mere possibility is never enough to establish a version of a fact. The trier of fact would again be dealing in mere speculation or conjecture (guessing).

Figure 7.2 Continued

How Convincing Is the Version of the Fact?	Use of This Standard
Highly Unbelievable: There is a high probability that the version of the fact is false.	Obviously enough to establish the falsity of a version of a fact.
Totally Unbelievable: The evidence leaves no doubt whatsoever that the version of the fact is false.	Obviously enough to establish the falsity of a version of a fact.

6. Presentation of Plaintiff's Case

After the opening statements, the plaintiff begins presenting evidence through witnesses and exhibits. The sequence for the use of lay and expert witnesses is as follows:

> **Direct examination:** Plaintiff's attorney calls his or her lay or expert witness to the stand for questioning.

> **Cross-examination:** Defendant's attorney questions this witness on the subject matters covered on direct examination.

> **Re-direct examination:** Plaintiff's attorney is often given the chance to ask further questions of the witness based on what was said during cross-examination.

Exhibits such as bills, photographs, etc. are marked for identification with a number and then offered into evidence. Plaintiff's objective is to use the witnesses and exhibits to prove each element of the tort by a *preponderance of the evidence.*

The most common objections made to the introduction of evidence are:

- the evidence is hearsay
- the evidence is irrelevant
- the evidence is inflammatory and prejudicial
- the evidence is protected by privilege

One of the basic rules of the trial is that if you fail to object to evidence, you are deemed to have **waived** the objection. A court reporter takes down every word of the proceeding, which becomes part of the **record** of the trial. (The record is the official collection of all the trial pleadings, exhibits, orders, and word-for-word testimony given during the trial.) It is the job of the attorney to see to it that every objection is stated "for the record." When the case is appealed to an appellate court, it is the record of the trial that is reviewed for errors.

7. Defendant's Motion for a Directed Verdict

After presenting the case, the plaintiff **rests.** Defendant's attorney then stands up and moves for a **directed verdict.** The motion is argued out of the hearing of the jury, usually in chambers. The basis of the motion is that the plaintiff has failed to prove a **prima facie case.** This means that the plaintiff has not introduced and proven sufficient evidence that would enable a jury to find for the plaintiff on each element of the cause of action. If more than one cause of action was asserted by the plaintiff, the directed verdict could cover one or all of them. If the defendant wins the motion for a directed verdict, the case is dismissed on the causes of action covered. If the plaintiff wins the motion, the trial proceeds with the next step—the presentation of the defendant's evidence.

To grant the motion for a directed verdict at this state of the trial is obviously a drastic step, which trial judges are reluctant to take. No evidence has yet been put on by the defendant. Thus far the defendant has done no more than make an opening statement (unless it was reserved) and cross-examine the plaintiff's witnesses.

The judge makes the ruling on the motion by examining the evidence *in the light most favorable to the plaintiff.* Any doubts that the judge may have about the credibility of the plaintiff's witnesses, for example, are resolved in favor of the plaintiff solely for purposes of this motion. Clearly, the cards are stacked against the defendant on this motion because of the drastic consequences of his or her winning it. The standard used by the judge in ruling on the motion is as follows:

- **Denial of Motion** Looking at the evidence in the light most favorable to the plaintiff, the judge will *deny* the defendant's motion for a directed verdict if the judge feels that a jury could find for the plaintiff on each element of the cause of action because there is sufficient evidence on each element. Of course, any doubt in the judge's mind about whether the evidence would be sufficient for this purpose is resolved in favor of the plaintiff and hence, in favor of denying the motion. Evidence is sufficient when there is some admissible evidence on each element which a reasonable jury *could* accept.
- **Granting of Motion** Looking at the evidence in the light most favorable to the plaintiff, the judge will *grant* the defendant's motion for a directed verdict only if there is a defect in the plaintiff's evidence. The defect exists only when there is no sufficient evidence (as defined above) to support any of the elements of the cause of action.

Suppose that the plaintiff is suing the defendant for negligence and introduces evidence on duty, breach of duty, and damages. All of this evidence is sufficient in that a jury could reasonably find for the plaintiff on each of these elements. On the element of causation, however, the plaintiff's evidence is so weak as to be almost non-existent. Even if the judge gives the plaintiff the benefit of the doubt on the facts constituting causation, the motion for a directed verdict will be granted if the judge concludes that there is no sufficient evidence that the defendant caused the plaintiff's injury. Again, however, it does not take much evidence for the judge to rule that it would be sufficient to support a favorable jury resolution. Hence, it is relatively rare for the defendant to win the motion for a directed verdict at this early stage of the trial. Of course, if the plaintiff has failed to fulfill the burden of production on any of the elements of the cause of action, the judge *will* grant the defendant's motion for a directed verdict since, by definition, there cannot be sufficient evidence on which a jury can reach a conclusion favorable to the plaintiff on that element.

Some judges may decline to rule on the defendant's motion for a directed verdict until after the defendant has presented his or her case and the rebuttal evidence from both sides is concluded. If so, the judge will postpone a ruling on the motion until that time.

8. Defendant's Opening Statement to the Jury if it Was Reserved

Defendant delivers his or her opening statement to the jury at the close of the plaintiff's case only if the defendant previously decided to postpone it until this time rather than deliver it at the normal time—after the plaintiff's opening statement.

9. Presentation of Defendant's Case

The defendant now presents his or her case (assuming the motion for a directed verdict has been postponed or denied). The defendant proceeds along the same lines as the plaintiff: direct examination by the defendant of the witnesses he or she calls, cross-examination by the plaintiff, re-direct by the defendant, introduction of exhibits by the defendant, evidentiary objections made by the plaintiff, etc.

The defendant's goal is to refute the evidence of the plaintiff and so fulfill the defendant's burden of production and burden of proof on each element of the defenses alleged.

10. Rebuttal Evidence by Plaintiff
11. Rebuttal Evidence by Defendant

At the close of the defendant's case, many courts allow the plaintiff to present **rebuttal evidence** to cover matters raised while the defendant presented his or her case. This can include recalling witnesses, calling new witnesses, introducing additional exhibits, etc. Then the defendant is given a similar chance to present evidence designed to rebut the plaintiff's rebuttal.

12. Motions for Directed Verdict by Plaintiff and Defendant

Both parties have now rested. Before the case goes to the jury, each side can move for a directed verdict. These motions are resolved the same way the judge resolved the defendant's motion for a directed verdict at the close of the plaintiff's case. Taking one motion at a time, the judge views the evidence in the light most favorable to the *non-moving* party and decides whether there is sufficient evidence to support a jury finding on every element for which the moving party had the burden of production and the burden of proof. The evidence is sufficient if admissible evidence has been introduced on every such element that a reasonable jury could accept. The test is not whether the judge thinks one party or the other should win the case. The judge does not weigh the evidence for this purpose. The test is what the judge feels a reasonable jury could accept.

Sometimes, the judge will refuse to rule on the motions for a directed verdict until the jury has rendered its verdict, at which time the judge will make the ruling through a motion for a judgment notwithstanding the verdict (judgment NOV) to be considered below. The reason for this relates to the consequences of a reversal of the judge's ruling on appeal. If the appellate court reverses the trial court's granting of a directed verdict, the entire trial will have to be repeated, since the case never got to the jury. If, however, the appellate court reverses a trial court's granting of a judgment NOV, there may not have to be a new trial, since all the appellate court would have to do is reinstate the verdict of the jury, which was set aside when the trial court granted the judgment NOV.

13. Closing Argument of Defendant to Jury
14. Closing Argument of Plaintiff to Jury

In some states, the **closing arguments** come after the judge has given instructions to the jury. In most states (and in the federal courts), the closing arguments precede the instructions, so that the judge has the last word. Depending on the complexity of the case, the judge will allot a designated amount of time for each party to speak.

What is said during closing argument? The attorneys try to sum up the case in the light most favorable to their client, highlighting the strengths and downplaying the weaknesses in the claims and defenses. With this objective in mind, the attorney reviews the evidence and relates the evidence to the law. It is sometimes said, "if the law is against you, argue the facts; if the facts are against you, argue the law; if both the law and the facts are against you, scream for justice!" Of course, there are limits on what can be said during closing argument. An attorney can object, for example, if the other attorney falsely states what the evidence was or refers to evidence that was never introduced at the trial. Equally objectionable would be pleas directed to the prejudices of the jurors.

15. Instructions to Jury by Judge

Before the jury retires to deliberate, it receives instructions (called the **charge**) from the judge on what law applies to the case. The instructions tell the jury which party has the burden of proof and the standard the jury must use in determining whether the burden has been met. Also, the elements of the causes of action and of the defenses are presented, with guidelines for determining whether the facts support the elements. If any presumptions or other evidentiary rules apply, they will be explained.

Before the judge "charges" the jury, each attorney is allowed to request that the judge give designated instructions to the jury. After considering and ruling on these requests, the judge gives the jury the instructions to use.

16. Kinds of Verdicts

There are three types of verdicts:

- general verdict
- general verdict with interrogatories
- special verdict

General Verdict

The jury simply states which party wins, and, if applicable, how much the party wins. A general verdict in favor of one of the parties means that party met its burden of proof in each of the elements of the cause of action or defense.

General Verdict with Interrogatories

The jury states which party wins, and if applicable, how much the party wins, as with any general verdict. In addition, the jury answers a series of specific fact questions concerning critical aspects of the case that are submitted by the court. This system enables the judge to determine whether the jury has been consistent with itself, and to some extent, whether it misunderstood the law it was given in the judge's charge. If there has been an inconsistency or a mistake, the judge will try to reconcile what the jury has said or ask the jury to go back to deliberate again.

Special Verdict

The jury does not state who wins in a special verdict. Rather, the jury answers a series of specific questions submitted by the judge who then concludes who wins on the basis of the answers given. The same effort is made to reconcile any inconsistencies.

17. Motion for Judgment Notwithstanding the Verdict (NOV)

If a **judgment NOV** is granted, the judge, in effect, is setting aside the verdict of the jury in order to grant a judgment to the party that lost the verdict. The difference between a motion for a directed verdict and a motion for a judgment NOV is the time the motions are made. The motion for a directed verdict is made before the verdict is rendered by the jury (at the close of the plaintiff's case or at the close of the defendant's case), while the motion for a judgment NOV is made after the verdict. The essence of both motions is the same: the judge is ruling that the evidence is insufficient to support a verdict. When this ruling is made after the jury has already rendered a verdict, the judge is saying that no reasonable jury could have reached the verdict that it reached because there was not sufficient evidence of all the elements on which to base a verdict. When the ruling is made before the verdict, the judge is saying that the jury should not even get the case because of insufficient evidence.

There are usually time limits during which the party that lost the verdict must make a motion for a judgment NOV, e.g., ten days after entry of the judgment.

18. Remittitur and Additur

A trial judge may be dissatisfied with the jury verdict but still be unwilling to grant a motion for judgment NOV because he or she concludes there was sufficient evidence for the jury to find all the elements. Rather, the dissatisfaction of the judge is over the amount of the damages award given by the jury to the plaintiff. If the judge feels that the award was too low, he or she will say to the defendant that unless the latter agrees to increase the award by a designated amount, the judge will order a new trial. If the judge feels that the award is too high, he or she will say to the plaintiff that unless the latter agrees to decrease the award by a designated amount, the judge will order a new trial. The judge conditions the requirement of a new trial on the consent of the party to either increase the damages award **(additur)** or decrease it **(remittitur)**.[1] The standard

---

[1] In the federal courts, an additur is not permitted. Remitturs, however, are proper in the federal system.

used by the judge in taking this course of action is whether the damages award in the verdict is manifestly against the weight of the evidence.

19. Entry of Judgment

After the verdict is rendered, the judge announces the judgment either in accordance with the verdict or contrary to the verdict, via a judgment NOV. The judgment is then "entered" in the court's official docket and filed. See Figure 7.3.

Figure 7.3   Judgment on Jury Verdict

United States District Court for the Southern District of New York
Civil Action, File Number _____

A. B., Plaintiff
    v.   JUDGMENT
C. D., Defendant

This action came on for trial before the Court and a jury, Honorable John Marshall, District Judge, presiding, and the issues having been duly tried and the jury having duly rendered its verdict,
It is Ordered and Adjudged
[that the plaintiff A. B. recover of the defendant C. D. the sum of _____ , with interest thereon at the rate of _____ per cent as provided by law, and his costs of action.
[that the plaintiff take nothing, that the action be dismissed on the merits, and that the defendant C. D. recover of the plaintiff A. B. his costs of action.]
Dated at New York, New York, this _____ day of _____ , 19___ .

_____
Clerk of Court

20. Motion for a New Trial

Within a set number of days after the entry of the judgment, the parties can make a **motion for a new trial.** An order for a new trial is quite different from granting a judgment NOV. With respect to the latter, there is no new trial; the judge simply sets aside the verdict and enters judgment in favor of the party that lost the verdict. When a new trial is granted, however, everything starts all over again unless the new trial was granted on limited issues only, e.g., a new trial on the issue of damages only.

A number of grounds exist for granting a motion for a new trial:

- prejudicial irregularities committed by the judge or by an attorney
- jury misconduct
- surprise
- fraud by a party
- the verdict is manifestly against the weight of the evidence

Prejudicial Irregularities Committed by the Judge or by an Attorney

The judge may now concede that he or she improperly badgered an attorney or made erroneous rulings of law on the evidence. Opposing counsel may have committed serious improprieties during the trial, such as discussing the case with one of the jurors during a break, or making reference during closing argument to the large amount of insurance carried by the defendant. The irregularity must be considered serious enough to warrant a new trial. Harmless errors or errors that were corrected during the trial are not enough.

Jury Misconduct

The attorney, for example, may learn after the trial that one of the jurors lied about knowing one of the parties during the voir dire examination. Misconduct may also occur during the time for jury deliberations, e.g., a juror may visit the scene of the accident in order to take measurements or assess visibility personally.

When the jury announces its verdict, the attorney has a right to **poll** jurors in order to ask them individually if the verdict announced was the one agreed upon. Not all states require unanimous agreement among all the jurors. In some states, for example, a three-fourths vote is sufficient. Polling jurors also determines whether the requisite number of jurors agreed on the verdict.

Certain kinds of verdicts are improper, e.g., **quotient verdicts,** in which each juror states the amount of damages he or she thinks should be awarded and the total of all these amounts is divided by the number of jurors to determine the damages award eventually submitted in court.

In some states, it is difficult to determine whether there has been jury misconduct. The attorney may be prevented from even questioning jurors (other than polling them as indicated above). Extrinsic misconduct must be distinguished from intrinsic misconduct. Some states will allow inquiry into the former, but not the latter. **Intrinsic misconduct** involves the juror's thinking process that went into the conclusions he or she reached in the jury room, e.g., he or she did not like the plaintiff's race, or felt the plaintiff was foolish for suing. Attorneys cannot use evidence of intrinsic misconduct to impeach (attack) a jury verdict in the hope of setting it aside. **Extrinsic misconduct,** on the other hand, primarily involves overt conduct such as visiting the scene of the accident. Attorneys can question jurors or seek their affidavits in search of such conduct in order to try to set aside the verdict.

Surprise

The surprise must be serious and not due to the attorney's neglect or inexperience. A common example of surprise is newly discovered evidence during or just after the trial. Courts are reluctant to grant a new trial because of newly discovered evidence unless the new facts are so significant that they would probably have changed the result of the trial. Also, the new facts must relate to facts already in existence at the time of the trial, rather than to facts occurring after the trial. Finally, the facts must be such that due diligence by the attorney would not have resulted in their discovery before trial.

Fraud by a Party

An example would be fraud by a party that prevented the other side from discovering crucial evidence. Not all courts agree, however, on the kind of fraud that will warrant the granting of a new trial. Courts differ, for example, on whether serious perjury committed by a party during trial is enough to warrant a new trial.

The Verdict is Manifestly Against the Weight of the Evidence

The standard used by a judge to determine whether the verdict is manifestly against the weight of the evidence (which will justify a new trial) is different from the standard used to decide whether to grant a judgment NOV. A judgment NOV is given if the evidence is insufficient in that no reasonable jury could have found the way it did. In making this decision, a judge does not weigh the evidence; he or she simply decides whether there was enough evidence to convince a reasonable jury. When, however, the judge is deciding a motion for a new trial because the verdict is manifestly against the weight of the evidence, he or she *does* weigh the evidence in order to determine whether it clearly or manifestly should not have led to the verdict reached by the jury.

21. Motion to Trial Court for Relief from Judgment

Once the judgment is rendered, many states allow a party a period of time to go back to the trial court that rendered the original judgment to seek relief from that judgment. The grounds for such relief vary from state to state. The most common grounds are: the court lacked jurisdiction to render the judgment, the other party committed fraud, there is newly discovered evidence that due diligence could not have uncovered earlier, reasonable mistakes or inadvertence led to a default judgment, etc. Trial courts, however, are reluctant to grant relief by ordering a new trial once the judgment has been rendered.

▪ ASSIGNMENT 7.1 ▪

Read the following statements. Determine whether they are true or false. For each false statement, indicate why it is false and correct it.

a. The party with the burden of proof on the main claims has the option of making the second opening statement to the jury.
b. The party with the burden of proof on the main claims has a choice on when to deliver the opening statement.
c. The burden of proof is the standard that enables the trier of fact to assess the admissibility of the evidence.
d. No tort case ever requires proof of any fact by clear and convincing evidence.
e. When trial judges rule on motions for a directed verdict, they use the same standard of evaluating the evidence as is used to determine whether a party has met his or her standard of proof.
f. The burden of production is always on the plaintiff. The defendant does not have the burden of production until the plaintiff has met his or her burden of proof.
g. A jury can accept a fact as true when there is enough evidence to enable it to conclude that there is a possibility that it is true.
h. The defendant has the burden of proof on all facts needed to prove each element of the cause of action in the complaint.
i. Another name for the burden of proof is the burden of coming forward with the evidence.

j. Generally, the party with the burden of pleading an issue has the burden of producing evidence on that issue.

k. The judge decides whether the burden of production has been met after resolving whether the burden of proof has been met.

l. Sustaining the burden of proof allows the party to get his or her case the to jury.

m. A party calls his or her own witnesses to the stand for cross-examination.

n. In ruling on a motion for a directed verdict, the trial judge will resolve all doubts in the evidence in favor of the non-moving party.

o. Appellate courts grant motions for directed verdict only when there is a jurisdictional defect.

p. A trial judge will always grant an immediate ruling on a party's motion for a directed verdict.

q. The trial judge instructs the jury on which party has the burden of production.

r. A special verdict indicates which party will win and also answers questions the attorneys feel are critical to the case.

s. A judgment NOV is granted when the judge feels that most of the witnesses for the party that won the verdict were believable.

t. In additur, the plaintiff must agree to a higher damages aware or be forced into a new trial, while in remittitur, the defendant must agree to a lower damages award or be forced into a new trial.

u. Any irregularity committed by a trial judge can be a ground for a new trial.

v. A quotient verdict, by definition, is a general verdict with interrogatories.

▪ ASSIGNMENT 7.2 ▪

Contact the court clerk's office of any trial court in your state that hears tort cases. Find out what jury trials are scheduled. Sit in on a trial to observe. Record your observations on as many of the following topics as you can. Describe what you saw, what was being attempted, how the judge responded, effectiveness of the attorneys, etc. It would be valuable to record all of your observations on one trial, but if this is not practical, sit in on more than one trial.

a. voir dire
b. opening statements of attorneys
c. use of exhibits
d. direct examination of a witness
e. cross-examination of a witness
f. re-direct examination of a witness
g. arguments over the admissibility of evidence
h. motion for a directed verdict
i. closing arguments of attorneys
j. instructions to the jury
k. polling of the jury
l. motion for judgment notwithstanding the verdict
m. motion for a new trial
n. other motions made
o. other events not listed above

▪ ASSIGNMENT 7.3 ▪

For each of the following questions or topics, find statutes, if any, or rules of court, if any, that pertain to a state trial court in your state. Give citations to and brief summaries of whatever you find. (See the General Instructions for the State Code Assignment in Chapter 2.)

a. opening statements by attorneys
b. motions that can be made after the opening statements
c. exhibits introduced into evidence
d. motions that can be made after the plaintiff has rested his or her case
e. standards governing the motion for a directed verdict
f. requests for instructions to the jury
g. laws governing jury deliberations
h. kinds of verdicts a jury can give
i. standards governing the motion for a judgment notwithstanding the verdict
j. grounds for a motion for a new trial; plus time at which this motion must be made
k. entering of judgments
l. after judgment is entered, ways parties can obtain from the trial court relief from the judgment of that trial court, and when this relief must be sought

■ RES JUDICATA AND COLLATERAL ESTOPPEL

Res Judicata

The doctrine of **res judicata** says, in effect, that if you have already had your day in court on a cause of action, you cannot relitigate it in a later suit. If this rule did not exist, litigation would never come to an end. The elements of res judicata are as follows:

1. The court in suit #1 rendered a final judgment.
2. The judgment in suit #1 was on the merits.
3. Suit #2 raises the same cause of action that was raised in suit #1.

When all of these elements are present, the defense of res judicata can be raised in suit #2. When the plaintiff wins suit #1, his or her cause of action in suit #1 is *merged* in the judgment rendered on that cause of action. The same cause of action cannot be relitigated. The plaintiff can go to court to enforce the judgment, but it cannot be relitigated. If the defendant won the case in suit #1, then the plaintiff in suit #1 is *barred* from relitigating the same cause of action in suit #2.

1. Final Judgment

The judgment in suit #1 must be *final* to have res judicata effect. Nothing must be left to be decided and the appeal process must be over or the time to appeal must have expired in order for the judgment to be final.

Example:

Suit #1: Tom sues Mary for conversion of a car. Mary wins. The judgment is affirmed on appeal.

Suit #2: Tom sues Mary for conversion of the same car, raising the same facts that were litigated in suit #1. Mary can successfully raise the defense of res judicata to suit #2 since the judgment in suit #1 was final. Tom is barred from relitigating the case.

It is important to distinguish between a direct attack and a collateral attack on a judgment. The final judgment rule in the first element of res judicata applies only to direct attacks. When a party (the appellant) appeals a judgment immediately after the trial in the time period allotted for such appeals, he or she is bringing a *direct* attack against the judgment. A **direct attack** is one brought as part of the regular appeal process. Suppose, however, the judgment is attacked in another proceeding brought to enforce the judgment, or is attacked in a totally separate litigation. This is a **collateral attack** against the judgment and can be brought only for jurisdictional defects in the judgment, e.g., the court that rendered the judgment lacked subject matter jurisdiction.

A judgment is final for purposes of res judicata when a *direct* appeal can no longer be brought because the appeal process is over or the time for appeal has expired. There is *no* time limit, however, for bringing a collateral attack. Hence, a judgment is final for purposes of res judicata when a direct appeal can no longer be brought, even though it may *still* be possible to collaterally attack the judgment for jurisdictional defects. Even a final judgment can be relitigated if it is jurisdictionally defective; res judicata does not bar the collateral attack of a judgment for jurisdictional defects.

2. On the Merits

A final judgment is **on the merits** when the court has ruled on the substance of the claims raised, e.g., the court has found negligence or contributory negligence, and has entered a judgment accordingly. Default judgments are on the merits. The cause of action raised in the pleadings cannot be relitigated, even though the default judgment was not reached after a full adversarial proceeding with both parties participating. A summary judgment is also on the merits.

Most judgments based on procedural technicalities, however, are not on the merits. A dismissal for lack of jurisdiction is not on the merits; the underlying cause of action can be relitigated. The same would be true of dismissals for improper venue. Most courts would say that a judgment based on a dismissal because of the defense of statute of limitations is not on the merits. Other courts, however, disagree. If an involuntary dismissal is imposed on the plaintiff for failure to comply with a court order or for failure to "prosecute" the claim, the judgment is on the merits.

3. Same Cause of Action

Not all courts use the same test to determine whether the cause of action that was litigated in suit #1 is the same cause of action that is raised in suit #2. The distinction is not based on the labels of the causes of action. The major tests are as follows:

- **Same wrong test**
  All claims raised in suit #2 based on the same wrong that was the focus of suit #1 cannot be relitigated because of the doctrine of res judicata.
- **Same transaction/occurrence test**
  All claims raised in suit #2 arising out of the same transaction or related series of occurrences that were the focus of suit #1 cannot be relitigated because of the doctrine of res judicata.
- **Same evidence test**
  All claims raised in suit #2 that call for the use of substantially the same evidence used to resolve the claims in suit #1 cannot be relitigated because of the doctrine of res judicata.

- **Same law test**

  All claims raised in suit #2 that call for the application of the same law applied in suit #1 cannot be relitigated because of the doctrine of res judicata.

  Example:

  Suit #1: Tom sues Mary for $400 for negligent damage to his car in a collision. Tom wins and the judgment is affirmed on appeal.

  Suit #2: Tom sues Mary for $10,000 for personal injuries received in the same accident involved in suit #1. The cause of action is negligence. Under several of the above tests, Mary can raise the defense of res judicata in most states to prevent suit #2. Suit #2 involves the same evidence and the same transaction. A few courts, however, say that a property damage claim is sufficiently different from a personal injury claim that the causes of action are not the same and res judicata would not prevent suit #2.

The practical effect of res judicata is to encourage parties to join all their claims and defenses in suit #1 for fear that res judicata may prevent them from raising them in a later suit. Res judicata is not limited to claims that were actually litigated in suit #1. In the example immediately above, the personal injury claim was never litigated in suit #1, but in most states res judicata will prevent it from being raised in suit #2 since the cause of action in both suits is considered the same under several of the tests listed.

Res judicata prevents the relitigation of causes of action that were litigated and *that could have been litigated* in the first suit.

Collateral Estoppel

Collateral estoppel prevents the relitigation of *issues* that were resolved in suit #1. The elements of collateral estoppel are as follows:

1. The same issue is raised in suit #2 that was raised in suit #1.
2. The issue was actually litigated and was essential to the determination of suit #1.

The two suits do not have to involve the same cause of action for collateral estoppel to apply, unlike res judicata. Res judicata is not limited to matters that were actually litigated in suit #1. Collateral estoppel, on the other hand, has this limitation. The target of res judicata is the prevention of the relitigation of the same cause of action or claim. The target of collateral estoppel is the prevention of the relitigation of the same issue.

- ASSIGNMENT 7.4 ·

Bill dies in an automobile accident with Fred. Fred is charged with manslaughter since he was allegedly drunk at the time of the accident. Bill's estate later sues Fred for negligence. Assume that Fred was convicted in the criminal case. Does collateral estoppel prevent the relitigation of any issues in the civil case that were litigated in the criminal case in your state? Would your answer differ if Fred were acquitted of the criminal charge? (See General Instructions for the State Court Opinion Assignment in Chapter 2.)

▪ APPEAL

The main way to challenge a judgment is to bring a direct appeal to the appellate court or courts with supervisory jurisdiction over the trial court. Some states have only one appellate court. Other states and the federal government, however, have two appeals courts: an intermediary appellate court and the highest court, often called the supreme court. (See Figures 5.1 and 5.2 in Chapter 5.)

Appellate courts do not try cases. New evidence is not taken and witnesses are not called. The function of appellate courts is to review lower court proceedings to make sure no errors of law were made.

With limited exceptions, the appellate court will review only final judgments. (Parties dissatisfied with rulings of the trial judge cannot stop the trial every time such a ruling is made in order to appeal it to a higher court.) A judgment is final when nothing is left to be decided by the trial judge. Up until that point, if a party disagrees with something the trial judge has done, the attorney must state his or her objection for the record and raise the matter later on appeal once the judgment is final. The rulings of the judge that resolve only portions of the trial are called **interlocutory orders.** There are some exceptions to the final judgment rule. The federal courts and some states do allow appellate review of some interlocutory orders. The trial judge may have to certify to the appellate court that the interlocutory order involves a controlling question of law. Generally, the appeal will be allowed only if the interlocutory order will have irremediable consequences if it is not appealed immediately.

The party seeking the appeal is called the **appellant.** The party against whom the appeal is brought is called the **appellee** or **respondent.** Sometimes, both parties will bring the appeal if both are dissatisfied with rulings the trial judge has made. The procedure for the appeal is as follows:

1. The party makes a formal request for an appeal (a **notice of appeal**) within a designated time after the trial judgment is rendered. See Figure 7.4 for a sample notice.
2. This request is filed in the appellate court and served on the other party.
3. The appellant files and serves an **appellate brief,** which is a written document covering the rulings objected to, the reasons for the objections with supporting authorities, the relevant portions of the record to which the objections pertain, and the action the appellant wants the appellate court to take.
4. The appellee files and serves an appellate brief responding to the points made in the appellant's brief and raising any other objections of the appellee to what the trial judge did or failed to do.
5. The appellant files and serves a **reply brief** responding to the appellee's brief.
6. The appellate court sets a date for oral argument, in which the attorneys state their basic positions and answer questions from the appellate judges.
7. The appellate court renders its decision. It may affirm, reverse, or modify the lower court judgment. The case may be **remanded** (sent back) to the lower court with instructions on how to proceed.

In some courts, a party cannot bring an appeal unless he or she posts a bond at the time the notice of appeal is filed. The bond is to cover the costs of appeal, e.g., filing fees, which will be paid to the appellee if the appellate court eventually affirms the lower court judgment. These costs do not include attorneys fees in-

Figure 7.4   Notice of Appeal

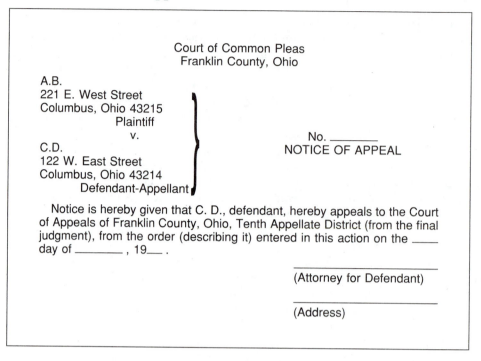

Court of Common Pleas
Franklin County, Ohio

A.B.
221 E. West Street
Columbus, Ohio 43215
        Plaintiff
            v.
C.D.
122 W. East Street
Columbus, Ohio 43214
        Defendant-Appellant

No. _____
NOTICE OF APPEAL

Notice is hereby given that C. D., defendant, hereby appeals to the Court of Appeals of Franklin County, Ohio, Tenth Appellate District (from the final judgment), from the order (describing it) entered in this action on the _____ day of _____ , 19___ .

_____
(Attorney for Defendant)

_____
(Address)

curred by the appellee in the appeal. A **supersedeas bond** is posed by the appellant covering the amount of the judgment and the costs of appeal if the appellant has asked the trial court to stay the execution (i.e., the carrying out) of the judgment pending the appeal.

As indicated, the scope of appellate review is limited to errors of law. The trial judge had to make numerous decisions on the pleadings, on jury selection, on pre-trial motions, on rules of evidence during the trial, on trial motions, on post-trial motions, etc. The error could involve the substantive law of torts (e.g., giving the jury the wrong instruction on proximate cause), or the technical law of procedure (e.g., improperly refusing to allow the plaintiff to amend the complaint).

The alleged errors must appear in the record. With very few exceptions, if parties do not state their objection on the record during the trial, the error is waived and cannot be raised on appeal. The major exception is a party's failure to object to the trial court's assertion of jurisdiction over the case. Appellate courts will usually review a challenge to the trial court's jurisdiction even if the challenge is raised for the first time on appeal.

Also, the error must be **prejudicial,** which means that the substantial rights of the aggrieved party must be affected by the error, e.g., the judge's instructions misled the jury. An error is **harmless** if it does not affect substantial rights. An appellate court will not grant relief from harmless errors.

- ASSIGNMENT 7.5 -

For each of the following questions, find statutes, if any, or rules of court, if any, from your state. (See the General Instructions for the State Code Assignment in Chapter 2.)

a. What courts have appellate jurisdiction to hear appeals from the trial of tort cases?
b. How is an appeal to such courts initiated?
c. Is the appellate court required to hear every appeal brought to it?
d. When, if ever, are interlocutory appeals allowed?
e. What bonds, if any, must be filed?
f. What laws govern the format, content, and sequence of appellate briefs and reply briefs?
g. What laws govern oral argument?
h. What options are available to an appellate court when it agrees or disagrees with the trial court?
i. What laws govern a motion to the appellate court to re-hear the case?
j. How many different appeal levels are there?

SUMMARY

The trial begins with an opening statement from the party with the burden of proof, the plaintiff. The defendant may then move for a dismissal on the ground that even if the plaintiff could prove everything stated in the opening statement, he or she would not have established a cause of action. Next comes the opening statement by the defendant, unless he or she reserves it for later. The party asserting a cause of action or a defense has the burden of production and the burden of proof on its elements. The burden of proof is the standard that tells the trier of fact how believable a party's evidence must be on a fact in order to accept that fact as true. In most tort cases the standard is preponderance of the evidence. The plaintiff's case is presented through exhibits and witnesses who are subjected to direct, cross, and re-direct examination. The defendant then moves for a directed verdict on the basis that the plaintiff has not proven a prima facie case. If this motion is denied, the defendant presents its case. Rebuttal evidence is often allowed after each side presents its case. After both parties rest, they can make a motion for a directed verdict. Next come closing arguments to the jury, followed by the judge's charge to the jury. The three kinds of verdicts are general verdict, general verdict with interrogatories, and special verdict. If the judge concludes that the evidence was not sufficient to support the verdict reached by the jury, he or she can order a judgment NOV. Through an additur or remittitur, the trial judge often has the power to pressure the parties to change the amount of a jury's award of damages. Among the grounds a judge will consider in a motion for a new trial are prejudicial irregularities of the judge or attorney, jury misconduct, surprise, fraud by a party, and the verdict being manifestly against the weight of the evidence.

Under res judicata, a judgment on the merits will prevent the same parties from relitigating the same cause of action. Collateral estoppel will prevent the relitigation of the same issue.

Appellate courts review final judgments for errors of law. Rarely will the appellate court review interlocutory orders. The appellant brings the appeal against the appellee (respondent) by filing a notice of appeal. The parties file appellate briefs that contain arguments on whether a lower court made errors of law and hence whether this judgment should be affirmed, reversed, or modified.

Key Terms

opening statement
burden of proof
beyond a reasonable
  doubt
clear and convincing
preponderance of the
  evidence
admissible
burden of production
direct examination
cross-examination
re-direct examination
waived
record
rests
directed verdict

prima facie case
rebuttal evidence
closing arguments
charge
general verdict
general verdict with
  interrogatories
special verdict
judgment NOV
additur
remittitur
motion for a new trial
poll
quotient verdicts
intrinsic misconduct
extrinsic misconduct

res judicata
direct attack
collateral attack
on the merits
collateral estoppel
interlocutory orders
appellant
appellee
respondent
notice of appeal
appellate brief
reply brief
remanded
supersedeas bond
prejudicial
harmless

CHAPTER 8

The Judgment Creditor: Enforcement of the Judgment

CHAPTER OUTLINE

- INTRODUCTION
- LOCATING THE ASSETS OF THE JUDGMENT DEBTOR

- COLLECTION OF THE JUDGMENT AWARD

▪ INTRODUCTION

Unfortunately, most cases are not over when the plaintiff receives a judgment award of a sum of money as damages from the defendant—even if the award is affirmed on appeal. The plaintiff simply becomes a **judgment creditor** against the defendant, who becomes the **judgment debtor.** The debt owed to the creditor is the amount of the damages award. The plaintiff must now go through what is sometimes a long and expensive process of enforcement to collect the damages award. For uncooperative judgment debtors, further litigation might be needed. Indeed, two of the major questions an attorney will ask in deciding whether to take a case are, "Can we win?" and "Can we collect what we win?" For a plaintiff whose main motivation in bringing the suit is to be compensated for the harm the defendant caused, it may make no sense to sue if it is known in advance that the defendant is **judgment proof,** which means that the defendant has few or no assets from which a judgment can be satisfied.

Suppose that at the beginning of the trial the defendant is not judgment proof, but there is a good possibility that he or she will *voluntarily* become judgment proof by destroying assets, giving them away, taking them out of the state, or otherwise hiding them. In such situations the plaintiff may be able to obtain a **pre-trial attachment** of the defendant's personal or real property. If the plaintiff can convince a court that pre-trial attachment is needed, the court will issue a **writ of attachment** to a sheriff or similar official, who will actually or symboli- **185** cally take custody of the property and preserve the status quo until a final judgment on the merits is reached by the court. Our concern in this chapter is the collection of a money judgment when no such pre-trial property orders are used.

The judgment may simply say that the defendant shall pay the plaintiff the sum of $75,000, or more elaborately:

> It is hereby Ordered and Adjudged that the plaintiff, Mary Smith, shall recover of the defendant, Fred Jones, the sum of $75,000 and her costs of the action.

Often the judge will **stay** the entry of the judgment or stay the execution on the judgment in order to give the losing party time to appeal the judgment. The stay prevents the judgment creditor from taking formal steps to collect. To obtain a stay, the judgment debtor may be forced to post a bond to protect the judgment creditor. (See the discussion of the *supersedeas bond* at the end of Chapter 7.)

Once the period of the stay and the appeal process is over, the judgment creditor is ready to try to collect. If the judgment debtor is relatively cooperative, a number of payment options might be voluntarily worked out between the judgment creditor and the judgment debtor:

- The judgment debtor pays in full immediately.
- An installment payment schedule is worked out.
- The judgment debtor signs a promissory note secured by a pledge of other real or personal property.
- The judgment debtor assigns to (i.e., transfers to) the judgment creditor any rights the judgment debtor has to money from other persons (e.g., accounts receivable).

The headaches begin, however, with the *uncooperative* judgment debtor. The judgment creditor has two concerns:

- How do you locate the assets of the judgment creditor?
- What enforcement mechanisms are available to reach the assets you have located?

■ LOCATING THE ASSETS OF THE JUDGMENT DEBTOR

Your objective is to compile a list of every asset of the judgment debtor. As you search for assets, you will want to obtain the following basic information for each asset:

- A description of the asset. Be specific as to quantity, color, size or other measurements, function, component parts, or any other data relevant to the kind of asset in question.
- Location. Where is the asset? Give the exact addresses and names of people who have possession of the asset or who recently had possession, including, of course, the judgment debtor.
- A record of how the judgment debtor obtained his or her interest in the asset. If by purchase, how much was paid, when was it acquired, etc.?
- Current fair market value of the asset. If the asset was sold on the open market today, how much would it probably bring?

When tracking assets in an attempt to obtain the above information, it is useful to think of the various possible categories of assets:

Categories of Assets

1. personal property; real property
2. property solely owned by the judgment debtor; property in which others also have an interest
3. tangible property; intangible property
4. property in the possession of the judgment debtor; property in the possession of a third person
5. property in the state where the judgment was rendered (forum state); property in another state (foreign state)
6. property the judgment debtor currently has; property that will be received in the future
7. property the judgment debtor currently has; property the judgment creditor disposed of since the litigation began or just before it began
8. property that is exempt from creditor collection; property not protected by exemption

Any single asset may fall into a variety of these categories.

1. Personal/Real Property

Personal property includes cash, bonds, securities, uncashed checks, cars, trucks, boats, jewelry, clothing, business inventory, equipment, pension rights, insurance policies, debts owed the judgment debtor (e.g., accounts receivable).

Real property includes current residence, vacation home, fixtures on the land, buildings (for business or personal use). Real property is land and everything attached to the land. All other property is personal property.

2. Solely Owned/Others with Interest

The judgment debtor may own many assets in his or her own name without anyone else having a property interest in the asset. On the other hand, there will usually be assets in which others will also have a property interest. For example:

- A spouse may jointly own a bank account or a home.
- A spouse may have a dower or community property interest in assets acquired during the marriage.
- An associate may have an equal partnership interest in a business.
- A tenant may have a property right to remain on land owned by the judgment debtor as landlord.
- The government may have a tax lien on property because of nonpayment of taxes.
- A bank or other creditor may have a security interest in property, e.g, the property was used as collateral to obtain a mortgage or to borrow money in some other way.
- A neighbor may have an easement over the judgment debtor's land allowing the neighbor to use the land for a limited purpose.

The following are some basic property terms that involve assets in which more than one person has a property interest:

> **Joint tenancy:** Individuals (called joint tenants) own the entire property together. They do not own parts of it; each individual owns all of the property. When one joint tenant dies, the property does not pass through the

deceased's estate. The property passes immediately to the surviving joint tenants. This is known as the **right of survivorship.** (A joint tenant is *not* a tenant who rents an apartment; this is a totally separate concept of tenancy.)

Tenancy by the entirety: This is a joint tenancy in which the joint tenants are husband and wife.

Tenancy in common: Individuals (called tenants in common) own a portion or a share of the whole property. There is no right of survivorship. When one tenant in common dies, his or her interest in the property passes through his or her estate and does not go to the surviving tenants in common.

Lien: This is a claim against property that is usually created to secure payment of a debt. The holder of the lien can force the sale of the property when the debt is not paid. The proceeds from the forced sale are used to satisfy the debt.

Mortgage: In some states, a mortgage is simply a lien on property used to secure the mortgage debt.

3. Tangible/Intangible Property

Tangible property has a physical form that can be seen or touched, e.g., land, car, equipment.

Intangible property is a ''right'' rather than a physical object, e.g., the right to receive money from an employer, the right to the exclusive use of an invention, the right to have money repaid with interest. These rights may be described in documents that are tangible, e.g., stock certificates, promissory notes, patents, but the rights represented by these documents are intangible.

4. Possession of Judgment Debtor/Possession of Others

Very often the judgment debtor will have assets in the possession of other persons or institutions. Banks and employers, for example, often hold money that belongs to the judgment debtor, which will be turned over upon request or when a set date arrives. Insurance companies, unions, and government agencies also hold assets (often called benefits) that will be given to the judgment debtor at a certain time or upon the happening of a designated condition, e.g., retirement.

A **bailment** exists when someone else's goods are being held for use, repair, or storage, e.g., furniture in storage, a borrowed or rented car, a car in a repair shop. The person holding the property (called the **bailee**) may or may not be receiving a profit for holding the goods of the other (called the **bailor**).

5. Property in Forum State/Property in Foreign State

The **forum state** is the state where the parties litigated (or are litigating) their dispute. For our purposes, the forum state is the state that rendered the judgment for the judgment creditor against the judgment debtor. A **foreign state** is any other state in the United States or any other country in the world. The judgment debtor may own land or other assets in a foreign state as well as in the forum state.

6. Current Property/Future Property

The judgment debtor will probably have many assets in his or her possession. Other assets, however, may be on their way to the judgment debtor through the mail or other means of shipment. Some assets will not be received until the occurrence of a designated event or condition, e.g., the judgment debtor reaches a certain age, retires, dies, etc.

Assets that the judgment debtor has a right to receive in the future can usually be assigned (transferred) to someone else so that the latter will be entitled to receive the asset. An **assignment** is simply a transfer of rights from one person to another.

7. Current Property/Property Recently Disposed Of

The great fear of a judgment creditor is that the judgment debtor will voluntarily become judgment proof by giving away, destroying, or otherwise disposing of assets before the trial is over. As mentioned earlier, a pre-trial attachment order might help in such situations. Even if this order was not obtained, the judgment creditor can still ask the court to invalidate any transfers of assets made by the judgment debtor just before and during the trial on the ground that they were sham transfers or were made with the intent to defraud the judgment winner.

8. Exempt Property/Nonexempt Property

All the assets owned by judgment debtors are not fair game to judgment creditors. By law, certain property is **exempt**, e.g., a designated percentage of the judgment debtor's salary, clothes, the tools of one's trade or profession, some furniture. Such property cannot be reached by a judgment creditor to satisfy the judgment debt.

▪ ASSIGNMENT 8.1 ▪

In your state, what assets of a judgment debtor are exempt from a judgment creditor? Check the state code of your state, rules of court, and opinions written by courts in your state. (See General Instructions for the State Code and the State Court Opinion Assignment in Chapter 2.)

How then does the judgment creditor go about locating the assets of the uncooperative judgment debtor that fall into one or more of the above eight categories of assets? There are some formal procedures that can be of assistance in discovering assets. Before discussing these, some thoughts will be presented on *informal* investigative techniques. See Figure 8.1. Reference should also be made back to Chapter 4 for general principles on the skill of investigation.

The judgment creditor has just been through a trial and perhaps on appeal with the judgment debtor. A good deal is already known about the latter. This data must be organized and evaluated at two levels. First, the data contains specific information on the possible assets and other debts of the judgment debtor. Second, the data tells you a lot about the lifestyle of the judgment debtor. One's lifestyle can be an excellent clue to available assets.

Figure 8.1 Informal Investigative Techniques to Discover the Assets and Liabilities of the Judgment Debtor

I. Financial Data That You Already Have about the Judgment Debtor from the Litigation to Date

A. Data in the Office Case File

1. Notes on the reasons why the attorney for the judgment creditor agreed to take the case initially. What led the attorney to believe that the defendant was not judgment proof?
2. Notes on the intake interview of the client. What did the client say or imply about the financial status of the defendant?
3. Notes on preliminary investigations done by the law firm.
4. Notes on early negotiations with opposing counsel to settle the case. What was said about the defendant? Did you learn about liability insurance limits?
5. Pleadings, e.g., the responses given in the answer to the complaint.
6. Correspondence in the file.
7. Data obtained through pre-trial discovery:
   • answers to interrogatories
   • deposition transcripts of the defendant and other witnesses
   • the contents of documents obtained through a motion to produce
   • the answers to requests for admissions
   • the results of physical and mental examinations
8. Transcripts of direct, cross, and re-direct examination of the defendant and other witnesses who testified about the defendant's past.
9. Exhibits introduced at trial, whether or not they were admitted into evidence, e.g., police reports on the accident, prior convictions.
10. Motions and briefs filed by the defendant.

B. Other Direct or Indirect Financial Data Based on Appearances as Clues to Lifestyle

1. Did the defendant hire an expensive law firm?
2. How well did the defendant dress? What kind of car did he or she drive?
3. Did the defendant appear successful and prominent in business?
4. What educational level was demonstrated?
5. To what kind of lifestyle did the defendant's family appear to be accustomed?
6. What level of integrity and openness was demonstrated? Did the defendant appear to be secretive?
7. Was it expensive for the defendant to defend this suit? Did the defendant use extensive resources, e.g., expert witnesses, demonstrations? Do you know who paid these expenses?

II. Leads to Additional Financial Data about Judgment Debtor

A. Data in Public Records

1. Telephone directory (how many phone numbers are listed?).
2. Land records in county offices.
3. Prior litigation brought by or against the defendant as revealed in court clerks' offices, e.g., breach-of-contract actions, divorce proceedings, bankruptcy proceedings.

Figure 8.1 Continued

---

    4. Index bureaus on prior claims made by the defendant.
    5. Credit bureaus with data on the defendant or on the defendant's business.
    6. Motor vehicle registration.
    7. Government license offices.
    8. Secretary of state's office for incorporation papers, financial statements.
    9. Newspaper stories on the defendant or on the defendant's business.
   10. Obituary column, if defendant is deceased.
   11. Government consumer protection agencies that might list consumer complaints against defendant's business.
   12. Government offices where liens and mortgages are filed (including filings pursuant to the Uniform Commercial Code).

B. Other leads
    1. Interviews with neighbors.
    2. Interviews with clients or other business associates of the defendant.
    3. Site visit to residencies.
    4. Site visit to places of business.

Formal Methods of Discovering Assets and Liabilities

We now turn to the more formal methods of post-trial discovery of assets and liabilities that might be available. Four major devices should be discussed, some of which overlap. These devices are often begun by the judgment creditor's service of a subpoena on the judgment debtor or on anyone else who may have information on the financial condition of the judgment debtor.

Post-Trial Deposition

In Chapter 6, we examined the *pre-trial* deposition used by attorneys to help prepare for trial. The procedures for the *post-trial* deposition are often very similar, including the availability of protection from the court against undue harassment by the judgment creditor who is using the deposition to discover assets.

Production of Documents

In a motion for production of documents, the judgment creditor is looking for bank statements, balance sheets, tax returns, dividend and royalty statements, separation agreements (check alimony and property division terms), antenuptial agreements, wills, insurance policies, trust instruments, mortgages, deeds, financial statements filed to obtain loans, etc.

Written Interrogatories

Much of the same information can be sought by sending written questions, which often must be answered under oath.

Supplementary Proceedings

The judgment creditor may be able to ask the court to order the judgment debtor to appear at a court hearing in order to answer questions about available assets and finances. In some states, such a hearing can be used in addition to the above three discovery devices.

▪ ASSIGNMENT 8.2 ▪

Check the rules of court, state code, and court opinions of your state to determine what post-trial discovery methods are available to a judgment creditor trying to locate financial information about the judgment debtor. What specifically can be used? When, if ever, is the court involved in the method used? What sanctions are available for non-cooperation? What specific methods, if any, are prohibited? (See General Instructions for the State Code and State Court Opinion Assignments in Chapter 2.)

▪ COLLECTION OF THE JUDGMENT AWARD

Again we are talking about collection mechanisms against an uncooperative judgment debtor who has not voluntarily satisfied the judgment award of a judgment creditor. In the preceding section, we examined discovery techniques designed to *locate* the assets of the judgment debtor. While now our focus is on the methods available to *collect* assets that are discovered, it should be pointed out that in the process of using these collection methods, the judgment creditor will often be able to uncover new financial data. Hence, the collection mechanisms can serve discovery and collection purposes.

Collection begins by **execution.** Execution is simply a process of carrying something out. When a judgment creditor wants to execute a judgment, a **writ of execution** is obtained from the court, which directs the sheriff (1) to take possession of (i.e., to **levy**) assets of the judgment debtor, (2) to sell these assets, (3) to deduct the costs of execution, (4) to give the judgment creditor enough proceeds from the sale to satisfy the judgment award plus interest, and (5) to return the remaining proceeds, if any, to the judgment debtor. This sale of assets is often referred to as a **forced sale** or a **judicial sale.**

The judgment creditor will not be able to obtain execution against all of the assets of the judgment debtor. We have already seen that certain property of the judgment debtor is exempt and beyond the reach of collection. Also, it may be that the original court acquired only limited jurisdiction over the case through the attachment of the judgment debtor's property in the state. If so, execution is limited to the attached property.

If the assets of the judgment debtor are in the possession of a third person such as a bank or employer, execution is accomplished by **garnishment.** Garnishment is the process of reaching the assets of a debtor in the possession of a third party in order to satisfy a debt. The judgment creditor seeks a **writ of garnishment** from a court after filing an affidavit stating that the judgment has not been satisfied and that a third person, called the **garnishee,** has assets of the judgment debtor. See Figure 8.2 for an example. The writ is then served on the garnishee, who must state what assets he or she has of the judgment debtor. The service of the writ creates a lien for the judgment creditor on the assets of the judgment debtor in the possession of the garnishee. If the garnishee contests the writ, a hearing is usually held.

Suppose that the judgment debtor owns land. How is execution achieved? The judgment creditor usually obtains a lien on real property by docketing the judg-

Figure 8.2   Writ of Garnishment

STATE OF COLORADO

City and County of Denver

_____ County of _____
State of Colorado
Civil Action No. _____

_____
_____
_____

Plaintiff,

vs.

_____
_____
_____

Defendant,

WRIT OF GARNISHMENT
WITH INTERROGATORIES

Served _____ , 19__
at _____ o'clock __
Manager of Safety and Excise and
Ex-officio Sheriff City and County of
Denver

By _____
       Deputy Sheriff

The People of the State of Colorado,
To _____ , Garnishee:

_____
_____

   You are hereby notified that you are attached as garnishee in the above entitled action, and

   You are required to answer the interrogatories attached hereto within twenty days from the date of the service of this writ upon you. If you fail to answer the interrogatories within twenty days of the service of this writ upon you, you will be in default and judgment may be entered against you.

INTERROGATORIES

1. On the date and at the time that this writ of garnishment was served on you, were you indebted to the defendant for wages, commissions, monies or credits, etc? If so, please state how much.
ANSWER: _____

_____

2. On the date and at the time that this writ of garnishment was served on you, did you have any property belonging to the defendant (1) in your possession, or (2) under your control? If so, give all particulars, including a description of the property, statement of its value or estimated value, and state why you have possession or control of the property.
ANSWER: _____

_____

_____
_____
Garnishee

I, _____ , being first duly sworn upon my oath, state (or affirm) that the answers to the foregoing interrogatories by me subscribed are true.

_____
Garnishee

Subscribed and sworn to before me this _____ day of _____ ,
A.D., 19__ .

_____
Notary Public

SOURCE: E. King, *Colorado Practice* § 2362 (1970).

ment in the clerk's office of the county where the real property is located. After the passage of a designated period of time, the land can be sold by a government official to help satisfy the judgment debt. If the land is located in another state, an authenticated ("exemplified") copy of the judgment is filed in the court of the other state, which will then issue its own writ of execution to enforce the judgment against the land. In this second court, the judgment debtor is not allowed to relitigate the tort case that initially led to the judgment in the first state. The second state is required under the United States Constitution to give full faith and credit to the judgments of the first state. The only objections that judgment debtors can raise in the second state are that the first state did not have jurisdiction to render the initial judgment or that they have in fact already satisfied the judgment.

▪ ASSIGNMENT 8.3 ▪

Check the rules of court and your state code to answer the following questions. (See General Instructions for the State Code Assignment in Chapter 2.)

a. Describe the specific methods, including garnishment, that are available in your state to a judgment creditor to enforce a judgment award against the personal property of the judgment debtor. List the steps that are required for each method.

b. How can the judgment be enforced against a judgment debtor's land located in your state? What happens if the land is located in another state?

c. Can a judgment debtor be fined, jailed, or held in contempt of court for failure to pay the judgment creditor?

SUMMARY

After wining in court, the judgment creditor next hopes that the judgment debtor is not judgment proof. A pre-trial attachment may be needed to prevent the judgment debtor from removing assets. Locating the assets can sometimes be difficult. The judgment debtor may have personal property, real property, solely owned property, property in which someone else also has an interest, tangible property, intangible property, property in the possession of another, property in the forum state, property in a foreign state, property that will be received in the future, exempt property, nonexempt property, etc. Among the informal methods of uncovering the assets of the judgment debtor are the notes already in the file, clues from his or her lifestyle, and data in public records. The formal methods might include post-trial deposition, production of documents, written interrogatories, and supplementary proceedings. Once assets are identified, they can be reached by a writ of execution, writ of garnishment, obtaining a lien against real property, etc.

Key Terms

judgment creditor	tenancy in common	assignment
judgment debtor	lien	exempt
judgment proof	mortgage	execution
pre-trial attachment	tangible property	writ of execution
writ of attachment	intangible property	levy
stay	bailment	forced sale
personal property	bailee	judicial sale
real property	bailor	garnishment
joint tenancy	forum state	writ of garnishment
right of survivorship	foreign state	garnishee
tenancy by the entirety		

CHAPTER 9

Negligence: A Summary

CHAPTER OUTLINE

- INTRODUCTION
- NEGLIGENCE AND BREACH OF DUTY
- NEGLIGENCE AND INSURANCE
- SHORTHAND DEFINITION
- NEGLIGENCE CHECKLIST

▪ INTRODUCTION

Negligence is one of the three major categories of torts (the other two being the intentional torts and the various kinds of strict liability). Negligence has been called a "catch-all" tort in that it encompasses a wide variety of unreasonable actions and inactions that cause injury. This chapter is an overview of negligence. Elsewhere, more specific negligence topics will be treated:

Figure 9.1   Coverage of Negligence Topics

Topic	Where Covered in This Book
Foreseeability	p. 203
Duty	p. 212
Breach of Duty	p. 230
Proximate Cause	p. 282
Damages	p. 302
Employer Liability	p. 259
Medical Malpractice	p. 266
Legal Malpractice	p. 273
Owners and Occupiers of Land	p. 495
Manufacturers and Retailers (products liability)	p. 345
Wrongful Death	p. 336
Negligent Infliction of Emotional Distress	p. 396
Defenses	p. 317

▪ NEGLIGENCE AND BREACH OF DUTY

The word "negligence" is used in two different senses. It can mean the entire tort or only one of its elements. In this book, **negligence** means the entire tort that exists when all four elements are present: duty, breach of duty, proximate cause, and damages. You will also sometimes see the word negligence used in the narrower sense of **unreasonableness,** which is another way of phrasing the breach-of-duty element. Hence the statement, "he acted negligently" either means that one of the elements **(breach of duty)** has been established, or that the tort has been committed. In this book, we mean the latter.

▪ NEGLIGENCE AND INSURANCE

It is commonly assumed by the public that if a driver hits a pedestrian on the street, the driver is responsible and must pay for the injuries suffered by the pedestrian. This is not necessarily so. We must be careful to distinguish **insurance** law from negligence law. The injured party may be automatically compensated if the terms of an insurance policy so provide. For many insurance policies, all that is needed is a covered injury, a covered person, and causation. Much more is needed to trigger the law of negligence. You are not considered negligent simply because you cause an injury. The hallmark of negligence is **fault**—sometimes referred to as **culpability,** or wrongfulness. By "fault" or "wrong," we do not necessarily mean moral blameworthiness. It is not necessary to show that the defendant caused an injury while violating a specific law such as the speed limit. The fault or wrong involved may be simple carelessness or momentary unreasonableness. But a lapse of some kind is required. We are *not* liable for every injury that we cause. We are liable under the law of negligence for those injuries we wrongfully cause in the sense that our conduct fell below a minimum standard of conduct when we caused the injury. One of our main objectives in the following chapters is to explore what this standard is. An important first step in achieving this objective is to avoid the trap of equating negligence with causation or with insurance.

▪ SHORTHAND DEFINITION

A shorthand definition of the tort of negligence is *injury caused by unreasonable conduct*. In the vast majority of negligence cases that are litigated, the sole questions before the court are:

· Was the defendant's conduct unreasonable?
· Did this unreasonableness cause the plaintiff's injury?

In the following pages, we will examine these questions along with a large number of others. As we do so, it is important that you not lose sight of the general definition of negligence as *injury caused by unreasonable conduct*. This definition will suffice for most negligence cases. While we must look at a maze of special rules in the law of negligence, there is a danger of thinking that the maze is the norm. It isn't.

▪ NEGLIGENCE CHECKLIST

Throughout the chapters of this book you will find checklists on the major torts. The checklists are designed to give you an analytical and research overview of the torts. A more comprehensive treatment of each tort is presented immediately after the checklist for that tort. The one exception to this is the tort of negligence. Because of the predominance of this tort, the explanation of the components of the negligence checklist spans the nine chapters that follow this checklist. While later chapters also cover aspects of negligence, these nine are the main negligence chapters.

Negligence Checklist:
Definitions, Relationships, and Research References

Category
Negligence is a category unto itself. It covers harm that is neither intentional nor the basis of strict liability.

Interest Protected by This Tort
The right to protect your person or property from harm caused by unreasonable conduct.

Elements of This Tort
1. Duty
2. Breach of duty
3. Proximate cause
4. Damages

Major Definitions of Words/Phrases in the Elements
Duty: The obligation to use reasonable care to avoid risks of injuring the person or property of others.

Breach of duty: Unreasonable conduct; the foreseeability of an accident causing serious injury outweighed the burden or inconvenience on the defendant to take precautions against the injury, and the defendant failed to take those precautions.

Proximate cause: The defendant is the cause in fact of the plaintiff's injury, the injury was the foreseeable consequence of the original risk, and there is no policy reason why the defendant should not be liable for what he or she caused in fact.

Damages: Actual harm or loss.

Major Defenses and Counter-Argument Possibilities That Need to Be Explored
1. The defendant owed the plaintiff no duty.
2. No injury was foreseeable.
3. No serious injury was foreseeable.
4. The burden or inconvenience on the defendant to avoid the injury was very substantial in view of the minimal risk of injury.
5. The activity of the defendant had great social importance or utility, which justified taking serious risks of injury.

6. The defendant was not the cause in fact of the plaintiff's injury. "But for" what the defendant did or failed to do, the injury would have occurred anyway. The defendant was not a substantial factor in producing the injury.
7. The injury was not within the forseeable risk originally created by the defendant.
8. The injury was produced by an intervening cause that was highly extraordinary.
9. The plaintiff suffered no actual harm or loss due to the unreasonable conduct of the defendant.
10. Contributory negligence by the plaintiff.
11. Assumption of risk by the plaintiff.
12. The plaintiff failed to mitigate damages.
13. Sovereign immunity.
14. Public official immunity.
15. Charitable immunity.
16. Intra-family immunity.
17. Satisfaction.
18. Release.

Damages

The damages must be actual. Nominal damages cannot be recovered in a negligence action. General damages and special damages can be recovered. Punitive damages are not available for ordinary negligence. Recklessness can be the basis of punitive damages.

Relationship to Criminal Law

There are some crimes based on negligence, e.g., negligent homicide. More than ordinary negligence, however, is usually required. Negligence in criminal law means recklessness.

Relationship to Other Torts

If you are not able to prove one of the intentional torts, explore the possibility of negligence. For example, if you cannot establish the tort of battery because you cannot prove that the defendant had the intent to cause a harmful or offensive contact, you may be able to establish the tort of negligence if you can prove that the harmful or offensive contact was caused by the defendant's unreasonable conduct. The same may be true of other intentional torts, such as conversion and false imprisonment. Whenever you are having difficulty establishing an intentional tort, determine whether the defendant created an unreasonable risk of the same injury occurring. If so, negligence may be an alternative cause of action.

Federal Law

Under the Federal Tort Claims Act, the United States government will be liable for negligence committed by a federal employee within the scope of employment as long as the employee's conduct did not involve discretion at the planning level. Under the Consumer Product Safety Act, damages can be recovered for certain violations of the rules of the Consumer Product Safety Commission concerning dangerous products on the market. Negligence does not have to be proved.

Employer-Employee (Agency) Law

Employers are liable for the negligent acts of their employees committed within the scope of employment. In addition to this vicarious liability, employers are independently liable for negligence in carelessly hiring incompetent employees (who pose a risk of injuring others) or for carelessly supervising employees if the risk of injury was foreseeable or should have been foreseeable.

Research References for This Tort

• Digests

In the digests of West, look for case summaries on negligence under key topics such as:

Negligence	Automobiles
Damages	Landlord and Tenant
Products Liability	Health and Environment
Master and Servant	Innkeepers
Physicians and Surgeons	Highways
Death	Nuisance
Animals	Contribution
Drugs and Narcotics	Carriers
Explosives	Telecommunications
Torts	

• *Corpus Juris Secundum*

In this legal encyclopedia, see the discussions on negligence under topic headings such as:

Negligence	Landlord and Tenant
Damages	Health and Environment
Products Liability	Inns, Hotels and Eating Places
Master and Servant	Highways
Physicians and Surgeons	Nuisance
Death	Contribution
Animals	Carriers
Drugs and Narcotics	Telegraphs, Telephones, Radio and
Explosives	Television
Motor Vehicles	

• *American Jurisprudence 2d*

In this legal encyclopedia, see the discussions on negligence under topic headings such as:

Negligence	Drugs, Narcotics and Poisons
Products Liability	Master and Servant
Premises Liability	Automobiles and Highway Traffic
Hospitals and Asylums	Occupations, Trades and Professions
Damages	Hotels, Motels and Restaurants
Contribution	Landlord and Tenant
Amusements and Exhibitions	Highways, Streets and Bridges
Animals	Physicians and Surgeons
Carriers	Health
Death	

Legal Periodical Literature

There are three index systems to use to locate legal periodical literature on negligence:

Index to Legal Periodicals (ILP)	*Current Law Index* (CLI)	*Legal Resource Index* (LRI)
See literature in ILP under subject headings such as:	See literature in CLI under subject headings such as:	See literature in LRI under subject headings such as:
Negligence	Negligence	Negligence
Accidents	Automobiles	Automobiles
Act of God	Bailments	Bailments
Automobile Insurance	Contribution	Contribution
Contributory Negligence	Damages	Damages
Damages	Death by Wrongful Act	Death by Wrongful Act
Highways and Streets	Exemplary Damages	Exemplary Damages
Inns and Innkeepers	Drugs	Drugs
Joint Tortfeasors	Employers' Liability	Employers' Liability
Landlord and Tenant	Food	Food
Last Clear Chance	Hospitals	Hospitals
Master and Servant	Informed Consent	Informed Consent
Motor Vehicles	Joint Tortfeasors	Joint Tortfeasors
Nuisance	Landlord and Tenant	Landlord and Tenant
Products Liability	Liability for Condition and Use of Land	Liability for Condition and Use of Land
Personal Injuries	Malpractice	Malpractice
Proximate Cause	Products Liability	Products Liability
Physicians and Surgeons	Respondeat Superior	Respondeat Superior
Res Ipsa Loquitur	Personal Injuries	Personal Injuries
Traffic Accidents	Physicians	Physicians
Vicarious Liability	Tort Liability	Tort Liability
Wrongful Death		

Example of a legal periodical article you will find on negligence by using ILP, CLI, or LRI:

> *Emergency Room Negligence,* 16 Trial 50 (May, 1980).

• ALR, ALR2d, ALR3d, ALR4th, ALR5th, ALR Fed.

Use the *Index to Annotations* to locate annotations on negligence. In this index, check subject headings such as:

Negligence	Landlord and Tenant
Aggravated Negligence	Products Liability
Attractive Nuisance	Rescue Doctrine
Comparative Negligence	Malpractice
Concurrent Negligence	Hospitals
Contributory Negligence or Assumption of Risk	Master and Servant
Corporate Officers, Directors and Agents	Res Ipsa Loquitur
	Mitigation or Aggravation of Damages
Governmental Immunity or Privilege	Federal Tort Claims Act
Gross Negligence	Health and Accident Insurance
Imputed Negligence and Liability	Policies and Provisions

Example of an annotation on negligence you can locate through the *Index to Annotations*:

> *Modern Development of Comparative Negligence Doctrine Having Applicability to Negligence Actions Generally,* 78 ALR3d 339.

• Words and Phrases

In this multi-volume legal dictionary, look up every word or phrase connected with negligence in order to find definitions from court opinions.

SUMMARY

Negligence is one of the three major categories of torts. It covers harm caused by unreasonableness as opposed to harm that is intentional or the basis of strict liability. The broad meaning of negligence is the tort that exists when all four of its elements have been established. More narrowly, it refers to the second element of the tort: breach of duty. Under the law of negligence, we are liable for the harm that we wrongfully cause. Insurance, on the other hand, often provides compensation for every covered injury that we cause, whether it was wrongful or not. A shorthand definition of negligence is injury caused by unreasonable conduct.

Key Terms

negligence	insurance	duty
unreasonableness	fault	proximate cause
breach of duty	culpability	damages

CHAPTER 10

Foreseeability in Tort Law

CHAPTER OUTLINE

- INTRODUCTION
- DEFINING FORESEEABILITY
- FORESEEABILITY SPECTRUM
- OBJECTIVE STANDARD
- PHRASING THE FORESEEABILITY
  QUESTION

- FORESEEABILITY DETERMINATION
  "FORMULA"
- REVIEW OF STEPS TO DETERMINE
  FORESEEABILITY

■ INTRODUCTION

Foreseeability is a critical concept in tort law. In three of the elements of negligence, for example, foreseeability often plays a major role:

- duty
- breach of duty
- proximate cause

In later chapters we will see that foreseeability is relevant to other torts as well.

Before beginning our detailed discussion of the elements of negligence, we will spend some time analyzing foreseeability because this concept is so critical. We will refer to this analysis of foreseeability throughout our discussion of negligence, and indeed, throughout the remainder of the book.

The central question of this chapter is, How do we determine foreseeability? This question is explored through the following topics:

- the meaning of foreseeability
- the spectrum of foreseeability
- foreseeability as an objective standard

g vs. generalizing the foreseeability question
ility determination "formula"

quences of foreseeability will be considered in later chapters. For
rn is the nature of foreseeability itself.

RESEEABILITY

nguage, **foresee** means "to see or know beforehand." **Foresee-** __, the adjective, simply describes "that which one can see or know before-hand." From a legal perspective, however, the emphasis is on the *extent* to which something can be known beforehand. It is important to understand that the question, "Is it foreseeable?", is less significant than the question, "How foreseeable is it?" Or, to combine the two questions: "How foreseeable is it, if at all?" Foreseeability is primarily a question of the *extent* to which something is predictable or "occur-able."

It is also important to understand that foreseeability is determined *before the fact.* If you want to know, for example, whether a fire was foreseeable, you mentally turn the clock back to the period of time *before* the fire occurred and ask: how likely was it, if at all, that a fire would occur? This determination is *not* made on the basis of what happens after the fact. An event or result is not foreseeable simply because it happened!

■ FORESEEABILITY SPECTRUM

To assess the foreseeability of an event or result, you must pinpoint it on a scale or **spectrum of foreseeability.** Figure 10.1 presents this spectrum. The threshold question is whether the event or result was foreseeable in any shape, fashion, or form. If the answer is no, the inquiry is ended. If, however, the answer

Figure 10.1   Foreseeability Spectrum: How Foreseeable, If at All?

(Suppose, for example, you are trying to determine how foreseeable it was that a child would dart in front of a car and be hit.)

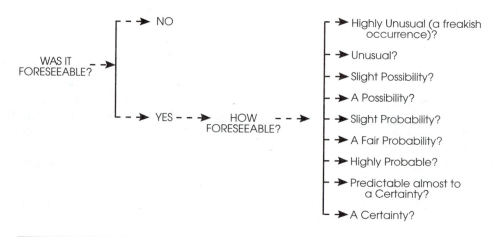

is yes, then the next and most important inquiry is *how* foreseeable the event or result was. Where on the spectrum did it fall before it happened?

The categories on the spectrum are not mutually exclusive. There is no scientific or measurable distinction among all the items on the spectrum. The categories are rough approximations on the higher-to-lower ranges of "occurability."

Note the last item on the spectrum: foreseeability to a certainty. When something is that foreseeable, the law says that you *intended* the event or result to occur. **Intent** has two meanings in the law: the desire to have something happen or the **knowledge with substantial certainty** that it will happen from what you do or fail to do. If you pull the trigger of a gun aimed at a crowd a few feet in front of where you are standing, you cannot claim that you did not intend to shoot the person who was hit. You may have hoped and prayed that no one would be hit, but a court will probably find that you had substantially certain knowledge that someone would be hit. In the eyes of the law, you intended this result. You have committed a battery, assuming the court also finds that you were sane enough at the time to have coherent knowledge of anything.

▪ OBJECTIVE STANDARD

When foreseeability is an issue in the law, it is usually measured by an **objective standard.** The question is not simply the extent to which the event or result was actually foreseeable to this particular defendant, but also to what extent the event or result should have been foreseeable to this defendant. For example, should someone in the defendant's position have known that the dog would attack the mail carrier? If a purely **subjective standard** were used, there would be an advantage to remaining ignorant about possible danger. When the danger occurred, you would simply say, "I didn't know it would happen." The question, however, is not whether you knew, but whether you should have known. This is an objective standard.

▪ PHRASING THE FORESEEABILITY QUESTION

When someone asks the question, "Was it foreseeable?" or "How foreseeable was it?" there is a need to break down what is meant by "it." A great deal depends on whether the focus of the question is *particular* or *general*. Compare the following two questions:

1. Was any harm foreseeable when Mrs. X allowed Tommy to take her Christmas tree that had just been thrown in the garbage two weeks after Christmas?
2. When Mrs. X allowed ten-year-old Tommy to take the Christmas tree that had just been thrown into the garbage two weeks after Christmas, how foreseeable was it:
   a. that an older child would steal the tree from Tommy?
   b. that the older child would organize a tree-collection project so that the trees could be burned together in a big bonfire at the local beach?
   c. that children in groups of ten or more would drag the trees across busy streets?
   d. that traffic would be interrupted?
   e. that the plaintiff's car would swerve into a lamp post in an effort to avoid hitting one of the kids crossing the street with the trees?

The first statement above is a very generalized foreseeability question: Is *any* harm foreseeable? The second statement, on the other hand, is particularized. Everything is segmented into events that raise isolated foreseeability questions or subquestions. Again our concern: When do you **generalize** the foreseeability question? When do you **particularize** the foreseeability question? The answer is governed, in part, by the following advocacy principles:

Advocacy Principles: Arguments on Foreseeability

· The party who wants to reach a conclusion that something was *foreseeable* will tend to phrase the foreseeability question in the most broad, *generalized* form possible.
· The party who wants to reach a conclusion that something was *unforeseeable* will tend to phrase the foreseeability question in the most narrow, *particularized* form possible.

A particularized statement of the foreseeability question itemizes the major chain of events that led up to the accident or injury. The more events listed, the more self-evident the answer becomes: a particularized question is stacked in favor of *un*foreseeability. After reading all the events in the question, we are often inclined to say that all of it could not possibly have been foreseen. Care must be used, however, not to overparticularize the question to the point of absurdity.

Later, we will learn what the courts have said on how foreseeable something must be in given areas of tort law such as proximate cause in negligence. Knowing the law, however, will not eliminate the need for advocacy in the statement of the foreseeability question. The more an advocate wants to conclude that something was very foreseeable on the foreseeability spectrum, the more generalized the advocate will try to make the foreseeability question. The more an advocate wants to conclude that there was low foreseeability, the more particularized the advocate will try to make the foreseeability question.

· ASSIGNMENT 10.1 ·

Read the following fact situation. Focus on the foreseeability of Pete's seizure. Phrase a broad, generalized statement of the foreseeability question for Pete. Then phrase a narrow, particularized statement of the foreseeability question for Dan. Assume that Dan wants to reach a conclusion that the seizure was very unforeseeable, and that Pete wants to reach a conclusion that an injury was foreseeable.

> *Dan has a weekend job operating a ferris wheel at the state fair. Pete buys a ticket and gets on. Soon after the ride begins, Dan notices that Pete is throwing objects onto the people below. Dan decides to stop the wheel in order to remove Pete. When Dan grabs the brake lever, he immediately notices it is stuck. He has an emergency brake, but is very reluctant to use it because it might cause the entire wheel to come to a jolting halt. He fears that some of the riders could be thrown out. The more he thinks about it, the more frantic he gets. This is only his first week on the job. While he stands there thinking about what to do, some of the people on the ground, who have been hit by the objects Pete threw on them, begin shouting at Dan to do something. Dan becomes more and more dizzy as he tries to think of what to do. Someone in the crowd yells out at Dan to turn the electricity off as a way to stop the wheel. Dan thinks*

it is a good idea, but by this time, he is so confused that he does not know what to do. Suddenly, he dashes away from the crowd so that he can try to collect his thoughts. Luckily, he spots his boss at the other end of the fair. He runs toward her for help. When he reaches her, he is so upset and frantic that it takes his boss close to a minute to figure out what he is talking about. When the boss finally does understand, she goes to the still-turning ferris wheel and stops it safety by skillfully using the emergency brake. When Pete gets off this twenty-eight-minute ride, he suffers a seizure. Later, he sues Dan.

■ FORESEEABILITY DETERMINATION ''FORMULA''

It is probably accurate to say that you will rarely have enough facts to help you make a determination of how foreseeable something was or was not. Hence, determining foreseeability often requires a probing for further facts. Questions need to be asked about the facts that you do not have, and sometimes more important, about the facts that you do have. For this reason, effective interviewing and investigation are often critical to reaching intelligent conclusions about foreseeability.

The foreseeability ''formula'' in Figure 10.2 is designed to provide a framework for asking the right questions about foreseeability. The starting point in the use of the ''formula'' is to identify the subject matter of the foreseeability question. What is the event or result whose foreseeability or unforeseeability you want to assess? As pointed out earlier, the subject matter of the foreseeability inquiry can be stated in *generalized* terms (e.g., was any harm or injury of any kind foreseeable), or in very *particularized* terms (e.g., was it foreseeable that customers in a department store would run toward an exit because of a light failure during the day, push each other in an effort to get out, and then fail to. . . .). After you have identified the question, you then apply the ''formula.''

There are eight factors to be considered: area, activity, people, preparation, human nature, history, sensory data, and common sense. Examine the factors separately, even though there will be considerable overlap among them. As you focus on each factor, ask your factual questions that relate to foreseeability. Do not, however, expect definitive answers at this point. The ''formula'' is not a mathematical equation. It is simply an aid to give you some direction as you try to place an event or result on the foreseeability spectrum. Later, you will want to pursue the questions during client interviews and field investigation.

Figure 10.2 Foreseeability Determination ''Formula''

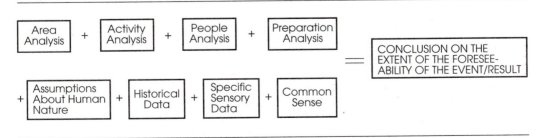

Area Analysis

The nature of the area can sometimes be very important. If, for example, a child is hit by a car, it is important to know whether the accident occurred in a residential area, near a school, at a playground, etc. From the nature of the area, how foreseeable is it that children will be around? If an accident occurs in a supermarket, it is equally important to assess the area. It is usually a crowded, closed area with many products stacked on shelves or on the floor. What is foreseeable given these conditions? A rotted tree branch falls and hits the plaintiff. Where did this occur? In the country? In a city? A suburb? A zoo? A park? How, if at all, would the area affect the foreseeability of what happened? An explosion occurs in a university lab. A lab is a place for experiments and the storage of chemicals. Danger is usually more foreseeable in a lab than in other areas.

Activity Analysis

Area and activity are intimately related. What specific activities were going on at the time of the accident or event whose foreseeability we are assessing? Swimming? Driving? Walking? Running? Eating? Dynamiting? Selling? What occurs during this activity? What is frequently foreseeable? Occasionally foreseeable? Rarely foreseeable? Examine the nature of the activity or activities themselves. What does human experience tell you (or what should it tell you) about what might be anticipated from this activity?

People Analysis

What kind of people were involved in the activities that led to the event or result whose foreseeability is being examined? How would you characterize them, and does this characterization tell you something about what should have been foreseeable by them or by others interacting with them? Were they children? Adults? Trespassers? Doctors? Mechanics or others with special knowledge and skills? What is normally expected from such people? What precautions do they usually take or fail to take? We have certain expectations from certain classes or kinds of people. What are the expectations in this case? Do these expectations help us determine what should have been foreseeable?

Preparation Analysis

What do people usually do before they engage in the activity you listed? Is any long-term preparation needed, e.g., testing? Short-term preparation, e.g., checking equipment, looking out for obstacles? No preparation? The data received from any preparation will usually be very relevant to foreseeability.

Assumptions About Human Nature

This factor is very similar to the people analysis, except that it is more general. What kind of behavior is usually expected of anyone engaged in the kind of activity in question? In driving a car, for example, can you assume that other drivers will *not* always obey all traffic laws? When people are in danger, can you assume that they will act in self-defense? Can you assume that people will gravitate toward pleasurable, attractive things or events? Can you assume that many people will not read five pages of fine-print instructions? Such assumptions, when they can be made, are often relevant to what might be anticipated from people.

This is not to say that any of these assumptions are to be condoned or that they justify conduct in any way. The law that applies to conduct is a separate matter that will be considered in later chapters. Here we are limiting ourselves to a consideration of the extent of foreseeability, independent of any legal consequences.

Historical Data

The more something has occurred in the past, the more foreseeable is its recurrence. Have incidents of a similar nature occurred in the past? If so, under what circumstances? How often? How well known were they? A customer sues a grocery store owner for injuries received when opening a can of tuna. We want to know if this injury was foreseeable to the owner of the store. Has the owner had similar complaints about this tuna brand in the past? Has the owner heard of problems other stores have had? Is this the first time the owner became aware of such a problem? Historical data can be quite relevant to foreseeability.

Specific Sensory Data

What did the eyes, ears, nose, fingers, feet, etc. tell the parties just before the incident? Did any of this sensory data provide signs of what might happen? Are certain things foreseeable in certain kinds of weather? (Was this kind of weather foreseeable?) Visibility is often relevant to foreseeability. What factors affected visibility, e.g., weather, time of day, presence of obstructions, etc.? Were there distractions that prevented people from being aware of a danger? If so, were these distractions foreseeable?

Common Sense

Common sense is a catch-all factor. All of the other factors should have led you to questions and observations grounded in common sense. Here we simply reinforce the central role of this factor and ask ourselves to what extent something was or was not foreseeable based on common sense.

Example: Jones builds a swimming pool in his backyard. The use of the pool is restricted to Jones family members and guests who are present when an adult is there to supervise. One hot, summer night, a neighbor's child opens an unlocked door of a fence that surrounds the Jones yard and goes into the pool. (There is no separate fence around the pool.) The child knows he is not supposed to be there without an adult. No one else is at the pool. The child drowns.

Foreseeability question (general): Was it foreseeable that someone would be injured in the pool?

Foreseeability question (particular): Was it foreseeable that a neighbor's child would violate a rule of the owner of the pool not to use it unless an adult was present, open a closed fence door to get to the pool, and drown in it?

From the facts, it appears that Jones built his pool in a residential area. If so, it certainly was foreseeable that children would be in the area. Jones should have anticipated that children would be drawn to the pool. The neighbor's child used the pool while no one was around. It would help to know whether people use each other's pools in this way in the neighborhood. If it is common, then it is more foreseeable to Jones that a child would use his pool without permission or supervision in spite of his rule to the contrary. Why did he impose this rule? Because of prior pool trespassing in the neighborhood? Swimming is generally considered a dangerous activity, particularly for children. It is foreseeable, however, that children will not be able to fully protect themselves in water, hence the need to take additional precautions when children could be swimming.

There was no separate fence around Jones's pool; there was simply an unlocked door to a fence around the yard. Was it foreseeable to Jones that this might be an inadequate precaution? Again, this may depend on the frequency with which children have made unauthorized use of pools in the area and the extent to which Jones knew about this or should have known about it. Are other pools in the area left unlocked and unguarded at night? Should Jones have checked on this? It is true that Jones had a rule that adults must be present. But is this rule enough? Shouldn't Jones have assumed that a child would *not* obey such a rule? Has any child ever violated this rule in the past? Have there ever been children using the Jones pool without adults present? If so, then Jones was on notice that it could happen again and that additional precautions would be needed. What steps did Jones take, if any, to make sure that neighborhood children knew about his rule?

We also need to know whether there have been any recent swimming pool accidents in the area. The drowning took place at night. (We do not know whether any of the Jones family members were at home at the time.) Common sense tells us that a child will be tempted to use an easily accessible swimming pool in the summer and that drowning is a fair probability when there is no supervision.

▪ REVIEW OF STEPS TO DETERMINE FORESEEABILITY

1. Turn the clock back to the time before the event/result in question occurred—foreseeability is determined *before* the fact.
2. Decide how broadly (generalized) or narrowly (particularized) you want to phrase the foreseeability question.
3. Apply those factors in the foreseeability determination ''formula'' that are applicable to the situation.
4. From the range of ''highly unusual'' to ''a certainty,'' draw your conclusion of where the event/result falls on the foreseeability spectrum.
5. Give a counteranalysis. If both sides are not going to agree on the extent to which the event/result was foreseeable, state the other side.

▪ ASSIGNMENT 10.2 ▪

Assess the foreseeability of the events listed in the following situations. Go through the five steps just listed. Include a large number of factual questions you would raise and state how these factual questions might be relevant to the foreseeability of the result or event in question.

a. The ABC Company manufactures kitchen stoves. Smith buys one of the stoves. There is no heat in Smith's kitchen. Hence, Smith often turns the stove on, opens the oven door, and rests his feet on the door while sitting on a chair in front of the stove. One day, the stove collapses forward onto Smith while he is warming his feet in this way. Smith is severely injured. Was this injury foreseeable to the ABC Company?

b. A hobo hitching a ride on a railroad train falls off and injures herself. Was this injury foreseeable to the railroad?

c. Examine the facts of Assignment 10.1. Was the injury foreseeable to Dan's boss?

SUMMARY

Foreseeability means the extent to which we can see or know something beforehand. It is determined on a before-the-fact basis. The spectrum of foreseeability ranges from "highly unusual" to "a virtual certainty." (If something falls into the latter category, in the eyes of the law it was intended.) We measure foreseeability by an objective standard by asking to what extent something should have been foreseeable. Advocates tend to generalize the foreseeability question when they want to argue that something was foreseeable; they particularize the question when they are hoping for a finding of unforeseeability. Assessing foreseeability requires an analysis of the area involved, the activity undertaken, the people involved, the preparation involved, assumptions about human nature, historical data, specific sensory data, and common sense.

Key Terms

foresee
foreseeable
spectrum of
    foreseeability

intent
knowledge with
    substantial certainty
objective standard

subjective standard
generalize
particularize

CHAPTER 11

Negligence: Element I: Duty

CHAPTER OUTLINE

- GENERAL RULE ON DUTY
- UNFORESEEABLE PLAINTIFF
- NONFEASANCE AND SPECIAL RELATIONSHIPS

- GRATUITOUS UNDERTAKING

■ GENERAL RULE ON DUTY

What is a **duty?** In its broadest sense:

> A duty is an obligation or a requirement to conform to a standard of conduct prescribed by law.

From this broad definition, we come to a series of very specific interrelated questions:

- Who owes this duty?
- To whom is it owed?
- When does the duty arise?
- What is the standard of conduct to which there must be conformity?—i.e., duty to do what?

All of these questions can be answered by the **general rule on duty,** which is outlined at the beginning of Figure 11.1. This general rule will be adequate to cover the vast majority of automobile collision cases, on-the-job mishaps, and similar occurrences. The chart will also outline those circumstances that call for limitations on or modifications of the general rule on duty.

You are driving down the road late at night. It is raining and the road is slippery. It is foreseeable that someone may be injured when driving under such conditions. Therefore, you owe a duty of reasonable care to take precautions to prevent such an injury—to slow down, turn on the headlights, watch extra care-

Figure 11.1 Duty in the Law of Negligence

General Rule on Duty:

> Whenever one's acts and omissions create a foreseeable risk of injury or damage to someone else's person or property, a duty of reasonable care arises to take precautions to prevent that injury or damage.

Exceptions and Special Circumstances:

1. The unforeseeable plaintiff, p. 213
   a. Zone-of-danger test of duty, p. 215
   b. World-at-large test of duty, p. 215
2. Nonfeasance and the special relationship, p. 216
3. Gratuitous undertaking, p. 223

---

fully for pedestrians and other cars, keep a safe distance between your car and the car in front of you, etc. The more foreseeable the injury, the greater is the need for precautions such as these.

Under the general rule, the duty is to use **reasonable care,** which will be discussed at length in the next chapter when we examine **breach of duty,** or unreasonableness. In the vast majority of cases, this duty is triggered by the **foreseeability** of injury or damage. We have already looked at foreseeability in tort law in Chapter 10, and we will examine it again when we discuss breach of duty and proximate cause. (A foreseeability analysis is needed to determine the applicability of three elements: duty, breach of duty, and proximate cause. In most cases, the foreseeability analysis is the same in all three elements. This is why foreseeability was treated separately in Chapter 10, with particular emphasis on the factors that go into the determination of foreseeability.)

For the remainder of this chapter, we will focus on those exceptions and special circumstances that have posed problems with the general rule on duty stated in Figure 11.1.

▪ UNFORESEEABLE PLAINTIFF

Consider the sequence of events in Figure 11.2, based on the famous *Palsgraf* case.[1] Plaintiff #1 in Figure 11.2 is a **foreseeable plaintiff** who will have no trouble suing the railroad for the negligence of its employee. A duty is clearly owed to the passenger. Since the employee carelessly pushed the passenger, some harm was foreseeable to the passenger's property or to the person of the passenger. What about the bystander, plaintiff #2? At the time the employee pushed the passenger onto the train, no one could foresee danger to the bystander from the falling package. Plaintiff #2 is an **unforeseeable plaintiff.** An essential question in plaintiff #2's negligence suit against the railroad is whether a *duty* was owed to this plaintiff. If not, then the first element of negligence cannot be established and hence the entire negligence cause of action will fall. How then

---

[1]The two tests covering plaintiff #2 in Figure 11.2 are based on two separate opinions written by Justice Cardozo and Justice Andrews in the case of *Palsgraf v. Long Island R.R.,* 248 N.Y. 339, 162 N.E. 99, 59 ALR 1253 (1928). *Palsgraf* is one of the most controversial and well-known cases in legal jurisprudence. Every law student spends a good deal of time in law school studying it.

Figure 11.2   The Unforeseeable Plaintiff

PLAINTIFF #1
THE FORESEEABLE PLAINTIFF
(The Passenger)

A passenger carrying a wrapped package tries to enter a crowded train. A railroad employee helps the passenger onto the train with a push. Unfortunately, the employee is careless in the push, resulting in the package falling out of the passenger's hands to the ground. The package is damaged.

PLAINTIFF #2
THE UNFORESEEABLE PLAINTIFF
(The Bystander)

To the surprise of everyone, the package explodes when it hits the ground. It contained fireworks which ignite upon impact. The concussion from the explosion causes a scale on the platform to fall over and injure a bystander.

Figure 11.3   Negligence: When Is a Duty Owed?

Zone-of-Danger Test (the Cardozo test)
A duty is owed a specific person (plaintiff) in the **zone of danger,** as determined by the test of foreseeability.

World-at-Large Test (the Andrews test)
A duty is owed to anyone in the **world at large** (any plaintiff) IF:
1. the plaintiff (who sues) suffers injury as a result of
2. unreasonable conduct of the defendant toward anyone, whether or not the plaintiff who sues was in the zone of danger. This plaintiff does not have to have been in the zone of danger as long as *someone* (in the world at large) was in this zone because of the action or inaction of the defendant.

do we determine whether a duty is owed to a person in plaintiff #2's position? Two major tests have been proposed: the **Cardozo test,** or zone-of-danger test, and the **Andrews test,** or world-at-large test. (See Figure 11.3.) States differ on which of these two tests is followed.

A number of points should be made about these two tests:

- The two tests focus only on the element of duty. All of the other elements of negligence must also be analyzed to determine whether the cause of action has been established.
- The Andrews test is broader than the Cardozo test. More plaintiffs can establish duty under the Andrews test because they do not have to be in the foreseeable zone of danger in order to be owed a duty. They only have to be injured as a result of the defendant's unreasonable conduct that created, and placed *someone* in, the zone of danger.
- A choice between the two tests must be made when the fact situation of the client (or of your teacher's hypothetical) involves a chain of events and an unanticipated person—an unforeseeable plaintiff. The two tests give two different standards on whether such a person is owed a duty. If, however, the facts do not involve a chain of events, then the great likelihood is that both tests would produce the *same* result on whether a duty is owed (i.e., it would make no difference in such cases which test is used).

Let us now apply the two different tests to the fact situation involving the passenger whose package was damaged and the bystander on whom the scale fell. What would happen in a state that has adopted the zone-of-danger (Cardozo) test? How does this compare with the outcome in a state that has adopted the world-at-large (Andrews) test?

1. **Zone-of-danger state:**
   Would a duty be owed to the passenger? YES. When the employee carelessly pushed the passenger, it was foreseeable that some injury or damage would result to this passenger. Hence, the passenger was in the zone of danger.

   Would a duty be owed to the bystander? NO. Pushing the passenger created no foreseeable risk to a bystander, since there was no indication to the employee that there were fireworks or any other dangerous object in the passenger's package. The bystander was outside the zone of danger.

2. **World-at-large state:**

Would a duty be owed to the passenger? YES. The two-part test has been met: the passenger suffered injury or damage (to the package) as a result of unreasonable conduct (the careless push) directed at someone (here, the passenger). While it is not necessary for the passenger to have been in the zone of danger under this test, in fact, the passenger was within this zone.

Would a duty be owed to the bystander? YES. The two-part test has been met: the bystander suffered an injury (the scale fell on the bystander) as a result of unreasonable conduct (the careless push) directed at someone (here, the passenger). Under this test, it is not necessary that the bystander be in the zone of danger as long as someone was in this zone as a result of the defendant's unreasonable conduct. The passenger is the "someone" who was in the zone of danger.

▪ ASSIGNMENT 11.1 ▪

Helen and Grace are on a subway train on the way home from an office where they work together. Both are standing near one of the doors of the crowded train. Suddenly, the door opens while the train is moving and Helen falls out. Moments later, the train stops when the driver realizes what has happened. (Assume that the reason the door opened was negligent maintenance by the subway.) Grace watches in horror as Helen falls out the door. When the train stops, Grace immediately climbs down through the open door onto the tracks in order to try to help Helen. As Grace searches in the dark, she slips on a live rail and dies from electrocution. Luckily, Helen finds her way to safety with only minor injury. Helen and Grace's estate now bring separate negligence actions against the subway. Focus solely on the issue of duty:

a. In a zone-of-danger (Cardozo) state, did the subway owe a duty to Helen? Explain. To Grace? Explain.
b. In a world at large (Andrews) state, did the subway owe a duty to Helen? Explain. To Grace? Explain.

(See also general Instructions for the Legal Analysis Assignment in Chapter 3.)

▪ ASSIGNMENT 11.2 ▪

In this assignment, you are asked to try to find one case in which your state has confronted the issue of the unforeseeable plaintiff. Give the citation of this case and a brief summary of its facts. To locate such a case for your state, check the following digests: your state digest, or the regional digest covering your state (if one exists), or the *American Digest System*. One of the key topics and numbers you should check in these digests is Negligence ⬷ 2. See General Instructions for the State Court Opinion Assignment in Chapter 2. (If your state is New York, select a case other than *Palsgraf*, cited in footnote 1 on p. 213.) Does the case you have located adopt the zone-of-danger test of duty (Cardozo), or the world-at-large test (Andrews)? Explain.

▪ **NONFEASANCE AND SPECIAL RELATIONSHIPS**

Most negligence liability is based on **affirmative conduct** that is improper or unreasonable. This is called **misfeasance.** With limited exceptions, negligence liability cannot be based on a mere omission or failure to act, called **nonfea-**

Figure 11.4   Misfeasance and Nonfeasance

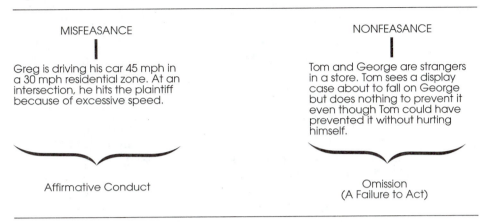

MISFEASANCE

Greg is driving his car 45 mph in a 30 mph residential zone. At an intersection, he hits the plaintiff because of excessive speed.

Affirmative Conduct

NONFEASANCE

Tom and George are strangers in a store. Tom sees a display case about to fall on George but does nothing to prevent it even though Tom could have prevented it without hurting himself.

Omission
(A Failure to Act)

sance.[2] Only if a **special relationship** existed between the plaintiff and defendant will nonfeasance by the defendant lead to negligence. Compare the two situations in Figure 11.4.

When Greg (in Figure 11.4) is sued by the plaintiff for negligence in the first situation, there will not be a problem establishing the existence of a duty. In such cases of *mis*feasance, there is almost never a duty problem. Affirmative conduct by Greg (his driving) created a risk of foreseeable injury to the plaintiff. It is very easy to establish the existence of a duty when affirmative conduct (alone or in combination with inaction) creates such a risk. The vast majority of negligence cases fall into the misfeasance category.

Now let us focus on the second hypothetical in Figure 11.4, involving Tom and George. Here we have *non*feasance. There was no affirmative conduct by Tom. Rather, there was an omission, a failure to act. In most states, there is no duty in such situations to exercise any kind of care unless a special relationship exists between the parties. These special relationships are outlined in Figure 11.6.

In most cases involving strangers such as Tom and George above, there is no such special relationship, and hence no duty to act with reasonable care. It is surprising to many to learn that *there is no duty to assist someone simply because it is possible for you to give assistance without harming yourself.* Nor does the mere foreseeability of injury give rise to a duty to give aid. According to the American Law Institute:

> The fact that the actor realizes or should realize that action on his part is necessary for another's aid or protection does not of itself impose upon him a duty to take such action.[3]

The classic example is the stranger who refuses to lift a finger to save the life of a drowning victim, even though the stranger would be under no jeopardy in making the effort. There is *no* requirement in our law to be a **Good Samaritan.** In fact, if someone voluntarily decides to be a Good Samaritan and renders assis-

---

[2]Do not confuse the following three words. *Nonfeasance* is the omission of an act, the failure to act. *Misfeasance* is improper or unreasonable action. **Malfeasance** is wrongful or illegal actions by a public official.
[3]*Restatement (Second) of Torts* § 314 (1965).

Figure 11.5   Duty in Nonfeasance Cases

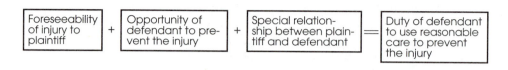

tance, even though there was no initial duty to do so, the Good Samaritan can be sued for negligence if he or she fails to use reasonable care in rendering this free assistance! (This rule and its exceptions will be discussed later in the section on Gratuitous Undertaking.)

Most accidents involve *both* affirmative conduct and omissions; for example, while driving on the highway (affirmative conduct), the defendant failed to slow down at the intersection and failed to use the horn to warn the inattentive plaintiff (omissions). This example would be considered a *mis*feasance case of negligence, even though there were components of *non*feasance in it. Generally, if there was *some* affirmative conduct that helped cause the injury, you will not need to worry about the existence or nonexistence of a special relationship, even though omissions were involved. The nonfeasance case usually arises when all the defendant "did" was to "decide" to do nothing to help the plaintiff. Here the special relationship will be critical. Without it, the plaintiff's negligence case falls because there is no duty to act.

In addition to the presence of a special relationship, the defendant's duty depends on the foreseeability of injury and the opportunity to do something about it, as diagrammed in Figure 11.5.

The duty is *not* to prevent the injury. The duty arising from the special relationship is simply to use *reasonable care* to avoid the injury. The duty does not guarantee anything. Here are some examples of what reasonable care entails:

- taking reasonable steps in advance to try to make the area safe
- taking reasonable steps to try to prevent third persons under the defendant's control from injuring the plaintiff
- taking reasonable steps immediately after the injury to try to prevent aggravation of the injury

What are the special relationships? They are outlined in Figure 11.6.

A good deal of controversy has recently centered around the problem of controlling the conduct of third parties who are not part of the special relationship itself.

> **Example:**   Tom is a patient of Dr. Smith, a therapist. During a session, Tom tells Dr. Smith that he is going to kill his girlfriend. The latter is not a patient of Dr. Smith. The next day, Tom carries out his threat and kills his girlfriend.

The girlfriend's estate now brings a negligence action against Dr. Smith. Again, we have a nonfeasance problem. We have omissions: Dr. Smith did not warn the girlfriend of Tom's threat, he did not tell the police of the threat, and he did not tell the girlfriend's family about the threat, etc. The questions is whether Dr. Smith owed a *duty* to the girlfriend. Dr. Smith engaged in no affirmative conduct toward the girlfriend that placed her in danger. Hence, we do not have misfeasance. There was no special relationship between Dr. Smith and the girlfriend. The traditional result, therefore, in such situations is that there is no duty and hence no liability for negligence. It should be noted, however, that not all states follow this traditional rule. Some states, and the Restatement,[4] will say that a duty of reasonable care *would* be owed by the doctor to the girlfriend in such a case.

_____

[4]*Restatement (Second) of Torts* § 315 (1965).

Figure 11.6 Special Relationships Creating a Duty to Use Reasonable Care in Nonfeasance Cases

Principle
There is no duty to use reasonable care (and hence no negligence) unless the plaintiff fits within one of the following categories of special relationships. If not, there is no duty to act, and hence omissions (nonfeasance) by the defendant cannot constitute negligence. This applies only to nonfeasance cases. If the defendant has engaged in affirmative conduct, there is usually a duty to use reasonable care whether or not a special relationship exists between plaintiff and defendant.

Special Relationships

1. Common Carrier/Passenger
   Example: A bus driver cannot ignore a passenger who becomes ill on the bus or who is in danger of being injured by another passenger. The bus driver must use reasonable care to help the passenger in trouble.

2. Innkeeper (hotel, motel, etc.)/Guest
   Example: A hotel employee must take steps to aid guests who become ill or who are injured (even if the illness or injury is caused totally by the guests themselves). The hotel employee must use reasonable care to help the guests.

3. Employer/Employee
   Example: When an employee is injured on the job, the employer must use reasonable care to aid the employee even if the injury was not due to any fault or action by the employer.

4. Land Owner or Possessor/Invitee
   Example: A department store employee cannot ignore a guest or customer who becomes ill in the store or who is in danger of being injured by another person in the store. The store employee must use reasonable care to help the customer in trouble even if the store itself did nothing to cause the illness or danger.

CASE

Soldano v. O'Daniels
141 Cal.App.3d 443, 190 Cal.Rptr. 310 (1983)
California Court of Appeal, Fifth District

Background: On August 9, 1977, Darrell Soldano was shot and killed at Happy Jack's Saloon. The defendant, O'Daniels, owns the

Circle Inn, an eating establishment across the street from Happy Jack's. A patron at Happy Jack's Saloon came into the Circle Inn and informed a Circle Inn bartender that a man had been threatened at Happy Jack's. He asked the bartender either to call the police or to allow him to use the Circle Inn phone to call the police. The bartender refused even though it would have been convenient to grant either request and would have cost the defendant nothing. The victim's son sued the defendant for negligence, alleging that the Circle Inn employee (the bartender) breached a legal duty owed to the decedent. At the trial, the court granted the defendant a summary judgment. The plaintiff has now appealed to the California Court of Appeals for the Fifth District.

Decision on Appeal: The trial court judgment is reversed. The defendant had a duty to call the police or to allow the phone to be used for this purpose.

Opinion of Court

Justice ANDREEN delivered the opinion of the court . . .

Does a business establishment incur liability . . . if it denies use of its telephone to a good samaritan who explains an emergency situation occurring without and wishes to call the police? . . .

There is a distinction, well rooted in the common law, between action and nonaction. It has found its way into the prestigious Restatement Second of Torts (hereafter cited as "Restatement"), which provides in section 314: "The fact that the actor realizes or should realize that action on his part is necessary for another's aid or protection does not of itself impose upon him a duty to take such action." . . .

Defendant argues that the request that its employee call the police is a request that it *do* something. He points to the established rule that one who has not created a peril ordinarily does not have a duty to take affirmative action to assist an imperiled person. It is urged that the alternative request of the patron from Happy Jack's Saloon that he be allowed to use defendant's telephone so that he personally could make the call is again a request that the defendant do something—assist another to give aid. . . .

The refusal of the law to recognize the moral obligation of one to aid another

when he is in peril and when such aid may be given without danger and at little cost in effort has been roundly criticized. Prosser describes the case law sanctioning such inaction as a "refus[al] to recognize the moral obligation of common decency and common humanity" and characterizes some of these decisions as "shocking in the extreme. . . ." (Prosser, Law of Torts (4th ed. 1971) § 56, pp. 340–341.) . . .

As noted in *Tarasoff v. Regents of University of California,* (1976) 17 Cal.3d 425, 435, 551 P.2d 334, the courts have increased the instances in which affirmative duties are imposed not by direct rejection of the common law rule, but by expanding the list of special relationships which will justify departure from that rule. For instance, California courts have found special relationships in *Ellis v. D'Angelo* (1953) 116 Cal.App.2d 310, 253 P.2d 675 (upholding a cause of action against parents who failed to warn a babysitter of the violent proclivities of their child), *Johnson v. State of California* (1968) 69 Cal.2d 782, 73 Cal.Rptr. 240, 447 P.2d 352 (upholding suit against the state for failure to warn foster parents of the dangerous tendencies of their ward), *Morgan v. County of Yuba* (1964) 230 Cal.App.2d 938, 41 Cal.Rptr. 508 (sustaining cause of action against a sheriff who had promised to warn decedent before releasing a dangerous prisoner, but failed to do so).

And in *Tarasoff,* a therapist was told by his patient that he intended to kill Tatiana Tarasoff [the patient's girlfriend]. The therapist and his supervisors predicted the patient presented a serious danger of violence. In fact he did, for he carried out his threat. The court held the patient-therapist relationship was enough to create duty to exercise reasonable care to protect others from the foreseeable result of the patient's illness.

Section 314A of the Restatement lists other special relationships which create a duty to render aid, such as that of a common carrier to its passengers, an innkeeper to his guest, possessors of land who hold it open to the public, or one who has a custodial relationship to another. A duty may be created by an undertaking to give assistance. (See Rest.2d Torts, § 321 et seq.)

Here there was no special relationship between the defendant and the deceased. It would be stretching the concept beyond recognition to assert there was a relationship between the defendant and the patron from Happy Jack's Saloon who wished to summon aid. But this does not end the matter. It is time to re-examine the common law rule of nonliability for nonfeasance in the special circumstances of the instant case. . . .

The [California] Supreme Court has identified certain factors to be considered in determining whether a duty is owed to third persons. These factors include: "the foreseeability of harm to the plaintiff, the degree of certainty that the plaintiff suffered injury, the closeness of the connection between the defendant's conduct and the injury suffered, the moral blame attached to the defendant's conduct, the policy of preventing future harm, the extent of the burden to the defendant and consequences to the community of imposing a duty to exercise care with resulting liability for breach, and the availability, cost, and prevalence of insurance for the risk involved." (*Rowland v. Christian* (1968) 69 Cal.2d 108, 113, 70 Cal.Rptr. 97, 443 P.2d 561.

We examine those factors in reference to this case. (1) The harm to the decedent was abundantly foreseeable; it was imminent. The employee was expressly told that a man had been threatened. The employee was a bartender. As such he knew it is foreseeable that some people who drink alcohol in the milieu of a bar setting are prone to violence. (2) The certainty of decedent's injury is undisputed. (3) There is arguably a close connection between the employee's conduct and the injury: the patron wanted to use the phone to summon the police to intervene. The employee's refusal to allow the use of the phone pre-

vented this anticipated intervention. If permitted to go to trial, the plaintiff may be able to show that the probable response time of the police would have been shorter than the time between the prohibited telephone call and the fatal shot. (4) The employee's conduct displayed a disregard for human life that can be characterized as morally wrong:* he was callously indifferent to the possibility that Darrell Soldano would die as the result of his refusal to allow a person to use the telephone. Under the circumstances before us the bartender's burden was minimal and exposed him to no risk: all he had to do was allow the use of the telephone. It would have cost him or his employer nothing. It could have saved a life. (5) Finding a duty in these circumstances would promote a policy of preventing future harm. A citizen would not be required to summon the police but would be required, in circumstances such as those before us, not to impede another who has chosen to summon aid. (6) We have no information on the question of the availability, cost, and prevalence of insurance for the risk, but note that the liability which is sought to be imposed here is that of employee negligence, which is covered by many insurance policies. (7) The extent of the burden on the defendant was minimal. . . .

As the Supreme Court has noted, the reluctance of the law to impose liability for nonfeasance, as distinguished from misfeasance, is in part due to the difficulties in setting standards and of making rules workable.

Many citizens simply "don't want to get involved." No rule should be adopted which would require a citizen to open up his or her house to a stranger so that the

---

*The moral right of plaintiff's decedent to have the defendant's bartender permit the telephone call is so apparent that legal philosophers treat such rights as given and requiring no supporting argument. (See Dworkin, *Taking Rights Seriously* (Harv.U.Press 1978) p. 99.) The concept flows from the principle that each member of a community has a right to have each other member treat him with a minimal respect due a fellow human being. (Id. at p. 98.)

latter may use the telephone to call for emergency assistance. As Mrs. Alexander in Anthony Burgess' *A Clockwork Orange* learned to her horror, such an action may be fraught with danger. It does not follow, however, that use of a telephone in a public portion of a business should be refused for a legitimate emergency call. Imposing liability for such a refusal would not subject innocent citizens to possible attack by the "good samaritan," for it would be limited to an establishment open to the public during times when it is open to business, and to places within the establishment ordinarily accessible to the public. Nor would a stranger's mere assertion that an "emergency" situation is occurring create the duty to utilize an accessible telephone because the duty would arise if and only if it were clearly conveyed that there exists an imminent danger of physical harm. (See Rest.2d Torts, supra, § 327.)

Such a holding would not involve difficulties in proof, overburden the courts or unduly hamper self-determination or enterprise.

A business establishment such as the Circle Inn is open for profit. The owner encourages the public to enter, for his earnings depend on it. A telephone is a necessary adjunct to such a place. It is not unusual in such circumstances for patrons to use the telephone to call a taxicab or family member.

We acknowledge that defendant contracted for the use of his telephone, and its use is a species of property. But if it exists in a public place as defined above, there is no privacy or ownership interest in it such that the owner should be permitted to interfere with a good faith attempt to use it by a third person to come to the aid of another. . . .

We conclude that the bartender owed a duty to the plaintiff's decedent to permit the patron from Happy Jack's to place a call to the police or to place the call himself. It bears emphasizing that the duty in this case does not require that one must go to the aid of another. That is not the issue here. The employee was not the good samaritan intent on aiding another. The patron was.

It would not be appropriate to await legislative action in this area. The rule was fashioned in the common law tradition, as were the exceptions to the rule. To the extent this opinion expands the reach of section 327 of the Restatement, it represents logical and needed growth, the hallmark of the common law. . . . "Although the Legislature may of course speak to the subject, in the common law system the primary instruments of this evolution are the courts, adjudicating on a regular basis the rich variety of individual cases brought before them." (*Rodriguez v. Bethlehem Steel Corp.* (1974) 12 Cal.3d 382, 394, 115 Cal.Rptr. 765, 525 P.2d 669.) . . .

The creative and regenerative power of the law has been strong enough to break chains imposed by outmoded former decisions. What the courts have power to create, they also have power to modify, reject and re-create in response to the needs of a dynamic society. The exercise of this power is an imperative function of the courts and is the strength of the common law. . . .

The possible imposition of liability on the defendant in this case is not a global change in the law. It is but a slight departure from the "morally questionable" rule of nonliability for inaction absent a special relationship. . . . It is a logical extension of Restatement section 327 which imposes liability for negligent interference with a third person who the defendant knows is attempting to render necessary aid. However small it may be, it is a step which should be taken.

We conclude there are sufficient justiciable issues to permit the case to go to trial and therefore reverse.

• ASSIGNMENT 11.3 •

a. Do you think the courts should provide a forum to redress every moral wrong? Should every moral duty be backed up by a legal duty? Does the *Soldano* court take this position?

b. What if the only phone at the Circle Inn were a pay phone. The Good Samaritan asks the bartender to let him borrow money for the emergency call. The bartender has the change readily available, but refuses to let him borrow the money. Does *Soldano* apply?

c. Your house is on fire. You do not have a phone. You run across the street and ask your neighbor to call 911 for help. The neighbor, who has never liked you, refuses. Later you sue the neighbor for refusing your request. Does *Soldano* apply?

▪ GRATUITOUS UNDERTAKING

Question: If you do something that you do not have to do, is there a duty to do it with reasonable care?

An **undertaking** is simply doing something. The undertaking is **gratuitous** if there was no obligation to do it—the defendant did it for free. Most undertakings are not for free. Rather, they result from "payment" of one kind or another. In the law of contracts, this payment is often referred to as **consideration.** A homeowner may enter a contract with an electrician to re-wire a house for a set fee. The work of the electrician on the wiring is an undertaking supported by consideration. There is no duty problem here. The electrician has the duty to perform the undertaking (the re-wiring) with reasonable care. Suppose, however, that the undertaking is *not* supported by consideration. Suppose that the undertaking is gratuitous.

> **Example:**
>
> • While the electrician in the above situation is re-wiring the house, he discovers a broken water valve in the bathroom. On his own, as a goodwill gesture, the electrician decides to fix the valve. Because of his inexperience with plumbing, the electrician causes additional damage to the pipes. Working on the pipes was a gratuitous undertaking. Did the electrician have a *duty* to use reasonable care in trying to fix the water valve?
>
> • Phil is an off-duty lifeguard driving by a lake in another state. He sees a small, unattended child drowning close to the shore. Phil stops his car and decides to help. While Phil is carrying the child out of the water, the child's arm is broken due to Phil's carelessness in holding the child. Phil did not have a duty to come to the aid of the child because no special relationship existed between them. Phil's act of help was a gratuitous undertaking. Did Phil owe a *duty* to use reasonable care in helping the child?

The answer to both questions is *yes.* Even though there may be no duty to do anything, if you decide to do something, you have the duty to do it reasonably. The duty arises from a gratuitous undertaking. The defendants (the electrician and Phil in the above examples) are said to have assumed the duty on their own.

A final dimension of this problem must be considered. Suppose a defendant, who has no special relationship with plaintiff, makes a gratuitous **promise** to the plaintiff.

> **Example:** Richard is injured on the road. A passerby sees Richard and says, "Don't do anything. Lie still. I'll get help." Soon another stranger comes by and asks Richard if he needs any help. He says, "No, someone has just gone for help." In fact, the original passerby did nothing, thinking (foolishly) that someone else would probably help Richard.

Did the original passerby owe Richard a *duty* to perform his gratuitous promise with reasonable care? The traditional answer has been no. More modern cases, however, are beginning to find that a duty does exist as long as there has been **reliance** by plaintiff on the defendant's promise. Such was clearly the case with Richard, who did not seek further help because of the first passerby's promise.

· ASSIGNMENT 11.4 ·

ABC Realty Company leases space to Jones, who uses it as a grocery store. The lease agreement provides that all repairs and maintenance are the responsibility of Jones. One day, an officer of the ABC Realty Company tells Jones that the company is thinking about installing smoke detectors to replace the rusty sprinkler system. Two days later, a customer is injured in Jones's store due to a fire. The sprinkler system did not work and smoke detectors had not been installed. Did ABC Realty Company owe a duty of reasonable care to the customer? (See General Instructions for the Legal Analysis Assignment in Chapter 3.)

· ASSIGNMENT 11.5 ·

The B & O Railroad (RR) has a track that crosses a county street. For years, the RR stationed one of its employees at this crossing in order to warn oncoming traffic using the county street of an approaching train. There is no law that requires the RR to keep this employee at this crossing. You may assume that if the RR had never placed an employee at this crossing, a claim of negligence against the RR would not be successful. The fact of the matter, however, is that the RR had an employee at this crossing for years. As a train approached, the employee stepped out onto the county street and warned all traffic to stop. The employee lived in the area, and hence knew many of the automobile drivers that used the crossing. For the last three years, the RR had been experiencing declining business and never had more than two trains crossing the county street on any given day. The poor business also led to employee layoffs. On December 3rd, the employee who had worked the county street crossing was laid off. She was not replaced. Hence, no RR employee now works at the county street crossing. In the view of the RR, the sound of an oncoming train would be warning enough to cars approaching the county street. On December 6th of the same year, Peter Blanchard was driving his truck on the county street in question. He was making a delivery from a neighboring state. He crashed into one of the RR's trains at the point where the county street and the RR track meet. At all times Peter was driving very carefully. It was a rainy night, and hence he did not hear the oncoming train. You may assume that Peter will be able to establish that the accident would not have happened if the RR employee (who was laid off on 12/3) had been on duty at the time of the accident. Peter Blanchard brings a negligence action against the B & O RR for its failure to have the employee present to warn traffic of oncoming trains at the crossing. Discuss the element of duty. (See General Instructions for the Legal Analysis Assignment in Chapter 3.)

▪ ASSIGNMENT 11.6 ▪

Rich is driving down the road carefully. Suddenly a storm begins. Visibility is very poor. Rich unavoidably hits a pedestrian, who suffers a broken leg. Rich gets out of the car and runs toward the pedestrian. When Rich sees the injury, he panics. He does not know what to do. Hours go by without Rich doing anything. The pedestrian dies. Did Rich owe the pedestrian a duty? Give an argument that he did. Give an argument that he did not. (See General Instructions for the Legal Analysis Assignment in Chapter 3.)

▪ ASSIGNMENT 11.7 ▪

On the facts of assignment 11.6:

a. What liability, if any, would Rich have to the estate of the pedestrian in your state? (See General Instructions for the State Code Assignment and for the State Court Opinion Assignment, both in Chapter 2.)
b. Prepare a negligence complaint for the estate of the pedestrian against Rich. (See General Instructions for the Complaint Drafting Assignment in Chapter 5.)

▪ ASSIGNMENT 11.8 ▪

Do you feel that society should encourage Good Samaritans to come to the aid of fellow citizens? Do the gratuitous undertaking principles have this effect?

▪ ASSIGNMENT 11.9 ▪

Prepare an annotated bibliography on the Good Samaritan rule for your state. (See General Instructions for the Annotated Bibliography Assignment in Chapter 2.)

CASE

Riss v. City of New York
22 N.Y.2d 579, 240 N.E.2d 860, 293 N.Y.S.2d 897 (1968)
Court of Appeals of New York

Background: For more than six months, Linda Riss was terrorized by a rejected suitor, Burton Pugach. This miscreant, masquerading as a respectable attorney, repeatedly threatened to have Linda killed or maimed if she did not yield to him: "If I can't have you, no one else will have you, and when I get through with you, no one else will want you." In fear for her life, she contacted the police. One detective told her that she would have to be hurt before the police could do anything. On June 14, 1959 Linda became engaged to another man. At a party held to celebrate the event, she received a phone call warning her that it was her "last chance." Completely distraught, she called the police, begging for help, but was refused. The next day Pugach carried out his dire threats in the very manner he had foretold by having a hired thug throw lye in Linda's face. She was blinded in one eye, lost a good portion of her vision in the other, and her face was permanently scarred. After this assault, the authorities concluded that there was some basis for Linda's fears, and for the next three and one-half years, she was given around-the-clock protection. She sued the city for negligence. The trial court dismissed the complaint. The Appellate Division affirmed. The plaintiff now appeals to the Court of Appeals of New York.

Decision on Appeal: The judgment for the city is affirmed. The city is not liable to an assault victim for failure to supply police protection upon request.

Opinion of Court

Judge BREITEL delivered the opinion of the court . . .

This appeal presents, in a very sympathetic framework, the issue of the liability of a municipality for failure to provide special protection to a member of the public who was repeatedly threatened with personal harm and eventually suffered dire personal injuries for lack of such protection. [The] . . . case involves the provision of a governmental service to protect the public generally from external hazards and particularly to control the activities of criminal wrongdoers. The amount of protection that may be provided is limited by the resources of the community and by a considered legislative-executive decision as to how those resources may be deployed. For the courts to proclaim a new and general duty of protection in the law of tort, even to those who may be the particular seekers of protection based on specific hazards, could and would inevitably determine how the limited police re-

sources of the community should be allocated and without predictable limits. This is quite different from the predictable allocation of resources and liabilities when public hospitals, rapid transit systems, or even highways are provided.

Before such extension of responsibilities should be dictated by the indirect imposition of tort liabilities, there should be a legislative determination that that should be the scope of public responsibility. . . . When one considers the greatly increased amount of crime committed throughout the cities, but especially in certain portions of them, with a repetitive and predictable pattern, it is easy to see the consequences of fixing municipal liability upon a showing of probable need for and request for protection. To be sure these are grave problems at the present time, exciting high priority activity on the part of the national, state and local governments, to which the answers are neither simple, known, or presently within reasonable controls. To foist a presumed cure for these problems by judicial innovation of a new kind of liability in tort would be foolhardy indeed and an assumption of judicial wisdom and power not possessed by the courts. . . .

For all of these reasons, there is no warrant in judicial tradition or in the proper allocation of the powers of government for the courts, in the absence of legislation, to carve out an area of tort liability for police protection to members of the public. Quite distinguishable, of course, is the situation where the police authorities undertake responsibilities to particular members of the public and expose them, without adequate protection, to the risks which then materialize into actual losses (*Schuster v. City of New York,* 5 N.Y.2d 75, 180 N.Y.S.2d 265, 154 N.E.2d 534).

Accordingly, the order of the Appellate Division affirming the judgment of dismissal should be affirmed.

KEATING, Judge (dissenting).

No one questions the proposition that the first duty of government is to assure its citizens the opportunity to live in personal security. And no one who reads the record of Linda's ordeal can reach a conclusion other than that the City of New York, acting through its agent, completely and negligently failed to fulfill this obligation to Linda.

Linda has turned to the courts of this State for redress, asking that the city be held liable in damages for its negligent failure to protect her from harm. . . . If a private detective acts carelessly, no one would deny that a jury could find such conduct unacceptable. Why then is the city not required to live up to at least the same minimal standards of professional competence which would be demanded of a private detective?

Linda's reasoning seems so eminently sensible that surely it must come as a shock to her and to every citizen to hear the city argue and to learn that this court decides that the city has no duty to provide police protection to any given individual. What makes the city's position particularly difficult to understand is that, in conformity to the dictates of the law, Linda did not carry any weapon for self-defense. Thus, by a rather bitter irony she was required to rely for protection on the City of New York which now denies all responsibility to her. . . .

The city invokes the specter of a "crushing burden" if we should depart from the existing rule and enunciate even the limited proposition that the State and its municipalities can be held liable for the negligent acts of their police employees in executing whatever police services they do in fact provide. The fear of financial disaster is a myth. . . [I]n the past four or five years, New York City has been presented with an average of some 10,000 claims each year. The figure would sound ominous except for the fact the city has been paying out less than $8,000,000 on tort claims each year and this amount includes all those sidewalk defect and snow and ice cases about which the courts fret so often. . . . Certainly this is a slight burden in a budget of more than six billion dollars (less than two tenths of 1%) and of no importance as compared to the injustice of permitting unredressed wrongs to continue to go unrepaired. That Linda Riss should be asked to bear the loss, which should properly fall on the city if . . . her injuries resulted from the city's failure to provide sufficient police to protect Linda is contrary to the most elementary notions of justice. . . .

No one would claim that, under the facts here, the police were negligent when they did not give Linda protection after her first calls or visits to the police station in February of 1959. The preliminary investigation was sufficient. If Linda had been attacked at this point, clearly there would be no liability here. When, however, as time went on and it was established that Linda was a reputable person, that other verifiable attempts to injure her or intimidate her had taken place, that other witnesses were available to support her claim that her life was being threatened, something more was required—either by way of further investigation or protection—than the statement that was made by one detective to Linda that she would have to be hurt before the police could do anything for her. . . .

If the police force of the City of New York is so understaffed that it is unable to cope with the everyday problem posed by the relatively few cases where single, known individuals threaten the lives of other persons, then indeed we have reached the danger line and the lives of all of us are in peril. If the police department is in such a deplorable state that the city, because of insufficient manpower, is truly unable to protect persons in Linda Riss' position, then liability not only should, but must be imposed. It will act as an effective inducement for public officials to provide at least a minimally adequate number of police.

. . .

[I]f we were to hold the city liable here for the negligence of the police, courts would no more be interfering with the operations of the police department than they "meddle" in the affairs of the highway department when they hold the municipality liable for personal injuries resulting from defective sidewalks, or a private employer for the negligence of his employees. In other words, all the courts do in these municipal negligence cases is require officials to weigh the consequences of their decisions. If Linda Riss' injury resulted from the failure of the city to pay sufficient salaries to attract qualified and sufficient personnel, the full cost of that choice should become acknowledged in the same way as it has in other areas of municipal tort liability. Perhaps officials will find it less costly to choose the alternative of paying damages than changing their existing practices. That may be well and good, but the price for the refusal to provide for an adequate police force should not be borne by Linda Riss and all the other innocent victims of such decisions. . . .

The methods of dealing with the problem of crime are left completely to the city's discretion. All that the courts can do is make sure that the costs of the city's and its employees' mistakes are placed where they properly belong. . . . The order of the Appellate Division should be reversed and a new trial granted.

■ ASSIGNMENT 11.10 ■

a. Is it relevant that eight months after Burton Pugach was released from a fourteen-year prison term, he married Linda Riss? *Love Story: Part II,* N.Y. Times, Feb. 22, 1987, at 26, col. 4.

b. Is the *Riss* case consistent with the *Soldano* case? Why or why not?

c. Smith is an informant who helps the police arrest a criminal. In a news interview, the police tell a reporter that Smith was helpful in making the arrest. Two weeks later, Smith tells the police that he needs special protection because his life has been threatened. He is denied this protection. When he is murdered, his estate sues the city for negligently failing to protect him. Does *Riss* apply?

SUMMARY

Whenever one's acts or omissions create a foreseeable risk of injury or damage to someone else's person or property, a duty of reasonable care arises to take precautions to prevent that injury or damage. Under the Cardozo test, a duty is owed to a specific person who is foreseeably in the zone of danger. Under the Andrews test, a duty is owed to someone who suffers injury as a result of the defendant's unreasonable conduct toward anyone, even if the person injured was not in the zone of danger. In most cases, nonfeasance alone does not create a duty unless there is a special relationship between the parties. Among the special relationships are common carrier and passenger, innkeeper and guest, employer and employee, and land owner or possessor and invitee. If the defendant undertakes a task, he or she assumes a duty to perform it with reasonable care, even though there was no initial duty to undertake it and even though the undertaking was gratuitous. If the defendant promises to undertake a task, he or she assumes a duty to perform it with reasonable care if the plaintiff relies on the promise, even though there was no initial duty to undertake it and even though the promise was gratuitous.

Key Terms

duty	Andrews test	special relationship
general rule on duty	zone of danger	Good Samaritan
reasonable care	world at large	undertaking
breach of duty	affirmative conduct	gratuitous
foreseeability	misfeasance	consideration
foreseeable plaintiff	nonfeasance	promise
unforeseeable plaintiff	malfeasance	reliance
Cardozo test		

CHAPTER 12

Negligence: Element II: Breach of Duty (Unreasonableness)

CHAPTER OUTLINE

- STANDARD OF CARE: REASONABLENESS
- BREACH-OF-DUTY (UNREASONABLENESS) EQUATION
- OBJECTIVE OR SUBJECTIVE STANDARD?
- RES IPSA LOQUITUR
- CUSTOM AND USAGE
- VIOLATION OF STATUTE, ORDINANCE, OR REGULATION (S/O/R)

- COMPLIANCE WITH STATUTE, ORDINANCE, OR REGULATION (S/O/R)
- GROSS NEGLIGENCE (UNREASONABLENESS) AND WILFUL, WANTON, AND RECKLESS CONDUCT
- VICARIOUS LIABILITY
- MEDICAL MALPRACTICE
- LEGAL MALPRACTICE

■ STANDARD OF CARE: REASONABLENESS

Thus far we have established through the first element of negligence that a duty exists. Our concern now is: duty to do what? The answer in the vast majority of cases is: to use **reasonable care** in order to avoid injuring others. There is a **breach of duty** (the second element of negligence) when the defendant engages in **unreasonable conduct.** Reasonableness, therefore, becomes the **standard of care** that we use in most cases to determine whether the second element of negligence applies to a given situation.

One of the most fascinating and troublesome problems in the law of torts is the difficulty of defining reasonableness. Addressing this difficulty is our challenge in this chapter.

230

Totality of Circumstances

The beauty of **reasonableness** as a standard is that it is flexible enough to accommodate an infinite variety of situations. It is very versatile. On the other hand, the nightmare of reasonableness as a standard is that its determination requires a juggling act. All of the circumstances leading to the accident and injury must be assessed. At times, a slight change in any of the circumstances can produce a different result.

What are these circumstances? Figure 12.1 identifies them as **factors** in the determination of reasonableness. A factor is one of the circumstances or considerations that will be weighed in making a decision, no one of which is usually conclusive. Some of the factors pertain to the data of the senses, others to the identity and characteristics of the participants, and still others to prior occurrences and expectations. We will examine these factors throughout the chapter.

Comparative Standard

We must go through five steps to try to establish a breach of duty due to unreasonable conduct on the part of the defendant in a negligence case.

> **Step 1:** State the injury the plaintiff claims to have suffered because of the defendant.
>
> **Step 2:** Identify the specific acts or omissions of the defendant about which the plaintiff is complaining.
>
> **Step 3:** Turn back the clock in your mind to the time just before the acts and omissions identified in Step 2. Ask yourself what a reasonable person would have done under the same or similar circumstances at that time.
>
> **Step 4:** Compare the specific acts and omissions of the defendant (see Step 2) with what you said a reasonable person would have done (see Step 3).
>
> **Step 5:** Reach your conclusion:
> a. If the comparison in Step 4 tells you that the defendant did exactly what a reasonable person would have done (or that there is a substantial similarity), then you can conclude that the defendant acted reasonably, and hence there is no breach of duty.
> b. If the comparison in Step 4 tells you that a reasonable person would have done the opposite of what the defendant did (or would have acted substantially differently from the defendant), then you can conclude that the defendant acted unreasonably, and hence there was a breach of duty.

In flowchart form, the comparative process is outlined in Figure 12.2.

Reasonableness vs. Perfection

What is a **reasonable person?** Unfortunately, it is easier to define what a reasonable person is *not* than to say definitively what one is. First, let us look at the traditional definition:

> A reasonable person is an ordinary, prudent person who uses reasonable care
> to avoid injuring others.

Figure 12.1 Factors to be Assessed in the Determination of Reasonableness

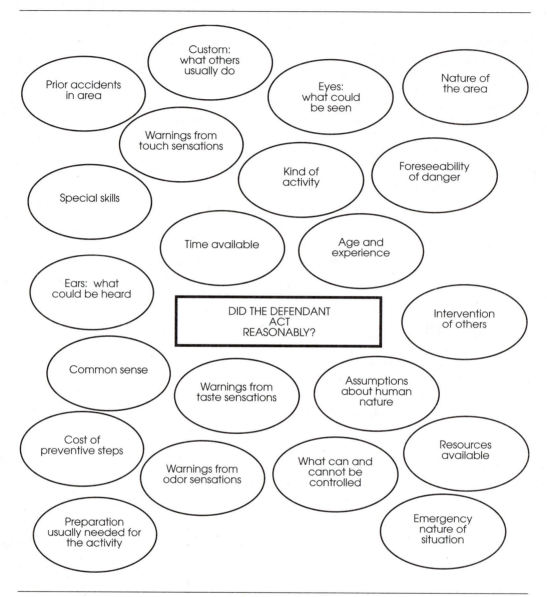

This definition, although commonly used, is not very satisfactory. We are still left with the questions of what is "ordinary," what is "prudent," what is "reasonable care." We will focus on these questions in great detail later. For now, we need to confront the major myth that the reasonable person is a perfect person, or more narrowly, that a reasonable person does not injure other people. Figure 12.3 gives an overview of some of the basic differences among the perfect person, the reasonable person, and the unreasonable person.

Figure 12.2 Reasonableness by Comparison

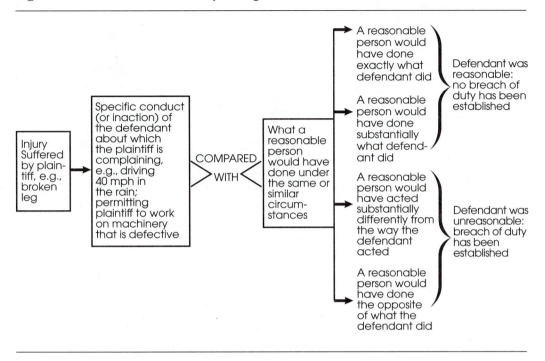

Figure 12.3 Perfect/Reasonable/Unreasonable Persons

Perfect Person	Reasonable Person	Unreasonable Person
1. Never causes an accident.	1. Does cause accidents, but they are never due to carelessness.	1. Causes accidents due to carelessness.
2. Never makes a mistake leading to an accident.	2. Does make mistakes leading to accidents, but the mistakes are never careless.	2. Makes careless mistakes leading to accidents.
3. Reacts perfectly in an emergency in order to prevent accidents.	3. Reacts as cautiously as possible in an emergency, but can still make a mistake in an emergency that causes an accident. These mistakes, however, are not careless.	3. Reacts carelessly in an emergency, causing accidents.

Figure 12.3   Continued

4. Has the right knowledge and experience needed to avoid accidents.	**4a.** Has the knowledge and experience common to everyone, and uses them to help avoid accidents. **b.** When more expert knowledge and experience are available, the reasonable person uses them to help avoid accidents. **Note:** even with the use of common or expert knowledge and experience, accidents can happen, but they are not due to carelessness.	**4a.** Does not have or fails to use the knowledge and experience common to everyone to help avoid accidents. **b.** When more expert knowledge and experience is available, does not adequately use them to help prevent accidents.
5. Will undergo any inconvenience or burden to avoid an accident.	**5.** Will undergo only reasonable inconvenience or burden to avoid an accident.	**5.** Refuses to undergo even reasonable inconvenience or burden to avoid an accident.

▪ BREACH-OF-DUTY (UNREASONABLENESS) EQUATION

To avoid injuring others, the reasonable person tries to avoid the dangers or risks of injury. How is this done? What mental process is used to decide what dangers to take precautions against? The reasonable person applies the **breach-of-duty equation** in Figure 12.4.

If the danger of a serious accident outweighed the burden or inconvenience of taking precautions to avoid the accident, the reasonable person would take

Figure 12.4   Breach-of-Duty Equation

Foreseeability of the danger of an accident occuring
———————————————
Foreseeability of the kind of injury or damage that will result if an accident occurs

} balanced against {

The burden or inconvenience on the defendant of taking precautions to avoid the accident
———————————————
The importance or social utility of what the defendant was trying to do before the accident

those precautions. The failure of the defendant to do so would mean that the defendant was unreasonable and committed a breach of duty in the law of negligence. If the danger of a serious accident were so slight that the danger would not outweigh the relatively high burden or inconvenience of the precautions that would be needed to avoid the accident, then the reasonable person would *not* take these precautions. The failure of the defendant, therefore, to take these precautions would not amount to a breach of duty, and the defendant would not be deemed to have been unreasonable in not taking them.

To better understand the breach-of-duty equation, we need to explore the following topics:

- danger/caution hypothesis
- foreseeability
- burden or inconvenience
- importance or social utility

Danger/Caution Hypothesis

A **hypothesis** is a theory or assumption. For every fact or group of facts, it is possible to state a hypothesis about the amount of danger present and the amount of caution needed to offset or eliminate the danger. The overriding principle is as follows: THE GREATER THE DANGER, THE GREATER THE CAUTION NEEDED. Here are some examples:

Facts: A sharp knife is on a table in a day care center.

Danger hypothesis: Knives are very attractive to children; knives are often easy for children to pick up; children do not appreciate the danger of knives; knives can seriously injure parts of the body with minimal force. Therefore, a sharp knife on a table in a day care center presents a VERY SERIOUS DANGER of injury to one of the children.

Caution: Given the serious nature of the potential danger, a GREAT DEAL of CAUTION is needed to avoid an injury from the knife.

Facts: A sharp knife is on a table in a factory.

Danger hypothesis: Factories are places for adults; adults know how to handle sharp knives, especially if the knife is used in a factory where the workers are skilled people. Therefore, a sharp knife on a table in a factory poses ALMOST NO DANGER of injury to anyone.

Caution: Given the minimal and almost nonexistent nature of the danger posed by the knife, VERY LITTLE CAUTION is needed to avoid an injury from the knife.

- ASSIGNMENT 12.1 ▪

Analyze the following fact situations. Assess the danger/caution hypothesis for each fact situation. Identify all possible dangers in each. How likely will each danger lead to an injury? What kind of injury? In the light of your assessment of each danger, state how much caution is needed to avoid the injury. What precautions need to be taken? (See General Instructions for the Legal Analysis Assignment in Chapter 3.)

a. A sign on a busy three-lane street says, ''USE TWO LANES GOING NORTH FROM 6 A.M. to 9:30 A.M. AND FROM 4:30 P.M. to 6:30 P.M. EXCEPT HOLIDAYS AND WEEKENDS. USE ONE LANE AT ALL OTHER TIMES.''

b. Mary owns a motorcycle. Her friend, Leo, does not know how to drive. Mary lets Leo drive the motorcycle while Mary is sitting right behind him, giving instructions as they drive in an empty lot.

c. The XYZ Chemical Company manufactures a new floor cleaner. On the label of the bottle containing the cleaner, there are very bright colors and the cartoon of a happy person cleaning the floor. The ingredients are listed on the label, plus a warning to keep the liquid away from eyes.

Of course, it can be argued that there is danger lurking in everything. It is possible to conceive of a set of acts in which any object (e.g., a tissue) could be used to injure someone in some way. This is not the kind of danger we are talking about in negligence law. It is not a breach of duty to fail to take precautions against every conceivable danger. Reasonableness does not require excessive caution.

How do we decide the amount of caution that *is* reasonable in a given set of circumstances? The answer depends on carefully weighing the elements of the breach-of-duty equation in Figure 12.4.

1. **The FORESEEABILITY of an accident occurring.**
   The more foreseeable the accident is, the more caution a reasonable person would take to try to prevent the accident.
2. **The FORESEEABILITY of the kind of injury or damage that would result from the accident if it occurred.**
   The more serious the kind of injury or damage that is foreseeable, the more caution a reasonable person would take to prevent the accident.
3. **The BURDEN or INCONVENIENCE that would be involved in taking the precautions necessary to avoid the accident.**
   The greater the burden or inconvenience, the less likely a reasonable person would take the precautions to avoid the accident.
4. **The IMPORTANCE or SOCIAL UTILITY of what the defendant was trying to do before the accident.**
   The more important or socially useful it is, the more likely a reasonable person would take risks in carrying it out.

Foreseeability

In Chapter 10 we took a detailed look at foreseeability and the methods by which it is determined. Review the foreseeability-determination formula in that chapter (see Figure 10.2). Our concern here is the foreseeability of the danger of an accident occurring (e.g., a customer slipping on a wet floor, an employee dropping a case of dynamite, an electric switch malfunctioning) and the danger of a particular kind of injury or damage occurring (e.g., death, crop destruction). As indicated in the formula, there are eight interrelated topics to be assessed:

- area analysis
- activity analysis
- people analysis
- preparation analysis
- assumptions about human nature
- historical data
- specific sensory data
- common sense

Assessing all of these topics will tell us what dangers a reasonable person would have foreseen. Once we know what a reasonable person would have foreseen, we know what the defendant *should* have foreseen.

Recall that we do not simply want to know *whether* the danger is foreseeable. The critical question is *how foreseeable* are the dangers. Review the foreseeability spectrum in Chapter 10, Figure 10.1. Are we talking about a danger that is only a slight possibility? A slight probability? A highly unusual danger? A certainty?

Burden or Inconvenience

Next, we examine the **burden or inconvenience** that would have to be borne in order to avoid the danger. What do we mean by burden or inconvenience? Suppose that the danger under discussion is that of a customer falling on a wet floor in a supermarket on a rainy day, and that the kind of injury posed by this danger is a broken or bruised limb. After going through the foreseeability-determination formula, assume we conclude that both dangers are fairly probable. Now let us focus on the burden or inconvenience on the supermarket of eliminating the danger. Burdens or inconveniences fall into several interrelated categories:

1. Costs
How much money would be needed to take steps to prevent the accident from happening? The cost of a sign saying, "CAUTION, WET FLOOR"? The cost of an employee whose job on a rainy day is to mop the floor all day long? Every other hour? The cost of a rug to absorb the water? The cost of closing the store on rainy days? Etc.

2. Time
How much time would be lost in having the sign painted? How much time would be lost in having an employee mop up all day? Every other hour? Etc.

3. Effectiveness
By effectiveness, we do *not* mean the effectiveness of the precautions in preventing the accident. Rather, the question is what impact any of the precautions would have on the overall effectiveness of what the defendant was doing. If the precautions were taken, how would they affect the defendant's operation or activity? Going through the modest trouble of making and using a "WET FLOOR" sign would certainly not alter the effectiveness of the supermarket's business very much. Closing every day that it rains, however, would substantially disrupt the effectiveness of the supermarket's business. Indeed, the burden might amount to having to go out of business.

4. Aesthetics
Would the precautionary steps be unsightly or unpleasant to the eye in any way?

Importance or Social Utility

Finally, we examine the **importance or social utility** of what the defendant was trying to do before the accident occurred. Was the defendant driving to work? Watching a football game? Playing a practical joke? Skydiving for fun? Trying to cure cancer? Saving a child from a fire? The more important or socially useful the activity, the more likely it is that a reasonable person would take risks to accomplish the goals involved. This does not mean that a reasonable person would never take any risks of injury if engaged in a mundane or frivolous task. It simply means that reasonable persons would take fewer risks of injuring someone else (or themselves) while engaged in such tasks than they would in tasks that we would all agree are more important and socially beneficial.

———————————————

The reasonable person, therefore, will juggle all four components of the equation in order to decide what risks should be taken and what precautions should be taken to avoid injury. The foreseeability of an accident, the foreseeability of the kind of injury or damage, the burden or inconvenience of the precautions, and the importance or social utility of the defendant's conduct must all be properly assessed. Defendants will be found to have breached their duty if these factors were not assessed in the same or in substantially the same manner as a reasonable person would have assessed them.

▪ OBJECTIVE OR SUBJECTIVE STANDARD?

It is important that you understand the distinction between a **subjective standard** and an **objective standard.** By ''standard'' we mean the method by which something is assessed or determined.

A subjective standard is being used when something is defined or resolved solely by reference to one person. When Bob says, ''that car is attractive,'' he is probably using a subjective standard: attractiveness *to Bob*. An objective standard is being used when something is defined or resolved solely by comparing one person to one or more other persons. When Bob says, ''Jane is an excellent athlete,'' he is probably using an objective standard. Jane is excellent because she performs as well as or better than *other* athletes. The quality of her athletic skills is determined by comparing her to other athletes—an objective standard. See Figure 12.5.

We said earlier that reasonableness was a comparative standard: we compared what the defendant did to what a reasonable person would have done. This suggests that reasonableness is an objective standard. In the main, this is so. To at least some extent, however, reasonableness is also a subjective standard, as we shall see.

There is, of course, no actual human being who holds the title of ''reasonable person.'' The concept of the reasonable person (sometimes called the ''reasonable man'') was invented in order to provide juries with guidance in trying to determine whether conduct that unintentionally caused injury was wrongful and hence negligent.[1] We now take a closer look at who this reasonable person is. We know that the reasonable person is not perfect. The reasonable person can and does cause accidents. Such accidents, however, are never due to carelessness or imprudent behavior. What else do we know about this person? We examine first the physical characteristics and then the mental characteristics of the reasonable person.

———————————————

[1] If the defendant *intended* the contact or the injury that the plaintiff suffered, then we are not talking about negligence as the cause of action. The plaintiff may be able to use one of the intentional torts, e.g., battery. Intentional conduct may even lead to prosecution for a crime (e.g., criminal trespass, manslaughter).

Figure 12.5   Objective and Subjective Standards

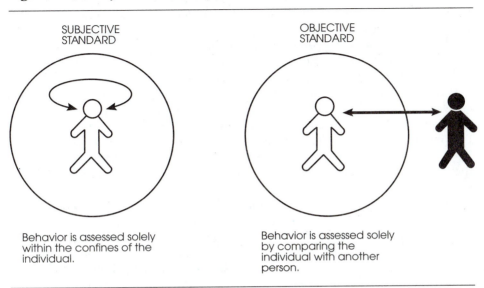

SUBJECTIVE STANDARD

OBJECTIVE STANDARD

Behavior is assessed solely within the confines of the individual.

Behavior is assessed solely by comparing the individual with another person.

Physical Characteristics

The reasonable person has the same physical strengths and weaknesses as the defendant. Hence, if a blind man causes an accident and is sued, the blind man's conduct will be measured against what a reasonable *blind* person would have done under the same or similar circumstances. In this sense, the reasonable person is both a subjective and an objective standard. If the standard were totally objective, the blind man's conduct would be compared to what a non-handicapped reasonable person would have done. If the standard were totally subjective, the blind man's conduct would not be compared with anyone else's conduct. We would simply ask whether we thought this particular blind person did everything he or she was capable of doing to avoid the accident. The actual test, however, is the *reasonable* person with the same handicap as the defendant. If, for example, a defendant with two broken legs tried to drive an ordinary car and had an accident, we would ask whether a reasonable person with two broken legs would have driven a car at all, given the obvious danger of serious injury.

Suppose, however, that the defendant had physical capacities *beyond* that of most people, e.g., superior vision, quicker reflexes. The test of reasonableness for this defendant is what a reasonable person *with these same physical strengths* would have done under the same or similar circumstances.

Mental Characteristics (When the Defendant is an Adult)

Here we are talking about knowledge, intelligence, and overall mental ability that comes from experience and learning. In this regard, the reasonable person is neither exceptionally bright, nor of low intelligence. The reasonable person has the basic knowledge and intelligence needed in everyday life to handle the common occurrences of living. For example, a reasonable person would know that an exposed electrical wire can be very dangerous, but is not expected to know how to repair wire cables. A reasonable person would know that a child in a large body of water can drown, but is not expected to know how to perform complicated medical procedures on a drowning victim.

Suppose that the defendant has a mental illness or deficiency that prevents him or her from knowing that electricity is dangerous or that water can drown people. Is this defendant still held to the standard of the reasonable person who has no such illness or deficiency? Yes. Such defendants are therefore held to a standard that they cannot meet. The standard as to mental characteristics is very objective. For physical handicaps, discussed above, the test is what the reasonable person *with defendant's physical handicap* would have done. For mental disabilities, the test is what a reasonable person *without defendant's mental disabilities* would have done.

Suppose, however, that the defendant has mental strengths beyond that expected of everyone. For example, the defendant may be a doctor, an electrician, a police officer, etc. When this individual causes an injury, the standard of performance will be the reasonable person *with this special knowledge or skill.* Hence, the standard is subjective in the sense that we are talking about the special knowledge or skill *of the defendant,* but is objective in that we are comparing the defendant's conduct with that *of a reasonable person* with that knowledge or skill.

The special problems involving a doctor's skills (medical malpractice) and an attorney's skills (legal malpractice) will be discussed later.

Mental characteristics (When the Defendant Is a Child)

An exception is made when the defendant is a child. When assessing breach of duty by a child, the standard is substantially subjective: What would a reasonable child of the age and intelligence of the defendant have done under the same or similar circumstances? Finally, however, there is an exception to this exception. When the child is engaging in an adult activity, such as driving a car, the child will be held to the standard of a reasonable *adult.*

▪ RES IPSA LOQUITUR

Res ipsa loquitur means "the event speaks for itself." It is a doctrine used by a plaintiff having trouble proving the defendant's breach of duty—the defendant's unreasonableness. It is an evidentiary tool designed to give the plaintiff a break in certain kinds of situations.

> **Example:**   Plaintiff sues the owner of a building for negligence after being injured in an elevator that suddenly crashed to the basement from the second floor. Assume that the *only* evidence plaintiff is able to introduce is the fact of being in the elevator when it collapsed.

Without the aid of res ipsa, the plaintiff would lose because of the failure to establish the second elements of negligence—breach of duty. Where is the specific evidence that the building owner was unreasonable in the maintenance of the elevator? There is none. All we know is that the accident happened. If res ipsa applies in such a case, the jury will be allowed to draw an inference of unreasonableness. In effect, res ipsa simply allows the plaintiff to get its case to the jury. It does not mean that the plaintiff has won the case.

What are the elements of a res ipsa case, in which the inference of unreasonableness can be drawn simply by reason of the fact that the accident happened? What does the plaintiff have to prove in order to get the case to the jury and require the latter to consider the inference of the defendant's unreasonableness? The three basic elements that must be established by the plaintiff are outlined in Figure 12.6.

More Likely Than Not Due to Someone's Unreasonableness

> **Example:** Tom is driving his car down the street. Suddenly, his front tire blows out. His car runs into plaintiff's car. Plaintiff sues Tom for negligence. The only evidence of unreasonableness introduced by the plaintiff is the fact of the tire blowout. Is this a res ipsa case?

No. The first element of a res ipsa case has not been satisfied. The most likely explanation of the tire blowout is *not* someone's unreasonableness. An equally likely explanation is that Tom unknowingly and quite innocently ran over a nail or other sharp object. To be sure, Tom's unreasonableness is a *possible* explanation. A mere possibility of unreasonableness, however, is not enough for the first element of a res ipsa case.

Compare the tire blowout case with the elevator case mentioned earlier. Can it be said that it is more likely than not that the explanation for an elevator falling from the second floor is someone's unreasonableness? The answer in this case is yes. One might indeed go so far as to say that it is highly likely that someone

Figure 12.6   Elements of a Res Ipsa Loquitur Case

Traditional Statement of the Elements	Statement of the Elements as Applied
1. The event must be of a kind that ordinarily does not occur in the absence of someone's negligence.	1. It must be more likely than not that the accident was due to someone's unreasonableness.
2. The event must be caused by an agency or instrumentality within the exclusive control of the defendant.	2a. It must be more likely than not that the accident was due to the *defendant's* unreasonableness. b. The possibility, if any, that the unreasonableness of others caused the accident must be adequately eliminated.
3. The event must not have been due to any voluntary action or contribution on the part of the plaintiff.	3. Plaintiff must not be a responsible cause of the accident.

Figure 12.7   Spectrum of Likelihood

HOW LIKELY IS IT THAT THE ACCIDENT WAS
DUE TO SOMEONE'S UNREASONABLENESS?

— A Certainty
— A Near Certainty
— Highly Likely
— More Likely Than Not
— A 50/50 Possibility
— A Slight Possibility
— A Possibility
— More Unlikely Than Not
— Highly Unlikely

---

was unreasonable. Here are some of the arguments that could be made in support of this conclusion:

- It is commonly known that elevators require frequent inspections.
- If the inspections are adequate, they should reveal defects.
- A falling elevator can cause severe damage to passengers.
- Given the severity of the potential damage, one would expect very careful maintenance by those in charge of the operation and safety of the elevator; when an elevator falls, the likelihood is that this kind of care was not given.
- Elevators have been in existence for a long time; they are not mysterious machines we know very little about; hence, we cannot say that the mishap was probably due to some unknown factor.
- There is safety equipment on an elevator system; if this equipment were being maintained properly (reasonably), it is unlikely that the collapse would occur.

The plaintiff does not have to prove that the *only* explanation for the accident was someone's unreasonableness. The plaintiff does not have to prove that no other cause is possible. The test for this first element is whether unreasonableness by someone is *more likely than not* the explanation. (See Figure 12.7.) Hence, a defendant does not defeat a res ipsa case simply by showing that it is *possible* that the accident was *not* due to unreasonableness.

■ ASSIGNMENT 12.2 ■

Examine the following list of accidents. How likely is it, if at all, that each accident was due to someone's unreasonableness? Where on the ''spectrum of likelihood'' does each accident fall? Give reasons for your answer. If more than one answer is possible, explain all the answers. In each case you can assume that the person injured is trying to get to the jury on a res ipsa theory. Assume that the only evidence available is the fact of the accident. (See the General Instructions for the Legal Analysis Assignment in Chapter 3.)

a. A passenger is injured when an airplane explodes on the runway before takeoff.
b. Electricity leaks from a wire and injures a child.

   c. A small insect is found in a can of soup, injuring a consumer.
   d. A large nail is found in a can of soup, injuring a consumer.
   e. Two cars collide on the street, injuring a pedestrian.
   f. A car collides into a parked car, damaging the latter.
   g. A bottle of soda explodes, injuring a customer.
   h. Cattle stray onto a road, damaging a parked car.

More Likely Than Not Due to Defendant's Unreasonableness

When the first element of res ipsa is established, we know that the accident was more likely than not due to *someone's* unreasonableness. In a lawsuit, of course, you do not sue a vague someone—you must sue the *defendant.* The second element of res ipsa requires the plaintiff to show that it is more likely than not that the accident was caused by the unreasonableness *of the defendant.* The "spectrum of likelihood" in Figure 12.7 for the first element applies here as well. If the unreasonableness of the defendant is a mere possibility, or if there is a 50/50 possibility that the accident was due to the unreasonableness of someone other than the defendant, then the second element of res ipsa has not been established.

> **Example:** Mary is a passenger on XYZ Airlines, which manufactures, assembles, and flies its own commercial planes. While Mary's plane is flying over the ocean, it disappears. Mary's estate sues XYZ for negligence and tries to get its case to the jury on a res ipsa theory. The only evidence of unreasonableness offered by the estate is the fact that the plane disappeared.

Can it be said that it is more likely than not that the defendant's (XYZ's) unreasonableness caused the disappearance of the plane, e.g., due to a defectively built or maintained plane? It is surely *possible* that other causes created the disappearance (e.g., a sudden violent storm that could not have been anticipated, a bomb concealed in luggage that could not be detected by current equipment, another passenger who went insane). It is possible that there was no unreasonableness by the defendant, XYZ Airlines. Yet, a jury could still conclude that the defendant's unreasonableness was more likely than not the cause of the accident leading to the disappearance. XYZ Airlines apparently had exclusive control of the plane—it built and operated the plane. Airplane travel is very common in our society. Crashes are thoroughly investigated and the results usually point to some defect in the design, construction, or operation of the plane—or at least one could reasonably argue this position. Given XYZ's exclusive control, a jury could, therefore, conclude that the disappearance was due to XYZ's unreasonableness in some respect.

Two other major issues need to be considered: 1. What if the defendant was not in exclusive control of what caused the accident? 2. What if more than one person is sued and not all of them could have caused the accident?

1. What if the defendant was not in exclusive control of what caused the accident? In spite of the traditional way in which the second element of res ipsa is commonly phrased (see first column of Figure 12.6), it is *not* always necessary for the defendant to be in exclusive control of what caused the accident. Exclusive control is simply *one* of the ways to prove that the unreasonableness causing the accident was that of the defendant. Assume that a soda bottle explodes in the plaintiff's hands. At the time of this accident, the bottle may no longer be in the exclusive control of the manufacturer. Yet, res ipsa loquitur is still possible in negligence suits of this kind.[2] It is true that before the bottle reached the consumer, it passed through several hands in addition to the manufacturer. A trucking company, for example, as well as one or more distributor/retailers will have made some contact with the bottle. It is admittedly difficult for the consumer to prove via res ipsa that it was the manufacturer's unreasonableness that was responsible for the explosion of the bottle. The law, however, tends to be somewhat lenient on plaintiffs in such cases, knowing the tremendous problem of proof that they have. The second element of res ipsa can still apply if the plaintiff submits enough evidence to enable a jury to conclude that the explosion was *probably not* due to anyone else in the chain between the manufacturer and consumer. Examples of such evidence include:

- evidence of careful handling of the bottle once it left the manufacturer, or the absence of evidence of careless handling during this time
- no evidence the bottle was dropped once it left the manufacturer
- no evidence of cracks on the bottle
- no improper storage indicated

ROBERT FARRELL

Such evidence, although fairly weak in itself, is usually sufficient to permit a jury to rationally eliminate other potential causes so as to conclude that it is more likely than not that the unreasonableness of the defendant (here, the manufacturer) caused the accident (exploding bottle). If, of course, there is strong specific evidence to the contrary (e.g., evidence of vandalism or dropping since it left the hands of the manufacturer), the plaintiff will have great difficulty establishing the second element of res ipsa.

---

[2]Additional theories of liability against the manufacturer include strict liability in tort and breach of warranty. See Chapter 17.

■ ASSIGNMENT 12.3 ■

Richard is a customer in Karen's supermarket. He slips on a banana peel near the door and is injured. What are the *possible* explanations for the banana peel being on the floor? Are all the explanations based upon someone's unreasonableness? Explain. What is the likelihood that the presence of the peel is due to the unreasonableness of Karen? What evidence would you try to use to eliminate other causal possibilities? (See General Instructions for the Legal Analysis Assignment in Chapter 3, and for the Investigation Strategy Assignment in Chapter 4.)

2. What if more than one person is sued and not all of them could have caused the accident? The classic res ipsa case involving multiple defendants is *Ybarra v. Spangard,*[3] in which a patient received an injury while unconscious. The patient sued all the doctors, nurses, and other hospital employees involved. Since the plaintiff was unconscious at the time of the injury, there was no way for the plaintiff to give direct testimony about which of the defendants was or was not responsible. Hence, according to our test on the second element of res ipsa, the plaintiff cannot show it is more likely than not that the unreasonableness of any of the individual defendants caused the injury. Remarkably, however, the court in *Ybarra* allowed the application of res ipsa loquitur against all of the defendants. This had the practical effect of forcing these defendants to decide among themselves who was responsible. Failing to do this, they would all be jointly and severally liable (p. 258) to the plaintiff.

Not all states follow the *Ybarra* case. Many would deny the application of res ipsa in such cases because of the difficulty of establishing the second element. It has been argued that the unusual ruling in *Ybarra* was due to the special duty of care medical personnel owe patients and to the fact that in *Ybarra* there was a pre-existing relationship among all the defendants.[4]

■ ASSIGNMENT 12.4 ■

Shepardize *Ybarra v. Spangard,* 25 Cal.2d 486, 154 P.2d 687 (1944) in order to find out if its ruling has been adopted in your state. (If your state is California, choose any other state to do this assignment.) Has *Ybarra* been cited by courts in your state? If so, go to the reporters to which *Shepard's* refers you and read what the cases in these reporters have said about *Ybarra.* Do any of these cases involve multiple defendants in a res ipsa issue? If so, summarize one of the opinions. Show how the court resolved this issue.

Plaintiff Is Not a Responsible Cause of the Accident

The final element of res ipsa the plaintiff must establish is that the plaintiff was not the responsible cause of the accident. In the vast majority of cases, this means little more than plaintiff's showing no contributory negligence (or more accurately, showing that the plaintiff's own unreasonableness, if any, did not cause the accident). In bottle explosion cases, for example, plaintiff must show that while holding the bottle, he or she did not mishandle or drop it.

---

[3]25 Cal.2d 486, 154 P.2d 687 (1944).
[4]*Prosser & Keeton on Torts,* 5th ed., 252 (1984).

▪ ASSIGNMENT 12.5 ▪

a. In the digests of West Publishing Company, find the key topics and numbers assigned to res ipsa loquitur. Use the American Digest System, or the regional digest covering your state (if any), or the digest devoted exclusively to your state in order to find any four cases on res ipsa loquitur decided by a court of your state. Try to find two cases in which res ipsa was applied and two in which it was denied. Go to the reporters containing these four cases. Briefly summarize the facts of each case and how each case handled the res ipsa issues.

b. Use the *ALR Index* covering *ALR, ALR2d, ALR3d, ALR4th, and ALR5th* to try to find one annotation in *each* of these five sets on res ipsa loquitur. Cite all five annotations. Flip through the pages of these annotations to try to find the citation to one case in each annotation written by a state court of your state or a federal court (other than the United States Supreme Court) with jurisdiction over your state.

c. Re-examine the eight fact situations (a)–(h) of assignment 12.2. Select any one of these fact situations and determine whether a court of your state would grant res ipsa loquitur in the fact situation you have selected. (See General Instructions for the State Court Opinion Assignment in Chapter 2.)

d. Draft a complaint covering the fact situation you selected in question (c) above. (See General Instructions for the Complaint Drafting Assignment in Chapter 5.)

CASE

Ward v. Forrester Day Care, Inc.
547 So.2d 410 (1989)
Supreme Court of Alabama

Background: The parents of an 11-week-old child sued a day care center for negligently causing the child's broken arm. The trial court entered summary judgment for the center. The case is now on appeal before the Supreme Court of Alabama.

Decision on Appeal: Reversed and remanded. Res ipsa loquitur can apply.

Opinion of Court

Justice MADDOX delivered the opinion of the court . . .

On April 29, 1987, Radney Garrett Ward, an 11-week-old baby boy, was left at Forrester day care center in Dothan, operated by the defendant. The parents of baby Garrett, Radney Ward, Sr., and Margaret Ward, did not see their child until approximately 5:30 or 6:00 that afternoon, when he was picked up by Radney Ward, Sr. When the child was lifted out of his chair that afternoon, he screamed "a very unusual scream," according to the plaintiffs, causing them to suspect that something was wrong with him. The Wards said they examined him to determine if something was wrong with him, but they could not discover what caused him to scream. The next day, the child was brought back to Forrester day care center and was left for the day. Mr. and Mrs. Ward said that when Garrett was taken home on the afternoon of April 30, they noticed swelling on his right wrist. The next morning, they took young Garrett to his pediatrician, Dr. Barron, who instructed them to take him to

Dr. Owen, a local orthopedic surgeon, and have his arm X-rayed. Dr. Owen examined the child and discovered that his arm had been broken. The parents sued Forrester Day Care, Inc.

Mr. and Mrs. Ward both testified in depositions that their child was not injured while under their care and that the only other place he had been cared for was Forrester day care center. Employees of Forrester testified that the baby was not injured while at the Forrester day care center. The same employees also testified about the operations of the center, the tendencies of their evidence being to indicate that there was no negligence.

In contrast to the testimony of the Forrester employees, Mr. and Mrs. Ward both testified in their depositions that they had witnessed conditions at the center that they contend showed the Center was improperly operated. The Wards testified in their depositions concerning several conditions that they say were potentially dangerous and could have caused the injury to their child, or to any other child under the care of the Forrester day care center. However, there is no evidence that shows the exact cause of the child's broken arm.

The plaintiffs' position is that the defendant's employees have adopted a "conspiracy of silence" and that that conspiracy should not remove their legal remedy for the injury suffered by Garrett while at the day care center. The Wards ask us to apply the doctrine of *res ipsa loquitur*. . . .

Defendant argues that "[w]here the act or instrumentality causing the injury is unknown, there is no basis for the application of the doctrine of res ipsa loquitur," citing *McClinton v. McClinton*, 258 Ala. 542, 63 So.2d 594 (1952), and *Viking Motor Lodge, Inc. v. American Tobacco Co.*, 286 Ala. 112, 237 So.2d 632 (1970). Defendant correctly states the plaintiff's usual burden of proof, but a plaintiff is not required in every case to show a specific instrumentality that caused the injury. The drafters of comments (f) and (g) to the Re-

statement (Second) of Torts § 328D (1965) state that in making the negligence point to the defendant, this is usually done by showing that a specific instrumentality has caused the event, or that *"all reasonably probable causes were under the exclusive control of the defendant."* (Emphasis added.) The commentators note that "[i]t is not, however, necessary to the inference that the defendant have such exclusive control; and exclusive control is merely one way of proving his responsibility." Restatement (Second) of Torts § 328D.

In this case, the plaintiffs claim that the defendant was guilty of negligent supervision. As a general rule, a plaintiff who can prove his case by specific acts of negligence cannot avail himself of the doctrine of *res ipsa loquitur*. We do not believe that rule is applicable here.

In *Zimmer v. Celebrities, Inc.*, 44 Colo. App. 515, 519, 615 P.2d 76, 79–80 (1980), the Court addressed this question, as follows:

"Defendant also contends that res ipsa loquitur is inapplicable in this case because plaintiffs have argued and introduced some evidence that defendant was negligent in supervision of the nursery. Defendant reasons that negligent supervision would be a specific act of negligence and therefore res ipsa is not applicable. We do not agree. *Kitto v. Gilbert*, 39 Colo.App. 374, 570 P.2d 544 (1977), is dispositive of this issue. In that case we held that:

" 'Res ipsa loquitur is a rule which presumes evidence which applies when it is judicially determined that a particular unexplained occurrence creates a prima facie case of negligence without proof of specific misfeasance. . . . A corollary requirement is that no direct evidence exists establishing that a specific act of negligence was *the only likely cause* for the harm. . . . *The mere introduction of evidence as to how an accident could have occurred and its possible causes* does not necessarily preclude application of res ipsa loquitur so long as that evidence does not clearly resolve the issue of culpability.' "

39 Colo.App. at 379, 570 P.2d at 548 (emphasis added except the word 'possible'.)

"Even though evidence was offered concerning the probabilities of the injury being caused by a piece of equipment or by inadequate supervision on the premises, there was no direct evidence establishing a specific act of negligence which was the only likely cause of the injury, and the evidence presented did not resolve the issue of culpability."

44 Colo.App. at 519, 615 P.2d at 79–80.

We hold that the mere introduction of evidence as to how an accident could have occurred and its possible causes does not necessarily preclude the application of the doctrine of *res ipsa loquitur* so long as that evidence does not clearly resolve the issue of culpability.

Based on the foregoing, we hold that the trial court erred in entering summary judgment for the defendant. Reversed and remanded.

▪ ASSIGNMENT 12.6 ▪

a. Who had exclusive control of the baby during the time of the injury? The Wards took the baby home and returned him to the center the next day after hearing the "very unusual scream" at the center. Was there exclusive control by the defendant? If not, how can the Wards use res ipsa loquitur?

b. The Smiths are about to go on a two-week vacation. They take their pet poodle to the Dog Vacation Home. When they return, the manager of the Home says that the dog unfortunately died and had to be cremated. The manager does not know why it died. The caretaker at the Dog Vacation Home came in one morning and found it dead in its cage. Does res ipsa loquitur apply?

▪ CUSTOM AND USAGE

Often in a negligence case the plaintiff alleges that the defendant failed to take specific precautionary steps and that this failure led to the plaintiff's injury. For example:

- the failure to place a safety guard on a bicycle wheel
- the failure to build a fence alongside a railroad track
- the failure to use a rubber mat in front of a store
- the failure to have two-way radios in tugboats
- the failure to perform a medical test to detect a certain disease

A common response of the defendant in these cases is that no one else in the field takes these steps. The defendant is saying: "a reasonable person in my position would not have taken these steps; it is the custom in the field to act the way I acted." Hence, the question becomes: When is it reasonable to do what everyone else is doing or to fail to do something when everyone else fails to do it as well?

As indicated in Figure 12.1, what is reasonable depends on a wide variety of circumstances. One of these circumstances is what others are doing. It may be unreasonable, for example, to expect a defendant to take a very expensive precaution that no other person in the defendant's position has ever taken and that is designed to avoid the small risk of very minor injury. On the other hand, it may be that an entire industry or profession is being unreasonable in failing to take a certain precautionary step. They may be acting unreasonably in spite of the fact that everyone is doing it. To let them off the hook would provide little incentive to raise their standards.

Recall the breach-of-duty equation: The foreseeability of injury must be balanced against the extent of the burden or inconvenience of taking precautions against the injury occurring. (See Figure 12.4.) The more foreseeable the danger of serious injury, the more reasonable it is for the defendant to bear the burden or inconvenience of trying to prevent the injury. This principle helps us assess the impact of **custom and usage.**

We need to ask *why* the business or profession acted or failed to act in a certain way. Suppose a company manufactures a product, but does not add a device that would protect the public against a particular kind of injury. Suppose further that this is the custom in the industry—no manufacturer adds the device. Why isn't the device added? Because the injury is very rare? If so, this is relevant to the foreseeability of danger in the breach-of-duty equation. Because of the cost of adding the device? Would the price to the consumer be so high that only the wealthy could afford the product with the device? Because of a loss of effectiveness? If the device were added, would the product be significantly less effective in its primary function? These questions are relevant to the burden/inconvenience component of the breach-of-duty equation.

In short, the most you can say is that custom and usage is *a* relevant factor in the law of negligence, but it almost never settles the question of what is reasonableness or unreasonableness.

▪ VIOLATION OF STATUTE, ORDINANCE, OR REGULATION (S/O/R)

When an accident occurs and the defendant is sued for negligence, the plaintiff tries to establish that the defendant acted unreasonably. The plaintiff may be successful even if the defendant did not violate a statute, regulation, or ordinance (referred to collectively as S/O/R). But suppose that there *was* a violation of an S/O/R, such as a traffic ordinance, a criminal statute on keeping a wild animal in the home, or a civil building code requirement. How does this affect the negligence suit? Does the violation make it easier for the plaintiff to establish that the defendant violated the standard of care of reasonableness? Unfortunately, the text of the S/O/R will almost never say anything explicit about negligence.

A seven-part analysis is used to determine how a court will handle an S/O/R in a negligence action:

1. State what the defendant did or failed to do that allegedly caused the accident.
2. Do legal research to find out if any statutes, ordinance, or regulations (S/O/Rs) might apply.
3. Carefully examine the text of any S/O/R uncovered in legal research. Thoroughly analyze it. Determine whether the S/O/R was *violated.*
4. If so, determine whether the violation of the S/O/R *caused* the accident.
5. If so, determine whether the plaintiff was within the *class of persons* the S/O/R was intended to protect.
6. If so, determine whether the S/O/R was intended to avoid the *kind of harm* the plaintiff suffered.
7. If so, do legal research to determine whether your state considers the violation of this type of S/O/R to be negligence (unreasonableness) per se, a presumption of negligence (unreasonableness), or simply some evidence of negligence (unreasonableness).

At the end of this section you will find a flowchart (Figure 12.8) on how these seven steps fit together.

It is important to keep in mind that a plaintiff's failure to establish the S/O/R as the standard of care does *not* mean that the defendant wins the case. What the defendant did or failed to do may be found by a court to have been unreasonable *independent* of any S/O/R. A given accident may involve hundreds or thousands of facts, only a small portion of which may be relevant to a certain S/O/R. Suppose a statute requires farmers to place a fence around certain kinds of animals. No fence is erected and the plaintiff is injured by one of the farmer's animals. It may be that after we go through the seven-part analysis listed above, we will come to the conclusion that a court would *not* adopt the statute as the standard of reasonable conduct because, for example, the plaintiff was not within the class of persons intended to be protected by the legislature when it wrote the statute. This would eliminate the statute from the case. It is *still* possible, however, that the court will find that the defendant acted unreasonably in failing to erect the fence. If so, it will not be due to the existence of the statute; it will be due to the court's application of the breach-of-duty equation, in which the absence of a fence is but one of the factors that enter into the balancing required by the equation (see Figure 12.4)

We now turn to an examination of the seven steps that are most likely to present difficulties.

Was the S/O/R Violated?

Suppose a local traffic statute reads: "No motor vehicle can travel more than 25 mph in a thickly settled district." An accident occurs when the defendant is driving his motorcycle downtown at 30 mph. The motorcycle collides with the car of the plaintiff, who then sues the defendant for negligence. The plaintiff wants the court to conclude that reasonable care under the circumstances would have been to drive 25 mph or less, according to the statute. The first question is whether the statute was violated. Is a motorcycle a "motor vehicle" under the statute? What is a "thickly settled district"? Was the defendant in such a district at the time of the accident? These are questions of **legislative intent:** what was the legislature's intention when it passed the law? Prior case law interpreting the statute may be helpful to determine legislative intent. Tracing the legislative history of the statute may also be helpful in finding intent.

The ball game is not over for the plaintiff if the defendant convinces a court that the statute was not violated. Independent of the statute, the plaintiff may be able to show that the defendant was driving unreasonably, given the totality of circumstances. Assume the defendant is successful in arguing that the legislature did not intend to include a motorcycle as a "motor vehicle." The statute is out of the case, but the plaintiff may still be able to show (by the breach-of-duty equation) that going 30 mph on a motorcycle was unreasonable in the circumstances (e.g., road conditions, the level of traffic).

Did the Violation Cause the Accident?

There was a time when all American males of a certain age were required by statute to carry a draft card on their person. Suppose such a person injures someone in a car accident while he is not carrying his draft card. The defendant has clearly violated the draft card statute. But this is not relevant to the accident. Not having a draft card certainly did not cause the car accident.

Use the but-for test or the substantial-factor test to determine whether the violation of the S/O/R caused the accident. If there had been no violation (i.e., "but for" the violation), would the accident still have occurred? If so, then the violation did not cause the accident. When more than one possible cause exists, the test is whether the violation was a substantial factor (along with other factors) in producing the accident. If not, then the violation did not cause the accident.

Licensing S/O/Rs often raise causation questions:

- You are in a traffic accident at a time when your driver's license is expired.
- You are a doctor whose license has been suspended and you are sued for a medical injury you caused while you were without a license.
- You are a contractor who fails to obtain the required permit to build a house; you are sued when the house collapses and injures the owner.

In most of these license cases, it cannot be said that the violation caused the harm. You may have had the same mishap if you had had the driver's license, doctor's license, or building permit. It is very weak to argue that because you did not have the license, you probably were incompetent in what you were doing. Competence is determined by a host of other factors, e.g., age, prior experience, training. It cannot be said that simply because you did not have a license, you acted unreasonably in doing what you did. Competent doctors, for example, do not automatically become incompetent the day after their medical licenses expire.

Let's look at a closer case. Assume that there is an ordinance requiring handrails on the stairs of every restaurant facility. A customer at a restaurant slips and falls on the stairs where there are no handrails. There appears to be a clear violation of the ordinance. But did the violation *cause* the fall? The answer appears to be yes. To be sure, however, we need to know more facts in order to determine whether the fall would have occurred even if there were handrails, or if their absence was a substantial factor in the fall. For example, how quickly did the accident happen? How wide were the steps, and where was the plaintiff at the time of the fall? If the plaintiff fell in the center of very wide steps, it may have been impossible to have reached handrails if they were available.

· ASSIGNMENT 12.7 ·

A statute requires department stores to report all accidents occurring on elevators to a city agency. Over the years, the XYZ department store has never reported accidents on some of its elevators. Recently, a customer was injured on one of the XYZ elevators. The customer sues the XYZ store for negligence. The customer bases its entire breach-of-duty claim on the violation of the statute. Discuss causation. (See General Instructions for the Legal Analysis Assignment in Chapter 3.)

Is Plaintiff Within the Class of Persons Protected by the S/O/R?

It is not enough that the plaintiff establishes a violation of an S/O/R, which is the cause of the injury suffered by the plaintiff. More analysis of the intent of the

S/O/R is needed to determine whether the plaintiff is the kind of person the S/O/R was designed to protect.

Suppose that you have a statute requiring factories to have certain safety devices on machines. A factory violates the statute by not installing these devices. One day a salesperson happens to be in the factory and is injured while walking past one of the machines. Assume that there is no causation problem, in that the salesperson can prove that "but for" the failure to have the safety device, the accident would not have occurred. The question then becomes: Who was the statute designed to protect? Only factory employees? If so, the breach of statute cannot be the basis of the salesperson's claim that the factory was unreasonable (negligent). Was it designed to protect *anyone* who is in the factory on business? If so, the salesperson can use the statute.

Your job is to raise these questions about the meaning of the statute (or ordinance or regulation) potentially involved in the accident. You try to obtain answers to such questions by your own common-sense reading of the S/O/R, by trying to find cases interpreting the S/O/R, and by tracing legislative history when the provision is a statute. The main point is: Do not assume plaintiff has established breach of duty (unreasonableness) just because he or she has shown a violation of an S/O/R that caused the injury.

▪ ASSIGNMENT 12.8 ▪

An ordinance in the city requires all vacant lots to be fenced at all times. Tom owns a vacant lot in the city, which has no fence. One day a stranger cuts through Tom's lot and injures himself by falling into a hole that is very difficult to see. The stranger sues Tom for negligence. What breach-of-duty argument will the stranger make based on the ordinance? What will Tom's response be? (See General Instructions for the Legal Analysis Assignment in Chapter 3.)

Again, it is important that you do careful legal research in order to find out how the S/O/R has been interpreted by the courts, if at all, and what historically was the reason for the passage of the S/O/R. Some courts will take very narrow readings of the S/O/R (called a **strict construction**) and limit the class of people the S/O/R was intended to protect. Other courts may be more inclined to a liberal reading of the S/O/R and include within its protection any person who reasonably fits within the language of the S/O/R and who might reasonably have been expected to be hurt in any way if there was a violation.

Was the S/O/R Intended to Avoid this Kind of Harm?

Closely related to the kind-of-plaintiff problem just discussed is the question of whether the S/O/R was meant to cover the kind of harm or injury the plaintiff suffered.

Examples:

▪ A statute requires all traffic to drive under 55 mph on the highways. Defendant crashes into plaintiff while defendant is driving 65 mph. *Is the purpose of statute* to:
  a. Save lives?
  b. Save gas?

▪ A statute requires employers to have sprinkler systems in good repair at all times. One day the sprinkler system at a plant malfunctions. It

is activated even though no fire exists. The entire plant is flooded. An employee, who is laid off because of the flood, sues the employer for lost wages due to the breach of the statute. *Is the purpose of statute* to:
a. Avoid personal injuries in case of fire?
b. Avoid economic loss due to flooding?

• A statute requires that all commercial poison be stored in properly designated containers. A business fails to use the right containers. One day the box containing the poison explodes because it was stored too close to heat. The explosion would not have occurred if the correct containers had been used. A customer is injured by the explosion. *Is the purpose of statute* to:
a. Prevent people (or animals) from being poisoned?
b. Prevent explosions?

If the S/O/R was not intended to cover the kind of harm that resulted, the plaintiff cannot use the breach of the S/O/R as the basis of the breach-of-duty argument. As we said before, however, even if the S/O/R was not intended to cover what happened, plaintiff should still try to establish unreasonableness as if the S/O/R did not exist. In the poison example, even if the statute was not intended to cover explosions, a court could still find that the defendant was unreasonable in the method used to store the poison if, according to the breach-of-duty equation, the danger of explosion was highly foreseeable and the burden or inconvenience on the defendant of preventing this danger by proper storage was minimal.

Negligence Per Se? Presumption of Negligence? Some Evidence of Negligence?

Once the plaintiff has gone through all the hurdles of establishing violation, causation, class of person protected, and kind of harm, how will the court use the statute, ordinance, or regulation (S/O/R)? Here again, legal research into the case law of your state is necessary. A number of possibilities exist:

Negligence (Unreasonableness) Per Se
The violation is **negligence per se** (or unreasonableness per se). This means that the jury *must* find unreasonableness. The jury will not be permitted to consider any arguments by the defendant that he or she was in fact reasonable in spite of the violation.

Presumption of Negligence (Unreasonableness)
The **presumption** is rebuttable. The jury must find that the violation by the defendant was unreasonable *unless* the defendant has introduced convincing evidence that she or he was reasonable in spite of the violation.

Evidence of Negligence (Unreasonableness)
The violation is simply some evidence of unreasonableness, which the jury is free to accept or reject, as with any other kind of evidence.

In many states, a court will find that the violation of the statute, ordinance, or regulation is negligence (unreasonableness) per se. Some courts, however, may not go this far if the provision is a regulation of an administrative agency, such as a health department. As indicated, legal research is needed in each state on this question.

Figure 12.8 presents an overview of the seven-part analytical process we have just examined.

Figure 12.8 How to Determine Whether a Statute, Ordinance, or Regulation (S/O/R) Will Become the Standard of Care in a Negligence Action

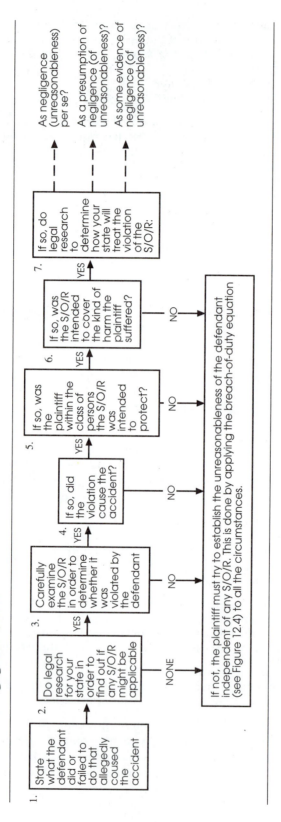

■ ASSIGNMENT 12.9 ■

a. Go to any digest published by West that covers the courts of your state. Use the Descriptive Word Index to find out what key topics and numbers cover breach of statute, ordinance, or regulation in a negligence case.

b. Select any three cases decided by courts of your state involving the alleged violation of a statute, ordinance, or regulation in a negligence action. Briefly summarize these cases.

c. On page 252 there are a number of examples involving the violation of a statute, ordinance, or regulation in a negligence action. Select any one of them and draft a complaint based upon the facts of that example. (See General Instructions for the Complaint Drafting Assignment in Chapter 5.)

■ ASSIGNMENT 12.10 ■

Prepare an annotated bibliography on violation of an S/O/R in a negligence case for your state. (See General Instructions for the Annotated Bibliography Assignment in Chapter 2.)

CASE

Potts v. Fidelity Fruit & Produce Co., Inc.
165 Ga.App. 546, 301 S.E.2d 903 (1983)
Court of Appeals of Georgia

Background: There are spiders on bananas of Fidelity Fruit & Produce Company in violation of the Georgia Food Act. An employee is bitten by one of the spiders while unloading them from a truck. He sues for negligence. The trial court enters a summary judgment in favor of the company. The employee, now the appellant, appeals to the Court of Appeals of Georgia.

Decision on Appeal: Judgment affirmed. Violation of the Georgia Food Act cannot be the basis of a negligence action by an employee.

Opinion of Court

Judge BANKE delivered the opinion of the court. . . .

In determining whether the violation of a statute or ordinance is negligence *per se* as to a particular person, it is necessary to examine the purposes of the legislation and decide (1) whether the injured person falls within the class of persons it was intended to protect and (2) whether the harm complained of was the harm it was intended to

guard against. *Rhodes v. Baker,* 116 Ga.App. 157, 160, 156 S.E.2d 545 (1967); *Huckabee v. Grace,* 48 Ga.App. 621, 636, 173 S.E. 744 (1933). Having examined the provisions of the Georgia Food Act, we agree fully with the following analysis made by the trial court: "Clearly, the Act is a consumer protection act, designed not to render the workplace a safe environment, but to prevent the sale and distribution of adulterated or misbranded foods to consumers. While safety in the workplace, and compensation for injuries arising out of work activities, are indeed matters of contemporary concern, they are the subject of other legislative enactments on both the state and federal level." Because the appellant's alleged injuries did not arise incident to his consumption of the bananas, we hold that the trial court was correct in concluding that the Act affords him no basis for recovery.

Judgment affirmed.

▪ ASSIGNMENT 12.11 ▪

a. What if the employee ate one of the bananas while unloading them from the truck, and then was bitten by the spider. Would the *Potts* case reach the same result?

b. Assume that there was no violation of a statute in this case. Would the company be liable for negligence due to the spider bite?

▪ COMPLIANCE WITH STATUTE, ORDINANCE, OR REGULATION (S/O/R)

Thus far we have seen that just because a defendant has *violated* an S/O/R, it does not necessarily mean the defendant was unreasonable. We now look at the converse problem. If a defendant can show *compliance* with an S/O/R, does it necessarily mean he or she acted reasonably at the time the accident occurred? *No*, but compliance can be strong evidence of reasonableness.

Suppose, for example, that a safety regulation of an administrative agency requires railroad companies to place flashing red lights at all points where tracks cross public highways. The fact that the railroad complies with this regulation and has the lights in place does not guarantee that a court will find that the railroad acted reasonably. Suppose an accident occurs at a corner where the lights are working, but it is clear that much more is needed by the railroad to prevent injuries because of the large number of accidents in the past at this same intersection. In such a case, the regulation amounts only to the *minimum* conduct expected of the railroad. Reasonableness may have called for additional precautions, e.g., a swing gate, an alarm, or an attendant on duty at the intersection during times of heavy traffic. The railroad is not off the hook simply by showing compliance with the regulation. Similarly, a motorist traveling 30 mph who causes an accident cannot claim that he or she was driving at a reasonable speed simply because he or she was well within the speed limit of 45 mph. Compliance is evidence of reasonableness, but it is not conclusive.

To summarize, the S/O/R merely sets the minimum standard of conduct, but reasonableness under the circumstances might call for more than what the S/O/R requires.

▪ GROSS NEGLIGENCE (UNREASONABLENESS) AND WILFUL, WANTON, AND RECKLESS CONDUCT

Statutes exist in many states covering special negligence cases, such as that of a *guest* injured in an automobile.

> **Example:** Mary is on her way to the post office. Her neighbor asks Mary if he could have a ride, since he also needs to go to the post office. Mary agrees. On the way, Mary negligently hits a tree. The neighbor is injured and sues Mary for negligence.

The neighbor is a guest in Mary's car—he did not pay for the ride and there is no indication that Mary derived any benefit from the neighbor's presence in the car other than social companionship. There are **guest statutes** in many states that make it difficult for guests to sue their automobile hosts. Such statutes require guests to prove a greater degree of negligence (unreasonableness) than in non-guest/host suits. **Ordinary negligence** (unreasonableness) is not enough. The following are some of the terms used to describe the degree of negligence (unreasonableness) a guest must prove:

Gross Negligence (Unreasonableness)
> The failure to use even a small amount of care to avoid foreseeable harm.

Wilful, Wanton, and Reckless Conduct
> Having knowledge that harm will probably result from one's actions or inactions (harm is *very* foreseeable).

In our tree case involving Mary and the neighbor, if Mary simply failed to do what an ordinary, reasonable person would have done to avoid the tree, the neighbor would lose his negligence action in a state that imposes standards such as those just listed. To be grossly negligent or reckless, Mary would have had to be drunk at the time, or be traveling 60 mph in a 20 mph zone before hitting the tree.

As we shall see later, **gross negligence** (unreasonableness) or **wilful, wanton, and reckless conduct** will often be the basis for awarding punitive damages in a negligence case.

▪ ASSIGNMENT 12.12 ▪

a. Is there a guest statute in your state? If so, give its citation and summarize its major provisions. If the word "guest" is defined in the statute, give the definition. (See General Instructions for the State Code Assignment in Chapter 2.)

b. Matthew is driving from one city to another in your state. The distance is 50 miles. His best friend, George, asks Matthew if he could drive him to a point midway between the two cities. Matthew is delighted to do him this favor, since he enjoys his company very much. When they reach the point where George is to get off, the latter gives Matthew $5 as a contribution toward the cost of gas. As George is getting out, Matthew carelessly steps on the accelerator, injuring George. George sues Matthew for negligence in your state. What is the standard of care that would apply in this case? (See General Instructions for the State Court Opinion Assignment and for the State Code Assignment, both in Chapter 2.)

c. Go to the multi-volume dictionary called *Words and Phrases*. Find out if there are any definitions of the following words written by courts of your state: gross negligence, wilful, wanton, and reckless. If so, state the definitions and the citations to the cases providing them.

d. Go to the *Index to Legal Periodicals*, the *Current Law Index*, or the *Legal Resource Index*. Find any three legal periodical articles dealing with any aspect of guest statutes. Give the citations of all three articles.

e. Go to *ALR, ALR2d, ALR3d, ALR4th, and ALR5th*. Try to find two annotations in any of these sets that cover any aspect of the guest statute. Give the citations of the annotations.

▪ VICARIOUS LIABILITY

"Vicarious" means taking the place of another. Vicarious negligence, or more accurately, vicarious unreasonableness, means that one person will be found to be unreasonable solely because someone else is unreasonable. Other terms used

Figure 12.9   Vicarious Unreasonableness

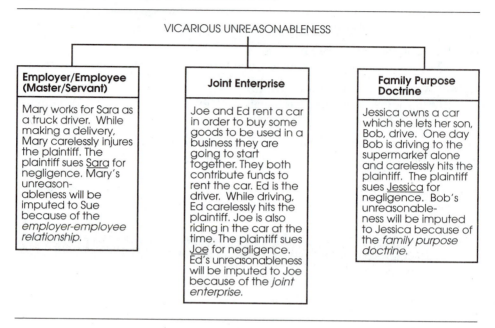

to mean the same thing include **vicarious liability** and **imputed negligence.** Again, since we are discussing only one element of negligence—breach of duty— it is more accurate to say: imputed unreasonableness. The unreasonableness of one person is imputed or *thrust upon* another person, even though the latter did nothing wrong or unreasonable. The three types of vicarious unreasonableness we will consider are outlined in Figure 12.9.

Vicarious liability is not automatic in the three situations of Figure 12.9. As we shall see, there are tests that must be applied before this liability can be imposed.

Two major points need to be kept in mind as we explore each of the three forms of vicarious unreasonableness. The first deals with who can be sued, and the second deals with the distinction between vicarious liability and independent liability:

Who Can Be Sued?

You will note in the three examples of Figure 12.9 that Sara, Joe, and Jessica were the defendants in the three negligence actions. What about the other three who were more directly responsible for the accidents: Mary, Ed, and Bob? Can they also be sued for negligence? Yes. **Joint and several liability** exists, meaning that the parties can be sued individually or together. Hence the possible actions are:

Plaintiff vs. Sara *or*	Plaintiff vs. Joe *or*	Plaintiff vs. Jessica *or*
Plaintiff vs. Mary *or*	Plaintiff vs. Ed *or*	Plaintiff vs. Bob *or*
Plaintiff vs. Sara and Mary	Plaintiff vs. Joe and Ed	Plaintiff vs. Jessica and Bob

Mary, Ed, and Bob are not off the hook simply because Sara, Joe, and Jessica are vicariously liable. Why then would the plaintiffs want to bring an action against Sara, Joe, and Jessica? The practical answer is the **deep pocket** reality: a plaintiff wants to go after the party with the deepest pocket, i.e., the one who probably has the most money from which a negligence judgment can be satisfied. If vicarious liability exists, the deep pocket strategy can be used. But again, this does not mean that the other parties cannot also be sued, or that both parties cannot be sued together.

Vicarious Liability and Independent Liability

In the three examples in Figure 12.9, there is no indication that the parties vicariously liable (Sara, Joe, and Jessica) did anything wrong, careless, or unreasonable themselves. They were not individually at fault. Suppose, however, that they were, as in the following scenarios.

Employer/Employee Case
- Sara knew that Mary was a poor driver, but let her drive anyway.
- Sara instructed Mary to make the delivery as fast as she could, even if it meant breaking the speed law.
- Sara never bothered to check to determine whether her drivers were properly trained.

Joint Enterprise Case
- Joe knew that Ed was a poor driver, but let him drive anyway.
- The accident happened because Joe carelessly distracted Ed.
- Joe knew that the car was defective; this defect contributed to the accident.

Family Purpose Doctrine Case
- Jessica knew that Bob was a poor driver, but let him drive anyway.
- Jessica instructed Bob to get to the supermarket and back as soon as possible, even if it meant breaking the speed law.
- Jessica knew that the car was defective; this defect contributed to the accident

Now we have *individual* fault on the part of the parties who were not driving. Sara, Joe, and Jessica may be liable for their own negligence as well as vicariously liable.

In the discussion that follows, we will assume that the defendants are not independently liable because of any unreasonableness of their own. Our focus is on vicarious liability only. You should always keep in mind, however, the distinction between vicarious and **independent liability,** because in any given case a defendant may be legitimately faced with both theories of liability.

Employer/Employee

Vicarious liability because of the **employer/employee relationship** (sometimes referred to as the **master/servant relationship**) is often given the Latin name, **respondeat superior,** meaning "look to the man higher up." The underlying principle has been phrased as follows: "He who does a thing through another does it himself."[5] The employer/employee relationship is one example

---

[5]*Prosser & Keeton on Torts,* 5th ed., 499 (1984).

of a broader category called **principal/agent relationships.** Generally, an *agent* is someone who agrees to do something on behalf of another. A *principal* is the person on whose behalf the agent is acting and who has some authority or control over the agent while so acting.

Our study of the vicarious liability of an employer shall center on two questions: 1. When is an employee acting within the scope of employment? and 2. When is defendant vicariously liable for the negligence of his or her independent contractor?

1. When is an employee acting within the scope of employment? The overriding principle is that the employer is vicariously liable for the torts of his or her employee if the latter was acting within the **scope of employment** at the time. A great deal of litigation has resulted from trying to define the phrase "scope of employment." (As we shall see in Chapter 30, the comparable phrase in the law of worker's compensation is, "arising out of and in the course of employment.")

There is no absolute definition of scope of employment. A working definition is as follows:

> Scope of employment is that which is foreseeably done by the employee for the employer under the employer's specific or general control.

Scope of employment is not determined by what the employer has authorized the employee to do, although authorization is one factor a court will consider. Suppose that a boss tells her hardware clerk not to allow a customer to operate the automatic paint mixer. The employee violates this instruction, resulting in an injury to a customer. This violation does not mean respondeat superior will not apply. The boss will still be liable for the negligence of her employee if the latter was acting for the boss, under the latter's control, and if what the employee did should have been foreseeable to the boss because of prior conduct of the employee and the nature of the work.

A major concern of the courts has been the so-called **frolic and detour** of an employee. There is no vicarious liability if the negligent act of the employee was committed while he or she was on a frolic and detour of his or her own. For example, while making a delivery for the company, the employee drives 25 miles out of the way to spend several hours with his girlfriend. While driving out of the latter's garage, he rams the company car into the plaintiff's fence. It is highly unlikely that the plaintiff can win a negligence action against the employer; the accident was not within the scope of employment—the employee was on a frolic and detour of his own. The plaintiff will be limited to a suit against the employee. On a frolic and detour, the employee is acting primarily for his or her personal objectives rather than for the employer's business.

There is a large gray area where courts have had difficulty determining what is within the scope of employment. A number of factors are considered in identifying this scope. The factors are outlined in the scope of employment checklist in Figure 12.10. No single factor is determinative; a court will weigh them all. Although our emphasis has been on negligence liability (vicarious unreasonableness), the factors in the checklist would also be used by a court to determine whether the employer would be liable for any intentional torts committed by the employee, such as battery, fraud, or false imprisonment.

Figure 12.10 Checklist of Factors Used to Define Scope of Employment

A "yes" answer to any of the following interrelated questions would help support a conclusion that the employee acted within the scope of employment. The "conduct" referred to in these questions is what the employee did that accidently resulted in the plaintiff's injury, which is now the basis of the plaintiff's negligence suit against the employer.

1. **Authorization**
   Was the employee's conduct substantially within what the employer authorized the employee to do?
2. **Purpose**
   Was the employee acting to pursue the business interests of the employer? If the employee also had personal objectives in what was done, can it nevertheless be said that the employee was acting *primarily* to pursue the business interests of the employer?
3. **Normalcy**
   Was the employee's conduct common or usual in the job being performed?
4. **Foreseeability**
   Was the conduct of the employee foreseeable to the employer?
5. **Time**
   Was the employee's conduct undertaken substantially within the time of work for the employer?
6. **Place**
   Was the employee's conduct undertaken substantially within the place or locale authorized by the employer for such conduct?
7. **Special Obligation**
   Was the employer engaged in the kind of business on which the courts have historically placed a special obligation for the protection of its customers, e.g., common carriers, innkeepers?
8. **Common Sense**
   As a matter of common sense, can we say that the employee's conduct was within the scope of employment?

▪ ASSIGNMENT 12.13 ▪

Apply the scope of employment checklist of factors in Figure 12.10 to determine whether the employees in the following situations were acting within the scope of their employment at the time of the accident. Identify further fact investigation you may need. In each instance, the plaintiff is suing the employer on a respondeat superior theory. (See General Instructions for the Legal Analysis Assignment in Chapter 3.)

a. The ashes from the employee's cigarette fall onto the plaintiff's fur coat, causing substantial damage. The plaintiff sues for negligence.
b. While making a delivery in a company truck, the employee travels five miles out of the way to visit his ailing mother. He stays three hours. On his way back to the company plant to return the truck, he injures plaintiff in a traffic accident. The plaintiff sues for negligence.

c. The employee is a door-to-door salesperson. At one house, the employee gets into an argument with the plaintiff, who owns the house. The plaintiff calls the employee ''stupid.'' The employee hits the plaintiff, who now sues for battery.

▪ ASSIGNMENT 12.14 ▪

a. In Assignment 12.13, you examined three fact situations. Select any one of them and determine how a court in your state would decide the scope of employment issue. (See General Instructions for the State Court Opinion Assignment in Chapter 2.)
b. Draft a complaint for the fact situation you selected for question (a) above. (See General Instructions for the Complaint Drafting Assignment in Chapter 5.)

2. When is the defendant vicariously liable for the negligence of his or her independent contractor? Different rules apply when the defendant hires an **independent contractor.** The distinction between an employee and an independent contractor is not always easy to draw. Some of the significant points of difference include:

▪ the defendant has less control over the independent contractor than over the employee
▪ the independent contractor has a great deal more discretion over the way the job is done than an employee
▪ the employee is on the payroll of the employer, while the independent contractor is hired primarily to produce a certain product or result without being on the payroll

If, for example, you hire an accountant to help you prepare your annual tax return, the accountant is an independent contractor because of the control, discretion, and payroll points made above. Suppose, however, you own a company and you have a staff of accountants and lawyers "in house." Then the accountants and lawyers would be employees.

The general rule of liability for the torts of independent contractors is presented in Figure 12.11. The exceptions listed in Figure 12.11 do not mean that you are forbidden to hire an independent contractor to perform a non-delegable duty or to undertake inherently dangerous work for you. It simply means that when the independent contractor is hired to do any of these things, you are vicariously liable for the torts of the independent contractor. When doing such work, therefore, the independent contractor is treated as an employee for purposes of vicarious responsibility.

Recall the distinction made above between vicarious liability and independent liability. If the employer is careless in selecting the independent contractor, or otherwise fails to prevent foreseeable harm due to the work of the independent contractor, the employer may be independently (rather than just vicariously) liable for what the independent contractor does.

Figure 12.11   Liability for Torts of Independent Contractors

General Rule
A defendant is not vicariously liable for the torts of his or her independent contractor.

Exceptions
There are two circumstances in which a defendant *will* be liable for the torts committed by his or her independent contractor:
1. the independent contractor is performing certain **non-delegable duties** of the defendant (e.g., a city's duty to keep its streets in repair, a landlord's duty to keep the leased premises safe for business visitors, a duty of a common carrier to transport passengers safely, and other special duties imposed by statute or regulation), or
2. the independent contractor is performing **inherently dangerous** work for the defendant, (e.g., transporting dynamite, keeping vicious animals, conducting fireworks exhibitions).[6]

▪ ASSIGNMENT 12.15 ▪

a. A business hires a construction company to erect a commercial building. While one of the company's executives is driving back from the job site in her car, she carelessly hits Tom's car.
b. A month later, the company is transporting a gigantic derrick along a small county road on the back of a massive trailer. An accident occurs when the derrick falls off the trailer and damages Mary's barn.

Who can sue whom and on what theories? Be sure to discuss vicarious liability, if applicable. (See General Instructions for the Legal Analysis Assignment in Chapter 3). Prepare investigation strategies for each case. (See General Instructions for the Investigation Strategy Assignment in Chapter 4.)

▪ ASSIGNMENT 12.16 ▪

Prepare an annotated bibliography on respondeat superior for your state. (See General Instructions for the Annotated Bibliography Assignment in Chapter 2.)

Joint Enterprise
For parties to be engaged in a **joint enterprise,** the following elements must be present:

1. an express or implied agreement to participate in the enterprise together
2. a common purpose (usually financial or business-related)
3. a mutual right to control the enterprise

In a few states, the agreement can be to go to a picnic or to the zoo. In most states, however, the common purpose must be financial or business-related.

---

[6]Some of these activities may also impose strict liability. See Chapter 17.

The third element has caused the courts the most difficulty. How, for example, do you establish that two people riding in a car for a common business purpose have the same (mutual) right to control the direction and operation of the car?

Mutuality of the right of control is not established simply because both are riding together for a business purpose. There must be more concrete indications that the passenger has the same right to control the direction and operation of the car as the driver. Such indications would include: they rented the car with their joint funds; both own the car; they share expenses on the maintenance of the car; both have driven the car in the past; on this trip they alternate the driving; the passenger is reading the road map and giving route instructions to the driver. The court must be able to find that there was a clear understanding between the parties that both had an equal say in the operation of the car, even if only one party did all the driving at the time the car had the accident injuring the plaintiff. Taking all the factors into consideration, the question is whether it would have been odd, unusual, or presumptuous for the passenger to have exercised the same authority as the driver in the operation of the car. If so, there probably was no joint control.

Once a joint enterprise is established, vicarious liability comes into play. In automobile cases, the passenger is vicariously unreasonable if the driver's unreasonableness caused the accident. In a sense, the joint enterprise is treated as a partnership in which one partner becomes personally liable for the acts of all the other partners. Most joint enterprises, however, are usually more limited in their duration and less structured than the traditional partnership.

▪ ASSIGNMENT 12.17 ▪

Husband and wife are in a car on their way to sign up for a motel training course in which couples are taught the motel business. The car is in both names. The wife is driving. An accident occurs. The third party sues the husband for negligence. How would you determine if there is a joint enterprise? (See General Instructions for the Legal Analysis Assignment in Chapter 3.) Prepare an investigation strategy. (See General Instructions for the Investigation Strategy Assignment in Chapter 4.)

▪ ASSIGNMENT 12.18 ▪

Dr. Jones and Dr. Smith practice medicine separately. During times of vacation, however, they cover for each other's patients. While Dr. Smith is on vacation, Dr. Jones sees one of Dr. Smith's patients. The patient suffers an injury because of negligent treatment by Dr. Jones. Assume that Dr. Jones, unlike Dr. Smith, has no liability insurance and almost no assets. Dr. Smith, therefore, is the ''deep pocket.'' Vicarious liability? Can the patient sue Dr. Smith for the negligence of Dr. Jones? Assume that Dr. Smith had no reason to suspect that Dr. Jones would ever commit negligence. (See General Instructions for the Legal Analysis Assignment in Chapter 2.)

Once a joint enterprise is established, there can also be **imputed contributory negligence.** Compare the following two cases:

Case I (Imputed Negligence)

Driver and passenger are engaged in a joint enterprise on a highway. Driver and third party crash. Third party sues passenger for negligence. The negligence (unreasonableness) of the driver is imputed to the passenger—vicarious unreasonableness.

Case II (Imputed Contributory Negligence)

Driver and passenger are engaged in a joint enterprise on a highway. Driver and third party crash. Both the driver and the third party are negligent (unreasonable). The *passenger* sues the third party for negligence. As a defense, the third party asserts the contributory negligence of the driver. This contributory negligence of the driver is imputed to the passenger-plaintiff in the latter's negligence action against the third party, which in many states will defeat the action. The contributory unreasonableness of the driver is vicariously imposed upon the otherwise innocent passenger-plaintiff solely because of the existence of the joint enterprise.

Family Purpose Doctrine

The final form of vicarious unreasonableness we want to discuss is the family purpose doctrine. Not all states have adopted it. Not all states that have the doctrine agree on the elements that will bring it into operation. Generally, the elements are as follows:

1. Defendant must own the car, or have an ownership interest in it (e.g., co-owner), or control the use of the car.
2. Defendant must make the car available for family use rather than for the defendant's business. (In some states, the defendant must make it available for general family use rather than for a particular occasion.)
3. The driver must be a member of the defendant's immediate household.
4. The driver must be using the car for a family purpose at the time of the accident.
5. The driver must have had the defendant's express or implied consent to be using the car at the time of the accident.

The defendant does not have to be the traditional head of the household and does not have to be in the car at the time of the accident. Again, individual states, by case law or by statute, may impose different elements to the doctrine or may reject it entirely.

■ ASSIGNMENT 12.19 ■

a. Is there a family purpose doctrine in your state? If so, what are its components or elements? (See General Instructions for the State Code Assignment and the State Court Opinion Assignment, both in Chapter 2.)
b. Fred has just bought a used car, but it will not be ready for a week. During the week he is waiting, he rents a car. He pays a per-mile charge on the car. He tells his family that the car is to be used only to drive to work. One day while the car is at home and Fred is at the supermarket, his child becomes sick. Fred's mother, who is staying with Fred until an opening comes up in a local nursing home, drives the child to the hospital. On the way, she has an accident, injuring the plaintiff, a pedestrian. The plaintiff sues Fred for negligence. Apply the five elements listed immediately above to determine whether the family purpose doctrine would apply. (See General Instructions for the Legal Analysis Assignment in Chapter 3.) How would this case be handled in your state? (See question (a) above.)

▪ ASSIGNMENT 12.20 ▪

Prepare an annotated bibliography on the family purpose doctrine for your state. (See General Instructions for the Annotated Bibliography Assignment in Chapter 2.)

NOTE	**The Vicarious Liability of a Parent for the Torts of His or Her Child**

The traditional rule is that a parent is not vicariously liable for the torts of his or her children. If a child commits negligence (or an intentional tort), the child is personally liable. The parent might be individually liable for his or her own negligence in failing to use available opportunities to control a child with known **dangerous propensities** or for actually participating in the unreasonable conduct of the child. This is quite separate from the parent being vicariously liable simply because he or she is the parent of the child who committed the tort. There are statutes in some states, however, that do impose vicarious liability on parents for the torts of their child, but only up to a limited dollar amount, e.g., $1,000. (See Chapter 26.)

▪ MEDICAL MALPRACTICE

Physician-Patient Relationship

A doctor is not required to accept every patient. The physician-patient relationship arises when the doctor undertakes to render services in response to an express or implied request for services by the patient or the patient's guardian. The relationship does not come into existence simply because the doctor provides emergency medical care to an injured person. Yet, in providing such services, the doctor is required to use reasonable care.

Once the physician-patient relationship exists, doctors cannot withdraw at will. They must give reasonable notice of withdrawal to their patients so that the latter have an opportunity to find alternative treatment. Of course, a patient is always free to end the relationship at any time. A client can fire his or her doctor, attorney, or anyone hired to provide a service.

Warranty

Normally a doctor does not warrant or promise a particular result or cure. If such a **warranty** or promise is given, the patient has a breach-of-warranty or breach-of-contract action against the doctor if the result or cure is not produced. Although doctors are understandably reluctant to give express guarantees, they sometimes use language to their patients that a court will interpret as a guarantee. Suppose, for example, that a doctor makes the following statements to a patient about an operation:

"The operation will take care of all your troubles."
"You'll be able to return to work in approximately three or four weeks at the most."

Such language has been interpreted as a promise to cure. If the patient is not cured, a breach-of-contract action may be successful against the doctor *even if the doctor was not negligent in performing the operation.*

A mere opinion by a doctor on the probable results of treatment is not a promise. It is sometimes very difficult, however, to distinguish between a prediction of probabilities and a promise.

Negligence

A doctor can make mistakes and cause injury while performing medical services without being liable. There is no **strict liability,** or liability without fault, for professional services. The patient must show that the mistake was caused wrongfully (e.g., by negligence).

Doctors are held to a standard of reasonable care under the circumstances. Because they have specialized knowledge and skill, the standard is what a reasonable person would have done with that specialized knowledge and skill. A doctor must have the skill and learning commonly possessed by members of the profession in good standing.[7] There is considerable controversy, however, on whether this standard is to be gauged from a national or from a local perspective:

- Is the doctor required to have and use the equipment, knowledge, and experience that doctors have and use nationally? **(national standard)** or,
- Is the doctor required to have and use the equipment, knowledge, and experience that doctors have and use locally or in localities similar to the community where the defendant-doctor practices? **(local standard)**

In assessing reasonable care, one of the considerations of the court is the custom of doctors in treating a particular ailment. Other doctors are often called as expert witnesses for this purpose. If a state has adopted a local standard, a doctor from a big medical facility in the city will not be allowed to give testimony on what sound medical practice is in a small rural town where a local doctor is being sued for malpractice. Most states impose a local standard rather than a national one, although a number of states have moved in the latter direction.

- ASSIGNMENT 12.21 •

Has your state adopted a national or a local standard as the standard of care for suing doctors? (See General Instructions for the State Code Assignment, and the State Court Opinion Assignment, both in Chapter 2.)

Of course, not all doctors agree on the treatment that should be provided in a given case. Schools of thought exist, as in any area. If there is more than one recognized method of diagnosis or treatment, and no one of them is used exclusively and uniformly by all practitioners in good standing, doctors, in the exercise of their best judgment, can select one of the approved methods. Negligence is not established simply because it turns out to be the wrong selection or because other doctors would have used other methods. Again, the test is reasonableness.

---

[7]*Prosser & Keeton on Torts,* 5th ed., 187 (1984).

If more than one approach is reasonable, doctors will not be liable if they make a mistake as long as due diligence and good judgment were otherwise used in the method selected and applied.

■ ASSIGNMENT 12.22 ■

a. What is the statute of limitations for suing doctors in your state?
b. What is the statute of limitations when a patient does not discover that a doctor made a negligent mistake until ten years after the doctor operated on this patient—and the doctor did not discover it until this time either?
c. Same question and facts as in (b), except that the doctor discovered the negligent mistake on the day of the operation, but kept silent about it.

(See General Instructions for the State Code Assignment and the State Court Opinion Assignment, both in Chapter 2.)

In the 1980s, the country faced what was called a medical malpractice crisis (Figure 12.12). Considerable publicity was given to the substantial increases that occurred in the liability insurance premiums paid by doctors. In some areas of the country, doctors withdrew from certain high-risk kinds of practice (e.g., delivering babies) because of the frequency of litigation and the high cost of malpractice insurance associated with these areas of practice. The legal system was given a large part of the blame for the skyrocketing cost of health care. For example, doctors allegedly ordered expensive tests solely to make them "look good" in court in the event of a later malpractice suit by the patient. This became known as the practice of **defensive medicine.**

Insurance companies blamed attorneys, particularly for the **percentage fee,** which allowed them to take a large percentage of a jury award as their fee. This arguably caused attorneys to be excessively aggressive in pursuing litigation for their clients. Attorneys, on the other hand, denied that there was a malpractice insurance crisis, arguing that if there was a problem, it was due to greedy insurance companies and incompetent doctors.

Figure 12.12   Top Ten Allegations of Medical Malpractice by Frequency

1. Surgery/postoperative complications
2. Improper treatment/birth-related
3. Failure to diagnose/cancer
4. Surgery/inadvertent act
5. Failure to diagnose/fracture or dislocation
6. Improper treatment/fracture or dislocation
7. Improper treatment/drug side effect
8. Failure to diagnose/infection
9. Surgery/inappropriate procedure
10. Improper treatment/infection

SOURCE: *St. Paul Fire and Marine Insurance 1988 Report to Policyholders.*

The turmoil has led to change. In some states,

- limitations on damage awards **(damage caps)** and on attorney fees **(fee caps)** were enacted;
- special screening panels or review boards were set up to try to resolve cases without litigation; a case would have to go through this procedure before the courts could be used.

The turmoil—along with proposals for further change and ''reform''—continues today.

- ▪ ASSIGNMENT 12.23 ▪

Has your state established any limitations on suing doctors, e.g., on the procedures that must be followed, on the amount in damages that can be recovered, on attorney fees? If so, summarize these limitations. Include citations to the statutes that imposed them. (See General Instructions for the State Code Assignment in chapter 2.)

Informed Consent

Doctors can commit a battery if they make physical contact with a part of the patient's body without the latter's consent. Most cases, however, are decided under a negligence theory. The patient argues that there was no **informed consent,** in that the doctor negligently failed to inform the patient of the risks involved in what was to be done. This failure allegedly prevented the patient from being able to make an intelligent decision on whether to seek the operation or treatment.

Consent forms are often used by doctors and hospitals as a way of providing information and avoiding liability. At times, however, these forms are inadequate. Suppose that a woman consents to a simple appendectomy. The surgeon, however, performs a total hysterectomy as a precautionary measure, because he feels that it would be a sound medical procedure even though no emergency existed. Before the operation, the woman signed the following statement:

> ''I hereby authorize the physician in charge to administer such treatment and the surgeon to administer such aesthetics as found necessary to perform this operation which is advisable in the treatment of this patient.''

A court would probably find this consent form to be invalid. It is very ambiguous. It does not designate the nature of the operation and therefore does not state what is being consented to. It is close to a blanket authorization to do whatever the doctor thinks is wise.

Suppose that the condition of the patient is such that it would be dangerous to inform him or her of all the details of a proposed treatment. Or suppose that the doctor discovers an unanticipated emergency after the patient is under anesthesia and an incision has been made. How is consent to be handled in these situations? A court will examine all of the circumstances in order to determine whether it was reasonable for the doctor not to obtain consent or even to ask for it. The factors to be considered include: the seriousness of the patient's condition, the patient's emotional stability, the availability of time, the extent of the emergency, the practice in the medical community in such cases. A court might conclude that it was reasonable for the doctor to proceed without consent.

▪ ASSIGNMENT 12.24 ▪

Prepare an annotated bibliography on medical malpractice for your state. (See General Instructions for the Annotated Bibliography Assignment in Chapter 2.)

CASE

Fein v. Permanente Medical Group
38 Cal.3d 137, 211 Cal.Rptr. 368, 695 P.2d 665 (1985)
Supreme Court of California

Background: A nurse practitioner and a doctor told the plaintiff that his chest pains were muscle spasms. Valium and other drugs were prescribed. In fact, the plaintiff was suffering a heart attack. In a medical malpractice action, he alleged negligence in the diagnosis. He was successful in the trial court. The case is now before the Supreme Court of California on appeal.

Decision on Appeal: Judgment affirmed.

Opinion of Court

Justice KAUS delivered the opinion of the court . . .

On Saturday, February 21, 1976, plaintiff Lawrence Fein, a 34-year-old attorney employed by the Legislative Counsel Bureau of the California State Legislature in Sacramento, felt a brief pain in his chest as he was riding his bicycle to work. The pain lasted a minute or two. He noticed a similar brief pain the following day while he was jogging, and then, three days later, experienced another episode while walking after lunch. When the chest pain returned again while he was working at his office that evening, he became concerned for his health and, the following morning, called the office of his regular physician, Dr. Arlene Brandwein, who was employed by defendant Permanente Medical Group, an affiliate of the Kaiser Health Foundation (Kaiser).

Dr. Brandwein had no open appointment available that day, and her receptionist advised plaintiff to call Kaiser's central appointment desk for a "short appointment." He did so and was given an appointment for 4 P.M. that afternoon, Thursday, February 26. Plaintiff testified that he did not feel that the problem was so severe as to require immediate treatment at Kaiser Hospital's emergency room, and that he worked until the time for his scheduled appointment.

When he appeared for his appointment, plaintiff was examined by a nurse practitioner, Cheryl Welch, who was working under the supervision of a physician-consultant, Dr. Wintrop Frantz; plaintiff was aware that Nurse Welch was a nurse practitioner and he did not ask to see a doctor. After examining plaintiff and taking a history, Nurse Welch left the room to consult with Dr. Frantz. When she returned, she advised plaintiff that she and Dr. Frantz believed his pain was due to muscle spasm and that the doctor had given him a prescription for Valium. Plaintiff went home, took the Valium, and went to sleep.

That night, about 1 A.M., plaintiff awoke with severe chest pains. His wife drove him to the Kaiser emergency room where he was examined by Dr. Lowell Redding about 1:30 A.M. Following an examination that the doctor felt showed no signs of a heart problem, Dr. Redding ordered a chest X-ray. On the basis of his examination and the X-ray results, Dr. Redding also concluded that plaintiff was experiencing muscle spasms and gave him an injection of Demerol and a prescription for a codeine medication.

Plaintiff went home but continued to experience intermittent chest pain. About noon that same day, the pain became more severe and constant and plaintiff returned to the Kaiser emergency room where he was seen by another physician, Dr. Donald Oliver. From his initial examination of plaintiff, Dr. Oliver also believed that plaintiff's problem was of muscular origin, but, after administering some pain medication, he directed that an electrocardiogram (EKG) be performed. The EKG showed that plaintiff was suffering from a heart attack (acute myocardial infarction). Plaintiff was then transferred to the cardiac care unit.

Following a period of hospitalization and medical treatment without surgery, plaintiff returned to his job on a part-time basis in October 1976, and resumed full-time work in September 1977. By the time of trial, he had been permitted to return to virtually all of his prior recreational activities—e.g., jogging, swimming, bicycling and skiing.

In February 1977, plaintiff filed the present action, alleging that his heart condition should have been diagnosed earlier and that treatment should have been given either to prevent the heart attack or, at least, to lessen its residual effects. The case went to judgment only against Permanente.

At trial, Dr. Harold Swan, the head of cardiology at the Cedars-Sinai Medical Center in Los Angeles, was the principal witness for plaintiff. Dr. Swan testified that an important signal that a heart attack may be imminent is chest pain which can radiate to other parts of the body. Such pain is not relieved by rest or pain medication. He stated that if the condition is properly diagnosed, a patient can be given Inderal to stabilize his condition, and that continued medication or surgery may relieve the condition.

Dr. Swan further testified that in his opinion any patient who appears with chest pains should be given an EKG to rule out the worst possibility, a heart problem. He stated that the symptoms that plaintiff had described to Nurse Welch at the 4 P.M. examination on Thursday, February 26, should have indicated to her that an EKG was in order. He also stated that when plaintiff returned to Kaiser late that same night with his chest pain unrelieved by the medication he had been given, Dr. Redding should also have ordered an EKG. According to Dr. Swan, if an EKG had been ordered at those times it could have revealed plaintiff's imminent heart attack, and treatment could have been administered which might have prevented or minimized the attack.

Dr. Swan also testified to the damage caused by the attack. He stated that as a result of the attack a large portion of plaintiff's heart muscle had died, reducing plaintiff's future life expectancy by about one-half, to about 16 or 17 years. Although Dr. Swan acknowledged that some of plaintiff's other coronary arteries also suffer from disease, he felt that if plaintiff had been properly treated his future life expectancy would be decreased by only 10 to 15 percent, rather than half.

Nurse Welch and Dr. Redding testified on behalf of the defense, indicating that the symptoms that plaintiff had reported to them at the time of the examinations were not the same symptoms he had described at trial. Defendant also introduced a number of expert witnesses—not employed by Kaiser—who stated that on the basis of the symptoms reported and observed before the heart attack, the medical personnel could not reasonably have determined that a heart attack was imminent. Additional defense evidence indicated (1) that an EKG would not have shown that a heart attack was imminent, (2) that because of the severe disease in the coronary arteries which caused plaintiff's heart attack, the attack could not have been prevented even had it been known that it was about to occur, and finally (3) that, given the deterioration in plaintiff's other coronary arteries, the heart attack had not affected plaintiff's life expectancy to the degree suggested by Dr. Swan.

In the face of this sharply conflicting evidence, the jury found in favor of plaintiff on the issue of liability and, pursuant to the trial court's instructions, returned special verdicts itemizing various elements of damages. The jury awarded $24,733 for wages lost by plaintiff to the time of trial, $63,000 for future medical expenses, and $700,000 for wages lost in the future as a result of the reduction in plaintiff's life expectancy. Finally, the jury awarded $500,000 for "noneconomic damages," to compensate for pain, suffering, inconvenience, physical impairment and other intangible damages sustained by plaintiff from the time of the injury until his death. . . .

[One of the issues on appeal is whether the trial judge properly instructed the jury in the duty of care owed by a nurse practitioner. The judge] told the jury that "the standard of care required of a nurse practitioner is that of a physician and surgeon . . . when the nurse practitioner is examining a patient or making a diagnosis."*

We agree with defendant that this instruction is inconsistent with recent legislation setting forth general guidelines for the services that may properly be performed by registered nurses in this state. Section 2725 of the Business and Professions Code . . . explicitly declares a legislative intent "to recognize the existence of overlapping functions between physicians and registered nurses and to permit additional sharing of functions within orga-

nized health care systems which provide for collaboration between physicians and registered nurses." Section 2725 also includes, among the functions that properly fall within "the practice of nursing" in California, the "[o]bservation of signs and symptoms of illness, reactions to treatment, general behavior, or general physical condition, and . . . determination of whether such signs, symptoms, reactions, behavior or general appearance exhibit abnormal characteristics. . . ." In light of these provisions, the "examination" or "diagnosis" of a patient cannot in all circumstances be said—as a matter of law— to be a function reserved to physicians, rather than registered nurses or nurse practitioners. Although plaintiff was certainly entitled to have the jury determine (1) whether defendant medical center was negligent in permitting a nurse practitioner to see a patient who exhibited the symptoms of which plaintiff complained and (2) whether Nurse Welch met the standard of care of a reasonably prudent nurse practitioner in conducting the examination and prescribing treatment in conjunction with her supervising physician, the court should not have told the jury that the nurse's conduct in this case must as a matter of law be measured by the standard of care of a physician or surgeon. (See *Fraijo v. Hartland Hospital* (1979) 99 Cal.App.3d 331, 340-344, *White—New Approaches in Treating Nurses as Professionals* (1977) 30 Vand.L.Rev. 839, 871-879.)

But while the instruction was erroneous, it is not reasonably probable that the error affected the judgment in this case. As noted, several hours after Nurse Welch examined plaintiff and gave him the Valium that her supervising doctor had prescribed, plaintiff returned to the medical center with similar complaints and was examined by a physician, Dr. Redding. Although there was considerable expert testimony that the failure of the medication to provide relief and the continued chest pain rendered the diagnosis of muscle spasm more questionable, Dr. Red-

---

*The relevant instruction read in full: "It is the duty of one who undertakes to perform the service of a trained or graduate nurse to have the knowledge and skill ordinarily possessed, and to exercise the care and skill ordinarily used in like cases, by trained and skilled members of the nursing profession practicing their profession in the same or similar locality and under similar circumstances. Failure to fulfill either of these duties is negligence. I instruct you that the standard of care required of a nurse practitioner is that of a physician and surgeon duly licensed to practice medicine in the state of California when the nurse practitioner is examining a patient or making a diagnosis." . . .

ding—like Nurse Welch—failed to order an EKG. Given these facts, the jury could not reasonably have found Nurse Welch negligent under the physician standard of care without also finding Dr. Redding—who had more information and to whom the physician standard of care was properly applicable—similarly negligent. Defendant does not point to any evidence which suggests that the award in this case was affected by whether defendant's liability was grounded solely on the negligence of Dr. Redding, rather than on the negligence of both Dr. Redding and Nurse Welch, and, from our review of the record, we conclude that it is not reasonably probable that the instructional error affected the judgment. Accordingly, the erroneous instruction on the standard of care of a nurse practitioner does not warrant reversal. . . .

- ASSIGNMENT 12.25 -

a. 1. What was the error committed by the trial judge on the standard of care of a nurse practitioner? 2. Why was it an error? 3. Why was this error harmless?
b. What implications does this case have for paralegals?

▪ LEGAL MALPRACTICE

When can an attorney be sued for negligence? What is the standard of care? Courts again use the reasonable person test. Because attorneys hold themselves out as persons with special skills, the standard of care will be a reasonable person possessing such skills. Liability for negligence will not automatically result when an attorney makes a mistake or loses the case. Unless the attorney specifically guarantees a result, the standard of care will be reasonableness, not warranty. Expressed in greater detail, the standard is as follows:[8]

> Ordinarily when an attorney engages in the practice of the law and contracts to prosecute an action in behalf of his client, he impliedly represents that (1) he possesses the requisite degree of learning, skill, and ability necessary to the practice of his profession and which others similarly situated ordinarily possess; (2) he will exert his best judgment in the prosecution of the litigation entrusted to him; and (3) he will exercise reasonable and ordinary care and diligence in the use of his skill and in the application of his knowledge to his client's cause.
>
> An attorney who acts in good faith and in an honest belief that his advice and acts are well founded and in the best interest of his client is not answerable for a mere error of judgment or for a mistake in a point of law which has not been settled by the court of last resort in his State and on which reasonable doubt may be entertained by well-informed lawyers.
>
> Conversely, he is answerable in damages for any loss to his client which proximately results from a want of that degree of knowledge and skill ordinarily possessed by others of his profession similarly situated, or from the omission to use reasonable care and diligence, or from the failure to exercise in good faith his best judgment in attending to the litigation committed to his care.

If attorneys hold themselves out to the public as specialists in a particular area of the law (e.g., criminal law or patent law), the standard of competence is not

---

[8]*Hodges v. Carter*, 239 N.C. 517, 519-20, 80 S.E.2d 144, 145-46 (1954).

the general practitioner handling such a case, but the specialist in good standing using the skills and knowledge normally possessed by such specialists. The *Restatement of Torts 2d* phrases the standard this way:[9]

> *Special representation.* An actor undertaking to render services may represent that he has superior skill or knowledge, beyond that common to his profession or trade. In that event he incurs an obligation to the person to whom he makes such a representation, to have, and to exercise, the skill and knowledge which he represents himself to have.

Mistakes

A distinction should be made between:

- a reasonable mistake that could have been made by any attorney in good standing using the skill and knowledge normally possessed by attorneys, and
- an unreasonable mistake that would not have been made by an attorney in good standing using the skill and knowledge normally possessed by attorneys.

Only the latter kinds of mistakes will lead to liability for negligence. (See Figure 12.13.) The test is not whether the average attorney would have made the mistake. The focus is on the attorney in good standing using the knowledge and skills normally found in attorneys.[10]

It is important to keep in mind that the lawyer is the agent of the client. While the lawyer is representing the client (within the scope of the attorney's "employment"), the client is bound by what the attorney does. This includes both successes and mistakes. Hence, if the attorney makes a mistake and the client loses the case as a result, the recourse of the client is to sue the attorney and try to establish that an unreasonable mistake was made that would not have been made by an attorney in good standing using the skill and knowledge normally possessed by attorneys.[11]

There are three basic interrelated errors in the way an attorney practices law that often lead to successful negligence actions against the attorney. Errors in practicing law that can make an attorney vulnerable include:

- **Taking Too Many Cases**
  There are strong temptations to keep adding new cases to the attorney's caseload. Although one might admire "busy" attorneys, the danger exists that they have more than they can competently handle.
- **Failure to Do More Than Minimal Legal Research**
  Legal research can be difficult and time-consuming. It is much easier "to practice out of one's hip pocket." Courts, however, have warned attorneys that the failure to do needed legal research is a strong indication of incompetence.
- **Failure to Consult and/or Associate with More Experienced Attorneys**
  The tendency in legal practice is for an attorney to concentrate on certain kinds of cases—to specialize. Even many general practitioners will emphasize one or two categories of cases in their practice. What happens when the client with

---

[9]*Restatement (Second) of Torts § 299A, comment d (1965).*
[10]*Restatement (Second) of Torts § 229A, comment e (1965).*
[11]Depending on the kind of mistake the attorney made, some courts might permit the client to "undo" the error by correcting it, e.g., permit a client to file a document even though the client's attorney had negligently allowed the deadline for its filing to pass. It is rare, however, that the courts will be this accommodating. A client will have to live with the mistakes of his or her attorney and seek relief solely by suing the attorney for negligence. See R. Mallen & V. Levit, *Legal Malpractice* 45ff (1977).

a new kind of case walks into the office? If the case is taken and the attorney does *not* have enough time to learn the theory and practicalities of a new area of the law, it is strong evidence of incompetence if the attorney fails to consult with attorneys who are experienced in that area of the law, and perhaps, with the client's consent, to work with such an attorney on the case.

Figure 12.13   Mistakes of Attorneys

Kind of Mistake	Examples	Negligence Consequences
1. Technical/mechanical mistake *not* involving the exercise of judgment.	• Attorney forgets to file an action and client is thereby barred by the statute of limitations. • Attorney forgets to appear in court and client thereby has a default judgment entered against him or her.	It is relatively easy for a client to win a negligence action against an attorney based on this kind of mistake. (See, however, the discussion on causation.)
2. Tactical mistake involving the exercise of judgment and discretion in a relatively uncomplicated area of the law.	• Attorney decides not to call a certain witness who would have been able to provide valuable testimony. • Attorney does not object to the introduction of certain evidence at trial from the other side and thereby waives the right to object on appeal.	It is difficult for a client to win a negligence action against an attorney based on this kind of mistake unless what the attorney did or failed to do was blatantly contrary to what would be considered good or competent practice. (See discussion on causation.)
3. Tactical mistake involving the exercise of judgment and discretion in a complicated area of the law.	• Attorney fails to challenge the constitutionality of a guest statute. • Attorney calls an expert witness on a design defect in a products-liability case and the witness gives very damaging testimony to the attorney's own case.	It is almost impossible for a client to win a negligence action against an attorney based on this kind of mistake. This is so not only because of the complexity of the area of the law, but also because of the difficulty of proving causation, i.e., that the mistake caused the client any harm. (See discussion on causation.)

Causation

To win a negligence case against an attorney, it is not enough to establish that the attorney made an unreasonable mistake; causation must also be proven. For certain kinds of attorney errors, a **trial within a trial** must occur.

> **Example:**   George hires John Taylor, Esq. to represent him in a products-liability case against XYZ Motor Company. The car George bought from XYZ exploded, causing $100,000 in injuries to George. John Taylor is so tied up with other cases that he neglects to file the action within the statute-of-limitations period. Hence, George can no longer sue XYZ Motor Company; the action is barred. George now sues John Taylor for negligence (malpractice) in letting the statute of limitations run. Assume that the error of John Taylor was quite unreasonable. What can George recover from John Taylor? $100,000? Is that what he lost? Did John Taylor *cause* $100,000 in damages? The answer is yes—but only if George can establish:
>
> **1.** that he would have won his case against XYZ Motor Company, and,
> **2.** that the recovery from XYZ would have been at least $100,000.
>
> In George's negligence suit against John Taylor, George must establish that he would have received $100,000 in his suit against the XYZ Motor Company if the suit had not been barred by the statute of limitations. This, then, is the suit within the suit, or the trial within a trial.

The difficulty of establishing causation can be further complicated: Suppose XYZ Motor Company is bankrupt. Even if George could have won a $100,000 judgment against XYZ, he would have been able to *collect* nothing or very little. Hence, it cannot be said that John Taylor's negligence in waiting too long to file the action caused George a $100,000 loss. In such circumstances, George would have to prove (in his action against John Taylor) that there would have been something to collect from XYZ Motor Company.

NOTE	Indemnity

Indemnity is the right to have another person pay you the amount you were forced to pay. In tort law, when one party is liable to a plaintiff solely because of what someone else has done (e.g., employer is liable because of what employee did), the party who is liable, and who pays as a result of the liability, can often receive indemnity from the person whose action produced the liability. Assume that an attorney is representing a *defendant* in a suit brought against the latter. Assume further that the defendant loses the suit and must pay the judgment solely because of the negligence of the attorney. In some states, the defendant can ask a court to force the attorney to *indemnify* him or her based upon the above definition of indemnity.[12]

---

[12]R. Mallen & V. Levit, *Legal Malpractice* 124 (1977).

■ ASSIGNMENT 12.26 ■

Karen Smith, Esq. represents Jim Noonan in the preparation of a will. It was Jim's intent that his friend Ralph Skidmore receive a bequest of $10,000. Karen Smith drafts the will. After Jim dies, it is discovered that Karen Smith made a mistake in drafting the will, with the result that Ralph received nothing.

a. Make an argument that Karen Smith did not *cause* a $10,000 loss to Ralph. Assume that Jim died at the age of 35, one year after the will was drafted, and that his death was a surprise to everyone—including Jim.
b. Are there any other problems that might prevent Ralph from being able to bring a negligence action against Karen Smith?

(See General Instructions for the Legal Analysis Assignment in Chapter 3.)

■ ASSIGNMENT 12.27 ■

Review the material in this chapter on res ipsa loquitur. Can you think of a fact situation involving attorney error in which res ipsa loquitur might apply? If so, state the facts and explain how res ipsa might apply.

■ ASSIGNMENT 12.28 ■

Use the digests covering your state courts to find two state court opinions in which an attorney was sued for negligence. Go to the reporter containing the full text of these opinions. Summarize the negligence rulings in them. (See General Instructions for the State Court Opinion Assignment in Chapter 2.)

■ ASSIGNMENT 12.29 ■

Prepare an annotated bibliography on suing attorneys in your state. (See General Instructions for the Annotated Bibliography Assignment in Chapter 2.)

CASE

Smith v. Lewis
13 Cal.3d 349, 118 Cal.Rptr. 621, 530 P.2d 589 (1975)
Supreme Court of California

Background: Rosemary Smith hired Jerome Lewis, Esq. to represent her in her divorce case. He advised her that her husband's state and federal retirement benefits were his separate property; they were not community property. Hence these benefits were not pleaded as items of community property, and therefore were not apportioned by the divorce court. After the divorce decree became final, Smith sued Lewis for legal malpractice in giving her negligent legal advice on the pensions. The trial court ruled for Smith (the plaintiff) against Lewis (the defendant). The case is now on appeal before the Supreme Court of California.

Decision on Appeal: Judgment affirmed. Lewis committed legal malpractice by failing to perform adequate research into the community property character of retirement benefits.

Opinion of Court

Justice MOSK delivered the opinion of the court . . .

In determining whether defendant exhibited the requisite degree of competence in his handling of plaintiff's divorce action, the crucial inquiry is whether his advice was so legally deficient when it was given that he may be found to have failed to use "such skill, prudence, and diligence as lawyers of ordinary skill and capacity commonly possess and exercise in the performance of the tasks which they undertake." *Lucas v. Hamm* (1961) 364 P.2d 685, 689. We must, therefore examine the indicia of the law which were readily available to defendant at the time he performed the legal services in question.

The major authoritative reference works which attorneys routinely consult for a brief and reliable exposition of the law relevant to a specific problem uniformly indicated in 1967 that vested retirement benefits earned during marriage were generally subject to community [property] treatment. See, e.g., 38 Cal.Jur.2d, Pensions, § 12, p. 325; 4 Witkin, Summary of Cal.Law (1960) pp. 2723-2724. . . .

Although it is true this court had not foreclosed all conflicts on some aspects of the issue at that time, the community character of retirement benefits had been reported in a number of appellate opinions often cited in the literature and readily accessible to defendant. *Benson v. City of Los Angeles* (1963) 384 P.2d 649; *French v. French* (1941) 112 P.2d 235. In Benson, decided four years before defendant was retained herein, we stated directly that "pension rights which are earned during the course of a marriage are the community property of the employee and his wife." 384 P.2d at p. 651. . . .

On the other hand, substantial uncertainty may have existed in 1967 with regard to the community character of [her husband's] *federal* pension. . . . [But] the fact that in 1967 a reasonable argument could have been offered to support the characterization of [her husband's] federal benefits as separate property does not indicate the trial court erred in submitting the issue of defendant's malpractice to the jury. The *state* benefits, the large majority of the payments at issue, were unquestionably community property according to all available authority and should have been claimed as such. As for the *federal* benefits, the record documents defendant's failure to conduct any reasonable research into their proper characterization under community property law. Instead, he dogmatically asserted his theory, which he was unable to support with authority, . . . that all noncontributory . . . retirement benefits, whether state or federal, were immune from community treatment upon divorce. The jury could well have found defendant's refusal to educate himself to the applicable principles of law constituted negligence which prevented him from exercising informed discretion with regard to his client's rights.

As the jury was correctly instructed, an attorney does not ordinarily guarantee the soundness of his opinions and, accordingly, is not liable for every mistake he may make in his practice. He is expected, however, to possess knowledge of those plain and elementary principles of law which are commonly known by well informed attorneys, and to discover those additional rules of law which, although not commonly known, may readily be found by standard research techniques. If the law on a particular subject is doubtful or debatable, an attorney will not be held responsible for failing to anticipate the manner in which the uncertainty will be resolved. But even with respect to an unsettled area of the law, we believe an attorney assumes an obligation to his client to undertake reasonable research in an effort to ascertain relevant legal principles and to make an informed decision as to a course of conduct based upon an intelligent assessment of the problem. In the instant case, ample evidence was introduced to support a jury finding that defendant failed to perform such adequate research into the question of the community character of retirement benefits and thus was unable to exercise the informed judgment to which his client was entitled.

We recognize, of course, that an attorney engaging in litigation may have occasion to choose among various alternative strategies available to his client, one of which may be to refrain from pressing a debatable point because potential benefit may not equal detriment in terms of expenditure of time and resources or because of calculated tactics to the advantage of his client. But, as the Ninth Circuit put it somewhat brutally in *Pineda v. Craven* (9th Cir. 1970) 424 F.2d 369, 372: "There is nothing strategic or tactical about ignorance. . . ." In the case before us it is difficult to conceive of tactical advantage which could have been served by neglecting to advance a claim so clearly in plaintiff's best interest, nor does defendant suggest any. The decision to forego litigation on the issue of plaintiff's community property right to a share of [her husband's] retirement benefits was apparently the product of a culpable misconception of the relevant principles of law, and the jury could have so found.

Furthermore, no lawyer would suggest the property characterization of [her husband's] retirement benefits to be so esoteric an issue that defendant could not reasonably have been expected to be aware of it or its probable resolution. *Lucas v. Hamm* (1961) 364 P.2d 685. In *Lucas* we held that the rule against perpetuities poses such complex and difficult problems for the draftsman that even careful and competent attorneys occasionally fall prey to its traps. The situation before us is not analogous. Certainly one of the central issues in any divorce proceeding is the extent and division of the community property. In this case the question reached monumental proportions, since [her husband's] retirement benefits constituted the only significant asset available to the community. In undertaking professional representation of plaintiff, defendant assumed the duty to familiarize himself with the law defining the character of retirement benefits; instead, he rendered erroneous advice contrary to the best interests of his client without the guidance through research of readily available authority. . . .

In any event, as indicated above, had defendant conducted minimal research into either hornbook or case law, he would have discovered with modest effort that [the husband's] state retirement benefits were likely to be treated as community property and that his federal benefits at least arguably belonged to the community as well. . . . Even as to doubtful matters, an attorney is expected to perform sufficient research to enable him to make an informed and intelligent judgment on behalf of his client. . . .

The judgment is affirmed.

• ASSIGNMENT 12.30 •

a. Assume that Rosemary Smith's husband had a federal pension, but no state pension. Would the court still have found Lewis negligent?

b. To avoid a charge of negligence, is every attorney obligated to own a comprehensive law library?

SUMMARY

In most negligence cases, the standard of care is reasonableness, which is determined by assessing the totality of circumstances. The defendant has breached this standard if his or her acts and omissions are substantially different from those of a reasonable person under the same or similar circumstances. Reasonableness is determined by comparing what this person would have done to what the defendant did or failed to do. A reasonable person is someone who makes mistakes and causes injury, but never due to carelessness. If the danger of a foreseeably serious accident outweighed the burden or inconvenience of taking precautions to avoid the accident, the reasonable person would take those precautions. In assessing a burden or inconvenience, the court will consider cost, time, effectiveness, and aesthetics. The more important or socially useful the activity, the more likely it is that a reasonable person would take the risks involved in the activity.

Physically, a reasonable person has the same strengths and weaknesses as the defendant. Mentally, the reasonable person has the basic knowledge and intelligence needed in everyday life, even if the defendant does not. If the defendant has more than the minimum (e.g., has professional) knowledge and skills, then the reasonable person is deemed to have the same knowledge and skills. If the defendant is a child, the standard is a reasonable child of the age and intelligence of the defendant, unless the defendant was engaging in an adult activity, in which case the standard is the reasonable adult.

Res ipsa loquitur allows a jury to infer unreasonableness simply by reason of the fact that the accident happened, even if there is no direct or specific evidence of unreasonableness. It must be more likely than not that the accident was due to someone's unreasonableness—the defendant's—and the plaintiff must not be a responsible cause of the accident.

Custom and usage (what others in the business or industry are doing) is one of the factors a court will consider in assessing reasonableness. Following custom and usage does not necessarily make a defendant reasonable. Under the breach-of-duty equation, a defendant may be required to do more than what everyone else is doing.

If the defendant has violated a statute, ordinance, or regulation (S/O/R), the violation might be considered negligence per se; create a presumption of negligence; or simply be some evidence of negligence if a) the violation caused the accident; b) the plaintiff is within the class of persons protected by the S/O/R; and c) the plaintiff has suffered the kind of harm the S/O/R was intended to avoid. Conversely, the defendant's compliance with an S/O/R does not automatically establish reasonableness. Compliance may merely constitute some evidence of reasonableness. Reasonable care under the circumstances may call for more than the minimum requirements imposed by the S/O/R.

Guest statutes often refuse to impose liability on hosts unless the latter have committed gross negligence or have been wilful, wanton, or reckless. Under the doctrine of respondeat superior, employers are vicariously liable for the negligence committed by their employees within the scope of employment. There is no vicarious liability for the negligence committed by independent contractors unless the latter are performing non-delegable duties or inherently dangerous work. Participants in a joint enterprise are vicariously liable for the negligence committed by each other in furtherance of the objective of the enterprise. Under the family purpose doctrine, the owner of a car who makes it available for family (nonbusiness) use will be vicariously liable for the negligence of a driver in the owner's immediate household who was using the car for a family purpose at the time of the accident with the express or implied consent of the owner.

Unless a doctor warrants his or her services, liability for injuries must be based on negligence. The standard of care in most states is the skill and learning commonly possessed by members of the medical profession in good standing in the same or a similar locality to that where the defendant-doctor practices. The standard of care for attorneys is the skill and knowledge normally used by attorneys in good standing. Every mistake by an attorney will not necessarily lead to negligence liability. It must be an unreasonable mistake that actually causes the client a loss.

Key Terms

reasonable care
breach of duty
unreasonable conduct
standard of care
reasonableness
factors
reasonable person
breach-of-duty equation
hypothesis
burden or
    inconvenience
importance or social
    utility
subjective standard
objective standard
res ipsa loquitur
custom and usage
legislative intent
strict construction
negligence per se

presumption
guest statutes
ordinary negligence
gross negligence
wilful, wanton, and
    reckless conduct
vicarious liability
imputed negligence
joint and several
    liability
deep pocket
independent liability
employer/employee
    relationship
master/servant
    relationship
respondeat superior
principal/agent
    relationships
scope of employment

frolic and detour
independent contractor
non-delegable duties
inherently dangerous
joint enterprise
imputed contributory
    negligence
dangerous propensities
warranty
strict liability
national standard
local standard
defensive medicine
percentage fee
damage caps
fee caps
informed consent
trial within a trial
indemnity

CHAPTER 13

Negligence: Element III: Proximate Cause

CHAPTER OUTLINE

- INTRODUCTION
- CAUSE IN FACT
  Evidence of Causation
  Causation by Market Share
- CUT-OFF TEST OF PROXIMATE CAUSE
  Exceptions to Test
  Unforeseeable Plaintiff
  Intervening Causes

- OVERVIEW OF STEPS NEEDED TO ANALYZE PROXIMATE CAUSE

■ INTRODUCTION

Proximate cause[1] involves two separate questions, only one of which deals with causation. The two questions are:

1. The causation question *(cause in fact):*
   Did the defendant cause the plaintiff's injury?
2. The policy question (a *cut-off test*):
   At what point will the law refuse to hold the defendant responsible for the injury or injuries that he or she has in fact caused?

In the vast majority of negligence cases, the policy question does not need to be considered. Defendant breaks plaintiff's leg in an automobile accident in which the defendant is driving at an excessive rate of speed. We do not need a cut-off test once we establish that the defendant in fact caused plaintiff's leg injury. There is no reason to refuse to hold the defendant responsible. The defendant is the

[1]Sometimes referred to as **legal cause.**

proximate cause of the leg injury in this case. The two-fold questions of proximate cause become critical in two main situations:

- when the injury suffered by the plaintiff appears to be unusual or unexpected, *or*
- when other causes join the defendant in a chain-type sequence

Assume that Sam unreasonably drives his car down the street at an excessive rate of speed and hits the plaintiff, breaking the latter's leg. While the plaintiff is lying in the road, a second car runs over the plaintiff's arm, and disappears. When the ambulance finally arrives and takes the plaintiff to the hospital, a nurse carelessly treats the plaintiff, causing injury to the plaintiff's knee. Assume that *only* Sam is sued for negligence. The proximate cause issue is two-fold:

1. **Cause in Fact:**
   a. Did Sam cause the original leg injury by hitting the plaintiff?
   b. Did Sam cause the arm injury when the second car ran over the plaintiff's arm?
   c. Did Sam cause the knee injury that resulted from the nurse's carelessness?

2. **Policy (cut-off):**
   Should Sam be responsible for *all* the injury or injuries that he has in fact caused? Should Sam be liable for what the nurse did and for what the second car did, as well as for what he directly did himself when he hit the plaintiff? Did Sam proximately cause the arm and knee injuries as well as the original leg injury?

The tests of proximate cause, outlined in Figure 13.1, will answer all of these questions. Later we will examine some modifications or exceptions to these tests.

▪ CAUSE IN FACT

The **but-for test** and the **substantial-factor test** are alternative tests that courts often use to determine whether the defendant was the cause in fact of the plaintiff's injury. As we shall see, the substantial-factor test is fully adequate and often easier for a plaintiff to establish. It is important, however, that you understand both tests.

Figure 13.1   The Tests of Proximate Cause

---

1. The Case-in-Fact Tests
   a. But-for test[2] (used when there is only one causal entity):
      Is it more likely than not that but for the defendant's unreasonable acts or omissions, the injury would not have been suffered by the plaintiff?
   b. Substantial-factor test (used when there is more than one causal entity):
      Is it more likely than not that the defendant's unreasonable acts or omissions were a substantial factor in producing the injury suffered by the plaintiff?
2. The Cut-off Test:
   Is the injury suffered by the plaintiff the **foreseeable consequence** of the **original risk** created by the defendant's unreasonable acts or omissions?

---

[2]Also referred to as the **sine qua non test.**

The but-for test asks the following question: Would the plaintiff have been injured but for what the defendant did or failed to do? Under this test, if the plaintiff would have been injured regardless of what the defendant did or failed to do, the defendant did not cause the injury.

Examples:

- Dwayne is an ambulance driver. One day he gets a call from the plaintiff's home for an ambulance to take the plaintiff to the hospital. Dwayne takes the call at 9:00 A.M. Because of Dwayne's careless driving, he arrives at the plaintiff's home 45 minutes later than he would have arrived if he had not been careless. When he does arrive, the plaintiff is already dead. According to the coroner's report, the plaintiff died at 9:01 A.M. Dwayne was not the cause in fact of the death. Dwayne was careless and unreasonable in driving to the plaintiff, but the plaintiff would have died even if Dwayne had driven with great caution and skill. But for what Dwayne did or failed to do, the plaintiff would still have been dead when he arrived to take her to the hospital. Hence, there was not cause in fact.

- Mary is a doctor whose license to practice medicine has been suspended for a year because of the illegal prescription of drugs to several patients. In secret, however, Mary continues her practice. During this time, she performs a routine operation on George. George suffers serious complications following the operation and dies. His estate sues Mary for negligence. At the trial there is no evidence that Mary was careless or unreasonable in performing the operation. The estate introduces evidence that Mary performed the operation while her license was suspended. The lack of a license, however, was not the cause in fact of George's death. Even if Mary had had a license, the death would still have occurred. But for Mary's not having a license, it cannot be said that George would not have died. There was no evidence that Mary did not use adequate professional skill in performing the operation. It may be that a separate criminal proceeding can be brought against Mary for practicing without a license, but the estate loses its negligence action for failure to establish cause in fact.

- Sam carelessly drives his car into Fred's barn. But for the way Sam drove, the damage to the barn would not have occurred. Sam, therefore, is the cause in fact of the damage to Fred's property.

The but-for test is sufficient for most tort cases on the issue of causation. This includes negligence cases as well as those charging intentional torts or strict liability, which we shall examine later. There is, however, an alternative test: the defendant will be considered the cause in fact of the plaintiff's injury if the defendant was *a substantial factor* in producing the injury. Every time you establish cause in fact by the but-for test, you certainly have established that the defendant was a substantial factor. But the converse is not necessarily true:

Example: Helen and Jane carelessly shoot their hunting guns at the same time through some bushes, trying to hit an animal. Both bullets, however, hit plaintiff, who is killed instantly. Either bullet would have killed the plaintiff. Here, the but-for test leads to a bizarre result. Helen says, correctly, that but for her bullet, the plaintiff would have died anyway. Jane says, correctly, that but for her bullet, the plaintiff would have died anyway. Hence, each uses the but-for test to show that she individually was not the cause in fact of the plaintiff's death.

The plaintiff's estate would not be able to win a negligence action against anyone if the but-for test were the only test to determine cause in fact in such a case. Hence the need for an alternative test. If either Helen or Jane was *a substantial factor* in producing the death, then either one is the cause in fact of the death. When two people fire a bullet at a person who is killed by the impacts, the law will say that they are both substantial factors in producing the death. In this case, therefore, the substantial-factor test leads to the establishment of cause in fact, even though the but-for test would not do so.

It is usually easier for a plaintiff to establish cause in fact by the substantial-factor test than by the but-for test, but in most cases, both tests will lead to the same result. In tort law, it is sufficient if the plaintiff proves cause in fact by the broader substantial-factor test. *In analyzing any tort problem on the issue of cause in fact, you should apply both tests, but always keep in mind that the substantial-factor test will be sufficient.* Plaintiffs will have a stronger case if they can show cause in fact by the but-for test. Hence, you should determine whether this can be done on the facts before you. If not, move on to the substantial-factor test, particularly when more than one causal entity has contributed to the plaintiff's injury.

Note that the substantial-factor test requires only that the defendant be *a* substantial factor. It is not necessary that the defendant be the *sole* or *only* cause of the plaintiff's injury in order to be the cause in fact of the injury. It is not even necessary to show that the defendant was the dominant factor in producing the injury. Being *a* substantial factor is enough.

Evidence of Causation

What do we mean when we say that there is evidence of causation—whether we're using the but-for test or the substantial-factor test? How does one establish a connection between cause and effect? For the vast majority of cases, our most sophisticated tool in assessing causation is common sense based upon everyday experience. Our common sense depends heavily on the factors of *time, space,* and *history.* These factors present us with some fundamental hypotheses about life and human nature.

Time

When did the injury occur? After the defendant's acts or omissions? The shorter the time between the plaintiff's injury and the acts or omissions of the defendant, the more convinced we are that those acts or omissions caused the injury. The more time that elapses between the defendant's acts or omissions and the injury of the plaintiff, the more skeptical we are that those acts or omissions caused the injury.

Space

Where did the injury occur? In the same area or vicinity where the defendant was acting or failing to act? The more closely we can place the defendant's acts or omissions to the area or vicinity of the plaintiff's injury, the more convinced we are that those acts or omissions caused the injury. The greater the distance between the area or vicinity of the injury and the area or vicinity of the defendant's acts or omissions, the more skeptical we are that those acts or omissions caused the injury.

These hypotheses, or assumptions, about life and human nature are but points of departure. The specific facts about a given case may lead us to a different conclusion about causation. Some illnesses, for example, may not appear until months or years after the accident, yet we can still be convinced that one caused the other. So, too, we can be convinced that actions taken in New York can lead to damage or injury in California. There is nothing ironclad about the hypotheses. Just as we can be convinced that the defendant has caused an injury that is far removed in time and space from what the defendant did or failed to do, so too, cases may arise in which we can be convinced that the defendant did not cause an injury that occurred immediately after the defendant's acts or omissions. The facts of each individual case must be carefully scrutinized. The predisposition of our common sense, however, tells us to begin this scrutiny with the hypotheses listed above on time and space.

Assume that for years a railroad has stationed a guard at a point where the track crosses a highway. One day, the railroad removes the guard. Two days later, a train crashes into a car at the intersection. Was the absence of the guard the cause in fact of the injury? Was the absence of the guard a substantial factor in producing the injury? Among the evidence to be introduced by the plaintiff's attorney are time and space evidence. The attorney will present evidence to show that the crash occurred soon after the guard was removed (time) and that the crash occurred at the very intersection where the guard was once stationed (space). Common sense tells us, according to this attorney, that the accident would not have happened if the guard had been there, or at the very least, that the absence of the guard was a substantial factor in producing the crash. Time-and-space evidence is critical on the issue of causation. But not necessarily determinative. Other evidence might show that the job function of the guard was not to try to prevent the kind of collision that occurred and that even if the guard had been present, the collision would have occurred anyway. Again, the time and space evidence is but a point of departure.

Another important source of causation evidence is *history*. Here again, a basic hypothesis is in play.

History

In the past, have the same or similar acts or omissions by the defendant or people like the defendant produced this kind of injury? The more often this kind of injury has resulted from such acts or omissions in the past, the more convinced we are that the acts or omissions of the defendant caused the injury. If this kind of injury has never or has rarely been produced by such acts or omissions, we are more skeptical that the defendant's acts or omissions caused the injury.

Of course, just because something has happened in the past does not necessarily mean that it happened in this particular case. The predisposition of our common sense, however, tells us that history does tend to repeat itself. Hence, our common sense leads us to inquire about the past. In the railroad crossing case discussed above, for example, the plaintiff's attorney may try to introduce evidence that collisions between trains and cars never occurred when the guard was on duty, as a way of proving that it is more likely than not that the absence of the guard caused the collision.

Hence, evidence of time, space, and history is critical in beginning to collect evidence of causation in fact. We are drawn to search out such evidence on the basis of some basic hypotheses about time, space, and history. Such evidence will not always be conclusive—either way—on the issue of causation in fact. All of the facts and circumstances of a given case must be examined. Start your examination, however, with the evidence of time, space, and history.

▪ ASSIGNMENT 13.1 ▪

Re-read the fact situation at the beginning of this chapter about the plaintiff whose leg, arm, and knee were injured. Was Sam the cause in fact of each of these injuries? (Sam is the driver who initially hit the plaintiff while driving at an excessive rate of speed.) (See General Instructions for the Legal Analysis Assignment in Chapter 3.)

Let us shift our focus for a moment away from the test for causation to the **standard of proof** for establishing causation in fact. By standard of proof we mean how convincing the plaintiff's evidence must be that the defendant was a substantial factor in producing the injury. (While the discussion that follows refers to the substantial-factor test, the discussion is equally applicable to the but-for test.) The standard of proof is the **preponderance of the evidence:**

> Plaintiff must produce evidence that is convincing enough for a fact finder to conclude that it is *more likely than not* that the defendant was a substantial factor in producing the injury.

Evidence can have different degrees of believability. This diversity is referred to as the **weight of the evidence.** The more-likely-than-not standard is the minimum degree of believability that the plaintiff must establish in order to prove cause in fact. A mere **possibility** that the defendant was a substantial factor is not enough. Anything is possible. A 50/50 possibility is also not enough. In mathematical terms, believability must be 51 percent or better. This is what is meant by the more-likely-than-not standard. (See Figure 13.2.)

Suppose the evidence is so overwhelming that defendant was a substantial factor that no reasonable jury could fail to find otherwise. If so, the judge will not even let the jury consider the question. The judge will rule *as a matter of law* that cause in fact exists. (When judges make rulings as a matter of law, they are saying that there is no factual dispute involved.) On the other hand, suppose there is very little, if any, evidence that the defendant was a substantial factor. If so, the judge may again refuse to let the jury consider the issue and resolve the causation issue as a matter of law against the plaintiff. This will occur when all that can be said from the evidence is that there is only a possibility that defendant was a substantial factor. Courts will not permit juries to speculate on mere possibilities. Plaintiff must prove causation in fact by a preponderance of the evidence, not by mere conjecture. Preponderance means, in mathematical terms, *at least* a 51-percent probability. A 50/50 probability is not enough to take the issue out of the realm of speculation and conjecture.

Figure 13.2 Preponderance of the Evidence on the Issue of Causation

Weight of the Evidence

Consequences

The evidence is overwhelming that the defendant was a substantial factor in producing the injury

From the evidence, it is highly likely that the defendant was a substantial factor in producing the injury

From the evidence, it is more likely than not that the defendant was a substantial factor in producing the injury

If the case falls into any one of these three categories, the plaintiff has carried the burden of proving at least by a preponderance of the evidence that the defendant was a substantial factor in producing the injury.

From the evidence, there is a 50/50 possibility that the defendant was a substantial factor in producing the injury

From the evidence, there is a possibility that the defendant was a substantial factor in producing the injury

The evidence is overwhelming that the defendant was not a substantial factor in producing the injury

If the case falls into any one of these three categories, the plaintiff has failed to carry the burden of proving at least by a preponderance of the evidence that the defendant was a substantial factor in producing the injury. Causation, therefore, cannot be established.

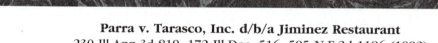

CASE

Parra v. Tarasco, Inc. d/b/a Jiminez Restaurant
230 Ill.App.3d 819, 172 Ill.Dec. 516, 595 N.E.2d 1186 (1992)
Appellate Court of Illinois, First District (1992)

Background: Ernest Parra died when he choked on a piece of food at Jiminez Restaurant. This suit alleges that the restaurant negligently failed to post instructions in the restaurant on how to aid a choking victim and negligently failed to summon emergency medical assistance. The Illinois Choke-Saving Methods Act requires every restaurant to "have posted in a conspicuous location that is visible to patrons and employees on the premises, but which location need not be in the actual dining areas, instructions concerning at least one method of first aid assistance to choking persons." Jiminez Restaurant failed to post these instructions. The trial court dismissed the complaint for failure to state a cause of action. The case is now on appeal before the Appellate Court of Illinois.

Decision on Appeal: Judgment affirmed. Plaintiff has not alleged causation.

Opinion of Court

Justice GORDON delivered the opinion of the court. . . .

[Plaintiff has] failed to adequately allege that failure to post the sign was the proximate cause of decedent's death. The violation of a statute or ordinance designed for the protection of human life or property can be *prima facie* evidence of negligence, but the injury must have a direct and proximate connection with the violation. Plaintiff must include sufficient factual allegations that such violation was the proximate cause of his injuries. It is not sufficient to merely plead conclusions. *Horcher v. Guerin,* 94 Ill.App.2d 244, 248–50, 236 N.E.2d 576 (complaint merely alleges conclusion that violation of building code [requiring windows in operating condition] was proximate cause of injury from fire; however, nothing indicates causal connection between inoperative windows and actual injury of plaintiff).

In order to state a cause of action, plaintiff must allege the ultimate facts which give rise to the cause of action, and liberality of pleading will not relieve plaintiff of the requirement that the complaint contain sufficient, factual averments and set out every fact essential to be proved.

In determining whether proximate cause has been sufficiently set forth, it is important to "distinguish the causal connection between what the defendant did and the plaintiff's injury from the connection between the plaintiff's injury and the class of the injuries from which the statute was intended to afford protection [choking to death]." (N.J. Singer, 2B *Sutherland Statutory Construction,* sec. 55.05, at 287–88 (5th ed. 1992) (footnotes omitted).) While clearly decedent's choking to death is precisely the class of injury for which the statute intends to afford protection; however, the necessary causal connection here runs between what defendant allegedly did— failure to post the sign, and plaintiff's injury—choking to death on his food.

The complaint here merely alleges that defendant: "5a. failed to post in a conspicuous location that was visible to patrons and employees in the premises instructions concerning first aid assistance to choking persons in violation of Illinois Revised statute; b. failed to instruct their employees in first aid assistance to choking persons; c. failed to assist the plaintiff decedent who was choking after failing to post in a con- spicuous place instructions concerning first aid assistance to choking persons. 6. That as a direct and proximte result of the aforesaid negligent acts or omissions of the defendants, the plaintiff decedent . . . suffered personal injuries and died on March 18, 1989."

This broad, conclusory language fails to provide the necessary factual allegations which would establish a causal relationship between not posting the sign and decedent's death. There is no allegation, for example, that anyone tried to perform the Heimlich Maneuver but performed it incorrectly because the sign was not posted, or failed to undertake such an attempt because of a failure to post the sign.

Plaintiff additionally alleges in the complaint that defendant "failed to promptly summon emergency medical personnel." . . . [But] there is no factual allegation in the complaint which even hints at a causal connection between decedent's death, and any action or inaction by defendant. In fact, there is no allegation that anyone in the restaurant had any knowledge that decedent was choking. There is no allegation that defendant's employees had discovered decedent choking and refused to call, or delayed calling, for medical assistance. There is no allegation that, but for the failure of defendant to summon an ambulance, decedent would have lived. Cf. *Acosta v. Fuentes,* 150 Misc.2d 1013, 571 N.Y.S. at 669 (if the patron choking on his food was "already doomed to die" before the restaurant's employees called an ambulance and moved him outside, then no causal connection has been shown between defendants' action or inaction and decedent's death).

We conclude that the trial court properly found that plaintiff's allegations of negligence based on defendant's failure to post a sign, or failure to secure or render first aid, did not state a cause of action. . . .

▪ ASSIGNMENT 13.2 ▪

a. Write a complaint for Parra that *adequately* alleges causation. Make up whatever facts you need to draft this complaint. Be sure that Justice Gordon would not have the same problems with your complaint that he had with the complaint actually used in the litigation, even if your state does not require the same kind of pleading specificity that Justice Gordon required. (See General Instructions for the Complaint Drafting Assignment in Chapter 5.)
b. Assume that none of the employees in the Illinois restaurant spoke English, and that none of the customers in the restaurant at the time of the choking spoke English. There are instructions clearly posted in the restaurant on what to do if someone chokes on food, but the instructions are in English. Would the result be the same? What would the complaint have to allege?

Causation by Market Share

In Chapter 12, we saw that the courts created the doctrine of res ipsa loquitur to help plaintiffs who would otherwise have great difficulty establishing the second element of negligence: breach of duty (unreasonableness). The doctrine allowed the jury to draw the inference of unreasonableness even though there was no direct or specific evidence of it.

We now look at a similar problem pertaining to another element of negligence: causation.

> **Example:**   During pregnancy a woman takes DES (diethylstilbestrol), a synthetic form of estrogen, designed to prevent miscarriage. She gives birth to a daughter. When the child grows up, she develops cervical cancer, which was caused by the DES taken by her mother. Which manufacturer of DES can the daughter sue? At least 200 manufacturers used an identical formula to produce DES. But the daughter cannot determine which manufacturer made the DES pills that her mother took. The pharmacist used by her mother is no longer in business, and no records are available.

The drug was obviously defective, and unreasonably so. A duty of reasonable care existed, the duty was breached, and an injury resulted. But *who caused the injury?* We know *what* caused the cancer, but we do not know *who* caused it. Under traditional rules, it is fundamental that the plaintiff establish which manufacturer made the defective pills taken by her mother. But she has no way of doing so on these facts.

In most states, she loses her case. A minority of states, however, are more sympathetic.

In *Sindell v. Abbott Laboratories,*[3] for example, a California court held that if the plaintiff:

▪ established that DES caused the cancer, and
▪ sued a substantial share of the DES manufacturers who were selling in the market in which her mother purchased the drug,

then each defendant/manufacturer would be liable for the proportion of the plaintiff's damages represented by its share of that market unless it could prove that

---

[3]26 Cal.3d 588, 607 P.2d 924, 163 Cal.Rptr. 132, 2 ALR 4th 1061 (1980).

it could not have made the DES pill that caused plaintiff's injuries.[4] If a particular defendant/manufacturer could not prove this, then it would be liable for that part of the judgment that was proportional to its market share. This approach has been called **market share** liability.

Using this method of handling causation has been highly controversial. Some fear that it might open a floodgate of liability.

Although *Sindell* was dramatic in its approach, there are limitations to its use. The product made by the manufacturers must be identical, or nearly so. If the products are simply similar and are not made in the same dangerous way, this approach cannot be used. *Sindell* arguably would not apply, for example, if different manufacturers used different proportions of ingredients to make what would otherwise be considered the same product. Also, a large number of manufacturers must be sued so that it can be said that they constitute a significant or substantial share of the market.

▪ CUT-OFF TEST OF PROXIMATE CAUSE

As we saw in Figure 13.1 at the beginning of this chapter, the basic cut-off test for when a defendant will or will not be held liable for what he or she has caused in fact is as follows: The injury must be the foreseeable consequence of the original risk created by the defendant's unreasonable acts or omissions.

> **Example:** Cliff speeds through a red light in his truck. He hits a car proceeding on a green light in the intersection. The plaintiff in the car suffers a broken arm from the collision, and the car is demolished.

> **Cause in fact:** "But-for" the way Cliff drove, the plaintiff would not have suffered property damage to the car, nor the broken arm; Cliff was certainly a substantial factor in producing the personal and property damage. Cliff is the cause in fact of both.

> **Proximate cause:** Cliff is also the proximate cause of the personal and property damage. The original risk created by speeding through a red light was the risk of hitting other cars and people. The plaintiff's broken arm and demolished car are foreseeable consequences of this original risk Cliff created. Hence, there is no need for a cut-off rule. Cliff is the proximate cause of what he caused in fact.

Suppose that a plaintiff suffers a second or third injury that is causally related to the first. For example, the defendant carelessly pushes the plaintiff, who breaks a leg. Two months later, while walking on crutches, the plaintiff falls and breaks her arm. Soon thereafter, the plaintiff catches pneumonia because of her general run-down condition. Assume that the defendant is the cause in fact of these injuries (i.e., assume that what the defendant did was a substantial factor in producing the broken leg, the broken arm, and the pneumonia). In this case, the defendant will be liable for all of the injuries and harm because they are all foreseeable consequences of the original risk defendant created. Defendant proximately caused them all.

This conclusion is subject to the general principle that the plaintiff must take reasonable steps to **mitigate the consequences** of the original injury caused by

---

[4]*Prosser & Keeton on the Law of Torts*, 5th ed., 271 (1984).

the defendant. Plaintiff, for example, cannot refuse all medical attention and then hold the defendant responsible for the *aggravation* of the injury that resulted from the plaintiff's refusal to see a doctor.

There are two major exceptions to the general cut-off test that we need to examine.

Exceptions to Test

"Eggshell Skull" Rule—Extent of Injury

If it is foreseeable that defendant's unreasonable acts or omissions will result in any *impact on plaintiff's body,* and this impact does occur, the defendant will be liable for the foreseeable *and the unforeseeable* personal injuries that follow. The cut-off test of proximate cause will not prevent liability for unforeseeable personal injuries that follow from any foreseeable impact on the plaintiff's body. Assume that the defendant is carelessly running down the corridor and bumps into the plaintiff as the latter is turning the corner. Plaintiff is one month pregnant at the time. The accidental bump causes a miscarriage. Or, assume the defendant is driving 15 mph in heavy traffic. For a second, the defendant carelessly takes his eyes off the road and runs into the rear of the plaintiff's car. Only a slight dent is put on the plaintiff's car. The plaintiff, however, dies because the collision activates a rare disease. In both of these examples, the plaintiff had an **eggshell skull,** meaning a very high vulnerability to injury to any part of the body. The extent of the injury was not foreseeable by the defendant. The extent of the injury was not within the risk originally created by the defendant. In both cases, it was foreseeable that the defendant would cause an impact on someone's body, but the injury itself that resulted was clearly not foreseeable. In such situations, however, the defendant "takes the plaintiff as he finds him." There is no cut-off of liability. Note again, however, that this exception to the cut-off test applies only when it is foreseeable that there will be at least some **body impact** on the plaintiff.

The eggshell-skull rule is not limited to impact caused by negligence or unreasonableness. If the defendant makes impact on the plaintiff's body through an intentional tort such as battery, the defendant will be liable for all resulting injuries, foreseeable or not.

Phrased another way, the eggshell-skull exception means that the defendant will be deemed to be the proximate cause of all foreseeable and unforeseeable personal injuries that result from any foreseeable impact due to unreasonable or intentional conduct by the defendant.

Often, the plaintiff with the eggshell skull has a pre-existing, disease, or injury, which has been aggravated by the defendant. The latter, of course, will not be responsible for the original existence of the pre-existing condition, disease, or injury, but will be responsible for its **aggravation.**

Suppose that the plaintiff goes insane or commits suicide because of despair over the original injuries caused by the defendant. Assume that there was a foreseeable impact on the plaintiff's person. Courts differ as to whether the defendant will be held responsible. Some courts would say that insanity or suicide is so extreme that the cut-off principle of proximate cause will prevent liability for such a drastic consequence. Other courts would consider the suicide to be a superseding cause (to be considered below), which would cut off liability. Many courts, on the other hand, will carry the eggshell-skull rule to its logical extreme and hold that the defendant is the proximate cause of the insanity or the death by suicide as long as there was a foreseeable impact on the body that the defendant carelessly or intentionally created.

Unforeseeability of Manner of Injury

In Chapter 10 on foreseeability, we saw that the advocate who wants the court to find that something was foreseeable will tend to phrase the foreseeability question in the broadest terms possible:

> "Was *any* injury whatsoever foreseeable to anyone from what the defendant did or failed to do?"

On the other hand, the advocate who wants a court to find that something was unforeseeable will try to phrase the foreseeability question in the narrowest, most particularized form possible:

> "Was it foreseeable that the plaintiff would be blinded by a blowtorch that he was using to repair a bridge when the defendant's carelessly navigated steamboat rammed into the bridge, causing the plaintiff to fall forward onto the torch, even though the plaintiff was not visible to anyone on the boat at the time of the collision?"

It is frequently the case that the precise **manner** in which the damage or injury would occur is not foreseeable. In the boat collision case, it was foreseeable that some damage to the bridge and some kind of injury to someone on the bridge would occur from the careless navigation of a steamboat in the area of the bridge. Personal and property damage was foreseeable. But the *manner* in which the injury would result in this particular plaintiff—falling on the blowtorch—was not foreseeable to the defendant, who did not even know that the plaintiff was there working with a torch. Drowning or a severe concussion to anyone on the bridge may have been foreseeable to the defendant, but not the manner in which the injury in fact occurred in this case. The rule in such cases is as follows:

> The manner in which an injury occurs does not have to be foreseeable in order for the defendant to be the proximate cause of the injury, as long as the harm that resulted was within the risk originally created by the defendant's acts or omissions.

This then is the second major exception to the rule that you are not the proximate cause of an injury that is unforeseeable. You can be the proximate cause of a foreseeable injury that occurs in an unforeseeable manner.

The American Law Institute, in its *Restatement of Torts,* would agree that the particular manner of the occurrence of the harm need not be foreseeable in order for the defendant to be the proximate cause of the injury (or as the Restatement would phrase it, the "legal cause" of the injury). It is important to the Restatement (and to the courts that follow it) to assess whether the injury was a normal or ordinary consequence of the risk that the defendant created. Liability should be cut off, according to this view, only if we can say that the harm that resulted was in fact **highly extraordinary.**[5]

---

[5]American Law Institute, *Restatement (Second) of Torts* § 435(2) (1965).

▪ ASSIGNMENT 13.3 ▪

Tom, an adult, gives a loaded gun to Bob, a young boy. Tom asks Bob to deliver the gun to Jack. Bob takes his friend Bill with him to make the delivery. Upon arrival, Bob accidentally drops the gun on Bill's toe. The toe breaks. When the gun falls, it discharges immediately, killing Jack. Bob suffers a nervous breakdown over the incident. Is Tom the proximate cause of Bill's broken toe? Of Jack's death? Of Bob's nervous breakdown? (See General Instructions for the Legal Analysis Assignment in Chapter 3. See also *Restatement (Second) of Torts* 281, illustration 3 (1965).)

As we examine proximate cause, it is important that this element be kept in perspective with the other elements of negligence discussed thus far—duty, and breach of duty. A discussion of proximate cause assumes that the plaintiff has already been able to establish that a duty of reasonable care (the first element) exists between the plaintiff and defendant, and that the defendant has breached that duty (the second element) by unreasonable conduct. Note the role that foreseeability plays in each element:

Element I: Duty

Defendant owes plaintiff a duty of reasonable care if the defendant's act or omission has created a *foreseeable* risk of injury to the plaintiff's person or property (the general rule).

Element II: Breach of Duty

Defendant breaches a duty of reasonable care by failing to take precautions against injury to the plaintiff when the *foreseeability* of serious injury outweighs the burden or inconvenience of taking those precautions.

Element III: Proximate Cause

Defendant is the proximate cause of every injury he or she in fact caused the plaintiff to suffer if those injuries were the *foreseeable* consequence of the original risk of injury created by the defendant's acts or omissions.

The foreseeability analysis that you must do to determine whether a duty exists (first element) is substantially the same foreseeability analysis that you must do to determine whether proximate cause exists (third element), or more accurately, whether the cut-off test of proximate cause will prevent the defendant from being liable for harm he or she has caused in fact. The very definition of the cut-off test requires you to refer back to the original risk created by the defendant. The relationship between the first element, duty, and the third element, proximate cause, is so close that you will sometimes see the proximate cause issue phrased in terms of duty: was the defendant under a duty to protect the plaintiff against the injury that resulted? Always keep in mind the two exceptions that operate to establish proximate cause for injuries that in extent or manner go beyond the original risk that was foreseeable. Aside from these two exceptions, you conduct the cut-off test of proximate cause by substantially repeating the same foreseeability analysis that you used to determine whether the first element of negligence (duty) applied.

Finally, we need to examine two special problem areas:

▪ the unforeseeable plaintiff
▪ intervening causes

Unforeseeable Plaintiff

We already looked at the problem of the *unforeseeable plaintiff* when we studied duty in Chapter 11. (See Figure 11.2.) What happens when injury to someone is foreseeable but not injury to the particular plaintiff who is injured? Is a duty (first element) owed to the unforeseeable plaintiff? As we saw in Figure 11.3, the Cardozo zone-of-danger test would say no, whereas the Andrews world-at-large test would say yes. If the Cardozo view is adopted in a state, the negligence case is over. The plaintiff loses for failure to establish one of the elements of negligence (duty). If the Andrews view is adopted in a state, the plaintiff will be successful in establishing the existence of a duty and must then move to the other elements of negligence, such as proximate cause. Because of the close relationship between duty and proximate cause, as we have seen, a plaintiff who successfully establishes duty is well on the way to establishing proximate cause as well. The cut-off principle of proximate cause will prevent liability only if the injury was beyond the scope of the foreseeable risk.

Intervening Causes

An **intervening cause** or force has been defined as:

> "a force which actively operates in producing harm to another after the [defendant's unreasonable] act or omission has been committed.[6]

Several different kinds of intervening causes or forces should be kept in mind:

Intervening Force of Nature
Example: The ABC company, the defendant, carelessly builds a dam. It is clear that the dam will not last more than two weeks before it breaks. The next day a hurricane hits the area and the dam collapses. The hurricane is an **intervening force of nature.**

Intervening Innocent Human Force
Example: Cynthia, the defendant, carelessly runs into the plaintiff, a bystander. It is dark out. A third party, driving carefully, fails to see the plaintiff on the road. Without knowing it, the third party runs over the plaintiff. The third party is an **intervening innocent human force.**

Intervening Negligent Human Force
Example: Alex, the defendant, carelessly runs into the plaintiff. Plaintiff is rushed to the hospital, but is given negligent medical treatment by the doctor, causing further injuries. The doctor is an **intervening negligent human force.**

Intervening Intentional or Criminal Human Force
Example: George, the defendant, carelessly hits the plaintiff in a highway collision. While at the hospital, the plaintiff sees his archenemy, who tries to kill him by poison. The plaintiff almost dies. The enemy is an **intervening intentional or criminal human force.**

If any of these intervening forces can be classified as a **superseding cause,** the cut-off test of proximate cause will prevent the defendant from being responsible for the harm caused by the intervening force. If the intervening force

---

[6]American Law Institute, *Restatement (Second) of Torts* § 441(1) (1965).

is not a superseding cause, then the defendant will be found to be the proximate cause of the harm caused by the intervening force. Our question, therefore, becomes: when is an intervening force a superseding cause?

> An intervening force becomes a superseding cause when the harm caused by the intervening force is beyond the foreseeable risk originally created by the defendant's unreasonable acts or omissions, and/or the harm caused by the intervening force is considered highly extraordinary.

Hence, foreseeability and the original risk created by the defendant again become critical factors. Alternatively, the "highly extraordinary" test of the Restatement that we saw earlier can be used as a guide.

Intervening intentional or criminal human forces are often considered superseding causes, because they are either outside the scope of the original risk or are highly extraordinary. Examine again the example just given involving the archenemy's attempt to poison the plaintiff in the hospital. George initially hit the plaintiff in an automobile collision and is the proximate cause of the plaintiff's injuries sustained in the collision, but he is not the proximate cause of the poisoning. The latter was highly extraordinary and far beyond the original risk that George created by his careless driving. The injuries are the natural and foreseeable consequence of bad driving. The intentional and criminal act of poisoning is not reasonably connected with George's bad driving.

Intervening intentional or criminal human forces are *not* always considered superseding causes. What the defendant does or fails to do may increase the risk of such an intervention, making the latter neither unforeseeable nor extraordinary. Suppose the defendant gives loaded guns to a group of juvenile delinquents, who intentionally shoot the plaintiff. Or suppose a motel fails to provide any security in a section of the motel where the burglary or robbery of patrons is highly likely, and such a burglary or robbery in fact occurs. In these cases, the intentional or criminal intervening force was part of the foreseeable risk created by the defendant's acts or omissions. Such intervening forces are not superseding; defendant is the proximate cause of the harm produced by them.

Intervening innocent or negligent human forces are treated the same way. If their intervention was part of the original risk, then they were foreseeable and do not become superseding causes. In those cases, for example, where the plaintiff is further injured in a hospital (whether innocently or negligently) after being brought there for treatment for the injury originally caused by the defendant, the hospital injuries are usually considered to be part of the original risk and not highly extraordinary. So, too, if the plaintiff receives a second injury by a third party (whether innocently or negligently) at the scene of the accident. In all these cases, the defendant has rendered the plaintiff highly vulnerable to further injury. It is not uncommon for individuals to receive injuries in hospitals or on the road after the first injury, although it may be highly unusual for such second injuries to be produced intentionally or criminally.

What about intervening forces of nature? Here it is important to ask whether the injury or damage is of the same kind as would have occurred if the intervening force of nature had not intervened at all. If the same kind of injury or damage results, the intervening force of nature is not a superseding cause. Suppose, for example, that the defendant carelessly leaves explosives in an area where people would be hurt by an explosion. Because of the manner of storage, assume that the explosives could detonate on their own. Hence, unreasonable storage creates a risk of serious personal and property damage to people in the area. One day, lightning strikes the explosives, leading to serious personal and property damage. The lightning was unforeseeable, but the damage and injury caused by the intervention of the lightning was the same kind of damage or injury that the defendant's method of storage risked. Defendant is the proximate cause of what the lightning produced. The resulting damage or injury is not highly extraordinary, even though it was unforeseeable that it would occur in this way.

A different result is reached in many, but not all, courts when the intervening force of nature causes a totally different kind of injury from that originally foreseeable by the defendant's act or omission. Suppose, for example, that a truck company carelessly delays the delivery of the plaintiff's goods, and the goods are destroyed by a storm. The destruction was not within the original risk created by the defendant, and some courts would therefore say that the intervening force of nature was a superseding cause.

■ OVERVIEW OF STEPS NEEDED TO ANALYZE PROXIMATE CAUSE

• **Cause in Fact**

Apply the two tests for cause in fact. First ask if the plaintiff's injury would have occurred but for the acts or omissions of the defendant. Then apply the substantial-factor test, especially when more than one cause may have produced the plaintiff's injury. Was the defendant's act or omission *a* substantial factor in producing the plaintiff's injury? Plaintiff can establish cause in fact by *either* test.

• **Burden of Proof**

Determine if there is enough evidence so that a jury could at least say that it is more likely than not that the defendant's act or omission was a substantial factor in producing the plaintiff's injury. Or determine if there is enough evidence so that a jury could say it is more likely than not that but for the defendant's act or omission, the injury would not have occurred.

• **Original Risk**

Turn the clock back to the time of the defendant's original act or omission. Identify the foreseeable risk as of that time. What kind of injury or damage was foreseeable or should have been foreseeable to the defendant? Phrase the foreseeability question, keeping in mind that the advocate who wants something to be foreseeable will try to phrase the question in the broadest terms possible, and the advocate who wants something to be unforeseeable will try to phrase the question in the narrowest, most particularized terms possible.

• **Eggshell Skull**

Determine whether the plaintiff has an "eggshell skull," or special vulnerability to injury or harm, and suffered personal injuries as a result of foreseeable impact on his or her body. If so, the injuries are proximately caused by the defendant, even if the extent of the injuries was unforeseeable.

• **Unforeseeable Manner**

Determine whether the general injury or damage was foreseeable because it was within the original risk created by the defendant and whether the only thing that was unforeseeable was the manner in which that injury or damage occurred. If so, the defendant is the proximate cause of the injury or damage, even though the manner of occurrence was unforeseeable.

- **Intervening Human Force**

  Determine whether any intervening human force was a causal factor in producing the injury or damage. If so, determine whether this human force was innocent, negligent, intentional, or criminal. Was the intervening human force within the scope of the original risk produced by the defendant? Was it foreseeable to the defendant? Did the human force proceed naturally out of what the defendant did or failed to do? Affirmative answers to these questions will make the defendant the proximate cause of what the intervening human force produced.

- **Intervening Force of Nature**

  Determine whether an intervening force of nature was a causal factor in producing the injury or damage. If so, ask whether the injury or damage that resulted was the same kind that would have occurred if the force of nature had not intervened. If so, the defendant is still the proximate cause of the injury or damage.

- **Highly Extraordinary**

  Can it be said that the injury or damage was highly extraordinary in view of what the defendant did or failed to do? If not, then the likelihood is that a court will find that the defendant was the proximate cause of the injury or damage.

- **Causation vs. Policy**

  Make sure that your analysis has not confused the causation question with the policy question of proximate cause. The causation question involves a straightforward but-for or substantial-factor assessment. The policy question involves the cut-off test that will prevent defendants from being responsible for injury or damage they have in fact caused. Do not worry about the policy question if cause in fact cannot be established.

▪ ASSIGNMENT 13.4 ▪

Examine both issues of proximate cause (cause in fact and the cut-off principle) in the following situations:

a. Tom carelessly drives his motorcycle into Dan's horse. The horse goes wild and jumps over a five-foot fence (which it has never done before) and runs into traffic. Henry tries to turn his car away from the horse and accidentally hits Pete, who is a pedestrian on the sidewalk at the time of the collision. Pete sues Tom for negligence.

b. Same facts as in (a) above, except that Henry just misses Pete, rather than hitting him with his car. Pete and Henry begin an argument over Henry's driving. Henry hits Pete in the jaw. Pete sues Tom for negligence.

c. Mary gives a loaded gun to a ten-year-old girl who is Mary's neighbor. The girl takes the gun home. The girl's father discovers the gun but fails to take it away from his daughter. The girl shoots Linda with the gun. Linda sues Mary for negligence.

d. Harry carelessly hits Helen, a pedestrian, with his car in a busy intersection downtown. While Helen is lying on the ground, a person in another car accidentally hits Helen, causing further injuries. This other person is a hit-and-run driver who does not stop after hitting Helen. Helen sues Harry for negligence.

e. Pat carelessly leaves her keys in her car. A thief gets in the car and starts to speed away. Moments later, the thief hits Kevin with the car one block away from where Pat parked the car. Kevin sues Pat for negligence.

f. Same facts as in (e) above, except that the thief hits Kevin one month after he has stolen the car, in another section of the city.

(See General Instructions for the Legal Analysis Assignment in Chapter 3.)

CASE

Mussivand v. David
45 Ohio St.3d 314, 544 N.E.2d 265 (1989)
Supreme Court of Ohio

Background: George David has a venereal disease, but does not tell the woman he is having an affair with. She contracts the disease from him and then gives it to her husband, Tofigh Mussivand. The latter sues David for negligence in failing to tell his wife that he had the disease. This failure allegedly caused Mussivand to contract the disease. The trial court granted David's motion to dismiss. The case is now on appeal before the Supreme Court of Ohio.

Decision on Appeal: The case should not have been dismissed. A husband can bring an action against his wife's paramour (lover), alleging that the paramour was negligent in failing to notify the wife that the paramour was at risk of passing venereal disease to the wife, who in turn could (and did) pass it to the husband.

Opinion of Court

Justice RESNICK delivered the opinion of the court. . . .

The complaint basically states that [Mussivand] contracted a venereal disease due to the acts of [David]. . . . A "venereal disease" is defined as "a contagious disease, most commonly acquired in sexual intercourse or other genital contact; the venereal diseases include syphilis, gonorrhea, chancroid, granuloma inguinale, lymphogranuloma venereum, genital herpesvirus infection, and balanitis gangraenosa." *Dorland's Illustrated Medical Dictionary* (26 Ed. 1985) 394. . . .

Recently several jurisdictions have allowed tort actions for negligent, fraudulent or intentional transmission of genital herpes where the person infected with genital herpes fails to disclose to his or her sexual partner that he or she is infected with such a disease. *Maharam v. Maharam* (1986), 123 A.D.2d 165, 510 N.Y.S.2d 104; *Long v. Adams* (1985), 175 Ga.App. 538, 333 S.E.2d 852. Thus, courts have placed upon

persons who have a venereal disease such as genital herpes or gonorrhea the duty to protect others who might be in danger of being infected by such a disease. In other words, people with a venereal disease have a duty to use reasonable care to avoid infecting others with whom they engage in sexual conduct. . . .

David argues that possibly Mussivand's wife, not he, was the cause of Mussivand's injuries. "Whether an intervening act breaks the causal connection between negligence and injury, thus relieving one of liability for his negligence, depends upon whether that intervening cause was a conscious and responsible agency which could or should have eliminated the hazard, and whether the intervening cause was reasonably foreseeable by the one who is guilty of the negligence. . . ." *Cascone v. Herb Kay Co.* (1983), 6 Ohio St.3d 155, 451 N.E.2d 815.

In *Jeffers v. Olexo* (1989), 43 Ohio St.3d 140, 144, 539 N.E.2d 614, 618, we equated foreseeability with proximate cause. This is misleading since they are not equatable. Rather, in order to establish proximate cause, foreseeability must be found. In determining whether an intervening cause "breaks the causal connection" between negligence and injury depends upon whether that intervening cause was reasonably foreseeable by one who was guilty of the negligence. If an injury is the natural and probable consequence of a negligent act and it is such as should have been foreseen in the light of all the attending circumstances, the injury is then the proximate result of the negligence. It is not necessary that the defendant should have anticipated the particular injury. It is sufficient that his act is likely to result in an injury to someone. Thus we do not equate foreseeability with proximate cause. Instead, if David knew his paramour was married, then it can be said that it was reasonably foreseeable that she would engage in sexual intercourse with her husband. In addition, if David did not inform her of the fact that he had a venereal disease, she could not be an intervening cause and, as such, David's liability to Mussivand would not be terminated. David's negligence would then be the proximate cause of Mussivand's injury.

We do not, however, mean to say that David, subsequent to his affair with Mussivand's wife, will be liable to any and all persons with whom she may have sexual contact. A spouse, however, is a foreseeable sexual partner. Furthermore, the liability of a person with a sexually transmissible disease to a third person, such as a spouse, would be extinguished as soon as the paramour spouse knew or should have

known that he or she was exposed to or had contracted a venereal disease. She or he then would become a "conscious and responsible agency which could or should have eliminated the hazard." *Cascone,* supra. For example, if David told Mussivand's wife he had a venereal disease or if she noticed symptoms of the disease on herself, she then would have the duty to abstain from sexual relations or warn her sexual partner. Whether Mussivand's wife knew, or should have known, of her exposure to a venereal disease is a question of fact to be decided by the trier of fact. . . .

For the foregoing reasons we cannot say that Mussivand could not prove any set of facts entitling him to recover in negligence from David. Accordingly, the trial court erred in granting David's motion to dismiss. . . .

▪ ASSIGNMENT 13.5 ▪

a. Why did the court say that Mrs. Mussivand may not have broken the chain of David's causation?
b. Suppose David does tell his paramour (Mrs. Mussivand) that he has VD. She tells him she doesn't care because this is the last time she will have sex with him before returning to her husband. She says, "I will never tell my husband about you or our affair." Mr. Mussivand contracts VD from her. Is David the proximate cause of Mr. Mussivand's VD?
c. Could Mr. Mussivand sue Mrs. Mussivand for negligence?

SUMMARY

Proximate cause raises a causation issue (who caused what?) and a policy issue (is there a point at which the law should cut off liability for the harm we have caused?) There are two cause-in-fact tests. First, it is more likely than not that but for the defendant's unreasonable acts or omissions, the injury would not have been suffered by the plaintiff? (This test is used when there is only one causal entity.) Second, is it more likely than not that the defendant's unreasonable acts or omissions were a substantial factor in producing the injury suffered by the plaintiff? (This test is used when there is more than one causal entity.) The policy test used to determine whether to cut off liability is as follows: Was the injury suffered by the plaintiff the foreseeable consequence of the original risk created by the defendant's unreasonable acts or omissions?

In assessing cause in fact, our common sense relies on time (how soon after the defendant's act or omission did the injury occur?), space (how close was the defendant's act or omission to the area where the injury occurred?), and historical data (in the past, have acts or omissions similar to the defendant's led to this kind of injury?). The standard of proof used by the jury to decide the cause-in-fact issue is preponderance of the evidence. Under certain conditions, a manufacturer will be liable for the part of a judgment that is proportional to its market share, even though the plaintiff cannot prove what that particular manufacturer in fact caused.

If it is foreseeable that the defendant's unreasonable (or intentional) acts or omissions will result in any impact on the plaintiff's body, the plaintiff will be responsible for the foreseeable and the unforeseeable personal injuries that follow. The manner in which an injury occurs does not have to be foreseeable in order for the defendant to be the proximate cause of the injury, as long as the harm that resulted was within the original risk created by the defendant's acts or omissions. Whether an intervening force is a superseding cause depends on whether the intervention was beyond the original risk or was highly extraordinary. Intervening intentional or criminal human forces are often considered superseding, unlike intervening innocent or negligent human forces. An intervening force of nature is not a superseding cause if it creates the same kind of injury or damage that the defendant's carelessness would have caused if nature had not intervened.

Key Terms

proximate cause
legal cause
cause in fact
but-for test
sine qua non test
substantial-factor test
foreseeable
   consequence
original risk
standard of proof
preponderance of the
   evidence

weight of the evidence
possibility
market share
mitigate the
   consequences
eggshell skull
body impact
aggravation
manner
highly extraordinary
intervening cause

intervening force of
   nature
intervening innocent
   human force
intervening negligent
   human force
intervening intentional
   or criminal human
   force
superseding cause

CHAPTER 14

Negligence: Element IV: Damages

CHAPTER OUTLINE

- KINDS OF DAMAGES
- PAIN AND SUFFERING
- PROPERTY DAMAGE
- DOCTRINE OF AVOIDABLE CONSEQUENCES
- COLLATERAL-SOURCE RULE

- JOINT TORTFEASORS
    Persons Acting in Concert
    Persons Not Acting in Concert
- RELEASE
- CONTRIBUTION
- INDEMNITY

■ KINDS OF DAMAGES

The plaintiff in a negligence action must suffer actual harm or loss to person or property. It is not enough that the defendant has engaged in unreasonable or even reckless conduct. Without actual harm or loss, the negligence action fails.

Although the focus of this chapter is on damages in a negligence action, most of the principles discussed here also apply to intentional and strict liability torts. First, some basic definitions:

Damages are pecuniary compensation—a money award for a legally recognized wrong. Damages are considered a *legal* remedy, unlike an injunction, for example, which is an *equitable* remedy.

Compensatory damages are designed to make plaintiffs whole, to compensate them for actual loss or injury. The primary purpose of tort law is to provide compensatory damages for harm caused by recognized torts. Through a money payment, plaintiffs are placed in the position they were in before the injury—or an effort is made to return to the status quo through this payment. **Out-of-pocket** (i.e., economic) losses are covered, such as medical bills and loss of wages. An attempt is also made to provide a money payment for noneconomic losses, such as **pain and suffering.**

Nominal damages consist of a small amount of money that is awarded when the defendant has committed a tort that has resulted in little or no

302

damage. Nominal damages can never be awarded in a negligence action since actual damages are required for the existence of this tort. Nominal damages are awarded in intentional and strict liability cases when the tort has been committed, but no actual harm has resulted other than the technical commission of the tort. Attorneys usually do not take cases that do not present the possibility of substantial damages, since fees are often a percentage of the damages received. Where only nominal damages are likely, the plaintiff's incentive to bring the case is to vindicate a right or to warn the defendant that future misconduct of the same kind will lead to further suits. An attorney taking such a case will probably be paid on an hourly or set fee basis rather than a percentage basis.

General damages are those compensatory damages that generally result from the kind of conduct in which the defendant was engaged. General damages usually and naturally follow from such conduct. Pain and suffering, for example, naturally follow from a severe head injury. In most states, the plaintiff's complaint does not have to allege general damages with specificity. The law will presume that general damages result from the wrong complained of.

Special damages are those compensatory damages that are peculiar to the particular plaintiff, for example, medical expenses, loss of earnings, loss of sales, insanity resulting from the tort. Special damages usually must be specifically pleaded in the complaint. They are also called **consequential damages.**

Punitive damages are a noncompensatory form of damages to punish the defendant and to deter similar conduct by others. Punitive damages are awarded when the defendant has acted with actual malice, ill will, or conscious disregard for others. Mere negligence is not enough, nor is intentional conduct enough, unless a court can conclude that the defendant has acted in a morally reprehensible way. Punitive damages are also called **exemplary damages.**

Hedonic damages are compensatory damages that cover the victim's loss of pleasure or enjoyment—in raising children, in experiencing the morning sun, in reading a good book, in singing in a choir, in attending college, etc. Many argue that hedonic damages are improper because they are already provided for in the award for pain and suffering. If, however, the victim dies immediately, there may have been no pain and suffering. The concept of hedonic damages is relatively new; it is unclear how many states will allow juries to consider it.

CASE

O'Shea v. Riverway Towing Co.
677 F.2d 1194 (7th Cir. 1982)
United States Court of Appeals for the Seventh Circuit

Background: Margaret O'Shea was a cook on a Mississippi towboat. After falling and breaking her leg getting off the boat, she sued her employer, Riverway, for negligently causing the fall. She won in the district court (the federal trial court), which awarded her over

$150,000 in damages for lost future wages. The case is now on appeal before the United States Court of Appeals for Seventh Circuit.

Decision on Appeal: The award of damages was proper.

Opinion of Court

Judge POSNER delivered the opinion of the court. . . .

When the harbor boat reached shore it tied up to a seawall the top of which was several feet above the boat's deck. There was no ladder. The other passengers, who were seamen, clambered up the seawall without difficulty, but Mrs. O'Shea, a 57-year-old woman who weighs 200 pounds (she is five foot seven), balked. According to Mrs. O'Shea testimony, which the district court believed, a deckhand instructed her to climb the stairs to a catwalk above the deck and disembark from there. But the catwalk was three feet above the top of the seawall, and again there was no ladder. The deckhand told her that she should jump and that the men who had already disembarked would help her land safely. She did as told, but fell in landing, carrying the assisting seamen down with her, and broke her leg. . . .

Mrs. O'Shea's job as a cook paid her $40 a day, and since the custom was to work 30 days consecutively and then have the next 30 days off, this comes to $7200 a year although, as we shall see, she never had earned that much in a single year. She testified that when the accident occurred she had been about to get another cook's job on a Mississippi towboat that would have paid her $60 a day ($10,800 a year). She also testified that she had been intending to work as a boat's cook until she was 70—longer if she was able. An economist who testified on Mrs. O'Shea's behalf used the foregoing testimony as the basis for estimating the wages that she lost because of the accident. He first subtracted federal income tax from yearly wage estimates based on alternative assumptions about her wage rate (that it would be either $40 or

$60 a day); assumed that this wage would have grown by between six and eight percent a year; assumed that she would have worked either to age 65 or to age 70; and then discounted the resulting lost-wage estimates to present value, using a discount rate of 8.5 percent a year. These calculations, being based on alternative assumptions concerning starting wage rate, annual wage increases, and length of employment, yielded a range of values rather than a single value. The bottom of the range was $50,000. This is the present value, computed at an 8.5 percent discount rate, of Mrs. O'Shea's lost future wages on the assumption that her starting wage was $40 a day and that it would have grown by six percent a year until she retired at the age of 65. The top of the range was $114,000, which is the present value (again discounted at 8.5 percent) of her lost future wages assuming she would have worked till she was 70 at a wage that would have started at $60 a day and increased by eight percent a year. The judge awarded a figure—$86,033—near the midpoint of this range. He did not explain in his written opinion how he had arrived at this figure, but in a preceding oral opinion he stated that he was "not certain that she would work until age 70 at this type of work," although "she certainly was entitled to" do so and "could have earned something"; and that he had not "felt bound by [the economist's] figure of eight per cent increase in wages" and had "not found the wages based on necessarily a 60 dollar a day job." If this can be taken to mean that he thought Mrs. O'Shea would probably have worked till she was 70, starting at $40 a day but moving up from there at six rather than eight percent a year, the economist's estimate of the present value of her lost future wages would be $75,000.

There is no doubt that the accident disabled Mrs. O'Shea from working as a cook on a boat. The break in her leg was very serious: it reduced the stability of the leg and caused her to fall frequently. It is impossible to see how she could have continued working as a cook, a job performed mostly while standing up, and especially on a boat, with its unsteady motion. But Riverway argues that Mrs. O'Shea (who has not worked at all since the accident, which occurred two years before the trial) could have gotten some sort of job and that the wages in that job should be deducted from the admittedly higher wages that she could have earned as a cook on a boat.

The question is not whether Mrs. O'Shea is totally disabled in the sense, relevant to social security disability cases but not tort cases, that there is no job in the American economy for which she is medically fit. It is whether she can by reasonable diligence find gainful employment, given the physical condition in which the accident left her. Here is a middle-aged woman, very overweight, badly scarred on one arm and one leg, unsteady on her feet, in constant and serious pain from the accident, with no education beyond high school and no work skills other than cooking, a job that happens to require standing for long periods which she is incapable of doing. It seems unlikely that someone in this condition could find gainful work at the minimum wage. True, the probability is not zero; and a better procedure, therefore, might have been to subtract from Mrs. O'Shea's lost future wages as a boat's cook the wages in some other job, discounted (i.e., multiplied) by the probability—very low—that she would in fact be able to get another job. But the district judge cannot be criticized for having failed to use a procedure not suggested by either party. The question put to him was the dichotomous one, would she or would she not get another job if she made reasonable efforts to do so? This required him to decide whether there was a more than 50 percent probability that she would. We cannot say that the negative answer he gave to that question was clearly erroneous.

Riverway argues next that it was wrong for the judge to award damages on the basis of a wage not validated, as it were, by at least a year's employment at that wage. Mrs. O'Shea had never worked full time, had never in fact earned more than $3600 in a full year, and in the year preceding the accident had earned only $900. But previous wages do not put a cap on an award of lost future wages. If a man who had never worked in his life graduated from law school, began working at a law firm at an annual salary of $35,000, and was killed the second day on the job, his lack of a past wage history would be irrelevant to computing his lost future wages. The present case is similar if less dramatic. Mrs. O'Shea did not work at all until 1974, when her husband died. She then lived on her inheritance and worked at a variety of part-time jobs till January 1979, when she started working as a cook on the towboat. According to her testimony, which the trial judge believed, she was then working full time. It is immaterial that this was her first full-time job and that the accident occurred before she had held it for a full year. Her job history was typical of women who return to the labor force after their children are grown or, as in Mrs. O'Shea's case, after their husband dies, and these women are, like any tort victims, entitled to damages based on what they would have earned in the future rather than on what they may or may not have earned in the past.

If we are correct so far, Mrs. O'Shea was entitled to have her lost wages determined on the assumption that she would have earned at least $7200 in the first year after the accident and that the accident caused her to lose that entire amount by disabling her from any gainful employment. And since Riverway neither challenges the district judge's (apparent) finding that Mrs. O'Shea would have worked till she was 70 nor contends that the lost wages for each year until then should be discounted by the probability that she would in fact have been alive and working as a boat's cook throughout the damage period, we may also assume that her wages would have been at least $7200 a year for the 12 years between the date of the accident and her seventieth birthday. But Riverway does argue that we cannot assume she might have earned $10,800 a year rather than $7200, despite her testimony that at the time of the accident she was about to take another job as a boat's cook where she would have been paid at the rate of $60 rather than $40 a day. The point is not terribly important since the trial judge gave little weight to this testimony, but we shall discuss it briefly. Mrs. O'Shea was asked on direct examination what "pay you would have worked" for in the new job. Riverway's counsel objected on the ground of hearsay, the judge overruled his objection, and she answered $60 a day. The objection was not well taken. Riverway argues that only her prospective employer knew what her wage was, and hence when she said it was $60 she was testifying to what he had told her. But an employee's wage is as much in the personal knowledge of the employee as of the employer. If Mrs. O'Shea's prospective employer had testified that he would have paid her $60, Riverway's counsel could have made the converse hearsay objection that the employer was really testifying to what Mrs. O'Shea had told him she was willing to work for. Riverway's counsel could on cross-examination have probed the basis for Mrs. O'Shea's belief that she was going to get $60 a day in a new job, but he did not do so and cannot complain now that the judge may have given her testimony some (though little) weight.

We come at last to the most important issue in the case, which is the proper treatment of inflation in calculating lost future wages. Mrs. O'Shea's economist based the six to eight percent range which he used to estimate future increases in the wages of a boat's cook on the general pattern of wage increases in service occupations over the past 25 years. During the second half of this period the rate of inflation has been substantial and has accounted for much of the increase in nominal wages in this period; and to use that increase to project future wage increases is therefore to assume that inflation will continue, and continue to push up wages. Riverway argues that it is improper as a matter of law to take inflation into account in projecting lost future wages. Yet Riverway itself wants to take inflation into account—one-sidedly, to reduce the amount of the damages computed. For Riverway does not object to the economist's choice of an 8.5 percent discount rate for reducing Mrs. O'Shea's lost future wages to present value, although the rate includes an allowance—a very large allowance—for inflation.

To explain, the object of discounting lost future wages to present value is to give the plaintiff an amount of money which, invested safely, will grow to a sum equal to those wages. So if we thought that but for the accident Mrs. O'Shea would have earned $7200 in 1990, and we were computing in 1980 (when this case was tried) her damages based on those lost earnings, we would need to determine the sum of money that, invested safely for a period of 10 years, would grow to $7200. Suppose that in 1980 the rate of interest on ultra-safe (i.e., federal government) bonds or notes maturing in 10 years was 12 percent. Then we would consult a table of present values to see what sum of money invested at 12 percent for 10 years would at the end of that time have grown to $7200. The answer is $2318. But a moment's reflection will show that to give Mrs. O'Shea $2318 to compensate her for lost wages in 1990 would grossly undercompensate her. People demand 12 percent to lend money risklessly for 10 years because they expect their principal to have much less purchasing power when they get it back at the end of the time. In other words, when long-term interest rates are high, they are high in order to compensate lenders for the fact that they will be repaid in cheaper dollars. In periods when no inflation is anticipated, the risk-free interest rate is between one and three percent. See references in *Doca v. Marina Mercante Nicaraguense, S.A.,* 634 F.2d 30, 39 n.2 (2d Cir. 1980). Additional percentage points above that level reflect inflation anticipated over the life of the loan. But if there is inflation it will affect wages as well as prices. Therefore to give Mrs. O'Shea $2318 today because that is the present value of $7200 10 years hence, computed at a discount rate—12 percent—that consists mainly of an allowance for anticipated inflation, is in fact to give her less than she would have been earning then if she was earning $7200 on the date of the accident, even if the only wage increases she would have received would have been those necessary to keep pace with inflation.

There are (at least) two ways to deal with inflation in computing the present value of lost future wages. One is to take it out of both the wages and the discount rate—to say to Mrs. O'Shea, "we are going to calculate your probable wage in 1990 on the assumption, unrealistic as it is, that there will be zero inflation between now and then; and, to be consistent, we are going to discount the amount thus calculated by the interest rate that would be charged under the same assumption of zero inflation." Thus, if we thought Mrs. O'Shea's real (i.e., inflation-free) wage rate would not rise in the future, we would fix her lost earnings in 1990 as $7200 and, to be consistent, we would discount that to present (1980) value using an estimate of the real interest rate. At two percent, this procedure would yield a present value of $5906. Of course, she would not invest this money at a mere two percent. She would invest it at the much higher prevailing interest rate. But that would not give her a windfall; it would just enable her to replace her lost 1990 earnings with an amount equal to what she would in fact have earned in that year if inflation continues, as most people expect it to do. (If people did not expect continued inflation,

long-term interest rates would be much lower; those rates impound investors' inflationary expectations.)

An alternative approach, which yields the same result, is to use a (higher) discount rate based on the current risk-free 10-year interest rate, but apply that rate to an estimate of lost future wages that includes expected inflation. Contrary to Riverway's argument, this projection would not require gazing into a crystal ball. The expected rate of inflation can, as just suggested, be read off from the current long-term interest rate. If that rate is 12 percent, and if as suggested earlier the real or inflation-free interest rate is only one to three percent, this implies that the market is anticipating 9–11 percent inflation over the next 10 years, for a long-term interest rate is simply the sum of the real interest rate and the anticipated rate of inflation during the term.

Either approach to dealing with inflation is acceptable (they are, in fact, equivalent) and we by no means rule out others; but it is illogical and indefensible to build inflation into the discount rate yet ignore it in calculating the lost future wages that are to be discounted. That results in systematic undercompensation, just as building inflation into the estimate of future lost earnings and then discounting using the real rate of interest would systematically overcompensate. The former error is committed, we respectfully suggest, by those circuits, notably the Fifth, that refuse to allow inflation to be used in projecting lost future earnings but then use a discount rate that has built into it a large allowance for inflation. See, e.g., *Culver v. Slater Boat Co.,* 644 F.2d 460, 464 (5th Cir. 1981) (using a 9.125 percent discount rate). We align ourselves instead with those circuits (a majority, see *Doca v. Marina Mercante Nicaraguense, S.A.,* supra, 634 F.2d at 35–36), notably the Second, that require that inflation be treated consistently in choosing a discount rate and in estimating the future lost wages to be discounted to present value using that rate. . . .

Applying our analysis to the present case, we cannot pronounce the approach taken by the plaintiff's economist unreasonable. He chose a discount rate—8.5 percent—well above the real rate of interest, and therefore containing an allowance for inflation. Consistency required him to inflate Mrs. O'Shea's starting wage as a boat's cook in calculating her lost future wages, and he did so at a rate of six to eight percent a year. If this rate had been intended as a forecast of purely inflationary wage changes, his approach would be open to question, especially at the upper end of his range. For if the estimated rate of inflation were eight percent, the use of a discount rate of 8.5 percent would imply that the real rate of interest was only .5 percent, which is lower than most economists believe it to be for any substantial period of time. But wages do not rise just because of inflation. Mrs. O'Shea could expect her real wages as a boat's cook to rise as she became more experienced and as average real wage rates throughout the economy rose, as they usually do over a decade or more. It would not be outlandish to assume that even if there were no inflation, Mrs. O'Shea's wages would have risen by three percent a year. If we subtract that from the economist's six to eight percent range, the inflation allowance built into his estimated future wage increases is only three to five percent; and when we subtract these figures from 8.5 percent we see that his implicit estimate of the real rate of interest was very high (3.5–5.5 percent). This means he was conservative, because the higher the discount rate used the lower the damages calculated.

If conservative in one sense, the economist was most liberal in another. He made no allowance for the fact that Mrs. O'Shea, whose health history quite apart from the accident is not outstanding, might very well not have survived—let alone survived and been working as a boat's cook or in an equivalent job—until the age of 70. The damage award is a sum certain, but the lost future wages to which that award is equated by means of the discount rate are mere probabilities. If the probability of her being employed as a boat's cook full time in 1990 was only 75 percent, for example, then her estimated wages in that year should have been multiplied by .75 to determine the value of the expectation that she lost as a result of the accident; and so with each of the other future years. The economist did not do this, and by failing to do this he overstated the loss due to the accident.

But Riverway does not make an issue of this aspect of the economist's analysis. Nor of another: the economist selected the 8.5 percent figure for the discount rate because that was the current interest rate on Triple A 10-year state and municipal bonds, but it would not make sense in Mrs. O'Shea's federal income tax bracket to invest in tax-free bonds. If he wanted to use nominal rather than real interest rates and wage increases (as we said was proper), the economist should have used a higher discount rate and a higher expected rate of inflation. But as these adjustments would have been largely or entirely offsetting, the failure to make them was not a critical error.

Although we are not entirely satisfied with the economic analysis on which the judge, in the absence of any other evidence of the present value of Mrs. O'Shea's lost future wages, must have relied heavily, we recognize that the exactness which economic analysis rigorously pursued appears to offer is, at least in the litigation setting, somewhat delusive. Therefore, we will not reverse an award of damages for lost wages because of questionable assumptions unless it yields an unreasonable result—especially when, as in the present case, the defendant does not offer any economic evidence himself and does not object to the questionable steps in the plaintiff's economic analysis. We cannot say the result here was unreasonable. If the economist's method of estimating damages was too generous to Mrs. O'Shea in one important respect it was, as we have seen, niggardly in another. Another error against Mrs. O'Shea should be noted: the economist should not have deducted her entire income tax liability in estimating her future lost wages. While it is true that the damage award is not taxable, the interest she earns on it will be (a point the economist may have ignored because of his erroneous assumption that she would invest the award in tax-exempt bonds), so that his method involved an element of double taxation.

If we assume that Mrs. O'Shea could have expected a three percent annual increase in her real wages from a base of $7200, that the real risk-free rate of interest (and therefore the appropriate discount rate if we are considering only real wage increases) is two percent, and that she would have worked till she was 70, the present value of her lost future wages would be $91,310. This figure ignores the fact that she did not have a 100 percent probability of actually working till age 70 as a boat's cook, and fails to make the appropriate (though probably, in her bracket, very small) net income tax adjustment; but it also ignores the possibility, small but not totally negligible, that the proper base is really $10,800 rather than $7200.

So we cannot say that the figure arrived at by the judge, $86,033, was unreasonably high. But we are distressed that he made no attempt to explain how he had arrived at that figure, since it was not one contained in the economist's testimony though it must in some way have been derived from that testimony. Unlike many other damage items in a personal injury case, notably pain and suffering, the calculation of damages for lost earnings can and should be an analytical rather than an intuitive undertaking. Therefore, compliance with Rule 52(a) of the Federal Rules of Civil Procedure requires that in a bench trial the district judge set out the steps by which he arrived at his award for lost future earnings, in order to assist the appellate court in reviewing the award. The district judge failed to do that here. We do not consider this reversible error, because our own analysis convinces us that the award of damages for lost future wages was reasonable. But for the future we ask the district judges in this circuit to indicate the steps by which they arrive at damage awards for lost future earnings.

Judgment Affirmed.

■ ASSIGNMENT 14.1 ■

a. What is meant by present value? What role does it play in an award of damages?
b. What tactical mistakes did the attorney representing the employer make in the trial of this case?

■ PAIN AND SUFFERING

Pain is often experienced when a tort is committed, at the time of medical treatment, and while recovering. During these periods, mental suffering or distress can also occur. For example:

- fright
- humiliation
- fear and anxiety

- loss of companionship
- unhappiness
- depression or other forms of mental illness

The amount recovered for pain and suffering will depend on the amount of time it was experienced and the intensity of the experience. Also considered are the age and condition of life of the plaintiff. It is, of course, very difficult to assign a dollar amount that will compensate the plaintiff for pain and suffering. The main guide available is the amount a reasonable person would estimate as fair. A minority of states permit counsel to make **per diem** arguments to the jury whereby a certain amount is requested for every day the pain and suffering has been endured and is expected to continue. Other states do not allow such arguments on the ground that they are too arbitrary. A few states have statutes limiting the amount of damages for pain and suffering that can be recovered in certain kinds of cases, e.g., medical malpractice.

▪ PROPERTY DAMAGE

The defendant can inflict loss to property through the commission of a number of torts, such as negligence, trespass to chattels, and conversion. The measure of damages depends on the extent of the loss caused by the tort.

> **Property destroyed:** The measure of damages is the fair market value of the property at the time of the destruction.

> **Property damaged but not destroyed:** The measure of damages is the difference between the fair market value of the property before the damage was done and its fair market value after the damage was done.

> **Deprivation of the use of the property:** The measure of damages is the fair market value of the use of the property during the time the plaintiff was wrongfully deprived of its use.

Fair market value is what the property could probably have been sold for in the ordinary course of a voluntary sale by a willing seller to a willing buyer.[1] The fair market value of the use of the property might be the cost that an unpressured lessee would have to pay to rent the property from a willing lessor.

There are times when the fair market value of property is not a proper measure of damages, for example, a family portrait that may have no exchange value or a dog trained to answer only one master. In such cases, other measures of damage might be used, e.g., replacement value, original cost, value of the time spent producing it.[2]

In addition, the plaintiff can recover for any mental distress that accompanied the destruction, damage, or deprivation of the property.

▪ ASSIGNMENT 14.2 ▪

Prepare an annotated bibliography on the rules that exist in your state governing damages in any tort case. Include rules for personal injury as well as property damage. For example, what is the measure of damages, are there

---

[1]McCormick, *Handbook on the Law of Damages* 165 (1975).
[2]*Restatement (Second) of Torts* § 911, comment e (1979).

limits on recovery, are there certain kinds of arguments that cannot be made to the jury, are there special rules for certain kinds of cases, etc.? (See General Instructions for the Annotated Bibliography Assignment in Chapter 2.)

▪ DOCTRINE OF AVOIDABLE CONSEQUENCES

Once plaintiffs have been injured, they must take reasonable steps to avoid further injury to themselves. A defendant will not be liable for those damages that could reasonably have been avoided by a plaintiff. This doctrine of **avoidable consequences** is different from contributory negligence. The latter is unreasonable conduct by the plaintiff that bars all recovery. It occurs before or simultaneously with the wrong committed by the defendant. The doctrine of avoidable consequences refers to unreasonable conduct by the plaintiff *after* the defendant has wronged the plaintiff. All recovery is not barred. The amount of the recovery is reduced to cover those damages the plaintiff brought on him- or herself by failing to use reasonable care after the initial injury was received.

The most obvious example is the plaintiff who fails to obtain medical help after being injured by the defendant. The plaintiff has thereby aggravated his or her own injury. The defendant will be liable for the initial injury, but not for the **aggravation** of that injury if the failure to seek medical assistance was unreasonable under the circumstances (e.g., such assistance was available, was known about by the plaintiff, and had a good chance of helping the plaintiff).

The same principles apply to harm to property. Suppose that the defendant negligently sets fire to a small portion of the plaintiff's barn. The plaintiff cannot sit by and watch the entire farm burn up if some reasonable steps by the plaintiff could have **mitigated** the loss (e.g., throwing an available bucket of water on the fire or calling the fire department).

▪ ASSIGNMENT 14.3 ▪

Mary negligently hits a pedestrian. The pedestrian is rushed to the hospital and told that a blood transfusion is necessary. The pedestrian refuses on religious grounds. The pedestrian dies. For what damages will Mary be responsible in the negligence action brought by the pedestrian's estate? (See General Instructions for the Legal Analysis Assignment in Chapter 3.) How would your state handle this problem? (See General Instructions for the State Court Opinion Assignment in Chapter 2.)

▪ COLLATERAL-SOURCE RULE

When a person is injured or dies, he or she often receives funds or services from a variety of sources other than the defendant:

- the plaintiff's own medical or life insurance
- company insurance
- veteran's benefits
- Social Security
- wage continuation plans
- free medical care provided by a relative

These are all **collateral sources**—sources to which the defendant did not contribute. When the time comes to calculate the total amount in damages owed by the defendant to the plaintiff, should this amount be reduced by what the plaintiff has received through collateral sources? Not in most states, even though the plaintiff, in effect, recovers twice for part or all of the injury. This is the collateral-source rule. The defendant is not given the benefit of the plaintiff's good luck or resourcefulness in being able to receive benefits from collateral sources.

▪ JOINT TORTFEASORS

Joint tortfeasors fall into two categories:

- persons acting in concert to produce a negligent or intentional wrong
- persons not acting in concert whose wrongs produce a single indivisible result[3]

The significance of being a joint tortfeasor is that each joint tortfeasor is **jointly and severally liable** for the entire harm suffered by the plaintiff. This means that the plaintiff can sue any individual joint tortfeasor for the entire harm or can join them all to recover for the entire harm. It does not mean that the plaintiff receives a multiple recovery. The plaintiff can receive only one satisfaction. Yet the plaintiff chooses whether to go after all of them or one of them. If the plaintiff sues one, but is unable to collect the full judgment, the plaintiff can sue the remaining tortfeasors until the full amount of the damages is recovered. Suppose only one joint tortfeasor pays the entire judgment. Can this person then collect anything from the other joint tortfeasors as their "share"? We will consider this separate topic later when we discuss contribution. It is of no concern to the plaintiff that the joint tortfeasors did not pay the judgment equally. They are left to fight this out among themselves. The plaintiff's only interest is in recovering full damages.

Persons Acting in Concert

Persons who act in **concert** to produce the negligent or intentional wrong are joint tortfeasors, and hence are jointly and severally liable for the harm they caused while on their **joint venture.**

Examples:

- Mary and Jane buy a truck together to make deliveries together. One day, they are late in making a delivery. Mary, the driver, starts speeding. Jane urges her to go even faster. The truck negligently hits the plaintiff. Both Mary and Jane are joint tortfeasors.
- Al and Donald agree to steal the plaintiff's goods. Al takes the goods while Donald acts as lookout. Both are joint tortfeasors.

There must be an express agreement or a tacit understanding that each will participate in the activity that produces the wrong. No such agreement or understanding would exist, for example, with a hitchhiker in the truck of Mary and Jane at the time of the accident in the first case above. The hitchhiker would not be a joint tortfeasor along with Mary and Jane. To be a joint tortfeasor, the person must cooperate in the wrong, encourage it, or otherwise be an active participant.

---

[3]Some authorities feel that it is a mistake to include such persons in the category of joint tortfeasors. Joint tortfeasors, according to this view, should be limited to defendants who act in concert and should not extend to independent defendants who concurrently produce the wrong.

Someone who approves or **ratifies** the wrong after it is done for his or her benefit can also be a joint tortfeasor.

Persons Not Acting in Concert

Here the defendants act independently of each other and produce a single, indivisible result; there is no joint venture. Each defendant, however, is a substantial factor in producing a harm that is **indivisible,** in that it comes from a single impact that cannot be divided.

> **Example:** Two cars carelessly collide on the highway. They both run into and kill the plaintiff, a pedestrian.

The drivers are jointly and severally liable for the death of the pedestrian. If the result cannot be practically divided, it is indivisible, and the defendants who independently and concurrently cause it are jointly and severally liable. They are treated in the same way as they would be if they acted in concert.

If the harm is divisible, there is no joint tortfeasorship and no joint and several liability. Suppose that two companies independently pollute a stream with different chemicals, which can be separately identified. Each company will be liable only for that portion of the damage it caused. Suppose, however, that it is difficult to apportion the damages, because the companies used the same chemicals or because the different chemicals cannot be separately identified. The plaintiff and the defendants are in difficult positions. The plaintiff must do more than show that "somebody caused me harm." How is the plaintiff to meet his or her burden of proving what the individual defendants caused? From the defendants' perspective, it is unfair to saddle any one of them with the harm caused by the other defendants. A few courts shift the burden to the defendants and require them to establish who caused what. Most courts do not go this far; yet, they will assist the plaintiff in such cases by accepting a rough approximation of the portion of the harm caused by each defendant.

▪ ASSIGNMENT 14.4 ▪

Ten families live in an apartment complex. They are very unhappy with the maintenance service provided by the landlord. Nine of the families begin throwing their garbage in a pile in one of the alleys next to the main building. The garbage draws many rats, which infest the apartment of the tenth family. This family sues the other nine families for negligence when it is forced to move out because of the rats.

a. Are the nine families jointly and severally liable? (See General Instructions for the Legal Analysis Assignment in Chapter 3.)
b. Prepare an investigation strategy to help you determine whether the nine families are jointly and severally liable. (See General Instructions for the Investigation Strategy Assignment in Chapter 4.)

▪ RELEASE

Satisfaction is the receipt of full payment or compensation by the plaintiff. If the satisfaction has been received from one joint tortfeasor, the others can no longer be sued by the plaintiff. A **release,** on the other hand, is the giving up of a claim. This may be done for "free" **(gratuitously)** or for money or something else of value **(consideration).**

> **Example:**   While Tim and Fred are fishing in a lake, they negligently destroy Diane's boat, which was moored at the dock. Because they were engaged in a joint enterprise, they are jointly and severally liable to her for the damage. Diane agrees, however, to give up (i.e., release) all her claims against Tim and Fred if they stop fishing in the lake where the accident occurred. They agree. If they abide by their agreement, Diane cannot later change her mind and sue them for the damage to her boat.

What happens if the plaintiff releases only one of the joint tortfeasors? Are the other joint tortfeasors likewise released? Yes. In most states, the release of one joint tortfeasor automatically releases the others. Statutes in some states change this result by providing that the release of one does not automatically discharge the others. The plaintiff under these statutes can still go after the other joint tortfeasors.

In states where the release of one discharges all the joint tortfeasors, there is a device designed to get around this result. The device works as follows: In the negotiation with one joint tortfeasor, the plaintiff does not provide a release. Rather, he or she makes a promise or **covenant not to sue** that joint tortfeasor. The covenant, unlike the release, does not act as a bar to go after the other joint tortfeasors.

• ASSIGNMENT 14.5 •

What happens in your state when the plaintiff wants to settle with and release one of the joint tortfeasors? Are the other joint tortfeasors automatically discharged? (See General Instructions for the State Code Assignment, and for the State Court Opinion Assignment, both in Chapter 2.)

■ CONTRIBUTION

Suppose that the plaintiff obtains satisfaction of the entire amount of damages from one of the joint tortfeasors. Can that tortfeasor now force the other joint tortfeasors to contribute their share of the amount paid? Can he or she obtain **contribution,** which is a proportional payment among joint tortfeasors? States answer this question differently:

- Some states deny contribution among joint tortfeasors.
- Some states allow contribution only among joint tortfeasors against whom the plaintiff has secured a judgment. Those not sued would not have to contribute.
- Some states allow contribution only among joint tortfeasors who were negligent. Intentional joint tortfeasors cannot obtain contribution.

When contribution is allowed, the allocation is usually pro rata, or proportionate to the number of joint tortfeasors: two would be responsible for fifty percent each, three for $33^{1}/_{3}$ each, etc. A few states, however, make the allocation according to the relative fault of the joint tortfeasors.

Again, contribution is not a concern of the plaintiff who has received satisfaction. Contribution is a battle among the joint tortfeasors.

■ ASSIGNMENT 14.6 ■

When, if ever, is contribution allowed among joint tortfeasors in your state? (See General Instructions for the State Code Assignment, and for the State Court Opinion Assignment, both in Chapter 2.)

■ INDEMNITY

Indemnity is a device whereby one party who has paid the plaintiff can force another party to reimburse him or her for the full amount paid. Unlike contribution, which usually calls for a proportionate sharing of the loss, indemnity shifts the entire loss from the defendant who has paid onto someone else. Indemnity can arise by contract, where one person agrees to indemnify the other for any loss that results if the latter is sued. Indemnity can also arise by operation of law independent of any agreement between the parties.

Examples:

- The defendant is found liable for a tort and pays solely because of vicarious liability. That defendant can then obtain indemnity from the person who actually committed the tort; for example, an employer vicariously liable for a tort committed by its employee within the scope of employment can be indemnified by the employee once the employer has paid the judgment.
- The supermarket, which is strictly liable for a product it sold, can obtain indemnity from the negligent manufacturer who made the product—once the supermarket pays the judgment.
- One who has been passively negligent may be able to obtain indemnity from the person who was actively negligent or who acted intentionally.

The person seeking indemnity is liable for the tort. This person, however, is allowed to make someone else reimburse him or her for the judgment he or she has paid when it appears equitable to do so. The relationship between the party who has paid and the party against whom indemnity is sought must be such that in fairness we can say that the latter should pay.

■ ASSIGNMENT 14.7 ■

Prepare an annotated bibliography on indemnity in tort cases for your state. (See General Instructions for the Annotated Bibliography Assignment in Chapter 2.)

SUMMARY

Different kinds of damages exist: compensatory damages, which make the victim whole; nominal damages, which provide a small amount when there has been no actual loss; general damages, which flow naturally from the wrong; special damages, which are peculiar to the victim; punitive damages, which punish the wrongdoer and deter others; and hedonic damages, which cover the loss of pleasure.

Damages for pain and suffering cover the unpleasant emotions that accompanied the wrong. The measure of damages to property is often the fair market value of the property before and after the wrong. A defendant will not be liable for the additional or aggravated damages that the victim's reasonable steps could have avoided. Under the collateral-source rule, the amount in damages owed by the defendant is not reduced by the injury-related funds received by the plaintiff from sources independent of the trial.

Joint tortfeasors are jointly and severally liable for the harm they wrongfully cause. They may have acted in concert or independently to produce an indivisible result. If the victim receives full payment (satisfaction) from one joint tortfeasor, the other joint tortfeasors cannot be sued. The relinquishment (release) of a claim against one joint tortfeasor usually acts to discharge the others. States differ on whether and when joint tortfeasors can seek contribution and thereby allocate the damages among themselves. Indemnity is the device whereby one party who has paid the plaintiff can force another party to reimburse him or her for the full amount paid.

Key Terms

damages
compensatory damages
out-of-pocket
pain and suffering
nominal damages
general damages
special damages
consequential damages
punitive damages
exemplary damages
hedonic damages

per diem
fair market value
avoidable consequences
aggravation
mitigated
collateral sources
joint tortfeasors
jointly and severally
  liable
concert

joint venture
ratifies
indivisible
satisfaction
release
gratuitously
consideration
covenant not to sue
contribution
indemnity

CHAPTER 15

Negligence: Defenses

CHAPTER OUTLINE

- INTRODUCTION
- CONTRIBUTORY NEGLIGENCE
    Plaintiff's Negligence
    Cause in Fact
- LAST CLEAR CHANCE
    Plaintiff in Helpless Peril
    Plaintiff in Inattentive Peril
- COMPARATIVE NEGLIGENCE
    Pure Comparative Negligence
    Restricted Comparative
        Negligence
- ASSUMPTION OF THE RISK
    Understanding the Risk
    Voluntarily Confronting the Risk

INTRODUCTION

In Chapter 31, we will discuss the defenses of sovereign immunity, public official immunity, intrafamily tort immunity, and charitable immunity.

In this chapter, our primary concern will be the two major defenses to negligence: contributory negligence and assumption of the risk. The doctrines of last clear chance and comparative negligence are also examined. As you will see, these defenses are all interrelated.

Contributory negligence: Acts as a complete defense to the plaintiff's negligence action against the defendant. If the plaintiff was unreasonable in avoiding risks for his or her own safety, and if this unreasonableness was a substantial factor in producing the plaintiff's own injury, the defendant is not liable, even though the defendant was also negligent by unreasonably creating risks for the plaintiff's safety, and even though the defendant's unreasonableness also was a substantial factor in producing the plaintiff's injury.

Last clear chance: Acts to offset the impact of contributory negligence and is designed to benefit the plaintiff only. It comes into play when the

317

defendant establishes the contributory negligence of the plaintiff. When this happens, the normal result, as indicated above, is that the plaintiff loses, because contributory negligence is a complete defense. The plaintiff wins, however, if the defendant had the last clear chance to avoid the injury of the plaintiff but failed to use this chance. In such a case the plaintiff wins, even though the plaintiff was contributorily negligent.

Comparative negligence: Acts to apportion the damages between the plaintiff and the defendant. Comparative negligence applies only in a state that has abolished contributory negligence partially or completely. In comparative negligence states, the contributory negligence of the plaintiff does not act as a complete bar to the plaintiff's action.

Assumption of the risk: Acts as a complete defense to the plaintiff's negligence action against the defendant. If the plaintiff knowingly and voluntarily accepts the risk of being injured by the negligence of the defendant, the latter is not liable for the injury it negligently caused the plaintiff.

The defenses of contributory negligence and assumption of the risk, particularly the former, are disliked by courts and legislatures. As a result, the law governing these defenses has gone through considerable change in an effort to avoid what is distasteful about them. In some states, the defenses have been abolished in whole or in part.

▪ CONTRIBUTORY NEGLIGENCE

Contributory negligence is a very drastic doctrine. It leaves the plaintiff to bear the full loss of his or her injury. The negligent defendant walks away without having to pay a penny because the plaintiff was also negligent, even if considerably less so than the defendant.

There are, however, some limitations on this defense. The contributory negligence of the plaintiff will prevent liability primarily when the defendant has committed **ordinary negligence.** If the defendant's negligence falls into the category of **wilful, wanton, or reckless conduct,** the contributory negligence of the plaintiff will not prevent the defendant's liability. Also, contributory negligence is never a defense to any of the intentional torts the defendant might commit.

In most states, contributory negligence must be pleaded and proven by a preponderance of the evidence by the defendant. It is an affirmative defense. In a few states, however, the *plaintiff* has the burden of pleading and proving that the injury was not caused by his or her negligence.

There are two major elements of contributory negligence:

▪ plaintiff's negligence (unreasonableness)
▪ cause in fact

Plaintiff's Negligence (Unreasonableness)

Example: Ben is driving 40 mph in a 40 mph zone in rainy weather at night. Fred runs through a red light and hits Ben's car. Ben sues Fred for negligence. In Fred's answer, he raises the defense of contributory negligence.

In Chapter 12, we considered the standard that would apply to a defendant such as Fred who is sued for negligence: a defendant will be liable for acting unrea-

Figure 15.1   Breach-of-Duty Equation

Foreseeability of the danger of an accident occuring

——————————————

Foreseeability of the kind of injury or damage that will result if an accident occurs

balanced against

The burden or inconvenience on the defendant of taking precautions to avoid the accident

——————————————

The importance or social utility of what the defendant was trying to do before the accident

sonably under the circumstances. This same test applies to determine whether a *plaintiff* has been contributorily negligent.

Plaintiffs must not take **unreasonable risks** of injuring themselves. There is a formula or equation that is used to determine whether someone has acted unreasonably. See Figure 15.1. This is the same equation used to determine whether the defendant was negligent or unreasonable. See Figure 12.4 in Chapter 12.

When you are charged with contributory negligence, the allegation is that you acted unreasonably for your own safety. To determine whether this was so, we apply the equation by asking a series of questions. How foreseeable was it to you that your conduct would contribute to an accident? How foreseeable should it have been to you? What kind of injury was foreseeable to you? What kind of injury should have been foreseeable to you? What kind of burden or inconvenience would you have had to endure in order to take added precautions to avoid injuring yourself? What were you trying to do before the accident? How important or socially beneficial was it? These are the questions that a reasonable person would ask in your position.

If the danger of an accident causing serious injury to yourself outweighs whatever burden or inconvenience you would have had to go through to avoid this injury, then you were unreasonable and hence negligent in failing to take those preventive steps. The equation also considers the importance or social utility of what you were trying to do at the time. A reasonable person is more likely to take risks of injuring him- or herself when engaged in socially useful tasks than when engaged in minor or frivolous activities.

In the example involving Ben and Fred, was Ben contributorily negligent? He was driving 40 mph in a 40 mph zone in rainy weather at night. All of the circumstances of the accident would have to be considered in applying the equation. To determine the foreseeability of an accident, for example, we must know the condition of the road, the amount of traffic, visibility, etc. We have to *particularize* the event. (See Figure 4.6 in Chapter 4.) It may be that Ben's speed was not unreasonable under the circumstances. What was Ben trying to do at the time? Simply get home as fast as possible to watch a football game, or get to a hospital as soon as possible to take a passenger to the emergency room? The more important or socially useful the goal of Ben at the time, the more reasonable it would be for him to take risks of his own safety. What was the burden or inconvenience on Ben of driving slower and hence taking less risk of injuring himself? All he had to do was not press down so hard on the accelerator. A minimal burden. What was the inconvenience of doing this? Arriving a few seconds or minutes later? Whether this is much of an inconvenience may depend on where he was going and whether the extra time was needed for an important or socially useful purpose.

You will recall that special allowances are made for a defendant who has a physical defect or who is a child (see the beginning of Chapter 12). The same allowances are made for a plaintiff who is alleged to be contributorily negligent. The test of reasonableness is what a reasonable person with the plaintiff's physical defects would have done under the circumstances, or what a reasonable person as young as the plaintiff would have done under the circumstances. Mental deficiencies of the party, however, are not taken into consideration. The standard of reasonableness is a mentally healthy person. Finally, if the plaintiff had any special knowledge or skills that would have helped to avoid the accident, the test of reasonableness is what a reasonable person with that knowledge or those skills would have done under the circumstances.

In assessing the contributory negligence of plaintiffs, it is important to identify the particular risks that they undertook in order to determine whether these risks were in fact the risks that contributed to their injuries. The general rule is that plaintiffs are contributorily negligent only if the risks they unreasonably created to their own safety are the *same* risks that eventually led to the injury.

> **Example:**   Tomas goes on Jim's land knowing that there are many dangerous animals on the land. While walking, Tomas falls into a concealed hole and breaks his leg. Tomas sues Jim for negligence. Jim raises the defense of contributory negligence.

Tomas was not contributorily negligent. Tomas may have created an unreasonable risk of injury to himself when he went on the land knowing dangerous animals were present, but this is not the particular risk that produced the broken leg—Tomas was not attacked by an animal. Nor is it significant that Tomas may have been a trespasser on Jim's land. Torts can be committed against trespassers, as we shall see.

Suppose that the plaintiff's negligence consists of a violation of a statute, ordinance, or regulation (S/O/R). For most statutes, ordinances, or regulations, a court will treat a violation by the plaintiff the same way that it will treat a violation by the defendant. The same analytical process is used whether we are assessing the negligence of the defendant (see Figure 12.8 in Chapter 12) or the contributory negligence of the plaintiff.

▪ ASSIGNMENT 15.1 ▪

In the following situation, will the defendant be successful in raising the defense of contributory negligence? (See General Instructions for the Legal Analysis Assignment in Chapter 3.)

A trucking company uses a public alley to load and unload its trucks. The manager warns a pedestrian to keep out because of the danger. The pedestrian ignores the warning and walks through. Two of the trucks collide. The collision causes a tremor in the alley. The tremor causes a large shovel to fall off a truck and hit the pedestrian. This truck was parked and was not part of the collision. The pedestrian sues the trucking company for negligence. The company asserts contributory negligence.

Cause in Fact

Once it is determined that the plaintiff was negligent (unreasonable), the next question is whether the plaintiff was a **cause in fact** of his or her own injury, along with the defendant. The question is whether both the plaintiff and the defendant caused the plaintiff's injury. The substantial-factor test is used to answer this question. The plaintiff caused his or her own injury if he or she was a substantial factor in producing the injury. The same test is used to determine whether the defendant caused the injury.

If the plaintiff acted unreasonably regarding his or her own safety, and this unreasonableness was a substantial factor in producing that injury, contributory negligence is established. It does not matter that the plaintiff's unreasonableness was only slight when compared to the unreasonableness of the defendant, unless, as indicated, the defendant's unreasonableness could be categorized as wilful, wanton, or reckless.

In Chapter 14, on damages, we considered the doctrine of **avoidable consequences.** Assume that the defendant is liable in a case where there is no contributory negligence. Once the accident occurs, the plaintiff must take reasonable steps to mitigate or avoid aggravated or increased damages (e.g., by seeking proper medical attention). If the plaintiff does not take these steps, the defendant will not be liable for the aggravated or increased damages that could have been avoided. This is a damages issue, not a contributory negligence issue.

▪ ASSIGNMENT 15.2 ▪

Go to the Descriptive Word Index of digests that cover opinions written by courts in your state. Examine the topics of contributory negligence, negligence, and pleading/procedure. Find a recent case written by a court in your state that will tell you whether contributory negligence is a defense in your state. If it is, who must plead and prove contributory negligence?

▪ ASSIGNMENT 15.3 ▪

How would the following cases be handled in your state? See General Instructions for the State Court Opinion Assignment, and for the State Code Assignment, both in Chapter 2.)

a. Dan negligently collides with Sam's car. Sam breaks his neck. He sues Dan for negligence. Sam was not wearing his seatbelt at the time of the collision. The evidence establishes that Sam would not have broken his neck if he had been wearing his seat belt. Dan claims that Sam's own negligence caused the injury.
b. Mary and Helen both negligently pollute the same stream. Mary sues Helen for negligence. Helen asserts that Mary was also negligent.

▪ ASSIGNMENT 15.4 ▪

Prepare an annotated bibliography on contributory negligence for your state. (See General Instructions for the Annotated Bibliography Assignment in Chapter 2.)

▪ LAST CLEAR CHANCE

Last clear chance is a pro-plaintiff doctrine that counteracts the drastic consequences of contributory negligence. A plaintiff found to be contributorily negligent can still recover if he or she can show that the defendant had the last clear chance to avoid the injury and failed to do so. Unfortunately, the doctrine is surrounded by a good deal of confusion, so that it is sometimes unclear whether a court will apply it.

It is important to distinguish the different predicaments in which plaintiffs can find themselves:

> **Plaintiff in helpless peril:** A plaintiff is in **helpless peril** when his contributory negligence has placed him in a predicament which he *cannot* get himself out of. Even if the plaintiff now used reasonable care, he could not get out of the danger (e.g., plaintiff's foot is carelessly caught in a machine or in a railroad track).

> **Plaintiff in inattentive peril:** A plaintiff is in **inattentive peril** when her contributory negligence has placed her in a predicament which she *could* get herself out of by the use of reasonable care, but the plaintiff remains negligently unaware of her peril up to the time of the accident (e.g., in a noisy section of town, plaintiff carelessly fails to hear or see a bus coming right at her on the street).

Plaintiff in Helpless Peril

If the defendant discovered the plaintiff in helpless peril and had an opportunity to avoid the accident but did not take it, then the plaintiff's contributory negligence will not bar recovery. The reason is that the defendant had and failed to take the last clear chance to avoid the injury.

Suppose, however, that the defendant did *not* discover the helpless plaintiff. Theoretically, the defendant did not have the last clear chance to avoid the accident. How can the defendant avoid what he or she does not know? Many states say that it is impossible, and hence deny the plaintiff the use of the last-clear-chance doctrine. This results in the plaintiff's loss of the case because of contributory negligence. Other states, however, take a different position, but only if the defendant *could have discovered* the helpless peril if the defendant had used reasonable care in his or her observation of the situation. For example, as the defendant railroad engineer approached the scene of the accident, the engineer failed to see the helpless plaintiff because the engineer negligently failed to maintain proper attention to the track directly in front. A few states treat "should-have-discovered" in the same way as "did-discover" and permit the plaintiff to recover in spite of the latter's contributory negligence if the defendant would have had a reasonable opportunity to prevent the accident at the last moment. The defendant must have been negligent in failing to discover the plaintiff and must have had a reasonable opportunity to prevent the accident if the plaintiff had been discovered.

Plaintiff in Inattentive Peril

If the defendant discovered the plaintiff in inattentive peril and had a reasonable opportunity to avoid the accident but did not take it, then the plaintiff's contributory negligence will not bar his or her recovery. The reason is that the defendant had and failed to take the last clear chance to avoid the injury. In other words, discovery of plaintiff in inattentive peril is treated in the same way as discovery of the plaintiff in helpless peril. The defendant does not have to have definite knowledge that the plaintiff was unaware of his or her peril, but the situation must be such that the defendant did see the plaintiff and should have known that the plaintiff was unaware or inattentive.

The most troublesome case is when the defendant failed to discover the plaintiff in inattentive peril because of the defendant's negligence at the time of the accident. Very few courts would permit the plaintiff to recover here. The negligence of both plaintiff and defendant resulted in their being ignorant of each other. Neither had the last clear chance. In most courts, therefore, the plaintiff's contributory negligence would bar his or her recovery.

▪ ASSIGNMENT 15.5 ▪

Peter is negligently driving his car, which collides with Bill's car at an intersection. Peter is not injured, but his car is thrown onto the other side of the road, upon which Dan's car is approaching from the opposite direction. Dan is driving carelessly. Dan sees Peter's car, but instead of stopping, unreasonably thinks he can cut around Peter's car. The space is too narrow and Dan collides with Peter's car, causing Peter to break his leg. Peter sues Dan for negligence. Dan raises the defense of contributory negligence.

a. Assess Dan's chances of succeeding with this defense. (See General Instructions for the Legal Analysis Assignment in Chapter 3.)
b. Prepare an investigation strategy. (See General Instructions for the Investigation Strategy Assignment in Chapter 4.)

▪ ASSIGNMENT 15.6 ▪

Does your state recognize the doctrine of last clear chance? If so, under what circumstances does it apply? Give the citation and facts of one case in which it was applied. (See General Instructions for the State Court Opinion Assignment and for the State Code Assignment, both in Chapter 2.)

▪ COMPARATIVE NEGLIGENCE

Many states have done away with contributory negligence in whole or in part. They have adopted comparative negligence principles that determine the total amount of the damages suffered by the plaintiff, and then apportion the damages between the negligent plaintiff and the negligent defendant. There are two main kinds of comparative negligence systems:

Pure Comparative Negligence

When the plaintiff sues the defendant for negligence and the defendant claims that the plaintiff's negligence contributed to the injury, a court will decide the percentage by which each side was negligent. Plaintiff's recovery is limited to that percentage of the award that was due to the defendant's negligence. If, for example, plaintiff suffered $100,000 in damages, and the court concludes that the defendant was 5 percent at fault and the plaintiff was 95 percent at fault in causing the injury, the plaintiff recovers $5,000 from the defendant—5 percent of $100,000. Plaintiff always recovers something if the injury was caused by the negligence of both parties, even if the plaintiff's fault was greater than the defendant's.

Restricted Comparative Negligence

Other states use different versions of comparative negligence that are not as comprehensive as the pure form. For example, some states will compare the negligence of the defendant and plaintiff in causing the plaintiff's injury and allow the plaintiff to recover only if the plaintiff's negligence was "slight" in comparison with the "gross" negligence of the defendant. Other states will compare the negligence of the defendant and that of the plaintiff in causing the plaintiff's injury, and allow the plaintiff to recover only if the plaintiff's negligence is less than that of the defendant. In the latter states, if they are equally negligent, the plaintiff recovers nothing; if the plaintiff is 51 percent negligent and the defendant is 49 percent negligent, the plaintiff recovers nothing.

▪ ASSIGNMENT 15.7 ▪

a. Is your state a comparative negligence state? If so, was this enacted by statute (give citation and effective date), or by court opinion (give citation)? Briefly describe how comparative negligence works.

b. What happens if the plaintiff sues more than one defendant in the negligence action? Can the plaintiff win if everyone—including the plaintiff—is found to have negligently caused the plaintiff's injury? (See General Instructions for the State Code Assignment and for the State Court Opinion Assignment, both in Chapter 2.)

▪ ASSUMPTION OF THE RISK

Assumption of the risk is another possible defense to negligence. The plaintiff's conduct may amount to both contributory negligence and assumption of the risk, so that the defendant can choose *either* theory to avoid liability. A basic difference between the two defenses, however, is that contributory negligence is determined by the **objective standard** of the reasonable person, whereas assumption of the risk is determined by a **subjective standard**—whether this particular plaintiff knowingly and voluntarily assumed the risk of the defendant's conduct.

> **Contributory negligence (objective test):** The plaintiff *should have known* that he or she was creating an unreasonable risk of injuring him- or herself and *should have taken* greater precautions against this risk.

> **Assumption of the risk (subjective test):** The plaintiff *actually knew* of the risk to his or her safety, but voluntarily chose to confront it.

There are two main elements of the defense of assumption of risk:

- Plaintiff understood the risks posed by the defendant's conduct to the plaintiff's safety.
- Plaintiff voluntarily chose to confront those risks.

Understanding the Risk

It is very easy to confuse assumption of the risk with contributory negligence. Suppose, for example, that Sam is injured in an electrical plant by coming into contact with large live wires that the plant negligently left on the floor. Sam did not see the wires, in spite of their size. In Sam's negligence suit against the plant, can the plant use the assumption-of-the-risk defense? No. How could Sam have understood a risk in something that he did not see? If the plant says that Sam *should have seen* the wires because they were so large, the plant is confusing assumption of the risk with contributory negligence. If Sam did not see the wires but should have seen them had he been acting reasonably as he walked, he was contributorily negligent, but it was impossible for him to have assumed the risk. Assumption of risk is subjective: the risk must be known and understood by a particular plaintiff before we can say that he or she assumed that risk. If all the defendant can say is that the plaintiff was stupid in failing to understand the risk, the defendant has conceded that assumption of the risk cannot apply.

To be sure, there will be some extreme cases in which no one will believe the plaintiff's claim that he or she did not understand the danger. A plaintiff, for example, who walks into a fire that was negligently set by the defendant may not be believed if the plaintiff says he or she did not know that the fire could cause serious injury.

▪ ASSIGNMENT 15.8 ▪

An Australian comes to America to visit a friend. The friend takes the visitor to a baseball game. The visitor is hit by a line drive foul ball and seriously injured. The visitor sues the ball park for negligence. The latter raises the defense of assumption of the risk. What result? (See General Instructions for the Legal Analysis Assignment in Chapter 3.)

Voluntarily Confronting the Risk

We need to examine two different situations:

- the plaintiff's **express assumption of the risk**
- the plaintiff's **implied assumption of the risk**

Express Assumption

People often enter into agreements limiting their liability to each other. For example, when someone stores a car or a coat in a warehouse or other business set up for this purpose, the parties may agree that the business will not be liable for certain kinds of damage to the car or coat. The owner of the car or coat in these situations is expressly assuming the risk of the damage.

But it must be clear that the parties agreed to such **limitation of liability.** The plaintiff must know about the limitation. A company may try to tell the customer that it will not be liable for negligence by putting a notice to this effect on a sign buried on a wall in the rear of a room, or in very small print on the back of a receipt check. Such communication will usually be insufficient. Customers do not agree to assume a risk of which they are unaware.

There are a number of situations in which the law will not permit or will restrict assumption-of-the-risk agreements even if the terms are made quite clear to both parties. This occurs mainly when there is a significantly unbalanced bargaining position between the parties. In such situations, the likelihood is that the weaker of the parties did not voluntarily agree to assume the risk. Considerable **coercion** or pressure took place. As a matter of **public policy,** the law will invalidate such "agreements."

Examples:

- An employer cannot ask an employee to assume all risks of injury on the job. The employer must provide a reasonably safe workplace.
- Someone engaged in a public service (e.g., common carrier, innkeeper, public utility) cannot ask a customer to assume all risks of injury or damage while using the public service—but it can seek to limit its liability if the terms of the limitation are clearly communicated to the customer so that the latter knows what he or she is getting into.

In ruling on the validity of an express assumption of risk by the plaintiff in these sensitive areas, the court will consider a number of factors:

- How clearly was the limitation communicated to the plaintiff?
- Does the limitation apply to all risks or to limited risks?
- Does the limitation apply to the total amount of the dollar loss or to a portion of it?
- What options were available to the plaintiff? Could the plaintiff have gone elsewhere to obtain the same service without having to agree to assume the risk? Does the defendant have a monopoly over the service?
- How vulnerable is the plaintiff? Is special protection needed for plaintiffs using this service?
- Is the defendant engaged in a vital service?

▪ ASSIGNMENT 15.9 ▪

Go to the digests covering court opinions of your state. Try to find and briefly summarize an opinion in which the court invalidated an express assumption of risk and another opinion in which such an express assumption was enforced. List the factors that the court considered in reaching its conclusion in each opinion.

Implied Assumption

The plaintiff can voluntarily assume the risk in ways other than by express agreement. If, for example, the plaintiff walks very close to the spot where fireworks are exploding and fully understands the dangers involved, the plaintiff has assumed the risk of injury due to the negligent setting off of the fireworks. This is an implied assumption of the risk. As with express assumption of the risk, however, there are some situations in which the law as a matter of public policy will not permit a plaintiff to impliedly assume the risk. Such a situation occurs when an employee works in an unsafe environment. The law may not permit express *or* implied assumption of the risk in such situations. With this qualification in mind, the rule on implied assumption of the risk, according to the Restatement, is as follows:

> A plaintiff who fully understands a risk of harm to himself or his things caused by the defendant's conduct or by the condition of the defendant's land, and

who nevertheless voluntarily chooses to enter or remain, or to permit his things to enter or remain in the area of that risk, under circumstances that manifest his willingness to accept it, is not entitled to recover for harm within that risk.[1]

In effect, once you understand the risks and voluntarily proceed to confront them, you have decided to take your chances on injury or damage caused by the negligence of the defendant. Suppose that you buy a lawn mower, but before using it, you discover that it is defective. The blade has been negligently fastened to the body of the machine. You see the defect and understand the consequences of the blade's flying off while in use. If you decide to use it anyway, and are injured when the blade does come off, your negligence suit against the manufacturer will be defeated because of assumption of the risk. You have impliedly assumed the risk.

▪ ASSIGNMENT 15.10 ▪

Examine the following situations to determine whether the plaintiff has voluntarily assumed the risk. (See General Instructions for the Legal Analysis Assignment in Chapter 3.)

a. Plaintiff runs out into the street in the path of cars that are exceeding the speed limit. One of the cars hits the plaintiff. Plaintiff sues the driver.
b. Plaintiff agrees to take a joy ride with the defendant, who will drive on the beach in very shallow water. Neither party knows that the brakes are defective. The brakes fail and the car goes out to deep water, almost drowning the plaintiff. Plaintiff sues the defendant.

There is a form of pressure that a defendant can place on the plaintiff that can negate what would otherwise be an assumption of the risk. The pressure comes in the form of negligently leaving the plaintiff no reasonable alternative in protecting the plaintiff's rights.

> **Example:** Defendant negligently sets fire to the plaintiff's car. The plaintiff tries to put out the fire and is burned. Plaintiff sues defendant for damage to the car and for personal injuries due to the burn. As to the personal injuries, the defendant raises the defense of assumption of the risk.

If the plaintiff acted reasonably in trying to put out the fire, he or she has not assumed the risk of being burned *even though the plaintiff fully understood the risks of being burned.* The risks were not voluntarily assumed. Defendant's tortious conduct put the plaintiff in the predicament of either watching the fire destroy the car or trying to stop the fire. The essential question is whether the plaintiff was reasonable in the course taken. This will depend on all the circumstances. How big was the fire at the time the plaintiff tried to put it out? How old was the car? What was its value? How close was a fire station, and how difficult or easy was it to contact the station? What was in the car? Nothing? Valuable papers? An infant? Would the plaintiff have been stranded in an inhospitable area if he or she were not able to use the car? Taking all of these factors into consideration, if the attempt to put out the fire was reasonable, there was

---

[1] *Restatement (Second) of Torts* § 496C (1965).

no voluntary assumption of the risk. If, on the other hand, the attempt was foolhardy because of the extraordinary danger of being seriously burned to protect a car of relatively little value, a court will conclude that there was an assumption of the risk. The plaintiff's protection of his or her rights or property must not be out of all proportion to the danger that the plaintiff walks or leaps into.

▪ ASSIGNMENT 15.11 ▪

In the following cases, determine whether the defendant can successfully raise the assumption-of-risk defense. (See General Instructions for the Legal Analysis Assignment in Chapter 3.)

a. Tony is building a new road in front of Alan's house. A ditch is dug in front of the house. Tony puts a thin piece of plywood across the ditch so that workers and Alan can cross over the ditch. A large "danger" sign is placed by Tony close to the plywood crossing. Alan sees the sign. While Alan is crossing over the plywood, it caves in, causing severe injuries. Alan sues Tony for negligence.

b. Bob's leg is injured in a hit-and-run accident. Along comes Tom in another car. Tom's car has defective brakes, and Bob knows this. Bob has no other way to get to a hospital for needed medical attention. Bob goes with Tom to the hospital. Along the way, the defective brakes cause another accident, in which Bob breaks his arm. Bob sues Tom for negligent injury to his arm.

Not all states allow the doctrine of assumption of risk in all cases. A state, for example, may have abolished this defense (as well as the defense of contributory negligence) in certain situations, such as that in which an employee is injured on the job. Statutes might require the defendant to give special protection to certain classes of plaintiffs, e.g., child labor laws, and such statutes have been interpreted as eliminating assumption of the risk as a defense to the defendant's violation of the statute.

Finally, in some states, the adoption of comparative negligence has led to a significant decline in the number of cases using the defense of implied assumption of the risk. Courts are more inclined to compare the fault of the parties in causing the plaintiff's injury, and to let the comparative negligence rules govern how much plaintiff's recovery should be proportionately reduced, or whether it should be completely wiped out due to the plaintiff's own negligence.

▪ ASSIGNMENT 15.12 ▪

To what extent is assumption of the risk available in your state? Has it been abolished? If so, in what circumstances? (See General Instructions for the State Code Assignment and for the State Court Opinion Assignment, both in Chapter 2.)

▪ ASSIGNMENT 15.13 ▪

Prepare an annotated bibliography on assumption of risk for your state. (See General Instructions for the Annotated Bibliography Assignment in Chapter 2.)

Hendricks v. Broderick
284 N.W.2d 209 (1979)
Supreme Court of Iowa

Background: Edward Broderick shot Billy
Hendricks while "working a turkey." They
were hunting in Shimek Forest, a dense and
dark woodland in Iowa. They did not know
each other. To hunt a "tom turkey," you imitate the softer yelp of a hen to entice the tom
turkey within gunshot. Hendricks was "working a turkey" in this way when Broderick shot
him by mistake. Both were camouflaged at the
time. At the trial Hendricks alleged that Broderick negligently failed to identify his target
before shooting at it with his shotgun. Broderick raised the defense of contributory negligence. The jury found for Broderick.
Hendricks appealed on the ground that the
judge's instruction to the jury confused the
defenses of contributory negligence and assumption of the risk. The case is now before
the Supreme Court of Iowa.

Decision on Appeal: Judgment reversed.
The trial judge improperly instructed the jury
on contributory negligence.

Opinion of Court

Justice UHLENHOPP delivered the opinion of the court. . . .

The jury could find that after Hendricks
entered the forest he heard the gobble of
a tom and worked the turkey by making
yelp sounds. He "spooked" (frightened
off) that bird, however, and proceeded on,
listening for another one.

Meanwhile Broderick also heard a tom
gobbling and proceeded to imitate the yelp
sounds of a hen turkey. He testified regarding his understanding of turkey hunting and
the specific events of that morning . . . :

Q. How long had it been that you had
been yelping before you saw the movement?
A. I had been yelping 20 or 25 minutes.
Q. Constantly? A. On and off.
Q. Now, what do you mean by on and
off. Do you wait? A. You don't call con-

stantly. You'll call and wait four or five
minutes and then you'll call again.
Q. So you had been waiting maybe four
or five minutes before you saw this move-
ment? A. Well, I could have been waiting a
longer period of time than that.
Q. Maybe ten minutes? A. Maybe even
ten minutes.
Q. Did you hear anything at the time you
saw the movement? A. No, I didn't.
Q. You only saw movement in the brush?
A. Yeah.
Q. Now, did you take any action then
when you saw that movement? A. The first
time?
Q. Yes. A. No.
Q. What did you do? A. I didn't do any-
thing because it disappeared and I didn't see
it anymore.
Q. Did you continue to look for more?
A. Yes, I did.
Q. And what did you see, if anything?
A. Well, then shortly after that about 25
yards or 30 yards further I saw this movement again and I assumed by me calling this
tom turkey and him answering me that.
Q. Just a moment. I don't want to know
what you assumed yet. A. Okay.
Q. You say you saw movement later.
A. Yes.
Q. Further away from you. Could you tell
what the movement was at that time? A. It
was my judgment that was the tom turkey.
Q. You say it was your judgment but
could you tell what it was? A. I couldn't tell
what it was. It was the same size as a turkey,
as much of it I saw was dark and it looked
the same size as a turkey, and I figured the
turkey had seen me the first time and he was
leaving and I shot.
Q. You shot at that movement. A. Yes, I
did.
Q. And you said it was about how far
from you at the time you shot? A. I'd say
about 60 yards.
Q. And did you hit anything? A. Sir?
Q. Did you hit anything? A. Yes, I did.
Q. What? A. I hit Mr. Hendricks. . . .

Q. Is the wild turkey a wary bird? A. Very wary.

Q. And must the hunter make a swift decision if he's going to get a shot? A. Yes, he does. . . .

Broderick pleaded contributory negligence as one of his defenses. The court submitted that defense to the jury in Instruction 11:

The law of Iowa provides that if a person who has been injured, was himself negligent, and such negligence was a proximate cause of his injury and resulting damages, then he cannot recover from another. This is known as the defense of contributory negligence and the burden of proof of such defense is upon the Defendant.

To sustain this defense the burden is upon the Defendant to prove by a preponderance of the evidence both of the following propositions:

1. That the Plaintiff, Billy Hendricks, was negligent in that he placed himself in a position of assuming whatever risk there would be when he voluntarily went turkey hunting in Shimek Forest.

2. That such negligence was a proximate cause of his injury and damages, if any. . . .

If the Defendant has proved both of the foregoing propositions, then . . . Plaintiff is [not] entitled to recover and your verdict should be for the Defendant.

Hendricks objected in district court and objects here to the language, "was negligent in that he placed himself in a position of assuming whatever risk there would be when he voluntarily went turkey hunting in Shimek Forest."

Hendricks of course accepted the hazards which naturally attend turkey hunting in Shimek Forest *without culpability on the part of other hunters. Rosenau v. City of Estherville,* 199 N.W.2d 125, 133 (Iowa 1972). . . . Under Rosenau, the defense is *contributory negligence* which, if supported by substantial evidence, should be submitted in the usual terms of the conduct of an ordinarily prudent person under the circumstances. Under the particular circumstances here the contributory negligence issue was whether, if Hendricks knew or in the exercise of due care should have known that Broderick was working a turkey at the place in question, Hendricks acted as an ordinarily prudent person in entering that place. If Broderick established by a preponderance of the evidence that Hendricks did not act as an ordinarily prudent person, and also that Hendricks' conduct constituted a proximate cause of the damages, Hendricks could not recover. Lively jury arguments could be made on both sides of this question.

The difficulty is that Instruction 11 does not proceed on this basis. Instead it permits the jury to find the defense established if Hendricks "placed himself in a position of assuming whatever risk there would be when he voluntarily went turkey hunting in Shimek Forest" and that such conduct constituted a proximate cause. In the absence of evidence which does not appear here, however, a hunter does not assume whatever risk there would be by voluntarily hunting in Shimek Forest. This court stated in *Gross v. Miller,* 93 Iowa 72, 82, 61 N.W. 385, 388 (1884): "Men go hunting every day, and no one reasonably anticipates that, as a result, one will negligently shoot the other."

Although Shimek is a dark and deep forest, Hendricks had a right to assume, until he knew otherwise or in the exercise of ordinary care should have known otherwise, that other hunters would exercise due care under the circumstances, including the circumstance of the nature of the forest. See *Conrad v. Board of Supervisors,* 199 N.W.2d 139, 144 (Iowa 1972).

This instruction was on a vital point in the case and requires reversal. . . . We return the case to district court for retrial.

▪ ASSIGNMENT 15.14 ▪

a. Did the Supreme Court of Iowa find that Hendricks committed contributory negligence?

b. Do you think Hendricks assumed the risk of being shot? To answer this question, what further facts would you like to know and why?

c. The court said "(l)ively jury arguments could be made" on the question of contributory negligence. Prepare two arguments that could be presented to the jury, one to be delivered by Hendricks' counsel, and the other by Broderick's counsel.

d. How would this case be handled in a comparative negligence state?

SUMMARY

Under the doctrine of contributory negligence, the plaintiff's unreasonableness in taking risks for his or her own safety is a complete bar to recovery of damages if it was a substantial factor in causing the injury. If, however, the defendant was wilful, wanton, or reckless, the contributory negligence of the plaintiff will not bar recovery. Plaintiff's contributory negligence is determined by the same formula used to determine the defendant's negligence: the foreseeability of the accident and of the kind of injury or damage that could result is weighed against the importance or social utility of what plaintiff was doing at the time and the burden or inconvenience of taking precautions to avoid the accident.

Contributory negligence does not bar recovery of damages if the defendant had the last clear chance to avoid the injury but failed to take it. If the defendant discovered (or could have discovered) the plaintiff in helpless peril and failed to take reasonable steps to avoid the accident, the plaintiff's contributory negligence is not a bar. The same is true if the defendant discovered the plaintiff in inattentive peril.

Comparative negligence apportions the damages between the plaintiff and the defendant based on the extent to which each acted unreasonably. In a state that has adopted pure comparative negligence, the plaintiff's recovery is limited to the percentage of the harm that was due to the defendant's negligence. In a state that has adopted restricted comparative negligence, there may be no recovery unless the plaintiff's negligence meets a designated standard, such as being "slight" as opposed to the "gross" negligence of the defendant.

The plaintiff recovers nothing if he or she knowingly and voluntarily accepted (i.e., assumed) the risk of being injured by the negligence of the defendant. There must be actual knowledge of the risk. Generally, parties are free to enter agreements that limit their liability to each other. This is an express assumption of the risk. If, however, there is a significantly unequal bargaining position between the parties, the law may place restrictions on such agreements. If there is no agreement between the parties, plaintiffs can impliedly assume the risk of dangers that they know, understand, and voluntarily undertake. In some states today, there are fewer cases of implied assumption of the risk because of the adoption of comparative negligence statutes.

Key Terms

contributory negligence
last clear chance
comparative negligence
assumption of the risk
ordinary negligence
wilful, wanton, or
    reckless conduct

unreasonable risks
cause in fact
avoidable consequences
helpless peril
inattentive peril
objective standard
subjective standard

express assumption of
    the risk
implied assumption of
    the risk
limitation of liability
coercion
public policy

CHAPTER 16

Survival and Wrongful Death

CHAPTER OUTLINE

- SURVIVAL
    Kinds of Torts That Survive
    Common Law and Statutory Law
    Characteristics of Actions That
        Survive

- WRONGFUL DEATH
    Common Law
    Recovery for Wrongful Death
- AVOIDING DOUBLE RECOVERY

■ SURVIVAL

Kinds of Torts That Survive

When one person commits a tort against another (and hence becomes a **tort-feasor**), the death of either person should logically not affect the right of the victim to bring the tort action against the tortfeasor. If the victim dies, the victim's **estate** or **representative** should be able to bring the action against the tortfea-sor. If the tortfeasor dies, the victim should be able to bring the action against the tortfeasor's estate or representative. The law, however, has not always been logical in this regard. Distinguish the following kinds of tort actions:

Personal torts: Tom invades Pete's privacy, or defames Pete, or intention-ally subjects Pete to severe emotional distress, or commits any other tort against Pete's *person.* Then:

- Tom dies from a cause unrelated to the tort, or
- Pete dies from a cause unrelated to the tort.

Personal property torts Mary converts Linda's car, or negligently dam-ages Linda's livestock, or commits any other tort against Linda's *personal property.* Then:

- Mary dies from a cause unrelated to the tort, or
- Linda dies from a cause unrelated to the tort.

Real property torts: Marvin trespasses on Jane's land, or negligently damages Jane's house, or commits any other tort against Jane's *real property.* Then:

- Marvin dies from a cause unrelated to the tort, or
- Jane dies from a cause unrelated to the tort.

The question is whether the tort action (or the right to bring the tort action) in any of the above three situations survives the death of either of the potential participants to the litigation. This question should be kept separate from the problem of what happens if the victim dies *because* of the tort committed by the tortfeasor. The latter question raises a wrongful-death issue, which we shall discuss later. A **survival** issue primarily involves the question of what happens to the tort action if one of the participants dies from a cause unconnected with that tort. Yet as we shall see, the line between survival and wrongful death can become blurred. For now, however, keep the two issues separate by asking whether the death was related to the commission of the tort.

Common Law and Statutory Law

Back to our survival question: can the tort action be brought even though one of the participants has died? The answer depends on the kind of tort that was committed. (A personal tort? A personal property tort? A real property tort?) Also, statutory law has made major changes in the situation that existed at common law:

Personal torts

Common law: At common law, torts against the *person* of the victim did not survive the death of either the victim or the tortfeasor. If the victim died, the action could not be brought by the victim's estate or representative. If the tortfeasor died, the action could not be brought against the estate or representative of the tortfeasor.

Statutory law: In most states, survival statutes have been passed that change the common law. These statutes, however, have not completely changed the common law with respect to torts against the person. Torts such as defamation, invasion of privacy, malicious prosecution, or similar torts involving invasions of intangible interests still do not survive the death of either the victim or the wrongdoer in some states. Other personal torts, however, particularly those involving invasions to tangible interests, do survive, e.g., battery. Hence, the statute may modify only some of the common law with respect to personal torts.

Personal property torts

Common law: At common law, torts against the *personal property* of the victim survived the death of the victim but did not survive the death of the tortfeasor.

Statutory law: Survival statutes have been passed that change the common law. In all states, torts against personal property survive the death of either the victim or the tortfeasor.

Real property torts

> **Common law:** At common law, torts against the *real property* of the victim did not survive the death of the victim or the tortfeasor.

> **Statutory law:** Survival statutes have been passed that change the common law. In all states, torts against real property survive the death of either the victim or the tortfeasor.

Hence, if a tort action survives today, it is because the action is one of the few that survived at common law, or because a survival statute has established that it survives.

Characteristics of Actions That Survive

Let us focus on a tort action that survives the death of the victim, again keeping in mind that we are not yet talking about a death that is caused by the tort. Before the victim brings any action against the tortfeasor, the victim dies from a cause unrelated to the tort. The action is brought after this death. Note the following characteristics of this action:

- The action is brought by the estate of the victim through the decedent's executor, court-appointed administrator, or other legal representative of the estate.
- The action is not a new or independent action. It is the same action that the victim would have had if he or she had lived.
- The plaintiff in the action is not an heir or relative of the victim unless the heir or relative happens to be the legal representative of the victim's estate.
- Heirs or relatives do not directly receive any benefit from a damage award in the tort action that survives. If they benefit from the award, they do so through the estate as beneficiaries of a will or via **intestacy** (the distribution of a decedent's estate when no valid will exists).
- There is no recovery for the death of the victim, because the tort did not cause the death of the victim; the decedent was the victim of a tort that did not cause death.
- Any defenses the tortfeasor would have had against the victim, had the latter lived (e.g., contributory negligence, assumption of the risk, self-defense), are available to the tortfeasor in the action that survives.

▪ ASSIGNMENT 16.1 ▪

In this assignment you are asked to check the law of survival in your state. Examine your state code and court opinions to determine whether the following tort actions survive the death of the victim or of the tortfeasor:

a. torts against the person involving invasions of tangible interests, e.g., assault, battery, negligence
b. torts against the person involving invasions of intangible interests, e.g., defamation, invasion of privacy
c. torts against personal property, e.g., conversion, negligence
d. torts against real property, e.g., trespass to land, ''nuisance''

Assume that none of these torts caused the death of the victim; the victim died from a cause unrelated to the tort of the defendant. As we shall see in the next section, some states combine a survival statute with a wrongful death law. For purposes of this assignment, however, do not discuss the survival of a tort action when the tort caused the death. (See General Instructions for the State Code Assignment and for the State Court Opinion Assignment, both in Chapter 2.)

■ WRONGFUL DEATH

Common Law

Now we move to the second issue referred to in the first section of this chapter: what happens when the victim of a tort dies *because* of the tort? Here we are talking about a **tortious** or **wrongful death.** At common law, a civil action for this death could not be brought against the wrongdoer. If the act that caused the death of the victim constituted a crime, the wrongdoer might be prosecuted in a criminal court, but no civil tort action could be brought. If the wrongdoer had committed a nondeadly tort against the victim, or had committed a tort against the property of a victim who was still alive, there could be recovery against the wrongdoer, but not if the latter had killed the victim. It was cheaper, therefore, to kill the victim!

Needless to say, statutes were passed to change this absurdity. Every state now has a remedy for wrongful death. The remedy is not the same in each state. Although your primary concern will be the law of your state, you will need to be aware of the major remedies available in other states, because it is not uncommon for an office to work on a case involving the death of someone in another state.

Elsewhere in this book, we discuss the law of worker's compensation (Chapter 30). If an employee dies from an injury that arises out of and in the course of employment, compensation to heirs or relatives is received through the worker's compensation statute, whether or not the employer wrongfully caused the death. In most states, worker's compensation replaces any other civil remedy. Hence, the following discussion does not apply to death due to an employment accident or disease.

Recovery for Wrongful Death

States differ on how they allow recovery for wrongful death. Two common methods include:

- enlarging the survival statute to include death, and
- enacting a wrongful-death statute (Lord Campbell's Act)

Enlarging the Survival Statute to Include Wrongful Death

We saw above that survival statutes have been passed to permit most kinds of tort actions to survive the death of the victim of the tort. In some states, the death of the victim by reason of the tort is handled as follows:

- the tort action of the victim survives his or her death and covers damages that accrued up to the moment of death
- damages resulting from the death can be recovered in the same survival action

No new cause of action is created because of the death. The victim's cause of action is continued by his or her estate or legal representative. In this action, any defense is available that could have been brought had the victim lived. The damages that are recoverable in this action usually include:

- pain and suffering of the victim from the time of the injury to the time of death
- medical, hospital, and funeral expenses

- lost net earnings and savings the victim would have accumulated if he or she had lived to his or her life expectancy.

Enacting a Wrongful-Death Statute (Lord Campbell's Act)

Most states create a new cause of action for designated relatives of the deceased victim, e.g., spouse and children. A statute creating this wrongful-death cause of action is usually modeled after **Lord Campbell's Act** in England and is sometimes referred to as a "pure" death action, as distinguished from the enlarged survival action, which continues the victim's claim. The new cause of action is brought by a representative for the benefit of the relatives or beneficiaries, or in some states, by the beneficiaries themselves. The damages that are recoverable in this action are usually limited to **pecuniary losses.** This covers the loss of the economic value of the support, services, and contributions that the beneficiaries would have received if the victim had lived to his or her life expectancy.

Damages are *not* recoverable in this action for:

- pain and suffering of the victim, medical bills, lost wages, or any other loss that the victim would have had against the tortfeasor (damages for such items are recoverable in a separate survival action, which is often brought along with the beneficiaries' action—see discussion below on Avoiding Double Recovery)
- mental suffering and grief experienced by the survivor-beneficiaries because of the death of the victim, and loss of consortium rights (see Chapter 26), particularly the right to the companionship and society of the deceased (some states, however, have changed this rule and allow recovery for such **nonpecuniary losses**)

Under most wrongful-death statutes, the defendant can raise any defense he or she would have had against the victim if death had not occurred. For example, the defendant may assert that the death was not wrongful. The defendant may have caused the death—but not tortiously. There must be an underlying intentional, negligence, or strict-liability tort before the beneficiaries can recover anything in the wrongful-death action. Also, defenses of contributory negligence, assumption of the risk, or any of the privileges will usually defeat the wrongful-death action. In most states, the statute of limitations runs from the time of death and not from the date of the injury.

■ AVOIDING DOUBLE RECOVERY

Some states have both a survival statute (covering the victim's pain and suffering, loss of earnings, medical expenses up to death, etc.) *and* a wrongful-death statute (covering the beneficiaries pecuniary loss of the support, services, and contributions that the victim would have provided them if he or she had not died). The survival action and the wrongful death action can usually be brought concurrently. When both actions are possible, there is a fear of double recovery, especially with respect to the lost earnings of the victim. The following describes the basic conflict and how it may be handled:

> An injured person's own cause of action in tort, which at common law would have ended abruptly at death, is now preserved and vested in his personal representative by means of a survival statute, one of which obtains in every jurisdiction. The existence of such a measure side by side with a wrongful death provision has proved to be a source of concern arising from fear that a duplication of damages could result. Indeed such a fear is not without foundation: Whenever an injured victim while still alive can demonstrate that the

impairment of his bodily condition is sufficiently serious to shorten his life expectancy he will become entitled to damages sufficient to replace the lost earnings that otherwise would have been in prospect for him. It is not to be expected that this right would be expunged in the event that death does indeed foreshorten his life before the award has been made. In theory, this element of loss should persist and remain available to his personal representative under a survival statute. If, however, to this survived claim for lost future earnings there were superadded a separate award for his dependents' loss of support under a [wrongful] death statute, the prospect of a duplication of damages would face the defendant. This dilemma has been dealt with in a bewildering variety of ways. In a few states a binding election must be made between a survival claim and an action for wrongful death (e.g., Ky. and Wyo.). Occasionally the survival suit is arbitrarily restricted to those claims of the deceased that were unrelated to his death (e.g., W.Va.). In other states the law makers have deliberately omitted a separate death statute, and lost future earnings in full are provided under the survival measure (e.g., Conn.). There are numerous other varieties in approach. The one that is most satisfactory and which has been most widely adopted is that of affording recognition of both the survival claim and the wrongful death claims but with damages for loss of earnings under the survival suit limited exclusively to those earnings that were lost between the time of accident and the moment of death. All pecuniary loss accruing thereafter must be recovered solely under the [wrongful] death statute. It is noteworthy, however, that funeral expenses, which do not accrue, of course, during the lifetime of the deceased, are frequently made recoverable by express provision in the survival statute.[1]

· ASSIGNMENT 16.2 ·

What remedies are available when the tort of a defendant causes the death of the victim in your state? What options exist? Is there an enlarged survival statute, a wrongful death statute, a combination of the two? Carefully examine the statutes that exist. Who can bring the action? What defenses are available to the defendant? What is the statute of limitations? What damages are recoverable? Can punitive damages be obtained? Is there a maximum limit to the recovery? Are damages for pain and suffering recoverable? What other limitations exist, if any? Briefly summarize the major provisions of the statute(s) of your state. (See General Instructions for the State Code Assignment in Chapter 2.)

· ASSIGNMENT 16.3 ·

Bill negligently kills George in an automobile accident. A wrongful death action is brought in your state. Draft a complaint for this action. Select any plaintiff or plaintiffs who would be able to sue in your state. (See General Instructions for the Complaint Drafting Assignment in Chapter 5.)

---

[1]W. Malone, *Injuries to Family, Social and Trade Relations* 44-45 (1979).

CASE

Cassano v. Durham

180 N.J.Super. 620, 436 A.2d 118 (1981)

Superior Court of New Jersey, Law Division, Passaic County

Background: The plaintiff had a "live-in" relationship with decedent; they never married. He died intestate—without leaving a will. Following his death, she claimed benefits as the equivalent of a "surviving spouse" under the New Jersey intestacy statute and Wrongful Death Act. In the trial court, a motion for summary judgment has been made that would strike plaintiff's claim.

Decision: The motion is granted. Only spouses can claim benefits under the Wrongful Death Act.

Opinion of Court

Judge SCHWARTZ delivered the opinion of the court . . .

In this case the [the plaintiff] had lived with decedent for seven years and they intended to get married. The court is asked to permit her to recover for her pecuniary loss as if she qualified as a "surviving spouse" under N.J.S.A. 3A:2A–34 of the intestacy statute. . . .

The "palimony" cases which have been decided in various states . . . have not been of aid to the court because they were not determined on the basis of the status of the live-in partner but on entirely contractual grounds.

In *Wood v. State Farm Mutual Automobile Ins. Co.,* 178 N.J.Super. 607, 429 A.2d 1082 (App.Div.1981) the court held that an economically independent companion who lived in the same home as the insured for three and one-half years before he suffered a vehicular accident and who married her almost two years later, had not been a member of her "family" residing in her household and therefore was not entitled to coverage under the personal injury protection provision of the insurance policy.

But even when a claimant relies upon the companion for support, the issue of dependency is irrelevant since the right of the spouse to partake of the benefits of the Wrongful Death Act is not conditioned on dependency. In this respect, it differs from the Worker's Compensation Act in which our Supreme Court in *Parkinson v. J. & S. Tool Co.,* 64 N.J. 159, 313 A.2d 609 (1974) recognized as a proper petitioner a live-in partner who had previously been married to and divorced from the decedent and who became entitled to the benefits of that statute having proved dependency upon the decedent who suffered death during and arising out of employment.

In *Bulloch v. United States,* 487 F.Supp. 1078 (1980) the U.S. District Court recognized the right of recovery for loss of consortium as residing in one who had intended to resume cohabitation with the injured party after having been previously married to and divorced from the injured party. The court reasoned that the intended cohabitant suffered as much as a consequence of the injuries suffered by her mate as a spouse did.

The court concluded that since the right of consortium is judge-made law, the court could readily expand it. The law of intestacy, however, is statutorily created and not subject to judicial amendment. . . .

Is it arbitrary to provide a remedy for a surviving spouse and to deny a like remedy for a live-in companion who may equally suffer as the result of the tort? There is no constitutional impediment to the legislative determination to designate one, who has entered into the bonds of matrimony with decedent, as a beneficiary under the Wrongful Death Act among those who will inherit under the intestacy statute. That is solely a legislative function and the court cannot enlarge the reach of the statute.

Changed attitudes toward marriage are temporal, reflecting the temper of the times as they may still relate to the permissiveness of the 1960s and the early '70s. But the reaction to freedom of thought as it extends to consensual sexual conduct outside of the family tradition has not found ready acceptance by the Legislature in areas where the stability and responsibility of family life may be affected.

It was in 1939 that the Legislature determined (now N.J.S.A. 37:1–10) that no marriage subsequently contracted shall be valid unless the contracting parties obtained a marriage license and the marriage was legally solemnized. This was an expression of public policy which precluded common law marital relationships acquired through cohabitation and matrimonial repute, and the statute has not been amended. . . .

The family has been the genesis of our society since the birth of civilization, and the laws of inheritance were intended to buttress the stability and continuance of the family unit. The preservation of familial law is so essential that where questions of inheritance, property, legitimacy of offspring and the like are involved, an adherence to conventional doctrine is demanded.

Since the live-in plaintiff cannot be classified as a "surviving spouse" under the legislative designation in the intestacy laws, and the Wrongful Death Act was intended to apply for the exclusive benefit of persons eligible to inherit under the succession provisions of the statute, the motion for summary judgment striking the claim of plaintiff shall be granted.

▪ ASSIGNMENT 16.4 ▪

a. Would this case be decided in the same way if the decedent died the moment before he said "I do" to the plaintiff at the altar?

b. Is this opinion consistent with *Bulloch v. United States* discussed in the opinion?

c. Is it consistent with *Parkinson v. J. & S. Tool Co.* discussed in the opinion?

SUMMARY

An action for a personal tort that does not cause death, such as defamation, does not survive the death of either the tortfeasor or the victim when the tort protects an intangible interest such as reputation or privacy. A personal tort that does not cause death, such as battery, and that protects tangible interests, does survive the death of either the tortfeasor or the victim. A personal property tort or a real property tort that does not cause death also survives the death of either. The tort action that survives is the same action that the victim would have brought if he or she had lived.

When the tort causes the death of the victim, a state might enlarge its survival statute to allow the estate or representative of the deceased to recover damages for wrongful death in the survival action. On the other hand, the state might create a separate cause of action for wrongful death for designated relatives of the deceased. Special provisions are often necessary to avoid double recovery for lost earnings (in the survival action) and loss of support (in the wrongful-death action).

Key Terms

tortfeasor
estate
representative
personal torts
personal property torts

real property torts
survival
intestacy
tortious

wrongful death
Lord Campbell's Act
pecuniary losses
nonpecuniary losses

CHAPTER 17

Products Liability

CHAPTER OUTLINE

- INTRODUCTION
- NEGLIGENCE
- MISREPRESENTATION
- WARRANTY AND STRICT LIABILITY
- EXPRESS WARRANTY

- SALE VS. SERVICE
- IMPLIED WARRANTIES
- STRICT LIABILITY IN TORT
- A FEDERAL PRODUCTS-LIABILITY LAW?

■ INTRODUCTION

The term **products liability** does not refer to a particular tort. Rather, it describes an entire area of potential liability for injury caused by products that have been placed on the market. (See Figure 17.1 for an idea of the scope of this area.)

Figure 17.1 Estimates of Hospital Emergency Room-Treated Injuries Associated with the Use of Certain Consumer Products October 1, 1990–September 30, 1991

Product Group	Total	Age Group			
		Under 5	5–24	25–64	65 and over
1. Child Nursery Equipment and Supplies	111,735	93,910	8,583	5,913	3,115
2. Toys	163,515	77,853	63,004	21,579	1,078
3. Sports and Recreational Activities and Equipment	4,260,576	212,748	3,008,623	989,928	48,329
4. Home Communication, Entertainment, and Hobby Equipment	118,095	31,636	38,724	35,504	12,194
5. Personal Use Items	521,879	164,696	190,268	136,785	29,886
6. Packaging and Containers for Household Products	324,469	48,283	127,609	130,863	17,574
7. Yard and Garden Equipment	271,659	13,009	67,423	154,976	35,911
8. Home Workshop Apparatus, Tools, and Attachments	359,492	15,604	95,722	212,680	35,443
9. Home and Family Maintenance Products	124,130	35,855	30,653	49,609	7,818
10. General Household Appliances	154,133	35,778	38,606	63,709	15,981
11. Space Heating, Cooling, and Ventilating Appliances	141,264	44,950	38,943	45,065	12,221
12. Housewares	824,973	63,131	302,790	415,518	43,448
13. Home Furnishings and Fixtures	1,841,275	543,598	444,853	541,366	310,816
14. Home Structures and Construction Materials	3,183,618	497,507	1,060,158	1,134,508	490,499
15. Miscellaneous	216,282	48,107	101,965	52,110	14,030

SOURCE: National Electronic Injury Surveillance System (NEISS) of the Consumer Product Safety Commission. Note: NEISS data indicate that a product was associated with an injury but not necessarily that the product caused the injury.

In this chapter, we shall discuss the theories or causes of action that are the basis of this liability. The causes of action are:

- negligence
- common law misrepresentation
- breach of express warranty
- breach of implied warranty of merchantability
- breach of implied warranty of fitness for a particular purpose
- strict liability in tort

When injured by a product, a plaintiff will often be able to sue under more than one of these causes of action. In most cases, it will make no difference which cause of action is used. In some cases, however, the choice can have a critical impact on the amount of damages recoverable and particularly on the defenses that may be available to the defendant. In practice, a plaintiff's attorney will usually bring the suit on more than one cause of action.

Some of the products liability causes of action (particularly negligence and strict liability in tort) involve a product that is **defective.** Something is wrong with the product that makes it dangerous, and an injury or damage to person or property is caused by the defect. As we shall see, however, every product that causes an injury is not necessarily defective. A bottle of milk that falls and breaks one's toe has caused an injury, but it is highly unlikely that the bottle fell because it was defective. The three broad categories of defectiveness are outlined in Figure 17.2.

Figure 17.2   Categories of Defects in Products

---

1. Manufacturing Defect
The product does not conform to its design. Something went wrong in the manufacturing or distribution process making the product dangerous. The defective product is different from the others. For example, the screws on the wheels of the car were not tightened, a foreign substance was left in the soda bottle, or a worker poured too much of a chemical into the mold.

---

2. Design Defect
The product conforms to the design, but the design is defective. Something went wrong at the planning stage making the product dangerous. The defective product is exactly like all the others, but something is wrong with all of them because of the very design of the product. For example, the kind of metal called for by the design is not strong enough to do the work of the product, a safety shield should have been built into the product, or vision through the rear view mirror is blocked because of the paneling of the back of the car.

---

3. Warning Defect
There are no effective instructions or warnings to go with the product. This defect makes the product dangerous. The design of the product is otherwise reasonable and there are no manufacturing flaws in it, but the consumer should have been told certain things about what the product can and cannot do. For example, consumers with a certain allergy should have been told not to use the drug, or should have been told to use it only under a doctor's supervision; consumers should have been told to keep the polish out of the reach of children.

As we examine the causes of action for products liability, we will see that it is sometimes important to determine the status of the plaintiff and of the defendant. The various combinations are presented in Figure 17.3. In some instances, when the status of a party changes, the applicable law will change.

▪ NEGLIGENCE

If the plaintiff tries to assert a negligence cause of action, he or she must establish the elements that would apply to any negligence case:

1. duty
2. breach of duty
3. proximate cause
4. damages

Let's review the first two elements as they apply to products liability cases. The element of **duty** is rarely difficult to establish. A defendant who brings a product on the market for sale has engaged in affirmative conduct, which gives rise to a duty to use reasonable care so that the product does not cause injury. There was a time when this duty was owed only to plaintiffs who were buyers of the product. A buyer was said to be in **privity** of contract with the seller. Privity simply means the relationship that exists between parties who have entered a contract with each other. The old rule was that if there was no privity, there could not be a duty. Jones buys a toaster from a department store. While a neighbor is visiting Jones one morning, the toaster catches fire and injures the neighbor. The neighbor could not sue the store for negligence because of the absence of privity between the neighbor and the store. Since the neighbor was not part of the original contract of sale to buy the toaster, the store owes no duty of reasonable care to the neighbor. The famous case of *MacPherson v. Buick*[1] changed this privity rule. Today, a duty of reasonable care is owed to all **foreseeable users** of the product whenever it can be anticipated that substantial harm to person or property will result if the product is defective. The neighbor in the toaster example is certainly a foreseeable user of the toaster that Jones bought. A toaster, like almost any product, can cause serious harm if it is defective. A duty of reasonable care, therefore, is owed by the store to the neighbor.

Figure 17.3   Status of Parties

Status Possibilities of the Injured Plaintiff	Status Possibilities of the Defendant
• buyer of product • user of product • lessee (renter) of product • bailee of product • bystander	• manufacturer of entire product • manufacturer of a part of product • assembler of product • supplier/wholesaler of product • retail seller of product • lessor of product • bailor of product

---

[1]217 N.Y. 382, 111 N.E. 1050 (1916).

Once the existence of the duty is clear, the next issue is **breach of duty.** As we saw in Chapter 12, a breach of duty is unreasonable conduct under the circumstances as measured by the equation in Figure 17.4.

Figure 17.4 ▪ Breach-of-Duty Equation

The defendant is unreasonable when the foreseeability of serious injury outweighs the burden or inconvenience of trying to avoid the accident and the defendant fails to go through that burden or inconvenience. Also, the more important or socially useful the defendant's objective or task, the more reasonable it is to take risks of injury. A wonder drug has considerable social importance. If, however, the drug has the potential of dangerous side effects, the defendant must act reasonably to test the drug and make it as safe as reasonably possible. Some risk may still exist—even if consumer warnings are also added. Given the social importance of the drug, however, the law is less inclined to call a manufacturer negligent (unreasonable) for taking such risks by putting the drug on the market.

The same analysis is used for a product such as a lawn mower. Is it foreseeable that rocks will be thrown from the blade onto a person? If so, reasonable steps, such as the addition of an extra safety guard, may be needed. Lawn mowers are arguably not as socially valuable as medicine, but they are not frivolous items, and it is important to have them on the market even though they pose some risk. In all these cases, we must ask how much of a burden or inconvenience it would be for the defendant to take steps to try to eliminate the danger. The greater the potential harm, the more burden or inconvenience the defendant should undergo. It may be unreasonable for a manufacturer to fail to take extra time to do more testing and perhaps to add a safety feature (even if this will increase the cost of the product) when the foreseeability of serious harm without this feature is very high. On the other hand, it would be unreasonable to go through considerable expense to avoid a small injury that has little chance of occurring.

It is important to remember that the defendant is not an insurer. Injury caused by a manufacturing defect, a design defect, or a warning defect will *not* impose negligence liability on the defendant if the latter has taken all reasonable precautions as to safety. Under the law of negligence, the defendant does not have an obligation to produce a safe product; the obligation is to provide a **reasonably safe** product. The defendant does not have an obligation to produce a product without defects; the obligation is to take reasonable steps to avoid defects.

Later in the chapter when we cover warranty and strict liability in tort, we will see that defendants are not always off the hook simply by showing that they acted reasonably. It is generally much easier to establish liability under these causes of action than under negligence.

We turn now to an examination of how the status of the defendant in a negligence action affects the determination of what is reasonable.

Manufacturer

A **manufacturer** is held to the standard of an expert in the product manufactured. It must use reasonable care to discover and correct manufacturing defects. This includes the requirement of inspection and testing. Reasonable care must be used in the training of employees and in the operation of machinery on the production line. If parts are used from other manufacturers, care must be used to be sure that the parts are safe. The packaging must also be reasonably safe with no misleading markings or advertising on it that could lead someone into a dangerous use. Defects that are discovered or that should have been discovered must be made known. A manufacturer cannot shift its inspection responsibility to someone else in the chain of distribution. For example, a manufacturer of a car is not relieved of its obligation to inspect simply because it knows that a dealer will later inspect the car before final sale.

Design defects pose more of a problem. There is no absolute answer to the question of when a design is unreasonable. What, for example, is a reasonable design of a car? It causes thousands of deaths every year. Theoretically, a car could be designed like a tank, which would vastly decrease its potential for accidents. But what would be the cost to build and buy such a car? How much gas would it use? Could anyone afford it? Would its practical utility be reduced to close to zero? A reasonable design does not require a manufacturer to do that which is ridiculous—even if it could be done.

▪ ASSIGNMENT 17.1 ▪

Is a car manufacturer unreasonable for making a car without air bags as standard equipment today? (See General Instructions for the Legal Analysis Assignment in Chapter 3.)

Warning defects also need to be considered. A reasonable manufacturer always provides adequate instructions on the use of the product and warns against dangers that may not be obvious. It must be emphasized, however, that a good warning is not a substitute for a reasonably safe product. Slapping a ''danger'' sign on an unreasonably dangerous product will not relieve the manufacturer from negligence liability. The product must be designed so that it is reasonably safe, even though it may still pose dangers.

A plaintiff's difficulty in establishing negligence against a manufacturer can sometimes be overcome by the doctrine of *res ipsa loquitur*. The elements of a res ipsa case require showing that:

1. the accident is one that ordinarily does not occur in the absence of someone's negligence (i.e., unreasonableness);
2. the accident was caused by an agency or instrumentality within the exclusive control of the defendant;
3. the accident was not due to any voluntary action or contribution of the plaintiff.

The doctrine helps the plaintiff in cases such as the following: a human toe is found in a soda bottle, an aspirin contains ten times the normal ingredients, a new car explodes while driving it off the dealer's lot. The special problems of applying the elements of res ipsa loquitur are discussed in Chapter 12.

Nonmanufacturer

A **merchant** who sells the product wholesale or retail directly to the consumer can also be liable for negligence when a defective product causes injury. The boundary line of liability is reasonableness. Again, the status of the defendant is relevant to our determination of what is reasonable. It may be unreasonable to ask a wholesaler or retailer to take certain safety precautions that would be quite reasonable for a manufacturer to take. A department store, for example, would not be under an obligation to safety-test every product it sells, whereas one would expect manufacturers to undertake safety tests for their products. The burden or inconvenience of this testing on a department store, a gas station, or a drugstore would be so great that it would probably mean going out of business.

It is admittedly difficult, but not impossible, to find a wholesaler or retailer negligent. (The difficulty is one reason a plaintiff will find the warranty and strict-liability-in-tort causes of action more attractive.) The major issue in a negligence case against a wholesaler or retailer is the foreseeability of injury. Such defendants must take action (e.g., remove the product from their shelves or stock) when they anticipate or should anticipate danger in the product. Specific factors affecting this foreseeability include:

Complaints
If merchants have received complaints of injury from customers, they are on notice that something should be done. A reasonable merchant would not take a business-as-usual attitude in the face of actual knowledge that the product is being attacked by prior customers, especially if they are claiming serious injury.

Reputation of the Manufacturer
A reasonable merchant who deals with a reputable manufacturer has less concern over the safety of the latter's product than he would when the manufacturer had had a history of problems or was relatively new on the market.

Packaging
A reasonable merchant is less likely to be concerned about packaged products than those that are sold without packaging. The package helps to prevent damage in most cases. A merchant is not expected to open every package to make sure there are no dangers.

Custom in the Trade
Although what other merchants do is never conclusive on the issue of reasonableness (see Chapter 12), the **custom in the trade** is relevant to determining what is reasonable. Is it the practice of similar merchants, for example, to sell the product without any inspection or warning? If so, then this may help persuade a court that a particular merchant was not unreasonable when it did not inspect or warn.

Common Sense
A reasonable merchant uses common sense. Obvious defects in the product, for example, would call for caution, especially if it is clear that the danger

would not be equally apparent to every consumer,
may not stick their heads in the sand and play dur
danger.

- ASSIGNMENT 17.2 -

Helen is the manager of the XYZ Supermarket. Wh
day, Helen is told that the neighbor began feelin'
she bought from the XYZ Supermarket. Helen say
these days.'' Two weeks later, another customer
the same brand. Prepare an investigation strate
XYZ Supermarket was negligent in selling the tampo.
tions for the Investigation Strategy Assignment in Chapter 4.)

- ASSIGNMENT 17.3 -

The ABC Company manufactures a chain saw. Assume that it is negligently
designed because the blade comes off while the saw is in operation. Jones
owns a hardware store that sells the saw. Many customers have complained to
Jones about this defect in the saw. Jones, however, keeps selling the product,
telling earlier customers to direct their complaints to ABC. A month later another
customer buys the saw and is injured because of the defect. Can this customer
successfully sue the ABC Company for negligence? (See General Instructions for
the Legal Analysis Assignment in Chapter 3.)

Defenses

Contributory negligence of the plaintiff is a complete defense in states where
the full force of this defense is still alive. If the state has adopted **comparative
negligence** (see Chapter 15), the court will compare the fault of the plaintiff
and defendant and apportion responsibility according to the applicable formula.

Plaintiffs must use reasonable care to protect themselves, particularly with respect to discovering reasonably detectable defects in the product. It is contributory negligence for a plaintiff to fail to discover a defect in a product if a
reasonable person in the plaintiff's position would have discovered it. Assume,
for example, that the plaintiff is injured by a lawn mower, which she kept using
even though she heard loud, unusual noises from the motor. These noises would
have alerted any reasonable user to the probability of serious malfunction. Consumers who have paid "good money" for a product tend to be reluctant to cease
using it, even when danger signs exist. The consumer keeps using the product
in the hope that the machine will correct itself. After the injury, the consumer
says, "I didn't know it was dangerous." If a reasonable user would have discovered the danger, the plaintiff loses the case in a contributory-negligence state in
spite of the fact that the product was negligently designed or manufactured. Of
course, consumers are not expected to conduct elaborate tests on a product in
order to discover defects. They are held only to what a reasonable user would
have discovered and done. (It is important to note that this negligent failure on
the part of the plaintiff to discover the danger will *not* be a defense when the
plaintiff sues under a warranty or strict-liability-in-tort cause of action, as we shall
see later.)

Suppose that the plaintiff *does* discover the defect in the product and fully
appreciates the danger. Continuing to use the product under such circumstances

ssumption of the risk, which is a defense to *any* cause of action in a
...cts-liability case. The plaintiff must have actual knowledge of the danger
...voluntarily encounter it. There is a difference between suspecting that a
...roblem might exist and knowing that it exists. The assumption-of-the-risk defense requires the latter.

▪ MISREPRESENTATION

The tort of **misrepresentation** is another cause of action that should be considered. Suppose that a merchant knowingly (intentionally) makes a false statement of fact to a consumer about a product, e.g., telling a customer that a liquid
is not flammable when the merchant knows otherwise. A customer who is injured
because the product is flammable could bring a deceit or misrepresentation action
against the merchant. The elements of misrepresentation are covered in Chapter 25.

▪ WARRANTY AND STRICT LIABILITY

A **warranty** action is a form of **strict liability,** meaning that a breach of the
warranty will lead to liability whether the defendant acted intentionally, negligently, or innocently. The historical development of warranty shows that it has
both contract and tort dimensions. The contract dimension is that the warranty
grows out of a contract relationship. The major tort dimension is that there are
consequences of violating or breaching the warranty that are imposed by law
irrespective of what the parties to the contract agreed to do.

Three warranties need to be considered:

- express warranty
- implied warranty of merchantability
- implied warranty of fitness for a particular purpose

A plaintiff using breach of any of these three warranties as a cause of action does
not have to show that the defendant was negligent (or acted intentionally) in
order to recover. In this sense, all three are *strict-liability* causes of action. Do
not confuse the terms *strict liability* and *strict liability in tort.* "Strict liability"
is a general term that means liability without fault—the imposition of liability
without having to show negligence or intent. When we say that a cause of action
imposes "strict liability," we are simply saying that there is no need to prove
negligence or intent. The phrase "strict liability in tort," on the other hand, has
a narrower meaning. It is an actual tort cause of action. Of course, the general
meaning of liability without fault also applies to this tort. But since "strict liability
in tort" is an actual cause of action, it has elements, as we shall see later in this
chapter. Think of "strict liability" as a phrase applying to different causes of
action, only one of which is "strict liability in tort."

▪ EXPRESS WARRANTY

The elements of an action for a breach of **express warranty** are as follows:

1. a statement of fact that is false
2. made with the intent or expectation that the statement will reach the plaintiff

3. reliance on the statement by the plaintiff
4. damage
5. causation

Many states have passed statutes on express warranties, e.g., § 2–313 of the **Uniform Commercial Code.**[2]

False Statement of Fact

The first element of a breach-of-express-warranty cause of action is that there must be a statement of **fact** that is false. The statement must be reasonably understood as a fact. Statements of opinion that fall into the category of **puffing** or seller's talk do not qualify. The following statements do not communicate facts:

"The car is a great buy."
"The tool is excellent."
"It is the best buy around."

It does state a fact, however, to say that the glass in the car is "shatter-proof," and the statement would be false if a rock broke the glass. Sometimes it will be difficult to classify a statement as fact or as seller's talk. Suppose that a merchant says that a chain saw is "durable." Has a fact been stated? The answer depends on how a reasonable listener would interpret the statement. It would be unreasonable to interpret the statement to mean that it will last forever. Arguably, however, the statement communicates the statement that the saw is safe.

The creation of the express warranty does not require the use of the words "warranty" or "guarantee." Any words describing a product can be sufficient as long as the words communicate statements of fact as indicated above. The warranty can also be created by showing the plaintiff a model or sample. The defendant is stating that the product sold conforms to the model or sample.

The plaintiff does not have to prove that the defendant knew that the statement was false; it simply must be false. (If the defendant knew it was false, a tort suit for misrepresentation would also be available.) Nor does the plaintiff have to show that the defendant acted negligently or intentionally in communicating the false statement.

▪ ASSIGNMENT 17.4 ▪

Which of the following statements, if any, communicate statements of fact? (See General Instructions for the Legal Analysis Assignment in Chapter 3.)

a. "The ladder will last a lifetime."
b. "The vaporizer is practically foolproof."
c. "These cigarettes are soothing."
d. "The detergent dissolves instantly."
e. "You can trust General Electric."

Intent or Expectation the Statement Will Reach the Plaintiff

The false statement of fact must be made to the plaintiff. If it is made to the public, the defendant must reasonably expect that the statement will reach some-

---

[2]See also *Restatement (Second) of Torts* § 402B (1965).

one like the plaintiff. Hence, statements made in general advertising would be covered. If the manufacturer makes statements in a manual that it distributes to retailers, the question will be whether the manufacturer could reasonably expect the retailer to tell consumers what is in the manual or to show the manual to them.

Reliance on Statement

Plaintiffs cannot rely on the statement unless they know about it. Hence, it must be shown that the plaintiff saw or heard the statement. **Reliance** means the plaintiff either bought the product because of the statement or used it because of the statement.

Damage and Causation

The reliance on the false statement of fact must cause the plaintiff's damage or injury. The plaintiff must show that "but for" the statement, the damage or injury would not have occurred, or that the statement was a substantial factor in producing the damage or injury.

CASE

Cipollone v. Liggett Group, Inc.
893 F.2d 541 (1990)
United States Court of Appeals for the Third Circuit

Background: Rose Cipollone smoked cigarettes from 1942 until her death from lung cancer in 1984. Her husband has brought a products liability action against three cigarette manufacturers, Liggett, Lorillard, and Philip Morris. One of the causes of action he raises is breach of express warranty. After five years of discovery and pre-trial motions, the case went to trial in the district court. The jury returned a verdict of $400,000 for the plaintiff on the breach-of-express-warranty claim. The case is now on appeal before the United States Court of Appeals for the Third Circuit. Many issues were raised in the trial and on appeal. The excerpts below relate solely to the breach-of-warranty claim.

Decision on Appeal: Affirmed in part, reversed in part, and remanded for a new trial. The charge to the jury on the express warranty claim was in error. The trial court should have allowed the cigarette manufacturer to try to prove that Mrs. Cipollone did not believe the manufacturer's advertisements. Advertisements constitute an express warranty as long they constitute a basis of the bargain.

Mrs. Cipollone must have been aware of the advertisements and must have believed them.

Opinion of the Court

Justice BECKER delivered the opinion of the court. . . .

Rose Cipollone . . . smoked Chesterfield brand cigarettes, manufactured by Liggett, until 1955. In her deposition, introduced into evidence at the trial, she stated that she smoked the Chesterfield brand to be "glamorous," to "imitate" the "pretty girls and movie stars" depicted in Chesterfield advertisements, and because the advertisements stated that Chesterfield cigarettes were "mild." Mrs. Cipollone stated that she understood the description of Chesterfield cigarettes as "mild" to mean that the cigarettes were safe.

Mrs. Cipollone also testified that she was an avid reader of a variety of magazines, frequently listened to the radio, and often watched television during the years that she smoked the Chesterfield brand. Although she could not specifically remember which Chesterfield advertisements she saw or heard during those years, Chesterfield advertisements appeared continuously in those media during that period. Several of these advertisements were introduced into evidence. The following copy appeared commonly in Chesterfield magazine advertisements during the year 1952:

PLAY SAFE Smoke Chesterfield.

NOSE, THROAT, and Accessory Organs not Adversely Affected by Smoking Chesterfields. First such report ever published about any cigarette. A responsible consulting organization has reported the results of a continuing study by a competent medical specialist and his staff on the effects of smoking Chesterfield cigarettes. A group of people from various walks of life was organized to smoke only Chesterfields. For six months this group of men and women smoked their normal amount of Chesterfields—10 to 40 a day. 45% of the group have smoked Chesterfields continually from one to thirty years for an average of 10 years each. At the beginning and at the end of the six-months period each smoker was given a thorough examination, including X-ray pictures, by the medical specialist and his assistants. The examination covered the sinuses as well as the nose, ears and throat. The medical specialist, after a thorough examination of every member of the group, stated: "It is my opinion that the ears, nose, throat and accessory organs of all participating subjects examined by me were not adversely affected in the six-month period by smoking the cigarettes provided."

The defendants stipulated that Mrs. Cipollone had seen many of these advertisements. . . .

Mrs. Cipollone testified that she frequently listened to the radio show "Arthur Godfrey and His Friends," sponsored by the Chesterfield brand. The Chesterfield brand was marketed on the show as follows (text read by Mr. Godfrey):

[Y]ou saw me read this last week but a lot of folks didn't and it's a very important mes-

sage—especially those of you who smoke Chesterfields—you probably been wonderin' about this. You hear stuff all the time about "cigarettes are harmful to you" this and that and the other thing. . . .

Here's an ad, you've seen it in the papers—please read it when you get it. If you smoke it will make you feel better, really.

"Nose, throat and accessory organs not adversely affected by smoking Chesterfield. This is the first such report ever published about any cigarette. A responsible consulting organization has reported the results of a continuing study by a competent medical specialist and his staff on the effects of smoking Chesterfield cigarettes.

"A group of people from various walks of life was organized to smoke only chesterfields. For six months this group of men and women smoked their normal amount of Chesterfields—10 to 40 a day. 45% of the group have smoked Chesterfields continually from one to thirty years for an average of 10 years each.

"At the beginning and at the end of the six months period each smoker was given a thorough examination, including X-Ray pictures, by the medical specialist and his assistants. The examination covered the sinuses as well as the nose, ears and throat.

"Now—here's the important thing. "The medical specialist, after a thorough examination of every member of the group, stated: 'It is my opinion that the ears, nose, throat and accessory organs of all participating subjects examined by me were not adversely affected in the six-months period by smoking the Chesterfield cigarettes provided.' "

Now that ought to make you feel better if you've had any worries at all about it. I never did. I smoke two or three packs of these things every day. I feel pretty good. I don't know, I never did believe they did you any harm and now, we've got the proof. So—Chesterfields are the cigarette for you to smoke, be they regular size or king-size. (Sept. 24, 1952).†

In 1955, Mrs. Cipollone stopped smoking Chesterfield cigarettes and began to smoke L&M filter cigarettes, also made by

---

†[Mr. Godfrey also told his listeners:] You know you hear all this applesause about—you'd better quit smoking, pal, or you won't be here long and stuff. . . . But . . . I never recall seein' on anybody's gravestone—He Smoked Too Much, did you? I never did. . . .

Liggett. In response to a question as to why she switched to the L&M brand, Mrs. Cipollone stated that "[w]ell, they were talking about the filter tip, that it was milder and a miracle it would keep the stuff inside a trap, whatever." When asked why she desired the filter tip, she testified that "it was the new thing and I figured, well, go along[, and that] it was better [because t]he bad stuff would stay in the filter then." When asked whether concern about the "bad stuff" was due to a concern about her health, she stated "[n]ot really. . . . It was the trend. Everybody was smoking the filter cigarettes and I changed, too."

She also stated that although she could not remember any specific advertisements, she did "recall the ads and . . . remember the tips [and] the messages of a filter, a safer, something to that effect. . . . That it would filter the nicotine and the tar and the tobacco . . . [and] be a cleaner and fresher smoke." Mrs. Cipollone also stated that she "recall[ed] seeing an ad that said doctors recommend you smoke . . . I think it was L&M's. . . . [T]hrough advertising, I was led to assume that they were safe and they wouldn't harm me. . . . There was lots of advertising. There was advertising everywhere. There was advertising in magazines, on billboards, in newspapers."

Mr. Cipollone also introduced evidence as to how the L&M brand was marketed during the years that Mrs. Cipollone smoked that brand. One series of advertisements that appeared on television and in magazines at the outset of L&M's introduction to the public stated that L&M "miracle tip" filters were "just what the doctor ordered!"; the "just what the doctor ordered" phrase often appeared in a large bold typescript in magazine advertisements. The "miracle tip" was advertised as "remov[ing] the heavy particles, leaving you a Light and Mild smoke."

In 1968, Mrs. Cipollone stopped smoking the L&M brand and started smoking the Virginia Slims brand, manufactured by

Philip Morris. She stated that she switched "because it was very glamorous and very attractive ads and it was a nice looking cigarette. That persuaded me." In the 1970's, Mrs. Cipollone switch[ed] to the Parliament brand, also manufactured by Philip Morris. She testified that this brand was advertised as having a "recessed" filter and that she thought that this made it healthier. In 1974, she changed from the Parliament to the True brand, a cigarette manufactured by Lorillard, Inc. ("Lorillard") and advertised as low tar, upon the advice of her doctor, who had told her son to stop smoking.

From 1942 until the early 1980's, Mrs. Cipollone smoked between one pack and two packs of cigarettes per day. The only exception to this pattern was that, at the urging of her husband, Mrs. Cipollone substantially reduced her smoking during her first pregnancy in the 1940's. In 1981, Mrs. Cipollone was diagnosed as having lung cancer, but even though her doctors advised her to stop smoking, she was unable to do so. Mrs. Cipollone continued to smoke until June of 1982 when her lung was removed. Even after that, she smoked occasionally, in secret. She testified that she was "addicted" to cigarette smoking and that it was terribly difficult for her to give it up. She stopped smoking in 1983 after her cancer had spread widely and she had become terminally ill. Mrs. Cipollone died on October 21, 1984.

Evidence was also introduced on the subject of Mrs. Cipollone's awareness of the health consequences of smoking cigarettes. Some of that evidence has already been alluded to: she switched to the L&M brand in part because she thought that brand safer than the Chesterfield brand, and she later switched to the Parliament and True brands out of concern for her health. In addition, from the beginning of the Cipollones' marriage in 1947, Mr. Cipollone repeatedly told his wife that she should stop smoking because it was unlady-like and bad for her health. When reports linking smoking with cancer and heart disease began to appear in the media, Mr. Cipollone repeatedly brought them to his wife's attention. Other members of the Cipollone family also told her that cigarette smoking was dangerous to her health and could cause cancer. After January 1, 1966, every package of cigarettes purchased by Mrs. Cipollone bore the Congressionally mandated warning labels.

There is also evidence that Mrs. Cipollone feared that her cigarette smoking would damage her health. When she developed a bad cough, her concern about the possible effect of smoking on her health led her, apparently prior to 1966, to make novenas to Saint Judge [Jude?] asking his intercession on her behalf to prevent her from developing cancer. There is also evidence, however, that Mrs. Cipollone disbelieved the reports linking cigarette smoking to cancer and other health problems. As explained above, there is evidence that she read the cigarette companies' advertisements, understood them as representing that the cigarettes were safe, and thus, as she put it, "was led to assume that [the cigarettes that I purchased] wouldn't harm me." She stated that she had often read cigarette company or Tobacco Institute statements, reported in articles about the health consequences of smoking or reproduced in advertisements, stating that the link between smoking and disease has not been proven. She also testified that because she found it so difficult to stop smoking, she "[m]aybe . . . didn't want to believe" the reports that she heard that smoking caused cancer or other diseases and that she "didn't believe" that her smoking would cause her to contract lung cancer. In addition, Mrs. Cipollone stated that she believed that "[t]obacco companies wouldn't do anything that was really going to kill you." . . .

Mr. Cipollone brought his express warranty claim under U.C.C. (Uniform Commercial Code) § 2–313(1), which provides:

(1) Express warranties by the seller are created as follows:

(a) Any affirmation of fact or promise made by the seller to the buyer which relates to the goods and becomes *part of the basis of the bargain* creates an express warranty that the goods shall conform to the affirmation or promise. (b) Any description of the goods which is made *part of the basis of the bargain* creates an express warranty that the goods shall conform to the description.

N.J.S.A. § 12A:2–313(1) (emphasis added). With respect to this issue, the district court gave the following instructions to the jury:

[P]laintiff must prove . . . that Liggett . . . made one or more of the statements claimed by the plaintiff and that such statements were affirmations of fact or promises by Liggett . . . [and] that such statements were part of the basis of the bargain between Liggett and consumers like Rose Cipollone. . . .

The law does not require plaintiff to show that Rose Cipollone specifically relied on Liggett's warranties.

Ordinarily a guarantee or promise in an advertisement or other description of the goods becomes part of the basis of the bargain if it would naturally induce the purchase of the product and no particular reliance by the buyer on such statement needs to be shown. However, if the evidence establishes that the claimed statement cannot fairly be viewed as entering into the bargain, that is, that the statement would not naturally induce the purchase of a product, then no express warranty has been created.

. . .

[T]he district court's jury instructions were erroneous for two reasons. First, they did not require the plaintiff to prove that Mrs. Cipollone had read, seen, or heard the advertisements at issue. Second, they did not permit the defendant to prove that although Mrs. Cipollone had read, seen, or heard the advertisements, she did not believe the safety assurances contained therein. We must therefore reverse and remand for a new trial on this issue.

There is ample evidence from which a jury could conclude that Mrs. Cipollone saw, read, or heard the advertisements. She frequently listened to the Arthur Godfrey show, and frequently read magazines that contained the advertisements. Thus, the awareness question is not problematic. However, there is also evidence that family members brought the hazards of smoking to her attention. Thus Liggett might be able to prove that she did not believe the advertisements that she saw. . . .

For the foregoing reasons we will . . . reverse the district court's judgment in favor of plaintiff and against defendant, Liggett, on plaintiff's express warranty claim . . . and . . . remand for a new trial.

▪ ASSIGNMENT 17.5 ▪

a. The Federal Cigarette Labeling and Advertising Act (15 U.S.C.A. §§ 1331–1340, which became effective January 1, 1966) required cigarette manufacturers to place warnings on their labels and advertising on the hazards of smoking. Do you think it is possible for a smoker to assert a breach-of-express-warranty claim covering smoking after 1966? What about a blind person who started smoking after 1966?
b. Can you think of any ads on TV or other media today on any product that make express or implied claims that could become the basis of breach-of-express-warranty claims? Explain them.

▪ SALE VS. SERVICE

The final three causes of action we will examine in this chapter are:

- breach of implied warranty of merchantability
- breach of implied warranty of fitness for a particular purpose
- strict liability in tort

A common component of all three is that they apply to **sales,** not to **services.** The distinction can be critical. If you are injured because of what the defendant *sold* you, the causes of action you can bring include negligence and the three strict-liability causes of action: breach of implied warranty of merchantability, breach of implied warranty of fitness for a particular purpose, and strict liability in tort. If, however, you are injured while the defendant is rendering a *service,* your cause of action is limited to negligence.[3] Phrased another way, if the defendant is engaged in a service, you must show that the defendant acted unreasonably; but if a sale is involved, you can use the strict-liability causes of actions without having to establish the defendant's unreasonableness, i.e. negligence. It is therefore to the plaintiff's advantage to be able to show that the defendant sold something.

Unfortunately, it is not always easy to distinguish between a sale and a service. The technical definition of a sale is the passing of title to goods or products from a seller to a buyer for a price.[4] Generally, if title doesn't pass, then what you

---

[3]You can also sue for misrepresentation if you can establish intent. Of course, if the service provider has made express statements of fact about the service, a breach-of-express-warranty suit is a possibility as well.
[4]Our focus here is on the sale of personal property—**chattels**—rather than on the sale of real property—land. There are some courts, however, that have allowed strict-liability causes of action in real estate transactions, particularly when the houses sold were mass-produced.

have paid for is a service. But courts don't always use this definition. For example, when you rent or lease property, title does not pass, but the courts treat such transactions as "sales" for purpose of using the strict-liability causes of action. Also, every sale does not qualify. The sale must be by a merchant—someone in the business of selling. Hence, the strict-liability causes of action would not apply to the sale of a car between neighbors who are not car merchants.

▪ ASSIGNMENT 17.6 ▪

Is there a sale in the following situations? (See General Instructions for the Legal Analysis Assignment in Chapter 3.)

a. Fred is at a supermarket. he takes a bottle of catsup from the shelf, puts it in his cart, and heads for the checkout counter. While he is picking up the bottle from the cart to place it on the counter, it explodes, injuring Fred.
b. Mary is test driving a car that she is considering purchasing. She is alone in the car five blocks from the dealer. On her way back to the dealer, she decides against purchasing the car. Just as she drives in to the dealer's lot, the brakes malfunction, causing an accident, in which she is injured.

▪ ASSIGNMENT 17.7 ▪

In the following situations, would your state impose strict liability or would negligence have to be shown? (See General Instructions for the State Court Opinion Assignment in Chapter 2.)

a. Tom rents a furnished apartment from George. The sofa collapses, injuring Tom.
b. Same problem as in (a) above, except that the injury is from plaster that falls on Tom.

The easiest services to recognize are the professional services: those provided by doctors, lawyers, and teachers. Such professionals are not strictly liable for the harm they cause. Suits against them must establish their negligence.[5]

A service does not become a sale simply because there is a sale dimension to what occurs. Suppose, for example, that a dentist uses a hypodermic needle in a patient's mouth. The needle is a product or "good" for which the patient is charged. Yet this does not change the character of the event from a service to a sale. There is no implied warranty that the needle is safe. There is no implied warranty that anything the dentist does is safe or effective. If the needle breaks in the patient's mouth, a suit against the dentist must show negligence.

What about a blood transfusion at a hospital? Assume that a hemophiliac contracts AIDS by receiving infected blood during a transfusion. Is the blood a "good" (a product) that has been purchased? Most courts say no. The blood transfusion is a service. (In some states this result is mandated by statute.) Negligence, therefore, must be shown, e.g., carelessness in the screening and testing procedures for those who donate blood.

---

[5]Unless, of course, they have guaranteed their service (in which case they may have breached an express warranty) or lied about their service (in which case they may have committed the tort of misrepresentation). See also footnote 3.

▪ ASSIGNMENT 17.8 ▪

If a patient contracts AIDS through a blood transfusion in your state, what theories of liability should be explored? (See General Instructions for the State Code Assignment and for the State Court Opinion Assignment, both in Chapter 2.)

Services are not limited to the professions. Hotels provide services, as do plumbers and carpenters. The gray area is again the situation where it appears that both a sale and a service exist. A beauty parlor, for example, provides a service. Yet, it uses and charges for products in rendering this service, e.g., a permanent-wave solution. Again, the general rule is that a service does not become a sale simply because a product is used or because there is a product component to what is predominantly a service. There are courts, however, that *are* willing to chip away at this rule when nonprofessional services are involved. In the beauty parlor case, for example, there is a well-known New Jersey opinion that held there was a sale of the permanent-wave solution by a beauty parlor. When the solution caused injury, strict liability was imposed without the need to prove negligence.[6] The same result would be reached if a plaintiff at a restaurant were injured by food or drink. They are sales.

Defendants understandably want to classify what they do as services in order to avoid any form of strict liability. If they are correct that they are engaged in a service, the plaintiff must prove that the injury was negligently produced.

▪ ASSIGNMENT 17.9 ▪

Jones is an optometrist. Smith buys a pair of contact lenses from Jones, who fits them on Smith. The lenses are defective, causing injury to Smith. Does Smith have to prove Jones's negligence in your state? Would your state consider this a sale or a service? (See General Instructions for the State Court Opinion Assignment in Chapter 2.)

▪ IMPLIED WARRANTIES

There are two implied warranties:

- implied warranty of merchantability
- implied warranty of fitness for a particular purpose

They are imposed by the law and not through agreement of the parties. You will find these warranties in state statutory codes. State legislatures created the warranties by modeling them on § 2-314 (merchantability) and § 2-315 (fitness) of the Uniform Commercial Code. Like the breach of an express warranty, the breach of these two implied warranties imposes strict liability, in that the plaintiff does not have to establish that the defendant intended to breach them nor that the defendant was negligent in breaching them.

Our discussion of the implied warranties will cover the following topics:

- elements of breach
- problems of privity
- defenses

---

[6]*Newmark v. Gimbel's Inc.* 102 N.J.Super. 279, 246 A.2d 11, *aff'd*, 54 N.J. 585, 258 A.2d 697 (1969).

Implied Warranty of Merchantability

The elements of a breach of an **implied warranty of merchantability** are:

1. sale of goods
2. by a merchant of goods of that kind
3. the goods are not merchantable
4. damage
5. causation

Sale of Goods

Sales are covered, but not services. See the earlier discussion in this chapter on the problems of distinguishing a sale (which does carry an implied warranty of merchantability) and a service (which does not).

Merchant of Goods of that Kind

This warranty does not apply to the occasional seller of goods, such as a cab driver who sells a watch to a fellow cab driver or to a customer in the cab. The defendant must be a merchant in the business of selling goods of the kind in question. There is an implied warranty of merchantability in a car sold by a car dealer, but not in a rifle sold by the car dealer.

Goods are not Merchantable

Goods are **merchantable** when they are fit for the ordinary purposes for which the goods are used. (As we shall see in the next section, this is a broader test than that used for *strict liability in tort,* which requires that the product be unreasonably dangerous.) The following are examples of products that are not merchantable:

- vinegar bottles that contain large particles of glass
- shoes with heels that break off with normal use soon after purchase
- aspirin that causes infertility

If, however, regular shoes fall apart when the plaintiff is mountain climbing, there is no implied warranty of merchantability, because the shoes were not being used for their ordinary purpose. If the plaintiff who bought the shoes can establish the elements of an implied warranty of fitness *for a particular purpose,* strict liability will be imposed on that theory. Otherwise, the defendant is not liable without a showing of negligence.

There is no requirement that plaintiffs prove they actually relied on the merchantability of the goods before purchase. This reliance is assumed. Suppose, however, that there are obvious defects in the product, which a reasonable inspection of the goods would reveal to the typical consumer. There is no implied warranty with respect to such defects as long as the consumer had full opportunity to inspect.

Damage and Causation

The damage or injury to the person or property of the plaintiff must be caused by the fact that the goods were not fit for their ordinary purpose. The traditional but-for or substantial-factor test will be applied to establish causation.

▪ ASSIGNMENT 17.10 ▪

Jim dies of lung cancer in your state. He smoked cigarettes for twenty-five years. Would a court in your state say that the cigarettes were not merchantable? (See General Instructions for the State Court Opinion Assignment in Chapter 2.)

Implied Warranty of Fitness for a Particular Purpose

Next we examine the **implied warranty of fitness for a particular purpose.** The elements of a breach of this warranty are:

1. sale of goods
2. seller has reason to know the buyer's particular purpose in buying the goods
3. seller has reason to know the buyer is relying on the seller's skill or judgment in buying the goods
4. the goods are not fit for the particular purpose
5. damage
6. causation

Particular purposes must be distinguished from the ordinary purposes of a product. Ordinary purposes are the customary uses of the product. The following are examples of particular purposes:

▪ shoes to be used to climb mountains
▪ sunglasses to be used by a professional baseball player
▪ a dog chain to hold a three-hundred-pound dog

The seller must know or have reason to know about the particular purpose, and know that the buyer is relying on the seller's skill and judgment. The buyer must in fact rely on this skill and judgment. A buyer who makes a careful inspection of the product may have difficulty proving reliance. A good deal will depend on the extent of the inspection and on the expertise of the buyer in the use of the product. If the buyer relies on his or her own skill and judgment rather than on that of the seller, the buyer cannot use this cause of action. Of course, if the product is also not fit for its *ordinary* purpose, the plaintiff can sue under the merchantability warranty. Otherwise, there is no recovery unless the plaintiff establishes negligence.

Privity

Privity describes the relationship that exists between parties to a contract. Our question is whether an express warranty and the two implied warranties apply *only* if the plaintiff and defendant are in privity with each other. The old rule was that privity was required. The plaintiff had to purchase the product from the defendant in order to sue the latter for a breach of warranty. To get around the rule, courts sometimes tried to use agency principles. For example, a wife who purchased a can of tuna that injured her husband was said to be the **agent** of the husband in making the purchase, so that theoretically the husband was the purchaser and hence in privity with the defendant.

Assume that you are in a state requiring privity in warranty actions. When Helen buys a car from the Fairfax Car Dealership, there is privity between Helen and the dealer. However:

- there is no privity between Helen and the car manufacturer
- there is no privity between someone borrowing Helen's car and the dealer or the manufacturer
- there is no privity between a passenger in Helen's car and the dealer or the manufacturer
- there is no privity between a bystander injured by Helen's car and the dealer or the manufacturer

The absence of privity prevented a good deal of litigation when a product violated the warranty. Particularly troublesome was the inability of nonprivity plaintiffs to reach the manufacturer—the "deep pocket" that is often most responsible for the injury. This did not mean the manufacturer was off the hook. As we saw earlier, negligence actions between parties does not require privity. To reach the manufacturer in a warranty action, the immediate buyer would sue the immediate seller, who in turn would sue the next person up the distribution chain, until the manufacturer was eventually sued by *its* immediate buyer. The process was very cumbersome. Even the gimmick of agency left much to be desired.

Today, there is considerable disagreement among the states on how the privity problem should be handled in warranty cases, i.e., who can sue and who can be sued.

Who can sue for breach of warranty

- A few states cling to the old rule that there must be privity, which can exist only between an immediate buyer and the immediate seller.
- Some states permit the immediate buyer and members of the buyer's family or household to bring the warranty action.
- Some states permit the immediate buyer and any person who may reasonably be expected to be affected by the goods to bring the warranty action, e.g., a bystander who is hit by a car.

Who can be sued for breach of warranty

- A few states cling to the old rule that there must be privity, which can exist only between an immediate buyer and the immediate seller.
- Some states permit designated nonprivity plaintiffs (see "who can sue") to bring direct warranty actions against the manufacturer when the product is designed to come into contact with the body, e.g., food, home permanent solution.
- Some states permit designated nonprivity plaintiffs (see "who can sue") to bring direct warranty actions against the manufacturer for any product.

• ASSIGNMENT 17.11 •

Tom buys a car in your state from a dealer. The brakes are defective due to their design. The defect causes an accident injuring Tom, Ed (his neighbor who was riding in the car at the time), and Sam (a pedestrian who was hit by the car when the brakes failed). Tom, Ed, and Sam want to bring separate suits against the manufacturer for breach of implied warranty of merchantability. Assume that the car was not merchantable. Which of these three individuals, if any, will be allowed to bring the suit? (See General Instructions for the State Code Assignment and for the State Court Opinion Assignment, both in Chapter 2.)

Defenses to Warranty Actions

The following defenses will be briefly discussed:

- disclaimer
- notice
- contributory negligence
- assumption of the risk

Disclaimer of Warranty

Under certain conditions, parties to a sales contract can agree that some or all warranties do not exist, i.e., the warranties have been disclaimed. The **disclaimer** must be conspicuous and unambiguous so that it is clearly communicated to the buyer. A disclaimer buried in small print on the back of a standardized contract form will probably be held to be ineffective against the ordinary consumer. A court may rule that the disclaimer is invalid because it is **unconscionable,** meaning that it is substantially unfair to a consumer in a highly unequal bargaining position against a defendant selling or manufacturing mass-produced goods. Also, disclaimers are generally ineffective against nonpurchasers, who are allowed to bring the warranty action. If none of these special situations or problems exist, however, express and implied warranties can be validly disclaimed.

Notice

It is a defense to a warranty action that the injured plaintiff failed to give **notice** to the defendant of the breach of the warranty within a reasonable time after the breach was discovered or should have been discovered. Since many plaintiffs wait a good deal of time before taking action, they fall into the trap of this defense. Some courts, however, disregard the notice requirement when the breach of warranty causes personal injury or when the plaintiff is a nonpurchaser. Even if a court will not go this far, the tendency is to be lenient to plaintiffs in deciding whether they waited an unreasonable time to notify the defendant.

Contributory Negligence

Generally, contributory negligence is not a defense to a breach-of-warranty action.

Assumption of Risk

Assumption of the risk *is* a defense to a breach-of-warranty action. The defendant must show that the plaintiff had actual knowledge and an appreciation of the danger and yet still voluntarily proceeded to use the product.

▪ STRICT LIABILITY IN TORT

Strict Liability in Tort Checklist:
Definitions, Relationships, and Research References

Category

Strict Liability in tort is a strict liability tort. There is no need to show intent or negligence. In many states, however, negligence concepts are relevant to design defects.

Interest Protected by This Tort

The right to be free from injuries due to products that are defective and unreasonably dangerous.

Elements of This Tort

1. seller
2. a defective product that is unreasonably dangerous to person or property
3. a user or consumer
4. physical harm
5. causation

Major Definitions of Words/Phrases in These Elements

Seller: A person engaged in the business of selling products for use or consumption.

Defective product: At the time the product leaves the seller's hands, it has a manufacturing, design, or warning defect.

Unreasonably dangerous: The product is dangerous to an extent beyond that which would be contemplated by the ordinary consumer who purchases it, with the ordinary knowledge common to the community as to its characteristics. (Note: Some courts use other tests.)

User or consumer: Anyone who uses or consumes the product (some courts have extended liability to bystanders).

Physical harm: Damage to person or property.

Causation: "But for" the defect, the physical harm would not have occurred, or the defect was a substantial factor in producing the physical harm.

Major Defenses and Counter-Argument Possibilities That Need to Be Explored

1. The defendant is not a seller.
2. The injury came from a service, not a product.
3. The product is not defective.
4. The product is not unreasonably dangerous.
5. The plaintiff is not a user or consumer.
6. There was no physical harm to person or property of the plaintiff.
7. The defendant did not cause the physical harm.
8. There was unforeseeable, extreme misuse of the product by the plaintiff.
9. The plaintiff assumed the risk of the danger in the product.
10. The plaintiff failed to mitigate damages.
11. Release.
12. Statute of limitations.
13. Res judicata or collateral estoppel.

Damages

In most states, damages cover persons or property, but not economic loss alone. Once physical harm to person or property is established, there can be recovery for consequential damages as well, e.g., medical bills. Pain and suffering can be included. Punitive damages are also possible.

Relationship to Criminal Law

A state might impose criminal penalties on a company for selling designated products, e.g., drugs, explosives. The company would also be subject to civil liability—strict liability in tort—if the product is defective (unreasonably dangerous) and causes injury.

Relationship to Other Causes of Action

Breach of Implied Warranty of Merchantability: Available if the product is not fit for the ordinary purpose for which the goods are used.

Misrepresentation: Defendant must have knowingly made false statements of fact about the product that led to the injury.

Negligence: Plaintiff must prove that the injury from the product was caused by absence of reasonable care on the part of the seller.

Wrongful Death: Available if the product leads to the death of plaintiff.

Federal Law

The Federal Tort Claims Act does not cover claims based on strict liability. The Consumer Products Safety Commission has authority to protect the public against unreasonable risks of injury associated with consumer products. Damages can be recovered by consumers injured by certain violations of the Commission's rules. There are other federal agencies in existence with jurisdiction over consumer products, e.g., the Food and Drug Administration. The standards of such agencies must be examined since they are relevant to strict-liability-in-tort issues, e.g., whether the defendant complied with safety regulations.

Employer-Employee (Agency) Law

An employer who is a seller is strictly liable in tort for products sold by one of its employees within the scope of employment.

Research References for This Tort

▪ Digests

In the digests of West, look for case summaries of court opinions on this tort under key topics such as:

Products liability	Damages
Drugs and narcotics	Torts
Food	Negligence
Sales	Death

▪ Corpus Juris Secundum

In this legal encyclopedia, look for discussions under topic headings such as:

Products liability	Damages
Drugs and narcotics	Torts
Food	Negligence
Sales	Death

• American Jurisprudence 2d

   In this legal encyclopedia, look for discussions under topic headings such as:

Products liability	Damages
Drugs, narcotics and poisons	Torts
Food	Negligence
Sales	Death

• Law Review Literature

   There are three index systems to use to locate articles on this tort:

Index to Legal Periodicals (ILP)	Current Law Index (CLI)	Legal Resource Index (LRI)
See literature in *ILP* under subject headings such as:	See literature in *CLI* under subject headings such as:	See literature in *LRI* under subject headings such as:
Products Liability	Products Liability	Products Liability
Insurance, Products Liability	Insurance, Products Liability	Insurance, Products Liability
Product Recall	Product Recall	Product Recall
Manufacturers	Manufacturers	Manufacturers
Torts	Torts	Torts
Damages	Damages	Damages
Negligence	Negligence	Negligence
	Warranty	Warranty

Example of a law review article you can locate on this tort by using ILP, CLI, or LRI:

> *Strict Liability in Tort: Reliance on Circumstantial Evidence to Prove a Defect,* 27 Federation of Insurance Counsel Quarterly 129 (1977).

• *ALR, ALR2D, ALR3D, ALR4TH, ALR5TH, ALR Fed*

   Use the *Index to Annotations* to locate annotations on this tort. In this index, check subject headings such as:

Products liability	Negligence
Warranty	Torts
Warnings	Damages
Drugs and narcotics	Death
Absolute liability	Repairs and maintenance

Example of an annotation you can locate through this index on strict liability in tort:

> *Products Liability: Modern Cases Determining Whether Product is Defectively Designed,* 96 ALR3d 22.

• *Words and Phrases*

   In this multivolume legal dictionary, look up every word or phrase discussed in this section to try to find definitions of the words or phrases from court opinions.

Strict liability in tort avoids many potential obstacles to recovery:

- The plaintiff does not have to prove the negligence of the defendant (although negligence concepts are relevant when the injury is caused by design defects).
- The plaintiff does not have to prove that the defendant knew of the defect.
- The plaintiff does not have to establish privity.
- The defendant cannot disclaim the obligation of safety.
- The plaintiff has no duty to notify the defendant after the injury caused by the product.

The elements of a **strict-liability-in-tort** cause of action are:

1. seller
2. a defective product that is unreasonably dangerous to person or property
3. a user or consumer
4. physical harm
5. causation

These elements are based on the highly influential § 402A of the *Restatement of Torts*.[7] Many courts have adopted the above elements of § 402A. As we shall see, however, there are a number of courts that have modified them.

Seller

The defendant must be a **seller.** Seller has a broad definition: any person engaged in the business of selling products for use or consumption. Not covered is the occasional seller of a product who is not engaged in selling as part of his or her business. If, for example, one student sells another student a car, there is no strict liability in tort, because the student is not in the business of selling products. If the student is liable at all, negligence will have to be shown. Isolated sales that are not part of the usual course of business of the seller are not covered.

The following would be sellers under the first element:

- manufacturer of entire product
- supplier
- assembler
- distributor
- wholesaler
- retailer
- operator of a restaurant

Some states do not impose strict liability in tort on the manufacturer of a **component part** of a product. Its liability would have to be based on negligence. Other courts, however, treat the manufacturer of a component part like everyone else in the **chain of distribution** and impose strict liability in tort.

At a small neighborhood hardware store you buy a defective hammer that is manufactured by a company a thousand miles away. Both the store (a retailer) and the manufacturer are subject to strict liability in tort. The store manager cannot say, "I didn't make the hammer; go sue the manufacturer." The store is a seller engaged in the business of selling, and hence is subject to strict liability in tort. The plaintiff does not have to prove that the store manager was negligent.

---

[7]*Restatement (Second) of Torts* § 402A (1965).

Someone who *rents* products as a business is also a seller. A company that rents cars, planes, or other equipment, for example, can be strictly liable in tort. Section 402A does not cover sales of real property. As we saw with implied warranty of merchantability, however, some states are willing to extend strict liability to some sellers of houses, particularly mass-produced structures. (See footnote 4.)

Strict liability in tort applies to the *sale of products,* not to *services.* See the earlier discussion of this distinction in this chapter, particularly with reference to the problem of transactions that have both sale and service components.

Defective Product that is Unreasonably Dangerous

There are two requirements for this element. The product must be both defective *and* unreasonably dangerous. Most states agree that both components must be established.

We have already see the three major categories of defects:

Manufacturing Defects: Something never intended went wrong when the product was being put together and delivered.

Design Defects: The product is as it was intended to be, but something is wrong with its design.

Warning Defects: The instructions or warnings are inadequate.

In theory, the plaintiff does not have to prove that the defendant was negligent in producing these defects. A defendant who has "sold" a defective product can be strictly liable in tort even if the defendant used all reasonable care. The problem, however, is that it is sometimes very difficult to define what is meant by defectiveness without using negligence concepts such as reasonableness and foreseeability, particularly with respect to design and warning defects.

According to the Restatement's § 402A, the product must be **unreasonably dangerous:**

A product is unreasonably dangerous when it is dangerous to an extent beyond that which would be contemplated by the ordinary consumer who purchases it, with the ordinary knowledge common to the community as to its characteristics.[8]

It is important to note that the test is not whether the injured plaintiff thinks the product is unreasonably dangerous. All injured plaintiffs undoubtedly do. The test is **objective:** what would an ordinary consumer think?

For many products, there is little difficulty establishing unreasonable danger. An ordinary consumer would not expect:

- a new television to explode
- a bottle of catsup to have arsenic in it
- the steering wheel of a new car to break off while driving
- the emergency door of a new school bus to suddenly fall off

An ordinary person possessing no more than the knowledge that any ordinary person in the community would have about the product would conclude that

---

[8]*Restatement (Second) of Torts* § 402A (1965).

the products just listed are unreasonably dangerous. You do not have to be an expert, for example, to know that catsup is not supposed to have arsenic in it.

Other products, however, are not so easy to assess. Assume, for example, that the plaintiff eats a bowl of fish chowder at a New England restaurant and suffers severe injuries when a fish bone gets caught in the throat. Is the product unreasonably dangerous? Probably not. An ordinary customer would expect to find some bones in this kind of soup. There is a danger from bones, but not an unreasonable danger. A court might reach a different result, however, if the plaintiff were a minor or were mentally ill. An ordinary consumer would think the product is unreasonably dangerous for such individuals.

There are some courts that argue that a product is unreasonably dangerous only when it contains a substance that is "foreign" to the product. Other courts, however, reject this view and say that even a substance that is "natural" to the product can also be unreasonably dangerous.

Note that we do not ask whether the restaurant used reasonable care to remove bones from the fish chowder. The use of reasonable care is a negligence standard. The test here is the expectation of the ordinary consumer.

▪ ASSIGNMENT 17.12 ▪

Linda goes into a bar and orders a martini. She breaks a tooth on an unpitted olive. Is the product unreasonably dangerous? What about a cherry pit in a vending machine pie? (See General Instructions for the Legal Analysis Assignment in Chapter 3.)

The danger in some products is obvious, e.g., knives, matches, bug sprays. Assuming that none of these products is defectively made or designed, they are not unreasonably dangerous. An ordinary consumer would expect the danger to be present and would take precautions.

An ordinary consumer is expected to know that certain products can be dangerous. A regular pair of shoes, for example, will slip when wet. A manufacturer or retailer is not required to sell a product that will never cause injury. Nor are they required to sell a product that is in the safest condition possible. A car built like a tank may be the safest vehicle on the road, but a car manufacturer is not strictly liable in tort for failing to build a car this way. Again, the test is the expectation of the ordinary consumer as to safety.

▪ ASSIGNMENT 17.13 ▪

Tom, aged twelve, buys a bicycle from the Cycle and Sports Store. The bike does not have a headlight on it. While carefully driving the bike at night, Tom is hit by a car. Assume that the accident would not have occurred if the bike had a headlight on it. Is the store strictly liable in tort? (See General Instructions for the Legal Analysis Assignment in Chapter 3.)

Many products can become dangerous to a consumer who overuses or overconsumes them, but they are not necessarily unreasonably dangerous. Good, "wholesome" whiskey is not unreasonably dangerous because it can be deadly to alcoholics. Uncontaminated butter is not unreasonably dangerous because it can bring on heart attacks for people who need a low-cholesterol diet.

Nor is a product unreasonably dangerous because it fails to warn against every possible danger that could be caused by its use.

> The seller may reasonably assume that those with common allergies, as for example to eggs or strawberries, will be aware of them, and he is not required to warn against them. Where, however, the product contains an ingredient to which a substantial number of the population are allergic, and the ingredient is one whose danger is not generally known, or if known is one which the consumer would reasonably not expect to find in the product, the seller is required to give warning against it, if he has knowledge, or by the application of reasonable, developed human skills and foresight should have knowledge, of the presence of the ingredient and the danger. Likewise in the case of poisonous drugs, or those unduly dangerous for other reasons, warning as to use may be required.[9]

Once a warning is clearly and conspicuously given, the seller can assume that it will be read and followed.

Unavoidably unsafe products are those that are incapable of being made safe due to the current state of technology and science. A certain drug, for example, may be extremely valuable, but have a high risk of dangerous side effects. If the drug is properly prepared and marketed, and an adequate warning is given of the risk, the drug is neither defective nor unreasonably dangerous. Properly prepared means that all feasible tests were conducted on the drug before it was placed on the market. Properly marketed might mean that it is sold only by prescription through a doctor.

Design defects pose the greatest headaches for the courts. The first problem is to make the distinction between the **intended use** and the **foreseeable use** of a product:

> **Intended Use:** What the manufacturer wanted the product used for; the purpose for which the product was built and placed on the market.

> **Foreseeable Use:** What the manufacturer anticipates or should be able to anticipate the product will be used for; a foreseeable use may not be the intended use.

A product must not be unreasonably dangerous both for its intended use *and* for its foreseeable use.

> **Examples:**
>
> • Chair
>
> | Intended Use: | To sit on |
> | Foreseeable Use: | To stand on in order to store things in a closet |
> | Unforeseeable Use: | To provide extra support for an elevated car while a tire is being changed |
>
> • Cleaning Fluid
>
> | Intended Use: | To clean floors |
> | Foreseeable Use: | To be swallowed by children |
> | Unforeseeable Use: | As a lighter fluid for a barbecue |

---

[9]*Restatement (Second) of Torts* § 402A, comment j (1965).

If a plaintiff is injured when a chair on which he or she is standing collapses, the manufacturer cannot escape strict liability in tort by arguing that the plaintiff was not using the product for its intended purpose. It is foreseeable that at least a fair number of users will stand on chairs. Therefore, the product must not be unreasonably dangerous for this foreseeable purpose—the chair must be built strongly enough to accommodate this purpose, or adequate warnings against use for this purpose must be provided. An ordinary consumer would expect the product to be reasonably safe for all foreseeable purposes, including, of course, its intended purposes.

Nor will the defendant be able to raise the defense that the plaintiff misused the product. It is not a **misuse** of a product to use it for a purpose that the manufacturer should have anticipated. Or, viewed from another perspective, if it is a misuse, it is a foreseeable misuse that should have been guarded against in the design or through a warning. Similarly, it is foreseeable that children will swallow cleaning liquid. Therefore the manufacturer should provide safety precautions against such use, e.g., a warning on the bottle addressed to parents that the substance is toxic and should be kept out of the reach of children.

Unforeseeable uses, however, are another matter. To make a manufacturer strictly liable in tort for injuries caused by products put to unforeseeable uses would be to make the manufacturer an insurer. Liability does not extend this far.

Of course, liability for unreasonably dangerous products put to foreseeable uses is not limited to the manufacturer that designed the defective product. The local department store is also strictly liable for such products. Anyone who is a ''seller'' in the chain of distribution has committed strict liability in tort.

• ASSIGNMENT 17.14 •

For the following products, identify what you think are:
  • the intended uses
  • possible unintended uses that are foreseeable
  • possible unintended uses that are unforeseeable
    a. a screwdriver
    b. shampoo for a dog
    c. a lawn mower
    d. bug spray

Assume that each time the product was used for one of the three categories of use, an injury occurred because the product was defective and dangerous for that use. (See General Instructions for the Legal Analysis Assignment in Chapter 3.)

Ordinary consumers do not expect that a product will last forever. Their expectation is that the product will be reasonably safe only during the life of the product's normal use. Tires, for example, are expected to wear out after being driven a certain number of miles. What is the expected life of a product? How long should the manufacturer design it to last? The problem of how long a product should be designed to last is similar to the problem of what uses a product should be designed for.

How much is a manufacturer expected to do in order to design out defects that are dangerous? How durable are the materials in a product expected to be? Because the manufacturer is not expected to design a product that is perfectly safe for everyone whenever it is used, how is the decision made as to what is reasonably safe? Most courts will answer this question by considering the same factors that go into a determination of negligence.

The foreseeability of serious harm: The greater the foreseeability of serious harm, the more care, time, and expense are needed to design the product to avoid the harm.

The importance or social utility of the product: How valuable or significant is the product? The more importance or social utility it has, the more reasonable it is to take risks in putting the product on the market.

The burden or inconvenience on the manufacturer of redesigning the product to make it safer: If the expense, for example, of the extra safety precaution is slight, it should be taken. If, however, the cost is so excessive as to make the product close to unmarketable, the precautions may not have to be taken—unless the foreseeability of serious harm is very high. The state of the art is important. Were alternative designs available? Were they feasible? Manufacturers cannot do the impossible. They can go only as far as technology and science will permit. Of course, the cheapest and least burdensome precaution may be a warning. A warning, however, is not a substitute for reasonable design changes that would take the unreasonable danger out of the product altogether.

Courts differ on how they phrase the test to determine whether there is a problem with the design. Not everyone agrees with the language of the test of the Restatement (see first item in following list). There is little uniformity:

- The product is defective and unreasonably dangerous—more dangerous than an ordinary consumer would expect (the Restatement test).
- The product is defective if it is unreasonably dangerous because of its design.
- The danger associated with the use of the product outweighs the utility of the product.
- The risks of the product are so great that a reasonable seller, knowing the risks, would not place the product on the market.
- The product is dangerously defective.
- The product fails to perform as safely as an ordinary consumer would expect when used in an intended or reasonably foreseeable manner.

The products-liability cases on design defects tend to be extremely lengthy as the courts wrestle with definitions. This area of the law is still in the process of development.

CASE

Patterson v. Gesellschaft
608 F. Supp. 1206 (1985)
United States District Court, Northern District, Texas

Background: Berlin Ransom used a Rohm .38 caliber revolver to murder James Patterson, a "7-Eleven" store clerk. The mother of the victim has brought a products liability action against the manufacturer of the gun. The case is before the United States District Court in Texas (Northern District). During the trial, the manufacturer has made a motion for a summary judgment.

Decision: Motion for summary judgment granted since the gun was not defective.

Opinion of Court

Judge BUCHMEYER delivered the opinion of the court. . . .

The handgun in question was manufactured and sold in 1967 by a West German company, the defendant Rohm Gesellschaft ("Rohm"). The gun is a .38 caliber revolver with a four-inch barrel and a total length of only nine inches. It is cheap, small, light, easy to conceal—and, for these reasons, is of the type commonly referred to as "snubbies" or "Saturday Night Specials."

On December 29, 1980—**over 13 years after the handgun was manufactured**—it was used by Berlin Ransom in the attempted robbery of a "7-Eleven" store in Dallas, Texas. During the crime, Ransom shot and killed James Patterson, the clerk at this convenience grocery. Later, Ransom was caught and convicted; he is now confined in the Texas Department of Corrections.

The plaintiff, Jett Edwards Patterson, is the mother of James Patterson, the murder victim. She seeks $500,000 in damages from Rohm, the manufacturer, and from R. G. Industries, a firearm distributor in Florida. . . . Although it is conceded that the Rohm .38 revolver did not malfunction—and performed exactly as it was intended—the plaintiff's attorneys nevertheless make these two "products liability" claims:

(i) *Design Defect:* that the handgun was "defective and unreasonably dangerous" in its design because handguns simply pose risks of injury and death that "far outweigh" any social utility they may have. (ii) *Defect in Distribution:* that the system of distributing and marketing handguns was "defective and unreasonably dangerous" because it is too easy for handguns to be obtained by criminals and others who misuse them.

Both of these theories are baseless. They have been rejected by almost every court that has considered them.* Since it is admitted that there was nothing wrong with the .38 caliber revolver, the plaintiff cannot recover under either of the purported "products liability" claims.

The Texas law of products liability controls this diversity case. Texas has adopted the Restatement (Second) of Torts § 402A—which provides that one who sells a product "in **a defective condition unreasonably dangerous**" is subject to liability for injuries caused by the product. *Turner v. General Motors Corp.*, 584 S.W.2d 844 (Tex.1979). However, under Texas law, the manufacturer is not required to insure that its products are completely safe or that they will not cause injury to anyone. Instead, the manufacturer is liable for injuries resulting from a product only if that product is "defective"—i.e., has a defect in the sense that something is wrong with it. *Syrie v. Knoll International*, 748 F.2d 304 (5th Cir.1984); *Davidson v. Stanadyne, Inc.*, 718 F.2d 1334 (5th Cir.1983). This required defect may be one of three distinct types:

(i) The product may malfunction because of some manufacturing defect. (ii) The product may be defective because it was sold without sufficient warning or instructions.** (iii) The product may be defective because its basic design is unsafe.

---

*[E]very *reported* decision to date—except one—has refused to permit shooting victims to recover damages from handgun manufacturers under "absolute or strict liability principles." The sole exception is *Richman v. Charter Arms Corp.*, 571 F.Supp. 192 (E.D.La.1983). Although this case holds that a nondefective handgun *is not* unreasonably dangerous, it found that selling such a gun to the public *could* constitute "an ultrahazardous activity" under Louisiana law. . . .

Although some commentators have argued that consumers must be warned about the dangers of handgun use and the possibility of handgun theft . . ., there is no duty to warn of "dangers" that are obvious and commonly known. Obviously, **it is not "necessary to tell a zookeeper to keep his head out of the hippopotamus' mouth." *Bartkewich v. Billinger*, 432 Pa. 351, 247 A.2d 603, 606 (1968).

In cases involving the third type of defect, that of defective design, Texas uses the "risk/utility balancing test": whether the product is "unreasonably" dangerous in the sense that "the danger-in-fact associated with the use of the product outweighs the utility of the product." *Davidson,* 718 F.2d at 1338. Typically, this requires the jury to weigh the risks involved in the defective product against the feasibility and cost of an improved design. For example, if placing the gasoline tank in the center of the car "would reduce the chances of fire in rear-end collisions without creating other risks, significantly reducing performance, or significantly increasing costs, then the risk of the rear-end design outweighs its utility, and the car is defective." Note, "Handguns and Product Liability," 97 Harv.L.Rev. 1912, 1913–1914 (1984).

In this case, it is admitted that the Rohm .38 caliber revolver did not malfunction and that it did not lack any essential safety features. Nevertheless, the plaintiff's attorneys argue (i) that Texas law no longer requires a showing that the product is defective; (ii) that the word "defective" in § 402A is merely synonymous with the phrase "unreasonably dangerous"; and (iii) **that the jury may simply apply the "risk/utility test" to *any* product (whether or not it has a defect).**

By this reasoning, the plaintiff's attorneys contend . . . that a nondefective handgun will be "defective and unreasonably dangerous" if the jury determines that the risks of injury and death outweigh any utility a handgun may have. Specifically, they argue that: "[h]andgun use results in 22,000 deaths every year in the United States and that medical care for gunshot victims costs approximately $500 million each year. Although handguns constitute only thirty percent of all firearms sold in the United States, ninety percent of all cases of firearm misuse involve handguns. Most murders are sudden crimes of passion; without the ready availability of handguns, such crimes would be less likely. Proponents of manufacturers' liability further argue that handguns are almost useless for self-protection: a handgun is six times more likely to be used to kill a friend or relative than to repel a burglar, and a person who uses a handgun in self-defense is eight times more likely to be killed than one who quietly acquiesces. Thus, handguns, at least as distributed to the general public, are said to be defective." These arguments, of course, apply to *all* handguns, not just the "Saturday Night Special" involved in this case.

Aside from the fact that contrary evidence can obviously be advanced to argue the "social utility" of handguns[†]—and despite this Court's admiration for such a delightfully nonsensical claim: **that a product which does not have a defect can nevertheless, under the law, be defective**[††]—the plaintiff's attorneys are simply wrong. Under Texas law, there can be no products liability recovery unless the product does have a defect. Without this essential predicate, that something is wrong with the product, the risk/utility balancing test does not even apply. . . . [T]he operative phrase used in § 402A of the Restatement (Second) of Torts—a product "in a defective condition unreasonably dangerous"—was deliberately chosen to make it

---

[†]"Handguns are collected as a hobby and are used for target shooting and hunting, as well as for self-defense. Despite the great movement in this country to ban or restrict handgun ownership, the failure of any state legislature to do so strongly suggests a general legislative agreement that handguns do have social utility. Furthermore, handguns provide their owners with a psychic security that cannot be easily measured. And although the chances that an intruder will be shot by a homeowner or merchant are small, the consequences of a gunshot wound are so serious that the possibility may deter many people from attempting crimes." Note, "Handguns and Product Liability," 97 Harv.L.Rev. 1912, 1915 (1984).

[††]Lewis Carroll would have certainly approved. In "Through the Looking Glass," he was very candid in Humpty Dumpty's statement: "When *I* use a word, it means just what *I* choose it to mean—neither more or less."

clear that the product must be defective, and that the manufacturer of a product that may involve some danger, but that is not defective, will not be held liable.

In addition, the theory advanced by the plaintiff's attorneys perverts the very purpose of the "risk/utility balancing test" used in Texas products liability cases. That test, itself, incorporates the idea that a defect is something that can be remedied or changed. Thus, in considering a design defect claim, the "very factors a jury is supposed to consider when weighing risk and utility includes the feasibility and cost of an improved design." Note, "Handguns," supra, 97 Harv.L.Rev. at 1916; *Davidson v. Stanadyne,* 718 F.2d at 1340.

But here, the plaintiff's attorneys offer no alternatives and no safer designs for a handgun. Nor can they do so—because a gun, by its very nature, must be dangerous and must have the capacity to discharge a bullet with deadly force. Accordingly, by their unconventional application of the risk/utility test to a nondefective product, **the plaintiff's attorneys simply want to eliminate handguns.**

Moreover, if this unconventional theory were correct, then it should apply equally to other products besides handguns—to rifles, to shotguns, to switchblade and kitchen and Swiss Army knives, to axes, to whiskey, to automobiles, etc.—even though these products are not defective. The possible consequences of expanding products liability in this manner have been described: "a plaintiff would need only to prove that the product was a factual cause in producing his injury. Thus, the manufacturer of a match would be liable for anything burned by a fire started by a match produced by him, an automobile manufacturer would be liable for all damages produced by the car, a gun maker would be liable to anyone shot by the gun, anyone cut by a knife could sue the maker, and a purchaser of food with high calories would have an action for his overweight condition and for an ensuing heart attack. The liability would

be like that created by a particularly stringent dramshop law." Wade, "On the Nature of Strict Tort Liability for Products," 44 Miss.L.J. 825, 828 (1973).

The plaintiff's attorneys argue that this drastic expansion need not occur—that a handgun is not serving its function when it is used for unlawful purposes, so at least the illegal use of handguns should be subject to the risk/utility balancing test. Obviously, this is wrong: "Virtually any product can be put to an illegal use: an automobile can be used in order to make a getaway from a bank robbery, or a ship in order to smuggle drugs, yet no one would suggest that those products were not performing their intended function of transportation. The argument that a jury should be permitted to subject a product to risk/utility scrutiny merely because it is often used illegally has no logical limit: the manufacturer of any product that is frequently put to illegal use could be called into court to defend his product." Note, "Handguns," supra, 97 Harv.L.Rev. at 1917.

The plaintiff's attorneys . . . assert that imposing this absolute liability upon handgun manufacturers simply furthers the products liability goal of placing the financial burden upon those who are best able to spread the loss. This is not correct. . . . Our tort law is premised upon fairness, making individuals responsible for their own acts. The ability of a gun manufacturer to "spread the loss" is not a sufficient basis for requiring guiltless purchasers of guns to subsidize the actions of those who use firearms wrongfully. If it were, then we should simply hold—contrary to established principles—that all manufacturers who cannot produce a "failsafe product" are insurers because of their ability to spread loss. Note, "Handguns," supra, 97 Harv.L.Rev. at 1920.

They argue that, if their theory is not accepted, handgun manufacturers will be given a "special immunity" from responsibility for physical harm caused by their products. This is not correct. If this unconventional and unfounded theory is accepted, then—contrary to one of the basic principles of products liability—**handgun manufacturers would become insurers** for all injuries resulting from their products. However, by its rejection, manufacturers of handguns, like the producers of any other product, will be responsible for injuries caused by defects in designing their products, in manufacturing them, and in distributing them. . . .

The plaintiff's attorneys also claim that the manner in which handguns are distributed is "defective and unreasonably dangerous" because it is too easy for handguns to be obtained by persons who misuse them (including criminals, such as Berlin Ransom in this case). Here, they rely upon *Richman v. Charter Arms Corp.*, 571 F.Supp. 192 (E.D.La.1983), in which the district court did hold that the sale of handguns indiscriminately to the public could constitute an "ultrahazardous activity under Louisiana law."†††

However, *Richman* . . . is contrary to Texas law. There is simply no such products liability principle as "defect in distribution." Under Texas law, the plaintiff in a products liability case must establish that the product was defective because of its unsafe design, or an error in manufacturing, or the failure to give adequate warnings or instructions.

Moreover, as discussed above, the risk/utility balancing test is founded upon the

premise that the alleged defect can be repaired or remedied. Yet, there is simply no way that a manufacturer could devise a safe and effective system of distributing handguns—without ceasing distribution entirely, even to persons who want them for legitimate reasons.

In addition, even if the alleged "defect in distribution" could be shown, there would be no liability unless the defect actually caused the injury. Yet: "In order to prove actual causation (cause in fact), the plaintiff would have to show that his assailant would not have acquired a handgun had the manufacturer used a 'nondefective' system of distribution. If the assailant would have been able to purchase a handgun despite a 'better' system of distribution, the plaintiff could not recover. Because many of the people who misuse handguns have no criminal record or established history of violence, a distributional system that attempted to weed out people who were likely to misuse handguns could not prevent distribution to most of those who actually did misuse them; hence the cause-in-fact requirement would be difficult to fulfill." (Note, "Handguns," supra, 97 Harv.L.Rev. at 1922–23.) . . .

Despite the well-documented dangers of **"Saturday Night Specials"** and other handguns, not a single state has seen fit to prohibit the manufacture and sale of handguns. Nor has Congress passed any meaningful gun-control measures. The increasing number of cases like this one are intended to change this and to accomplish gun control under the guise of products liability law—by trying to subject handgun manufacturers to liability for all injuries caused by their products. Presumably, the proponents of these suits feel that "judges and juries enjoy immunity from the political pressures of the gun control lobby," and that handgun control "is not going to come legislatively any time soon, if ever." Note, "Handguns," supra, 97 Harv.L.Rev. at 1925.

---

†††This argument does find some support in *Moning v. Alfono*, 254 N.W.2d 759 (Mich.1979). There, the Michigan Supreme Court held that "if a jury finds that the risks of selling slingshots to young children outweigh the utility of permitting the children to have slingshots, the manufacturer can be held liable for the injury that results when one child shoots another with a slingshot." Note, "Handguns," supra, 97 Harv.L.Rev. at 1920. However, the *Moning* opinion points out that "special rules for children are not unusual." 254 N.W.2d at 768. And, in any event, there are contrary decisions—see *Bojorquez v. House of Toys, Inc.*, 62 Cal.App.3d 930, 133 Cal.Rptr. 483, 484 (1976)—so it has been noted that "the view expressed in *Moning* is not universally accepted, however, and will not easily be extended." Note, "Handguns," supra, 97 Harv.L.Rev. at 1920–21.

But the unconventional theories advanced in this case (and others) are totally without merit, a misuse of products liability laws. It makes no sense to characterize any product as "defective"—even a handgun"—if it performs as intended and causes injury only because it is intentionally misused. Similarly, the claim that handgun manufacturers should be held responsible for keeping their products out of the hands of criminals—an admittedly impossible task—is an unsupported, tortured extension of products liability principles. Both theories are contrary to the established law that a manufacturer is not an insurer of its products; and both theories would, unless logic is abandoned, be applicable to other products besides handguns.

Moreover, **the judicial system is, at best, ill-equipped to deal with the emotional issues of handgun control.** Certainly, there can be no effective handgun control imposed on an ad hoc basis by six or twelve jurors sitting in judgment on a single case. Decisions in these suits—made on the basis of a particular record developing a unique set of facts—will necessarily be inconsistent, and there can only be varying and uneven results in different jurisdictions. Thus, an overwhelming number of cases—and tremendous expenditure of judicial resources—would be required before the proponents of these unconventional theories could even begin to accomplish their ultimate goal: driving all handgun manufacturers out of business.

As an individual, I believe, very strongly, that handguns should be banned and that there should be stringent, effective control of other firearms. **However, as a judge, I know full well that the question of whether handguns can be sold is a political one,** not an issue of products liability law—**and that this is a matter for the legislatures, not the courts.**

Accordingly, this case is Dismissed.

• ASSIGNMENT 17.15 •

a. You start a business in Houston to make small bombs that will be sold to the public. In fact, your only customers are terrorists throughout the world. Someone injured by such a terrorist bomb brings a products liability claim against you. Does *Patterson* apply?

b. You invent a "fraternity funnel" whose sole function is to allow college students to pour liquor directly into their throats during parties. The parents of a student who died using this device bring a products liability case against you. Does *Patterson* apply?

c. Read the following opinion: *Kelley v. R. G. Industries,* 304 Md. 124, 497 A.2d 1143 (1985). Why does it reach a different conclusion on "Saturday Night Specials"?

d. What test or tests for design defect are used by your state when the cause of action is strict liability in tort? You need to find the latest opinion through the digests that cover your state court opinions. When you have a recent opinion, be sure to Shepardize it in order to determine if there are more current opinions on the issue. When you have the latest opinion on point, give its citation, state the test or tests of the court, summarize the facts of the case, state whether the court found a design defect on those facts, and give the reasons why or why not. (For other techniques on finding court opinions, see General Instructions for the State Court Opinion Assignment in Chapter 2.)

One of the major design defect issues in the courts today concerns the **crashworthiness** of automobiles—the problem of the second injury or the second collision. An automobile accident often involves two events: the impact with the other car or object and the impact of the plaintiff *inside* the car with the steering wheel, window, dashboard, or car roof. The design of the car may have nothing to do with the initial accident, yet have a great deal to do with the extent of the injury suffered by the plaintiff. The question is: how crashworthy does the car have to be? Does the manufacturer have the responsibility of designing the car so that the plaintiff is not injured through internal impact with the car's steering wheel, dashboard, gas tank, or other component? Most courts apply the traditional tests of foreseeability, social utility, and burden. It is highly foreseeable that a plaintiff will receive serious injury following an initial crash. This risk must be weighed against the cost of designing the car to minimize the risk. A court may conclude, for example, that a dashboard made out of steel is unreasonably dangerous, or that the placement of the gas tank is unreasonably dangerous because alternative designs were feasible and would have lessened the danger of the second injury.

Many state and federal statutes and regulations exist on consumer products. Is a product that conforms to all of them automatically deemed to be reasonably safe even though it causes an injury? Yes, according to some courts, particularly if the statute explicitly exempts the defendant from liability when there is compliance. Many courts, however, say that a product that conforms to all of the statutes and regulations can still be unreasonably dangerous, because they may cover only what is minimally required for safety. Compliance is merely some evidence—or at most, raises a presumption—that the product is not defective or unreasonably dangerous.

User or Consumer

Who can be a plaintiff in a case brought on a theory of strict liability in tort? The plaintiff does not have to be in privity with the seller. The plaintiff, therefore, does not have to be the purchaser of the product. Section 402A requires only that the plaintiff be a user or a consumer. This would not cover the **bystander** who does not purchase, use, or consume the product but who is injured by it. Suppose, for example, that Tom is driving a car that is unreasonably dangerous because of defective brakes. The car goes out of control and hits Mary, a pedestrian. Mary is not a user or consumer of the car. She is a bystander. If a state adopts the Restatement position, she could not sue the car manufacturer for strict liability in tort. There are states, however, that extend strict liability in tort to anyone who is foreseeably injured by the unreasonably dangerous product. This would cover Mary.

▪ ASSIGNMENT 17.16 ▪

In the fact situation just mentioned involving Tom, Mary, and the defective brakes, could Mary sue Tom for strict liability in tort? (See General Instructions for the Legal Analysis Assignment in Chapter 3.)

Physical Harm

The tort covers actual damage to property (e.g., demolished car) or to person (e.g., broken arm, death). If no such damage has occurred, and the plaintiff has suffered economic damage only, most courts do not allow recovery under this cause of action. If the plaintiff is the purchaser, he or she may be able to sue under some other cause of action. The plaintiff, for example, buys a boat that is defective and unreasonably dangerous because of the design of the motor. The boat cannot be used in the plaintiff's business. No one is injured and no damage occurs to the boat itself. Only an economic loss has been suffered. The plaintiff may be able to sue for breach of contract, for breach of warranty, or perhaps even for misrepresentation. Most courts, however, do not provide strict liability in tort as a remedy for purely economic loss.

Causation

The plaintiff must show that the product was defective at the time it left the hands of the defendant and that this defect caused the physical harm. Causation is established by the but-for test (but for the defect, the harm would not have resulted), or the substantial-factor test when more than one causal entity is involved (the defect was a substantial factor in producing the harm).

> The seller is not liable when he delivers the product in a safe condition, and subsequent mishandling or other causes make it harmful by the time it is consumed. . . . If the injury results from abnormal handling, as where a bottled beverage is knocked against a radiator to remove a cap, or from abnormal preparation for use, as where too much salt is added to food, or from abnormal consumption, as where a child eats too much candy and is made ill, the seller is not liable.[10]

Causation can sometimes be difficult to prove when the defendant is a remote manufacturer and the product had passed through many hands before it injured the plaintiff. A court will not allow causation to be established by mere speculation. This does not mean that the plaintiff must eliminate every possible cause other than the defendant. Where there is some evidence of other causes, however, the plaintiff must either negate them or show that the defendant was at least a substantial factor along with the other causes in producing the injury.

For a sample products-liability complaint and a sample answer, see Figures 17.5 and 17.6.

Defenses to Strict Liability in Tort

Misuse

Every misuse of the product is not a defense. As indicated earlier, the simple fact that a consumer does not use a product for its intended purpose does not necessarily mean that it has been misused. A product must be reasonably safe for the foreseeable uses of the product. Furthermore, a manufacturer must plan for a certain amount of foreseeable misuse. Misuse is a defense when it is unforeseeable and when it is extreme. Such misuse occurs, for example, when the plaintiff knowingly violates the plain, unambiguous instructions on using the product or ignores the clear warnings provided.

---

[10]*Restatement (Second) of Torts* § 402A, comment g (1965).

Figure 17.5   Sample Products-Liability Complaint

SUPREME COURT OF THE STATE OF NEW
YORK
COUNTY OF NASSAU

————————————————————X

STEVEN HURT   Index No.

                              Plaintiff,   VERIFIED
                                          COMPLAINT

            v.

NICE CUT MOWER CORP., GETWELL
HOSPITAL, INC., AND SAMUEL BONZ, M.D.,

                          Defendants.

————————————————————X

    Plaintiff, STEVEN HURT, by his attorney, ADAM ABEL, as and for his complaint against the defendants, respectfully sets forth:

    1. That plaintiff was and is a resident of the State of New York, County of Nassau.

    2. That defendant NICE CUT MOWER CORP. (hereinafter "NICE CUT") was and is a New York corporation having a place of business in Suffolk County, New York.

    3. That defendant GETWELL HOSPITAL, INC. (hereinafter "HOSPITAL") was and is a New York proprietary hospital corporation having its principal place of business in Nassau County, New York.

    4. That defendant SAMUEL BONZ, M.D., (hereinafter "DOCTOR") was and is a physician duly licensed to practice medicine in the State of New York.

    5. That defendant DOCTOR was and is a resident of the State of New York, County of Suffolk.

As and for a First Cause of Action

    6. That defendant NICE CUT was and is engaged in the manufacture of lawn mowers and the sale of same to the public.

    7. That on or about May 1, 1991, plaintiff purchased a lawn mower from defendant NICE CUT at its retail store in Stony Brook, New York bearing Model No. A-1.

    8. That on June 13, 1992, while plaintiff was operating said mower in accordance with its instructions, plaintiff sustained personal injury.

    9. That defendant NICE CUT was negligent in the design, manufacture, and sale of said mower to the plaintiff.

    10. That the aforementioned occurrence was caused by the negligence, carelessness, and recklessness of the defendants.

    11. That by reason of the foregoing, plaintiff has been damaged.

As and for a Second Cause of Action

    12. Plaintiff repeats and realleges each and every allegation contained in paragraphs "6" through "8" of the complaint as if set forth more fully at length herein.

    13. That defendant NICE CUT expressly and impliedly warranted that said mower was fit for its intended use, was safe, and was of merchantable quality.

    14. That the plaintiff relied upon the warranties of defendant NICE CUT.

    15. That defendant NICE CUT breached its warranties in that said mower was unsafe and unsuitable for its intended purpose, and not of merchantable quality.

16. That by reason of the foregoing, plaintiff has been damaged.

As and for a Third Cause of Action

17. Plaintiff repeats and realleges each and every allegation contained in paragraphs "6" through "8" of the complaint as if set forth more fully at length herein.

18. That said mower was manufactured and sold in a dangerous and defective condition.

19. That said mower was an inherently dangerous product.

20. That said defects resulted in injury to the plaintiff.

21. That by reason of the foregoing, defendant NICE CUT is strictly liable in tort to the plaintiff.

22. That by reason of the foregoing, plaintiff has been damaged.

23. That defendant NICE CUT knew or should have known that said mower was dangerous and that defendant NICE CUT engaged in conduct which amounted to a deliberate, reckless, and outrageous disregard and indifference to the lives and safety of the public.

24. That by reason of the foregoing, plaintiff is entitled to an award of punitive damages.

As and for a Fourth Cause of Action

25. Plaintiff repeats and realleges each and every allegation contained in paragraphs "6" through "8" of the complaint as if set forth more fully at length herein.

26. That on or about June 13, 1992, and after the plaintiff utilized his lawn mower, the plaintiff sought medical care and treatment at the emergency room of defendant HOSPITAL.

27. That on or about June 13, 1992, the plaintiff was admitted to defendant HOSPITAL and came under the care of defendant DOCTOR.

28. That defendant DOCTOR was an agent, servant, employee, or was otherwise an affiliate of defendant HOSPITAL.

29. That plaintiff remained under the care of defendant HOSPITAL and defendant DOCTOR until he was discharged on July 15, 1992.

30. That defendant HOSPITAL, defendant DOCTOR, and their agents, servants, and employees negligently, carelessly, and recklessly failed to diagnose, treat, and care for the plaintiff, failed to obtain the plaintiff's informed consent to treatment, and deviated from the reasonable and accepted standard of medical care and skill prevailing among other hospitals and physicians in the community.

31. That as a result of the negligence and medical malpractice of defendant HOSPITAL and defendant DOCTOR, the plaintiff was caused to sustain a injury.

32. That by reason of the foregoing, plaintiff has been damaged in a sum which exceeds the jurisdictional limit of all other courts which would otherwise have jurisdiction over this matter.

WHEREFORE, plaintiff demands judgment against the defendant as follows:

1. On the first Cause of Action, judgment against defendant NICE CUT for the sum of $2,000,000.

2. On the Second Cause of Action, judgment against defendant NICE CUT for the sum of 2,000,000.

3. On the Third Cause of Action, judgment against defendant NICE CUT for the sum of 2,000,000.

4. Judgment against defendant NICE CUT for the sum of $6,000,000 in punitive damages.

5. On the Fourth Cause of Action, judgment against defendant HOSPITAL and defendant DOCTOR for a sum in excess of the jurisdictional limit of all other courts which would otherwise have jurisdiction over this matter;

all together with the costs and disbursements of this action.

Dated: Mineola, New York
        August 21, 1994

Yours, etc.

ADAM ABEL, ESQ.
Attorney for Plaintiff
1 Retainer Plaza
Mineola, New York

SOURCE: New York State Bar Association, *Trial of a Personal Injury Case-1984, Case Study 27–38*
(1984).

Figure 17.6 Sample Products-Liability Answer

SUPREME COURT OF THE STATE OF
NEW YORK
COUNTY OF NASSAU

——————————————————— X

STEVEN HURT,

                        Plaintiff,   VERIFIED ANSWER

                  v.
NICE CUT MOWER CORP., GETWELL
HOSPITAL, INC., and SAMUEL BONZ,
M.D.

                  Defendants.
——————————————————— X

Defendant, NICE CUT MOWER CORP., by its attorneys, ROBERT BLACK, P.C., as and for its answer to the complaint of the plaintiff, respectfully sets forth:

1. Denies knowledge or information sufficient to form a belief as to the truth of the allegations contained in paragraphs "1", "3", "4", and "5" of the complaint.

As and for an Answer to the First Cause of Action

2. Denies the allegations contained in paragraphs "9", "10" and "11" of the complaint.

3. Denies knowledge or information sufficient to form a belief as to the truth of the allegations contained in paragraphs "7" and "8" of the complaint.

As and for an Answer to the Second Cause of Action

4. Repeats and reiterates the denials to each and every allegation contained in paragraph "12" of the complaint as if more fully set forth at length herein.

5. Denies the allegations contained in paragraphs "15" and "16" of the complaint.

6. Denies knowledge or information sufficient to form a belief as to the truth of the allegations contained in paragraphs "13" and "14" of the complaint.

As and for an Answer to the Third Cause of Action

7. Repeats and reiterates the denials to each and every allegation contained in paragraph "17" of the complaint as if more fully set forth at length herein.

8. Denies the allegations contained in paragraphs "18", "19", "20", "21", "22", "23" and "24" of the complaint.

As and for an Answer to the Fourth Cause of Action

9. Repeats and reiterates the denials to each and every allegation contained in paragraph "25" of the complaint as if more fully set forth at length herein.

10. Denies knowledge or information sufficient to form a belief as to the truth of the allegations contained in paragraphs "26", "27", "28", "29", "30", "31" and "32" of the complaint.

As and for a First Affirmative Defense

11. Upon information and belief, any damage or damages sustained by the plaintiff herein were not caused by the wrongdoing on the part of the answering defendant, his servants, agents or employees, but were caused solely by the wrongdoing of the plaintiff and that such conduct requires diminution of any award, verdict or judgment that plaintiff may recover against said answering defendant.

As and for a Cross-Claim Against Co-Defendants Getwell Hospital, Inc. and Samuel Bonz, M.D.

12. That although NICE CUT MOWER CORP. has denied the allegations of plaintiff with respect to any wrongdoing on the part of said defendant, nevertheless, in the event that there is a verdict or judgment in favor of the plaintiff as against NICE CUT MOWER CORP., then, and in that event, said defendant demands judgment over and against co-defendants, GETWELL HOSPITAL, INC. and SAMUEL BONZ, M.D., by reason of their wrongful conduct being primary and/or active while any wrongdoing of NICE CUT MOWER CORP., if any, was secondary and/or passive and the indemnity is to be full and complete.

As and for a Second Cross Claim against Co-Defendants Getwell Hospital, Inc. and Samuel Bonz, M.D.

13. Although NICE CUT MOWER CORP. has denied allegations of plaintiff with respect to any alleged wrongdoing on the part of NICE CUT MOWER CORP., nevertheless, if it is found that NICE CUT MOWER CORP. is liable to the plaintiff-herein, all of which is denied, said defendant, on the basis of apportionment of responsibility for the alleged occurrence, is entitled to contribution from and judgment over and against co-defendants, GETWELL HOSPITAL, INC. and SAMUEL BONZ, M.D., for all or part of any verdict or judgment plaintiff may recover against NICE CUT MOWER CORP.

WHEREFORE, defendant, NICE CUT MOWER CORP., demands:

1. Judgment dismissing the complaint;

2. In the event that the complaint is not dismissed, then full indemnity with respect to the first cross-claim;

3. In the event that full indemnity is not granted, then contribution pursuant to the second cross-claim in accordance with degrees of wrongdoing; together with the costs and disbursements of this action.

Dated: Commack, New York
      September 5, 1984

Yours, etc.,

ROBERT BLACK, P.C.
Attorneys for Defendant
NICE CUT MOWER CORP.
Defense Street
Commack, New York

SOURCE: New York State Bar Association, *Trial of a Personal Injury Case-1984, Case Study 27-38* (1984).

Contributory Negligence

In most states, contributory negligence is *not* a defense when the plaintiff's conduct consists of failing to discover the danger. Assume the defendant rents a defective car to Bob Smith. On the dashboard, there is a red light signaling trouble to the driver. Smith does not see the light and keeps driving. An accident occurs because of the defect in the car that makes it unreasonably dangerous. It is no defense that Smith failed to discover the danger—even if a reasonable person would have discovered it by checking the dashboard and seeing the red light. Smith's own negligence in failing to discover the danger to himself is not a defense.

Contributory negligence is a defense only when it constitutes the extreme, unforeseeable misuse described above, or an assumption of the risk described below.

Comparative Negligence

There are some states that apply their comparative negligence rules to strict-liability-in-tort cases, even though there is no need for the plaintiff in such cases to establish the negligence of the defendant. The damages suffered by the plaintiffs are proportionately reduced by whatever percentage of the harm the plaintiffs caused themselves through carelessness.

Assumption of the Risk

If the plaintiff has actual knowledge of the danger and voluntarily proceeds to use the product in spite of the danger, there has been an assumption of the risk, which *is* a defense to strict liability in tort. The plaintiff must have actually discovered the danger.

• ASSIGNMENT 17.17 •

Tom buys a lawn mower from a department store. A string is tied around the top of the mower attached to a tag that says "WARNING: BEFORE USING, READ INSTRUCTION BOOK CAREFULLY." Tom sees this sign but fails to read the instruction book. In the book, the consumer is told never to use the mower on a steep hill. Tom is injured while mowing on a steep hill in his yard. The mower tips over and falls on him. Is the department store strictly liable in tort? (See General Instructions for the Legal Analysis Assignment in Chapter 3.)

• ASSIGNMENT 17.18 •

Prepare an annotated bibliography on strict liability in tort for your state. (See General Instructions for the Annotated Bibliography Assignment in Chapter 2.)

• A FEDERAL PRODUCTS-LIABILITY LAW?

Federal involvement in this area of the law has been relatively minor, including the work of the Consumer Product Safety Commission, whose role has primarily been that of a monitor and information collector. The Commission recalls about 250 products a year, but almost all of these recalls are handled voluntarily under the Commission's supervision.

Most products-liability law is created and applied at the state level, which is true for most of tort law. This, of course, means that each state is free to develop its own products-liability law. Critics say that this system has produced chaos, and that we need a federal products-liability law. Although Congress has considered a number of proposals to implement such a law, none has been enacted to date. Here are selected aspects of some of the proposed reforms:

- The creation of federal standards governing the litigation of disputes arising out of injuries caused by defective products. These standards would preempt state law.
- The creation of an expedited settlement system to be available at the outset of every case.
- The imposition of a cap on noneconomic damages that can be awarded.
- The creation of standards for when punitive damages can be obtained from a defendant.
- A uniform statute of limitations for bringing a case.

SUMMARY

Products liability is not a cause of action. It is a general term that covers different causes of action based on products that cause harm. These causes of action are negligence, misrepresentation, breach of express warranty, breach of implied warranty of merchantability, breach of implied warranty of fitness for a particular purpose, and strict liability in tort. There are three categories of defects in products: manufacturing defects, design defects, and warning defects.

For purposes of a negligence suit, the defendant owes a duty of reasonable care to all foreseeable users of the product if it can be anticipated that substantial harm to person or property will result if the product is defective. Privity is not necessary. Breach of duty is established when the defendant fails to take reasonable steps to prevent injury caused by the product. Contributory negligence is a complete defense unless the state had adopted comparative negligence as the standard. Assumption of the risk is also a complete defense. Another traditional cause of action is misrepresentation, which can be used when the defendant makes an intentionally false statement about a product that causes injury.

Breach of express warranty requires proof of a false statement of fact, the intent or expectation that the statement will reach the plaintiff, reliance on the statement by the plaintiff, and causation of damage or injury.

The following causes of action apply to sales rather than to services: breach of implied warranty of merchantability, breach of implied warranty of fitness for a particular purpose, and strict liability in tort. For a breach of implied warranty of merchantability, goods must be sold by a merchant of that kind. The goods are not merchantable and cause damage or injury. For a breach of implied warranty of fitness for a particular purpose, goods must be sold by a seller who has reason to know that the buyer has a particular purpose in buying the goods and is relying on the seller's skill or judgment. The goods cause damage or injury because they are not fit for that particular purpose.

To bring a warranty action, the general rule is that there must be privity, or a contractual relationship, between the defendant and the person injured. Some states get around this requirement by agency principles or by abolishing the privity requirement in designated kinds of cases. Defenses to actions for breach of warranty include valid disclaimers, failure of the plaintiff to provide notice within a reasonable time after the breach was discovered or should have been discovered, and assumption of the risk. Contributory negligence is generally not a defense.

In an action for strict liability in tort, the defendant must be a seller, which includes most companies in the chain of distribution. Companies in the business of renting products are also included. The product must be defective and unreasonably dangerous for its intended use and its foreseeable use. States differ on the tests they use to determine when a defect is unreasonably dangerous. The unreasonably dangerous defect in the product must cause physical harm in the plaintiff, who is either a user or consumer of the product, or, in some states, a bystander. Misuse is a defense when it is unforeseeable and is extreme. Assumption of the risk is also a defense. Generally, contributory negligence is not. A state may compare the fault of the plaintiff and the defendant and apportion the damages according to its applicable formula.

Key Terms

products liability
defective
manufacturing defect
design defect
warning defect
duty
privity
MacPherson v. Buick
foreseeable users
breach of duty
reasonably safe
manufacturer
res ipsa loquitur
merchant
custom in the trade
contributory negligence
comparative negligence
assumption of the risk
misrepresentation

warranty
strict liability
express warranty
Uniform Commercial
 Code
fact
puffing
reliance
sales
services
chattels
implied warranty of
 merchantability
merchantable
implied warranty of
 fitness for a
 particular purpose
agent
disclaimer

unconscionable
notice
strict liability in tort
seller
defective product
user or consumer
physical harm
causation
component part
chain of distribution
unreasonably dangerous
objective
unavoidably unsafe
 products
intended use
foreseeable use
misuse
crashworthiness
bystander

CHAPTER 18

Infliction of Emotional Distress

CHAPTER OUTLINE

- INTENTIONAL INFLICTION OF
  EMOTIONAL DISTRESS
  - Intentional Infliction of Emotional
    Distress Checklist
  - Extreme or Outrageous Conduct
  - Intent
  - Severe Emotional Distress
  - Causation

- NEGLIGENT INFLICTION OF
  EMOTIONAL DISTRESS (NIED)
  - Traditional Negligence
  - No Physical Harm or Injury
  - Later Physical Harm or Injury
  - Witnessing Someone Else's Injury

■ INTENTIONAL INFLICTION OF EMOTIONAL DISTRESS

Intentional Infliction of Emotional Distress Checklist
Definitions, Relationships, and Research References

Category
Intentional Infliction of Emotional Distress is a relatively new intentional tort. (It is also called the tort of **outrage**.) Some courts have expanded it to include recovery for reckless infliction of emotional distress.

Interest Protected by This Tort
   The right to be free from emotional distress that is intentionally (or recklessly) caused by someone else.

Elements of This Tort
1. An act of extreme or outrageous conduct
2. Intent to cause severe emotional distress

3. Plaintiff suffers severe emotional distress
4. Defendant is the cause of this distress

Major Definitions of Words/Phrases in These Elements

Act: Voluntary movement of the defendant's body.

Extreme or outrageous conduct: Atrocious and totally intolerable behavior—shocking conduct.

Intent: The desire to inflict severe emotional distress on the plaintiff or the knowledge with substantial certainty that such distress will result from what the defendant does. (In some states, recklessness, or wanton and willful conduct, will be sufficient.)

Severe emotional distress: Substantial mental anguish.

Cause: "But for" what the defendant did, the plaintiff would not have suffered severe emotional distress, or the defendant was a substantial factor in producing such distress.

Major Defense and Counter-Argument Possibilities That Need to Be Explored

1. The defendant did not act voluntarily.
2. The defendant's conduct may have been unpleasant and wrongful, but it was not extreme or outrageous.
3. The defendant had no reason to know that the plaintiff was unusually sensitive; a reasonable person would not have reacted the way the plaintiff did.
4. The plaintiff consented to the defendant's conduct.
5. The defendant did not desire the plaintiff to suffer extreme emotional distress or know with substantial certainty that it would result.
6. The defendant was not reckless in causing the emotional distress.
7. The plaintiff was embarrassed and annoyed, but did not experience substantial emotional distress.
8. "But for" what the defendant did, the plaintiff would still have suffered severe emotional distress, or, the defendant was not a substantial factor in producing this distress. (No causation.)
9. The defendant may have caused the plaintiff to suffer severe emotional distress, but the defendant's intent was to cause this in someone else.
10. Privilege of arrest.
11. Privilege of discipline.
12. Privilege of self-defense.
13. Privilege of defense of others.
14. Privilege of defense of property.
15. Privilege to recapture chattels.
16. Privilege to retake possession of land.
17. Constitutional freedom of speech and press.
18. Sovereign immunity.
19. Public official immunity.

Damages

The plaintiff can recover for the mental distress suffered as well as for any physical harm or illness that may have resulted from the defendant's conduct. Punitive damages are also likely if the defendant acted out of hatred or malice.

Relationship to Criminal Law

The defendant's conduct may also constitute the crime of extortion, criminal assault, breach of the peace, criminal battery, etc.

Relationship to Other Torts

Abuse of process: While using the criminal process for an improper purpose, the defendant may have intended to cause the plaintiff severe emotional distress.

Alienation of affections: When the defendant alienated the affections of one spouse to the other, the defendant may have intended to cause severe emotional distress in the aggrieved spouse.

Assault: While intending to cause severe emotional distress in the plaintiff, the defendant may have placed the plaintiff in apprehension of an imminent harmful or offensive contact.

Battery: While intending to cause severe emotional distress in the plaintiff, the defendant may have intentionally made harmful or offensive contact with the plaintiff.

Conversion: Defendant may have intended to have the plaintiff suffer severe emotional distress by destroying plaintiff's personal property.

Defamation: While intentionally causing the plaintiff to suffer severe emotional distress, the defendant may have published derogatory statements that injured the reputation of the plaintiff.

False imprisonment: By locking the plaintiff up or otherwise restricting his or her movement, the defendant may have had the intent to cause the plaintiff severe emotional distress.

False light: By giving unreasonable publicity to false private facts, the defendant may have had the intent to cause the plaintiff severe emotional distress.

Intrusion: By unreasonably intruding on the plaintiff's privacy, the defendant may have had the intent to cause the plaintiff severe emotional distress.

Malicious prosecution: The defendant may have initiated legal proceedings against the plaintiff with the intent to cause the plaintiff severe emotional distress.

Negligence: If the defendant negligently caused physical harm to the plaintiff, the latter can also recover for resulting emotional distress that was not intended. Some states also allow recovery for negligent infliction of emotional distress.

Trespass to land: While trespassing on the plaintiff's land, the defendant may have had the intent to subject the plaintiff to severe emotional distress.

Wrongful death: If the plaintiff died as a result of intentional infliction of emotional distress, designated survivors may be able to bring a wrongful-death action.

Federal Law

1. There is no explicit exclusion of the tort of intentional infliction of emotional distress from coverage under the Federal Tort Claims Act. Hence the federal government can be sued for this tort if a federal employee commits it.

2. There can be recovery under the Federal Civil Rights Act if the defendant, while intending to cause severe emotional distress in the plaintiff, deprived the plaintiff of a federal constitutional or statutory right under color of law.

Employer-Employee (Agency) Law

A private employer will be liable for intentional infliction of emotional distress committed by its employee within the scope of employment if the tort was committed by the employee while furthering the business objective of the employer.

Research References for This Tort

- Digests

In the digests of West, look for case summaries on this tort under key topics such as:

Torts	Death
Threats	Damages

- *Corpus Juris Secundum*

In this legal encyclopedia, look for discussions on this tort under topic headings such as:

Torts	Telegraph, telephone, radio
Threats and unlawful	and television
communications	Death
Damages	

- *American Jurisprudence 2d*

In this legal encyclopedia, look for discussions on this tort under topic headings such as:

Torts	Damages
Fright, shock and	Death
mental disturbance	

- Legal Periodical Literature

There are three index systems to use to try to locate articles on this tort:

Index to Legal Periodicals (ILP) See literature in *ILP* under subject headings such as:	*Current Law Index (CLI)* See literature in *CLI* under subject headings such as:	*Legal Resource Index (LRI)* See literature in *LRI* under subject headings such as:
Torts	Privacy, Right of	Privacy, Right of
Collection	Mental Distress	Mental Distress
Agencies	Negligence	Negligence
Damages	Damages	Damages
Negligence	Torts	Torts
Personal Injuries	Personal Injuries	Personal Injuries
Privacy	Death by	Death by
Wrongful Death	Wrongful Act	Wrongful Act
	Collection	Collection
	Agencies	Agencies

Example of legal periodical literature you can locate through the *ILP, CLI,* or *LRI* on this tort:

Intentional Infliction of Mental Distress—Seventeen Years Later, 66 Illinois Bar Journal 248 (1978).

▪ *ALR, ALR2d, ALR3d, ALR4th, ALR5th, ALRFed*

Use the *Index to Annotations* to locate annotations on this tort. In this index, check subject headings such as:

Mental Anguish	Torts
Shock	Death
Emotional Disturbance	Intentional Tort
Debtors and Creditors	

Example of an annotation you can locate through this index on this tort:

Recovery by Debtor, under Tort of Intentional or Reckless Infliction of Emotional Distress, for Damages Resulting from Collection Methods, 87 ALR3d 201.

▪ *Words and Phrases*

In this multivolume legal dictionary, look up every word or phrase discussed in this chapter connected with infliction of emotional distress in order to find definitions of the words or phrases from court opinions.

Extreme or Outrageous Conduct

The conduct of the defendant must be so **extreme or outrageous** that it would be regarded as atrocious and totally intolerable. Avoid the mistake of concluding that it is atrocious and intolerable to commit any intentional tort, and that therefore, any battery, assault, false imprisonment, or malicious prosecution is *also* the tort of intentional infliction of emotional distress. This is not always so. As indicated in the chart, it is possible for the tort of intentional infliction of emotional distress to be committed simultaneously with other torts. This, however, is not necessarily the case. The act required for intentional infliction of emotional distress must shock the conscience of society.

Examples:

- playing a practical joke on a mother by telling her that her son has just committed suicide
- putting a knife to the throat of a ten-year-old child as a threat
- surrounding a debtor and threatening to kill him and to destroy all of his business machinery if he does not pay a debt
- pushing a pregnant woman down a flight of stairs or threatening to do so

If the defendant knows that the plaintiff is vulnerable because of age, mental illness, or physical illness, it is usually easier to establish that the conduct was extreme or outrageous. Yet, vulnerability in this sense is not required. It would be extreme or outrageous, for example, for a defendant to drive a car at a high rate of speed on the sidewalk in order to scare a pedestrian directly in front of the car, whether the pedestrian is on crutches or is a healthy boxer.

As we have seen elsewhere in this book, common carriers, innkeepers, and public utilities are more likely to be found liable for a tort than other categories of defendants. This is particularly true with the tort of intentional infliction of emotional distress. For most defendants, the first element of this tort is not established by mere insults, threats, or obscenities directed at the plaintiff—they are not atrocious enough. Yet, such conduct might be sufficient if the defendant is a hotel or a public transit facility.

■ ASSIGNMENT 18.1 ■

Has extreme or outrageous conduct taken place in the following cases? (See General Instructions for the Legal Analysis Assignment in Chapter 3.)

a. A creditor threatens to force the debtor into involuntary bankruptcy if a debt is not paid immediately.
b. The principal of the school suspects that a student has been smoking marijuana in the restroom. The principal threatens to use the student as an example of delinquency before the entire school assembly if the student does not confess to smoking the marijuana.
c. Defendant pretends to be a police detective and threatens to arrest the plaintiff for espionage if the plaintiff does not turn over letters received by the plaintiff from a friend in Asia.
d. A bus driver tells a seventy-five year old passenger that her hat is so ridiculous that she would look better bald.

Intent

In most states, the defendant must have the **intent** to cause the severe emotional distress. This means that the defendant must either desire such a consequence or know with substantial certainty that it will result from what he or she does.

In a few states, **recklessness** (or willful and wanton conduct) is enough. In such states, the second element is met if the defendant knows that his or her conduct creates a very great risk that the plaintiff will suffer severe emotional distress. The following is the classic example of the kind of case that meets this standard:

> **Example:** Bob is a good friend of Mary's. They are roommates. While Mary is at work, Bob attempts to commit suicide with a knife in their kitchen. Mary suffers severe emotional distress upon seeing the blood and gore.

Mary sues Bob for intentional infliction of emotional distress. In a state that requires intent, Mary loses because there is no indication that Bob desired Mary to suffer this distress or that Bob knew with certainty that it would result. Mary has a better chance in a state where recklessness will suffice, because a strong argument can be made that Bob knew he created a very great risk that Mary would suffer this distress.

The line between desiring something or knowing something with substantial certainty (intent), and knowing that you create a very great risk of something (recklessness) is sometimes very difficult to draw. Yet the line may have to be drawn in a state where recklessness is not enough to establish the second element of this tort.

If the defendant is merely *negligent* in causing the severe emotional distress, there is no intentional infliction of emotional distress. In the next section, we will consider the question of whether the plaintiff might be able to recover under a theory of negligence.

What happens if the defendant intends to cause severe emotional distress in one person, but in fact causes such distress in another person whom the defendant had no intent to bother? What happens if two individuals suffer severe emotional distress, even though defendant's intent was directed at only one of them? Rodney, for example, intentionally terrifies Mary and then maims her. Mary's mother suffers severe emotional distress because of this injury and the way it was brought about. Can both Mary and her mother sue Rodney for intentional infliction of emotional distress? Mary certainly can. In most states, however, her mother cannot sue unless the defendant either desired to cause her severe emotional distress or knew with substantial certainty that it would result from what he did. The doctrine of **transferred intent** (to be considered in Chapter 24) does not apply to this tort. If, however, Rodney knew that the mother was present when he terrified and maimed Mary, a good argument can be made that he was at least reckless in creating a very grave risk that the mother would suffer severe emotional distress along with the daughter. In those states where reck-lessness is sufficient, the mother would be able to sue for intentional infliction of emotional distress if she could convince a jury that Rodney knew that he was creating this very grave risk.

Even states that accept recklessness, however, are reluctant to permit third persons to sue under this tort, and sometimes impose the requirements that the third person be a close relative of the person whom the defendant intends to injure, that this third person be present at the time of the act, and that the defendant know this third person is present.

Whether the mother can sue under a theory of negligence will be considered in the next section of this chapter.

Severe Emotional Distress

It is not enough that the defendant commit an outrageous act intended to cause **severe emotional distress** in the plaintiff. The plaintiff must in fact experience such distress. Minor inconvenience or annoyance is not enough. There must be severe fright, horror, grief, humiliation, embarrassment, anger, worry, or nausea. The severity of these feelings is, of course, measured by their intensity and du-ration as well as other factors, such as the relative size and weight of the plaintiff and defendant, and how the defendant approached the plaintiff. It is not neces-sary in the vast majority of states that the plaintiff suffer any **physical illness or harm** as a result of what the defendant did. Such physical illness or harm, if it exists, will increase the damages and help to prove that the plaintiff is telling the truth about the severity of the emotional distress that is alleged, but the plaintiff need not prove physical illness or harm in order to establish the tort.

Suppose the plaintiff is unusually sensitive and experiences severe emotional distress even though anyone else would not, e.g., the plaintiff goes into shock when the defendant plays a practical joke by telling the plaintiff that one of his flowers has just died. If the defendant knew of this vulnerability and still proceeded with the intent to cause severe emotional distress, the third element of the tort is established. Otherwise, the test is objective: the plaintiff will not be able to recover unless an ordinary person, not unduly sensitive, would have suffered severe emotional distress from what the defendant did.

• ASSIGNMENT 18.2 •

For months Tom has been having difficulty finding work. Finally he gets a job at the XYZ gym as a judo instructor. It is the first time he has had a job in over a year and a half. A collection agency has been after Tom to pay a $500 debt. An employee of the agency calls Tom and says, ''I understand that you now have a job and that you have had to go through a lot to get it. Don't do anything silly, which might cost you that job. Don't make me call your new boss to let him know that you're the kind of guy who doesn't pay his debts. You've got one week to pay up or else.'' Tom is terrified at the thought of losing his job. He has many sleepless nights worrying about the possibility that the collection agency might call his boss. Tom sues the agency for intentional infliction of emotional distress. What result? (See General Instructions for the Legal Analysis Assignment in Chapter 3.)

Causation

Plaintiff can use either of the following tests to establish **causation:**

- But for what the defendant did, the plaintiff would not have suffered severe emotional distress.
- The defendant was a substantial factor in producing the plaintiff's severe emotional distress.

The second test is used when there is more than one causal factor producing the severe emotional distress. There is more than one defendant even though only one defendant is sued. The plaintiff is not required to prove causation by the but-for test. The broader substantial-factor test is sufficient.

CASE

White v. Monsanto Co.
585 So.2d 1205 (1991)
Supreme Court of Louisiana

Background: Irma White worked for Monsanto Company under the supervision of Gary McDermott. After an ''outburst of profanity'' by McDermott against White (and two other employees), she sued him and the company for intentional infliction of emotional distress. The trial court found for White and awarded her $60,000. The Court of Appeals affirmed

this judgment. The case is now before the Supreme Court of Louisiana on appeal.

Decision on Appeal: Lower courts reversed. Judgment for the defendants. McDermott's conduct was crude and uncalled for, but did not amount to intentional infliction of emotional distress.

Opinion of Court

Justice HALL delivered the opinion of the court . . .

Plaintiff, Irma White, a church-going woman in her late forties with grown children, was employed in the labor pool at Monsanto Company's refinery for several years. In the spring of 1986, she had been assigned to work in the canning department for several weeks. Defendant, Gary McDermott, a long-time Monsanto employee, was industrial foreman of that department. On the date of the incident in question, plaintiff and three other employees were assigned at the beginning of the work day to transfer a certain chemical from a large container into smaller containers. When they arrived at their work station and noticed that the container was marked "hazardous-corrosive," they requested rubber gloves and goggles before starting their assigned task. A supervisor sent for the safety equipment. Shop rules required that employees busy themselves while waiting for equipment. One of the employees went to another area to do some work. Plaintiff started doing some clean-up or pick-up work around the area. The other two employees were apparently sitting around waiting for the equipment. Someone reported to McDermott that the group was idle, causing McDermott to become angry. He went to the work station and launched a profane tirade at the three workers present, including plaintiff, referring to them as "mother fuckers," accusing them of sitting on their "fucking asses," and threatening to "show them to the gate." The tirade lasted for about a minute, and then McDermott left the area.

Plaintiff was upset and began to experience pain in her chest, pounding in her head, and had difficulty breathing. She went to McDermott's office to discuss the incident. He said he apologized to her; she said he did not. She went to the company nurse, who suggested that plaintiff see a doctor. Plaintiff's family physician met her at the hospital, at which time plaintiff had chest pains, shortness of breath, and cold clammy hands. Fearing that she was having a heart attack, the doctor admitted her to the hospital. Plaintiff spent two days in the coronary care unit and another day in a regular room, during which time she had intravenous fluids, had blood drawn, and had an EKG and other tests done. A heart attack was ruled out and the doctor's diagnosis was acute anxiety reaction, a panic attack. Plaintiff was released from the hospital after three days without restriction, but with medication to take if she had further trouble.

Ms. White returned to work within a week. She was paid her regular pay while off from work, and her medical bills, totaling about $3,200, were paid by the company's medical benefits program. Plaintiff has continued to work at Monsanto, later transferring to McDermott's department at her own request. She occasionally becomes upset thinking about or dreaming about the incident, and has occasionally taken the prescribed medicine, but is not one to take medication. . . .

[I]n order to recover for intentional infliction of emotional distress, a plaintiff must establish (1) that the conduct of the defendant was extreme and outrageous; (2) that the emotional distress suffered by the plaintiff was severe; and (3) that the defendant desired to inflict severe emotional distress or knew that severe emotional distress would be certain or substantially certain to result from his conduct.

The conduct must be so outrageous in character, and so extreme in degree, as to go beyond all possible bounds of decency, and to be regarded as atrocious and utterly intolerable in a civilized community. Liability does not extend to mere insults, indignities, threats, annoyances, petty oppressions, or other trivialities. Persons must necessarily be expected to be hardened to a certain amount of rough language, and to occasional acts that are definitely inconsiderate and unkind. Not every verbal encounter may be converted into a tort; on the contrary, "some safety valve must be left through which irascible tempers may blow off relatively harmless steam." Restatement (Second) Torts, § 46, comment d; Prosser and Keeton, *The Law of Torts,* § 12, p. 59 (5th ed. 1984).

The extreme and outrageous character of the conduct may arise from an abuse by the actor of a position, or a relation with the other, which gives him actual or apparent authority over the other, or power to affect his interests. *Restatement, supra,* comment e, § 46. Thus, many of the cases have involved circumstances arising in the workplace. A plaintiff's status as an employee may entitle him to a greater degree of protection from insult and outrage by a supervisor with authority over him than if he were a stranger.

On the other hand, conduct which may otherwise be extreme and outrageous, may be privileged under the circumstances. Liability does not attach where the actor has done no more than to insist upon his legal rights in a permissible way, even though he is aware that such insistence is certain to cause emotional stress. *Restatement, supra,* comment g, § 46. Thus, disciplinary action and conflict in a pressure-packed workplace environment, although calculated to cause some degree of mental anguish, is not ordinarily actionable. Recognition of a cause of action for intentional infliction of emotion distress in a workplace environment has usually been limited to cases involving a pattern of deliberate, repeated harassment over a period of time.

The distress suffered must be such that no reasonable person could be expected to endure it. Liability arises only where the mental suffering or anguish is extreme. *Restatement, supra,* comment j, § 46.

The defendant's knowledge that plaintiff is particularly susceptible to emotional distress is a factor to be considered. But the mere fact that the actor knows that the other will regard the conduct as insulting, or will have his feelings hurt, is not enough. *Restatement, supra,* comment f, § 46. It follows that unless the actor has knowledge of the other's particular susceptibility to emotional distress, the actor's conduct should be judged in the light of the effect such conduct would ordinarily have on a person of ordinary sensibilities.

Liability can arise only where the actor desires to inflict severe emotional distress or where he knows that such distress is certain or substantially certain to result from his conduct. *Restatement, supra,* comment i, § 46. The conduct must be intended or calculated to cause severe emotional distress and not just some lesser degree of fright, humiliation, embarrassment, worry, or the like.

Applying these precepts of law to the facts of the instant case, we find that plaintiff has failed to establish her right to recover from the defendants for an intentional tort.

The one-minute outburst of profanity directed at three employees by a supervisor in the course of dressing them down for not working as he thought they should does not amount to such extreme and outrageous conduct as to give rise to recovery for intentional infliction of emotional distress. The vile language used was not so extreme or outrageous as to go beyond all possible bounds of decency and to be regarded as utterly intolerable in a civilized community. Such conduct, although crude, rough and uncalled for, was not tortious, that is, did not give rise to a cause of action. . . . The brief, isolated instance of improper behavior by the supervisor who lost his temper was the kind of unpleasant experience persons must expect to endure form time to time. The conduct was not more than a person of ordinary sensibilities can be expected to endure. The tirade was directed to all three employees and not just to plaintiff specifically. Although the evidence certainly supports a finding that plaintiff was a de-cent person and a diligent employee who would not condone the use of vulgar language and who would be upset at being unjustifiably called down at her place of work, there was no evidence that she was particularly susceptible to emotional distress, or that McDermott had knowledge of any such susceptibility. It was obviously his intention to cause some degree of dis-tress on the part of the employees, but there is no indication that his spontaneous, brief, intemperate outburst was intended to cause emotional distress of a severe nature. . . .

For the reasons expressed in this opinion, the judgments . . . are reversed, and judgment is rendered in favor of defendants. . . .

■ ASSIGNMENT 18.3 ■

a. Is the court saying that a single incident of harassment cannot amount to intentional infliction of emotional distress?
b. Would the result be different if McDermott did any of the following while uttering the profanities at White?
  1. wagged his finger at her
  2. placed his fist within an inch of her face
  3. poked her in the right shoulder
  4. pushed her so hard that she fell over

■ NEGLIGENT INFLICTION OF EMOTIONAL DISTRESS (NIED)

Traditional Negligence

No problem arises when the plaintiff can prove that he or she has suffered emotional distress arising out of direct and immediate physical harm or injury caused by **negligence.**

> **Example:** Dan negligently drives his car into Rose, a pedestrian crossing the street. She suffers a broken back and extensive pain and suffering.

Rose can recover damages for the injury to the back (which is a direct physical injury) as well as for her **pain and suffering** (which is emotional distress) up to the date of the trial and into the future.

No Physical Harm or Injury

Suppose, however, that the defendant's negligently driven car just misses the plaintiff. The latter suffers no *physical* harm or injury at any time, but does suffer substantial fright, anxiety, or other emotional distress. There can be no recovery according to the traditional rule. Courts take the position that the emotional distress is too trivial if it does not grow out of or cause a physical harm or injury, e.g., a heart attack. Courts are also concerned that it would be too easy to fabricate the emotional distress if it were not connected to physical harm or injury. A small number of courts provide an exception to this rule in certain kinds of cases, e.g., the defendant is a telegraph company that has negligently misdelivered a message (e.g., of death) to the wrong relative; the defendant is a funeral home that has negligently handled the body of the deceased. Relatives suffering emotional distress in such cases *can* recover even if they did not also suffer direct physical harm or injury. These are exceptions, however. In the vast majority of other cases, recovery is denied.

Later Physical Harm or Injury

Next we examine the case in which the negligence of the defendant causes emotional distress that *later* leads to physical harm or injury. The negligence does not directly produce this harm or injury. The classic case is the woman who suffers a miscarriage due to anxiety two weeks after the defendant *almost* hit her while negligently driving a truck close to the sidewalk. Assuming that the plaintiff can establish the causal link between the emotional distress and the physical harm or injury (not an easy task), can there be recovery? Courts answer this question differently; considerably confusion exists.

- Some courts will deny recovery unless the emotional distress and physical harm or injury are simultaneous.
- Some courts will allow recovery, but only if there is some **physical impact** on the plaintiff at the time of the defendant's negligence; the impact need not be substantial (a slight jar, or smoke in the face will be sufficient); the impact itself does not have to produce any physical harm or injury, as long as harm or injury is caused by the emotional distress.
- Some courts allow recovery even if there is no impact, as long as the evidence is strong enough to establish the causal connection between the emotional distress and the physical harm or injury that later develops.
- Some courts will allow recovery, but only if the plaintiff is in the **zone of danger** of physical impact due to the defendant's negligence, even if there is no actual impact on the plaintiff.

When recovery is denied, it is sometimes based on the theory that the defendant owed no duty to the plaintiff to prevent the injury that resulted, or that the defendant was not the proximate cause of the injury.

Witnessing Someone Else's Injury

The situation becomes even more complicated when the plaintiff is a witness to an injury negligently caused to someone else. What happens when the plaintiff suffers emotional distress in such a case (e.g., the plaintiff witnesses her son being hit by the defendant's negligently driven truck) and there is no impact on the plaintiff? Can the plaintiff recover damages for physical injury caused by such emotional distress? Again, the courts differ in answering this question.

- Some courts deny recovery in all such cases.
- Some courts will allow recovery, but only if the plaintiff was also in the zone of danger, which means that the plaintiff would have had to be present at the time the other person was injured, and close enough to also be in danger.
- A few courts will allow recovery even if the plaintiff was not in the zone of danger, as long as the plaintiff is very closely related to the other person injured and as long as the plaintiff's physical injury resulting from the emotional distress occurred soon after witnessing the injury suffered by the other person.

When recovery is denied, it is sometimes based on the theory that the defendant owed no duty to a plaintiff witnessing an accident, or that the defendant was not the proximate cause of the physical injury that resulted from the emotional distress in witnessing someone else's injury.

▪ ASSIGNMENT 18.4 ▪

In the following situations, determine whether there can be recovery for emotional distress in a negligence action. (See General Instructions for the Legal Analysis Assignment in Chapter 3.)

a. While eating a sandwich, Bill senses something strange in the mustard. He immediately spits out what is in his mouth and discovers very small glass particles in the mustard. Bill suffers great anxiety at the thought of the glass in his mouth. He sues the manufacturer of the mustard for negligence.

b. Helen and Laura work for the railroad. Due to Laura's negligence, Helen's foot is trapped for a few seconds on a track with a train approaching directly at her. At the last moment, Helen is able to move out of the way. Helen is numb from fright. At home that night and for three nights thereafter, she suffers excruciating anguish at the thought of almost being hit by a train. Helen sues Laura for negligence.

c. Fred is on a hill overlooking his house. He watches a huge truck being carelessly driven by Jim heading right for his house. Fred knows that there is no one in the house, but is extremely concerned because he just had $50,000 in repairs made on the front of the house. Jim smashes into the front of the house. Fred is frantic. He starts running toward the house, trips, and has a heart attack. Fred sues Jim for negligence.

CASE

Thing v. La Chusa
48 Cal.3d 644, 771 P.2d 814 (1989)
Supreme Court of California

Background: Maria Thing's son, John, was injured in an automobile accident that was negligently caused by the defendant, James V. La Chusa. The son sued the defendant separately for his injuries. Maria Thing brought her own suit for negligent infliction of emotional distress (NIED) based on the distress she suffered when she came to the scene of the accident and saw the condition of her son. She did not observe the accident itself. There was no physical impact on her and she suffered no physical injury herself at the scene. The trial court dismissed her claim by granting a summary judgment for the defendant because she did not contemporaneously perceive the accident. On appeal, however, the Court of Appeals reversed and allowed her to recover for NIED. The case is now on further appeal before the Supreme Court of California.

Decision on Appeal: Judgment for the defendant. Maria Thing has failed to establish negligent infliction of emotional distress since she did not witness the accident.

Opinion of Court

Justice EAGLESON delivered the opinion of the court . . .

On December 8, 1980, John Thing, a minor, was injured when struck by an automobile operated by defendant James V. La Chusa. His mother, plaintiff Maria Thing, was nearby, but neither saw nor heard the accident. She became aware of the injury to her son when told by a daughter that John had been struck by a car. She rushed

to the scene where she saw her bloody and unconscious child, whom she believed was dead, lying in the roadway. Maria sued defendant, alleging that she suffered great emotional disturbance, shock, and injury to her nervous system as a result of these events, and that the injury to John and emotional distress she suffered were proximately caused by defendant's negligence.
. . .

The impact of personally observing the injury-producing event in most, although concededly not all, cases distinguishes the plaintiff's resultant emotional distress from the emotion felt when one learns of the injury or death of a loved one from another, or observes pain and suffering but not the traumatic cause of the injury. Greater certainty and a more reasonable limit on the exposure to liability for negligent conduct is possible by limiting the right to recover for negligently caused emotional distress to plaintiffs who personally and contemporaneously perceive the injury-producing event and its traumatic consequences.*

Similar reasoning justifies limiting recover to persons closely related by blood or marriage since, in common experience, it is more likely that they will suffer a greater degree of emotional distress than a disinterested witness to negligently caused pain and suffering or death. Such limita-

tions are indisputably arbitrary since it is foreseeable that in some cases unrelated persons have a relationship to the victim or are so affected by the traumatic event that they suffer equivalent emotional distress. As we have observed, however, drawing arbitrary lines is unavoidable if we are to limit liability and establish meaningful rules for application by litigants and lower courts.

No policy supports extension of the right to recover for NIED to a larger class of plaintiffs. Emotional distress is an intangible condition experienced by most persons, even absent negligence, at some time during their lives. Close relatives suffer serious, even debilitating, emotional reactions to the injury, death, serious illness, and evident suffering of loved ones. These reactions occur regardless of the cause of the loved one's illness, injury, or death. That relatives will have severe emotional distress is an unavoidable aspect of the "human condition." The emotional distress for which monetary damages may be recovered, however, ought not to be that form of acute emotional distress or the transient emotional reaction to the occasional gruesome or horrible incident to which every person may potentially be exposed in an industrial and sometimes violent society. Regardless of the depth of feeling or the resultant physical or mental illness that results from witnessing violent events, persons unrelated to those injured or killed may not now recover for such emotional upheaval even if negligently caused. Close relatives who witness the accidental injury or death of a loved one and suffer emotional trauma may not recover when the loved one's conduct was the cause of that emotional trauma. The overwhelming majority of "emotional distress" which we endure, therefore, is not compensable.

Unlike an award of damages for intentionally caused emotional distress which is punitive, the award for NIED simply reflects society's belief that a negligent actor

---

*"[A] distinction between distress caused by personal observation of the injury and by hearing of the tragedy from another is justified because compensation should be limited to abnormal life experiences which cause emotional distress. While receiving news that a loved one has been injured or has died may cause emotional distress, it is the type of experience for which in a general way one is prepared, an experience which is common. By contrast few persons are forced to witness the death or injury of a loved one or to suddenly come upon the scene without warning in situations where tortious conduct is involved. In the present case, for example, while it is common to visit a loved one in a hospital and to be distressed by the loved one's pain and suffering, it is highly uncommon to witness the apparent neglect of the patient's immediate medical needs by medical personnel." (*Ochoa v. Superior Court* (1985) 39 Cal.3d 159, 165, fn. 6, 703 P.2d 1.)

bears some responsibility for the effect of his conduct on persons other than those who suffer physical injury. In identifying those persons and the circumstances in which the defendant will be held to redress the injury, it is appropriate to restrict recovery to those persons who will suffer an emotional impact beyond the impact that can be anticipated whenever one learns that a relative is injured, or dies, or the emotion felt by a "disinterested" witness. The class of potential plaintiffs should be limited to those who because of their relationship suffer the greatest emotional distress. When the right to recover is limited in this manner, the liability bears a reasonable relationship to the culpability of the negligent defendant. . . . Even if it is "foreseeable" that persons other than closely related percipient witnesses may suffer emotional distress, this fact does not justify the imposition of what threatens to become unlimited liability for emotional distress on a defendant whose conduct is simply negligent. . . .

We conclude, therefore, that a plaintiff may recover damages for emotional distress caused by observing the negligently inflicted injury of a third person if, but only if, said plaintiff: (1) is closely related to the injury victim;** (2) is present at the scene of the injury-producing event at the time it occurs and is then aware that it is causing injury to the victim; and (3) as a result suffers serious emotional distress—a reaction beyond that which would be anticipated in a disinterested witness and which is not an abnormal response to the circumstances. . . .†

The merely negligent actor does not owe a duty the law will recognize to make monetary amends to all persons who may have suffered emotional distress on viewing or learning about the injurious consequences of his conduct. . . .

The undisputed facts establish that [Maria Thing] was not present at the scene of the accident in which her son was injured. She did not observe defendant's conduct and was not aware that her son was being injured. She could not, therefore, establish a right to recover for the emotional distress she suffered when she subsequently learned of the accident and observed its consequences. The order granting summary judgment was proper. The judgment of the Court of Appeal is reversed.

**In most cases no justification exists for permitting recovery for NIED by persons who are only distantly related to the injury victim. Absent exceptional circumstances, recovery should be limited to relatives residing in the same household, or parents, siblings, children, and grandparents of the victim.

†As explained by the Hawaii Supreme Court, "serious mental distress may be found where a reasonable [person] normally constituted, would be unable to adequately cope with the mental distress engendered by the circumstances of the case." (*Rodrigues v. State* (1970) 52 Hawaii 156, 173, 472 P.2d 509, 519-520.)

▪ ASSIGNMENT 18.5 ▪

Jim Nester drowns while swimming in a pool operated by Fun Center, Inc. The death is solely due to the negligence of Fun Center, Inc. Jim was at the pool with his stepfather, Frank Carter. (Frank married Jim's mother a month before Jim's death. Frank had lived with the mother about three weeks before the marriage.) Jim was accidentally pushed into the pool by a careless lifeguard. Frank did not see this, but he heard a stranger scream when Jim fell in the water. When he heard the scream, Fred looked over in the direction of Jim. Since people had gathered around, he was not certain what had happened. He walked over and saw Jim being pulled from the water. Frank gasped in horror when he saw Jim's face turn blue. As a lifeguard started carrying Jim to an ambulance, Frank panicked. He felt dizzy and almost fainted. He has been unable to sleep because of Jim's death. After the funeral, Frank sued Fun Center, Inc. for negligent infliction of emotional distress. What are his chances of success?

SUMMARY

The tort of intentional infliction of emotional distress requires an act of extreme or outrageous conduct. It must shock the conscience. For defendants such as common carriers and innkeepers, however, courts sometimes say that less severe conduct will suffice. In most states, there must be intent to cause the severe emotional distress; in some states, recklessness is enough. The defendant's intent to cause distress in one person will not be transferred to another person who suffered the distress if the defendant did not intend to harm the latter. The plaintiff must in fact suffer severe emotional distress. Physical illness or harm is not required. The test of whether the distress was severe is an objective test unless the defendant is aware of (and takes advantage of) the plaintiff's unusual susceptibility to such distress. The plaintiff must show either that but for what the defendant did the distress would not have resulted, or that the defendant was a substantial factor in producing it.

In a standard negligence action, the plaintiff can recover for emotional distress arising out of direct and immediate physical harm or injury. With few exceptions, if the plaintiff never suffers physical harm or injury, courts deny recovery for the negligently caused emotional distress. If this distress later results in physical harm or injury, courts sometimes grant recovery. It may depend on whether there was some physical impact on the plaintiff or whether the plaintiff was in the zone of danger of impact. If the plaintiff witnesses someone else's injury, the plaintiff's ability to recover damages for his or her own emotional distress and physical injury may depend on factors such as whether the plaintiff is present and in the zone of danger of impact when the other person is injured and whether the latter is closely related to the plaintiff.

Key Terms

intentional infliction of
  emotional distress
outrage
extreme or outrageous
intent
recklessness
transferred intent

severe emotional
  distress
physical illness or harm
causation
negligent infliction of
  emotional distress

NIED
negligence
pain and suffering
physical impact
zone of danger

CHAPTER 19

False Imprison-
ment and False
Arrest

CHAPTER OUTLINE

- FALSE IMPRISONMENT
  - False Imprisonment Checklist
  - Confinement
  - Intent
  - Causation
  - Consciousness or Harm

- FALSE ARREST
  - Peace Officer's Privilege to Arrest
  - Private Citizen's Privilege to Arrest

■ FALSE IMPRISONMENT

False Imprisonment Checklist
Definitions, Relationships, and Research References

Category
False Imprisonment is an intentional tort.

Interest Protected by This Tort
   The right to be free from intentional restraints on one's freedom of movement.

Elements of This Tort
1. An act that completely confines the plaintiff within fixed boundaries set by the defendant
2. Intent to confine the plaintiff or a third party
3. Causation of the confinement
4. The plaintiff was either conscious of the confinement *or* was physically harmed by it

Major Definitions of Words/Phrases in These Elements

> **Act:** A volitional movement of the defendant's body by words or other conduct.

> **Confine:** To restrain the plaintiff's freedom of movement:
>
> **a.** by physical barriers, or
> **b.** by physical force, or
> **c.** by the threat of present physical force, or
> **d.** by asserting legal authority to confine, or
> **e.** by refusing to release the plaintiff.

> **Complete:** A total confinement where the plaintiff knows of no safe or inoffensive means of escape.

> **Intent to Confine:** The desire to confine the plaintiff or the knowledge with substantial certainty that the defendant's act will result in the confinement.

> **Causation:** But for the defendant's act, the plaintiff would not have been confined, or the defendant was a substantial factor in producing the confinement.

> **Harmed:** Actual damage or injury in addition to the confinement itself.

Major Defense and Counter-Argument Possibilities That Need to Be Explored

1. There was no confinement.
2. The confinement was not total; there was a safe and inoffensive means of escape that the plaintiff did not take.
3. The threat of force related to the future.
4. The confinement was accidental. It may have been negligently or recklessly caused, but it was not intentional.
5. The defendant was not a substantial factor in producing the confinement.
6. The plaintiff either did not know about the confinement or was not physically harmed by it.
7. The plaintiff consented to the confinement.
8. The defendant acted in self-defense against the plaintiff.
9. The defendant acted in defense of others against the plaintiff.
10. The defendant had a shopkeeper's privilege to detain the plaintiff.
11. The defendant had a privilege to discipline the plaintiff.
12. The defendant had a privilege to arrest the plaintiff.
13. Sovereign immunity.
14. Public official immunity.
15. Charitable immunity.
16. Intrafamily immunity.

Damages

No actual damages need to be shown to prove a prima facie case (unless the plaintiff was unaware of the confinement). In most cases, the confinement is damage enough. Once the elements have been proven, the jury will be allowed to consider damages for humiliation, physical discomfort, illness, injury to the plaintiff's reputation, or loss of earnings or other personal property due to the confinement. If the defendant acted out of hatred or malice, punitive damages are also possible.

Relationship to Criminal Law

In many states, false imprisonment is also a crime if the confinement is serious enough. The crime may be called false imprisonment, abduction, kidnapping, etc.

Relationship to Other Torts

Assault: An assault may also be committed if the defendant puts the plaintiff in apprehension of a harmful or offensive contact while falsely imprisoning him or her.

Battery: It is common for the defendant to touch the plaintiff while falsely imprisoning him or her. If this touching was without consent, the defendant may also be liable for a battery.

Defamation: Defamation may occur during the false imprisonment. For example, the defendant may use derogatory language while confining the plaintiff. Also, the very act of being confined may be a derogatory "communication," especially if the defendant is a police officer.

Intentional Infliction of Emotional Distress: This tort may also be committed if the intent of the defendant who falsely imprisoned the plaintiff was to subject the plaintiff to severe emotional trauma by the confinement.

Malicious Prosecution: If the defendant has instigated an unlawful arrest of the plaintiff, the defendant may be liable for false imprisonment and for malicious prosecution if the defendant acted with malice, without probable cause, and if the criminal case terminated in a way favorable to the plaintiff.

Negligence: The defendant may have caused the confinement of the plaintiff by carelessness or recklessness rather than with the intent to confine him or her. If so, there is no false imprisonment, but there may be negligence if the plaintiff has suffered actual damages in addition to the confinement itself.

Federal Law

1. Under the Federal Tort Claims Act, the United States Government is *not* liable if a federal employee falsely imprisons the plaintiff *unless* the employee is a federal investigative or law enforcement officer.
2. When the defendant deprives the plaintiff of a federal constitutional or statutory right, the defendant is liable under the Civil Rights Act if the defendant acted under color of law.

Employer-Employee (Agency) Law

A private employer will be liable for false imprisonment committed by employees if it occurs within the scope of employment. Intentional torts such as false imprisonment are often considered outside this scope unless it can be shown that the employee acted while furthering the business objectives of the employer.

Research References for This Tort

▪ Digests

In the digests of West, look for case summaries on false imprisonment under key topics such as:

False Imprisonment	Torts
Arrest	Damages

▪ *Corpus Juris Secundum*

In this legal encyclopedia, look for discussions under topic headings such as:

False Imprisonment	Torts
Arrest	Damages

▪ *American Jurisprudence 2d*

In this legal encyclopedia, look for discussions under topic headings such as:

False Imprisonment	Torts
Arrest	Damages

▪ Legal Periodical Literature

There are three index systems to use to try to locate legal periodical literature on false imprisonment:

Index to Legal Periodicals (ILP)	*Current Law Index (CLI)*	*Legal Resource Index (LRI)*
See literature in *ILP* under subject headings such as:	See literature in *CLI* under subject headings such as:	See literature in *LRI* under subject headings such as:
False Imprisonment	False Imprisonment	False Imprisonment
Arrest	Arrest	Arrest
Damages	Tort	Tort
Torts	Damages	Damages
Personal Injuries	Duress	Duress
	Personal Injuries	Personal Injuries
	Privileges and Immunities	Privileges and Immunities

Example of a legal periodical article on this tort you will find by using *ILP, CLI,* or *LRI:*

> *"Nowhere to Go and Chose to Stay"; Using the Tort of False Imprisonment to Redress Involuntary Confinement of the Elderly in Nursing Homes and Hospitals* by C. Razin, 137 University of Pennsylvania Law Review 903 (1989).

▪ *ALR, ALR2D, ALR3D, ALR4th, ALR5th, ALR Fed*

Use the *Index to Annotations* to locate annotations on false imprisonment. In this index, check subject headings such as:

False Imprisonment	Shoplifting
Arrest	Torts
Privileges and Immunities	Damages

Example of an annotation on false imprisonment you can locate through this index:

Liability of Attorney Acting for Client for False Imprisonment or Malicious Prosecution of Third Party, 27 ALR3d 1113.

▪ *Words and Phrases*

In this multivolume legal dictionary, look up every word or phrase discussed in this chapter connected with false imprisonment and false arrest to try to locate definitions of these words or phrases from court opinions.

False Imprisonment consists of an illegal confinement. One of the ways in which the plaintiff can be falsely imprisoned is through a false arrest, which we will consider separately later in the chapter. Here, our main focus will be other kinds of false imprisonment.

Confinement

The first element of false imprisonment is an act that completely confines the plaintiff within fixed boundaries set by the defendant. The word "imprisonment" is very misleading. To commit this tort, you do not have to place someone behind bars without authority. Such an act will constitute false imprisonment, as will an illegal delay in releasing someone from jail or prison. But false imprisonment is not limited to such extreme situations. It can also occur when there is a **confinement** of one's freedom of movement. This confinement or restraint can happen in five ways:

Confinement by Physical Barrier

Tangible, physical restraints or barriers are imposed on the plaintiff.

Examples:

- The defendant locks the plaintiff in a room.
- The defendant takes away the plaintiff's wheelchair.
- The defendant takes away a ladder the plaintiff needs to climb out of a deep ditch.

Confinement by Physical Force Against the Plaintiff, the Plaintiff's Immediate Family, or the Plaintiff's Property

Examples:

- If the defendant grabs or holds the plaintiff, confinement results from physical force on the plaintiff's body.
- The plaintiff can also be confined if the defendant uses physical force on the plaintiff's child or other members of his or her immediate family. Suppose that the defendant ties up the plaintiff's son. The plaintiff may be able to escape, but it is highly unlikely that he or she will do so while the child is in danger. Hence, the defendant has confined *both* the child and the plaintiff. The physical force used against the child has also resulted in the confinement of the parent.
- Finally, suppose that the defendant uses physical force against the plaintiff's valuable property, such as by seizing the plaintiff's watch.

The plaintiff stays in order to try to get the watch back. (As we will see in Chapter 31, the plaintiff has a **privilege to recapture** such property.)

In the last two examples, the parent who remains because his or her child is tied up and the plaintiff who remains to see about a watch that has been taken have "agreed" to stay, but they have done so under such severe **duress** that the confinement is not voluntary. The confinement is imposed on the plaintiffs as effectively in these situations as when actual physical force is used on a plaintiff's body.

Confinement by Present Threat of Physical Force Against the Plaintiff, the Plaintiff's Immediate Family, or Against the Plaintiff's Property

A plaintiff's freedom of movement is certainly restricted if the defendant threatens immediate force or violence against the plaintiff, against a member of the plaintiff's immediate family, or against the plaintiff's valuable property if the plaintiff tries to escape or move out of an area designated by the defendant. If the plaintiff submits to the threat and remains, a confinement has occurred for purposes of establishing the first element of the tort of false imprisonment. The plaintiff does not have to be reasonable in submitting as long as the defendant has the intent to confine the plaintiff through the threat of immediate physical force.[1]

Confinement by Asserted Legal Authority

Here the defendant claims the **legal authority** to confine or arrest the plaintiff. Confinement occurs when the plaintiff is taken into custody. If the defendant does not have the privilege of arresting the plaintiff, as defined later in the chapter, the first element of false imprisonment has been met. No physical force or touching need be used as long as the plaintiff has reason to believe that such force will be used if the plaintiff either moves outside an area designated by the defendant or fails to follow the defendant.

Confinement by Refusal to Release

Assume that the plaintiff has been validly confined, e.g., imprisoned. At the time when the plaintiff has a right to be released, he or she has been improperly confined if the defendant interferes with the release.

Confinement in any of the above five ways must be **complete** or total, meaning that the plaintiff must know of no safe or inoffensive means of escape out of the fixed boundaries set by the defendant. There is no confinement, for example, if the defendant blocks the plaintiff's path when there is a clear and accessible way around the defendant. Nor is there confinement if the defendant locks all the doors of a house, if the plaintiff is able to escape by climbing out of a window that is very close to the ground, and if the inconvenience in climbing out is very slight. A different result would follow, however, if the plaintiff had little or no clothing on, or would have substantial difficulty climbing out because of age or illness.

---

[1]*Restatement (Second) of Torts* § 40 comment d (1965).

Finally, there is no set length of time that the confinement must last. A person can be confined for a brief or a prolonged period.

A great many false imprisonment cases result from detention in shops and department stores when a customer is suspected of stealing merchandise. A **shopkeeper's privilege** gives a shopkeeper the right to detain someone temporarily for the sole purpose of investigating whether theft has occurred. Reasonable force can be used to carry out this temporary investigation. The shopkeeper must be reasonable in suspecting that the person has committed the crime. If it turns out that the person is innocent and that the shopkeeper has made a mistake, the latter is still protected if the mistake was reasonable.

Intent

False imprisonment is an intentional tort. To establish **intent,** the defendant must desire to confine or know with substantial certainty that confinement will result from what he or she does. If the defendant is merely negligent or reckless in causing the confinement, the intentional tort of false imprisonment has not been committed. The tort of **negligence** might be possible. A negligence suit, however, requires proof of actual damages, whereas for false imprisonment, no more damages than the confinement itself need be shown. (See, however, an exception in the next section on causation covering cases in which the plaintiff was unaware of the confinement.)

> **Example:** The defendant locks up an old building and carelessly or even recklessly fails to check whether anyone is still inside. This is not enough to establish intent to confine, because the defendant neither desired nor knew with substantial certainty that someone would be confined.

The doctrine of **transferred intent** applies. If the defendant intends to confine one person, but mistakingly confines a plaintiff whom the defendant never even knew existed, the requisite intent has been established. The defendant's intent to confine one person is transferred to another person who is in fact confined by the defendant's intentional conduct.

Causation

To establish the element of **causation,** the plaintiff must be able to show that either:

- but for the act of the defendant the plaintiff would not have been confined, or
- the defendant was a substantial factor in producing the plaintiff's confinement.

The defendant need not be the sole cause of the confinement.

> **Example:** A citizen makes a complaint about a person to a police officer. The latter makes an arrest of the person—a false arrest, because the privilege to arrest, to be discussed later, does not apply.

The question arises whether the citizen who made the complaint to the police officer is liable for the false imprisonment that resulted from the false arrest. Was the citizen a substantial factor in the false arrest? The answer depends on whether the citizen instigated the arrest, as opposed to simply reporting the facts to the police officer who made up his or her own mind on whether to arrest. **Insti-**

gation consists of insisting, directing, encouraging, or participating in the arrest. There must be persuasion or influencing of some kind in order for the citizen to have been a substantial factor in producing the arrest by the police officer. Without this instigation, the citizen has not caused the confinement.

Consciousness or Harm

The courts are split on whether the plaintiff must *know* that he or she is being confined. Some courts, for example, conclude that no tort exists if someone is locked in a room for a period of time without ever knowing that he or she could not get out. If, however, physical harm is suffered by the plaintiff other than the mere restriction of movement, there are courts that will provide recovery under false imprisonment even if the plaintiff was not aware of the confinement. The general rule is that actual damage or harm—in addition to the confinement itself—is not an element of the tort of false imprisonment. An exception exists if the plaintiff was not aware of the confinement.

▪ ASSIGNMENT 19.1 ▪

In each of the following situations, determine whether false imprisonment has been committed. (For the first three questions, see General Instructions for the Legal Analysis Assignment in Chapter 3.)

a. Luis is driving a car down a highway. His two-year-old son, Fred, is in the back seat playing. It is a three-lane highway, and Luis is in the middle lane. Dan's car is in the far right lane. Luis gives a right turn signal. He wants to go to the far right lane in order to take the next exit ramp on the right. Dan is driving to the immediate right of Luis. Dan refuses to yield, forcing Luis to miss his right turn. Luis loses fifteen minutes in taking an alternate route to where he was headed. Luis and Fred sue Dan for false imprisonment.

b. Mary calls John on the phone and threatens to kill him by 2:00 P.M. tomorrow unless John goes downtown today to pay a debt that John owes Mary's company. John does so. He later sues Mary for false imprisonment.

c. Jim is soliciting religious contributions in Leo's department store. Leo tells Jim that this is not allowed in his store. Jim nevertheless continues. Leo and four of his security guards surround Jim and tell him to come to the manager's office. Jim does so. In the manager's office, Leo shouts at Jim and tells him that he has thirty seconds to get out the back door. Jim leaves and sues Leo for false imprisonment.

d. Draft a complaint for Luis, John, or Jim in any of the above three situations. (See General Instructions for the Complaint Drafting Assignment in Chapter 5.)

▪ ASSIGNMENT 19.2 ▪

How would a court in your state handle the facts posed in problem (c) in Assignment 19.1? (See General Instructions for the State Code and the State Court Opinion Assignments, both in Chapter 2.)

▪ ASSIGNMENT 19.3 ▪

Prepare an annotated bibliography on false imprisonment for your state. (See General Instructions for the Annotated Bibliography Assignment in Chapter 2.)

CASE

Andrews v. Piedmont Air Lines
297 S.C. 367, 377 S.E.2d 127 (1989)
Court of Appeals of South Carolina

Background: Clarence Andrews was not allowed to board an airplane due to the restrictions the airline imposed on customers in wheelchairs. He sued for false imprisonment. The lower court granted summary judgment for the airlines. The case is now before the Court of Appeals of South Carolina.

Decision of Appeal: Judgment for the airlines. There was no false imprisonment.

Opinion of Court

PER CURIAM.

. . . Clarence Andrews sued Piedmont Air Lines for an incident which occurred after Piedmont denied him boarding on a flight due to his physical incapacity to travel unaccompanied . . . In 1984, Andrews, a diabetic who had previously suffered a stroke, was admitted to Greenville Memorial Hospital for circulatory problems in his right leg. As a result of the stroke, his speech was slurred, he drooled, and his left side was paralyzed. Unfortunately, the treatment for his leg was unsuccessful and it had to be amputated above the knee. During the recovery period, the hospital contacted Andrews' daughter in Florida and asked if her father could live with her. She agreed and the hospital arranged the trip.

A hospital social worker, Andrew Irwin, telephoned Piedmont and reserved a seat for Andrews. Piedmont informed Irwin that the airline had guidelines governing travel by unaccompanied physically handicapped passengers. Under the guidelines, Piedmont would accept the passenger if he (1) could use the lavatory without assistance, (2) was able to sit in a normal sitting position with the seatbelt properly fastened, and (3) required no assistance eating.

In December 1984, the hospital discharged Andrews and took him by ambulance to the Greenville/Spartanburg Airport. He was placed in an airport wheelchair and taken to the Piedmont ticket counter. He purchased a ticket and was wheeled to the gate area to wait for his flight. While waiting to embark, Andrews asked other passengers for cigarettes and asked a passenger to tie his leg to the wheelchair. The supervisor of airport security notified Milton Ward, the Piedmont station manager, of a potential problem at the departure gate.

When Ward arrived at the gate, he found Andrews slumped over in the wheelchair with saliva drooling out of the side of his mouth. Ward questioned Andrews about his ability to go to the bathroom by himself. He received a negative answer. Since Andrews did not meet Piedmont's guidelines, Ward kept him off the flight. Andrews was removed from the passenger waiting area to an area adjacent to the Piedmont office and ticket counter. Piedmont telephoned the hospital to come get Andrews.

Upon receipt of Piedmont's call, Irwin went to the airport and found Andrews in a wheelchair. He called the hospital requesting an ambulance and remained with Andrews, one and a half to two hours, until it arrived. Andrews returned to the hospital and alternate travel plans were arranged. . . .

False imprisonment is depriving the plaintiff of his liberty without lawful justification. In order to establish a cause of action, the evidence must prove: (1) that the defendant restrained the plaintiff; (2) that the restraint was intentional; and (3) that the restraint was unlawful.

The facts of the case do not support a cause of action for false imprisonment. Assuming Piedmont restrained Andrews, there is no evidence that the restraint was unlawful. Common carriers have a higher duty of care towards noticeably handicapped passengers. See *Singletary v. Atlantic Coast Line Railroad Co.,* 217 S.C. 212, 60 S.E.2d 305 (1950). Due to his physical condition, Andrews was not ambulatory. Piedmont placed Andrews in the area adjacent to the ticket counter so they could periodically check on him and find him when the ambulance arrived. There is no evidence that he protested waiting there or that he asked to be moved to another location. Further, after Irwin arrived, Andrews did not leave in Irwin's personal car, but chose to wait for the ambulance in this same area. In light of Andrews' condition, the alleged restraint was reasonable and it might well have been a breach of a Piedmont's duty if they had not detained him until Irwin arrived. The trial court correctly granted the motion for summary judgment on the cause of action for false imprisonment.

▪ ASSIGNMENT 19.4 ▪

a. Was Andrews restrained by the airline? Was he confined by Greenville Memorial Hospital?
b. Assume Andrews met all the requirements for boarding the airplane. Would it have been false imprisonment for the airline to refuse to allow him to board?

▪ FALSE ARREST

One way to commit false imprisonment is to make a **false arrest.** An arrest is false when it is not privileged. Private citizens as well as peace officers have a privilege to arrest. We shall consider the extent of the privilege each enjoys in Figure 19.1.

Throughout this discussion, our concern is the **personal liability** of the individual making the arrest. When someone is personally liable for a wrong, the consequence is that an adverse judgment is paid out of the pocket of the wrongdoer. When the defendant is a peace officer, a separate question arises as to whether the government that employs the officer is *also* liable for the tort on a theory of **respondeat superior.** The answer depends upon whether the government has waived its sovereign immunity for this kind of claim. Sovereign immunity is considered in Chapter 31.

Peace Officer's Privilege to Arrest

When a **peace officer** has a **warrant** to arrest someone, the arrest is privileged as long as the warrant is **fair on its face.** Courts differ on the meaning of this phrase. Most courts give it a broad interpretation in order to protect the officer. In such courts, the warrant is not fair on its face if it is obviously defective, such as a warrant that does not name the party to be arrested or does not state the crime charged. An officer is not required to be an attorney who knows how to analyze the warrant in all its technicalities. The officer is required, however, to be able to recognize blatant irregularities.

If the officer arrests the wrong person under the warrant, the privilege is lost in most states. In some states, however, the privilege is not lost if the officer's mistake was reasonable under the circumstances.

An officer may also make an arrest without a warrant. As Figure 19.1 shows, the principles of the privilege to arrest without a warrant differ depending on why the arrest is being made:

- criminal arrest for a felony
- criminal arrest for a misdemeanor
- civil arrest for treatment or protection rather than for the commission of an alleged crime

• ASSIGNMENT 19.5 •

At a rock concert, a police officer smells marijuana coming from a section where Mary and her seven friends are sitting. The officer arrests all of them. The officer thinks that one or two are doing the smoking, but he wants to take them all in for questioning so that he can find out which ones are guilty. Mary tries to run away. The officer shoots her. An investigation reveals that none of the arrested individuals possessed or used any drugs. The police officer is sued for false arrest, false imprisonment, and battery. What result based on the principles in Figure 19.1? (See General Instructions for the Legal Analysis Assignment in Chapter 3.)

Private Citizen's Privilege to Arrest

The privilege of a **private citizen** to make an arrest without a warrant must be considered under the same three categories covered in Figure 19.1 for peace officers:

- criminal arrest for a felony
- criminal arrest for a misdemeanor
- criminal arrest for treatment or protection rather than for the commission of an alleged crime

• ASSIGNMENT 19.6 •

For this assignment, the facts are the same as in Assignment 19.5, except that the person who made the arrests, did the shooting, and is sued is a private citizen, rather than a peace officer. What result based on the principles in Figure 19.1? (See General Instructions for the Legal Analysis Assignment in Chapter 3.)

• ASSIGNMENT 19.7 •

Find out if your state has passed any laws that alter any of the principles listed in Figure 19.1 on the privilege of a peace officer or a private citizen to make an arrest. (See General Instructions for the State Code Assignment in Chapter 2.) Also check to see if any courts in your state have made changes of their own in any of these principles. (See General Instructions for the State Court Opinion Assignment in Chapter 2.)

• ASSIGNMENT 19.8 •

Sam is a private citizen. Someone has just stolen his $200 watch, but he is not sure who did it. Len, a stranger, comes up to Sam and tells him that he just saw a woman named Cindy steal the watch. Len points Cindy out to Sam as she is about to board a train. Sam follows the train in his car until Cindy gets off. He arrests her immediately. When she resists, he pushes her into his car. At the trial,

Cindy is found innocent of the crime. Cindy now sues Sam for battery and false imprisonment. Does Sam have any defense? Prepare an investigation strategy. (See General Instructions for the Investigation Strategy Assignment in Chapter 4.)

Figure 19.1 **Comparison of Peace Officer's and Private Citizen's Privilege to Arrest without a Warrant**

Elements of Privilege

Peace Officer's Privilege	Private Citizen's Privilege

1. Criminal Arrest: Felony

a. The peace officer has reasonable grounds to believe a felony has been committed.

b. The peace officer has reasonable grounds to suspect that the person arrested by the peace officer probably committed the felony.

c. The peace officer uses reasonable force in making the arrest or in preventing the person from fleeing.

Notes:

• States differ on whether deadly force can be used to make the arrest or to prevent fleeing.

• Deadly force can be used if the peace officer's life becomes endangered while making the arrest or preventing fleeing (self-defense).

• A reasonable mistake on any of the three elements will still protect the officer.

2. Criminal Arrest: Misdemeanor

a. The misdemeanor must be a breach of the peace.

b. The misdemeanor must be committed in the presence of the officer.

c. The arrest must be made immediately or in fresh pursuit.

d. Reasonable force is used to make the arrest or to prevent fleeing.

Notes:

• The peace officer's privilege to arrest for a misdemeanor is the same as that of a private citizen.

• In most states, a mistake on the first three elements will not protect the peace officer, even if the mistake was reasonable.

1. Criminal Arrest: Felony

a. A felony has in fact been committed.

b. The felony committed is the one for which the citizen has made the arrest.

c. The citizen has reasonable grounds to suspect that the person arrested by the citizen probably committed the felony.

d. The citizen uses reasonable force in making the arrest or in preventing the person from fleeing.

Notes:

• States differ on whether deadly force can be used to make the arrest or to prevent fleeing.

• Deadly force can be used if the citizen's life becomes endangered while making the arrest or preventing fleeing (self-defense).

• Some states have passed statutes that change the above law. Under these statutes, the privilege is not lost if the citizen has reasonable grounds to believe that a felony has been committed by the person arrested—a reasonable mistake will protect the citizen.

2. Criminal Arrest: Misdemeanor

a. The misdemeanor must be a breach of the peace.

b. The misdemeanor must be committed in the presence of the citizen.

c. The arrest must be made immediately or in fresh pursuit.

d. Reasonable force is used to make the arrest or to prevent fleeing.

Figure 19.1   Continued

Elements of Privilege	
Peace Officer's Privilege	**Private Citizen's Privilege**
• The officer can use deadly force only if the officer's life is in danger in making the arrest or in preventing fleeing (self-defense).	Notes:
	• The citizen's privilege to arrest for a misdemeanor is the same as that of a peace officer.
• Statutes may exist in a state to extend the privilege to arrest for misdemeanors not committed in the officer's presence and for misdemeanors that are not breaches of the peace.	• In most states, a mistake on the first three elements will not protect the citizen, even if the mistake was reasonable.
3. Civil Arrest	• The citizen can use deadly force only if the citizen's own life was in danger in making the arrest or in preventing fleeing (self-defense).
a. The officer must reasonably believe that an insane or mentally ill person poses a serious threat of danger to him- or herself or to others.	• Statutes may exist in a state to extend the privilege to arrest for misdemeanors not committed in the citizen's presence and for misdemeanors that are not breaches of the peace.
b. Reasonable force is used to bring the person to the authorities for medical attention.	**3. Civil Arrest**
	a. The citizen must reasonably believe that an insane or mentally ill person poses a serious threat of danger to him- or herself or to others.
	b. Reasonable force is used to bring the person to the authorities for medical attention.

Factors That Destroy the Privilege	
Peace Officer's Privilege	**Private Citizen's Privilege**
• The officer did not have reasonable grounds to suspect that a felony had probably been committed.	• No felony was in fact committed (D's reasonable mistake will not protect D).
• The officer did not have reasonable grounds to suspect that P had probably committed a felony.	• A felony was committed but it was not the felony for which D arrested P (D's reasonable mistake will not protect D).
• The officer used a disproportionate amount of force to make the arrest or to prevent P from fleeing.	• D did not have reasonable grounds to suspect that P probably committed the felony.
• The officer failed to take P before the proper authorities after taking P into custody.	• D used a disproportionate amount of force to make the arrest or to prevent P from fleeing.
• The misdemeanor was not a breach of the peace.	• D failed to take P before the proper authorities after taking P into custody.
• The misdemeanor was not committed in the presence of the officer.	

Figure 19.1 Continued

Factors That Destroy the Privilege	
Peace Officer's Privilege	**Private Citizen's Privilege**
• The arrest for the misdemeanor was not made immediately or in fresh pursuit. • P (in a civil arrest case) posed no threat of harm to P or to others.	• The misdemeanor was not a breach of the peace. • The misdemeanor was not committed in the presence of D (the citizen). • The arrest for the misdemeanor was not made immediately or in fresh pursuit. • P (in a civil arrest case) posed no threat of harm to P or to others.

Major Definitions

• WARRANT: a written order issued by an authorized government body directing the arrest of a person.
• PEACE OFFICER: a person appointed by the government to keep the peace.
• ARREST: taking another into custody to bring before the proper authorities.
• FELONY: a serious crime that is defined as a felony by the government. The common definition is a crime punishable by incarceration for a term exceeding a year.
• MISDEMEANOR: a less serious crime that is defined as a misdemeanor by the government. The common definition is a crime punishable by incarceration of a year or less, or a crime that is less serious than a felony.
• BREACH OF THE PEACE: an offense committed by violence or by acts likely to cause immediate disturbance of the public order.
• FRESH PURSUIT: promptly, without undue delay.
• CIVIL ARREST: arrest for the purpose of treatment or protection, and not because of the alleged commission of a crime.

The Torts Involved: Examples

Peace Officer's Privilege	**Private Citizen's Privilege**
• BATTERY Ex: P has just tried to pass a check that P has forged. The officer arrests P. When P resists, the officer handcuffs P. P sues the officer for battery. The officer can raise the defense of the privilege to arrest. • ASSAULT Ex: A traffic cop stops P for speeding and finds that P is driving a car that P has stolen. The officer tries to arrest P. P resists by trying to run away. The officer raises his club in front of P's face and says, "Don't	• BATTERY Ex: P has stolen a watch in D's presence (D is a private citizen). D tries to arrest P. P resists. D ties P's hands and takes P to the police station. P sues D for battery. D can raise the defense of the privilege to arrest. • FALSE IMPRISONMENT Ex: Same facts as above. P sues D for false imprisonment because of the confinement D caused. D can raise the defense of the privilege to arrest.

Figure 19.1 Continued

The Torts Involved: Examples	
Peace Officer's Privilege	**Private Citizen's Privilege**

make another move.'' P sues the officer for assault. The officer can use the defense of the privilege to arrest.
· FALSE ARREST OR FALSE IMPRISONMENT
Ex: Same facts as above. The officer takes P to the police station. P sues the officer for false arrest or for false imprisonment. The officer can use the defense of the privilege to arrest.

Note: In each of the above examples, the officer must establish all the elements of the privilege to arrest. The elements that apply depend on what the officer was arresting P for. See "Elements of Privilege" column at the beginning of Figure 19.1.

· ASSAULT
Ex: Same facts as above. D raises his fist and threatens to hit P if P resists the arrest. P sues D for assault. D can raise the defense of the privilege to arrest.

Note: In each of the above examples, the citizen must establish all the elements of the privilege to arrest. The elements that apply depend on what the citizen was arresting P for. See "Elements of Privilege" column at the beginning of Figure 19.1.

Investigation Tasks	

· What crime was suspected or reported?
· Who can verify that a crime was committed?
· What is this crime called in the state?
· Why did D think that P committed this crime?
· Did D know P?
· Did P have a reputation for criminal behavior in the area?
· What did P commit the crime with?
· What did P say before and during P's act?
· Did P admit to D that P committed a crime?
· Did others besides D suspect P of a crime?
· Who was present when the crime was committed?

· How soon was the arrest made?
· What caused the delay, if any?
· Did P resist the arrest?
· How did P resist?
· What force did D use?
· Was less force possible? Why or why not?
· What age and strength differences existed between P and D?
· Where did D take P after the arrest and how long did it take to get there?
· If D made a civil arrest, what indications were there that P was a threat to P's own safety or to that of others?
· Was P's mental illness harmful to anyone?

SUMMARY

False imprisonment is an intentional confinement within fixed boundaries set by the defendant. The confinement can be by physical barriers; by physical force or threat of physical force against the plaintiff, against his or her immediate family, or against his or her property; by asserted legal authority; or by a refusal to release someone who was initially confined properly. The confinement must be complete or total. Shopkeepers have a limited privilege to detain someone temporarily to investigate whether merchandise has been stolen.

The defendant must desire to confine the plaintiff or know with substantial certainty that the confinement will result from what the defendant does. The plaintiff must either be aware of the confinement or suffer physical harm as a result of it.

An arrest is false when it is unprivileged. A peace officer has a privilege to arrest someone if the officer is acting on a warrant that is fair on its face. If no warrant exists, the peace officer has a privilege to make a felony arrest if there are reasonable grounds to believe the plaintiff committed the felony and if the officer uses reasonable force; to make a misdemeanor arrest if the misdemeanor is a breach of the peace, if it is committed in the officer's presence, if the arrest is made immediately or in fresh pursuit, and if the officer uses reasonable force; or to make a civil arrest if the officer reasonably believes the insane or mentally ill plaintiff poses a serious danger to him- or herself or to others, and if the officer uses reasonable force.

A private citizen has a privilege to make a felony arrest if a felony has in fact been committed, if it is the felony the citizen arrested the plaintiff for, if the citizen has reasonable grounds to believe the plaintiff committed the felony, and if the citizen uses reasonable force; to make a misdemeanor arrest if the misdemeanor is a breach of the peace, if it is committed in the citizen's presence, if the arrest is made immediately or in fresh pursuit, and if the citizen uses reasonable force; or to make a civil arrest if the citizen reasonably believes the insane or mentally ill plaintiff poses a serious danger to him- or herself or to others, and if the citizen uses reasonable force.

Key Terms

false imprisonment	transferred intent	fair on its face
confinement	causation	private citizen
privilege to recapture	instigation	arrest
duress	false arrest	felony
legal authority	personal liability	misdemeanor
complete	respondeat superior	breach of the peace
shopkeeper's privilege	peace officer	fresh pursuit
intent	warrant	civil arrest
negligence		

CHAPTER 20

Misuse of Legal Proceedings

CHAPTER OUTLINE

- MALICIOUS PROSECUTION
    Malicious Prosecution Checklist
    Initiate or Procure the Initiation
        of Criminal Proceedings
    Without Probable Cause
    With Malice

    Criminal Proceedings Terminate in
        Favor of the Accused
- WRONGFUL OR UNJUSTIFIED CIVIL
    PROCEEDINGS
- ABUSE OF PROCESS

▪ MALICIOUS PROSECUTION

Malicious Prosecution Checklist
Definitions, Relationships, and Research References

Category
Malicious Prosecution is an intentional tort.

Interest Prosecuted by This Tort
    The right to be free from unreasonable or unjustifiable criminal litigation brought against you. Secondarily, the tort protects your interest in not having your reputation harmed by such litigation.

Elements of This Tort
1. Initiate or procure the initiation of criminal proceedings
2. Without probable cause
3. With malice
4. The criminal proceedings terminate in favor of the accused

Major Definitions of Words/Phrases in These Elements

Initiate: Instigate, urge on, incite, exert pressure to begin something.

Criminal Proceedings: Formal action commenced by criminal justice officials.

Probable Cause: A suspicion based upon the appearance of circumstances that are strong enough to allow a reasonable person to believe that a criminal charge against an individual is true.

Malice: An improper motive. If the primary motive for initiating criminal proceedings is not the desire to bring the accused to justice, then the motive is improper.

Terminate in Favor of the Accused: The ending expressly or by fair implication shows that the accused is innocent of the charge.

Major Defense and Counter-Argument Possibilities That Need to Be Explored

1. Legal proceedings never actually began.
2. The accuser did not instigate the prosecution, but simply gave the facts to the authorities, who decided to prosecute without urging from the accuser.
3. There was probable cause.
4. The primary purpose of the accuser was to bring the accused to justice (i.e., to use the court for its proper purpose).
5. The legal proceedings have not yet terminated.
6. The legal proceedings did not terminate in favor of the accused.
7. Absolute privilege of a public prosecutor to prosecute.
8. Privilege of arrest.
9. Sovereign immunity.
10. Public official immunity.
11. Intrafamily immunity.

Damages

Unlike negligence, malicious prosecution does not require proof of actual damages. The jury will be allowed to assume what the damages are if the elements of the tort are established. These are general damages, such as for mental suffering and humiliation or injury to reputation. Special damages must be specifically pleaded and proven, e.g., costs of defending the underlying criminal (or civil) case, medical bills, loss of employment. Punitive damages are possible when the accuser acted out of hatred for the accused.

Relationship to Criminal Law

One of the main purposes of the malicious prosecution tort is to provide a remedy against a person who has unjustifiably caused the criminal justice system ''to go after you'' because of an accusation that you have committed a crime.

Relationship to Other Torts

Abuse of Process: Abuse of process is the improper use of legal proceedings that may have been properly initiated. If proceedings have been properly initiated, there is no malicious prosecution, but there may be abuse of process if the proceedings are used for an improper goal, e.g., to coerce the accused to pay a debt.

Battery: If the accused was touched, e.g., as part of an arrest, as criminal proceedings were initiated, the tort of battery as well as malicious prosecution may have been committed.

Defamation: Defamation (libel or slander) as well as malicious prosecution may be committed when the accuser initiates legal proceedings against the accused. Things may be said or written that are derogatory of the accused's character.

Disparagement: In the process of initiating criminal proceedings against the accused, the accuser may utter false statements injurious to the accused's business or property. The tort of disparagement as well as malicious prosecution may have been committed.

False Imprisonment: The accused may have been improperly restrained in his or her liberty while being maliciously prosecuted.

Intentional Infliction of Emotional Distress: It may be that the objective of the accuser was to subject the accused to severe emotional trauma by initiating criminal proceedings against the accused. A court might consider such conduct sufficiently outrageous so that the tort of intentional infliction of emotional distress is committed along with malicious prosecution.

Federal Law

Under the Federal Tort Claims Act, the United States Government will not be liable for malicious prosecution committed by one of its employees unless the employee is an investigative or law enforcement officer acting within the scope of employment. An action for a civil rights violation may be possible if the defendant deprived the plaintiff of federal rights under color of law.

Employer-Employee (Agency) Law

A private employer will be liable for malicious prosecution committed by an employee when the malicious prosecution falls within the scope of employment. Intentional torts such as malicious prosecution are often considered outside this scope unless it can be shown that the employee committed the malicious prosecution while furthering the business objectives of the employer.

Research References for This Tort
• Digests of West such as the *American Digest System*

In these digests, check key topics such as:

Malicious Prosecution	Arrest (especially key number
False Imprisonment	63.4 on probable cause)
Torts	Damages
Extortion	Compromise and Settlement
Indictment and Information	Attorney and Client (especially
	key number 159)

- *Corpus Juris Secundum*

    In this legal encyclopedia, see the discussions under topic headings such as:

Malicious Prosecution	Indictment and Information
Malice	Arrest
False Imprisonment	Damages
Agency	Accord and Satisfaction
Torts	Compromise and Settlement
Extortion	

- *American Jurisprudence 2d*

    In this legal encyclopedia, see the discussions under topic headings such as:

Malicious Prosecution	Torts
Abuse of Process	Master and Servant
Attachment and	Damages
Garnishment (see sections 596ff)	Arrest
	Criminal Law
Executions (sections 750ff)	Extortion, Blackmail and Threats
Malice	Indictment and Information
False Imprisonment	Compromise and Settlement
	Prosecuting Attorneys

- Legal Periodical Literature

Index to Legal Periodicals	*Legal Resource Index* *Current Law Index*
Look for legal periodical literature through this index. Check subject headings such as:	Look for legal periodical literature through these indexes. Check subject headings such as:
Malicious Prosecution	Malicious Prosecution
Damages	False Imprisonment
False Imprisonment	Torts
Master and Servant	Damages
Personal Injuries	Personal Injuries
Settlements	Employers' Liability
Torts	

Example of a legal periodical article you can locate by using these index systems:

> *Damages for Injury to Feelings in Malicious Prosecution and Abuse of Process*, 15 Cleveland Marshall Law Review 15 (1966).

- *ALR, ALR2d, ALR3d, ALR4th, ALR5th, ALR Fed*

    Use the *Index to Annotations* to find annotations relevant to malicious prosecution. In this index, check headings such as:

Malicious Prosecution	Libel and Slander
Malice	Master and Servant
Malicious Use of Process	Federal Tort Claims Act
Torts	Criminal Law
Damages	

Example of an annotation you can locate by using this index:

Malicious Prosecution: Effect of Grand Jury Indictment on Issue of Probable Cause, 28 ALR3d 748 (1969).

▪ *Words and Phrases*

In this multivolume dictionary you will find definitions from court opinions of words and phrases such as:

Malicious Prosecution	Malice
Abuse of Legal Process	Nolle Prosequi
False Imprisonment	Probable Cause in General
Favorable Termination	Probable Cause in Malicious
Initiate	Prosecution
	Terminate; Termination

Initiate or Procure the Initiation of Criminal Proceedings

The first element of **malicious prosecution** is that the wrongdoer initiates or procures the initiation of criminal proceedings.

> **Example:**   Dan calls the police to complain that Linda stole his car. The police then arrest Linda. After an investigation, she is indicted for grand larceny.

Dan has set official action in motion against Linda. To **initiate** means to instigate, urge on, or incite. Dan certainly instigated the arrest and indictment of Linda. Hence he has initiated criminal proceedings. If all the other elements are established, Dan will later become the defendant in a malicious prosecution action brought by Linda.

Without Probable Cause

The legal proceedings must be initiated without **probable cause.** Probable cause is a suspicion based on the appearance of circumstances that are strong enough to allow a reasonable person to believe that a criminal charge against a person is true. If there *is* probable cause, then the tort of malicious prosecution cannot succeed, no matter how much ill will or malice the initiator may have against the accused.

Some of the factors that a court will use to determine whether probable cause exists are outlined in Figure 20.1.

With Malice

Malice means doing something for an improper motive. It does not necessarily require a showing of hatred or ill will. The proper motive for initiating criminal proceedings is to bring an alleged criminal to justice. If this is not the initiator's primary purpose, then he or she is acting with malice. Examples of improper (and hence malicious) purposes are to exert pressure on the accused to pay a debt, to return property, or to vote a certain way in an election. Often the initiator

Figure 20.1 Probable Cause in Malicious Prosecution Suits

Factors Considered by the Court in Determining Whether the Accuser Had Probable Cause to Initiate the Criminal Process against the Accused.

1. Did the accuser honestly believe that the accused committed the crime charged?
2. Did the accuser have first-hand knowledge/observation of what the accused allegedly did?
3. If the accuser used second-hand knowledge/observation, how reliable was the source used? If, for example, an informer gave information to the accuser (which the latter used in initiating the criminal case against the accused), what was the informer's reputation for reliability? Did the accuser check into this before initiating the criminal case?
4. What was the accused's reputation in the community? Notorious? The type of person who would commit this kind of crime? Or an honest, upright citizen?
5. Did the accuser know of the accused's reputation? If not, was there time to find out?
6. Did the accuser first confront the accused before going to the authorities? If not, why not? Impractical? No time? Danger to the accuser? Fear the accused would flee?
7. Was there any time for the accuser to do any further informal or formal investigation before contacting the authorities? If there was time, was it practical to use it?
8. Did the accuser seek the advice of his or her own attorney on whether there was a basis for the accuser to initiate criminal proceedings against the accused? If so, and if the advice was that the accuser should go to the authorities, did the accuser give the attorney all the relevant facts known to the accuser so that the attorney could provide informed advice?
9. Was there any other information that was reasonably available to the accuser that should have been obtained by the accuser before he or she initiated the criminal case against the accused?

---

has more than one motive; if the primary motive is proper, the contemporaneous presence of improper incidental motives will not lead to the conclusion that the proceeding was initiated with malice.

Criminal Proceedings Terminate in Favor of the Accused

The criminal proceedings must be over, and the accused must have won the case. Most states require the victory to be on the merits, rather than be a mere technical or procedural victory. If there is no such victory, the strong likelihood is that the initial prosecution against the accused was made with probable cause rather than with malice.

▪ ASSIGNMENT 20.1 ▪

Elaine arrives home one night to find that her home has been burglarized. She calls the police. When questioned by the police, she says she does not know who did it, but that her uncle Bob recently threatened to harm her. The police conduct an investigation of Bob. He is indicted for burglary. At his trial, Elaine testifies that he once threatened her. The jury is deadlocked, and a mistrial is declared. The District Attorney (D.A.) is unsure whether to reprosecute him. By this time, Elaine is convinced Bob is guilty of the burglary. She urges the D.A. to retry Bob for the burglary. She constantly calls the D.A. Once she carries a sign outside the D.A.'s office urging prosecution. The D.A.'s decision, however, is to drop the charges. After the case is dismissed, Bob sues Elaine for malicious prosecution. What result? (See General Instructions for the Legal Analysis Assignment in Chapter 3.)

▪ WRONGFUL OR UNJUSTIFIED CIVIL PROCEEDINGS

The tort of malicious prosecution covers wrongful criminal litigation. Suppose that **wrongful civil proceedings** are initiated.

> **Example:**   Charles files a complaint against Ted for negligence. Ted is served with process, which orders Ted to file an answer within thirty days.

Charles has initiated civil proceedings against Ted. Many states will allow Ted to assert a tort action against Charles for bringing wrongful civil proceedings. The action may still be called malicious prosecution, although this term is more appropriate when the underlying proceedings are criminal.

Generally, the same elements apply for the causes of action of wrongful civil proceedings and wrongful criminal proceedings. The defendant must maliciously initiate civil proceedings without probable cause, and the proceedings must terminate in favor of the person charged in the civil proceedings. (The latter was the defendant in the civil proceedings case and is now the plaintiff in the wrongful civil proceedings case.) Probable cause here means a reasonable belief that good grounds exist for initiating the civil proceeding. Some courts impose an additional requirement for parties bringing wrongful civil proceedings suits: they must show some special interference with person or property as a result of the wrongful civil proceedings. Evidence of such a special injury or grievance is not required of parties suing because of wrongful criminal proceedings.

▪ ABUSE OF PROCESS

The elements of the tort of **abuse of process** are:

1. Use of civil or criminal proceedings, and
2. Improper or ulterior motive.

Some states also require a showing of injury to person or property beyond mere injury to name or reputation.

Unlike malicious prosecution, abuse of process involves a civil or criminal case that was *properly* initiated. Probable cause may exist, and the proceeding does not have to terminate in favor of the person now bringing the abuse-of-process action. Yet, the civil or criminal proceeding was used for an improper or ulterior motive.

Example: Reggie has probable cause to believe that Fred has stolen Reggie's car. Reggie tells Fred that if Fred pays Reggie $1,000, Reggie will not tell the police. Fred refuses. Reggie goes to the police. Fred is arrested, tried, and convicted of stealing the car. Fred now sues Reggie for abuse of process.

Fred would win. Reggie had an ulterior motive in initiating the criminal case against Fred. Reggie was using the courts for a purpose for which they are not designed. It is improper to use the threat of legal action to extort money.

CASE

Raine v. Drasin
621 S.W.2d 895 (1981)
Supreme Court of Kentucky

Background: Robert Browning sued a hospital and Doctors Drasin and Fadel for medical malpractice. Browning was represented by two attorneys, Raine and Highfield. The doctors won the malpractice case by a voluntary dismissal, which meant that Browning agreed to terminate his suit. Since the dismissal was with prejudice, the same claims could not be brought again on the same facts. The doctors then sued Raine and Highfield for malicious prosecution and abuse of process. The trial court dismissed the abuse of process claim, but found that both attorneys committed malicious prosecution (wrongful civil proceedings). The Court of Appeals affirmed the judgment against Raine, but dismissed all claims against Highfield. The case is now before the Supreme Court of Kentucky on appeal.

Decision on Appeal: There was no abuse of process. Raine committed malicious prosecution; Highfield did not.

Opinion of Court

Justice STEPHENS delivered the opinion of the court . . .

On July 19, 1975, Robert Browning . . . suffered a massive heart attack at his home. He was taken, unconscious, to Sts. Mary and Elizabeth Hospital. Following treatment in the emergency room, he was examined by Dr. James Fitzpatrick. During his initial examination of Browning, Dr. Fitzpatrick discovered an injury to Browning's shoulder. He ordered X-rays taken which revealed that the shoulder was fractured. Dr. Fitzpatrick then called in Dr. Fadel, an orthopedic surgeon, to treat the shoulder. Dr. Drasin, a radiologist, had read the X-ray but never saw or treated Browning.

Following his release from the hospital, Browning contacted attorney Raine regarding a possible suit for the fracture of his shoulder. On September 15, 1975, Raine visited the hospital and reviewed its records which clearly showed that the fracture of the shoulder occurred before Drs. Drasin and Fadel were involved.

On November 21, 1975, a complaint was filed in the Jefferson Circuit Court against the hospital for allegedly breaking Browning's shoulder. Raine prepared the complaint, but because he represented another hospital he did not wish to sign the complaint. At his request attorney James H. Highfield, a long-time associate of Raine's, with space in his office, signed it. He did so without reading it and without investigating any of the facts. In March of 1976, the attorneys served interrogatories on the hospital, the answers to which revealed that . . . both doctors were contacted after Browning's shoulder injury was discovered. On May 24, 1976, the deposition of Dr. Fitzpatrick was taken. It is clearly shown that the deponent told the attorneys that the injury occurred before he saw Browning in the emergency room and moreover that, after he discovered the injury, he then called in Drs. Fadel and Drasin. In spite of this clear and cumulative evidence, on July 15, 1976, Raine filed an amended complaint (signed by Highfield), in which the two doctors were joined as parties defendant, and were charged with malpractice in that they negligently broke Browning's shoulder. Highfield did not read the amended complaint.

[Soon thereafter, however, an order for voluntary dismissal was entered. It dismissed the medical malpractice case against the doctors with prejudice.]

Subsequent to the dismissal, the doctors filed this suit against both attorneys, alleging both malicious prosecution and abuse of process. . . . At the trial, no evidence was introduced by the doctors concerning any out-of-pocket expenses. They did testify as to their embarrassment, humiliation, mortification and mental anguish at having been publicly accused of malpractice. Dr. Fadel testified that he suffered an acute anxiety reaction.

Both doctors stated that the malpractice accusation (even though specious), became a permanent part of their professional and insurance records. The attorneys testified that they had no evidence to implicate the doctors. Raine had access to and was aware of this fact even when he filed the malpractice action. . . .

On this appeal Raine argues that the order of dismissal was not a favorable determination of the action, thus eliminating a key ingredient in a malicious prosecution action . . . [and] that the testimony of an expert concerning violations of an ethical code was improperly admitted in evidence. . . . [T]he doctors argue [on appeal] that the dismissal of the . . . claim against Highfield was improper. . . .

The doctrine of malicious prosecution is an old one in our Commonwealth. Historically, it has not been favored in the law. Public policy requires that all persons be able to freely resort to the courts for redress of a wrong, and the law should and does protect them when they commence a civil or criminal action in good faith and upon reasonable grounds. It is for this reason that one must strictly comply with the prerequisites of maintaining an action for malicious prosecution.

Generally speaking, there are six basic elements necessary to the maintenance of an action for malicious prosecution, in response to both criminal prosecutions and civil action. They are: (1) the institution or continuation of original judicial proceedings, either civil or criminal, or of administrative or disciplinary proceedings, (2) by, or at the instance, of the plaintiff, (3) the termination of such proceedings in defendant's favor, (4) malice in the institution of such proceeding, (5) want or lack of probable cause for the proceeding, and (6) the suffering of damage as a result of the proceeding. With these principles in mind, we will examine the arguments.

Shortly after the malpractice action against the doctors was filed, the order of dismissal was filed. It was, by its terms, an "agreed order of dismissal." The order provided that the amended complaint against the doctors was dismissed, with prejudice. It was signed by the plaintiff, Browning, and by his counsel, Raine and Highfield, and by counsel for the doctors. The document did not entail any compromise or settlement; it simply and effectively terminated the lawsuit as far as the defendant doctors were concerned. The dismissal declared, in effect, that there was no malpractice on the part of the defendants.

The purpose of this prerequisite to a malicious prosecution suit is to show that the action against the defendant was unsuccessful. The basis for the requirement is that courts will not tolerate inconsistent judgments on the same action between the same parties. In Kentucky, no particular form of termination in civil actions has been required. Since the order of dismissal effectively terminates the litigation, with respect to the doctors, . . . the order constituted a favorable termination so as to support this action. . . .

The deposition of Professor David Leibson, a member of the Ethics Committee of the Louisville Bar Association, was apparently read to the jury. Professor Leibson stated that, in his opinion, the actions of both Raine and Highfield did not comply with the standard of care for ordinary and prudent lawyers. Raine complains that the admission was improper. We believe that such evidence was properly introduced to show one of the key ingredients of a malicious prosecution action; viz., lack of probable cause. . . .

The cause of action for abuse of process has been defined as "the technical designation of the irregular or wrongful employment of a judicial proceeding." *Stoll Oil Refining Co. v. Pierce, Ky.,* 337 S.W.2d 263, 266 (1970). The distinction between an action for malicious prosecution and an action for abuse of process is that a malicious prosecution consists in maliciously causing process to be issued, whereas an abuse of process is the employment of legal process for some other purpose other than that which it was intended by the law to effect. Moreover, an action for abuse of process will not lie unless there has been an injury to the person or his property. Injury to name or reputation is not sufficient. The trial court and the Court of Appeals were correct in dismissing that part of the doctors' complaint relating to an alleged abuse of process.

Attorney Highfield, it will be remembered, signed the complaint and amended complaint without reading them. He literally knew nothing about the allegations therein, the parties therein, the factual background or the law. The evidence shows that he was a long-time friend, associate of attorney Raine and has space in Raine's office. Undoubtedly, he signed the documents as a convenience and as a favor to Raine. . . . [S]uch action does not constitute malice. At worst it was a breach of ethics, and at least, it was poor judgment on his part.

The only evidence, relative to probable cause and malice against Highfield, is his signing the amended complaint. He was given a plausible reason why Raine did not want to sign the complaint, and based on years of fellowship and association, he signed it. . . . [T]his is not sufficient evidence, as a matter of law, for a jury to find the necessary malice upon which to base a malicious prosecution action.

[The decision dismissing the claim for abuse of process is affirmed. The decision affirming the malicious prosecution claim against Raine but reversing it against Highfield is affirmed.]

■ ASSIGNMENT 20.2 ■

a. The court does not like malicious prosecution cases. They have "not been favored in the law." Why?

b. Raine did not want to sign the complaint "because he represented another hospital." Why would this make any difference?

c. Do you agree with the dismissal of all claims against attorney Highfield? What message does this send out to attorneys? Suppose that an attorney brings a case solely to pressure the defendant to settle. The attorney refuses to do any research or investigation on the case. Does this make the attorney immune from a malicious prosecution suit later by the defendant?

■ ASSIGNMENT 20.3 ■

Prepare an annotated bibliography on misuse of legal proceedings for your state. (See General Instructions for the Annotated Bibliography Assignment in Chapter 2.)

SUMMARY

Malicious prosecution requires initiating, or procuring the initiation of, criminal proceedings against an accused. There must be no probable cause to initiate the proceedings. This means that a reasonable person would not have suspected that the accused was guilty. Malice is also required, meaning that the primary purpose in initiating the proceedings was improper because the purpose was something other than to bring someone to justice. Finally, the legal proceedings must terminate in favor of the accused, usually on the merits.

Initiating wrongful civil proceedings is a tort in many states. The defendant must maliciously initiate civil proceedings without probable cause, and the proceedings must terminate in favor of the person charged in the civil proceedings. Some courts also require the defendant to show that he or she suffered a special injury or grievance as a result of the wrongdoing civil proceedings.

Abuse of process covers criminal or civil litigation that is properly initiated because probable cause exists, but it is used for an improper motive or purpose. To bring an action for abuse of process, some states require proof of injury to person or property beyond injury to name or reputation. The civil or criminal litigation does not have to terminate in favor of the defendant in the litigation.

Key Terms

malicious prosecution	malice	abuse of process
initiate	wrongful civil	
probable cause	proceedings	

Defamation

CHAPTER OUTLINE

- TWO TORTS
- DEFAMATION CHECKLIST
- DEFAMATORY STATEMENT
  Fact
  Opinion
- EXTRINSIC FACTS
- FALSITY OF THE STATEMENT
- OF AND CONCERNING THE
  PLAINTIFF
- PUBLICATION
- DAMAGES
  Libel
  Slander
- PRIVILEGE
  Absolute Privilege
  Qualified Privilege

■ TWO TORTS

Defamation covers two torts: libel and slander. **Libel** consists of defamation that is written (e.g., a book) or embodied in a physical form (e.g., a photograph, an effigy). **Slander** consists of defamation that is spoken (e.g., a conversation) or gestured as a substitute for speech (e.g., a nod of the head, a wave of the hand).[1] The elements of these two torts are essentially the same, although some differences exist in the element of damages, as we will see later.

Defamation Checklist
Definitions, Relationships, and Research References

Category
At common law, defamation was a strict liability tort except for the element of publication. For some defendants (e.g., media defendants), this has been

---

[1]If the defamation is broadcast on radio or television, it is sometimes referred to as **defamacast.**

changed by constitutional law. For such defendants, defamation is now a tort that requires a showing of fault.

Interest Protected
The right to one's good name and reputation.

Elements
Defamation consists of two torts: libel and slander. The elements of these torts are the same except for the element of damages.

1. A defamatory statement by the defendant
2. Of and concerning the plaintiff
3. Publication
4. Damages
5. Causation

Major Definitions of Words/Phrases in These Elements

Defamatory Statement: A statement of fact that would tend to harm the reputation of the plaintiff in the eyes of at least a substantial and respectable minority of people by lowering the plaintiff in the estimation of those people or by deterring them from associating with the plaintiff.

Of and Concerning the Plaintiff: A statement reasonably understood to refer to the plaintiff.

Publication: A communication of the statement to someone other than the plaintiff.

Damages: Slander:
  a. Special damages are not required if the slander is *slander per se*.
  b. Special damages must be proven if the slander is *slander per quod*.

  Libel:
  a. In some states libel never requires special damages.
  b. In other states only libel on its face does not require special damages. In such states, libel per quod requires special damages.

Causation: But for the defendant's statement, the plaintiff would not have suffered harm to reputation; or, the defendant's statement was a substantial factor in bringing about the harm to the plaintiff's reputation.

Major Defenses and Counter-Argument Possibilities That Need to Be Explored
(Constitutional law has changed a good deal of the common law of defamation as it applies to the media. It is not clear, however, whether the constitutional principles will apply to all defamation defendants or only to media defamation defendants. To date, the Supreme Court has not extended the constitution beyond media defendants, but many expect that it will. In the following list, if the item has been applied only to media defendants, it will so indicate.)

1. The statement did not tend to harm the reputation of the plaintiff in the eyes of at least a respectable and substantial minority of the community.
2. Only the plaintiff thought that the statement harmed his or her reputation, or that it had a tendency to do so.

3. The defendant's statement cannot reasonably be understood in a defamatory sense.
4. The defendant's statement was not in fact understood in a defamatory sense.
5. The defendant merely stated an opinion, which did not expressly or impliedly communicate any statements of fact.
6. The defendant neither intentionally nor negligently communicated a statement that was defamatory (for media defendants only).
7. The defendant's statement could not reasonably be understood to refer to the plaintiff.
8. The group the defendant defamed was too large for the plaintiff (who was part of the group) to be able to reasonably say that the statement was of and concerning the plaintiff.
9. The defendant neither intended to refer to the plaintiff nor was negligent in referring to the plaintiff (for media defendants only).
10. The defendant's statement was not communicated to someone other than the plaintiff.
11. The defendant neither intended to communicate the statement to someone other than the plaintiff nor was negligent in this regard.
12. The defendant's oral defamatory statement is not slander per se and the plaintiff has failed to prove special damages.
13. The defendant's statement is libel per quod and the plaintiff has failed to prove special damages.
14. The plaintiff has failed to prove actual injury (for media defendants only).
15. The harm suffered by the plaintiff was not caused by the defendant's defamatory statement.
16. The defendant's defamatory statement was true.
17. The plaintiff is a public official or a public figure who has failed to prove constitutional malice, i.e., that the defendant knew the statement was false or was reckless as to its truth or falsity (for media defendants only).
18. The plaintiff is a private person who has failed to show whatever degree of fault (constitutional malice or negligence) the state has selected as to the truth or falsity of the statement (for media defendants only).
19. The defendant had an absolute privilege to utter the defamatory statement.
20. The defendant had a qualified privilege to utter the defamatory statement and the privilege was not abused.
21. The plaintiff consented to the publication of the defamatory statement.
22. Sovereign immunity.
23. Public official immunity.
24. Charitable immunity.
25. Intrafamily tort immunity.

Damages

Special damages must be shown if the defamation is not slander per se. In many states, special damages must also be shown if the defamation is libel per quod. Special damages are proven pecuniary losses.

For media defendants, the constitution requires proof of actual injury, which may be tangible (e.g., pecuniary) or intangible.

Relationship to Criminal Law

Certain forms of defamation are crimes in some states if the defamatory statement is intentionally published. Truth is usually not a defense to such crimes.

Relationship to Other Torts

Abuse of Process: While abusing legal process, the defendant may also defame the plaintiff.

Alienation of Affections: While alienating the affections of a spouse, the defendant probably also defamed the aggrieved spouse.

Assault: While assaulting the plaintiff, the defendant may have also defamed the plaintiff.

Battery: While committing a battery, the defendant may have also defamed the plaintiff.

Disparagement: Defamation protects the personal reputation of the plaintiff. Disparagement is an attack against the goods or property of the plaintiff. Both torts may be committed if the defendant's attack against the plaintiff's goods is also an express or implied attack on the reputation of the plaintiff personally.

False Imprisonment: While committing false imprisonment, the defendant may have also defamed the plaintiff.

Intentional Infliction of Emotional Distress: The defendant's defamatory statement may not be actionable as defamation because the statement is true, but may be so outrageous as to constitute the tort of intentional infliction of emotional distress.

Invasion of Privacy: False light invasion of privacy often involves the same facts that constitute defamation.

Malicious Prosecution: Defamation often occurs while the defendant is committing the tort of malicious prosecution.

Federal Law

Under the Federal Tort Claims Act, the federal government is not liable for libel or slander committed by one of its employees.

Employer-Employee (Agency) Law

A private employer is liable for libel or slander committed by one of its employees within the scope of employment when the employee was furthering a business objective of the employer at the time.

Research References for Defamation

· Digests

In the digests of West, look for case summaries on defamation under key topics such as:

Libel and Slander	Damages
Constitutional Law (90)	Torts

· *Corpus Juris Secundum*

In this legal encyclopedia, see the discussions under topic headings such as:

Libel and Slander	Damages
Constitutional Law (585)	Torts

- *American Jurisprudence 2d*

    In this legal encyclopedia, see the discussions under topic headings such as:

Libel and Slander	Constitutional Law
Damages	Torts

- Legal Periodical Literature

    There are three index systems to use to try to locate articles on defamation:

Index to Legal Periodicals (ILP)	*Current Law Index (CLI)*	*Legal Resource Index (LRI)*
See literature in *ILP* under subject headings such as:	See literature in *CLI* under subject headings such as:	See literature in *LRI* under subject headings such as:
Libel and Slander	Libel and Slander	Libel and Slander
Constitutional Law	Liberty of the Press	Liberty of the Press
Freedom of the Press	Constitutional Law	Constitutional Law
Liability without Fault	Strict Liability	Strict Liability
Radio and Television	Torts	Torts
Torts	Damages	Damages
Damages		

    Example of a legal periodical article that you will find by using *ILP, CLI* or *LRI:*

    > *Pornography as Defamation and Discrimination* by Catharine MacKinnon, 71 Boston University Law Review 793 (1991).

- *ALR, ALR2d, ALR3d, ALR4th, ALR5th, ALR Fed*

    Use the *Index to Annotations* to find annotations on defamation. In this index, check subject headings such as:

Libel and Slander	Radio and Television
Freedom of Speech and Press	Damages
Privileges and Immunities	Torts
Newspapers	New York Times Rule

    Example of an annotation on defamation that you can find by using this index:

    > *Libel and Slander: Who is 'Public Figure' in the Light of Gertz v. Robert Welch, Inc.,* 75 ALR3d 616.

- *Words and Phrases*

    In this multivolume legal dictionary look up every word or phrase connected with defamation to try to locate definitions of these words or phrases from court opinions.

As we examine the common-law elements of defamation, we need to keep in mind that the U.S. Supreme Court has significantly changed the law of defamation when the defendant is part of the media. It is difficult to sue media defendants because of their constitutional freedom-of-the-press protections.

▪ DEFAMATORY STATEMENT

Fact

A **defamatory statement** is a statement of fact that would tend to harm the reputation of the plaintiff in the eyes of at least a substantial and respectable minority of people by lowering the plaintiff in the estimation of those people or by deterring them from associating with the plaintiff. More specifically, it is a statement of fact that tends to disgrace a person by holding him or her up to hatred or ridicule, or by causing others to avoid him or her. The people who express this hatred or ridicule must not be extreme or antisocial in their reaction. For example, although it is possible to find people who hate members of a particular race, it is not defamatory for someone to say that you like or support the rights of members of that race, even if a large number of bigots hold you in contempt for this position.

Opinion

In general, a **defamatory opinion** is not actionable. There is a difference between saying, "Helen's conduct was disgraceful" and saying, "Helen stole one hundred dollars." Only the latter is a statement of fact. A major distinction between a fact and an opinion is that it is possible to prove the truth or falsity of a fact, whereas an opinion can often be the subject of endless debate.

Two other reasons the law discourages defamation suits for defamatory opinions are: 1) At common law, opinions on matters of public interest were regarded as **fair comment,** and hence could not be the basis of defamation suits, and 2) The constitutional right of free speech gives us wide latitude in the expression of ideas and opinions. "Under the First Amendment, there is no such thing as a false idea."[2] If, however, an opinion implies the existence of objective facts, a defamation action may still be possible.

▪ ASSIGNMENT 21.1 ▪

Are any of the following statements defamatory? (See General Instructions for the Legal Analysis Assignment in Chapter 3.)

a. Vince calls Nick a "closet Republican." Nick is a registered Democrat.
b. Tom calls Juanita a "Socialist."
c. Ed calls Bill a "tree-hugger."
d. Rich is a member of the union who returns to work during a strike. Hank, another union member, calls Rich a "traitor."

▪ EXTRINSIC FACTS

Statements are not defamatory on their face if you cannot understand the defamatory meaning simply by examining the words or images used. For example, to say that "Mary gave birth to a child today" is not defamatory **on its face** because you need to know the **extrinsic fact** that Mary has been married only a month. When extrinsic facts are needed, they are alleged in the part of the

---

[2]*Gertz v. Robert Welch, Inc.,* 418 U.S. 323, 339, 94 S.Ct. 2997, 3007, 41 L.Ed.2d 789, 805 (1974).

complaint called the **inducement.** The explanation of the defamatory meaning of words alleged by inducement is called the **innuendo.**

■ FALSITY OF THE STATEMENT

At common law, the plaintiff did not have to prove the statement was false. It was assumed to be false. Truth was an **affirmative defense,** which meant that the defendant had to allege and prove it. The U.S. Supreme Court, however, has changed the common law when the defendant is part of the media. In such cases, plaintiffs can fall into three possible categories: public officials, public figures, and private persons. See Figure 21.1

If the plaintiff is a **public official** or a **public figure,** he or she must establish **constitutional malice** (also called **actual malice**), which is proof by clear and convincing evidence that the defendant knew the statement was false or was reckless in regard to its truth or falsity. Public officials are public employees who have significant government authority, e.g., mayors and police officers. Public figures are people who have assumed special prominence in the affairs of society because of power or influence (e.g., celebrities) or because of voluntary involvement in controversy of interest to the general public (e.g., death-penalty activists). It is not enough to prove that the media published a carelessly or negligently false defamatory statement about public officials and figures. The media must know that it is false or be reckless as to its truth or falsity. In effect, the media has a constitutional right to negligently publish defamation about such plaintiffs!

If the plaintiff is not a public official or figure, he or she is a **private person.** If the media defames a private person, a state court can either require the plaintiff to establish the same degree of fault as public officials or figures (knowledge of falsity or recklessness), or impose a less demanding standard, such as proving that the media defendant was negligent in determining the truth or falsity of the defamatory statement. A state cannot impose strict liability for the defamation; some degree of fault is required.

Suppose that the defendant is not part of the media and that the plaintiff is neither a public official nor a public figure. Is there a constitutional requirement that the plaintiff prove fault on the part of the defendant? The law is still evolving on this point. If the subject matter of the defamation involves a matter of public

Figure 21.1 Fault in Defamation Actions against Media Defendants

Status of Plaintiff:	What Plaintiff Must Prove:
Public Official or Public Figure	The defendant knew the statement was false or was reckless in regard to its truth or falsity.
Private Person	The defendant knew the statement was false or was reckless in regard to its truth or falsity, or the defendant was negligent in determining the truth or falsity of the statement.

interest or controversy, the courts will probably require the plaintiff to establish some degree of fault in the defendant.

▪ OF AND CONCERNING THE PLAINTIFF

The defamatory statement must be **of and concerning the plaintiff.** This requires proof by the plaintiff that a recipient of the statement reasonably understood that it referred to the plaintiff. Occasionally, extrinsic facts are needed to make this determination. Suppose the defendant says that "the head guard at Fulton Prison has stolen state funds." On the face of this statement, we cannot identify who was defamed. We need to know who was the head guard at the time the statement was made. The plaintiff can introduce the extrinsic fact that he or she was the head guard at the time, and that, therefore, the statement was reasonably understood to refer to the plaintiff. The part of the complaint in which the plaintiff alleges that the defamatory statement was of and concerning the plaintiff is called the **colloquium.**

Suppose that the defendant defames a group, e.g., "all Italians are thieves" or "Boston doctors are quacks." The groups defamed here are too large; no individual Italian or Boston doctor can say that the statement can be reasonably understood to refer to him or her as an individual. The larger the group, the less reasonable such an understanding would be.

▪ ASSIGNMENT 21.2 ▪

Can defamation actions be brought because of the following statements? If so, by whom? (See General Instructions for the Legal Analysis Assignment in Chapter 3.)

a. "The jury that acquitted John Gotti was bribed."
b. "Cab drivers always cheat."
c. "The Titon University football players take steroids."
d. "The money was stolen by Tom or Fred."

▪ PUBLICATION

There must be a **publication** of the defamatory statement, meaning that the statement must be communicated to someone other than the plaintiff. The defendant must intentionally or negligently allow someone else to read, hear, or see the statement. If Ted telephones Paulette to call her a thief, there is no publication if Paulette is the only person to hear this statement. If, however, Ted sends her a postcard containing this allegation, there may be publication if Ted knows or should know that it is being sent to an address where more than one person picks up the mail and that one of them could read the statement on the card before Paulette does.

▪ DAMAGES

Libel

In most libel cases, the jury is allowed to presume that the plaintiff suffered humiliation or harm to reputation. These are called **presumed damages.** The plaintiff does not have to prove that he or she suffered **special damages,** which are actual economic or pecuniary losses such as medical expenses and lost wages. In some states, however, if the plaintiff is alleging **libel per quod,** special damages must be shown. Libel per quod is a written statement that requires the reader to know extrinsic facts (see earlier section on extrinsic facts) to understand its defamatory meaning or to understand its reference to the plaintiff. Special damages in libel cases are not required in any state if the statement is defamatory on its face.

Slander

Slander per se does not require proof of special damages; slander per quod does.

Slander per se is an oral statement that is defamatory in one of the following four ways: it accuses the plaintiff of a crime (e.g., ''Ed stole a car''); it accuses the plaintiff of having a communicable disease (e.g., ''Ed has venereal disease''); it accuses the plaintiff of sexual misconduct (e.g., ''Ed is an adulterer'') it adversely affects the plaintiff's trade, profession, or office (e.g., ''Ed forged his license to sell liquor''). A slanderous statement that does *not* fall into one of these four categories (e.g., ''Ed is illegitimate'') is called **slander per quod.** The latter requires proof of special damages.

▪ PRIVILEGE

There are a number of situations in which the defendant has, in effect, a **privilege to defame.** Two kinds of privileges are recognized: an *absolute privilege,* which cannot be lost by the defendant's unreasonableness in exercising it or by having an improper purpose or motive in exercising it, and a *qualified privilege,* which can be lost by the defendant's abusing it. (For more on privileges, see Chapter 31.)

Absolute Privilege

Judges, lawyers, parties, and witnesses have an **absolute privilege** to make defamatory statements in judicial proceedings. The same is true of legislators and high executive officers while performing their duties.

Qualified Privilege

A person has a **qualified privilege** to publish defamatory statements in order to protect his or her own legitimate interests.

> **Example:** Tony calls Diane a ''liar'' after Diane says Tony stole her money.

Tony has defamed Diane. If she sues him for defamation, his defense is the qualified privilege of protecting his interest in his own good name. This privilege is lost if Tony goes beyond the scope of protecting his interest by, for instance, calling Diane a prostitute or responding solely out of revenge.

Under certain circumstances, a person also has a qualified privilege to publish defamatory statements in order to protect the interests of others. The person must be under a legal or moral obligation to protect the other and act reasonably in believing that the protection is necessary.

> **Example:** Lena tells her daughter that it would be disastrous for her to marry "a bum and a gigolo like Paul."

CASE

Van Duyn v. Smith
173 Ill.App.3d 523, 123 Ill.Dec. 367, 527 N.E.2d 1005 (1988)
Appellate Court of Illinois, Third District

Background: Margaret Van Duyn directs an abortion clinic. Smith is a pro-life activist who distributed a "Wanted" poster and a "Face The American Holocaust" poster to Van Duyn's friends, neighbors and acquaintances living in the three block area surrounding Van Duyn's residence. She sued Smith for defamation and other causes of action. Her complaint was dismissed by the trial court for failure to state a cause of action. The case is now before the Third District Appellate Court of Illinois.

Decision on Appeal: Defamation was not committed because there was no statement of fact; the posters contained opinions.

Opinion of Court

Justice SCOTT delivered the opinion of the court . . .

Plaintiff claims that the "Wanted" poster . . . resembling those used by the Federal bureau of Investigation and seen on bulletin boards in public places, states: that plaintiff is a wanted person "for prenatal killing in violation of the Hippocratic oath and Geneva Code"; that plaintiff uses the alias "Margaret the Malignant"; that plaintiff has participated in killing for profit and has presided over more than 50,000 killings; and the plaintiff's modus operandi is a small round tube attached to a powerful suction machine that tears the developing child limb from limb. The poster further contains a statement at the bottom which indicates in part, that "(n)othing in this poster should be considered unethical. Once abortion was a crime but it is not now considered a crime."

The "Face The American Holocaust" poster . . . contains pictures of fetuses between 22 and 29 weeks gestational age that have been aborted. Under each picture the "cause of death" of the fetus is listed; referring to the method used to perform the abortion. Among the techniques listed are dismemberment, salt poisoning, and massive hemorrhaging. The poster also contains four paragraphs of information regarding the discovery of some 17,000 fetuses stored in a 3½ ton container in California, the number of abortions performed per day in "America's abortion mills", and how "America's Holocaust is the responsibility of us all." The poster additionally gives the name and address of Pro-Life Action League and lists the defendant's name and telephone number for those who choose to call locally. . . . [Plaintiff alleges] that as a result of defendant's actions, her good name, character and reputation were impaired and brought into disrepute before her friends and acquaintances. . . .

Generally, defamation, which consists of the identically treated branches of libel and slander, is the publication of anything injurious to the good name or reputation of another, or which tends to bring him into disrepute. Illinois courts have held that a statement is defamatory if it impeaches a person's integrity, virtue, human decency, respect for others, or reputation and thereby lowers that person in the estimation of the community or deters third parties from dealing with that person. Each defamation case must be decided on its own facts. . . .

Plaintiff maintains that the "Wanted" poster, when read alone, or in conjunction with the "Face the American Holocaust" poster, contains false statements of fact that are libelous. . . . In particular, plaintiff argues that defendant's use of the word "killing" would cause the average reader to believe that plaintiff has committed a criminal offense. . . .

We acknowledge, however, that the Supreme Court has recognized a constitutional privilege for expressions of opinion. (*Gertz v. Welch,* 418 U.S. 323.) Whether a statement is one of opinion or fact is a matter of law. Moreover, the alleged defamatory language must be considered in context to determine whether or not it is an expression of opinion. . . .

In *Ollman v. Evans,* the court drew upon theories used in prior cases to devise the totality of the circumstances analysis for determining whether a publication is a statement of fact or an expression of opinion. The four part analysis is explained as follows: "First, we will analyze the common usage or meaning of the specific language of the challenged statement itself. Our analysis of the specific language under scrutiny will be aimed at determining whether the statement has a precise core of meaning for which a consensus of understanding exists or, conversely, whether the statement is indefinite and ambiguous. Readers are, in our judgment, considerably less likely to infer facts from an indefinite or ambiguous statement than one with a commonly understood meaning. Second, we will consider the statement's verifiability—is the statement capable of being objectively characterized as true or false? Insofar as a statement lacks a plausible method of verification, a reasonable reader will not believe that the statement has specific factual content. And, in the setting of litigation, the trier of fact obliged in a defamation action to assess the truth of an unverifiable statement will have considerable difficulty returning a verdict based upon

anything but speculation. Third, moving from the challenged language itself, we will consider the full context of the statement—the entire article or column, for example—inasmuch as other, unchallenged language surrounding the allegedly defamatory statement will influence the average reader's readiness to infer that a particular statement has factual content. Finally, we will consider the broader context or setting in which the statement appears. Different types of writing have . . . widely varying social conventions which signal to the reader the likelihood of a statement's being either fact or opinion." (*Ollman v. Evans,* 750 F.2d 970, 979 (D.C.Cir.1984).

We believe defendant's statement that plaintiff is involved in "killing" can be commonly understood as meaning that plaintiff has terminated a life of something or someone that was previously living. In itself the accusation that plaintiff is involved with "killing the unwanted and unprotected" is a potentially damaging fact. Our difficulty, however, is that the type of killing being referred to in this instance is not, in our opinion, objectively capable of being proven or disproven. This is especially true when the allegedly defamatory statements are read in the context in which the statements occur. It becomes apparent when looking at the "Wanted" poster in its entirety that defendant's use of the word "killing" is his description of what takes place during an abortion procedure. We are not prepared to find that the word "killing" in this context is verifiable and, thus, a defamatory statement of fact. Additionally, when the statements are considered within the social context, it becomes quite clear that defendant's use of the word "killing" merely describes his opinion of the results of an abortion procedure. Since the Supreme Court decision of *Roe v. Wade* (1973), 410 U.S. 113, wherein a woman's right to have an abortion was determined to be constitutionally protected, one of the primary issues has been, and still is, whether or not there is an actual killing of a human life as the result of an abortion. Pro-life activists certainly maintain that abortion is a killing, however, pro-choice activists believe the contrary, especially before the fetus has reached viability. Regardless of which position may ultimately be considered correct, at the present we find that the average reasonable reader of the "Wanted" poster would not believe as an actual fact that plaintiff has been involved in killing, as that word is commonly understood by our society. In fact, we believe that the average reader would quickly realize that the central theme of the "Wanted" poster is that abortion is a killing, to which plaintiff plays a part, and should be a crime in the opinion of those siding with the pro-life movement.

Although we consider the "Wanted" poster repulsive, explicit, unnecessary and in bad taste, we adhere to the belief that "(u)nder the First Amendment there is no such thing as a false idea. However pernicious an opinion may seem, we depend for its correction not on the conscience of judges and juries but on the competition of other ideas." (*Gertz v. Welch,* 418 U.S. at 339–40.) As elaboration, we cite *Sloan v. Hatton,* wherein the court stated: "Free speech is not restricted to compliments. Were this not so there could be no verbal give and take, no meaningful exchange of ideas, and we would be forced to confine ourselves to platitudes and compliments. But members of a free society must be able to express candid opinions and make personal judgments. And those opinions and judgments may be harsh or critical—even abusive—yet still not subject the speaker or writer to civil liability." (*Sloan v. Hatton* (1978), 383 N.E.2d 259, 260.)

We consider the above rationale applicable to all the other allegedly defamatory statements with the exception of the allegedly false statement that plaintiff performs abortions on 29 week gestationally old fetuses. This alleged statement requires reading the two posters in conjunction. In this regard we perceive plaintiff's reasoning to be that the two posters were distributed at the same time, therefore, the average reader would look at the pictures of apparently aborted fetuses on the "Face the American Holocaust" poster and infer that plaintiff was involved with abortions involving fetuses as old as 29 weeks gestationally. Without more information, we note that an abortion at 29 weeks may be a crime. (Ill.Rev.Stat.1987, ch. 38, ¶ 81–21 et seq. . . .) [Yet defendant did not state] that plaintiff performs abortions on 29 week gestationally old fetuses. . . . First, there is absolutely no cross-referencing between the two posters which would lead the average reader to infer that the two posters should be read and considered together. Second, the "Face the American Holocaust" poster tells the story of how 17,000 fetuses were found in a 3½ ton container in Los Angeles, California. Nowhere does it state that plaintiff was responsible for any of the fetuses found in the container. . . .

The average reasonable reader would realize that the "Wanted" poster is referring to the practice of abortion and that the basis for defendant's opinion that plaintiff is "killing for profit the unwanted and unprotected" is that plaintiff is somehow involved in the abortion process. Moreover, the average reader of the "Wanted" poster would recognize that it is merely another restatement of the pro-life movement's opinion regarding abortion; an opinion that has been publicized since at least the *Roe v. Wade* decision in 1973. The "Wanted" poster does not imply that plaintiff has been involved in any "killing for profit" outside of her involvement with abortions. The "Face the American Holocaust" poster simply does not refer to plaintiff and cannot be read in conjunction with the "Wanted" poster for reasons previously stated. Accordingly, we affirm the trial court's dismissal. . . .

■ ASSIGNMENT 21.3 ■

Has defamation been committed in the following circumstances?

a. Sam is the mayor. Because he refuses to say in advance that he will never raise taxes, Alice calls him a ``coward and a fraud.'' ``It's highway robbery what you're doing,'' she says to him in a corridor in front of many people.
b. George Harrison is a doctor who performs abortions. Ed carries a poster in front of Harrison's office that reads, ``Dr. Harrison is a murderer who pressures young women to kill their babies.''

■ ASSIGNMENT 21.4 ■

Prepare an annotated bibliography on defamation for your state. (See General Instructions for the Annotated Bibliography Assignment in Chapter 2.)

SUMMARY

There are two defamation torts: libel (written or pictorial defamation) and slander (spoken or gestural defamation). A statement of fact is defamatory if it would tend to harm the reputation of the plaintiff in the eyes of at least a substantial and respectable minority of people by lowering the plaintiff in the estimation of those people or by deterring them from associating with the plaintiff. Defamatory opinions are not actionable unless they imply the existence of objective facts.

At common law, truth was a defense. Recent constitutional law, however, requires public officials or public figures suing a media defendant to prove that the latter knew the defamatory statement was false or was reckless in regard to its truth or falsity. If the plaintiff is a private person, he or she must prove that the media defendant was at least negligent as to the truth or falsity of the statement.

The defamatory statement must be of and concerning the plaintiff. If needed, extrinsic facts must be pleaded and proved to establish the defamatory meaning of the statement and that it was of and concerning the plaintiff. Libel on its face does not require special damages. In some states, libel per quod does. Slander per se does not require special damages; slander per quod does.

Judges, lawyers, parties, and witnesses have an absolute privilege to make defamatory statements in judicial proceedings. The same is true of legislators and high executive officers while performing their duties. Under certain circumstances, defendants have a qualified privilege to defame in order to protect their own legitimate interests or the interests of others.

Key Terms

defamation	innuendo	publication
libel	affirmative defense	presumed damages
slander	public official	special damages
defamacast	public figure	libel per quod
defamatory statement	constitutional malice	slander per se
defamatory opinion	actual malice	slander per quod
fair comment	private person	privilege to defame
on its face	of and concerning the	absolute privilege
extrinsic fact	plaintiff	qualified privilege
inducement	colloquium	

CHAPTER 22

Invasion of Privacy

CHAPTER OUTLINE

- FOUR TORTS
- INVASION OF PRIVACY CHECKLIST
- INTRUSION
- APPROPRIATION

- PUBLIC DISCLOSURE OF PRIVATE FACT
- FALSE LIGHT

■ FOUR TORTS

Invasion of privacy consists of four torts: intrusion, appropriation, public disclosure of private fact, and false light. Each has its own elements. In general, the torts are designed to protect an individual's interest in being left alone that is violated because of an unreasonable form of attention or publicity.

Invasion of Privacy Checklist
Definitions, Relationships, and Research References

Interests Protected by These Torts

Intrusion: The right to be free from unreasonable intrusions into one's private affairs or concerns.

Appropriation: The right to prevent the unauthorized use of one's name, likeness, or personality for someone else's benefit.

Public Disclosure of Private Facts: The right to be free from unreasonable disclosures of private facts about one's life that are not matters of legitimate public concern.

False Light: The right to be free from false statements that unreasonably place one in a false light in the public eye.

Elements of These Torts

1. Intrusion:
   a. An act of intrusion into someone's private affairs or concerns
   b. highly offensive to a reasonable person
2. Appropriation:
   a. the use of the plaintiff's name, likeness, or personality
   b. for the benefit of the defendant
3. Public disclosure of private fact:
   a. publicity
   b. concerning the private life of the plaintiff
   c. highly offensive to a reasonable person
4. False light:
   a. publicity
   b. placing the plaintiff in a false light
   c. highly offensive to a reasonable person

Major Definitions of Words/Phrases in These Elements

Intrusion: Prying, peering, or probing.

Private: Pertaining to facts about an individual's personal life that have no reasonable or logical connection to what the person does in public and that the person does not consent to reveal.

Reasonable Person: An ordinary person who is not unduly sensitive.

Benefit: Deriving of some advantage.

Publicity: Communication to the public at large or to a large group of people.

Major Defense and Counter-Argument Possibilities That Need to Be Explored

1. The plaintiff consented to what the defendant did (for all four torts).
2. There was no prying, peering, or probing (for Intrusion).
3. What the defendant did related to the public activities of the defendant (for Intrusion, Public Disclosure of Private Fact, and False Light).
4. The defendant did not use plaintiff's name, likeness, or personality (for Appropriation).
5. The defendant did not derive benefit from the use of the plaintiff's name, likeness, or personality—or derived only incidental benefit (for Appropriation).
6. The statement about the plaintiff was not communicated to the public at large nor to a large group of people (for Public Disclosure of Private Fact and False Light).
7. The plaintiff was not placed in a false light; no inaccurate impression or statement was made about the plaintiff (for False Light).

8. The defendant had a privilege: in arresting the plaintiff, in protecting the defendant's own property, or in giving testimony at a public proceeding (for Intrusion, Public Disclosure of Private Fact, and False Light).
9. Sovereign immunity.
10. Public official immunity.
11. Charitable immunity.
12. Intrafamily immunity.

Damages

The plaintiff can recover for humiliation or embarrassment caused by the defendant. If the plaintiff suffered mental or physical illness due to the tort committed by the defendant, recovery can also include damages for the illness. If the defendant's conduct constituted more than one of the four torts, there can be only one recovery. If the defendant acted with a malicious motive to harm or injure the plaintiff, punitive damages are possible.

Relationship to Criminal Law

If the defendant committed Intrusion by wiretapping or other electronic devices, the conduct may also violate the criminal law.

Relationship to Other Torts

Defamation: Libel or slander may be committed along with False Light if the statement is also derogatory and harms the plaintiff's reputation.

Intentional Infliction of Emotional Distress: This tort is committed along with any of the four invasion-of-privacy torts if the defendant committed an outrageous act with the intent to cause severe emotional distress.

Malicious Prosecution: One example of Intrusion is to pry into the plaintiff's private affairs through procedural devices such as subpoenas. In such cases, malicious prosecution may also be committed.

Misrepresentation: Misrepresentation may be committed along with False Light when the following elements can be established: a false statement of fact, intent to deceive, intent that the plaintiff rely, justifiable reliance, and actual damages.

Prima Facie Torts: If the plaintiff cannot establish the elements of any of the four invasion-of-privacy torts, the plaintiff should check prima facie tort in those states that recognize it.

Federal Law

Under the Federal Tort Claims Act, the United States Government can be liable for invasion of privacy committed by a federal employee within the course of employment. A defendant may be liable under the Civil Rights Act if invasion of privacy is committed while depriving the plaintiff of federal rights under color of law.

Employer-Employee (Agency) Law

A private employer will be liable for invasion of privacy committed by its employee within the scope of employment. The employee must have been furthering the business objectives of the employer at the time.

Research References for These Torts

- Digests

    In the digests of West, Look for case summaries on these torts under key topics such as:

    Torts   Constitutional Law (274)
    Damages

- *Corpus Juris Secundum*

    In this legal encyclopedia, see the discussions under topic headings such as:

    Constitutional Law (582)   Torts
    Right of Privacy   Damages

- *American Jurisprudence 2d*

    In this legal encyclopedia, see the discussions under topic headings such as:

    Privacy   Damages
    Constitutional Law (503)   Fright, Shock, and Mental Disturbance
    Torts

- Legal Periodical Literature

    There are three index systems to use to locate articles and other legal periodical literature on these torts:

Index to Legal Periodicals (ILP)	*Current Law Index (CLI)*	*Legal Resource Index (LRI)*
See literature in *ILP* under subject headings such as:	See literature in *CLI* under subject headings such as:	See literature in *LRI* under subject headings such as:
Right of Privacy	Privacy, Right of	Privacy, Right of
Eavesdropping	Liberty of the Press	Liberty of the Press
Torts	Torts	Torts
Freedom of the Press	Damages	Damages
Damages		

    Example of a legal periodical article you can find by using *ILP, CLI* or *LRI:*

    > *Invasion of Privacy: New Guidelines for the Public Disclosure Tort,* 6 Capitol University Law Review 95 (1976).

- *ALR, ALR2d, ALR3d, ALR4th, ALR5th, ALR Fed*

    Use the *Index to Annotations* to locate annotations on these torts. In this index, check subject headings such as:

    Privacy   Newspapers
    Harassment   Torts
    Eavesdropping   Damages

    Example of an annotation you can locate through this index on these torts:

    > *Publication of Address as well as Name of Person as Invasion of Privacy,* 84 ALR3d 1159.

• *Words and Phrases*

In this multivolume legal dictionary look up every word or phrase discussed in this chapter on the four torts to try to locate court opinions that have defined these words or phrases.

■ INTRUSION

The elements of the tort of **intrusion** are:

1. an act of intrusion into someone's private affairs or concerns
2. highly offensive to a reasonable person

Intrusion consists of prying, peering, or probing of some kind, e.g., wiretapping, opening mail, filing subpoenas that require disclosure of records, making persistent phone calls. Such methods of intrusion must be directed at something that is considered one's **private affairs.** It is usually not an intrusion to follow the plaintiff in a department store or to photograph him or her in a park. In these settings, the plaintiff is engaging in public activity. There are a number of factors a court will consider in determining whether something is private, none of which is usually conclusive alone. These factors are outlined in Figure 22.1.

Not every intrusion into private matters is tortious. The intrusion must be highly offensive to a **reasonable person.** The test is objective—what the reasonable person considers **highly offensive.** The plaintiff may be greatly offended by a call from a bill collector at the plaintiff's workplace. But a reasonable person would probably not be highly offended by such a call. The case may be different, however, if calls are made every fifteen minutes starting at midnight while the plaintiff is trying to sleep at home.

Figure 22.1   Factors Considered by Courts to Determine Whether Something is Private

• Was the plaintiff in a public place at the time?
• Was the subject of the defendant's attention already a matter of public record?
• Was the activity of the plaintiff observable by normal methods of observation?
• Was the plaintiff doing something that society would consider none of anyone else's business?
• Was the plaintiff drawing attention to him- or herself?
• Was the defendant trying to obtain information about the plaintiff?
• Was the plaintiff caught off guard through no fault of his or her own?
• Did the defendant take advantage of a vulnerable position of the plaintiff?

■ ASSIGNMENT 22.1 ■

Has the tort of intrusion been committed in any of the following situations? (See General Instructions for the Legal Analysis Assignment in Chapter 3.)

a. Tim photographs Karla at an amusement park in the fun house at the moment an air vent on the floor blows up her dress.

b. At a bus terminal, a television monitor is clearly visible in the men's room.
c. General Motors hires a prostitute to solicit Ralph Nader to engage in sexual activities. Ralph refuses.

■ APPROPRIATION

The elements of the tort of **appropriation** are:

1. the use of the plaintiff's name, likeness, or personality
2. for the benefit of the defendant

The first element is present if the plaintiff is specifically identifiable through the use of his or her name, likeness, or personality. To make a statute or mannequin of the plaintiff is not sufficient unless the plaintiff is clearly recognizable.

The defendant must derive benefit from the use. In some states, the benefit must be commercial or pecuniary, e.g., impersonating the plaintiff to obtain credit, or using the plaintiff's name or picture in an ad to give the appearance of an endorsement. But in most states the benefit does not have to be financial. The second element would be met, for example, if the defendant pretended to be a famous photographer as part of his effort to seduce women.

Of course, photographs or films of people, and people's names, are used by the media without permission all the time. This does not constitute the tort of appropriation, even though the media clearly derives economic benefit from its activities. The **First Amendment** freedoms of the press and speech give broad constitutional protection to communications by the media and by artists.

■ ASSIGNMENT 22.2 ■

The plaintiff is a ''human cannonball'' who shoots himself out of a cannon at county fairs. Do either of the following situations constitute appropriation? (See General Instructions for the Legal Analysis Assignment in Chapter 3.)

a. The defendant tapes a video of the stunt and shows it at home to friends and relatives.
b. The defendant is a television station. One of its employees videotapes the stunt and shows it both on the evening news and on its ''Incredible People'' variety show.

■ PUBLIC DISCLOSURE OF PRIVATE FACT

The elements of the tort of **public disclosure of private fact** are:

1. publicity
2. concerning the private life of the plaintiff
3. highly offensive to a reasonable person

For purposes of this tort, ''publicity'' has a different meaning from ''publication'' in the law of defamation. **Publication** is the communication of the defamatory statement to at least one person other than the plaintiff. **Publicity,** however, means communication to the public at large. More than a few people must hear or read the statement.

Review the eight factors mentioned in the section on intrusion that are used to determine whether something is private (see Figure 22.1). Most of these factors are also relevant to determine whether there has been a public disclosure of a private fact.

There is no disclosure of a private fact when publicity is given to something that is already a matter of public record (e.g., a document filed in court, the names of contributors to a political candidate). Some subject matter, however, is clearly private, either by law or by custom. Data provided on income tax returns and census forms, for example, are protected from disclosure by law. Also legally protected are confidential communications between attorney and client, doctor and patient, and minister and penitent. One's sexual inclinations are also private, because in our society such matters are considered no one's business. Of course, if a plaintiff flaunts such information, he or she may be considered to have consented to the disclosure.

If there has been a disclosure of a private fact, it is no defense that the fact is true. Falsity is not one of the elements of this tort.

It is not enough that the plaintiff considers the publicity discomforting or embarrassing. It must be highly offensive to a reasonable person. A reasonable person, for example, would not be highly offended by a story about an individual's having his deceased dog cremated, but would probably be offended by a story about the individual's three unsuccessful operations to cure his impotency. Here are some other disclosures that might be highly offensive to a reasonable person:

- a sign placed in the defendant's window that the plaintiff does not pay his or her debts
- an interoffice memo sent to thirty employees that a fellow employee is lesbian
- a video shown in a barroom of a woman nursing her baby on her backyard porch

If the defendant is part of the media, the constitutional freedoms of the press and speech may bar recovery for this tort if publicity is given to a matter of **legitimate public interest** and hence is **newsworthy.** A great deal of private information about **public figures** falls into this category. A public figure is a celebrity, someone in whom the public has a legitimate interest because of his or her achievements, reputation, or occupation.

▪ ASSIGNMENT 22.3 ▪

Tom is an ex-convict who served time for murder twenty-five years ago. He is now a reformed citizen living an outstanding life in a new community. Bill finds out about Tom's past and lets everyone know at a town meeting. Does Tom have a cause of action against Bill? (See General Instructions for the Legal Analysis Assignment in Chapter 3.)

▪ FALSE LIGHT

The elements of the tort of **false light** are:

1. publicity
2. placing the plaintiff in a false light
3. highly offensive to a reasonable person

False light is similar to defamation in that the statement about the plaintiff must be false. Unlike defamation, however, false light can be established without the statement harming the plaintiff's reputation, although most usually do.

When is a person placed in a false light? Broadly speaking, whenever an impression or conclusion is given about a person that is not accurate.

Examples:

- falsely stating in a report that a doctor has given AIDS to one of his patients during an operation
- falsely claiming that the plaintiff has written a pornographic novel
- signing the name of a pro-choice plaintiff on a pro-life petition without permission.

These cases of false light would be considered highly offensive by a reasonable person. Not all false light, however, falls into this category. Misspelling the plaintiff's name on a notice places him or her in a false light, but this would hardly be deemed highly offensive, even if the plaintiff was very embarrassed by the incident. A reasonable person would not take such offense.

If the defendant is part of the media, constitutional law requires the plaintiff to prove **actual malice.** This means that the defendant either knew the statement placed the plaintiff in a false light or acted in reckless disregard of whether it did so.

▪ ASSIGNMENT 22.4 ▪

At a banquet honoring the retirement of Linda, her boss rises to make a speech. The boss gives some details of Linda's life, including the fact that she was married on June 26, 1968 and gave birth to her first child on July 1, 1968. In fact, the child was born on June 30, 1969. Linda sues her boss for false light. What result? (See General Instructions for the Legal Analysis Assignment in Chapter 3.)

CASE

Peoples Bank and Trust Co. of Mountain Home, Conservator of the Estate of Nellie Mitchell, an Aged Person

v.

Globe International Publishing, Inc. doing business as "Sun"
978 F.2d 1065 (1992)
United States Court of Appeals for the Eighth Circuit

Background: The *Sun,* a supermarket tabloid owned by Globe International, published photographs of Nellie Mitchell to illustrate a story about a 101-year old pregnant woman. Mitchell sued for false light invasion of privacy and won a jury verdict in federal district court. Globe now appeals to the United States Court of Appeals for the Eighth Circuit.

Decision on Appeal: Globe committed false light invasion of privacy. A judgment against Globe does not violate the First Amendment.

Opinion of Court

Judge HEANEY delivered the opinion of the court . . .

Plaintiff Mitchell is a ninety-seven-year-old woman from the city of Mountain Home, in Baxter County, Arkansas. After having operated a newsstand and delivered newspapers in Mountain Home for almost fifty years, Mitchell has become a well-recognized figure in her community and something of a local legend. She was recognized for her long service in 1980 when major newspapers ran human interest stories about her and she appeared for interviews on television talk shows.

Defendant Globe publishes several supermarket tabloids, including the *National Examiner* and the *Sun*. Globe published a fairly accurate account of Mitchell in the November 25, 1980, issue of the *National Examiner*. A photograph of Mitchell, purchased from the Baxter County News, accompanied that story.

The same photograph appeared again on the cover page of the October 2, 1990, edition of the *Sun* with the headline "Pregnancy forces granny to quit work at age 101." Customers at supermarket checkout lines in Baxter County who scanned the cover page of the *Sun* saw only that Nellie Mitchell was featured next to a headline about a "granny" forced to quit work because of pregnancy. Purchasers of the tabloid who turned to the story on page eleven also would have seen a second photograph of Mitchell next to a fictitious story about a woman named "Audrey Wiles," living in Australia, who quit her paper route at the age of 101 because an extramarital affair with a millionaire client on her route had left her pregnant.

Word spread quickly in Mountain Home that Nellie Mitchell, "the paper lady," was featured in the offending edition of the *Sun*. This edition of the *Sun* was a "sell-out" in the northern region of Arkansas where Mitchell lives. . . .

The district court gave the following instruction regarding "false light" invasion of privacy:

> to prevail on this claim, the plaintiff has the burden of proving by clear and convincing evidence the following: one, that the false light in which she was placed by the publicity would be highly offensive to a reasonable person; and two, that the defendant acted with actual malice in publishing the statements at issue in this case. Actual malice means that Globe International intended, or

recklessly failed to anticipate, that readers would construe the publicized matter as conveying actual facts or events concerning Mrs. Mitchell. A finding of actual malice requires a showing of more than mere negligence.

Globe does not dispute that the published story was false; indeed, its principal defense is that the story was "pure fiction." Nor does Globe dispute that the story would be highly offensive to a reasonable person, or that it was in fact highly offensive to Mitchell. The central issue on appeal is the existence of actual malice: whether Globe intended, or recklessly failed to anticipate, that readers would construe the story as conveying actual facts or events concerning Mitchell. Globe contends that, as a matter of law, no reader reasonably could construe the story as conveying actual facts about Mitchell, and that no evidence supports a finding that Globe intended that result.

Globe . . . asserts it is biologically impossible for a woman of either 101 or 95 years of age to become pregnant, and therefore, as a matter of law, no reasonable reader could have believed the story represented true facts about Mitchell. . . .

Every other aspect of the charged story, however—such as the implication of sexual impropriety and that Mitchell was quitting her life-long profession—is subject to reasonable belief. Even the report of the pregnancy—a physical condition, not an opinion, metaphor, fantasy, or surrealism—could be proved either true or false. In the context of this case, therefore, we cannot say as a matter of law that readers could not reasonably have believed that the charged story portrayed actual facts or events concerning Mitchell. . . .

The circumstances of the instant case suggest the story in the *Sun* may well be believed by readers as conveying actual facts about Mitchell despite the apparent absurdity of a pregnant centenarian. Indeed, there is more than sufficient evidence to conclude that Globe intends its readers to believe the *Sun* generally. Although there is less evidence to conclude that Globe intended its readers to believe facts specifically about Mitchell, we conclude there is sufficient evidence to find that it recklessly failed to anticipate that result. . . .

The format and style of the *Sun* suggest it is a factual newspaper. Globe advertises the *Sun* as publishing "the weird, the strange, and the outlandish *news* from around the globe," and nowhere in the publication does it suggest its stories are false or exaggerated. The *Sun* also mingles factual, fictional, and hybrid stories without overtly identifying one from the other. At trial, even its own writers could not tell which stories were true and which were completely fabricated.

In the October 2, 1990, issue submitted as evidence, the *Sun* consistently alerted its readers to advertisements with small-print caveats above the text of those advertisements. The *Sun* even published a disclaimer above certain personal advertisements warning its readers that those notices had not been investigated—implying that other advertisements and the news stories had been investigated. These disclaimers and caveats on advertisements, and the absence of any warning or explanation on the admittedly fictional "news" stories, bolster our conclusion that Globe intends for its 366,000 readers to believe the *Sun* prints factual material. It is the

kind of *calculated* falsehood against which the First Amendment can tolerate sanctions without significant impairment of its function. See *Time, Inc. v. Hill,* 385 U.S. 374 (1967).

Globe was on notice that the photographs of Mitchell it published in its October 2, 1990, issue of the *Sun* were purchased from Baxter County, Arkansas— an area where Globe circulated the *Sun.* Counsel at oral argument conceded that the photographs were identified on the back as having been purchased from the Baxter County Bulletin. The editor who chose the photograph testified that he knew the individual pictured in the photograph was a real person, but that he assumed she was dead. This was the same editor who, ten years before, had worked for the Examiner when it published the essentially truthful story about Mitchell.

Although Globe's failure to investigate and confirm its assumption of Mitchell's death will not alone support a finding of actual malice, the purposeful avoidance of the truth is in a different category. Globe contends it made a simple mistake, and that it was not on notice that Mitchell was alive. The jury, however, had sufficient evidence to determine that Globe purposefully avoided the truth about Mitchell.

[Judgment affirmed. The case is remanded, however, to reconsider the issue of damages.]

■ ASSIGNMENT 22.5 ■

a. Was Nellie Mitchell a public figure? If so, is this relevant to her invasion-of-privacy claim?
b. Was the case correctly decided? Some may think that tabloids deserve to be sued, but is it accurate to say that readers could interpret the photos and story as conveying actual facts or events concerning Mrs. Mitchell?
c. What other torts do you think Globe may have committed?

▪ ASSIGNMENT 22.6 ▪

Prepare an annotated bibliography on the four invasion of privacy torts for your state. (See General Instructions for the Annotated Bibliography Assignment in Chapter 2.)

SUMMARY

There are four invasion-of-privacy torts that protect an individual's interest in being left alone: intrusion, appropriation, public disclosure of private fact, and false light.

Intrusion is prying, peering, or probing into the plaintiff's private affairs or concerns when it is considered highly offensive to a reasonable person. Appropriation is the use of the plaintiff's name, likeness, or personality for the benefit of the defendant. In most states, this benefit does not have to be pecuniary. Public disclosure of private fact is a communication of a statement to the public at large (publicity) concerning the private life of the plaintiff when such publicity is considered highly offensive to a reasonable person. False light is publicity that inaccurately portrays the plaintiff when such publicity is considered highly offensive to a reasonable person.

Media defendants in an action for appropriation or for public disclosure of private fact often have the defense that the information was a matter of legitimate public interest, which the media has a constitutional right to make public. In an action for false light against a media defendant, the plaintiff must prove that the defendant knew the statement placed the plaintiff in a false light or acted in reckless disregard of whether it did so.

Key Terms

intrusion	public disclosure of	newsworthy
private affairs	private fact	public figures
reasonable person	publication	false light
highly offensive	publicity	actual malice
appropriation	legitimate public	
First Amendment	interest	

CHAPTER

23

Battery

CHAPTER OUTLINE

- INTRODUCTION
- BATTERY CHECKLIST
- ACT
- PERSON
    Consciousness
- INTENT
    Transferred Intent
    Motive
- HARMFUL OR OFFENSIVE
    CONTACT
- CONSENT AND PRIVILEGE

■ INTRODUCTION

A **battery** is a harmful or offensive contact with a person that results from the defendant's intent to cause this contact or the intent to cause apprehension of an imminent contact. The easiest case is when the defendant punches the plaintiff in the nose. Many make the mistake in such a case of saying that the defendant "assaulted" the plaintiff. As we will see later, however, assault is a separate tort that does not require actual contact with the plaintiff.

Battery Checklist
Definitions, Relationships, and Research References

Category
Battery is an intentional tort.

Interest Protected by This Tort
The right to be free from a harmful or offensive bodily contact.

Elements

1. Act
2. Intent to cause a harmful or offensive contact
3. Harmful or offensive contact with the plaintiff's person
4. Causation of the harmful or offensive contact

Major Definitions of Words/Phrases in the Elements

Act: A voluntary movement of the defendant's body.

Intent: Either
    a. the desire to bring about the consequences of the act (i.e., the desire to cause the contact or to cause an apprehension of an imminent contact), or
    b. the substantially certain knowledge that the consequences (i.e., the contact) will follow from the act.

Harmful: Involving physical damage, impairment, pain, or illness to the body.

Offensive: Offending the personal dignity of an ordinary person who is not unduly sensitive.

Person: One's body, something attached to the body, or something so closely associated with the body as to be identified with it.

Causation: Either
    a. but for the defendant's act, the consequences would not have occurred (i.e., the contact would not have occurred), or
    b. the defendant's act was a substantial factor in bringing about the consequences (i.e., the contact).

Major Defense and Counter-Argument Possibilities That Need to be Explored

1. There was no voluntary movement of the defendant's body (no act).
2. The defendant had no desire to make contact with the plaintiff, nor any substantially certain knowledge that such contact would result from what the defendant did (no intent).
3. The defendant had no desire to cause an apprehension of an imminent contact.
4. The contact was neither harmful nor offensive.
5. But for what the defendant did, the contact would have resulted anyway. The defendant was not a substantial factor in producing the contact. (No causation.)
6. The plaintiff consented to the contact.
7. Privilege of self-defense.
8. Privilege to defend others.
9. Privilege to defend property.
10. Privilege to recapture chattels.
11. Privilege of discipline.
12. Privilege of arrest.
13. Sovereign immunity.
14. Official immunity.
15. Charitable immunity.
16. Intrafamily immunity.

Damages

The plaintiff can recover damages for the contact, including pain and suffering, medical bills, and loss of wages. If the defendant acted out of hatred or malice, punitive damages can be recovered as well.

Relationship to Criminal Law

The same act of the defendant may constitute a civil battery (for which damages can be recovered) and a criminal battery (for which a fine or imprisonment may be imposed). The crime may be called aggravated assault, assault with intent to kill, assault and battery, etc.

Relationship to Other Torts

Assault: If the defendant intended a battery, but merely put the plaintiff in apprehension of a battery, the tort of assault may have been committed.

False Imprisonment: While committing the tort of false imprisonment, battery may also have been committed if contact was made with the plaintiff's person just before or during the confinement.

Negligence: There may have been a harmful or offensive contact that was not intentional, hence no battery. If the contact was due to unreasonable conduct by the defendant, negligence should be explored.

Wrongful Death: A wrongful-death action can be brought by the survivors of the plaintiff if a death results from the battery.

Federal Law

Under the Federal Tort Claims Act, the United States Government will not be liable for a battery committed by one of its federal employees unless the federal employee is an investigative or law enforcement officer. There may be liability under the Civil Rights Act if the battery was committed while the defendant was depriving the plaintiff of federal rights under color of law.

Employer-Employee (Agency) Law

A private employer will be liable for a battery committed by its employee within the scope of employment. The employee must be furthering a business objective of the employer at the time. Intentional torts such as battery are often outside the scope of employment. If so, only the employee is liable for the battery.

Research References for Battery

• Digests

In the digests of West, look for case summaries on battery under key topics such as:

Assault and Battery	Damages
Torts	Death

• *Corpus Juris Secundum*

In this legal encyclopedia, see the discussion under topic headings such as:

Assault and Battery	Damages
Torts	Death

• *American Jurisprudence 2d*

In this legal encyclopedia, see the discussion under topic headings such as:

Assault and Battery	Damages
Torts	Death

• Legal Periodical Literature

There are three index systems to use to try to locate legal periodical literature on battery:

Index to Legal Periodicals (ILP)	*Current Law Index (CLI)*	*Legal Resource Index (LRI)*
See literature in *ILP* under subject headings such as:	See literature in *CLI* under subject headings such as:	See literature in *LRI* under subject headings such as:
Assault and Battery	Assault and Battery	Assault and Battery
Damages	Torts	Torts
Federal Tort Claims Act	Damages	Damages
Personal Injuries	Personal Injuries	Personal Injuries
Torts		
Wrongful Death		

Example of a legal periodical article you will find by using *ILP, CLI,* or *LRI:*

D. Ezra, *Smoker Battery: An Antidote to Second-Hand Smoke,* 63 Southern California Law Review 1061 (1991).

• *ALR, ALR2d, ALR3d, ALR4th, ALR5th, ALR Fed*

Use the *Index to Annotations* to locate annotations on battery. In this index, check subject headings such as:

Assault and Battery
Damages
Torts

Example of an annotation on battery you can locate through this index:

Civil Liability of Insane or Other Disordered Person for Assault or Battery, 77 ALR2d 625 (1961).

• *Words and Phrases*

In this multivolume legal dictionary, look up every word of phrase connected with battery to try to locate summaries of court opinions that have defined these words or phrases.

■ ACT

There must be an **act** by the defendant that leads to contact with the plaintiff's person. An act is a voluntary movement of the body. Not all harmful or offensive contacts are the result of acts. For example, if Dan's arm hits Linda during a violent sneeze, no battery exists because there is no act—no voluntary movement of Dan's body that caused the contact.

▪ PERSON

The definition of **person** is broad. It means one's body, anything attached to one's body, or anything so closely associated with one's body as to be identified with it. A kick in the shin is clearly a contact with the body. So is a yank on a tie or other item of clothing worn by the plaintiff. The following cases also illustrate the broader definition of person:

- the defendant knocks off the plaintiff's hat
- the defendant pulls a plate out of the plaintiff's hand
- the defendant stabs or shoots a horse while the plaintiff is riding it

The hat, plate, and horse are so closely associated with the body in these cases as to be practically identified with it at the time of the contact. There does not have to be contact with the physical body.

Consciousness

The tort of battery is designed to protect the personal integrity of one's body against intentional invasions, which can occur even if one does not know it at the time.

Example: Jim kisses Lena while she is asleep or under anesthesia.

Lena has been battered by Jim.

▪ INTENT

For purposes of battery, **intent** is the desire to bring about harmful or offensive contact or to bring about apprehension of that contact. In most cases, intent is not difficult to prove, because it is clear that the defendant wants to make contact with the plaintiff, e.g., the defendant picks up a bucket of water and pours it on the plaintiff's head. It is more difficult to prove intent when the defendant does not want contact to occur, but merely wants the plaintiff to think it will occur.

Example: Mary throws a hammer at George. She aims it several feet above George's head, hoping to scare him. Unfortunately, it hits him in the eye.

Mary can accurately say that she did not intend to hit George, but this is not a defense. She wanted him to think he was about to be hit. She intended to cause an **apprehension** (i.e., an understanding or awareness) of an **imminent contact.** This is sufficient to establish the element of intent.

Suppose that there is no desire to cause a contact or even an apprehension of one.

Example: Fred throws a stone through an open window of a crowded moving bus. His purpose is to have it pass through another open window at the other side of the bus without anyone noticing. One of the passengers, however, is hit by the stone.

Did Fred intend to hit the passenger? In general, intent is the desire to bring about the consequences of an act or the **substantially certain knowledge** that the consequences will follow from the act. If Fred had substantially certain knowledge that a passenger would be hit (or would have an apprehension of being hit), then he intended that result. Being careless or even reckless is not enough to establish intent. There must be substantially certain knowledge. If all you can show is carelessness or recklessness, the tort to bring is negligence in creating an unreasonable risk of injuring someone, not the intentional tort of battery.

Transferred Intent

It is no defense to argue that the person hit is not the one the defendant intended to hit.

> **Example:**   Helen fires a gun at Paul. She misses him, but strikes Rich, whom she did not see.

Helen has battered Rich. Under the rule of **transferred intent,** her intent to hit Paul is transferred to Rich. (For more on transferred intent, see Figure 24.1 in chapter 24.)

Motive

Motive is irrelevant. If the defendant intends a harmful or offensive contact, a battery has been committed, even if the defendant was trying to help the plaintiff through the contact.

> **Example:**   A doctor injects medicine into a patient after being asked not to do so.

The doctor has battered the patient. The fact that the motive may have been to help the patient is no defense. As long as the content is harmful or offensive (see discussion below), the tort has been committed.

■ HARMFUL OR OFFENSIVE CONTACT

Contact is **harmful** if it brings about physical damage, impairment, pain, or illness. It is **offensive** if it offends the personal dignity of an ordinary person who is not unduly sensitive.

Any physical damage, impairment, pain, or illness—no matter how trivial or slight—is considered harmful. The jury award that the plaintiff can recover for modest harm is usually nominal, but even technical violations will give rise to a cause of action for battery. It makes no difference if the pain or impairment is in fact beneficial for the plaintiff.

> **Example:**   A nurse puts a tourniquet on the arm of the plaintiff, who has refused medical treatment.

The nurse had battered the plaintiff. The fact that the contact benefited the plaintiff is not a defense.

If there is no harmful contact, the plaintiff may still be able to recover if the contact is offensive. An **objective standard** is used to determine when contact is offensive. The test is whether a reasonable person—someone not unduly sensitive—would be offended by the contact. If not, there is no battery, even though the plaintiff considered the contact offensive.

Example: In a noisy, crowded subway, Jim approaches Cecile, a stranger. He gently taps her on the shoulder and says, "Would you please tell me the time?" Cecile is absolutely outraged by this contact, and screams.

A reasonable person would not consider this contact offensive, even though Cecile clearly does. In city life, a reasonable person expects a certain amount of contact as part of everyday living.

There is an exception to this rule when the defendant knows that the plaintiff has peculiar—even unreasonable—sensibilities about being touched. In such a case, the court will find the contact to be offensive, even though someone of ordinary sensibilities would not be offended by it. The test of offensiveness is no longer objective when the defendant has such knowledge.

Example: Same situation involving Jim and Cecile, except that she is not a stranger, and Jim knows that she would be angered by the tap.

Here the contact is offensive. Jim's knowledge of her idiosyncrasy makes it so. (Depending on the severity of the circumstances, she may even have an action for the separate tort of intentional infliction of emotional distress. See Chapter 18.)

■ CONSENT AND PRIVILEGE

Consent is a complete defense. There is no liability for battery if the plaintiff permitted the contact.

> **Example:**   The plaintiff offers her arm to a doctor who is inoculating everyone in line.

The plaintiff cannot later say that the doctor battered her. She consents to the contact if certain conditions are met, e.g., she has the capacity to consent, she voluntarily does so, and she knows what she is consenting to. For a discussion of consent, see Chapter 31.

Similarly, if the plaintiff has a **privilege** to cause a contact with the plaintiff, the latter cannot win a suit for battery. The privileges include self-defense, the defense of others, the defense of property, discipline, and arrest. The elements of these privileges are discussed in Chapters 19 and 31.

■ ASSIGNMENT 23.1 ■

a. Bill is behind the steering wheel of his parked car. He sees Helen take a baseball bat and swing it at the windshield directly in front of him. The windshield cracks but does not shatter. Has a battery been committed? Why or why not? What other torts, if any, might have been committed?

b. Ed throws a snowball at Dan's house, knowing that Dan is inside. The moment Dan hears the snowball, he is afraid that he will be hit. Battery?

c. Dan makes a batch of cookies with poison in them. He leaves them in a hall next to a telephone booth. A stranger eats one after making a call. Has Dan battered the stranger? If not, has another tort been committed?

d. Diane and Bob are walking across the street. Bob is daydreaming and doesn't see a car about to hit him. Diane pushes him away from the path of the car into safety. But he falls and breaks his ankle from the push. Bob sues Diane for battery. What result?

(See General Instructions for the Legal Analysis Assignment in Chapter 3.)

■ ASSIGNMENT 23.2 ■

In the case discussed in the text, in which Fred threw a stone through the window of a moving bus, do you think that intent can be established? What further facts would you like to have? (See General Instructions for the Investigation Strategy Assignment in Chapter 4.)

CASE

Funeral Services by Gregory, Inc.,
v.
Bluefield Community Hospital
186 W.Va. 424, 413 S.E.2d 79 (1991)
Supreme Court of Appeals of West Virginia

Background: "John Doe" died of AIDS in the Bluefield Hospital. His body was embalmed by Keith Gregory who runs Gregory Funeral Services. At the time of the embalming, Gregory did not know that Doe died of AIDS. When he found out, he (and his wife) sued the Hospital for battery, claiming that the silence of the hospital had caused an "offensive contact" with an infected body. He lost in the lower courts. The case is now on appeal before the Supreme Court of Appeals of West Virginia.

Decision on Appeal: Judgment for the Hospital. No battery was committed.

Opinion of Court

Justice BROTHERTON delivered the opinion of the Court:

In this case, we are asked to determine whether a mortician who embalmed a corpse, unaware that it was infected with Acquired Immune Deficiency Syndrome, was subjected to a battery. . . . Keith Gregory is a mortician who embalmed the body of "John Doe," a man who died at Bluefield Community Hospital on June 5, 1986. According to the hospital, when John Doe was admitted on May 25, 1986, the only medical history he reported was having had pneumonia in the past week and using antibiotics. He denied ever having any major medical problems. . . .

The facts contained in the record now before this Court reveal that after John Doe died on June 5, 1986, the hospital released the body . . . for embalming and funeral services. Michael Nowlin and Daniel Gregory, the plaintiff's brother, picked up the body at the hospital morgue. Hospital personnel told the men to wear protective gloves, masks, aprons, hats, and booties. Although they found these precautions a bit unusual, both men maintain that they were not told that John Doe was an AIDS-infected corpse, and that neither the toe tag,* the body nor the death certificate mentioned AIDS as a possible cause of death. Nowlin and Daniel Gregory stated that the body was bloody because it has been subjected to a full autopsy, so they wrapped it in garbage bags to prevent it from soiling their cot and blanket any more than necessary. They subsequently delivered the body and the death certificate to the preparation room of the Gregory Funeral Home in Williamson, West Virginia.
. . .

Keith Gregory . . . states that he was not unduly concerned when he began the embalming procedure on John Doe, because the death certificate did not list AIDS as a cause of death and the toe tag on the body did not indicate that an infectious disease was involved. However, after working on the body for about ninety minutes, Gregory took a break, at which time his brother Daniel related his perception that hospital personnel were acting strange in making him and Nowlin wear so much protective gear before removing the body. Gregory was suspicious, but because he did not want to stop in the middle of embalming the body, he went back to the preparation room and put on additional protective

_____

*The plaintiffs allege that the hospital used a plain tag instead of the red infectious body tag which it normally uses and which Keith Gregory relied upon for notification.

clothing.** Upon completing the embalming procedure, he washed his arms with Clorox bleach and took his clothes off and later burned them. He immediately showered and then washed his hands and fingernails with Clorox. . . .

[O]n the morning of John Doe's funeral on June 11, 1986, the hospital called Keith Gregory and informed him that John Doe had probably died from AIDS. Gregory states that if he had known from the beginning that John Doe was infected with the AIDS virus, he would have suggested that the family arrange a burial within twenty-four hours, cremation, or a closed casket funeral service. These procedures would not require embalming the body. If the family had insisted upon embalming, Gregory would have taken steps to minimize his exposure, such as wearing additional protective clothing, asking another mortician to assist in the procedure in order to reduce preparation time, or sending the body to an embalming service.

Gregory and his wife allege that as a result of the [hospital's] tortious conduct, they now live with the fear that one or both of them will someday be diagnosed as having AIDS. The Gregorys state that they "have suffered severe emotional distress and humiliation, and their marriage has all but fallen apart." . . .

Noting that this Court has held that damages for emotional distress may be recovered in a battery action, *Criss v. Criss,* 177 W.Va. 749, 356 S.E.2d 620 (1987), [Gregory] argues first that the lower court erred when it held that exposing someone to intimate physical contact with the bodily fluids and tissues of an AIDS-infected corpse, without his knowledge or consent, did not constitute an "offensive touching" sufficient to support a claim of battery. How-

ever, we agree that the [actions of the hospital] cannot be construed as a battery. . . .

The Restatement (Second) of Torts, § 13(a) and (b) (1965), states that: "[a]n actor is subject to liability to another for battery if (a) he acts *intending* to cause a harmful or offensive contact with the person of the other or a third person, or an imminent apprehension of such a contact, and (b) a harmful contact with the person of the other directly or indirectly results." (Emphasis added.) The word "intent" in the Restatement denotes that "the actor desires to cause the consequences of his act, or that he believes that the consequences are substantially certain to result from it." Id. at § 8A.

In this case, the hospital simply released the body to the plaintiff's funeral home for preparation. The plaintiff alleges that this act resulted in an "offensive touching" which constituted a battery, because he was subsequently "exposed to body fluids and mucus membranes of the deceased 'John Doe' which were infected with the AIDS virus thereby being exposed by the extreme and outrageous conduct of the defendants intentionally or recklessly to the AIDS virus. . . ." However, the plaintiff does not allege that the hospital acted with the intention of causing him a harmful or offensive contact, nor is there any evidence which might support such a charge. Whether the hospital negligently caused Gregory to come into contact with the body of John Doe is a separate inquiry.

We also note that the plaintiff did not allege that he suffered actual physical impairment as a result of what he refers to as an "exposure" to the AIDS virus.† All of the plaintiffs' claims are based solely on a fear of contracting the AIDS virus. However, Gregory has been tested for AIDS antibodies on four occasions with negative

---

**When he began the embalming procedure, Gregory states that he was wearing a surgical scrub suit, athletic socks, deck shoes, and latex surgical gloves. He later added a mask, rubber sleeves, shoe covers, and an additional apron.

---

†"Bodily harm" is defined as "any physical impairment of the condition of another's body, or physical pain or illness." Restatement (Second) of Torts § 15.

results. Thus, there is no evidence that Gregory has been infected with the Human Immunodeficiency Virus (HIV), a retrovirus that causes AIDS. "It is extremely unlikely that a patient who tests HIV-negative more than six months after a potential exposure will contract the disease as a result of that exposure." *Burk v. Sage Products, Inc.,* 747 F.Supp. 285, 287 (E.D.Pa. 1990), citing Morbidity and Mortality Weekly Report, July 21, 1989, Vol. 38, No. S-7 at 5.

Although the plaintiff undoubtedly came into contact with bodily fluids during the embalming procedure, there is no evidence indicating that he was actually exposed to a disease-causing agent. It is a well-established medical fact that the AIDS virus is transmitted through the exchange of bodily fluids, primarily blood or semen. The plaintiff admits that he was wearing proper protective gear, and he merely hypothesizes as to how a potential exposure to the virus may have occurred without offering any substantiating evidence.‡ For example, the plaintiff did not recall sticking himself or puncturing his gloves during the embalming procedure. . . .

For the reasons set forth above, the orders of the [lower courts in dismissing the] claims are hereby affirmed.

---

‡William Robinson, M.D., an expert retained by the Gregorys, stated in an affidavit that "to a reasonable degree of medical certainty" Gregory "was exposed to the AIDS virus as a result of the aerosolizing of the fluids of the corpse during the embalming process." When plaintiff's counsel raised this point with this Court during oral arguments, he was asked exactly how this may have resulted in an exposure, since Gregory had no open wounds or sores and was, in fact, wearing protective clothing. Counsel stated that Gregory had chapped lips, presumably implying that infected aerosols or droplets could have come into contact with chapped lips.

▪ ASSIGNMENT 23.3 ▪

a. Why did the court say that there was no intent in this case? Do you agree with the court?

b. Tom and Linda are drug addicts. Tom knows he has AIDS, but Linda does not know this. They have sexual relations and share each other's drug needles. Has either of them committed a battery?

▪ ASSIGNMENT 23.4 ▪

Prepare an annotated bibliography on civil battery for your state. (See General Instructions for the Annotated Bibliography Assignment in Chapter 2.)

SUMMARY

Battery is a harmful or offensive contact with a person that results from the defendant's intent to cause either contact or apprehension of imminent contact. There must be a voluntary movement of the defendant's body—an act. There must be actual contact with the person of the plaintiff. The plaintiff's person can include the plaintiff's body, anything attached to it, or anything so closely associated with the body as to be identified with it. The plaintiff does not have to be aware of the contact. The intent must be either the desire to bring about the contact or an imminent apprehension of the contact.

The law presumes the defendant had the requisite intent if he or she knew with substantial certainty that the contact or apprehension would result from his or her act. If the defendant intended to make contact with one person but in fact hit another, the law will transfer the intent to cover the latter. The defendant's motive is not relevant, even if it was to help (and even if the defendant does in fact help) the plaintiff through the contact.

The contact is harmful if it brings about physical damage, impairment, pain, or illness. It is offensive if it offends the personal dignity of an ordinary person who is not unduly sensitive. This objective test of offensiveness is used unless the defendant has reason to know that the plaintiff has an overly sensitive reaction to contact.

Consent and privilege are defenses to the cause of action of battery.

Key Terms

battery	imminent contact	harmful
act	substantially certain	offensive
person	knowledge	objective standard
intent	transferred intent	consent
apprehension	motive	privilege

CHAPTER 24

Assault

CHAPTER OUTLINE

- INTRODUCTION
- ASSAULT CHECKLIST
- ACT
- APPREHENSION

- HARMFUL OR OFFENSIVE
  - Reasonable
  - Imminent
- TRANSFERRED INTENT

■ INTRODUCTION

Assault is an act that intentionally causes an apprehension of a harmful or offensive contact. Phrased another way, it means intentionally causing an awareness of a battery. The average citizen thinks of assault as an unwanted, and usually violent, contact with someone. But the tort of assault does not require actual contact. If someone hits you with a stick, you have been battered. If you were aware of the stick coming at you, you have also been assaulted. The contact and the apprehension of the contact constitute separate torts. In criminal law, assault often means a violent contact; in the law of torts, it is the apprehension of a harmful or offensive contact.

> **Assault Checklist**
> **Definitions, Relationships, and Research References**

Category
   Assault is an intentional tort.

Interest Protected by This Tort
   The right to be free from the apprehension of a harmful or offensive contact.

Elements of This Tort

1. Act
2. Intent either:
   a. to cause a harmful or offensive contact, or
   b. to cause an apprehension of a harmful or offensive contact
3. Apprehension of an imminent harmful or offensive contact to the plaintiff's own person.
4. Causation of the apprehension.

Major Definitions of Words/Phrases in the Elements

Act: A voluntary movement of the defendant's body.

Intent: Either:
   a. the desire to bring about the consequence of the act (i.e., the desire to cause the apprehension), or
   b. the substantially certain knowledge that the consequence (i.e., the apprehension) will follow from the act.

Apprehension: Anticipation, knowledge, or belief (fear is *not* required).

Imminent: Immediate in the sense of no significant delay (something can be imminent without being instantaneous).

Harmful: Involving physical impairment, pain, or illness.

Offensive: Offending the personal dignity of an ordinary person who is not unduly sensitive.

Causation: Either:
   a. but for the defendant's act, the consequence would not have occurred (i.e., the apprehension would not have occurred), or
   b. the defendant's act was a substantial factor in bringing about the consequence (i.e., the apprehension).

Major Defense and Counter-Argument Possibilities That Need to Be Explored

1. Defendant's conduct was involuntary (no act).
2. Defendant did not desire a contact or apprehension, or know with substantial certainty that the apprehension would result from what he or she did (no intent).
3. There was no apprehension.
4. The apprehension was for a future contact (no imminence).
5. The apprehension would have occurred even if the defendant did not do what he or she did. The defendant was not a substantial factor in producing the apprehension. (No causation.)
6. The plaintiff consented to the conduct of the defendant that led to the apprehension.
7. The defendant acted in self-defense.
8. The defendant acted in defense of others.
9. Privilege of necessity.
10. Privilege of the defense of property.
11. Privilege to recapture property.
12. Privilege of arrest.
13. Sovereign immunity.
14. Official immunity.

15. Charitable immunity.
16. Intrafamily immunity.

Damages

The defendant is liable for the injuries, if any, resulting from the assault, in addition to any mental suffering or fear experienced. Punitive damages are also a possibility, as with all intentional torts.

Relationship to Criminal Law

The same act of the defendant may be both a civil assault and a criminal assault. The word "assault" in criminal law is often used interchangeably with the word "battery."

Relationship to Other Torts

Battery: The defendant may intend to batter the plaintiff, but fail to do so. If, in the process, the plaintiff is aware of the attempted battery, the tort of assault is probably committed.

False Imprisonment: If the plaintiff is aware of the defendant's attempt to confine the plaintiff, there may be an apprehension of contact, and hence an assault as well as false imprisonment.

Intentional Infliction of Emotional Distress: Assaults frequently accompany this tort.

Negligence: If the defendant does not intentionally cause apprehension in the plaintiff, the defendant may be negligent in causing it. For the negligence action to succeed, there must be actual harm in addition to the apprehension.

Wrongful Death: A wrongful-death action can be brought by the survivors of the plaintiff if death results from the assault.

Federal Law

Under the Federal Tort Claims Act, the United States will not be liable for an assault committed by one of its federal employees unless the federal employee is an investigative or law enforcement officer. There may be liability under the Civil Rights Act if the assault was committed while the defendant was depriving the plaintiff of federal rights under color of law.

Employer-Employee (Agency) Law

A private employer will be liable for an assault committed by its employee within the scope of employment. The employee must be furthering a business objective of the employer at the time. Intentional torts such as assault are often outside the scope of employment. If so, only the employee is liable for the tort.

Research References for Assault

▪ Digests

In the digests of West, look for case summaries on assault under key topics such as:

Assault and Battery   Damages
Torts

▪ *Corpus Juris Secundum*

In this legal encyclopedia, see the discussions under topic headings such as:

Assault and Battery   Damages
Torts

▪ *American Jurisprudence 2d*

In this legal encyclopedia, see the discussions under the topic heading such as:

Assault and Battery   Damages
Torts

▪ Legal Periodical Literature

There are three index systems to use to try to locate legal periodical literature on assault:

Index to Legal Periodicals (ILP)	*Current Law Index (CLI)*	*Legal Resource Index (LRI)*
See literature in *ILP* under subject headings such as:	See literature in *CLI* under subject headings such as:	See literature in *LRI* under subject headings such as:
Assault and Battery	Assault and Battery	Assault and Battery
Damages	Torts	Torts
Federal Tort Claims Act	Damages	Damages
Personal Injuries	Personal Injuries	Personal Injuries
Torts		
Wrongful Death		

Example of a legal periodical article you will find by using *ILP, CLI, or LRI*:

Respondeat Superior and the Intentional Tort: A Short Discourse on How to Make Assault and Battery a Part of the Job, 45 University of Cincinnati Law Review 235 (1976).

▪ *ALR, ALR2d, ALR3d, ALR4th, ALR5th, ALR Fed*

Use the *Index to Annotations* to locate annotations on assault. In this index, check subject headings such as:

Assault and Battery   Damages
Torts

Example of an annotation on assault you can locate through this index:

Federal Tort Claims Act Provision Exempting from Coverage Claim Arising out of Assault, Battery, False Imprisonment, False Arrest, Malicious Prosecution, etc. 23 ALR2d 574.

▪ *Words and Phrases*

In this multivolume legal dictionary, look up every word or phrase discussed in this chapter connected with assault to try to locate court opinions that have defined these words or phrases.

▪ ACT

The apprehension of a harmful or offensive contact must be caused by an **act,** which is a voluntary movement of the body.

> **Example:**   A stranger pushes Jim, who then falls toward Ed. When Ed sees Jim coming, he quickly gets out of the way.

Ed, concerned about being hit by Jim, clearly had an apprehension of a harmful or offensive contact. But Jim did not commit an act that caused this apprehension. Because of the stranger's push, Jim involuntarily moved toward Ed.

▪ APPREHENSION

Apprehension is an understanding, awareness, anticipation, belief, or knowledge of something. It is not the equivalent of fear, although fear certainly qualifies as apprehension.

> **Examples:**
>
> - Greg (a 300-pound wrestler) swings his fist at Martha (a seventy-year-old, petite widow) because she called him a ''bum'' at a match. Terrified, Martha ducks just in time to avoid his punch.
> - Later, Martha raises her newspaper to strike Greg in the stomach. Laughing, Greg steps back to avoid Martha's swing.

Greg and Martha have assaulted each other. Both had an awareness—an apprehension—of a harmful or offensive contact. Martha was afraid; Greg wasn't. But fear or intimidation is not required.

Greg laughed. Doesn't this mean he didn't think Martha was going to do something harmful or offensive? It depends on the meaning of harmful and offensive.

▪ HARMFUL OR OFFENSIVE

As we saw in Chapter 23 on battery, **harmful** means bringing about physical damage, impairment, pain, or illness; and **offensive** means offending the dignity of an ordinary person who is not unduly sensitive. A smack on the stomach with a newspaper could cause pain, no matter how slight. Also, it is hardly a friendly gesture. Furthermore, most people would take offense at being hit under these circumstances. Greg may have thought it was all a big joke. Yet note that he stepped back to avoid the newspaper. To him, the idea of a fight with an old lady may have been ludicrous, but he clearly didn't appreciate being hit. Most people wouldn't. He was not *afraid* of a harmful or offensive contact, but he surely had an *apprehension* of one, however minor it might have been.

Reasonable

The plaintiff must be **reasonable** in claiming that he or she experienced an apprehension of the contact. The plaintiff may actually feel that a harmful or offensive contact is coming, but if this concern is exaggerated, there is no tort of assault. There may, however, be an exception if the defendant knows that the plaintiff is subject to unreasonable reactions but proceeds to cause the apprehension anyway.

Imminent

The apprehension must be of an **imminent** harmful or offensive contact. A future or **conditional threat** is not enough.

> **Example:**   On Monday, Ted calls Don on the phone and says, "If you don't pay your debt to me by this Friday, I'll be by Saturday to kill you." When Don hangs up the phone, he breaks out in a sweat because he knows Ted can be very violent.

There is no doubt that Don apprehends a very dangerous harmful and offensive contact. Yet it is not an imminent contact. It is scheduled to happen in the future (Saturday), and is conditional (on not paying the debt by Friday). Imminent means immediate, without significant delay. Verbal threats alone are often not sufficient when they explicitly relate to future conduct. Furthermore, the defendant must have the **apparent present ability** to carry out the threat. If the defendant points a toy gun at the plaintiff and threatens to shoot, there is no imminent apprehension if the plaintiff knows that the gun is a toy that is incapable of firing anything.

▪ TRANSFERRED INTENT

Assume that the defendant intends to assault one person, but in fact assaults the plaintiff, whom the defendant never knew existed. In spite of this mistake, the plaintiff has been assaulted by the defendant. This result is due to the doctrine of **transferred intent** which covers specified unintended plaintiffs and unintended torts. See Figure 24.1.

Figure 24.1   Doctrine of Transferred Intent: What to Do about an Unintended Plaintiff and/or an Unintended Tort?

Unintended Plaintiff	Unintended Tort

a. Defendant (D) intends to commit one of the following five torts against P_1:
    Assault
    Battery
    False Imprisonment
    Trespass to Land
    Trespass to Chattel
b. In fact, this tort is committed against P_2.
c. D did not intend to commit this tort against P_2.
 	
Result: The law will transfer D's intent from P_1 to P_2 in order to make D liable for this tort to P_2.
	a. Defendant (D) intends to commit acts that would constitute one of the following five torts:
	    Assault
	    Battery
	    False Imprisonment
	    Trespass to Land
	    Trespass to Chattel
	b. In fact, D commits one of the other four torts.
	c. D did not intend to commit the tort that occurred.
	
	Result: The law will transfer D's intent from the tort D intended to commit to the tort that in fact resulted in order to make D liable for the latter tort.

Figure 24.1 Continued

Unintended Plaintiff	Unintended Tort
Examples: • D wants to lock Mary in a room. D mistakes Fran for Mary and falsely imprisons Fran. Fran can sue D for false imprisonment. • D throws a rock, intending to hit Paul's car. The rock misses Paul's car and hits Bill's van. Bill can sue D for trespass to chattels. In the above two examples, it is irrelevant that D did not intend to commit any tort against Fran or Bill. They are unintended plaintiffs to whom D is liable under the doctrine of transferred intent.	**Example:** • D wants to lock Joe in a room. D does not succeed. By mistake, however, D causes Joe to be in apprehension of being hit. Joe can sue D for assault In the above example, it is irrelevant that D did not intend to commit assault against Joe. An unintended tort has been committed for which D is liable under the doctrine of transferred intent.

▪ ASSIGNMENT 24.1 ▪

Recall this example: A stranger pushes Jim, who then falls toward Ed. When Ed sees Jim coming toward him, he quickly gets out of the way. As we said in the text, Jim did not commit an assault against Ed. What torts, if any, has the stranger committed?

CASE

Allen v. Walker
569 So.2d 350 (1990)
Supreme Court of Alabama

Background: Kathryn Allen and Richard Walker both work for Gulf States Paper Company. Following an argument, she sued him for assault. The lower court granted Walker a summary judgment. The case is now on appeal before the Supreme Court of Alabama.

Decision on Appeal: Judgment for Kathryn Allen. There is sufficient evidence to support an action for assault.

Opinion of Court

Justice ALMON delivered the opinion of the court. . . .

Kathryn and Walker were employed at Gulf States' plant in Demopolis and were members of the same union. During a conversation concerning the proper method of filing a grievance against Gulf States with the union, Walker allegedly shook his finger at Kathryn's face. Kathryn told Walker that the last man who pointed his finger at her "was sorry that he did it." Walker then allegedly stated that he would "whip [Kathryn's] ass anytime, anywhere." The conversation then ended and Kathryn returned to work. The next day she and

Walker had a second confrontation, during which Walker allegedly repeated his earlier threat. Following that second incident Kathryn became "agitated and upset" and reported Walker's threats to her supervisor.

"An assault consists of '. . . an intentional, unlawful, offer to touch the person of another in a rude or angry manner under such circumstances as to create in the mind of the party alleging the assault a well-founded fear of an imminent battery, coupled with the apparent present ability to effectuate the attempt, if not prevented.' *Western Union Telegraph Co. v. Hill,* 25 Ala.App. 540, 542, 150 So. 709, 710 (1933)." *Holcombe v. Whitaker,* 294 Ala. 430, 435, 318 So.2d 289, 294 (1975). Words standing alone cannot constitute an assault. However, they may give meaning to an act, and when both are taken together they may create a well-founded fear of a battery in the mind of the person at whom they are directed, thereby constituting an assault.

Kathryn argues that Walker's alleged threats, when combined with the fact that he shook his finger in her face during their first conversation, created a question for the jury on the issue of assault. . . .

[W]e cannot say that, as a matter of law, Walker's acts and threats could not create a reasonable or well-founded apprehension of imminent physical harm. There was evidence that, after Walker's first alleged threat, Allen walked away. That evidence is not conclusive, however, as to whether she discounted the threat or whether she left to avoid the threatened harm. She also testified that, after the second alleged assault the next day, she had to leave work because she was so frightened and upset. . . .

[W]e conclude that Kathryn presented sufficient evidence that Walker's alleged threats created a well-founded fear of imminent harm and created a jury question on her claim of assault. Therefore, the summary judgment on that claim will be reversed. . . .

■ ASSIGNMENT 24.2 ■

a. If someone says he can or will harm you "anytime, anywhere," isn't this a threat to do something to you in the future *if* you keep bothering him? Isn't that what Walker meant? Why did the court say otherwise?

b. Kathryn told Walker that the last man who pointed his finger at her "was sorry that he did it." If she pointed her finger at Walker when she said this, would he have an assault case against her?

SUMMARY

An assault is an act (usually attempted battery) that causes apprehension of a harmful or offensive contact. There is no requirement that the plaintiff fear—he or she need only be aware of—a coming harmful or offensive contact. "Harmful" means bringing about physical damage, impairment, pain, or illness; "offensive" means offending the dignity of an ordinary person who is not unduly sensitive.

The plaintiff must be reasonable in claiming that he or she experienced the apprehension. Furthermore, the apprehension must be of an imminent (not a future) harmful or offensive contact.

If the defendant intends to assault one person but accidently assaults another, or intends to commit one tort but accidently commits another, the doctrine of transferred intent makes the defendant liable for the tort committed.

Key Terms

assault	offensive	conditional threat
act	reasonable	apparent present ability
apprehension	imminent	transferred intent
harmful		

CHAPTER 25

Misrepresenta-tion

CHAPTER OUTLINE

- INTRODUCTION
- MISREPRESENTATION CHECKLIST
- STATEMENT OF FACT THAT IS FALSE
- SCIENTER
- NEGLIGENT MISREPRESENTATION
- JUSTIFIABLE RELIANCE

▪ INTRODUCTION

The tort of **misrepresentation** (sometimes called **deceit**) covers primarily economic or **pecuniary loss** caused by false statements of fact. If someone suffers **physical loss** such as injury to the body or destruction of property, other torts are often available, e.g., negligence or conversion.

Misrepresentation Checklist
Definitions, Relationships, and Research References

Category
Misrepresentation is an intentional tort. (In some states, however, negligence is also a basis for liability—negligent misrepresentation—in this area.)

Interest Protected by This Tort
The right to be free from pecuniary or economic loss resulting from false statements.

Elements of This Tort

1. **a.** Statement of fact
   b. Some statements of opinion (e.g., when a fiduciary relationship exists between the parties)
2. Statement is false
3. Scienter (intent to mislead)
4. Justifiable reliance
5. Actual damages

Major Definitions of Words/Phrases in These Elements

Statement of Fact: An express or implied communication covering the existence of tangible things, the happening of events, or a state of mind.

Opinion: A communication expressing the belief of the defendant as to the existence of a fact, or, the defendant's judgment as to quality or value of something.

Intent to Mislead (Scienter): The defendant knows his or her statement is false, or knows or believes that the statement is not accurate as stated or implied, or acts in reckless disregard for its truth or falsity, and wants the audience of the statement to believe it and rely on it.

Causation in Fact: The plaintiff would not have acted or refrained from acting if the defendant had not made the statement, or the defendant's statement was a substantial factor in the action or inaction of the plaintiff.

Justifiable Reliance: A reasonable person in the plaintiff's position would have relied on the defendant's statement.

Major Defense and Counter-Argument Possibilities That Need to Be Explored

1. The defendant made no statement of past or present fact.
2. The defendant concealed no past or present fact.
3. The defendant had no duty to disclose the fact.
4. No fiduciary or other relationship of trust and confidence existed between the parties (concerning statements of opinion).
5. The statement was not false, incomplete, ambiguous, or misleading.
6. The defendant did not have a state of mind that differed from what he or she expressed.
7. The defendant did not know or believe the statement was false or inaccurate.
8. The defendant did not act in reckless disregard of the truth or falsity of his or her statement.
9. The defendant did not intend the plaintiff to rely on the defendant's statement, and had no reason to expect that the plaintiff would rely on it.
10. The plaintiff did not in fact rely on the defendant's statement.
11. The defendant's statement was not a substantial factor in the plaintiff's action or inaction.
12. The plaintiff's reliance was not justifiable.
13. The defendant did not take advantage of idiosyncrasies of the plaintiff.

14. A cursory investigation by the plaintiff would have revealed the truth or falsity of the defendant's statement.
15. The plaintiff suffered no actual damages.
16. Sovereign immunity.
17. Public official immunity.
18. Charitable immunity.

Damages

Actual damages must be proved. Some courts use the out-of-pocket measure of damages, while other courts allow a benefit-of-the-bargain measure of damages. Traditionally, misrepresentation covered only pecuniary or economic damages. Many courts now also allow recovery for injury to person or property caused by the false statement.

Relationship to Criminal Law

In all states embezzlement is a crime. In many states there is a crime called false pretenses. False statements of fact are often made by the defendant in the commission of both crimes.

Relationship to Other Torts

Battery: One way to commit battery is to induce the plaintiff to give consent to a touching by falsely stating facts (e.g., defendant falsely claims to be a doctor and examines the plaintiff).

Conversion: One way to commit this tort is to take possession of the plaintiff's property by falsely stating the authority to do so.

Defamation: Defendant can defame the character of the plaintiff by making false statements about the plaintiff.

False Imprisonment: One way to commit this tort is to confine the plaintiff by falsely stating the authority to do so.

Intentional Infliction of Emotional Distress: One way to commit this tort is to tell a particularly vicious lie to an unsuspecting plaintiff.

Negligence: The tort of negligence can be committed when the defendant causes injury to plaintiff's person or property by falsely and carelessly stating facts (e.g., falsely and carelessly telling the plaintiff that the milk is safe to drink).

Trespass to Land: One way to commit this tort is to get someone to go onto the plaintiff's land by making false statements about who owns the land.

Federal Law

Under the Federal Tort Claims Act, the United States is *not* liable for a claim arising out of deceit or misrepresentation.

Employer-Employee (Agency) Law

An employer will be liable for misrepresentation committed by an employee when the acts of the latter occurred within the scope of employment in furtherance of the business objectives of the employer.

Research References for Misrepresentation

• Digests

In the digests of West look for case summaries on this tort under the following key topics:

Fraud	Torts
Vendor and Purchaser	Damages
Negligence	

• *Corpus Juris Secundum*

In this legal encyclopedia, see the discussion under topic headings such as:

Fraud	Torts
Vendor and Purchaser	Damages
Negligence	

• *American Jurisprudence 2d*

In this legal encyclopedia, see the discussion under topic headings such as:

Fraud and Deceit	Sales
Fraudulent Conveyances	Damages
Vendor and Purchaser	Torts
Negligence	

• Legal Periodical Literature

There are three index systems to use to locate legal periodical articles on this tort:

Index to Legal Periodicals (ILP)	*Current Law Index (CLI)*	*Legal Resource Index (LRI)*
See Literature in *ILP* under subject headings such as:	See literature in *CLI* under subject headings such as:	See literature in *LRI* under subject headings such as:
Fraud	Fraud	Fraud
Damages	Fraudulent	Fraudulent
Fraudulent	Conveyance	Conveyance
Conveyance	Debtor and Creditor	Debtor and Creditor
Negligence	Negligence	Negligence
Torts	Torts	Torts
Debtor and	Damages	Damages
Creditor		

Example of a legal periodical article you can find by using *ILP, CLI,* or *LRI:*

J. Mann, *Misrepresentation of Sterility or of Use of Birth Control*, 26 Journal of Family Law 623 (1987–88).

• *ALR, ALR2d, ALR3d, ALR4th, ALR5th, ALR Fed*

Use the *Index to Annotations* to locate annotations on this tort. In this index, check subject headings such as:

Fraud and Deceit	Negligence
Fraudulent Conveyance	Torts
Vendor and Purchaser	Damages
Debtors and Creditors	

Example of an annotation you can find through this index:

Consumer Class Action Based on Fraud or Misrepresentations, 53 ALR3d 534.

▪ *Words and Phrases*

In this multivolume legal dictionary look up every word or phrase mentioned in this chapter connected with deceit and misrepresentation to try to find court opinions that have defined those words or phrases.

▪ STATEMENT OF FACT THAT IS FALSE

Words are not always necessary to communicate a **fact.** For example, someone who turns back the odometer is making a factual statement about the number of miles the vehicle has traveled to date. Also, the active **concealment** of a fact can sometimes lead to liability for misrepresentation. For example, the defendant paints over cracks in an engine in order to conceal its defects from a potential buyer.

Liability can also be based on silence if an obligation exists to disclose certain facts. When there is a **confidential or fiduciary relationship** between the parties (e.g., two business partners, doctor and patient, bank and depositor, husband and wife, principal and agent), **nondisclosure** of facts can lead to liability for misrepresentation.

Generally, a statement of **opinion** between two strangers cannot be the basis of liability, e.g., a used car salesman tells a customer that a particular car is an "excellent value." Reliance on obviously exaggerated statements—often called **puffing**—is not considered justifiable. Unless facts are clearly communicated or implied in the opinion, there is no misrepresentation. On the other hand, if a confidential or fiduciary relationship exists between the parties, reliance on an opinion may be actionable.

▪ SCIENTER

Scienter is the intent to mislead. This means that the defendant knows the statement is false, or does not believe in its truth, or acts in **reckless disregard** for its truth or falsity. Scienter also includes an intent that the audience of the statement believe it and act in reliance on its truth. The audience consists of those individuals the defendant intends to reach with the statement. Some states go further and extend liability to those individuals the defendant has reason to expect will learn about and act on the statement, even though the defendant never actually intended to reach them.

▪ NEGLIGENT MISREPRESENTATION

Suppose the defendant's misrepresentation does not encompass scienter because there was no knowledge of the statement's falsity, no lack of belief in its truth, or no reckless disregard for truth or falsity. The defendant may simply have been careless in making the false statement, such as by not taking reasonable steps to check the accuracy of the statement before making it. If this leads to physical harm (e.g., plaintiff is injured because the car brakes failed after defendant carelessly told the plaintiff that the brakes were safe), a traditional negligence suit can be brought. If, however, only pecuniary harm results (e.g., the plaintiff loses $10,000 because of a careless statement by the defendant on the value of a painting), the plaintiff can sue for **negligent misrepresentation** as long as he or she was one of the individuals the defendant intended to reach by the careless statement. In many states, individuals within a relatively small group can also sue if the defendant knows that at least someone in a group will learn about the statement and rely on it, even if the defendant does not know which specific individual will do so.

▪ JUSTIFIABLE RELIANCE

To recover, the plaintiff must rely on the statement of the defendant, and it must be a **justifiable reliance.** If the plaintiff is foolish in believing and acting on the defendant's statement, recovery for misrepresentation may be denied unless the defendant knew about and took advantage of the plaintiff's intellectual vulnerabilities. The fact on which the plaintiff relies must be **material,** meaning that it was important to the transaction. In selling the plaintiff a car, for example, it is not material that the defendant falsely tells the plaintiff that the defendant likes bananas, if all the statements about the car itself are accurate. If, however, the defendant knows that the plaintiff attaches significance to a peculiar fact and intentionally misleads him or her as to that fact, recovery may be allowed.

▪ ASSIGNMENT 25.1 ▪

Diane has just been hired as a telemarketer for a museum. She calls Harry, a stranger, to solicit a contribution. She tells Harry that the museum has important works of art in it and therefore deserves the support of the community. In fact, none of the works of art is valued over $500. During the conversation, Diane learns that Harry is a Catholic. She tells Harry that she too is a Catholic. In fact, she has always been a practicing Lutheran. She is married to a Catholic and attends Catholic church services once or twice a year. Harry tells his wife about the museum. His wife decides to donate $10,000. When she finds out that the museum has a very weak collection and that Diane is not a Catholic, she sues Diane for misrepresentation. What result? (See General Instructions for the Legal Analysis Assignment in Chapter 3.)

CASE

Vokes v. Arthur Murray, Inc.
212 So.2d 906 (1968)
District Court of Appeal of Florida, Second District

Background: After spending over $31,000 for 2302 hours of dancing lessons, Audry Vokes sued the dancing school for misrepresentation. The trial dismissed the complaint for failure to state a cause of action. The case is now before the Florida District Court of Appeal.

Decision on Appeal: The dismissal is reversed. Audry Vokes has alleged enough to state a cause of action.

Opinion of Court

Judge PIERCE delivered the opinion of the court . . .

Defendant Arthur Murray, Inc., a corporation, authorizes the operation throughout the nation of dancing schools under the name of "Arthur Murray School of Dancing" through local franchised operators, one of whom was defendant J. P. Davenport whose dancing establishment was in Clearwater.

Plaintiff Mrs. Audry E. Vokes, a widow of 51 years and without family, had a yen to be "an accomplished dancer" with the hopes of finding "new interest in life". So, on February 10, 1961, a dubious fate, with the assist of a motivated acquaintance, procured her to attend a "dance party" at Davenport's "School of Dancing" where she whiled away the pleasant hours, sometimes in a private room, absorbing his accomplished sales technique, during which her grace and poise were elaborated upon and her rosy future as "an excellent dancer" was painted for her in vivid and glowing colors. As an incident to this interlude, he sold her eight ½-hour dance lessons to be utilized within one calendar month therefrom, for the sum of $14.50 cash in hand paid, obviously a baited "comeon".

Thus she embarked upon an almost endless pursuit of the terpsichorean art during which, over a period of less than sixteen months, she was sold fourteen "dance courses" totalling in the aggregate 2302 hours of dancing lessons for a total cash outlay of $31,090.45, all at Davenport's dance emporium. All of these fourteen courses were evidenced by execution of a written "Enrollment Agreement—Arthur Murray's School of Dancing" with the addendum in heavy black print, "No one will be informed that you are taking dancing lessons. Your relations with us are held in strict confidence", setting forth the number of "dancing lessons" and the "lessons in rhythm sessions" currently sold to her from time to time, and always of course accompanied by payment of cash of the realm.

These dance lesson contracts and the monetary consideration therefor of over $31,000 were procured from her by means and methods of Davenport and his associates which went beyond the unsavory, yet legally permissible, perimeter of "sales puffing" and intruded well into the forbidden area of undue influence, the suggestion of falsehood, the suppression of truth, and the free exercise of rational judgment, if what plaintiff alleged in her complaint was true. From the time of her first contact with the dancing school in February, 1961, she was influenced unwittingly by a constant and continuous barrage of flattery, false praise, excessive compliments, and panegyric encomiums, to such extent that it would be not only inequitable, but unconscionable, for a Court exercising inherent chancery power to allow such contracts to stand.

She was incessantly subjected to overreaching blandishment and cajolery. She was assured she had "grace and poise"; that she was "rapidly improving and developing in her dancing skill"; that the additional lessons would "make her a beautiful dancer, capable of dancing with the most accomplished dancers"; that she was "rapidly progressing in the development of her dancing skill and gracefulness", etc., etc. She was given "dance aptitude tests" for the ostensible purpose of "determining" the number of remaining hours instructions needed by her from time to time.

At one point she was sold 545 additional hours of dancing lessons to be entitled to award of the "Bronze Medal" signifying that she had reached "the Bronze Standard", a supposed designation of dance achievement by students of Arthur Murray, Inc. Later she was sold an additional 926 hours in order to gain the "Silver Medal", indicating she had reached "the Silver Standard", at a cost of $12,501.35. At one point, while she still had to her credit about 900 unused hours of instructions, she was induced to purchase an additional 24 hours of lessons to participate in a trip to Miami at her own expense, where she would be "given the opportunity to dance with members of the Miami Studio". She was induced at another point to purchase an additional 123 hours of lessons in order to be not only eligible for the Miami trip but also to become "a life member of the Arthur Murray Studio", carrying with it certain dubious emoluments, at a further cost of $1,752.30. At another point, while she still had over 1,000 unused hours of instruction she was induced to buy 151 additional hours at a cost of $2,049.00 to be eligible for a "Student Trip to Trinidad", at her own expense as she later learned. Also, when she still had 1100 unused hours to her credit, she was prevailed upon to purchase an additional 347 hours at a cost of $4,235.74, to qualify her to receive a "Gold Medal" for achievement, indicating she had advanced to "the Gold Standard". On another occasion, while she still had over 1200 unused hours, she was induced to buy an additional 175 hours of instruction at a cost of $2,472.75 to be eligible "to take a trip to Mexico". Finally, sandwiched in between other lesser sales promotions, she was influenced to buy an additional 481 hours of instruction at a cost of $6,523.81 in order to "be classified as a Gold Bar member, the ultimate achievement of the dancing studio".

All the foregoing sales promotions, illustrative of the entire fourteen separate contracts, were procured by defendant Davenport and Arthur Murray, Inc., by false representations to her that she was improving in her dancing ability, that she had excellent potential, that they were developing her into a beautiful dancer, whereas in truth and in fact she did not develop in her dancing ability, she had no "dance aptitude", and in fact had difficulty in "hearing that musical beat". The complaint alleged that such representations to her "were in fact false and known by the defendant to be false and contrary to the plaintiff's true ability, the truth of plaintiff's ability being fully known to the defendants, but withheld from the plaintiff for the sole and specific intent to deceive and defraud the plaintiff and to induce her in the purchasing of additional hours of dance lessons". It was averred that the lessons were sold to her "in total disregard to the true physical, rhythm, and mental ability of the plaintiff". In other words, while she first exulted that she was entering the "spring of her life", she finally was awakened to the fact there was "spring" neither in her life nor in her feet.

The complaint prayed that the Court decree the dance contracts to be null and void and to be cancelled, that an accounting be had, and judgment entered against, the defendants "for that portion of the $31,090.45 not charged against specific hours of instruction given to the plaintiff". The Court held the complaint not to state a cause of action and dismissed it with prejudice. We disagree and reverse.

The material allegations of the complaint must, of course, be accepted as true for the purpose of testing its legal sufficiency. Defendants contend that contracts can only be rescinded for fraud or misrepresentation when the alleged misrepresentation is as to a material fact, rather than an opinion, prediction or expectation, and that the statements and representations set forth at length in the complaint were in the category of "trade puffing", within its legal orbit.

It is true that "generally a misrepresentation, to be actionable, must be one of fact rather than of opinion". *Tonkovich v. South Florida Citrus Industries, Inc.*, Fla.App.1966, 185 So.2d 710. But this rule has significant qualifications, applicable here. It does not apply where there is a fiduciary relationship between the parties, or where there has been some artifice or trick employed by the representor, or where the parties do not in general deal at "arm's length" as we understand the phrase, or where the representee does not have equal opportunity to become apprised of the truth or falsity of the fact represented. As stated by Judge Allen of this Court in *Ramel v. Chasebrook Construction Company*, Fla.App.1961, 135 So.2d 876: "A statement of a party having . . . superior knowledge may be regarded as a statement of fact although it would be considered as opinion if the parties were dealing on equal terms."

It could be reasonably supposed here that defendants had "superior knowledge" as to whether plaintiff had "dance potential" and as to whether she was noticeably improving in the art of terpsichore. And it would be a reasonable inference from the undenied averments of the complaint that the flowery eulogiums heaped upon her by defendants as a prelude to her contracting for 1944 additional hours of instruction in order to attain the rank of the Bronze Standard, thence to the bracket of the Silver Standard, thence to the class of the Gold Bar Standard, and finally to the crowning plateau of a Life Member of the Studio, proceeded as much or more from the urge to "ring the cash register" as from any honest or realistic appraisal of her dancing prowess or a factual representation of her progress.

Even in contractual situations where a party to a transaction owes no duty to disclose facts within his knowledge or to answer inquiries respecting such facts, the law is if he undertakes to do so he must disclose the *whole truth*. From the face of the complaint, it should have been reasonably apparent to defendants that her vast outlay of cash for the many hundreds of additional hours of instruction was not justified by her slow and awkward progress, which she would have been made well aware of it they had spoken the "whole truth".

In *Hirschman v. Hodges, etc.,* 1910, 59 Fla. 517, 51 So. 550, it was said that— "what is plainly injurious to good faith ought to be considered as a fraud sufficient to impeach a contract", and that an improvident agreement may be avoided— "because of surprise, or mistake, *want of freedom, undue influence, the suggestion of falsehood, or the suppression of truth*". (Emphasis supplied.)

We repeat that where parties are dealing on a contractual basis at arm's length with no inequities or inherently unfair practices employed, the Courts will in general "leave the parties where they find themselves". But in the case sub judice, from the allegations of the unanswered complaint, we cannot say that enough of the accompanying ingredients, as mentioned in the foregoing authorities, were not present which otherwise would have barred the equitable arm of the Court to her. In our view from the showing made in her complaint, plaintiff is entitled to her day in Court.

It accordingly follows that the order dismissing plaintiff's . . . complaint . . . is reversed.

▪ ASSIGNMENT 25.2 ▪

a. If you owned a small struggling business, how would you feel about *Vokes v. Arthur Murray, Inc.?* Consumers love it. What do you think the business community feels about this opinion?

b. What should the defendants have done to avoid liability for misrepresentation in *Vokes v. Arthur Murray, Inc.?* Should they have told Audry Vokes that she has two left feet? (Wouldn't she then be able to sue for slander?) Should they have refused to take her money for more lessons? (Wouldn't she then charge them with some form of discrimination or violation of her consumer right to spend her money as she pleased?) Assume that she is determined to become a good dancer no matter how much it costs. Where is she supposed to turn? Is it true that Arthur Murray, Inc. can continue to take her money forever as long as it explicitly insults her by telling her that she is wasting her time and money?

c. Ted Salinger has a problem losing weight. He attends the Avis Weight Reduction Center. The literature of the Center says, "We guarantee nothing, but eventually, we will help you lose it all." The Center costs $1,000 a week. Ted has been attending every week for the past six years. Center personnel work regularly with Ted. They encourage him to keep a good attitude and never give up. Is the Center liable under the reasoning of *Vokes v. Arthur Murray, Inc.?*

▪ ASSIGNMENT 25.3 ▪

Prepare an annotated bibliography on civil deceit, fraud, and misrepresentation for your state. (See General Instructions for the Annotated Bibliography Assignment in Chapter 2.)

SUMMARY

Misrepresentation covers pecuniary loss caused by false statements of fact, by the active concealment of facts, by the nondisclosure of facts that should have been disclosed, and in some instances, by the statement of a false opinion (either based on false implied facts or offered within a fiduciary relationship).

The intent to mislead (scienter) consists of the defendant's knowledge that the statement is false, lack of belief in its truth, or reckless disregard for its truth or falsity, as well as the defendant's intent that the audience of the statement believe the statement and act in reliance on it.

If there is no scienter, the individuals the defendant intended to reach by his or her careless statement may be able to recover for negligent misrepresentation. So can individuals within a relatively small group if the defendant knows that at least someone in the group will learn about the statement and rely on it.

The plaintiff's reliance on the statement of the defendant must be justifiable, and the statement must pertain to something material to the transaction.

Key Terms

misrepresentation	confidential or fiduciary	reckless disregard
deceit	relationship	negligent
pecuniary loss	nondisclosure	misrepresentation
physical loss	opinion	justifiable reliance
fact	puffing	material
concealment	scienter	

CHAPTER 26

Torts Against the Family

CHAPTER OUTLINE

- TORTS DERIVED FROM OTHER TORTS
  - Loss of Consortium
  - Loss of Services
- TORTS NOT DERIVED FROM OTHER TORTS
  - Alienation of Affections
  - Criminal Conversation
  - Enticement of Spouse
  - Abduction or Enticement of a Child
  - Seduction
- WRONGFUL LIFE, BIRTH, PREGNANCY

■ TORTS DERIVED FROM OTHER TORTS

Loss of Consortium

Consortium is the companionship, love, affection, sexual relationship, and services (e.g., cooking, making repairs around the house) that one spouse provides another. There can be a recovery for a tortious injury to consortium. At one time, only the husband could recover for loss of consortium. In every state, this view has been changed by statute or has been ruled unconstitutional as a denial of the equal protection of the law. Either spouse can now recover for loss of consortium.

Example:

- Rich and Ann are married.
- Paul, a stranger, injures Ann by negligently hitting her with his car.

484

- Ann sues Paul for negligence. She receives damages to cover her medical bills, lost wages, and pain and suffering, and also receives punitive damages.
- Rich then brings a *separate* suit against Paul for loss of his wife's consortium. He receives damages to compensate him for whatever loss or impairment he can prove to the companionship he had with Ann before the accident—to the love, affection, sexual intercourse, and services that she gave him as his wife before the accident.

In Rich's action against Paul, Rich cannot recover for injuries sustained by Ann. Ann must recover for such injuries in her own action against Paul. Paul's liability to Rich is limited to the specific injuries sustained by Rich—the loss or impairment of his wife's consortium. If Ann loses her suit against Paul, e.g., because she was contributorily negligent, Rich will not be able to bring his consortium suit. To recover for loss of consortium, there must be an underlying successfully litigated tort.

Of course, parties do not have to be married for consortium to exist between them.

Examples:

- Jim and Rachel are engaged to be married. The defendant negligently injured Rachel before the wedding. Can Jim sue the defendant for loss of consortium?
- Barbara and Paul are living together; they are not married. The defendant negligently injures Paul. Can Barbara sue the defendant for loss of consortium?
- Gabe is the son of Bill. The defendant negligently injures Bill. Can Gabe sue the defendant for loss of parental society (partial consortium, sometimes called **parental consortium**)?

In the vast majority of states, the answer is *no* to each of these questions. A marriage license is a precondition to a suit for loss of consortium. This conclusion has been criticized. Because the essence of consortium is the emotional commitment and devotion between two people, and not the formality of the relationship, a serious interference with this commitment and devotion should be the basis of recovery, according to the critics. The loss suffered by Jim, Barbara, and Gabe is just as real as the loss suffered by a person whose spouse has been injured. There is a fear, however, of opening the floodgate of litigation if anyone with consortium losses or consortium-like losses can sue. What about a homosexual plaintiff whose lover has been injured by the defendant?

Loss of Services

Suppose that an unemancipated child is tortiously injured by the defendant.[1] A parent has a right to services from the child. In most states, the parent can recover separate damages from the defendant for interference with this right, i.e., for **loss of services.** If, for example, a minor child is crippled by a battery committed by the defendant, the child will be able to recover for the injuries sustained as a result of the battery. The parent can receive separate damages due

---

[1]An **unemancipated** child is one who is still under the control and authority of his or her parents.

to the fact that the child is no longer able to provide the same services to the home that were possible prior to the accident, e.g., cutting the grass and running errands.

▪ ASSIGNMENT 26.1 ▪

a. Who can sue for loss of consortium in your state? Use the digests to find one case in which a party successfully sued for loss of consortium. Give the citation of the case and summarize its facts and holding.
b. Who can sue for loss of services in your state?

(See General Instructions for the State Code Assignment and the State Court Opinion Assignment, both in Chapter 2.)

▪ ASSIGNMENT 26.2 ▪

Prepare an annotated bibliography on loss of consortium in your state. (See General Instructions for the Annotated Bibliography Assignment in Chapter 2.)

▪ TORTS NOT DERIVED FROM OTHER TORTS

Other tort actions that can be brought by one family member because of what the defendant did with or to another family member include the following:

- **alienation of affections**
- **criminal conversation**
- **enticement of spouse**
- **abduction or enticement of a child**
- **seduction**

To establish one of these causes of action, there is no need to prove an underlying tort; they are torts in their own right. A number of states, however, have passed statutes (sometimes called **heart-balm statutes**) that have abolished some or all of these tort actions.

Alienation of Affections

Elements

1. The defendant intended to diminish the marital relationship (love, companionship, and comfort) between the plaintiff and the latter's spouse.
2. Affirmative conduct by the defendant.
3. Affections between the plaintiff and spouse were in fact alienated.
4. The defendant caused the alienation (but for the defendant, the alienation would not have occurred, or the defendant was a substantial factor in producing the alienation).

Criminal Conversation

Element

The defendant had sex with the plaintiff's spouse (adultery).

Enticement of Spouse

Elements

1. The defendant intended to diminish the marital relationship between the plaintiff and the latter's spouse.
2. Affirmative conduct by the defendant either:
   a. to entice or encourage the spouse to leave the plaintiff's home, or
   b. to harbor the spouse and encourage the latter to stay away from the plaintiff's home.
3. The plaintiff's spouse left home.
4. The defendant caused the plaintiff to leave home or to stay away (but for what defendant did, the plaintiff would not have left home or stayed away; or, the defendant was a substantial factor in the spouse's leaving or staying away).

Abduction or Enticement of a Child

Elements

1. The defendant intended to interfere with the parent's custody of the child.
2. Affirmative conduct by the defendant:
   a. to abduct or force the child from the parent's custody,
   b. to entice or encourage the child to leave the parent, or
   c. to harbor the child and encourage the latter to stay away from the parent's custody.
3. The child left the custody of the parent.
4. The defendant caused the child to leave or to stay away (but for what the defendant did, the child would not have left or stayed away; or, the defendant was a substantial factor in the child's leaving or staying away).

Seduction

Element

The defendant had sex with the plaintiff's minor daughter by force or with the consent of the daughter.

▪ ASSIGNMENT 26.3 ▪

Olivia is the mother of Irene, who is married to George. Olivia begged Irene not to marry George—to no avail. After the marriage and the birth of a son, Olivia warns Irene that George has a violent disposition. Irene and George separate. Irene takes their son to live with Olivia. Has Olivia committed any torts? (See General Instructions for the Legal Analysis Assignment in Chapter 3.)

▪ ASSIGNMENT 26.4 ▪

Can any of the above five causes of action be brought in your state? Check your state code (e.g., heart balm statute) and opinions written by courts in your state. If you find older cases that have permitted any of these actions, shepardize them to be sure that they still represent good law in your state. (See General Instructions for the State Code Assignment and the State Court Opinion Assignments, both in Chapter 2.)

▪ WRONGFUL LIFE, BIRTH, PREGNANCY

Doctors have been sued in three different kinds of cases for causing the birth of an unwanted child due to negligence, e.g., the doctor made a careless mistake performing a sterilization operation or an abortion.

Wrongful life: An action by or on behalf of an unwanted deformed or impaired child for its own damages

Wrongful birth: An action by parents of an unwanted deformed or impaired child for their own damages

Wrongful pregnancy: An action by parents of a healthy child they did not want

Most states deny a child the right to bring a **wrongful life** case for the anguish of being born deformed. A major reason for this decision is the enormous difficulty of calculating the damages that should be awarded in such a case. (See *Berman* case below.) One court worried that allowing the infant to sue might encourage other infants to sue for being "born into the world under conditions they might regard as adverse. One might seek damages for inheriting unfortunate family conditions; one for being born into a large and destitute family, another because a parent has an unsavory reputation."[2]

Wrongful birth cases by parents have been more successful.

Example: A woman contracts German measles early in her pregnancy. Her doctor negligently advises her that the disease will not affect the health of the child. In fact, the child is born with severe defects caused by the disease. If she had known the risks, the woman would have aborted the pregnancy.

States disagree on whether parents can bring a wrongful birth action in such a case. Those that allow it are not reluctant to try to assess the financial and emotional damages of the parents in giving birth to the deformed or impaired child. They can recover their monetary losses attributed to the child's condition and damages for emotional distress.

When the unwanted child is born healthy, a **wrongful pregnancy** action (also called a **wrongful conception** action) by the parents is often allowed. The damages, however, are usually limited to the costs of prenatal care and delivery; they rarely extend to the costs of raising the healthy child. The healthy child is usually not allowed to bring the same kind of action in his or her own right.

▪ ASSIGNMENT 26.5 ▪

a. A pregnant woman in your state has a genetic disease that could lead to the birth of a deformed child. Her doctor negligently fails to diagnose and inform the woman. The child is born deformed with this disease. If she had known of the disease, she would have aborted the pregnancy. Who can bring an action in your state against the doctor for negligence and for what damages? (See General Instructions for the State Court Opinion Assignment in Chapter 2.)

---

[2]*Zepeda v. Zepeda,* 190 N.E.2d 849, 858 (Ill. App. Ct. 1963).

b. A pharmacist in your state sells an unmarried couple birth control pills. The pills are negligently defective. A healthy, illegitimate child is born to this couple. Who can bring an action in your state against the pharmacist for negligence and for what damages? (See General Instructions for the State Court Opinion Assignment in Chapter 2.)

CASE

Berman v. Allen
80 N.J. 421, 404 A.2d 8 (1979)
Supreme Court of New Jersey

Background: Sharon Berman was born with Down's Syndrome, a genetic defect commonly referred to as mongolism. The mother would have had an abortion if she had known this before birth. Doctors Allen and Attardi, specialists in gynecology and obstetrics, failed to tell her about the availability of amniocentesis as a technique to discover the presence of Down's Syndrome. In this medical malpractice action, the parents sue for wrongful life on behalf of Sharon and for wrongful birth on their own behalf. The trial court granted the doctors a summary judgment because the plaintiffs failed to state a cause of action. The case is now on appeal before the Supreme Court of New Jersey.

Decision on Appeal: The child cannot sue for wrongful life, but the parents can sue for wrongful birth.

Opinion of Court

Justice PASHMAN delivered the opinion of the court . . .

Plaintiffs allege that defendants deviated from accepted medical standards by failing to inform Mrs. Berman during her pregnancy of the existence of a procedure known as amniocentesis. This procedure involves the insertion of a long needle into a mother's uterus and the removal therefrom of a sample of amniotic fluid containing living fetal cells. Through "karyotype analysis" a procedure in which the number and structure of the cells' chromosomes are examined, the sex of the fetus as well as the presence of gross chromosomal defects can be detected. Prenatal diagnosis of genetic abnormalities is potentially available for approximately 60 to 90 metabolic defects, including Tay-Sachs Disease and Down's Syndrome. Recent studies indicate that amniocentesis is highly accurate in predicting the presence of chromosomal defects, and that the risk of even minor damage to mother or fetus deriving from the procedure is less than one percent.

Due to Mrs. Berman's age at the time of her conception [38], plaintiffs contend that the risk that her child, if born, would be afflicted with Down's Syndrome was sufficiently great that sound medical practice at the time of pregnancy required defendants to inform her both of this risk and the availability of amniocentesis as a method of determining whether in her particular case that risk would come to fruition. Had defendants so informed Mrs. Berman, the complaint continues, she would have submitted to the amniocentesis procedure, discovered that the child, if born, would suffer from Down's Syndrome, and had the fetus aborted.

As a result of defendants' alleged negligence, the infant Sharon, through her Guardian *ad litem,* seeks compensation for the physical and emotional pain and suffering which she will endure throughout life because of her mongoloid condition. Mr. and Mrs. Berman, the child's parents, request damages in their own right both for the emotional anguish which they have experienced and will continue to experience on account of Sharon's birth defect, and the medical and other costs which they will incur in order to properly raise, educate and supervise the child. . . .

The claim for damages asserted on behalf of the infant Sharon has aptly been labeled a cause of action grounded upon "wrongful life." Sharon does not contend that absent defendants' negligence she would have come into the world in a normal and healthy state. There is no suggestion in either the pleadings below or the medical literature which we have scrutinized that any therapy could have been prescribed which would have decreased the risk that, upon birth, Sharon would suffer from Down's Syndrome. Rather, the gist of the infant's complaint is that had defendants informed her mother of the availability of amniocentesis, Sharon would never have come into existence.

As such, this case presents issues different from those involved in malpractice actions where a plaintiff asserts that a defendant's deviation from sound medical practices increased the probability that an infant would be born with defects. Nor are we here confronted with a situation in which an individual's negligence while a child was in gestation caused what otherwise would have been a normal and healthy child to come into the world in an impaired condition. Here, defendants' alleged negligence neither caused the mongoloid condition nor increased the risk that such a condition would occur. . . . In essence, Sharon claims that her very life is "wrongful. . . ."

The primary purpose of tort law is that of compensating plaintiffs for the injuries they have suffered wrongfully at the hands of others. As such, damages are ordinarily computed by "comparing the condition plaintiff would have been in, had the defendants not been negligent, with plaintiff's impaired condition as a result of the negligence." *Gleitman v. Cosgrove,* 49 N.J. 22, 28, 227 A.2d 689, 692. In the case of a claim predicated upon wrongful life, such a computation would require the trier of fact to measure the difference in value between life in an impaired condition and the "utter void of nonexistence." *Gleitman,* supra. Such an endeavor, however, is literally impossible. As Chief Justice Weintraub noted, man, "who knows nothing of death or nothingness," simply cannot affix a price tag to non-life. *Gleitman* at 63.

Nevertheless, although relevant to our determination, we would be extremely reluctant today to deny the validity of Sharon's complaint solely because damages are difficult to ascertain. The courts of this and other jurisdictions have long held that where a wrong itself is of such a nature as to preclude the computation of damages with precise exactitude, it would be a "perversion of fundamental principles of justice to deny all relief to the injured [party], and thereby relieve the wrongdoer from making any amend for his acts." *Story Parchment Co. v. Paterson Parchment Paper Co.,* 282 U.S. 555, 563, (1931). To be sure, damages may not be determined by mere speculation or guess and, as defendants emphasize, placing a value upon non-life is not simply difficult—it is humanly impossible. Nonetheless, were the measure of damages our sole concern, it is possible that some judicial remedy could be fashioned which would redress plaintiff, if only in part, for injuries suffered.

Difficulty in the measure of damages is not, however, our sole or even primary concern. Although we conclude, as did the . . . majority [in *Gleitman v. Cosgrove*] that Sharon has failed to state an actionable claim for relief, we base our result upon a different premise[:] that Sharon has not suffered any damage cognizable at law by being brought into existence.

One of the most deeply held beliefs of our society is that life whether experienced with or without a major physical handicap is more precious than non-life. See *In re Quinlin,* 70 N.J. 10, 19 & n. 1, 355 A.2d 647 (1976). Concrete manifestations of this belief are not difficult to discover. The documents which set forth the principles upon which our society is founded are replete with references to the sanctity of life. The federal constitution characterizes life as one of three fundamental rights of which no man can be deprived without due process of law. U.S. Const., Amends. V and XIV. Our own state constitution proclaims that the "enjoying and defending (of) life" is a natural right. N.J. Const. (1947), Art. I, § 1. The Declaration of Independence states that the primacy of man's "unalienable" right to life is a "self-evident truth." Nowhere in these documents is there to be found an indication that the lives of persons suffering from physical handicaps are to be less cherished than those of non-handicapped human beings.

State legislatures and thus the people as a whole have universally reserved the most severe criminal penalties for individuals who have unjustifiably deprived others of life. Indeed, so valued is this commodity that even one who has committed first degree murder cannot be sentenced to death unless he is accorded special procedural protections in addition to those given all criminal defendants. Moreover, it appears that execution is constitutionally impermissible unless the crime which a defendant has perpetrated was one which involved the taking of another's life. Again, these procedural protections and penalties do not vary according to the presence or absence of physical deformities in the victim or defendant. It is life itself that is jealously safeguarded, not life in a perfect state.

Finally, we would be remiss if we did not take judicial notice of the high esteem which our society accords to those involved in the medical profession. The reason for this is clear. Physicians are the preservers of life.

No man is perfect. Each of us suffers from some ailments or defects, whether major or minor, which make impossible participation in all the activities the world has to offer. But our lives are not thereby rendered less precious than those of others whose defects are less pervasive or less severe.

We recognize that as a mongoloid child, Sharon's abilities will be more circumscribed than those of normal, healthy children and that she, unlike them, will experience a great deal of physical and emotional pain and anguish. We sympathize with her plight. We cannot, however, say that she would have been better off had she never been brought into the world. Notwithstanding her affliction with Down's Syndrome, Sharon, by virtue of her birth, will be able to love and be loved and to experience happiness and pleasure[,] emotions which are truly the essence of life and which are far more valuable than the suffering she may endure. To rule otherwise would require us to disavow the basic assumption upon which our society is based. This we cannot do.

Accordingly, we hold that Sharon has failed to state a valid cause of action founded upon "wrongful life."

The validity of the parents' claim for relief calls into play considerations different from those involved in the infant's complaint. As in the case of the infant, Mr. and Mrs. Berman do not assert that defendants increased the risk that Sharon, if born, would be afflicted with Down's Syndrome. Rather, at bottom, they allege that they were tortiously injured because Mrs. Berman was deprived of the option of making a meaningful decision as to whether to abort the fetus, a decision which, at least during the first trimester of pregnancy, is not subject to state interference. See *Roe v. Wade,* 410 U.S. 113, 93 S.Ct. 705, 35 L.Ed.2d 147 (1973). They thus claim that Sharon's "birth" as opposed to her "life" was wrongful.

Two items of damage are requested in order to redress this allegedly tortious injury: (1) the medical and other costs that will be incurred in order to properly raise, supervise and educate the child; and

(2) compensation for the emotional anguish that has been and will continue to be experienced on account of Sharon's condition.

The . . . majority [in *Gleitman v. Cosgrove*] refused to recognize as valid a cause of action grounded upon wrongful birth. Two reasons underlay its determination. The first related to measure of damages should such a claim be allowed. In its view,

> In order to determine [the parents'] compensatory damages a court would have to evaluate the denial to them of the intangible, unmeasurable, and complex human benefits of motherhood and fatherhood and weigh these against the alleged emotional and money injuries. Such a proposed weighing is . . . impossible to perform. . . . [*Gleitman,* 49 N.J. at 29, 227 A.2d at 693]

Second, even though the Court's opinion was premised upon the assumption that Mrs. Gleitman could have legally secured an abortion, the majority concluded that "substantial [public] policy reasons" precluded the judicial allowance of tort damages "for the denial of the opportunity to take an embryonic life." 49 N.J. at 30, 227 A.2d at 693.

In light of changes in the law which have occurred in the 12 years since *Gleitman* was decided, the second ground relied upon by the *Gleitman* majority can no longer stand in the way of judicial recognition of a cause of action founded upon wrongful birth. The Supreme Court's ruling in *Roe v. Wade* clearly establishes that a woman possesses a constitutional right to decide whether her fetus should be aborted, at least during the first trimester of pregnancy. Public policy now supports, rather than militates against, the proposition that she not be impermissibly denied a meaningful opportunity to make that decision.

As in all other cases of tortious injury, a physician whose negligence has deprived a mother of this opportunity should be required to make amends for the damage which he has proximately caused. Any other ruling would in effect immunize from liability those in the medical field providing inadequate guidance to persons who would choose to exercise their constitutional right to abort fetuses which, if born, would suffer from genetic defects. Accordingly, we hold that a cause of action founded upon wrongful birth is a legally cognizable claim.

Troublesome, however, is the measure of damages. As noted earlier, the first item sought to be recompensed is the medical and other expenses that will be incurred in order to properly raise, educate and supervise the child. Although these costs were "caused" by defendants' negligence in the sense that but for the failure to inform, the child would not have come into existence, we conclude that this item of damage should not be recoverable. In essence, Mr. and Mrs. Berman desire to retain all the benefits inhering in the birth of the child, i.e., the love and joy they will experience as parents while saddling defendants with the enormous expenses attendant upon her rearing. Under the facts and circumstances here alleged, we find that such an award would be wholly disproportionate to the culpability involved, and that allowance of such a recovery would both constitute a windfall to the parents and place too unreasonable a financial burden upon physicians.

The parents' claim for emotional damages stands upon a different footing. In failing to inform Mrs. Berman of the availability of amniocentesis, defendants directly deprived her and, derivatively, her husband of the option to accept or reject a parental relationship with the child and thus caused them to experience mental and emotional anguish upon their realization that they had given birth to a child afflicted with Down's Syndrome. We feel that the monetary equivalent of this distress is an appropriate measure of the harm suffered by the parents deriving from Mrs. Berman's loss of her right to abort the fetus. . . .

[W]e do not feel that placing a monetary value upon the emotional suffering that Mr. and Mrs. Berman have and will continue to experience is an impossible task for the trier of fact. . . . [C]ourts have come to recognize that mental and emotional distress is just as "real" as physical pain, and that its valuation is no more difficult. Consequently, damages for such distress have been ruled allowable in an increasing number of contexts. Moreover . . . to deny Mr. and Mrs. Berman redress for their in-

juries merely because damages cannot be measured with precise exactitude would constitute a perversion of fundamental principles of justice.

Consequently, we hold that Mr. and Mrs. Berman have stated actionable claims for relief. Should their allegations be prove at trial, they are entitled to be recompensed for the mental and emotional anguish they have suffered and will continue to suffer on account of Sharon's condition. Accordingly, the judgment of the trial court is affirmed in part and reversed in part, and this case remanded for a plenary trial.

■ ASSIGNMENT 26.6 ■

a. Did the two doctors owe a duty of care to Sharon Berman? Why or why not?
b. Assume that the doctors owed Sharon a duty and that it was breached by a failure to render competent medical advice and services in connection with the pregnancy. What harm did the doctors cause? They clearly did not cause the Down's Syndrome. What was Sharon's loss?

SUMMARY

Loss of consortium is an independent action brought by a person whose spouse has been tortiously injured. The action covers the loss of love, affection, sexual relationship, and services that one spouse normally provides another. An action for loss of services is brought by a parent against a defendant who has committed a tort against the parent's unemancipated child that has diminished or interfered with the parent's right to the services of the child.

Other torts against the family include: alienation of affections (the defendant causes the deprivation of love, companionship, and comfort between the plaintiff and the plaintiff's spouse); criminal conversation (the defendant has sex with the plaintiff's spouse); enticement of spouse (the defendant causes the plaintiff's spouse to leave home or to stay away); abduction or enticement of a child (the defendant causes the plaintiff's child to leave home or to stay away); and seduction (the defendant has sex with the plaintiff's minor daughter, with or without the latter's consent).

Courts are reluctant to allow an unwanted deformed or impaired child to bring an action for wrongful life for his or her own damages in being negligently born. Wrongful birth actions, in which parents seek damages for the negligent birth of such a child, are permitted in some states, as are wrongful pregnancy actions, in which the parents seek damages for the negligent birth of an unwanted healthy child.

Key Terms

consortium
parental consortium
unemancipated
loss of services
alienation of affections
criminal conversation

enticement of spouse
abduction or
   enticement of a
   child
seduction

heart-balm statutes
wrongful life
wrongful birth
wrongful pregnancy
wrongful conception

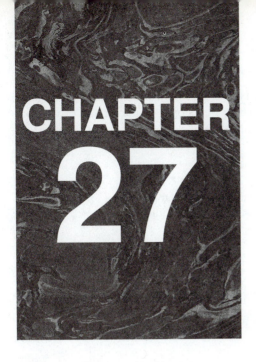

CHAPTER 27

Torts Connected with Land

CHAPTER OUTLINE

· INTRODUCTION
· TRESPASS TO LAND
    Trespass to Land Checklist
    Land
    Damages
· STRICT LIABILITY FOR
  ABNORMALLY DANGEROUS
  CONDITIONS OR ACTIVITIES
    Strict Liability for Abnormally
      Dangerous Conditions or
      Activities Checklist
    Abnormally Dangerous Condition
      or Activity
    Knowledge of the Condition or
      Activity
    Causation: Cause in Fact and
      Proximate Cause
    Defenses

· NUISANCE
    Private Nuisance
    Public Nuisance
· TRADITIONAL NEGLIGENCE
  LIABILITY
    Persons Outside the Land
    Trespassers, Licensees, and
      Invitees
    The Special Problems of the Seller
      and Buyer of Land (Vendor and
      Vendee)
    The Special Problems of the
      Landlord and Tenant (Lessor
      and Lessee)

■ INTRODUCTION

There are a variety of **interests** that a person can have in land based on his or her relationship to it:

· owner occupying the land
· nonoccupying owner as landlord (i.e., lessor) of the land
· tenant (i.e., lessee) of the land
· someone claiming to be an owner of the land (such as an adverse possessor)

495

This chapter is primarily about the torts that can be committed by and against individuals with these relationships to land. The single characteristic of the torts is that they are somehow related to the way land is used or abused. Our discussion will center on the following topics:

- trespass to land
- negligence
- strict liability due to abnormally dangerous use of land
- nuisance based on trespass, negligence, or strict liability

■ TRESPASS TO LAND

Trespass to Land Checklist
Definitions, Relationships, and Research References

Category
   Trespass to land is an intentional tort.

Interest Protected by This Tort
   The interest in the exclusive possession of land in its present physical condition.

Elements of This Tort
1. An act
2. Intrusion on land
3. In possession of another
4. Intent to intrude
5. Causation of the intrusion

Major Definitions of Words/Phrases in These Elements

    Act: A voluntary movement of the body that leads to the intrusion.

    Intrusion: a. Physically going on the land,
            b. Remaining on the land,
            c. Going to a prohibited portion of the land, or
            d. Failing to remove goods from the land.

    Possession: a. Actual occupancy with intent to have exclusive control over the land, or
            b. The right to immediate occupancy when no one else is actually occupying it with intent to control it.

    Intent to Intrude: The desire to intrude on the land or the knowledge with substantial certainty that an intrusion will result from what you do or fail to do.

    Causation: a. But for what the defendant did, the intrusion would not have occurred, or
            b. The defendant was a substantial factor in producing the intrusion.

Major Defenses and Counter-Argument Possibilities That Need to Be Explored

1. The defendant did not voluntarily go on the land, remain on the land, go to a prohibited portion of the land, or fail to remove goods from the land.
2. The plaintiff did not have possession of the land.
3. The plaintiff had no reasonably beneficial use of the land that the defendant entered (e.g., the air space over the land).
4. There was no intent to intrude: the defendant did not desire to intrude or know with substantial certainty that an intrusion would result from what the defendant did—the intrusion was either accidental or negligent.
5. The defendant did not cause the intrusion.
6. The plaintiff consented to the intrusion.
7. The privilege of necessity.
8. The privilege to abate a nuisance.
9. The privilege to retake possession of land forcibly.
10. Sovereign immunity.
11. Public official immunity.
12. Charitable immunity.

Damages

The plaintiff can receive nominal damages if no actual damages were committed by the trespass to land. Punitive damages are also possible if malice is present.

Relationship to Criminal Law

It may be a crime in certain states to enter designated land, e.g., government property.

Relationship to Other Torts

Negligence: If the defendant does not intentionally enter the plaintiff's land, the defendant may have entered negligently, e.g., due to an unreasonable mistake. The tort of negligence is committed if actual damage results from the negligent entry.

Nuisance: The defendant may commit a private or public nuisance while entering the plaintiff's land.

Strict Liability for Abnormally Dangerous Activities: The defendant may enter the land while engaged in abnormally dangerous activities, which could be the basis of strict liability.

Federal Law

Under the Federal Tort Claims Act, the federal government will be liable for trespass to land committed by a federal employee within the scope of employment. A violation of the Civil Rights Act may also be possible if there is a violation of the plaintiff's federal rights under color of law during or because of the trespass to land.

Employer-Employee (Agency) Law

A private employer will be liable for the trespass to land committed by its employee within the scope of employment. The employee must have acted to further a business objective of the employer to make the latter vicariously liable for the employee's trespass to land.

Research References for Trespass to Land

• Digests

In the digests of West, look for case summaries on trespass to land under key topics such as:

Trespass	Torts
Forcible Entry and Detainer	Damages
Ejectment	Adverse Possession
Landlord and Tenant	Animals

• *Corpus Juris Secundum*

In this legal encyclopedia, see the discussions under topic headings such as:

Trespass	Landlord and Tenant
Forcible Entry and Detainer	Torts
Ejectment	Damages
	Adverse Possession

• *American Jurisprudence 2d*

In this legal encyclopedia see the discussions under topic headings such as:

Trespass	Ejectment
Property	Landlord and Tenant
Damages	Torts
Forcible Entry and Detainer	Adverse Possession
	Animals

• Legal Periodical Literature

There are three index systems to use to locate legal periodical literature on trespass to land:

Index to Legal Periodicals (ILP)	Current Law Index (CLI)	Legal Resource Index (LRI)
See literature in *ILP* under subject headings such as:	See literature in *CLI* under subject headings such as:	See literature in *LRI* under subject headings such as:
Trespass	Trespass	Trespass
Forcible Entry and Detainer	Torts	Torts
Real Property	Riparian Rights	Riparian Rights
Air Law	Real Property	Real Property
Torts	Damages	Damages
Damages		
Adjoining Landowners		

Example of a legal periodical article you will find using *ILP*, *CLI*, or *LRI:*

Invasion of Radioactive Particulates as a Common Law Trespass, 3 Urban Law Review 206 (1980).

• *ALR, ALR2d, ALR3d, ALR4th, ALR5th, ALR Fed*

Use the *Index to Annotations* to locate annotations on trespass to land. In this index check subject headings such as:

Trespass	Adverse possession
Forcible Entry and Detainer	Torts
Real property	Damages
	Air Space

Example of an annotation on trespass to land you can locate through this index:

> *Liability for Personal Injury or Death Caused by Trespassing or Intruding Livestock*, 49 ALR4th 710 (1980).

• *Words and Phrases*

In this multivolume legal dictionary, look up every word or phrase mentioned in this checklist to try to locate summaries of court opinions that have defined these words or phrases.

Land

Land does not consist solely of ground. It also includes that portion of the air space above the ground over which the plaintiff can claim a **reasonable beneficial use.** If a defendant throws a brick over the plaintiff's land, a trespass has occurred even if the brick never touches the plaintiff's home or ground. Assume that it finally lands beyond the plaintiff's property line. The plaintiff has the use of the air space immediately above the ground. Hence there has been a trespass to land. The case is different, however, for the space one mile above the ground that is used by airplanes. The latter do not commit trespass.

Damages

Actual destruction or harm to the land does not have to be shown. The actual entry is damage enough. If nothing more has occurred, the plaintiff can at least recover **nominal damages.**

▪ ASSIGNMENT 27.1 ▪

Prepare an annotated bibliography on trespass to land for your state. (See General Instructions for the Annotated Bibliography Assignment in Chapter 2.)

▪ STRICT LIABILITY FOR ABNORMALLY DANGEROUS CONDITIONS OR ACTIVITIES

Strict Liability for Abnormally Dangerous Conditions or Activities Checklist
Definitions, Relationships, and Research References

Category

   Strict liability for abnormally dangerous conditions or activities is a strict liability tort (neither negligence nor intent must be shown).

Interest Protected by This Tort

   The right to be free from harm caused by abnormally dangerous conditions or activities.

Elements of This Tort

1. The existence of an abnormally dangerous condition or activity
2. Knowledge of the condition or activity by the defendant
3. Damages
4. Proximate cause

Major Definitions of Words/Phrases in the Elements

   Abnormal: Unusual or non-natural for the area.

   Dangerous: Creating a substantial likelihood of great harm to persons or property, which cannot be eliminated by the use of reasonable care by the defendant.

   Proximate Cause: The defendant is the cause in fact of the harm that results. The kind of harm that results was foreseeable by the defendant, or should have been foreseeable. The plaintiff was within the class of people who were foreseeably endangered by the condition or activity.

Major Defenses and Counter-Argument Possibilities That Need to Be Explored

1. The condition or activity was not abnormally dangerous. (NOTE: The objective of the defendant is to try to force the plaintiff to prove negligence. This is accomplished if the plaintiff fails to show that the condition or activity was abnormally dangerous. Items 2 to 4 below try to establish that the condition or activity was not abnormally dangerous.)
2. The condition or activity was usual or natural for the environment in question.
3. The likelihood of serious harm from the condition or activity was small.
4. The danger in the condition or activity could have been eliminated by the use of reasonable care. (Defendant does not admit, however, that such care was not used.)
5. A statute required or authorized the condition or activity.
6. The value of the condition or activity to the community outweighed any possible danger.
7. The defendant or defendant's agents were not aware of the condition or activity.
8. The defendant was not the cause in fact of the harm suffered by the plaintiff.
9. The kind of harm that resulted was not foreseeable.
10. The person injured was not a foreseeable plaintiff.
11. The plaintiff was aware of the danger, understood it, and unreasonably encountered it (assumption of the risk).
12. The plaintiff consented to what the defendant did.
13. Sovereign immunity.

14. Public official immunity.
15. Charitable immunity.

Damages

The plaintiff can recover for the harm proximately caused by the defendant. It is rare that punitive damages can be recovered, since it is difficult to establish that the defendant was malicious or intended the harm that resulted.

Relationship to Criminal Law

There may be a criminal statute that prohibits the defendant from maintaining the condition or engaging in the activity involved, e.g., a statute making it a crime to explode fireworks in public areas. The consequences of violating such a statute may include criminal penalties as well as civil liability for the strict liability tort under discussion in this section.

Relationships to Other Torts

Negligence: If the condition or activity of the defendant does not qualify for strict liability status because the condition or activity is not abnormally dangerous, the plaintiff may be able to show that the defendant was negligent in connection with the condition or activity.

Nuisance: Nuisance should be considered when the condition or activity of the defendant interferes with the use and enjoyment of the plaintiff's land. In some states, there is liability for an absolute nuisance for the same facts that would constitute strict liability for an abnormally dangerous condition or activity.

Trespass to Land: This tort is used when there is an entry of a physical object on the land of the plaintiff due to the abnormally dangerous condition or activity of the defendant.

Wrongful Death: This action can be brought by the survivors of the plaintiff if death results from the abnormally dangerous condition or activity of the defendant.

Federal Law

Under the Federal Tort Claims Act, the federal government will not be liable for a claim based on strict liability.

Employer-Employee (Agency) Law

An employer will be strictly liable for an abnormally dangerous condition or activity maintained or undertaken by an employee within the scope of the latter's employment.

Research References for This Tort

· Digests

In the digests of West, look for case summaries on this tort under key topics such as:

Explosives	Damages
Trespass	Torts
Waters and Water Courses	Death
	Nuisance

· *Corpus Juris Secundum*

In this legal encyclopedia, see the discussion under topic headings such as:

Explosives	Damages
Trespass	Torts
Waters and Water Courses	Death
	Nuisance

· *American Jurisprudence 2d*

In this legal encyclopedia, see the discussion under topic headings such as:

Explosions and Explosives	Damages
Waters	Torts
Premises Liability	Nuisance
Adjoining Landowners	Death

· Legal Periodical Literature

There are three index systems to use to locate legal periodical literature on this tort:

Index to Legal Periodicals (ILP)	*Current Law Index (CLI)*	*Legal Resource Index (LRI)*
See literature in *ILP* under subject headings such as:	See literature in *CLI* under subject headings such as:	See literature in *LRI* under subject headings such as:
Water and Water Courses	Strict Liability	Strict Liability
Liability without Fault	Explosives	Explosives
Animals	Water	Water
Trespass	Damages	Damages
Real Property	Torts	Real Property
Torts	Real Property	Liability for Landslide Damages
Damages	Liability for Landslide Damages	Liability for Condition and Use of Land
Adjoining Landowners	Liability for Condition and Use of Land	

Example of a legal periodical article you will find by using *ILP, CLI,* or *LRI:*

Common Carriers and Risk Distribution: Absolute Liability for Transporting Hazardous Materials, 67 Kentucky Law Journal 441 (1978-79).

· *ALR, ALR2d, ALR3d, ALR4th, ALR5th, ALR Fed*

Use the *Index to Annotations* to locate annotations on this tort. In this index, check subject headings such as:

Absolute Liability	Torts
Floods and Flooding	Damages
Explosions and Explosives	Water

Example of an annotation you can locate through this index:

Liability for Property Damage caused by Vibrations, or the like, Without Blasting or Explosion, 79 ALR2d 966.

• *Words and Phrases*

In this multivolume legal dictionary, look up every word or phrase discussed in this section connected with the tort in order to try to locate court opinions that have defined these words or phrases.

When discussing the tort of strict liability (or **absolute liability**) for abnormally dangerous conditions or activities, it is important to keep in mind the related actions of trespass to land and nuisance. If the court finds strict liability for abnormally dangerous conditions or activities, it is highly likely that trespass to land or nuisance could also have been committed.

Most of the cases on strict liability for abnormally dangerous conditions or activities involve the way in which the defendant uses or abuses land. It is also possible, however, to commit this tort while on someone else's land, e.g., transporting a large quantity of explosives on a public highway.

Abnormally Dangerous Condition or Activity

The first element is the existence of an **abnormally dangerous condition or activity.** Some conditions or activities are so dangerous to persons or property that the defendant will be liable for the harm they cause even if the defendant neither intended the harm nor was negligent in producing the harm. It is not a defense for the defendant to show that he or she used the greatest of care—strict liability will still be imposed.

A great deal of the law in this area stems from a famous English case, ***Rylands v. Fletcher.***[1] The defendants built a reservoir on their land. The plaintiff owned a mine nearby. This mine was flooded when water from the defendant's reservoir broke through and reached the mine. The rule from this case, which has been accepted in most American states, is that a defendant is strictly liable for harm caused by:

1. A non-natural or abnormal use of land
2. which creates increased danger to persons or property

In short, there is strict liability for abnormally dangerous conditions or activities.

The determination of what is abnormal or non-natural will, of course, depend on the environment. The following are examples that have been found to be abnormally dangerous:

• storing large quantities of inflammable liquids in an urban area
• blasting in a residential area
• extensive pile driving
• emitting noxious gases from a factory in a residential area

The activity or condition must be unusual for the area and present a serious threat of harm. The following are examples of cases that were *not* found to be abnormally dangerous because they did not meet both criteria:

• electric wiring in a business
• gasoline stored at a gas station underground

---

[1] L.R. 3 H.L. 330 (1868).

- a small amount of dynamite stored in a factory
- an oil well dug in a Texas field

Although damage caused by such activities may not be considered abnormally dangerous enough to qualify for strict liability status, a plaintiff may still be able to recover under other theories. If the defendant acted unreasonably, a negligence case is possible, perhaps with the help of res ipsa loquitur (see Chapter 12). Nuisance and trespass to land should also be explored.

Is airplane flying an abnormally dangerous activity? Suppose a plane crashes onto someone's land, causing substantial damage to people and property below. Strict liability? Years ago, many courts would say yes. As aviation became more common and accepted, however, modern courts were inclined to say no. A plaintiff must establish negligence in order to recover.

Statutes often play a role in this area of strict liability. A statute, for example, might require or simply authorize a common carrier to transport dangerous substances. In such cases, strict liability is usually not applied when damage results from the activity. Liability will result only if negligence can be shown. On the other hand, there may be statutes that prohibit certain activity, e.g., blasting in certain areas or selling drugs to minors. It is sometimes unclear what civil consequences, if any, the legislature intended for a violation of such statutes. Research into the legislative history of the statute must be undertaken. A court might interpret the statute as calling for strict liability, negligence liability, or no civil liability at all for its violation.

The *Restatement of Torts* lists a number of factors that a court should analyze in determining whether something is abnormally dangerous:[2]

- the degree of risk of some harm to people, land, or chattels of others
- the likelihood that the harm that results from the activity will be great
- the inability to eliminate the risk by the exercise of reasonable care
- the extent to which the activity is not a matter of common usage
- the inappropriateness of the activity to the place where the activity is carried on
- the extent to which the value of the activity to the community is outweighed by its dangerous attributes

None of these factors is usually conclusive in deciding whether an activity is abnormally dangerous. The factors are simply aids for a court to determine the extent of the abnormality and the extent of the danger posed by the defendant.

In balancing these factors, if a court tips the scale against strict liability, it does not necessarily mean that the defendant has won the case. It simply means that the plaintiff must try to fit the facts of the case under the elements of other torts: negligence, nuisance, trespass to land, etc.

▪ ASSIGNMENT 27.2 ▪

In each of the following situations, assume that the object or activity in question has resulted in damage or harm to someone. Do you think a court will impose strict liability? Why or why not? (See General Instructions for the Legal Analysis Assignment in Chapter 3.)

---

[2]*Restatement (Second) of Torts § 520 (1965).*

a. Tom is moving his own barn. He places it on a huge truck platform and drives it on a public highway. It crashes into a bridge.

b. The XYZ Company has installed a large steam boiler in its factory. It explodes.

c. The large lake on Linda's land overflows into neighboring land after a thunderstorm.

d. From an army base in Florida, scientists send up a satellite. Unfortunately it lands in Newark, New Jersey.

Knowledge of the Condition or Activity

A defendant will not be strictly liable for an abnormally dangerous condition or activity of which the defendant is unaware. The plaintiff must establish knowledge on the part of the defendant.

Causation: Cause in Fact and Proximate Cause

The harm that the plaintiff's person or property has suffered must have been caused by the defendant's abnormally dangerous condition or activity. The **cause-in-fact** tests are as follows:

- **but for** the defendant's conduct, the plaintiff would not have been harmed, or
- the defendant's conduct was a **substantial factor** in producing the harm suffered by the plaintiff

The second test is used when there is more than one causal factor involved.

Once cause in fact has been established, **proximate cause** must be explored. As indicated in the discussion on negligence, the rules of proximate cause establish a cut-off point beyond which the defendant will not be liable for the harm he or she caused in fact (see Chapter 13). Proximate cause, therefore, is more of a policy question than a causation question.

As we will see when we study the case involving the mink and her kittens, the harm that results must be within the type of harm that was initially foreseeable, and the individual injured must be part of a group or class of people that were included in the foreseeable risk posed by the abnormally dangerous activity. The foreseeability of both is required in order to establish proximate cause.

The proximate cause rules for strict liability are not as broad as the proximate cause rules we discussed for negligence. A court is more willing to find proximate cause in a negligence case than in a strict liability case involving abnormally dangerous activities. Unforeseeable **intervening causes** such as an **act of God** or an act of a third person are more likely to cut off liability in a strict liability case than in a negligence case. Courts are willing to limit the extent of liability in this way when there is an absence of fault in a defendant who is strictly liable. No such reluctance is shown toward defendants who are negligent or intentional wrongdoers. Suppose, for example, that the defendant maintains a lake that is abnormally dangerous. An unusual frost results in leakage, causing damage to neighboring land. In many courts, this act of God (the frost) would cut off the defendant's *strict liability*, whereas if the defendant had been careless in maintaining the lake, the act of God would probably not terminate *negligence* liability.

Defenses

Contributory negligence on the part of the plaintiff is not a defense to the tort of maintaining an abnormally dangerous condition or activity. This is so with all strict liability torts—the negligence of the plaintiff will not defeat liability. Suppose, for example, that Tom carelessly walks into an area where construction blasting is occurring. Tom fails to realize that blasting is going on, but if he had been exercising reasonable care for his own safety, he should have realized this. Tom is injured by the blasting. There is clear contributory negligence. This is not a defense, however, when the plaintiff is suing under the strict liability tort of maintaining an abnormally dangerous condition or activity.

If, however, the plaintiff knows of and understands the danger posed by the defendant and voluntarily proceeds to encounter it, then the plaintiff has assumed the risk of the danger. **Assumption of the risk** *is* a defense to a strict liability tort. To avoid permitting a defendant to use this defense as an unfair weapon against a plaintiff, however, the defendant must establish that the plaintiff's assumption of the risk was unreasonable. A plaintiff has a right to the reasonable use and enjoyment of his or her property. A defendant cannot encircle the plaintiff's land with a dangerous condition or activity and then claim assumption of the risk when the plaintiff uses his or her land and is injured because of the condition or activity. The defendant must show that this use was unreasonable, and courts are reluctant to make such a finding when the defendant has prevented the plaintiff from making ordinary and reasonable use of his or her property.

CASE

Foster v. Preston Mill Co.
44 Wash.2d 440, 268 P.2d 645 (1954).
Supreme Court of Washington

Background: Blasting for road construction frightened mother mink owned by B. W. Foster, which caused the mink to kill their kittens. Foster brought this action against the company doing the blasting (Preston Mill) to recover damages on the theory of absolute liability. The trial court found for Foster in the sum of $1,953.68. The case is now on appeal before the Supreme Court of Washington where Preston Mill is the appellant and Foster is the respondent.

Decision on Appeal: Judgment reversed. Damages for absolute liability does not extend this far.

Opinion of Court

Justice HAMLEY delivered the opinion of the court . . .

Respondent's mink ranch is located in a rural area one and one-half miles east of North Bend, in King County, Washington. The ranch occupies seven and one half acres on which are located seven sheds for growing mink. The cages are of welded wire, but have wood roofs covered with composition roofing. The ranch is located about two blocks from U.S. highway No. 10, which is a main east-west thoroughfare across the state. Northern Pacific Railway Company tracks are located between the ranch and the highway, and Chicago, Milwaukee, St. Paul & Pacific Railroad Company tracks are located on the other side of the highway about fifteen hundred feet from the ranch.

The period of each year during which mink kittens are born, known as the whelping season, begins about May 1st. The kittens are born during a period of about two and one-half weeks, and are left with their mothers until they are six weeks old. During this period, the mothers are very excitable. If disturbed by noises, smoke, or dogs and cats, they run back and forth in their cages and frequently destroy their young. However, mink become accustomed to disturbances of this kind, if continued over a period of time. This explains why the mink in question were apparently not bothered, even during the whelping season, by the heavy traffic on U.S. highway No. 10, and by the noise and vibration caused by passing trains. There was testimony to the effect that mink would even become accustomed to the vibration and noise of blasting, if it were carried on in a regular and continuous manner.

Appellant and several other companies have been engaged in logging in the adjacent area for more than fifty years. Early in May, 1951, appellant began the construction of a road to gain access to certain timber which it desired to cut. The road was located about two and one-quarter miles southwest of the mink ranch, and about twenty-five hundred feet above the ranch, along the side of what is known as Rattlesnake Ledge.

It was necessary to use explosives to build the road. The customary types of explosives were used, and the customary methods of blasting were followed. The most powder used in one shooting was one hundred pounds, and usually the charge was limited to fifty pounds. The procedure used was to set off blasts twice a day—at noon and at the end of the work day.

Roy A. Peterson, the manager of the ranch in 1951, testified that the blasting resulted in "a tremendous vibration, is all. Boxes would rattle on the cages." The mother mink would then run back and forth in their cages and many of them would kill their kittens. Peterson also testified that on two occasions the blasts had broken windows.

Appellant's expert, Professor Drury Augustus Pfeiffer, of the University of Washington, testified as to tests made with a pin seismometer, using blasts as large as those used by appellant. He reported that no ef-

fect on the delicate apparatus was shown at distances comparable to those involved in this case. He said that it would be impossible to break a window at two and one-fourth miles with a hundred-pound shot, but that it could cause vibration of a lightly-supported cage. It would also be audible. Charles E. Erickson, who had charge of the road construction for appellant in 1951, testified that there was no glass breakage in the portable storage and filing shed which the company kept within a thousand feet of where the blasting was done. There were windows on the roof as well as on the sides of this shed.

Before the 1951 whelping season had far progressed, the mink mothers, according to Peterson's estimate, had killed thirty-five or forty of their kittens. He then told the manager of appellant company what had happened. He did not request that the blasting be stopped. After some discussion, however, appellant's manager indicated that the shots would be made as light as possible. The amount of explosives used in a normal shot was then reduced from nineteen or twenty sticks to fourteen sticks.

Officials of appellant company testified that it would have been impractical to entirely cease road-building during the several weeks required for the mink to whelp and wean their young. Such a delay would have made it necessary to run the logging operation another season, with attendant expense. It would also have disrupted the company's log production schedule and consequently the operation of its lumber mill.

In this action, respondent sought and recovered judgment only for such damages as were claimed to have been sustained as a result of blasting operations conducted after appellant received notice that its activity was causing loss of mink kittens.

The primary question presented by appellant's assignments of error is whether, on these facts, the judgment against appellant [Preston Mill] is sustainable on the theory of absolute liability.

The modern doctrine of strict liability for dangerous substances and activities stems from Justice Blackburn's decision in *Rylands v. Fletcher,* L.R. 3 H.L. 330 (1868). *Prosser on Torts,* 449, § 59. As applied to blasting operations, the doctrine has quite uniformly been held to establish liability, irrespective of negligence, for property damage sustained as a result of casting rocks or other debris on adjoining or neighboring premises. *Patrick v. Smith,* 75 Wash. 407, 134 P. 1076. . . . However . . . strict liability should be confined to consequences which lie within the extraordinary risk whose existence calls for such responsibility. *Prosser on Torts,* 458, § 60; 3 *Restatement of Torts,* 41, § 519. . . . This restriction which has been placed upon the application of the doctrine of absolute liability is based upon considerations of policy. As Professor Prosser has said:

"It is one thing to say that a dangerous enterprise must pay its way within reasonable limits, and quite another to say that it must bear responsibility for every extreme of harm that it may cause. . . . *Prosser on Torts,* 457, § 60.

Applying this principle to the case before us, the question comes down to this: Is the risk that any unusual vibration or noise may cause wild animals, which are being raised for commercial purposes, to kill their young, one of the things which make the activity of blasting ultrahazardous?

We have found nothing in the decisional law which would support an affirmative answer to this question. The decided cases, as well as common experience, indicate that the thing which makes blasting ultrahazardous is the risk that property or persons may be damaged or injured by coming into direct contact with flying debris, or by being directly affected by vibrations of the earth or concussions of the air.

Where, as a result of blasting operations, a horse has become frightened and has trampled or otherwise injured a person, recovery of damages has been upheld on the theory of negligence. *Klein v. Phelps Lumber Co.,* 75 Wash. 500, 135 P. 226. Contra: *Uvalde Construction Co. v. Hill,* 142 Tex. 19, 175 S.W.2d 247, where a milkmaid was injured by a frightened cow. But we have found no case where recovery of damages caused by a frightened farm animal has been sustained on the ground of absolute liability.

If, however, the possibility that a violent vibration, concussion, or noise might frighten domestic animals and lead to property damages or personal injuries be considered one of the harms which makes the activity of blasting ultrahazardous, this would still not include the case we have here.

The relatively moderate vibration and noise which appellant's blasting produced at a distance of two and a quarter miles was no more than a usual incident of the ordinary life of the community. See 3 Restatement of Torts, 48, § 522, comment a. The trial court specifically found that the blasting did not unreasonably interfere with the enjoyment of their property by nearby landowners, except in the case of respondent's mink ranch.

It is the exceedingly nervous disposition of mink, rather than the normal risks inherent in blasting operations, which therefore must, as a matter of sound policy, bear the responsibility for the loss here sustained. [T]he policy of the law does not impose the rule of strict liability to protect against harms incident to the . . . extraordinary and unusual use of land. . . .

It is our conclusion that the risk of causing harm of the kind here experienced, as a result of the relatively minor vibration, concussion, and noise from distant blasting, is not the kind of risk which makes the activity of blasting ultrahazardous. The doctrine of absolute liability is therefore inapplicable under the facts of this case, and respondent is not entitled to recover damages. The judgment is reversed.

• ASSIGNMENT 27.3 •

a. What other theories of recovery could Foster try to use against Preston Mill Co. to recover for the damages the blasting did to its mink kittens? What difficulties would Foster have in establishing recovery on these other theories?
b. A company blasts in an area. This excites a horse, which then runs into and kills a prize cow. The owner of the cow sues the blasting company on a theory of absolute liability. What result?

• ASSIGNMENT 27.4 •

Prepare an annotated bibliography on strict liability for abnormally dangerous conditions or activities for your state. (See General Instructions for the Annotated Bibliography Assignment in Chapter 2.)

NOTE	**Strict Liability for Harm Caused by Animals**

Different rules apply for **domestic animals** (e.g., dogs and horses) and for **wild animals** (e.g., monkeys and bears). As with all strict liability cases, the objective of the plaintiff is to establish that the facts fit within the conditions for the imposition of strict liability. If the plaintiff fails to do so, then the plaintiff must explore other theories of liability, particularly negligence.

Domestic Animals
Unless modified by statute, an owner (or keeper) of a domestic animal will be strictly liable for the harm that it causes if:

1. the owner/keeper had reason to know the animal had specific propensities to harm others, and
2. the harm caused by the animal was due to that specific propensity.

Hence, if an owner/keeper of a dog knows that the dog likes to bite people, the owner/keeper will be strictly liable when the dog bites the plaintiff. If, however, the dog knocks someone down, and this was not a known propensity of the dog, the owner/keeper will be liable only if the plaintiff can prove negligence or intent on the part of the owner/keeper.

Wild Animals
The owner (or keeper) of a wild animal will be strictly liable for the harm it causes whether or not the owner/keeper knew of the animal's dangerous propensities and irrespective of how well-trained the animal was.

• ASSIGNMENT 27.5 •

Prepare an annotated bibliography on harm caused by animals in your state. (See General Instructions for the Annotated Bibliography Assignment in Chapter 2.)

• **NUISANCE**

The first obstacle in understanding this topic is to realize that the word **nuisance** has been very loosely used throughout the law. There is *no* separate tort of nuisance, although the language of many opinions would appear to indicate otherwise. Nuisance is a word that describes two different kinds of harm that are produced by some other tortious or wrongful conduct. The two kinds of harm are **private** and **public nuisance:**

> **Private nuisance:** An unreasonable interference with the use and enjoyment of private land.

> **Public nuisance:** An unreasonable interference with a right common to the general public.

There are a variety of ways that these interferences can be brought about:

- The interferences may be due to negligence.
- The interferences may be due to abnormally dangerous conditions or activities that impose strict liability.
- The interferences may be intentional.
- The interferences may be due to a violation of a statute.

Although nuisance is often thought to apply to land, only private nuisance is primarily concerned with land. In the main, public nuisance is a separate category of injury that often has nothing to do with land. As we shall see, however, there are some public nuisances that can also constitute private nuisances.

Private Nuisance

A private nuisance is different from a trespass to land in that the latter protects one's interest in the exclusive possession of land, whereas the former protects one's right to the reasonable use and enjoyment of land. Of course, the same conduct of the defendant may constitute a private nuisance and a trespass to land, e.g., building a fence on the plaintiff's land. In such cases, the plaintiff can sue either for trespass to land or for a private nuisance.

We approach the subject of private nuisance through five basic questions:

1. What is the nature of a private nuisance? What type of harm does it cover?
2. How is it created?
3. Who can sue?
4. What remedies are available?
5. What defenses are available?

See Figure 27.1 for an overview of these questions.

1. What is the Nature of a Private Nuisance and What Type of Harm Does It Cover?

There are a number of forms that the interference can take:

- loud noises
- vibrations from blasting
- odors or gases
- pollution of air, land, or water
- flooding
- damage to crops or to structures on the land
- keeping a house of prostitution next door
- constant knocking on the door, constant telephone calls

Any of these examples can interfere with the use and enjoyment of one's land. It is not necessary that the physical condition of the land be altered or damaged,

Figure 27.1   Private Nuisance: An Overview

1. What type of harm does private nuisance cover?	**1.** Unreasonable interference with the use and enjoyment of private land.
2. What are the ways in which a private nuisance can be created?	**2.** a. Negligently causing the unreasonable interference with the use and enjoyment of land. b. Intentionally causing the unreasonable interference with the use and enjoyment of land. c. Strict liability in maintaining an abnormally dangerous condition or activity, which causes an unreasonable interference with the use and enjoyment of land.
3. Who can sue for the private nuisance?	**3.** Anyone who has a right to the use and enjoyment of the land.
4. What remedies can be obtained when a private nuisance has been committed?	**4.** a. Damages (money). b. Injunction—if the reasonable interference is threatened or is continuous. c. The plaintiff can exercise the privilege to abate the nuisance (self-help).
5. What defenses are available?	**5.** a. Contributory negligence. This is a defense if the defendant negligently created the unreasonable interference with the use and enjoyment of the land. Contributory negligence is not a defense if the defendant recklessly or intentionally created the unreasonable interference with the use and enjoyment of the land. b. Assumption of the risk. This is a defense no matter how the defendant produced the unreasonable interference with the use and enjoyment of the land. c. Failure to mitigate damages. A plaintiff must mitigate damages no matter how the defendant produced the unreasonable interference with the use and enjoyment of the land. d. Official authorization. The government has authorized or required the defendant's activity.

although this will certainly qualify. Interference with use and enjoyment of land also occurs when the plaintiff's **peace of mind** is disturbed while on the land because of what the defendant has done or failed to do.

Of course, every interference with the use and enjoyment of land is not a private nuisance. It is not a private nuisance for one's relative to move into the state, no matter how upsetting this might be! The interference must be **unreasonable.** The determination of when this is so has caused the greatest difficulty in this area of the law. The difficulty arises from the fact that *both* plaintiff and defendant are claiming the reasonable use and enjoyment of their own land. A delicate balancing process must be used to determine unreasonableness. There are a number of factors that a court will consider.

Factors to Consider When Determining Unreasonableness

- the gravity and character of the harm
- the social value of the use that the plaintiff is making of the land
- the character of the locality
- the extent of the burden on the plaintiff of avoiding or minimizing the interference
- the motive of the defendant
- the social value of the defendant's conduct that led to the interference
- the extent of the burden on the defendant of avoiding or minimizing the interference

The gravity and character of the harm   The interference must be substantial. There is a certain level of annoyance that we are all required to endure in society. A restaurant next door that occasionally makes noises or a neighbor whose garden sprinkler occasionally throws drops of water on someone else's land does not constitute substantial interference with the use and enjoyment of land.

It is important to know the extent of the harm in order to assess its gravity. Has there been serious physical damage done to the land? Even if the physical condition of the land has not been altered, is the plaintiff experiencing significant mental discomfort as a result of what the defendant has done? Can such discomfort be passed off as the whining of a grouchy neighbor, or would most people agree that plaintiff's adverse reaction is justified? The duration of the harm is also important to measure. Is the interference momentary or is it continuous?

The spectrum of the gravity and character of harm can be viewed in Figure 27.2. Of course, something less than total interruption can qualify as a private

Figure 27.2   Spectrum of Interference

Interference with Use and Enjoyment of Land

Slight Interruption or Inconvenience		Total Interruption of Use and Enjoyment

nuisance. How much less? This question can never be answered in isolation. All of the other factors, to be discussed below, would also have to be examined.

When the physical condition of the land has been damaged, a court will usually have little trouble measuring the gravity of the interference. When, however, the interference involves personal discomfort or annoyance alone, the difficulties of assessment are sometimes acute. A rough objective standard is used in such cases. The test is: How would a normal person in that locality view the interference? Would a person who is not unduly sensitive be substantially annoyed or disturbed? Suppose that a halfway house is opened next door to the plaintiff. The halfway house will provide rehabilitation services for men just released from prison as a transition to parole. The plaintiff fears that his children may be molested and that property values in the area will go down as a result of the halfway house. Has there been a substantial interference with the use and enjoyment of the plaintiff's land? This question is answered by determining how a normal person, who is not hypersensitive, would react to the halfway house. If the fears of the plaintiff are based on sheer speculation on what *might* happen, then a normal person would not consider the interference to be a serious one. If, however, the fears are based on substantive data, e.g., the fact that the men in the house will receive very little supervision from trained staff, or the fact that many of the ex-inmates have a history of child molestation, or the fact that property assessments have actually gone down due to the halfway house, then a normal person might agree that the interference is a substantial one.

The social value of the use that the plaintiff is making of the land   For what purpose is the plaintiff using his or her land? How valuable is that use to society? The following uses have considerable **social value:** use as a residence, use for business purposes, and use for recreational purposes. This is not to say that vacant or unoccupied land has no social value. In balancing all of the factors, however, a court is less likely to conclude that an interference with such land is unreasonable than an interference with land actively used for residential, commercial, or recreational purposes.

The character of the locality   This factor is one of the most important in determining the reasonableness or unreasonableness of the interference. How suitable is the use the plaintiff is making of his or her land to the environment? Zoning ordinances are one measure of suitability. Even if no such ordinances exist, however, a court will still ask whether an area is used primarily or exclusively for residences, for heavy industry, for small businesses, for agriculture, etc. Having made this determination, a court will then use the following rough equation:

> If the plaintiff's use of his or her land is suitable to the locality, a court will be more likely to conclude that an interference with this use is unreasonable than if the use is not suitable or compatible.

If, for example, the plaintiff is using land as a home in an area that is predominantly residential, a court will be more inclined to find that noise, odor, or other pollution from a nearby business is unreasonable than if the area is predominantly commercial. Of course, the equation becomes more difficult to apply when an area consists of a significant mixture of residential, commercial, and recreational structures, such as in many of our cities, where use patterns change over the years. When there is such a mixture, it simply means that a plaintiff cannot be as sensitive to interferences as a plaintiff living in a purer or more homogeneous area.

The character of the locality can also be looked at from the perspective of the defendant's conduct. How compatible is the conduct with the predominant nature of the environment? The more incompatible it is, the more likely that a court would find that the interference with the plaintiff's use and enjoyment of land is unreasonable.

The extent of the burden on the plaintiff of avoiding or minimizing the interference   A court will probably be unwilling to find an interference by the defendant to be unreasonable if the burden on the plaintiff of avoiding or minimizing the interference is modest. The plaintiff, in effect, has an obligation to avoid the consequences of the defendant's tort when it is practical to do so. Suppose, for example, that all the plaintiff had to do to prevent occasional factory odors from coming into the house was to close some of the windows at certain times of the day. The minor nature of this burden would weigh against calling the interference unreasonable. On the other hand, if the only way for the plaintiff to avoid or minimize the interference were to rebuild the house or business or to move away, then the substantial nature of the burden might help tip the scale toward concluding that the interference is unreasonable.

The motive of the defendant   Why has the defendant interfered with the plaintiff's use and enjoyment of his or her land? If it can be shown that the defendant acted out of spite to harm the plaintiff, then it is highly likely that a court will conclude that any significant interference is unreasonable. On the other hand, if the interference is simply the product of the defendant's pursuit of his or her own self-interest, unreasonableness will be more difficult to establish.

The social value of the defendant's conduct that led to the interference   Just as we needed to ask about the social value of the plaintiff's use of his or her land, so too we must ask about the social utility of the defendant's conduct that produced the interference. Conduct can have social utility even if the defendant is acting for his or her own private interests, e.g., using his or her backyard for a barbecue or running a machine in a farm or other business. Social value concerns the general public good in its broadest sense. From this perspective, there is little that the defendant can do that does not have at least some social value, as long as the defendant is not acting out of malice or in violation of some criminal or civil statute. No absolute conclusions can be made for every situation. The question is rarely: does the defendant's conduct have social value or utility? Rather, the question is: *how much* social value or utility does it have? How much is the general public good advanced by the conduct? Operating a hospital or school has high social value. Operating a farm or living in a home also has social value. The court must assess where on the scale the activity falls. The greater the social value, the less likely that a court will conclude that the conduct or condition causing the interference is unreasonable. This does not mean, however, that a cancer-curing hospital cannot commit a private nuisance. Again, all of the factors must be considered. The ultimate test is whether the social value or utility of the defendant's conduct outweighs the hardship of the interference the plaintiff is suffering.

The extent of the burden on the defendant of avoiding or minimizing the interference What would the defendant have to do to stop or minimize the interference? Install an inexpensive shield? Close down? Radically change the nature of the business? The more minimal the burden, the more likely the court will find the continued interference to be unreasonable. This does not mean, however, that the defendant is home free simply by showing that the burden of avoiding or minimizing the interference would be great. The extent of the burden is but one factor that must be weighed.

■ ASSIGNMENT 27.6 ■

Examine the following situations. What questions would you want answered in order to make a determination of whether there has been an unreasonable interference with the use and enjoyment of land for purposes of establishing a private nuisance? (See General Instructions for the Investigation Strategy Assignment in Chapter 4.)

a. The plaintiff lives next door to a small nursing home. The home has a large air conditioner motor in the back yard. The plaintiff is very upset about the noise given off by this motor.
b. The defendant is an excellent mechanic. She works on cars as a hobby after her regular job hours. She frequently works on her car and the cars of her friends until late at night. The plaintiff, a neighbor, is bothered by the bright lights the defendant uses while working on the cars and by the constant coming and going of her friends who visit to talk about cars.
c. The local church runs a bingo game every Thursday night. This is extremely upsetting to the plaintiff, who lives next door to the church.
d. A factory employing five hundred people has a chimney that sends black smoke into the air. Particles in the smoke sometimes fall on the plaintiff's house. The plaintiff is worried that the particles will damage her property.

2. What Are the Ways in Which a Private Nuisance Can Be Committed?

First, the unreasonable interference can be created negligently. Here, there is no intent to interfere. The defendant creates an unreasonable risk of interfering. Suppose, for example, the defendants dump what they think is harmless waste into a stream that flows through the plaintiff's land before going out to sea. In fact, the waste is not harmless. As a result, the plaintiff's land becomes totally useless. If the defendants had taken reasonable precautions, they would have discovered the harmful nature of the waste. The defendants have negligently created an unreasonable interference with the plaintiff's use and enjoyment of land.

Second, the unreasonable interference can be created intentionally. Intent here means that the defendant knows the interference will occur or has knowledge with substantial certainty that the interference will result from what the defendant does or fails to do. If the defendant, for example, knows that foul pollutants are coming from its factory to the plaintiff's land, the defendant, in the eyes of the law, has intended this interference.

Finally, the unreasonable interference can be created through conduct that would impose strict liability—an abnormally dangerous condition or activity, such as blasting.

3. Who Can Sue for a Private Nuisance?

Since private nuisance protects the use and enjoyment of private land, anyone who has rights to the use and enjoyment of the land can sue for a private nuisance. This includes individuals in possession of the land, such as tenants, who are claiming an interest in the land, as well as their families. Landlords who do not live on or use the land themselves can bring the suit when the damages caused by the defendant are permanent.

4. What Remedies can Be Obtained When a Private Nuisance Has Been Committed?

Damages can be awarded for the harm caused by the private nuisance. The measure of damages is usually the difference between the value of the land before the harm and its value after the harm. Some courts will permit a plaintiff to choose as the measure of damages the **cost of restoration.** Additional compensatory damages include the loss in the rental value of the land, the loss of the plaintiff's own personal use of the land, and an amount to compensate the plaintiff for any discomfort or annoyance that has been experienced.

There are times when a damage award is not adequate, particularly when the interference is threatened or is continuous. The issue will be whether the plaintiff can obtain an **injunction** against the defendants to prevent or stop the interference. Most courts are reluctant to grant the equitable relief of an injunction because of its drastic nature. The court must first be satisfied that a damage award will not be adequate to remedy the problem. If the interference is threatened, the court will want to be convinced that there is a high likelihood that the interference will in fact occur. The effect of an injunction could be to close down a defendant's business. This may lead to the loss of many jobs. Hence, before a court will grant an injunction, it will weigh (a) the economic hardship that will be suffered by the defendant due to an injunction, and (b) the nature of the interference the plaintiff is suffering. The court will also consider the hardship that the entire community might suffer if the injunction is granted. In short, the court will go through a kind of analysis on the injunction issue similar to the process it went through to determine whether the interference was unreasonable. A court may decide that the interference is unreasonable, but that injunctive relief against it is unwarranted because it is too drastic. If so, the court will permit the defendant to proceed, but require damages to be paid to the plaintiff. This is an unsatisfactory result, because the practical effect of refusing to grant the injunction is a kind of court "permission" to continue with an unreasonable interference with the plaintiff's land.

Another remedy that might be available to the plaintiff is **self-help.** This would include the common-law privilege to **abate the nuisance** without going through court proceedings. The plaintiff must act within a reasonable amount of time after the interference is discovered. If practical, the plaintiff must first notify the defendants of the interference to see if the latter will correct it on their own. Only reasonable force can be used by the plaintiff to abate the nuisance. The plaintiff will not be permitted to blow up a factory in order to shut it down.

5. What Defenses Are Available to a Defendant?

Contributory negligence   The contributory negligence of the plaintiff in helping to cause his or her own injury or interference is a defense if the defendant produced the private nuisance negligently. Contributory negligence of the plaintiff is not a defense if the defendant produced the private nuisance recklessly or intentionally.

Assumption of the risk   Assumption of the risk is a defense if the plaintiff voluntarily accepted a risk from the nuisance that he or she fully understands. It is not often that a defendant can establish that the plaintiff assumed the risk of a private nuisance. The defense is more frequently raised in cases of a public nuisance, to be discussed below.

Suppose that the plaintiff has "moved to the nuisance," e.g., the plaintiff moves to an industrial town knowing that a lot of noise and pollution exists. Hasn't the plaintiff assumed the risk of the private nuisance? No. A plaintiff is not barred from complaining about a nuisance simply because the nuisance was there before the plaintiff arrived. To say that someone has "moved to the nuisance" may beg the question of whether there is in fact a private nuisance. All of the factors discussed above must be analyzed to determine whether there is an unreasonable interference, e.g., the suitability of the activity to the locale.

An interference may be unreasonable in an exclusively residential area, but quite reasonable in an industrial area. On the separate question of whether a court will grant an injunction against what it has found to be a nuisance, the fact that the plaintiff has "come to the nuisance" will be a factor to be weighed *against* the granting of the injunction. This is different, however, from the problem of whether a private nuisance in fact exists.

Mitigation of damages   If the plaintiff knows that the defendant's private nuisance has resulted in the poisoning of the plaintiff's drinking water, the plaintiff cannot proceed to drink the water anyway or continue to let his or her animals drink it. The defendant will be responsible for the poisoning of the water, but not for the consequences of the poisoning that the plaintiff could have eliminated. The plaintiff has failed to **mitigate the damages.** The rule of **avoidable consequences** requires the plaintiff to take reasonable steps to avoid the harmful consequences of the defendant's tort.

Official authorization   Special statutes, ordinances, or regulations may exist that either authorize or require the defendant to engage in the activity that is later being challenged as a nuisance. For example, zoning ordinances authorize certain kinds of activities and structures, and statutes may exist requiring public utilities to transport dangerous substances. Such official sanction, however, is never an authorization to carry on the activity carelessly or negligently. Damages and injunctive relief will be granted only to the extent that harm is caused or threatened by carrying on the activity in an unreasonable manner. The entire operation will rarely be enjoined, because that would have the effect of rescinding the official authorization.

Even if the defendant is not conducting the activity unreasonably, a plaintiff may have an argument that the official sanction of the activity has, in effect, resulted in a **taking of property** for which the government is responsible and therefore liable for just compensation.

Public Nuisance

We examine public nuisance by the same five basic questions we used to discuss a private nuisance:

1. What is the nature of a public nuisance? What type of harm does it cover?
2. How is it created?
3. Who can sue?
4. What remedies are available?
5. What defenses are available?

For some of the questions, the answers are very similar to those given for private nuisance. The answers to the first and third questions, however, are substantially different.

1. What is the Nature of a Public Nuisance and What Type of Harm Does It Cover?

A public nuisance often has nothing to do with the use and enjoyment of land. It is an unreasonable interference with a right that is common to the public.

Examples:

- keeping diseased animals that will be sold for food
- operating a house of prostitution
- operating an illegal gambling parlor
- obstructing a public highway
- polluting a public river
- wiretapping conversations in a judge's chambers or in a jury room
- maintaining unsafe apartment buildings used by many people
- using public profanity

Very often, the conduct of the defendant constitutes a crime.

For an interference to be a public nuisance, there must be some public right involved. Every member of the public does not have to be actually affected by it. If only a small number of people are affected, however, there is usually no public nuisance. To obstruct a public highway, e.g., by leaving a truck on it or by causing boulders to be placed on it, is a public nuisance, because there is a public right to use the highway, and this right is taken away from everyone who tries to use it.

The interference with the public right must be unreasonable. If the defendant has violated a specific statute, ordinance, or regulation, there is usually little difficulty establishing unreasonableness. Otherwise, many of the same factors described earlier to determine the reasonableness of an alleged private nuisance must also be used to determine the reasonableness of an alleged public nuisance, e.g., the gravity of the interference and the burden of removal or mitigation.

2. What Are the Ways in Which a Public Nuisance Can Be Created?

Negligence: The defendant can negligently create the public nuisance, e.g., carelessly allowing logs to fall off a truck, which obstruct a public highway.

Intent: Here the defendant knows that the interference with a public right will occur or is substantially certain that it will occur based on what the defendant does or fails to do, e.g., the defendant knows that the pollutants being poured into a lake will make the lake unusable by the public for fishing.

Abnormally dangerous condition or activity: The defendant, for example, conducts blasting in an area, which causes substantial damage to all surrounding buildings through vibrations.

Violation of a statute, ordinance, or regulation: The defendant, for example, opens a house of prostitution.

3. Who Can Sue for the Public Nuisance?

Because public rights are involved, a public official can always either bring a civil action against the defendant or prosecute him or her in the criminal courts.

When can a *private* citizen bring a suit for a public nuisance? A private person can sue only when he or she suffered in a way that is different from the suffering of every other member of the public affected by the public nuisance. The plaintiff must have suffered special or particular damage. The harm must be different in kind. If the plaintiff has only suffered more of the same harm everyone else has suffered (a difference in degree only), few courts will allow the plaintiff to bring an independent action for the public nuisance. If the defendant obstructs a public highway, resulting in the need for a substantial detour, the citizens who must suffer this inconvenience have *not* suffered an inconvenience that is different in kind from that of everyone else. Hence, a private suit cannot be brought. All that a citizen can do is ask the public authorities to take the defendant to court. Suppose, however, that one citizen crashes into obstruction. This individual has suffered personal or property damage that is different in kind from having to make a detour. Such an individual, therefore, *can* bring a private action for the public nuisance. Also, if the plaintiff can show special financial damage that other members of the public do not suffer, the plaintiff will usually be able to bring the public nuisance action.

Some public nuisances are also private nuisances when the conduct of the defendant interferes with a public right *and* interferes with the use and enjoyment of a particular plaintiff's land. For example, the defendant builds a dam that prevents the public from using the water that would otherwise flow into a lake used for recreational purposes, and the dam also floods the plaintiff's land; or the defendant opens a gambling establishment next door to the plaintiff, whose peace of mind is substantially disrupted as a result.

Occasionally, environmental legislation will give private citizens **standing,** which is the right to initiate a court proceeding to redress a wrong such as the violation of the environmental legislation. The violation might constitute a public nuisance. The legislation will often be limited to injunctive relief, so that the individual plaintiff who is acting on behalf of a class or group of citizens cannot recover personal damages. Sometimes the legislation will authorize the plaintiff to collect the litigation costs from the defendant, including attorney fees.

4. What Remedies Can Be Obtained When a Public Nuisance Has Been Committed?

When a public official brings the public nuisance action, the remedies often include a fine or imprisonment. The government may also be able to collect damages that may have been done to public property.

As with a private nuisance, it is sometimes difficult to obtain an injunction against a public nuisance, particularly when a crime has been committed or is threatened. There is an elaborate trial procedure governing crimes that a court cannot bypass through an injunction against a public nuisance allegedly involving criminal behavior. Where this problem does not exist, a court will go through a balancing analysis similar to the one it uses in deciding whether to issue an injunction against a private nuisance.

Self-help is also a possible remedy—the privilege to abate a nuisance. Only reasonable force can be used, and the steps taken by the plaintiff to stop the nuisance must occur very soon after the nuisance is discovered and after notice is given to the defendant, unless such notice is impractical under the circumstances.

5. What Defenses Are Available to a Defendant in a Public Nuisance Case?

The four main categories of defenses discussed under private nuisance apply equally to public nuisances:

- contributory negligence
- assumption of the risk
- mitigation of damages
- official authorization

CASE

Armory Park Neighborhood Assn v. Episcopal Community Services
148 Ariz. 1, 712 P.2d 914 (1985)
Supreme Court of Arizona

Background: St. Martin's Center is run by Episcopal Community Services (ECS). The Center operates a free food distribution program for indigent persons in Tuscon. The Armory Park Neighborhood Association sought an injunction against this program as a public nuisance. Although the program did not violate any zoning or health codes, the trial court granted a preliminary injunction against the Center on the ground that its activities constituted a public and a private nuisance. The case is now on appeal before the Supreme Court of Arizona.

Decision on Appeal: The injunction against the Center's free meal program is appropriate.

Opinion of Court

Justice FELDMAN delivered the opinion of the court . . .

Before the Center opened, the area had been primarily residential with a few small businesses. When the Center began operating in December 1982, many transients crossed the area daily on their way to and from the Center. Although the Center was only open from 5:00 to 6:00 p.m., patrons lined up well before this hour and often lingered in the neighborhood long after finishing their meal. The Center rented an adjacent fenced lot for a waiting area and organized neighborhood cleaning projects, but the trial judge apparently felt these efforts were inadequate to control the activity stemming from the Center. Transients frequently trespassed onto residents' yards, sometimes urinating, defecating, drinking and littering on the residents' property. A few broke into storage areas and unoccupied homes, and some asked residents for handouts. The number of arrests in the area increased dramatically. Many residents were frightened or annoyed by the transients and altered their lifestyles to avoid them. . . .

We have previously distinguished public and private nuisances. In *City of Phoenix v. Johnson,* 51 Ariz. 115, 75 P.2d 30 (1938), we noted that a nuisance is public when it affects rights of "citizens as a part of the public, while a private nuisance is one which affects a single individual or a definite number of persons on the enjoyment of some private right which is not common to the public." Id. at 123, 75 P.2d 34. A public nuisance must also affect a considerable number of people. . . .

Defendant claims that its business should not be held responsible for acts committed by its patrons off the premises of the Center. It argues that since it has no control over the patrons when they are not on the Center's premises, it cannot be enjoined because of their acts. We do not believe this position is supported either by precedent or theory.

In *Shambart v. Morrison Cafeteria Co.,* 159 Fla. 629, 32 So.2d 727 (1947), the defendant operated a well frequented cafeteria. Each day customers waiting to enter the business would line up on the sidewalk, blocking the entrances to the neighboring establishments. The dissenting justices argued that the defendant had not actually caused the lines to form and that the duty to prevent the harm to the plaintiffs should be left to the police through regulation of the public streets. The majority of the court rejected this argument, and remanded the case for a determination of the damages. See, also, *Reid v. Brodsky,* 397 Pa. 463, 156 A.2d 334 (1959) (operation of a bar enjoined because its patrons were often noisy and intoxicated; they frequently used the neighboring properties for toilet purposes and sexual misconduct); *Barrett v. Lopez,* 57 N.M. 697, 262 P.2d 981, 983

(1953) (operation of a dance hall enjoined, the court finding that "mere possibility of relief from another source [police] does not relieve the courts of their responsibilities"); *Wade v. Fuller,* 12 Utah 2d 299, 365 P.2d 802 (1961) (operation of drive-in cafe enjoined where patrons created disturbances to nearby residents); *McQuade v. Tucson Tiller Apartments,* 25 Ariz.App. 312, 543 P.2d 150 (1975) (music concerts at mall designed to attract customers enjoined because of increased crowds and noise in residential area). . . .

Since the rules of a civilized society require us to tolerate our neighbors, the law requires our neighbors to keep their activities within the limits of what is tolerable by a reasonable person. However, what is reasonably tolerable must be tolerated; not all interferences with public rights are public nuisances. As Dean Prosser explains, "[t]he law does not concern itself with trifles, or seek to remedy all of the petty annoyances and disturbances of everyday life in a civilized community even from conduct committed with knowledge that annoyance and inconvenience will result." Prosser, W. and W. P. Keeton, *Handbook on the Law of Torts,* § 88, at 626 (5th ed. 1984). Thus, to constitute a nuisance, the complained-of interference must be substantial, intentional and unreasonable under the circumstances. *Restatement (Second) of Torts,* § 826 comment c and § 821F. Our courts have generally used a balancing test in deciding the reasonableness of an interference. The trial court should look at the utility and reasonableness of the conduct and balance these factors against the extent of harm inflicted and the nature of the affected neighborhood. We noted in the early case of *MacDonald v. Perry:*

> What might amount to a serious nuisance in one locality by reason of the density of the population, or character of the neighborhood affected, may in another place and under different surroundings be deemed proper and unobjectionable. What amount

of annoyance or inconvenience caused by others in the lawful use of their property will constitute a nuisance depends upon varying circumstances and cannot be precisely defined.

32 Ariz. 39, 50, 255 P. 494 (1927).

The trial judge did not ignore the balancing test and was well aware of the social utility of defendant's operation. His words are illuminating:

> It is distressing to this Court that an activity such as defendants [sic] should be restrained. Providing for the poor and the homeless is certainly a worthwhile, praisworthy [sic] activity. It is particularly distressing to this Court because it [defendant] has no control over those who are attracted to the kitchen while they are either coming or leaving the premises. However, the right to the comfortable enjoyment of one's property is something that another's activities should not affect, the harm being suffered by the Armory Park Neighborhood and the residents therein is irreparable and substantial, for which they have no adequate legal remedy. . . .

We believe that a determination made by weighing and balancing conflicting interests or principles is truly one which lies within the discretion of the trial judge. We defer to that discretion here. The evidence of the multiple trespasses upon and defacement of the residents' property supports the trial court's conclusion that the interference caused by defendant's operation was unreasonable despite its charitable cause.

The common law has long recognized that the usefulness of a particular activity may outweigh the inconveniences, discomforts and changes it causes some persons to suffer. We, too, acknowledge the social value of the Center. Its charitable purpose, that of feeding the hungry, is entitled to greater deference than pursuits of lesser intrinsic value. It appears from the record that ECS purposes in operating the Center were entirely admirable. However, even admirable ventures may cause unreasonable interferences. See e.g., *Assembly of God Church of Tahoka v. Bradley,* 196 S.W.2d 696 (Tex. Civ. App. 1946). We do not believe that the law allows the costs of a charitable enterprise to be visited in their entirety upon the residents of a single neighborhood. The problems of dealing with the unemployed, the homeless and the mentally ill are also matters of community or governmental responsibility.

ECS argues that its compliance with City of Tucson zoning regulations is a conclusive determination of reasonableness. We agree that compliance with zoning provisions has some bearing in nuisance cases. . . . We decline, however, to find that ECS' compliance with the applicable zoning provisions precludes a court from enjoining its activities. The equitable power of the judiciary exists independent of statute. Although zoning and criminal provisions are binding with respect to the type of activity, they do not limit the power of a court acting in equity to enjoin an unreasonable, albeit permitted, activity as a public nuisance. . . .

The trial court's order granting the preliminary injunction is affirmed. By affirming the trial court's preliminary orders, we do not require that he close the Center permanently. It is of course, within the equitable discretion of the trial court to fashion a less severe remedy, if possible. . . .

▪ ASSIGNMENT 27.7 ▪

a. Suppose that a church operated the same kind of free meal program in New York City. Would the result be the same?

b. What is the logical consequence of this opinion? That programs such as those operated by St. Martin's Center will always be kept in the inner city and never be allowed in the suburbs?

▪ ASSIGNMENT 27.8 ▪

Prepare an annotated bibliography on nuisance (public and private) in your state. (See General Instructions for the Annotated Bibliography Assignment in Chapter 2.)

▪ TRADITIONAL NEGLIGENCE LIABILITY

In this section, we consider negligence liability to persons who are injured on someone's premises or in the immediate environment. In Chapters 11 through 14, we studied the elements of negligence:

- duty
- breach of duty
- proximate cause
- damages

The major headache in the area of premises liability is the first element: duty. In chapter 11 the general rule on duty is stated as follows:

> Whenever one's acts or omissions create a foreseeable risk of injury or damage to someone else's person or property, a duty of reasonable care arises to take precautions to prevent that injury or damage.

When discussing the negligence liability of occupiers of land, this general rule on duty is unfortunately riddled with exceptions depending on the status of the plaintiff:

- adult trespasser
- child trespasser
- licensee
- invitee

and the status of the defendant:

- owner-seller
- owner-buyer
- tenant

Every time the status of the plaintiff or defendant changes, we must ask whether the court will apply a different standard of duty (other than the general duty of reasonable care) for purposes of negligence liability.

A few courts have recently discarded all these special rules and exceptions, and have declared that the duty is reasonable care for all categories of plaintiffs and defendants. The status of the plaintiff or defendant is simply one of the factors to be taken into consideration in deciding whether there has been a breach of this duty. The status of the plaintiff as trespasser, licensee, or invitee, for example, would be relevant solely in determining the extent to which their presence on the land was foreseeable to the defendant. A separate duty would not exist for each category of plaintiff under this minority view. Because most courts, however, do not take this position, we must examine each status separately.

Throughout the discussion, we will be asking whether a **duty of reasonable care** is owed by the defendant, and if not, what **lesser standard of care** is owed. In some situations, it may be that *no duty* of care is owed, so that the defendant will not be liable for the injury suffered by the plaintiff.

The following themes will guide our discussion:

1. the duty of occupiers of land to persons outside the land
2. the duty of occupiers of land to trespassers, licensees, and invitees on the land
3. the special problems of the seller and buyer of land (vendor and vendee)
4. the special problems of the landlord and tenant (lessor and lessee)

By **occupier** we mean anyone in possession of the land claiming a right to possession, e.g., an owner personally using the premises, a tenant, or an adverse possessor.

1. Persons Outside the Land

A person traveling in front of the defendant's land or living close by can be injured in a number of ways. The injury can come from a natural condition on the defendant's land (e.g., a tree limb falls on the plaintiff who is walking on a sidewalk), or from a non-natural condition on the defendant's land (e.g., a building collapses on a car parked on a street in front of the defendant's land), or from some business or personal activity taking place on the defendant's land (e.g., a bucket falls from a plank used by painters, and the bucket hits a pedestrian). See Figure 27.3 for the defendant's duty with respect to each category.

The rules in Figure 27.3 apply if the injury results from anything that the defendant's employees do or fail to do within the scope of their employment. Suppose, however, the defendant hires an **independent contractor** over whom the

Figure 27.3   Standard of Care Owed by Occupiers of Land to Persons Outside the Land

The Condition or Activity	The Duty Owed
1. *Natural conditions on the defendant's land* (e.g., natural lakes, trees, rocks)	1. Generally, the defendant owes *no* duty of care to prevent injury to persons outside the land who might be injured by natural conditions on the defendant's land. If, however, the defendant owns *trees* in an *urban* area, he or she does owe a *duty of reasonable care* to inspect the trees and make sure that they are safe to persons outside the land. In most states, there is *no* duty owed if the trees are in a *rural* area.
2. *Non-natural or artificial conditions on the defendant's land* (e.g., fence, swimming pool, building)	2. The defendant owes a *duty of reasonable care* to prevent injury to persons outside the land who might be injured by non-natural or artificial conditions on the defendant's land.

Figure 27.3   Continued

The Condition or Activity	The Duty Owed
3. *Business or personal activity taking place on the defendant's land* (e.g., steam blasting the side of a building)	**3.** The defendant owes a *duty of reasonable care* to prevent injury to persons outside the land who might be injured by business or personal activities being conducted by the defendant on the land.

defendant usually has little control concerning the manner in which the work is done. If injury occurs to plaintiffs not on the land due to the activity of independent contractors on the land, the independent contractor and not the defendant will be liable for the negligence. An exception exists when the defendant hires the independent contractor to do inherently dangerous work. The defendant will be liable for injuries resulting from such activities. When, however, the injury results from the manner or method of work of the independent contractor not involved in inherently dangerous work, the defendant-occupier of the land is not liable.

2. Trespassers, Licensees, and Invitees

Everyone who comes on the land will fall into one of the three categories of trespasser, licensee, or invitee. The highest standard of care is owed the invitee, who must be accorded full reasonable-care treatment by the land occupier. While the trespasser is given the lowest standard of care of the three, there are important exceptions that have the effect of elevating the amount of care owed the trespasser.

The basic definitions of the three categories of persons on the land are given in Figure 27.4.

Trespassers

Trespassers have neither consent nor privilege to be on the land or on designated portions of the land. The privileges would include necessity, recapture of chattels, and abatement of a nuisance. (See Chapter 31.)

The general rule is that the occupier owes *no duty of care* to a trespasser unless the trespasser falls into one of the following categories:

- discovered trespasser anywhere on the land
- foreseeable constant trespassers on limited areas of the land
- child trespasser anywhere on the land

Discovered trespasser anywhere on the land   An occupier cannot commit any *intentional* harm on a known trespasser except in self-defense, defense of another, or some other recognized privilege of using such force. A spring gun, for example, cannot be used to catch an unsuspecting trespasser. What about

Figure 27.4   Trespasser, Licensee, and Invitee

Trespasser: A person who enters the land without the consent of the occupier and without any privilege to do so.

Licensee: A person who enters the land for his or her own purposes, but with the express or implied consent of the occupier. A licensee does not enter to pursue a purpose of the occupier.

Invitee: A person who enters the land upon the express or implied invitation of the occupier in order to use the land for the purposes for which it is held open to the public or to pursue the business of the occupier.

---

negligence liability? A known trespasser is owed a duty of reasonable care by the occupier. If, for example, a railroad engineer sees a trespasser ahead, reasonable care must be used to avoid hitting the trespasser. Actual knowledge of the trespasser is not necessary as long as the occupier has enough information to lead a reasonable person to know that a trespasser is present.

Reasonable care does not mean that the occupier must make the land safe for the trespasser. It simply means that once discovered, the occupier must use reasonable care to avoid injuring the trespasser. Ordinary care under the circumstances will be sufficient. A warning, for example, may be required to alert the trespasser to dangerous activities or conditions on the land, which the trespasser might not be expected to notice. No such warning would be needed, however, for natural conditions on the land, such as a lake or clearly visible ice.

A few courts take a more simplistic view and argue that the only duty of the occupier to the known trespasser is to avoid injuring the trespasser by willful or wanton conduct.

Foreseeable constant trespassers on limited portions of the land   The occupier has a duty of reasonable care to discover and provide protection for trespassers who frequently enter limited areas of the land. For example, a railroad may know (or should know) that large numbers of people regularly walk across the track at a designated spot. The area must be limited and the trespassing in that area must be constant. As with the known trespasser, the occupier does not have a duty to inspect his or her land in order to make it injury-proof. The duty is to use reasonable care under the circumstances, which may include a warning, fencing, extra lighting—but only on the limited area where constant trespassers are foreseeable. The more dangerous the condition or activity in that area, the greater the precaution the occupier must take to prevent the injury. No such precautions are usually needed for natural conditions on the limited area of the land that the trespassers can be expected to protect themselves against. If the trespasser is injured in spite of the reasonable steps taken by the occupier, the latter will not be liable for negligence.

Child trespassers anywhere on the land   Children are given special protection in the law of premises liability. A **child** is usually defined as someone who is too young to appreciate the dangers that could be involved in a given situation.

There is no age limit that sets the boundary line for the level of immaturity that is required, but in the vast majority of cases that have provided this special protection, the plaintiff has been under fifteen.

The special protection is embodied in the **attractive nuisance doctrine,** which says a duty of reasonable care is owed to prevent injury:

1. to a trespassing child unable to appreciate the danger
2. from an artificial condition or activity on land
3. to which the child can be expected to be attracted

The word "nuisance" is used in its generic sense of something that is mischievous; it has no reference to the rules on private and public nuisance discussed earlier.

A more modern statement of the "attractive nuisance" rule or doctrine has been provided by the *Restatement of Torts*[3], which provides that an occupier of land is liable for physical harm caused by artificial conditions on the land if:

1. the artificial condition is on a place on the land that the occupier knows or has reason to know that children will trespass upon, and
2. the occupier knows or has reason to know that the artificial condition will involve an unreasonable risk of serious injury to the trespassing children, and
3. the trespassing children are too young to discover the artificial condition or to appreciate the danger within it, and
4. the utility to the occupier of maintaining the condition and the burden or inconvenience of eliminating the danger are slight when compared to the risk to the trespassing children, and
5. the occupier fails to take those reasonable steps that would protect the child

This list of conditions is a specific application of the traditional breach-of-duty equation we examined in Chapter 12, which balances the factors that help the court determine what is and is not unreasonable conduct:

Figure 27.5   Breach-of-Duty Equation

Foreseeability of the danger of an accident occuring

———————————————

Foreseeability of the kind of injury or damage that will result if an accident occurs

balanced against

The burden or inconvenience on the defendant of taking precautions to avoid the accident

———————————————

The importance or social utility of what the defendant was trying to do before the accident

The foreseeability of serious injury to the child is measured or weighed against what the defendant was trying to accomplish by the artificial condition, and the burden or inconvenience on the defendant to protect the child against this condition.

---

[3]*Restatement (Second) of Torts § 339 (1965).*

Artificial conditions include tracks, vehicles, rope, fences, barns, and factories. Under the Restatement's formula, the attractiveness of the condition is important mainly on the issue of the foreseeability of the child's presence.

The duty of reasonable care is usually not applied when the child is injured by natural conditions on the land (e.g., lakes, rivers, and natural rock formations) unless the defendant has significantly altered these conditions through strip-mining or other processes.

▪ ASSIGNMENT 27.9 ▪

What questions would you investigate to decide whether the defendant in the following cases owed and breached a duty of reasonable care to the plaintiff? (See General Instructions for the Investigation Strategy Assignment in Chapter 4.)

a. A ten-year-old boy is trespassing on the defendant's land. He leans against a fence on the land and badly injures his back against a protruding nail.
b. A nine-year-old girl is trespassing on the defendant's land. She watches workers climb a pole on the land. After the workers leave, the girl puts on a pair of spiked or cleated shoes that she owns and tries to climb the pole. She falls and severely injures herself.

Licensees

Licensees are on the land with the express or implied permission of the occupier. The licensees, however, are present for their own purposes.

Examples:

- someone taking a shortcut through the land
- someone soliciting money for charity
- a trespasser who has been allowed to remain, e.g., a loiterer
- a person who comes to borrow a tool
- a social guest, even if invited

The last example has caused some difficulty. Because **social guests** are invited, one would normally tend to classify them as invitees. Only a few courts, however, take this position. In most states, a social guest is a mere licensee, no matter how much urging the occupier may have used to get the guest to come and even though the guest may perform some incidental chores or tasks for the occupier while there. A **business guest,** however, who comes for the purpose of doing business with the occupier, *is* an invitee.

What standard of care is owed by the occupier to the licensee?

1. First, the occupier owes the licensee at least the same duty of care that he or she owes the trespasser discussed above.
2. Second, the occupier must warn the licensee of dangerous natural *or* artificial conditions of which the occupier has actual knowledge. (Note: the occupier does not have a duty to inspect his or her premises to discover such danger. This duty to inspect *will* exist for the protection of an invitee.)
3. Third, if the condition is extremely dangerous, the occupier's duty may be to take active, reasonable precautions to protect the licensee rather than to simply warn him or her of the condition.
4. Fourth, for any activities being conducted on the land, the occupier owes the licensee a duty of reasonable care to avoid injuring the licensee, which may call for a warning or for more active safety precautions.

Suppose that there is a fence on the land in a state of disrepair. The occupier has no actual knowledge of this artificial condition but should know about it if he or she were acting reasonably. The licensee is injured when the fence falls on him or her. The occupier is not liable to the licensee for negligence. The occupier has no duty to inspect for dangerous *conditions*. If the occupier has actual knowledge of the dangerous condition (artificial or natural), then he or she must either warn the licensee of it or make it safe, depending on the nature of the danger. *Activities,* such as operating machinery on the land, however, call for reasonable care.

If the occupier knows that third persons are on the land who are likely to injure the licensee, the occupier has a duty to at least warn the licensee of the presence of such third persons, e.g., known criminals or individuals who have told the occupier that they want to harm the licensee.

An analogous situation involves automobiles. If the social guest is a licensee in an automobile, the same rules apply: the driver has a duty to use reasonable care in driving the car (an activity), but has no duty to inspect the car to make sure that it is safe. When the driver knows of defective conditions in the car, he or she must warn the guest of them. As indicated in Chapter 12, however, there are automobile guest statutes in many states that change this common law, often making the driver liable only for wanton or reckless conduct in driving the car. Such statutes usually do not apply if the plaintiff is a **passenger** rather than a guest. To be a passenger, the plaintiff's presence must confer some benefit on the driver other than the benefit of his or her company or the mere sharing of expenses, although the latter can be a factor to show that the plaintiff is a passenger if other benefit to the driver is also shown. If the plaintiff is paying for the ride, or if the driver is trying to solicit business from the plaintiff, the latter is a passenger to whom a duty of reasonable care is owed.

▪ ASSIGNMENT 27.10 ▪

A door-to-door salesperson slips and falls on a child's skate upon approaching the front door of a residence. What standard of care would the occupier owe this person in your state? (See General Instructions for the State Court Opinion Assignment in Chapter 2.)

Invitees

The highest degree of care by the occupier of land is owed an invitee. An invitee is someone present on the land with the express or implied invitation of the occupier to use the land for a purpose for which it is open to the public or to use the land to pursue the business of the occupier.

Examples:

- a customer in a department store
- someone browsing in a department store, even if nothing is purchased
- a user of a laundromat to wash clothes (a person present in the laundromat to wait for a bus or to get out of the rain, however, is probably a licensee only)
- someone attending a free public lecture on religion
- a user of a library (a person who is there to meet a friend, however, is probably only a licensee)

- a patron at a restaurant, theater, amusement park, or other establishment
- someone who goes to a garage to find out if it sells a certain part for a car

There must be an element of invitation that is much stronger than mere permission or consent that the person be on the land. The invitation is an implied or direct statement of a desire by the occupier that the person be present. A greater standard of care is owed to an invitee than to a trespasser or a licensee because the invitation justifies the invitee's belief that the premises are safe.

Public employees injured on the premises often pose a problem. They include police officers, fire fighters, sanitation workers, postal workers, and meter readers. What is their status? If they are not present in their official capacity within working hours, their status is determined like that of any other citizen. Indeed, they could have the status of trespasser. When present in an *official* role, are they invitees or licensees?

In most states, police officers and fire fighters are licensees only, to whom a duty of reasonable care is owed for activities conducted on the premises, but no duty concerning dangerous conditions unknown to the occupier. The theory behind this position is that these public employees are likely to go to parts of the premises that the occupier has no reason to expect, especially in emergency situations. As to such areas, the occupier has made no implied or direct representation that they are safe. Other public official entrants, however, are given the status of invitees on the somewhat strained theory they are present for a business purpose of the occupier.

A few states disregard the above distinction and classify all public entrants as invitees.

▪ ASSIGNMENT 27.11 ▪

Are the following individuals invitees, licensees, or trespassers? (See General Instructions for the Legal Analysis Assignment in Chapter 3.)

a. Tom enters a restaurant solely to use its bathroom. He slips on the bathroom floor.
b. Mary wants to visit a friend who is staying at a hotel. She goes to the room of the friend. While there, she is assaulted by another guest.
c. Fred goes to a railroad station to meet a passenger. While there, he falls over a hose on the ramp.
d. Linda goes to a soccer game to pass out religious literature. She falls down a flight of steps.
e. Jim is in a restaurant eating. He notices that there are cries of distress coming from the kitchen. He passes through the kitchen door on which a sign is posted reading, ``Authorized Personnel Only.'' He discovers that nothing is wrong, but slips on the kitchen floor.

What is the duty of care owed by an occupier to an invitee?

1. First, the occupier owes the invitee at least the same standard of care owed the trespasser discussed above.
2. Second, the occupier owes the invitee at least the same standard of care owed the licensee discussed above.

3. Third, the occupier owes the invitee a duty of reasonable care to inspect *and discover* dangerous artificial conditions on the land, dangerous natural conditions on the land, and dangerous activities on the land.
4. Fourth, depending on the extent of the danger in the condition or activity, the occupier must either warn the invitee or make the condition or activity safe.

Again, no more than reasonable care is required to discover the danger and protect the invitee from it. The occupier is not the insurer of the invitee.

3. The Special Problems of the Seller and Buyer of Land (Vendor and Vendee)

When land is sold, the general rule is that the seller **(vendor)** has no further tort liability for injuries that occur on the land, either to the buyer **(vendee)** or to a third person. The buyer, under the theory of **caveat emptor** (buyer beware), takes the land as he or she finds it. The buyer is expected to make an inspection of the premises before purchasing. The seller will not be liable if the buyer is injured by a condition on the land, even if the condition was present when the land was sold. Third parties injured by such conditions must look to the new owner for liability.

A number of exceptions exist to this rule. If there is a hidden or **latent** condition on the land that is dangerous and that is known to the seller, the latter has a duty to either warn the buyer of the condition or repair it before turning the land over to the buyer. Examples of latent conditions include holes in the yard covered by thin plywood, and ceilings infested with termites not visible on the surface. The seller does not have a duty to inspect the premises to discover such defects, and must do something about them only if he or she knows about them or has reason to believe that they are present. A failure to warn the buyer of these latent defects or to repair them will impose negligence liability on the seller for injuries caused by them. In some states, a suit for misrepresentation may also be available. (See Chapter 25.)

Another exception concerns conditions on the land that are dangerous to persons *outside the land* at the time of the sale. These conditions sometimes amount to a public or private nuisance, although the seller's liability for injury caused to a plaintiff outside the land is not dependent on the existence of a nuisance. The seller's liability exists only for a reasonable time to enable the buyer to discover such conditions and therefore assume responsibility for them.

4. The Special Problems of the Landlord and Tenant (Lessor and Lessee)

Normally, a landlord **(lessor)** is not entitled to possession of the land, but has a **reversionary interest** in the land, which comes into effect after the tenancy is over. As a result, the general rule is that the tenant **(lessee)** assumes all liability for injuries caused by conditions or activities on the land. There are a number of exceptions to this general rule.

Statutes may exist in a state requiring the landlord to maintain the premises, particularly apartment houses, in a safe condition. The violation of such statutes may impose negligence (and maybe criminal) liability on the landlord.

The landlord will be liable to the tenant and to third parties for injuries caused by latent dangerous conditions on the land at the time of the lease which the landlord has actual knowledge of or has reason to believe exist. In most states, the landlord has no duty to inspect and discover such conditions, but must know of them or have reason to believe that they are present. The conditions must be latent or concealed—not obvious to the tenant.

Often the landlord does not lease the entire building or land to the tenant(s). The landlord may retain control over certain **common areas,** such as hallways, stairways, elevators, boiler rooms. The landlord has a duty of reasonable care to inspect these common areas and make sure that they are safe for those who are entitled to use them, e.g., the tenants and people using the land as invitees.

If, at the time of the lease, there are conditions on the land that are dangerous to people outside the land, the landlord (like the vendor) has a duty for a reasonable period of time to prevent injury from these conditions.

Another exception occurs when the landlord leases the premises for a purpose that involves the admission of the public, e.g., theater, pier, hotel, and department store. In such cases, the landlord has a duty to inspect the premises and to repair any dangerous conditions that exist at the time of the lease, *before* the tenant takes over. Reasonable care must be used to make sure that the land is not turned over in a dangerous condition. If a member of the public is injured by such a condition that was unreasonably not discovered and repaired by the landlord before the tenant took over, the landlord will be liable, even if the lease agreement provides that the tenant shall assume all responsibility for repairs. The landlord cannot shift the responsibility to the tenant in this way. The duty is nondelegable.

Suppose that the dangerous condition arises *after* the land is leased. The general rule is that injured third parties must look to the tenant for liability rather than to the landlord. If, however, the landlord is obligated to make repairs by the terms of the lease, failure to do so will lead to negligence liability in most states. In such cases, the tenant can argue that the tenant did not make the repairs because of reasonable reliance on the landlord's contract obligation to do so. There are some states, however, that do not impose tort liability on the landlord for a failure to make agreed-upon repairs. In such states, the tenant is liable in tort to injured third parties. The tenant's only recourse in such states is a breach-of-contract action against the landlord. If the landlord does undertake the repairs but performs them negligently, the landlord will be liable in tort.

▪ ASSIGNMENT 27.12 ▪

Prepare an annotated bibliography on the negligence liability of owners and occupiers of land in your state. (See General Instructions for the Annotated Bibliography Assignment in Chapter 2.)

SUMMARY

Trespass to land is an intentional intrusion on land in possession of another. Land includes the ground and the air space above the ground over which the plaintiff has reasonable beneficial use. Actual harm to the land does not have to be shown.

A condition or activity is abnormal (for purposes of establishing strict liability for abnormally dangerous conditions or activities) if it is unusual or non-natural for the area. It is dangerous when it poses a substantial likelihood of great harm to persons or property that cannot be eliminated by the use of reasonable care by the defendant. If the abnormal condition or activity does not meet this definition of "dangerous," there can be no strict liability; in order to recover, the plaintiff must establish that the defendant created a nuisance, caused a trespass to land, or acted negligently with the condition or activity. For strict liability, the defendant must know that the condition or activity is dangerous, must be the cause in fact of the harm, and must be the proximate cause of the harm. For proximate cause, the harm that results must be within the type of harm that was initially foreseeable, and the plaintiffs must be part of the group within the foreseeable risk posed by the abnormally dangerous condition or activity. Contributory negligence is not a defense, but unreasonable assumption of the risk is.

A private nuisance is a substantial interference with the reasonable use and enjoyment of private land. This occurs when one's peace of mind is disturbed while on the land. In determining whether the interference is unreasonable, the court will consider a number of factors: the gravity and character of the harm, the social value of the use the plaintiff is making of the land, the character of the locality, the extent of the burden on the plaintiff of avoiding or minimizing the interference, the motive of the defendant, the social value of the defendant's conduct, and the extent of the burden on the defendant of avoiding or minimizing the interference. A private nuisance can be created negligently, intentionally, or through an abnormally dangerous condition or activity. Any person who has the right to the use and enjoyment of the land can bring the action. The remedies might include money damages, injunction, and self-help via the privilege to abate the nuisance. Depending on how the nuisance was created, the defenses include contributory negligence, assumption of the risk, the failure to mitigate damages, and official authorization.

A public nuisance is an unreasonable interference with a right common to the general public. It can be created negligently; intentionally; through an abnormally dangerous condition or activity; or by violating a statute, ordinance, or regulation. A public official can sue the wrongdoer. A private citizen can also sue if he or she has suffered in a way that is different in kind from every other member of the public affected by the public nuisance. The remedies are similar to those for a private nuisance, and the government may also be able to impose a fine or imprisonment. The defenses to a public nuisance are similar to those available in private nuisance cases.

Traditional negligence liability may depend on the status of the parties. To persons outside the land, occupiers owe a duty of reasonable care as to non-natural or artificial conditions on the land and as to business or personal activity taking place on the land. No duty of care is owed to trespassers unless they are discovered on the land, are constant trespassers on limited areas of the land, or are trespassing children (under the attractive nuisance doctrine). Licensees must be warned of dangerous natural or artificial conditions on the land of which the occupier has actual knowledge. More than a warning is needed if the condition is extremely dangerous. Licensees must be accorded reasonable care as to activities on the land. For invitees, the occupier must take reasonable steps to inspect and discover dangerous artificial or natural conditions and dangerous activities on the land. The occupier must then use reasonable care to protect the invitee from such conditions and activities. The seller of land can be liable for known latent defects that injure the buyer or a third person on the land. A landlord can be liable to tenants and others injured by latent dangerous conditions on the land that the landlord knows about or should know about. The landlord must use reasonable care to make common areas safe.

Key Terms

interests
trespass to land
reasonable beneficial
    use
nominal damages
absolute liability
strict liability for
    abnormally
    dangerous conditions
    or activities
abnormally dangerous
    condition or activity
Rylands v. Fletcher
cause in fact
but for
substantial factor
proximate cause
intervening causes
act of God
contributory negligence

assumption of the risk
domestic animals
wild animals
nuisance
private nuisance
public nuisance
peace of mind
unreasonable
social value
damages
cost of restoration
injunction
self-help
abate the nuisance
mitigate the damages
avoidable consequences
taking of property
standing
duty of reasonable care
lesser standard of care

occupier
independent contractor
trespasser
licensee
invitee
child
attractive nuisance
    doctrine
social guests
business guest
passenger
vendor
vendee
caveat emptor
latent
lessor
reversionary interest
lessee
common areas

CHAPTER 28

Conversion and Trespass to Chattels

CHAPTER OUTLINE

- INTRODUCTION
- CONVERSION AND TRESPASS TO CHATTELS CHECKLIST
- DAMAGES
- KIND OF INTERFERENCE
- MISTAKE DEFENSE

▪ INTRODUCTION

If someone accidently damages your personal property (also called a **chattel**), you may be able to sue for negligence, e.g., a motorist dents the right fender of your car in a collision. Suppose, however, that the interference is *intentional* rather than accidental, e.g., someone steals your fountain pen from your bag or decides to "borrow" your car for an hour without your permission. Your remedy in such cases is the tort of **conversion** or the tort of **trespass to chattels.** The major distinction between the two torts is the degree of interference involved. If the interference is relatively minor, the tort to use is trespass to chattels. A more serious interference justifies an action for conversion.

Conversion and Trespass to Chattels Checklist
Definitions, Relationships, and Research References

Category of These Torts

They are intentional torts. They are also strict liability torts, in that the defendant's reasonable mistake is generally not a defense.

Interests Protected by These Torts

Conversion: The right to be free from serious intentional interferences with personal property.

535

Trespass to Chattels: The right to be free from intentional interferences with personal property resulting in dispossession or intermeddling.

Elements of These Torts
Conversion:

1. Personal property (chattel)
2. The plaintiff is in possession of the chattel or is entitled to immediate possession
3. Intent to exercise dominion or control over the chattel
4. Serious interference with plaintiff's possession
5. Causation (of element 4)

Trespass to Chattels:

1. Personal property (chattel)
2. The plaintiff is in possession of the chattel or is entitled to immediate possession
3. Intent to dispossess or to intermeddle with the chattel
4. Dispossession or intermeddling
5. Causation (of element 4)

Major Definitions of Words/Phrases in the Elements

Chattel: Tangible or intangible property other than land or things attached to land (for both torts).

Intent: The desire to exercise control or dominion over the chattel, or the knowledge with substantial certainty that this control or dominion will result from what the defendant does (for conversion). The desire to dispossess or to intermeddle, or the knowledge with substantial certainty that dispossession or intermeddling will result from what the defendant does (for trespass to chattels).

Control: Exerting power over something (for conversion).

Dominion: Asserting supreme power or authority over something (for conversion).

Dispossess: Take nontrivial physical control of the chattel without the consent of the person who has possession, or prevent access to the chattel by the person who has possession (for trespass to chattel).

Intermeddle: Make physical contact with the chattel (for trespass to chattel).

Causation: But for what the defendant did, the serious interference with the chattel would not have occurred, or the defendant was a substantial factor in producing the serious interference (for conversion). But for what the defendant did, the plaintiff would not have been dispossessed of the chattel or had it intermeddled with, or the defendant was a substantial factor in producing the dispossession or intermeddling (for trespass to chattel).

Major Defense and Counter-Argument Possibilities That Need to Be Explored
1. The property involved was not personal property (not a chattel).
2. The plaintiff was not in possession or entitled to immediate possession.

3. There was no intent to exercise dominion or control (for conversion), nor to dispossess or intermeddle (for trespass to chattels).
4. The interference was not serious enough (for both torts).
5. The defendant's control over the chattel was trivial. There was no impairment. The plaintiff was not deprived of the use of the chattel for a substantial time (for both torts).
6. The defendant did not cause the interference with the plaintiff's possession of the chattel.
7. The plaintiff consented to what the defendant did with the chattel and the defendant did not exceed that consent.
8. The defense of avoidable consequences.
9. The privilege of defense of property.
10. The privilege of recapture of chattels.
11. The privilege of necessity.
12. The privilege to abate a nuisance.
13. Sovereign immunity.
14. Public official immunity.
15. Charitable immunity.

Damages

In conversion, the plaintiff recovers the full fair market value of the chattel at the time and place of the conversion. In trespass to chattels, the plaintiff's recovery is limited to harm or injury caused the chattel, e.g., repair costs and cost of renting a substitute. If malice or hatred existed, punitive damages are also possible.

Relationship to Criminal Law

A number of crimes may also be involved in addition to these torts: theft or larceny, embezzlement, false pretenses, receiving stolen property, robbery, extortion, blackmail, burglary, etc.

Relationship to Other Torts

Misrepresentation: The defendant's interference with the chattel of plaintiff may have occurred through misrepresentation, so that this tort plus conversion or trespass to chattels are committed.

Negligence: If the plaintiff cannot establish that the interference with his or her property was intentional, he or she may be able to show negligence if there was unreasonable conduct by the defendant and actual harm to the property.

Federal Law

Under the Federal Tort Claims Act, the United States will be liable for claims arising out of conversion or trespass to chattels when committed by a federal employee within the scope of employment.

Employer-Employee (Agency) Law

A private employer will be liable for conversion or trespass to chattels committed by its employees within the scope of employment. The employee must be furthering the business objectives of the employer at the time the torts were committed.

Research References for These Torts

- Digests

In the digests of West, look for case summaries on these torts under key topics such as:

Conversion	Bailments
Trover and Conversion	Torts
Property	Damages

- *Corpus Juris Secundum*

In this legal encyclopedia, see the discussion under topic headings such as:

Conversion	Bailments
Trover and Conversion	Torts
Property	Damages

- *American Jurisprudence 2d*

In this legal encyclopedia, see the discussion under topic headings such as:

Conversion	Abandoned, Lost and Unclaimed Property
Property	Damages
Bailments	Torts

- Legal Periodical Literature

There are three index systems to use to locate legal periodical literature on these torts:

Index to Legal Periodicals (ILP)	*Current Legal Index (CLI)*	*Legal Resource Index (LRI)*
See literature in *ILP* under subject headings such as:	See literature in *CLI* under subject headings such as:	See literature in *LRI* under subject headings such as:
Conversion	Personal Property	Personal Property
Personal Property	Torts	Torts
Property	Property	Property
Torts	Bailments	Bailments
Damages	Intangible Property	Intangible Property
Bailments	Damages	Damages
	Fraudulent Conveyances	Fraudulent Conveyances

Example of a legal periodical article you will find by using *ILP* or *CLI* or *LRI:*

A Co-payee Has a Cause of Action in Conversion against Both the Collecting and Payor Banks for Payment of a Check over His Missing Endorsement, 13 Georgia Law Review 677 (1979).

- *ALR, ALR2d, ALR3d, ALR4th, ALR5th, ALRFed*

Use the *Index to Annotations* to locate annotations on these torts. In this index, check subject headings such as:

Trover and Conversion	Property Damages
Conversion	Personal Property
Damages	Torts

Example of an annotation you can locate through this index on these torts:

> *Punitive or Exemplary Damages for Conversion of Personalty by One Other Than Chattel Mortgagee or Conditional Seller,* 54 ALR2d 1361.

• *Words and Phrases*

In this multivolume legal dictionary, look up every word or phrase connected with conversion and trespass to chattels to try to locate court opinions that have defined these words or phrases.

■ DAMAGES

A successful plaintiff in an action for trespass to chattels can recover the cost of repairs or the cost of temporarily renting a replacement for the chattel. For major or aggravated interferences, the plaintiff can sue for conversion, for which the recovery is the full value of the chattel at the time it was converted. In effect, the party that interfered with the chattel is forced to buy it—even if this wrongdoer later offers to return the chattel in its original condition.

■ KIND OF INTERFERENCE

When is an interference serious enough for conversion? There is no absolute answer to this question that will cover every case. The court will consider a number of factors, no one of which is conclusive. The factors are outlined in Figure 28.1.

In general, the interferences of **dispossession** and **intermeddling** are not considered serious enough for conversion, but would constitute trespass to chattels:

Dispossession

> **Example:** Dan takes Jim's book for an afternoon and reads it without permission. No damage is done to the book. It is returned. Dan

---

Figure 28.1 Factors Considered by a Court to Determine Whether an Interference with a Chattel is Serious Enough for Conversion[1]

• The extent and duration of the defendant's exercise of control or dominion over the chattel; the more substantial and lengthy the interference, the more likely it will constitute conversion.
• Whether the defendant intended to assert a right in the chattel that was inconsistent with the plaintiff's right of control.
• Whether the defendant acted in good faith or bad faith when interfering with the chattel.
• Whether the interference caused any damage or harm to the chattel.
• Whether the plaintiff suffered any inconvenience or expense as a result of the interference.

---

[1]*Prosser and Keeton on the Law of Torts* 90 (W. Page Keeton et al. eds., 5th Ed. 1984).

never claims that he owned the book. Jim did not need the book while Dan had it.

Intermeddling

> **Example:**   Tom is sitting in the park with his new puppy. Paula comes over and starts petting it, even though Tom asks her to stop. The dog growls a little, but is not harmed.

In the intermeddling example, suppose that Paul accidently got a little ink on the white fur of the puppy. The case is still not serious enough to constitute conversion. In a trespass-to-chattels action, Tom would be limited to recovering any cost associated with cleaning the dog.

▪ MISTAKE DEFENSE

It is not a defense that the defendant acted in good faith or made a reasonable **mistake,** although this is one of the overall factors that the court will take into consideration in determining whether the interference is serious enough for conversion.

> **Example:**   Lena steals Sam's rifle. She offers to sell the rifle to Ed, who has no idea where she got it. Ed buys it for $200. Lena disappears. When Sam finds out what happened, he demands that Ed return the rifle. Ed refuses. Sam then sues Ed for conversion.

Sam will win. It is no defense that Ed is a **bona fide purchaser** who bought the rifle thinking that Lena had the right to sell it. Ed intended to exercise total ownership and control over the gun when he bought it. This was in full contradiction to Sam's rights in the rifle.

To the extent that an honest mistake is not a defense to conversion or trespass to chattels, these two torts can be classified as **strict liability** torts.

▪ ASSIGNMENT 28.1 ▪

Ted grows valuable and expensive orchids in his back yard. It is the end of the growing season. He has two orchids remaining from his most expensive variety. He cuts one and places it in a basket in the yard next to the one still growing. Later that afternoon, Janice, one of Ted's house guests, mistakenly thinks Ted is throwing away the orchid in the basket. She takes it from the basket and also cuts the one still growing. She puts them both in her suitcase. The next morning she wonders whether she made a mistake in taking the orchids without asking Ted. When Ted finds out what Janice did, he sues her for conversion. What result? (See General Instructions for the Legal Analysis Assignment in Chapter 3.)

CASE

Moore v. The Regents of the University of California
51 Cal.3d 120, 793 P.2d 479, 271 Cal.Rptr. 146 (1990)
Supreme Court of California

Background: John Moore underwent treatment for hairy-cell leukemia at the UCLA Medical Center. The doctors withdrew blood, skin, bone marrow aspirate, sperm, and his spleen.

Unknown to Moore, the defendants were using his cells in research on regulating the immune system through the techniques of recombinant DNA. The research was successful. The defendants established a cell line from Moore's T-lymphocytes and applied for a patent on the cell line, which they received. Some biotechnology reports predict a potential market of over three billion dollars in this area. When Moore found out what role his cells played in this development, he sued for breach of a duty to disclose and for conversion. The trial court ruled against Moore. The case is now on appeal before the Supreme Court of California.

Decision on Appeal: The use of excised human cells in medical research does not amount to a conversion. Moore, however, can sue for breach of a physician's fiduciary duty of disclosure of information needed by a patient to make an informed consent to treatment.

Opinion of Court

Justice PANELLI delivered the opinion of the court . . .

Moore . . . attempts to characterize the invasion of his rights as a conversion—a tort that protects against interference with possessory and ownership interests in personal property. He theorizes that he continued to own his cells following their removal from his body, at least for the purpose of directing their use, and that he never consented to their use in potentially lucrative medical research. Thus, to complete Moore's argument, defendants' unauthorized use of his cells constitutes a conversion. As a result of the alleged conversion, Moore claims a proprietary interest in each of the products that any of the defendants might ever create from his cells or the patented cell line. . . .

In effect, what Moore is asking us to do is to impose a tort duty on scientists to investigate the consensual pedigree of each human cell sample used in research. To impose such a duty, which would affect medical research of importance to all of society, implicates policy concerns far removed from the traditional, two-party ownership disputes in which the law of conversion arose. Invoking a tort theory originally used to determine whether the loser or the finder of a horse had the better title, Moore claims ownership of the results of socially important medical research, including the genetic code for chemicals that regulate the functions of every human being's immune system. . . .

"To establish a conversion, plaintiff must establish an actual interference with his *ownership* or *right of possession.* . . . Where plaintiff neither has title to the property alleged to have been converted, nor possession thereof, he cannot maintain an action for conversion." (*Del E. Webb Corp. v. Structural Materials Co.* (1981) 123 Cal.App.3d 593, 610–611.

Since Moore clearly did not expect to retain possession of his cells following their removal, to sue for their conversion he must have retained an ownership interest in them. But . . . California statutory law . . . drastically limits a patient's control over excised cells. Pursuant to Health and Safety Code section 7054.4, "[n]otwithstanding any other provision of law, recognizable anatomical parts, human tissues, anatomical human remains, or infectious waste following conclusion of scientific use shall be disposed of by interment, incineration, or any other method determined by the state department [of health services] to protect the public health and safety." Clearly the Legislature did not specifically intend this statute to resolve the question of whether a patient is entitled to compensation for the nonconsensual use of excised cells. A primary object of the statute is to ensure the safe handling of potentially hazardous biological waste materials. Yet one cannot escape the conclusion that the statute's practical effect is to limit, drastically, a patient's control over excised cells. By restricting how excised cells may be used and requiring their eventual destruction, the statute eliminates so many of the rights ordinarily attached to property that one cannot simply assume that what is left amounts to "property" or "ownership" for purposes of conversion law.

It may be that some limited right to control the use of excised cells does survive the operation of this statute. There is, for example, no need to read the statute to permit "scientific use" contrary to the patient's expressed wish. A fully informed patient may always withhold consent to treatment by a physician whose research plans the patient does not approve. That right, however . . . is protected by the fiduciary-duty and informed-consent theories.

Finally, the subject matter of the Regents' patent—the patented cell line and the products derived from it—cannot be Moore's property. This is because the patented cell line is both factually and legally distinct from the cells taken from Moore's body. Federal law permits the patenting of organisms that represent the product of "human ingenuity," but not naturally occurring organisms. . . . It is this *inventive effort* that patent law rewards, not the discovery of naturally occurring raw materials. Thus, Moore's allegations that he owns the cell line and the products derived from it are inconsistent with the patent, which constitutes an authoritative determination that the cell line is the product of invention. . . .

[A competent patient does have a right] to make autonomous medical decisions. That right . . . is grounded in well-recognized and long-standing principles of fiduciary duty and informed consent. This policy weighs in favor of providing a remedy to patients when physicians act with undisclosed motives that may affect their professional judgment. . . . [But we should] not threaten with disabling civil liability innocent parties who are engaged in socially useful activities, such as researchers who have no reason to believe that their use of a particular cell sample is, or may be, against a donor's wishes. . . .

We need not, however, make an arbitrary choice between liability and nonliability. Instead, an examination of the relevant policy considerations suggests an appropriate balance: Liability based upon existing disclosure obligations, rather than

an unprecedented extension of the conversion theory, protects patients' rights of privacy and autonomy without unnecessarily hindering research.

To be sure, the threat of liability for conversion might help to enforce patients' rights indirectly. This is because physicians might be able to avoid liability by obtaining patients' consent, in the broadest possible terms, to any conceivable subsequent research use of excised cells. Unfortunately, to extend the conversion theory would utterly sacrifice the other goal of protecting innocent parties. Since conversion is a strict liability tort,[*] it would impose liability on all those into whose hands the cells come, whether or not the particular defendant participated in, or knew of, the inadequate disclosures that violated the patient's right to make an informed decision. In contrast to the conversion theory, the fiduciary-duty and informed-consent theories protect the patient directly, without punishing innocent parties or creating disincentives to the conduct of socially beneficial research. . . .

[T]he theory of liability that Moore urges us to endorse threatens to destroy the economic incentive to conduct important medical research. If the use of cells in research is a conversion, then with every cell sample a researcher purchases a ticket in a litigation lottery. . . .

If the scientific users of human cells are to be held liable for failing to investigate the consensual pedigree of their raw materials, we believe the Legislature should make that decision. Complex policy choices affecting all society are involved, and "[l]egislatures,

---

[*] " 'The foundation for the action for conversion rests neither in the knowledge nor the intent of the defendant. . . . [Instead,] "the tort consists in the breach of what may be called an absolute duty; the act itself . . . is unlawful and redressible as a tort." ' [Citation.]" (*Byer v. Canadian Bank of Commerce* (1937) 8 Cal.2d 297, 300, 65 P.2d 67, quoting *Poggi v. Scott* (1914) 167 Cal. 372, 375, 139 P. 815. See also *City of Los Angeles v. Superior Court* (1978) 85 Cal.App.3d 143, 149, 149 Cal.Rptr. 320 ["[c]onversion is a species of strict liability in which questions of good faith, lack of knowledge and motive are ordinarily immaterial."].)

in making such policy decisions, have the ability to gather empirical evidence, solicit the advice of experts, and hold hearings at which all interested parties present evidence and express their views. . . ." (*Foley v. Interactive Data Corp.* (1988) 47 Cal.3d 654, 694, 765 P.2d 373.)

Finally, there is no pressing need to impose a judicially created rule of strict liability, since enforcement of physicians' disclosure obligations will protect patients against the very type of harm with which Moore was threatened. So long as a physician discloses research and economic interests that may affect his judgment, the patient is protected from conflicts of interest. Aware of any conflicts, the patient can make an informed decision to consent to treatment, or to withhold consent and look elsewhere for medical assistance. As already discussed, enforcement of physicians' disclosure obligations protects patients directly, without hindering the socially useful activities of innocent researchers.

For these reasons, we hold that the allegations of Moore's . . . complaint state a cause of action for breach of fiduciary duty or lack of informed consent, but not conversion. . . .

▪ ASSIGNMENT 28.2 ▪

a. The doctors that treated Moore had a conflict of interest. What was the conflict?

b. In most states, you have the right to make a gift of your eyes or other organs. Is the decision in *Moore* inconsistent with this right?

c. Assume that after the UCLA Medical Center doctor extracts blood, skin, bone marrow aspirate, and sperm from Moore (plus his spleen), a doctor from another hospital breaks into the UCLA Medical Center and steals everything extracted from Moore. The doctors and researchers in this other hospital then use it in their own research, which leads to the patent. Do the UCLA doctor and the UCLA Medical Center have an action for conversion?

▪ ASSIGNMENT 28.3 ▪

Prepare an annotated bibliography on conversion and trespass to chattels in your state. (See General Instructions for the Legal Analysis Assignment in Chapter 2.)

SUMMARY

The torts of conversion and trespass to chattels are designed to provide a remedy for intentional interferences with personal property. If the interference is serious, conversion is the appropriate remedy, requiring the wrongdoer to pay the plaintiff the full value of the chattel converted. Trespass to chattels covers less serious interferences. If the act constituting interference is intentional, it is no defense that the interference was an innocent mistake, as in the case of a bona fide purchaser.

Key Terms

chattel	dispossession	bona fide purchaser
conversion	intermeddling	strict liability
trespass to chattels	mistake	

CHAPTER 29

Business Torts

CHAPTER OUTLINE

- INTRODUCTION
- DISPARAGEMENT
  False Statement of Fact
  Disparaging the Plaintiff's Business
    or Property
  Publication
  Intent
  Special Damages
  Causation
  Privilege to Disparage
- INJURIOUS FALSEHOOD
- INTERFERENCE WITH CONTRACT
  RELATIONS
  Existing Contract
  Interference
  Intent
  Damages
  Causation
  Privilege to Interfere with
    Contract Relations

- INTERFERENCE WITH
  PROSPECTIVE ADVANTAGE
- PRIMA FACIE TORT
- BAD FAITH LIABILITY
- DRAM SHOP LIABILITY
- TORTIOUS INTERFERENCE WITH
  EMPLOYMENT

▪ INTRODUCTION

A very large percentage of tort actions are brought against businesses. They represent the **deep pocket** in our litigious society—the ones to go after because they are perceived to have the money.

A business acts through its employees. Under the doctrine of **respondeat superior,** the business (the employer) is liable for the torts committed by its employees within the scope of their employment. This is a form of **vicarious**

544

liability, by which one party is liable for what another party has done or failed to do. We have already examined the factors that go into a court's determination of whether an employee has acted within the scope of employment (see Figure 12.10 in Chapter 12). Companies have been found liable for a large variety of torts because they were committed by employees who were serving the interests of the company and hence were within the **scope of employment.**

Examples:

Abuse of Process	Strict Liability for Abnormally Dangerous
Assault	Conditions or Activities
Battery	Malicious Prosecution
Conversion	Negligence
Deceit	"Nuisance"
Defamation	Private Nuisance
False Imprisonment	Public Nuisance
Intentional Infliction of	"Products Liability"
Emotional Distress	Negligence
Invasion of Privacy	Strict Liability in Tort
Appropriation	Misrepresentation
False Light	Breach of Warranty
Intrusion	Trespass to Chattels
Public Disclosure of	Trespass to Land
Private Fact	Wrongful Death

In this chapter we will consider other areas of civil liability that can be imposed on businesses:

- disparagement
- injurious falsehood
- interference with contract relations
- interference with prospective advantage
- prima facie tort

■ DISPARAGEMENT

The tort of **disparagement** covers attacks made against the business or property of the plaintiff. It has some similarity with defamation, although, as we shall see, there are important differences. The common law of defamation has gone through tremendous change because of recent interpretations of the First Amendment of the Constitution. The same may eventually happen with disparagement, because this tort also concerns speech in one form or another.

The common law elements of disparagement are:

1. false statement of fact
2. disparaging the plaintiff's business or property
3. publication
4. intent
5. special damages
6. causation

False Statement of Fact

The plaintiff must prove that a **statement of fact** made by the defendant was false. This, of course, is quite different from most common law *defamation* cases, in which the truth of the statement was established by the defendant by way of defense. As we shall see in the next element, the statements must attack or disparage the quality of the plaintiff's property or the conduct of its business, e.g., a statement that "the XYZ company is selling stolen goods." Mere statements of opinion or **puffing** by the plaintiff about the plaintiff's goods that do not communicate statements of fact about them are not actionable. Compare the following two statements by the plaintiff who sells stamps:

> "My stamps are the best that money can buy on the market today."
> "My stamps are the only genuine stamps available on the market today."

The first statement is puffing. It is an exaggerated claim of quality that is not reasonably understood as a statement of fact about anyone else's goods. Or, viewed from another perspective, to the extent that the first statement communicates the "fact" that other sellers do not sell the same quality product, the statement is simply part of **privileged competition** in the marketplace. The second statement, however, is quite different. It goes beyond puffing; it implies the statement of fact that the stamps sold by others are not genuine—that they are fakes, forgeries, or other than what they are represented to be. To be sure, there is a component of puffing in the statement as well. But the statement does clearly imply a statement of fact.

Disparaging the Plaintiff's Business or Property

The false statement must be disparaging. It must cast doubt on the plaintiff's title to the property (sometimes called **slander of title**) or attribute a quality to goods that makes them undesirable for sale or other commercial use (sometimes called **trade libel**). The effect of the disparaging statement is to cause others not to deal with the plaintiff or to cause some other similar disadvantage.

Examples:

- Omar falsely states that he holds a mortgage on the plaintiff's farm, which the latter has on the market for sale.
- Tom falsely says that he owns the land being sold by Jim.
- Sarah falsely states that the tires being sold by XYZ as radials are not radials.

Either the defendant must intend the disparaging meaning, or the disparaging meaning must be reasonably understood as such by the persons to whom it is published or communicated, even if the defendant did not intend that meaning.

Some statements constitute the torts of both disparagement and defamation. Disparagement discredits the quality of or title to *goods or property*. Defamation consists of a derogatory statement about the *person* of the plaintiff. Compare the following statements:

> "Prostitutes regularly use the XYZ Hotel for their clients."
> "Fred, the manager of the XYZ Hotel, takes a cut of the fee charged by prostitutes in exchange for the use of the hotel for their clients."

The first statement disparages the hotel—the business. The second statement disparages the hotel *and* personally defames the manager.

Publication

Publication has the same technical meaning in disparagement as it has in defamation: communication of the statement to someone other than the plaintiff. It must be communicated intentionally or negligently.

Intent

The defendant might make a false statement of fact **intentionally** (knowing it is false), **recklessly** (acting in conscious disregard of whether the statement is true or false), **negligently** (taking unreasonable risks that the statement might be false), or **innocently** (no reasonable person in the plaintiff's position would realize that the statement is false). Is the defendant off the hook if he or she acted innocently with respect to the truth or falsity of the statement? Does the plaintiff have to show intent, recklessness, or negligence?

The law does not provide clear answers to these questions. Many of the common law cases require a showing of **malice** on the part of the defendant. Unfortunately, the word "malice" is not given a consistent meaning by the courts. By malice, some courts mean ill will or hatred toward the plaintiff. Other courts mean a desire to harm the plaintiff by wanting others to rely on the false statements about the plaintiff's property or business. In still other courts, malice simply means making an intentionally or recklessly false statement.

Note that under the new constitutional law of defamation, the plaintiff must prove that the statement was negligently false, and in some cases, knowingly or recklessly false. It is arguable that the United States Supreme Court will eventually impose the same requirements on a disparagement action.[1] There is reason to believe that the **commercial speech** involved in disparagement litigation will receive protection similar to what the Court has provided in defamation.

Special Damages

The plaintiff must plead and prove **special damages,** which are specific economic or pecuniary losses. It is usually not enough for the plaintiff to prove that there was a general loss of business following the disparaging statements of the defendant. The plaintiff must show specifically identified contracts or customers that were lost. Or, the plaintiff must show he or she had to sell goods at a lower price to specific customers as a result of the disparagement.

There are some courts, however, that will not require the plaintiff to identify specifically lost customers if it would be obviously impossible to do so, e.g., when the disparagement is very widely disseminated. In such cases, a showing of a more general loss of business or of a market will be sufficient for this element.

Causation

The special damages must be caused by the defendant. The plaintiff must show that but for the disparagement, the plaintiff would not have suffered the special damages. Alternatively, if more than one causal factor was involved, the plaintiff can establish this element by showing that the defendant's disparaging statement

---

[1] *Restatement (Second) of Torts §§ 623A, 629 (1965).*

was a substantial factor in producing the special damages. The disparagement, for example, does not have to be the sole cause of a customer's breaking a contract with the plaintiff or refusing to exercise an option to buy from the plaintiff, as long as the disparagement was a substantial factor in producing this result.

Privilege to Disparage

All of the absolute and qualified privileges that apply to defamation also apply to disparagement. To protect his or her own interest, for example, a defendant can state that he or she owns property the plaintiff is trying to sell. This disparages the property of the plaintiff, but it is privileged as long as the defendant is acting in the honest belief that he or she is protecting his or her own interest. Malice, however, defeats the privilege.

There is also a general privilege to compete in the business world by exaggerating the qualities of your own products compared to the products of others. There is a privilege, for example, to say that "no car is more economical" than the car being offered for sale. As indicated earlier, such statements are viewed either as nonfactual statements (hence not qualifying as the first element of disparagement) or as **fair competition.**

▪ ASSIGNMENT 29.1 ▪

a. Select any fact situation discussed in this section on disparagement. Prepare a set of interrogatories to be sent by the defendant to the plaintiff in the case. (See General Instructions for the Interrogatories Assignment in Chapter 6.) Also make a list of separate questions that the plaintiff would send the defendant as interrogatories.
b. For the fact situation you selected in (a), draft a complaint for disparagement for your state. (See General Instructions for the Complaint Drafting Assignment in Chapter 5.)
c. Prepare an annotated bibliography on disparagement for your state. (See General Instructions for the Annotated Bibliography Assignment in Chapter 2.)

▪ INJURIOUS FALSEHOOD

The phrase **injurious falsehood** is sometimes used interchangeably with the word "disparagement," but injurious falsehood is a broader concept; disparagement is an example of an injurious falsehood. An injurious falsehood can consist of a statement of fact that injures someone economically in a way other than disparaging goods or a business.

Examples:

- a false statement to the immigration officials that results in the deportation of the plaintiff
- a false statement that someone has been hospitalized and is no longer paying child support
- a false statement by an employer of the income paid to an employee, resulting in tax evasion charges against the employee

The same elements discussed for disparagement are required for injurious false-hood, except for the second element: disparaging the plaintiff's business or property. Instead of showing that the statement disparages the business or products of the plaintiff, the broader tort of injurious falsehood requires only that the statement be harmful to the interests of the plaintiff. The other elements are the same: false statement of fact, publication, intent, special damages, and causation.

▪ ASSIGNMENT 29.2 ▪

Tom dies intestate, i.e., without a valid will. There are only two survivors: Mary, a daughter, and George, a nephew. Under the intestate law of the state, all property goes to legitimate children. If no legitimate children survive, the property goes to other relatives. George claims that Mary is illegitimate. Mary hires a lawyer who helps establish that she is legitimate. What tort or torts, if any, has George committed? (See General Instructions for the Legal Analysis Assignment in Chapter 3.)

▪ INTERFERENCE WITH CONTRACT RELATIONS

Suppose that Fred has a contract to build a bridge for Sam. If Fred fails, without justification, to build the bridge, Sam can sue Fred in a *contract* action—for breach of contract. If Dan persuades Fred not to build Sam's bridge so that Fred can build one for Dan, then Sam also has a *tort* action against Dan for inducing a breach of contract, or, more broadly, for **interference with contract relations.** The elements of this tort are:

1. an existing contract
2. interference with the contract by defendant
3. intent
4. damages
5. causation

Existing Contract

There must be a contract with which the defendant interferes. The enforcement of the contract must not violate public policy. A contract to marry, for example, cannot be the subject of a breach-of-contract action in most states. It is against public policy to enforce such contracts. Therefore, it would not be a tort to induce someone to breach a contract to marry in these states. So too, it is not a tort to induce the breach of an illegal gambling contract or a prostitution contract.

Suppose that the contract is **voidable,** i.e., unenforceable at the option of one of the parties. A contract might be voidable because it is not in writing or because one of the parties is a minor. Is it a tort to interfere with such a contract? Yes, as long as the contract is in existence and is not contrary to public policy as just discussed. The contract does not have to be enforceable to be the foundation of this tort. There is always the possibility that the parties to the contract will *not* exercise their option to get out of it; hence, it is a wrong (a tort) for a third party (the defendant) to induce its breach.

Many contracts, particularly employment contracts, are **terminable at will,** meaning that either party can get out at any time. Some courts conclude that it is not a tort to induce the termination of a contract at will since the parties to the contract are always free to terminate it without committing a breach of contract to each other. Most courts, however, disagree. It is a tort in most states to interfere with a contract at will. The injured party to the contract had a valuable expectation that the other party would not terminate—until the defendant came along. It is a tort to upset the contract relationship that existed.

Interference

The interference with the contract can take a number of forms:

- inducing one party to the contract to breach it
- making it impossible for one party to perform the contract
- making it more difficult for one party to perform the contract

Intent

The plaintiff must show that the defendant intended to interfere with the contract relation by inducing the breach, or by rendering performance impossible or more burdensome. The defendant must desire this interference or know with substantial certainty that the interference will result from what the defendant does or fails to do. Negligence is not enough. Suppose that the XYZ Company has a contract to supply lake water to a city, and the defendant (a third party) negligently pollutes this water before delivery. The defendant has surely interfered with XYZ's contract with the city, but no intentional tort has been committed by the defendant because there was no intent to interfere with the contract. The XYZ Company or the city may be able to sue the defendant for negligence in polluting the water, but there can be no suit for interference with contract. The defendant must know about the contract and intend to interfere with it. Courts sometimes refer to this requirement as the need to prove malice.

One narrow exception to the intent rule concerns servants. It is a tort to interfere with the relationship between a master and his or her servant by injuring the servant, even though the interference is not intentional. Negligent injury to the servant (resulting in a loss of service to the master) is enough.

Damages

The damages for this tort cover the loss of the contract or the diminished value of its performance. Most courts require a showing of actual damages, even though they may be nominal. In addition, damages for mental suffering and punitive damages are usually allowed. As indicated in the bridge example at the beginning of this section, the plaintiff may have a breach-of-contract action against the other party to the contract *and* a tort action against the third party for inducing the breach or for diminishing the value of performance. To avoid double recovery, however, the amount recovered in the tort action is reduced by whatever the plaintiff recovers in the contract action. When the defendant has threatened an interference with the contract, or when the interference is continuing, many courts will grant an **injunction** against the defendant because of the inadequacy of damages as a remedy.

Causation

The plaintiff must show that either:

- but for the action or inaction of the defendant, the plaintiff would not have suffered the damages that are provable, or
- the defendant was a substantial factor in producing these damages

Privilege to Interfere with Contract Relations

To claim the privilege, the defendant must show that the interference was justified or privileged. If the only objective of the defendant was to interfere with the contract, then the interference was **malicious,** and therefore not privileged. The privileges for defamation also apply to this tort, e.g., the privilege to protect one's own interest, the privilege to protect the interest of another, the privilege to protect the public interest. Assume, for example, that Len has a contract to furnish goods to Ted. Len is to obtain the goods under a separate contract with Mary. If Mary believes that Len is violating his contract with her, she can protect her own interest. This may include stopping delivery of the goods. This, of course, would have the effect of interfering with Ted's contract with Len. Mary has not committed a tort, however, as long as she is acting reasonably to protect her own interest. Similarly, if someone has a legal or moral duty to protect another person (e.g., a doctor caring for a patient, a lawyer advising a client), there is a privilege to protect the interest of this other person. This could include recommendations that the person remove him- or herself from certain contract obligations that are reasonably thought to be detrimental to the welfare of that person. Again, in all these situations the defendant must be acting reasonably and not out of a desire simply to interfere with contract relations, or to encourage that which is clearly illegal or improper.

- ASSIGNMENT 29.3 -

Helen works for Linda. One day, Helen borrows $500 from Linda to repair a fence at Helen's home. Linda has difficulty collecting this money from Helen. Linda tells her that she will lose her job if she does not repay the money within a week. Helen is fired when she does not make the payment at the time designated.

a. Does Helen have a cause of action against Linda?
b. Some facts as for (a), except that it is Linda's mother who convinces Linda to fire Helen if the repayment is not made. Does Helen have a cause of action against Linda's mother?

(See General Instructions for the Legal Analysis Assignment in Chapter 3.)

CASE

Texaco, Inc. v. Pennzoil Co.
729 S.W.2d 768 (1987)
Court of Appeals of Texas, Houston (1st District)

Background: This case involves a multi*billion* dollar verdict for committing the tort of interference with contract relations. In 1984 Getty Oil was for sale. It agreed "in principle" to be purchased by Pennzoil in a leveraged buyout for $110 per share (plus a $5 "stub," payable later). Although there was no formal contract between Getty and Pennzoil, both issued a "news release" that announced an "agreement in principle" based on a Memorandum of Agreement. The day after this announcement, Texaco offered to buy Getty for $125 per share. Getty withdrew from its relationship with Pennzoil and agreed to merge with Texaco. Pennzoil then sued Texaco for the tort of interfering with its contract with Getty. A Houston jury found that: (1) at the end of a board meeting on January 3, 1984, the Getty entities intended to bind themselves to an agreement providing for the purchase of Getty Oil stock by Pennzoil; (2) Texaco knowingly interfered with the agreement between Pennzoil and the Getty entities; (3) As a result of Texaco's interference, Pennzoil suffered damages of $7.53 billion; (4) Texaco's actions were intentional, willful, and in wanton disregard of Pennzoil's rights; and, (5) Pennzoil was entitled to punitive damages of $3 billion. The case is now on appeal before the Court of Appeals of Texas.

Decision on Appeal: The Court of Appeals affirmed the trial court and held that Texaco did commit the tort. Following this opinion, the parties negotiated to try to settle the case. After further court proceedings (including a Chapter 11 bankruptcy by Texaco) Pennzoil and Texaco agreed to a settlement of $3 billion dollars to be paid by Texaco.

Opinion of Court

Justice WARREN delivered the opinion of the court. . . .

Texaco argues first that there was no evidence [Getty intended to bind itself] to an agreement with Pennzoil. . . . Second, Texaco asserts that the evidence is legally and factually insufficient to support the . . .

[finding that] it had actual knowledge of a legally enforceable contract, or that Texaco actively induced a breach of the alleged contract. . . . Pennzoil contends that the evidence showed that the parties intended to be bound to the terms in the Memorandum of Agreement plus price terms of $110 plus a $5 stub, even though the parties may have contemplated a later, more formal document to memorialize the agreement already reached. . . .

[If] parties do not intend to be bound to an agreement until it is reduced to writing and signed by both parties, then there is no contract until that event occurs. If there is no understanding that a signed writing is necessary before the parties will be bound, and the parties have agreed upon all substantial terms, then an informal agreement can be binding, even though the parties contemplate evidencing their agreement in a formal document later. . . .

Texaco states that the use of the term "agreement in principle" in the press release was a conscious and deliberate choice of words to convey that there was not yet any binding agreement. . . . There was sufficient evidence at trial on the common business usage of the expression "agreement in principle" and on its meaning in this case for the jury reasonably to decide that its use in the press release did not necessarily establish that the parties did not intend to be bound before signing a formal document. . . . There was sufficient evidence for the jury to conclude that the parties had reached agreement on all essential terms of the transaction with only the mechanics and details left to be supplied by the parties' attorneys. Although there may have been many specific items relating to the transaction agreement draft that had yet to be put in final form, there is sufficient evidence to support a conclusion by the jury that the parties did not consider any of Texaco's asserted "open items" significant obstacles precluding an intent to be bound. . . .

Texaco asserts that Pennzoil failed to prove that Texaco had actual knowledge that a contract existed. [There must be] knowledge by a defendant of the existence of contractual rights as an element of the tort of inducing a breach of that contract. However, the defendant need not have full knowledge of all the detailed terms of the contract. . . . Since there was no direct evidence of Texaco's knowledge of a contract in this case, the question is whether there was legally and factually sufficient circumstantial evidence from which the trier of fact reasonably could have inferred knowledge. . . .

Pennzoil responds that there was legally and factually sufficient evidence to support the jury's finding of knowledge, because the jury could reasonably infer that Texaco knew about the Pennzoil deal from the evidence of (1) how Texaco carefully mapped its strategy to defeat Pennzoil's deal by acting to "stop the train" or "stop the signing"; (2) the notice of a contract given by a January 5 Wall Street Journal article reporting on the Pennzoil agreement—an article that Texaco denied anyone at Texaco had seen; [and] (3) the knowledge of an agreement that would arise from comparing the Memorandum of Agreement with the Getty press release. . . . Pennzoil contends that these circumstances indicated Texaco's knowledge of Pennzoil's deal too strongly to be overcome by Texaco's "self-serving verbal protestations at trial" that

Texaco was told and believed that there was no agreement. We find that an inference could arise that Texaco had some knowledge of Pennzoil's agreement with the Getty entities, given the evidence of Texaco's detailed studies of the Pennzoil plan, its knowledge that some members of the Getty board were not happy with Pennzoil's price, and its subsequent formulation of strategy to "stop the [Pennzoil] train". . . .

The second major issue Texaco raises . . . is that the evidence was legally and factually insufficient to show that Texaco actively induced breach of the alleged Pennzoil/Getty contract. A necessary element of the plaintiff's cause of action is a showing that the defendant took an active part in persuading a party to a contract to breach it. Merely entering into a contract with a party with the knowledge of that party's contractual obligations to someone else is not the same as inducing a breach. It is necessary that there be some act of interference or of persuading a party to breach, for example by offering better terms or other incentives, for tort liability to arise. . . .

The evidence . . . on Texaco's calculated formulation and implementation of its ideal strategy to acquire Getty is . . . inconsistent with its contention that it was merely the passive target of Getty's aggressive solicitation campaign and did nothing more than to accept terms that Getty Oil . . . proposed. The evidence showed that Texaco knew it had to act quickly, and that it had "24 hours" to "stop the train." . . .

[The judgment of the trial court is affirmed.]

• ASSIGNMENT 29.4 •

You and Bob are applying for the job of president of a major corporation. The contract will be for three years. Both of you are equally qualified. After the chairman of the board of the corporation meets with Bob, the chairman tells the press that the board is very impressed with Bob and that "no one should be surprised if the formality of an announcement is made soon that Bob will be joining us very soon.'' This announcement troubles you. You immediately call the chairman and tell him that Bob is not serious about joining the corporation. ''He is really using an offer by you as leverage to negotiate better employment terms with a rival company where he really wants to work.'' The chairman investigates and finds out that in fact Bob is actively pursuing a position there. The corporation decides to give you the job. Have you committed the tort of interference with contract relations?

■ ASSIGNMENT 29.5 ■

Prepare an annotated bibliography on interference with contract relations for your state. (See General Instructions for the Annotated Bibliography Assignment in Chapter 2.)

■ INTERFERENCE WITH PROSPECTIVE ADVANTAGE

Recall our discussion of the following two torts:

Disparagement: Making false statements of fact causing special damages to another's property or business

Interference with Contract: Inducing the breach of an existing contract or impairing the value of its performance

Now we consider the problem of interfering with *potential* or prospective benefits when no such false statements are made and when no existing contract has been breached or diminished. Such interference can also constitute a tort, the elements of which are:

1. reasonable expectation of an economic advantage
2. interference with this exception
3. intent
4. damages
5. causation

The defendant usually has committed other torts that have led to this interference, e.g., assault, battery, deceit, or defamation. The tort of **interference with prospective advantage** is often said to require such an underlying tort to make the interference wrongful.

In the business world, most of the cases that have arisen under the tort of interference with prospective advantage have involved what is loosely called **unfair competition.**

Examples:

- The plaintiff is trying to lure ducks at a public pond, which he or she will then kill and try to sell. The defendant intentionally fires a gun into the air in order to scare the ducks out of the plaintiff's range. The defendant is a competitor of the plaintiff in the sale of ducks.
- The defendant threatens a third party not to go to work for the plaintiff (no employment contract yet exists). The goal of the defendant is to get the third party to go to work for the defendant.

- The defendant pours some foul-smelling chemicals on his or her own property, which is next door to the plaintiff's, in order to scare the latter's potential customers away. The defendant wants the plaintiff to leave the area so that the defendant can rent the premises now occupied by the plaintiff.

The defendant has a privilege to protect his or her own business interests by engaging in fair competitive practices. Deceptive advertising and monopolistic steps, of course, constitute unfair (and illegal) competition. When these devices are not used, the defendant is free to use tactics such as high pressure advertising, price cutting, and rebates in order to lure prospective customers away from other merchants.

Courts are often reluctant to allow the tort of interference with prospective advantage when business or commercial interests are not involved, e.g., a defendant pressures a person to remove the plaintiff as the beneficiary of a will. There are a few courts, however, that will allow recovery in such situations, when there is a reasonable degree of certainty that the plaintiff would have received the expected benefit if there had been no interference by the defendant. In most cases of interference with prospective advantage, causation is a problem. It can be very difficult to prove that the benefit would have been obtained but for what the defendant did, or that the defendant was a substantial factor in the loss of the benefit. This is because the plaintiff had no contract right to the benefit at the time of the interference. Yet, if causation can be shown with reasonable certainty, recovery is allowed.

▪ PRIMA FACIE TORT

Negligence is a catch-all tort that encompasses a very wide variety of wrongful conduct that is considered unreasonable. There is no comparable catch-all tort for conduct that is intentional. We cannot say that all intentional conduct causing harm is tortious. If the defendant's actions or inactions do not fall within the elements of negligence, the plaintiff must look to the approximately thirty other torts, e.g., battery, deceit, malicious prosecution, and others listed in Figure 1.1 of Chapter 1. If these torts do not fit, then the plaintiff must suffer the loss, unless, of course, worker's compensation and no-fault insurance provide some form of relief.

Some consider it unfortunate that the law does not provide a clear tort remedy for a defendant's intentional conduct that harms someone, even though the facts do not fit within the traditional torts. In a sense, the torts of injurious falsehood and interference with prospective advantage try to fill some of the holes left by the traditional torts. Yet, as we have seen, even these torts have limitations on what intentional conduct they will or will not cover. Because interference with prospective advantage often requires proof of an underlying traditional tort, for example, it adds little that does not already exist.

▪ ASSIGNMENT 29.6 ▪

Select one of the three examples listed above—the duck case, the threat case, or the foul-smelling chemical case. Draft a complaint for the plaintiff in the case you select. (See General Instructions for the Complaint Drafting Assignment in Chapter 5.)

In a few states (including New York), small efforts toward the creation of a generic intentional tort have been made in the form of the **prima facie tort.** While this tort is not limited to the business world, most of the cases applying it have involved commercial matters. The elements of the prima facie tort are:

1. infliction of harm
2. intent to do harm (malice)
3. special damages
4. causation

It is sometimes said that the tort does not exist unless the defendant acted "maliciously and without justification." It is not always clear whether malice means a desire to harm someone or simply an intentional act or omission.

In theory, the prima facie tort is available when the facts of the case do not fit the pigeonholes of any of the traditional torts. It does not follow, however, that the prima facie tort will apply every time the other torts do not. The requirement of special damages, for example, tends to limit the applicability of the prima facie tort, due to the difficulty of proving specific economic or pecuniary loss (i.e., special damages).

The vast majority of states do *not* recognize the prima facie tort. Too many problems exist in defining it and in defining the defenses to it. There is also a danger of a party trying to bypass important public policy through this tort. Suppose, for example, that the statute of limitations has run out on a defamation action. A plaintiff should not be able to circumvent the defamation statute of limitations by suing under the theory of prima facie tort when the facts of the case would lend themselves to both torts, and when the statute of limitations on the prima facie tort had not yet run out. Rather than create a new tort, most states would prefer to try to stretch the boundaries of the existing torts so that plaintiffs will not be without a remedy when defendants have intentionally caused injury.

▪ ASSIGNMENT 29.7 ▪

Does your state recognize a prima facie tort? If so, define its elements and prepare an annotated bibliography on the tort. (See General Instructions for the State Court Opinion Assignment, and General Instructions for the Annotated Bibliography Assignment, both in Chapter 2.)

▪ BAD FAITH LIABILITY

A relatively recent basis of liability against insurance companies is called bad faith liability. For example, Jackson has a $100,000 liability policy with an insurance company. He has an accident and is sued for $250,000 by Pamela. The latter offers to settle for $80,000. Jackson's attorney notifies the insurance company of the offer, but the company takes an unreasonable amount of time to respond. Pamela proceeds with the litigation and obtains a $200,000 judgment against Jackson. The insurance company pays $100,000 of this judgment, the maximum under the policy. Jackson can now successfully argue that the insurance company acted in **bad faith** in failing to settle the case for an amount within policy limits.

▪ ASSIGNMENT 29.8 ▪

How would the Jackson case be resolved in your state? (See General Instructions for the State Court Opinion Assignment in Chapter 2.)

▪ DRAM SHOP LIABILITY

A number of states have what is called a Civil Liability Act or Dram Shop Act that imposes liability on those who give liquor to someone who is visibly intoxicated when the intoxication causes an injury to a third person. The basis of **dram shop liability** can differ from state to state. Negligence may have to be shown, in that the person giving the liquor created an unreasonable risk that the person receiving the liquor might injure others. Some states impose strict liability, especially if the person receiving the liquor is a minor. In such states there is no need for the injured third party to show that the person giving the liquor was negligent.

Many states impose dram shop liability only when the liquor is *sold* and only when the buyer is already visibly intoxicated. In a few states, however, liability is not dependent on a sale. A social host can also be held to dram shop liability when a *gift* of intoxicating liquor causes an injury.

> **Example:** Bob holds a high school graduation party in his home for his daughter and her friends. He serves intoxicating liquor at the party. One of the guests is Kelly, who becomes intoxicated. While driving home from the party, Kelly hits a pedestrian. Kelly became intoxicated at the party and the intoxication was a substantial factor in causing the pedestrian's injury. The latter can now seek civil, dram shop liability against Bob.

▪ ASSIGNMENT 29.9 ▪

The XYZ Supermarket has a liquor section. Davidson, an adult, buys two six-packs of beer. At the time of the purchase, he is not intoxicated. After the purchase, Davidson goes to his car in the parking lot of the XYZ Supermarket and drinks all of the beer he has just bought. How would a state court in your state handle the following cases? Assume that in each situation, Davidson's actions were caused by the intoxication that resulted from his drinking this beer:

a. After Davidson drives out of the XYZ lot, he accidentally hits a pedestrian, who now wants to sue the XYZ Supermarket.

b. Davidson drives out of the XYZ lot. In another parking lot, he has an argument with a truck driver over a parking spot. Davidson knocks the truck driver unconscious. The truck driver now wants to sue the XYZ Supermarket.

c. Davidson drives out of the XYZ lot and hits a tree. He is severely injured and can no longer support his family. His family now wants to sue the XYZ Supermarket.

d. Davidson drives out of the XYZ lot and goes to the Townhouse Restaurant in the area. Townhouse has a parking valet service. Davidson, visibly intoxicated, gives his key to the Townhouse valet and goes into the restaurant. A minute later he comes out, having changed his mind about eating at the restaurant. He tells the valet to get his car. The valet does so and hands the key to Davidson. A block from the restaurant, Davidson injures a pedestrian in an accident. The pedestrian now wants to sue Townhouse Restaurant for giving the keys back to Davidson.

(See General Instructions for the State Code Assignment and General Instructions for the State Court Opinion Assignment, both in Chapter 2.)

■ TORTIOUS INTERFERENCE WITH EMPLOYMENT

Most people are employed "at will," which, as indicated earlier, simply means that either the employee or the employer can terminate the relationship at any time and for any reason. There is no obligation to explain why or to state a cause. If, on the other hand, an express contract of employment exists for a designated period of time (e.g., a one-year union contract), the termination of the relationship within this period must comply with the terms of the contract. This usually means that terminations are allowed only for cause; employees with contract protection cannot be fired at will. In this context, **cause** means a justifiable reason.

The traditional rule on **employment at will** has been undergoing some modification. There are now some circumstances in which the law *will* protect the employee at will. Suppose, for example, that the employer fires the employee because the latter reported fire hazards in the employer's building to the city, or because the employee filed a worker's compensation claim. This **retaliatory discharge** violates public policy, because it obviously discourages employees from engaging in important activity such as fire prevention and in exercising rights such as those provided by the worker's compensation system.

What is the remedy for such retaliation? It is difficult to categorize the remedy within the traditional causes of action. A breach-of-contract action is somewhat strained, because there is no express contract that was violated. Some courts say that in the employment relationship there is an implied condition that forbids the employer from terminating the relationship for a reason that violates public policy. Most courts take a different approach by concluding that a tort has been committed—the **tortious interference with employment.** This tort differs from the tort of interference with contract relations (discussed earlier), in which a *third party* has wrongfully caused the interference.

■ ASSIGNMENT 29.10 ■

Bill works at an electrical power plant. He is laid off two days after he notified the state health agency that the plant was emitting poisonous gases into the air. His supervisor was very angry at him for contacting the agency. Bill believes that this anger led to his termination. Does Bill have any remedy in your state? (See General Instructions for the State Court Opinion Assignment in Chapter 2.)

SUMMARY

To commit the tort of disparagement, the defendant must publish an express or implied false statement of fact that casts doubt on the plaintiff's title to property (slander of title) or attributes a quality to the plaintiff's goods that makes them undesirable for commercial use (trade libel). Many courts say that the defendant must act out of malice in publishing the false statement, although the courts do not all agree on what is meant by malice. The consequence of the statement must be special (i.e., economic) damages suffered by the plaintiff. Among the defenses to disparagement are the privilege to protect one's own interest and to engage in fair competition in the business world.

Injurious falsehood is a broader tort by which the plaintiff suffers special damages to his or her interests due to the publication of a false statement by the defendant. Unlike disparagement, the statement does not have to attack the plaintiff's property or business.

It is a tort to interfere with contract relations by intentionally inducing another to breach a contract, or to make it impossible or more difficult to perform. The plaintiff's damages include compensation to cover the loss of the contract or the diminished value of its performance. One of the defenses to this tort is the privilege to protect one's own interest.

If the plaintiff does not have a contract, but the defendant interferes with the plaintiff's reasonable expectation of an economic advantage, the defendant has committed the tort of interference with prospective advantage. Most such cases in the business world involve unfair competition.

If the defendant causes special damages by intentionally inflicting harm, the plaintiff may be able to bring an action for prima facie tort, even if the conduct does not fit within any of the traditional torts.

Insurance companies that do not act in good faith in trying to settle claims within policy limits can be subject to liability for bad faith. Businesses that sell liquor to intoxicated persons who then injure others can be subject to dram shop liability. Some states also impose this liability on hosts that serve liquor to intoxicated guests at social gatherings. Finally, some states allow an employee at will to sue an employer for tortious interference with an employment relationship through a retaliatory discharge.

Key Terms

deep pocket
respondeat superior
vicarious liability
scope of employment
disparagement
statement of fact
puffing
privileged competition
slander of title
trade libel
publication
intentionally
recklessly

negligently
innocently
malice
commercial speech
special damages
fair competition
injurious falsehood
interference with
    contract relations
voidable
terminable at will
injunction
malicious

interference with
    prospective
    advantage
unfair competition
prima facie tort
bad faith
dram shop liability
cause
employment at will
retaliatory discharge
tortious interference
    with employment

CHAPTER 30

Worker's Compensation

CHAPTER OUTLINE

- ON-THE-JOB INJURIES AT COMMON LAW
- WORKER'S COMPENSATION STATUTES
- INJURIES AND DISEASES COVERED
  In the Course of Employment
  Arising Out of Employment

- FILING A CLAIM
- BENEFITS AVAILABLE

■ ON-THE-JOB INJURIES AT COMMON LAW

When an employee is injured on the job, his or her traditional remedy has been a negligence suit, brought on the theory that the employer unreasonably failed to provide a safe work environment. This is, of course, a common law tort remedy. For years, there was widespread criticism of this remedy, primarily because it was difficult for an employee to win a negligence case.

The difficulty was due to the employer's ability to establish one of the following three defenses:

Contributory negligence: The employee acted unreasonably, which contributed to his or her own injury, along with the negligence of the employer. The contributory negligence of the employee will prevent recovery against the employer (unless the latter's negligence was willful or wanton, or unless the employer failed to take the last clear chance (see Chapter 12) to avoid the injury).

Assumption of the risk: The employee knew about the hazards of the job and voluntarily took the job and/or remained on the job, even though the employee understood the dangers involved. Assumption of the risk defeats the employee's recovery for the employer's negligence.

Fellow-employee rule: The employer will not be liable for the injuries received by an employee if the injury was caused by the negligence of a fellow employee. An exception exists when the fellow employee is a **vice principal,** i.e., an employee with supervisory authority over other employees or an employee of any rank who has been given some responsibility for the safety of the work environment; the employer *will* be liable if the employee is injured because of the negligence of a fellow employee who is a vice principal.

■ WORKER'S COMPENSATION STATUTES

Throughout the country, **worker's compensation** statutes have been passed by the legislatures as an alternative to the common law negligence system. Under these statutes, an employee will receive compensation for an industrial accident without having to prove that the employer was negligent. Hence, the liability of the employer under such a statute is a form of **strict liability.** This means there is no need to prove that the employer caused the injury negligently. It is a **no-fault system.** The defenses of contributory negligence, assumption of the risk, and the fellow-servant rule are abolished.

Not all employers and employees are covered under worker's compensation. When employees are not covered, they are left with a traditional negligence action against the employer, in which they must face the defenses of contributory negligence, assumption of the risk, and the fellow-servant rule.

Benefits of Worker's Compensation to the Employee

- no need to prove the employer was negligent
- contributory negligence, assumption of the risk, and the fellow-servant rule do not apply
- recovery usually takes much longer in a negligence suit than in a worker's compensation case

Disadvantage of Worker's Compensation to the Employee

- If the employee is successful in a negligence action against the employer, the employee often receives considerably more than would be received under worker's compensation.

The primary way in which the worker's compensation system is financed is through insurance. An employer must either purchase insurance or prove that it is financially able to cover any risks on its own. The latter is called **self-insurance.** When insurance is purchased, it comes either from a state-operated insurance fund or from a private insurer or carrier.

Most states have an agency or commission to administer the worker's compensation law. It may be an independent entity or be part of the state's department of labor. Worker's compensation for civil employees of the federal government is administered by the United States Department of Labor. In this chapter, our primary concern is worker's compensation for employees in the *private* sector.

The state code will list the categories of employers and employees covered by worker's compensation in the private sector. It is important to note the definitions of employer, employee, employment, and any other word that will tell you who is and who is not covered. Some codes may say that everyone is covered except those specifically excluded, such as domestic workers, farm workers, casual workers, or people who work for employers with fewer than a certain number of employees.

· ASSIGNMENT 30.1 ·

What is the name, address, and phone number of the central office of the agency in your state that administers the worker's compensation law for employees in the private sector? You can obtain this information in a number of ways: Check with the personnel department of any large employer in the private sector in your state, ask any union officer in your state, call information for your state government, contact the office of a politician, ask any library if it has an organizational chart or a list of state agencies (e.g., *The National Directory of State Agencies*). Write or call this agency to request a brochure describing benefits and other information about the system. Also request sample application forms used by the agency.

· ASSIGNMENT 30.2 ·

What employers and employees in the private sector are covered by worker's compensation in your state? Who is excluded? (Summarize, if the list of inclusions and exclusions is extensive.) What choices exist, if any, on being covered? What choices exist, if any, on the manner of financing the employer's participation in the program? What penalties exist for a covered employer who fails to obtain insurance or who fails to qualify as a self-insurer? (See General Instructions for the State Code Assignment in Chapter 2.)

• ASSIGNMENT 30.3 •

The XYZ trucking firm does business and has an office in your state. It has 264 employees. At tax time, it hires an accountant to come in to examine all its books and prepare its returns. The job is expected to take two weeks, for which the accountant is paid $800 per week. While in the bookkeeping office of XYZ, the accountant trips and breaks a leg. Can the accountant recover worker's compensation through the XYZ trucking firm in your state? (See General Instructions for the State Code Assignment and the General Instructions for the State Court Opinion Assignment, both in Chapter 2.)

• ASSIGNMENT 30.4 •

Who administers the worker's compensation system for *state* employees injured on the job in your state? Is it the same system for city and county employees? Who administers the worker's compensation system for *federal* employees who are working in your state? To obtain answers to these questions, call a state personnel office in any state agency, call the office of any local politician, call any union office covering civil servants, or ask any state employee. For federal employees, call the personnel office of any federal agency with a branch in your state, call the office of any United States senator or United States congressperson in your state, or ask any federal employee. Try to obtain a copy of any brochures that are available on coverage for such government workers.

▪ INJURIES AND DISEASES COVERED

Every industrial misfortune is not covered under worker's compensation. A few states, for example, do not cover certain diseases that occur as a result of long-term exposure to conditions or hazards at a job. In most states, however, diseases as well as accidents are covered.

The basic requirement is that the employee's injury must **arise out of** and occur **in the course of** employment. "Arising out of" refers to the causal connection between the injury and the employment; "in the course of" refers to the time, place, and circumstances of the injury in connection with the employment. We will explore both issues through the following themes:

In the Course of Employment

1. while clearly at work
2. while going to or coming from work
3. during mixed-purpose trips
4. during horseplay and misconduct
5. while engaged in personal comfort

Arising Out of Employment

1. causal connection tests
2. acts of nature

3. street risks
4. assault and battery
5. personal risks

In the Course of Employment

1. While Clearly at Work

The vast majority of injuries pose little or no difficulty, e.g., a hand is injured while operating a printing press, or death results from an explosion while the worker is in a mine. Liability under the worker's compensation statute is clear for most cases of this kind.

2. While Going to and Coming from Work

A **going-and-coming rule** exists in most states: worker's compensation is denied if the employee is injured "off the premises" while going to or coming back from work or while going to or coming back from lunch. The company parking lot is usually considered part of the employer's premises, so that there *is* coverage if the employee is injured while on the lot. A number of exceptions have been created to the going-and-coming rule. For example, if the route to work exposes the worker to special dangers or risks (e.g., passing through a "rough" neighborhood to get to the plant), the injury will be considered within the "course of employment" even though it technically occurred beyond the premises owned or leased by the employer. Such risks are said to be **incident to the job.** The court will conclude that there is a close association between the access route and the premises of the employer.[1] Some courts also make an exception if the injury occurs when the employee is on a public sidewalk or street that is close to the premises of the employer.

3. During Mixed-Purpose Trips

Of course, any trip made by the employee that is part of a job responsibility is within the course of employment, and an injury that occurs on such a trip will be covered by worker's compensation, e.g., injury while making a sales trip or a delivery. Even if the employee is going to or from work, the trip will be considered part of the employment if the trip is a special assignment from or service to the employer, e.g., an employee is injured when asked to return to the shop after work hours to check on an alarm or to let someone in. It is not always necessary to show that the employee is paid extra compensation for such a trip, but when such compensation is paid, the argument is strengthened that the trip is within the course of employment.

Suppose, however, that the trip serves a *personal* purpose of the employee as well as a business purpose of the employer. This is a **mixed-purpose trip,** also called a **dual-purpose trip.**

> **Example:** Helen is asked to deliver a package to a certain city. She rents a car for the purpose at company expense. She takes along two of her friends so that the three of them can attend a party after Helen makes the delivery. While on her way to the city, Helen is injured in a traffic accident.

---

[1] Larson, *Workmen's Compensation Law* § 15.13, p. 4-22 (1978).

Helen had a business purpose for the trip (make the delivery) and a personal purpose (go to a party with her friends). The criteria a court will use to determine whether the trip is business (and hence covered by worker's compensation) or personal (and not covered) are as follows:

· The trip is considered a business trip if it would have been made even if the personal objective did not exist.
· The trip is considered a personal trip if it would have been made even if the business objective did not exist.

Therefore, the characterization of the trip depends on what would have happened if one of the purposes failed or did not materialize. The business nature of the trip is established once it can be said that the trip would have to be made at some time by someone, whether or not the person making the trip will also attend to some personal matters.

Suppose that an employee is on a purely business trip. While on the trip, however, the employee decides to take a detour for personal reasons, e.g., to visit a relative or to inquire into another job. The general rule is that the employee is not covered by worker's compensation if injured while on the detour. Once the personal detour has been completed and the employee is once more attending to the business purpose of the trip, coverage under the compensation statute resumes.

4. During Horseplay and Misconduct

It is not uncommon for workers on the job to be playful with each other or to engage in horseplay. What happens if an employee is injured during such horseplay? If the employee is the innocent victim of the horseplay, he or she will be covered by worker's compensation, e.g., the employee is hit on the head by a hard aluminum-foil ball that other employees were using to "play catch," in which the injured employee was not participating.

Suppose, however, that one of the employees participating in or instigating the horseplay is injured. Such injuries are often not covered by worker's compensation, unless it can be shown that the horseplay was a very minor departure from normal work responsibilities, or that the horseplay had been occurring over a long period of time and had, in effect, become customary.

The employee's injury may be caused by his or her own misconduct on the job. Recall what was said earlier about the defense of contributory negligence: the employee's own negligence is not a defense to recovery under worker's compensation. Some worker's compensation statutes, however, provide that if the employee is injured while engaged in **willful** misconduct, such as the willful failure to use a safety device, worker's compensation benefits *will* be denied or reduced.

It is important to distinguish between the following:

· what the employee has been asked to do—the **objective** of the job, and
· the **method** that the employee uses to carry out the objective

The general rule is that employee misconduct related to the objective of a job leads to no coverage under worker's compensation, but misconduct related to method is still covered.

Objective: A bus ticket clerk violates specific instructions never to drive a bus, and is injured. The injury is not covered under worker's compensation.

Method: A bus driver is injured because of careless operation of the bus. The injury is covered by worker's compensation.

Other examples of injuries that grow out of the method of doing the job and hence are covered under worker's compensation include: reaching into a machine before stopping it, climbing over a fence rather than walking around it, repairing a machine while it is still operating, and using a machine with its safety guard removed.[2] Even if these methods of doing the job were specifically prohibited by the employer, worker's compensation will still be allowed unless the statute has an exception for certain willful violations, as already mentioned.

5. While Engaged in Personal Comfort

The simple fact that an employee is injured while taking care of a personal need on the job does not mean that coverage is denied under worker's compensation. Here is how one court described this aspect of the law:

> For the purposes of the [worker's] compensation act the concept of course of employment is more comprehensive than the assigned work at the lathe. It includes an employee's ministrations to his own human needs: he must eat; concessions to his own human frailties: he must rest, must now and then have a break, and he sometimes, even on the job, plays practical jokes on his fellows. Course of employment is not scope of employment. The former, as the cases so clearly reveal, is a way of life in a working environment. If the injury results from the work itself, or from the stresses, the tensions, the associations of the working environments, human as well as material, it is compensable. Why? because those are the ingredients of the product itself. It carries to the market with it, on its price tag stained and scarred, its human as well as its material costs.[3]

When an injury occurs while a worker is taking a lunch break, going to the restroom, or stepping out for a moment of fresh air, worker's compensation usually applies. Factors that will be considered in reaching this result include whether the accident occurred on the premises and within an authorized area for the activity, whether it occurred within working hours, whether the hazard that led to the accident is considered normal for that work environment, and whether the employer prohibited the activity that led to the accident.

Suppose that the employee is injured while engaged in a sports contest at a picnic or other social event involving coworkers. Worker's compensation is applicable if the activity is sponsored by the employer or if the workers are otherwise encouraged to participate by the employer. The more benefit the employer is likely to derive from the activity, the more inclined an agency or a court will be to conclude that the activity was within the course of employment and hence covered by worker's compensation.

---

[2]Larson, *Workmen's Compensation Law* § 31.22, p. 6–20 (1978).
[3]*Crilly v. Ballou*, 353 Mich. 303, 326, 91 N.W.2d 493, 505 (1958). See also Malone, Plant, & Little, *Workers' Compensation and Employment Rights* 126 (2d. 3d. 1980).

▪ ASSIGNMENT 30.5 ▪

Examine the following situations to determine whether the injury was within the "course of employment." (See General Instructions for the Legal Analysis Assignment in Chapter 3.)

a. An employee is killed while crossing a public street immediately in front of her office. She is on her way home when hit by the car of another employee on the way to work.

b. The street in front of the company building is over 50 feet wide and is heavily traveled. An employee, walking to a restaurant during a lunch break, is hit by a car on this street. Another route to the restaurant is available through the rear of the company building. If the employee had used this other route, the trip would have taken an extra twelve minutes.

c. An employee is injured in a public parking lot 800 feet form his place of work. The company parking lot has spaces for only 200 of its 500 employees. The public parking lot is the closest alternative parking lot available.

d. During the work day, the employee is given an old company radio and allowed to take it home on company time. While putting the radio in her car in the company parking lot, she drops the radio and injures her foot.

e. An employee is a company salesperson who travels extensively throughout the city. At 6:00 P.M., the employee makes the last call and is on the way home. The employee is killed in an automobile collision one mile from home.

f. A teacher attends an evening PTA meeting and is on the way home. The teacher stops for a few minutes at a tavern and has half a glass of beer. After leaving the tavern, the teacher is injured in an automobile collision one mile from home.

g. An employee is a lawyer who works for a title insurance company. She usually takes a bus to work. On Tuesday, her employer asks her to come to work as soon as possible. The lawyer takes her car and has a collision on the way to work.

h. A real estate agent leaves home to inspect property listed by his employer. On the way, he stops at a jewelry store to buy a present for his wife. He slips in the store and injures his back.

i. An employee is a salesperson. While on a sales trip, she stops at a store to buy some groceries for that evening. The stop takes her ten miles out of the way. While in the store buying her groceries, she meets a prospective customer. After a brief discussion about a possible sale, she injures herself in a fall just outside the store.

j. An employee injures his back while putting out a cigarette in the lunchroom during his lunch break. The employee was leaning down to extinguish the cigarette in a bucket that had sand in it.

k. An employee has a heart attack while dancing at a Christmas party in the company hall.

l. An employee is injured while playing handball in the rear of the plant during a break. Employees have been playing handball there for months in spite of a company sign forbidding play in that area.

m. During a break, an employee is injured while trying to lift another employee.

n. The elevator door in a company building is broken. All employees are forbidden to use it until it is repaired. Two employees use this elevator and are both injured during a friendly wrestling match while the elevator is in motion.

▪ ASSIGNMENT 30.6 ▪

Select any three fact situations examined in Assignment 30.5. Determine whether worker's compensation would be granted in your state for the three situations you select. (See also General Instructions for the State Code Assignment and for the State Court Opinion Assignment, both in Chapter 2.)

Arising Out of Employment

1. Causal Connection Tests

"Arising out of employment" refers to the worker's compensation requirement that the injury must be caused by the employment. Various tests have been used by the courts to determine whether the requisite causal connection exists between the conditions under which the employee works and the injury sustained.[4]

> **Peculiar-risk test:** The source of the harm is peculiar to the employment. The danger must be incidental to the character of the business and dependent on the existence of an employer-employee relationship. The risk must not be one that the employee shares with every citizen, e.g., injury due to cold weather. The risk must differ in quality.

> **Increased-risk test:** The risk of injury to the employee is quantitatively greater than the risk of injury to nonemployees. The employment must increase the risk of an injury, even if others are also exposed to the risk of the injury.

> **Positional-risk test:** The injury of the employee would not have occurred but for the fact that the job placed the employee in a position where the employee could be injured.

> **Proximate-cause test:** The injury is foreseeable, and no intervening factor breaks the chain of causation between the conditions of employment and the injury.

> **Actual-risk test:** The injury is a risk of this employment. Whether or not the employment increases the risk, there is causation if the injury comes from a risk that is actually present in this employment.

Most states use the increased-risk test to determine whether the injury arises out of the employment. You must be aware of the other tests, however, because they are used by some states as sole tests, and they are sometimes used along with the increased-risk test.

2. Acts of Nature

There is usually no problem showing that an injury arose out of (was caused by) the employment when it was due to an **act of God** such as a storm or freezing weather that occurred during work. The increased-risk test is most often applied to reach this result. An injury received by an employee by lightning, for example, arises out of the employment if the job places the employee on an elevation, near metal, or in any place where there is an increased risk of this injury's occurring.

---

[4]Larson, *Workmen's Compensation Law* § 6, p. 3-1 (1978).

Suppose, however, that the act of nature delivers the same harm to everyone, e.g., a tornado levels an entire town. In such a case, it cannot be said that the employee was subjected to any increased risk by being on the job as opposed to being at home. Worker's compensation will be denied, because the injury did not arise out of the employment. Many courts make an exception to this rule if there is contact with the premises: if the act of God produces a force that makes actual contact with the employment premises, e.g., the hurricane blows down a company pole that hits the employee.

Exposure to the elements may bring on diseases such as Rocky Mountain spotted fever, which many people in an area may contract. If the employment increases the employee's chances of getting the disease, causation is established.

3. Street Risks

Traveling salespersons and employees making deliveries or soliciting sales are sometimes injured by falls or traffic accidents. Even though everyone is exposed to the risk of such injuries, most states will say that if the job increases the risk of their occurring, compensation will be allowed. Other courts will go even further and say that worker's compensation will be awarded simply by the plaintiff's showing that the job requires that public streets be used.

4. Assault and Battery

What happens if the employee is injured because of an assault or a battery? If the employee is the aggressor and the quarrel is personal, having nothing to do with the job, the injury does not arise out of the employment and worker's compensation is denied. It does not take much, however, for the assault or battery to be connected with the employment. The following are examples of injuries due to assault or battery that are sufficiently connected with the employment so that it can be said that the injury arises out of the employment:

- a police officer is hit by someone under arrest
- a cashier is killed in a robbery attempt
- a lawyer is raped in an office located in a dangerous area
- a supervisor is struck by a subordinate being disciplined
- a worker is struck by a coworker in an argument over who is supposed to perform a certain task
- a union member and a nonunion member have a fight over whether the latter should join the union

Fights on the job pose some difficulty. It is not always easy to determine whether a fight is due solely to personal animosity or vengeance (not compensable under worker's compensation) or has its origin in the employment, so that it can be said that the employment is a contributing factor to the fight (compensable under worker's compensation). In most states, the fact that the injured employee is the aggressor in the fight does not mean that compensation will be denied to him or her, as long as the employment itself contributed to the fight.

5. Personal Risks

Some employees are more susceptible to injury or disease than others, e.g., someone with a heart condition or epilepsy. An on-the-job injury or disease suffered by such an employee will be said to arise out of the employment only if it can be shown that the employment increased the risk of the injury or disease occurring, or if the employment **aggravated** the extent of the harm resulting from the injury or disease. Worker's compensation, of course, cannot be awarded for any **pre-existing injuries or diseases** that the employee brings to the job, because the job did not cause them. Such injuries or diseases are personal to the employee, unrelated to the occupation. Worker's compensation will be granted, however, when the job contributes to the risk or aggravates the resulting injury or disease. For example, an employee might fall on a machine after blacking out due to a pre-existing condition. The dangerous consequences of a blackout have been increased by the employer because the employee was stationed next to such a machine. Since the employer increased the risk of serious injury, worker's compensation will be awarded. Most courts, however, would reach a different result if the injury resulted from a fall onto the floor (without hitting any objects) while the employee was standing on a level surface. The injury following the blackout was not increased by the employment; it is the same injury that would have occurred if the employee had blacked out at home.

An employer cannot insist that all employees be fully healthy or normal at the time of employment. The employer takes employees as he or she finds them. If the employment produces stress, exertion, or strain that activates or aggravates a pre-existing condition, the resulting injury or disease is said to arise out of the employment. Worker's compensation will be awarded.

▪ ASSIGNMENT 30.7 ▪

Examine the following situations to determine whether the injury ''arises out of the employment.'' (See General Instructions for the Legal Analysis Assignment in Chapter 3.)

a. A caddie is struck by lightning while under a tree on a golf course during a sudden storm.

b. While digging a ditch, an employee is stung by a wasp, resulting in a severe fever.

c. A professor contracts infectious hepatitis due to exposure to an infected student.

d. An employee is killed in an airplane explosion on the way to a business meeting. The plane exploded because of a bomb planted by another passenger.

e. An employee had an ulcer before taking her job. She becomes worried about being laid off. The employee is hospitalized for further treatment on the ulcer during a period of depression about the possible loss of the job.

f. An employee is a door-to-door salesperson. While at a home trying to make a sale, he asks the prospective customer if she would go out with him to a dance that evening. She breaks his arm.

g. Two employees have an intense argument on the job over which employee is entitled to go to lunch first. Thirty minutes after the argument, one of the employees walks up behind the other and hits him over the head.

h. An employee has a weak leg due to an injury sustained before she began her present employment. As part of her job, she is required to use a ladder to store supplies on shelves. While on the second rung of the ladder, she falls due to the weak condition of her bad leg.

▪ ASSIGNMENT 30.8 ▪

Select any three fact situations examined in Assignment 30.7. Determine whether worker's compensation would be granted in your state for the three situations you select. (See also General Instructions for the State Code Assignment and for the State Court Opinion Assignment, both in Chapter 2.)

CASE

Seitz v. L&R Industries, Inc.
437 A.2d 1345 (1981)
Supreme Court of Rhode Island

Background: Beulah Seitz (referred to in the opinion as "the employee") sought worker's compensation for mental distress allegedly caused by her job. Under § 28-33-1 of the Rhode Island statute, benefits can be awarded if there has been a "personal injury arising out of and in the course of employment." The Rhode Island Worker's Compensation Commission awarded her compensation. The case is now before the Supreme Court of Rhode Island on appeal.

Decision on Appeal: Her mental injury was the result of the ordinary stresses of her job, not a physical or unexpected emotional trauma. Worker's compensation, therefore, is denied.

Opinion of Court

Justice WEISBERGER delivered the opinion of the court. . . .

The employee had worked as secretary to the vice president and general manager of the Worcester Pressed Aluminum Corporation (Worcester) for approximately six years. The place of employment during this period was Worcester, Massachusetts. In 1975 portions of the Worcester enterprise were placed on the market for sale. One of the divisions known as Palco Products Division was sold to L&R Industries, Inc. (employer). At some time during the month of September 1975, the employer ordered the Palco operations to be moved from Worcester, Massachusetts, to Smith-

field, Rhode Island. This change necessitated physical movement of office equipment, furniture, inventory, records, movement of office equipment, furniture, inventory, records, invoices, and machinery. The moving operation began on a Friday afternoon and was completed in a thirty-six-hour period. The employee and a former vice president of Palco Products Division, one Francis Maguire, were active in supervising and implementing the moving activities.

When Palco Products, under the new ownership, began operation on the following Monday, conditions in the new location were confusing and abnormal to a marked degree. Records were unavailable, the telephone service was inadequate, the previous tenants had not vacated the premises, and personnel were untrained. The employee sought to perform duties as office manager and secretary to Mr. Maguire but was also required to do janitorial and cleaning work and to protect office equipment from potential damage due to a leaking roof. She encountered difficulties in interpersonal relations with other employees in the new location. Her authority as office manager was not recognized, and office protocol was not satisfactory to her. She attempted to arrange a meeting with Mr. Maguire and other key personnel in order to work out these difficulties and to improve the organization of the employer's business at the new location. The meeting was scheduled for October 3, 1975, but because of the intervention of another employee, the meeting did not take place. As a result, the employee became so upset that she terminated her employment on the afternoon of October 3, 1975, and has not returned to work since that time.

Dr. Elliot R. Reiner, a psychiatrist who practices in the city of Worcester, had earlier begun treatment of the employee on June 10, 1967, for a condition he described as a depressive neurosis. After three office visits, the employee was discharged. The employee next visited the doctor on October 9, 1975, and described the emotional disruption she had experienced in association with occupational problems and conflicts during the period she had worked with the employer in Smithfield. The doctor diagnosed the employee's condition as an "obsessive compulsive personality disorder." The doctor stated, and the [worker's compensation] commission found, that the employee's rigid personality characteristic had been of long standing but had been aggravated by her employment from September 15, 1975 to October 3, 1975. The doctor testified that the employee had sustained an emotional trauma but had not experienced any physical trauma as the result of her employment.

The commission found that this aggravation qualified within the terms of G.L. 1956 (1979 Reenactment) § 28-33-1 as a "personal injury arising out of and in the course of [her] employment." Although the commission determined the aggravation to be entirely psychic, it found as a matter of fact and held as a matter of law that the conditions under which the employee had been required to work resulted in a malfunction of the body which gave rise to an incapacity to perform her customary work. Therefore, the appellate commission, with one dissenting member, sustained the decree of the trial commissioner

and ordered that compensation for total disability be paid to the employee. We reverse.

Professor Larson in this treatise . . . has set forth an analysis of three broad types of psychic injury. 1b Larson, *The Law of Workmen's Compensation* §§ 42.21–.23 (1980). The first type is a physical injury caused by mental stimulus. An analysis of case law on this subject leads Professor Larson to conclude that the "decisions uniformly find compensability." . . . The second broad type of psychic injury is that caused by physical trauma. The courts, including this court, have almost universally awarded compensation for this type of physically produced psychic injury upon an appropriate showing of causal connection. *Greenville Finishing Co. v. Pezza,* 81 R.I. 20, 98 A.2d 825 (1953) (neurosis produced by traumatic loss of eye). . . .

The third type of psychiatric injury mentioned by Professor Larson is a mental injury produced by mental stimulus in which there are neither physical causes nor physical results. Professor Larson finds "a distinct majority position supporting compensability in these cases" but concedes that "[t]he contra view, denying compensation in the 'mental-mental' category continues, however, to command a substantial following." 1B Larson, *The Law of Workmen's Compensation* §§ 42.23 at 7-628 (1980). In this field, of course, it is difficult to compare holdings in various jurisdictions because of the variation among the statutory provisions. Some statutes require accidental injuries. Other statutes, such as that of Rhode Island, require "personal injury" without the necessity of an accident. . . .

The Supreme Court of Wisconsin has succinctly encapsulated the distinction in *School District No. 1 v. Department of Industry, Labor & Human Relations,* 62 Wis.2d 370, 215 N.W.2d 373 (1974), in which it stated: "Thus it is the opinion of this court that mental injury nontraumatically caused must have resulted from a situation of greater dimensions than the day-to-day emotional strain and tension which all employees must experience. Only if the 'fortuitous event unexpected and unforeseen' can be said to be so out of the ordinary from the countless emotional strains and differences that employees encounter daily without serious mental injury will liability . . . be found." Id. at 377–78, 215 N.W.2d at 377.

In *School District No. 1 v. Department of Industry, Labor & Human Relations,* compensation was denied to a school guidance teacher who suffered psychic injury in the form of an acute anxiety reaction upon seeing a recommendation from a group of students that she be dismissed from her position as a member of the guidance counseling staff of the school. . . .

The courts are reluctant to deny compensation for genuine disability arising out of psychic injury. However, since screening of such claims is a difficult process, the courts recognize the burden that may be placed upon commerce and industry by allowing compensation for neurotic reaction to the ordinary everyday stresses that are found in most areas of employment. Indeed, it is a rare situation in which some adverse interpersonal relations among employees are not encountered from time to time. Employers and managers must admonish their subordinates and correct perceived shortcomings. The stress of competitive enterprise is ever present and attendant upon all types of commercial and industrial activity.

Great care must be taken in order to avoid the creation of voluntary "retirement" programs that may be seized upon by an employee at an early age if he or she is willing or, indeed, even eager to give up active employment and assert a neurotic inability to continue.

It is all very well to say that the adversary system will expose the difference between the genuine neurotic and the malingerer. We have great fears that neither the science of psychiatry nor the adversary judicial process is equal to this task on the type of claim here presented. An examination of the evidence in the instant case discloses that the employee's psychiatrist largely accepted her statement that she was unable to return to work. The patient, who had exhibited neurotic tendencies, arising out of family relationships as early as 1967, apparently suffered an aggravation during her sixteen-day period of employment with the employer. An analysis of the testimony in the case would clearly indicate that this stressful period contained conditions that, though scarcely tranquil did not exceed the intensity of stimuli encountered by thousands of other employees and management personnel every day. If psychic injury is to be compensable, a more dramatically stressful stimulus must be established. . . .

[The decision of the Worker's Compensation Commission is reversed.]

KELLEHER, Justice, with whom BEVILACQUA, Chief Justice, joins, dissenting. . . .

An overriding objective of workers' compensation legislation is to impose upon the employer the burden of caring for the casualties occurring in its employment by preventing an employee who has suffered a job-related loss of earning capacity from becoming a public charge. . . . An employer takes its workers as it finds them, and when the employee aggravates an existing condition and the result is an incapacity for work, the employee is entitled to compensation for such incapacity. Here, the commission, in awarding Beulah compensation, believed her psychiatrist when he testified that the office chaos that ensued following her employer's weekend move from Massachusetts to Rhode Island aggravated a preexisting psychiatric condition. Credibility and fact-finding are part of the commission's job. However, this award goes for naught because of the . . . imposition by my brother of a standard calling for a "more dramatically stressful stimulus." With all due deference to my learned associate, this standard represents judicial legislation. . . .

▪ ASSIGNMENT 30.9 ▪

Can worker's compensation be granted in the following situations?

a. Smith and Jones are working on a scaffold when one end gives way. Jones falls to his death as Smith watches. Smith had the sensation that he might fall himself, but he didn't. After this experience, Smith is unable to continue in this employment as a structural steelworker. He blanks out and freezes, experiencing complete paralysis when attempting work in a high place.

b. Edward works as an assistant manager at a food processing plant. Last year has been very stressful. For three months he was temporarily laid off because of a small fire that seriously damaged the plant's electrical system. He was accused of stealing and of sexually harassing another worker. (After an investigation, the owners of the plant concluded that he was innocent of both charges.) Due to declining profits, the plant seriously considered filing for bankruptcy. All of these events led to Edward's having a mental breakdown requiring hospitalization.

▪ FILING A CLAIM

States differ on the steps involved in making a worker's compensation claim. (See Figure 30.1 for an example.) The basic procedure is often as follows:

1. The worker reports the injury or disease to the supervisor and/or to the insurance carrier.
2. The worker receives medical attention.
3. The doctor, worker, and employer fill out forms provided by the worker's compensation agency and/or insurance carrier.
4. The worker receives disability benefits after a waiting period following the injury, e.g., seven days.

Each state has a statute of limitations within which the worker must make a claim, e.g., two years from the date of the injury or accident.

Most claims for worker's compensation are uncontested. No questions of liability for compensation arise. The employer or insurance carrier and the employee sign an agreement on the benefits to be received consistent with any state laws on the extent of such benefits. The state worker's compensation agency will usually approve such agreements as a matter of course. Some states do not use this agreement system. In such states, the employer or insurance carrier simply begins to make direct payments to the employee or to the dependents of the employee.

If there is a dispute, it will be resolved by the agency responsible for the worker's compensation program, often a board or commission. The procedure is frequently as follows:

▪ A hearing is held before a hearing officer, arbitrator, or referee of the agency. The proceeding is usually informal, unlike a court trial.
▪ A decision is made by the hearing officer, arbitrator, or referee. A party disagreeing with the decision can appeal it to the agency's commission or board.
▪ The commission or board makes the final decision of the agency. This decision can then be appealed to a court.

▪ ASSIGNMENT 30.10 ▪

Once a worker in the private sector has an injury or disease, how is a claim filed for worker's compensation benefits in your state? What are the steps that

Figure 30.1   Filing a Claim

WORKERS'
COMPENSATION NOTICE
And Instructions to
Employers & Employees

All employees of this establishment, entitled to benefits under the provisions of the Arkansas Workers' Compensation Law, are hereby notified that their Employer has secured the payment of such compensation as may at any time be due a disabled employee or his dependents.

IN CASE OF JOB-RELATED INJURIES OR OCCUPATIONAL DISEASES
The Employer Shall:

1. Provide all necessary medical, surgical and hospital treatment, as required by the Law, following the disability and for such additional time as ordered by the Commission.

2. Keep a record of all injuries received by his employees, and make a prompt report thereof in writing to the Arkansas Workers' Compensation Commission on blanks procured for this purpose.

3. Determine the average weekly wage of the employee and provide compensation in accordance with the provisions of the Act. The first installment of compensation becomes due on the 15th day after the employer has notice of the injury or death, except in those cases where liability has been denied by the employer. Additional compensation shall be paid every two weeks, except where the Commission directs that installment payments be made at other periods.

The Employee Should:

1. Immediately give or cause to be given to the employer notice in writing of disability or upon the first distinct manifestation of an occupational disease and request medical services. Failure to give notice within sixty (60) days after an accident or injury or ninety (90) days after the first distinct manifestation of an occupational disease, or to accept the medical services provided, may deprive the employee of the right to compensation.

2. Give promptly to the employer and to the Workers' Compensation Commission, on forms approved by the latter, notice of any claim for compensation for the period of disability. In case of fatal injuries, notice must be given by one or more dependents of the deceased or by a person in their behalf. (Act, Sec. 17.)

ARKANSAS WORKERS' COMPENSATION COMMISSION
Justice Building
State Capitol Grounds
Little Rock, Ark. 72201

All employers, who come within the operation of the Arkansas Workers' Compensation Law, and have complied with its provisions, MUST POST THIS NOTICE IN A CONSPICUOUS PLACE in or about his place or places of business, in addition to the prescribed notice as required by the Commission for insured employers.

ALLYN C. TATUM, Chairman
JOHN E. COWNE, JR., Commissioner
JIMMIE D. CLARK, Commissioner
OGDEN BERRY, Executive Director

INSURED EMPLOYERS make all reports to the insurance carrier in all cases where the employee loses time or is sent to the doctor. The insurance carrier then makes the necessary reports to the Commission. SELF-INSURED employers, State agencies, counties and cities under the State Plan, and public schools shall report directly to the Workers' Compensation Commission.

REVISED 6-1-76

must be followed? What forms must be prepared and who must prepare them? What is the waiting period before the employee can receive disability benefits? Once the benefits start coming, are they retroactive to the date of the injury? What is the statute of limitations? What is the appeal process? (See General Instructions for the State Code Assignment in Chapter 2.)

■ BENEFITS AVAILABLE

Most statutes are very specific on the number of weeks of disability benefits that are available to an employee who establishes a worker's compensation claim. For an example, see Figure 30.2.

The weekly disability benefit is usually based on a percentage of the employee's weekly pay over a designated period of time. The percentage is often $66^{2}/_{3}$ percent. This benefit is in addition to the cost of medical services. Different benefit periods, percentages, and amounts are provided depending on which of the following the employee has suffered:

- permanent total disability
- temporary total disability
- permanent partial disability
- temporary partial disability
- disfigurement
- death

Figure 30.2   Example of a Schedule of Weeks of Benefits

Injury	Weeks of Compensation Benefits
Loss of thumb	60
Loss of first finger	35
Loss of second finger	30
Loss of third finger	25
Loss of fourth finger	20
Loss of hand	190
Loss of arm	250
Loss of great toe	40
Loss of any other toe	15
Loss of foot	150
Loss of leg	220
Loss of eye	140
Loss of hearing in one ear	50
Loss of hearing in both ears	175
Permanent disfigurement, face or head	150

Note: The schedule of weeks is based on a 100 percent loss of the body member indicated. If the disability rating is less than 100 percent, the percentage rated should be multiplied by the number of weeks shown. For example a 20 percent loss of function of a thumb would be computed as 20 percent of sixty weeks, or twelve weeks of compensation benefits.

▪ ASSIGNMENT 30.11 ▪

Briefly describe the major kinds of benefits that an employee can receive under worker's compensation in your state. (See General Instructions for the State Code Assignment in Chapter 2.)

▪ ASSIGNMENT 30.12 ▪

Do an annotated bibliography on worker's compensation for employees in the private sector in your state. (See General Instructions for the Annotated Bibliography Assignment in Chapter 2.)

SUMMARY

Traditional negligence actions brought by employees injured on the job were often won by employers who used the defenses of contributory negligence, assumption of the risk, or the fellow-employee rule. An alternative remedy is worker's compensation, which is a form of strict liability, because recovery is not dependent on establishing the negligence of the employer. To be covered, the injury or disease must arise out of and occur in the course of employment.

Generally injuries off the premises while going to or coming back from work or lunch are not within the course of employment and hence are not covered. Injuries that occur while on a mixed-purpose trip are covered if the trip is primarily business, because the trip would have been made even if the employee did not also have a personal purpose in making the trip. But an injury that occurs during a personal detour while on a business trip is not covered.

An employee who is the innocent victim of horseplay is covered, but not the employee who participated in or instigated the horseplay, unless the horseplay was a very minor departure from normal work responsibility or had become customary. The employee's own misconduct is usually not a bar to recovery unless it amounted to a willful failure to use a safety device. An injury that results from misconduct in the method of doing a job is covered, whereas one that results from misconduct in what the employee has been asked to do, or the objective of the job, is not. Whether there is coverage for an injury that occurs while an employee is engaged in personal comfort on the job, e.g., during a break, depends on factors such as whether the injury occurred on the premises, within an authorized area for the activity, and within working hours.

Courts use different tests to determine whether the injury arose out of, and hence was caused by, the employment. The most common is the increased-risk test, whereby the risk of injury to the employee is quantitatively greater than the risk of injury to nonemployees. An injury that results from an act of nature is covered if the job increased the risk of that injury occurring. The same is true of injuries incurred from street risks. An employee who is injured from an assault and battery or a fight is covered if the event was connected with the employment. Worker's compensation does not cover pre-existing injury or disease, but does cover their aggravation due to the job.

Claims are made to the employer, to the insurance carrier, or both. If the claim is disputed, the worker's compensation agency will attempt to resolve it. If this is unsuccessful, the claim can be appealed in court.

Key Terms

contributory negligence
assumption of the risk
fellow-employee rule
vice principal
worker's compensation
strict liability
no-fault system
self-insurance
arise out of

in the course of
going-and-coming rule
incident to the job
mixed-purpose trip
dual-purpose trip
willful
objective
method
peculiar-risk test

increased-risk test
positional-risk test
proximate-cause test
actual-risk test
act of God
aggravated
pre-existing injuries or
    diseases

CHAPTER 31

Privileges and Immunities: Defenses That Avoid Tort Liability

---

CHAPTER OUTLINE

- INTRODUCTION
- CONSENT IN TORT LAW
  - Capacity to Consent
  - Manifestation of Willingness
  - Voluntariness
  - Reasonable Belief
  - Knowledge
  - Substantially the Same Conduct
- SELF-HELP PRIVILEGES
  - Introduction
  - Self-Defense
  - Defense of Others
  - Necessity
  - Abating a Nuisance
  - Defense of Property
  - Recapture of Chattels

- Retaking Possession of Land Forcibly
- Discipline
- Protecting Safety or Morals of a Close Relative, Friend, or Client
- Arrest
- SOVEREIGN IMMUNITY
  - Federal Government
  - State Government
  - Local Government
- OFFICIAL IMMUNITY: THE PERSONAL LIABILITY OF GOVERNMENT EMPLOYEES
- CHARITABLE IMMUNITY
- INTRAFAMILY TORT IMMUNITY

■ INTRODUCTION

A **privilege** is a justification for what would otherwise be wrongful or tortious conduct. Technically, the tort cannot exist if there was a privilege to act. An **immunity** is a special protection given to someone who has committed a tort. The practical effect of privileges and immunities is the same: they both are defenses that prevent the actor from being liable for the damage or injury that the actor has caused. Because of this similarity of effect, you will often see the words "privilege" and "immunity" used interchangeably.

The privileges to be discussed in this chapter are different from *evidentiary* privileges, which operate to exclude evidence from being considered in litigation, e.g., the privilege against self-incrimination, the attorney-client privilege, the doctor-patient privilege, the husband-wife privilege. The tort privileges that are our concern in this chapter operate to prevent liability altogether.

▪ CONSENT IN TORT LAW

A basic principle of the law is **volenti non fit injuria:** no wrong is done to one who consents. If the plaintiff consented to the defendant's conduct, the latter cannot be liable for the resulting harm. We have already discussed consent in a negligence case as ''assumption of the risk'' (see Chapter 15). In strict liability cases, assumption of the risk equals consent and hence, no liability. In most intentional tort cases, consent also defeats liability.

The basic elements of **consent** are presented in Figure 31.1.

Figure 31.1   Elements of Consent

1. Plaintiff (P) has the capacity to consent to the conduct of Defendant (D).
2. There is an express or implied manifestation from P of a willingness to let the conduct of D occur.
3. P's willingness is voluntary.
4. D reasonably believes that P is willing to let D's conduct occur.
5. P has knowledge of the nature and consequences of D's conduct.
6. D's conduct is substantially the same as the conduct P agreed to.

Capacity to Consent

The person giving consent must have the capacity to consent. A young girl, for example, may agree to sexual intercourse with an older male, but the latter can still be guilty of statutory rape. If the girl later sues the male for battery in a civil case, the male cannot raise the defense of consent, just as he could not raise it in the criminal case. The young girl does not have the capacity to consent if she is below the age designated by law. So too, there are statutes intended to protect children from working in dangerous conditions. If a child is injured in working conditions that violate the statute, the employer will not be able to say that the child consented to work there and took the risk of being injured—even if the child understood those risks and willingly proceeded. The statutes will probably be interpreted as taking away the child's capacity to consent.

A person can also lack the capacity to consent by being too young or ill to understand the conduct involved. Unless an authorized parent or guardian gives consent for this person, the consent is invalid.

Suppose that the conduct to which consent is given is criminal conduct. Paul and Dan agree to a duel or boxing match that is illegal. Both are prosecuted under criminal law. Paul then sues Dan for damages in a civil battery case. Dan's defense is that Paul consented to being hit. Courts differ on how they handle this problem. Some hold that the consent will be a good defense, barring the civil action. Other courts, however, do not recognize the consent as valid, on the theory that no one has the power or capacity to consent to a crime. Since the consent is invalid, the civil battery action can be brought. As a consequence, a plaintiff can receive damages growing out of a criminal act in which the plaintiff willingly participated. Of course, if both Paul and Dan were injured in their illegal fight with each other, each of them could sue the other for civil battery in a state where the consent will not be recognized.

▪ ASSIGNMENT 31.1 ▪

Henry and Fred are having an argument. Henry is about to hit Fred with a baseball bat. In self-defense Fred punches Henry with his fist and breaks Henry's jaw. While Henry is unconscious on the ground, Fred stabs him in the leg. Henry later sues Fred for injury to his leg in a civil battery case. Fred raises the defense of consent. What result and why? (See General Instructions for the Legal Analysis Assignment in Chapter 3.)

▪ ASSIGNMENT 31.2 ▪

a. Go to the criminal code in your state statutes. Try to find crimes to which the consent of the victim or the other person involved is *not* a defense to the criminal prosecution. For example, check statutes involving drugs, sex, or children. (See General Instructions for the State Code Assignment in Chapter 2.)
b. For any of the statutes you identified in answer to (a) above, assume that a civil action is later brought against the defendant for the same acts that were classified as crimes in the criminal code. Would the plaintiff's consent be a valid defense in the civil suit? (See General instructions for the State Court Opinion Assignment in Chapter 2.)

Manifestation of Willingness

A person can express or manifest willingness other than verbally. The wave of a hand can indicate consent to come on one's land. Consent by silence is also common, if the person would normally be expected to speak if he or she objected to conduct about to occur. If a trespasser enters your yard and you fail to object or fail to take steps to remove the individual, your silence or nonaction is strong evidence that you do not object. This is an **implied consent.** If you voluntarily agree to play football, you are implying consent to the kind of rugged contact that is usually associated with this sport. If you walk downtown into a crowded store, you are implying consent to the kind of everyday contact that is normal in crowds.

▪ ASSIGNMENT 31.3 ▪

At a college dance, Jessica asks Dan, a stranger, to dance. After the dance, Jessica kisses Dan on the cheek and walks away. Dan sues Jessica for battery. Does she have a defense? (See General Instructions for the Legal Analysis Assignment in Chapter 3.)

Voluntariness

Of course, if the plaintiff has been coerced into agreeing to the defendant's conduct, the consent is invalid. Being coerced into agreeing is different from being pressured into agreeing. The latter is generally not sufficient to invalidate the consent. **Coercion** means that the plaintiff's consent was not the product of his or her own will. Suppose that a foreign passenger about to enter port does not want to be vaccinated, but nevertheless rolls up her sleeve to the doctor injecting the needle. Her conduct led the doctor to believe that she consented. She may have been under pressure to be vaccinated in order to avoid the hassle of being detained at port, yet the consent was still the product of a free will. The consent was voluntary.

Extreme or drastic pressure, however, can be enough to invalidate consent, e.g., a threat of force against the plaintiff or a member of the plaintiff's family, or a threat against the valuable property of the plaintiff. The plaintiff's agreement as a result of such pressure would not be voluntary.

• ASSIGNMENT 31.4 •

Tom calls Linda on the phone and tells her that he has her very valuable painting, which he will destroy if she does not come to his apartment and engage in sexual intercourse. Linda is frantic about the painting. She goes to his apartment and has sex with him. He then gives her the painting. Later, she brings a civil battery action against him. Does he have a defense? Would it make any difference if his threat was to harm Linda's neighbor? (See General Instructions for the Legal Analysis Assignment in Chapter 3.)

Reasonable Belief

The defendant must be reasonable in believing that the plaintiff has consented to the conduct in question. Problems often arise when the defendant claims to have relied on the plaintiff's implied consent. Suppose that the defendant has always played practical jokes on the plaintiff, to the latter's great amusement, e.g., squirting the plaintiff with a water pistol or pretending to steal the plaintiff's hat. It would be reasonable for the defendant to believe that the plaintiff would continue to agree to such jokes as long as they were of the same kind as practiced in the past. If the plaintiff has decided that enough is enough and does not want to be subjected to such jokes anymore, he or she must communicate this to the defendant. Otherwise, the defendant is justified in believing that plaintiff continues to consent. The test of consent is not what the plaintiff subjectively thinks, but what someone reasonably interprets the plaintiff to be communicating based upon the latter's words, actions, and silence, and upon the customs of the area.

• ASSIGNMENT 31.5 •

Mary is riding in her car when she spots Alex injured on the side of the road. Mary pulls over to try to help. She sees that his arm is broken and puts it in a sling. Later, Alex sues Mary for battery. Does she have a defense? Does it make any difference that Mary is a doctor? Why or why not? (See General Instructions for the Legal Analysis Assignment in Chapter 3.)

Knowledge

The plaintiff must know what conduct is being consented to and its probable consequences, in order for the consent to be an effective bar to a later tort action against the defendant. If a doctor obtains the consent of a patient to undergo an operation, but fails to tell the patient of the very serious probable side effects of the operation, the patient has not consented to the operation. The defendant has not provided the patient with the basic knowledge to enable the patient to give an **informed consent.** As we saw in Chapter 12, if an emergency exists, the doctor can proceed with treatment to save the patient's life or to avoid serious further injuries if it is not possible or practical to obtain the patient's consent and the doctor does not have an express prior direction to the contrary from the patient.

Consent obtained by trickery or misrepresentation is not effective. The classic case is the plaintiff who buys candy that turns out to be poisoned. The implied representation of the seller is that the candy is wholesome. The plaintiff consented to eat candy, not poison. So too if the defendant entices the plaintiff to play a game of ice hockey in order to get the plaintiff into a position where the defendant can intentionally cut the plaintiff with skates, the defendant cannot later claim that the plaintiff consented to such contact. The plaintiff's consent was obtained by misrepresentation.

When the plaintiff has made a mistake about what he or she is consenting to, it is important to know whether the defendant caused the plaintiff's mistake and whether the defendant knew about it. If the mistake was not caused by and was not known to the defendant, the consent is still valid, as long as the defendant was reasonable in believing that the plaintiff consented. If, for example, the plaintiff agrees to let the defendant ride a truck over one parcel of land, but makes a mistake and lets the defendant ride over a different parcel of land, the consent is valid and defeats a trespass action as long as the defendant neither knew about nor procured the error that the plaintiff made. The consent is invalid if the defendant either knew about or caused the plaintiff to make the mistake, as through misrepresentation.

The mistake must relate to the essence of the transaction rather than to something collateral. If the plaintiff agrees to pay the defendant $200 for a massage, the plaintiff cannot later sue the defendant for battery when the money turns out to be counterfeit, if the defendant did not know the money was counterfeit. If the defendant did know the money was phony, the consent is not valid because it was obtained by the defendant's own misrepresentation.

Substantially the Same Conduct

If the defendant's conduct deviates in a minor way from the conduct the plaintiff consented to, the consent is still effective. The deviation must be substantial for the consent to be invalid. If, for example, the plaintiff agrees to let the defendant throw a bucket of water on him or her, the consent is still effective if approximately the same amount of water is poured on the plaintiff by using a garden hose. The defendant's conduct is substantially different, however, if the bucket of water contains rocks, unknown to the plaintiff.

The defendant must also substantially comply with any restrictions or conditions imposed on the consent by the plaintiff that are communicated to the defendant. If, for example, the plaintiff tells the defendant that he or she can cut one truckload of timber from the plaintiff's land on January 3 or 4, the defendant will be liable for trespass to land if he or she cuts three truckloads on those dates, or cuts any timber on January 10.

▪ ASSIGNMENT 31.6 ▪

Tom and Mary agree to have sexual intercourse. Mary gets venereal disease from Tom and sues him for battery. How, if at all, would the following factors affect Tom's defense of consent?

a. Tom was a prostitute and Mary knew it.
b. Tom led Mary to believe that he was a virgin.
c. Tom and Mary confided to each other that both had had many lovers before.
d. Tom lied to Mary about wanting to marry her.
e. Mary lied to Tom about wanting to marry him.
f. This was the first time Tom and Mary met.
g. Tom and Mary are married to each other.

CASE

Peterson v. Sorlien
299 N.W.2d 123 (1980)
Supreme Court of Minnesota

Background: Susan Jungclaus Peterson joined a religion called The Way Ministry. Her father, Norman Jungclaus, enlisted the support of Susan's former minister, Paul Sorlien, and of deprogrammers to try to separate her from what the father believed was a cult. Later Susan sued for false imprisonment. The lower courts dismissed the suit. The case is now on appeal in the Supreme Court of Minnesota.

Decision on Appeal: Judgment affirmed. There was no false imprisonment.

Opinion of Court

Chief Justice SHERAN delivered the opinion of the court. . . .

This action by plaintiff Susan Jungclaus Peterson for false imprisonment . . . arises from an effort by her parents . . . to prompt her disaffiliation from an organization known as The Way Ministry. . . . [T]his case marks the emergence of a new cultural phenomenon: youth-oriented religious or psuedo-religious groups which utilize the techniques of what has been termed "coercive persuasion" or "mind control" to cultivate an uncritical and devoted following. Commentators have used the term "coercive persuasion," originally coined to identify the experience of American prisoners of war during the Korean conflict to describe the cult-induction process. The word "cult" is not used pejoratively but in its dictionary sense to describe an unorthodox system of belief characterized by "[g]reat or excessive devotion or dedication to some person, idea, or thing." Webster's *New International Dictionary of the English Language Unabridged* 552 (1976). Coercive persuasion is fostered through the creation of a controlled environment that heightens the susceptibility of a subject to suggestion and manipulation through sensory deprivation, physiological depletion, cognitive dissonance, peer pressure, and a clear assertion of authority and dominion. The aftermath of indoctrination is a severe impairment of autonomy and the ability to think independently, which induces a subject's unyielding compliance and the rupture of past connections, affiliations and associations. See generally Delgado, *Religious Totalism: Gentle and Ungentle Persuasion under the First Amendment,* 51 S.Cal.L.Rev. 1 (1977). One psychologist characterized the process of cult indoctrination as "psychological kidnapping." Id. at 23.

At the time of the events in question, Susan Jungclaus Peterson was 21 years old. For most of her life, she lived with her family on a farm near Bird Island, Minnesota. In 1973, she graduated with honors from high school, ranking second in her class. She matriculated that fall at Moorhead State College. A dean's list student during her first year, her academic performance declined and her interests narrowed after she joined the local chapter of a group organized internationally and identified locally as The Way of Minnesota, Inc.

The operation of The Way is predicated on the fund-raising activities of its members. The Way's fund-raising strategy centers upon the sale of pre-recorded learning programs. Members are instructed to elicit the interest of a group of ten or twelve people and then play for them, at a charge of $85 per participant, a taped introductory course produced by The Way International. Advanced tape courses are then offered to the participants at additional cost, and training sessions are conducted to more fully acquaint recruits with the orientation of the group and the obligations of membership. Recruits must contribute a minimum of 10 percent of their earnings to the organization; to meet the tithe, student members are expected to obtain part-time employment. Members are also required to purchase books and other materials published by the ministry, and are encouraged to make larger financial contributions and to engage in more sustained efforts at solicitation.

By the end of her freshman year, Susan was devoting many hours to The Way, listening to instructional tapes, soliciting new members and assisting in training sessions. As her sophomore year began, Susan committed herself significantly, selling the car her father had given her and working part-time as a waitress to finance her contribu-

tions to The Way. Susan spent the following summer in South Dakota, living in conditions described as appalling and over-crowded, while recruiting, raising money and conducting training sessions for The Way.

As her junior year in college drew to a close, the Jungclauses grew increasingly alarmed by the personality changes they witnessed in their daughter; overly tired, unusually pale, distraught, and irritable, she exhibited an increasing alienation from family, diminished interest in education and decline in academic performance. The Jungclauses, versed in the literature of youth cults and based on conversations with former members of The Way, concluded that through a calculated process of manipulation and exploitation Susan had been reduced to a condition of psychological bondage.

On May 24, 1976, defendant Norman Jungclaus, father of plaintiff, arrived at Moorhead to pick up Susan following the end of the third college quarter. Instead of returning to their family home, defendant drove with Susan to Minneapolis to the home of Veronica Morgel. Entering the home of Mrs. Morgel, Susan was greeted by Kathy Mills and several young people who wished to discuss Susan's involvement in the ministry. Each of those present had been in some way touched by the cult phenomenon. Kathy Mills, the leader of the group, had treated a number of former cult members, including Veronica Morgel's son. It was Kathy Mills a self-styled professional deprogrammer, to whom the Jungclauses turned, and intermittently for the next sixteen days, it was in the home of Veronica Morgel that Susan stayed.

The avowed purpose of deprogramming is to break the hold of the cult over the individual through reason and confrontation. Initially, Susan was unwilling to discuss her involvement; she lay curled in a fetal position, in the downstairs bedroom where she first stayed, plugging her ears and crying while her father pleaded with her to listen to what was being said. This behavior persisted for two days during which she intermittently engaged in conversation, at one point screaming hysterically and flailing at her father. But by Wednesday Susan's demeanor had changed completely; she was friendly and vivacious and that night slept in an upstairs bedroom. Susan spent all day Thursday reading and conversing with her father and on Saturday night went roller-skating. On Sunday she played softball at a nearby park, afterwards enjoying a picnic lunch. The next week Susan spent in Columbus, Ohio, flying there with a former cult member who had shared with her the experiences of the previous week. While in Columbus, she spoke every day by telephone to her fiance who, playing tapes and songs from the ministry's headquarters in Minneapolis, begged that she return to the fold. Susan expressed the desire to extricate her fiance from the dominion of the cult.

Susan returned to Minneapolis on June 9. Unable to arrange a controlled meeting so that Susan could see her fiance outside the presence of other members of the ministry, her parents asked that she sign an agreement releasing them from liability for their past weeks' actions. Refusing to do so, Susan stepped outside the Morgel residence with the puppy she had purchased in Ohio, motioned to a passing police car and shortly thereafter was reunited with her fiance in the Minneapolis headquarters of The Way. Following her return to the ministry, she was directed to counsel and initiated the present action.

Plaintiff [alleges] that defendants unlawfully interfered with her personal liberty by words or acts which induced a reasonable apprehension that force would be used against her if she did not otherwise comply. The jury, instructed that an informed and reasoned consent is a defense to an allegation of false imprisonment and that a nonconsensual detention could be deemed consensual if one's behavior so indicated, exonerated defendants with respect to the false imprisonment claim.

The period in question began on Monday, May 24, 1976, and ceased on Wednesday, June 9, 1976, a period of 16 days. The record clearly demonstrates that Susan willingly remained in the company of defendants for at least 13 of those days. During that time she took many excursions into the public sphere, playing softball and picnicking in a city park, roller-skating at a public rink, flying aboard public aircraft and shopping and swimming while relaxing in Ohio. Had Susan desired, manifold opportunities existed for her to alert the authorities of her allegedly unlawful detention; in Minneapolis, two police officers observed at close range the softball game in which she engaged; en route to Ohio, she passed through the security areas of the Twin Cities and Columbus airports in the presence of security guards and uniformed police; in Columbus she transacted business at a bank, went for walks in solitude and was interviewed by an F.B.I. agent who sought assurances of her safety. At no time during the 13-day period did she complain of her treatment or suggest that defendants were holding her against her will. If one is aware of a reasonable means of escape that does not present a danger of bodily or material harm, a restriction is not total and complete and does not constitute unlawful imprisonment. Damages may not be assessed for any period of detention to which one freely consents.

In his summation to the jury, the trial judge instructed that to deem consent a defense to the charge of false imprisonment for the entire period or for any part therein, a preponderance of the evidence must demonstrate that such plaintiff voluntarily consented. The central issue for the jury, then, was whether Susan voluntarily participated in the activities of the first three days. The jury concluded that her behavior constituted a waiver.

We believe the determination to have been consistent with the evidence. See *Faniel v. Chesapeake & Potomac Telephone Co.,* 404 A.2d 147 (D.C.1979); *Schneckloth v. Bustamonte,* 412 U.S. 218, 93 S.Ct 2041,

36 L.Ed.2d 854 (1973); F. Harper & F. James, *The Law of Torts* § 3.10, at 235 (1956). Were the relationship other than that of parent and child, the consent would have less significance.

To determine whether the findings of the jury can be supported upon review, the behavior Susan manifested during the initial three days at issue must be considered in light of her actions in the remainder of the period. Because, it is argued, the cult conditioning process induces dramatic and non-consensual change giving rise to a new temporary identity on the part of the individuals whose consent is under examination, Susan's volitional capacity prior to treatment may well have been impaired. Following her readjustment, the evidence suggests that Susan was a different person, "like her old self." As such, the question of Susan's consent becomes a function of time. We therefore deem Susan's subsequent affirmation of defendants' actions dispositive.

In *Weiss v. Patrick*, 453 F.Supp. 717 (D.R.I.), aff'd, 588 F.2d 818 (1st Cir. 1978), the federal district court in Rhode Island confronted a situation similar to that which faces us. Plaintiff, a devotee of the Unification Church, brought an action for false imprisonment against individuals hired by her parents to prompt her disassociation from the church. Because plaintiff's mother was dying of cancer, the church authorities permitted her to join her family for the Thanksgiving holiday. Met at the airport by her mother, she testified that she was restrained against her will in the home of one of the defendants and subjected to vituperative attacks against the church until she seized an opportunity to flee. Despite the evidently traumatic experience sustained by plaintiff, the district court found that she failed to demonstrate a meaningful deprivation of personal liberty, reasoning that "any limitation upon personal mobility was not her primary concern." Id. at 722. In so reasoning, the court underscored a parental right to advocate freely a point of view to one's child, "be

she minor or adult." To assure freedom, the court observed, "the right of every person 'to be left alone' must be placed in the scales with the right of others to communicate." Id. (quoting *Rowan v. United States Post Office Department*, 397 U.S. 728, 736, 90 S.Ct. 1484, 1490, 25 L.Ed.2d 736 (1970).

In light of our examination of the record and rules of construction providing that upon review the evidence must be viewed in a manner most favorable to the prevailing party, we find that a reasonable basis existed for the verdict exonerating defendants of the charge of false imprisonment. Although carried out under colorably religious auspices, the method of cult indoctrination, viewed in a light most favorable to the prevailing party, is predicated on a strategy of coercive persuasion that undermines the capacity for informed consent. While we acknowledge that other social institutions may utilize a degree of coercion in promoting their objectives, none do so to the same extent or intend the same consequences. Society, therefore, has a compelling interest favoring intervention. The facts in this case support the conclusion that plaintiff only regained her volitional capacity to consent after engaging in the first three days of the deprogramming process. As such, we hold that when parents, or their agents, acting under the conviction that the judgmental capacity of their adult child is impaired, seek to extricate that child from what they reasonably believe to be a religious or psuedo-religious cult, and the child at some juncture assents to the actions in question, limitations upon the child's mobility do not constitute meaningful deprivations of personal liberty sufficient to support a judgment for false imprisonment. But owing to the threat that deprogramming poses to public order, we do not endorse self-help as a preferred alternative. In fashioning a remedy, the First Amendment requires resort to the least restrictive alternative so as to not impinge upon religious belief. *Cantwell v. Connecticut*, 310

U.S. 296, 60 S.Ct. 900, 84 L.Ed.2d 1213 (1940). . . .*

Affirmed.

Justice WAHL (dissenting in part).

I must respectfully dissent. In every generation, parents have viewed their children's religious and political beliefs with alarm and dismay if those beliefs were different from their own. Under the First Amendment, however, adults in our society enjoy freedoms of association and belief. In my view, it is unwise to tamper with those freedoms and with longstanding principles of tort law out of sympathy for parents seeking to help their "misguided" offspring, however well-intentioned and loving their acts may be. . . .

Any imprisonment "which is not legally justifiable" is false imprisonment; *Kleidon v. Glascock,* 215 Minn. 417, 10 N.W.2d 394 (1943); therefore, the fact that the tortfeasor acted in good faith is no defense to a charge of false imprisonment. . . .

---

*While we decline at this time to suggest a particular alternative, we observe that some courts have permitted the creation of temporary guardianships to allow the removal of cult members to therapeutic settings. If the individuals desire, at the end of the conservatorship they may return to the cult. Actions have also been initiated against cult leaders on the basis of criminal liability. See generally Delgado, supra, at 73-97.

The majority opinion finds, in plaintiff's behavior during the remainder of the 16-day period of "deprogramming," a reasonable basis for acquitting [her father] of the false imprisonment charge for the initial three days, during which time he admittedly held plaintiff against her will. Under this theory, plaintiff's "acquiescence" in the later stages of deprogramming operates as consent which "relates back" to the events of the earlier three days, and constitutes a "waiver" of her claim for those days. . . . Certainly, parents who disapprove of or disagree with the religious beliefs of their adult offspring are free to exercise their own First Amendment rights in an attempt, by speech and persuasion without physical restraints, to change their adult children's minds. But parents who engage in tortious conduct in their "deprogramming" attempts do so at the risk that the deprogramming will be unsuccessful and the adult children will pursue tort remedies against their parents. To allow parents' "conviction that the judgmental capacity of their [adult] child is impaired [by her religious indoctrination]" to excuse their tortious conduct sets a dangerous precedent.

Here, the evidence clearly supported a verdict against Norman Jungclaus on the false imprisonment claim. . . .

▪ ASSIGNMENT 31.7 ▪

a. Explain why the court said Susan consented to the confinement during the first three days. Or is the court saying that she did not have the capacity to consent during these three days? Or is the court saying that there really was no confinement during these three days?

b. Susan's parents asked her to sign an agreement releasing them from liability for their past weeks' actions. Suppose she had signed. Would the agreement have had legal effect?

c. Can you falsely imprison someone who is mentally retarded?

d. Does this opinion set good social policy? Why or why not?

▪ SELF-HELP PRIVILEGES

Introduction

When serious conflict arises, our society encourages people to use the legal system—the courts—to resolve the conflict. In effect, we say, "don't take the law into your own hands; tell it to a judge!'' There are situations, however, where it simply is not practical to ask the courts to intervene. A person may need to act immediately to protect an interest or a right. Such immediate, protective action is called **self-help.** Self-help is justified when there is a privilege to act without first obtaining the permission or involvement of the court.

We shall consider ten self-help privileges:

1. self-defense
2. defense of others
3. necessity
4. abating a nuisance
5. defense of property
6. recapture of chattels
7. retaking possession of land forcibly
8. discipline
9. protection of safety or morals of a close relative, friend, or client
10. arrest

The question often arises whether a defendant loses the protection of a privilege because the defendant has made a *mistake*. As we shall see in the charts that follow, some reasonable mistakes do not destroy the privilege, whereas other mistakes—even if reasonably made—do destroy it.

Self-Defense

Figure 31.2   An Overview of the Privilege of Self-Defense

Elements of the Privilege of Self-Defense	The Torts Involved (Examples)	Investigation Tasks	Factors That Destroy the Privilege
a. Reasonable belief by D that P will immediately inflict harmful or offensive contact on D. **b.** Reasonable force used by D with the intent to prevent P's apparent threat of an immediate harmful or offensive contact on D.	• *Battery* P is about to hit D. To prevent this, D knocks P down. P sues D for battery. D can raise the defense of **self-defense.** • *Assault* P is about to hit D. To prevent this, D threatens to hit P. P sues D for assault. D can raise the defense of self-defense.	• Has P threatened D in the past? • Has P hit D in the past? • Does P have a reputation for aggressiveness? • What age and strength differences, if any, exist between P and D? • How close was P to D at the time of the threat? • What did P threaten D with?	• D's response to the threat of P was disproportionate to the danger posed by P. (D cannot kill P to prevent a shove by P when the shove does not threaten D's life or limb with serious bodily harm). • P's threat was to inflict future harm on D. • P was merely insulting D and

Figure 31.2 Continued

Elements of the Privilege of Self-Defense	The Torts Involved (Examples)	Investigation Tasks	Factors That Destroy the Privilege
	· *False Imprisonment* P is about to hit D. To prevent this, D locks P in a room. P sues D for false imprisonment. D can raise the defense of self-defense.	· Did the threat occur in D's residence? · Did P say anything to indicate how serious the threat was? · How much time did D have before P would carry out P's threat? · Was P's threat to inflict future or present harm on D? · Did D know or believe that P was only bluffing? · Did D have time to warn P that D would inflict force on P? · In the past, has D ever consented to the kind of contact that P threatened?	not threatening D with bodily harm or offensive contact. · D was acting solely to protect D's honor and not to prevent a harmful or offensive contact by P. · D was acting out of revenge and not to prevent immediate harm to D. · D was not threatened at D's residence and could have retreated without responding with deadly force or force calculated to impose serious bodily harm on P. · D knew or believed that P was only bluffing.

Notes:
· If D makes a mistake on whether P is about to inflict an immediate harmful or offensive contact on D, or if D makes a mistake on the amount of force needed to prevent the immediate threat, the privilege of self-defense is still valid if the mistake was reasonable under the circumstances.
· Reasonable force can include deadly force or force calculated to cause serious bodily harm *if* D reasonably believes D is threatened with death or serious bodily harm from P.
· If D is in his or her residence, D does not have to retreat before inflicting deadly force or force calculated to cause serious bodily harm if such force is otherwise reasonable.
· States differ on whether such retreat is needed if D is *not* in his or her residence.

▪ ASSIGNMENT 31.8 ▪

In the following situations, assess whether the defendant can successfully raise the privilege of self-defense. (See General Instructions for the Legal Analysis Assignment in Chapter 3.)

a. Richard raises his cane over his head and shouts at Gary, saying, "If my daughter wasn't here with me, I'd smash you in the head." Gary is afraid. He grabs Richard's cane and knocks him down. Richard then sues Gary for battery.

b. Jane asks Clayton to leave Jane's store because she does not like the color of Clayton's clothes. Clayton refuses to leave. Jane comes at Clayton with a broom. Jane is over twenty-five feet away and is on crutches. As Jane approaches, Clayton shoots her. Jane sues Clayton for battery.

c. Lou, the plaintiff, is in Robin's home. Lou starts yelling obscenities at Robin in front of the latter's family. Lou spits in Robin's face and throws the latter's coat out the window. Just as Lou is about to spit in Robin's face again, Robin stabs Lou. Lou sues Robin for battery.

▪ ASSIGNMENT 31.9 ▪

Prepare an annotated bibliography on self-defense in a civil action in your state. (See General Instructions for the Annotated Bibliography Assignment in Chapter 2.)

Defense of Others

Figure 31.3   An Overview of the Privilege of Defense of Others

Elements of the Privilege of Defense of Others	The Torts Involved (Examples)	Investigation Tasks	Factors That Destroy the Privilege
a. Belief by D that P will immediately inflict harmful or offensive contact on a third person. **b.** Reasonable force used by D with the intent to prevent P's threat to the third person.	• *Battery* P is about to hit a third person. D sees this and hits P to prevent P's attack on the third person. P sues D for battery. D can raise the defense of **defense of others.**	• Has P threatened the third person in the past? • Has P hit the third person in the past? • Does P have a reputation for aggressiveness? • What age and strength differences, if any, appear to exist	• D's response was disproportionate to the harm P was threatening the third person with. • P's threat was to impose future harm on the third person. • P was merely insulting the

Figure 31.3 Continued

Elements of the Privilege of Defense of Others	The Torts Involved (Examples)	Investigation Tasks	Factors That Destroy the Privilege
c. The third person was not in fact the aggressor against P, i.e., P did not have a privilege to threaten the third person.	• *Assault* P is about to hit a third person. D sees this and threatens to hit P if P does not stop. P sues D for assault. D can raise the defense of defense of others. • *False Imprisonment* P is about to hit a third person. D sees this and locks P in a "bear hug" until the third person can escape. P sues D for false imprisonment (and for battery). D can raise the defense of others.	between P and the third person? Between P and D? • How close was P to the third person at the time of P's threat? • What gestures or words were used by P to the third person that D could observe or hear? • How much time appeared to exist before P would carry out P's threat against the third person? • Was P's threat against the third person immediate or for the future? • Did P appear to be bluffing? • Did D have time to warn P that D would use force against P if the latter did not stop trying to harm the third person? • Did the third person appear to be consenting to contact from P, e.g., in a football game?	third person and not threatening the latter with immediate harm • D knew P was bluffing. • D was acting out of revenge and not to prevent immediate harm to the third person. • In most states, D loses the privilege if D made a mistake and the third person turns out to have been the aggressor against P. This is so even if the mistake was reasonable. In a minority of states, the privilege is *not* lost if D's mistake was reasonable.

Figure 31.3   Continued

Notes:
- A minority of states do not include the third element listed in the first column (c) as long as D was reasonable in what turns out to be a mistake as to the third party's right to be protected. In the states that *do* include this element, D takes the risk that he or she has made a mistake about the third person's right to be protected. Even if D's belief is reasonable, D will not be protected in such states if in fact the third party turns out to have been the aggressor against P.
- As to the amount of force that is reasonable, D stands in the shoes of the third person. D can use the amount of force that the third person could have reasonably used to protect him- or herself. This could include deadly force if the third person was in danger of death or serious bodily harm from P.
- The third person does not have to be a member of D's family. In most states, the third person D tried to protect can be a stranger.

• ASSIGNMENT 31.10 •

Bill is walking down the street and sees a man and a woman engaged in a heated argument. Bill does not know either of these individuals. Bill thinks the man is trying to attack or molest the woman. Bill quickly knocks the man down. In fact, it turns out that the woman was trying to rob the man. The man sues Bill for battery. How would this case be handled in your state? (See General Instructions for the State Court Opinion Assignment in Chapter 2.)

Necessity

Figure 31.4   An Overview of the Privilege of Necessity

Elements of the Privilege of Necessity	The Torts Involved (Examples)	Investigation Tasks	Factors That Destroy the Privilege
a. Reasonable belief by D that persons or property will be immediately injured or damaged. **b.** Reasonable *use* by D of P's **chattels** (personal property) or land to prevent the	• *Conversion* D destroys P's liquor to prevent it from getting into the hands of an invading army. P sues D for conversion. D can raise the defense of public necessity and avoid paying P for the loss D caused.	• What alternatives, if any, were available to D and how realistic were they? • How much time did D have to act? • How much damage did D do? • What were the indications that the public was	• D's belief in the existence of the danger was unreasonable. • D's use of P's chattels or land was disproportionate to the danger. (For example, D cannot blow up P's house to prevent the spread of a fire

Figure 31.4   Continued

Elements of the Privilege of Necessity	The Torts Involved (Examples)	Investigation Tasks	Factors That Destroy the Privilege
immediate injury or damage.	• *Conversion* D is injured in a car accident and uses P's scarf as a tourniquet. The scarf is ruined. P sues D for conversion. D can raise the defense of private necessity, but must compensate P for any damage done to P's scarf. • *Trespass to Land* D runs onto P's land to escape a bear. P sues D for trespass to land. D can raise the defense of private necessity but must compensate P for any damage D does to P's land, e.g., to a fence.	in danger (for public necessity)? • Did D seek advice on what to do—if any time was available?	when the fire is minor and water is available to put it out.)

Notes:
- Reasonable use (see the second element in the first column) can include the damage or destruction of P's chattels or damage to P's land. Must D compensate P for the loss? Yes, if a private necessity existed; no, if a public necessity existed.
- A **public necessity** exists when a public danger is threatened, e.g., flood, large fire. D must be acting to prevent a public danger and not a purely private danger. If D damages or destroys P's property, D does not have to compensate P if D acted reasonably otherwise.
- A **private necessity** exists if D is acting to prevent a private danger, e.g., to protect D's crops. If D damages or destroys P's property, D must compensate P.
- Some states have statutes that compensate D for losses stemming from a public necessity.

▪ ASSIGNMENT 31.11 ▪

Tom has a contagious disease. He has no money to buy medicine and no hospitals are in the area. Tom breaks into a doctor's office at night and steals what he thinks is medicine that will help. In fact, he takes the wrong medicine. The doctor sues Tom for conversion. Does Tom have a defense? If Tom has a defense, does he still have to pay the doctor for losses sustained due to the break-in? (See General Instructions for the Legal Analysis Assignment in Chapter 3.)

Abating a Nuisance

There are times when a defendant has a privilege to enter someone's land in order to **abate a nuisance.** This privilege is discussed elsewhere in the book (see Chapter 27). When the privilege applies, it is a defense to the tort of trespass to land.

Defense of Property

Figure 31.5   Overview of the Privilege of Defense of Property

Elements of the Privilege of Defense of Property	The Torts Involved (Examples)	Investigation Tasks	Factors That Destroy the Privilege
a. D has possession of land or chattel (personal property). **b.** D's right to possession is superior to P's claim of possession, if any. **c.** D has a reasonable belief that immediate force is needed to prevent P's present threat to or continued interference with D's possession. **d.** D uses reasonable force against P to prevent the threatened or	▪ *Battery* P enters D's land and refuses to leave when D asks him to do so. D takes P by the collar and pushes him out. P sues D for battery. D can raise the defense of **defense of property.** ▪ *Assault* P reaches for D's purse on the table. D raises her fist at P and shouts at him to keep away from her purse. P sues D for assault. D can raise the defense of	▪ Did D have possession of the land or chattel? ▪ What indications were there that P was going to interfere immediately or was going to continue the interference? ▪ What did P say or do? ▪ What alternatives to force, if any, were available to D? ▪ What age and strength differences existed between P and D? ▪ What harm was P subjected to by	▪ P had a privilege to be on the land or to possess the chattel. ▪ P's right to possession was superior to D's. ▪ P's threat to interfere was in the future—it was not an immediate threat. ▪ D's use of force was disproportionate to the threat posed by P to D's possession. ▪ D was motivated solely by hatred and revenge. D was not trying to prevent interference by P.

Figure 31.5   Continued

Elements of the Privilege of Defense of Property	The Torts Involved (Examples)	Investigation Tasks	Factors That Destroy the Privilege
continued interference by P of D's possession. e. D requests that P cease the threatened or continued interference, unless the request would be unsafe or impractical for D.	defense of property.	D's use of force to prevent P's threatened or continued interference? · Did D ask P to stop the interference? Would such a request have been realistic? · Did P's interference with D's land or chattel in any way threaten D's personal safety or that of others?	· D knew that P was bluffing when P threatened interference. · D did not ask P to cease the threatened or actual interference by P. The request would have been reasonable or practical. · D used deadly force or force calculated to cause serious bodily harm even though neither D nor anyone else was threatened with death or serious bodily harm by P.

Notes:

· In most states, D cannot use deadly force or force calculated to cause serious bodily harm, (e.g., shoot P), even if D adequately warns P that such force will be used. D has a privilege to use great force *only* if P's interference with property also threatens life or limb of others.

· D is still protected by the privilege if D makes a reasonable mistake on the amount of force needed, but not if D makes even a reasonable mistake on D's right to possession of the land or the chattel, unless P caused D to make the mistake.

· In this privilege, we are not talking about D's privilege to *recapture* possession from P. Recapture will be considered later in Figure 31.6.

CASE

Katko v. Briney
183 N.W.2d 657 (1971)
Supreme Court of Iowa

Background: The Brineys own an unoccupied farm house that had been broken into several times. Boarding up the windows and posting no-trespassing signs did not deter the break-ins. On June 11, 1967 Mr. Briney set "a shotgun trap" in the north bedroom. He secured the gun to an iron bed with the barrel pointed at the bedroom door. It was rigged with wire from the doorknob to the gun's trigger so it would fire when the door was opened. He first pointed the gun so an intruder would be hit in the stomach. At Mrs. Briney's suggestion, however, it was lowered to hit the legs. He admitted he did so "because I was mad and tired of being tormented" but "he did not intend to injure anyone." Tin was nailed over the bedroom window. The spring gun could not be seen from the outside and no warning of its presence was posted. When Katko and a companion tried to break in, Katko was seriously injured when he triggered the gun. Much of his leg, including part of the tibia, was blown away. In a criminal proceeding, Katko pled guilty to larceny, was fined $50, and was paroled during good behavior from a sixty-day jail sentence. He then brought a civil suit against the Brineys for damages. At the trial, the jury returned a verdict for Katko for $20,000 actual and $10,000 punitive damages. The case is now on appeal before the Supreme Court of Iowa.

Decision on Appeal: Judgment affirmed. Deadly force cannot be used to protect uninhabited property.

Opinion of Court

Chief Justice MOORE delivered the opinion of the court.

The primary issue presented here is whether an owner may protect personal property in an unoccupied boarded-up farm house against trespassers and thieves by a spring gun capable of inflicting death or serious injury. We are not here concerned with a man's right to protect his home and members of his family. Defendants' home was several miles from the scene of the incident. . . .

In the statement of issues the trial court stated plaintiff and his companion committed a felony when they broke and entered defendants' house. In instruction 2 the court referred to the early case history of the use of spring guns and stated under the law their use was prohibited except to prevent the commission of felonies of violence and where human life is in danger. The instruction included a statement [that] breaking and entering is not a felony of violence.

Instruction 5 stated: "You are hereby instructed that one may use reasonable force in the protection of his property, but such right is subject to the qualification that one may not use such means of force as will take human life or inflict great bodily injury. Such is the rule even though the injured party is a trespasser and is in violation of the law himself."

Instruction 6 stated: "An owner of premises is prohibited from willfully or intentionally injuring a trespasser by means of force that either takes life or inflicts great bodily injury; and therefore a person owning a premise is prohibited from setting out 'spring guns' and like dangerous devices which will likely take life or inflict great bodily injury, for the purpose of harming trespassers. The fact that the trespasser may be acting in violation of the law does not change the rule. The only time when such conduct of setting a 'spring gun' or a like dangerous device is justified would be when the trespasser was committing a felony of violence or a felony punishable by death, or where the trespasser was endangering human life by his act." . . .

The overwhelming weight of authority, both textbook and case law, supports the trial court's statement of the applicable principles of law.

Prosser on Torts, Third Edition, pages 116–118, states: "the law has always placed a higher value upon human safety than upon mere rights in property. [It] is the accepted rule that there is no privilege to use any force calculated to cause death or serious bodily injury to repel the threat to land or chattels, unless there is also such a threat to the defendant's personal safety as to justify a self-defense. . . . [S]pring guns and other mankilling devices are not justifiable against a mere trespasser, or even a petty thief. They are privileged only against those upon whom the landowner, if he were present in person would be free to inflict injury of the same kind." . . .

Affirmed.

▪ ASSIGNMENT 31.12 ▪

a. Do you agree with the result in this case? Why or why not?
b. Would the case have been decided differently if the Brineys had posted a large sign on the farm property saying, "WARNING: Property Protected by Spring Guns"?
c. Smith owns a liquor store that has been burglarized often. He buys a pit bull dog to stay in the store after he closes. A midnight burglar is mauled by the dog. Does *Katko* apply?

▪ ASSIGNMENT 31.13 ▪

In the following situations, examine what defenses, if any, can be raised in the suits brought. (See General Instructions for the Legal Analysis Assignment in Chapter 3.)

a. George is invited to Henry's house for dinner. They have an argument and Henry asks George to leave. George refuses. Henry pushes George through a glass window. George sues Henry for battery.
b. Tom is terrified by dogs. Leo's little dog starts barking at Tom in the street. Tom picks up a stick and is about to hit the dog. Leo sees this and clubs Tom with a baseball bat. Tom sues Leo for battery.
c. Helen is in her boat when a storm suddenly begins. Helen takes the boat to Kevin's private dock in order to prevent the destruction of her boat. When Kevin sees Helen's boat at his dock, he tells her to leave immediately or he will punch her in the nose. Helen leaves even though the storm is still raging. Helen sues Kevin for assault.

Recapture of Chattels

Figure 31.6   Overview of the Privilege of Recapture of Chattels (Personal Property)

Elements of the Privilege of Recapture of Chattels	The Torts Involved (Examples)	Investigation Tasks	Factors That Destroy the Privilege
a. P acquired possession of the chattel wrongfully, e.g., by fraud or force. **b.** D has the right to immediate possession. **c.** D requests that P return the chattel. This request is made before D uses force to recapture it, unless the request would be unrealistic or unsafe for D. **d.** D's use of force to recapture the chattel occurs promptly after P took possession of the chattel (sometimes referred to as **fresh pursuit**), or promptly after D discovered that P took possession.	• *Battery* P has just stolen D's television, and refuses to return it. D pushes P aside in order to take the television back. P sues D for battery. D can raise the defense of **recapture of chattels.** • *Assault* Same facts as above, except that instead of pushing P, D raises his fist and threatens to hit P if P does not return the television. P sues D for assault. D can raise the defense of recapture of chattels. • *Trespass to Land* Same facts as above on the television. P has the television in his garage. When D finds out, D	• How did P get possession of the chattel? • Did P claim P had a right to possession? If so, on what basis? • What is D's basis for the claim that D had a right to possess the chattel? • Did either P or D claim that they owned the chattel, that they had properly rented it, or that they were properly holding it for someone else? • Did P originally get possession with the consent of D? • Did D request P to return the chattel? Was such a request realistic? • When did D discover that P had possession, and how long after discovery did D try to recapture it?	• P did not have actual possession nor did P control possession. • D made a mistake about whether P had acquired possession wrongfully. (It makes no difference that D's mistake was reasonable—unless P caused D to make the mistake.) • P in fact got possession rightfully (even though P's *continued* possession may now be wrongful, in which case D does not have the privilege of recapture—D must use the courts to get the chattel back) • D has no right to possession. • D failed to request a return when such a request was practical.

Figure 31.6   Continued

Elements of the Privilege of Recapture of Chattels	The Torts Involved (Examples)	Investigation Tasks	Factors That Destroy the Privilege
e. D uses reasonable force (not force calculated to cause death or serious bodily injury) with the intent to recapture the chattel from P.	immediately goes into the garage to recapture the television. P sues D for trespass to land. D can raise the defense of recapture of chattels.	▪ Could D have discovered that P had possession sooner? Why or why not? ▪ Could D have acted sooner to recapture the chattel? Why or why not? ▪ How much force was necessary to take the chattel back from P? Could less force have been used? Why or why not? ▪ What did P and D say to each other just prior to D's use of force?	▪ D took too long to discover that P had possession. ▪ D took too long to recapture after D knew or should have known that P had possession. ▪ D used a disproportionate amount of force to recapture the chattel. ▪ D was acting solely from the motive of hatred and revenge and did not limit the force to what was necessary to recapture the chattel.

Notes:
▪ D's mistake about P's right to possession destroys the privilege even if the mistake was reasonable (unless P caused D to make the mistake).
▪ The **shopkeeper privilege** allows a merchant to detain a person for a reasonably short time for the purpose of investigating whether there has been a theft. The merchant must reasonably believe the person detained is a thief.
▪ For each example in the second column, D must establish compliance with the five elements of the privilege listed in the first column, e.g., the demand for a return is made when realistic.

▪ ASSIGNMENT 31.14 ▪

In the following situations, determine whether the defendant can claim the defense of recapture of chattels. (See General Instructions for the Legal Analysis Assignments in Chapter 3.)

a. Tom is playing football. He asks Fred to hold his watch. While Tom is on the field, Fred suddenly must leave. Fred asks Joe to hold the watch for Tom. Fred does not know that Joe is Tom's archenemy. When Tom finds out that Joe has the watch, he asks for it back. Joe refuses. Tom hits Joe over the head with a football helmet and takes the watch back. Joe sues Tom for battery.

b. Sam steals John's ring and sells it for $1 in a dark alley to Fred, who does not know Sam. Two weeks after John finds out that Fred has the ring. John breaks into Fred's house and takes the ring from Fred's jewelry box. Fred sues John for trespass to land.

▪ ASSIGNMENT 31.15 ▪

Jim buys a car in your state on credit. Jim stops making payments. Under what circumstances, if any, can the seller of the car repossess it from Jim with the use of force? Check statutes and court opinions in your state. (See General Instructions for the State Code Assignment, and General Instructions for the State Court Opinion Assignment, both in Chapter 2.)

▪ ASSIGNMENT 31.16 ▪

Prepare an annotated bibliography on the defense of recapture of chattels for your state. (See General Instructions for the Annotated Bibliography Assignment in Chapter 2.)

Retaking Possession of Land Forcibly

Only under limited circumstances is a defendant entitled to retake possession of *land* from a plaintiff with the use of force, e.g., the plaintiff him- or herself has directly and wrongfully dispossessed the defendant. State statutes exist in most states governing the repossession of land through the use of court proceedings, particularly when a landlord is trying to remove (evict) a tenant.

▪ ASSIGNMENT 31.17 ▪

Pat owns the house she is renting to Charles. Charles has not paid rent for months.

a. Can Pat use force to remove Charles and all his personal property from the house? What steps must Pat go through in your state to do this? (See General Instructions for the State Code Assignment, and General Instructions for the State Court Opinion, both in Chapter 2.)

b. Assume that Pat does not proceed through proper channels. Make a list of all the torts for which Pat might be liable. You can assume additional facts that you think might be likely to occur in these circumstances. (See General Instructions for the Legal Analysis Assignment in Chapter 3.)

Discipline

Parents have the privilege of disciplining their children. This can include physically hitting and confining the children, as long as such force is reasonable. (Teachers and others who stand in the place of parents—*in loco parentis*—also have this privilege.) Suits within the family are discussed later in this chapter, in the section on Intrafamily Tort Immunity.

Protecting Safety or Morals of a Close Relative, Friend, or Client

In some states, it is a tort to alienate the affections of one spouse for another (see Chapter 26). This might be done, for example, by a mother-in-law or father-in-law counseling a child to leave the child's spouse. Close relatives, professional counselors, and close friends have a privilege to intervene if they are acting to protect the safety or morals of the spouse. The privilege is also a defense to the tort of enticing one spouse to leave the home of the other spouse. The privilege is lost, however, if they act maliciously, fraudulently, or otherwise excessively in trying to assist the spouse.

Arrest

When a public officer or a private citizen tries to arrest someone, the latter might respond with a suit for battery, assault, or false imprisonment. The privilege of **arrest** can be raised as a defense to such suits. The elements of this privilege and its special circumstances are considered in Chapter 19, "False Imprisonment and False Arrest." The arrest of an individual can also raise issues of defamation, invasion of privacy, malicious prosecution, and abuse of process. Finally, the arrested person might claim a violation of his or her civil rights.

▪ SOVEREIGN IMMUNITY

When is the government liable for its torts? The old answer was: never. The King cannot be sued because the King can do no wrong. This was the essence of the doctrine of **sovereign immunity.** Over the years, however, the government (i.e., the sovereign) has agreed to be sued for torts in limited situations. In this section, we will discuss the boundaries of what is now a limited sovereign immunity. Government, of course, acts only through its agents or employees. Hence, when the government is liable, it will be on a theory of **respondeat superior:** let the master answer for the acts of its servant. The servant is the government employee. We also need to explore when this employee is *personally* liable for the torts he or she commits while carrying out governmental functions. In summary, the issues are:

1. When has the *federal* government agreed to be liable for the torts of its employees?
2. When has the *state* government agreed to be liable for the torts of its employees?
3. When have *local* governments agreed (on their own or on order from the state government) to be liable for the torts of their employees?
4. When is any government employee (federal, state, or local) independently and personally liable for the torts he or she commits on the job?

In the next section, we shall consider the last issue—the immunity of the public official as an individual against personal liability. This is separate from the question of sovereign immunity.

In this section, we are not talking about contract actions in which the government is being sued by a citizen for breach of contract. Sovereign immunity is almost always waived to permit such contract actions.

Before analyzing the issues of sovereign immunity for torts, two major exceptions to immunity need to be kept in mind. First, legislatures sometimes pass private bills that allow private individuals to sue the government when the individuals would otherwise be prevented from suing because of sovereign immunity. This waiver of immunity is different from the more general waiver that exists for designated classes of torts or claims. Second, constitutions often contain provisions forbidding the government from **taking private property** for public purposes without **just compensation.** This "taking" can consist of forcing the private person to give up his or her land. It can also consist of damage the government does to private property that is serious enough to warrant just compensation under the constitution. To the extent that the government is forced by the constitution to provide compensation for a "taking," the government is waiving its sovereign immunity.

Federal Government

The basic law containing the federal government's consent to be sued is the **Federal Tort Claims Act.**[1] By no means does the Act abolish sovereign immunity for the federal government. The general rule established by the Act says that the United States will be liable for torts according to the local law in the place where the tort occurs in the same manner as a private individual would be liable. But there are enormous exceptions to this general rule.

Figure 31.7 presents an overview of what the Federal Tort Claims Act excludes and covers. As you can see from Figure 31.7, the *exclusions* column is much longer than the *coverage* column. Claimants often seek to get around the exclusions by trying to switch labels. This usually does not work. A federal government doctor, for example, who performs surgery on the wrong part of the patient's body has committed a battery, for which sovereign immunity is not waived under the Federal Tort Claims Act. The federal government cannot be sued for the harm caused by this doctor even if the patient pleads negligence rather than battery, and even if there was negligence in addition to a battery. The essence of the claim arises out of an excluded tort—battery. (See the first column of Figure 31.7.)

Most of the litigation under the Act has involved the distinction between planning and operational discretion. The government will often try to avoid liability via sovereign immunity by claiming that the negligent act of its employee involved *planning* discretion. Suppose that the United States Coast Guard negligently maintains a lighthouse, causing a private ship to crash into rocks. Do we have planning or *operational* discretion? Surely the initial decision to install the lighthouse involves a great deal of planning discretion, for which the government will not be liable, even if the Coast Guard was negligent in that planning. But the maintenance of the lighthouse itself is an operational function. To be sure, discretion is needed in running the lighthouse, but this discretion is at the operational level. Negligence at this level *will* impose liability under the Act. The same would be true of negligent operation of government motor vehicles.

Before a citizen tries to bring a claim under the Federal Tort Claims Act, the administrative agency involved must be given the chance to settle the case on its

---

[1] 28 U.S.C. § 1291, 1346, 1402, 1504, 2110, 2401–2, 2411–2, 2671–8, 2680 (1946).

Figure 31.7   Federal Tort Claims Act

Exclusions	Coverage
(Claims for which the United States will *not* be liable; sovereign immunity is *not* waived)	(Claims for which the United States *will* be liable; sovereign immunity *is* waived)

I. Explicitly Excluded Torts

Claims arising out of
1. assault
2. battery
3. false imprisonment
4. false arrest
5. malicious prosecution
6. abuse of process
7. libel
8. slander
9. misrepresentation
10. deceit
11. interference with contract rights

A limited exception to this list of exclusions is created for investigative or law enforcement officers. The United States government *will* be liable when such officers commit assault, battery, false imprisonment, false arrest, abuse of process, or malicious prosecution. (See item I. 3. in the "Coverage" column.)

II. Discretion

Claims arising out of the non-negligent or negligent exercise of discretion by the employee at the **planning** level, involving judgment on whether or not to perform a government task. Also excluded are claims based on the execution or administration of a statute or regulation, even if invalid.

III. Strict Liabillity

Claims based on liability without fault, such as acts or omissions involving ultrahazardous activities. To make the federal government liable for such activities, fault (i.e., negligence or intent) must be shown.

I. Covered Torts

1. Negligence: negligent acts or omissions committed within the scope of employment, as long as the claim for negligence does not arise out of one of the eleven excluded torts or involve any of the other exclusions mentioned in the "Exclusions" column.
2. Trespass to land, trespass to chattels, conversion, invasion of privacy, or other tort, as long as the claim does not also arise out of one of the eleven excluded torts or involve any of the other exclusions mentioned in the "Exclusions" column.
3. Assault, battery, false imprisonment, false arrest, abuse of process, or malicious prosecution committed by investigative or law enforcement officers.

II. Ministerial/Operational Level

Claims arising out of acts or omissions of the employee at the **ministerial** level, where no discretion is involved, or at the **operational** level, where the discretion involved, if any, relates only to the carrying out of the planning decisions.

Figure 31.7   Continued

Exclusions	Coverage

IV. Other Exclusions

1. Claims arising out of the
   following activities: war, mail
   delivery, admiralty, customs, tax
   collection. (Government liability
   for some of these activities is
   covered under *other* waiver-of-
   immunity statutes.)
2. Claims by members of the
   armed forces in the course of
   their duties.

own within certain dollar limits. If the citizen is still dissatisfied, he or she can sue under the Act in a federal court. (See a sample complaint in Figure 31.8.)

Federal employees themselves are generally excluded as claimants under the Federal Tort Claims Act. Injuries that they receive on the job are covered by other statutory schemes, such as the Federal Employees' Compensation Act.[2]

▪ ASSIGNMENT 31.18 ▪

In this assignment, you will be asked to go to the Federal Torts Claims Act in the United States Code Annotated (U.S.C.A.) or in the United States Code Service (U.S.C.S.).

a. Find the Federal Tort Claims Act in the U.S.C.A. or the U.S.C.S. Use the case summaries found after the statute sections in U.S.C.A. or U.S.C.S. to locate any two cases in which the federal government was found liable under the Act for the negligence of its employees. Go to these cases in the reporters and briefly summarize the opinions.
b. Use the case summaries found after the statute sections in U.S.C.A. or U.S.C.S. to locate one case in which the federal government was found not liable because the act or omission of the employee involved discretion at the planning level. Also locate one case in which the federal government was found liable because the wrongful act or omission of the employee involved discretion at the operational level. Go to these cases in the reporters and briefly summarize the opinions. (Do not use the same cases you found in part (a) of this assignment.)

State Government

The state government consists of the governor's office, state agencies such as the state police, state hospitals, and state commissions and boards. To what ex-

---

[2]5 U.S.C. § 8116.

tent has a state government waived its own sovereign immunity so that citizens can sue the state for the torts of state employees? States differ in their answers to this question. Some states have come close to abolishing sovereign immunity. Other states have schemes modeled in whole or in part on the Federal Tort Claims Act. Finally, other states have retained most of the traditional immunity.

Special protection is always given to agencies and offices when they are carrying out policy deliberations involving considerable judgment and discretion. It is sometimes said that it is not a tort for a government to govern! Rarely, for

Figure 31.8   Sample Federal Tort Claims Act Complaint

IN THE UNITED STATES DISTRICT COURT FOR THE WESTERN DISTRICT OF _____

_____ , Plaintiff

v.

[U.S.], Defendant

Complaint[3]

Plaintiff for his claim for relief states:

1. The action arises under the Federal Tort Claims Act, 60 Stat. 842, 843, 28 U.S.C.A. § 1346(b) and § 2671 et. seq.

2. Plaintiff resides in the City of _____ , _____ County, State of _____ , the same being within the Western District of _____ .

3. On July 1, 1967, in a public highway called _____ Street in _____ , _____ , _____ , an employee of defendant, negligently drove a motor vehicle against plaintiff who was then crossing said highway.

4. At the above time and place the said _____ was acting within the scope of his employment as an employee of the United States _____ Department, one of the departments of defendant, in that he was operating a truck owned by that Department.

5. On November 4, 1967, plaintiff presented to the Secretary of the Department in _____ a claim for his personal injuries on Standard Form 95 in the amount of ten thousand dollars.

6. On February 7, 1968, such claim was finally denied by the _____ Department of the United States.

7. As a result of said accident plaintiff was thrown down and had his leg broken and was otherwise injured, was prevented from transacting his business, suffered great pain of body and mind, and incurred expenses for medical attention and hospitalization in the sum of six thousand dollars.

Wherefore plaintiff demands judgment against defendant in the sum of sixteen thousand dollars and costs.

_____ ,
Attorney for Plaintiff,
_____ Building,

_____ , _____ ,

---

[3]*West's Federal Practice Manual*, § 2031 (1970).

example, will any government waive immunity for tortious injury caused a citizen by a judge, legislator, or high administrative officer. Negligence by a lower-level employee in the judicial, legislative, or executive branches, however, may constitute an act or omission for which the state will waive immunity e.g., a court clerk negligently loses a pleading that was properly filed. Acts that do not involve much discretion and that do not involve the formulation of policy will often subject the state to tort liability because the state has waived immunity for such acts.

Keep in mind that we are not talking about individual or personal liability of the government employee at this point. Personal liability will be discussed later. Our focus is on the government's liability via respondeat superior for the torts of its employees committed within the scope of their employment.

• ASSIGNMENT 31.19 •

To answer the following questions, you need to check the statutes in your state code and perhaps your state constitution as well. (See General Instructions for the State Code Assignment in Chapter 2.)

a. For what torts can your state be sued? Phrased another way, for what torts or claims has your state waived sovereign immunity? Do not discuss suits against counties, cities, or municipalities. Limit yourself to suits against the state itself or against state agencies.
b. What kinds of suits cannot be brought? What specific exclusions exist?
c. In what court or courts can tort claims against the state be brought?
d. What statute of limitations applies to such suits?

• ASSIGNMENT 31.20 •

a. Find one case in which a citizen won a tort action (involving any tort) against your state. Read the opinion and briefly summarize it.
b. Find one case in which a citizen was prevented from bringing a tort action against your state because of sovereign immunity. Read the opinion and briefly summarize it.

(See General Instructions for the Court Opinion Assignment in Chapter 2.)

Local Government

Local government units have a variety of names: cities, municipalities, municipal corporations, counties, towns, villages, etc. Also part of many local governments are the schools, transportation agencies, hospitals, recreational agencies, and some utilities. Whether any of these local units of government can be sued in tort is again a problem of sovereign immunity. A number of possibilities exist:

- Sovereign immunity has been completely or almost completely waived.
- The sovereign immunity of the local units of government is the same as that enjoyed by the state government.
- The sovereign immunity of the local units of government is different from that of the state government.
- Different local units of government have different sovereign immunity rules.

In short, extensive legal research must be done every time you sue a local unit of government. You must determine its category or status. What is it called? Who created it? Why was it created? What are its powers? Is it really part of the state government? Is it separate from the state government? Is it a hybrid combination of both state and local government? Many cities and counties receive substantial state aid. Does such aid entitle them to the same sovereign immunity protection as the state? You may find that for some purposes, the unit of government is considered part of the state, whereas for other purposes it is considered entirely separate and local. Over the years, a great deal of litigation has dealt with the problem of determining the nature of the unit of government in order to decide what sovereign immunity principles apply.

Local units of government perform many different kinds of functions. These functions are often grouped into two classifications: **governmental** and **propri- etary.** The sovereign immunity rules may differ depending on what category of function the employee was carrying out when the tort was committed. The gen- eral rule is that sovereign immunity is *not* waived when the tort grows out of a *governmental* function, while it *is* waived when it grows out of a *proprietary* function. (An important exception is when the city, county, town, or other unit has created a public or a private nuisance. Even if this nuisance grows out of a governmental function, sovereign immunity will usually not prevent the suit.) Of course, there is always the possibility that a government will waive its sovereign immunity for torts arising out of both governmental and proprietary functions. The waiver, however, is usually limited to proprietary functions.

Unfortunately, there are few clear rules on the distinction between a govern- mental and a proprietary function.

Governmental Functions

A governmental function is one that can be performed adequately only by the government.[4] The operation of local courts and local legislatures (e.g., a city council) is considered governmental. The same is true of the chief administrative offices of the local government (e.g., office of the mayor, office of the county commissioner) where basic policy is made. Police and fire departments, jails, schools, and sanitation also fall into the category of governmental functions where sovereign immunity will prevent suits for the torts that grow out of these functions.

Proprietary Functions

These are functions that generally cannot be performed adequately *only* by the government. Examples include government-run airports, docks, garages, and util- ities such as water and gas. For some of these functions, the local government often collects special fees or revenue. The test for a proprietary function, how- ever, is not whether a "profit" is made. This is simply one factor that tends to indicate a proprietary function.

Some functions are very difficult to classify, such as the operation of a city hospital. You will find courts going both ways for these and similar functions.

There are courts that do not rely totally on the distinction between govern- mental and proprietary functions to decide whether sovereign immunity prevents the suit against the local government. Some courts make the same distinction we

---

[4]Prosser, *Handbook of the Law of Torts* 1053 (4th ed., 1971). See also *Restatement (Second) of Torts* § 895C (1965).

saw earlier under the Federal Tort Claims Act between a claim arising out of planning decisions made by the government (for which sovereign immunity will not be waived), and claims arising out of the operation or implementation of the planning decisions at the ministerial level (for which sovereign immunity will be waived). In such courts, a city may be immune from liability for damages resulting from its negligent decision on where to construct sewers, but would be liable for damages resulting from the negligent construction or repair of a particular sewer.

Finally, some governments have purchased liability insurance and have waived sovereign immunity, but only to the extent of this coverage.

▪ ASSIGNMENT 31.21 ▪

a. The statutory code of the state legislature and the state constitution will often say when sovereign immunity is waived for local units of government. Check both to determine when a local unit of government in your state can be sued for a tort. What torts are included in the waiver of immunity? Where does the immunity still apply? Does the waiver differ depending on what unit of government is being sued? (See General Instructions for the State Code Assignment in Chapter 2.)

b. A city-owned garbage truck negligently hits a citizen. Does sovereign immunity prevent the suit in your state? (See General Instructions for the State Court Opinion Assignment in Chapter 2.) Is the distinction between a governmental and a proprietary function relevant in your state in determining when a local unit of government can be sued in tort?

c. Find one annotation in either *ALR, ALR2d, ALR3d, ALR4th,* or *ALR5th* that deals with the distinction between proprietary and governmental functions in sovereign immunity cases. List all cases written by courts in your state, if any, that are cited in the annotation.

d. In *Words and Phrases,* look up the word ``proprietary.'' Are there any definitions written by courts in your state? If so, what are the definitions? Cite the cases you use.

▪ OFFICIAL IMMUNITY: THE PERSONAL LIABILITY OF GOVERNMENT EMPLOYEES

What about a suit against the *individual* government employee as opposed to one against the sovereign, or the government itself? If the employee is sued *personally,* any judgment is paid out of the employee's own pocket. While there are circumstances in which **personal liability** is imposed on government employees, it should be pointed out that the law is reluctant to impose such liability. Public employees must be "free to exercise their duties unembarrassed by the fear of damage suits in respect of acts done in the course of those duties—suits which would consume time and energies which would otherwise be devoted to governmental service and the threat of which might appreciably inhibit the fearless, vigorous, and effective administration of policies of government."[5] On the other hand, critics argue that public employees should not be treated differently from employees in the private sector. When an employee of a business commits

---

[5]*Barr v. Matteo,* 360 U.S. 564, 571, 79 S.Ct. 1335, 3 L.Ed.2d 1434 (1959).

a tort, for example, the employer is **vicariously liable** if the tort was committed within the scope of employment, but the employee is usually also *personally liable.*[6] The critics say that the same rule should apply to government employees. For the most part, however, it does not.

If government employees are *not* liable for the torts they commit in the course of their employment, it is usually due to what is called **official immunity**—the immunity of a public official. Of course, the first question that must always be asked is whether a tort was in fact committed. It may be that the employee had a privilege to act so that there was no tort. For example, a police officer has a privilege to arrest under certain circumstances. This privilege prevents liability for battery or false imprisonment. If there is no privilege and a tort is committed, we then must ask whether the public official will be immune from personal liability under the doctrine of official immunity.

A citizen who has been the victim of a government tort may face one of several scenarios in looking for a defendant to sue:

- Sovereign immunity may prevent a suit against the government, and official immunity may prevent a suit against the employee; the citizen is without remedy.
- Sovereign immunity may have been waived so that the government can be sued, and official immunity may not apply so that the employee can also be sued; the citizen can sue either or both.
- Sovereign immunity may have been waived so that the government can be sued, but official immunity may prevent a suit against the employee; the citizen can sue only the government.
- Sovereign immunity may prevent a suit against the government, but official immunity may not apply so that the employee can be sued; the citizen can sue only the employee.

If the citizen can sue both the government and the employee, and successfully does so, the citizen does not receive double damages for the same injury. There is one recovery only. The plaintiff can usually collect from either defendant until there has been a satisfaction of the judgment.

Official immunity must be examined under two main categories: the employee's personal liability for the common law torts (e.g., negligence, battery, defamation), and the employee's personal liability under the **Civil Rights Act** of 1871. The latter liability exists when the employee deprives someone of his or her rights under the United States Constitution or under any federal statute of Congress, if the employee acted under "color" of any law or custom of the states or territories. The employee acts under **color of law** or custom whenever the employee is acting or pretending to act in an official capacity.

Liability for a common law tort is separate from liability for violation of the Civil Rights Act. It is possible for a government employee to have committed a common law tort without depriving anyone of federal constitutional and statutory rights, just as it is possible for a deprivation under the Civil Rights Act to be nontortious. On the other hand, a government employee can commit a common law tort that is also a violation of the Act.

---

[6]For exceptions to this general rule, see *Restatement (Second) of Agency* § 343 (1958).

Examples:

- A police officer commits a battery and a false arrest to prevent a citizen from voting.
- A state trooper destroys a citizen's flag (conversion) in order to stop the citizen from participating in a lawful demonstration.

When will a government employee be personally liable for common law torts and for civil rights violations? As Figure 31.9 demonstrates, the answer depends on whether the employee has an **absolute official immunity,** a **qualified official immunity,** or no immunity at all. An immunity is qualified if it can be lost because of malice; it is absolute if malice will not defeat it. Whether the government employee can claim the protection of one of these immunities depends in large measure on the nature of his or her job. The more ministerial or operational the job, the less protection the employee is given. Of course, it is difficult to think of any job that does not involve at least some measure of discretion. The difference between a job that is primarily judgmental and discretionary, on the one hand, and a job that is primarily ministerial or operational, on the other, is often a matter of degree. Some jobs clearly involve a great deal of discretion, e.g., those of high administrative officers, judges, or legislators. Jobs such as repairing roads, driving trucks, and collecting taxes also pose little difficulty; they are clearly ministerial jobs. The gray area between these two extremes has produced a good deal of litigation.

Congress and the state legislatures are always free to pass special legislation that changes the basic rules outlined in Figure 31.9, on the official's immunity for common-law torts. For example, a statute might be passed to extend the qualified immunity to employees who act at the ministerial or operational level. Also, Congress has passed a law under which a federal employee will not be personally liable for damages caused while driving a government vehicle in the course of his or her employment.[7]

- ASSIGNMENT 31.22 •

a. To what extent will government employees in your state at any level of government be personally liable for the common law torts that they commit in the course of their employment? Check your state constitution, state code, and case law through digests that cover your state courts. (See General Instructions for the State Code Assignments, and the General Instructions for the State Court Opinion Assignments, both in Chapter 2.)
b. A police officer has a warrant for the arrest of an individual in your state. A reasonable mistake is made and the officer arrests the wrong person. The person arrested brings a tort action against the officer. To what extent, if at all, can the officer avoid personal liability in your state under the doctrine of official immunity? (See General Instructions for the State Code Assignment, and General Instructions for the State Court Opinion Assignment, both in Chapter 2.)
c. Find one annotation in *ALR, ALR2d, ALR3d, ALR4th, or ALR5th* that deals with the distinction between ministerial and discretionary jobs in the area of official immunity. List all cases written by courts in your state, if any, that are cited in the annotation.
d. In *Words and Phrases,* find definitions, if any, of the words "ministerial" and "discretionary" written by courts in your state. Cite the cases you use.

---

[7]28 U.S.C. § 2679.

Figure 31.9 Official Immunity of Government Employees for Common Law Torts and for Violations of the Civil Rights Act

The Government Employees	Official Immunity for Common Law Torts	How the Official Immunity for Common Law Torts Can Be Lost	Official Immunity for Violations of the Civil Rights Act
Judges and legislators	Absolute official immunity for torts committed in the course of their employment, even if they acted maliciously.	a. They did not commit the tort in the course of their employment b. They acted totally outside their authority or jurisdiction. **Note:** The immunity is not lost if they acted merely in excess of their authority or jurisdiction.	Absolute official immunity for violations of the Act committed under color of state law or custom, even if they acted maliciously.
High administrative officials	Same as for judges and legislators	Same as for judges and legislators. In some states, however, the immunity *is* defeated by malice.	Qualified official immunity, which is lost if a reasonable official would have believed that the conduct violated a clearly established constitutional or statutory right.
Lower administrative officials who exercise considerable discretion in their job	Qualified official immunity for torts committed in the course of their employment.	a. They did not commit the tort in the course of their employment. b. They acted totally outside their authority or jurisdiction. c. They acted maliciously or not in good faith.	Qualified official immunity. Same as for high administrative officials.

Figure 31.9 Continued

The Government Employees	Official Immunity for Common Law Torts	How the Official Immunity for Common Law Torts Can Be Lost	Official Immunity for Violations of the Civil Rights Act
Lower administrative officials who function at the ministerial level with little or no discretion	No immunity in most states. They are personally liable for their torts, whether or not they acted in good faith or without malice. Some states, however, have statutes providing limited immunity for such employees.		Qualified official immunity. Same as for high administrative officials.

Note: As indicated earlier, the words "immunity" and "privilege" are sometimes used interchangeably in this area of the law. Absolute immunity, for example, is often referred to as absolute privilege, and qualified immunity as qualified privilege. In this chapter, we use the word "immunity" as a doctrine that prevents liability for a tort that was committed, and the word "privilege" as a doctrine that prevents the defendant's conduct from being a tort. The practical effect of either word, however, is the same with respect to the ultimate question of whether the government official will be personally liable.

▪ ASSIGNMENT 31.23 ▪

Can a *private* citizen violate the Civil Rights Act and be liable for damages under the Act? If so, give two examples from cases that have so held. Give the facts of the cases and a brief summary of what the court decided. (See General Instructions for the Federal Code Assignment and General Instructions for the Federal Court Opinion Assignment, both in Chapter 2.)

▪ CHARITABLE IMMUNITY

There was a time when a charitable, educational, religious, or other benevolent organization enjoyed an immunity for the torts it committed in the course of its work. This **charitable immunity,** however, was never complete. An organization, for example, was liable for its negligence in selecting personnel and in raising money. Most states, however, have abolished the immunity altogether, and other states have severely restricted its applicability.

▪ ASSIGNMENT 31.24 ▪

To what extent, if at all, does your state provide an immunity for the torts committed by charitable, educational, or similar organizations? (See General

Instructions for the State Code Assignment and General Instructions for the State Court Opinion Assignment, both in Chapter 2.)

■ INTRAFAMILY TORT IMMUNITY

Here our concern is a tort committed by one family member against another. Elsewhere we considered the special problems involved when one family member is injured because a *stranger* committed a tort against another family member (see Chapter 26).

Courts have always been reluctant to permit tort actions among any combination of wife, husband, and unemancipated child (a child is **emancipated** when a parent gives up his or her control over the child—usually when the child has married, is in the armed services, or is living independently). This reluctance is based on the theory that family harmony will be threatened if members know they can sue each other in tort. If the family carries liability insurance, there is also a fear that family members will fraudulently try to collect under the policy by fabricating tort actions against each other. A more technical and brutal reason was given at common law for why husbands and wives could not sue each other—the husband and wife were considered to be one person, and that one person was the husband! Hence, to allow a suit between spouses would theoretically amount to one person suing himself. With the passage of the Married Women's Property Acts and the enforcement of the laws against sex discrimination, a wife now retains her separate identity so that she can sue and be sued like anyone else.

Reform in the law, however, has not meant that **intrafamily tort immunity** no longer exists. A distinction must be made between a suit against the person (such as battery) and a suit against property (such as conversion). For torts against property, most states allow suits between spouses and between parent and child. Most states, however, retain the immunity in some form when the suit involves a tort against the person. The state of the law is outlined in Figure 31.10.

Figure 31.10   Intrafamily Torts

Spouse against Spouse

1. In most states, spouses can sue each other for intentional or negligent injury to their property, e.g., negligence, trespass, conversion.
2. In many states, spouses cannot sue each other for intentional or negligent injury to their person—a personal tort action, e.g., negligence, assault, battery.
3. Some states will permit personal tort actions if the man and woman are divorced or if the tort is covered by liability insurance.
4. Some states will permit intentional tort actions against the person to be brought by spouses against each other, but continue to forbid negligence actions for injury to the person.

Figure 31.10 Continued

Child against Parent(s)

1. In all states, a child can sue the parent for intentional or negligent injury caused by the parent to the child's property, e.g., negligence, trespass, conversion.
2. In many states, a child cannot sue a parent for intentional or negligent injury caused by the parent to the child's person, e.g., negligence, assault, battery.
3. If the child is emancipated (e.g., married, member of the armed forces, self-supporting), the child in all states can sue the parent for intentional or negligent injury caused by the parent to the child's person, e.g., negligence, assault, battery.
4. Some states will permit any child (emancipated or not) to sue the parent for intentional torts causing injury to the person, but continue to forbid actions for negligence causing injury to the person.
5. A few states allow the child to sue the parent for all intentional torts causing injury to the person, except where a tort arises out of the parent's exercise of discipline over the child.

Other Related Persons

Brothers and sisters, aunts and uncles, grandparents and grandchildren, and other relatives can sue each other in tort. The restrictions imposed on spouse suits and child suits do not apply to tort actions involving other relatives.

■ ASSIGNMENT 31.25 ■

To answer the following questions, you may have to check both the state code and the opinions of state courts in your state. (See General Instructions for the State Code Assignment, and General Instructions for the State Court Opinion Assignment, both in Chapter 2.)

a. Under what circumstances, if any, can one spouse bring a tort action against the other spouse in your state?
b. Can divorced spouses sue each other in tort?
c. Under what circumstances, if any, can a child bring a tort action against a parent in your state?
d. Pick any tort action that one family member can bring against another in your state. Draft a complaint in which the cause of action is this tort. (See General Instructions for the Complaint Drafting Assignment in Chapter 5.)

■ ASSIGNMENT 31.26 ■

a. Dave knows that he has contagious genital herpes, but does not tell Alice, who contracts the disease from Dave. Can Alice sue Dave for battery? For intentional infliction of emotional distress? For deceit or fraud? Does it make any difference whether the disease was communicated before or after Dave and Alice were married? Does it make any difference that they are now divorced? (See General Instructions for the Legal Analysis Assignment in Chapter 3.)

b. Jim and Helen live together for a year before they are married. They separate two years after the marriage. While preparing to file for divorce, Helen discovers that she has contracted chlamydia trachomatis, a serious venereal disease that attacks the ovaries. Her reproductive system is permanently damaged. Assume that Jim gave her this disease through intercourse. Jim carelessly thought that he was not capable of infecting Helen. Can she sue Jim for negligence in your state? (See General Instructions for the State Court Opinion Assignment in Chapter 2.)

SUMMARY

If defendants have an immunity, they will not be liable for the torts they commit. If they have a privilege, their conduct does not constitute a tort.

Consent is a defense to most torts. The plaintiff must have the capacity to consent and must voluntarily manifest the consent. The test is the reasonableness of the defendant's belief that the plaintiff consented, not the plaintiff's subjective state of mind. For the consent to be valid, the plaintiff must know the nature and consequences of what the defendant wants to do; gaining consent by misrepresentation renders the consent invalid.

There are several self-help privileges. The defendant can use reasonable force to protect him- or herself in the reasonable belief that the plaintiff will immediately inflict harmful or offensive contact on the defendant (self-defense). The defendant can use reasonable force to prevent the plaintiff from immediately inflicting on a third person harmful or offensive contact which the plaintiff does not have the privilege to inflict (defense of others). If the defendant reasonably believes that persons or property will be immediately injured or damaged, he or she can make reasonable use of the plaintiff's chattels or land to prevent it (necessity). If the defendant possesses land or chattels and this right of possession is superior to the plaintiff's claim of possession, the defendant can use reasonable force to prevent the plaintiff's threatened or continued interference with the defendant's possession (defense of property). If the plaintiff wrongfully acquires possession of a chattel and the defendant has the immediate right to possession, the defendant can use reasonable force to recapture it promptly after the plaintiff takes possession or promptly after discovering that the plaintiff has taken possession. There must be a request that it be returned before force is used, unless this would be unrealistic or unsafe (recapture of chattels).

Under the Federal Tort Claims Act, the federal government has waived sovereign immunity for designated torts. Examples include negligence at the ministerial or operational level, trespass to land or invasion of privacy committed by any federal employee, and battery or false arrest committed by a federal law enforcement officer.

State governments differ on the extent to which sovereign immunity is waived. The state often retains its immunity to cover the conduct of its judges, legislators, and high administrative officers. The less discretion and policy involvement a state employee has, the more likely the state will waive its sovereign immunity for harm caused by that employee. Local governments often waive their sovereign immunity for the proprietary functions they perform, but not for their governmental functions.

Government employees with official immunity cannot be personally liable for the torts they commit within the scope of their employment. Generally, judges, legislators, and high administrative officers have an absolute official immunity; lower officials who exercise considerable discretion on their jobs have a qualified official immunity; lower officials who exercise little or no discretion in their jobs have no official immunity.

Most states have eliminated the charitable immunity that once relieved charities and similar organizations of liability for their torts. Generally, there is no intrafamily tort immunity concerning property tort litigation between spouses or between parent and child. But in many states, the immunity prevents spouses from bringing personal tort actions against each other. The same is true for personal tort actions between parent and unemancipated child.

Key Terms

privilege
immunity
volenti non fit injuria
consent
implied consent
coercion
informed consent
self-help
self-defense
defense of others
chattels
public necessity
private necessity
abate a nuisance
defense of property

fresh pursuit
recapture of chattels
shopkeeper privilege
in loco parentis
arrest
sovereign immunity
respondeat superior
taking private property
just compensation
Federal Tort Claims Act
planning
ministerial
operational
governmental

proprietary
personal liability
vicariously liable
official immunity
Civil Rights Act
color of law
absolute official
immunity
qualified official
immunity
charitable immunity
emancipated
intrafamily tort
immunity

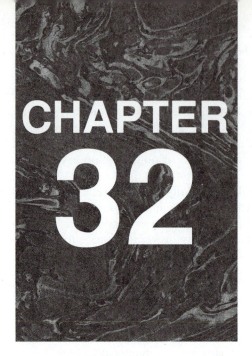

CHAPTER 32   Settlement

CHAPTER OUTLINE

- INTRODUCTION
- SETTLEMENT PRECIS
- SETTLEMENT BROCHURE

■ INTRODUCTION

The vast majority of legal disputes are settled in one form or another without the need for a complete trial. In fact, the moment a case is initiated, the opposing attorneys are usually thinking about the possibilities of **settlement.** There are substantial incentives for the parties to settle, such as the enormity of the cost of a trial and of the amount of time needed to complete the litigation through the appeal process.

This chapter presents two documents used by attorneys to encourage settlement—the settlement precis[1] and the settlement brochure. They are documents presented by one attorney to the other side and to the insurance company in an effort to settle the case. A **settlement precis** is a relatively brief document used by a party to advocate a settlement. It states an amount the party is willing to settle the case for. To support this request, the precis summarizes facts, theories of recovery, medical expenses, lost wages or profits, and other components of damages. If the document is more elaborate, it is often called a **settlement brochure.**

---

[1]The following discussion and illustration of a settlement precis is taken in large part from J. Jeans, *Trial Advocacy* 438–44 (1975).

▪ SETTLEMENT PRECIS

Lawyers are constantly reminded that theirs is "a profession, not a business." Unfortunately this plea for competence and high ethical standards has been interpreted by some to mean that lawyers should give no thought to the economic realities of their profession. Obviously a case with a potential settlement value of less than one thousand dollars cannot be handled in the same fashion as one with a settlement value of ten or twenty or a hundred times that much. The client is concerned with the net amount of the settlement. A lawyer who diverts a substantial percentage of that settlement for photographs, plats, etc., when the potential of the case does not deserve it, is guilty of dissipating his or her time and the money of his or her client. Neither client nor lawyer can afford to swat flies with sledgehammers.

But the smaller case has the same need of effective presentation as the larger one. Some format should be adopted that will have the advantages of a persuasive disclosure without the expense of time and money in its preparation.

The use of a *settlement precis* seeks to meet that need. Its primary purpose is to present the claim in as persuasive a fashion as possible. It is divided into six main sections:

- Identity of the plaintiff
- Facts of the case
- Theories of liability
- Medical
- Expenses
- Analysis of evaluation

The preparation of such a precis has two secondary advantages: it will discipline attorneys to analyze their liability, marshall their evidence and appraise the case; and it will provide a dress rehearsal for trial in the event that efforts at settlement are fruitless.

Settlement Precis—Illustration

Identity of the Plaintiff

Sharon Williams was born July 10, 1983, the fourth of four children born to John and Virginia Williams. The family lives at 2305 Grand Vista, Columbus, Missouri. Mr. Williams is employed as a machinist at Eagle Air Craft Co., a position he has held for six years.

Sharon is a student in the second grade of Middleton Grade School. She is a member of Girl Scout Troop 378 and is a member of the YMCA girl's swimming team.

Sharon had a normal prenatal history and a normal birth. She has been attended by Dr. Grant Fry, a pediatrician, from birth. She has suffered from the childhood diseases of chicken pox and measles. She has never suffered any disability to her lower limbs and has never sustained any injuries to her legs, back, or spine. Dr. Fry's medical report is attached.

Facts of the Case

On April 5, 1990 Sharon was en route from her home to school. The attached police report confirms that the day was clear and warm and the streets were dry.

Sharon was by herself and crossing Grand Avenue at its intersection with Washington Street moving westwardly from the southeast to the southwest corner approximately six feet south of the south curb line and within the designated crosswalk. Grand Avenue is forty feet wide with two lanes of traffic moving in each direction. It is straight and level and surfaced with asphalt. There were no cars parked within sixty feet of the intersection. A sign located one hundred feet south of the intersection on Grand has a legend "Caution Children." A police report confirming the description of the scene of the accident is attached.

Sharon was struck by the north bound automobile of defendant at a point five feet from the center line. The attached photographs show the following:

Photo 1: skid marks ten feet long, blood on street.

Photo 2: damage to left headlight.

Sharon states that when she left the southeast corner of the intersection the light was in her favor. She never looked at the light again. She walked at a normal pace until she was hit. She was looking forward and never saw or heard the defendant's automobile. The accident occurred at 8:35 A.M. The school is two blocks away and convenes at 8:45 A.M.

A statement taken from the defendant, a copy of which is attached, acknowledges that he didn't see the plaintiff until she was fifteen feet from him and that his automobile came to a stop twenty feet after impact.

Theories of Recovery

The plaintiff has three theories of recover:

1. That defendant violated a red light
2. That defendant failed to keep a lookout
3. That defendant failed to exercise the highest degree of care to bring his automobile to a stop or slacken after plaintiff came into a position of immediate danger.

The proof of the first theory is supported by plaintiff's testimony that when she left the curb the light was green for westbound traffic. By reason of the plaintiff's age the court might decide not to permit her to testify. In that event, the defendant's failure to keep a lookout could be submitted as an alternate theory of recovery. Defendant has acknowledged that he didn't see plaintiff until he was fifteen feet away from her and she was already in his path. This would place Sharon at least twelve feet from the curb. The court will judicially notice that the pace of walk is approximately two or three miles an hour or 2.9 to 4.4 feet per second. *Wofford v. St. Louis Public Service Co., Mo.,* 252 S.W.2d 529. Sharon was in the street and visible to defendant for almost three seconds before the accident. At defendant's acknowledged speed of twenty-five miles per hour he was traveling at approximately thirty-six feet per second or was approximately one hundred feet away when he should have seen Sharon. He was further alerted by the warning sign as he approached the intersection.

By reason of her age, it is questionable whether Sharon would be held responsible for her own actions. *Mallot v. Harvey,* 199 Mo.App. 615, 204 S.W. 940; *Quirk v. Metropolitan St. Ry. Co.,* 200 Mo.App. 585, 210 S.W. 103.

In the event Sharon could be held accountable for not maintaining a proper lookout a third theory of recovery is available: defendant's failure to stop or slacken after plaintiff came into a position of immediate danger. By defendant's admission he came to a stop twenty feet after the impact and he did not attempt evasive action until he was fifteen feet from Sharon; therefore, his overall stopping distance was thirty-five feet. A jury could find that by reason of Sharon's obliviousness that she was in immediate danger as she approached the path of the vehicle and when defendant's automobile was more than the thirty-five feet that was available to bring his vehicle to a stop.

The skid marks indicate that no slackening took place until the defendant's vehicle was within ten feet of the impact. The damage to the automobile indicates it was the left front headlight which struck Sharon. Sharon was within two feet of safety beyond the path of the car when she was struck. Moving at 4.4 feet per second, in one-half second she would have escaped injury. From this the jury could assume that a failure to slacken at an earlier time was the proximate cause of the injury.

Medical

The police report states that Sharon was "bleeding about the face and mouth" complaining of "pain in the right hip." She was taken by police cruiser to Welfare Hospital where it was discovered that she had suffered the loss of a front upper left tooth which was permanent, a laceration of the lip necessitating six stitches and a bruise of the right hip. Portions of the hospital record are attached. She was examined by her pediatrician, Dr. Fry, who referred her to Dr. William Jones, a dentist, for examination. He confirms the loss of the permanent tooth and outlines the dental prostheses which will be needed throughout her growth stage and into adulthood. His report is attached. The stitches were removed after six days by Dr. Fry, leaving a hairline scar one-fourth inch long near the upper lip.

Expenses

Emergency room Welfare Hospital	$1,250.00
Dr. Grant Fry	$750.00
Dr. William Jones	$550.00
Anticipated treatment	$4,000.00

Analysis of Evaluation

The loss of the tooth is permanent and will necessitate special prophylactic care to maintain the prosthetic devices which must be employed. The scar above the lip is discernible and will be permanent.

It is anticipated that a jury verdict could fall within the $13,000 to $20,000 range. If the case could be settled without further legal procedure I would recommend a settlement of $10,000.

▪ SETTLEMENT BROCHURE

Larger cases often require more than a settlement precis. If the case is of sufficient potential to warrant the necessary time and expense, a **settlement brochure** should be utilized in pretrial settlement negotiations. It will attempt to serve the same functions as outlined above for the settlement precis, but on a larger scale.

A settlement brochure presents the plaintiff's case in a written documentary form. It is based on facts—statements, reports, exhibits. There is little oratorical flourish or emotional argument. The claims agent or representative of the insurance company receives the information "in cold blood" and can appraise the case rationally.

A well-ordered, carefully planned settlement brochure carries with it an aura of importance. The bulk alone suggests value. Plaintiff files might not be sold by the pound, but there seems to be some correlation between the bigness of the file and the bigness of the case. The preparation of a brochure demonstrates that the plaintiff has sufficient confidence in the magnitude of the case to warrant a detailed presentation. It immediately creates an impression of importance.

Settlement Brochure—Illustration

DEMAND FOR SETTLEMENT

TO: ALL-RISK INSURANCE COMPANY

IN THE MATTER OF THE CLAIM OF

SARAH ANDERSON

CLAIMANT AND POTENTIAL PLAINTIFF

VERSUS

DONALD M. SWANSON

AND

JACK G. SWANSON D/B/A
SWANSON LOGGING

PRESENTED BY:

REX PALMER
ATTORNEYS, INC., P.C.
PO BOX 7742
MISSOULA, MT 59807
(406) 738-4514
ATTORNEY FOR CLAIMANT

DISCLAIMER

The matters set forth herein are stated solely for purposes of expediting possible settlement at this stage of this claim, and as such, are not to be used or referred to in any way should these matters proceed to trial, except as set forth in the paragraph immediately below. All photographs, attachments and other exhibits set forth herein shall remain the property of Claimant and Claimant's attorney, the originals of which are to be returned promptly upon oral or written request. All figures utilized herein are subject to change without notice, as discovery and investigation are continuing, medical attention continues to be required, and all figures will accordingly require supplementation and updating at or prior to trial, and are not to be construed as final figures should these matters proceed to trial.

Potential plaintiff, Sarah Anderson, and her legal counsel, reserve the right to present a copy of this Settlement Brochure as evidence in a secondary action directly against All-Risk Insurance Company to recover compensatory and punitive damages if the Claimant and her legal counsel, in their sole discretion, deem that All-Risk has violated the provisions of the Montana Fair Claims Practices Act, Sec. 33-18-201(6), MCA, or the Montana common law obligation of good faith and fair dealing in insurance claims settlement practices. For readers unfamiliar with Montana law regarding settlement practices, a review of applicable statutory and case law is set forth in Appendix I to this brochure.

SUMMARY

This is a personal injury claim resulting from an automobile collision in Yellowstone County, Montana. On August 20, 1985, Sarah Anderson was making a left turn off a secondary highway into her driveway. Donald Swanson, who was delivering a check for his father's logging company, Swanson Logging, tried to pass Sarah Anderson's vehicle in a no-passing zone as she was completing her turn. Swanson's pickup hit Anderson's Datsun station wagon in the left rear corner, knocking it sideways and off the roadway into a power pole. In the wreck, Sarah Anderson was injured. For the direct medical costs resulting from these injuries, for the pain and suffering, for her continued impairment and future losses, she demands compensation in the amount of One Hundred Eighty-five Thousand and no/100 Dollars ($185,000.00).

Liability, jointly and severally, of the prospective defendants is clearly demonstrated by the facts set forth in this brochure. All-Risk, the insurer for the potential defendants, is therefore under a legal obligation to effectuate a settlement at or near the figure set forth above, or the policy limits of their insurance policies, whichever is less, within a reasonable period of time.

If All-Risk disagrees with the evaluation of this claim as set forth herein, it should respond within a reasonable period of time by providing Sarah Anderson's counsel with a written statement of its analysis and evaluation of this claim, together with its payment of the sum supported by its own evaluation.

For the purposes of this brochure, we consider thirty (30) days a reasonable period of time. This period will end on the 20th day of April, 1987. Thereafter, no further settlement negotiations will be initiated by Claimant, and Claimant will initiate legal action against the insurance carrier and its insured under the provisions of Montana statutory and case law, in an action for compensatory, general, and punitive damages in courts of appropriate jurisdiction.

RESPECTFULLY SUBMITTED, this 20th day of March, 1987.

ATTORNEYS, INC., P.C.

Rex Palmer

Rex Palmer Esq.
P.O. Box 7742
Missoula, MT 59807
(406) 728-4514
ATTORNEY FOR CLAIMANT

3

SETTLEMENT BROCHURE
TABLE OF CONTENTS

Disclaimer 2
Summary 3
Table of Contents 4
Statement of Facts 5
— Family Background 5
— Prior Medical History 5
— The Collision 5
— The Injuries 6
— Medical Expenses 9
Evaluation of the Case 9
— Legal issues 9
— Damages 10
Conclusion 12
Appendix I: Good Faith and Fair Claims Practices
  in Montana 14
Appendix II: Diagnostic Pain Clinic Reports 16
Appendix III: Witnesses and Testimony 45
  Exhibit A: Sid Silker, M.D., letter of Sept. 23,
    1986 53
  Exhibit B: Keith Makie, Ph.D.
    Pain Clinic Director, letter of January 21, 1987 54
  Exhibit C: Photographs Relevant to the Accident 56
    — Photographs 1–9
  Exhibit D: Accident Report, Montana Highway
    Patrol 60
  Exhibit E: Oil Paintings by Sarah Anderson 61
  Exhibit F: Newspaper Clipping Showing
    Sharon Anderson Painting Miniature
    Figures on Fingernails 62

STATEMENT OF FACTS

Family Background

Sarah Anderson was born March 10, 1941. At the time of this collision, Sarah was 44 years old. She resides with her husband, Ross and her family approximately 1 mile east of Laurel, Montana, on Devlin Rd. Sarah and Ross have two (2) daughters, namely: Marsha, age 17, who still resides in the family home, and Teresa, age 20, who is currently residing in the family home but has lived outside the home on occasion. Sarah has two (2) other children from a prior marriage which ended in divorce: Jerry Landquer, who has been on his own for the past ten (10) years, and Roxanne Aist, who is married and resides in Red Lodge, Montana. Sarah has a close relationship with Roxanne and generally sees her once each week. Sarah also enjoys her relationship with her grandchild, Roxanne's daughter.

Prior Medical History

Sarah has had a complex medical history including surgeries on her pituitary gland, bladder, and colon. As well, she has had bilateral carpel tunnel repairs and a complete hysterectomy. In spite of this checkered medical history, she has always been able to return to her normal activities without restriction after a reasonable healing period.

The Collision

On August 20, 1985, Sarah Anderson drove her house guests, Lisa Weston and Lisa's children, Samuel and Laura, to visit a friend. After this visit, Sarah and her guests drove to the grocery store. After purchasing groceries, Sarah and her guests returned to the car and drove away from Laurel east on Devlin Road toward home, which is a little over 1 mile from Superior. (See Appendix III.)

Devlin Road is a paved two-lane secondary highway. Sarah's home is immediately north of Devlin Road so that she must cross over the center line to turn into her driveway whenever she is returning home from town. When traveling east from town, Devlin Road dips down to cross a bridge, then immediately develops an uphill grade throughout the approach to Sarah Anderson's driveway and beyond. These physical characteristics of the road make passing very unsafe. The Highway Department has marked the entire area with solid double yellow lines, indicating that this is a no-passing zone.

On the day of this collision, it was daylight, approximately 5:00 P.M. Though the sky was somewhat overcast with patchy clouds, the road was dry. (See Exhibit D.)

At the time of the collision, Sarah was driving a 1975 Datsun 710 station wagon. She had driven this vehicle for some time and was completely familiar with its operation.

5

She is a cautious driver, and as a matter of practice she turns on her left turn indicator several hundred feet before turning into her driveway from Devlin Road. She is so regular in this practice that, a few days before this collision, Laura Weston asked Sarah why she began signaling her turn so early, referring to the fact that Sarah turns on her blinker before crossing the bridge.

On the day of this collision, Sarah followed her normal routine and triggered her left-turn indicator before crossing the bridge and before beginning the uphill grade to her driveway. Sarah slowed from approximately 45 m.p.h. at the bridge to approximately 3–4 m.p.h. at the immediate approach to her driveway. Immediately before initiating her turn, she checked her rear-view mirrors for approaching vehicles and saw none. (See Appendix III.)

After she had completely crossed the center line with the front tires of her compact vehicle completely off the paved roadway, Donald Swanson smashed into the left rear corner of Sarah's car with the left front corner of his 1980 four-wheel-drive Chevrolet pickup. (See Exhibit C.)

Donald Swanson was traveling at an excessive rate of speed (passing speed) with his vehicle traveling east in the passing lane when he collided with Sarah Anderson's vehicle. At the time of the collision, he was on an errand, delivering a check for his father Jack G. Swanson, d/b/a Swanson Logging.

If Donald Swanson had remained in his own lane of traffic, there would have been no collision even at his excessive rate of speed.

Donald Swanson left skid marks of over 60 feet prior to the point of impact. After impact, his vehicle continued to skid, leaving skid marks with a total length of approximately 119 feet. The impact of the collision threw Sarah Anderson's vehicle into a violent spin, off the roadway, and into a telephone pole approximately 65 feet from the point of impact. The force of the impact and the sudden stop against the telephone pole was so great that it broke the front passenger's seat belt and threw Lisa Weston completely out of the vehicle. Fortunately for Sarah Anderson, her seat belt did not break. Nevertheless, she was seriously injured when the car smashed into the telephone pole at precisely the point where her shoulder and left side were inside the car.

The Anderson vehicle was a total loss. (See Exhibit C.)

The Injuries

The hospital records and medical reports now in your possession, as well as the medical reports that have been furnished to you herewith, are self-explanatory as to the injuries received. Basically, Sarah sustained musculo-skeletal strain and chronic myofascitis of the left shoulder and neck region. As well, her dentures were broken, and she suffered an injury to her left side

6

temporomandibular joint. The above were apparently the direct result of the rear-end collision and her subsequent left side contact with the telephone pole. She also required the surgical repair of a rectocele. Sarah had suffered a previous rectocele which had required surgical repair, and this recurrence was apparently due to the pressure exerted on her abdomen by her seat belt.

Immediately following the accident, Sarah was admitted to Billings Community Hospital on August 20, 1985, and was discharged five (5) days later on August 25, 1985. She was subsequently admitted to Deaconess Hospital on October 2, 1985 for repair of her rectocele. She was discharged five (5) days later on October 7, 1985. Over the eighteen (18) months since the accident, she has undergone an extensive regimen of physical therapy in an attempt to control her pain and return to her normal activities. Her primary treating physician, Sid Silker, M.D., was not satisfied with Sarah's progress and referred her to the Pain Center at Billings Community Rehabilitation Center for evaluation. (See Dr. Silker's Sept. 23, 1986 letter, Exhibit A).

Sarah appeared for evaluation at the Billings Community Hospital Diagnostic Pain Clinic on December 9, 1986. She was evaluated by a team of six (6) professionals: Physiatric evaluation by Sandy T. Bickett, M.D.; Psychological evaluation by Keith Makie, Ph.D.; Neurologic evaluation by Edward B. Runk, M.D.; Orthopedic evaluation by W. J. McConnell, M.D.; Physical Therapy evaluation by Todd Rockler, R.P.T.; and Social Service Intake Interview by Rick Wysil, B.S.W. The results of this diagnostic evaluation are attached hereto in full as Appendix II. In addition to the diagnostic team's results, the Pain Clinic Director, Keith Makie, Ph.D., provided a letter dated January 21, 1987, summarizing the process and costs of the Pain Clinic program. (See attached letter, Exhibit B.)

The Pain Clinic team unanimously recommends that Sarah seek out a highly structured, interdisciplinary, chronic pain treatment program such as that offered by the Billings Community Hospital Pain Clinic.

Prior to the accident, Sarah and her family routinely engaged in such activities as camping, gold mining, digging crystals, hiking, and searching for arrowheads. Through all these activities, whether summer or winter, Sarah would bring her easel and create portrait paintings. (See Exhibit E.) She particularly excelled in painting miniatures. Until the accident, Sarah usually entered the Yellowstone County Art Fair. One year she even painted small figures on people's fingernails at the art and craft show in Laurel. (See Exhibit F.) Often she sold and bartered her art work.

The pain, stiffness, and muscle spasms resulting from Sarah's injuries preclude her participation in the family's outdoor activities described above. The injuries also interfere with her indoor activities.

7

Now, Sarah is almost entirely unable to engage in her art work. The muscle spasms and stiffness in her shoulder and neck interfere with the delicate work generally required in her paintings. Aside from these physical restrictions, her ongoing pain substantialy precludes the intricate detail and concentration required by her art work. As well, these restrictions and pain make it impossible to enjoy her art work even when she is physically able to do it.

Before the accident, Sarah was constantly sewing. She sewed for her family as well as for others. Sarah not only enjoyed sewing as an activity, her sewing saved her family clothing expense and provided her income from the sale of some of her work. This in turn gave her satisfaction and fulfillment from contributing to her family's welfare. Now, Sarah cannot even bend over the sewing machine and concentrate on her sewing work in any meaningful fashion.

The same is true of her cake decorating activities. Before the accident, she was able to engage in such activities to augment her family's income and to fulfill her creative desires. Now, her pain and physical limitations simply preclude any substantial participation in such activities.

Sarah has calculated that her income from cake decorating, paintings, jewelry, and sewing of shirts and coats for sale and barter has grown from between $700–$800 in 1982 to approximately $2,000 in 1985. From this we have calculated that her injuries have diminished her income by approximately $2,000 to date. These losses will continue into the future unless the Pain Clinic program is as successful as expected by Dr. Makie.

To date, Sarah has been primarily a housewife. Through her services she has nurtured and cared for her children and husband. Now that her children have reached adulthood, she could easily begin to pursue her sewing, cake decorating, and art as full-time occupations, or even work outside the home if she chose. But this is not possible because of the pain and restrictions she suffers from the accident.

Sarah's current diagnosis remains: musculo-skeletal strain and chronic myofascitis of the left shoulder and neck region, and chronic pain syndrome. We understand that the proposed treatment at the Pain Clinic will not relieve her of ongoing pain. The muscle problem and pain are probably a fact of life for her. However, with the treatment recommended by the pain evaluation team, the pain should no longer dominate her life. She should be able to substantially return to her previous active lifestyle by learning to manage her pain.

The next Pain Clinic starts April 27, 1987. As is evident from Dr. Keith Makie's January 21st letter, it is urgent that she receive the funds to participate in this or a similar program.

All indications are that Sarah's pain and physical limitations are a direct result of the accident which either caused the particular condition or significantly aggravated a pre-existing condition such as with the aggravation of her prior depression and the recurrence of her rectocele.

Medical Expenses

As a result of the injuries sustained by Sarah Anderson, the following medical expenses were incurred:

Billings Community Hospital	$ 1,786.75
Yellowstone Co. Hospital	1,921.14
Laurel Vol. Fire Dept.	177.30
Jason Pharmacy	135.95
Doug Bard (dentures 1 TMJ)	850.00
Billings Radiology	125.70
Matterson Surgical Supply	40.00
Dr. B. J. Halst (glasses)	288.00
John Raysmer (dentist)	35.00
R. K. Hersh, M.D., P.C. (Radiologist)	16.00
Billings Medical Clinic	273.00
Deaconess Hosp. (Rectocele)	1,841.75
Family Practice Clinic	906.90
Vern Chase, M.D., (Anesthesiologist)	330.00
Neurological Associates	180.00
Medical reports	45.00
Billings Clinic Pharmacy	163.60
Edward B. Runk, M.D.	148.00**
Community Hosp., Diag. Pain Clinic	845.00**
Yellowstone Co. Hospital	253.50**
Yellowstone Co. Hospital	122.50**
Yellowstone Co. Hospital	45.00**
Billings Medical Clinic	20.00**
TOTAL:	$10,550.09

The sums indicated ''**'' have not yet been paid. In addition, as stated in Dr. Makie's letter of January 21st (see Exhibit B), Sarah is in urgent need of enrollment in the Pain Clinic program at a cost of between $25,000.00–$27,000.00 for a seven (7) week treatment program.

EVALUATION OF THE CASE

Legal Issues

From our investigation and our understanding of the facts, we feel that we will obtain a directed verdict in this case in favor of the Plaintiff, leaving only the issue of damages for the jury. We base this upon our research and briefing of the law.

Under Sec. 61-8-326 MCA, your insured should not have been driving on the left side of the roadway within the no-passing zone as indicated by the double yellow striping on the pavement. Furthermore, your insured was very familiar with this particular area; he knew that it was a low-visibility area with a no-passing zone throughout, and that several homes adjoined the roadway, requiring residents to enter and leave the highway to reach their homes. In this instance, the Andersons' driveway was clearly marked by their mailbox, which would call for additional caution on the part of a would-be passing vehicle. (See Exhibit C, photos 6-9).

It has been held repeatedly that the primary duty of avoiding a collision rests upon the following driver (*Custer Broadcasting Corp. v. Brewer*, 163 Mont. 519, 518 P.2d 257 (1974)). In a case directly on point with the present claim, a jury entered a verdict for the defendant where the defendant rear-ended the plaintiff while the plaintiff was turning into his driveway. *Garza v. Peppard*, 51 St. Rptr. 1922 (Mont.). In *Garza*, as with this claim, both vehicles were proceeding in the same direction, and both vehicles had passed over the double yellow lines on the pavement. The District Court entered judgment for the plaintiff notwithstanding the verdict. On appeal the Supreme Court affirmed the District Court and found that the defendant, who had been driving the following vehicle, was guilty of negligence as a matter of law for failing to keep a proper lookout. The Court stated:

> Under Montana law, a motorist has a duty to look not only straight ahead but laterally ahead as well and to see that which is in plain sight. Furthermore, a motorist is presumed to see that which he could see by looking, and he will not be permitted to escape the penalty of his negligence by saying that he did not see that which is in plain view. *Nissen v. Johnson*, 135 Mont. 329, 333, 339 P.2d 651, 653 (1959); *Sorrells v. Ryan*, 129 Mont. 29, 289 P.2d 1028 (1955); *Koppang v. Sevier*, 106 Mont. 79, 75 P.2d 790 (1938).
>
> Clearly, a person is negligent in either not looking or looking but not seeing if he claims not to have seen an object which is so clearly visible that all reasonable minds would agree the person must see the object if he were to look with reasonable diligence. *Payne v. Sorenson*, 183 Mont. 323, 326-327, 599 P.2d 362, 364 (1979).

Having these cases and other cases in mind, we strongly feel that this is a case in which the only issue will be the amount of damages to be awarded the plaintiff.

Damages

As to the question of damages, we have taken into

10

consideration the initial hospitalization as well as the subsequent hospitalization for surgical repair of the rectocele, the extreme pain at the outset and during the initial recovery period, the continuing pain in therapy as well as the permanent pain which Sarah hopes to manage with the assistance of the Pain Clinic program. We have also considered Sarah's lost income and changed course of life.

Sarah still receives treatment in connection with this injury, and even if the Pain Clinic program is successful in managing the pain, it is expected that she will continue to require intermittent physical therapy indefinitely. She will continue to suffer the effects of this injury, and we have considered her life expectancy, which at the present age of 46 is 34.5 years.

We have considered the substantial medical testimony indicating the relationship between Sarah's injuries and the automobile accident. We have considered the magnitude of medical expenses already incurred and those immediately required. We have adjusted our calculations downward to recognize the preexisting nature of her rectocele problem and intermittent depression.

We feel that in our evaluation of this matter, a probable jury verdict in this case would be the sum of Two Hundred Thousand Dollars ($200,000.00). This figure includes the following:

Pain and suffering: PAST:

10 days or 240 hours for the 2 hospital stays of 5 days each:

Physical Pain at $25.00/hour (muscular and skeletal strain and sprain, tempormandi-bular joint injury, headaches, surgical rectocele repair): $ 6,000.00

Mental anguish at $25.00/hour (restricted to hospital and trauma of surgery): $ 6,000.00

Lost pleasure at $5.00/hour (inability to perform any activities): $ 3,000.00

Remaining 18 months since the accident, approx. 12,960 hours:

Physical pain at $2.00/hour (therapy, re-habilitation, pain related to muscle and skeletal strain and sprain, TMJ and sur-gery, etc.): $25,920.00

Mental anguish at $3.00/hour (depression from pain and inability to pursue normal activities, 16 waking hours/day = 8,640 hours): $17,280.00

11

Lost pleasure at $2.00/hour (limitations 8 hours/day = 4,320 hours, on sports, physical activities with friends, and self-fulfillment in pursuing established course of life, etc.): $ 8,640.00

                     TOTAL PAST PAIN AND SUFFERING: $66,840.00

Pain and suffering: FUTURE:

Sarah Anderson is 46 years old and has a life expectancy of 34.5 years pursuant to the life expectancy tables prepared by the U.S. Department of Health & Human Services. 34.5 years is 12,592 days or 302,220 hours:

Physical pain at $.10/hour (muscular and skeletal strain and sprain, myofascitis syndrome and chronic pain syndrome, future arthritis, etc.): $30,222.00

Mental anguish at $.10/hour (includes concerns for diminished active physical relationship with immediate family and grandchildren, etc., for 16 waking hours/day = 199,465 hours): $19,946.00

Lost pleasure at $.10/hour (this recognizes partial limitations in active sports and intricate detail work, and the need to be careful due to the injury, for 16 waking hours each day): $19,946.00

                    TOTAL FUTURE PAIN AND SUFFERING: $70,114.00

MEDICAL SPECIALS:
  Past: $10,550.00

  Future — Pain Clinic: $27,000.00
         — Occasional physical
             therapy etc., @
             $500.00/year: $17,250.00
                    TOTAL MEDICAL SPECIALS: $54,800.00

INCOME AND PRODUCTIVITY LOSSES:
  Past — outside earnings and barter: $ 2,000.00
       — household activities: 6,000.00
       TOTAL INCOME AND PRODUCTIVITY LOSSES: $ 8,000.00

The calculations of pain, suffering, medical expenses, income and productivity losses anticipate successful pain management by the Pain Clinic program as is expected by Dr. Makie in his January 21, 1987 letter.

Conclusion
As we have stated, our investigation discloses that the liability of your insured is certain in our opinion, and

the injuries and actual damages sustained by our client are in excess of the amount of One Hundred Eighty-five Thousand Dollars ($185,000.00) for which we now offer to settle. In the event that you do not notify us to the contrary, we will proceed on the assumption that the offer of settlement made in this case is within the coverage of your insurance contract with your insured.

This offer and material is submitted in good faith and we expect you to carefully examine the material contained and honestly evaluate the same, responding to it in the same good faith with which it is submitted to you. Thank you for your cooperation.

Sincerely yours,

Rex Palmer

Rex Palmer
ATTORNEYS, INC., P.C.

Encs.

13

APPENDIX I: GOOD FAITH AND FAIR CLAIMS PRACTICES IN MONTANA

Public policy in the State of Montana encourages timely settlement of insurance claims without litigation. Montana statutory and case law history support this conclusion. Sec. 33-18-201(6), MCA, states:

> Unfair claims settlement practices prohibited. No person may, with such frequency as to indicate a general business practice, do any of the following: . . . (6) neglect to attempt in good faith to effectuate prompt, fair, and equitable settlements of claims in which liability has become reasonably clear. . . .

The above statute creates a duty which runs from the insurer to the insured as well as to third party claimants. The duty includes an obligation to negotiate in good faith and promptly settle claims when liability has become ''reasonably clear.'' An action based upon a breach of this obligation by the insurer may be prosecuted by a third-party claimant after an action against the insured to determine liability.

The case generally cited for the above proposition is *Klaudt v. Flink,* 658 P.2d 1065 (Mont., 1983). Justice Daley for the majority wrote:

> We therefore hold that Sec. 33-18-201(6), MCA, does create an obligation running from the insurer to the claimant. When such an obligation is breached, the claimant has a basis for a civil action.

> The obligation to negotiate in good faith and to promptly settle claims does not mean that liability has been determined. Sec. 33-18-201(6) states that the insurer's obligation arises when liability has become ''reasonably clear''. . . . 658 P.2d 1065, 1067.

The *Klaudt* result was to be expected. In Montana, the State District Courts and Supreme Court have accepted the principle of third-party liability and the duty to deal in good faith in *Fowler v. State Farm Mutual Automobile Ins. Co.,* 153 Mont. 74, 454 P.2d 76 (1969), and *Thompson v. State Farm Mutual Automobile Ins. Co.,* 161 Mont. 207, 505 P.2d 423 (1973). *Klaudt* was immediately followed by *St. Paul Fire & Marine Ins. Co. v. Kumiskey,* 665 P.2d 223 (Mont. 1983); *Reno v. Erickstein,* 679 P.2d 1204 (Mont. 1984); and *Gibson v. Western Fire Ins. Co.,* 682 P.2d 725 (Mont. 1984). In this rapidly expanding area of tort law, the relatively old federal case of *Jensen v. O'Daniel,* 210 F.Supp. 317 (D. Mont. 1962), hereinafter *Jensen,* establishes six (6)

14

''elements of bad faith.'' In that case by an insured against his carrier, the carrier refused a pretrial settlement offer below policy limits.

The six (6) elements examined in *Jensen* and cited with approval by the court in *Gibson v. Western Fire Insurance Co., supra,* are as follows:

1. the likelihood of a verdict in excess of policy limits
2. whether a defendant's verdict is doubtful
3. the company's trial counsel's own recommendations
4. whether insured has been informed of all settlement offers
5. whether there has been a demand for settlement within policy limits, and
6. whether any offer of contribution has been made by the insured.

The *Gibson* court easily discarded the *Jensen* factors which were inapplicable, and relied upon as many of them as are clearly applicable.

> As the court said in *Jensen,* no one factor is decisive, and all of the circumstances must be considered as to whether the insurance company acted in good faith . . . [T]he failure of *Western* through its agents to follow established standards of investigation, evaluation, negotiation, and communication with its insured are the deciding factors upon which we base this conclusion . . . (682 P.2d 725, 737).

> Among the ''standards of evaluation'' mentioned in the *Gibson* decision is the fact that the insured's attorney evaluated the claim as being reasonably worth the amount demanded by the claimant in the insured's malpractice case.
> The second issue is raised by the statute, namely, the requirement that bad faith be shown to be ''general business practice'' of that particular company.

> [I]t is possible that multiple violations occurring in the same claim could be sufficient to show a frequent business practice, as would violations by the same company in different cases. (*Klaudt v. Flink,* 658 P.2d 1065, 1068).

The court concedes that its ruling in *Klaudt* could be viewed by many as ''harsh,'' but offers the following rationale:

> [T]he legislature has reacted to what it perceives to be an important problem. Insurance companies have, and are able to exert, leverage against individual claimants because of the disparity in resource base. Justice delayed is often justice denied. Public policy calls for a meaningful solution. The legislature has spoken and we, by this decision, breathe life into the legislative product. (*Ibid.*)

15

APPENDIX II: DIAGNOSTIC PAIN CLINIC REPORTS

Billings Community Hospital Rehabilitation Center

Gregory M. Wies, EXECUTIVE DIRECTOR
January 9, 1987

Sid R. Silker, M.D.
Post Office Box 1045
Laurel, Montana 59248

Dear Dr. Silker:

  Sarah Anderson was evaluated at Billings Community Rehabilitation Center's Outpatient Diagnostic Pain Clinic on December 9, 1986, by the following clinic team members: Keith Makie, Ph.D., Psychologist; Sandy Bickett, M.D., Physiatrist; Todd Rockler, R.P.T., Physical Therapist; Rick Wysil, B.S.W., Social Worker; and the following consultants: Edward B. Runk, M.D., Neurologist, and W. J. McConnell, M.D., Orthopedist.

  Enclosed for your review are their reports, together with the Summary and Recommendations. If you wish to follow through with the recommendations, please contact the Pain Program Secretary at 248-2400 extension 3634 or by letter.

  Thank you for referring your patient to the Billings Community Rehabilitation Center's Outpatient Diagnostic Pain Clinic.

  Sincerely,

  Keith Makie

  Keith Makie, Ph.D.
  Pain Program Director

  KCM:pdr
  enclosures
  xc: Rex Palmer, Attorney

16

REPORTS
Billings Community Rehabilitation Center
OUTPATIENT DIAGNOSTIC PAIN CLINIC

December 9, 1986

SUMMARY AND RECOMMENDATIONS ......   Keith Makie, Ph.D.
                                       Albert Fremont, M.D.

PHYSIATRIC EVALUATION ....   Sandy Bickett, M.D.

PSYCHOLOGICAL EVALUATION ....   Keith Makie, Ph.D.

NEUROLOGIC EVALUATION ....   Edward Runk, M.D.

ORTHOPEDIC EVALUATION ....   W. J. McConnell, M.D.

PHYSICAL THERAPY EVALUATION ......   Todd Rockler, R.P.T.

SOCIAL SERVICE INTAKE INTERVIEW ...   Rick Wysil, B.S.W.

17

SUMMARY AND RECOMMENDATIONS
(DIAGNOSTIC PAIN CLINIC)

Billings Community Rehabilitation Center

PATIENT: Sarah Anderson
MEDICAL RECORD NUMBER: 0113075
DATE OF EVALUATION: 12-9-86
PROGRAM: Diagnostic Pain Clinic

On December 9, 1986 Sarah Anderson and her husband, Ross, participated in a comprehensive pain evaluation. Sarah was seen by an orthopedic surgeon, a physiatrist, a psychologist, a physical therapist, and a neurologist; Ross was seen by a social worker. The reports from these various people are included; this will serve as a summary of their findings and the recommendations of the Diagnostic Pain Clinic Team.

It was the consensus of the individuals who examined Sarah from a physical standpoint that she was suffering from a rather long-standing problem with chronic shoulder, neck, and headache pain. Those who examined her agreed that the pain was of a musculo-skeletal chronic myofascitis origin and there was a consensus that Sarah was in the midst of what they would term chronic pain syndrome. Upon examination there was evidence of rather marked limitation and range of motion in her neck due to pain. There was a good deal of evidence of muscle tightness and some tenderness. There was no evidence of radiculopathy or other neurologic involvement upon examination and in general those who examined her from a physical standpoint saw her problem as mainly musculoskeletal with resultant problems in muscle tightness, deconditioning, and general inactivity. There were comments upon the large number of treatments that had been tried with Sarah to no avail and suggestions that an interdisciplinary, highly structured, intensive treatment program would be necessary to turn around the problem.

The Psychological Evaluation indicates that Sarah is a woman who, at the present time, is in a great deal of obvious psychological distress. She reports being extremely agitated and nervous. She clearly states that the stresses in her life that are enumerable at this time tend to directly contribute to her pain. She has many, many family and relationship problems with her husband, from her standpoint. She gave the impression during the psychological evaluation of being distressed to the point

18

of being desperate and not being in control of her life and this very high level of general psychological distress was definitely reflected on the MMPI. She appeared to be very motivated to do something about her problem because, as she said in the evaluation, she was coming to the ''end of her rope,'' and very much wanted something to change.

In the social worker's interview with Ross, there was a marked discrepancy between Ross's report of the problem situation with Sarah's chronic pain and Sarah's own report. Ross appeared to be a rather poor historian and to be relatively uninvolved in Sarah's chronic pain problem. He continued to have past expectations of her even though she reports to be in great pain and is unable to do many things physically. The social worker commented that their relationship is quite traditional with Ross's expectations being that Sarah carry her load as a traditional wife. The social worker noted that Ross was quite ambivalent about supporting an intensive treatment program that could remove her from home, even if Sarah decided that was the best thing for her. The social worker questioned Ross's involvement and motivation to work with Sarah on solving this problem.

It was the overwhelming consensus of the Diagnostic Pain Clinic Team that Sarah seek out an inpatient, interdisciplinary, behaviorally oriented, chronic-pain treatment program. The team felt it was imperative that such a program be implemented very soon. They were concerned not only with Sarah's obvious decline physically and lack of ability to engage in most activities in her daily life, but also about the extreme degree of psychological distress reflected in the evaluation. The Team agreed that unless such an interdisciplinary, highly structured pain treatment program were implemented, Sarah's situation would continue to deteriorate to the point where she became more and more distressed psychologically and already serious family concerns would become even more serious. The Team felt that given Sarah's level of motivation to do something about her problem, she would be a good candidate for chronic pain treatment.

Keith Makie

Keith Makie, Ph.D.
Pain Program Director

Albert Fremont

Albert Fremont, M.D.
Medical Director
Community Rehabilitation Center

KCM/brm
dic 1/8/87
tran 1/8/87

19

PHYSIATRIC EVALUATION
(SANDY BICKETT, M.D.)

Billings Community Hospital

DIAGNOSTIC PAIN CLINIC

NAME: Sarah Anderson
MEDICAL RECORD NUMBER: 0113075
EVALUATION: Psysiatrist Evaluation
EVALUATOR: Sandy Bickett, M.D.
DATE OF EVALUATION: December 9, 1986

Sarah is a 45-year-old woman who was involved in a motor vehicle accident in August of 1985. She reports that at that time she was pulling into her driveway when a four-wheel-drive pickup truck was passing in a no-passing zone and struck the rear of her car going approximately 80 to 90 miles an hour. The impact was sufficient to break the seat belt that the passenger was wearing and the passenger was thrown from the car. Sarah stayed in the car; she did have her seat belt on. The car was spun around and wrapped around the telephone pole on the driver's side and Sarah was wedged in the car and found herself wrapped around the telephone pole as well. She reports that she lost consciousness briefly and when she came to, the daughter of the woman who had been thrown from the car was calling out for her mother. Sarah reports being able to get out of the car though she felt like she was in slow motion and walked over to her friend who was injured and there passed out. They were taken initially to the Emergency Room in Laurel and from there to the Emergency Room in Billings. She remembers having no feeling in her left leg or foot at the time of the accident and for the rest of that night. She was initially seen by Dr. Coots who evaluated her and managed her during that stay, which he reports as a few days. She reports that from the moment she began to be fully conscious she had numbness in her left leg, but an aching feeling as well; she had an aching, burning pain in her left arm and shoulder and neck. She reports having been bruised over that entire shoulder and upper-arm region. She was sent home from the hospital and the pain was still there. She reports that the pain has continued to be present continuously ever since. It may wax and wane in intensity, but is always present in her shoulder and neck. Her leg and low back pain has subsided and only recurs once in a while. She notices pain in her lower back and leg when she has to do anything bending or stooping. She attempted to pick some

20

strawberries this summer and had the recurrence of her back and leg pain. She was unable to have a garden as she usually does.

When Sarah describes her shoulder and neck pain, which is her chief complaint, she reports that the pain is always present. It has a nagging, burning quality as well as a deep itching. It is not an itch which can be scratched on the surface, but is an itch or a tingle deep within. When she moves or stretches, she has a pulling, burning pain throughout that area that is being stretched. She has currently been instructed in some exercises for stretching her neck and shoulder and when she does those it brings on the pulling, burning pain, which does not subside during that hour. She also reports having headaches since the time of the accident, at least one a day. She reports she cannot remember a day since the accident when she did not have a headache. There are days when it is worse than others and some days where she is unable to function because of the headache and neck pain, but in general, the intensity waxes and wanes.

Sarah reports that things that increase the intensity of her pain include activity and stress. Activities that she describes that are particularly painful or pain-producing include doing paperwork, when she leans forward and concentrates. Vacuuming is particularly painful. She reports having been an avid seamstress prior to her accident and would finish two or three garments per day. Now, if she sews a half a garment she will hurt for the entire week. She does not do heavy housekeeping including mopping or vacuuming, but does do dishes, cooking, baking, and washing. Her husband is self-employed, so she does some of his bookwork on a daily basis. Sarah reports having tried multiple medications at the recommendation of her physicians and this includes Valium, which she reports ''put her in outer space,'' but helped the pain. She discontinued that because although it reduced the pain she was unable to function. Xanax she will take on occasion when the pain is particularly severe and she is unable to relax and go to sleep at night. The Xanax causes her bad dreams and so she takes it only rarely, but will take it when the pain is severe. She reports having tried Naprosyn, which was not helpful, and is now taking Clinoril, which she finds somewhat better than Tylenol. In addition to the medications which she has tried, she has also tried physical therapy. The ultrasound helped and made her feel better and lasted approximately one-half an hour. She has tried hot baths and hot showers and finds that if she can lie down in the tub and relax and get the water as hot as possible, this will help for a short period of time. She had a Cortisone injection into her left shoulder by Dr. Todd on two occasions, both of which helped; however, she is

21

fearful of having too much Cortisone and Dr. Todd warned against having too many injections. She was seen by Dr. Dowell, who placed her on exercises for stretching, which she is supposed to do on an hourly basis. However, the exercise consistently makes her worse and so she is reluctant to do it hourly and does it somewhat less than that.

Sarah Anderson reports that her sleeping has been poor since the time of the accident. She reports she cannot remember sleeping through a whole night and is up three or four times a night because of the pain waking her, and she cannot get back to sleep. At these times, she will get up, read a little or walk around, or have a glass of warm milk in an attempt to go back to bed and go to sleep. She is finding that she will fall asleep during the day if she is sitting, because of her fitful night sleep. She reports occasionally staying in bed the whole day and sleeping essentially all day. This has only begun to occur in the last two months and she feels that this is an indication of her becoming worn out by the pain. She reports a bad appetite, comments that this seems unreasonable given her overweight condition, but reports not really having a good appetite or enjoying food, but that she considers herself a nervous eater and that when she is in pain, in order to make herself feel better she begins to eat and eat and not even taste what she is eating. She reports that after the injury, her weight got down to 155 pounds for a period of time; however, her usual weight is between 172 and 184 and has remained there for the last several years, and she is in that range at the present time. Sarah also reports that her social life and recreational life have taken a real reduction since her accident. She went to a Bible study both Tuesday and Wednesday nights and to church on Sunday regularly before her accident and now occasionally gets to Sunday services, which is a dramatic reduction for her. She used to visit people regularly; however, now she reports being anxious and hating to be around people. She finds they make her nervous and she thinks she rattles on. She also does not like to talk about her pain and yet people will comment on how bad she looks and this makes her feel worse. She also reports that she dislikes being around people because she has lost touch with the activities that she used to do and to do with them, and feels like she has nothing to talk about anymore. Prior to her accident, she liked to do a variety of activities, including camping, some gold mining, searching for arrowheads, hiking. She reports that she usually does a lot of activities with her family in the summer. However, last summer after the accident, she was left at home alone frequently while they went off to do their usual activities. She has done oil painting in the past, doing both miniatures and canvas. Since the time of the accident, she is unable to do

22

miniatures because she cannot lean forward and concentrate or do the fine work. She has been unable to do her canvas oil painting because of the pain and the nervousness. Sewing was one of Sarah Anderson's other areas of release and enjoyment, as well as substantially contributing to the family's well-being. She finds she cannot do that anymore. She not only made her own clothing and that of her children, she also made jeans for her husband and did the winter coats for her adult daughters, as well as undergarments. The cost of doing it herself was so much less than the cost of purchasing that she and her family are experiencing a substantial burden by her inability to continue to do this activity and she is feeling a particular loss because this was an area of outlet for her.

Physical examination reveals a very short, stout woman in no apparent distress.

HEENT: The pupils are equal and react to light and accommodate. Extraocular muscles are intact. Sensation over the face is intact as are facial movements.
BACK: Back was examined and though there is no back deformity, the left shoulder is carried approximately an inch lower than the right without causing a spinal curve. Hips and pelvis are equal and level. Palpation of the back, neck, and shoulders reveals multiple areas of tautness of muscle and trigger point tenderness as demonstrated on the attached diagram.
NECK: Neck range of motion is limited in flexion to chin one inch from the chest. Extension is essentially normal. Rotation is approximately 60 degrees in both directions.
UPPER EXTREMITIES: Upper extremity strength is Grade V minus on the right and IV on the left including grip. These are all reduced because of the pain that they reportedly produce in the left shoulder. Range of motion of the left upper extremity is also limited by pain produced in the left shoulder area and limited to 120 degrees of flexion, 100 degrees of abduction, external rotation lacks 45 degrees.
NEUROLOGIC: Deep tendon reflexes and coordination are intact in both upper and lower extremities as is sensation to pin prick and light touch.

IMPRESSION:
1. Musculo-skeletal strain and chronic myofascitis of the left shoulder and neck region.
2. Chronic pain syndrome.

RECOMMENDATIONS: Sarah Anderson has had good episodic physical therapy, which produced short-term relief. All of the previous persons who have examined her have recommended physical therapy and stretch which have produced some positive results, but have not fully resolved this problem. For this reason, it is recommended

that she become involved in an inpatient program that
combines treatment for her myofascitis, tenseness,
tightness as well as her chronic pain syndrome in order to
achieve maximal results.

Sandy Bickett

Sandy Bickett, M.D.

STB: ajf

24

PSYCHOLOGICAL EVALUATION
(KEITH MAKIE, PH.D.)

Billings Community Rehabilitation Center

Psychological Evaluation

PATIENT: Sarah Anderson
DATE OF EVALUATION: 12/9/86
EVALUATION PROCEDURES: Review of records and
questionnaires, interview, Minnesota Multiphasic
Personality Inventory (MMPI)
STATUS: outpatient
AGE: 45
PROGRAM: Diagnostic Pain Clinic
EVALUATOR: Keith Makie, Ph.D.

Background Information

Sarah is a 45-year-old married woman who lives with her husband and family in Laurel, Montana. She was referred for this Psychological Evaluation, which is part of a larger interdisciplinary pain evaluation because of her long-standing debilitating problem with chronic shoulder, neck, and headache pain. It was obvious from the onset of the interview part of this evaluation that Sarah was extremely agitated and distressed. She came into the interview reporting that she was very nervous, that her pain is getting worse, that she had numerous family and personal problems, and was even having a hard time concentrating on the evaluation. She talked at a rapid rate, much of her thinking was confused, her speech was forced at times, she became quite emotional in several parts of the interview and in general presents herself as someone who is operating under a great deal of pressure and that pressure was steadily mounting to the point where she was feeling out of control.

She presented a history of her injury which happened in August of 1985 as a result of a motor vehicle accident. She indicated that since that time she has had rather excruciating and constant pain in her shoulder and neck and has had headaches. She says that this pain increases with any kind of activity, but definitely increases when she has problems with anxieties and worries at home. She said that nothing really helps the pain, other than taking medication and getting rest and quiet, which she never gets in her rather crisis-filled, tumultuous life. At the present time she takes Xanax, Tylenol Extra-Strength, and Clinoril. She says that these medications tend to help her somewhat, although the pain is usually there. She says that

25

the pain does disturb her sleep but is not sure whether the disturbance is due to the pain, per se, or the many other worries and rapid thoughts she has going through her mind most of the time.

I did not have to ask her how the chronic pain had affected her life because she quickly launched into a long description of how out of control she feels and how awful her life has become since the accident. She indicated that before the accident she still had a number of concerns and problems, but was able to ''roll with the punches'' and handle the situations as they arose. She said that since the accident, her physical limitations, and the constant pain, she is just unable to handle the pressures in her life and finds herself wishing things like going to sleep and never waking up and then her family just all going away, which are very disturbing to her. She describes herself as a very responsible, caring, caretaking kind of person who watches out for the needs of everybody else before she takes care of her own needs. She again said that it was fine for her to operate that way before the chronic pain situation, but now she is finding she is ''at her wit's end,'' she is losing control of her emotions, she feels that her life is a mass of confusion and she doesn't know which way to turn. All of this was presented in a rather distressed, agitated manner with Sarah shifting around in her chair, talking rapidly, and in general appearing as if she was having a difficult time. At several points during the interview she commented on the fact that she didn't know why she was telling me all these details because usually she presents a rather calm, stoic front when underneath she is seething with distress and agitation.

One of the things that came out clearly in the interview is that Sarah is a woman who takes responsibility for almost everybody she comes in contact with. She described her relationship with her husband as extremely problematic. She said that she does the work around the house, even though she has days where she cannot get out of bed; her husband still pretty much demands that she keep up the pace. She says at times she feels like a slave in her own home, and then again feels very badly for even having those unacceptable thoughts. She says there has been some recent trouble in her home because of a 21-year-old who has been living with them because he has nowhere else to go; this individual has gotten in trouble with the law and caused a great deal of stress and conflict in her life. She described her home as a motel for anybody who wants to stay there.

She doesn't feel like she has control over who impinges on her life. She said that she constantly works hard and doesn't seem to get anywhere and is feeling quite desperate. In general, it appeared that she was unable to draw any limits on what people in her life could expect from her and she did not know how she was going to get out of a situation that she definitely saw herself as getting into because of her wanting to help other people and meet their needs. There was a definite tone in the whole interview of her being trapped in a situation that she does not know how to get out of.

We talked about alternative treatments to chronic pain, including structured chronic pain treatment. She said she had heard about such a program and thought that would be exactly what she needed. She thought she needed to be removed from the very stressful environment she now lives in. She thought her family needed to learn more about her pain and the effects of stress on her pain and she seemed very interested in anything that could relieve what she describes as a desperate, intolerable situation.

TEST RESULTS: The Welsh Code for Sarah's MMPI is as follows: 83**1*76"429'0/5# F'K/L:

The first thing about this Welsh Code is the significantly elevated 'F' Scale, suggesting that Sarah is in a good deal of general psychological distress, which she is openly admitting. There are a number of extremely elevated clinical scales, suggesting a number of themes for this profile. The two high points suggest an individual who appears to be in a great deal of psychological turmoil. These individuals report feeling anxious, tense, nervous, fearful, and worried. They tend to be very dependent in interpersonal relationships and seek attention and affection; they tend to be depressed with feelings of hopelessness. They tend to present a large number of physical complaints of a vague nature. There tends to be a disturbance in their thinking and they often report memory lapses, poor concentration, and intrusive thoughts. A second theme is that of someone who is overly involved in her physical complaints and bodily functions; these complaints tend to increase in times of stress. There is also a suggestion of an individual who tends to convert psychological problems into physical symptoms. Other suggestions from the profile are someone who is quite distrustful and suspicious of the motives of others. There is a suggestion from this profile of an individual who is quite dependent in interpersonal relationships and tends to defer in decision-making matters, especially to males. This MMPI Profile fits in very well with my interview observations of Sarah, that of an extremely distressed, obviously upset, rather desperate woman who sees herself as trapped in a situation that she cannot solve with her own resources.

SUMMARY AND RECOMMENDATIONS: This evaluation indicates that Sarah has a rather long-standing, complicated, chronic pain problem that is made even more complicated by an obviously stressful family and social situation. She comes across as quite desperate, confused, and psychologically distressed. This distress definitely worsens her chronic pain, which then, in a circular fashion, increases her distress. My main recommendation at this point is that she seek out an inpatient, interdisciplinary, behaviorally oriented, chronic pain treatment program. Only in such a program could the multiplicity of factors contributing to her chronic pain problem be reasonably addressed. I would think without such an intervention she will continue to deteriorate and eventually the family situation will most likely collapse.

Keith Makie

Keith Makie, Ph.D.
Licensed psychologist

KCM/brm
dic 12/12/86
tran 12/16/86

28

NEUROLOGIC EVALUATION (EDWARD RUNK, M.D.)

HX: This 45 YOWF is referred via the Pain Clinic for evaluation. Apparently she was injured in a MVA in 8/85. She was a driver wearing a belt, but apparently it was not tight. She was struck from behind by another vehicle that caused her vehicle to go into a spin and strike a tree. Apparently the tree was struck on the driver's door. The patient feels that her head struck a telephone pole through the open window and her shoulder was pinched between the seat and the door. The patient thinks she may have been unconscious for one minute, and was subsequently hospitalized for four days. She had a CAT scan that was reportedly negative. The patient had residual neck, shoulder, and trapezius pain on the left, with continued symptoms until this time. This consists of a burning in the left arm, with some numbness in the hand. This is called a constant nagging pain. This is worse with bending, vacuuming, and other activity and better with rest. Heat seems to help, such as in the bath.

  The patient has had an ultrasound, heat, massage, etc. via PT, without any continued benefit. Shoulder injection seems to help temporarily. Various checks in the past have shown spasm but no clear neurologic changes. The patient had nightmares on Xanax and amitriptyline. Imipramine apparently helped some, but it was DC'd for reasons that are unclear to the patient. Of the anti-inflammatories, she has had the best response on Clinoril but currently is only taking it intermittently, about three times per week. The patient is not currently in PT, and has never had a TENS unit.

PMH: The patient has had a transphenoidal hypophysectomy for a micropituitary tumor. She has had a prior hysterectomy, bil. carpal tunnel repairs, Marshall-Marketti procedure, and T and A. She has been treated in the past for depression. Current meds include the Clinoril, HCTZ, Premarin, K+, and occasional Xanax or Tylenol. The patient has no allergies. The patient had a grade eight education, but later received a GED. She is right-handed.
PH: Neg.
SH: The patient did sewing and painting for work in the past, is having difficulty pursuing these at the current time due to her problems. The patient's husband is out of work and currently is trying to get SSI for secondary to low-back pain and reported emotional problems. The patient denies use of tobacco and drinks alcohol rarely.

EXAM: Weight is 183 pounds. Height is 4'11". BP is 120-78. General: pleasant, obese 45 YOWF who appears quite comfortable at rest. Head: normocephalic, atraumatic

29

without bruits. ENT: unremarkable. Neck: reasonably supple
with full active ROM. Carotids 2+ without bruits.
Lhermitte's sign was negative. Chest: clear. Cor: S1, S2
without murmur. Abdomen: soft. The patient had bil. CTS
scars. The patient was very tight and tender throughout the
left trapezius area.
Mental Status: The patient was alert and oriented ×3. She
knew the recent presidents, was minimally right-left
confused, but had normal praxis and naming skills. She read
a grade 6 passage well with good recall. Serial 3's were
well done. The patient remembered two of three objects
after five minutes and confabulated on the third. With a
hint she came up with it. The patient's speech was normal.
The patient had a lot of nervous laughter. Cranial nerves:
1. intact. 2. fields and OKN's were normal. Fundi: benign.
PERRL. The patient had full EOM's but seemed to have a
minimal right exotropia at rest. Remaining cranial nerves
are unremarkable. On motor exam, the patient has pain
around the left shoulder girdle, leading to difficulty
testing the biceps, deltoids. There was no winging of the
scapula or other clear weakness. Sensation was intact to
fine touch, sharp/dull, vibration, position, and
graphesthesia testing throughout. A Romberg test was neg.

 On coordination testing, the patient performed finger to
nose, heel to shin, and rapid alternating movement tests
well. Gait including toe and tandem was normal. Reflexes
were 2-3+ and symmetrical with down going toes.
A: 45 YOWF seems to have a myofascial pain syndrome. I see
no evidence of specific radiculopathy or other neurologic
involvement at this time. The patient might respond to
another round of PT, especially including such modalities
as a TENS Unit. She might benefit additionally from
imipramine as it has been used in the past. More frequent
use of Clinoril might be of value as well. I will discuss
the situation further with other members of the Pain Clinic
team.

Edward Runk

Edward Runk, MD/jh
trans: 12/12/86

30

ORTHOPEDIC EVALUATION
(W. J. McCONNELL, M.D.)

Billings Community Rehabilitation Center

OUTPATIENT DIAGNOSTIC PAIN CLINIC

NAME: Sarah Anderson
MEDICAL RECORD NUMBER: 0113075
AGE: 45
PROGRAM: Outpatient Diagnostic Pain Clinic
EVALUATION: Orthopedic Evaluation
EVALUATOR: W. J. McConnell, M.D., Orthopedic Surgeon
EVALUATION: December 9, 1986

Sarah Anderson, a 45-year-old, Caucasian female, was evaluated on December 9, 1986 for purpose of the Pain Clinic Evaluation Unit.

She reported that on August 20, 1985, she was the driver of a Datsun pickup which was rear-ended by a 4 X 4 Chevy while she was turning into her driveway near Laurel, Montana. She reported injuring her left shoulder, neck and head as well as her left leg. According to her, she went to the Laurel Hospital where Dr. Gosten saw her and then was transferred to Billings Community Hospital. She further reported that Dr. Coots saw her upon her entrance to the Community X-Ray Department. She further stated that since that time she has been bothered by a lot of headaches, left neck, and shoulder pain extending down into the posterior aspect of the left arm to above the elbow; also to the front of her chest, indicating the anterior pectoral region.

In addition to being seen by Dr. Coots, she has also had neurosurgical consultation by Dr. Dowell, orthopedic consultation by Dr. Todd, and has also been seen by Dr. Sid Silker of Laurel. Dr. Silker is her doctor of record, according to her.

Past medical history is quite complex surgically as she reported that she has had a brain tumor removed by Dr. Grost in Seattle. She has had bilateral carpal tunnel three to four years ago, a number of D & C's, followed by a complete hysterectomy.

PRESENT CONDITION: According to her, she continues having frequent headaches, which she localizes by placing the

31

palm of her hand to the occipital region, which she
indicated progressed upwards and forwards, indicating the
parietal-temporal regions, continuing into the frontal
area. She characterized the pain as dull, deep, aching pain
that she can partially alleviate when severe, by taking
Xanax or Tylenol. She also reported other medical intake,
including blood pressure medications and Premarin.

In regards to her headaches she denied any oral or
auditory auras and denied any memory loss, type of
seizures, dizziness, or syncope. She also indicated that
the left shoulder bothered her and here, again, placing the
palm of her hand onto the trapezii areas, extending up into
the cervical region to the occiput on the left. She also
reported that this pain extended into the posterior arm
area, by her description and stopping at a level just above
the elbow. She further related that the plain also extended
forward, indicating the pectoralis area on the left. She
also indicated that her upper back, and here indicated the
infrascapular region, mainly on the left paraspinal
musculature, bothers her at times when she is tense or with
extended arm use.

She also indicated to this evaluator that actually her
back is doing pretty well now and that she is not having any
particular leg problem currently, at the time she was being
seen here.

According to her, her last medical attention was provided
by Dr. Silker who saw her approximately one month to her
being seen here. Examination revealed a rather short,
moderately obese female of stated age who did not appear in
acute or chronic distress. She appeared awake, alert, and
oriented and proved to be a good historian. She was noted to
move about without a visible gait disturbance and offered
no complaints during the interview, with her sitting on the
examining table throughout.

She was able to stand in the mode of attention upon request
and the spine appeared to be in good alignment when viewed
posteriorly and laterally. The scapular angles were noted
to be level and scapular motion was full in all planes, as
was range of motion of the upper extremities and the
cervical spine. She produced forward flexion to
approximately 60°, extension to 15°, right and left lateral
flexion and rotation to 25° each. Motor power of the upper
extremities, including grip, was considered to be within
normal limits throughout. Digit dexterity was opinioned to
be intact. There was no atrophy, in opinion noted, with
special reference to the hand intrinsics.

32

She was able to stand and walk on toes and heels and tandem walk without apparent difficulty or complaint. Sitting straight-leg raise was negative, bilaterally, to beyond 90°. Passive ankle dorsiflexion was performed readily. Motor power of the lower extremities was considered to be within normal limits throughout, with special reference to the great toe extensors and feet evertors.

Deep tendon reflexes of the upper and lower extremities were considered to be bilaterally equal and active and produced without clonus. There were no sensory changes elicited to pin involving the upper extremities, with special reference to the left upper extremity.

It should be noted that while passive range of motion of the left shoulder was able to be performed fully, she was unable, according to her, to lift her arm in lateral elevation to above 90° and was able to forward elevate to approximately 120° with complaints of pain and pulling. At this point in time, palpation of this shoulder was accomplished and she indicated that the greatest amount of tenderness lay in the specific region of the bicipital groove on this side.

The question of left bicipital tendonitis is unanswered at this point and it may prove beneficial to form appropriate injection(s). Other than this suggestion, no other opinions to any further treatment, medically or surgically are able to be projected by this evaluator.

Following further X-ray reviews and file review, will discuss at the appropriate scheduled conference.

W. J. McConnell

W. J. McConnell, M.D.
Orthopedic Surgeon

WJM/brm
dic 12/16/86
tran 12/22/86

33

PHYSICAL THERAPY EVALUATION
(TODD ROCKLER, R.P.T.)
Billings Community Rehabilitation Center

PHYSICAL THERAPY EVALUATION

NAME: Sarah Anderson
MEDICAL RECORD NUMBER: 113075
AGE: 45
DIAGNOSIS: Chronic left arm and cervical pain.
PHYSICIAN ORDERS: Evaluation
PHYSICIAN: Dr. Sandy Bickett
FREQUENCY/DURATION: one time only
DATE OF EVAL: 12/9/86
STATUS: Outpatient Diagnostic Pain Clinic

HISTORY: This is a 45-year-old woman who was involved in a motor vehicle accident in August of 1985 in which she was hit from behind and spun around and struck a telephone pole. The patient stated she had immediate onset of shoulder and neck pain, and left upper extremity pain. She describes this pain as a nagging, dull, constant pain. She is worse with forward bending and doing desk work, lifting over 5 pounds. Patient said she is better with heat and ultrasound temporarily side bending to the right. She stated her upper extremity pain comes and goes, and that she has a problem sleeping and is up walking around, three to four times a night. She has been treated with stretching exercises, hot packs, ultrasound, and massage. Isometric exercises made her worse. She has been treated by a osteopath who gave her acupressure which temporarily helped relieve her pain. She has had two cortisone shots in the cervical area which she stated helped her pain for approximately one month. She currently has hypertension and is on medication for this. She feels that her pain is staying about the same over the last several months.

SUBJECTIVE: Patient's chief complaint is of dull, nagging, constant pain in her cervical area and left shoulder with intermittent radiations down her left upper extremity.

OBJECTIVE: Evaluation of patient showed her to have good posture with a slightly forward head. Range of motion of her cervical spine was approximately 75% in backward bending, approximately 90% in forward bending, within normal limits in left rotation and left side bending, approximately 75% of right rotation and right side

34

bending. Palpation of patient's upper cervical and thoracic area showed her to be sore over her left sterno-calvicular joint and over the left clavicle, the subacrominal triangle, the sterno-cleidomastoids, and the scalenes on the left were all tender to palpation. The facet joints, bilaterally were tender to palpation and patient had a difficult time swallowing. Passive mobility of her cervical spine was difficult due to muscle guarding, but did show some significant tightness in the muscles on the left cervical and thoracic area. Temporomandibular test showed patient to have a late opening click on the left with a late closing click. She also had a late opening click on the right with an early closing click on the right. The patient has dentures and has had dentures since she was fifteen years old. Soft tissue testing showed her to be extremely tight on the left upper thoracic area and cervical area. Upper extremity range of motion was decreased on the left, both actively and passively, and internal and external rotation and abduction. Her strength was decreased to good-minus and sensation seemed to be increased on the left. Evaluation of her cervical spine was difficult due to her obesity.

PROBLEMS: Soft tissue tightness on the left in her upper thoracic and cervical area. Decreased strength. Decreased range of motion and increased sensation in the left upper extremity. Possible TMJ problems and slightly poor posture with a forward head.

GOALS: Not applicable.

TREATMENT RECOMMENDATIONS: Patient would probably do well with an intensive physical therapy program for stretching, strengthening, and mobilization of her left upper extremity. It is recommended that patient would do well with inpatient, behavioral modification pain program with extensive physical therapy.

Todd Rockler

Todd Rockler, RPT
12/10/86

TR/brm
dic 12/10/86
tran 12/12/86

SOCIAL SERVICE INTAKE INTERVIEW
(RICK WYSIL, B.S.W.)

Billings Community Rehabilitation Center

OUTPATIENT DIAGNOSTIC PAIN CLINIC EVALUATION

NAME: Sarah Anderson
MEDICAL RECORD NUMBER: 113075
PROGRAM: Chronic Pain Program

EVALUATION: Social Services
EVALUATOR: Rick Wysil, BSW
SIGNIFICANT OTHER: Ross Anderson, husband
DATE OF INTAKE: 12/9/86

DESCRIPTIVE STATEMENT: The following information was obtained from a personal interview with Sarah's husband, Ross Anderson. He was a poor historian; he had particular trouble providing details or estimation of dates. Ross shared he is hard of hearing. He also stated he is ''absent-minded'' and if he is required to ''think fast'' he gets confused. Sarah Anderson, a 45-year-old married female, was injured in a two-vehicle accident during the summer of 1985. According to Ross the other driver was at fault. Ross stated that Sarah was hospitalized for a number of days following this accident. He said she suffered injury to her left shoulder, neck, and upper back. As a result of the accident, Ross said she has had numerous surgeries and suffers from headaches.

Ross said Sarah has had a complicated medical history for the past twenty years, which has included surgeries on her bladder, intestines, and pituitary gland (he said she has had many other surgeries, but he couldn't remember them all).

FAMILY COMPOSITION AND SUPPORT NETWORK: Sarah and her 49-year-old husband, Ross, have been married between 20 and 25 years; this is the second marriage for both people. Ross indicated their attraction for each other was the cause of dissolvement of both their first marriages. He indicated this was a traumatic period for all parties involved; in fact, Sarah's husband somehow convinced her to go to Warm Springs State Mental Hospital for a month or so. Sarah has two adult children from her first union: Jerry Landquer, and Roxanne Aist, who is married and resides in Red Lodge (Ross adopted her). Ross and Sarah see Roxanne at least once a week. Roxanne has one daughter. Ross stated Sarah is very close to her daughter and grandchild and enjoys spending time with them. Sarah's son by her first marriage, Jerry Landquer, is in the Service and has been out of the family

36

home for the past ten years. Ross had two children from his first marriage: his son died in an accident shortly after the divorce; his daughter Jolene, lives in Florida. He has little contact with his daughter. Ross and Sarah have two daughters, Theresa, age 20 who occasionally still resides in the family home and Marsha, age 17 who is still in the family home. Ross reports Sarah has close relationships with both daughters. He added they are having typical trouble with Marsha that one would expect from a teenager; he indicated he and Sarah both believe in physical punishment when they cannot manage Marsha in any other manner. Ross described Sarah as a good mother and stated she has very close family ties.

Ross stated his relationship with Sarah has had the ''usual ups-and-downs,'' but ''nothing terrible.'' He added they have always been able to overcome their problems. As far as communication between the two, Ross admitted Sarah probably feels he does not talk to her enough. He shared he tends not to discuss his feelings, but instead tends to keep things to himself. Ross said he and Sarah believe in traditional male/female values in their marriage, i.e., her place is in the home caring for the children and he is responsible for providing for their financial security. Ross added, ''I'm in charge, I don't believe in a woman leading a family.''

Sarah's father is deceased, her mother, Lisa Scoon, lives in Laurel. Ross stated Sarah sees her mother weekly, but does not believe they are terribly close; he stated Sarah's relationship with her mother has improved over the years. Ross said he believes Sarah's childhood was difficult. He said because her parents were divorced, the children (he did not know how many siblings she has) were ''shoved around in the family.'' He believes Sarah's mother was physically and mentally abusive to her. He stated Sarah came from an extremely poor family. Sarah was born and raised in Wyoming. Ross said Sarah married at age 15 or 16; he suspects she married at such a young age as a means of getting out of her family situation.

Ross's father is deceased, his mother, Donna Anderson, resides in Laurel except during the summer when she lives with her daughter in Oregon. Ross believes his mother provides Sarah with much emotional support, but does not interfere.

Sarah apparently receives good emotional support from her sister, Lena Morgal, who lives in Laurel. Ross stated that she sees her at least weekly and they talk on the phone frequently.

37

According to Ross, Sarah has many friends, but none of them are particularly close. He has noticed her friends seem to come over less often; Sarah also does less with friends because of her pain.

Ross stated he has no one that he confides in; probably for emotional support he depends on Sarah.

CURRENT LIVING ARRANGEMENTS: Sarah and her family reside approximately one mile east of Laurel, Montana, on Devlin Road. They have lived in this home for the past ten years. Ross stated it is a two-bedroom, single-story home with a basement. They use the basement for storage, particularly of their canned goods; Sarah is able to go up and down the basement stairs without problems. They are buying their home.

Prior to her injury, Sarah was responsible for all homemaking tasks, including housework, laundry, meal preparation, and grocery shopping. Ross stated, as far as her homemaking duties, he always felt she enjoyed this work but now she asks the girls to share more in the chores. Ross stated the children do assist with cooking, dishes, and are responsible for their own rooms. He has noticed they are doing more of the home chores than they did before Sarah's accident. Ross stated, ''I have never done housework, and never changed a baby's diapers.''

Ross stated Sarah typically gets up around 7 A.M., at which time she may cook breakfast for Marsha (Teresa often does her own). After Marsha goes to school, Sarah may go back to bed. She then gets up around 8:30 and prepares Ross's breakfast. After that she does housework and may work on sewing projects for the children. Ross has noticed her housework is not at the level it used to be and he added, ''she is not the greatest housekeeper.'' At noon Sarah prepares lunch for Ross. After lunch he is uncertain what she does with her time; he suspects she may lie down if the pain is severe. The evening meal is prepared by either Sarah or one of the daughters. Sarah tends to spend her evening time reading, watching television, or working on a craft project. She usually retires by 10:30 P.M.

Ross has noticed since her accident Sarah is less ''energetic.'' He explained she still does the day-to-day tasks, but not all the extras she used to do. He has noticed she has given more responsibility to their daughters. When the daughters prepare a meal she usually sits in the kitchen with them and provides instructions.

EFFECT OF CHRONIC PAIN: Ross said Sarah's pain is constant; however, he has noticed the degree does vary. He

38

is uncertain what makes her pain worse, but has noticed that when she uses her left arm during housework, her pain seems to increase. Ross believes Sarah's pain has progressively worsened. Ross said it is hard to know what her pain level is because she is not a complainer. He stated, ''she doesn't tell me that much, and I haven't tried to find out.'' He believes Sarah continues to do her homemaking tasks even when she is in a lot of pain. He stated that Sarah has ''an iron constitution.'' He added, ''I don't try to keep her from doing her tasks, because I think she needs to as things would fall apart if she didn't.'' Ross stated her pain is primarily in her shoulders and neck area and that she is also bothered with extreme headaches. He was uncertain how often she gets the headaches, but they are frequent. Unless Sarah has had an extremely bad day as far as her pain goes, she does not talk about it. Ross believes she has a very high pain tolerance.

Ross stated he can tell when Sarah's pain is worse because she becomes short-tempered with him and the girls, she grimaces, or she may hold the back of her neck or put her hand on her forehead.

Ross believes Sarah attempts to manage her pain by lying down with a pillow under her neck and a cold washcloth on her forehead, and with the use of medication. Ross was uncertain what type of medication Sarah is on, but he believes it is a muscle relaxant. He stated she is not taking any pain medication, as she does not wish to be ''zonked out.''

Ross stated there is little he does to assist Sarah when she is in pain. He said he seldom waits on her. Occasionally he will ask if there is something she needs. However, for the most part, he will ask the children to assist her. Ross shared it is emotionally difficult for him to provide the comfort she may wish.

Sarah is suffering from sleep disturbance due to her chronic pain. Ross said she changes position often during the night and she is up and down frequently. When she is up she may sit and have a cup of tea. Ross said she has been bothered with sleep disturbance for many years, but since the accident it has gotten worse. She is unable to sleep on her left side, due to the shoulder pain.

Ross was uncertain if Sarah's injury has affected her appetite. He stated he does not know what she weighs, but she may be losing some weight. He stated she has always had a weight problem and diets frequently. He believes she is 4'11" tall.

39

Ross believes the only way Sarah's chronic pain has changed her relationship with their daughters is that she is shorter-tempered with them. He stated the girls often complain to him about this, but he reminds them of what Sarah is going through. He said when Sarah is particularly upset with Marsha, she may slap her or hit her with a belt. Ross stated Sarah does not overuse physical punishment, nor does he believe this has increased since her injury. He stated when Sarah physically punishes Marsha, he believes Marsha ''has it coming.'' He stated, ''I sit in the background to see if it is justified.'' Ross believes Sarah has difficulty with Marsha because Marsha is ''headstrong and talks back.''

Ross believes he is able to understand Sarah's chronic pain because of the pain he has suffered in his back since he injured it skiing when he was in his twenties. Apparently because of his back injury, Ross has been self-employed for the past ten years so he is able to work at his own pace and for the number of hours he feels physically capable. Ross said when his back pain becomes severe he may be down for two or three days; however, this does not happen very often. He stated, ''I have learned to live with it and know when to take it easy.'' He added he is uncertain whether Sarah has learned her physical limitations. Ross also senses because of his back pain he, too, is shorter-tempered. He stated, ''If people leave me alone I get over it fast.'' When he is upset he tends to yell, swear, and throw objects. He stated he does not physically abuse Sarah when he is upset. He explained they used to fight a lot and in the early days occasionally hit each other; he added that this was many years ago.

When this worker asked Ross what he would do if their situation does not change, he indicated he can continue to cope and he does not plan to leave Sarah. He added he tends to look at the situation a day at a time, and does not plan ahead.

COMMUNITY AGENCIES AND TRANSPORTATION: Ross stated their family is receiving assistance through County Social Services and Human Resources.

Sarah is capable of driving; however, she often has one of the daughters run errands for her. Ross has noticed she does not want to go out of the house as much as she used to; he stated he is unsure why.

INCOME, FINANCIAL RESOURCES, AND MEDICAL COVERAGE:
- Ross stated his income varies from month to month, but probably averages around $500 a month.
- The family receives $100+ a month in food stamps.

- They are receiving energy assistance for their utility costs through Human Resources
- Sarah's medical costs that relate to the accident are covered by the other driver's insurance, All-Risk.
- Ross thinks Sarah is considering applying for Social Security.
- Ross said their finances are extremely tight, and it is a stress area for the couple—he said that it tends to create friction between them.
- Sarah manages the family's finances; however, Ross oversees their money and makes the decisions as to how it will be spent.

EDUCATION AND MILITARY SERVICE:
- Sarah did not complete high school; Ross believes she was an average student; she quit school to get married.
- Sarah has her GED.
- Ross completed the ninth grade.
- Ross served in the Air Force for three years and received an Honorable Discharge.
- Sarah has no military experience.

EMPLOYMENT:
- Sarah has primarily been a homemaker throughout their marriage. Ross stated she has on several occasions worked as a waitress. This lasted for a short period of time as he was opposed to her working outside the home. Ross believes Sarah enjoyed working as a waitress, but stated, ''a woman's place is in the home raising children.''
- Ross has been self-employed as a ''handyman'' for the past ten years. He works four to five hours a day doing such things as plumbing, carpentry, welding, and furniture construction.
- Until ten years ago he worked as a welder. He held this position until he could no longer tolerate the pain. Prior to working as a welder he worked in the sawmills.

LEISURE ACTIVITIES AND ORGANIZATIONS: Sarah enjoys the following:
- cards (Pinochle)
- board games with the children
- sewing
- reading (romance novels)
- television
- knitting and crocheting
- listening to music (classical and country-western)
- working crossword puzzles

  Prior to her injury she also enjoyed spending her time camping, going on short car trips, rock hunting, painting (oil and acrylics), and making jewelry. Ross has attempted to encourage her to do her art work, but stated, ''mentally

41

she can't get into it.'' Ross shared they do little as a couple. He said he tends to watch television a lot.

Sarah is a member of the Jehovah's Witnesses; she attends meetings at least once a week. Prior to her accident she attended Jehovah's Witnesses meetings five times a week.

PATIENT AND FAMILY COPING HISTORY: Ross described Sarah in the following terms:
- friendly and easy to get along with
- even-tempered
- optimistic
- poorly organized in housework and generally; this has been a friction area for the couple
- has always ''bounded back'' from surgeries; seems to endure ''a lot''
- a humanitarian

Ross has noticed the following changes in Sarah since her accident:
- mentally seems less able to tolerate the pain; Ross believes it may be too much after all of the medical problems she has had to deal with
- cries much more easily
- more irritable
- moody
- seems withdrawn

Ross believes Sarah copes with her situation through the support she receives from her family and her strong religious faith. Ross indicated he has always relied strongly on Sarah's optimistic attitude to help him get through difficult times. Ross shared he often feels anxious due to the amount of stress in his life caused by his inability to work, their limited financial resources and during peak work times, the number of jobs he has to do. Ross stated he had a mild heart attack some time after Sarah's accident; he believes it was brought on by stress.

HISTORY OF DRUG AND ALCOHOL USE: Ross stated Sarah does not have a problem with drugs or alcohol. He said at times he has been concerned that she may ''get hooked on prescription drugs.'' However, he does not believe this has, as yet, been a problem. Ross shared that in the past he has been a heavy drinker; he believes in the past year or so he has decreased his amount of consumption. He stated, he at times uses alcohol to relax. When he drinks it is beer or whiskey.

Sarah drinks approximately three to four cups of coffee a day, and also often drinks black tea; she is not a smoker.

42

Ross indicated both his father and Sarah's mother were problem drinkers.

ASSESSMENT OF CURRENT SOCIAL SITUATION AND PROBLEMS: From this report, Ross adamantly believes in traditional male and female roles within the marriage. He very clearly views himself as the head of the family and the individual who makes the major decisions. According to Ross it is out of the question that Sarah will work outside of the home because he does not approve of it. Apparently when Sarah has worked in the past she has acquiesced to his wishes for her to quit. Ross believes they have a strong relationship, although the communication is limited. He indicated there are some problems regarding their 17-year-old daughter; however, he minimized these problems by indicating they are typical teenage concerns. Ross and Sarah both subscribe to physical punishment when they feel their youngest daughter is out of line. This family does appear to be experiencing financial stress. Nonetheless, Ross does not consider it appropriate for Sarah to work to help ease the financial burden.

Sarah has apparently dealt with many medical problems over the last twenty years. Ross described her as highly resilient through all of her medical concerns. However, at this point he does not feel she is dealing with her injuries from the accident with the same mental strength and attitude she has demonstrated in the past. Ross is concerned she may ''give up.'' Ross has noticed the following changes in Sarah since her accident: increased irritability, moodiness, more withdrawn behavior, and a change in her mental attitude (less optimistic). These changes, particularly the mental attitude, are probably very frightening to Ross as he indicated he has always depended on her to help him manage his own stress. By Ross's admission, his use of alcohol in the past has been heavy; it's possible he may revert back to that if he feels overwhelmed with the situation.

GOALS OF CLIENT AND FAMILY: Ross stated his primary goal for Sarah is for her to be more comfortable and for her to again pursue past projects such as her painting. Ross strongly indicated he does not plan for her to go to work (even though she has indicated a desire to). As far as her working goes, he said, ''I just wouldn't let her; what I say is what happens.''

Ross said they hope to receive a settlement from the other driver's insurance company.

SOCIAL SERVICE PLAN: This worker provided Ross with information on a residential chronic pain program. Ross

43

was particularly troubled by the thought of Sarah being out of their home for six to seven weeks. He said it would be extremely hard on both of them. He was unwilling to commit himself to supporting such a program, even if Sarah would choose to participate. Unless Sarah is highly motivated to work in such a program (if one is deemed appropriate) and is able to solicit Ross's support, I suspect her chances of succeeding are slim. If Ross's perception is accurate of his being the final decision-maker, his support is crucial. If Ross's concern about Sarah's mental attitude and thus her inability to provide him with the kind of support he found uplifting is strong enough, this may be an issue that would push him to seek change. In general, I believe Ross would find the separation and the program highly threatening.

If Sarah takes part in the pain program, weekly sessions with Ross and occasional sessions with their daughters would be necessary to:

1. assist them to understand Sarah's chronic pain and behavior
2. assist them to understand their roles in Sarah's chronic pain
3. help them to understand the program's goals and expectations
4. help promote generalization of progress Sarah would make in a pain program to their home environment

Rick Wysil

Rick Wysil, BSW
Medical Social Services
12/18/86

RW/brm
dic 12/18/86
tran 12/29/86

44

APPENDIX III: WITNESSES AND TESTIMONY

Transcript of Telephone Interview Between Insurance Agent and Sarah Anderson

This is Tim Taner recording a telephone interview with Sarah Anderson who is speaking from her attorney's office in Missoula, Montana. The date of this conversation is September 4, 1985. The time is 9:50 A.M. and we're going to be talking about an accident that Mrs. Anderson was involved in on or about August 20, 1985.

Q. Mrs. Anderson, would you give me your full name and spell your last name?
A. Sarah Anderson. A-n-d-e-r-s-o-n

Q. And Mrs. Anderson, you're aware that I'm recording this conversation?
A. Yes.

Q. It's being done with your consent?
A. Yes.

Q. Your age?
A. 44.

Q. You're married. Your husband's first name?
A. Ross.

Q. And what is your home address and phone number?
A. It's Box 336, Laurel, Montana, 59044. And my phone number's 248-6733.

Q. Are you employed other than as a housewife?
A. No.

Q. And were you operator of a car involved in this accident?
A. Yes, I was.

Q. What kind of a car is it and who is the owner of it?
A. It's a 1975 Datsun 710 station wagon, and my husband and I own it.

Q. What was the purpose of your trip that day? Where had you been? Where were you going?
A. Okay, we were, we went to a friend's house. Then we went to the store to get groceries and came home. And we were on the way home when this happened.

Q. What was the date and time of this accident as near as you an recollect?
A. It was on a Tuesday, August 20th.

Q. This year?
A. 1985.

45

Q. And the time?
A. About 5:00.

Q. And where did this accident occur?
A. Just right near my driveway on Devlin Road as we were, as I was almost turned in to go into the drive.

Q. All right. Where is this accident location relative to Laurel, Montana?
A. It's a mile-and-three-tenths from the Town Pump station.

Q. It's not in the city limits then?
A. No.

Q. It's in the county?
A. Um huh.

Q. And the county is?
A. Yellowstone.

Q. Devlin Road at this point, what direction does it run?
A. East and west.

Q. Is this a two-lane, two-way road or is it wider than that?
A. It's a two-lane road.

Q. Paved?
A. Yes.

Q. Were there any traffic controls in the immediate vicinity that regulated the flow of traffic, like stop signs?
A. There was no stop signs. There was a double yellow line.

Q. The double yellow line which indicated no passing?
A. Right.

Q. Is there a speed limit in the area?
A. Yes, it's 50.

Q. At the time this accident occurred, what other traffic was in the vicinity?
A. Coming to the town of Laurel, there was none. But going out, there was myself and there was a semi behind us, way behind us. And that's all I could see.

Q. All right. The terrain where this happened, is it level or is there a hill crest or curve involved?
A. Well there's a hill crest, but it's, uh, oh, how many— about 2200 feet to the crest of the hill. Oh it's more than that, but you can see. You can see the crest of the hill from my drive real easy.

46

Q. The road isn't level then. Are you going uphill or
downhill?
A. It's going uphill as you turn into my drive.

Q. All right.
A. Just starting to go uphill.

Q. Would you classify this as a business, residential, or
rural area?
A. A rural area.

Q. Were there any obstructions to your view either in your
vehicle or outside it which would cause you or the other
driver to fail to see each other?
A. No. My mirror was, I even looked in my rear-view mirror,
and there was a truck coming just over the crest of the
hill, but it was a semi.

Q. This was an oncoming vehicle or one that . . .
A. It was an oncoming one behind me. And my side mirror,
there was nothing coming from it when I turned either.

Q. I see. This was a vehicle behind you, not coming at you?
A. Right.

Q. All right.
A. And it's not the vehicle that hit us.

Q. Yes. We've established that you were the driver of the
car you were in. Would you indicate your passengers and
their position in the vehicle?
A. Okay. Mrs. Weston was in the front seat with a seat belt
on. And I had my seat belt on. And her son, Samuel, was
behind her and her daughter, Laura, was behind me.

Q. So you had a total of three people besides yourself?
A. Right.

Q. Who was the operator of the other vehicle involved in
this accident?
A. Donald Swanson.

Q. Was he alone in his vehicle?
A. Yes.

Q. And what kind of a vehicle was he operating?
A. It was a pickup truck, and I have no idea what kind. It's
a four-wheel-drive, but what the make was I don't know.

Q. What was the weather like that day?
A. Clear.

Q. Pavement's dry?
A. Um huh.

47

Q. And at that time of day, it's still daylight?
A. Oh yeah.

Q. What was your direction of travel and speed?
A. Okay, I was going east. At the time of the accident, I wasn't going, oh maybe, three or four miles an hour because I had to turn in.

Q. Okay. You were making a turn, what direction?
A. To the left.

Q. Were you signaling for that turn?
A. Yes, I was.

Q. For what interval of time did you give your signal?
A. It started at the, the other side of the bridge, and, how far was the bridge from there? . . .

Q. That would be adequate for me. The other side of the bridge?
A. Um huh.

Q. All right. That's as you approach the bridge and before you crossed it you started . . .
A. I started signaling.

Q. And what was your speed at the time you started signaling and then again as you were in your turn?
A. Well, I started, well I started slowing it down right at the bridge to about, oh 45 maybe. And then I slowed continually down till I came to where we turn in. And then I looked and nobody's coming up. And then as I turned in I don't think I was going more than two or three miles an hour.

Q. Did you at any time reduce your speed suddenly?
A. No It was just all gradual.

Q. When were you first aware of the Swanson's vehicle?
A. I never was.

Q. You didn't see it before the impact?
A. No, I didn't. And I had looked behind me and I looked in my rear-view mirror, too, and I didn't see him at all. I, in the side mirror I looked.

Q. How far into your turn or, well, you indicated that your intention was to turn. Had you started that turn?
A. Yes, I'd started the turn and I was almost down into my driveway. I was across the double yellow line.

Q. All right, so your car would be, would you say entirely in the left-hand lane or westbound lane when it was hit?
A. Well, I think part of my wheels were on my own driveway.

48

Q. So you had completed more than half of your turn?
A. Oh yeah.

Q. When were you first aware, you said you weren't aware of the other vehicle. Were you aware of it at impact?
A. Well, yes (inaudible).

Q. You didn't lose consciousness?
A. I did. I heard a crash and glass breaking. And um, I saw my friend going past me through my window. And then I must have hit the telephone pole because I blacked out completely.

Q. The Swanson vehicle as far as you're able to deduce at this time was traveling what direction?
A. East towards Billings.

Q. Overtaking you then, apparently?
A. Um huh.

Q. To your knowledge, was it apparent that Swanson had done anything to try and avoid this impact?
A. Well, no. As a matter of fact, I felt that he was going so fast, he'd have to have been going so fast that there's no way he could have avoided it except staying in his own lane. Staying in the right lane instead of turning into my passing lane.

Q. On what basis do you come to the conclusion that he was traveling too fast or that he was traveling fast?
A. Because I hadn't seen him as I turned. And he'd have to have been coming at a tremendous amount of speed in order for him to get up on us so close and so fast.

Q. Was there anything going on inside of the car that might have been a momentary distraction to you?
A. No, cause I don't play the radio or the, I don't even have a tape deck in the car, so I don't play that when I'm driving cause I don't like . . .

Q. Any conversation going on at the time?
A. No, nothing heavy. Just, in fact I can't even remember anything with it going on as far as conversations go that would even begin to cause a distraction.

Q. What was the point of impact on your car?
A. Okay. It was on the driver's side in the rear.

Q. Did you observe the other vehicle, the Swanson pickup, after the accident?
A. Yes, I've been down to see it.

Q. Where was the impact on it?
A. Okay, the right front fender on his.

49

Q. Following . . .
A. (Is that right?)

Q. Following this impact, where did your vehicle end up?
A. Well, just a minute. It's the left front fender.

Q. On the Swanson truck?
A. Yes.

Q. All right.
A. And where did my vehicle end up?

Q. Um huh.
A. Against the telephone pole.

Q. It actually came in contact with the pole?
A. Yes, and it dented the car. And the pole pushed it in quite a bit.

Q. Are you completely off the road?
A. Yes.

Q. And headed what direction?
A. Okay, headed north, nope, just a minute. I think south.

Q. All right, if you're not sure.
A. Okay.

Q. Yet, this would be on the right or left side of the road?
A. On the left side.

Q. Are you beyond your driveway?
A. Yes, well, a few feet off of the driveway if that. Yeah, a few feet off the driveway.

Q. Where was the Swanson pickup when it came to rest?
A. I have no idea because I didn't see it.

Q. Did you have any conversation with Mr. Swanson after the accident?
A. I didn't, no.

Q. To your knowledge, was it, had Mr. Swanson had anything intoxicating to drink?
A. No.

Q. Had you or your passengers?
A. No.

Q. Do you know of any witnesses to this accident other than the people involved?
A. My daughter seen a car get hit, but it was down in our yard. And she, she just knew there was an accident because our yard sits down a ways from where the highway was.

50

Q. You mentioned a semi.
A. Um huh.

Q. Is there, has that party been identified?
A. I don't think so. It was chip truck from, uh, . . .

Q. I see. Would it have been in a position to have seen the accident?
A. I think so, yes.

Q. Mrs. Anderson, I still have a few questions. I'm coming to the end of this side of the tape. I'll have to stop the recorder and turn over to the other side. Before I do, you are aware that I've recorded the entire conversation thus far?
A. Yes.

Q. And it's been done with your consent?
A. If you will hold, I'll change over the tape.

(End Tape, Side 1)

This is Tim Taner recording an in-person interview with Sarah Anderson on September 4, 1985. It concerns her accident on August 20, '85.

Q. All right, Mrs. Anderson, you're still with me?
A. Yes.

Q. And you're aware I'm once again recording?
A. Right.

Q. Was either car driveable following this accident?
A. I don't know if his was, but I know mine is completely totaled out.

Q. All right. Were, what injuries were sustained in your car to you and your passengers? Now that, anything that you're actually aware of by personal knowledge. Doesn't have to be anything too great.
A. Okay, I had a concussion, um, all my left side is bruised internally, all the soft tissue is bruised, um, my shoulder and my neck. Okay, and then I'm going to go in today and I think there's been damage to my bladder and to my colon. And then, um, Mrs. Weston, she had three broken ribs. Her leg was broke in two places. She has a broken clavical, a concussion, and problems with her neck, too, I think. I'm not, I'm not sure. Then to Laura Weston, she had a whiplash and Samuel did also. And Laura had bruises, a concussion too.

Q. Following the accident, where did you receive your first medical attention?
A. At Yellowstone County Hospital.

51

Q. Your doctor there?
A. Dr. Gosten.

Q. And how did you get to the hospital?
A. Ambulance.

Q. You had subsequent medical attention, you personally.
Where did you receive that?
A. They put an I.V. in me in the emergency room and got Mrs.
Weston ready, and they took some X-rays of me there. And
then they took us both into Billings.

Q. Did the, the police were at the scene?
A. I think they were, yes.

Q. You don't recall them specifically?
A. Yeah, I do. I recall Alice, um, Pracel there.

Q. The vehicles to your knowledge had not been moved by the
time the police arrived?
A. Oh no, nothing had been.

Q. What relation is Mrs. Weston to you?
A. She's just a good friend.

Q. I see. Does she live in this area?
A. No, she lives in Spokane, Washington.

Q. She had come to visit you?
A. Right.

Q. A social-type visit?
A. Yes. She just came for a vacation.

Q. Had your passengers registered any kind of complaint
about your driving prior to this accident?
A. No.

Q. Mrs. Anderson, I think that completes my interview, but
is there anything further you would comment on? Something
we haven't discussed to this point?
A. No, there isn't.

Q. You are aware that I've recorded this entire
conversation using one side of a tape and part of another?
A. Yes, I have.

Q. It was done with your full knowledge and consent?
A. Right.

Q. Everything you've told me in the course of this
interview is true?
A. Yes.

Q. Then that completes the recording and I'll turn off the
machine.

52

EXHIBIT A: SID SILKER, M.D., LETTER OF SEPTEMBER 23, 1986

September 23, 1986

Attorneys, Inc. P.C.
126 E Broadway, Suite 25
P.O. Box 7742
Missoula, MT 59807

RE: Sarah Anderson

To Whom It May Concern:

I have referred Sarah Anderson to the Pain Center at Billings Community Rehabilitation Center for evaluation of her shoulder pain and neck pain. This pain she initially began experiencing as the result of a rear end automobile collision in the summer of 1985.

Despite multiple modalities of treatment locally, we have not succeeded in reducing her pain to an acceptable degree, either for her or for us. It is my belief that the pain that she is currently experiencing is the result of the motor vehicle accident that occurred last year.

If you have any other questions please feel free to contact me.

Sincerely,

Sid Silker

Sid Silker, M.D.
P.O. Box 1045
Laurel, MT 59248

SRS/bd
C: File

53

EXHIBIT B: KEITH MAKIE, PH.D.
PAIN CLINIC DIRECTOR, LETTER OF
JANUARY 21, 1987

January 21, 1987

Mr. Rex Palmer
Attorneys, Inc.
126 East Broadway
Missoula, Montana
59802

RE: Sarah Anderson

Dear Mr. Palmer:

The purpose of this letter is to answer your questions about the program we have recommended for your client, Sarah Anderson and the cost of that program. Sarah, as you know, was evaluated in our Diagnostic Pain Clinic on 12/9/86; it was the unanimous recommendation of the Evaluation Team that she seek out a highly structured, interdisciplinary, chronic pain treatment program. The evaluation suggested that not only does Sarah have an extremely complicated physical pain problem, but this physical pain problem is exacerbated by a great deal of general emotional distress and enumerable family problems.

Your specific question about our program was what exactly would we be recommending for Sarah and what would the cost be, and what outcomes might be expected. Our program is truly interdisciplinary and residential. We have the best of both worlds in that we have a highly trained interdisciplinary team affiliated with Billings Community Rehabilitation Center to do the treatment while we have the people stay in a home-like residential facility with twenty-four hour nursing care. Our program is aimed specifically at increasing activity level, returning people to as much of their function, prior to the injury, as possible, given the physical effects of the injury. Our goal is to get people active, to strengthen, stretch their muscles, to get them back into activities of daily living, and to eventually, in most cases, return them to work. Our program is seven weeks in length, involves a large vocational component, and addresses not only physical factors, but also psychological and family factors. The cost of the program at the present time is between $25,000 and $27,000 for the seven-week program. By the end of the program the Evaluation Team felt that Sarah would very likely be able to return to her former, fairly active lifestyle, and even work outside the home, if she chose to. The Evaluation Team predicted that by the end of the

54

program the chronic pain and its attendant problems would cease to dominate Sarah's life. Much of the psychological upheaval we found in the evaluation would be reduced and we would also be able to improve her family situation. There was no doubt in the minds of the Evaluation Team that Sarah would not only find some relief from her seemingly unrelenting pain, but she would also be able to resume the activities of her life very close to what they had been before the accident.

The Evaluation Team was also unanimous in their prediction that unless Sarah took advantage of such an interdisciplinary, highly structured, intensive pain treatment program, she would continue to deteriorate. The Team felt this deterioration not only would manifest itself in decreased activity level, increased deconditioning, lack of mobility, but also that the great deal of psychological distress she reports at the present time, would worsen; her family situation would worsen to the point where the prediction was that the family would break down.

I hope this general description provides you with the information you need. If you need any more specific information I would be more than happy to provide it to you. You can either write to me or call me at 248-2400, extension 3634.

Sincerely,

Keith Makie

Keith C. Makie, Ph.D.
Pain Clinic Director

KCM/brm

EXHIBIT C: PHOTOGRAPHS RELEVANT TO THE ACCIDENT

Photo 1: Sarah Anderson's Vehicle

Photos 2-5: Sarah Anderson's Vehicle; Donald Swanson's Vehicle

56

Photo 3

Photo 4

Photo 5

Photos 6-9: Devlin Road

Photo 6

Photo 7

Photo 8

Photo 9

Exhibit D: Accident Report, of Montana Highway Patrol

STATE OF MONTANA   ACCIDENT INVESTIGATOR'S REPORT

ACCIDENT NUMBER	YEAR	AGENCY	BADGE	MONTH	SEQ NO	DATE OF ACCIDENT	TIME	CITY	COUNTY
	8 5	0 0 0 1	5 5 0	8	0 2	0 8 2 0 8 5	1 6 5 5	YELLOWSTONE	5 4

OCCURRED ON DEVLIN ROAD   AT INTERSECTION OF PVT. ROAD   MILES -|-|7 N S |K| W   OF LAUREL

IF NOT AT INTERSECTION	OF	FUNCTIONAL CLASS	HIGHWAY	MILEPOST
FEET MILES N S E W			5 2 5 7 0 0 1	+ 0 5 0 0

INDICATE NORTH WITH ARROW ↑   131

FIRST HARMFUL EVENT	C	4
FIRST OBJECT HIT OFF RDWY	0	7
INJURY SEVERITY		2
DAMAGE SEVERITY		1
CLASS OF TRAFFICWAY		4
BIKEWAY		0
GRADE & HORIZ ALIGN		3
ROADWAY RELATED LOC		0
RELATIONSHIP TO JUNCTION		0
NUMBER OF VEHICLES	C	2
NUMBER OF PEDESTRIANS	0	0
NUMBER OF FATALITIES	0	0
NUMBER OF INJURIES	0	5
WEATHER CONDITION		5
ROAD CONDITION		1
LIGHT CONDITION		1
TRAFFIC CONTROLS	1	4

RANGE 2 6 W TOWNSHIP 1 7 N SECTION 3 5 ACCIDENT NARRATIVE

VEH. #1 WAS MAKING LEFT TURN AND VEH. #2 WAS ATTEMPTING TO
PASS #1 IN A NO PASSING ZONE. #2 IN PASSING LANE STEPPED ON
BRAKES AND TURNED TO RIGHT. VEH #2 HIT #1 IN THE LEFT REAR
CORNER, KNOCKING #1 SIDEWAYS AND OFF RDWY, & INTO POWER POLE.
#2 WENT STRAIGHT AHEAD AND STOPPED IN MIDDLE OF ROAD

DAMAGE TO OTHER PROPERTY		
TYPE	0	0
SEVERITY		0
OWNERSHIP		0
POSTED SPEED	5	0
ENGINEERING STUDY REQUEST		0
ACCIDENT ANALYSIS I	0	2
ACCIDENT ANALYSIS II	0	0
TYPE OF COLLISION		3

OFFICER'S SIGNATURE	BADGE NO.	DEPT.	DATE	DATE NOTIFIED	TIME	DATE ARRIVED	TIME
Alice Pracel	155	MHP	8/22/85	0 8 2 0 8 5	1 7 0 9	0 8 2 0 8 5	1 7 5 5

DRIVER / PEDESTRIAN	NAME (LAST)	FIRST	MIDDLE	ADDRESS
	ANDERSON	SARAH	T.	Box 336, LAUREL, MT

DRIVER LICENSE NUMBER	STATE	OPER CHAUF OTHER	DRIVER LICENSE STATUS	DATE OF BIRTH
5 1 9 4 6 8 5 0 5	MONTANA	M T	i RESTRICTION COMPLIANCE 1	0 3 1 0 4 1

VIOLATION CODE	SUMMONS NO.	CONTRIBUTING	DRIVER
VIOLATION CODE	SUMMONS NO.	FACTORS 0 0 0 0 0	0 44 F 1 0 2

SEAT POSITION	NAME	ADDRESS	ALC	AGE	SEX	BELT	LOC	INJ
FRONT CENTER								
FRONT RIGHT	LISA WESTON		0	37	F	0	2	2
REAR LEFT	LAURA WESTON		0	16	F	0	0	2
REAR CENTER								
REAR RIGHT	SAMUEL WESTON		0	17	M	0	2	3

INSURANCE CARRIER STATE FARM   THIS DRIVER/PEDESTRIAN, WAS HEADED N S (E) W ON DEVLIN RD.

POLICY NO. 5062-3-13-43

	VEHICLE NO.	0 1	INTENDED TO	0 4	WRECKER CO	GREGORY'S
PROPERTY DAMAGED BY THIS VEHICLE	PEDESTRIAN NO.		INTENDED TO	0 4	REQUESTED BY	

OWNER _____ VEHICLE MAKE DATSUN   BODY 23 TRLR 0 VEH YEAR 75   VEHICLE DAMAGE (x) IF OVER $4 00 ☒

ADDRESS _____

VEHICLE ID NUMBER	LICENSE PLATE NO.	STATE	LIC YEAR	
J H L 7 6 0 8 4 5 8 6	5 9 - 3 9 8 1	MONTANA M T	85	DAMAGE SEVERITY 1

OWNER OF VEHICLE ROSS ANDERSON   ADDRESS BOX 336 LAUREL MT

DRIVER / PEDESTRIAN	NAME (LAST)	FIRST	MIDDLE	ADDRESS
	SWANSON	DONALD	M.	212 CREEK LOOP RD, LAUREL MT

DRIVER LICENSE NUMBER	STATE	OPER CHAUF OTHER	DRIVER LICENSE STATUS	DATE OF BIRTH
5 6 7 0 7 0 3	MONTANA	M T	1 RESTRICTION COMPLIANCE 1	0 7 0 3 6 7

VIOLATION CODE	SUMMONS NO.	CONTRIBUTING	DRIVER
5 2 6 0 0 2	5 1 0 M 0 1 2 0 2 5	FACTORS 0 0 0 0 5	0 18 M 2 0 4

SEAT POSITION	NAME	ADDRESS	ALC	AGE	SEX	BELT	LOC	INJ
FRONT CENTER								
FRONT RIGHT								
REAR LEFT								
REAR CENTER								
REAR RIGHT								

INSURANCE CARRIER ALL-RISK   THIS DRIVER/PEDESTRIAN, WAS HEADED N S (E) W ON DEVLIN RD.

POLICY NO. 020626048

	VEHICLE NO.	0 2	INTENDED TO	0 2	WRECKER CO	GREGORY'S
PROPERTY DAMAGED BY THIS VEHICLE	PEDESTRIAN NO.		INTENDED TO	0 2	REQUESTED BY	

OWNER _____ VEHICLE MAKE CHEVROLET   BODY 18 TRLR 0 VEH YEAR 80   VEHICLE DAMAGE (x) IF OVER $ 1 00 X

ADDRESS _____

VEHICLE ID NUMBER	LICENSE PLATE NO.	STATE	LIC YEAR	
C K L 1 H A 7 7 8 3 5 7 7	D 0 0 G 1 E	MONTANA M T	86	DAMAGE SEVERITY 1

OWNER OF VEHICLE _____   ADDRESS _____

HQ-1599

60

EXHIBIT E: OIL PAINTINGS BY SARAH ANDERSON

Four (4) Original Oil Paintings by Sarah Anderson

EXHIBIT F: NEWSPAPER CLIPPING SHOWING SARAH ANDERSON PAINTING MINIATURE FIGURES ON FINGERNAILS

PAGE TWELVE–THURSDAY, NOVEMBER 10, 1983

Jacki Sander took home a miniature souvenir from the Art and Craft show over the weekend. Sarah Anderson paints a very small figure on her finger nail. A continuous slide show, toys, stained glass work and other beautiful examples of Mineral county crafts were on display.

62

SUMMARY

A settlement is a resolution of a legal dispute without the need for a complete trial. To achieve this goal, a party may use a settlement precis. This is an advocacy document that tries to persuade the opponent (or the insurance company of the opponent) to settle the case in a certain way—or more accurately, for a certain amount. The precis presents the facts of the case, the theories of liability, the nature of past and anticipated expenses, and other matters that pertain to damages. If the case is more complex or elaborate, the advocacy document is often called a settlement brochure.

Key Terms

settlement
settlement precis
settlement brochure

Appendix A
Nonfault Insurance

R. Keeton & A. Widiss, *Insurance Law* 410–13 (Student Ed. 1988).

Insurance policies typically provide for the payment of benefits upon the occurrence of described events and without regard to whether those events were caused by the fault of either the insured or another person. Thus, most coverages are appropriately characterized as "no-fault insurance." For example, several of the coverages commonly included in automobile insurance policies provide such protection. The principal coverages of this type—that have been and continue to be selected for inclusion by most vehicle owners—are collision coverage (for damage to the insured vehicle as a result of a "collision" with another object), comprehensive coverage (for damage to an insured vehicle caused by falling objects, fire, theft, explosions, earthquakes and a variety of other risks), and medical payments coverage.

In general, the interests protected by "first party" motor vehicle insurance coverages have been those of the named insureds, persons who are closely associated with named insureds such as family members who live in a named insured's household, and persons who are authorized either to drive or to be passengers in an insured vehicle—that is, insurers are committed to provide benefits designed to indemnify such insureds when losses are sustained either by them or by property owned by them unless coverage is subject to a specific exclusion or other restriction. Each of these coverages is appropriately viewed as a first-party, no-fault insurance because the insurance benefits are paid to the insured without regard to any fault determination.

During the first half of the twentieth century, every state enacted some type of legislation that was either designed to encourage or that required motorists to acquire liability insurance which would assure accident victims that the insured would be able to provide at least minimum levels of financial responsibility in regard to injuries resulting from the negligent operation of an automobile. Liability insurance is a third-party, fault based insurance—that is, the insurance company agrees to provide indemnification for an insured in the event that the insured is legally obligated to a third party who is injured as a consequence of the insured's negligence.

In the 1960s, every state enacted legislation which required that uninsured motorist insurance (which provides indemnification to an insured who is injured by an uninsured motorist) either be included in all automobile insurance policies or that it be offered to all purchasers of automobile insurance policies. In the 1970s and 1980s, legislation in many states has required insurers to afford purchasers underinsured motorist insurance. Uninsured and underinsured motorist insurance . . . are fault-based, first-party insurance: the insurer is only obligated to an insured when the insured is legally entitled to recover from the uninsured or underinsured motorist.

In the latter portion of the 1960s, proposals for the substantial expansion of the use of no-fault automobile insurance coverage became the center of an active controversy over reform of the automobile accident reparations system. In August of 1970, Massachusetts enacted the first no-fault automobile insurance law in the United States. Thereafter, approximately half the states adopted legislation which mandated that some form of no-fault coverage be included in automobile or motor vehicle insurance policies. The requirements imposed by these statutes served to broaden the extent of no-fault protection that had been afforded by the medical payments coverages which had been commonly included in automobile insurance policies for many years.

Many first-party insurance coverages—such as life insurance, health insurance, disability insurance, sick leave, etc.—provide individuals with protection at all times, and these coverages frequently are sources of indemnification when persons are injured in motor vehicle accidents without regard to a determination of fault. Each of these sources of compensation or indemnification is provided without regard to any fault determination.

Consequently, when an individual is injured in a motor vehicle accident, several sources or types of insurance coverage may apply to the occurrence. In some situations, accident victims may be entitled to secure compensation by some insurance that is fault based. In most circumstances, indemnification will be provided by motor vehicle insurance coverages that are not predicated on any determination of fault, as well as first-party insurance coverages that are not limited to injuries that result from motor vehicle accidents. For example, most motor vehicle insurance policies have included medical payments coverage which provides a limited amount of no-fault, first-party insurance. And no-fault legislation has increased the amount of first-party, no-fault insurance coverage for accident victims in approximately half the states.

Figure A.1.   Provisions of State "No-Fault" Laws

State	No-Fault Benefits	Limitation on Damages For Pain and Suffering	Vehicle Damage	Effective Date
Arkansas	Purchase is optional. $5,000 per person for medical and hospital expenses. Wage loss: 70% of lost wages up to $140 a week, beginning 8 days after accident, for up to 52 weeks. Essential services: up to $70 a week for up to 52 weeks, subject to 8-day waiting period. Death benefit: $5,000.	None.	Stays under tort system.	July 1, 1974.
Colorado	$50,000 for medical expenses. $50,000 for rehabilitation. Lost income: Benefits for 100% of the first $125 per week, 70% of the next $125, and 60% of the remainder up to $400 per week, limited to 52 weeks. Essential services: Up to $25 a day for up to 52 weeks. Death benefit: $1,000.	Cannot recover unless medical and rehabilitation services have reasonable value of more than $2,500, or injury causes permanent disfigurement, permanent disability, dismemberment, loss of earnings for more than 52 weeks, or death.	Stays under tort system.	April 1, 1974. These provisions effective Jan. 1, 1985.

	Benefits	Restrictions on lawsuits		Effective date
Connecticut	$5,000 benefits for medical, hospital, funeral (limit $2,000), lost wages, survivors' loss, and substitute service expenses. Wage loss, substitute service, and survivors' benefits limited to 85% of actual loss.	Cannot recover unless economic loss exceeds $400, or there is permanent injury, bone fracture, disfigurement, dismemberment, or death.	Stays under tort system.	Jan. 1, 1973.
Delaware	$15,000 per person and $30,000 per accident. Covers medical costs, loss of income, loss of services, and funeral expenses (limited to $3,000).	None. But amount of no-fault benefits received can't be used as evidence in suits for general damages.	Stays under tort system.	Jan. 1, 1972.
District of Columbia	Medical and rehabilitation benefits of $50,000 or $100,000. Work loss benefits of $12,000 or $24,000. Up to $4,000 in funeral benefits. Purchase is optional. Motorists can buy any combination they choose.	Victims who are covered by no-fault benefits have 60 days after accident to decide whether to receive no-fault benefits. Victims who choose to get no-fault benefits cannot recover damages unless injury resulted in substantial permanent scarring or disfigurement; substantial and medically demonstrable permanent impairment which has significantly affected the	Stays under tort system.	Original law effective Oct. 1, 1983. This version effective June 2, 1986.

Figure A.1.   Continued

State	No-Fault Benefits	Limitation on Damages For Pain and Suffering	Vehicle Damage	Effective Date
District of Columbia (continued)		ability of the victim to perform professional activities or usual and customary daily activities; a medically demonstrable impairment that prevents victim from performing substantially all of his or her usual customary daily activities for more than 180 continuous days; or medical and rehabilitation expenses or work loss exceeding the amount of no-fault benefits available.		
Florida	$10,000 per person. Pays 80% of medical costs; 60% of lost income; replacement services; and funeral costs (limited to $5,000). Deductibles of $250, $500, $1,000, and $2,000 available.	Cannot recover unless injury results in significant, permanent loss of important body function; permanent injury; significant and permanent scarring or disfigurement; or death.	Stays under tort system.	Jan. 1, 1972, for original law. Provisions at left effective Oct. 1, 1982.

Georgia **The Georgia no-fault law was repealed April 17, 1991.**	Aggregate limit of $5,000. Up to $2,500 for medical costs. 85% of lost income with maximum $200 week. $20 day for necessary services. Survivors' benefits same as lost income benefits had victim lived. $1,500 funeral benefit.	Could not recover unless medical costs exceeded $500, disability lasted 10 days, or injury resulted in death, fractured bone, permanent disfigurement, dismemberment, permanent loss of body function, permanent, partial or total loss of sight or hearing.	Stayed under tort system.	Mar. 1, 1975. Repeal effective Oct. 1, 1991.
Hawaii	Aggregate limit of $15,000. Pays for medical and hospital services; rehabilitation; occupational, psychiatric, and physical therapy; up to $900 monthly for income loss, substitute services and survivors' loss; and up to $1,500 for funeral expenses.	Cannot recover unless medical and rehabilitation expenses exceed a floating threshold established annually by the insurance commissioner. Can also recover if injury results in death; significant permanent loss of use of body part or function; or permanent and serious disfigurement that subjects injured person to mental or emotional suffering.	Stays under tort system.	Sept. 1, 1974.

Figure A.1.   Continued

State	No-Fault Benefits	Limitation on Damages For Pain and Suffering	Vehicle Damage	Effective Date
Kansas	$4,500 per person for medical expenses. Wage loss: up to $900 a month for one year. $4,500 for rehabilitation costs. Substitute service benefits of $25 a day for 365 days. Survivor's benefits: Up to $900 a month for lost income, $25 a day for substitution benefits, for not over one year after death, minus any disability benefits victim received before death. Funeral benefit: $2,000.	Cannot recover unless medical costs exceed $2,000, or injury results in permanent disfigurement, fracture to a weight-bearing bone, a compound, comminuted, displaced or compressed fracture, loss of a body member, permanent injury, permanent loss of a body function, or death.	Stays under tort system.	Jan. 1, 1974.
Kentucky	Aggregate limit of $10,000. Covers medical expense; funeral expense up to $1,000; Income loss up to $200 weekly, with as much as 15% deducted for income tax savings; up to $200 a week each for replacement services loss, survivors economic loss, and survivors replacement	Cannot recover unless medical expenses exceed $1,000, or injury results in permanent disfigurement; fracture of a bone; a compound, comminuted, displaced or compressed fracture; loss of a body member; permanent injury; permanent loss of a body function; or death. But	Stays under tort system.	July 1, 1975.

State	Benefits	Limitations on tort recovery	Tort system	Effective date
Kentucky (Continued)	services loss. Motorist has right to reject no-fault.	limitation does not apply to those who reject no-fault system or to those injured by driver who has rejected it.		
Maryland	$2,500 in benefits for medical, hospital, funeral, wage loss, and substitute service expenses.	None.	Stays under tort system.	Jan. 1, 1973.
Massachusetts	$8,000 in benefits for medical, funeral, wage loss, and substitute service expenses. Wage loss and substitute service benefits are limited to 75% of actual loss.	Can recover only if medical costs exceed $2,000, or in case of death, loss of all or part of body member, permanent and serious disfigurement, loss of sight or hearing, or a fracture.	Stays under tort system after Jan. 1, 1977. Prior to then, no tort liability for vehicle damage.	Jan. 1, 1971. This version effective Jan. 1, 1989.
Michigan	Unlimited medical & hospital benefits; funeral benefits not less than $1,750 nor more than $5,000; lost wages up to $1,475 per month, adjusted annually to keep up with cost of living; substitute services of $20 a day payable to victim or survivor.	Cannot recover unless injuries result in death, serious impairment of body function, or permanent serious disfigurement.	Tort liability abolished, except in cases where damage is not over $400.	Oct. 1, 1973, for original law; Oct. 1, 1988, for this version.

Figure A.1. Continued

State	No-Fault Benefits	Limitation on Damages For Pain and Suffering	Vehicle Damage	Effective Date
Minnesota	$20,000 for medical expense. $20,000 for other benefits, including 85% of lost income up to $250 weekly; $200 a week for replacement services, with 8-day waiting period; up to $200 weekly in survivors economic loss benefits; up to $200 weekly for survivors replacement service loss; and $2,000 for funeral benefits.	Cannot recover unless medical expenses (not including X-rays and rehabilitation) exceed $4,000; or disability exceeds 60 days; or the injury results in permanent disfigurement; permanent injury; or death.	Stays under tort system.	Jan. 1, 1975.
Nevada **The Nevada no-fault law was repealed June 5, 1979.**	Aggregate limit was $10,000. Paid for medical and rehabilitation expenses; up to $175 a week for loss of income; up to $18 a day for 104 weeks for replacement services; survivors' benefits of not less than $5,000 and not more than victim would have gotten in disability benefits for 1 year; and $1,000 for death.	Could not recover unless medical benefits exceeded $750 or injury caused chronic or permanent injury, permanent partial or permanent total disability, disfigurement, more than 180 days of inability to work at occupation, fracture of a major bone, dismemberment, permanent loss of a body function, or death.	Stayed under tort system.	Feb. 1, 1974. Repeal effective Jan. 1, 1980.

State	Benefits	Restrictions on tort actions		Effective date
New Jersey	Up to $250,000 for medical and hospital costs, subject to a $250 deductible and 20 percent co-insurance between $250 and $5,000. Wage loss up to $100 a week for one year. Substitute services up to $12 a day for maximum of $4,380 per person. Funeral expenses of $1,000. Survivors' benefits equal to amount victim would have received if he had not died. Motorist may exclude all benefits except medical and hospital. Medical coverage may be bought with deductibles of $500, $1,000, or $2,500.	Motorist selects one of these two options: (1) Will be liable for any non-economic loss that he causes as result of motor vehicle accident. (2) Will not be liable for non-economic loss unless victim suffers death, dismemberment, permanent loss of use of body organ, member, function or system, permanent consequential limitation of use of a body organ or member, significant limitation of use of body function or system, non-permanent impairment that disables victim for at least 90 of the 180 days following injury. Motorists choosing second option pay a lower insurance premium.	Stays under tort system.	Jan. 1, 1973, for original law. Jan. 1, 1991, for this version.
New York	Aggregate limit of $50,000 for medical, wage loss, and substitute service benefits. Wage loss: 80% of actual loss with benefit limited to $2,000 per month. Substitute services benefits: $25 a day for one year. In	Cannot recover unless disabled for 90 of the 180 days after accident, or injury causes dismemberment; significant disfigurement; fracture; loss of a fetus; permanent loss of use of body organ,	Stays under tort system.	Feb. 1, 1974, for original law.

Figure A.1.   Continued

State	No-Fault Benefits	Limitation on Damages For Pain and Suffering	Vehicle Damage	Effective Date
New York (continued)	fatal cases, estate gets $2,000 in addition to above benefits.	member, function, or system; permanent consequential limitation of use of body organ or member; significant limitation of use of body function or system; or death.		
North Dakota	Overall limit of $30,000 per person. Covers medical and rehabilitation costs, up to $150 a week for income loss, up to $15 a day for replacement services, up to $150 a week for survivors income loss, up to $15 a day for survivors replacement services loss, and up to $3,500 for funeral expenses.	Cannot recover from insured person unless injury results in more than $2,500 in medical expenses, more than 60 days of disability, serious and permanent disfigurement, dismemberment, or death.	Stays under tort system.	Jan. 1, 1976. This version effective 1991.
Oregon	$10,000 medical benefits. 70% of lost wages up to $1,250 a month. $30 a day for substitute services. $15 a day for child care, to maximum of $450. Wage	None.	Stays under tort system.	Jan. 1, 1972. Jan. 1, 1990, for benefits at left.

State	Benefits	Tort Restrictions	Effective Date
Oregon (continued)	loss and substitute services paid from first day if disability lasts 14 days; are limited to 52 weeks.		
Pennsylvania	$5,000 for medical expenses. Optional coverages are available up to $177,500, including income loss benefits, accidental death benefits, and funeral benefits, in addition to medical benefits. An extraordinary medical benefit coverage up to $1,100,000 is available.	Motorist chooses between a full-tort option, with no limit on general damages, and a limited-tort option. Those choosing the limited-tort option cannot recover for non-economic loss unless injury results in serious impairment of body function, permanent serious disfigurement, or death.	July 1, 1990.
South Carolina	Aggregate limit of $1,000. Covers medical and funeral costs, loss of earnings (if desired), loss of essential services. Purchase is optional.	None.	Oct. 1, 1974.
South Dakota	Purchase is optional. $2,000 in medical expense. $60 a week for wage loss, starting 14 days after injury, for up to 52 weeks. $10,000 death benefit.	None.	Jan. 1, 1972.

Figure A.1. Continued

State	No-Fault Benefits	Limitation on Damages For Pain and Suffering	Vehicle Damage	Effective Date
Texas	$2,500 per person overall limit. Covers medical and funeral expenses, lost income, and loss of services. Purchase optional.	None.	Stays under tort system.	90 days after adjournment of 1973 regular session.
Utah	$3,000 per person for medical and hospital expenses. 85% of gross income loss, up to $250 a week, for up to 52 weeks. $20 a day for loss of services for up to 365 days. Both wage loss and service loss coverages subject to 3-day waiting periods that disappear if disability lasts longer than two weeks. $1,500 funeral benefit. $3,000 survivor's benefit.	Cannot recover unless medical expenses exceed $3,000, or injury results in dismemberment or fracture, permanent disfigurement, permanent disability, or death.	Stays under tort system.	Jan. 1, 1974. Revision effective July 1, 1986.
Virginia	Purchase is optional. $2,000 for medical and funeral costs. $100 a week for wage loss with limit of 52 weeks.	None.	Stays under tort system.	July 1, 1972.

SOURCE: State Farm Insurance Companies, *No Fault Press Release Manual*, E-100 to E-106 (1977—).

Appendix B
Accident Reports and Financial Responsibility

State	ACCIDENT REPORT FILING REQUIREMENTS			FINANCIAL RESPONSIBILITY (FR) REQUIREMENTS	
	Property Damage in Excess of	Personal Injury or Death	Days to File Report	Minimum Policy Coverage Limits (in Thousands)	Length of Time Proof of FR must be Maintained
Alabama	$250 (§32–7–5)	Yes	10	20/40/10 (§32–7–2)	3 years (§32–7–31)
Alaska	$500 (§28.20,230)	Yes	10	50/100/25 (§28.20.070)	3 years (§28.20.540)
Arizona	$500 (§28–606)	Yes	5	15/30/10 (§28–1102)	3 years (§28–1178)
Arkansas	$500 (§27–19–501)	Yes	30	25/50/15 (§27–19–701)	3 years (§27–19–721)
California[1]	$500 (§16000 Vehicle Code) (V.C.)	Yes	10	15/30/5 (§16056 V.C.)	3 years (§16480 V.C.)
Colorado	$1,000 (§42–7–202)[2]	Yes	10	25/50/15 (§42–7–103)	3 years (§42–7–408)
Connecticut	$1,000 (§14–108a)	Yes	5	20/40/10 (§14–112)	12 months (§14–112i)
Delaware	$500 (21 §4203)[3]	Yes	Immediately	15/30/10 (21 §101)	N/A[4]
District of Columbia	$200 (18 §803)	Yes	5	25/50/10 (40 §435)	3 years (18 §805)
Florida	$500 (§316.066)[5]	Yes	5	10/20/10 (§324.021)	3 years (§324.131)

State	Amount	Report Required	Days	FR Limits	Report Retention
Georgia	$250 (§40-9-20)	Yes	10	15/30/10 (§40-9-2)	1 year (§40-9-80)
Hawaii	$1,000 (§287-4)	Yes	1	25/unlimited/10 (§294-10)	3 years (§287-40)
Idaho	$750 (§49-1305)	Yes	Immediately	25/50/15 (§49-117)	3 years (§49-1220)
Illinois	$500 (625 §5/11-406)	Yes	10	20/40/15 (625 §5/7-202)	3 years (625 §5/7-304)
Indiana	$750 (§9-26-1-2)	Yes	10	25/50/10 (§9-25-4-5)	3 years (§9-25-7-3)
Iowa	$500 (§321.266)	Yes	3	20/40/15 (§321A.1)	2 years (§321A.29)
Kansas	$500 (§8-1606)	Yes	Immediately	25/50/10 (§40-3107)	3 years (§40-3118)
Kentucky	$500 (§189.635)	Yes	10	10/20/5 (§187.290)	N/A
Louisiana	$500 (32 §871)	Yes	10	10/20/10 (32 §900)	3 years (32 §908)
Maine	$500 (29 §783)	Yes	5	20/40/10 (29 §787)	3 years (29 §783)
Maryland	See note 6 (§20-107)	Yes	15	20/40/10 (§17-103)	N/A
Massachusetts	$1,000 (90 §26)	Yes	5	20/40/5 (90 §34A)	N/A

[1]California requires the person responsible for the property damage to provide evidence of FR to the other driver, owner or person in charge of the damaged property.
[2]§42-7-202 also requires a police officer to submit an accident report (regardless of the amount of property damage) if one of the participants cannot show proof of insurance.
[3]21 §4203 also requires the filing of an accident report if it appears that an alcohol-impaired driver was involved in the accident.
[4]N/A = Not Applicable.
[5]§316.066 stipulates that a driver need not submit an accident report if a police officer submits the report as required by §324.051.
[6]No accident reports are required if: (1) the accident results in property damage only; (2) a police officer files a report; or (3) a person is physically unable to make a report.

State	ACCIDENT REPORT FILING REQUIREMENTS			FINANCIAL RESPONSIBILITY (FR) REQUIREMENTS	
	Property Damage in Excess of	Personal Injury or Death	Days to File Report	Minimum Policy Coverage Limits (in Thousands)	Length of Time Proof of FR must be Maintained
Michigan	$400 (§257.622)	Yes	Immediately[7]	20/40/10 (§257.520)	3 years (§257.528)
Minnesota	$500 (§169.09)	Yes	10	30/60/10 (§65B.49)	N/A
Mississippi	$250 (§63-15-9)	Yes	10	10/20/5 (§63-15-3)	3 years (§63-15-61)
Missouri	$500 (§303.040)	Yes	30	25/50/10 (§303.020)	3 years (§303.044)
Montana	$400 (§61-7-109)	Yes	10	25/50/10 (§61-6-103)	3 years (§61-6-142)
Nebraska	$500 (§60-505)	Yes	10	25/50/25 (§60-501)	3 years (§60-524)
Nevada	$350 (§484.229)	Yes	10	15/30/10 (§485.105)	3 years (§485.3099)
New Hampshire	$1,000 (§264:25)	Yes	15	25/50/25 (§264:20)	3 years (§264:7)
New Jersey	$500 (§39:4-130)	Yes	10	15/30/5 (§39:6-25)[8]	3 years (§39:6-45)
New Mexico	$50 (§66-3-1014)	Yes	5	25/50/10 (§66-5-208)	1 year (§66-5-229)
New York	$1,000 (§605, Vehicle and Traffic Law) (V.T.L.)	Yes	10	10/20/5 (§311, V.T.L.)[9]	3 years (§330, V.T.L.)

North Carolina	$500 (§20–166.1)	Yes	Immediately	25/50/15 (§20–279.11)	2 years (§20–279.29)
North Dakota	$1,000 (§38–08–09)	Yes	Immediately	25/50/25 (§39–16.1–02)	3 years (§39–16.1–19)
Ohio	$400 (§4509.01, §4509.06)	Yes	30	12.5/25/7.5 (§4509.01)	3 years (§4509.45)
Oklahoma	$300 (47.7–201)	Yes	10	10/20/10 (§47:7–204)	3 years (§47:7–335)
Oregon	$500 (§811.720)	Yes	3	25/50/10[10] (§806.070)	3 years (§806.245)
Pennsylvania[11]	Any acc. not investigated by a police officer. (75 §3747)	Yes	5	15/30/5 (75 §1702)	See footnote 11
Rhode Island	$500 (§31–26–6)	Yes	10	25/50/25 (§31–32–2)	1 year (§31–32–35)
South Carolina	$400 (§56–9–350)	Yes	15	15/30/5 (§56–9–353)	3 years (§56–9–620)
South Dakota	$500/per person or $1,000/per accident (32–34–7)	Yes	Immediately	25/50/25 (§32–35–2)	3 years (§32–35–95)

[7]Accident reports are to be submitted to the investigating police officer who then shall forward the report to the Director of the State Police.
[8]§39:6–25 requires the filing of proof of FR if a driver is involved in an accident resulting in injury, death, or property damage to one person greater than $200.
[9]§311 also requires wrongful death coverage in the amount of 50/100.
[10]§806.075 requires coverage in the amounts of 50/100/10 for those previously convicted of DUI, proof of which shall be maintained for three years.
[11]Pennsylvania law is a combination of financial responsibility, compulsory liability and no-fault insurance reparation systems.

| State | ACCIDENT REPORT FILING REQUIREMENTS | | | FINANCIAL RESPONSIBILITY (FR) REQUIREMENTS | |
	Property Damage in Excess of	Personal Injury or Death	Days to File Report	Minimum Policy Coverage Limits (in Thousands)	Length of Time Proof of FR must be Maintained
Tennessee	$400 §55-12-104)	Yes	20	25/50/10 (§55-12-102)	5 years (§55-12-114)
Texas[12]	$500 (6701h §4)	Yes	10	20/40/15 (6701h §1)	2 years (6701h §1f)
Utah[13]	$750 (§41-6-35)	Yes	5	25/50/15 (§31A-22-302)	3 years (§41-12a-411)
Vermont	$500 (23 §1129)	Yes	3	20/40/10 (23 §800)	3 years (23 §809)
Virginia	$1,000 (§46.2-373)	Yes	5	25/50/20 (§46.2-472)	3 years
Washington	$500 §46.52.030	Yes	1	25/50/10 (§46.29.260)	3 years (§46.29.600)
West Virginia	$250 (§17C-4-7)	Yes	5	20/40/10 (§17D-4-2)	N/A
Wisconsin	$200; $500 for state- or government-owned vehicles. (§346.70)	Yes	10	25/50/10 (§344.01)	3 years (§344.25)
Wyoming	$500 (§31-5-1106)	Yes	10	25/50/20 (§31-9-405)	3 years (31-9-413)

(SOURCE: National Association of Independent Insurers (1994))

[12]6701 §5 requires the filing of proof of FR if a driver is involved in an accident resulting in injury, death or property damage to one person greater than $1,000.
[13]Requires peace officer to file the original accident report with the Department of Public Safety.

Most personal injury attorneys want to have very current information on cases that have been recently litigated in the courts. They need something more current than what is printed in the reporter volumes examined in Chapter 2. Furthermore, only selected cases are printed in the reporters. Attorneys who want a broader overview of courtroom litigation "today" must turn elsewhere. One source is the section containing case summaries printed in daily and weekly legal newspapers. Here are some samples from the feature called "Verdicts & Settlements" in the *San Francisco Daily Journal.*

PERSONAL INJURY

Tow Truck Accident
Rear End Collision

Verdict: $157,000
Case: Scott Butterfield v. Riggs Jones, et al., No. 670,495-7
Court: Alameda Superior
Date: November 23, 1993
Judge: Hon. William L. Dunbar, Dept. 40
Attorneys: Plaintiff—Char Sachson (Law Offices of Bruce Krell, San Francisco). Defendant—Michael C. Osborne (Dryden, Margoles. et al., San Francisco)
Technical experts: Plaintiff—Dr. Bahram Ravani, biomechanical engineer, Sunnyvale
Medical experts: Plaintiff—Patrick S. Zaccalini, M.D., orthopedic surgeon, San Francisco. Defendant—Aubrey Swartz, M.D. treating orthopedic surgeon, San Francisco; Carl Borders, Jr., M.D., orthopedic surgeon, San Francisco; Lisa Jungelas, Ph.D., treating psychologist, Oakland
Facts: On April 6, 1988, Plaintiff Scott Butterfield's vehicle was struck in a rear end collision by a tow truck owned by Defendant Rube and Dan's Body Shop. Their driver was Defendant Rees Riggs Jones. Plaintiff was a 31-year-old carpenter at the time. Defendant admitted liability.
Contentions: Plaintiff contended that the injuries he claimed were the result of this collision and the negligent operation of a motor vehicle by Defendant Jones. Defendants contended that the injuries claimed by Plaintiff were not caused by this accident.
Injuries: 3mm bulge at L4-5 and 3mm bulge at L5/S1 requiring future surgeries; impotence.
Specials in evidence: MEDS $11,636; Future MEDS $20,000; LOE $84,000.
Trial jury: Length 4 days; Poll 12–0; Deliberation 2 days.
Settlement discussions: Plaintiff contends their demand was $107,000 and Defendants offer was $35,000.

PERSONAL INJURY

Van Accident
Broadside Collision

Settlement: $170,000
Case: Case I.D. Confidential
Court: L.A. Superior Pomona
Date: December 1, 1993
Attorneys: Plaintiff—Michael J. Hemming (Diamond Bar), Defendant—Confidential
Medical experts: Plaintiff—Frank Sorrentino, M.D., orthopedic surgeon, City of Industry. Defendant—Dr. William Zaayer, M.D., orthopedic surgeon, Ontario; Paul Northrop, M.D., neurosurgeon, Pomona
Facts: On November 27, 1991, Plaintiff, a 69-year-old retiree driving her automobile, was

struck in a broadside collision by Defendant's Astro van. Defendant denied that he ran the red light.

Contentions: Plaintiff contended that the collision and all injuries were caused by the negligent operation of a motor vehicle by Defendant. Defendant disputed the nature and extent of injuries, claiming that most of Plaintiff's physical conditions were preexisting and not caused by this collision.

Injuries: Plaintiff claimed the following disk herniations; L1-2 (4mm); L2-3 (5mm); L3-4 (7mm); L-4-5 (7mm); and L5-S1 (7mm)—all requiring physical therapy, MRI's, and probable future surgeries.

Specials in evidence: MEDS $17,044; Future MEDS $55,000 (disputed).

Settlement discussions: Plaintiff contends their demand was $250,000 and Defendant offer was $100,000.

PERSONAL INJURY

Medical Malpractice
Sexual Battery

Verdict: $427,194

Case: Tammy Howsmon v. Dr. Dominick A. Ricci, M.D., No. 650,194

Court: San Diego Superior

Date: August 17, 1993

Judge: Hon. Lawrence Kapiloff, Dept. 36

Attorneys: Plaintiff—Cynthia R. Chihak (Cynthia R. Chihak & Associates, San Diego). Defendant—Paul J. Pfingst (Higgs, Fletcher, et al., San Diego)

Technical experts: Plaintiff—Ed McShane, social worker, Escondido

Medical experts: Plaintiff—Nancy Gamble, Ph.D., psychologist, Escondido; Jeffrey Shapiro, M.D., gastroenterologist, Orange. Defendant—Alan Larson, M.D., gastroenterologist, Poway; Lidia Everett, M.D., internal medicine, San Marcos

Facts: On February 24, 1992, Plaintiff Tammy Howsmon, a 31-year-old nurse, went to Defendant Dr. Dominick A. Ricci, a gastroenterologist, for medical advice and examination.

Contentions: Plaintiff contended that Dr. Ricci unnecessarily and negligently performed a rectal examination on her and

that, during the course of the exam, the Defendant committed a sexual battery. Plaintiff claimed that Defendant falsely represented the medical reasonableness, necessity, and appropriateness of the repeated rectal examinations. Defendant Dr. Ricci claimed that his examination of Plaintiff was at all times medically indicated. He further contended that his care met the applicable standards at all times and that any damages alleged by the Plaintiff were not the result of his acts or omissions. Defendant denied sexual misconduct and blamed the Plaintiff's injury on preexisting psychological problems. Defendant also contended that there was anatomical confusion which created a cervical mimicking sensation, causing Plaintiff to feel as if her vagina had been penetrated when the rectum was entered.

Injuries: Severe emotional distress requiring counseling. Plaintiff's spouse claimed a loss of consortium injuries.

Specials in evidence: MEDS $8,040; Future MEDS $1,200.

Trial jury: Length 11 days; Poll 9-3; Deliberation 2 days.

Settlement discussions: Plaintiff contends they demanded $100,000 and Defendant offered nothing.

PERSONAL INJURY

Tropical Vacation Hurricane
Failure to Warn

Verdict: Defense Verdict

Case: Chris Brasseur, Elizabeth Oare v. Empire Tours, Mexicana Airlines, No. C89-3826

Court: USDC Northern

Date: December 10, 1993

Judge: Hon. Charles A. Legge

Attorneys: Plaintiff—Rocky V. Ortega (San Rafael). Defendant—Anthony O. Ricucci (Healey & Taylor, San Francisco) for Empire Tours, Empire Travel Service Inc., and Gisele Freedman; Robert King (Condon & Forsyth, L.A.) for Mexicana Airlines

Technical experts: Plaintiff—Russell Ellsberry, meterologist, Monterey; Val Tupy, travel agent, Sausalito; Bruce Abbott, airline pilot. Defendant—Alexander Anolik, travel industry (for Empire Tours), San Francisco; Ricardo Olea Rodriguez, pilot, Mexicana Airlines, Mexico City, MX

Facts: Defendant Empire Tours and Mexicana Airlines planned Plaintiff's vacation to Cancun, Mexico. The vacation was in September of 1988, during Hurricane Gilbert, with winds of 150 mph and hurricane conditions in the worst storm of the century. Plaintiffs Elizabeth Oare and Christine Brasseur were approximately 45 and 53 years of age when they booked the trip through a local agent in Mill Valley. They spent one week in Puerto Vallarta before departing on a flight to Guadalajara to change planes and on to Cancun on September 10, 1988.

Contentions: Plaintiffs contended that both Empire Tours and Mexicana should have known and warned Plaintiff of an approaching tropical storm in the Caribbean that battered Jamaica before record winds reached Cancun. Plaintiffs contended that the effects of the storm were felt in Cancun before they left Puerto Vallarta and that they should have received warnings from the Defendants. Defendants contested that the area was not in fact a tropical storm region, but a resort area renowned for its weather and that they did not have sufficient advance warning of the "storm of the century" in order to warn Plaintiffs not to proceed to Cancun or to the Yucatan Peninsula. Defendant Empire Tours further contended that once they learned of the severity of the storm, they chartered a private plane, flew into the danger zone onto an airport runway still lacking radio communications, and helped evacuate Plaintiffs (along with 100 other stranded vacationers) from Cancun before commercial flights resumed operations. In addition, Defendants referred to Plaintiffs' brochure and tickets which stated Empire would not be responsible for the clients' weather conditions at the travel destination.

Injuries: Anxiety, emotional distress, fear for their lives, and minor property damages.

Trial jury: Length 2 weeks; Poll 6-0; Deliberation 1 hour.

Settlement discussions: Defendants contend Mexicana offered $5,000 to each Plaintiff, Empire Tours made an indication of $5,000 to each Plaintiff, and Plaintiffs demanded $325,000 (one week before trial).

Other information: A prior arbitration resulted in a Defense ruling; trial de novo by Plaintiffs.

PERSONAL INJURY

Automobile Accident
Drunk Driver

Settlement: $135,000
Case: Case I.D. Confidential
Court: San Diego Superior
Date: December 6, 1993
Judge: Hon. Herbert B. Hoffman, Dept. B
Attorneys: Plaintiff—Jeffrey P. Jacobs (Berglund & Johnson, Granada Hills). Defendant—Thomas Stoddard (Borton, Petrini, et al., San Diego)
Technical experts: Plaintiff—David Toppino, vocational evaluator, L.A.; Joyce Pickersgill, economist, Irvine. Defendant—Paul P. Lees-Haley, vocational counselor, Encino; Roberta Spoon, economist, San Diego
Medical experts: Plaintiff—Daniel Robertson, M.D., orthopedic surgeon, San Diego; Isaac Baskt, M.D., neurologist, San Diego. Defendant—Frederick W. Close, M.D., orthopedic surgeon, La Mesa; Allen Nahum, M.D., biomechanics, San Diego.
Facts: On August 5, 1991, Plaintiff, a 19-year-old warehouse worker, spent the day in Mexico with four teenagers. One of the teenagers, the daughter of the owner of the vehicle, was the group's "designated driver" and did not drink, while the others consumed prodigious amounts of beer and tequila. After returning to Oceanside late in the evening, Plaintiff was asleep in the back seat of the automobile. The "designated driver's" boyfriend, also a Defendant, was driving at a high speed on a residential road, lost control, and struck a telephone pole. Defendant "designated driver" told the investigating police officer that it was she, not her boyfriend, who was driving (in her deposition, she admitted that she had lied so that her mother would not know that it had been her boyfriend who drove at the time of the collision).
Contentions: Plaintiff contended that the Defendant "designated driver" of the vehicle negligently entrusted her vehicle to the in-

toxicated, unlicensed Defendant boyfriend and that both Defendant "designated driver" and her mother (the registered owner) had prior knowledge of the boyfriend's DUI history. Defendant owner of the vehicle claimed no permissive use, no negligent entrustment. The Defendant "designated driver" contended that her boyfriend forcibly took the keys from her and drove against her protests. Defendants also contended that Plaintiff was contributorily negligent for riding in a car with an intoxicated driver and for not wearing a seat belt. (Defendant boyfriend defaulted and was not represented by counsel.)

Injuries: Compound, comminuted fracture of the left (non-major) upper arm requiring open reduction internal fixation; left ulnar radiculopathy requiring physical therapy.

Specials in evidence: MEDS $27,672; LOE $7,000; Future LOE $250,000.

Settlement discussions: Offers and demands were not disclosed.

Other information: This settlement included a release of all claims against the drunk driver/boyfriend and a waiver by Plaintiff of any claim to uninsured motorist benefits from Defendants' insurance company.

PERSONAL INJURY

Product and Premises Liability
Dangerous Condition

Settlement: $1,040,000
Case: Case I.D. Confidential
Court: L.A. Superior Central
Date: October 7, 1994
Disbursement: $1,040,000 to Plaintiff
Contributions: the division of contributions by the three Defendants is confidential.
Attorneys: Plaintiff—Edmont T. Barrett, Matthew B.F. Biren (Matthew B.F. Biren & Associates, L.A.). Defendant—Jeffrey S. Behar, Joseph A. Heath (Ford, Walker, et al., Long Beach); Cheryl J. Faris (L.A.); Louis E. Goldberg (Bragg, Short, et al., West Hollywood)
Technical experts: Plaintiff—Malcolm C. Robbins, forensic engineer, San Diego; Richard H. Anderson, M.S., vocational rehabilitation, Westminster; Peter Formuzis, Ph.D. economist, Santa Ana. Defendant—

Mack Quan, Ph.D., engineer, L.A.
Medical experts: Plaintiff—Franklin Kozin, M.D., rheumatology, La Jolla; Israel Chambi, M.D., neurosurgeon, Orange; Kenneth L. Nudleman, M.D., neurologist, Orange. Defendant—Barry I. Ludwig, M.D., neurologist, Inglewood; Orrin M. Troum, M.D., rheumatology, Santa Monica
Facts: On June 13, 1991, Plaintiff, a 30-year-old peace officer at a medical center, and her sister went to the Defendant hotel to make arrangements for a family Father's Day outing. While there, they went to the public telephones to make a call. When Plaintiff sat down on the seat in the telephone booth, the seat came off, and Plaintiff fell to the floor. The booth and phone belonged to the Defendant phone company, which shared the public telephone revenues with the defendant hotel. The booth was designed and manufactured by a third Defendant.
Contentions: Plaintiff contended that the Defendants hotel and phone company each neglected the booth, assuming that the other Defendant would inspect and maintain it; therefore both failed to inspect or agree between themselves who would inspect. Plaintiff further contended that Defendant manufacturer of the booth was liable because the seat and bracket assembly was defectively designed so as to create a teeter-totter effect; each time that someone sat on the seat, it caused flexion and extension in one direction, thereby causing the bolts to loosen with time. Plaintiff further contended that the Defendant manufacturer also failed to test its product before placing it in the stream of commerce and failed to warn and/or instruct the purchasers of the life expectancy and proper maintenance of the seat and bracket assembly. Plaintiff also held the Defendant phone company on a products theory as a distributor of the product. Defendant hotel took the position that it had no duty to either inspect to maintain or to inspect to request maintenance. Defendant phone company admitted that it had a duty to repair the phone booth, but that it relied upon its customer (the hotel) to inspect and request maintenance. Defendant manufacturer contended that the seat was not their product, but instead was a replacement seat that was attached to its bracket with the wrong bolts; they also contended

that proper maintenance would have avoided this accident. All Defendants agreed that Plaintiff's condition was not RSD, but instead a condition called Reynaud's disease, a disease of unknown etiology which causes vasal spasm and a blue color in the extremities; Defendants contended that Plaintiff's condition, whether RSD or Reynaud's disease, was not related to the fall in the phone booth, but was related to her prior lengthy medical and multiple accidents history.

Injuries: Reflex sympathetic dystrophy (RSD) of the right arm with attendant pain, swelling, and blue color due to vasal spasm requiring 11 stellate ganglion blocks, brachialplexus release surgery, and sympathectomy; Plaintiff claimed permanent and complete disability.

Specials in evidence: MEDS $66,496; Future MEDS not yet determined; LOE $60,694 (including loss of benefits); Future LOE $1,065,103 (total future economic losses).

Settlement discussions: Plaintiff contends she demanded $2,250,000 and Defendants initially offered $85,000.

PERSONAL INJURY

Toxic Tort
Chlorine Gas Exposure

Settlement: $1,400,000
Case: Case I.D. Confidential
Court: L.A. Superior Norwalk
Date: December 21, 1993
Judges: Hon. Lois Anderson Smaltz; Hon. John K. Trotter, Dept. C
Attorneys: Plaintiff—Garo Mardirossian, Joseph Martin Barrett (Mardirossian & Associates, Inc., L.A.). Defendant—Moris A. Thurston, Keith M. Parker, Jon L. Praed, Joseph L. Stanganelli (Latham & Watkins, Costa Mesa)
Facts: On October 19, 1990, a chlorine container (150 pounds) began leaking gaseous chlorine into the atmosphere directly adjacent to a parking lot in La Mirada where 22 primary Plaintiffs (and approximately 60 more people) were coming to work at a nearby wheel assembly plant. L.A. County HAZMAT personnel arrived and stopped

the leak. Victims were taken to nearby clinics and hospitals. All the exposed people went back to work on Monday (the accident occurred on a Friday).

Contentions: Twenty-two primary Plaintiffs and 5 of their spouses argued that Defendant acted recklessly in their failure to have leak-detection equipment. Plaintiffs also argued that Defendant improperly assembled, employed poorly trained personnel, and used PVC bushing instead of steel—all in an effort to economize, constituting gross negligence. Plaintiffs further contended that their exposure to dangerous quantities of chlorine gas resulted from Defendant's negligence and that the effects of such toxic exposure can be latent, subtle, and chronic. Defendant acknowledged negligence, but denied conduct justifying punitive damages. Defendant also contended that the Plaintiffs were exposed to insignificant amounts of chlorine gas, their injuries, if they existed, were transitory.

Injuries: Plaintiffs claimed headaches, rhinitis, sinusitis, dyspnea, RADS, organic brain damage and emotional distress requiring ongoing and future physiological and psychological evaluations. Five spouses claimed loss of consortium injuries.

Specials in evidence: MEDS $5–10,000 each (on the average); Future LOE unspecified.

Settlement discussions: Plaintiffs contend their demand was a 998 for $3,700,000 and early in 1993 Defendants made a 998 offer of $242,000 total.

Other information: This settlement was reached before Hon. John F. Trotter, retired.

PERSONAL INJURY

Automobile Accident
Mountain Road Collision

Settlement: $1,900,000 (present cash value, partially structured)
Case: I.D. Confidential
Court: L.A. Superior Santa Monica
Date: January 7, 1994
Judge: Hon. Jack Newman, Dept. S
Disbursement: $1,400,000 cash; $500,000 present cash value, structured

Attorneys: Plaintiff—Patrick G. Vastano, Steven V. Angarella (Vastano & Angarella, L.A.). Defendant—Fred Krakauer (Krakauer, Castaldi, et al., Burbank)

Technical experts: Plaintiff—Robert L. Tarozzi, accident reconstruction, Carmel Valley; Phillip Allman, Ph.D., economist, San Francisco; Sandra Schneider, vocational rehabilitation, L.A. Defendant—Robert Crommelin, road design, Palm Desert; Richard Andersen, vocational rehabilitation, Westminster; Raymond G. Schultz, Ph.D., economist, San Marino

Medical experts: Plaintiff—Herbert S. Gross, M.D., neuropsychiatrist, Culver City; Karen Schiltz, Ph.D., neuropsychologist, Thousand Oaks; Henry Kirsch, M.D., internist, Culver City. Defendant—Michael Weinir, M.D., neurologist, Encino; Jay B. Cohn, M.D., neuropsychiatrist, Beverly Hills

Facts: On March 2, 1992, Plaintiff, a 37-year-old paramedic, was proceeding southbound, in the rain, on Kanan Dune Road approximately 3/10 of a mile south of Mulholland Highway. Defendant's vehicle was traveling northbound at approximately 35–40 miles per hour. Defendant lost control of the vehicle through a right-hand curve. The speed limit is 50 miles per hour, and the subject curve had a speed advisory sign of 35 miles per hour. Defendant's vehicle crossed over the center line into oncoming traffic. Plaintiff swerved to avoid the collision, but was struck on the passenger side by Defendant's vehicle.

Contentions: Plaintiff contended that the Defendant driver was traveling too fast for the wet roadway conditions, was operating a vehicle with minimal rear tire-tread depth, and was the sole cause of the subject accident. Defendant contended that the County of Los Angeles failed to properly design the subject roadway in that the drainage of rain water caused a water buildup at the location where the Defendant's vehicle went out of control. (Rainfall was measured at 2.39 inches on the date of the accident.) Defendant claimed its vehicle hydroplaned across the water draining from the roadway, thereby causing the subject accident. (The County of Los Angeles was not a party to the action.) Defendant also contended that Plaintiff was proceeding too fast and that the tires on Plaintiff's vehicle had minimal tread depth, thereby causing Plaintiff to spin

out when Plaintiff tried to take evasive action. (The police report noted both vehicles to have minimal tire tread depth.) In addition, Defendant disputed Plaintiff's loss-of-earning capacity claim.

Injuries: Multiple rib fractures; fractured pelvis requiring open reduction internal fixation; closed-head trauma resulting in brain damage displayed in cognitive impairment and post-trauma seizures requiring ongoing monitoring and medication and disabling Plaintiff's return to his occupation.

Specials in evidence: MEDS $130,000 (per Plaintiff), $150,000 (per Defedant); Future MEDS $50,000; LOE & Future LOE $600,000 capacity (per Plaintiff); $30–40,000 LOE to date and Future LOE $6–700,000 (per Defendant).

Settlement discussions: Plaintiff contends there were no offers or demands exchanged prior to the Mandatory Settlement Conference. Defendant contends their initial offer was $1,150,000 and Plaintiff demanded $2,500,000 at the MSC.

PERSONAL INJURY

Truck Accident
Multiple Collisions

Settlement: $1,100,000 partial
Case: Case I.D. Confidential
Court: L.A. Superior Norwalk
Date: October 1, 1993
Attorneys: Plaintiff—David H. Greenberg, Stephen B. Simon (Greenberg & Simon, Santa Monica). Defendant—Alan G. Saler (Jones, Hirsch, et al., L.A.)
Technical experts: Plaintiff—Ira Lipsius, truck insurance coverage, New York, NY
Facts: On July 7, 1992, Plaintiff, a 46-year-old airline reservation supervisor, was traveling northbound in the number one lane of the 710 Freeway. Defendant's tractor/trailer rig was in the number 4 lane. This Defendant was transporting a load for Defendant corporation (the settling Defendant) at the time. Defendant's auto (case still pending) came into contact with the tractor/trailer rig. Defendant auto then lost control and struck Plaintiff's vehicle, which was thrown out of control and impacted with the concrete median. As a result of the collision with Defen-

dant's auto, the fuel tank in Plaintiff's vehicle ruptured and ignited. Plaintiff was forced to exit her vehicle through the driver's window and as a result was severely burned. Plaintiff claimed negligent operation of motor vehicles by Defendant drivers of both the truck and the auto.

Contentions: Plaintiff also claimed liability was imputed to Defendant corporation through the Doctrine of Respondeat Superior. Defendant corporation contended that the collisions were caused by the auto driver. Defendant corporation further contended the driver of its vehicle was an independent contractor and the duty of care was delegable.

Injuries: Second and third degree burns over 40% of the body, requiring burn center treatments, skin grafts; residual scarring will require future surgeries. Plaintiff's husband claimed loss of consortium injuries.

Specials in evidence: MEDS $160,000; Future MEDS Unknown; LOE $15,421 Plaintiff; $3,500 spouse.

Settlement discussions: Plaintiff contends they demanded the policy limits and this Defendant corporation offered nothing. Defendant corporation contends their offer was $500,000 increased to $1,100,000.

Other information: Case is still pending against Defendant auto driver and his employer.

PERSONAL INJURY

Medical Malpractice
Surgical Negligence

Verdict: Defense Verdict
Case: Kimberly Weemering v. John Muir Hospital, et al., No. C91 04345
Court: Contra Costa Superior
Date: November 9, 1993
Judge: Hon. David A. Dolgin, Dept. 6
Attorneys: Plaintiff—Bruce E. Krell, E. Robert Wallach (San Francisco). Defendant—Robert K. Lawrence (Bjork, Lawrence, et al., Oakland) for John Muir Medical Center and Dr. Robert Mueller; Richard E. Dodge (McNamara, Houston, et al., Walnut Creek) for Dr. Howard Taekman; Ralph C. Smith (Anderson, Galloway, et al., Walnut Creek) for Dr. Cavett Robert

Technical experts: Plaintiff—Anthony Gamboa, Ph.D., economist, Memphis, TN. Defendant—Lawrence J. Deneen, Ph.D., rehabilitation, Oakland

Medical experts: Plaintiff—Michael Smolens, M.D., emergency medicine, L.A.; Archimedes Ramirez, M.D., neurosurgeon, San Rafael; Lucien L. Trigiano, M.D., psychiatrist, San Francisco; Brendan Carroll, M.D., trauma surgeon, L.A.; Donald Trunkey, M.D., trauma surgeon, Portland; Elisa D'Gean, M.D., neuroradiologist, San Francisco. Defendant—Albert Yellin, M.D. trauma surgeon, L.A.; F. William Blaisdell, M.D., trauma surgeon, Davis; Peter B. Slabaugh, M.D. orthopedic surgeon, Oakland; Harry Genant, M.D., radiologist, San Francisco; Alan Gelb, M.D., emergency medicine, San Francisco; Daniel Meub, M.D., neurosurgery, Palo Alto; Ayub K. Ommaya, M.D., neurosurgery, Washington, D.C.; Gretchen Parker, R.N., emergency room nurse, Hayward; Paul Nottingham, M.D., orthopedic surgeon, Walnut Creek; William K. Hoddick, M.D., radiology, Walnut Creek; Thomas Thomason, M.D., anesthesiology, Walnut Creek; DeWitt Gifford, M.D., neurosurgery, Oakland

Facts: Plaintiff Kimberly Weemering, a 29-year-old sales representative and stocking clerk for outdoor sports equipment, received head and facial injuries in an automobile v. bicycle accident on September 18, 1990. Plaintiff was taken to defendant hospital and underwent 10 hours of facial surgery by Defendant doctor. Following the facial surgery, Plaintiff was found to be a paraplegic. Defense admission medical records had shown Plaintiff's spinal cord intact. The records also documented Plaintiff as being able to move all extremities, having full range of motion, and displaying response to pain stimulus.

Contentions: Plaintiff contends that she entered the hospital following the accident with her spinal cord intact and that her paraplegia was completely due to medical malpractice by the Defendants. Defendants contended that the medical records were wrong and that mistaken entries were erroneously made regarding Plaintiff's abilities. The Defendants claimed that Plaintiff had no ability to move sphincter muscles or limbs at the scene of the accident, and that Plaintiff was already a paraplegic prior to surgery.

Injuries: T-6 paraplegia.

Specials in evidence: MEDS $650,000; Future MEDS $1,900,000; LOE $50,000; Future LOE $650,000.

Trial jury: Length 8 weeks; Poll 10–2; Deliberation 3 hours.

Settlement discussions: Plaintiff contends their demand was $2,300,000 and Defendant hospital offered $75,000.

PERSONAL INJURY

Medical Malpractice
Misdiagnosis

Settlement: $564,408 (present cash value structured)

Case: Case I.D. Confidential

Court: Orange Superior

Date: October 18, 1993

Judge: Hon. James P. Gray, Dept. 15

Attorneys: Plaintiff—Kenneth M. Sigelman (Kenneth M. Sigelman & Associates, Santa Monica). Defendant—Confidential

Facts: In April of 1990, Plaintiff, a 66-year-old retiree was diagnosed as having esophageal cancer, for which surgery was performed in May of 1990, followed by 2 courses of chemotherapy. In August 1990, Plaintiff suffered a mild stroke. In September of 1990, Plaintiff moved to California to be with her family. She initially presented to Defendant medical center shortly after her arrival. Defendant interpreted a CT scan of her brain as showing metastatic cancer. Plaintiff underwent radiation therapy to her brain. On October 17, 1990, Plaintiff suffered a major stroke, which rendered her totally incapacitated.

Contentions: Plaintiff contended that the diagnosis of metastatic cancer was incorrect and that the abnormalities on the CT scan of the brain were due to the prior stroke. Plaintiff contended that this diagnosis was corroborated by the CT scan done of Plaintiff's brain at the time of her initial stroke, prior to her moving to California. Defendant contended that the misdiagnosis was within the standard of care, given the radiographic similarities of both conditions and Plaintiff's history of esophageal cancer.

Injuries: Major stoke resulting in total incapacitation, requiring full-time attendant care.

Settlement discussions: Plaintiff contends their demand was $700,000 and Defendant offered $300,000.

Other information: The Court approved the creation of a special needs trust for the benefit of Plaintiff, pursuant to Probate Code, Sections 3602 and 3604. This enabled Plaintiff to retain her eligibility for Medicare and Medi-Cal, which currently pay a total of approximately $3,000 per month for Plaintiff's care.

PERSONAL INJURY

Bus Accident
Passenger

Verdict: $42,600

Case: Adelaida Bravo v. S.C.R.T.D., No. BC 063,943

Court: L.A. Superior Central

Date: December 30, 1993

Judge: Hon. Ricardo A. Torres, Dept. 64

Attorneys: Plaintiff—Andrew L. Wright (Law Offices of Michael A. Cohen, L.A.) Defendant—Roslily H. Mitchell (Law Offices of Melanie E. Lomax & Associates, L.A.)

Medical experts: Plaintiff—Eugene Harris, M.D., orthopedic surgeon, L.A. Defendant—Henry Jones, M.D., orthopedic surgeon, Santa Monica

Facts: On November 3, 1991, Plaintiff Adelaida Bravo, a 68-year-old retiree, was exiting the front doors of Defendant Southern California Rapid Transit District's bus. Before Plaintiff could exit, the front doors closed, and the bus began moving. Plaintiff screamed, the bus stopped, and the doors were opened. Plaintiff fell to the sidewalk, striking her right shoulder, head, and elbows.

Contentions: Plaintiff contended that as a result of the negligence of the Defendant's driver, she suffered severe exacerbation of preexisting degenerative disease, causing an asymptomatic condition to become symptomatic. Defendants disputed the cause of the incident and the claim for injuries.

Injuries: Exacerbation of preexisting degenerative rotator cuff disease of the right shoulder, requiring physical therapy and possible future arthoscopic surgery.

Damages: Domestic help expenses of $2,400; pain and suffering.

Specials in evidence: MEDS $5,974; Future MEDS $3,000–4,000.

Trial jury: Length 3 days; Poll 12–0; Deliberation 3 hours.

Settlement discussions: Plaintiff contends they demanded $75,000 and Defendant offered $30,000.

Other information: prior arbitration before Donald R. Jacobs on July 8, 1993, resulted in a Plaintiff's award of $27,610; trial de novo by Plaintiff.

PERSONAL INJURY

Premises Liability
Dangerous Condition
Verdict: $511,000

Case: Edward Sirignano v. City of Bellflower, No. VC012,178

Court: L.A. Superior Norwalk

Date: December 27, 1993

Judge: Hon. J. Kimball Walker, Dept. A

Attorneys: Plaintiff—Dennis M. Elber (Stolpman, Krissman, et al., Long Beach). Defendant—John C. Barber (Barber & Bauermeister, Santa Ana)

Technical experts: Plaintiff—Peter Formuzis, Ph.D., economist, Santa Ana

Medical experts: Plaintiff—Reynolds Romaldi, M.D., orthopedic surgeon, Downey; David Wall, M.D., orthopedic surgeon, Bellflower. Defendant—James Moore, M.D., orthopedic surgeon, Santa Ana

Facts: On February 7, 1992, Plaintiff Edward Siragnano was a disabled, 31-year-old plumber. While walking in a public park in the Defendant City of Bellflower, his left leg went into a 12-inch by 18-inch-deep hole, causing him to twist his right knee. At the time, Plaintiff was recovering from right knee surgery which had been performed on January 24, 1992, as the result of a work-related injury that occurred in June of 1991.

Contentions: Plaintiff contended that the hole was a dangerous condition of public property, which had been created by a city employee who was doing sprinkler repair. Plaintiff contended that Defendant failed to barricade and the injury sustained prevented his scheduled return to the work force. Plaintiff continued to receive workers' compensation benefits (from the original injury), and his treating physicians attributed the subject incident with 50% of his current disability. Defendant contended that its employee had barricaded the hole and checked the barricade within 30 minutes of the accident; Defendant claimed that the barricade had been removed by someone other than park personnel. Defendant suggested that the accident may have been staged. The Defendant also contended that the MRI films taken before and after the subject incident, did not show any new injury or aggravation, nor could the treating physician specifically opine that there was a new injury or aggravation; therefore, Plaintiff's original injury of June, 1991, had resulted in limitations that prevented Plaintiff's continuing to work as a plumber, not the subject incident.

Injuries: Exacerbation of preexisting knee injury causing internal derangement of the knee and resulting in complete disability as a plumber.

Specials in evidence: MEDS $11,000 (per Plaintiff), $14,000 (per Defendant); Future MEDS not specified; LOE & Future LOE $700,000 to $1,000,000.

Trial jury: Length 6 days; Poll 12–0; Deliberation 6 hours.

Settlement discussions: Plaintiff contends there were no offers or demands exchanged prior to trial; Plaintiff indicated it would take "six figures" to settle and Defendant said that it would not pay six figures; at the conclusion of testimony, the Defendant offered $75,000 and asked Plaintiff for a formal demand, which Plaintiff did not provide.

Appendix D
Basic Medical Anatomy

Association of Trial Lawyers of America, *Anatomy of a Personal Injury Law Suit* 69–89 (1968). Reprinted with the permission of the Association of Trial Lawyers of America. Material also adapted from Bureau of Medicine and Surgery, *Handbook of the Hospital Corps* (1959). Illustrations adapted from Richard Sloane, *The Sloan-Dorland Annotated Medical-Legal Dictionary* (1987). Reprinted with permission of West Publishing Company and W. B. Saunders.

TERMINOLOGY

Medical terms are derived mainly from Greek and Latin. In learning a relatively small number of roots, suffixes and prefixes, you can acquire a basic understanding of medical terms. For example, the root for nerve is "neur" and the suffix, "itis," means inflammation. Thus, the term "neuritis" means inflammation of nerves.

A facet of the medical language which must be mastered at the outset is the terminology related to the positions, directions, and movements of the body. The following describe positions:

1. Anterior, posterior; front, back.

2. Ventral, dorsal; front, back.

3. Lateral, medial; away from the midline, toward the midline.

4. Proximal, distal; toward the source, away from the source.

5. Cranial, caudal; toward the head, toward the tail.

6. Superior, inferior; above, below.

The following describe movements of various portions of the body.

1. Abduction, adduction; away from the center of the body, toward the center of the body.

2. Flexion, extension; bending of a joint, straightening of a joint.

3. Supination, pronation; turning upward, turning downward.

4. Eversion, inversion; turning outward, turning inward.

"Anatomical planes" identify "views" of the body. The more common anatomical planes include:

1. Frontal: A section to the side of the body, passing at right angles to the median plane. This divides the body into anterior and posterior portions.

2. Median or midline: An imaginary plane which passes from the front to the back through the center of the body, dividing the body into right and left equal portions.

3. Sagittal: A section parallel to the long axis of the body or parallel to the median plane, dividing the body into right and left unequal parts.

4. Transverse: A horizontal plane, passing at right angles to both the frontal and median planes, dividing the body into cranial and caudal parts.

Some anatomical postures to which doctors have frequent reference are as follows:

1. Erect: the body is in a standing position.

2. Supine: the body is lying flat on the back.

3. Prone: the body is lying face and trunk down.

4. Laterally recumbent: the body is lying horizontally, either on the right or left side.

BASIC UNITS OF THE BODY

The human body is made up of four basic units: cells, tissues, organs and systems. Cells are the building blocks of the body; they are the ultimate unit of the body, and are not of immediate importance. Tissues are masses of cells which are similar in structure and function. The primary tissues are:

1. Epithelial: These cover internal and external surfaces of the body.

2. Connective: These hold organs in place and bind all parts of the body together.

3. Muscular: These largely carry out activities of motion.

4. Nervous: These are the most highly specialized in the body; they convey impulses from and to the central nervous system.

Organs are combinations of groups of different tissues, e.g., the liver, the heart, lungs, pancreas, etc. Organs do not function independently, for they operate within the framework of systems. Systems are groupings of organs which perform specific functions. The body may be divided into ten basic systems:

1. Skeletal;

2. Muscular;

3. Nervous;

4. Cardiovascular;

5. Lymphatic;

6. Gastrointestinal;

7. Genitourinary;

8. Respiratory;

9. Endocrine; and

10. Integumentary.

The greater part of those injuries the lawyer and paralegal will deal with have their primary effect upon one, or all, of the first four systems.

SKELETAL SYSTEM

A. General Considerations:

The skeletal system is the jointed framework of the body which makes movement possible. This system is made up of some 200 bones and connective fibers. The purpose of the skeletal system is to give support and shape to the body, and provide attachment points for bones, muscles and ligaments.

B. Anatomical Classification of Skeletal System:

1. The axial skeleton is comprised of those bones lying near the midline of the body, such as the skull and spinal column.

2. The appendicular skeleton is comprised of those bones which support the limbs.

C. Major Bones:

Lawyers and paralegals should learn the following portions of the skeletal systems:

1. The skull:
   a. Frontal;
   b. Temporal;
   c. Parietal;
   d. Occipital;
   e. Maxilla; and
   f. Mandible.

2. Vertebral column and associated structures:

   The importance of understanding the basic anatomy of the vertebral column and its associated structures cannot be over-emphasized. There are three major areas of the vertebral column: The cervical area, the thoracic or dorsal area, and the lumbar area. The bony structures which make up the vertebral column are known as vertebrae.

   The cervical area contains seven vertebrae. The first of these is termed the "atlas." This structure supports the skull. The second cervical vertebra is called the "axis." This provides a point of rotation of the skull on the neck. The thoracic or dorsal area of the vertebral column is made up of twelve vertebrae. The lumbar area has five vertebrae. It is the lumbar area which is responsible for carrying most of the weight of the trunk. Immediately below the lumbar area is the sacrum. This structure consists of five fused vertebrae. Immediately below the sacrum is the coccyx, or "tail bone."

   Between each pair of vertebrae there is an intervertebral disc. The outer portion of the disc, or the annulus fibrosus, is made up of cartilaginous substance. Within the annulus fibrosus is a jelly-like substance known as the nucleus pulposus. Intervertebral discs serve a highly important, cushioning function.

3. Upper trunk:

   The ribs are made up of twelve pairs of flat curved bones which are attached posteriorly to the thoracic portion of the vertebral column. Anteriorly the first seven pairs are attached to the sternum, the broad flat bone located in the midline of the chest (the "breast bone"). The eighth, ninth and tenth ribs are joined to the cartilage of the seventh rib. The eleventh and twelfth are unattached anteriorly and are the so called "floating ribs." Basically, the ribs, plus the sternum, comprise the thoracic cage. This bony structure protects the vital organs of the chest and makes possible the movement which permits expansion and contraction in breathing.

4. Upper extremities:
   a. Clavicle, the collar bone;
   b. Scapula, the shoulder blade;
   c. Humerus, the upper arm bone;
   d. Ulna and Radius, bones of the lower arm;
   e. Carpals, eight wrist bones;
   f. Metacarpals, bones of the palm and posterior hand; and
   g. Phalanges, finger bones.

5. Lower extremities:
   a. Pelvis: The pelvis may be divided into three principal parts: The ilium, the ischium, and the pubis. These three bones join to form the pelvic girdle.
   b. Acetabulum: This is not actually bone, but a large cup-shaped socket in the lateral aspect of the hip, into which the head of the femur fits.
   c. Greater and Lesser Trochanters: These are bony prominences located on the lateral and medial sides of the femur. These prominences are for the purpose of attachment of muscles.
   d. Femur: This is the longest bone in the body; it is the bone of the upper leg.
   e. Patella: This is the kneecap.
   f. Tibia and Fibula: These are the bones of the lower leg. The tibia is the larger, and is located medially.
   g. The Lateral Malleolus is the lower end of the fibula; the Medial Malleolus is the lower end of the tibia.

Figure D.1   The Human Skeleton

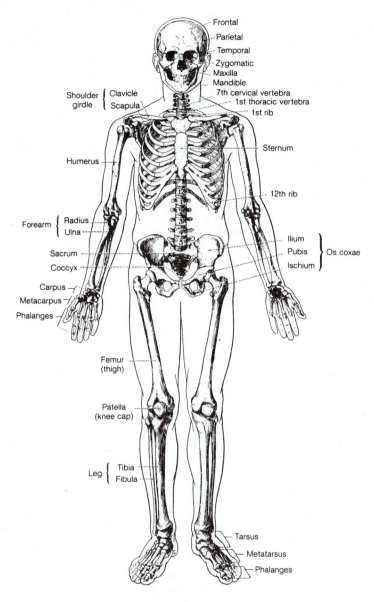

Frontal
Parietal
Temporal
Zygomatic
Maxilla
Mandible
7th cervical vertebra
1st thoracic vertebra
1st rib
Sternum
12th rib
Ilium
Pubis
Ischium
Os coxae
Shoulder girdle { Clavicle, Scapula
Humerus
Forearm { Radius, Ulna
Sacrum
Coccyx
Carpus
Metacarpus
Phalanges
Femur (thigh)
Patella (knee cap)
Leg { Tibia, Fibula
Tarsus
Metatarsus
Phalanges

---

h. Tarsals: These are the seven bones of the ankle.

i. Metatarsals: These are the five bones in the sole and instep of the foot.

j. Phalanges: These are the bones of the toes.

D. Joints:

A joint may be defined as a structure which holds bones together, permitting certain movements while prohibiting others. There are three types of joints:

1. Fibrous: united by Fibrous tissues; there are two types:

    a. Sutures: connected by several fibrous layers;

    b. Syndesmoses: a fibrous joint in which the intervening connective tissue is much more than in a suture;

2. Cartilaginous: united by fibrocartilage;

3. Synovial: often termed diathrodial joints; these possess a fluid filled space and are specialized to permit more or less free movements. The articular surfaces are covered with cartilage and the bones are united by the joint capsule and ligaments.

In classifying the joints with respect to movement, there are also three major classifications:

1. Synarthroses: These are immovable;

2. Amphiarthroses: These have limited movement; and

3. Diarthroses:
   a. Plane Joint (articular surfaces are slightly curved, and permit gliding or slipping in any direction).
   b. Hinge Joint (uni-axial and permits movement in only one place: an example is an interphalangeal joint).
   c. Condylar Joint (articular area consists of two district articular surfaces: knee joint is an example).
   d. Ball and Socket Joint (shoulder joint is an example).
   e. Ellipsoidal Joint (articulating surfaces are much longer in one direction than in another; radiocarpal joint is an example).
   f. Pivot Joint (uni-axial; axis is vertical).
   g. Saddle Joint (biaxial joint carpometacarpal joint of the thumb is an example).

MUSCULAR SYSTEM

A. General Considerations:

All human activity is carried on by operation of the muscles. The human body contains five hundred muscles which are large enough to be seen by the naked eye, and thousands more which are capable of visualization only through a microscope. Muscles constitute about one-half of the weight of the body; the form of the body is largely due to the muscle covering of the skeletal framework. Muscles are made up of tissues composed of long slender cells. In considering the muscular system, one should also consider tendons. There are strong bands which attach muscles to bones or to other structures.

B. Movement of Muscles:

Basically, muscles fall into the following categories with respect to movement:

1. Prime movers: These muscles actively produce movement.

2. Antagonists: These muscles operate in opposition to prime movers.

3. Fixation muscles: These muscles steady a part while others execute movement.

4. Synergists: These muscles control movement of a proximal joint so that a prime mover may obtain movement of a distal joint.

C. Primary Muscles:

1. The neck:
   a. Sternocleidomastoid: This muscle is frequently involved in cervical sprains.
   b. Paravertebral: These muscles run the length of the spine.

2. The Upper Trunk:
   a. Trapezius: The triangular-shaped muscle located in the back of the neck and the upper trunk.
   b. Pectoralis Major and Minor: These muscles are located on the chest.
   c. Latissimus: This is the broadest muscle on the back.
   d. Deltoid: This is a muscle capping the shoulder.
   e. Triceps: This is a muscle located on the posterior aspect of the upper arm.
   f. Biceps: This is a muscle located on the anterior aspect of the upper arm.

Figure D.2   Muscles of Trunk, Anterior View

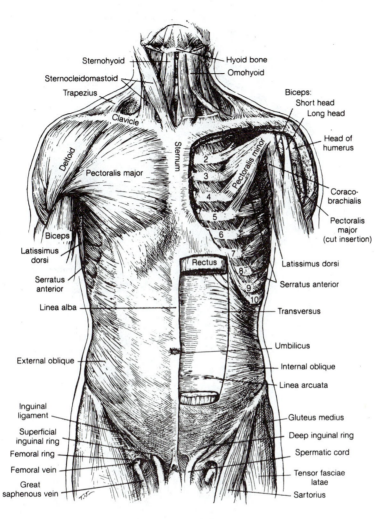

3. Thoracic Wall and Abdomen:
   a. Intercostals;
   b. Subcostals;
   c. Sternocostals;
   d. External and Internal Obliques;
   e. Rectus Abdominus; and
   f. Transversus Abdominus.

4. Hip and Thigh:
   a. Gluteus Minimus, Medius and Maximus;
   b. Pectineus;
   c. Adductur, Longus, Brevis and Magnus;
   d. Quadriceps Femoris;
   e. Sartorius;

Figure D.3   Muscles of Trunk, Posterior View

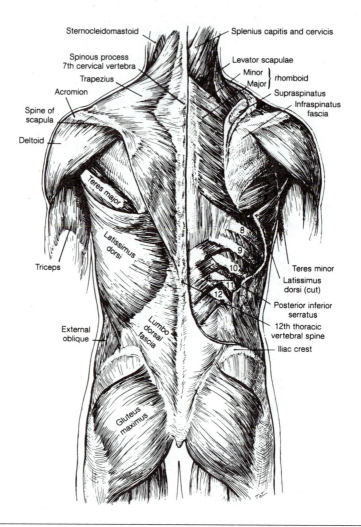

f. "Ham Strings":
    (1) Semimembranosus,
    (2) Semitendinosus,
    (3) Biceps Femoris; and

5. Lower Leg and Foot:
    a. Tibialis Anterior and Posterior;
    b. Peroneus Longus and Brevis;
    c. Soleus;
    d. Gastrocnemius.

NERVOUS SYSTEM

The human body has a "central authority" which issues orders to the rest of the body. The function of the nervous system, then, is to coordinate all of the activities of

Figure D.4 Superficial Muscles of Right Lower Extremity

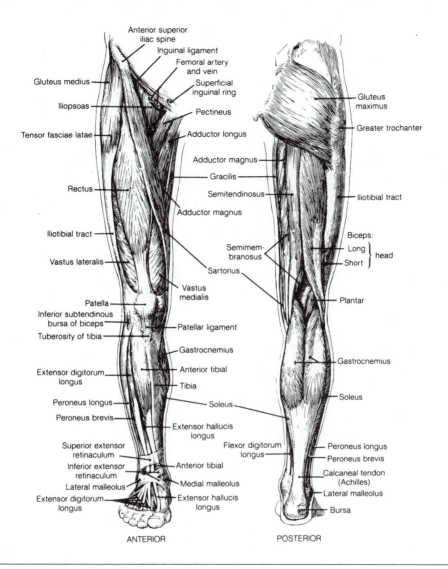

ANTERIOR

POSTERIOR

the body. The basic functional units of the nervous system are known as neurons. These are specifically designed to carry impulses or messages rapidly over relatively long distances. There are basically two types of neurons: sensory neurons, which conduct impulses from sense organs to the spinal cord and brain; and motor neurons, which conduct impulses from the brain and spinal cord to the muscles and glands.

The nervous system may be divided into three main parts: the central nervous system, the peripheral nervous system and the autonomic nervous system.

A. Central Nervous System:

There is no more important part of the body than the central nervous system. When one sustains serious trauma to this system, damage will be gross. The basic components

Figure D.5 Superficial Muscles of Right Upper Extremity

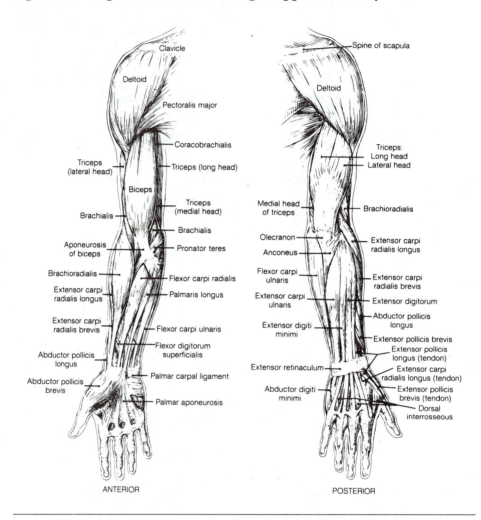

ANTERIOR

POSTERIOR

---

of the central nervous system are the brain and spinal cord. Three membranes, known as the meninges, ensheath the central nervous system. The meninges serve supportive and protective roles. The meninges, from the outer- to the innermost, are designated as the dura, the arachnoid, and the pia.

1. The Brain: The brain comprises 98% of the central nervous system, and lies within the bony protection of the skull. One may designate the following major divisions of the brain:

    a. Medulla Oblongata: A truncated cone of nervous tissue continuous above with the pons and below with the spinal cord. It lies anterior to the cerebellum. The medulla contains highly specialized nerve centers regulating heart action, breathing, circulation, and control of body temperature. It is in this area that many of the nerves cross over to the other side of the body. Thus, the right side of the brain controls the left side of the body, while left side of the brain controls the right side.

    b. Pons (meaning bridge): This connects the medulla and the midbrain.

    c. Midbrain: This is the upper part of the brain stem, located just above the pons.

    d. Cerebellum: This is the second largest portion of the brain; it is located in the posterior aspect of the skull. The chief function of the cerebellum is to bring balance, harmony, and coordination to motions of the body initiated by the cerebrum. The cerebellum integrates and correlates nerve impulses.

    e. Diencephalon: This is the portion of the brain lying between the midbrain and cerebrum. It contains the following:

        (1) Thalamus: The integrating center of the brain, where tactile, olfactory, painful, and gustatory impulses are correlated with motor reactions.

        (2) Epithalmus.

        (3) Subthalamus: This regulates the muscles of emotional expression.

        (4) Hypothalamus: This controls emotions that effect the heartbeat and blood pressure, as well as body temperature, carbohydrate metabolism, food metabolism, appetite and sexual reflexes.

    f. Cerebrum: This occupies most of the cranial cavity; it may be divided into cerebral hemispheres, and each hemisphere is, in turn, divided into four lobes:

        (1) Occipital: This is visual in function.

        (2) Frontal: This is the center of voluntary movement and is also the seat of intellect and memory.

        (3) Temporal: This is auditory in function.

        (4) Parietal: This is sensory and motor in function.

2. The Cerebral Spinal Fluid: a clear transparent fluid found in the spinal canal. When a history of central nervous system pathology is suspected, physicians will draw out, or "tap," some of the fluid for the purpose of analysis. This fluid surrounds the brain and spinal cord, and is in large measure protective in function.

3. The Spinal Cord: One may compare the spinal cord to a highly complex telephone cable. It is enclosed in the vertebral column and has the three membranous coverings: the dura, the pia and the arachnoid. Cerebral spinal fluid also surrounds the spinal cord.

    One may demonstrate an "ascending tract" (responsible for conducting impulses to the brain), and a "descending tract" (responsible for conducting impulses from the brain). It is through the spinal cord that the brain maintains its intimate functional relationship with the organs of the body. Thirty-one pairs of spinal nerves which protrude from the lateral aspects of the cord, through the vertebral foramina, and into the peripheral areas of the body, constitute the specific means of accomplishing this highly complex system of intra-communication. Spinal nerves are attached to the spinal cord by anterior and posterior roots. The nerves, after leaving the cord, are named after their corresponding vertebrae. Thus, the first eight spinal nerves are known as cervical; the next twelve, dorsal; the next five, lumbar; the next five, sacral; and the last pair, coccygeal.

    Actual trauma to the cord itself may produce serious injury. If there is any severing of the cord, the body will function normally above the level of the injury, while the portion below the injury will be paralyzed.

B. Peripheral Nervous System:

    The peripheral nervous system is made up of nerves outside of the brain and spinal column. The thirty-one pairs of spinal nerves and twelve pairs of cranial nerves which branch out into the body for the purpose of sending and receiving messages to and from the brain are known as the peripheral nerves.

    There are twelve pairs of cranial nerves which arise on each side of the brain. They are as follows:

1. First cranial nerve: This is olfactory in function; i.e., it is the nerve for the sense of smell.

2. Second cranial nerve: This is the optic nerve.

3. Third cranial nerve: This is oculomotor in function.

4. Fourth cranial nerve (also called the trochlear nerve): This serves the eye muscles.

5. Fifth cranial nerve: This is the largest of the cranial nerves. It serves both a sensory and a motor function. It has three portions:
   a. Ophalmic, serving the forehead;
   b. Maxillary, serving the upper cheek; and
   c. Mandibular, innervating the jaw and lower face.

6. Sixth cranial nerve (also called the abducens): This is visual in function and serves a purely motor function.

7. Seventh cranial nerve: This is both sensory and motor in function, and controls the muscles of the face, ears and scalp.

8. Eighth cranial nerve: This is primarily acoustic or auditory. This is the sensory nerve of hearing and equilibrium.

9. Ninth cranial nerve: Known as glossopharyngeal nerve: it serves both a motor and sensory function, carrying messages from the pharynx and back part of the tongue to the brain.

10. Tenth cranial nerve: This is the vagus nerve, serving both a motor and sensory function to the thorax and abdomen.

11. Eleventh cranial nerve: It is a motor nerve which supplies the muscles of the neck and shoulders.

12. Twelfth cranial nerve: This is the hypoglossal nerve. It is a motor nerve controlling the muscles of the tongue.

C. Autonomic Nervous System:

The automatic nervous system functions automatically; it activates involuntary, smooth, and cardiac muscles, as well as glands. It serves the vital systems which function automatically, i.e., the digestive, circulatory, respiratory, urinary, and endocrine systems.

The automatic nervous system is broken down into two major divisions: sympathetic nervous system and parasympathetic nervous system. These two systems work in opposition and maintain balanced activity in the body mechanisms. For example, the sympathetic system will dilate the pupils, while the parasympathic system contracts them.

The trunk of the sympathetic system lies in close proximity to the vertebral bodies and is composed of a series of ganglia on either side of the spinal column. The ganglia extend from the base of the skull to the coccyx.

The ganglia of the parasympathetic system are located in the mid-portion of the brain, and the sacral region of the spinal cord.

CARDIOVASCULAR SYSTEM

There are five principal components of the cardiovascular system: heart, arteries, veins, capillaries, and blood.

A. Blood:

Blood is a tissue fluid pumped by the heart, which courses through miles of arteries, veins, and capillaries. The function of blood is to carry oxygen, food and water to all of the cells of the body, and to return carbon dioxide to the lungs for disposal.

B. The Heart:

The heart is a hollow, muscular pump. It is located in the front of the chest, slightly to the left, between the lungs. A large portion of the heart is located directly behind the sternum. The heart is enclosed in a membranous sac called the pericardium.

The heart is divided longitudinally into left and right chambers by the septum passing through the apex at the base of the heart. Each side of the heart is subdivided into chambers; an atrium above, and a ventricle below.

C. Arteries:

Blood is carried from the heart to all of the structures of the body by arteries; these are elastic tubes. The arteries branch and rebranch as they course through the body becoming smaller and smaller, until they finally are called arterioles. The arterioles feed blood directly into the capillaries. As the blood circulates through the capillary net, it gives off oxygen and picks up waste products.

The aorta is the largest artery in the body. It arises directly from the left ventricle of the heart, arches upward and passes down along the spinal column through the diaphragm. All along its route, the aorta branches off into other arteries which supply blood to the head, neck, arms, chest, abdomen, and then it divides into arteries supplying the legs. Some of the larger arteries include the following:

1. Innominate artery;

2. Right subclavian, which supplies the right arm;

3. Right carotid, which supplies the right side of the head;

4. Internal carotid, which supplies the brain and eyes;

5. External carotid, which supplies the muscles and skin of the face;

6. Left carotid, which supplies the left side of the head;

7. Left subclavian, which supplies the left arm;

8. Axillary, which is an artery supplying the arm;

9. Brachial, which supplies the upper arm;

10. Radial and Ulnar, which supply the lower arm;

11. Coronary, which supplies the heart;

12. Pulmonary, which takes blood to be oxygenated;

13. Gastric, which supplies the stomach;

14. Splenic, which supplies the spleen;

15. Hepatic, which supplies the liver;

16. Superior mesenteric, which supplies the small intestine and proximal colon;

17. Inferior mesenteric, which supplies the lower half of the colon and rectum;

18. Renal, which supplies the kidneys;

19. Abdominal aorta, which divides into the right and left common iliacs which supply blood to the lower extremities;

20. Femoral, which supplies the thigh;

21. Popliteal, which is located just behind of, and supplies, the knee;

22. Anterior and posterior tibial, which supplies the area of the tibia;

23. Peroneal, which supplies blood to the lower leg; and

24. Dorsalis pedis, which supplies blood to the foot.

D. Veins:

The veins carry blood back to the heart. They are hollow tubes, like arteries, though their walls are much thinner and less muscular. The small veins are known as venules; these venules collect blood from the capillary nets, join larger veins, and finally return to the heart. There are two major systems of veins:

1. Pulmonary System:

This is comprised of four veins which carry blood from the lungs to the left atrium of the heart. These veins are the only ones in the entire body which carry freshly oxygenated blood. The systemic venous system carries deoxygenated blood to the right atrium of the heart. The blood then flows into the right ventricle from which it is pumped into the lungs. The pulmonary veins then carry the blood to the left atrium. From the left atrium, the blood flows to the left ventricle, from whence it is pumped into the aorta for distribution throughout the body.

2. Systemic Venous System:

This system returns blood to the right atrium from the entire body.

LYMPHATIC SYSTEM

The lymphatic system is closely associated and confluent with the vascular system. Lymph is an almost colorless fluid which is rich in white blood cells. It is circulated throughout the body by the lymph vessels, which are located in every part of the body except the brain, spinal cord, eyeball, internal ear, nails, and hair.

The lymph vessels and lymph glands form a vast network throughout the body; they collect the lymph and carry it toward the heart, eventually opening into the thoracic duct and right lymphatic duct, which in turn empty into the left internal jugular and right subclavian veins. Lymph vessels, like blood vessels, carry nourishment to the organs of the body and in turn collect waste products from them.

The lymph glands serve a filtering function; that is, they remove bacteria from the lymph stream. Lymph glands are also important in the production of white blood cells (lymphocytes). The lymphatic system is highly important in defense against infection. The lymphoid organs include the spleen, tonsils, and thymus, and lymph nodes (glands).

RESPIRATORY SYSTEM

Respiration refers to the interchange of oxygen and carbon dioxide between humans and their external world.

The principal structures of the respiratory system are:

A. Nose:

This serves both respiratory and sensory functions.

B. Pharynx:

This serves as an airway between the nasal chambers, the mouth, and larynx. It aids in both respiration and digestion.

C. Larynx:

This is the "voice box." It is located just below the pharynx, and serves as a passageway for air, aids in swallowing, and serves in the phonation or vocalization function.

D. Trachea:

This is the "windpipe." It is a tube, approximately four inches long, formed of cartilaginous rings.

E. Bronchi:

These are the branches of the trachea which carry air into the lungs. As the bronchi further branch within the lungs, they are known as bronchioles.

F. Lungs:

The lungs are two large, closed membranous sacs located on either side of the chest; they are enclosed in a sac called the pleura.

G. Mediastinum:

This separates the chest into two cavities. It is, actually, a space between the two plural cavities.

Figure D.6 Principal Arteries of the Body and Pulmonary Veins

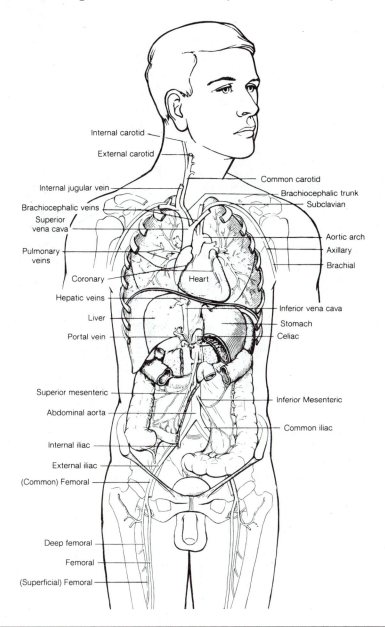

Internal carotid

External carotid

Common carotid

Internal jugular vein

Brachiocephalic trunk

Subclavian

Brachiocephalic veins

Superior
vena cava

Aortic arch

Axillary

Brachial

Pulmonary
veins

Coronary

Heart

Hepatic veins

Inferior vena cava

Liver

Stomach

Portal vein

Celiac

Superior mesenteric

Inferior Mesenteric

Abdominal aorta

Common iliac

Internal iliac

External iliac

(Common) Femoral

Deep femoral

Femoral

(Superficial) Femoral

H. Diaphragm:

This is a thin, muscular tendinous partition separating the thoracic cavity from the abdominal cavity; it is the chief muscle of respiration.

GASTROINTESTINAL SYSTEM

The gastrointestinal or digestive system includes the alimentary canal and its accessory organs. It extends from the mouth to the anus. The two major functions of the system are the digestion of food and the elimination of waste.

Figure D.7 Principal Veins of the Body

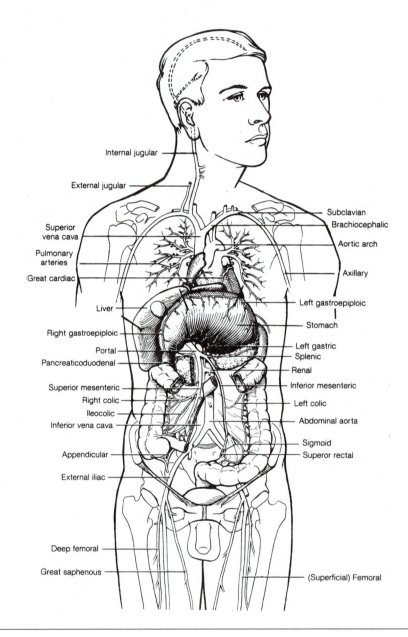

The principal components of the gastrointestinal system are as follows:

A. Mouth.

B. Pharynx:

This is an oval, fibromuscular sac about five inches long. It serves a dual function as a passageway for food and an air passageway.

C. Esophagus:

This is a narrow muscular tube about ten inches long. It connects the pharynx with the stomach.

D. Stomach:

This is the widest part of the alimentary canal. It digests masticated food to a fluid consistency and passes it along to the duodenum. There are millions of gastric glands in the stomach and these secrete juices which aid in the chemical breakdown of food.

E. Small Intestine:

This is a coiled twenty-foot tube which occupies the center and lower parts of the abdominal cavity. The greater part of digestion is completed in the small intestine, with three major divisions:

1. Duodenum: This is the widest, shortest and most fixed part. Three accessory organs bear consideration at this point.
   a. Pancreas: This is a gland extending across the posterior aspect of the abdomen. It empties an alkaline digestive juice into the duodenum.
   b. Liver: this is the largest gland in the body. It lies in the upper abdomen, under the diaphragm and above the duodenum. It secretes bile into the duodenum.
   c. Gall Bladder: This is a sac adhering to the lower aspect of the liver in a hollow space. The main function of the gall bladder is storage and concentration of bile.
2. Jejunum: The first part of the small intestine.

3. Ileum: This is the longest part of the small intestine. Most of the absorption of food takes place in the ileum.

F. Large Intestine:

This organ is about five feet long. The large intestine receives the products of digestion from the small intestine. The major divisions of the large intestine include the following:

1. Cecum: This is a blind sac located on the lower right side of the abdomen.

2. Vermiform Appendix: This is a narrow projection attached to the cecum.

3. Ascending Colon: This long tubular structure is fixed in the right flank.

4. Transverse Colon: This structure runs across the upper portion of the abdominal cavity.

5. Descending Colon: This structure runs down the left flank of the brim of the true pelvis.

6. Sigmoid Colon: The sigmoid colon communicates with the rectum.

7. Rectum: This communicates with the anus.

8. Anus.

GENITOURINARY SYSTEM

The genitourinary system is comprised of two major parts: urinary organs and reproductive organs.

A. Urinary Organs:

The urinary organs are common to both male and female, and are essentially similar in both. The major components of the urinary system are as follows:

1. Kidneys: These are bean-shaped organs situated in the posterior part of the abdomen on either side of the vertebral column.

2. Ureters: These are tubes about fifteen to eighteen inches long, extending from the kidneys down the back of the abdominal cavity and emptying into the urinary bladder.

Figure D.8 Thoracic and Abdominal Viscera

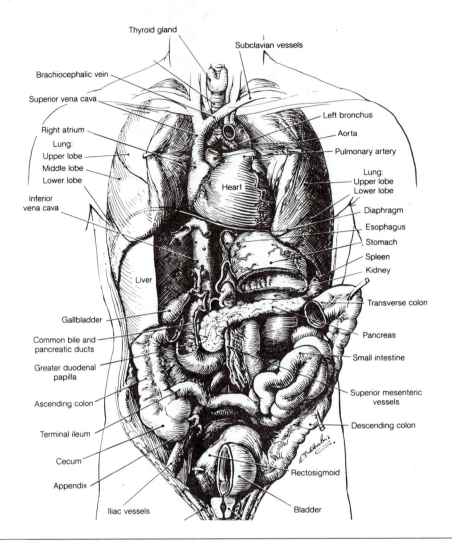

3. Urinary Bladder: This is a musculo-membranous sac lying in the pelvis. It serves as a reservoir for urine.

4. Urethra: This structure serves a different function in the male and female:
   a. In the male, this is a membranous tube running from the urinary bladder to the penis and ending in a foramina. The urethra conveys both urine and the produce of the male reproductive organs.
   b. The female urethra opens near the front of a slit in the middle of the vulva. The function of the urethra in the female is solely for voiding.

B. Reproductive Systems:

1. The Male Reproductive System:
   The essential organs of the male reproductive system are as follows:
   a. Testes: These are two organs suspended in a sack of skin (the scrotum). The epithelial cells of the testes produce sperm.

b. Epididymis: This is a cord-like, elongated structure located outside of, but hugging the posterior portion of the testis. Its function is to store sperm.

c. Vas Deferens: This tiny tube extends from the epididymis up through the inguinal canal toward the bladder. Its function is to carry sperm to the ejaculatory duct.

d. Spermatic Cord: Two spermatic cords comprise the vas deferens, arteries, veins, lymphatic ducts and nerves. The ejaculatory duct is formed by union of the ductus deferens and the duct of the seminal vesicle.

e. Ejaculatory Duct: This is a short, narrow tube, less than an inch long, which is formed just above the prostate by the union of seminal vesicles and the vas deferens.

f. Prostate Gland: This gland secretes a thin alkaline substance which precedes the sperm and secretion of the vesicles during sexual intercourse.

g. Cowper's Gland: These two structures are yellowish, rounded, lobulated, pea-size bodies on each side of the membranous urethra opening into the urethra.

h. Urethra: This is a canal about eight inches long which extends from the urinary bladder to the external foramina of the penis.

i. Penis: This is made up of three masses of tissue.

2. The Female Reproductive System:
   The essential organs of the female reproductive system include:

   a. Ovaries: These almond-shaped organs are approximately an inch and one-half in length, and an inch thick. They lie on each side of the pelvis and are responsible for the production of the germ cells.

   b. Uterus (womb): This is a thick-walled, hollow, pear-shaped organ about three inches long and three inches wide at the upper, widest portion. It lies between the bladder and the rectum. It tapers to a lower part called the cervix and projects into the anterior wall of the vagina.

   c. Fallopian Tubes: These are two musculo-membranous tubes about four inches long. They transmit the egg to the uterus where it meets the sperm.

   d. Vagina: This is a fibromuscular tube which extends from the cervix or neck of the uterus to the external genitalia part of the vagina.

   e. External Genitalia or Vulva.

ENDOCRINE SYSTEM

The complex activities of the body are carried on by the operation of the central nervous system and the endocrine system. The central nervous system is keyed to act instantaneously through the operation of the nerve impulses. The action of endocrine glands is more subtle, however; they slowly discharge secretions into blood and control the activities of the body more by "inference." The endocrine system is comprised of ductless glands of internal secretion; these glands secrete hormones.

The principle endocrine glands include:

A. Thyroid:

The thyroid is composed of two pear-shaped lobes separated by a strip of tissue; it is located immediately in front of the trachea. The main function of the thyroid gland is in the secretion of the Thyroid Hormone. The thyroid functions within the framework of growth and metabolism.

B. Parathyroids:

These are four glands, two on each side, lying posterior to the thyroid gland and usually found embedded in the thyroid. The parathyroid's function is to secrete hormones which regulate the calcium and phosphorus content of blood and bone.

C. Pituitary:

The pituitary gland exercises control over all of the other glands. It is attached to the base of the brain and is divided into an anterior and posterior lobe.

Figure D.9 The Endocrine Glands

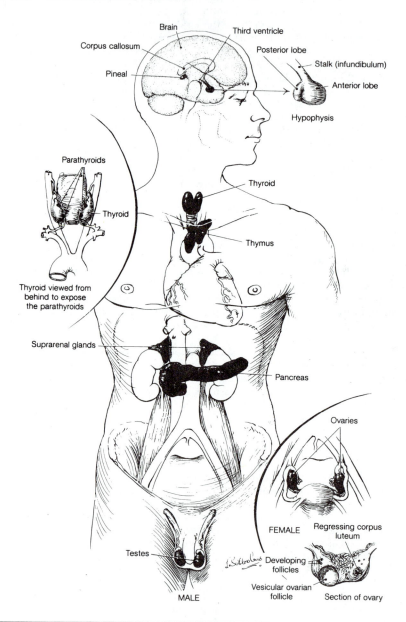

D. Adrenals:

The adrenal glands are located on the top of each kidney. These glands secrete hormones which are active in metabolism and sex development; adrenalin also is secreted. This is one of the body's most important hormones, since it is a great stimulant.

E. Gonads:

The female ovaries and male testes produce hormones important for function of the reproductive system.

F. Pineal:

This gland is located near the base of the brain: its exact functions are not understood.

G. Thymus:

This gland is situated in the front of the trachea, partly in the neck and partly in the thorax. It is believed to be associated with immunological activities.

H. Pancreas:

Specialized cells, called the Islets of Langerhans, secrete insulin into the blood stream.

INTEGUMENTARY SYSTEM

The Integumentary System includes the skin, hair, nails, mammary glands, sweat and sebaceous glands. Its main function is protective.

MEDICAL SYMBOLS

@	at	℞	prescription
Ⓛ	left	2x	twice
Ⓜ	murmur	x2	twice
Ⓡ	right	lx	once
x	end of operation	°	degree
∅	assisted respiration	'	foot; minute
⊗	controlled respiration	''	inch; second
♂	male	/	per; ratio
♀	female	bn:	ratio
p̄	after	+	positive
ā	before	−	negative
c̄	with	∝	is proportional to
s̄	without	=	equals
x̄	except	≠	does not equal
?	question of	>	greater than
~	approximate	<	less than
±	not definite	μ	micron; micro
↓	decreased, down	∅	none
↑	increased, elevated	&	and
→	causes	∫	direct arterial systolic blood pressure
∨	systolic blood pressure		
∧	distolic blood pressure	⊥	direct arterial diastolic blood pressure
#	gauge; number; pounds		
		∴	therefore

MEDICAL ABBREVIATIONS

ABG arterial blood gas
ABN abnormal
A/C anterior chamber
AC before meals
ADL activities of daily living
ADM admission
AMA against medical advice
AMT amount
ANT anterior
ASx asymptomatic
BG blood glucose
BID twice a day
BM bowel movement
B/P blood pressure
BS blood sugar
BX biopsy
C centigrade
c capillary
CBC complete blood count
CL clear
C/O complaints of
CVA cardiovascular accident
CXR chest x-ray
DC discontinue
DIS disease
DNR do not resuscitate
DOS day of surgery
DU diagnosis undetermined
DX diagnosis
EBL estimated blood loss
ECG electrocardiogram
EDC estimated date of confinement
EENT eye, ear, nose, and throat
FB foreign body
FH family history
F/U follow up
FX fracture
gm gram
HEENT head, eye, ear, nose, and throat
HR heart rate
HS hours of sleep
IM intramuscular
INT internal
I&O intake and output
IV intravenous

LAC laceration
LMP last menstrual period
M male
mg milligram
Na sodium
NAD no acute distress
NB newborn
N/C no complaints
NK not known
NOC night
NPO nothing by mouth
OCC occasional
OP operation
OZ ounce
P pulse
PE physical examination
PG pregnant
PERL pupils equal and reactive to light
PH past history
PI present illness
PO by mouth
PRN as necessary
PT physical therapy
Q every
QD every day
QID four times a day
QOD every other day
R respirations
RBC red blood count
RR recovery room
RT respiratory therapy
SAA same as above
SL serious list
STD standard
STAT immediately
T temperature
TID three times a day
TKO to keep open
U unit
UA urinalysis
UNK unknown
VS vital signs
WBC white blood count
WT weight
W/U work up

Appendix E
Products Liability Class Action Settlement Notice

In a class action, an individual member of a group or class brings a suit on behalf of every member of that class. Such suits are common in products-liability cases involving a potentially large number of plaintiffs. The recent breast implant controversy is an example. In this case, the parties negotiated a proposed settlement of $4,225,070,000 to resolve current and future claims. The problem then became trying to reach the large number of women who might have claims to find out if they wanted to participate in the settlement or to "opt out." To reach such individuals, courts often authorize the publication of advertisements in general circulation newspapers throughout the country. Here is the ad that appeared in *The Washington Post* (April 24, 1994, p. A27).

FAIRNESS HEARING

Judge Pointer will hold a hearing in the United States Courthouse, 1729 Fifth Avenue North, Birmingham, Alabama, on August 18, 1994, at 9:00 a.m. to determine whether the proposed settlement is fair, reasonable, and adequate and should be approved. You do **NOT** need to attend the hearing. You may comment by mail as this notice explains.

WHO IS A CLASS MEMBER

Except as noted below, the Settlement Class includes
• all persons who have been implanted with one or more breast implants before June 1, 1993 (whether or not later removed)
• all children of such Class Members born after a breast implant and before April 1, 1994, who may now or later have claims for their own personal injury resulting from their mother's breast implants
• all other persons or entities (including estates, representatives, spouses, children, relatives, and "significant others") who, because of a personal relationship with such Class Members, may now or later have claims (such as for loss of services) based on injuries to such Class Members.
Class membership includes all such persons, whether or not they have brought their own lawsuit, whether or not they are members of (or have excluded themselves from) another class action, and whether or not they now suffer from a medical condition associated with a breast implant.

The Settlement Notice describes conditions under which some persons **may be excluded** from class membership because they have received compensation or reimbursement as a result of a settlement, as a result of a judgment in federal or state court, or under the laws or procedures of another country, or because after a trial a final judgment has been rendered against them in favor of a settling defendant.

Also excluded at the present time are persons all of whose breast implants can be identified as having been manufactured or distributed by Porex Medical Technologies Corp. or by Koken Co., Ltd. or other foreign manufacturers. (These companies are not currently parties to the settlement. The Settlement Notice describes circumstances, including the possibility that one or more of them might later become parties to the settlement, under which eligibility to participate in the settlement may be extended to persons with implants manufactured by those companies.)

YOUR RIGHTS AND OPTIONS

Participation in the settlement class is optional, not mandatory. If you come within the class definition, you will automatically be a class member unless you exclude yourself and your family members from the class ("opt out"). To opt out, you must complete and return an "Exclusion Form," postmarked no later than June 17, 1994.
• If you opt out, you will **NOT** receive any benefits under the settlement. You would be free to file or pursue breast implant claims against all persons and companies in your own lawsuit at your own expense. Statutes of limitation or repose may limit the time for filing such lawsuits; any tolling of these periods due to pendency of a federal class action would cease 30 days after you opt out.
• If you remain in the class (by not opting out), you may make a claim to all benefits for which you are eligible under the settlement. You would give up any present or future claims against the settling defendants, subject to later opt out rights. You would retain any rights to file lawsuits against non–settling manufacturers and suppliers and against doctors, hospitals, and other health-care providers, subject to applicable statutes of limitation or repose.

TO RECEIVE SETTLEMENT NOTICE, FORMS, AND MORE INFORMATION

To make sure you receive the Settlement Notice (including details concerning the Disease Compensation Program and Disease Compensation Schedule, and the Claim, Registration, and Exclusion Forms) as well as future notices concerning the settlement, complete and return the attached Information Request Form, or call the 24–hour Settlement Information Line, 1–800–887–6828 (toll–free U.S.) or 312–609–9680, without delay. Your request will not be a matter of public record and your identity will be protected against disclosure except to the extent necessary to administer the settlement. The Settlement Notice and Forms will be mailed to you by April 18th (or within 5 days after your request), and in the interest of privacy will show the sender as "MDL 926."

TO MAKE A CLAIM OR REGISTER FOR FUTURE CLAIMS

To make a claim under the Current Disease Compensation Program, you must complete and return a Claim Form, with any necessary supporting documents,

postmarked no later than September 16, 1994. To preserve your right to make claims under the Designated Funds or under the Ongoing Disease Compensation Program, you should complete and return a Registration Form, postmarked no later than December 1, 1994.

LATER OPT OUT RIGHTS

Persons who remain in the class will have additional opportunities to opt out at a later date if the projected compensation amounts payable for covered diseases under the Disease Compensation Program must be reduced because the available funds are insufficient to pay the full amount of the claims approved under the Program. Should such a reduction occur during processing of Current Disease claims, persons electing at that time to opt out would be entitled to pursue all individual damages claims, including punitive and statutory multiple damages, against the settling defendants. Should a reduction occur during processing of Ongoing Disease claims, persons electing at that time to opt out would be entitled to pursue individual claims for all damages, except punitive or statutory multiple damages, against any or all settling defendants. The Settlement Notice describes additional opt out rights afforded to Class Members who are the children of breast implant recipients, with respect to claims of their own personal injury resulting from their mother's breast implants.

TO COMMENT ON OR OBJECT TO THE SETTLEMENT

Class members who do not opt out may comment in support of or in objection to the proposed settlement. To be considered, written comments or objections must be postmarked by June 17, 1994, and mailed to:

> MDL 926
> P. O. Box 11683
> Birmingham, AL 35202–1683

REPRESENTATION BY COUNSEL

You may retain an attorney of your choice. You are not, however, required to have a private lawyer in order to comment on the settlement or make a claim, and Settlement Class Counsel designated by the court will automatically represent Class Members who do not have their own lawyers. Class counsel support the settlement and will assist you in the settlement claims process at your request. All fees and expenses of attorneys (whether court–appointed or individually–retained) are subject to court approval and are to be paid from the Designated Fund established for that purpose, rather than from the other Designated Funds or from the Disease Compensation Program. The court has indicated that no more than 25% of the total settlement should be used to pay fees and expenses of attorneys and the cost of notice and claims administration. Because all legal expenses will be paid from this special Fund, the amount of money you receive will not be affected by whether or not you have a lawyer. The Settlement Notice contains further details concerning attorneys' fees and costs.

THIS NOTICE HAS BEEN APPROVED BY:

> Sam C. Pointer, Jr.
> United States District Judge

INFORMATION REQUEST FORM
Please send me the Settlement Notice with Registration, Claim, and Exclusion Forms

Name: _____

Telephone Number: (_____) _____

Address: _____

_____

_____

Type or Print Legibly and Mail to:

> **MDL 926**
> **P.O. Box 11683**
> **Birmingham, AL 35202-1683**

Glossary

A

abuse of process. The proper initiation of legal proceedings for an improper purpose.

act. A voluntary movement of the body.

actual malice. *See* Constitutional Malice.

additur. The power of a trial court to increase the amount of a jury's award of damages. The defendant is told that a new trial will be ordered if the defendant does not agree to the increase.

adjudication. The process by which a court or administrative agency resolves a legal dispute through litigation.

administrative code. A collection of administrative regulations organized by subject matter. Also called code of regulations.

administrative decision. An administrative agency's resolution of a specific controversy involving the application of the agency's regulations or its governing statutes and executive orders.

administrative regulation. A law of an administrative agency designed to explain or carry out the statutes and executive orders that govern the agency.

admissible. Allowable for consideration.

adverse possessor. Someone who gains title to the land of another after openly using the land in a manner that is hostile to the original owner for a designated number of continuous years.

agent. Someone who agrees to do something on behalf of another.

annotated statutes. A collection of statutes organized by subject matter, along with notes and commentary. Annotate means to provide notes and commentary.

annotation. The notes and commentary on issues in selected opinions. The annotations and opinions are published in *ALR, ALR2d, ALR3d, ALR4th, ALR5th,* and *ALR Fed.*

answer. The defendant's response to the plaintiff's complaint.

appellant. The party bringing an appeal.

appellate brief. A document submitted to an appellate court containing arguments on whether a lower court made errors of law.

appellee. The party against whom an appeal is brought. Also called the respondent.

apprehension. An understanding, awareness, anticipation, belief, or knowledge of something.

appropriation. The unauthorized use of one's name, likeness, or personality for someone else's benefit.

arrest. Take another into custody or bring before the proper authorities.

assault. An act that intentionally causes an apprehension of a harmful or offensive contact.

assignee. The person to whom someone transfers rights.

assignment. The transfer of rights.

assignor. The person who transfers rights to another.

assumption of the risk. Knowing and voluntary acceptance by the plaintiff of the risk of being injured by the acts or omissions of the defendant. The plaintiff recovers nothing.

attachment. The taking of control or seizure of the property or assets of someone. The court may order it through a writ of attachment.

attestation clause. A statement that a person personally observed a witness sign something.

authority. Any written material a court could rely on to reach its decision. *Primary* authority is any law and *secondary* authority is any nonlaw that a court could rely on to reach its decision.

B

bailment. The delivery of personal property to someone under an express or implied agreement to accept and later redeliver the prop-

---

Note: See William Statsky, *Legal Thesaurus/Dictionary* (West 1985); "Glossary of Insurance Terms," *No Fault Press Release Manual* (State Farm Insurance Companies, 1977-   ).

737

erty. The bailor delivers the property; the bailee receives it.

battery.   A harmful or offensive contact with a person resulting from the defendant's intent to cause this contact or to cause an imminent apprehension of this contact.

benefit of the bargain.   A measure of damages that gives the plaintiff the benefit of what he or she was promised.

bias.   A leaning in favor of or against someone; a prejudgment; a lack of open-mindedness.

bill.   A proposed statute. *See also* Monitor a Bill.

bill of particulars.   A request for more specific information than is contained in a complaint or other pleading that asserts a claim.

boilerplate.   Adjective describing standard language that is often used in a particular kind of document.

bona fide purchaser.   One who purchases property for value without notice of defects in the title of the seller.

breach of duty.   Unreasonable conduct; the foreseeability of an accident causing serious injury outweighed the burden or inconvenience on the defendant to take precautions against the injury, and the defendant failed to take those precautions.

breach of the peace.   An offense committed by violence or by acts likely to cause immediate disturbance of the public order.

breach of warranty.   *See* the entries under Warranty.

brief.   A summary of a court opinion. *See also* Appellate Brief.

burden of proof.   The standard that tells the trier of fact how believable a party's evidence must be on a fact in order to accept that fact as true.

but-for test.   One of the tests to determine causation: Without (i.e., "but for") the act or omissions, the event in question would not have occurred. Also referred to as the sine qua non test.

C

caption.   The heading of a pleading, appellate brief, or other document.

CARTWHEEL.   A technique to help you think of more words to look up in the indexes of law books.

case.   *See* Opinion.

causation in fact.   "But for" the act or omission, the event in question would not have occurred. The act or omission was a substantial factor in bringing about the event in question.

cause of action.   A legally acceptable reason for bringing a suit. To state a cause of action means to allege enough facts in the complaint to show that relief should be granted.

caveat emptor.   "Buyer beware."

challenge for cause.   A request that someone be excluded from a jury for a specified reason.

charge.   The judge's instructions to the jury on how to reach a verdict.

charter.   The fundamental law of a municipality or other local unit of government authorizing it to perform designated governmental functions.

chattel.   Personal property; property other than land or things attached to land.

civil arrest.   Arrest for the purpose of treatment or protection, not because of the alleged commission of a crime.

class action.   Suit brought by or brought against one or more persons who are members of a class on behalf of every other member of that class.

cognizable.   Capable of being examined or tried by a court; being within the jurisdiction of the court.

cohabitant.   One person who lives together with another as husband or wife without being married.

collateral attack.   A challenge to a judgment brought after the normal time for a direct appeal has expired.

collateral estoppel.   The same issue cannot be relitigated in a later suit.

collateral source rule.   The amount of damages caused by the defendant is not reduced by the injury-related funds received by the plaintiff from sources independent of the trial, e.g., employer, insurance.

colloquium. The part of the complaint in which the plaintiff alleges that the defamatory statement was of and concerning the plaintiff.

color of law. Acting or pretending to act in an official, governmental capacity.

common law. Judge-made law in the absence of statutes or other higher law to the contrary.

compensatory damages. Money compensation designed to make plaintiffs whole, to compensate them for actual loss or injury. They are designed to restore an injured party to his or her position prior to the injury or wrong.

complaint. A pre-trial document filed in court by the plaintiff that tries to state a claim or cause of action against the defendant. (Also called the petition.) It is one of the pleadings in the case.

confinement. The restraint of the plaintiff's physical movement.

conflict of interest. Divided loyalty that actually or potentially places one of the participants to whom undivided loyalty is owed at a disadvantage.

conflicts of law. An area of law that determines what law applies when a choice must be made between the laws of different, co-equal legal systems, e.g., two states.

consequential damages. *See* Special Damages.

conservator. Someone appointed by the court to manage the affairs of an adult who is not competent to do so on his or her own.

consideration. Something of value that is exchanged between parties, e.g., an exchange of money for accounting services; an exchange of promises to do something or to refrain from doing something.

consortium. Love, affection, sexual relationship, and services that one spouse provides another.

constitution. The fundamental law that creates the branches of government and identifies basic rights and obligations.

constitutional malice. Knowledge that a defamatory statement is false, or recklessness as to its truth or falsity. Also called actual malice.

contention interrogatories. *See* Interrogatories.

contingent fee. A fee that is dependent on the outcome of the case.

contribution. A proportional payment among joint tortfeasors.

conversion. An intentional interference with personal property that is serious enough to force the wrongdoer to pay its full value.

counterclaim. The defendant's statement of a claim or cause of action against the plaintiff.

cross-claim. The defendant's statement of a claim against a co-defendant.

cumulative. Adding to what has already been established or is already there; growing by addition.

D

damages. (1) Monetary compensation awarded for harm suffered. (2) Actual harm or loss. *See also* Compensatory Damages, General Damages, Hedonic Damages, Nominal Damages, Punitive Damages, Special Damages.

deceit. *See* Misrepresentation.

deep pocket. A defendant who has resources with which to pay a judgment.

defamacast. Defamation communicated on the radio or TV.

defamation. The publication of a written defamatory statement (libel) or an oral defamatory statement (slander) of and concerning the plaintiff that causes damages. *See also* Defamatory Statement, Disparagement.

defamatory statement. A statement of fact that would tend to harm the reputation of the plaintiff in the eyes of at least a substantial and respectable minority of people by lowering the plaintiff in the estimation of those people or by deterring them from associating with the plaintiff.

default judgment. A judgment for the plaintiff because the defendant failed to appear, file an answer, or otherwise defend the action.

demurrer. A challenge that says that even if a party can prove every fact alleged, there can be no recovery, since these facts do not constitute a cause of action.

deponent. *See* Deposition.

deposition.   A pretrial discovery device consisting of a question-and-answer session involving a party or witness. The session is designed to assist the other party in preparing for trial. The person who is questioned is called the deponent. *See also* Discovery.

derivative action.   A plaintiff's action against a defendant to recover for a loss which is dependent on an underlying tort committed by that defendant against another plaintiff.

derogation of common law, statutes in.   Statutes that change the common law.

digest.   (1) (n.) A set of volumes of small-paragraph summaries of court opinions. (2) (v.) To summarize a document according to a given organizational principle.

directed verdict.   An order by the trial court that the jury return a verdict for the party making the motion for the directed verdict.

discovery.   Pre-trial, out-of-court devices designed to assist a party prepare for trial. *See also* Deposition, Interrogatories.

dismissal.   (1) A termination or disposition of a lawsuit or motion without a trial. A plaintiff can have a voluntary dismissal without leave of court if sought before the answer is filed or by stipulation of all parties after the answer is filed. An involuntary dismissal occurs on the court's own motion for lack of prosecution, or on motion of defendant for lack of prosecution or for failure to introduce evidence of facts on which relief can be granted. (2) a release or discharge from employment.

disparagement.   The intentional discrediting of a plaintiff's business (sometimes called trade libel) or title to property (sometimes called slander of title).

diversity of citizenship.   A basis of federal jurisdiction that exists when the parties to a litigation are from different states, and the amount in controversy exceeds the amount specified by federal statute.

domicile.   The place where a person has been physically present and intends to stay indefinitely. It is the place to which the person intends to return when away.

domiciliary.   A person domiciled in a given place.

dram shop liability.   Civil liability imposed on the seller of intoxicating liquor to a buyer who then injures a third person. Sometimes applied also to social host who gives intoxicating liquor.

duty.   An obligation to conform to a standard of conduct prescribed by law. In negligence law, duty is the obligation to use reasonable care to avoid risks of injuring the person or property of others.

E

eggshell skull.   An unusually high vulnerability to injury.

element.   A component of a rule. A precondition to the applicability of a rule. *See also* Factor.

emancipated child.   A child who is married or otherwise living independently of his or her parent; a child whose parent has given up or renounced parental rights in the child.

emotional distress.   Mental anguish such as fright, horror, grief, shame, humiliation, and worry.

employment at will.   An employment arrangement that either the employee or the employer can terminate at any time without liability.

entirety.   *See* Joint Tenancy.

execution.   The process of carrying something out. In a writ of execution, the sheriff takes possession of the judgment debtor's assets, sells them, deducts the costs of execution, pays the judgment creditor, and gives anything left over back to the judgment debtor.

executive order.   A law issued by the chief executive (e.g., president, governor, mayor) pursuant to specific statutory authority or to the executive's inherent authority (e.g., to direct the operation of governmental agencies).

exemplary damages.   *See* Punitive Damages.

exempt.   Not reachable to satisfy a debt or other obligation.

exhaustion of administrative remedies   Using all available methods of resolving a dispute within an administrative agency before asking a court to take action.

express warranty.   *See* Warranty.

extreme or outrageous conduct. Atrocious, totally intolerable, shocking behavior.

F

fact, statement of. An express or implied communication covering the existence of tangible things, the happening of events, or a state of mind.

factor. One of the circumstances or considerations that will be weighed in making a decision, no one of which is usually conclusive. One of the considerations a court will examine to help it make a decision on whether a rule applies. Unlike elements, factors are not preconditions to the applicability of a rule.

fact pleading. A statement of every ultimate (i.e., essential) fact in the complaint.

fair market value. What something would probably sell for in the ordinary course of a voluntary sale by a willing seller and a willing buyer.

fair on its face. No obvious or blatant flaws or irregularities.

false arrest. An arrest for which the person taking someone into custody has no privilege.

false imprisonment. An intentional confinement within fixed boundaries set by the defendant.

false light. An inaccurate impression made by publicity about a person. It is highly offensive to a reasonable person.

felony. A crime that is punishable by incarceration for a term exceeding a year.

fiduciary. (1) (n.) Someone who owes another good faith, loyalty, trust, and candor. (2) (adj.) Based on trust.

financial responsibility law. Law requiring an operator or owner of a motor vehicle to give evidence of financial ability to meet claims for damages when he or she is involved in an accident.

first-party coverage. An insurance coverage under which policyholders collect compensation for their losses from their own insurer rather than from the insurer of the person who caused the accident.

fitness for a particular purpose. *See* Warranty of Fitness for a Particular Purpose.

foreseeable. Having the quality of being seen or known beforehand.

forum. The court where a case is brought.

fresh pursuit. Pursuit which is prompt, without undue delay.

frolic and detour. Conduct by an employee motivated by his or her personal objectives rather than by the business objectives of the employer.

G

garnishment. Reaching the assets of a debtor in the possession of a third party in order to satisfy a debt.

general damages. Compensatory damages that generally result from the wrongful conduct of the defendant. Damages that usually and naturally flow from this wrong, e.g., pain and suffering. The law implies or presumes that such damages result from the wrong complained of. General damages differ from special damages, which are awarded for actual economic loss, such as medical costs and loss of income.

general verdict. *See* Verdict.

governmental function. A function that can be performed adequately *only* by the government. Unlike a proprietary function.

gratuitous. Not involving payment or consideration; free.

gross negligence. The failure to use even a small amount of care to avoid foreseeable harm.

guardian. An individual appointed by a court to protect a minor, a sick person, or anyone else who needs special protection. If the protection is needed in a court suit, the guardian is called a guardian ad litem, a guardian "for the suit."

guest. Someone who is present for a nonbusiness reason.

H

harmful. Involving physical or actual damage, impairment, pain, or illness in the body.

harmless. Not affecting substantial rights.

heart-balm statute. A statute that has abolished actions for breach of promise to marry, alienation of affections, criminal conversation, enticement, and seduction of a person under the age of consent.

hedonic damages. Damages that cover the victim's loss of pleasure or enjoyment.

hypothetical. (1) (n.) A set of facts that are assumed to exist for the purposes of discussion. (The teacher asked the students to analyze the hypothetical she gave them.) (2) (adj.) Assumed or based on conjecture. (The lawyer asked the witness a hypothetical question.)

I

imminent. Immediate in the sense of no significant or undue delay.

immunity. A defense that renders otherwise tortious conduct nontortious. The right to be free from civil or criminal prosecution.

impeach. Discredit.

implead. To bring a new party into the action.

implied warranty. *See* entries under Warranty.

imputed. Attributed to or imposed on someone or something.

imputed negligence. Negligence liability imposed solely because of the wrongdoing of others.

indemnity. The right to have another person pay you the full amount you were forced to pay. In the law of insurance, indemnity is the transfer of loss from an insured to an insurer to the extent of the agreed-upon insurance proceeds to cover the loss.

independent contractor. Someone who is hired or retained to produce a certain product or result. This person has considerable discretion in the methods used to achieve that product or result. The person is not an employee.

indivisible. Not separable into parts; pertaining to that which cannot be divided.

inducement. The part of the complaint alleging extrinsic facts in a defamation action.

inferior court. A lower court.

injurious falsehood. The publication of a false statement which causes special damages.

in loco parentis. "In the place of the parent"; assuming some or all the duties of a parent.

innuendo. The explanation of the defamatory meaning of words alleged by inducement in the complaint.

in personam jurisdiction. *See* Jurisdiction.

instigation. Insisting, directing, encouraging, or participating.

insured. The person designated as being protected against specified loss under an insurance policy.

intangible property. Property without physical form; a right.

intent. In general, the desire to bring about the consequences of an act (or omission), or the substantially certain knowledge that the consequences will follow from the act (or omission).

intentional infliction of emotional distress. Intentionally causing severe emotional distress by an act of extreme or outrageous conduct. This tort is also called the tort of outrage.

interlocutory order. A ruling of a trial court that resolves only part of the dispute.

interpleader. The practice whereby someone who holds property joins all claimants to the property in one action in order to avoid multiple liability if all claimants sued separately. The holder of the property (called the stakeholder) usually makes no claim to the property.

interrogatories. A pretrial discovery device consisting of written questions sent by one party to another to assist the sender of the questions in preparing for trial. Contention interrogatories ask for the application of law to facts. *See also* Verdict.

intervening cause. A force that actively operates in producing harm to another after the defendant's omission or act has been committed.

intestate. Without leaving a valid will.

intrusion. (a) An unreasonable encroachment into an individual's private affairs or concerns. One of the invasion of privacy torts. (b) Physically going on land, remaining on the land, going to a prohibited portion of the land, or failing to remove goods from the land. One of the elements of trespass to land.

invasion of privacy. *See* Appropriation, False Light, Intrusion, and Public Disclosure of Private Fact.

invitee. One who enters the land upon the express or implied invitation of the occupier of the land, in order to use the land for the purposes for which it is held open to the public or to pursue the business of the occupier.

involuntary dismissal. *See* Dismissal.

IRAC. An acronym that stands for the components of legal analysis. Issue (I), rule (R), analysis of the rule in light of the facts (A), and conclusion (C).

issue. A question about how one or more rules apply to facts. Also called a question of law. A question of fact, by contrast, is a question of what happened.

J

joint and several liability. Liability by more than one defendant, each of whom is liable for all of the damages.

joint enterprise. An express or implied agreement to participate in a common enterprise (usually of a financial or business nature) in which the participants have a mutual right of control.

joint tenancy. Property owned by two or more persons in undivided equal shares with a right of survivorship. If the parties are married, it is called a tenancy by the entirety.

joint tortfeasors. Persons who together produce a tortious wrong.

judgment creditor. The person to whom a money judgment is owed.

judgment debtor. The person who owes a money judgment to another.

judgment NOV. A judgment notwithstanding the jury. It is a judgment ordered by the trial judge that is contrary to the verdict reached by the jury.

judgment proof. Having few or no assets from which a money judgment can be satisfied.

jurisdiction. The power of the court. Its subject matter jurisdiction is its power to hear certain kinds of cases. Its geographic jurisdiction is its power over a certain area of the country. Its personal jurisdiction (also called in personam jurisdiction) is its power to order a particular defendant to do something or to refrain from doing something.

L

legal analysis. The application of rules to facts in order to solve a legal problem or to prevent one from arising.

legal cause. *See* Proximate Cause.

legal encyclopedia. A multivolume set of books that alphabetically summarizes almost every legal topic.

legal issue. *See* Issue.

legal malpractice. Negligence or other misconduct committed by an attorney.

legal memorandum. An in-house (interoffice) presentation of legal analysis to a colleague or supervisor.

legal periodical. An ongoing publication (e.g., published six times a year) containing articles, case notes or studies, and other information on legal topics.

legal treatise. A book written by a private individual (or by a public official writing as a private citizen) that provides an overview, summary, or commentary on a legal topic.

legislative history. All the events that occur in the legislature before a bill is enacted into law as a statute.

lessee. Person renting property from another.

lessor. Person renting property to another.

lex loci delicti. The place of the wrong; place where the wrong occurred.

liability insurance. Insurance in which the insurer agrees to pay, on behalf of an insured, damages the latter is obligated to pay to a third party because of his or her legal liability to the third person for committing a tort or other wrong.

liable. Legally responsible; under an obligation to pay for a wrong committed.

libel. *See* Defamation, Libel Per Quod, Libel Per Se.

libel per quod.   A written statement that requires extrinsic facts for its defamatory meaning to be understood or for its reference to the plaintiff to be understood.

libel per se.   A written statement that is defamatory on its face.

licensee.   One who enters the land for his or her own purposes, but with the express or implied consent of the occupier.

lien.   A security or encumbrance on property; a claim or charge on property for the payment of a debt.

local action.   A lawsuit that can be brought in only one place, namely where the *res* or subject matter of the suit is located.

Lord Campbell's Act.   A statute that allowed a separate cause of action for a tort that caused the death of the victim.

loss of consortium.   *See* Consortium.

M

malfeasance.   Wrongful or illegal actions by a public official.

malice, acting with.   (1) Doing something with ill will, hatred, or a desire to harm. (2) Doing something recklessly. (3) Doing something knowingly. (4) Doing something with an improper motive.

malicious prosecution.   The malicious initiation or procurement of legal proceedings without probable cause. The proceedings terminate in favor of the accused.

malpractice.   Wrongful or illegal actions by a service provider such as a lawyer or doctor.

material.   Important to a transaction or event.

medical malpractice.   Negligence or other misconduct committed by a doctor. *See also* Malpractice.

memorandum.   *See* Legal Memorandum.

merchantable.   Fit for the ordinary purposes for which the goods are used. *See also* Warranty of Merchantability.

misdemeanor.   A crime that is punishable by incarceration for a term of a year or less.

misfeasance.   Improper or unreasonable action.

misrepresentation.   A false statement of fact made with the intent to mislead and to have the plaintiff rely on the statement. The plaintiff suffers actual damage due to a justifiable reliance on the statement.

monitor a bill.   To find out the current status of a proposed statute (i.e., a bill) in the legislature and to keep track of all the forces that are trying to enact, defeat, or modify the bill.

movant.   The party making a motion to the court.

N

necessity.   The privilege to use the property of others in order to prevent immediate harm or damage to persons or property.

negligence.   Harm caused by unreasonable conduct.

negligence per se.   Negligence as a matter of law. There is no need to present evidence that the acts and omissions were unreasonable.

no-fault insurance.   An auto insurance plan in which each person's own insurance company pays for injury or damage up to a certain limit, regardless of whether its insured was at fault.

nominal damages.   A small amount of money awarded when there has been no actual loss or injury.

nonfeasance.   The failure to act; an omission.

notes to decisions.   Summaries of court opinions interpreting a statute. The summaries are printed beneath the text of the statute in annotated codes.

notice of appeal.   A formal statement by a party to an appellate court that he or she is appealing a judgment.

notice pleading.   A short and plain statement of a claim showing that the pleader is entitled to relief.

NOV.   *See* Judgment NOV.

nuisance.   A private nuisance is a substantial interference with the reasonable use and enjoyment of private land. A public nuisance is an unreasonable interference with a right common to the general public.

O

occupier of land.   Anyone in possession of land claiming a right to possession.

offensive. Offending the personal dignity of an ordinary person who is not unduly sensitive.

official immunity. A government employee cannot be liable for torts he or she commits within the scope of employment.

on all fours. Expression meaning that the facts are exactly (or overwhelmingly) the same.

opinion. (1) A court's written explanation of how it applied the law to the facts before it to resolve a legal dispute. Also called a case. (2) A belief as to the existence of a fact or a judgment as to the value or quality of something.

opinion of the attorney general. Legal advice given by the attorney general to government officials on legal issues such as the legality of a proposed agency action.

ordinance. A law passed by the local legislative branch of government (e.g., city council, county commission).

out-of-pocket rule. A measure of damages that gives the plaintiff the difference between the value of what he or she parted with and the value of what was received.

outrage, tort of. *See* Intentional Infliction of Emotional Distress.

outrageous and extreme conduct. Atrocious, totally intolerable, shocking behavior.

P

pain and suffering. Disagreeable mental or emotional experience. Part of general damages.

palimony. A nonlegal term that means payments made by one unmarried party to another after they cease living together, usually because of an enforceable contract to do so while they were together.

parasitic. Attached to something else, e.g., another tort.

parasitic damages. Damages for mental anguish (pain and suffering) that attach to a physical injury.

peace officer. A person appointed by the government to keep the peace.

per curiam. "By the court." A per curiam opinion is one that does not name the particular judge who wrote it.

peremptory challenge. A request that someone be excluded from a jury without any reasons stated for this request.

person. For purposes of battery, one's body, something attached to the body, or something so closely associated with the body as to be identified with it.

personal jurisdiction. *See* Jurisdiction.

personal property. *See* Property.

petition. *See* Complaint.

pleading. A pre-trial paper or document filed in court stating the position of one of the parties on the cause(s) of action or on the defense(s).

prejudice. (1) Pertaining to what cannot be relitigated. If a motion or lawsuit is dismissed with prejudice, it cannot be relitigated on the same facts. If a motion or lawsuit is dismissed without prejudice, it can be relitigated on the same facts if the original problem with it is cured. (2) Having a bias, which is a preconceived feeling or opinion.

preponderance of the evidence. It is more likely than not that the defendant's act or omission was a substantial factor in producing the injury. Or, it is more likely than not that "but for" what the defendant did or failed to do, the injury would not have occurred.

presumption. An assumption that a certain fact is true.

prima facie case. Enough factual allegations by a party to cover every element of a cause of action.

prima facie tort. Intentionally inflicting harm that causes special damages.

primary authority. Any law that a court could rely on to reach a decision. *See also* Authority.

primary insurance. Insurance that pays compensation for a loss ahead of any other insurance coverage the policyholder may have.

principal. The person on whose behalf an agent is acting and who has some authority or control over the agent who is so acting.

privilege. A defense to the commission of a tort.

privity. The relationship that exists between two parties who directly enter a contract with each other.

probable cause. (a) A suspicion based upon the appearance of circumstances that are strong enough to allow a reasonable person to believe that a criminal charge against a person is true. (b) Reasonable cause to believe that good grounds exist to initiate a civil proceeding.

procedural law. The set of rules that govern the mechanics of resolving a dispute in court or an administrative agency, e.g., a rule on how to ask for an extension of time to file something.

products liability. A general term that covers different causes of action based on products that cause harm: negligence, breach of express warranty, misrepresentation, breach of implied warranty of fitness for a particular purpose, breach of implied warranty of merchantability, and strict liability in tort.

property. Real property is land and anything attached to the land. Personal property is every other kind of property. *See also* Intangible Property, Tangible Property.

proprietary function. A function that cannot be performed adequately *only* by the government—unlike a governmental function.

proximate cause. The defendant is the cause in fact of the plaintiff's injury, the injury was the foreseeable consequence of the original risk, and there is no policy reason why the defendant should not be liable for what he or she caused in fact. Proximate cause is also referred to as the legal cause.

publication. Communication of a statement to someone other than the plaintiff.

public disclosure of private fact. Unreasonable disclosure of private facts about an individual's life that are not matters of legitimate public concern.

public figure. Someone in whom the public has a legitimate interest because of his or her achievements, reputation, or occupation.

punitive damages. Non-compensatory damages designed to punish the defendant and deter similar conduct by others. Also called exemplary damages.

R

real property. *See* Property.

reasonable person. An ordinary, prudent person who uses reasonable care to avoid injuring others. An ordinary person who is not unduly sensitive.

reckless. Wanton and wilful; creating a very great risk that something will happen. Acting with the knowledge that harm will probably result.

record. The official collection of all the trial pleadings, exhibits, orders, and word-for-word testimony given during a trial.

release. The giving up or relinquishing of a claim.

remand. To send back.

remittitur. The power of a trial court to decrease the amount of a jury's award of damages. The plaintiff is told that a new trial will be ordered if the plaintiff does not agree to the decrease.

reporter. A volume containing the full text of court opinions.

request for admissions. A request by one party of another that the latter admit or deny certain facts; the facts admitted do not then have to be established at trial.

res. Subject matter.

res ipsa loquitur. "The event speaks for itself." The event would not have happened without negligence.

res judicata. A judgment on the merits, which will prevent the same parties from relitigating the same cause of action.

respondeat superior. "Let the master answer." Rule by which an employer is liable for the torts of the employee committed within the scope of employment.

respondent. The party against whom an appeal is brought. Also called the appellee.

retainer. An agreement to hire someone.

reversionary interest. A right to the future enjoyment of land that is presently being enjoyed by another. The property that reverts to the grantor after the expiration of an intervening interest.

review. To examine in order to determine whether any errors of law were made.

rule. A standard of conduct. A government rule is enforceable, in that its violation can lead to sanctions.

rules of court. The procedural laws (often called court rules or procedural court rules) that govern the mechanics of litigation before a particular court.

S

sale. The passing of title to property from a seller to a buyer for a price.

satisfaction. Full payment or compensation.

scienter. The intent to mislead. Making a statement while having the knowledge or belief that the statement is false, or acting in reckless disregard for its truth or falsity. Scienter includes an intent that the audience of the statement believe it and act in reliance on its truth.

scope of employment. That which is foreseeably done by an employee for the employer under the employer's specific or general control.

secondary authority. *See* Authority.

self-help. Conduct designed to protect rights on one's own without resort to the courts.

seller. (a) Someone in the business of selling. (b) Anyone who sells something.

service of process. The delivery to a defendant of a formal notice ordering him or her to appear in court to answer the allegations of the plaintiff.

settlement. A resolution of a legal dispute without the need for a complete trial. If the case has already begun in court, the judge may have to approve the terms of the settlement. A settlement precis is a relatively brief document used by a party to advocate a settlement. It states an amount the party is willing to settle the case for. To support this request, the precis summarizes facts, theories of recovery, medical expenses, lost wages or profits, and other components of damages. If the document is more elaborate, it is often called a settlement brochure.

shepardize. To use the volumes of *Shepard's Citations* to check the history and validity of what you are shepardizing, and in the process, to obtain leads to other relevant material.

sine qua non test. *See* But-For Test.

slander. *See* Defamation, Disparagement, Slander Per Quod, Slander Per Se.

slander of title. *See* Disparagement.

slander per quod. An oral defamatory statement that does not fit into one of the four categories that constitute slander per se.

slander per se. A statement that is defamatory in one of the following four ways: it accuses the plaintiff of a crime; it accuses the plaintiff of having a communicable disease; it accuses the plaintiff of sexual misconduct; it adversely affects the plaintiff's trade, profession, or calling.

sovereign immunity. Protection of the state from being sued without its permission.

special damages. Actual economic or pecuniary losses, such as medical expenses and lost wages. Also called consequential damages.

special verdict. *See* Verdict.

stakeholder. *See* Interpleader.

standing. The legal right to initiate a court proceeding.

statute. A law passed by the legislature declaring, commanding, or prohibiting something.

statutory code. A collection of statutes organized by subject matter.

stay. To stop or halt.

stipulated. Agreed upon. There is no need to have a trial on what the parties stipulate.

strict liability. Liability or responsibility for a result, even if there was no fault or moral impropriety in causing the result.

strict liability in tort. Physical harm caused by a defective product that is unreasonably dangerous. The plaintiff must be a user or consumer; the defendant must be a seller.

subject matter jurisdiction. *See* Jurisdiction.

subpoena duces tecum. A command that specific documents or other items be produced.

subrogation. The process by which one insurance company seeks reimbursement from another company or person for a claim it has already paid.

subscription. (a) The act of writing one's name. (b) The signature of the attorney who prepared the complaint.

substantive law. The nonprocedural rules that govern rights and obligations.

sui generis.   Unique; of its own kind or class.

summary judgment.   A decision reached on the basis of the pleadings alone without going through an entire trial, because there is no dispute on any material facts.

supersedeas **bond.**   A bond posted by the party that seeks to set aside a judgment covering the amount of the judgment.

superseding cause.   An intervening cause that is beyond the foreseeable risk originally created by the defendant's unreasonable acts or omissions. An intervening cause that creates a highly extraordinary harm.

survival.   When a tortfeasor or the victim dies from a cause unrelated to the tort, certain kinds of tort actions survive and can be brought by the estate or representative of the deceased.

T

tangible property.   Property that has a physical form that can be seen or touched.

tenancy by the entirety.   *See* Joint tenancy.

tenancy in common.   Property owned by two or more persons in shares that may or may not be equal, with no right of survivorship.

term of art.   A word or phrase that has a special or technical meaning.

testate.   Leaving a valid will.

tort.   A civil wrong that has caused harm to person or property for which a court will provide a remedy. While tort and breach of contract are separate theories of recovery, there are circumstances in which it is a tort to induce a breach of contract.

tortfeasor.   A wrongdoer who has committed a tort.

trade libel.   *See* Disparagement.

transcribe.   To provide a word-for-word account or recording of what was said.

transferred intent.   The defendant's intent to commit a tortious act against one person is transferred to the person who was in fact the object of this intent. Also, if the defendant intends to commit one tort but in fact commits another, the law may transfer the intent to cover the tort that was committed.

transitory action.   A lawsuit that may be brought in more than one place.

treatise.   *See* Legal Treatise.

treaty.   An international agreement between two or more countries. In the United States, the president makes treaties by and with the consent of the Senate.

trespasser.   One who enters land without the consent of the occupier and without any privilege to do so.

trespass to chattels.   An intentional interference with personal property resulting in dispossession, impairment, or deprivation of use.

trespass to land.   An intentional intrusion on land in possession of another.

U

unconscionable.   Substantially unfair because of highly unequal bargaining positions of the parties.

unemancipated child.   *See* Emancipated Child.

United States.   A term that usually refers to the federal government in legal references.

V

vendee.   Buyer.

vendor.   Seller.

venue.   The place of a trial.

verdict.   The decision of a jury. A general verdict simply states which party wins. A general verdict with interrogatories states which party wins and answers several specific fact questions posed by the judge. A special verdict answers several specific fact questions posed by the judge, but does not state who wins.

verification.   An affidavit signed by a party stating that he or she has read a complaint or other pleading and that it is accurate to the best of his or her knowledge, information, and belief.

vicarious liability.   Liability imposed solely because of the wrongdoing of others.

voidable.   Unenforceable at the option of someone.

voir dire.   The oral examination of prospective jurors for purposes of selecting a jury.

volenti non fit injuria.   "No wrong is done to one who consents."

voluntary dismissal.   *See* Dismissal.

W

waiver. The loss of a right or privilege because of an explicit rejection of it or because of a failure to claim it at the appropriate time.

wanton conduct. *See* Willful Conduct.

warrant. A written order issued by an authorized government body directing the arrest of a person.

warranty, breach of express. Damage caused by a false statement of fact relied on by the plaintiff and made with the intention or expectation that the statement will reach the plaintiff.

warranty of fitness for a particular purpose, breach of implied. Damage caused by a sale of goods by a seller who had reason to know the buyer was relying on the expertise of the seller in selecting the goods for a particular purpose. The goods were not fit for that purpose.

warranty of merchantability, breach of implied. Damage caused by a sale of goods by a merchant of goods of that kind. The goods were not fit for the ordinary purposes for which they are used.

willful conduct. Acting with the knowledge that harm will probably result.

with prejudice. *See* Prejudice.

without prejudice. *See* Prejudice.

worker's compensation. A system of providing for the cost of medical care and weekly payments to cover income loss of an insured employee if he or she is injured or killed on the job, regardless of blame for the accident.

writ of attachment. *See* Attachment.

writ of execution. *See* Execution.

wrongful birth. An action by parents of an unwanted deformed or impaired child for their own damages in the birth of the child.

wrongful conception or pregnancy. An action by parents of a healthy child they did not want.

wrongful death. A death caused by a tort. *See also* Lord Campbell's Act.

wrongful life. An action by or on behalf of an unwanted deformed or impaired child for its own damages in being born.

Index

Abate a Nuisance, Privilege to, 516, 595
Abduction of a Child, 4, 487
Ability, Apparent Present, 470
Abnormal Activity or Condition, 516
Abnormally Dangerous, 497, 500, 519
Abnormally Dangerous Activity, Strict Liability for, 6, 499, 519
Abortion, 438, 488
Absolute Liability, 542
Absolute Nuisance, 501
Absolute Official Immunity, 611
Absolute Privilege, 437, 548
Abuse of Process, 3, 388, 419, 424, 432, 604
Accident Checklist, 65
Accident Facts, 151, 619, 682
Account Receivable, 187
Accused, 423
Act, 456, 469
Acting in Concert, 312
Action, Local, 100
Action, Non-Derivative, 486
Action, Survival of, 333
Activity, Abnormally Dangerous, 499, 519
Activity, Public, 444
Act of God, 505, 568
Acts of Nature, 568
Actual Damage, 409, 419, 424, 478
Actual Knowledge, 526, 528
Actual Malice, 303, 449
Additur, 173
Administrative Agency, 12, 91
Administrative Code, 16
Administrative Decisions, 12, 17
Administrative Official, 612
Administrative Regulations. See Regulation
Admiralty, 605
Admissible, 79, 122, 167
Admissions, Request for, 128, 131
Adult Trespasser, 523
Adultery, 3, 486
Advantage, Economic, 554
Advantage, Interference with Prospective, 5, 554
Adverse Possessor, 495

Advertising, 353, 555
Advice, Attorney, 423
Advocacy, 38, 206
Aesthetics, 237
Affairs, Private, 443
Affection, Society, and Companionship, 485
Affections, Alienation of, 3, 388, 486
Affidavit, 108
Affirmative Conduct, 216
Affirmative Defense, 116, 435
Age, 589
Agency, 40, 432, 444, 467, 476, 497, 501. See also Administrative Agency
Agent and Principal, 260, 360, 478
Aggravated Damages or Injury, 292, 311, 539, 570
Agreement to Assume the Risk, 325
Aggressive, 589, 591
Aggressor, 592
A.H. Robins, 2
AIDS, 357, 449, 461
Air Pollution. See Pollution
Airlines, 243, 410, 504
Airport, 608
Alabama, 246
Alcohol, 368, 557
Alienation of Affections, 3, 388, 432, 486
Allegation of Jurisdiction, 105
Allergy, 369
ALR, 22, 49
Alter Conditions of Land, 528
Ambiguity in Consent Forms, 269
American Colonies, 13
American Digest System, 25, 49
American Jurisprudence, 2d, 19, 27, 49
American Law Institute. See Restatement
American Law Reports, 22, 49
American Revolution, 13
Amusement Park, 530
Analysis. See Legal Analysis
Analysis, Factor, 55, 231
Andrews Test, 215, 295
Anesthetics, Consent to, 269
Anger, 392
Animals, Diseased, 518

Animals, Strict Liability for, 6, 509
Animosity, 569
Annotated Bibliography, 30
Annotated Code, 15
Annotation, 21, 201
Annoyance, 392, 516
Answer, 104, 116, 381
Answers to Interrogatories, 143
Apartment, 518, 531
Apparent Present Ability, 470
Appeal, 181
Appeal Bond, 186
Appeal, Courts of, 91
Appeal, Direct, 179
Appeal, Notice of, 181
Appeal of Right, 90
Appeal of Worker's Compensation Case, 574
Appellant, 181
Appellate Brief, 181
Appellate Court, 181
Appellate Jurisdiction, 90
Appellate Review, 182
Appellee, 181
Appliances, Orthopedic, 142
Apprehension, 3, 457, 465, 469
Appropriation, 5, 442, 447, 448
Area, Commercial, 513
Area, Common, 532
Area, Residential, 517
Argument, Closing, 172
Arising out of Employment, 563, 568
Arkansas, 449, 688
Armed Forces, 137, 615
Arrest, 406, 411, 413, 415, 460, 602, 604, 611
Arrest, False, 406, 411, 604, 611
Arrest, Privilege to, 407
Arrest Warrant, 413
Artificial Condition, 524, 527
Arts, 447
Asbestos, 2
Assault, 3, 8, 388, 404, 415, 432, 455, 465, 467, 470, 569, 589, 592, 595, 599, 604
Assault and Transferred Intent, 470
Assault, Criminal, 455, 467

750

Assembler, 366
Assets, 187, 190
Assignment of Rights, 103, 189
Assignments, Research, 26
Assistant Role in Litigation,
 123
Association, Freedom of, 588
Assumption of Risk, 318, 324,
 335, 337, 362, 383, 506,
 511, 517, 580
Assumptions about Human
 Nature, 208
At Common Law, 13
Attack, Collateral, 179
Attempted Suicide, 391
Attestation Clause, 85
Attorney. See Lawyer
Attractive Nuisance, 527
At Will Employment, 558
Authentication, 194
Authority, Confinement by
 Legal, 407
Authority, Primary, 11
Authority, Secondary, 17
Authorization, 261, 511, 517
Automobile, 1, 65, 98, 264,
 376, 398, 529, 603, 686
Automobile Accident, 65, 398
Automobile Guest, 529
Aviation, 504
Avoidable Consequences, 311,
 321
Award, Jury, 1

Background Information, 63
Bad Faith, 539, 556
Bailment, 188, 345
Bankruptcy Court, 2
Barn, 528
Barriers, Physical, 406
Battery, 3, 8, 388, 404, 415,
 420, 453, 455, 470, 485,
 569, 580, 589, 591, 595,
 599, 604, 610, 611, 614
Battery and Transferred Intent,
 470
Battery by Doctor, 269
Beauty Parlor, 358
Belief, Reasonable, 582, 589,
 591, 595. See also
 Probable Cause.
Believability, 168, 548
Beneficiary-Survivor, 337
Benefit, 311, 443, 447, 458,
 554
Beyond a Reasonable Doubt,
 168
Bias, 117

Bibliography, Annotated, 30
Bill Collection, 446
Bill, Legislative, 32
Bill, Medical, 363, 419
Bill of Particulars, 120
Birth, Wrongful, 488
Biting by Animal, 509
Blackmail, 537
Blasting, 7, 503, 504, 506, 510,
 516
Blood, 357, 540
Bluffing, 590, 592
Board, Medical Review, 269
Board, Worker's
 Compensation, 574
Bodily Contact, Offensive, 454
Body Impact, 292, 397
Body of Complaint, 105
Boilerplate Language, 109, 115
Bona Fide Purchaser, 540
Bond, Appeal, 186
Bond, Supersedeas, 182
Bottle, Exploding, 244
Braces, 142
Breach of Contract, 377, 549
Breach of Duty, 203, 230, 294,
 319, 346, 523, 527
Breach of Duty Equation, 319
Breach of Peace, 415
Breach of Warranty. See
 Warranty
Brief, Appellate, 181
Broad vs. Narrow, 39
Brothers, 615
Building, Apartment, 518, 531
Burden of Avoiding the Harm,
 512, 514
Burden of Persuasion, 167
Burden of Production, 167
Burden of Proof, 167
Burden or Inconvenience, 234,
 237, 371
Business Disparagement, 545
Business Guest, 528
Business Objective, 455, 476,
 498, 513, 537, 564
Business of Selling, 359
Business Partners, 478
Business Torts, 9, 544
But-For Test, 52, 251, 283,
 321, 378, 393, 408
Buyer, Home, 531
Bystander, 215, 345, 377

California, 219, 270, 277, 398
Campbell, Lord, 337
Capacity to Consent, 580
Capacity to Sue, 103

Cap, Damage, 269, 384
Caption of Complaint, 105
Car. See Automobile
Cardozo, 215, 295
Care, Ordinary, 231
Care, Reasonable, 213, 230,
 504, 523
Care, Standard of, 523
Careless, 458
Carrier, Common, 219, 326,
 391, 504
CARTWHEEL, 22, 28
Case File, 190
Case Law. See Court Opinion
Causation, 53, 203, 245, 250,
 276, 282, 286, 294, 321,
 378, 393, 397, 408, 454,
 475, 505, 547, 551, 567
Causation and Res Ipsa, 245
Causation of Emotional
 Distress, 393
Cause, Challenge for, 118
Cause in Fact, 282, 321, 475,
 505
Cause, Intervening, 295
Cause, Legal, 282, 293
Cause of Action, 2, 62, 179
Cause, Probable, 419, 422
Cause, Proximate, 203, 282,
 294, 397, 505, 568
Cause, Speculative, 378
Cause, Superseding, 293, 295
Caution, 235
Caveat Emptor, 531
Cells, 541
Certainty, 205, 242
Chain of Distribution, 366
Chain Sequence, Causation,
 283
Challenge for Cause, 118
Challenge, Peremptory, 118
Characteristics, Mental or
 Physical, 239
Charge to Jury, 172
Charitable Immunity, 613
Charity, 528, 613
Charter, 12, 17
Chattels, 3, 470, 535, 593,
 595, 599, 604
Chattels, Recapture of, 599
Chattels, Trespass to, 6, 470,
 535, 604
Checklist in Interviewing, 65
Child, Abduction of, 4, 487
Child, Deformed, 488
Child, Discipline of, 601
Child, Emancipated, 485
Child, Enticement of, 4, 487

Child, Parent, Liability, 266
Child, Services of, 485
Child, Standard of Care for, 240
Child Suing Parents, 615
Child Trespasser, 523, 526
Child, Unwanted, 488
Choice of Law, 101
Church, 520, 587
Cigarettes, 352
Circuit Courts, 27, 93
Circumstances, Totality of, 231
Citation, 29
Citizen, Private, 412, 413, 519
Citizenship, Diversity of, 95
City, 40, 607
Civil Arrest, 415
Civil Assault, 3, 465. See also Assault
Civil Battery, 3, 455, 580. See also Battery
Civil Law and Common Law, 13
Civil Liability, 501
Civil Procedure, 8, 88, 122
Civil Proceedings, Wrongful, 424
Civil Rights Act, 3, 95, 420, 444, 455, 467, 497, 610, 612
Civil Standard, 250
Civil Wrong, 2
Claims Act, Federal Tort, 603
Claim for Worker's Compensation, 574
Claims, Insurance, 556, 636
Class Action, 104
Clear and Convincing Evidence, 168
Clear Chance, Last, 317, 322
Client, Background Information on, 63
Client Intake Memorandum, 76
Client Interview and Legal Analysis, 43
Client Verification, 78
Client-Attorney Privilege, 132, 580
Closing Argument, 172
Coast Guard, 603
Code, 12, 15
Co-Defendant, 105
Code Napoléon, 13
Code of Federal Regulations, 16
Code of Justinian, 13
Coercion, 582, 584
Cohabitation, 339
Collateral Attack, 179
Collateral Estoppel, 178, 180

Collateral Matter, 583
Collateral Source Rule, 311
Collection, 62, 185, 192
Collision, 23, 625
Colloquium, 436
Colonies, American, 13
Colorado, 688
Color of Law, 420, 444, 455, 467, 497, 610
Comfort, Personal, 566
Comment, Fair, 434
Commercial Area, 513
Commercial Speech, 547
Commission, Worker's Compensation, 574
Common Area, 532
Common Carrier, 219, 326, 391, 504
Common Law, 13, 15, 40, 334, 433
Common Law and Civil Law, 13
Common Law and Statutes, 15
Common Law Defamation, 433
Common Law Survival of Actions, 334
Common Pleas, 90
Common Sense, 80, 209, 261, 286, 348
Common, Tenancy in, 188
Communicable Disease, 437
Communication Checklist, 74
Communication, Confidential, 448
Communication, Intentional, 436
Community Property, 187
Community Values, 14
Companionship, Affection, and Society, 485
Comparative Negligence, 318, 323, 328, 383
Comparative Standard, 231, 238
Compensation, 560, 594, 603
Compensatory Damages, 302
Competence, Lawyer, 274
Competition, Fair, 546, 554
Complaint, 44, 96, 104, 106, 110, 114, 379, 424
Complete Confinement, 407
Compliance with Statute, 256
Component Part Manufacturer, 366
Compulsory Joinder, 103
Concealment of Fact, 478
Concert, Acting in, 312
Conclusion of Law, Pleading, 107

Conclusion of Memo, 53, 58
Conclusory Legal Analysis, 57
Concurrent Jurisdiction, 90
Condition, Abnormal, 516
Conditional Threat, 470
Condition, Artificial, 524, 527
Condition, Dangerous, 500
Condition, Known, 505
Condition, Latent, 531
Condition, Natural or Non-Natural, 524, 526
Condition, Pre-existing, 292, 570
Conduct, Affirmative, 216
Conduct, Extreme, 390
Conduct, Standard of, 249
Conduct, Reckless or Wanton, 256, 318, 391
Conduct, Willful, 256, 318, 391
Conference, Pre-Trial, 118
Confidentiality, 150, 448
Confinement, 403, 407, 409
Conflict of Law, 9, 101
Connecticut, 689
Congress, 34, 383, 611, 612
Conscious Disregard, 303
Consciousness, 457
Consent, 98, 269, 443, 460, 542, 525, 580, 583
Consent, Informed, 269, 583
Consent to Enter, 525
Consent to Jurisdiction, 98
Consequence, Extraordinary, 293
Consequence, Normal, 293
Consequences, Avoidable, 311, 321
Consequential Damages, 303, 363
Consideration, Contract, 223
Consortium, Loss of, 484
Consortium, Parental, 485
Constitutional Law, 9, 12, 16, 40, 430, 447, 449, 603
Construction, 506
Consumer, 363, 367, 377
Consumer Product Safety Act, 95
Consumer Product Safety Commission, 343, 364, 383
Contact, Apprehension of, 465
Contact, Harmful or Offensive, 454, 465, 469
Contact, Imminent, 457, 465
Contact, Physical, 536
Contacts, Minimum, 99
Containers, 343

Contention Interrogatories, 132

Contingent Fee, 62, 268

Continuing Interrogatories, 143

Continuous Interference, 512

Contract and Tort, 8

Contract, Breach of, 2, 378

Contract Consideration, 223

Contract, Government, 602

Contractor, Independent, 262, 524

Contract, Privity of, 345, 360

Contract Relations, Interference with, 5, 549, 604

Contract, Standardized, 362

Contract, Voidable, 549

Contribution, 314

Contributory Negligence, 245, 265, 317, 335, 349, 362, 378, 505, 511, 517, 560

Contributory Negligence, Imputed, 265

Control and Dominion, 536

Control, Exclusive, 243, 496

Control, Mutual, 264

Control, Physical, 536

Controversy, 435

Conversation, Criminal, 3

Conversion, 3, 114, 388, 535, 476, 593, 604, 611, 614

Copying and Inspection, 126

Corpus Juris Secundum, 19, 27, 49

Cost of Litigation, 1, 419

Cost of Redesign, 371

Cost of Repair, 537

Cost of Restoration, 516

Cost of Taking Precautions, 237

Counteranalysis, 38, 40, 56

Counterclaim, 105

Counts in Complaint, 105, 115

County Court, 92

Course of Employment, 563. See also Scope of Employment

Court, Appellate, 182

Court, Bankruptcy, 2

Court, County, 92

Court, Divisions of, 91

Court, Federal, 91

Court Functions, 608

Court, Justice of the Peace, 92

Court, Municipal, 92

Court of Appeal, 27, 91, 93, 303, 352

Court of First Instance, 90

Court of Original Jurisdiction, 90

Court Opinion, 12, 13, 26, 28, 434

Court, Probate, 92

Court Rules, 13, 17, 40

Court, State, 90

Court Stenographer, 145

Court, Supreme, 181

Court, Surrogate, 92

Crashworthiness, 376

Credit, 447

Creditor, Judgment, 185

Crime and Tort, 2, 8

Crimes, 2, 8, 138, 249, 388, 415, 419, 423, 437, 455, 467, 518, 580

Criminal Arrest, 415

Criminal Assault, 467

Criminal Battery, 455

Criminal Conversation, 3

Criminal Human Force, Intervening, 295

Criminal Liability, 531

Criminal Statute, 249

Cross-Claim, 105

Cross-Complaint, 105

Cross-Examination, 124, 169, 171

Culpability, 197

Cults, 584

Cure, Promise to, 266

Current Law Index, 27, 29

Custody, 407

Custom and Usage, 248, 267, 348, 582, 605

Customer, 219, 529

Cut-Off Test, 282, 291

Dalkon Shields, 2

Dam, 519

Damage, Actual, 409, 419, 424, 476

Damage Caps, 269, 384

Damage, Physical, 458

Damage, Property, 310, 539

Damages, 71, 156, 302, 337, 352, 391, 403, 436, 444, 488, 511, 517, 539, 516, 519, 550, 547, 554, 556, 632

Damages and Legal Interviewing, 61

Damages, Compensatory, 302

Damages, Complaint for, 113

Damages, Consequential, 303, 363

Damages, Economic, 476

Damages, Exemplary or Punative, 303, 387, 404, 444, 455, 497, 537

Damages for Nuisance, 516, 519

Damages for Wrongful Death, 337

Damages for Wrongful Life, 488

Damages, General, 303, 419

Damages, Hedonic, 303

Damages, Mitigation of, 511, 517

Damages, Negligence, 302

Damages, Nominal, 302, 497

Damages, Out-of-Pocket, 476

Damages, Pecuniary, 476

Damages, Presumed, 436

Damages, Punitive, 303, 387, 404, 444, 455, 497, 537

Damages, Special, 4, 303, 436, 519, 547, 554, 556

Damages to Reputation, 403

Danger, 235, 589

Danger, Discovery of the, 349

Danger, Inherent, 263

Danger, Obvious, 368

Danger Sign, 348

Danger, Zone of, 214, 397

Dangerous, Abnormally, 497, 499

Dangerous Activity, 500

Dangerous Condition, 500, 519

Dangerous Lake, 505

Dangerous Propensities, 266, 509

Dangerous, Unreasonably, 363, 367

Data, Digesting and Indexing, 157

Daughter, 487. See also Child

Deadly Force, 413, 590, 593, 596

Dealer and Privity, 360

Death, Wrongful, 333, 335

Debts, 185, 446, 448

Deceit. See Misrepresentation

Decennial Digests, 26

Deceptive Advertising, 555

Decisions, Administrative, 12, 17

Deep Pocket, 1, 62, 259, 361, 544

Defamacast, 429

Defamation, 3, 388, 404, 420, 429, 444, 447, 545, 546

Defamation and Disparagement, 545

Defamation, Group, 436

Defamatory Statement, 430, 434, 546
Default Judgment, 116
Defect, Design, 344, 367, 369
Defect, Discovery of the, 349
Defect, Kinds of, 344
Defect, Manufacturing, 344, 367
Defect, Warning, 344, 367
Defective Product, 344, 363, 367
Defendant's Case, 171
Defendants, Multiple, 245
Defenses, 116, 198, 317, 378, 419, 435, 460, 505, 579, 589, 591, 595
Defense, Affirmative, 116, 435
Defense Costs, 419
Defense of Others, 460, 591
Defense of Property, 595
Defenses, Negligence, 198, 317
Defenses, Products Liability, 378
Defenses, Strict Liability, 505
Defensive Medicine, 268
Deficiencies, Mental, 320
Definitions in Legal Analysis, 46
Deformed Child, 488
Delaware, 689
Delegable Duty, 263
Delicti, Lex Loci, 101
Delivery of Babies, 268
Demonstration, 611
Demurrer, 105
Denial, 116
Dentists, 357
Department Store, 219, 408, 446, 529, 532
Dependents, 338
Deposition, 44, 124, 144, 191, 199
Depravation of Use of Personal Property, 539
Depression, 309
Derogation of Common Law, 15
Derogatory Language, 404
DES, 290
Descriptive Word Index, 26
Design Defect, 344, 367, 369
Detain, Privilege to, 408
Detour, 260, 565
Diagnostic, 639
Diethylstilbestrol, 290
Digest by Person, 161
Digest by Subject Matter, 162
Digest Library, 25, 27, 28, 49

Digesting Discovery Data, 157
Direct Appeal, 179
Direct Examination, 169, 171
Direct Harm, 397
Directed Verdict, 169, 171
Disability, 239, 305, 576
Discharge, Retaliatory, 558
Discipline of Children, 601
Disclaimer of Warranty, 362
Disclose, Duty to, 478
Disclosure of Private Fact, Public, 442, 447
Discomfort, 403, 516
Discount for Present Value, 306
Discovered Trespasser, 525
Discover the Danger, Duty to, 531
Discover the Defect, 349
Discover the Peril, 322
Discovery, 120
Discovery Data, Digesting, 157
Discovery, Scope of, 122
Discretion, 90, 275, 604, 606, 611
Discretionary Appeal, 90
Discrimination, 614
Disease, Communicable, 437
Diseased Animals, 518
Diseases, Work-Related, 563
Disfigurement, 576
Dismiss, Motion to, 165
Dismissal, 117, 179
Disparagement, 4, 420, 432, 545, 546, 554
Dispossession, 6, 536, 539, 601
Disproportionate Force, 591, 595
Disregard, Reckless, 478
Distress, 309, 386, 392, 571
Distress, Intentional Infliction of Emotional, 5, 386
Distribution, Chain of, 366
Distributor, 366
District Court, 27, 91
Diversity Cases, 95, 100
DNA, 541
Doctor, 70, 218, 266, 284, 357, 425, 448, 458, 460, 478, 540, 551, 583, 603, 621
Doctor Guarantee, 266
Doctor Liability, 266
Doctor-Patient Privilege, 132, 266, 580
Documents, Production of, 126, 130, 191
Documents, Request for

Production of, 130
Doing Business, 98
Domestic Animals, 6, 509
Domestic Relations and Torts, 8
Domestic Relations Court, 92
Domestic Workers, 562
Domicile, 95, 98
Dominion and Control, 536
Double Recovery, 337, 550
Dower, 187
Drafting a Complaint, 114
Drafting Interrogatories, 131, 143
Dram Shop Liability, 557
Driver and Passenger, 264
Drivers License, 138
Drugs, 369
Duty, 203, 212, 263, 294, 397, 478, 526, 531. See also Breach of Duty
Duty and Emotional Distress, 397
Duty and Proximate Cause, 294
Duty, Delegable, 263
Duty, Negligence, 212
Duty, Non-Delegable, 263
Duty to Disclose, 478
Duty to Discover the Danger, 531
Duty to Inspect, 526
Duty to Warn, 218
Dynamite, 7, 503

Earnings, Lost, 338, 403
Easement, 187
Economic Advantage, 554
Economic Hardship, 516
Economic Loss, 302, 363, 476
Effectiveness, 237
Eggshell Skull, 292, 297
Element Breakdown, 44
Elements, 2, 41, 46, 62, 133, 198
Elevator, 532
Emancipated Child, 485, 615
Embarrassment, 392, 395, 444
Embezzlement, 476
Emergencies, 233, 269, 583
Emergency Room, 343
Emotional Distress, Infliction of, 5, 386, 392
Employer-Employee, 135, 219, 259, 315, 326, 364, 394, 419, 432, 444, 455, 467, 471, 476, 497, 501, 537, 544, 558, 560, 563, 568, 571, 605

Employment, Arising out of, 563, 568
Employment At Will, 558
Employment, Course of, 563
Employment, Scope of, 260, 315, 389, 404, 420, 455, 537, 610
Employment, Tortious Interference with, 558
Encyclopedias, 18, 49
Enforcement of a Judgment, 185
Enforcement Officer, Law, 404, 420, 455, 467
England, 13
Enjoyment of Land, 506
Enter Land, Consent to, 526
Enterprise, Joint, 259, 263
Enticement of Child, 4, 487
Enticement of Spouse, 4, 487
Entirety, Tenancy by the, 188
Entry Land for Inspection, 126, 130
Environment, Character of the, 513
Environment Law, 9, 519
Equipment, Injury Caused by, 343
Equitable, 302, 315
Error, Harmless, 182
Error of Law, 91, 182
Error, Technical, 275
Escape and False Imprisonment, 403
Estate Law, 9
Estate, Representative of, 334
Estoppel, Collateral, 180
Eviction, 601
Evidence, 8, 79, 140, 168, 171, 175
Evidence, Clear and Convincing, 168
Evidence, Medical, 140
Evidence, Newly-Discovered, 175
Evidence, Prejudicial, 169
Evidence, Preponderance of the, 168
Evidence, Preserving, 122
Evidence, Rebuttal, 171
Evidence, Weight of the, 176
Evidentiary Privilege, 579
Exam Answer, 44, 50
Examination, Cross, 169, 171
Examination, Direct, 169, 171
Examination, Mental and Physical, 127, 645
Examination, Re-Direct, 169, 171

Exclusive Control, 243, 496
Exclusive Jurisdiction, 89
Execution, 186, 192
Exemplary Damages, 303, 387, 404, 444, 455, 497, 537
Exemplified, 194
Exempt Property, 189
Exhaustion of Administrative Remedies, 17
Exhibits, 142
Expectancy, Life, 338
Expectation of Benefit, 554
Expert Evidence, 140, 267
Explosion, 7, 244, 597
Express Assumption of the Risk, 325
Express Invitation, 526, 529
Express Warranty. See Warranty
Extortion, 425
Extraordinary Consequence, 293
Extraordinary, Highly, 293
Extreme Conduct, 390
Extrinsic Facts, 434, 437
Extrinsic Misconduct, 175

Face, On its, 430, 434
Facts, 42, 55, 50, 62, 81, 107, 116, 121, 151, 350, 434, 437, 447, 475, 478, 545, 619, 627
Fact, Concealment, 478
Fact Disputes, 116
Fact, Extrinsic, 434, 437
Fact, False Statement of, 350, 478, 545
Fact, Material, 116
Factor Analysis, 55
Factor, Substantial, 321. See also Cause in Fact
Factory, 515, 528
Fact Particularization, 82
Fact Pleading, 107
Fact, Public Disclosure of Private, 447
Failure to Act, 216
Fair Comment, 434
Fair Competition, 546
Fair Market Value, 310, 537
Faith, Bad, 539, 556
Faith, Good, 539, 556
False Arrest, 406, 411, 604, 611
False Statement of Fact, 545
Falsehood, Injurious, 548
False Imprisonment, 4, 388, 402, 420, 455, 470, 584, 590, 592, 604

False Light, 5, 388, 443, 448
False Pretenses, 476
False Statement of Fact, 350, 478, 545
Falsity, 435, 448, 478
Family Law, 8, 92, 484
Family Purpose Doctrine, 259, 265
Family, Threat to Immediate, 407
Family Tort Immunity, 614
Family, Torts Against, 484
Farm Workers, 562
Fault, 197, 435, 604
Fault, Liability without, 7, 356
Fear, 469
Federal Court Opinion, 27. See also Court Opinion
Federal Court System, 91
Federal Employees' Compensation Act, 605
Federal Employers' Liability Act, 95
Federal Food and Drug Administration, 364
Federal Law, 27, 34, 89, 91, 95, 100, 122, 364, 383, 404, 603
Federal Products Liability Law, 383
Federal Question, 89, 100
Federal Rules of Civil Procedure, 122
Federal Standards, 383
Federal Statute, 29, 34, 95
Federal Tort Claims Act, 95, 199, 364, 388, 404, 420, 432, 444, 455, 467, 476, 497, 501, 537, 603
Fee, Attorney, 268, 519
Fee Cap, 269, 384
Fee, Contingent, 62, 268
Fellow-Employee Rule, 561
Felony, 413, 415
Fences, 528
Fiduciary Relationship, 478
Figure, Public, 435, 448
Filing a Worker's Compensation Claim, 574
Final Judgment, 178
Final Resort, Court of, 91
Financial Data, 190
Fire, 530, 593, 608
Fire Department, 530, 608
Fireworks, 501
Firing, 558
First Amendment, 9, 447
First Instance, 90
First Party Insurance, 686

Fitness for a Particular
    Purpose. See Warranty
Fleeing and False Arrest, 413
Flooding, 503, 510
Florida, 690
Food and Drug Administration,
    Federal, 364
Football, 581
Force, 407, 413, 582, 590,
    593, 596
Force, Deadly, 413, 590, 593,
    596
Force, Disproportionate, 591,
    595
Force, Immediate, 407
Force of Nature, Intervening,
    295
Force, Physical, 407
Force, Reasonable, 413, 589,
    591, 595
Forced Sale, 192
Foreign Object, 368
Foreseeability, 203, 213, 234,
    236, 319, 369, 370, 505,
    526
Foreseeable Misuse, 370
Foreseeable Plaintiff, 213
Foreseeable Purpose, 369
Foreseeable Risk, 213, 296,
    505
Foreseeable Trespasser, 526
Foreseeable Use and Users,
    345, 369, 378
Formbooks, 18
Forms, Standard, 109
Forum Non Conveniens, 99
Forum State, 101, 188
Fours, On All, 27
France, 13
Fraud, 175, 614. See also
    Misrepresentation
FRCP, 122
Free Speech, 434
Freedom of Association, 588
Freedom of Movement, 406
Freedom of Press, 9, 430, 447
Freedom of Speech, 447
Fresh Pursuit, 415, 599
Fright, 392
Frolic and Detour, 260
Frost, 505
Full Faith and Credit, 194
Function, Governmental, 608
Function, Proprietary, 608
Future Harm, 589, 591
Funeral Home, 396
Future Earnings, 338

Gambling, 518
Garage, 530, 608

Garnishment, 192
General Damages, 303, 419
General Denial, 116
General Digest, 26
General Jurisdiction, 89
General Practitioner, 274
General Verdict, 172
Geographic Jurisdiction, 89
Georgia, 255, 691
Gertz v. Robert Welch, 434
Gestures, 429, 592
Gift of Liquor, 557
God, Act of, 505, 568
Going-and-Coming Rule, 564
Good Faith, 539, 556, 636
Good Samaritan, 217, 222
Good Standing, Medical, 267
Goods, Disparagement of, 546
Goods, Mass-Produced, 362
Goods, Merchantable, 359
Goods, Sale of, 7
Government, 9, 511, 602, 605,
    607, 608
Government as Defendant, 9
Government Authorization,
    511
Government, Federal, 603
Government, Local, 607
Government, State, 605
Governmental Function, 608
Governor, 605
Gratuitous Promise or
    Undertaking, 223
Gravity of Harm, 512
Grief, 392
Gross Negligence, 256
Grounds, Reasonable, 413
Group Defamation, 436
Guarantee, 266, 351
Guardian, 580
Guest, Automobile, 529
Guest, Business, 528
Guest in Inn, 219
Guest, Social, 528
Gun, 368, 371, 525, 597
Gun, Spring, 525, 597

Hallway, 532
Handguns. See Gun
Handicap, Physical, 239
Hardship, Economic, 516
Harm and Confinement, 403,
    409
Harm Caused by Animals, 509
Harm, Direct, 397
Harm, Foreseeable, 505
Harmful Contact, 454, 458,
    465, 469
Harm, Future, 589, 591
Harm, Gravity of the, 512

Harm, Immediate, 397
Harm, Intentional, 525
Harm, Kind of, 252
Harm, Physical, 363, 377
Harmless Error, 182
Hatred, 387, 404, 455, 537
Hawaii, 691
Heading of Memo, 54
Health Care Costs, 268
Hearsay, 122, 169
Heart-Balm Statute, 486
Hedonic Damages, 303
Heirs, 335
Helpless Peril, 322
Highly Extraordinary, 293
Highly Offensive, 443, 446,
    448
Highways, 518
Historical Data and
    Foreseeability, 209
History and Causation, 286
History, Legislative. See
    Legislative History
Hobbies, 137
Hockey, 583
Home Buyer, 531
Honest Belief, 548
Horror, 392
Horseplay, 565
Hospital, 70, 154, 245, 269,
    296, 343, 514, 605, 608,
    629, 633. See also Doctor
Hospital Emergency Room
    Injuries, 343
Hostility, 569. See also Malice
Host, Social, 557. See also
    Guest
Hotel, 219
House, Apartment, 531
House of Prostitution, 510,
    518
Human Force, Intervening
    Criminal, 295
Human Force, Intervening
    Innocent, 295
Human Nature, Assumptions
    about, 208
Humiliation, 392, 395, 403,
    419, 444
Hunting, 329
Husband, 132, 478, 486, 485,
    580, 614
Husband, Consortium Rights
    of, 485
Husband-Wife Privilege, 132,
    580
Hypothetical, 41

Idiosyncrasy, 459
Illegal Confinement, 406

Illinois, 15, 288, 438
Illness, 239, 309, 458
Ill Will, 303. See also Malice
Immediacy, 592
Immediate Family, Threats
    Against, 407
Immediate Force or Harm,
    397, 407
Immediate Possession, 536
Imminent, 457, 465, 470
Immunity, 9, 411, 579, 602,
    609, 611, 613, 614
Immunity, Absolute official,
    611
Immunity, Charitable, 613
Immunity, Intrafamily Tort,
    614
Immunity, Official, 609
Immunity, Qualified official,
    611
Immunity, Sovereign, 9, 411,
    602
Impact, Body, 397
Impairment, 458, 465, 539
Impeach, 121
Impersonation, 447
Impleader, 104
Implied Assumption of the
    Risk, 326
Implied Consent, 581
Implied Invitation, 526, 529
Implied Warranty. See
    Warranty
Importance, Social, 346, 371
Imprisonment. See False
    Imprisonment.
Imputed Contributory
    Negligence, 265
Imputed Negligence, 258, 264
Inducing a Breach of Contract,
    549
Inattentive Peril, 322
Incident to the Job, 564
Income Tax Returns, 136
Inconvenience, 234, 237, 371,
    392, 512, 539
Increased Risk, 568
Indemnity, 276, 314, 315
Independent Contractor, 262,
    524
Independent Liability, 259
Index, 22, 23, 157
Index to Legal Periodicals, 27,
    29
Indexing Discovery Data, 157
Indispensable Party, 103
Indivisible Result, 313
Inducement, 435
Industry, Heavy, 513
Inference of Negligence, 240

Inflammable Liquids, 503
Inflammatory Evidence, 169
Inflation, 304
Infliction of Emotional
    Distress, 386, 396
Informed Consent, 269, 583
Inherent Danger, 263
Initiation of Legal Proceedings,
    419, 422
Injunction, 302, 511, 516, 519,
    520, 550
Injurious Falsehood, 548
Injury, 2, 137, 141, 292, 311,
    343, 397, 419, 560, 570,
    628
Injury, Aggravation of, 292,
    311, 570
Injury, Emergency, 343
Injury, Latent, 2
Injury on the Job, 560
Injury, Physical, 397
Injury, Pre-Existing, 570
Injury, Subsequent, 137
Injury to Reputation, 419
Injury, Witness to, 397
In Loco Parentis, 601
Innkeeper, 219, 326, 391
Innocent Human Force,
    Intervening, 295
Innuendo, 435
In Personam Jurisdiction, 89,
    95
Insanity, 240, 292
Inspect, Duty to, 526
Inspection of Premises, 528
Instructions to the Jury, 172
Insults, 391, 589
Insurance, 9, 138, 156, 148,
    197, 268, 311, 346, 556,
    609, 614, 618, 623, 686
Insurance and Negligence,
    197, 686
Insurance Claims, 556, 618
Insurance, Liability, 609, 614,
    686
Insurance, Medical, 311
Insurance, Medical
    Malpractice, 268
Insurance Settlement, 556
Intake Memorandum, 76
Intangible Property, 188, 536
Integrity, Personal, 457
Intended Purpose, 369, 378
Intent, 3, 52, 205, 250, 351,
    391, 392, 403, 408, 454,
    457, 458, 465, 470, 478,
    496, 515, 519, 525, 536,
    547, 604, 614
Intent and Foreseeability, 205
Intentional Harm, 525

Intentional Human Force,
    Intervening, 295
Intentional Infliction of
    Emotional Distress, 5,
    386, 404, 420, 444, 467
Intentional Tort, 2, 614
Intentional Tortfeasor, 314
Intent, Legislative, 250
Intent to Disparage, 547
Intent to Mislead, 478
Intent, Transferred, 392, 408,
    458, 470
Inter-Office Memorandum of
    Law, 52, 77
Interests in Land, 495
Interference, 5, 510, 512, 513,
    539
Interference, Continuous, 512
Interference, Serious, 513, 539
Interference, Unreasonable,
    510
Interference with Contract
    Relations, 5, 549, 604
Interference with Employment,
    Tortious, 558
Interference with Property,
    596
Interference with Prospective
    Advantage, 5, 554
Interlocutory Order, 181
Intermeddle, 536, 540
Intermediate Appellate Court,
    91, 181
Interpleader, 104
Interrogatories, 191, 123, 131,
    132, 134, 143, 172
Interrogatories, Answers to,
    143
Interrogatories, Contention,
    132
Interrogatories, Continuing,
    143
Interrogatories, General
    Verdict with, 172
Intervening Cause, 295
Intervening Criminal Human
    Force, 295
Intervening Force of Nature, 295
Intervening Innocent Human
    Force, 295
Intervening Intentional Human
    Force, 295
Intervenor, 104
Interview Memorandum, 76
Interviewing, 8, 10, 42, 55, 61,
    134, 658
Interviewing and
    Interrogatories, 134
Interviewing and Legal
    Analysis, 42, 55

Intestacy, 335
Intolerable Conduct, 390
Intoxication, 557
Intrafamily Tort Immunity, 614
Intrinsic Misconduct, 175
Intrusion, 5, 52, 388, 442, 443, 446, 496
Invasion of Privacy, 5, 388, 432, 442, 604
Investigation, 8, 10, 42, 55, 61, 78, 84, 134, 189, 190, 416, 589, 591, 593, 595, 599, 631
Investigation Strategy, 84
Investigative Officer, 404, 420, 455, 467, 604
Invitation, Express or Implied, 526, 529
Invitee, 219, 523, 525, 529
Involuntary Dismissal, 117, 179
Iowa, 329, 597
IRAC, 38
Irrelevance, 169
Issue, 38, 631

Jail, 406
Joinder of Parties, 103
Joint and Several Liability, 258, 312, 625
Joint Enterprise, 259, 263
Joint Tenancy, 187
Joint Tortfeasor, 312, 314
Joke, 393, 469, 582
Journal, Law, 21
Judge, 437, 611, 612
Judgment, 172, 173, 176, 185, 275, 610, 611
Judgment and Discretion, Mistake Involving, 275
Judgment Creditor, 185
Judgment Debtor, 185
Judgment, Enforcement of, 185
Judgment, Entry of, 173
Judgment, Final, 178
Judgment NOV, 172, 173, 176
Judgment Proof, 185
Judgment, Satisfaction of, 610
Judgment, Summary. See Summary Judgment
Judicial Sale, 192
Jurisdiction, 16, 88, 89, 90, 95, 105, 612
Jurisdiction, Allegation of, 105
Jurisdiction, Appellate, 90
Jurisdiction, Diversity, 95
Jurisdiction, In Personam/ Personal, 89, 95

Jurisdiction, Subject Matter, 89
Jury, 1, 44, 117, 172, 175
Jury Misconduct, 175
Jury Selection, 117
Just Compensation, 603
Justice of the Peace Court, 92
Justifiable Reliance, 479
Justinian, Code of, 13
Juvenile Court, 92

Kansas, 692
Keeping a Wild Animal, 6, 509
Kentucky, 425, 692
Key Topic and Number, 25
Kill, Intent to, 455
Knife, 368
Knowledge, 205, 240, 267, 423, 458, 505, 526, 528, 582
Knowledge, Actual, 526, 528
Knowledge, First-Hand, 423
Knowledge of Conditions, 505
Knowledge, Special, 240, 267
Knowledge, Substantially Certain, 205, 458
Known Risks, 326
Known Trespasser, 526

Lake, 505, 519, 524, 526
Land, 9, 100, 126, 130, 219, 495, 503, 506, 510, 516, 595
Land and Jurisdiction, 100
Land, Enjoyment of, 506
Land, Entry for Inspection, 126, 130
Land Interests, 495
Land Occupiers, 9
Land, Ordinary Use of, 506
Land Owner, 9, 219, 495
Land, Possession of, 219, 510
Land, Recapture of, 601
Land Torts, 495
Land Trespass. See Trespass to Land
Land Use, 503
Landlord, 495, 516, 531, 601
Larceny, 537
Last Clear Chance, 317, 322
Latent Condition, 531
Latent Injury, 2
Laundromat, 529
Law Books, 11
Law, Conflict of, 9, 101
Law Enforcement Officer, 404, 420, 455, 467, 604
Law Journal, 21
Law, Kinds of, 12
Law, Procedural, 101

Law Review, 21
Law, Substantive, 101
Lawn Mower, 327
Lawyer, 268, 273, 274, 276, 357, 423, 437, 448, 519
Lawyer, Breach of Warranty by, 273
Lawyer-Client Privilege, 132, 580
Lawyer Competence, 274
Lawyer Fee, 268, 519
Lawyer Malpractice, 273, 276
Lawyer Specialization, 274
Lawyer Work Product, 123, 132
Leased Premises, 263, 357, 531
Legal Analysis, 37, 40, 42, 44, 46, 55, 81, 231
Legal Analysis and Legal Research, 42, 55
Legal Cause, 282, 293
Legal Encyclopedia, 18, 49
Legal Interviewing. See Interviewing
Legal Investigation. See Investigation.
Legal Malpractice, 273, 276
Legal Memorandum, 38, 50, 54
Legal Periodicals, 21, 27, 29, 50
Legal Proceedings for Malicious Prosecution, 418
Legal Remedy, 302
Legal Representative, 334
Legal Research, 42, 55, 200, 274
Legal Research on Negligence, 200
Legal Resource Index, 27, 29, 201
Legal Skill, 274
Legal Treatise, 20, 50
Legislation. See Statutes
Legislative History. See Statutes
Legislative Intent. See Statutes
Legislator, 611, 612
Legitimate Public Interest, 448
Lessee, 345, 495
Levy, 192
Lex Loci Delicti, 101
Liability, 7, 37, 61, 259, 266, 312, 325, 501, 531, 556
Liability, Civil, 501
Liability, Criminal, 531
Liability, Doctor. See Medical Malpractice
Liability Insurance, 556, 609, 614

Liability, Joint and Several, 312
Liability, Lawyer. See Legal
    Malpractice
Liability, Limitation of, 325
Liability of Parent for Child,
    266
Liability, Personal, 602, 609
Liability, Products, 1, 342
Liability, Strict, 267, 356, 561,
    604
Liability, Vicarious, 258, 259,
    498, 544, 610
Liability without Fault, 7, 356
Liable. See Liability
Libel, 3, 9, 429, 436, 546, 604
Libel Per Quod, 437
Libel, Trade, 546
Liberty, 586
License, 138, 284
Licensee, 523, 525, 528
Lien, 188
Life Expectancy, 338
Life Insurance, 138, 311
Life, Private, 443
Life, Wrongful, 488
Lifeguard, 223
Light, False, 443
Likeness, Unauthorized Use of,
    443
Limitation. See Statute of
    Limitation
Limitation of Liability, 325
Limited Jurisdiction, 89
Limited Privilege, 408
Liquor, 557
Litigation and Discovery, 120
Litigation Assistant Role, 123
Litigation, Automobile, 1
Litigation, Pre-Trial, 88
Live-In Partner, 339
Local Actions, 100
Local Government, 9, 607
Local Standard, 267
Loiterer, 528
Long-Arm Statutes, 99
Lord Campbell, 337
Loss, Economic, 302, 363
Loss of Consortium, 484
Loss of Earnings, 338, 403
Loss of Employment, 419
Loss of Services, 485
Loss of Support, 338
Loss, Pecuniary, 474
Loss, Property, 474
Loud Noises, 510
Louisiana, 13, 393

Machinery, 529
MacPherson v. Buick, 345

Magistrate, Police, 92
Mail, 605
Malfeasance, 217
Malice, 303, 387, 404, 419,
    444, 449, 455, 537, 547,
    548, 550, 551, 602, 611,
    611, 612
Malicious Prosecution, 5, 388,
    404, 418, 432, 444, 604
Malpractice. See Legal
    Malpractice, Medical
    Malpractice
Manifestation of Willingness,
    581
Manifestly against the Weight
    of the Evidence, 176
Manner, Unforeseeability of,
    293
Manuals, 18
Manufacturer, 345, 347, 366
Manufacturing Defect, 344,
    367
Maps, 141
Marital Relationship. See
    Husband, Marriage,
    Spouse, Wife
Market Share, 290
Market Value, Fair, 537
Marks, Skid, 66
Marriage, 602. See also
    Husband, Spouse, Wife
Marriage, Torts Against, 484
Married Women's Property
    Act, 614
Maryland, 693
Massachusetts, 693
Mass-Produced Goods, 362
Master Servant, 259
Material, 116, 479
Mayor, 435
Measure of Damages, 310
Mechanical Mistake, 275
Media, 429, 447, 449
Medical Battery, 269
Medical Bills, 302, 363, 419,
    631
Medical Evidence, 140
Medical Examination, 156. See
    also Doctor
Medical Insurance, 311
Medical Malpractice, 1, 266,
    268, 425, 488. See also
    Doctor
Medical Mistakes, 267. See also
    Doctor
Medical Research, 542
Medical Review Boards, 269
Medical Services, Consent to,
    269

Medical Tests, 268
Medical Treatment, 70, 154.
    See also Doctor
Medicine, 142, 268. See also
    Doctor
Medicine, Defensive, 268
Memorandum, 38, 44, 50, 54,
    76
Mental Characteristics, 239
Mental Deficiencies or
    Disability, 239, 320
Mental Examination, 127
Mental Illness, 239, 309
Mental Suffering or Distress,
    309, 392, 419, 550, 571,
    633
Merchant, 348, 359
Merchantability. See Warranty
Merchantable Goods, 359
Merger, 178
Method of Doing a Job, 565
Michigan, 693
Middle Appeals Court, 91
Minimum Conduct, 99, 256
Minister, 448
Ministerial, 604, 611
Minnesota, 584, 694
Minor, 557. See also Child
Misconduct, 175, 437, 565
Misconduct, Jury, 175
Misconduct, Sexual, 437
Misconduct, Willful, 565
Misdelivery, 396
Misdemeanor, 413, 415
Misfeasance, 216
Mislead, Intent to, 478
Misrepresentation, 5, 350, 364,
    378, 474, 478, 531, 537,
    583, 604
Misrepresentation, Negligent,
    478
Mississippi, 303
Mistake, 233, 267, 275, 408,
    413, 540, 583, 589, 593,
    596, 600
Mistake and False
    Imprisonment, 408
Mistake, Medical, 267
Mistake, Reasonable, 275, 413
Mistake, Tactical, 275
Mistake, Unreasonable, 275
Misuse, 370, 378
Mitigation of Damages, 511,
    517
Mixed-Purpose Trip, 564
Money Judgment, Collection
    of, 185
Monitoring Legislation, 10, 32
Monopoly, 326

Montana, 636
Moral Duty, 551
Morals, 602
Mortgage, 188
Motel, 219
Motion for a Directed Verdict, 169, 171
Motion for a Judgment NOV, 173
Motion for a New Trial, 173 221
Motion to Dismiss, 105, 165
Motive, 424, 437, 458, 514
Motor Vehicles. See Automobile
Move to the Nuisance, 517
Movement, Freedom of, 406
Multiple Defendants, 245
Multiple Recovery, 312
Municipal Code, 17
Municipal Court, 92
Municipality, 607
Mutual Control, 264

Name, Unauthorized Use of, 443
Napoléon, Code, 13
Narrow vs. Broad, 39
National Standard, 267
Natural Condition, 526
Natural Use, 503
Natural vs. Foreign, 368
Nature, Acts of, 568
Nature, Intervening Force of, 295
Nausea, 392
Necessary Party, 103
Necessity, Private, 594
Necessity, Privilege of, 497
Necessity, Public, 594
Negligence, 6, 7, 106, 112, 196, 197, 198, 212, 230, 240, 253, 256, 258, 264, 282, 302, 317, 318, 323, 335, 337, 349, 362, 364, 378, 383, 388, 396, 404, 435, 436, 432, 455, 467, 476, 478, 485, 497, 501, 505, 510, 518, 523, 537, 547, 560, 604, 614
Negligence and Fault, 197
Negligence and Strict Liability in Tort, 364
Negligence, Breach of Duty, 230. See also Duty
Negligence, Comparative, 318, 323, 383
Negligence Complaint, 106, 112

Negligence, Contributory, 317, 335, 337, 349, 362, 378, 505, 511, 560
Negligence Damages, 302
Negligence Defenses, 198, 317
Negligence Duty, 212. See also Duty
Negligence, Elements of, 198
Negligence, Gross, 256
Negligence, Imputed, 258, 264
Negligence, Lawyer. See Legal Malpractice
Negligence, Malpractice. See Medical Malpractice
Negligence, Ordinary, 318
Negligence Per Se, 253
Negligence, Presumption of, 253
Negligence, Proximate Cause, 282. See also Proximate Cause
Negligence, Res Ipsa Loquitur, 240
Negligence, Vicarious, 257
Negligence, Worker's Compensation, 560
Negligent Infliction of Emotional Distress, 396
Negligent Misrepresentation, 478
Neighborhood, Residential, 517
Neighborhood, Urban, 524
NEISS, 343
Neurologic Evaluation, 651
Nevada, 694
New Jersey, 339, 489
New Trial, Motion for a, 173 221
New York, 90, 225, 556, 695
Newly-Discovered Evidence, 175
Newsworthy, 448
No-Fault, 561, 686
Noises, 510, 512
Nominal Damages, 62, 302, 497
Non-Delegable Duty, 263
Nondisclosure, 478
Non-Natural Condition, 524
Non-Natural Use of Land, 503
Nonfeasance, 216
Normal Consequence, 293
North Dakota, 696
Notes to Decisions, 28, 30, 49
Notice of Appeal, 181
Notice of Breach of Warranty, 362
Notice Pleading, 107
NOV, Judgment, 172, 173, 176

Nuisance, 6, 9, 501, 504, 509, 516, 427
Nuisance, Abate a, 516, 595
Nuisance, Absolute, 501
Nuisance and Strict Liability, 501, 504
Nuisance and Trespass to Land, 497, 510
Nuisance, Attractive, 527
Nuisance, Private, 6, 510, 515
Nuisance, Public, 6, 510, 518
Nursery Equipment, 343

Objection to Deposition Question, 149
Objection to Interrogatories, 144
Objective, Business, 455, 476, 498, 537
Objective, Job, 565
Objective Standard or Test, 205, 238, 324, 367, 393, 458, 513
Obscenities, 391
Obstruction, 518
Obvious Danger, 368
Occupier of Land, 9, 523
Odors, 510, 514
Of and Concerning the Plaintiff, 430, 436
Offensive Contact, 443, 446, 448, 454, 458, 465, 469, 454
Officer, Investigative, 420, 455, 467, 604
Officer, Law Enforcement, 604
Officer, Peace, 411, 413
Officer, Police, 153, 411, 435, 530, 610
Official, Administrative, 612
Official Authorization, 511, 517
Official Immunity, 609
Official Malfeasance, 216
Official, Public, 435
Ohio, 299
Omission, 216
On all Fours, 27
On its Face, 430, 434
On the Merits, 179
Opening Statement, 165, 171
Operational Level, 604, 609, 611
Operation, Consent to, 269
Opinion. See Court Opinion
Opinion vs. Fact, 475, 478. See also Facts
Oral Deposition, 124
Order, Interlocutory, 181

Ordinance, 13, 17, 40, 249, 320, 513, 517
Ordinary Care, 231
Ordinary Consequence, 293
Ordinary Consumer, 367
Ordinary Negligence, 318
Ordinary Person, 454
Ordinary Purposes, 359
Ordinary Use of Land, 506
Oregon, 14, 696
Original Jurisdiction, 90
Original Risk, 283, 292, 296, 297
Orthopedic Needs, 142, 653
Others, Defense of, 591
Out-of-Pocket Damages, 476
Outrageous Conduct, 390
Owner of Land, 495, 523
Owner-Seller, 523
Ownership, 541

Pacific Reporter, 14
Packaging, 343, 348
Pain, 458
Pain and Suffering, 302, 309, 455, 630, 634, 688
Palsgraff, 213
Panel, Special Medical, 269
Paraphrasing Testimony, 159
Parent, 266, 485, 580
Parent-Child Liability, 266
Parental Consortium, 485
Park, Amusement, 530
Partial Disability, 576
Particular Purpose. See Warranty
Particularization, Fact, 82
Particularize, 75, 206, 319
Parties, 103, 437
Passenger, 219, 264, 529
Patent and Trademark Office, 93
Patient, 448, 458, 478, 583. See also Doctor
Patient-Physician Privilege, 132
Patient-Physician Relationship, 266
Patron, 530
Peace, Breach of the, 415
Peace of Mind, 512
Peace Officer, 411, 413
Peculiar Risk, 568
Pecuniary Benefit, 447
Pecuniary Damages, 476
Pecuniary Loss, 474
Peering, 443
Penitent, 448
Pennsylvania, 697

Peremptory Challenge, 118
Perfection, Reasonableness and, 231
Peril, Helpless, 322
Peril, Inattentive, 322
Periodicals, Legal, 21, 50
Permanent Disability, 576
Permissive Joinder, 104
Per Quod, Slander, 430
Per Se, Negligence, 253
Per Se, Slander, 430
Person, 430, 435, 457, 454
Person, Ordinary, 454
Person, Private, 435
Person, Reasonable, 231, 320, 443, 458
Person, Unreasonable, 232
Personal Comfort, 566
Personal Integrity, 457
Personal Jurisdiction, 89, 95
Personal Liability, 411, 602, 609
Personal Life, 443
Personal Property, 3, 6, 187, 357, 535, 593, 595, 599
Personal Property Torts, Survival of, 333
Personal Purpose, 564
Personal Risks, 569
Personal Service, 96
Personal Torts, 333, 614
Personal Torts, Survival of, 333
Personality, Unauthorized Use of, 443
Personam, In, 89, 95
Persuasion, Burden of, 167
Pesticides Act,
Photograph, 141, 446, 450, 678
Physical Barriers, 406
Physical Characteristics, 239
Physical Contact, 536
Physical Control, 536
Physical Damage, 458
Physical Discomfort, 403
Physical Examination, 127
Physical Force, 407
Physical Handicap, 239
Physical Harm, Injury or Impairment, 363, 377, 388, 397, 465
Physical Strengths, 239
Physical Therapy, 656
Physical Threat, 407
Physician. See Doctor
PI, 62
Plaintiff, Foreseeable, 213
Plaintiff, Unforeseeable, 212, 295
Plaintiff, Unintended, 470

Plaintiff's Case, Presentation of, 169
Planning Level, 604, 609
Pleading, 104, 107
Pocket, Deep, 1, 62, 259, 361, 544
Pocket Parts, 28
Poison, 369, 517, 583
Police Magistrate, 92
Police Officer, 411, 435, 530, 605, 608, 610
Police Protection, 225
Policy, 283, 326, 505, 556, 558, 606
Policy and Causation, 283
Policy, Liability Insurance, 556, 637, 686
Policy, Public, 326, 558
Poll the Jury, 175
Pollution, 510, 515, 518
Pool, Swimming, 524
Popular Name Table, 30
Positional Risk, 568
Possession, 52, 219, 495, 496, 510, 536, 595, 599
Possession, Immediate, 536
Possession of Land, 219, 510
Possessor, Adverse, 495
Possibilities and Foreseeability, 204
Post-Trial Deposition, 191
Postal Workers, 530
Potential Benefit, 554
Power. See Jurisdiction
Practical Joke, 393, 582
Practice Books, 18, 73
Practitioner, General, 274
Prayer for Relief, 108, 115
Precaution, 234, 384
Precis, 619
Pre-existing Condition, 292, 570
Pregnancy, Wrongful, 488
Prejudice, 117, 169, 174, 221
Prejudice, Dismissal with, 117
Prejudicial Evidence, 169
Preliminary Analysis, 40
Premises, 263, 523, 528, 530, 531
Preponderance of the Evidence, 168, 287
Prescription Drugs, 369
Presence, Arrest in One's, 413
Present Ability, Apparent, 470
Present Value, 306
Press, 9, 433, 447
Pressure, 422, 581
Presumed Damages, 436
Presumption of Negligence, 253

Pre-Trial Conference, 118
Pre-Trial Litigation, 88
Pre-Trial Protection, 185
Prima Facie Case, 2, 170
Prima Facie Tort, 6, 444, 555
Primary Authority, 11
Principal and Agent, 260, 478
Prison, 406
Privacy, Invasion of, 5, 388, 432, 442, 604
Private, 412, 443, 446, 519
Private Affairs, 443, 446
Private Citizen, 412, 519
Private Fact, Public Disclosure of, 5, 442, 447
Private Life, 443
Private Necessity, 594
Private Nuisance, 6, 510, 515
Private Person and Defamation, 435
Privilege, 337, 437, 444, 454, 460, 466, 539, 579, 589, 600, 611, 613
Privilege, Absolute, 437, 548
Privilege, Attorney-Client, 123, 132
Privilege, Husband-Wife, 132
Privilege, Limited, 408
Privilege of Necessity, 497
Privilege, Qualified, 437, 548
Privilege, Shopkeeper, 408, 600
Privilege to Abate a Nuisance, 516
Privilege to Arrest, 407, 411, 413
Privilege to Disparage, 548
Privilege to Enter Land, 525
Privilege to Interfere with Contract Relations, 551
Privilege to Recapture, 407
Privity of Contract, 345, 360
Probability, 204, 242
Probable Cause, 419, 422
Probate Court, 92
Probing, 443
Procedure, 88, 101
Proceedings, Supplementary, 191
Process, Abuse of, 3, 419, 424
Process, Service of, 96
Production, Burden of, 167
Production of Documents, 126, 130, 191
Products, Defective, 344, 363, 367
Products Liability, 1, 15, 342, 344, 379, 383

Products Liability Complaint, 379
Products Recall, 383
Products, Redesign of, 371
Products Safety Commission, 364, 383
Profanity, 393, 518
Profession, Medical, 267. See also Doctor
Profession, Slander of One's, 437
Professional Services, 273, 357
Promise, Gratuitous, 224
Promise to Cure, 266
Proof, Burden of, 167
Proof, Judgment, 185
Proof, Standard of, 287
Propensities, Dangerous, 266, 509
Property Damage, 72, 310
Property, Defense of, 595
Property Disparagement, 546
Property, Exempt, 189
Property, Intangible, 188, 536
Property, Leasing, 357
Property Loss, 474
Property, Personal, 6, 187, 357, 535, 593, 595, 599
Property, Real, 9, 187, 495
Property, Recapture, 408
Property, Stolen, 537
Property, Taking of, 518, 603
Property, Tangible, 188, 536
Property, Threat to, 407
Property Torts, 333, 614
Proprietary Function, 608
Prosecute, Failure to, 179
Prosecution, Malicious, 5, 418
Prosecutor, 8
Prospective Advantage, Interference with, 5, 554
Prosser, 20
Prostitution, 437, 510, 518
Protection of Others, 437, 551
Protection of Police, 225
Proximate Cause, 203, 282, 294, 397, 505, 568
Prudent Person, 231
Prying, 443
Psychiatrist, 219
Psychological Evaluation, 640, 647
Public Activity, 443
Public Disclosure of Private Fact, 5, 442, 447
Public Employee, Standard of Care toward, 530
Public Figure, 435, 448

Public Good, 514
Public Highway, 518
Public Interest, Legitimate, 448
Public Necessity, 594
Public Nuisance, 6, 510, 518
Public Official, 216, 435
Public Policy, 326, 283, 549, 558
Public Profanity, 518
Public Right and Nuisance, 518
Public Service, 326
Public Transit, 391
Public Utility, 326
Publication, 3, 4, 430, 436, 447, 547
Publication of Defamation, 3, 430
Publication of Disparagement, 547
Publicity, 443, 447
Publicity, Invasion of Privacy, 443
Puffing, 351, 478, 546
Punitive Damages, 303, 387, 404, 444, 455, 497, 537
Pure Comparative Negligence, 323
Purpose, Business, 513, 564
Purpose, Family, 259, 265
Purpose, Foreseeable, 369
Purpose, Intended, 369, 378
Purpose, Ordinary, 359
Purpose, Personal, 564
Purpose, Recreational, 513
Purpose, Unforeseeable, 369
Purpose, Unintended, 369
Pursuit, Fresh, 415, 599

Qualified Official Immunity, 611
Qualified Privilege, 437, 548
Quasi-Public Employee, 530
Question of Law, 38
Questionnaire, 65
Quotient Verdict, 175

Radio, 429
Railroad, 526
Rape, Statutory, 580
Real Parties in Interest, 103
Real Property, 9, 187
Real Property Torts, 334, 495
Reasonable Belief, 582, 589, 591, 595
Reasonable Care, 213, 230, 504, 523
Reasonable Doubt, 168

Reasonable Force, 413, 589, 591, 595
Reasonable Grounds, 413
Reasonable Mistake, 233, 275, 413, 540
Reasonable Person, 231, 320, 443, 446, 458, 469
Reasonable Use of Land, 506
Reasonableness, 230
Reasonableness and Perfection, 231
Reasonableness Factors, 231
Reasonably Safe, 346
Rebuttal Evidence, 171
Recall, Product, 383
Recapture of Chattels, 407, 599
Recapture of Land, 601
Recapture, Privilege to, 407
Reckless, 256, 318, 391, 408, 435, 449, 458, 478, 517, 547
Reckless Disregard, 478
Record, Public, 446, 448
Recovery, Double, 337, 550
Recovery, Multiple, 312
Recreation, 137, 343, 513
Recreational Equipment, 343
Recreational Purpose, 513
Re-Direct Examination, 169, 171
Reform, Malpractice, 268
Registrar of Motor Vehicles, 98
Regulation, 12, 16, 40, 49, 249, 320, 517
Rehabilitation, 640
Relationship, Fiduciary, 478
Relationship, Marital, 486
Relationship, Special, 216, 218
Relatives, 335, 602, 615
Release, 313, 406
Relevance, 169,
Reliance, 224, 352, 478, 479, 582
Relitigation, 178
Remedy, 17, 302, 335, 511, 516, 519, 610
Remedy, Equitable, 302
Remedy for Wrongful Death, 335
Remittitur, 173
Repairs, 139, 523, 537
Reply, 104, 181
Reporter, 14, 145
Repossession, 601
Representative, Legal, 334
Reputation, 348, 403, 419, 448, 591

Request for Admissions, 128, 131
Request for Production of Documents, 130
Res, 100
Res Ipsa Loquitur, 240, 290, 347, 504
Res Judicata, 178
Research Assignments, 26
Research, Legal, 42, 55
Research on Negligence, 200
Residence, 98, 101, 590
Residential Area, 503, 517, 521
Respondeat Superior, 259, 411, 544, 607
Respondent, 181
Restatement, 19, 217, 367, 371, 504, 527
Restaurant, 366, 512, 530
Restoration Cost, 516
Restricted Comparative Negligence, 323
Restrictions, 583
Result, Indivisible, 313
Retailer, 348, 366
Retainer, 63
Retaliatory Discharge, 558
Return of Service, 98
Revenge, 589
Reversionary Interest, 531
Review, Appellate, 91
Review Boards, Medical, 269
Review, Law, 21
Revolution, American, 13
Rhode Island, 571
Ridicule, 434
Right of Control, 536
Right, Public, 518
Risk, Actual, 568
Risk, Assumption of, 318, 324, 335, 337, 362, 383, 506, 511, 517, 560
Risk, Degree of, 504
Risk, Foreseeable, 213, 296, 505
Risk, Increased, 568
Risk, Known, 326
Risk, Original, 283, 292, 296
Risk, Peculiar, 568
Risk, Personal, 569
Risk, Positional, 568
Risk, Street, 569
Risk, Understanding of the, 327
Risk, Unreasonable, 319, 527
Risk/Utility Test, 373
River, 518, 528
Robbery, 296, 537

Robins, A.H., 2
Rocks, 524
Roman Empire, 13
Rules and Elements, 44
Rules in Legal Analysis, 39
Rules of Court, 13, 17, 40
Rylands v. Fletcher, 503, 508

Safety, 252, 348, 602
Safety Devices, 252
Safety Test, 348
Sale of Goods, 7
Sale, Service, 356, 367
Samaritan, Good, 217
Sanctions in Discovery, 123
Sanitation Workers, 530
Satisfaction, 313, 610
Scars, 155
School, 514, 608
Science, 371
Scienter, 5, 475, 478
Scope of Discovery, 122
Scope of Employment, 260, 315, 389, 420, 432, 455, 467, 537, 610
Screening, 357
Secondary Authority, 17
Secretary of State, 98
Security Interest, 187
Seduction, 6, 447, 487
Self-Defense, 335, 413, 460, 589
Self-Help, 511, 516, 520, 588
Self-Incrimination, 123, 132, 580
Self-Insurance, 562
Seller, 351, 359, 363, 366
Seller's Talk, 351
Sensitive, Unduly, 393, 443, 454, 513
Sensitivity, 392
Sensory Data and Foreseeability, 209
Serious Interference, 539
Servant, Master, 259
Several. See Joint and Several
Service of Process, 96
Service, Personal, 96
Service, Professional, 273, 357
Service, Public, 326
Service, Sale, 356, 367
Service, Substituted, 96
Services, Loss of, 485
Services of Child, 485
Settlement, 118, 122, 556, 618
Settlement Brochure, 623
Settlement, Insurance, 556, 623

Settlement Precis, 619
Several Liability, 258, 312
Severe Emotional Distress, 392
Sewer, 609
Sex Discrimination, 614
Sexual Intercourse, 580
Sexual Matters, 3, 299, 437, 448, 580
Sexual Misconduct, 299, 437
Shame, 392
Shepard's, 27, 49
Sheriff, 192
Shields, Dalkon, 2
Shopkeeper Privilege, 408, 600
Should Have Discovered, 322
Should Have Known, 349
Side Effects, 583
Signs, Danger, 348
Sine Que Non, 283
Sisters, 615
Skid Marks, 66, 153
Skill Assignments, 9
Skill, Legal, 274
Skill, Special, 240, 267
Slander, 4, 113, 429, 437, 546, 604
Slander Complaint, 113
Slander of Title, 546
Slander Per Quod, 430, 437
Slander Per Se, 437
Social Guest, 528
Social Host, 557
Social Importance, 346, 371
Social Security, 136, 311
Social Utility, 234, 237, 346, 371
Social Value, 512
Social Worker, 658
Society, Companionship, and Affection, 485
Solely Owned Property, 187
Solicitation, 528
Source Rule, Collateral, 311
Sources of Tort Law, 11, 40
South Carolina, 410, 697
South Dakota, 697
Sovereign Immunity, 9, 17, 411, 602
Space and Causation, 285
Special Damages, 4, 303, 430, 436, 519, 547, 554, 556
Special Jurisdiction, 89
Special Knowledge, 240, 267
Special Medical Panels, 269
Special Relationship, 216, 218
Special Skill, 240, 267
Special Verdict, 172
Specialization, Lawyer, 274

Speculation, 378
Speculative Cause, 378
Speech, Commercial, 547
Speech, Free, 434, 447
Speed Limit, 152, 628
Sports, 343, 581, 583
Spousal Privilege, 132
Spouse, 4, 339, 487, 602
Spouse, Enticement of, 4, 487
Spouse, Surviving, 339
Spring Gun, 525, 597
Stairway, 532
Stakeholder, 104
Standard, Civil, 250
Standard, Comparative, 231, 238
Standard Contract, 362
Standard, Federal, 383
Standard Forms, 109
Standard, Local, 267
Standard, National, 267
Standard, Objective, 238
Standard of Care, 14, 240, 249, 267, 523, 528
Standard of Care for Children, 240
Standard of Care, Medical, 267
Standard of Proof, 168, 287
Standard, Product, 384
Standard, Subjective, 238
State, 28, 33, 602, 605
State a Cause of Action, 2
State Court Opinion, 26. See also Court Opinion
State Court Systems, 90
State Government, 605. See also Government
State Questions, 89
State Statute, 28, 33
Statement, Defamatory or Derogatory, 430, 434, 546
Statement, False, 478, 545
Statement of Participants and Witnesses, 139
Statute, 12, 14, 15, 32, 34, 40, 49, 95, 116, 249, 256, 320, 437, 517, 519, 556, 608, 611
Statute at Large, 34
Statute, Compliance with, 256
Statute, Criminal, 249
Statute, Federal, 34, 95
Statute in Derogation of Common Law, 15
Statute, Legislative History of, 33, 49
Statute, Legislative Intent of, 250

Statute Monitoring, 32
Statute of Limitation, 116, 556
Statute, State, 33
Statutory Code, 15
Statutory Rape, 580
Stay of Execution, 186
Stenographer, 124, 145
Stipulated, 118
Stolen Property, 537
Store, Department, 408, 529, 532
Strategy, 84, 121
Street Risks, 569
Strengths, Physical, 239
Strict Construction, 252
Strict Liability, 6, 7, 267, 315, 356, 362, 429, 497, 499, 505, 509, 540, 542, 557, 561, 604
Strict Liability and Alcohol, 557
Strict Liability and Conversion, 540, 542
Strict Liability and Indemnity, 315
Strict Liability Defenses, 505
Strict Liability for Abnormally Dangerous Activity, 6, 499
Strict Liability for Harm Caused by Animals, 6, 509
Strict Liability in Tort, 6, 356, 362
Strict Liability, Medical, 267
Students, 584
Subject Matter Digest, 162
Subject Matter Jurisdiction, 16, 89, 99
Subjective, 205, 238, 324, 582
Subjective Standard, 205, 238
Subjective Test, 324
Subpoena Duces tecum, 124, 130
Subpoenas, 446
Subscription, 108
Subsequent Injuries, 137
Substantial Factor, 283, 321, 378, 393, 408
Substantial Interference, 513
Substantially Certain Knowledge, 458
Substantive Law, 101
Substituted Service, 96
Suffering, Pain and, 302, 309, 419, 455, 550, 634
Suicide, 292, 391
Summary Judgment, 116, 122, 179
Summons, 96

Superior Court, 90
Supersedeas Bond, 181, 186
Superseding Cause, 293, 295
Supplementary Proceedings, 191
Supplier, 366
Support, Loss of, 338
Supreme Court, 90, 181, 430, 435
Surprise, 175
Surrogate Court, 92
Surveys, 141
Survival of Action, 333
Surviving Spouse, 339
Survivor-Beneficiary, 337
Survivorship, 188
Swimming Pool, 524

Tabloids, 449
Tactical Mistake, 275
Taking of Property, 518, 603
Talk, Seller's, 351
Tangible Property, 188, 536
Tax Collection, 605
Tax Lien, 187
Tax Returns, 136
Teachers, 357, 601
Technical Mistake, 275
Technical Wrong, 302
Technology, 371
Television, 429
Temporary Disability, 576
Tenancy by the Entirety, 188
Tenancy in Common, 188
Tenancy, Joint, 187
Tenant, 495, 523, 531, 601
Terminable at Will, 549
Termination of Employment, 558
Termination of Legal Proceedings, 419
Termites, 531
Terms of Art, 48
Terror, 392
Test, Medical, 268
Test, Objective, 367, 393
Test, Safety, 348
Testing, 357
Texas, 371, 504, 698
Theater, 530, 532
Theft, 537
Things, Production of, 126
Threat, 391, 407, 470, 589, 591
Threat, Conditional, 470
Threat, Physical, 407
Threat to Immediate Family, 407

Threat to Property, 407
Tickler System, 144
Time, 123, 237, 285
Title, Passing, 356
Title, Slander of, 546
Tools, 343
Tort Against the Family, 8, 484
Tort and Contract, 2, 8
Tort and Crime, 2, 8
Tort, Business, 1, 544
Tort Categories, 2
Tort Claims Act, Federal, 364, 603
Tort, Complaints, 110
Tort Connected with Land, 495
Tort Damages, 302
Tort Defined, 2
Tort Elements, 2
Tort, Federal, 95
Tort, Intentional, 2, 614
Tort Law and Investigation, 79
Tort Law, Scope of, 1
Tort Law Sources, 11, 40
Tort Legislation, 33
Tort, Personal, 334, 614
Tort, Prima Facie, 555
Tort, Property, 334, 614
Tort, Underlying, 485
Tort, Unintended, 470
Tortfeasor, Death of, 334
Tortfeasor, Intentional, 314
Tortfeasor, Joint, 312, 314
Tortious Interference with Employment, 558
Torts, Restatement of, 19. See also Restatement
Total Confinement, 403, 407
Town, 607
Toys, 343
Trade, 437
Trade Custom, 348
Trade Libel, 546
Traffic Violation, 138
Transcribed, 148
Transcript, 32, 124, 158
Transferred Intent, 392, 408, 458, 470
Transfusion, Blood, 357
Transit, Public, 391
Transitory Actions, 100
Treatise, 18, 20, 50
Treatment, Medical, 70, 154, 633
Trees, 524
Trespass to Chattels, 6, 470, 535, 604

Trespass to Chattels and Transferred Intent, 470
Trespass to Land, 7, 50, 52, 388, 470, 496, 583, 594, 599, 604
Trespasser, 523, 525, 526
Trespasser, Adult, 523
Trespasser, Child, 523, 526
Trespasser, Discovered, 525
Trespasser, Foreseeable, 526
Trespasser, Known, 526
Trial Court, 90
Trial, Motion for a New, 173 221
Trial Procedure, 164
Trial Within a Trial, 276
Trip, Mixed-Purpose, 564
Truth, 448, 478
TV, 429

Ulterior Motive, 424
Ultimate Facts, 107
Ultrahazardous, 500, 604
Unavoidably Unsafe, 369
Unconscionable, 362
Understanding of the Risks, 327
Undertaking, Gratuitous, 223
Unduly Sensitive, 393, 443, 454, 513
Unemancipated Child, 485
Unfair Competition, 554
Unforeseeability, 203, 212, 293, 295, 369, 378
Unforeseeability of Manner, 293
Unforeseeable Plaintiff, 213, 295
Unforeseeable Purpose, 369
Unforeseeable Use, 369, 378
Uniform Commercial Code, 355, 358
Unintended Plaintiff, 470
Unintended Purpose, 369
Unintended Tort, 470
Unintended Use, 369
Union, 471, 558
United States Claims Court, 93
United States Code, 28, 30
United States Court of Appeals, 27, 93, 303, 352
United States Court of Appeals for the Federal Circuit, 93
United States District Court, 27, 91
United States Supreme Court, 430, 435
Unreasonable Interference, 510

Unreasonable Intrusion, 443
Unreasonable Mistake, 275
Unreasonable Person, 232
Unreasonable Risk, 319, 527
Unreasonableness, 230, 241, 253, 256, 363, 367
Unreasonableness, Gross, 256
Unreasonableness, Vicarious, 257
Unreasonably Dangerous, 363, 367
Unsafe, Unavoidably, 369
Unwanted Child, 488
Urban Neighborhood, 524
Usage, Custom and, 248
USC, 28
Use, Depravation of, 310
Use, Foreseeable, 369, 378
Use, Intended, 369
Use, Natural, 503
Use of Land, Reasonable, 506
Use, Unforeseeable, 369, 378
Use, Unintended, 369
User, 345, 363, 377
Utah, 698
Utility, Public, 326
Utility/Risk Test, 373
Utility, Social, 346, 371

Value, Fair Market, 537
Value, Present, 306
Value, Social, 512
Values, Community, 14
Vehicle Repairs, 139
Vendor of Home, 531
Venereal Disease, 299
Vengeance, 569
Venue, 99, 105
Verdict, Directed, 169, 171
Verdict, Kinds of, 172
Verdict, Quotient, 175
Verification, 78, 108, 115
Veterans' Benefits, 311
Vicarious Liability, 257, 259, 498, 544, 610
Vicarious Negligence, 257
Vicarious Unreasonableness, 257

Vice Principal, 561
Village, 607
Violation of Civil Rights, 3. See also Civil Rights Act
Violation of Statute, 249
Violation, Traffic, 138
Virginia, 698
Voidable Contract, 549
Voir Dire, 117
Volenti Non Fit Injuria, 580
Voluntary, 325, 327, 456, 469, 580, 581
Voluntary Dismissal, 117

Waiver, 100, 602, 606
Wanton Conduct, 256, 318, 391, 526
War, 605
Warning, 344, 367, 371, 516, 528, 596
Warning Defect, 344, 367
Warning to Trespasser, 526
Warrant, 413
Warranty, 7, 266, 273, 350, 358, 359, 360, 362, 378
Warranty and Causation, 359
Warranty by Lawyer, 273
Warranty, Disclaimer of, 362
Warranty, Express, 7, 350
Warranty of Fitness for a Particular Purpose, Implied, 7, 360
Warranty of Merchantability, Implied, 7, 358
Warranty, Physician, 266
Waste, 515
Water Pollution, 510
Weight of the Evidence, 176
West Publishing Co., 25
West Virginia, 461
Wheelchair, 406, 410
Wholesaler, 348, 366
Wife, 132, 478, 614
Wife-Husband Privilege, 132, 580
Wild Animals, 6, 509
Will, 335

Will, Employment At, 558
Will, Terminable at, 549
Willful Conduct, 256, 318, 391, 565
Willingness, Manifestation of, 581
Wiretapping, 446, 518
Withdrawal of Physician, 266
Witness, 85, 140, 143, 267, 397, 437, 667
Witness, Expert, 267
Witness Statement, Taking a, 85
Witness to Injury, 397
Wives and Consortium Rights, 485
Words and Phrases, 27, 28
Worker, Domestic, 562
Worker, Farm, 562
Worker's Compensation, 136, 336, 558, 560
Work-Product, Attorney, 123, 132
Work-Related, Diseases, 563
World at Large Test, 215, 295
Worry, 392
Writ of Execution, 192
Writ of Garnishment, 192
Written Deposition, 125
Written Interrogatories, 123, 191
Wrong, Technical, 302
Wrongful Birth, 488
Wrongful Civil Proceedings, 424
Wrongful Death, 333, 335, 364, 388, 455
Wrongful Life, 488
Wrongful Pregnancy, 488
Wrongfulness and Negligence, 197

Ybarra v. Spangard, 245

Zone of Danger, 215, 295, 397
Zoning, 513, 517, 520